The Sunday Telegraph

GOLF COURSE GUIDE
TO
BRITAIN & IRELAND

DONALD STEEL

12th Edition

Sponsored by the CSMA

CollinsWillow
An Imprint of HarperCollins*Publishers*

*The publishers would like to acknowledge the help of the following
in the compilation of the 12th edition of this book:*

Text updating and revision:
Howard Beale
Val Coxon
Gaynor Harding
Delyth Jones
Research coordination:
Tricia Gibson
Technical support
Howard Scott

Map compilation and artwork:
Graeme Murdoch
Katie Murray

Cover photographs
The London Golf Club
by Tim Edwards

This edition published 1996 by
CollinsWillow
an imprint of HarperCollins*Publishers*
London

First published 1968
Twelfth revised edition 1996

A CIP catalogue record for this book
is available from the British Library

ISBN 0-00-218729-9

This edition jointly produced by
Robert MacDonald Publishing, London SW1
Peter MacDonald Publishing, Twickenham

Printed and bound in Great Britain by
The Bath Press

CONTENTS

KEY TO THE MAPS

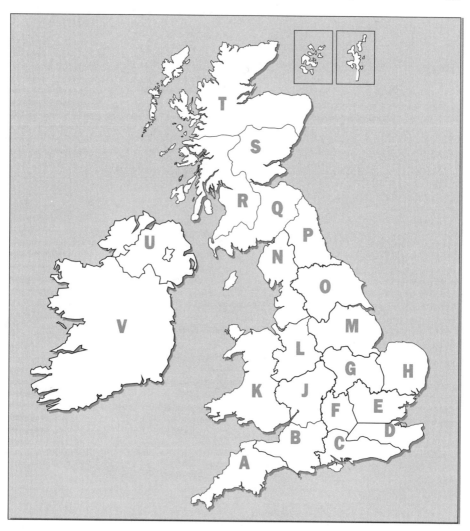

FOREWORD

When the first edition of the Golf Course Guide was published in 1968, it contained a list of just under 1,650 Clubs; the winner of the Open championship received a cheque for £3,000 and the cost of a round over the West course at Wentworth was twenty five shillings.

In 1996, the number of courses covered by the book has risen by more than eight hundred, the Open champion at Royal Lytham and St Annes will be richer by £200,000 while 18 holes on Wentworth's West course during the summer will set you back £120. Much has changed.

However, one of the few things that never changes is the spirit of adventure among golfers to explore and find new places to play. That sets it apart from other sports. Tennis players, for instance, cannot indulge in a knock-up on Wimbledon's Centre Court. You cannot stroll into Murrayfield and attempt a few conversions, and facing a few overs at Lord's is out of the question; but you can pay a green fee at St Andrews, Carnoustie or the Belfry and play exactly the same shots that Nick Faldo and Greg Norman confronted when you watched them on television or in the flesh. What is more, in spite of different circumstances, you might even hit them better.

The essential purpose of the Guide is to help provide the information essential in planning a day out or a few days away. First of all comes help in finding your destination, then there is an indication of the cost of a round and, finally, some local recommendations about where to stay. The names of new Clubs obviously expand the limits and widen the choice, thereby allowing visitors to seek the best value for money. A new air of competition about the rates for green fees and Society charges is no bad thing.

Commercialism is more readily apparent but, compared to equivalent charges in many other parts of the world, Great Britain and Ireland remain relatively inexpensive; and certainly nowhere else does such variety exist as around our shores. Happy hunting.

Donald Steel
March 1996

THE SUNDAY TELEGRAPH GOLF COURSE GUIDE
Sponsored By The CSMA

What is the CSMA ?

The CSMA - Civil Service Motoring Association - is Britain's premier private motoring club. As a non-profit making organisation, the Association is run by members for members and strives to provide good quality value-for-money benefits to satisfy members' motoring and leisure needs. Our success is demonstrated by the fact that we now offer a wide range of varied benefits to over 323,000 members.

What can the CSMA do for you ?

The benefits of CSMA membership are diverse and unique. Our considerable resources ensure that our members are guaranteed competitive prices on tried and tested products and services - not just in the motoring field but also in insurance, financial services, travel and leisure.

MOTORING BENEFITS:

As a CSMA member you are entitled to exclusively low premiums on membership to **Britannia Rescue** - widely regarded as the UK's fourth largest road rescue organisation and wholly owned by the CSMA. Independent research says our 34 minute average response time is the fastest and our latest survey shows that 95% of all calls are attended within the hour. *If you are not eligible for CSMA membership you can still enjoy the peace of mind of belonging to Britannia Rescue: call 0800 591563 for more information.*

If you are thinking of buying a car, the CSMA can help with our popular **New and Used Car Discount Scheme.** Not only can you make substantial savings on most makes and models, but we are also pleased to offer help and advice if required. CSMA members are also entitled to **free legal and technical advice.**

INSURANCE AND FINANCIAL SERVICES:

We have, on behalf of our members, negotiated privileged rates of **motor and home insurance** as well as on **personal loans, savings and financial planning** through the Frizzell group of companies. The exclusive **CSMA Visa and MasterCard** also provide extremely competitive rates of interest, are free from commission charges abroad and give you the opportunity to earn Plus Points every time you use your card/s.

TRAVEL BENEFITS:

You can enjoy complete peace of mind when travelling abroad with or without your car, with the CSMA's unrivalled travel insurance - **Britannia Continental.** Members can obtain instant discounts on holidays and travel when booking through the **CSMA Traveldesk** at all branches of *Going Places* travel agents. Furthermore, our **Social and Travel Programme** organises trips such as weekend breaks in the UK through to cruises and full scale holidays abroad - all at highly competitive prices.

LEISURE BENEFITS:

Enjoy the luxury and attentive service at **Eaves Hall** our exclusive country club in Lancashire or unwind in the peaceful splendour of **Ghyll Manor** our country hotel in Sussex. For those who prefer the outdoor life **Whitemead Leisure Park**, a picturesque camping, caravanning and chalet park in the Forest of Dean and **Sherwood Forest Caravan Park** deep in the heart of Robin Hood country provide the perfect get-away-from-it-all locations.

Our network of 50 plus **Local Groups** spread across the country arrange a variety of social events for members in the area. **Special events**, family weekends and adult entertainment weekends are also regularly organised by the CSMA.

You can keep in touch with all that the CSMA has to offer through our very own magazine - *Motoring & Leisure* - which is delivered straight to your door ten times a year, absolutely free.

Who Can Join the CSMA ?

CIVIL SERVICE EMPLOYEES:

As our name implies, if you are a current member of the Civil Service - including Next Step Government Agencies - or any ex-Civil Service organisation such as BT, the Post Office, Mercury, BAA or the CAA you are eligible to join the CSMA.

NON-CIVIL SERVICE EMPLOYEES:

You may also qualify for CSMA membership even if you are not currently employed within any eligible organisation. Membership to the CSMA is "portable" and for life. In fact anyone who has ever been eligible for membership never loses their entitlement to join. This means that if at one time in your life you have been employed by the Civil Service or any ex-Civil Service organisation, you can still become a member of the CSMA. **This includes anyone who has retired from these organisations.**

If you are not sure of your eligibility, if you want to find out more or if you want to join simply call us free on 0800 669944.

If you are not eligible to join the CSMA, you can still join Britannia Rescue and enjoy the reassurance and peace of mind that comes with the knowledge that fast and dependable road assistance and recovery is only a phone call away.

Call 0800 591563 for more information.

INTRODUCTION

This 12th edition of the Golf Course Guide contains several new features. Most noteworthy is the addition of a short section dealing with golf courses in northern France (p.88), now accessible through the Channel Tunnel. The maps have been completely revised and redrawn, and each is now accompanied by a key, allowing the reader instantly to match the numbers on the map to the names of the courses.

As in previous editions, the introductions to the county areas have been revised and updated, and several new profiles of individual courses have been included. For the first time, the author has also provided a preview of the venues for the 1996 and 1997 Open championships (Royal Lytham & St Annes and Royal Troon (see p.10).

Although great care has been taken to ensure the accuracy of the Guide, one golf course has been included that has no counterpart in reality. It exists only in the mind of the author. This is the "Dream Course" composed of the best 18 holes that Britain can offer, and based on the author's popular series in *The Sunday Telegraph*. The only way to enjoy this particular course is to turn to page 14 and read on.

Organisation. The book is divided into 21 areas or county groupings, retaining the changes introduced in the 11th edition. The areas have been defined on the basis of golfing affinities and familiarity of use rather than being dictated by cartographic convenience or beaurocratic definition. In particular, the purely administrative boundaries created by past local government reorganisation have been ignored. Thus, the golf courses of Humberside will be found in Lincolnshire or Yorkshire, those of the West Midlands in Warwickshire or Staffordshire, and those of Avon in Gloucestershire and Somerset. Middlesex has been resurrected.

As before, the areas are labelled alphabetically, from A to V – the letter I has not been used because of its similarity to the numeral 1. Each area has a map indicating the location of courses within it (see page 4 for a key to the county groupings and pages on which individual area maps are to be found). Within each section, courses are listed alphabetically and numbered in sequence; the combination of letter and number is used to identify each course in the overall index (page 372).

Course information. This is a guide to golf courses rather than golf clubs, and course rather than club names have been used throughout. However, where a course is uniquely associated with a particular club, the name of the club has generally been used. For each golf course the following information is normally provided: the name of the course; telephone number; address; travel directions to the course; a brief description of the type of course; the number of holes, length and Standard Scratch Score; the course architect and date of foundation; restriction on visiting golfers – when they may play and whether reservations, club membership, or handicap certificates are required; green fees (valid at the time of going to press but liable to change); terms for parties, company days or visiting societies, if applicable; what catering and other facilities (putting greens, driving ranges, tennis courts, for example) are available, and finally recommendations for local hotels (particularly where golfing breaks or holidays can be arranged). Where no information is given for a particular category – for example, societies or catering – it can be assumed that the facilities are not available to visitors or don't exist.

The information in this book has been compiled with the help of club secretaries, professionals and course managers, whose assistance is gratefully acknowledged.

Comments. The publishers would welcome information about any courses that are not in the book, and about any errors or alterations relating to the current contents, so that they can be incorporated in the next edition. Comments and suggestions should be sent to: The Golf Course Guide, The Sunday Telegraph, 1 Canada Square, Canary Wharf, London E14 5DT, where they will be gratefully received.

Donald Steel and Co. Ltd.

International Golf Course Architects

Designs currently under construction or completed in sixteen countries

York House, City Fields, Chichester, West Sussex PO20 6FR
Telephone: (01243) 531901/532582
Fax: (01243) 532581

Member of British Institute of Golf Course Architects

FIT FOR A CHAMPIONSHIP

ROYAL LYTHAM & ST ANNES

Royal Lytham & St. Annes eight championship Opens have yet to rank an American professional amongst the winners. 1926, their inaugural event, saw Bobby Jones triumphant in an era when the world's leading player was an amateur. Jones put his law practice in Atlanta first and golf second.

Jones was the Open's last amateur winner (he also won in 1927 and 1930) and 60 years later the breaking of the spell is no more likely than John Daly sporting a Norfolk jacket and hickory shafts.

Daly will find the demands of Lytham very different to the Old course at St Andrews where a feeling of space gave him the encouragement to open his shoulders and let rip. Lytham is a course on which you miss the fairway at your peril. Of all the Open championship courses, it is the most liberally bunkered. However, Daly may be heartened by the tale of Severiano Ballesteros in 1979, whose winning recipe was to ignore both fairways and bunkers. The Americans called him the parking lot champion although there was a measure of sour grapes about their claim. Nevertheless, Ballesteros saw the funny side, joking prophetically at his Press conference after a 2nd round 65, "one day they should play the Open on a course with no fairways, then I win".

For Lytham's most recent Open in 1988, Ballesteros was something of a reformed character, having very definitely the first and last words. After breakfast on the first morning, he opened with three birdies and, on the last afternoon, played a round he rated as his greatest.

In between, the main talking point was the weather which postponed the finish until Monday when his 65 captivated everyone, denying Nick Price whose 68 was magnificent in the circumstances.

Ballesteros backed up his bold driving with well judged iron play and moments of pure magic on and around the greens. Even now, it is easy to conjure up the deftness of his little chip from beside the 18th green which assured his victory. It is too much to hope that he will win a third Lytham Open in a row but, whatever it has in store, nothing will match his excitement and supernatural golfing powers. They are certainly a rich part of Lytham's folklore.

ROYAL TROON

Until 1989, post-war Open championships at Royal Troon (Royal since 1978), had been notable for comfortable winning margins rather than hairsbreadth finishes, although Tom Watson's fourth success in 1982 was a slight exception. It was the least glorious of the five he won, a number of players letting slip better chances than Watson.

Of Troon's three previous Opens, Bobby Locke won by two strokes in 1950, Arnold Palmer by six in 1962 and Tom Weiskopf by three in 1973. However, it was all change in 1989. Not only did that Open see the first three-way tie in the championship's history, it witnessed the first foreshortened play-off over four holes.

The 18th was certainly the place to be for the last hour and half, first as the play-off took shape and then as it reached its climax. Until the final few minutes, Mark Calcavecchia had not exactly looked the likely winner. Having pitched his ball full toss into the cup for an eagle 2 at the 12th and added birdies on the 16th and 18th, he was one behind Greg Norman with two holes of the play-off remaining. Then, Norman took three from the back of the 17th green, drove into a far distant bunker from the 18th tee and Calcavecchia, keeping out of trouble, was home.

In 1997, Norman is still likely to be a contender although, if so, he would give much to repeat his final round of 64 in 1989, in which his only dropped stroke occurred at The Postage Stamp, the shortest hole in Open championship golf. However, Troon will have other ideas about the 1997 winner. Colin Montgomerie's father, James, is the Club's Secretary/Manager and victory by the best and most consistent player in Europe for the last three years would see the start of local and national celebration.

Troon is a fair and honest course which begins along the beach and reaches its peak, to my mind, with the stretch from the 7th to the 13th. The start and finish are good but I like the variety which these middle holes provide. It is a curious fact that when Palmer spreadeagled the field in 1962, he failed to get a birdie on any of the first three holes in the four rounds but the 11th was where the drama unfurled.

The hole, hugging the railway line, had only recently been increased from a short-ish par four to a par five. It quickly proved a hole to be feared, as Palmer recalled on the eve of the championship 27 years later. "My motive was to get it behind me as quickly as I could." But, unlike Jack Nick-laus who ran up a ten there on the final day, Palmer got the 11th before it got him.

Having had to qualify with everyone else, Palmer had an eagle and three birdies in five rounds, his only par coming when he hit perhaps his best second shot and just overran the green. The 1997 champion may not match that brilliance but the 11th will still be a key hole.

ACCIDENT OR DESIGN?

In December 1993, Nick Price won the Sun City Million Dollar Challenge on a course measuring around 7,600 yards with a total of 264, 24 under par. Admittedly, al-lowance has to be made for the ball going further through the thinner air at high alti-tude, but it showed unmistakably how length alone poses few barriers to the leading players these days.

Naturally enough, most new courses have had to be stretched to accommodate the dramatic advances in technique and equipment which have resulted in every golfer achieving extra length. However, the search to combat power in golf has led to a regrettable fashion amongst some develop-ers and architects, who maintain that every new course must have a par of 72 with four par 5s, four par 3s and a championship label irrespective of whether a champi-onship is ever housed on it.

What lifts golf onto a higher plane than games that are played on courts or pitches with prescribed dimensions is that golf courses come in all shapes and sizes. Statistics cannot distinguish between the good and the bad. True judgement is based on interest, enjoyment and use of the terrain which, in turn, is a reflection of the skill and ingenuity of the architect.

The architect is cheered – or should be – by the comfort that there are no rights and wrongs, particularly with regard to the make-up and balance of his designs. The Old course at St Andrews – still hailed as a model for all architects – has only two par 3s and two par 5s. It has the 11th hole cross-ing the 7th and is unique in having many of its holes sharing fairways. At Royal Wor-lington and Newmarket which Bernard Darwin described as "The Sacred Nine", you drive on three occasions over the green which you have just played. Even at Royal Porthcawl, venue of the 1995 Walker Cup, the opening tee shot plays straight across the 18th fairway. Elsewhere in Britain, it is not uncommon to drive over roads or even fast flowing rivers or streams.

Clearly, the scale of a course is dictated by the quantity and character of land at the achitect's disposal. He has to cut his coat according to his cloth, a fact that leads to all sorts of different balances between the pars of holes and the make-up of new 18, 27 or 36 – hole courses.

Where possible, the par 3s, 4s and 5s are arranged so that they don't all come at once, but the list of design oddities which follows has been drawn up to counter some of the suggestions so frequently put forward, and so often received as conven-tional wisdom, about the par and S.S.S. of courses, courses beginning or ending with a par 3, courses having consecutive par 3s or par 5s and those maintaining a roughly equal balance in length between the two 9s on an 18-hole course.

It is not meant to be a comprehensive catalogue, but it does show that there are precedents for practically everything that a golf course architect might think of incor-porating in his designs. Before that, how-ever, it is worth reflecting that, of our seven current Open Championship links courses, only St Andrews and Royal Troon have a par of 72.

18-hole courses over 5,800 yards beginning with a par 3
Aboyne
Accrington
Addington
Anglesey
Ashburnham
Ballards Gore
Berkshire (Blue)
Churston
City of Derry
Cochrane Castle
Colville Park
Crow Wood
Dartford
Davenport
Davyhulme Park
Deer Park
Easingwold
Eastham Lodge
Falkirk Tryst
Hayling
Hollingbury Park
Horam Park
Houldsworth
Huntercombe
Kettering
Kingsknowe
Knole Park
Largs
La Moye
Liphook
Llandudno (Maesdu)
Llanymynech
Longcliffe
Macroom
Manor of Groves
Meyrick Park
Monkstown
Pebbles
Preston
Purley Downs
Royal Lytham and St Annes
Royal Mid-Surrey
Royal Norwich

Southport and Ainsdale
South Moor
Thetford
Upton by Chester
Wearside
Wellow
West Bowling
West Cornwall
Whitchurch (Cardiff)
Withington
Yelverton

18-hole courses over 5,800 yards ending with a par 3
Aberystwyth
Airdrie
Alloa
Arkley
Ashford (Kent)
Bandon
Barnard Castle
Beadlow Manor
Berkshire (Red)
Boyce Hill
Breightmet
Bremhill Park
Bright Castle
Brinkworth
Brora
Carlyon Bay
Cawder (Cawder)
Chapel-en-le-Frith
Chelmsford
Cold Ashby
Courtown
Darenth Valley
Deeside
Dewsbury
Douglaston
Downes Crediton
Dunstable Downs
Dunwood Manor
East Herts
Ellesmere
Erewash Valley
Fairlop Waters

Forest of Arden (Arden)
Fortrose and Rosemarkie
Glamorganshire (Penarth)
Goodwood
Great Barr
Hayston
Hoebridge
Howley Hall
Ilfracombe
Kennilworth
Killarney (Mahony's Point)
Kilsyth Lennox
Kirkcaldy
Lancaster
Langley Park
Leasowe
Leeds
Lindrick
Lochwinnoch
Louth
Milford Haven
Moor Park (High)
Mount Oswald
Northcliffe
Nottingham City
Old Padeswood
Old Ranfurly
Padeswood and Buckley
Parkstone
Penwortham
Piltdown
Prestwick St Nicholas
Royal Eastbourne
Royal Guernsey
Royal St David's
Ryton
Saffron Walden
St Pierre
Saltburn-by-the-Sea
Sandy Lodge
Shanklin and Sandown
Sickleholme

Stocksfield
Stoke by Nayland (both)
Stone
Tredegar Park
Wallsend
Welwyn Garden City
West Linton
Wetherby
Whitburn
Woodbury (Oaks)
Woodhall Hills (both)
Worksop

18-hole courses beginning and ending with a par 3
Aboyne
Aldwark Manor
Bala
Bearsted
Bingley St Ives
Didsbury
Eltham Warren
Harpenden Common
Hawick
Peacehaven
Southwold
Upminster

18-hole courses over 5,800 yards with two consecutive par 3s
Ashford Manor
Ballybunion (Old)
Balmoral
Bandon
Barnard Castle
Bawburgh
Birr
Bishop Auckland
Brancepeth Castle
Bristol & Clifton
Brough
Burntisland
Chester-le-Street
Clonmel

DALRIADA SPORTS HOLIDAYS
IRELAND, FRANCE, PORTUGAL, SPAIN AND UK

We have selected areas of each country to offer you golf with choices of
courses, starting times, hotel accommodation and car hire.

Phone, fax or write to us for details and receive our brochure.

DALRIADA SPORTS HOLIDAYS, P.O. BOX 24, PERTH. PH2 0SZ
Tel: 01738 622716 Fax: 01738 639392

Consett and District
Cruden Bay
Elgin
Erewash Valley
Harburn
Hartsbourne
Hayston
Holywood
Ganstead Park
Glamorganshire
 (Penarth)
Haywards Heath
Ilkley
Kidderminster
Killymoon
Knott End
Lee-on-the-Solent
Leyland
Linlithgow
Loudoun (twice)
Lurgan
Machrihanish
Market Rasen
Millport
North Oxford
Potters Bar
Roehampton
Royal Eastbourne
Royal Jersey
Rushmere
Sandy Lodge
Stoneham
Tain
Thurlestone
The Manor, Laceby
Tredegar Park
Waterlooville
West Linton
West Monmouthshire
West Sussex
Willesley Park

**18-hole courses over
6,000 yards with
fewer than 3 par 3s**
St Andrews (Old) – 2
Golf House Club,
 Elie – 2

**18-hole courses over
5,900 yards with more
than five par 3s**
Barnard Castle – 6
Berkshire (Red) – 6
Bigbury – 6
Darlington – 6
Downes Crediton – 6
Killymore – 6
Richmond – 6
Sandy Lodge – 6
Tredegar Park – 6
Note: Red at Berkshire
has six par 3s six par
4s and six par 5s.

**Courses with holes
over 600 yards**
Aldenham Golf &
 Country Club (13th,
 636 yards)
Belton Woods
 (Wellington) (18th,
 613 yards)
Bright Castle (16th,
 735 yards)
East Dorset (6th, 604
 yards)
Gedney Hill (2nd, 671
 yards)
Manor of Groves
 (18th, 614 yards)
Overstone Park (11th,
 601 yards)
Portal (6th, 603 yards)
Welwyn Garden City
 (17th, 601 yards)

**Courses over 7,000
yards**
Austin Lodge (7,118
 yards)
Ballards Gore (7,062
 yards)
Barkway Park (7,000
 yards)
Bidford Grange (7,233
 yards)

The Belfry (Brabazon)
 (7,177 yards)
Belton Woods
 (Lancaster) (7,021
 yards)
Bowood (7,317 yards)
Bright Castle (7,143
 yards)
Carnoustie (7,272
 yards)
Chart Hills (7,086
 yards)
Dartmouth (7,012
 yards)
East Dorset (7,027
 yards)
East Sussex (West)
 (7,154 yards)
Forest of Arden
 (Arden) (7,102
 yards)
Gleneagles (The
 Monarch's Course)
 (7,081 yards)
Hanbury Manor
 (7,011 yards)
Killarney (Killeen)
 (7,079 yards)
Loch Lomond (7,053
 yards)
The London Club
 (Heritage 7,208
 yards)
 (International 7,005
 yards)
Millbrook (7,100
 yards)
Moatlands (7,060
 yards)
Mount Juliet (7,100
 yards)
The Oxfordshire
 (7,143 yards)
Notts (Hollinwell)
 (7,020 yards)
Perton Park (7,007
 yards)
Portal (7,145 yards)

Royal Liverpool (7,100
 yards)
Slaley Hall (7,038
 yards)
Stocks Hotel (7,016
 yards)
Thorpe Wood (7,086
 yards)
Waterville (7,184
 yards)
West Berkshire (7,059
 yards)
Loch Lomond (7,053
 yards)

**18-hole courses with
holes under 100 yards**
Bridport and West
 Dorset (2nd, 81
 yards)
Dun Laoghaire (7th,
 95 yards)
Erewash Valley (4th,
 89 yards)
Ilfracombe (4th, 81
 yards)
Tilsworth (13th, 97
 yards)

**Courses with par 3s
numbered all odds or
all evens**
Addington
Auchterarder
Cape Cornwall
Cirencester
County Armagh
County Louth
Hoebridge
Liphook
Lyme Regis
Oake Manor
Scunthorpe
Stockwood Park
Sundridge Park
 (West)
West Cornwall
Uttoxeter

A DREAM COURSE

HOLE 1: **PRESTWICK**
Railway, Par 4, 346 yards
Most opening holes break golfers in gently. Prestwick throws them in at the deep end – without a lifebelt! For some, medal rounds are over before they leave the tee and fierce debate surrounds its suitability as a first hole. The main fear is the slice. The Railway and the stone wall that guards it run the entire length of the hole and are, as Bernard Darwin said, "quite unpleasantly near us."

The wall marks the edge of the tee, the edge of the fairway and the edge of the green, an immediate strain on nerve and judgement. First tees are never the most convivial of places but at Prestwick the feelings of unease are compounded by the knowledge that no leeway exists to the left either. It is rough ground, undulating and unfriendly. The fairway is not the best option; it is the only option.

One of the most spectacular examples of overguarding against the slice was provided in 1956 by Eric Brown who, six strokes ahead starting the final round of the Dunlop Masters, ran up to a seven, although, having driven into the heather on the left, it was more his skirmish with the burnt gorse on the bank of the second tee that proved his undoing. Brown lost by one stroke to Christy O'Connor.

If there are those who deny its charm as a first hole, it is a splendid 19th or 37th. John Ball won the 37th in three in his final of the Amateur championship of 1899, an act of high, competitive courage.

A birdie of a different kind at extra holes came in the final of the club's Jubilee foursomes for the Prince of Wales Cup in the early Fifties when J.O. MacAndrew and Robert Walker, a President of the Seniors GS, saw their second shot rebound off the railway to within a yard of the pin. This beat the conventional four of Sir Charles MacAndrew and the then Willie Whitelaw.

HOLE 2 : **ROYAL PORTHCAWL**
Par 4, 447 yards
Second holes are either seen as stepping up the tempo after relatively modest beginnings or catching you on the rebound after

a stern start. Royal Porthcawl's second contains an element of these extremes but claims admirers as a classic individual hole so typical of the seaside. For stern challenge and scenic beauty, it is impossible to beat.

The sea is visible from every hole at Porthcawl, where many of the upland holes form avenues between gorse.

Second holes rivalling Porthcawl as a challenge are those at Royal Aberdeen, running invitingly downhill between giant sandhills, and that at St Andrews or Royal Lytham & St Annes, both of which command admiration and respect.

The ideal at Porthcawl is a wind off the sea brisk enough to ensure that a solid drive is necessary to clear the bunker yet controlled enough to establish a position on the left of the fairway, which possesses some attractive changes of level.

The perfect line of attack to the two-tiered green is from the left, frequently a long-iron or wood to carry the bunker on the approach and negotiate a putting surface set at a slight angle. Allow too much for the wind and the beach awaits; allow too little and the ball may be swept past the bunker guarding the right of the green and into the rough.

Second holes rarely witness the drama of those coming later in the round, though it is easy to burden a score irretrievably early on. Despite holding the 1961 Dunlop Masters, which Peter Thomson won by eight strokes, Porthcawl is more at home with matchplay events for amateurs.

HOLE 3 : **ROYAL WEST NORFOLK**
Par 4, 405 yards
Brancaster, the more familiar name for Royal West Norfolk, is an echo of the past; yet, in another sense, it was ahead of its time. In America, it is all the rage nowadays for new courses to have lakes framed by railroad ties, as they call them. But the fashion is merely a copy of the vast sleeper-faced bunkers made famous long ago at Prestwick, Westward Ho! and Brancaster.

The formidable example on Brancaster's third shapes the strategy for a hole that offers many options. Situated on a crest about 60 yards short of the green, the sleepered bunker determines whether a drive is good enough to attempt the green with a second shot or whether it must be laid up short, leaving a demanding pitch of which all you can see is the dark wall of sleepers and perhaps the top of the flag. It is the avoidance of that shot that prompts many ill-advised attempts at the impossible.

From start to finish, the hole is a wonderful test of nerve. The elbow in the fence line that flanks the marsh, which is such a unique feature of Brancaster, is a psychological landmark that seems to encourage a policy of safety first. Although two bunkers await those who over-indulge, the fairway width is generous enough to draw comparison with St Andrews but, as at St Andrews, the more cowardly the drive the sterner the shot that follows.

Much of Brancaster's appeal and fame surrounds the tidal marsh which comes into view on the narrow lane leading to the club. At the highest tides, the clubhouse can be marooned and an exciting dimension added by the water to the holes, particularly the eighth, which flank the marsh.

HOLE 4 : ROYAL DORNOCH
Par 4, 430 yards

Appeal, subtlety and deception are the ingredients of the greatness of the fourth at Royal Dornoch, the northernmost of the world's outstanding courses. Apart from its playing challenge, its appeal is largely scenic. The line from the tee can be fixed on the distant monument to the 1st Duke of Sutherland, but the hole itself lies in the lee of the vast bank of gorse, stretching a mile or more, which in summer, is a sea of gold.

Subtlety takes the form of the balance between power and control. The angled green is easier to hit with a seven-iron than a five-iron but the positioning of the drive is the key to the secrets of the second shot. Where deception plays its hand is in the large depression in front of the enormous green which tends to make it look nearer – hence the local saying " to choose a club, add two and you"ll still be short.

The gorse is a real threat to the hook and there are a number of grassy hollows between the gorse and the left edge of the fairway which then slopes gradually before flattening out on the right. Perfection is a case of just enough fade or roll though it is easily overdone; in which case, the lower ground to the right of the fairway takes over. This comprises a further series of humps and hollows which can soon put a dampener on thoughts of hitting a green.

One of the joys of links golf is the variety and type of shot that can be played into different greens, Dornoch's fourth acting as a shining example of that assortment. Even on a links, the seemingly universal preferences for the high dropping approach has gained momentum but the low, running shot still has its advocates and, on the fourth, the size and contouring of the green ensure that judgement of bounce remains an integral part of the game at the seaside.

HOLE 5 : ROYAL WORLINGTON & NEWMARKET
Par 3, 157 yards

It wouldn't do for all golf's short holes to be as severe as the fifth at Royal Worlington & Newmarket, but severity lies at the root of its fun and fame. It is also something of an architectural freak. A hole so designed today might be condemned out of hand.

The tee shot plays across the path of two other holes and it is perfectly possible for it to overshoot onto the eighth green which lies behind the familiar line of pine trees at the back of the green.

The fact that the hole has no bunkers does not in itself qualify it as freakish, although bunkerless holes are pretty rare. However, its other defences are so strong that it surely doesn't need them. Henry Longhurst described it "as perhaps the best short hole in Britain".

Numerically and actually, it is the centrepiece of the nine but it retains a remarkable freshness. It sets thoughts racing well in advance and never disappoints. A three is always to be prized, a sure sign that its challenge is demanding, yet fair.

HOLE 6 : CRUDEN BAY
Bluidy Burn, Par 5, 529 yards

Cruden Bay, on the Aberdeenshire coast, is not the fashionable place for holidays it once was. Much has changed but happily not the golf links, which were bought by the club in 1950 for £2,750 – a figure that is currently more representative of a good day's takings.

There are some wonderful holes amid turbulent hills and valleys, the fifth providing a notable prelude to the sixth – a par-five with many options as to how it can be tackled. Bluidy Burn speaks for itself, the centrepiece that dictates every policy, prefacing the best of all golfing decisions: "Can I, can't I? Shall I, shan't I?"

However, the sixth is more than just a long hole with a sting in the tail. Unless the drive is powerful and well-positioned, better players have no thought of getting home in two and, unless the drive and second shots of the poorer golfers are well-positioned, there is little prospect of getting home in three. For those on the sixth who believe in taking one step at a time, there is a fairway to the right beyond the burn, the disadvantage here being that the pitch is full of pitfalls.

Holes that push you on the defensive strike a dull note, but the sixth is the opposite, encouraging guarded aggression that lends the game its challenge, enjoyment and gambling streak. The stakes are high; the rewards great.

HOLE 7 : **TURNBERRY**
Roon The Ben, Par 5, 529 yards
In my ignorance during my first round on the Ailsa course in 1961, I interpreted Roon the Ben to mean round the bend. My Scottish ancestry should have told me that it meant round the mountain. However I still believe my version is the better because the hole is far more bend than mountain.

It is the classic dog-leg, inviting the age-old decision between daring and discretion. One of the earliest examples was the fourth at Prestwick where the central feature of the dog-leg is the Pow Burn. At Turnberry, it is the lovely, wild country, reinforcing low dunes, that provides the danger.

When people think of Turnberry, it is perhaps the fourth, eighth, ninth and 10th that first spring to mind. Each would be a candidate for any Dream Course but the seventh fits perfectly into the category of great par-fives. To be great, a par-five should be reachable in two for the best players under normal conditions but getting home in two should involve a risk, a thin line between success and failure.

In order to preserve the authenticity of the dog-leg, a new back tee was constructed

for the 1986 Open, a perch from which the scenic splendours of Turnberry are fully apparent. The line is close to the War Memorial on the distant hill above the 12th but most find it all they can manage to clear Wilson's Burn and get a sight of the green.

HOLE 8: **ROYAL TROON**
Postage Stamp, Par 3, 123 yards
It is believed that good things come wrapped in small parcels, Royal Troon's Postage Stamp is a splendid example. Golf course design is a question of moderation and balance. Any "perfect" lay-out should therefore include one short, short hole, a hole to tease and taunt, a test of judgment not strength. Included in such a category are the seventh at Royal Porthcawl and the 16th at Formby, but greater fame surrounds the Postage Stamp, which, for all its lack of yards, is a holy terror.

Yet the Club's history, by I. M. Mackintosh, reveals that when it was brought into play more than 80 years ago, "it was almost universally condemned in the West of Scotland as being a bad hole." The Glasgow Herald correspondent went further, classing it "the worst hole I ever saw". There have been refinements since then and modern equipment has made it easier to hold greens with high shots, but opinion has undoubtedly swung in its favour.

Not surprisingly, it has been at the centre of much drama in the Open, and its reputation is largely based on that, but it is a hole to be feared, respected and enjoyed by all. The size of the putting surface is the element which gives the hole its name, but the need for precision in any tee shot is also lent by the tight cluster of deep bunkers which surround it.

HOLE 9 : **ROYAL ST GEORGE'S**
Par 4, 389 yards
Whenever I play Royal St George's, which isn't often enough, the holes to which I look forward most are the ninth and 10th. Both are par fours and under 400 yards, rare in itself on Open Championship courses these days, and both therefore reachable in two under most circumstances for most people.

What is more, they run in opposite directions, so if one is downwind the other is against it; and if one is in the left to right wind, for the other it is right to left. Even downwind, the task of stopping a ball on the exposed, 10th green is a test of cunning, but the ninth is blessed with a green whose eccentric contouring makes the second shot just as much of a joyous puzzle.

The first thing to know is that any ball missing the green to the left will require the touch of an angel to get it anywhere near the flag. The left part of the green is high-sided and the putting surface very much longer than it is wide. In the middle, there is a hump which calls for precise judgement and away to the right a drop which can be exasperating. Many is the golfer who has approached the green thinking he has a putt for a birdie only to find he is chipping back up a sharp bank.

Few courses have undergone greater change in their history than Royal St George's, the ninth being no exception, though the current version is old enough for nobody to remember its predecessor.

The present green is actually the original 16th, a rare example of how a green can be adapted without modification to receive shots from an entirely different direction. It certainly explains its configuration, but I am sure it is a hole on which Greg Norman can look back fondly, the ninth featuring among the many birdies he had in his remarkable final round of 64 in winning the 1993 Open.

HOLE 10 : **MUIRFIELD**
Par 4, 475 yards

Reactions to reaching the turn run the gamut of emotions. Those who have prospered on the front nine are determined that the rot shall not set in, while those whose hopes and ambitions have been prematurely dashed look upon the 10th as offering a fresh start.

On the 10th of the Old at St Andrews, a short par-four, the powerful have the chance of driving the green. Sunningdale's Old course starts home from a tee that makes you feel on top of the world. Wentworth, on the other hand, has a short hole over the trees. Saunton (East) and Woodhall Spa are further examples where length is not everything, but Muirfield's 10th stretches you to the limit, though forward tees provide some respite.

Muirfield is fuller of fine holes than most courses, the first, sixth, ninth, 12th,

13th and 18th perhaps the pick. The ninth is certainly to be feared, causing a lowering of the guard for some surviving it unscathed. Even Arnold Palmer may have been guilty of this in the final round of the 1966 Open. Having reached the turn in 35, and hell bent in his pursuit of Jack Nicklaus, he drove into the rough on the 10th and, aiming a howitzer at the green, failed to get it launched. He left it in the rough not once but twice, a seven signalling that his threat had passed. Sadly, he never came as close again.

Nevertheless, its greens are full of subtle borrows that are hard to fathom, and the 10th is one such. The 10th's influence on the outcome of Open Championships has been profound, although, in his final round in 1980, the champion, Tom Watson, could afford a five, which is more than could be said of 1987 when seven of the first 10 in the finishing order – Nick Faldo excluded – dropped a stroke there on the last day.

So, let Jack Nicklaus, a professed lover of Muirfield, provide the footnote. In Norman Mair's recent book, *Muirfield, Home of the Honourable Company (1744-1994)*, he quotes him as describing the 10th as "a great hole, one of my all-time favourites". Anyone disposed to argue?

HOLE 11: **ROYAL LIVERPOOL**
Alps, Par 3, 200 yards

Hoylake's 11th inherited its name, Alps, from the old version of the hole. In that, it has much in common with the Maiden at Royal St George's, which used to consist of a tee shot over the giant sandhill bearing its name, a shot that would be regarded by many as formidable even today. In the era of hickory shafts and gutty balls, it must have been mind-blowing.

No doubt Hoylake, the second-oldest seaside links in England, took the title, Alps, from the similarly named 17th at Prestwick, although the scale of Hoylake's Alps is a little less grandiose. It was Harry Colt who sounded the death knell of the old hole during the 1920s when he gave Hoylake a decided facelift, his magic having the twin benefit of allowing the 12th to become one of the finest par fours anywhere. It was written that the old 11th hole "had little but its romantic name to commend it"; the new 11th, as with the

Maiden, being less contentious than its predecessor. It quickly became a force in its own right, blending easily into a landscape that elsewhere at Hoylake is largely flat.

Hoylake is a course of kops and out of bounds; the Alps possessing the latter, a fairly distant fence guarding the shore. But the 11th is also part of the stretch of four holes from the ninth which follows the coast and therefore enjoys views denied the start and finish.

The Dee estuary and its sands dominate the scene that encompasses Hilbre Island, a haven of birdlife, and the more distant Welsh hills. The Open Championship's departure means that, sadly, the world's top players are no longer as familiar with Hoylake as were generations of professionals long ago, but the freshness of the challenge remains – not least on the 11th which is an absolutely first-class short hole.

HOLE 12: **ST ANDREWS OLD COURSE**
Heathery In, Par 4, 316 yards

With the 12th on the Old course at St Andrews, appearances are deceptive. From the tee, it has a wide-eyed innocence that, hard on the heels of the terrors of the short 11th, is, at first, welcome. However, behind its bland looks lies a web of intrigue.

All fine golf courses should contain a short par·four with the capacity to offer a birdie or, occasionally, in feats of great daring, an eagle. In an age when some courses have no par fours under 400 yards, it is more important than ever. Variety and balance are essential ingredients but, to be a really memorable, short par four, there must be the capacity for disaster to strike if an incorrect decision is made or a slightly wayward shot hit. The margin for error must be slender.

There are hidden bunkers galore, particularly on what appears on the tee to be the perfect line to pursue. Incidentally, on a lighter side, it was into one of these that a distinguished naval member of the R&A disappeared many years ago when, having had his eye caught by two attractively trim young ladies on the nearby Eden course, his navigation failed. To complete his embarrassment, his trolley finished on top of him as he was "lost" with all hands!

On account of this minefield of bunkers, a wary path must be trodden. There are three options depending on your power, skill and the conditions prevailing. The most direct line is between the heathery hill on the left and one of the most central of the hidden bunkers which number about half a dozen. They are deep and devilish.

It is sometimes possible for the strongest and longest to carry the heathery hill but, for those whose horizons are more restricted, the best tactic is to play to the right – and as far right as you like – or to nestle in short of the hill on the left – one of the few safe havens.

HOLE 13 : **ROYAL COUNTY DOWN**
Par 4, 445 yards

One of the problems in writing about Royal County Down is that it exhausts the supply of superlatives.

If there is a top 10 of the most beautiful places where the game is played, it would be in it. Golfers come from far and wide to sample its scenic delights, but they are lured more by the challenge of a links which is relentless in its demands.

There are no poor holes, merely some which are less excellent than others. Tom Watson is an unashamed admirer, feeling that the first 13 holes are as tough a stretch as anywhere. His failure to extend the accolade to the last five is perhaps explained by the fact that they lack the imposing sense of avenues between mighty dunes although that is splitting hairs.

Newcastle, as it is familiarly known, is, above all, a supreme test of driving. If you miss the fairway, heather is sprinkled liberally as a contrast to the vast banks of gorse which adorn and stabilise the sandhills. Nowhere is the enclosed look, which gives each hole its own identity, more marked than on the 13th. With gorse everywhere, it is hard to focus from the tee on the narrow fairway as it funnels down at the distance of the best drives.

At 445 yards, it is a man-sized par four and a long drive can have the added advantage of being able to see the green from the landing area, the hill on the right jutting into the fairway at the point where the hole doglegs slightly.

Certainly, those opting for less adventure with the drive have to hit blind over the corner of the hill and the bunkers set into it; and the line is important (there is a marker post behind the green) since the approach to the green slopes from the right. The green itself is open on the right but the bunker on the left can have a strong, magnetic effect.

HOLE 14 : **ROYAL PORTRUSH**
Calamity Corner, Par 3, 213 yards

Calamity Corner and Purgatory (the 15th) at Royal Portrush are wonderfully evocative names, expressing the full punishment that both holes can inflict. Portrush is a noble links, two or three miles from another gem, Portstewart, and the other side of Belfast from Royal County Down, with which it is constantly compared.

Calamity Corner is a short hole of rare grandeur which, once seen, is never forgotten. There is occasionally a sense of helplessness against the wind at the realisation, on the tee, that it is all too much. To the right is a chasm, running diagonally, which becomes deeper the closer it gets to the green; to the left are a series of low hills which, if allowed to grow rough, can engulf as easily as a quicksand. The only ray of hope takes the form of a narrow 30-yard approach with the green angled to accentuate the drop to perdition on the right.

The fact that the green is slightly higher than the tee gives it an inviting look that makes it even more tantalising. The author of those calendars of horrifically impossible holes set across ravines must have got his ideas from Calamity Corner.

The nearest equivalent is perhaps the 15th at Turnberry, but the key feature, the drop on the right, is more alarming at Portrush. The best description of it comes from the late Patric Dickinson in his book *A Round of Golf Courses*. "A yard to the right and over you go, sheer down this grass cliff whose gradient must be 1:1. It is a romantic chasm, an opening of hell, and to escape from it, it is necessary to defy gravity, taking your stance almost like a fly on the wall and striking a rocket-shot up to the zenith of heaven."

HOLE 15: **ROYAL LYTHAM & ST ANNES**
Par 4, 468 yards

One factor shared by the Open Championship courses of the North-West of England is the severity of their last four holes. It is debatable which is the hardest;

Royal Lytham & St Annes, Royal Liverpool or Royal Birkdale. The 15th hole on all three would make a stout contribution to the Dream Course, as indeed would the 15th at Formby but, after a difficult choice, my preference is for Royal Lytham's.

It is a par four of formidable proportions, stretching even the mightiest to show their powers of flight, control and courage. In a Dream Course, the holes that precede and follow it are taken out of context, but in the reality of the Fylde coast, the biggest adjustment necessary on the 15th is one of judgement to fathom two shots in a direction not hitherto encountered in the round. In his foreword to Tony Nickson's history, *The Lytham Century*, Gerald Micklem asked the question: "How many people in the Open have gone out in 32 or less to return in 40 or more?" Then he conveniently supplied part of the answer. "It is just the sheer length of some of the par fours."

Royal Lytham relies heavily on fairway bunkers to supplement its defences and the 15th has two important ones to influence the drive. Fours on Lytham's 15th have won Opens and fives have lost them and never was the latter more true than in 1963 when Jack Nicklaus was chasing the crown of Arnold Palmer, who had won the title for the previous two years.

HOLE 16 : **ROYAL CINQUE PORTS, DEAL**
Par 5, 508 yards

Long ago, on the course at Machrie on the Island of Islay off the west coast of Scotland, there was a famous hole, now defunct, called Mount Zion. It was so named on account of its green standing isolated, stoutly defended and defiant, but it is a title that could appropriately be adopted by the 16th at Deal.

Unlike many greens at the seaside, it stands in full view from afar, though there is no hint of the strong contouring and mounding that bedevil the putting until the crest of the large bank in front of the green has been scaled. This is also the first indication of whether a very long second shot or a pitch has been kindly or cruelly treated by the bounce, but it doesn't take much playing of the hole to realise the huge advantage of being up on top.

The penalty for finishing just short, or rolling back down the slope, can be out of all proportion to the shortcomings of the attempt. There is a particularly nasty hollow at the front left of the green with an almost vertical wall in front of it from where a shot of ingenuity and invention is necessary to get it close to the flag.

There are few more satisfying greens to hit with a wood or, for the young lions, a long iron, but there is a clear need for the right gameplan to be adopted if a good drive is in play. The left-hand side near the green is well guarded by bunkers and dunes while the prospects of a recovery to a raised green from the rough and rushes on the right are not bright. It can be all you can do to find your ball.

It is not an easy fairway to hit, but there is great satisfaction when it is boldly accomplished. There is a raised plateau from which to survey the scene and compose the strategy. Often the hole is three full shots, an indication of the extremes of seaside golf. Downwind, it may even be a drive and mid-iron but the ideal is a crosswind or a slight headwind to accentuate the shot-making values and allow it to be seen in its full challenging glory.

HOLE 17 : **CARNOUSTIE**
The Island, Par 4, 455 yards
Drama, it seems, is more likely to unfurl on 17th holes than on 18ths. A book could be written about the Road Hole at St Andrews, while golfing history is liberally punctuated with tales of the penultimate holes at Hoylake and Royal Lytham. Turnberry's 17th brought joy to Nick Price in 1994, as did Muirfield's to Lee Trevino in 1972. However, by contrast to Trevino, Tony Jacklin will carry to his grave thoughts of what might have been.

All the holes mentioned would grace the Dream Course and there would be consideration for the 17th at Sunningdale (Old), Royal St George's and Hillside. Short holes feature prominently in the reckoning of fine 17ths; in passing, Javier Arana, the supreme Spanish architect, adopted the trademark of making the 17th a par-three on all his courses, a list that includes El Saler (Valencia), El Prat (Barcelona), La Galea (Bilbao) and Club de Campo (Madrid).

My idea of the perfect 17th is The Island at Carnoustie, it winning my confidence and vote on the grounds of the challenge of

the drive. It is a great and treacherous hole. No matter what the circumstances or conditions, it is an achievement to keep the ball out of the Barry Burn which coils like a serpent around the fairway.

On the Road Hole at St Andrews, players can, and do, go left from the tee and, though there is little to compare with the difficulties of the second shot, even it has been eroded somewhat by making recovery from the Road Bunker and the Road less fearsome than it used to be.

At Carnoustie, there is a feeling of unease on the tee which everyone senses; a feeling that would have been more publicised had the Open been held there in last 20 years.

HOLE 18 : **RYE**
Par 4, 438 yards
It is probably the majority view that the ideal finishing hole is a tough par four, a hole where glory beckons and disaster lurks. Members of such a category are the 18ths at Muirfield, Royal Troon, Carnoustie, Royal Lytham and St Annes, Woodhall Spa, Royal St George's, Royal Porthcawl, St Enodoc and Royal Cinque Ports.

All demand a drive with a touch of daring, a well judged second and a sure touch on the green. Sounds easy, although doing it when it matters is anything but. Was there ever a better illustration of finishing than Tony Jacklin at Lytham in the Open in 1969, Nick Faldo at Muirfield in 1987 (and again in 1992), or Tom Watson at Royal Birkdale in 1983?

A four to win the Open is the ultimate test, an experience of which we can only dream, but, if the Open had been held at Rye on a regular basis – (preferably in January!) – many stirring and sad tales would surround the 18th with its elevated fairway that can be mighty hard to hit. On account of the fact that I have played it in competition far more often than any other 18th, it wins my vote for the Dream Course finale.

A

CORNWALL, DEVON, CHANNEL ISLANDS

There is about the courses in this region an unmistakable air of holiday golf although it is thoroughly easy to appreciate how the members of Clubs heave a sigh of relief when the holiday-makers have gone for the year and they are left in peace.

For the historical contribution that its golfers have made to the game it is appropriate to start in Jersey where Harry Vardon and Ted Ray were born, Vardon in a cottage on the edge of Royal Jersey's Links at Grouville. It is remarkable that, of the tiny handful of British winners of the US Open, two were born within a mile or so of each on an island that represents a mere dot on the world map. Vardon, who did not take up the game until he was 21 and yet was Open chanpion four years later, forged his game on a course that begins along the shore of Grouville Bay under the watchful, distant eye of Mont Argeuil.

Elsewhere, particularly on the second nine, recent change has eliminated one or two architectural shortcomings but nothing compared to the new broom that has transformed La Moye, set on Jersey's exposed western headland. In less than 20 years, it has been turned from a test of sporting eccentricities into one which, given the aid of a stiff breeze, can have a field of top class professionals at full stretch.

Les Mielles, on St Ouen's Bay, is relatively new and there are plans for a Jersey Golf Centre just down the road from La Moye. Over the water on Guernsey, there has been no such upheaval on the charming Royal Guernsey which has to shoulder and satisfy almost the entire golfing demand of the community.

On the mainland, St Mellion and Bodmin have boosted the courses in Cornwall, a county whose traditional delights surround West Cornwall at Lelant, Trevose and St Enodoc, the latter with a fine new clubhouse on land purchased from the Duchy in their centenary year in 1990.

Local interest in Devon was given a boost when their men's team won the English Counties championship for the first time in 1985, a tribute to the courses on which many were raised.

East Devon, a sort of elevated seaside Sunningdale, is the pick in the South, the Manor House at Morehampstead dominates the central heart while Saunton and Royal North Devon guard the northern coast with justifiable pride. Saunton, which has always been one of my favourite spots, boasts arguably the best pair of courses in Britain, the West upgraded a year or two back to rival its neighbour – a regular and deserved choice for championships.

Across the estuary at Westward Ho!, Royal North Devon is an ageless monument, the oldest seaside course in England although one where invasion of the sea is proving hard to repel. Nevertheless, ground that may appear plain from a distance comes compellingly to life as the holes penetrate land that is full of character down nearer the famous Pebble Ridge. No golfer with a grain of romance in his soul should pass it by, particularly as journeys to that part of the world have been made so much simpler by a new road from Tiverton and by a new bridge that crosses the estuary at Bideford.

A hearty word, too, for Yelverton on the edge of Dartmoor, north of Plymouth and for Thurlestone and Churston; and there are the comparatively recent complexes at Dartmouth and Woodbury Common. Woodbury, near Budleigh Salterton, is now in the ownership of Nigel Mansell, an accomplished golfer, who has built his home there.

A1 Alderney

☎(01481) 822835
Routes des Carriers, Alderney,
Channel Islands
1 mile E of St Annes.
Undulating seaside course.
9 holes (18 tees), 2528 yards,
S.S.S.65
Designed by Frank Pennink.
Visitors: welcome at all times, except
competition days.
Green Fee: WD £12.50; WE £17.50.
Societies: catered for on weekdays

by arrangement and weekends for
special events.
Catering: by arrangement.
Hotels: Bellevue; Sea View;
Deveraux.

A2 Ashbury

☎(01837) 55453, Fax 55468
Higher Maddaford, Southcott,
Okehampton, Devon EX20 4NL
4 miles W of Okehampton, 0.5 mile N
of A3079 to Ashbury.

Moorland course.
18 holes, S.S.S.68; 18 holes Par 3,
2000 yards. Opening 1996 new 18
hole course.
Designed by D.J. Fenson.
Founded 1991
Visitors: welcome at all times; busy
most days, must book tee-off times.
Green Fee: WD £12, WE £15.
Societies: small societies welcome,
preferably pm; free golf at all times for
residential societies (see below).
Catering: full clubhouse facilities; bar

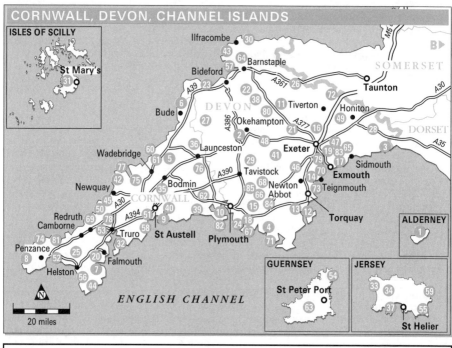

CORNWALL, DEVON, CHANNEL ISLANDS

ENGLISH CHANNEL

20 miles

KEY		17	East Devon	35	Lanhydrock (Bodmin	50	Perranporth	69	Tehidy Park
1	Alderney	18	Elfordleigh Hotel G &		G & CC)	51	Porthpean	70	Teignmouth
2	Ashbury		CC	36	Launceston	52	Praa Sands	71	Thurlestone
3	Axe Cliff	19	Exeter G & CC	37	Les Mielles Golf	53	Radnor Golf Centre	72	Tiverton
4	Bigbury	20	Falmouth		Centre	54	Royal Guernsey	73	Torquay
5	Bowood	21	Fingle Glen	38	Libbaton	55	Royal Jersey	74	Tregenna Castle
6	Bude and	22	Great Torrington	39	Looe	56	Royal Naval Air		Hotel
	N Cornwall	23	Hartland Forest Golf &	40	Lostwithiel G & CC		Station Culdrose	75	Treloy
7	Budock Vean		Leisure Park	41	Manor House Hotel &	57	Royal North Devon	76	Trethorne
	Hotel	24	Hele Park		Golf Course	58	St Austell	77	Trevose Country Club
8	Cape Cornwall G &	25	Helston Golf and	42	Merlin	59	St Clements	78	Truro
	CC		Leisure	43	Mortehoe &	60	St Enodoc	79	Warren
9	Carlyon Bay Hotel	26	Highbullen Hotel		Woolacombe	61	St Kew	80	Waterbridge
10	China Fleet Country	27	Holsworthy	44	Mullion	62	St Mellion	81	West Cornwall
	Club	28	Honiton	45	Newquay		International	82	Whitsand Bay Hotel
11	Chulmleigh	29	Hurdwick	46	Newton Abbot	63	St Pierre Park Hotel		Golf and Country Club
12	Churston	30	Ilfracombe		(Stover)	64	Saunton	83	Woodbury Park G &
13	Dainton Park	31	Isles of Scilly	47	Northbrook	65	Sidmouth		CC
14	Dartmoor G & CC	32	Killiow	48	Okehampton	66	Sparkwell	84	Wrangaton
15	Dinnaton	33	La Grande Mare	49	Padbrook Park	67	Staddon Heights	85	Yelverton
16	Downes Crediton	34	La Moye		(Cullompton)	68	Tavistock		

A beautiful 18 hole course overlooking the sea in South Devon

BIGBURY GOLF CLUB LIMITED

Bigbury, Kingsbridge, South Devon TQ7 4BB (01548) 810207

No golfer visiting the South Hams should miss the opportunity of playing at Bigbury. It's an ideal holiday course – challenging enough for low handicappers but not too daunting for the average golfer. There are outstanding views from almost everywhere on the course – with Dartmoor to the North, the river Avon running near a number of holes and breathtaking scenes of Bantham Beach and Burgh Island.

and bar snacks to 5pm every day. Indoor pool, sauna, solaria, snooker, indoor bowls, 10-pin bowling. **Hotels:** Ashbury GC; Manor House Hotel (Okehampton); both offer free golf for residents booking 3 nights.

A3 Axe Cliff

☎(01297) 20499, Sec 24371 Squires Lane, Axmouth, Seaton, Devon EX12 4AB Through village of Axmouth, along riverside, turn left just before Axmouth bridge and straight up lane. Coastal course one side, country the other. 18 holes, 4867 yards, S.S.S.64. Extension planned 1997. Founded 1892 **Visitors:** h/cap cert and membership of recognised club required; own clubs, no sharing; course closed until 11.00am Wed; with member only 12am-2pm Sat and 1pm-2pm Sun; competitions Sun before 11.30am. **Green Fee:** WD £17; WE & BH £19. **Societies:** welcome, must book in advance. **Catering:** bar and catering arrangements. **Hotels:** Shrubbery (Rousdon), Anchor (Beer).

A4 Bigbury

☎(01548) 810207, Sec 810557, Pro 810412. Bigbury-on-Sea, Kingsbridge, Devon TQ7 4BB Take A379 Plymouth-Kingsbridge road; turn right 2 miles from Modbury at Harraton Cross, signposted Bigbury-on-Sea; club is a further 5 miles from here. Undulating seaside course. 18 holes, 6048 yards, S.S.S.69. Designed by J.H. Taylor. Founded 1926 **Visitors:** welcome with h/cap certificate. **Green Fee:** WD £20; WE £24. **Societies:** welcome by prior arrangement. **Catering:** full facilities. **Hotels:** Thurlestone; Cottage Hotel (Hope Cove).

A5 Bowood

☎(01840) 213017, Fax 212622 Bowood Park, Valley Truckle, Camelford, Cornwall PL32 9RT A39 through Camelford to Valley Truckle, then right onto B3266 Boscastle-Tintagel road, 1st left after garage towards Lanteglos; entrance 0.5 mile on left. Parkland course with woodland and numerous ponds and lakes. 18 holes, 6692 yards, S.S.S.72 Founded June 1992 **Visitors:** welcome, starting times can be booked. **Green Fee:** £20 per round, £30 per day. **Societies:** catered for by prior arrangement. **Catering:** full facilities. Driving range, practice areas. **Hotels:** Lanteglos, Cornish Arms.

A6 Bude and N Cornwall

☎(01288) 352006 (Sec), Catering 353176, Pro 353635, Fax 356855 Burn View, Bude, Cornwall EX23 8DA A39, 1 minute from town centre. Seaside links course. 18 holes, 6205 yards, S.S.S.70 Designed by Tom Dunn. Founded 1891 **Visitors:** 1st tee reserved for members until 9.30am, 12.30pm-2pm, 5pm-6.30pm; times may be booked in advance. **Green Fee:** WD £20; WE £25. **Societies:** welcome; 1st tee can be reserved (Mon-Fri). **Catering:** wide selection of meals available throughout the day. **Hotels:** Camelot; Grosvenor; Falcon; Penarvor; Burn Court; Chough; Cliff; Langfield Manor; Stamford Hill.

A7 Budock Vean Hotel

☎(01326) 250288 Nr Mawnan Smith, Falmouth, Cornwall TR11 5LG On main road between Falmouth and Helston; head for Mabe then go through Mawnan Smith; golf course approx 1.5 miles on right. Undulating parkland course.

9 holes (18 tees), 5222 yards, S.S.S.65 Designed by James Braid, D. Cook and P.H. Whiteside. Founded 1932 **Visitors:** welcome with h/cap certs; phone for start time am only. **Green Fee:** WD & Sat £14; Sun & BH £18. **Societies:** on application. **Catering:** snacks, lunch and table d'hote or a la carte dinner. Snooker, swimming, tennis. **Hotels:** Budock Vean.

A8 Cape Cornwall Golf & Country Club

☎(01736) 788611 (Club/fax) Cape Cornwall, St Just, Penzance, Cornwall TR19 7NL A3071 to St Just-in-Penwith, turn left at memorial clock, 1 mile down road on left. Coastal parkland course. 18 holes, 5650 yards, S.S.S.68 Founded May 1990 **Visitors:** welcome except Sat and Sun between 8am and 11.30am. **Green Fee:** WD £20 per round, £25 per day; WE £20. **Societies:** welcome by arrangement. **Catering:** full bar all week, lunch 12am-2pm, dinner 7-10pm Wed-Sat (winter), every day (summer). Indoor heated pool, sauna, solarium, snooker, gym, practice area, putting green, on site accommodation.

A9 Carlyon Bay Hotel

☎(01726) 812304, Tee times 814228, Fax 814938. Carlyon Bay, St Austell, Cornwall PL25 3RD Main Plymouth-Truro road 1 mile W of St Blazey. Clifftop/parkland course. 18 holes, 6463 yards, S.S.S.71 Designed by J. Hamilton Stutt. Founded 1926 **Visitors:** h/cap certs required; ring for starting times. **Green Fee:** WD £20; WE £25. **Societies:** welcome by arrangement. **Catering:** full facilities. **Hotels:** Carlyon Bay.

A10 China Fleet Country Club

☎(01752) 848668, Fax 848456.
Saltash, Cornwall PL12 6LJ
1 mile from Tamar Bridge, leave A38
before tunnel and follow signs.
Parkland course.
18 holes, 6551 yards, S.S.S.72
Designed by Martin Hawtree.
Founded June 1991
Visitors: welcome by prior arrangement only.
Green Fee: WD £20; WE £25.
Societies: by arrangement with Sec (golf).
Catering: full facilities.
Driving range.
Hotels: accommodation available; off-peak packages; telephone for details.

A11 Chulmleigh

☎(01769) 580519
Leigh Rd, Chulmleigh, N Devon EX18 7BL
From Barnstaple follow Tourist Route Exeter signs; from Exeter follow A377 Crediton road, continue through Crediton, after approx 12 miles turn right into Chulmleigh.
Meadowland course.
18 holes, 1450 yards, S.S.S.54; winter (Dec-Mar), 9 holes, 2360 yards, S.S.S.56
Designed by J.W.D. Goodban OBE.
Founded 1976
Visitors: welcome.
Green Fee: £5.50.
Societies: welcome by prior arrangement.
Catering: light snacks, licensed bar.
Hotels: Thelbridge Cross Inn; Cottage available that sleeps 4; telephone for details.

A12 Churston

☎(01803) 842751 (Sec), Club 842218, Fax 845738.
Churston, Nr Brixham, Devon TQ5 0LA
On A379 3 miles from Paignton.
Downland course overlooking Torbay.
18 holes, 6219 yards, S.S.S.70
Designed by H.S. Colt.
Founded 1890
Visitors: members of recognised golf clubs only; h/cap certs required.
Green Fee: WD £22; WE £27.
Societies: welcome by prior arrangement.
Catering: bar and dining room facilities available all day.
Hotels: Broadsands Links.

A13 Dainton Park

☎(01803) 813812
Ipplepen, Newton Abbot, Devon TQ12 5TN
On A381 Newton Abbot-Totnes road.
Parkland course.
18 holes, 6207 yards, S.S.S.71
Designed by Adrian Stiff.
Founded 1993
Visitors: welcome, pay-as-you-play, booking advisable up to 4 days in advance; usual dress standards apply.
Green Fee: WD £12; WE £15.
Societies: welcome.
Catering: full facilities.
Driving range.

A14 Dartmouth Golf & Country Club

☎(01803) 712686, Fax 712628
Blackawton, Totnes, Devon TQ9 7DG
Off A3122 between Totnes and Dartmouth, 5 miles W of Dartmouth.
Moorland/parkland course.
18 holes, 7191 yards, SSS 74; 9 holes, 2583 yards, SSS 65.
Designed by Jeremy Pern.
Founded 1992
Visitors: requested to book starting times at the club and produce h/cap certs.
Green Fee: WD £26 per round, £32 per day; WE £32 per round, £35 per day.
Societies: Mon-Fri, phone for confirmation of date, start times, fees etc.
Catering: bar meals, restaurant, lounge/spike bar; function room for 240.
Hotels: Fingals (Dittisham).

A15 Dinnaton

☎(01752) 892512, 892452, Golf shop 691288, Fax 698334
Dinnaton Sporting and Country Club, Ivybridge, Devon PL21 9HU
At A38 Ivybridge follow Dinnaton Golf signs.
Parkland course.
9 hole, twin tee, 4089 yards, S.S.S.59
Founded 1989
Visitors: welcome at all times.
Green Fee: WD £10; WE £12.50.
Societies: welcome at all times by arrangement.
Catering: Club bar, coffee lounge, Haywain restaurant.
Driving nets, badminton, squash, volleyball, solarium, sauna, fitness suite, pool, tennis, snooker.
Hotels: accommodation on site; telephone for details.

A16 Downes Crediton

☎(01363) 773025 (Sec), Clubhouse 773991, Pro 774464
The Clubhouse, Hookway, Crediton, Devon EX17 3PT
Off A377 Exeter-Crediton road, 8 miles NW of Exeter; turn off at Crediton railway station (by Shell garage), then left at crossroads towards Hookway.
Parkland/meadowland course with water features.
18 holes, 5859 yards, S.S.S.68
Founded 1976
Visitors: welcome by arrangement, telephone Sec or Pro; h/cap cert required or proof of membership of recognised club.
Green Fee: WD £16; WE £22.
Societies: welcome by appointmenti.
Catering: coffee, breakfast, lunch, dinners available.
Hotels: Rosemont, New Inn (Coleford), Taw Vale GH (Crediton)

A17 East Devon

☎(01395) 443370, Pro 445195
North View Rd, Budleigh Salterton, Devon, EX12 2JB
5 miles E of Exmouth on A376.
Heathland seaside course.
18 holes, 6239 yards, S.S.S.70
Founded 1902
Visitors: welcome with letter of introduction.
Green Fee: WD £25; WE £30.
Societies: welcome by prior arrangement.
Catering: full facilities every day from 10am.

A18 Elfordleigh Hotel Golf & Country Club

☎(01752) 336428 (Pro), Sec 348425, Fax 344581.
Colebrook, Plympton, Plymouth, Devon PL7 5EB
Off A38, 5 miles NE of Plymouth, 2 miles from Marsh Mills roundabout.
Undulating parkland course.
9 holes (18 tees), 5664 yards, S.S.S.67
Designed by J.H. Taylor.
Founded 1932
Visitors: weekdays unrestricted, weekends phone first; h/cap cert required.
Green Fee: on application
Societies: weekdays, telephone in advance.
Catering: full facilities.
Swimming, snooker, squash, tennis etc.
Hotels: Elfordleigh.

A19 Exeter Golf & Country Club

☎(01392) 874139 (Tel/Fax)
Countess Wear, Exeter, Devon EX2 7AE
Topsham road off Countess Wear roundabout.
Parkland course.
18 holes, 6000 yards, S.S.S.69
Designed by James Braid.
Founded 1929
Visitors: welcome on weekdays with h/cap cert.
Green Fee: £22.
Societies: Thurs only by arrangement.
Catering: lunch and evening meals all week.
Snooker, indoor and outdoor swimming pools, tennis courts, squash, fitness centre.
Hotels: Devon Motel; Countess Wear Lodge; Buckerell Lodge.

A20 Falmouth

☎(01326) 311262 (Sec/fax), Pro 316229
Swanpool Road, Falmouth, Cornwall TR11 5BQ
0.5 mile W of Swanpool Beach, Falmouth, on road to Maenporth.
Seaside parkland course.
18 holes, 5680 yards, S.S.S.68
Founded 1928
Visitors: welcome, h/caps required.
Green Fee: £20 per round, £25 per day, £90 per week.
Societies: welcome by written application; 4 weeks notice required.
Catering: bar, lunch and tea all week, evening meals by arrangement.
Driving range..
Hotels: Royal Duchy; St Michael's; Penmere Manor; Greenlawns; Falmouth Beach; Meudon Vean; Park Grove; Falmouth: all offer reduced fees or free golf and golfing breaks/packages.

A21 Fingle Glen

☎(01647) 61817, Fax 61135
Fingle Glen Family Golf Centre, Tedburn St Mary, Nr Exeter, Devon EX6 6AF
4 miles from Exeter on A30 to Okehampton, 400 yards from Fingle Glen junction.
Public parkland course.
9 holes, 2483 yards, S.S.S.63
Designed by W. Pile.
Founded July 1989
Visitors: welcome.
Green Fee: WD £6 (9 holes), £10 (18 holes); WE £8.50 (9 holes), £13.50 (18 holes).
Societies: welcome.
Catering: bar, lounge, restaurant, 10am-10pm.
Driving range, fishing by arrangement.
Hotels: own 9-bed hotel; golfing breaks/packages available.

A22 Great Torrington

☎(01805) 622229
Weare Trees, Torrington, Devon EX38 7EZ
1 mile from Torrington on Weare Giffard road.
Undulating commonland course.
9 holes, 4418 yards, S.S.S.62
Founded 1932
Visitors: welcome except Sat and Sun am.
Green Fee: £10.
Societies: by arrangement except Sat and Sun am.
Catering: full meals by arrangement.

A23 Hartland Forest Golf & Leisure Park

☎(01237) 431442, 431448, Fax 431777
Woolsery, Bideford, Devon EX39 5RA
6 miles S of Clovelly off A39.
Parkland course.
18 holes 6015 yards, S.S.S.69
Designed by John Hepplewhite.
Founded 1987
Visitors: no restrictions except acceptable standard of golf.
Green Fee: £15 per round, £20 per day, £75 a week (Special rates for residents).
Societies: by prior arrangement
Catering: bar and restaurant.
Swimming, snooker, pool, tennis, fishing.
Hotels: 34 units of accommodation available on site sleeping 130.

A24 Hele Park

☎(01626) 336060
Ashburton Road, Newton Abbot, Devon, TQ12 6JN
From Newton Abbot take the Plymouth road and the club is on Ashburton Road one mile outside town
Parkland course with water features
9 holes 5000 yards S.S.S. 65
Founded 1993
Designed by M Craig
Visitors: welcome; pay as you play
Green Fee: WD £6.50 (9 holes), £11 (18 holes); WE £8.50 (9 holes),
£13.50 (18 holes).
Societies: welcome weekdays.
Corporate days.
Catering: full facilities
Driving range, indoor teaching studio

A25 Helston Golf and Leisure

☎(01326) 572518
Wendron, Helston, Cornwall TR13 0LX
1 mile N of Helston on B3297 Redruth road.
Short park and downland course, holes 70-170 yards, duration 2 hrs.
18 holes, 2000 yards, Par 3
Founded 1988
Visitors: welcome any time, open daily year round 9 am to dusk (7 am summer)
Green Fee: £5 pay and play.
Societies: Mon-Sat before 11 am or after 5 pm, book in advance.
Catering: at Homestead Bar.
Crazy golf, tennis, croquet, boule, horseshoes, crown bowls.
Hotels: Angel; Gwealdues; Nansloe Manor. Self catering accommodation.

A26 Highbullen Hotel

☎(01769) 540561, Fax 540492
Chittlehamholt, Umberleigh, Devon EX37 9HD
10 mins W on A361 from South Molton.
Parkland course.
18 holes, 5700 yards, S.S.S.68
Designed by Hugh Neil. New extension by M Neil & H. Stutt Design.
Founded 1960
Visitors: welcome.
Green Fee: £8 per day.
Catering: full hotel facilities.
Full leisure facilities.
Hotels: Highbullen.

A27 Holsworthy

☎(01409) 253177
Kilatree, Holsworthy, N Devon, EX22 6LP
1.5 miles W of Holsworthy on A3072 Bude road.
Parkland course.
18 holes, 6059 yards, S.S.S.69
Founded 1937
Visitors: welcome except Sun am.
Green Fee: WD £15; WE £20.
Societies: welcome by arrangement.
Catering: bar; dining facilities.
Practice area.
Hotels: Coles Mill; Court Barn (Clawton).

SALSTON MANOR HOTEL
Ottery St Mary, Near Exeter
Devon EX11 1RQ

A FIVE COURSE MENU IN EAST DEVON
Woodbury Park, Honiton, Sidmouth, Budleigh Salterton, Axe Cliff

A warm welcome awaits with En suite Rooms,
Indoor Heated Swimming Pool, Squash, Sauna, Solarium
and plenty of interest for Golfing Widows.

For Golfing Breaks, phone or Fax us now on: (01404) 815581

A28 Honiton
☎(01404) 44422 (Sec), Pro/Fax 42943, Bar & **Catering:** 47167 Middlehills, Honiton, Devon EX14 8TR
2 miles S of Honiton on minor road from town centre, past railway station and up steep hill signposted Northleigh and Seaton; caravans should approach from A35.
Parkland course.
18 holes, 5902 yards, S.S.S.68
Founded 1896
Visitors: members of a recognised golf club welcome any time except competition days.
Green Fee: WD £20; WE £23.
Societies: Thurs
Catering: lunch, high tea and dinner, except Sun.
Touring caravan park for golfers.
Hotels: Deer Park Hotel; Heathfield.

A29 Hurdwick
☎(01822) 612746
Tavistock Hamlets, Tavistock, Devon PL19 8PZ
1 mile N of Tavistock on road to Brentor.
Parkland course.
18 holes, 4628 yards, S.S.S.62
Designed by Hawtree.
Founded Aug 1990
Visitors: welcome.
Green Fee: £12 .
Societies: welcome.
Catering: snacks.
Hotels: Bedford (Tavistock); Castle Inn (Lydford).

A30 Ilfracombe
☎(01271) 862176, Fax 867731
Hele Bay, Ilfracombe, N Devon EX34 9RT
On A399 Ilfracombe to Combe Martin road.
Undulating heathland course with spectacular views over sea and moors.
18 holes, 5893 yards, S.S.S.69
Designed by T.K. Weir
Founded 1892
Visitors: welcome; start sheets April-Oct; h/cap certificate preferred.
Green Fee: WD £17 per day; WE

£20 per day £75 Mon-Fri 5 day ticket.
Societies: by arrangement with Sec.
Catering: normal bar; full time catering.
Pool table.
Hotels: Avalon, Cliff Hydro, Collingdale, Floyd, St Brannock's, St Helier, Wembley, Woodlands.

A31 Isles of Scilly
☎(01720) 422692
St Mary's, Isles of Scilly, TR21 0NF
1.5 miles from Hugh Town in St Mary's.
Moorland/seaside course.
9 holes, 6001 yards, S.S.S.69
Designed by Horace Hutchinson.
Founded 1904
Visitors: welcome Mon-Sat. Ring one hour before.
Green Fee: £15 per day.
Catering: available.

A32 Killiow
☎(01872) 70246, Pro 40915
Killiow, Kea, Nr Truro, Cornwall TR3 6AG
Leave Truro on A39 Truro/Falmouth road; turn right at 1st roundabout 3 miles from Truro, clearly signposted thereafter.
Picturesque parkland course.
18 holes, 3829 yards, S.S.S.59
Founded 1987
Visitors: welcome at all times; course restricted for members' use until 10.30am weekends and Bank Holidays; in main season advisable to ring for availability.
Green Fee: £10.
Catering: Lounge bar
Hotels: Hospitality Hotels (St Agnes).

A33 La Grande Mare
☎(01481) 53544
Vazon Bay, Castel, Guernsey, CI GY5 7LL
On West coast of island
Seaside course
18 holes, 5026 yards, S.S.S. 63
Visitors: welcome except on comp and corporate days.
Green Fee: £25 per day
Societies: welcome

Catering: full facilities on site
Hotels: La Grande Mare on site

A34 La Moye
☎(01534) 43401 (Sec/Manager), Course ranger: 47166, Pro 43130, Fax 42789
La Moye, St Brelade, Jersey, Channel Islands, JE3 8GQ
From airport turn right at crossroads, follow main road to main junction, turn right at crossroads; club about 1 mile down road, private lane on right.
Links course.
18 holes, 6741 yards, S.S.S.72
Founded 1902
Visitors: welcome 9.30-11.30am, 2.30-4pm except competition days; must have h/cap cert.
Green Fee: £35 per round, £55 per day (incl. lunch).
Societies: on request.
Catering: full restaurant facilities.
Practice ground, indoor practice net, driving range.
Hotels: Atlantic; L'Horizon; Le Chalet etc.

A35 Lanhydrock (Bodmin Golf & Country Club)
☎(01208) 73600, Fax 77325
Lostwithiel Rd, Bodmin, Cornwall PL30 5AQ
1 mile S of Bodmin, easy access from B3268 via A38/A30 Bodmin/Liskeard road.
Parkland course.
18 holes, 6185 yards, S.S.S.69
Designed by J. Hamilton Stutt.
Founded 1990
Visitors: welcome.
Green Fee: WD £24; WE £33
Societies: welcome on application (weekend dates available).
Catering: full facilities
Driving range opening 1996.

A36 Launceston
☎(01566) 773442
St Stephens, Launceston, Cornwall PL15 8HF
1 mile N of Launceston on Bude road (B3254).
Parkland course.

LANHYDROCK GOLF CLUB
for
CONNOISSEURS OF FINE GOLF

ACCOMMODATION AVAILABLE
for further details & bookings contact:
LANHYDROCK GOLF CLUB
Lostwithiel Road, Bodmin, Cornwall.
Tel: 01208 73600

18 holes, 6407 yards, S.S.S.71
Designed by J. Hamilton Stutt.
Founded 1927
Visitors: welcome weekdays by arrangement.
Green Fee: £20.
Societies: Mon-Fri by arrangement.
Catering: available by arrangement.
Hotels: White Hart.

A37 Les Mielles Golf Centre
☎(01534) 82787
The Mount, Valde la Mare, St Ouen's, Jersey, Channel Islands
In the middle of St Ouen's Bay.
Public seaside course
12 holes, 4200 yards, S.S.S.60
Founded 1976
Visitors: welcome.
Green Fee: apply for details.
Societies: welcome weekdays by prior arrangement.
Catering: cafeteria.
Driving range.
Hotels: Lobster Pot; La Place.

A38 Libbaton
☎(01769) 560269, Pro 560167, Fax 560342
High Bickington, Umberleigh, N Devon EX37 9BS
On B3217 1 mile through High Bickington towards Winkleigh, adjacent to A377 Barnstaple-Crediton road.
Parkland course.
18 holes, 6494 yards, S.S.S.72
Founded 1988
Visitors: welcome.
Green Fee: WD £14 per round, £18 per day; WE £16 per round, £20 per day.
Societies: welcome Mon, Tues, Wed, Fri; society package (golf and food) £27.50 per head.
Catering: food all day
Driving range, trout fishing.
Hotels: Beaford House; Northcote Manor.

A39 Looe
☎(01503) 240239 (Sec/fax)
Bin Down, Looe, Cornwall PL13 1PX

3 miles E of Looe.
Downland/parkland course.
18 holes, 5940 yards, S.S.S.68
Designed by Harry Vardon.
Founded 1934
Visitors: welcome 7 days per week.
Green Fee: £18 per round, £24 per day. 5 and 7 day tickets available.
Societies: welcome, arranged to suit requirements.
Catering: refreshments all day.
Shop, tuition available

A40 Lostwithiel Golf & Country Club
☎(01208) 873550, Greenkeepers: 872061, Fax 873479
Lower Polscoe, Lostwithiel, Cornwall PL22 0HQ
On A390 12 miles W of Liskeard, signposted.
Parkland course.
18 holes, 5984 yards, S.S.S.72
Designed by Stewart Wood R.I.B.A.
Founded 1991
Visitors: welcome with current h/cap cert; booking advised for starting time.
Green Fee: WD £18; WE £20.
Societies: welcome, not Bank Holidays.
Catering: bar and bar snacks all day; restaurant evenings and Sun lunch.
Tennis, indoor pool
Hotels: Lostwithiel G & CC on course; golf inclusive bargain breaks available.

A41 Manor House Hotel & Golf Course
☎(01647) 440355, 440961, Course ranger: 440998
Moretonhampstead, Newton Abbot, Devon TQ13 8RE
M5-A30-A382 or M5-B3212, on Dartmoor National Park, 17 miles from Exeter.
Parkland/moorland course.
18 holes, 6016 yards, S.S.S.69
Designed by J.F. Abercromby.
Founded 1934
Visitors: welcome by arrangement.
Green Fee: WD £22.50 per round, £30 per day; WE £28 per round, £35 per day.

Societies: catered for 7 days by arrangement.
Catering: full facilities.
Fishing, game and lake, croquet, tennis, snooker, driving range, Par 3 6 hole practice ground.
Hotels: Manor House Hotel and Golf Course.

A42 Merlin
☎(01637) 880257, Fax 881057
Mawgan Porth, Newquay, TR8 4AD
Mawgan Porth to St Eval road.
Links type course.
18 holes, 5227 yards, S.S.S. 67
Designed by Ross Oliver
Founded July 1991
Visitors: welcome any time.
Green Fee: WD £7; WE £10.
Societies: parties of 12 or more by arrangement.
Catering: at Merrymoor Inn and Falcon Inn. Club house opening 1996
Floodlit driving range: 6 bays.
Hotels: White Lodge, Tredragon (Golf packages).

A43 Mortehoe & Woolacombe
☎(01271) 870225 Course Owners, Sec 870745
Easewell, Mortehoe, N Devon EX34 7EH
Take Mortehoe turning on main Mullacott Cross to Woolacombe road; course approx. 1 mile on right, just before village of Mortehoe.
Open parkland course, views of sea from every tee and green.
9 holes (18 tees), 4638 yards, S.S.S.63
Designed by Hans Ellis.
Founded Jan 1992
Visitors: welcome at all times; no restrictions.
Green Fee: £6 (9 holes), £10 (18 holes).
Societies: welcome at all times, terms by negotiation.
Catering: full catering
Practice nets, putting green, indoor swimming pool.
Hotels: Woolacombe Bay; The Cleave; Watersmeet; camping facilities on site.

A44 **Mullion**

☎(01326) 240685 (Sec), Clubhouse 240276, Pro 241176
Cury, Helston, Cornwall TR12 7BP
5 miles from Helston on A3083 Lizard road.
Links and clifftop course.
18 holes, 6022 yards, S.S.S.69
Founded 1895
Visitors: welcome, h/cap required.
Green Fee: £20 per day, £70 for 5 days
Societies: welcome.
Catering: bar snacks, restaurant.
Hotels: Polurrian; Mullion Cove; Mullion Holiday Park; Cornwallis (St Ives).

A45 **Newquay**

☎(01637) 874354 (Tel/Fax), Pro 874830
Tower Rd, Newquay, Cornwall TR7 1LT
From ring road down Tower Rd to end, adjacent to Fistral beach.
Seaside course.
18 holes, 6136 yards, S.S.S.69
Designed by H.S. Colt.
Founded 1890
Visitors: welcome.
Green Fee: £20
Societies: weekdays, minimum 12 persons
Catering: full facilities.
Tennis, snooker, gym.
Hotels: Bristol; Barrowfield; Palma Nova.

A46 **Newton Abbot (Stover)**

☎(01626) 52460
Bovey Rd, Newton Abbot, S Devon TQ12 6QQ
On A382 Newton Abbot-Bovey Tracey road, N of Newton Abbot.
Parkland course.
18 holes, 5862 yards, S.S.S.68
Designed by James Braid
Founded 1931
Visitors: must be introduced or have proof of membership of recognised club.
Green Fee: £22
Societies: Thurs only, minimum 24.
Catering: full catering daily from 10.30am.
Hotels: Edgemoor, Dolphin (Bovey Tracey).

A47 **Northbrook**

☎(01392) 57436
Topsham Rd, Exeter, Devon EX2 6EU

From M5 junction 30 take A379; at 1st roundabout take 3rd exit onto B3182 Topsham road, course 0.5 mile on left.
Public, wooded parkland course.
18 holes, 1078 yards, S.S.S.54
Founded 1968
Visitors: open to all, Pay-as-you-Play.
Green Fee: £2 per round (clubs provided).
Catering: vending and confectionery.

A48 **Okehampton**

☎(01837) 52113, Fax 52724
Okehampton, Devon EX20 1EF
A30 to Okehampton centre from where club is clearly signposted.
Undulating moorland course.
18 holes, 5243 yards, S.S.S.67
Founded 1913
Visitors: weekdays only
Green Fee: £16.
Societies: welcome.
Catering: available.

A49 **Padbrook Park (Cullompton)**

☎(01884) 38286, Fax 34359
Padbrook Park, Cullompton, Devon EX15 1RU
1 mile from M5 Junction 28.
Parkland course; pay-as-you-play.
9 holes (double tees), 6108 yards, S.S.S.70.
Designed by Bob Sandow
Founded 1991
Visitors: welcome at all times.
Green Fee: WD £7 (9 holes), £10 (18 holes); WE £8 (9 holes), £16 (18 holes).
Societies: welcome by prior arrangement.
Catering: bar and catering all day.
Full practice facilities, 3-rink indoor bowling arena, fishing lake and nature trail.
Hotels: can be arranged through manager.

A50 **Perranporth**

☎(01872) 573701 (Sec), Club 572454, Pro 572317
Budnic Hill, Perranporth, Cornwall TR6 0AB
A3075 from Newquay then B3285; club is on fringe of town adjacent to beach.
Links course with panoramic sea views.
18 holes, 6208 yards, S.S.S.72
Designed by James Braid.
Founded 1929

Visitors: welcome but ring before arrival.
Green Fee: WD £20; WE £25.
Societies: welcome by prior arrangement.
Catering: 7 days a week from 7 am.
Hotels: Beach Dunes; Dunsmere.

A51 **Porthpean**

☎(01726 64613)
Porthpean, St Austell, Cornwall PL26 6AY
1.5 miles out of St Austell on the by pass turn off for Porthpean
Cliff top/ parkland course
9 holes (extended to 18 in 1996)
6532 yards, S.S.S. 72
Founded Aug 1992
Designed by R Oliver/ A Leather
Visitors: welcome
Green Fee: £6.50 (9 holes), £10 (18 holes)
Societies: welcome
Catering: Bar and light lunches

A52 **Praa Sands**

☎(01736) 763445, Fax 763399
Germoe Crossroads, Praa Sands, Penzance, Cornwall TR20 9TQ
7 miles E of Penzance on A394.
Scenic seaside parkland course.
9 holes, 4104 yards, S.S.S.60
Founded May 1971
Visitors: welcome except Sunday am.
Green Fee: £15 (18 holes).
Societies: welcome by prior arrangement.
Catering: open all day for meals or snacks.
Pool, darts.
Hotels: Mount Prospect (Penzance); Lobster Pot (Mousehole); Praa Sands.

A53 **Radnor Golf Centre**

☎(01209) 211059
Radnor Road, Redruth, Cornwall.
2 miles NE of Redruth, signposted from A3047 – the old Redruth by-pass and North Country Cross roads.
Public heathland type course created on derelict land.
9 holes Par 3, 1326 yards.
Designed by Gordon Wallbank.
Founded 1988
Visitors: no restrictions but own clubs required; phone first.
Green Fee: £4.80 (9 holes), £7.50 (18 holes).
Catering: bar.
Driving range, indoor ski training machine, snooker.

A54 Royal Guernsey
☎(01481) 47022, Sec 46523, Pro 45070, Fax 43960
L'Ancresse Vale, Guernsey, Channel Islands
3 miles from St Peter Port.
Seaside course.
18 holes, 6206 yards, S.S.S.70
Designed by Mackenzie Ross.
Founded 1890
Visitors: not after 12am Thurs and Sat; not Sun:h/cap cert required.
Green Fee: £28 (£18 with member).
Societies: small societies on application between Oct and Mar.
Catering: morning coffee, afternoon tea, lunch, evening meals Tues-Sat.
Driving range, snooker.
Hotels: Pembroke; L'Ancresse Lodge.

A55 Royal Jersey
☎(01534) 854416, Sec 851042, Pro 852234, Fax 854684
Grouville, Jersey, Channel Islands
4 miles E of St Helier on road to Gorey.
Seaside course.
18 holes, 6059 yards, S.S.S.70
Founded 1878
Visitors: welcome weekdays after 10am, weekends and Bank Holidays after 2.30pm (BST) or 12.30pm (GMT).
Green Fee: WD £35; WE £40.
Societies: small parties only.
Catering: full facilities by prior arrangement with Steward.
Hotels: Beachcomber; Grouville Bay.

A56 Royal Naval Air Station Culdrose
☎(01326) 574121 extn 2413
RNAS Culdrose, Helston, Cornwall TR12 8QY
2.5 miles from Helston on Lizard road.
Part of military airfield; members only.
11 holes (18 tees), S.S.S.71
Founded 1962
Visitors: through Sec or as guest of member, daily play restricted to weekends and leave periods.
Green Fee: on application

A57 Royal North Devon
☎(01237) 473817 (Sec), Clubhouse 473824
Golf Links Rd, Westward Ho!, Bideford, Devon EX39 1HD
From Northam village take the road down Bone Hill past the P.O. keeping left; clubhouse is visible from the hill.

Links course.
18 holes, 6662 yards, S.S.S.72
Designed by Tom Morris.
Founded 1864
Visitors: welcome; booking required.
Green Fee: £24 per round, £28 per day.
Societies: by booking.
Catering: full facilities.
Snooker.
Hotels: Culloden House; Durrant House; Anchorage.

A58 St Austell
☎(01726) 74756 (Sec), Clubhouse 72649, Pro 68621.
Tregongeeves Lane, St Austell, Cornwall PL26 7DS
On A390 St Austell-Truro road, 1 mile W of St Austell; the Tregongeeves Lane junction is clearly signposted just below St Mewan school.
Heathland/parkland course.
18 holes, 6089 yards, S.S.S.69
Founded 1911
Visitors: welcome with reservation; must be club members and hold h/cap certs.
Green Fee: WD £15; WE £18.
Societies: catered for weekdays by arrangement.
Catering: full service; hot meals, bar snacks daily; evening meals available, phone first.
Hotels: Cliff Head; Carlyon Bay.

A59 St Clements
☎(01534) 21938
Jersey Recreation Grounds Co Ltd, Graeve d'azette, St Clements, Jersey, Channel Islands JE2 6QN
Close to St Helier.
Public meadowland course
9 holes, 2244 yards, Par 30.
Alterations planned in 1996.
Founded 1913
Visitors: open to public every day except before 11.30 Tuesday and 1pm on Sun
Green Fee: £13 (18 holes).
Societies: any day except Sun am.
Catering: buffet bar and restaurant.
Tennis (16 courts), bowling, putting green etc.
Hotels: Hotel de Normandy, Merton.

A60 St Enodoc
☎(01208) 863216 (Sec), Pro 862402
Rock, Wadebridge, Cornwall PL27 6LB
From Wadebridge take B3314 Port Isaac road for 3 miles and then turn left to Rock.

Classic links course.
Church Course, 18 holes, 6243 yards, S.S.S.70; Holywell Course, 18 holes, 4134 yards, S.S.S.61
Designed by James Braid.
Founded 1890
Visitors: h/cap cert required for Church course, 24 max.
Green Fee: Church: WD £25 per round, £35 per day; WE £30 per round, £40 per day. Holywell course, £12 per round, £18 per day,
Societies: all year round, but avoid public holidays and main holiday periods.
Catering: full facilities available every day.
practice ground with driving, bunker and putting facilities.
Hotels: St Moritz; Bodare; Port Gaverne.

A61 St Kew
☎(01208) 841500
St Kew Highway, Bodmin, Cornwall PL30 3EF
Take the A39 and exit at Wadebridge
Parkland course
9 holes (18 tees) 4543 S.S.S. 62
Founded 1992
Designed by D Derry
Visitors: welcome
Green Fee: £7 (9 holes), £11 (18 holes)
Societies: by prior arrangement
Catering: full facilities. Bar
Driving range

A62 St Mellion International
☎(01579) 351351, Fax 350116, Pro 350724, Starter: 351182
St Mellion, Nr Saltash, Cornwall PL12 6SD
3 miles S of Callington on A388.
Parkland course.
Nicklaus course, 18 holes, 6651 yards, S.S.S.72; Old course, 18 holes, 5782 yards, S.S.S.68
Designed by Jack Nicklaus (International course), J. Hamilton Stutt (Old Course).
Founded 1976
Visitors: welcome. H/cap certificate required on Nicklaus course.
Green Fee: WD £45 singles, £120 for 4 ball; WE £50
Societies: welcome.
Catering: restaurant, coffee shop, grill room.
Swimming pool, sauna, solarium, mulitgym, badminton, tennis, snooker, banqueting and conferences.
Hotels: St Mellion.

Thurlestone

Thurlestone is situated by the sea but it is not a course of mighty dunes. With the exception of the 1st hole, its character is best described as clifftop and downland. It is certainly exposed to the wind and that is its main defence. At the same time, an elevated setting is its greatest attraction, with views that are as fine and varied as any in the land.

The approach, through narrow, high-hedged lanes, so typical of many small towns in Devon, has a timeless air about it, reinforced by the excellent hotel and by the simple welcome to the Golf Club which has kept hospitable doors open since the last century.

There is challenge here as well as a welcome, although no impossible carries or a series of lakes to engulf a dozen balls. Old fashioned it may be in parts but that is its strength.

Not that it all dates back to the age of hickory when a brewer, a doctor and a so-licitor discussed tentative plans for a course on an area of scrub, gorse and brambles alive with rabbits. Nine holes was the limit then with a stone wall marking the western boundary – rather like the one at Prestwick which marked the end of the famous old 12-hole course. No doubt there was fierce debate at Thurlestone as to whether to obtain land beyond the wall to extend to 18 holes; but the progressives won the argument, even if the acquisition introduced an altogether different type of golf. Further land was obtained fairly recently to complete the course as it is today but; but it is a curious fact that the 1st hole remains the only one at sea level.

It provides an unusual opening, a short par 4 from a high tee above the club-house, the drive having to cross the road and avoid a number of bunkers. There is then an awkward pitch to a green broader than it is deep, a green that can on occa-sions be driven by those with the neces-sary daring.

Ambitions on the first tee are inclined to be more modest and Thurlestone's 1st might be a more enticing hole later in the round but the drive at the 2nd has the face of a hill to scale and must be soundly struck to have any hope of making a four. The force of the wind is increasingly felt, and rare are the days in the year when there is none.

Flighting the ball well is the key to success at the seaside and nowhere is that truer than on the short 3rd which heads towards the point of the cliff. By now, the full flavour of the setting can be experi-enced, the splendour of the Devon coast in both directions, the quaintly shaped rock on Thurlestone beach and always sight and sound of the sea. The first seven holes are not overlong but they are the best and most varied in terms of stroke-making and appeal. After a splendid par four at the 4th, consecutive short holes at the 5th and 6th call for widely differing tee shots. At the 5th, the emphasis is on power, on the 6th it is more a case of art and judgement to clear the bunker and hold the green.

An inviting drive on the 7th is the prelude to a demanding second beside the original boundary wall but, as a further climb takes us on to more open territory, the yardages on the card show a marked uplift. The second nine is over 800 yards longer than the first.

Stout hitting, and the stouter the better, is increasingly the order of of the day, the 9th and 11th nevertheless falling within the range of most in two shots. The line from the tee at the 9th is down the left while the revised 11th offers ad-vantage from that side as well. However, the position of the 11th green is the most spectacular of all, Bigbury Bay and Burgh Island adding a new dimension to the panorama.

Starting with the 12th, the longest par 4, the finish poses stern demands with three par fives in the last six holes and a par 3 of over 200 yards. It lacks the charm of the earlier holes but the 17th is an at-tractive short hole in spite of being encir-cled by bunkers and the 18th poses the threat of out of bounds in the gardens of houses down the left. But it is hardly likely that their occupants would resent any intrusion, for they look out on a truly memorable sight that is mercifully, un-changing.

A63 St Pierre Park Hotel

☎(01481) 727039, **Hotels:** 728282
Rohais, St Peter Port, Guernsey,
Channel Islands
1 mile W of St Peter Port on Rohais
road.
Hilly course with water hazards.
9 holes, 1500 yards, S.S.S.48
Designed by Tony Jacklin.
Founded 1984
Visitors: welcome except during
competitions (Sun am).
Green Fee: WD £14(18 holes); WE
£16 (18 holes) special rates for Hotel
guests.
Societies: by arrangement.
Catering: full facilities at St Pierre
Park Hotel.
Driving range, indoor swimming pool,
health suite, etc.
Hotels: St Pierre Park.

A64 Saunton

☎(01271) 812436, Fax 814241, Pro
812013
Saunton, Nr Braunton, N Devon
EX33 1LG
On B3231 from Braunton to Croyde,
7 miles from Barnstaple.
Traditional links course.
East, 18 holes, 6701 yards, S.S.S.73;
West, 18 holes, 6356 yards, S.S.S.71
Designed by Herbert Fowler (East
Course), Frank Pennink (West
Course).
Founded 1897
Visitors: must be members of clubs
with h/cap certs.
Green Fee: WD £30; WE £35.
Societies: any time booked in
advance.
Catering: full restaurant meals
available all day.
Hotels: Saunton Sands; Kittiwell
House; Preston House, Croyde Bay
House, Woolacombe Bay.

A65 Sidmouth

☎(01395) 513451 (Sec), Club
513023, Pro 516407
Cotmaton Road, Peak Hill, Sidmouth,
Devon EX10 8SX
Take Exeter Station Rd to Woodlands
Hotel, then turn right on Cotmaton
Rd.
Undulating parkland course.
18 holes, 5068 yards, S.S.S.65
Founded Oct 1889
Visitors: welcome by arrangement
with Sec.
Green Fee: £18.
Societies: welcome by prior
arrangement.
Catering: Full facilities

A66 Sparkwell

☎(01752) 837219
Welbeck Manor Hotel, Sparkwell,
Plymouth, Devon PL7 5DF
From Plymouth take A38 turn left at
Plympton and then signposted to
Sparkwell
Parkland
9 holes, 5772 yards S.S.S. 68
Founded Aug 1993
Visitors: welcome pay as you play
Green Fee: WD £5 (9 holes) £9 (18
holes); WE £6 (9 holes), £11 (18
holes)
Societies: welcome
Catering: Hotel has restaurant and
bar facilities
9 hole pitch and putt, putting green
Hotels: Welbeck Manor

A67 Staddon Heights

☎(01752) 402475, Club 401998, Pro
492630
Staddon Heights, Plymstock,
Plymouth, Devon PL9 9SP
Leave Plymouth city on the
Plymstock road; clubhouse is 5 miles
S of city near Royal Navy aerial
towers.
Seaside course.
18 holes, 5869 yards, S.S.S.68
Founded 1895
Visitors: welcome weekdays with
h/cap cert.
Green Fee: WD £15; WE £20.
Societies: weekdays.
Catering: every day.

A68 Tavistock

☎(01822) 612049 (Club), Sec/Fax
612344, Pro 612316
Down Rd, Tavistock, Devon PL19
9AQ
Take the Whitchurch road, turning
into Down Rd, and onto Whitchurch
Down.
Moorland course.
18 holes, 6250 yards, S.S.S.70
Founded 1890
Visitors: welcome, telephone in
advance.
Green Fee: WD £18; WE £23.
Societies: by arrangement.
Catering: lunch, bar snacks, evening
meals.
Hotels: Bedford; Moorland Links;
Arundel Arms.

A69 Tehidy Park

☎(01209) 842208, Pro 842914
Nr Camborne, Cornwall TR14 0HH
Off A30, 2 miles NE of Camborne on
the Portreath road.

Parkland course.
18 holes, 6241 yards, S.S.S.71
Founded 1922
Visitors: h/cap cert required.
Green Fee: WD £21 per round, £27
per day; WE £26 per round, £32 per
day.
Societies: weekdays only.
Catering: full range bar snacks, a la
carte restaurant mornings and
evenings.
Snooker.
Hotels: Penventon, Glenfeadon, Old
Shire Inn, Tyacks.

A70 Teignmouth

☎(01626) 774194 Sec, Pro 772894,
Club 773614
Exeter Rd, Teignmouth, Devon TQ14
9NY
2 miles from Teignmouth on Exeter
road B3192.
Moorland course.
18 holes, 6142 yards, S.S.S. 70
Designed by Dr Alister Mackenzie.
Founded 1924
Visitors: must be members of a club
and have h/cap cert.
Green Fee: WD £22; WE £25.
Societies: by appointment, not
weekends or Wed.
Catering: full service every day.
Hotels: London; Venn Farm.

A71 Thurlestone

☎(01548) 560405, Pro 560715
Thurlestone, Nr Kingsbridge, S Devon
TQ7 3NZ
Take Thurlestone turning from A379
Plymouth-Salcombe road; club
situated 4 miles S of Kingsbridge.
Downland course.
18 holes, 6340 yards, S.S.S.70
Founded 1897
Visitors: must produce a current
h/cap cert from recognised club.
Green Fee: £24.
Societies: not catered for.
Catering: full facilities available all
day.
12 tennis courts (3 hard, 9 grass).
Hotels: Thurlestone.

A72 Tiverton

☎(01884) 252187, Pro 254836,
Steward: 252114
Post Hill, Tiverton, Devon EX16 4NE
5 miles from junction 27 on M5
towards Tiverton on A373; take 1st
exit left on dual carriageway through
Samford Peverell to Halberton.
Parkland/meadowland course.
18 holes, 6236 yards, S.S.S.71

TREVOSE GOLF & COUNTRY CLUB
Constantine Bay, Padstow, Cornwall. Tel: (01841) 520208 Fax: (01841) 521057

- Championship Golf Course of 18 holes. S.S.S.71. Fully automatic watering on all greens.
- 2 x 9 hole courses. One 3100 yds, par 35, the other 1369 yds par 29.
- Excellent appointed Club House with Bar and Restaurant providing full catering facilities. A/C throughout.

- Superior Accom. in 7 Chalets, 6 Bungalows, 11 Luxury Flats & 12 Dormy Suites. Daily Rates available. Mid-week bookings encouraged. **Open all Year.**
- 3 Hard Tennis Courts.
- Heated Swimming Pool open from mid May to mid September.

- In addition to Membership for Golf and Tennis, Social Membership of the Club is also available with full use of the Club House facilities.
- 6 glorious sandy bays within about a mile of the Club House, with pools, open sea and surf bathing.
- 8 miles from Civil Airport.

Designed by James Braid.
Founded 1931
Visitors: letter of intro. or h/cap cert required; no visitors Wed pm, weekends or Bank Holidays, or during Championship, Club and Open meetings.
Green Fee: WD £21; WE £27.
Societies: no, unless already a standard fixture.
Catering: lunch, teas available.
Hotels: Tiverton; Green Headland; Hartnoll.

A73 **Torquay**
☎(01803) 314591, Pro 329113
Petitor Rd, St Marychurch, Torquay, Devon TQ1 4QF
N of Torquay on A379 Teignmouth road, on outskirts of town.
Parkland course.
18 holes, 6175 yards, S.S.S.70
Founded 1910
Visitors: h/cap certs required.
Green Fee: WD £20; WE £25.
Societies: welcome by prior arrangement.
Catering: Full facilities

A74 **Tregenna Castle Hotel**
☎(01736) 795254, Fax 796066
St Ives, Cornwall TR26 2DE
In grounds of Tregenna Castle Hotel, signposted to left just before St Ives on A3074 from Hayle.
Parkland course
18 holes, 3549 yards, S.S.S.57
Founded 1982
Visitors: welcome; ring for tee times.
Green Fee: £12.50
Societies: welcome by prior arrangement.
Catering: full bar and restaurant facilities at hotel.
Tennis, squash, badminton, swimming etc.
Hotels: Tregenna Castle.

A75 **Treloy**
☎(01637) 878554
Newquay, Cornwall TR7 4JN
On A3059 St Columb Major-Newquay road, 3 miles from Newquay.
Public heathland/parkland course.
9 holes, 2143 yards, S.S.S.31
Designed by M.R.M. Sandow
Founded 1991
Visitors: welcome.
Green Fee: £15 per day.
Societies: welcome.
Hotels: Barrowfield, Hotel California (Newquay); White Lodge, Tredragon (Mawgan Porth).

A76 **Trethorne**
☎(01566) 86324
Kennards House, Launceston, Cornwall PL15 8QE
3 miles west of Launceston on A30.
Take Camelford/Wadebridge turn off
Undulating parkland course
9 holes (18 tees) 6338 yards S.S.S. 72
Opened Aug 1993
Visitors: welcome
Green Fee: £8 (9 holes), £12.75 (18 holes), £16 per day
Societies: welcome
Catering: bar, full facilities
Driving range

A77 **Trevose Country Club**
☎(01841) 520208; Fax 521057, Pro 520261
Constantine Bay, Padstow, Cornwall PL28 8JB
4 miles W of Padstow off B3276.
Seaside links course.
18 holes, 6608 yards, S.S.S.71; 9 holes, 3108 yards, Par 35; short course 1357 yards, Par 29
Designed by H.S. Colt.
Founded 1925
Visitors: welcome; 3 and 4 ball matches restricted; phone first.

A78 **Truro**
☎(01872) 78684, Pro 76595
Treliske, Truro, Cornwall TR1 3LG
From Truro follow A390 to Redruth, after 2 miles turn right at small roundabout; course signposted.
Undulating parkland course.
18 holes, 5306 yards, S.S.S.66
Designed by Colt, Alison & Morrison.
Founded 1937
Visitors: welcome, phone to ascertain any tee reservations.
Green Fee: WD £18; WE £22.
Societies: welcome except weekends and Tues.
Catering: full bar and restaurant facilities every day.
Snooker.
Hotels: special arrangements with Hospitality Hotels.

A79 **Warren**
☎(01626) 862255, Pro 864002
Dawlish Warren, Dawlish, Devon EX7 0NF
Take A379 from Exeter to Dawlish Warren.
Links course.
18 holes, 5965 yards, S.S.S.69
Founded 1892
Visitors: welcome, h/cap certs required.
Green Fee: WD £21; WE £24.
Societies: weekdays by arrangement with Sec.
Catering: bar snacks and meals all week.
Hotels: Langstone Cliff.

Green Fee: WD £25; WE £30
Societies: welcome any time except July-Sept.
Catering: all meals, good restaurant. Outdoor swimming pool, tennis courts, snooker.
Hotels: Own self-catering accommodation available, telephone for details.

A80 Waterbridge

☎(01363) 85111
Down St Mary, Nr Crediton, Devon
EX17 5LG
Off A377 Barnstaple-Exeter road
between Down St Mary and
Copplestone.
Parkland course.
9 holes, 3908 yards, Par 62
Designed by David Taylor.
Founded July 1992
Visitors: welcome; times bookable
24 hrs in advance.
Green Fee: WD £5 (9 holes), £9 (18 holes); WE £6.50 (9 holes), £12 (18 holes).
Societies: welcome by prior arrangement.
Catering: light snacks, meals by arrangement.
Hotels: Fox & Hounds (Eggesford).

A81 West Cornwall

☎(01736) 753401 (Sec), Pro
753177, Members: 753319
Lelant, St Ives, Cornwall TR26 3DZ
A30 to Hayle, then take A3074 to St
Ives.
Seaside links course.
18 holes, 5884 yards, S.S.S.69
Founded Dec 1889
Visitors: welcome by arrangement;
h/cap cert required.
Green Fee: WD £20; WE £25.
Societies: welcome on application to
Sec.
Catering: lunch and dinner except
Mon.
Snooker.
Hotels: Badger Inn (Lelant);
Boskerris (Carbis Bay); Pedn Olva
(St. Ives).

A82 Whitsand Bay Hotel Golf and Country Club

☎(01503) 230276 (Club), Fax
230329, Pro 230778
Portwrinkle, Torpoint, Cornwall PL11
3BU
On B3247, 6 miles off A38 from
Plymouth.
Clifftop course.
18 holes, 5796 yards, S.S.S.69
Designed by William Fernie of Troon.
Founded 1905
Visitors: h/cap cert required.
Green Fee: WD £15; WE £17.50.
Residents £35 per week.
Societies: welcome all year by
arrangement.
Catering: 2 bars, 3 restaurants.
Indoor swimming pool, sauna,
solarium etc.
Hotels: Whitsand Bay; Sconner

A83 Woodbury Park Golf & Country Club

☎(01395) 233382, Fax 233384
Woodbury Castle, Woodbury, Exeter
EX5 1JJ
From M5 junction 30 take A3052
Sidmouth road, turn right onto B3180,
after approx. 1 mile turn right to
Woodbury Salterton, then
immediately turn right to course.
Public parkland/moorland/heathland
course.
Oaks course: 18 holes, 6707 yards,
S.S.S.72; Acorns course: 9 holes,
2297 yards, Par 32.
Extension planned for 1996
Designed by J. Hamilton Stutt
Founded 1992
Visitors: welcome, h/cap cert
required.

Green Fee: Oaks: WD £35; WE £45;
Acorns: WD £12; WE £14.
Societies: all times by arrangement.
Catering: catering available, 2 bars.
Driving range, practice area.

A84 Wrangaton

☎(01364) 73229 (Sec), Pro 72161
Wrangaton, South Brent, S Devon
TQ10 9HJ
Turn off A38 between South Brent
and Bittaford at Wrangaton P.O.
Moorland/parkland course.
18 holes, 6041 yards, S.S.S.69
Designed by Donald Steel.
Founded 1895
Visitors: welcome; h/cap cert req.
Green Fee: WD £16; WE £20.
Societies: weclome by arrangement
Catering: bar and catering (except
Mon in winter) daily.
Hotels: The Coach House Inn;
Glazebrook.

A85 Yelverton

☎(01822) 852824, Pro 853593
Golf Links Rd, Yelverton, Devon
PL20 6BN
8 miles N of Plymouth and 5 miles S
of Tavistock on A386.
Moorland course.
18 holes, 6363 yards, S.S.S.70
Designed by Herbert Fowler.
Founded 1904
Visitors: accredited golfers welcome;
h/cap cert required.
Green Fee: £20
Societies: welcome by arrangement.
Catering: by arrangement.
Hotels: Manor House, Moorland
Links; Rosemont.

B

SOMERSET, DORSET, WILTSHIRE, SOUTH AVON

This is a region which has seen more expansion than most in the last ten years. Bowood, Castle Coombe and, more recently, Orchardleigh near Frome have boosted the resources of Somerset and Wiltshire while Woodsprings has provided Bristol with a welcome new 27-hole enterprise just down the road from the airport. Orchardleigh is a particular success story, the Brian Huggett designed course happily being rescued from abandonment in 1990.

Dorset has also seen its share of new developments in recent years, one of them being Dudsbury at Longham which has a splendid clubhouse position looking down on the River Stour. Converted from farmland and boasting lakes, well established trees and pleasant contours, it fills an obvious need in an area where the demand is great. A few miles away are even newer ventures at Crane Valley and Hamptworth. Slightly more remote are the settings of Sherborne in the midst of rural splendour and Lyme Regis on its clifftop perch close to the border with Devon. However, both of them typify the variety that exists on British courses.

In Wiltshire, Marlborough and High Post deserve mention, together with Broome Manor at Swindon which is certainly among the busiest courses. A public complex, it operates a booking system to cater for the enormous demand. Wiltshire can claim in Bowood the longest course in Britain but the one true championship course in Dorset, Wiltshire, Somerset and Avon is Burnham and Berrow, looking out on the Bristol Channel and the distant coastline of Wales. Its dunes used to be among the most mountainous, the arrangement of the holes taking somewhat eccentric benefit of them until modern amendments ironed out a few quirks and kinks.

Burnham's most recent changes surrounded the loss of the Church hole and the old 13th, which is now a housing estate. In consequence, the 14th is a short hole in the opposite direction but, for all its undoubted challenge, Burnham and Berrow is unchanging in its appeal.

Weston Super Mare is worth a visit, one memory of my first acquaintance of it thirty years ago being the comparison of one hole with the Road Hole at St Andrews. In spite of the persuasiveness of my guide, I remained unconvinced but that is no criticism of a course whose original design was by Tom Dunn, one of the early professionals who was among the first to turn his hand to golf course architecture.

Bristol and Bath each have several courses, with pleasant rounds awaiting at Long Ashton, Bristol, Clifton, Knowle; and, in the Gloucestershire area, Lansdown and Tracy Park. Mendip, north of Shepton Mallett, displays the best of Frank Pennink's art.

Last and, by no means least, a reminder that the area around Bournemouth, rich in natural heathland, is ideal for golfing holidays. Ferndown, Parkstone and Broadstone are traditional favourites. Isle of Purbeck is a scenic delight while both Queen's Park and Meyrick Park feature some of the best public facilities in the country.

Lanteglos Country House Hotel

The Lanteglos Country House Hotel has long been established as one of the major golfing centres in Cornwall with a very real understanding and appreciation of the holiday golfer's requirements.

Tucked away in a secluded valley in one of the most beautiful and unspoilt parts of Cornwall, yet situated on the very edge of the superb Bowood Park Golf Club, our aim is to provide quality accommodation, good food and friendly service in a relaxed and enjoyable atmosphere.

We have special arrangements and concessionary rates at most of the leading courses – ranging from glorious parkland courses such as Bowood, Launceston and Lanhydrock to some of the finest links outside Scotland including St Enodoc, Trevose and Perrenporth the ultimate challenge in the south west of the Jack Nicklaus Championship course at St Mellion.

You can choose from our golf packages or for any length of stay with a golf itinery tailor made to suit your own requirements. We make all the tee reservations for you so all you have to do is just turn up to play whether it is a party of two or a society of 22.

On the days when perhaps you want a rest from breaking par, there is an abundance of other attractions: golden beaches, picture postcard fishing villages, lovely gardens and great historic houses, coastal and moorland walks, not to mention the facilities of the hotel which include; squash and tennis courts, swimming pool, a snooker lounge and a delightful conservatory lounge.

Lanteglos Country House Hotel & Villas Ltd
Camelford, Cornwall PL32 9RF
Tel & Fax: (01840) 213551

B1 The Ashley Wood

☎(01258) 452253 (Sec), Pro 480379, Fax 450590
Wimborne Rd, Blandford, Dorset DT11 9HN
From Blandford 1 mile S along B3082 Wimborne road.
Undulating meadowland course.
18 holes, 6237 yards, S.S.S.70
Designed by Patrick Tallack.
Founded 1896
Visitors: welcome by arrangement except Tues am.
Green Fee: WD £24; WE £35.
Societies: welcome by arrangement with Sec.
Catering: Stewardess welcomes applications.
Hotels: Anvil (Pimperne)

B2 Bath

☎(01225) 425182, Sec 463834 , Pro 466953
Sham Castle, North Rd, Bath, Avon BA2 6JG
Take A36 Bath to Warminster road, up North Rd and club is about 800 yards on left, 1.5 miles SE of Bath.
Downland course.
18 holes, 6369 yards, S.S.S.71
Founded 1880

Visitors: Weekdays only (with member at weekend)
Green Fee: £25 per round; £30 per day
Societies: catered for Wed and Fri.
Catering: every day; bar snacks on Thurs.
Hotels: Bath; Beaufort; Dukes; Spa.

B3 Blue Circle

☎(01373) 822481
Trowbridge Rd, Westbury, Wilts
Parkland course; part of Blue Circle Works Sports Complex.
9 holes, 5600 yards, S.S.S.66
Visitors: with member only, or on county card system.
Green Fee: WD £6; WE £10.
Societies: welcome by prior arrangement.
Catering: by arrangement.

B4 Bournemouth & Meyrick Park

☎(01202) 290307 (Office), Manager: 292425, Bookings: 290862 or 290871.
Central Drive, Meyrick Park, Bournemouth BH2 6LH
In centre of Bournemouth.
Municipal parkland course (Meyrick Park), very picturesque.
18 holes, 5663 yards, S.S.S.68
Founded 1890
Visitors: welcome any time; advisable to book previous day.
Green Fee: WD £11; WE £12.
Societies: welcome by prior arrangement.
Catering: Clubhouse restaurant and bars.
Squash.

B5 Bowood Golf & Country Club

☎(01249) 822228, Fax 822218.
Calne, Wilts SN11 9PQ
Follow signs off M4 and A4 to Bowood House.
Public course in Grade 1 listed parkland.
18 holes, 7317 yards, S.S.S.74 (from Championship tees)
Designed by Dave Thomas
Founded May 1992
Visitors: open to anyone with proof of h/cap.
Green Fee: £30 per round, £35 for 27 holes, £40 for 36 holes.
Societies: weekdays and after 12 noon at weekends.

Bowood Golf & Country Club

Derry Hill, Calne, Wilts. SN11 9PQ
Tel: **01249 822228** Fax: **01249 822218**

BOWOOD

An 18 hole Championship Course set in the splendour of Bowood Park. Join us for first class golf with academy course, driving range, bar and a variety of catering options. Also ask about Queenwood Golf Lodge for parties of up to 8. **Call us now to book!**

Catering: private dining room, restaurant, lounge bar.
Driving range, 3 Academy holes £5 per hour.
Hotels: fully serviced house in centre of course (sleeps 8) for rent, free golf; apply for details.

B6 **Bradford-on-Avon**
☎(01225) 868268
Avon Close, Trowbridge Rd, Bradford-on-Avon, Wilts
From Bradford towards Trowbridge, on left near Police Station.
Parkland course next to River Avon.
9 holes, 2109 metres, S.S.S.61
Founded June 1991
Visitors: welcome, not Sat/Sun am.
Green Fee: apply for details.
Catering: on application.

B7 **Brean**
☎(01278) 751570 Pro shop/bookings
Coast Rd, Brean, Burnham-on-Sea, Somerset TA8 2RF
Leave M5 at junction 22, follow signs for Brean Leisure Park, course 4 miles N of Burnham, 6 miles M5.
Level moorland course.
18 holes, 5715 yards, S.S.S.68
Founded 1975
Visitors: members of other golf clubs welcome, not Sat or Sun am.
Green Fee: £12 WD; £15 WE.
Societies: welcome weekdays with prior notice.
Catering: bar and snacks, meals can be arranged in adjacent Leisure Centre.
Course adjoins Leisure Park and 6-mile sandy beach.

Hotels: Queens (Burnham-on-Sea); caravan park (touring & static) adjacent.

B8 **Bridport & West Dorset**
☎(01308) 422597 (Members), Sec 421095, Pro 421491.
East Cliff, West Bay, Bridport, Dorset DT6 4EP
Off A35, 1.5 miles S of Bridport on B3157.
Clifftop links course.
18 holes, 5246 yards, S.S.S.66. Re designed course opening 1996.
Designed by G.S.P. Salmon.
Founded 1891
Visitors: welcome.
Green Fee: £20.
Societies: as arranged.

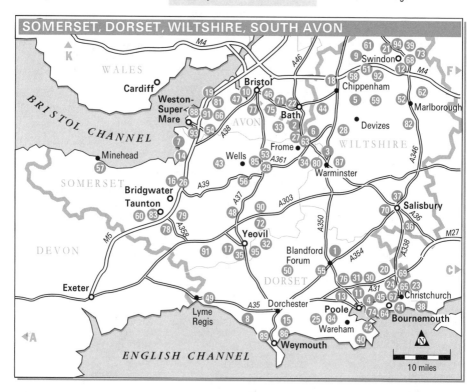

SOMERSET, DORSET, WILTSHIRE, SOUTH AVON

Catering: full, plus licensed bar. 9 hole Pitch & Putt.
Hotels: Haddon House.

B9 Brinkworth
☎(01666) 510277
Longmans Farm, Brinkworth, Chippenham, Wilts SN15 5DG
Between Swindon and Malmesbury on B4042.
Meadowland course.
18 holes, 5884 yards, S.S.S.69
Founded 1984
Visitors: welcome any time.
Green Fee: WD £6; WE £8.
Societies: by arrangement.
Catering: available.

B10 Bristol & Clifton
☎(01275) 393474, Pro 393031
House Manager: 393117, Fax 394611.
Beggar Bush Lane, Failand, Nr Clifton, Bristol BS8 3TH
Junction 19 off M5, 4 miles along A369 to Bristol turn right at traffic lights, then further 1.5 miles.
Parkland course.
18 holes, 6316 yards, S.S.S.70
Founded 1891
Visitors: weekdays with club h/cap cert; weekends restricted times.
Green Fee: WD £30; WE £38.
Societies: by arrangement, not WE.
Catering: normal golf club catering.
Hotels: Redwood Lodge; Beggar Bush Land; Failand.

B11 Broadstone
☎(01202) 692595, Pro 692835.
Wentworth Drive, Broadstone, Dorset BH 18 8DQ.

Off A349 half-way between Wimborne and Poole.
Heathland course.
18 holes, 6315 yards, S.S.S.70
Designed by George Dunn and H.S. Colt.
Founded 1898
Visitors: weekdays after 9.30am.
Green Fee: WD £28..
Societies: weekdays only by prior arrangement.
Catering: full facilities by prior arrangement.
Hotels: King's Head.

B12 Broome Manor
☎(01793) 532403, Fax 433255.
Piper's Way, Swindon, Wilts SN3 1RG
2 miles from M4 junction 15 to Swindon; follow signs for Golf Complex.
Public parkland course.
18 holes, 6283 yards, S.S.S.70; 9 holes, 2690 yards, S.S.S.66
Designed by Hawtree & Son.
Founded 1976
Visitors: welcome; booking system in operation (course very busy throughout the year).
Green Fee: WD £8.50; WE £10. 9hole: WD £5; WE £6.
Societies: welcome Mon-Thurs only by arrangement.
Catering: full facilities all week.
Floodlit driving range.
Hotels: Marriott, Forte Crest; Goddard Arms.

B13 Bulbury Woods
☎(01929) 459574, Fax 459000.
Halls Rd, Lytchett Matravers, Nr Poole, Dorset BH16 6EP

Off Poole-Bere Regis road A35.
Parkland course.
18 holes, 6065 yards, S.S.S.69
Designed by J. Sharkey.
Founded 1989
Visitors: welcome.
Green Fee: WD & WE £18.
Societies: welcome.
Catering: full catering and bar facilities.
Practice ground.
Hotels: on site accommodation.

B14 Burnham & Berrow
☎(01278) 785760, Pro 784545, Fax 795440.
St Christopher's Way, Burnham-on-Sea, Somerset TA8 2PE
M5 junction 22, 1 mile N of Burnham-on-Sea.
Seaside links, championship course.
18 holes, 6824 yards, S.S.S.74; 9 holes, 6332 yards, S.S.S.70
Founded 1890
Visitors: must be members of recognised club with h/caps of 22 or under (ladies 30) for championship course; book in advance.
Green Fee: WD £34; WE £48. 9-holes: £10 per day.
Societies: as for visitors.
Catering: every day 11am-6pm; breakfast and evening meals available on prior booking.
Hotels: Dormy House at club, golf inclusive prices; Batch Farm (Lympsham); Lulworth GH.

B15 Came Down
☎(01305) 812531 (Steward/club), Manager/Fax 813494, Pro 812670.
Came Down, Dorchester, Dorset DT2 8NR

2 miles S of Dorchester off A354.
Undulating downland course.
18 holes, 6244 yards, S.S.S.71
Designed by J.H. Taylor.
Founded 1896
Visitors: midweek from 9am, Sat
from 9am, Sun from 11am, h/cap
required, please phone.
Green Fee: WD £20; WE £25.
Societies: society day Wed, coffee,
lunch, 36 holes approx £30.
Catering: bar, restaurant.
Driving/practice area, putting green.

B16 Cannington
☎(01278) 652394
Cannington College, Nr Bridgewater,
Somerset TA5 2LS
M5 junction 23; course 3 miles W of
Bridgewater.
Parkland course.
9 holes, 2929 yards S.S.S.68
Designed by Martin Hawtree.
Founded July 1993
Visitors: welcome, no restrictions;
reservations for matches and
societies.
Green Fee: WD £10 (18 holes); WE
£12 (18 holes).
Societies: welcome by arrangement
with golf course manager/pro.
Catering: bar and restaurant.

B17 Chedington Court
☎(01935) 891413 (Bookings),
Manager: 891265, Fax 891442
South Perrott, Beaminster, Dorset
DT8 3HU
0.5 mile E of South Perrott on A356
Crewkerne-Dorchester road.
Parkland course.
9 holes, 6754 yards, S.S.S.72. 18
hole course opens mid 1996
(Designed by Donald Steel).
Designed by D. Hemstock, P. & H.
Chapman.
Founded 1991
Visitors: welcome; proper dress.
Green Fee: WD £15; WE £18.
9holes: WD £10; WE £12.
Societies: by arrangement.
Catering: refreshments available.
Basic Pitch & Putt course, driving and
practice areas.
Hotels: Chedington Court (01935
891265), bargain breaks all year, half
board with unlimited golf available.

B18 Chippenham
☎(01249) 652040 (Sec), Pro
655519, Fax 446681.
Malmesbury Rd, Chippenham, Wilts
SN15 5LT

Junction 17 off M4, 1 mile from town
centre on A350.
Meadowland course.
18 holes, 5559 yards, S.S.S.67
Founded 1896
Visitors: welcome with restrictions.
Green Fee: WD £20; WE £25.
Societies: welcome with prior
arrangement Tuesday, Thursday,
Friday only.
Catering: lunch (limited catering
Mon).
Hotels: Old Bell (Malmesbury).

B19 Clevedon
☎(01275) 874057 (Sec), Pro
874704, Steward: 873140 Fax
341228.
Castle Rd, Clevedon, Avon BS21
7AA
Leave M5 at junction 20, follow signs
to Clevedon; on outskirts of Clevedon
turn left into Holly Lane, at top of hill
turn right into private lane to golf club
and castle.
Undulating parkland course.
18 holes, 6050 yards, S.S.S.69
Designed by Sandy Herd.
Founded 1908
Visitors: every day, not Wed am;
must be playing members of a golf
club and must produce h/cap certs.
Green Fee: WD £22; WE & BH £35.
Societies: Mon & Tues only, not
Bank Holidays.
Catering: every day (bar snacks only
Mon).
Snooker.
Hotels: Highcliffe; Walton Park.

B20 Crane Valley
☎(01202) 814088, Fax 813407
West Farm, Romford, Verwood,
Dorset BH31 7LE
From A31 take B3081 signposted
Verwood, course is on left hand side
on northern outskirts of Verwood.
Parkland course, part public.
18 holes, Valley course: 6425 yards,
S.S.S.71; 9 holes (Woodland public
course), 2060 yards, S.S.S.60.
Designed by Donald Steel.
Founded 1992
Visitors: members of recognised
clubs with h/cap certs on 18 hole
course; all welcome on 9 hole
course.
Green Fee: WD £18; WE £25. 9
holes: WD £5.50; WE £6.50.
Societies: welcome by prior
appointment.
Catering: full restaurant and bar,
spikes bar and snacks.
Driving range.

B21 Cricklade Hotel & Country Club
☎(01793) 750751, Fax 751767
Common Hill, Cricklade, Wilts SN6
6HA
B4040 Cricklade-Malmesbury road,
15 mins from M4 junctions 15/16.
Parkland course.
9 holes, 1830 yards, S.S.S. 57.
Designed by Ian Bolt.
Founded 1992
Visitors: welcome Mon-Fri.
Green Fee: £16 per 18 holes; £25
per day.
Societies: welcome by arrangement.
Catering: full facilities, a la carte
restaurant.
Indoor swimming pool (residents
only), snooker, tennis, health and
fitness facilities.
Hotels: Cricklade.

B22 Cumberwell Park
☎(01225) 863322
Bradford on Avon, Wiltshire BA15
2PQ
From Bradford on Avon take the
A363 to Bath. Course 1 mile outside
town
Parkland course
18 holes, 6472 yards S.S.S. 71
Designed by A Stiff
Founded in 1994
Visitors: welcome with h/cap cert
Green Fee: WD £18; WE £25
Societies: welcome
Catering: 2 bars, 2 restaurants
10 acre practice ground
Hotels: Swan (Bradford).

B23 Dudmoor Farm
☎(01202) 483980
Dudmoor Farm Rd, Christchurch,
Dorset BH23 6AQ
Off A35 W of Christchurch.
Woodland course.
9 holes, 1428 metres, Par 31
Founded 1974
Visitors: welcome 7 days.
Green Fee: £4.50 for 18 holes.
Societies: advisable to phone.
Catering: snacks and soft drinks.
Squash, fishing.
Hotels: Avon Causeway; B&B on
site.

B24 Dudsbury
☎(01202) 593499, Pro 594488, Fax
594555.
Christchurch Rd, Ferndown, Dorset
BH22 8ST
From A31 at Ferndown take A348 for
approx 2 miles, then turn left down

B3073, entrance on right after approx 500 yards.
Parkland course.
18 holes, 6742 yards, S.S.S.72; 5 hole Academy course.
Designed by Donald Steel.
Founded April 1992
Visitors: details of visitor requirements and fees not available at time of going to press; phone for information.
Green Fee: WD £25; WE £30.
Societies: welcome any weekday (if free), package varies according to choice of catering/number of holes etc.
Catering: Spike bar, lounge bar, restaurant (open to non-members), function suite.
Driving range.

B25 East Dorset
☎(01929) 472244 (Sec), Shop/Reservations: 472272, Fax 471294.
Hyde, Wareham, Dorset BH20 7NT
A35 from Poole to Dorchester. At Bere Regis take left turning signed to Wool/ Bovington, 2-3 miles left into Puddletown Road signed at Wareham. Approx 0.75 miles turn left signed EDGC. 300 yards to club.
18 hole championship Lakeland course, 18 holes, 7027 yards, S.S.S.75; Woodland, 9 holes, 2440 yards, Par 33
Designed by Martin Hawtree.
Founded 1978
Visitors: welcome with prior reservation.
Green Fee: WD £21 per round, £26 per day; WE £26 per round, £31 per day. Woodland course: WD £15; WE £19.
Societies: welcome any day on application.
Catering: full bar and restaurant service, open to non-golfers.
Driving range, computerised fitting service and analyser, large golf shop, dormy bungalow.
Hotels: Golf lodge, dormy bungalow.

B26 Enmore Park
☎(01278) 671481, Pro/ bookings: 671519.
Enmore, Bridgewater, Somerset TA5 2AN
3 miles W of Bridgewater on Durleigh road.
Undulating parkland course.
18 holes, 6406 yards, S.S.S.71
Designed by Hawtree and Son.
Founded 1906, redesigned 1971

Visitors: welcome weekdays, check weekends.
Green Fee: WD £18 per round, £25 per day; WE £25 per round, £30 per day.
Societies: welcome Mon, Thurs, Fri by arrangement with Sec.
Catering: available.
Hotels: Club can advise.

B27 Entry Hill
☎(01225) 834248
Entry Hill, Bath, Avon BA2 5NA
Take A367 Wells road from city centre, fork left into Entry Hill Rd after 1 mile; course is about 0.5 mile on right.
Compact, hilly parkland course (private club playing on public course).
9 holes, 2103 yards, S.S.S.61
Founded 1984
Visitors: no restrictions but pre-booking up to 7 days in advance essential for weekends, Bank Holidays and peak periods.
Green Fee: WD £4.50 for 9 holes, £7.50 for 18; WE £5.40 for 9 holes, £8.50 for 18.
Societies: weekdays by arrangement with Pro

B28 Erlestoke Sands
☎(01380) 831069 (Office/Fax), Pro 831027 , Catering Steward: 830507.
Erlestoke, Devizes, Wiltshire SN10 5VA
On B3098 off A350 at Westbury signposted Bratton, course 6 miles on left before village of Erlestoke: or, on B3098 off A360 at Wes. '_avington signposted Erlestoke (3 miles) on right after Erlestoke village.
Parkland course.
18 holes, 6649 yards, S.S.S.72 (Extension in 1996)
Designed by Adrian Stiff.
Founded May 1992.
Visitors: welcome.
Green Fee: WD £12; WE £18.
Societies: weekdays preferably, phone Steward.
Catering: full facilities.
3 Academy holes and 5 acre driving/practice area
Hotels: local B&B.

B29 Farrington
☎(01761) 241274, Pro 241787.
Marsh Lane, Farrington Gurney, Bristol BS18 5TS
On A37/A39 from Bath and Bristol towards Wells.

Undulating downland course.
18 holes 6689 yards S.S.S. 72
Designed by Peter Thompson
Founded Aug 1993
Visitors: welcome, advance booking required; no jeans.
Green Fee: WD £12; WE £15.
Societies: welcome at all times, please book.
Catering: full facilities open all day every day.
Driving range, practice bunker, putting and chipping green 300 yard practice ground.

B30 Ferndown
☎(01202) 874602, Pro 873825, Fax 873926.
119 Golf Links Rd, Ferndown, Dorset BH22 8BU
A31 to Trickett's Cross and A348 to Ferndown.
Heathland course.
Old Course, 18 holes, 6462 yards, S.S.S.71; New Course, 9 holes, 5604 yards, S.S.S.68
Designed by Harold Hilton (Old Course).
Founded 1913
Visitors: prior permission, h/cap cert required; limited weekends.
Green Fee: Old course: WD £40; WE £45.: WD £15; WE £20.
Societies: Tues and Fri only.
Catering: full facilities all week.
Hotels: Coach House Motel; Dormy; Bridge House.

B31 Ferndown Forest
☎(01202) 876096
Forest Links Road, Ferndown, Dorset BH22 9QE
Take A31 and the course is just off the Ferndown by-pass
Parkland
18 holes, 4621 yards, S.S.S. 63
Designed by G Hunt & R Grafham
Founded 1994
Visitors: welcome
Green Fee: WD £12; WE £15
Societies: welcome
Catering: 2 bars, high class restaurant, snack bar, large golf shop.
Driving range
Hotels: Bridge House.

B32 Folke
Folke Golf Centre, Alewston, Sherborne, Dorset DT9 5HR
From Sherborne head towards Sturminster Newton, 2 miles from Sherborne turn off towards Alweston.
Course is 200 yards away

Parkland course.
9 holes (18 tees) 5430 yards,
S.S.S.66
Founded 1993
Visitors: welcome
Green Fee: WD £4 (9 holes), £7 (18 holes); WE £5 (9 holes), £9 (18 holes).
Societies: welcome
Catering: sandwiches, snacks, bar
Driving range

B33 Fosseway Country Club
☎(01761) 412214, Fax 418357.
Charlton Lane, Midsomer Norton, Bath, Somerset BA3 4BD
Off A367 10 miles S of Bath, through Radstock and turn left at Charlton roundabout.
Parkland course.
9 holes, 4608 yards, S.S.S.65
Founded 1971
Visitors: members only on Sat until 12 noon, Sun until 2pm and Wed after 5pm.
Green Fee: WD £8, WE and Weds until 5pm £10
Societies: details on application.
Catering: full facilities in Centurion Restaurant; bar meals.
Conferences, banqueting, indoor and outdoor swimming, bowls, squash, snooker.
Hotels: Centurion (part of Fosseway complex).

B34 Frome Golf Centre
☎(01373) 453410
Critchill Manor, Frome, Somerset BA 11 4LJ
Take Nunney Catch roundabout, head for Nunney village, take Frome road and course is 2 miles on left
Parkland/Meadowland
18 holes, 5220 yards, S.S.S. 66
Visitors: welcome
Green Fee: WD £8; WE £8.50
Societies: with prior booking
Catering: snacks and soft drinks available

B35 Halstock
☎(01935) 891689, Fax 891839.
Halstock Golf Enterprises, Common Lane, Halstock, Nr Yeovil, Somerset BA22 9SF
300 yards from centre of Halstock village; turn right at green, from Quiet Woman pub, 50 yards on left past village shop/P.O., signposted.
18 holes, 4351 yards, S.S.S.63
Founded 1988

Visitors: welcome.
Green Fee: WD £9.50; WE £11.50.
Societies: by arrangement.
Catering: limited at present to light refreshments.

B36 Hamptworth Golf & Country Club
☎(01794) 390155, Fax 390022.
Hamptworth Rd, Hamptworth , Wilts SP5 2DU
6 miles from M27 junctions 1 and 2, off A36 to Salisbury, follow Landford and then Downton road signs.
Parkland, ancient woodlands and lakes and river throughout.
18 hole championship quality course yards 6516 S.S.S. 71 ; 9 hole practice academy.
Designed by Brian Pierson and D. Saunders.
Founded May 1994
Visitors: by prior arrangment only; h/cap certs required.
Green Fee: WD £17.50; WE £22.50.
Societies: by prior arrangement only; h/cap certs required for all in group.
Catering: bar and light refreshments available.
Hotels: Crown (Lindhurst), Woodfalls Inn.

B37 High Post
☎(01722) 782356, Pro 782219.
Great Durnford, Salisbury, Wilts SP4 6AT
Half-way between Salisbury and Amesbury on the A345, opposite the Inn at High Post.
Downland course.
18 holes, 6297 yards, S.S.S.70
Founded 1922
Visitors: welcome weekdays without restriction; h/cap cert required weekends.
Green Fee: WD £23 per round, £30 per day; WE £28 per round, £35 per day.
Societies: catered for weekdays.
Catering: full catering facilities.
Hotels: The Inn; High Post; Milford Hall (Salisbury).

B38 Highcliffe Castle
☎(01425) 272210, Pro 276640
107 Lymington Rd, Highcliffe on Sea, Dorset BH23 4LA
A35 to Hinton Admiral, follow signpost to Highcliffe, approx 1 mile; on A337 3 miles E of Christchurch.
Seaside course.
18 holes, 4762 yards, S.S.S.63
Founded 1913

Visitors: welcome if member of recognised golf club.
Green Fee: WD £19.50; WE £27.50.
Societies: Tues only, with prior arrangement.
Catering: bar and restaurant facilities available.
Hotels: Avonmouth; Waterford Lodge, Old Vicarage.

B39 Highworth Golf Centre
☎(01793) 766014
Highworth Community Golf Centre, Swindon Rd, Highworth, Wilts SN6 7SJ
A361 Swindon Highworth road, in village.
Public, undulating downland course.
9 holes, 3120 yards, S.S.S.35
Designed by Borough of Thamesdown.
Founded 1990
Visitors: welcome.
Green Fee: WD £4.85; WE £5.90.
Societies: welcome.
Catering: none.
9 hole Pitch & Putt, 4 hole practice course.
Hotels: Blunsdon House, Jesmond House.

B40 Hyde House Country Club
☎(01929) 471847, Fax 471849.
Forest Lodge, Hyde, Nr Wareham, Dorset
Woodland/parkland courses with river and lakes.
Old, 18 holes, 6469 yards, S.S.S.72; New, 18 holes, 6204 yards, S.S.S.71
Designed by J. Hamilton Stutt & Chris Reynard.
Visitors: Welcome on application
Green Fee: £15 per round, £20 a day.
Societies: welcome weekdays and weekends.
Catering: available
Hotels: accommodation available.

B41 Iford Bridge Sports Complex
☎(01202) 473817
Iford Bridge Sports Centre, Barrack Rd, Iford, Christchurch, Dorset BH23 2BA
Off A35 between Bournemouth and Christchurch, then signposted.
Public parkland/meadowland course next to River Stour.
9 holes, 4290 yards, S.S.S.62
Founded 1977

Visitors: welcome.
Green Fee: WD £5.70; WE £6.45.
Societies: welcome.
Catering: bar facilities and snacks available.
Driving range, tennis, bowling.
Hotels: for bargain breaks contact Christchurch Information Centre (01202 471780).

B42 Isle of Purbeck
☎(01929) 450361, Pro 450354 Pro, Fax 450501.
Studland, Dorset BH19 3AB
Either by ferry from Sandbanks or by road through Wareham, turning left onto B3351 signposted Studland at Corfe Castle.
Undulating heathland course.
Purbeck Course, 18 holes, 6295 yards, S.S.S.71; Dene Course, 9 holes, 2007 yards, S.S.S.30
Designed by H.S. Colt.
Founded August 1892
Visitors: welcome; h/cap cert required for Purbeck Course.
Green Fee: Purbeck Course, WD £25 per round, £32.50 per day; WE £30 per round, £37.50 per day. Dene Course, WD £10; WE £12
Societies: welcome by arrangement.
Catering: bar open from 10.30am daily, restaurant open Tues-Sun.
Hotels: Knoll House; Pines (Swanage).

B43 Isle of Wedmore
☎(01934) 712452 (Pro), Office: 713649, Fax 713696.
Lineage, Lascots Hill, Wedmore, Somerset BS28 4QT
1st right past church in Wedmore, 0.5 mile on right.
Parkland course.
18 holes, 5900 yards, S.S.S.68
Designed by Terry Murray.
Founded July 1992
Visitors: welcome, usual standards of dress, no jeans T-shirts etc.
Green Fee: WD £15; WE £20.
Societies: welcome by prior arrangement, groups up to 100, weekdays only.
Catering: full bar and restaurant facilities
Hotels: Webbington (Loxton)

B44 Kingsdown
☎(01225) 742530, Pro 742634.
Kingsdown, Corsham, Wilts SN13 8BS
Turn off A4 onto A363, left at Crown Inn 250 yards, uphill for 2 miles.

Heathland course.
18 holes, 6445 yards, S.S.S.71
Founded 1880
Visitors: welcome with h/caps, not weekends.
Green Fee: WD £22.
Societies: by arrangement with Sec.
Catering: dining room meals or bar snacks.
Hotels: Beaufort (Bath); Conigre Farm (Melksham); Orchard (Bathford). Leigh Park Hotel (Bradford).

B45 Knighton Heath
☎(01202) 572633, Pro 578275, Fax 590774.
Francis Ave, Bournemouth, Dorset B11 8NX
On main A348 Poole-Ringwood road, junction with A3049 at Wallisdown roundabout.
Heathland course.
18 holes, 6064 yards, S.S.S.69
Founded 1976
Visitors: after 9.30am weekdays, not weekends or Bank Holidays, h/cap cert required.
Green Fee: WD £20 per round, £25 per day.
Societies: weekdays by prior arrangement.
Catering: lunch daily except Mon.
Hotels: Bridge House (Longham).

B46 Knowle
☎(0117) 9770660, Pro 9779193, Fax 9720615.
Fairway, Brislington, Bristol BS4 5DF
3 miles S of city centre on the A4 to junction with West Town Lane, entrance on left 800 yards along West Town Lane.
Parkland course.
18 holes, 6061 yards, S.S.S.69
Designed by Hawtree & J.H. Taylor.
Founded 1905
Visitors: welcome weekdays, weekends by special arrangement; h/cap certs required.
Green Fee: WD £22 per round, £27 per day; WE £27 per round, £32 per day.
Societies: Thurs only.
Catering: lunch daily, evening meals by arrangement.
Hotels: Grange (Keynsham).

B47 Long Ashton
☎(01275) 392316 (Sec), Pro 392265, Fax 394395
Clarken Combe, Long Ashton, Bristol BS18 9DW

Leave M5 at junction 19, take A369 to Bristol, turn right into B3129 at traffic lights and then left onto B3128; club is 0.5 mile on right.
Undulating moorland/parkland course.
18 holes, 6077 yards, S.S.S.70
Designed by Hawtree & Taylor.
Founded 1893
Visitors: must have official club h/cap.
Green Fee: WD £26; WE £35.
Societies: by arrangement.
Catering: full facilities daily until 6pm; evening meal by arrangement.
Hotels: Redwood Lodge.

B48 Long Sutton
☎(01458) 241017, Fax 241022.
Long Load, Nr Langport, Somerset TA10 9JU
Take Langport road from A303, after 3 miles turn left into Long Sutton, course 1 mile on left.
Parkland course.
18 holes, 6368 yards, S.S.S. 70.
Designed by Patrick Dawson.
Founded Sept 1991
Visitors: pay-as-you-play course, tees must be booked at weekends.
Green Fee: WD £12; WE £16.
Societies: by prior arrangement.
Catering: bar and restaurant.
Driving range.
Hotels: arrange through Sec.

B49 Lyme Regis
☎(01297) 442963, Pro 443822, Catering: 442043.
Timber Hill, Lyme Regis, Dorset DT7 3HQ
Off A3052 Charmouth road 1 mile E of town.
Clifftop course.
18 holes, 6220 yards, S.S.S.70
Founded 1893
Visitors: welcome, must have h/cap cert or proof of membership of recognised club; restrictions on Thurs and Sun.
Green Fee: £20 per round, £17 after 2pm.
Societies: apply for booking; Mon, Tues, Wed, Fri, Sat.
Catering: full à la carte, hot and cold snacks all day.
Hotels: Alexander; Bay; Buena Vista; Devon; Fairwater Head; Tudor House; all offer reduced green fees.

B50 Lyons Gate
☎(01300) 345239
Lyons Gate Farm, Lyons Gate, Dorchester DT2 7AZ

3 miles N of Cerne Abbas on A352
Sherborne-Dorchester road.
Wooded farmland course.
9 holes, 3838 yards, S.S.S.60
Designed by Ken Abel.
Founded 1991
Visitors: welcome by arrangement,
8am-5pm summer, 8.30am-4.30pm
Oct-Mar.
Green Fee: WD £4.50 (9 holes),
£7.50 (18 holes); WE £5 (9 holes),
£8.50 (18).
Societies: unrestricted
Catering: light refreshments;
clubhouse.
Practice nets.
Hotels: Kings Arms.

B51 **Manor House Golf Club (at Castle Combe)**
☎(01249) 782982, Fax 782992, Pro
783101
Castle Combe, Wilts SN14 7PL
On B4039 to N of Castle Combe
village.
Ancient woodland/parkland course
18 holes, 6340 yards, Par 73
Designed by Peter Alliss and Clive
Clark.
Founded 1992. Re named 1994
Visitors: welcome any time, with
h/cap cert and prior tee reservation
.required,
Green Fee: WD £30; WE £40.
Societies: Available with prior
booking.
Catering: 2 bars, restaurant, private
dining facilities, bar snacks available
all day.
Snooker room, practice range.
Hotels: Manor House.

B52 **Marlborough**
☎(01672) 512147, Pro 512493, Fax
513164.
The Common, Marlborough, Wilts
SN8 1DU
0.75 mile from town centre on A345
to Swindon.
Downland course.
18 holes, 6505 yards, S.S.S.71
Founded 1888
Visitors: welcome weekdays and
weekends on non-competition days,
ring in advance for details; h/cap
certs required.
Green Fee: WD £21 per round, £32
per day; WE on application,
telephone for details.
Societies: with prior booking,
weekdays only.
Catering: full catering facilities all
week.
Hotels: Castle & Ball; Ivy House.

B53 **Mendip**
☎(01749) 840570 (Sec), Pro
840793, Fax 841439.
Gurney Slade, Bath, Somerset BA3
4UT
3 miles N of Shepton Mallet off A37.
Undulating downland course.
18 holes, 6330 yards, S.S.S.70
Designed by H. Vardon with an
extension by F. Pennink.
Founded 1908
Visitors: with member only at
weekends unless member of affiliated
club; phone Pro to check availability.
Green Fee: WD £20 per round, £25
per day; WE £30.
Societies: welcome Mon and Thurs
Catering: full facilities every day.

B54 **Mendip Spring**
☎(01934) 853337, Club 852322, Fax
853021.
Honeyhall Lane, Congresbury, Avon
BS19 5JT
From M5 junction 21 take A370
towards Bristol, turn right in
Congresbury onto B3133.
Parkland course with hill views.
Brinsea, 18 holes, 6328 yards,
S.S.S.70; Lakeside, 9 holes, 2260
yards
Designed by Terry Murray.
Founded 1991
Visitors: starting times may be
reserved.
Green Fee: WD £17; WE £19. 9
holes £6.
Societies: apply to director of golf.
Catering: bar and restaurant.
Driving range.

B55 **Mid-Dorset**
☎(01258) 861386.
Belchalwell, Blandford Forum, Dorset
DT11 0EG
9 miles SW of Blandford between
Okeford Fitzpaine and Ibberton.
Parkland course.
18 holes, 6162 yards S.S.S. 71.
Designed by Project Golf (D.W.
Asthill).
Founded 1990
Visitors: all welcome.
Green Fee: WD £12 per round, £20
per day; WE £17 per round, £27 per
day.
Societies: welcome by prior
arrangement.
Catering: lunches, tea, evening
meals, 7-day bar open all day. Large
practice facilities.
Hotels: Swan (Sturminster Newton);
Crown (Blandford); telephone for
details on B&B.

B56 **Millfield School**
☎(01458) 442291 ext.279
Nr Glastonbury, Somerset
1 mile SE of Butleigh.
Parkland course.
9 holes, 4519 yards, S.S.S.62
Founded 1970
Visitors: members and guests only
and when not required by school.
Green Fee: £4.

B57 **Minehead & West Somerset**
☎(01643) 702057, Pro 704378, Fax
705095.
The Warren, Minehead, Somerset
TA24 5SJ
E end of sea front.
Links course.
18 holes, 6228 yards, S.S.S.71
Designed by Johnny Alan.
Founded 1882
Visitors: welcome.
Green Fee: WD £22; WE £25.
Societies: welcome on written
application.
Catering: by prior arrangement with
caterer; snacks always available.
Hotels: York; Northfield; Marshfield.

B58 **Monkton Park Par 3**
☎(01249) 653928 (Tel/Fax)
Monkton Park, Chippenham, Wilts
SN15 3PE
Into Chippenham, past railway
station, turn right.
Parkland course.
9 holes, Par 3 (longest hole 175
yards)
Designed by M. Dawson.
Founded 1960
Visitors: welcome.
Green Fee: WD £3 (9 holes), £4.50
(18 holes); WE £3.20 (9 holes), £4.80
(18 holes).
Catering: refreshments available.

B59 **North Wilts**
☎(01380) 860627 (Sec), Pro
860330, Fax 860061.
Bishops Cannings, Devizes, Wilts
SN10 2LP
1 mile from A4 E of Calne.
Downland course.
18 holes, 6333 yards, S.S.S.71
Founded 1890
Visitors: welcome, h/cap cert
required at weekends.
Green Fee: WD £18; WE £30.
Societies: welcome by arrangement.
Catering: full facilities available.
Hotels: Bear (Devizes); Lansdowne
Strand (Calne).

B60 Oake Manor

☎(01823) 461993, Fax 461995.
Oake, Taunton, Somerset TA4 1BA
M5 northbound, exit 26, then A38 to
Taunton, signs to Oake; 10 mins from
motorway. M5 southbound, exit 25
onto B3227, 5 miles W of Taunton.
Parkland course with lakes.
18 holes, 6109 yards, S.S.S.70
Designed by Adrian Stiff.
Founded July 1993
Visitors: welcome 7 days, phone for
start times.
Green Fee: WD £13.50; WE £15.
Societies: golf days and societies
welcome weekdays by arrangement.
Catering: bar and bar snacks,
restaurant, 8am-10pm daily.
Driving range.
Hotels: Rumwell Manor.

B61 Oaksey Park

☎(01666) 577995, Fax 577174.
Oaksey, Nr Malmesbury, Wilts SN16
9SB
Off A419 between Swindon and
Cirencester, W of Cotswold Water
Park.
Public parkland course.
9 holes, 2904 yards, S.S.S.68
Designed by Chapman & Warren.
Founded 1991
Visitors: welcome.
Green Fee: WD £8; WE £13.
Societies: welcome.
Catering: full facilities.
Driving range, practice ground, clay
pigeon shoot, children's play area,
archery, hot air ballooning.
Hotels: Oaksey Park Country
Cottages Hotel (10 farm cottages).

B62 Ogbourne Downs (Swindon)

☎(01672) 841327 (Sec), Pro 841287
Ogbourne St George, Marlborough,
Wilts SN8 1TB
Junction 15 off M4, on A345 to
Marlborough.
Undulating downland course.
18 holes, 6226 yards, S.S.S.70
Designed by Taylor, Hawtree and
Cotton.
Founded 1907-25 N Wilts, 25-95
Swindon 1995 Ogbourne Downs.
Visitors: welcome on weekdays.
Green Fee: £20
Societies: weekdays.
Catering: restaurant, bar snacks.

B63 Orchardleigh

☎(01373) 454200
Frome, Somerset BA11 2PH
On A362 1 mile NW of Frome.
Parkland course.
18 holes, 6,800 yards, S.S.S.73
Brian Huggett.
Founded 1995
Visitors: welcome; after 10am WE.
Green Fee: WD ú15, WE ú20.
Societies: welcome.
Catering: clubhouse opening 1996.
Hotels: Bishopstrow House.

B64 Parkstone

☎(01202) 707138, Pro 708092.
Links Rd, Parkstone, Poole, Dorset
BH14 9JU
A35 Bournemouth-Poole road, turn
left at St Osmond's Church.
Undulating heathland course.
18 holes, 6250 yards, S.S.S.70
Designed by Willie Park and James
Braid.
Founded 1910
Visitors: welcome (book in advance);
h/cap certs required.
Green Fee: WD £25 per round, £34
per day; WE £30 per round, £40 per
day.
Societies: welcome.
Catering: lunch available every day.

B65 Parley

☎(01202) 593131
Parley Green Lane, Hurn,
Christchurch, Dorset BH23 6BB
Opposite Bournemouth International
Airport.
Parkland course.
9 holes 4584 yards, Par 69
Designed by Paul Goodfellow.
Founded 1992
Visitors: welcome.
Green Fee: £3.50 (9 holes), £6.50
(18 holes).
Societies: contact in advance.
Catering: bar and snacks.

B66 Puxton Park

☎(01934) 876942
Woodspring Golf & Leisure Park,
Puxton, Nr Weston-Super-Mare, Avon
BS24 6TA
2 miles E of M5 junction 21 on A370
Bristol-Weston road.
Moorland course.
18 holes, 6559 yards, Par 72
Designed by R. Hemmingway &
Partner.
Founded 1992
Visitors: pay-and-play course, all
welcome.
Green Fee: WD £8; WE £10.
Societies: welcome.
Catering: bar.

B67 Queen's Park (Bournemouth)

☎(01202) 302611, Pro 396817.
Queen's Park West Drive,
Bournemouth, Dorset BH8 9BY
From Ringwood, proceed along
Wessex Way (A338), leave by 1st
junction, turn right at roundabout and
right again into Queens Park West
Drive.
Undulating public parkland course
18 holes, 6319 yards, S.S.S.71
Founded 1906
Visitors: welcome any time.
Green Fee: £12.
Societies: by prior arrangement.
Catering: bar and restaurant
facilities.

B68 RMCS Shrivenham

☎(01793) 785725
RMCS Shrivenham, Swindon, Wilts
SN6 8LA
In grounds of Royal Military College
of Science on A420 1 mile NE of
Shrivenham.
Parkland course
18 holes, 5547 yards, S.S.S.69
Founded 1953
Visitors: restricted access; with
member only; entry to grounds must
be arranged with Manager.
Green Fee: WD £8; WE £10.
Societies: limited access weekdays,
green fees + £1/day.
Catering: coffee/tea/soft drinks.

B69 Riversmeet

☎(01202) 477987
Two Riversmeet Leisure Centre,
Stony Lane South, Christchurch,
Dorset BH23 1HW
Left at mini-roundabout at end of
Christchurch High St, on to
crossroads, turn right to Leisure
Centre.
Picturesque public seaside course.
18 holes, 1455 yards, Par 3
Visitors: welcome any time.
Green Fee: £4 adults, £2.25 OAPs
and jnrs.
Catering: bar and restaurant.
Squash, badminton, swimming pool,
gym.

B70 Salisbury & South Wiltshire

☎(01722) 742645 (Sec), Pro 742929
Netherhampton, Salisbury, Wilts SP2
8PR
On A3094 2 miles from Salisbury and
from Wilton.
Downland course.

Sherborne

Sherborne belongs to that category of courses that provides the right degree of testing quality, without in any way impairing the enjoyment of a round in an incomparable setting – views, on a good day, across two or three counties. Taking the road up the hill out of a town famous for its abbey and its schools, you reach the club down a narrow country lane. Before the club's founding in 1894, the whole area was part of the fertile agricultural plain that surrounds it, but the second nine in particular covers some gently rolling land of which Harry Colt would most certainly have approved. He believed that undulations and hummocks are of great value through the green as they provide difficult stances and lies, without which no golf course can be deemed to be perfect.

Judged from the first six holes, Sherborne suggests a non-stop assault with woods and long irons. The first nine is, in fact, more than 800 yards longer than the second, though that does not necessarily mean that the second nine is any easier in relation to par. What it does mean is that the first six holes, including three par 5s, hold the key to a good score, the 1st and 3rd being notable par 4s.

It is easy enough though to have your card in tatters almost before you have started. There is plenty of scope for going out of bounds with an opening drive to a fairway which tapers cleverly to ensure that the further you hit the ball, the straighter you have to be. Control is essential too with the second shot to the 2nd, doglegging round the practice ground, while the 3rd and 4th, running up and back, are two of the best.

The 5th is the first of an excellent batch of short holes which vary in length and character, as all good short holes should, the 5th being perhaps the finest and the 7th the most daunting. In between, the par 5 6th demands a well positioned drive to allow a flat stance for what is most likely to be a long second; and the second, too, requires both care and thought in order to leave the easiest pitch when the pin is tucked away at the back of the green.

Nothing less than the most truly-hit tee shot will suffice at the 7th but there is a little respite at the 8th and 9th, which epitomises the compact nature of the layout on a limited acreage. It accommodates one more hole, the third par 3, before crossing back and passing the clubhouse and on down the excellent 459 yard 11th where the sloping terrain demands that, to hold both fairway and green, there is a very definite, if narrow, line to adopt.

It is from the tee that the full panorama of the view unfolds, an unmistakable slice of England at its greenest and best. There are other chances to stand and stare but not until the business in hand is complete and the ridge up the 18th fairway has been safely scaled.

In the meantime, the tiny 12th is not to be taken lightly. It is an admirable illustration that short holes don't have to be 200 yards to give a sense of achievement at hitting the green; and, though of modest length also, the 13th and 14th, one up and one back down again, permit little error in judging the pitches comprising the second shots.

The 15th has much in common with the 7th, a tee shot with the emphasis on carry, while the drive at the 16th must be well flighted to clear the trees guarding the wooded menace on the right. It may be wiser to take the safer line to the left and to rub shoulders with those turning back up the 17th with its hopes of a birdie. But, by now, thoughts will be on negotiating the final slope to the 18th.

This is done preferably with a drive and crisp iron, but for those flagging physically and in spirit, the sight of the clubhouse has the same effect as an oasis in the desert and it's no mirage. It has splendid reviving powers and if, on reflection, your golf is best forgotten, look not on the dark side. A further glimpse at the scenic splendour will promptly persuade you that it has been amply worthwhile.

18 holes, 6528 yards, S.S.S.71; 9 hole course.
Designed by J.H. Taylor. Extra 9 holes by S Gidman 1991
Founded 1888
Visitors: welcome; h/cap cert required weekends.
Green Fee: WD £25; WE £40.
Societies: welcome by arrangement.
Catering: full bar and catering facilities.
Snooker.
Hotels: Rose & Crown, Kings Arms (both Salisbury); Pembroke Arms (Wilton).

B71 Saltford
☎(01225) 873513, Pro 872043
Golf Club Lane, Saltford, Bristol BS18 3AA
Off A4 between Bath and Bristol.
Meadowland course.
18 holes, 6046 yards, S.S.S.69
Founded 1904
Visitors: welcome; h/cap cert required.
Green Fee: WD £22; WE £30.
Societies: Mon and Thurs by arrangement.
Catering: meals served daily.
Snooker.
Hotels: Grange (Keynsham); Crown; Tunnel House.

B72 Sherborne
☎(01935) 812475 (Club), Sec 814431, Pro 812274.
Higher Clatcombe, Sherborne, Dorset DT9 4RN
1 mile N of Sherborne off B3145 to Wincanton.
Parkland course.
18 holes, 5949 yards, S.S.S.68
Designed by James Braid.
Founded 1894
Visitors: weekdays and weekends dependent on Club Diary.
Green Fee: WD £25; WE £30.
Societies: Tues and Wed by arrangement.
Catering: comprehensive range of facilities available.
Hotels: Sherborne; Eastbury; Antelope.

B73 Shrivenham Park
☎(01793) 783853, Fax 782999.
Pennyhooks, Shrivenham, Swindon, Wilts SN6 8EX
A420 Swindon-Oxford road 6 miles from Swindon, leave by-pass for Shrivenham; on E edge of village.
Public undulating parkland course.

18 holes, 6100 yards, S.S.S.70
Designed by Roger Mace, Glen Johnson.
Visitors: welcome, pay-as-you-play.
Green Fee: WD £10.50; WE £12.50.
Societies: at all times.
Catering: full bar and restaurant facilities.

B74 Solent Meads Par 3
☎(01202) 420795
Rolls Drive, Nr Hengistbury Head, Bournemouth, Dorset
In Selfridge Avenue, off Broadway at Hengistbury Head.
Public seaside course.
18 holes, Par 3, 2235 yards
Visitors: welcome at all times.
Green Fee: £4.
Catering: light refreshments, cafe.
Driving range.

B75 Stockwood Vale
☎(0117) 9866505, Sec 9860509.
Stockwood Lane, Keynsham, Bristol BS18 2ER
In Stockwood Lane off A4.
Public, undulating parkland course.
9 holes, 5520 yards, S.S.S.67
Designed by J. Wade & M. Ramsay.
Founded 1991
Visitors: no restrictions; proper dress required; tee times bookable 7 days in advance.
Green Fee: £6
Societies: by prior arrangement..
Driving range.
Hotels: The Grange.

B76 Sturminster Marshall
☎(01258) 858444
Moor Lane, Sturminster Marshall, Dorset BH21 4AH
Off A350 Poole-Blandford road, signposted from middle of village.
Meadowland course.
9 holes, 4650 yards, S.S.S.63
Designed by John Sharkey.
Founded 1992
Visitors: welcome, no restrictions.
Green Fee: £6 (9 holes), £8 (18 holes).
Societies: welcome.
Catering: cafeteria, soft drinks.

B77 Tall Pines
☎(01275) 472076 Tel/Fax
Cooks Bridle Path, Downside, Backwell, Bristol BS19 3DJ
0.5 mile N of Bristol Airport.
Public parkland course.
18 holes, 5857 yards, S.S.S.68

Designed by Terry Murray.
Founded 1990
Visitors: welcome, booking at weekends only.
Green Fee: WD £12; WE £14.
Societies: Mon-Fri.
Catering: Bar and restaurant.
Hotels: Town and Country Lodge

B78 Taunton & Pickeridge
☎(01823) 421537 (Sec), Fax 521742, Pro 421790
Corfe, Taunton, Somerset TA3 7BY
B3170, 4 miles S of Taunton, through Corfe village, then 1st left.
Undulating course.
18 holes, 5926 yards, S.S.S.68
Designed by Hawtree
Founded 1892
Visitors: welcome weekdays by arrangement, h/cap cert required.
Green Fee: WD £20; WE £25.
Societies: by arrangement
Catering: full facilities.
Hotels: Castle.

B79 Taunton Vale
☎(01823) 412220 (Sec), Pro/reservations: 412880, Fax 413583.
Creech Heathfield, Taunton, Somerset TA3 5EY
Just off A361 at junction with A38, exits 24 or 25 from M5.
Parkland course.
18 holes, 6142 yards, S.S.S 69; 9 holes, 2000 yards, S.S.S.60
Designed by John Pyne.
Founded July 1991
Visitors: welcome, appropriate dress and etiquette.
Green Fee: WD £14; WE £17.50. 9 holes, WD £7; WE £8.75.
Societies: welcome weekdays.
Catering: full bar and catering in clubhouse.
Driving range.
Hotels: Walnut Tree (N Petherton - Best Western packages); Post House, Castle(Taunton); Falcon (Henlade).

B80 Thoulstone Park
☎(01373) 832825, Pro 832808, Fax 832821
Chapmanslade, Nr Westbury, Wilts BA13 4AQ
2.5 miles W of Warminster on A36.
Parkland course with spectacular views.
18 holes, 6312 yards, S.S.S.70
Designed by M.R.M. Sandow
Founded Oct 1991

Visitors: welcome.
Green Fee: WD £15; WE £20.
Societies: welcome weekdays; special arrangements for weekends, contact General Manager.
Catering: Restaurants, bars; conference facilities, function rooms, offices.
Driving range, sauna.

B81 Tickenham
☎(01275) 856626
Clevedon Rd, Tickenham, Avon BS21 6SB
From M5 junc 20 go rt at the first 2 roundabouts towards Nailsea and the course is just after the village of Tickenham
Parkland course
9 holes 3600 yards, Par 58
Re opened Dec 95
Visitors: welcome
Green Fee: WD £5 (9 holes), £9 (18 holes); WE £6 (9 holes), £10 (18 holes)
Societies: welcome
Catering: club house planned.

B82 Upavon (RAF)
☎(01980) 630787 (Club Manager), Pro 630281
Douglas Avenue, Upavon, Nr. Pewsey, Wilts SN9 6BQ
2 miles SE of Upavon village on A342 Andover-Devizes road.
Undulating downland course.
9 holes, 5589 yards, S.S.S.67
Founded 1918
Visitors: welcome on weekdays, weekends with member or after 11am with h/cap certificate.
Green Fee: WD £12 per round, £16 per day; WE £24.
Societies: welcome, call for details.
Catering: by special arrangement.
Hotels: Shears; Crown; Woodbridge Inn.

B83 Vivary
☎(01823) 289274, Bookings/Manager: 333875.
Taunton, Somerset
In centre of Taunton.
Municipal parkland course.
18 holes, 4620 yards, S.S.S.63
Designed by Herbert Fowler.
Founded 1928
Visitors: welcome.
Green Fee: £7.50 per round.
Societies: welcome weekdays only; special rates for groups of 16+; Company days available.
Catering: available.

B84 Wareham
☎(01929) 554147, Fax 554147.
Sandford Rd, Wareham, Dorset BH20 4DH
On A351 near railway station, 8 miles from Poole.
Undulating parkland course with fine views.
18 holes, 5603 yards, S.S.S.67
Designed by C. Whitcome
Founded 1908
Visitors: welcome 9.30am to 5pm Mon-Fri, phone in advance; h/cap certs required.
Green Fee: £15 per round, £20 per day.
Societies: by arrangement.
Catering: full bar and catering facilities.
Hotels: Springfield.

B85 Wells (Somerset)
☎(01749) 675005, Pro 679059
East Horrington Rd, Wells, Somerset BA5 3DS
1.5 miles from city centre off B3139.
Meadowland/parkland course.
18 holes, 6015 yards, S.S.S.69
Founded 1893 (extended course opened 1993)
Visitors: welcome, current h/cap card required weekends; no visitors before 9.30am weekends.
Green Fee: WD £18; WE £20.
Societies: welcome with advance booking, weekdays only.
Catering: bar, midday and evening meals available 7 days.
Hotels: Caravan facilities adjacent to course.

B86 Wessex Golf Centre
☎(01305) 784737
Radipole Lane, Weymouth, Dorset
Behind Weymouth football ground.
9 holes, Par 3
Visitors: welcome any time.
Green Fee: £3.85 per round (£5.50 inc. club hire).
Driving range.

B87 West Wilts
☎(01985) 212702 (Steward), Pro 212110, Sec 213133
Elm Hill, Warminster, Wilts BA12 0AU
Towards Westbury, on edge of town, on old road, not on the new by-pass; 1 mile from centre of Warminster.
Downland course, scenic views.
18 holes, 5709 yards, S.S.S.68
Designed by J.H. Taylor.
Founded 1891
Visitors: welcome with h/cap cert, except Sat and Sun am.
Green Fee: WD £24; WE £35.
Societies: accepted Wed/Thurs/Fri, contact Sec.
Catering: available.
Hotels: The Bell.

B88 Weston-super-Mare
☎(01934) 626968 (Office), Pro 633360
Uphill Rd North, Weston-super-Mare, Avon BS23 4NQ
M5 or A370 from Bristol.
Seaside links course.
18 holes, 6208 yards, S.S.S.70
Designed by T. Dunn.
Founded July 1892
Visitors: welcome, h/cap cert required at weekends and Bank Holidays.
Green Fee: WD £20; WE £28.
Societies: by arrangement.
Catering: bar and restaurant, snacks and meals daily.
Snooker.
Hotels: Grand Atlantic; Beachlands; Arosfa; Rozel.

B89 Weymouth
☎(01305) 773981, Pro 773997.
Links Rd, Weymouth, Dorset DT4 0PF
From Dorchester take A354, at Wessex roundabout take Town Centre exit, signposted at next exit.
Seaside/parkland course.
18 holes, 5976 yards, S.S.S.69
Designed by originally by James Braid; redesigned by J. Hamilton Stutt.
Founded 1909
Visitors: welcome with h/cap cert or proof of club membership.
Green Fee: WD £25; WE £30.
Societies: Tues and Thurs by arrangement.
Catering: full bar and restaurant facilities.
Practice area.
Hotels: Moonfleet Manor, weekday packages.

B90 Wheathill
☎(01963) 240667, Fax 240230
Wheathill, Somerton, Somerset TA11 7HG
Take A37 towards Yeovil. At village of Lydford Cross turn left. Course 1 mile on left
Parkland
18 holes 5362 yards S.S.S. 66
Designed J Payne
Opened; May 1993

Visitors: welcome
Green Fee: WD £10; WE £12
Societies: welcome.
Catering: bar and full catering facilities
12 acre practice ground. 4 hole academy course opening spring 1996
Hotels: George (Castle Carey); Lydford House

B91 Windwhistle

☎(01460) 30231, Fax 30055
Windwhistle, Cricket St Thomas, Nr Chard, Somerset TA20 4DG
On N side of A30 5 miles from Crewkerne, 3 miles from Chard, opposite wildlife park; follow signs from M5 junction 25.
Downland/parkland course.
18 holes, 6470 yards, S.S.S.71; 9 holes, 2542 yards par 3.
Designed by J.H. Taylor (1932), Leonard Fisher (1992).
Founded 1932
Visitors: welcome but advisable to phone first.
Green Fee: WD £12; WE £16.
Societies: welcome by appointment, phone for information.
Catering: comprehensive catering facilities.
International standard squash courts.
Hotels: information on request.

B92 Wootton Bassett

☎(01793) 849999, Pro 851360, Fax 849988
Wootton Basset, Swindon, Wilts SN4 7PB
Parkland course with 10 large lakes.
18 holes, 6496 yards, S.S.S. 71
Designed by Peter Alliss and Clive Clark.
Founded April 1992

B93 Worlebury

☎(01934) 623214 (Clubhouse), Sec/Fax 625789
Monks Hill, Worlebury, Weston-super-Mare, Avon BS22 9SX
2 miles from M5 at top of hill (off A370); 2 miles from centre of Weston-super-Mare.
Seaside meadowland course.
18 holes, 5936 yards, S.S.S.69
Designed by W. Hawtree & Son.
Founded 1908
Visitors: welcome on weekdays after 9am; h/cap certificate and membership of recognised club or society.
Green Fee: WD £20; WE £30.
Societies: catered for on weekdays, other weekdays by special arrangement.
Catering: licenced bar, restaurant serving snacks, lunch and evening meal.
Snooker.
Hotels: Beachlands; Commodore; Rozel; Queenswood.

B94 Wrag Barn Golf & Country Club

☎(01793) 861327 (Sec), Pro 766027, Fax 861325
Shrivenham Rd, Highworth, Wilts SN6 7QQ
10 miles from M4 Junction 15; take A419 towards Cirencester, left turn to Highworth, follow A316 to Highworth then 3rd exit at roundabout onto B4000 to Shrivenham; course is 0.5 mile on right.
Undulating, scenic, parkland course.
18 holes, 6548 yards, S.S.S.71
Designed by Hawtree & Sons.
Founded July 1990
Visitors: welcome; some restrictions at weekends, advisable to ring Pro.
Green Fee: WD £18; WE £23.
Societies: by arrangement with Sec.
Catering: full bar and restaurant facilities; catering for companies, parties, receptions.
Hotels: Blunsden House Hotel & Leisure Centre (Blunsden); Jesmond House (Highworth).

B95 Yeovil

☎(01935) 22965 (Sec), Clubhouse 75949, Pro 73763, Fax 411283.
Sherborne Rd, Yeovil, Somerset BA21 5BW
1 mile E of Yeovil on A30 Yeovil to Sherborne.
Undulating parkland course.
Old course, 18 holes, 6144 yards, S.S.S.70; Newton course, 9 holes, 4891 yards, S.S.S.66
Designed by 18 hole, Fowler & Alison; 9 hole, Sports Turf Research Institute.
Founded 1919
Visitors: welcome weekdays, both courses 9.30am-12.30pm and 2pm onwards (h/cap cert required for Old Course).
Green Fee: on application
Societies: must be affiliated to EGU or bona-fide members of a golf club.
Catering: full bar and restaurant facilities available.
Driving/practice area, snooker.
Hotels: Yeovil Court, Manor House (Yeovil); Northover House (Ilchester); Sherborne.

Visitors: telephone in advancefor availability.
Green Fee: WD £20; WE £25
Societies: phone for availability.
Catering: full bar and restaurant facilities.

C

HAMPSHIRE, SUSSEX, ISLE OF WIGHT

The connoisseur, making his way east from Brokenhurst Manor in the New Forest to Rye on the East Sussex border with Kent, passes through as good and varied a golfing tapestry as could be imagined – a veritable Aladdin's Cave. Compared with other parts of the country, the volume of courses is none too dense but any shortcomings in quantity are more than absorbed by quality.

For the purposes of playing qualification at county level, Hampshire embraces the Channel Islands, the Isle of Wight and Hayling Island, the latter a links, or part links, which Tom Simpson rated enormously highly. I also remember Henry Longhurst singing its praises and I can join in the chorus. Hampshire's inland gems are North Hants at Fleet, Blackmoor and Liphook – all extensions of the rich seam of heather, gorse and silver birch country which starts with Wentworth and Sunningdale in the east and continues down through Swinley Forest and Camberley Heath.

Liphook, straddling the busy A3 and involving one or two mad dashes to cross it, has had strong naval connections in view of its proximity to Portsmouth but it has remained essentially a refuge for the Club golfer in spite of being able to test the best.

Hockley and Royal Winchester typify downland golf at its best, while Stoneham at Southampton is more in the mould of Liphook. Sussex, too, is full of variety with something for everyone. West Sussex at Pulborough is a particular favourite, ideal for any occasion and giving the chance of a good score with its five short holes although, like Rye, the par of 68 can be tantalisingly elusive.

Straight hitting has more merit than unharnessed power, for the heather is punishing, but the unique charms of Rye centre more on a battle with the winds that sweep off the sea or across the exposed and chilly reaches of Romney Marsh.

There is a charm about Rye that never varies or fades. Expectation begins with departure from the ancient town and its cobbled streets and heightens as the road to Camber twists and turns through fields of grazing sheep. The character of the golf is distinctive in the range of shots it demands, the ability to flight the ball and gauge how it will run on landing being infinitely more valuable than memorising yardage charts and clubbing by numbers.

Rye is a monument to the links style of British golf but the new East Sussex National is the opposite, an expensive machine-shaped exercise in creating a new landscape over which the European Open was played in 1993.

There are those who prefer courses which preserve nature rather than fighting it, and nowhere is that aspect better illustrated than at Royal Ashdown Forest or at Crowborough, which run hither and thither across the Sussex Downs, Ashdown Forest notably without bunkers.

Goodwood is another from whose highest points scenic splendour unfurls, a contrast to its neighbour, the Goodwood Park Hotel Golf and Country Club which occupies a large part of the grounds of Goodwood House. Bognor Regis, Selsey and Littlehampton lie a few miles to the south while Chichester Golf Centre is a recently opened venture at Hunston – ideal for those wishing to learn the ropes.

Worthing, Brighton and Eastbourne are well served while Cooden Beach has its host of admirers, along with a particular favourite in Seaford, another downland course overlooking the Channel.

C1 Alresford

☎(01962) 733746 (Sec), Pro 733998, Fax 736040
Cheriton Rd, Tichborne Down, Alresford, Hants SO24 0PN
1 mile S of A31 Winchester-Alton road, 2 miles N of A272 Winchester-Petersfield road.
Undulating parkland course.
18 holes, 5905 yards, S.S.S.68
Designed by Scott Webb Young
Founded 16 Nov 1890
Visitors: welcome; not before 12am weekends and Bank Holidays.
Green Fee: WD £18; WE £35.
Societies: Tues-Thurs; book via Sec.
Catering: full catering except Mon.
Hotels: Swan; Bell.

C2 Alton

☎(01420) 82042, Pro 86518
Old Odiham Rd, Alton, Hants GU34 4BU
2 miles N of Alton on A32 turn right at Golden Pot public house, 1st right again, 0.5 mile on right.
Undulating parkland course.
9 holes, 5744 yards, S.S.S.68
Founded 1908
Visitors: welcome Mon-Fri; weekends 18 h/cap or with member.
Green Fee: WD £9 per round, £14 per day; WE £16.
Societies: WD by prior arrangement.
Catering: bar and snacks available.
Hotels: Alton House; Swan.

C3 Ampfield Par 3

☎(01794) 368480, Pro 368750
Winchester Rd, Ampfield, Romsey, Hants SO51 9BQ
On A31 2.5 miles W of Hursley, next door to White Horse public house.
Parkland course.
18 holes, 2478 yards, S.S.S.53
Designed by Henry Cotton.
Founded 1963
Visitors: welcome but advisable to telephone first; h/cap cert required weekends and Bank Holidays.
Green Fee: £9
Societies: small societies welcome weekdays by prior arrangement.
Catering: light lunch, snacks and society dinners by prior arrangement.
Hotels: Potters Heron (Ampfield); White Horse (Romsey).

C4 Andover

☎(01264) 358040 (Sec), Members: 323980, Pro 324151
Winchester Rd, Andover, Hants SP10 2EF

Just off A303 on Andover by-pass, entrance to club about 500 yards after leaving A303 on A3057.
Undulating parkland course.
9 holes, 6096 yards, S.S.S.69
Designed by J.H. Taylor.
Founded 1907
Visitors: welcome.
Green Fee: WD £10; WE £22.
Societies: welcome Mon-Wed.
Catering: snacks, lunch, evening meal.
Hotels: Danebury; White Hart.

C5 Army

☎(01252) 540638 (Sec), Club 541104, Pro 547232
Laffans Rd, Aldershot, Hants GU11 2HF
Access from Eelmoor Bridge off A323 Aldershot-Fleet road.
Heathland course.
18 holes, 6550 yards, S.S.S.71
Designed by Frank Pennink.
Founded 1883
Visitors: welcome Mon-Fri, h/cap cert required.
Green Fee: £22 per round, £30 per day
Societies: Mon, Thurs only.
Catering: available 9am to 5pm.
Hotels: Queens, Potters International.

C6 Ashdown Forest Hotel

☎(01342) 824866, Fax 824869
Chapel Lane, Forest Row, E Sussex RH18 5BB
3 miles S of East Grinstead on A22 in village of Forest Row, E on B2110; Chapel Lane 4th on right.
Heathland/woodland course.
18 holes, 5586 yards, S.S.S.67
Designed by Horace Hutchinson (1930s); Henry Luff (1965).
Founded 1985 (Anderida Golfers).
Visitors: welcome but advisable to check, particularly at weekends.
Green Fee: WD £16; WE £21.
Societies: catered for 7 days.
Catering: full restaurant service and bar snacks 7 days. Banqueting facilities up to 100.
Hotels: Ashdown Forest.

C7 Avisford Park

☎(01243) 554611, Fax 555580
Avisford Park, Yapton Lane,Walberton, Arundel, W Sussex BN18 0LS
On A27 4 miles W of Arundel, 6 miles E of Chichester.
Parkland course.

9 holes, 5703 yards, S.S.S.68 (18 holes May 1996)
Visitors: welcome, pay-as-you-play system.
Green Fee: WD £14; WE £18.
Societies: any time, terms on application.
Catering: bar.
Tennis, swimming, squash, snooker etc.
Hotels: Stakis Arundel.

C8 Barton-on-Sea

☎(01425) 615308 (Sec), Pro 611210, Members: 610189, Steward: 639092, Fax 621457.
Milford Road, New Milton, Hants BH25 8PP.
On B3057
Seaside course.
27 holes played in 3 combinations of 9. Needles/ Beckton 6492 SSS 71; Beckton/ Stroller 6276 SSS 70; Needles/ Stroller 6444 SSS 71
Designed by H.S. Colt/ J Hamilton Stutt.
Founded 1898. New course 1993.
Visitors: welcome weekdays after 9.30am and weekends and Bank Holidays after 11.15am; advisable to ring to ascertain programme for day.
Green Fee: apply for details.
Societies: societies 12 and over accepted weekdays.
Catering: snacks and teas available, evening catering for societies by arrangement.
Hotels: Chewton Glen; Old Coastguard; Passford House.

C9 Basingstoke

☎(01256) 465990, Pro 51332, Fax 331793.
Kempshott Park, Basingstoke, Hants RG23 7LL
On A30 3 miles W of Basingstoke, M3 junction 7.
Parkland course.
18 holes, 6350 yards, S.S.S.70
Designed by James Braid.
Founded 1928
Visitors: weekdays with h/cap cert, weekends with member.
Green Fee: £20.
Societies: welcome Wed and Thurs.
Catering: full every day.
Hotels: Wheatsheaf; Audley Wood.

C10 Basingstoke Golf Centre

☎(01256) 50054
Worting Rd, West Ham, Basingstoke, Hants RG23 0TY

M3 junction 7; 0.5 mile from Basingstoke town centre. Public parkland course. 9 holes Par 3, 908 yards. **Visitors:** welcome. **Green Fee:** WD £2.50; WE £2.90. Driving range.

C11 **Bishopswood**

☎(01734) 815213, 812200
Bishopswood Lane, Tadley, Basingstoke, Hants RG26 6AT
6 miles N of Basingstoke, off A340.
Public parkland course.
9 holes, 6474 yards, S.S.S.71
Designed by Blake and Phillips.
Founded 1976
Visitors: welcome, Mon to Fri, no h/cap cert required.
Green Fee: WD £8 (9 holes), £13 (18 holes).
Societies: welcome by arrangement (weekdays only)
Catering: bar snacks and restaurant.
Driving range.

C12 **Blackmoor**

☎(01420) 472775, Pro 472345, Fax 477666
Golf Lane, Whitehill, Bordon, Hants GU35 9EH

Off A325 between Farnham and Petersfield, turn into Firgrove Rd at Whitehill crossroads.
Parkland/heathland course.
18 holes, 6232 yards, S.S.S.70
Designed by H.S. Colt.
Founded 1913
Visitors: welcome weekdays with h/cap cert.
Green Fee: £40, after 1pm £30.
Societies: welcome Mon, Wed, Thurs and Fri.
Catering: full facilities, available every day.
Hotels: Silver Birch at Greatham.

C13 **Blacknest**

☎(01420) 22888
Binstead Rd, Binstead, Alton, Hants GU34 4QL
Take A31 to Bentley then the Bordon Road and course is immediately on right
Parkland
9 holes, 6726 yards, S.S.S. 72
9 hole par 3 course
Designed by P Nicholson
Founded 1994
Visitors: welcome, no jeans
Green Fee: WD £7.50 (9 holes), £14 (18 holes); WE £9 (9 holes), £16 (18 holes)

Societies: welcome **Catering:** Bar and restaurant facilities
Driving range

C14 **Blackwater Valley**

☎(01252) 874725
Fox Lane, Eversley Cross, Basingstoke, Hants RG27 0NZ
5 miles from Camberley on the Reading road in Eversley Cross just before the cricket club on right
Parkland/ Lakes
9 holes 4744 yards S.S.S. 62
Founded 1994
Visitors: welcome
Green Fee: WD £8 (9 holes) £10 (18 holes); WE £10 (9 holes), £12 (18 holes)
Socieites: welcome
Catering: full facilities

C15 **Bognor Regis**

☎(01243) 821929, Pro 865209, Fax 860719
Downview Rd, Felpham, Bognor Regis, W Sussex PO22 8JD
A259 Littlehampton-Bognor road, from Bognor Regis to traffic lights at Felpham, turn left, clubhouse 0.5 mile at end of road.
Parkland course

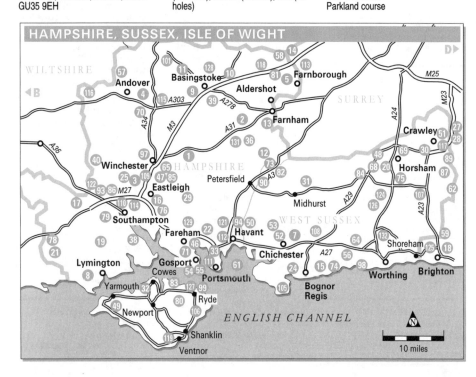

18 holes, 6238 yards, S.S.S.70
Designed by James Braid.
Founded 1 Jan 1892
Visitors: with h/cap cert, weekends
April-Oct with member only.
Green Fee: WD £25; WE £30.
Societies: by arrangement only.
Catering: meals by arrangement.

C16 **Botley Park Hotel & Country Club**

☎(01489) 780888, Fax 789242
Winchester Road, Boorley Green,
Botley, Hants SO32 2UA
NW of Botley on B3354 Winchester
road, within easy reach of M27
junction 7, or M3/A33.

Parkland course.
18 holes, 6341 yards, S.S.S.70
Designed by Charles Potterton.
Re-designed by E Murray in July
1995
Founded Feb 1990
Visitors: phone bookings required;
also h/cap cert or letter of
introduction.
Green Fee: £30 (£20 for residents).
Societies: available Wed and Thurs.
Catering: full restaurant facilities,
bars and bar snacks; banqueting
service.
Driving range, indoor swimming pool,
squash, tennis, croquet, snooker,
petanque, sauna etc.
Hotels: Hotel in complex.

C17 **Bramshaw**

☎(01703) 813433 (Manager), Pro
813434, **Hotels:** 812214, Fax
813958.
Brook, Lyndhurst, Hants SO4 7HE
Exit from M27 (Cadnam) at junction
1, take B3078 for 1 mile, club on right
behind Bell Inn.
Manor course, parkland; Forest
course, undulating.
Manor, 18 holes, 6517 yards,
S.S.S.71; Forest, 18 holes, 5774
yards, S.S.S.68
Founded 1880
Visitors: not weekends unless with
member or Bell Inn resident.
Green Fee: £20 per round, £30 per
day.
Societies: any weekday, bookings
only.
Catering: full catering.
Hotels: Bell Inn within Golf Complex
(golf inclusive breaks available with
reserved tee times at Bramshaw and
Dunwood Manor).

C18 **Brighton & Hove**

☎(01273) 556482 (Sec), Pro 540560
Devil's Dyke Rd, Brighton, E Sussex
BN1 8YJ
N of Brighton centre, 2.5 miles up
Dyke Rd on left side.
Downland course.
9 holes, 5601 yards, S.S.S.68
Designed by James Braid.
Founded 1887
Visitors: welcome; not before 12am
Wed, 10am Fri, 12am Sun.

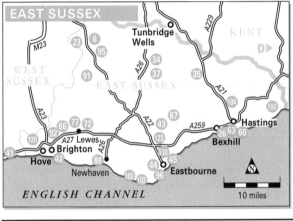
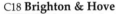

KEY							
1	Alresford	26	Cooden Beach	53	Goodwood Park Hotel G & CC	80	Newport
2	Alton	27	Copthorne			81	North Hants
3	Ampfield Par 3	28	Copthorne Effingham Park	54	Gosport & Stokes Bay	82	Old Thorns
4	Andover			55	Great Salterns	83	Osborne
5	Army	29	Corhampton	56	Ham Manor	84	Osiers Farm
6	Ashdown Forest Hotel	30	Cottesmore	57	Hampshire	85	Otterbourne GC
7	Avisford Park	31	Cowdray Park	58	Hartley Wintney	86	Paultons Golf Centre
8	Barton-on-Sea	32	Cowes	59	Hassocks	87	Paxhill Park
9	Basingstoke	33	Crookhorn Golf Centre	60	Hastings	88	Peacehaven
10	Basingstoke Golf Centre	34	Crowborough Beacon	61	Hayling	89	Pease Pottage GC & Driving Range
		35	Dale Hill Hotel	62	Haywards Heath		
11	Bishopswood	36	Dean Farm (Kingsley)	63	Highwoods	90	Petersfield
12	Blackmoor	37	Dewlands Manor Golf Course	64	Hill Barn	91	Piltdown
13	Blacknest			65	Hockley	92	Pyecombe
14	Blackwater Valley	38	Dibden	66	Hollingbury Park	93	Romsey
15	Bognor Regis	39	Dummer	67	Horam Park	94	Rowlands Castle
16	Botley Park Hotel & Country Club	40	Dunwood Manor	68	Horsham Golf Park	95	Royal Ashdown Forest
		41	Dyke	69	Ifield G & CC	96	Royal Eastbourne
17	Bramshaw	42	East Brighton	70	Leckford & Longstock	97	Royal Winchester
18	Brighton & Hove	43	East Sussex National	71	Lee-on-the-Solent	98	Rustington Golf Centre
19	Brockenhurst Manor	44	Eastbourne Downs	72	Lewes		
20	Brookfield	45	Eastbourne Golfing Park	73	Liphook	99	Ryde
21	Burley			74	Littlehampton	100	Rye
22	Cams Hall Estates Golf	46	Fleetlands	75	Mannings Heath	101	Sandford Springs
		47	Fleming Park	76	Meon Valley Hotel G & CC	102	Seaford
23	Chartham Park	48	Foxbridge			103	Seaford Head
24	Chichester Golf Centre	49	Freshwater Bay	77	Mid-Sussex	104	Sedlescombe (Aldershaw)
		50	Furzeley	78	Moors Valley Golf Centre		
25	Chilworth Golf Centre	51	Gatwick Manor Hotel			105	Selsey
		52	Goodwood	79	New Forest	106	Shanklin & Sandown
107	Singing Hills Golf Course						
108	Slinfold Park G & CC						
109	South Winchester						
110	Southampton						
111	Southsea						
112	Southwick Park						
113	Southwood						
114	Stoneham						
115	Test Valley						
116	Tidworth Garrison						
117	Tilgate Forest Golf Centre						
118	Tylney Park						
119	Ventnor						
120	Waterhall						
121	Waterlooville						
122	Wellow						
123	Wellshurst Golf & Country Club						
124	West Chiltington						
125	West Hove						
126	West Sussex						
127	Westridge						
128	Weybrook Park						
129	Wickham Park						
130	Willingdon						
131	Worldham Park						
132	Worthing						

Green Fee: WD £12.50 (18 holes); WE £21.
Societies: catered for weekdays.
Catering: full service available; snooker.
Hotels: Old Ship.

C19 Brockenhurst Manor

☎(01590) 623332 (Sec), Pro 623092, Fax 624140
Sway Rd, Brockenhurst, Hants SO42 7SG
A337 to Brockenhurst, then B3055 S from village centre, club 1 mile on right.
Gently undulating forest/parkland course.
18 holes, 6222 yards, S.S.S.70
Designed by H.S. Colt, with recent alterations by J. Hamilton Stutt.
Founded 1919
Visitors: phone booking in advance; must have current h/cap cert.
Green Fee: WD £28 per round, £35 per day; WE £40.
Societies: Thurs; book with Sec; small parties welcome on Mon, Wed and Fri, details from Sec.
Catering: bar and meals every day.
Hotels: information on request.

C20 Brookfield

☎(01403) 891568, Answerphone: 891891, Fax 891499
Winterpit Lane, Plummer's Plain, Horsham, W Sussex RH13 6LU
From M23 take A279 to Handcross, through village, then 2nd right and 1st left; from Horsham take A281 towards Brighton, at Manning's Heath Dun Horse pub turn left, over crossroads into Winterpit Lane.
Public parkland course.
9 holes, 4000 yards in Spring 1996
Designed by P. Webster and Associates.
Founded March 1991
Visitors: welcome at all times, no restrictions.
Green Fee: £10.
Societies: always welcome, also corporate day brochure available.
Catering: 2 bars, lounge, restaurants.
Driving range, pool/games room, sauna, gardens, children's play area.
Hotels: Brookfield Farm

C21 Burley

☎(01425) 402431 (Sec)
Cott Lane, Burley, Ringwood, Hants BH24 4BB
Leave A31 Ringwood-Cadnam road at Picket Post, through Burley Street

and Burley; club at top of hill, 400 yards from village centre on Lymington road.
Undulating heathland course.
9 holes, 6149 yards, S.S.S.69
Founded 1905
Visitors: welcome with h/cap cert and required standard of dress; not Wed until 1.45pm (Ladies Day); members only most Sat, some Sun.
Green Fee: WD £14; WE £16.
Societies: not catered for.
Catering: bar and catering available lunch time most days.
Hotels: Moorhill House; Burley Manor; White Buck; Toad Hall.

C22 Cams Hall Estates Golf

☎(01329) 827222, Fax 827111
Cams Hall, Fareham, Hants PO16 8UP
Close to M27 exit 11.
Parkland and coastal courses.
18 holes, 6244 yards, SSS 71; 9 holes, 3247 yards, Par 36.
Designed by Peter Alliss & Clive Clark.
Founded 1993
Visitors: welcome, h/cap certs required, phone in advance; restricted at weekends.
Green Fee: WD £15; WE £25. 9 hole WD £9.50; WE £12.
Societies: arranged in advance.
Catering: full facilities.
Sauna

C23 Chartham Park

☎(01342) 870340 Fax 870719
Felcourt Rd, Felcourt, E Grinstead, W Sussex RH19 2JT
1 miles out of E Grinstead town centre on the Lingfield Rd
Mature Parkland
18 holes, 6680 yards, S.S.S. 72
Designed by N Coles
Founded 1992
Visitors: welcome but not before 12 noon at weekends
Green Fee: WD £25 per round, £38 per day; WE £38
Societies: welcome Mon, Tues, Thurs
Catering: full facilities
Hotels: Felbridge

C24 Chichester Golf Centre

☎(01243) 533833 (Reservations), Admin: 536666, Fax 539922
Hoe Farm, Hunston, Chichester, W Sussex PO20 6AX

3 miles S of Chichester (A27) on B2145 to Selsey, on left hand side after village of Hunston.
Public course with membership; parkland with lakes.
Tower, 18 holes, 6174 yards, S.S.S.70; Cathedral, `Florida' style course, 6461 yards, SSS 71. 9 hole par 3.
Designed by Philip Sanders
Founded August 1990
Visitors: welcome, h/cap required on Cathedral course; tee reservations required; strict dress code.
Green Fee: WD Tower £14, Cathedral £20; WE Tower £19.50, Cathedral £28 . Par 3: WD £3.50; WE £4.50.
Societies: welcome by prior arrangement, society clubroom available.
Catering: full catering/refreshments available.
driving range, Academy hole, 825 yard Par 3 course.
Hotels: Millstream (Bosham); Hunston Mill B&B (Hunston); Post House (Hayling Island).

C25 Chilworth Golf Centre

☎(01703) 740544
Manor Farm, Botley Rd, Chilworth, Southampton, Hants SO16 7JP
On A27 between Southampton and Romsey.
Public parkland course.
18 holes, 5740 yards, S.S.S.69
Founded 1989
Visitors: pay-as-you-play with advance booking system, only 12 players per hour allowed.
Green Fee: WD £12; WE £18
Societies: by arrangement.
Catering: Full restaurant facilities; Driving range.

C26 Cooden Beach

☎(01424) 842040 (Sec), **Catering:** 843936, Pro 843938
Cooden Sea Rd, Nr Bexhill-on-Sea, E Sussex TN39 4TR
A259 Eastbourne-Hastings road, follow Cooden Beach sign at Little Common roundabout.
Seaside course.
18 holes, 6450 yards, S.S.S.71
Designed by Herbert Fowler.
Founded 1912
Visitors: h/cap certs required; prior arrangement preferred.
Green Fee: WD £26; WE £33.
Societies: Mon, Thurs, Fri by arrangement.

Catering: full services available.
Snooker.
Hotels: Cooden Resort.

C27 **Copthorne**
☎(01342) 712508, Pro 712405, Fax
717682
Borers Arms Rd, Copthorne, Crawley,
W Sussex RH10 3LL
On A264, 4 miles E of Crawley; 2
miles E of exit 10 from M23.
Parkland course.
18 holes, 6505 yards, S.S.S.71
Designed by James Braid.
Founded 1892
Visitors: welcome weekdays and
afternoons at weekends.
Green Fee: WD £27; WE £30 after
1pm.
Societies: on application.
Catering: lunch Mon-Fri and Sun.
Hotels: Copthorne Effingham Park.

C28 **Copthorne Effingham Park**
☎(01342) 716528, Fax 716039
West Park Rd, Copthorne, W Sussex
RH10 3EU
From M23 junction 10 onto A264.
Parkland course.
9 holes, 3498 yards, S.S.S.57
Designed by Francisco Escario
Founded 1980
Visitors: welcome, after 12 noon pm
Sat/Sun, not after 4pm Tues.
Green Fee: WD £8 (9 holes), £11.50
(18 holes); WE £9, £13.50.
Societies: on application.
Catering: 2 restaurants, clubhouse
bar.
Leisure Club; swimming, sauna, gym
etc; Golf academy, corporate days.
Hotels: Copthorne Effingham Park;
Copthorne Gatwick.

C29 **Corhampton**
☎(01489) 877279, Pro 877638
Sheeps Pond Lane, Droxford,
Southampton, Hants SO32 1QZ
Right off A32 at Corhampton on
B3135 for 1 mile.
Downland course.
18 holes, 6444 yards, S.S.S.71
Founded 1891
Visitors: welcome weekdays, with
member at weekends.
Green Fee: £20 per round £30 per
day.
Societies: welcome Mon and Thurs.
Catering: lunch, tea, dinners except
Tues.
Hotels: Little Uplands Country Guest
House; Coach House Motel.

C30 **Cottesmore**
☎(01293) 528256, Pro 535399, Fax
522819
Buchan Hill, Pease Pottage, Crawley,
Sussex RH11 9AT
M23 exit to Pease Pottage, 1 mile
down Horsham road from Pease
Pottage, on right.
Undulating meadowland course.
Griffin, 18 holes, 6280 yards,
S.S.S.70; Phoenix, 18 holes, 5489
yards, S.S.S.68
Designed by M.D. Rogerson.
Founded 1974
Visitors: welcome.
Green Fee: WD Griffin £24, Phoenix
£15; WE Griffin £30, Phoenix £20.
Societies: weekdays only; weekend
breaks in club accommodation.
Catering: full facilities.
Tennis, squash, indoor swimming
pool, health club, saunas etc.
Hotels: accommodation at club.

C31 **Cowdray Park**
☎(01730) 813599 (Sec/fax), Pro
812091
Midhurst, W Sussex GU29 0BB
About 1 mile E of Midhurst on A272.
Parkland course.
18 holes, 6212 yards, S.S.S.70
Founded 1920
Visitors: welcome.
Green Fee: WD £20; WE £25.
Societies: weekdays except Tues
and Fri.
Catering: bar snacks daily, evening
meals by arrangement, restaurant.
Hotels: Angel; Spread Eagle.

C32 **Cowes**
☎(01983) 292303, Members:
280135.
Crossfield Ave, Cowes, PO31 8HN
Make for Cowes High School; course
is at far end of school playing field.
Parkland course, Solent views.
9 holes, 5934 yards, S.S.S.68
Founded 1908
Visitors: by arrangement; not before
11.30am Sun or 10.30am-3pm Thurs.
Green Fee: WD £15; WE £18.
Societies: on application to Sec.
Catering: bar snacks from 11.30am
to 1pm except Sun, summer only.
Hotels: Fountain; New Holmwood.

C33 **Crookhorn Golf Centre**
☎(01705) 372210, 372299, Fax
200766
Crookhorn Lane, Widley, Portsmouth,
Hants PO7 5QL

Located on the hills overlooking
Portsmouth Harbour on N of the city,
within 1 mile of A3M.
Municipal undulating parkland course.
18 holes, 6200 yards, S.S.S.69
Founded 1926
Visitors: welcome.
Green Fee: Summer: £9.90; Winter
£7.25.
Societies: please arrange weekdays.
Catering: full facilities available

C34 **Crowborough Beacon**
☎(01892) 661511, Pro 653877, Fax
667339
Beacon Rd, Crowborough, E Sussex
TN6 1UJ
8 miles S of Tunbridge Wells on A26.
Heathland course.
18 holes, 6275 yards, S.S.S.70
Founded 1895
Visitors: weekdays; h/cap cert or
letter of intro. required.
Green Fee: WD £25 per round, £40
per day.
Societies: Mon, Tues, Wed, Fri by
prior arrangement with Sec.
Catering: for up to 60; breakfast
available by prior arrangement.
Hotels: Winston Manor.

C35 **Dale Hill Hotel**
☎(01580) 200112, Fax 201249
Ticehurst, Wadhurst, E Sussex TN5
7DQ
35 mins Gatwick Airport; A21 to
Flimwell crossroads, then B2087
towards Ticehurst 2 miles on the left.
Parkland course.
18 holes, 6106 yards, S.S.S.69; new
course opens 1997.
Founded 1974
Visitors: visitors welcome after
10am, ring to book times.
Green Fee: WD £20; WE £30.
Societies: welcome weekdays, ring
for Soc. form. Packages £50.
Catering: clubhouse bar/restaurant
and hotel restaurant, brasserie, spike
bar, pool, practice area, health club
(residents only), beauty salon
Hotels: Dale Hill, golf breaks and
packages; all day golf £15.

C36 **Dean Farm (Kingsley)**
☎(01420) 489478, 472313
Main Rd, Kingsley, Bordon, Hants
GU35 9NG
Off A325 Farnham-Petersfield road, 3
miles E of Bordon on the B3004.
Public pay-and-play parkland course.
9 holes, 1797 yards, S.S.S.27
Founded 1984

THE IDEAL 19th HOLE

Charming, fully licenced, privately owned, 4 Crown Commended hotel. 20 bedrooms all en-suite. The hotel is situated within the vicinity of 6 golf courses at the junction of A22/B2192, 2 miles South of the East Sussex National. Some concessions on green fees available via the hotel. Prices on request.

HOTEL & RESTAURANT
Halland, Nr Lewes, East Sussex BN8 6PW

TELEPHONE 01825 840456

Visitors: welcome any time.
Green Fee: £4 (9 holes), £6.50 (18 holes).
Catering: bar and snacks.

C37 Dewlands Manor Golf Course

☎(01892) 852266, 853308, Fax 853015
Cottage Hill, Rotherfield, E Sussex, TN6 3JN
0.5 mile S of village of Rotherfield just off B2101 to Five Ashes; 10 miles from Tunbridge Wells.
Pay-and-play parkland/woodland course with water hazards.
9 holes, 3186 yards, S.S.S.70
Designed by R.M. and Nick Godin.
Founded 1991
Visitors: welcome all year. 15 min tee intervals.
Green Fee: WD £12.50 (9 holes), £23 (18 holes); WE £14.50 (9 holes), £27.50 (18 holes)
Societies: small business groups welcome at all times, upper limit 20 persons.
Catering: fully licensed bar, light snacks at all times, special orders by pre-arrangement.
Practice net, putting green, practice hole.
Hotels: Spa, Royal Wells (Tunbridge Wells); Winston Manor (Crowborough).

C38 Dibden

☎(01703) 207508 (Bookings), Shop 845596, **Catering:** 845060
Main Rd, Dibden, Southampton, Hants SO45 5TB
Turn off A326 at Dibden roundabout, course situated 0.5 mile on right hand side.
Public parkland course.
18 holes, 5986 yards, S.S.S.69; 9 holes, 1520 yards Par 29
Designed by J. Hamilton Stutt.
Founded 1974
Visitors: welcome, no restrictions.
Green Fee: WD £7.25; WE £10.50.
Societies: by arrangement with Pro
Catering: full catering facilities available.
Driving range.

C39 Dummer

☎(01256) 397888, Pro 397950, Fax 397889
Dummer, Nr Basingstoke, Hants RG25 2AR
M3 exit 7.
Parkland course.
18 holes, 6513 yards S.S.S. 71
Designed by Peter Alliss and Clive Clark.
Founded 1992
Visitors: Mon-Fri only.
Green Fee: Before 12 noon £21, after 12 noon £18.
Societies: Golf days arranged.
Catering: full facilities.
Sauna
Hotels: Audley's Wood; Hilton National (Basingstoke).

C40 Dunwood Manor

☎(01794) 340549 (Office), Pro 340663, Fax 341215
Shootash Hill, Romsey, Hants SO51 0GF
Off A27 Romsey to Salisbury road, after 2 miles turn right at Shootash crossroads into Danes Rd, club is on left.
Undulating parkland course.
18 holes, 5925 yards, S.S.S.68
Founded 1972
Visitors: welcome weekdays by arrangement.
Green Fee: WD £20 per round, £28 per day; WE £30.
Societies: by arrangement.
Catering: bar meals 12am-2pm and 7-9.30pm or by arrangement.
Hotels: Bell Inn (discounts available).

C41 Dyke

☎(01273) 857296, Pro 857260, Fax 857078
Devil's Dyke, Dyke Rd, Brighton, E Sussex BN1 8YJ
5 miles N of Brighton between A23 and A27, 2 miles off Brighton by-pass.
Premier downland course.
18 holes, 6611 yards, S.S.S.72
Founded 1906
Visitors: welcome by appointment.
Green Fee: WD £25; WE £35.
Societies: full day inc. meals £47.

Catering: licensed bar and restaurant.
Snooker.
Hotels: Old Ship (Brighton); Tottington Manor nr Henfield.

C42 East Brighton

☎(01273) 604838, Pro 603989, Fax 680277.
Roedean Rd, Brighton, E Sussex BN2 5RA
Follow A259 from Brighton towards Newhaven, then signs for Marina. Left into Arundel Road, 300 yards beyond mini-roundabout turn right, over lights and 50 yards on the left.
Downland course.
18 holes, 6346 yards, S.S.S.70
Designed by James Braid
Founded 1893
Visitors: welcome on weekdays, weekends by appointment; h/cap cert required.
Green Fee: WD £22; WE £30 after 11 am.
Societies: by arrangement Mon, Tues pm, Thurs, Fri.
Catering: full bar, lunch/tea served every day, evening meals by arrangement. Light snacks on Monday only.
Snooker
Hotels: Old Ship, golf inclusive packages; Grand; Metropole; Brighton Thistle. White Horse, Rottingdean.

C43 East Sussex National

☎(01825) 880088, Pro 880229, Fax 880066.
Little Horsted, Uckfield, East Sussex TN22 5ES
2 miles S of Uckfield on A22.
Part (18 holes) public course: England's "Augusta" – bent grass tees, fairways and greens.
East, 18 holes, 7158 yards, S.S.S.74; West, 18 holes, 7154 yards, S.S.S.74; National Academy, 3 holes, 1155 yards, S.S.S.12
Designed by Bob Cupp
Founded 1989
Visitors: welcome; reservations advised.

Green Fee: East £49.50 per round, £65 per day; West £39.50, £49.50 per day.
Societies: welcome daily by arrangement.
Catering: bar and restaurant. Academy of Golf Teaching Centre; 2 double ended practice ranges; chipping, pitching, putting greens. Driving range.
Hotels: Horsted Place Hotel on site (golfers privileges).

C44 Eastbourne Downs
☎(01323) 720827, Pro 732264
East Dean Rd, Eastbourne, E Sussex BN20 8ES
On A259 0.5 miles W of Eastbourne.
Downland course.
18 holes, 6645 yards, S.S.S.72
Designed by J.H. Taylor.
Founded 1907
Visitors: welcome.
Green Fee: WD £14 per round, £18 per day; WE £18 per round, £20 per day.
Societies: welcome.
Catering: Every day 7.30am-8.30pm.
Hotels: Glastonbury; Lansdowne.

C45 Eastbourne Golfing Park
☎(01323) 520400
Lottbridge Drove, Eastbourne, E Sussex BN23 6QJ
Take coast road and turn left at Sovereign Centre
Lakeland course
9 holes
Founded 1993
Visitors: welcome
Green Fee: £7
Societies: welcome
Catering: full facilities

C46 Fleetlands
☎(01705) 722351 extn 44384 (Sec)
R.N.A.Y. Fleetlands, Gosport, Hants PO13 0AW
Off A32 2 miles S of Fareham.
9 holes, 4852 yards, S.S.S.64
Founded 1963
Visitors: with members only.
Green Fee: WD £5; WE £7.
Societies: by appointment.
Catering: bar.

C47 Fleming Park
☎(01703) 612797 (Pro), Sec 327110.
Magpie Lane, Eastleigh, Hants SO50 3LH

A27/M27, turn off at Eastleigh sign, 1 mile to course.
Parkland course.
18 holes, 4378 yards, S.S.S.61
Designed by Charles Lawrie.
Founded 1973
Visitors: welcome, phone in advance.
Green Fee: WD £6.45; WE £9.60.
Societies: apply to Pro.
Catering: bar snacks and meals.

C48 Foxbridge
☎(01403) 753303, Pro 753343
Foxbridge Lane, Plaistow, W Sussex RH14 0LB
Take B2133 from Billingshurst to Lockswood then take Plaistow road and course signposted
Parkland
9 holes (18 flags) 6236 yards, S.S.S. 70
Designed P Clark
Founded 1991
Visitors: weekdays only
Green Fee: from £12
Socieities: welcome weekdays by arrangement
Catering: full facilities and bar service

C49 Freshwater Bay
☎(01983) 752955
Afton Down, Freshwater Bay, Isle of Wight PO40 9TZ
3 miles from Yarmouth on A3055 overlooking Freshwater Bay.
Seaside downland course with views over Solent and English Channel.
18 holes, 5725 yards, S.S.S.68
Founded 1893
Visitors: welcome after 9.30am on weekdays and 10am on Sun.
Green Fee: WD £20; WE £24.
Societies: welcome at times shown for visitors; advance bookings required.
Catering: full catering, licenced bar
Hotels: Albion; Country Garden; Farringford.

C50 Furzeley
☎(01705) 231180
Furzeley Road, Denmead, Hants PO7 6TX
Off the Hambledon road 1.5m north of Waterlooville
Parkland course
18 holes, 4247 yards, Par 61
Designed by M Sale
Opened 1992 (extended 1995)
Visitors: pay and play course; tee times bookable 48 hours in advance

Green Fee: WD £9.80; WE £11.50
Societies: welcome weekdays by prior arrangement
Catering: Mead Inn local pub offer meals and bar facilities. Coffee and snacks available at club.

C51 Gatwick Manor Hotel
☎(01293) 526301, Fax 513077
London Rd, Lowfield Heath, Nr Crawley, W Sussex
0.75 miles S of Gatwick Airport on A23.
Refurbished parkland course.
9 holes, 1118 yards, Par 28
Designed by Patrick Tallack.
Visitors: welcome; priority to guests of Hotel.
Green Fee: apply for details.
Societies: societies and Company days welcome by prior arrangement.
Catering: 2 bars and 2 restaurants.
Hotels: Gatwick Manor.

C52 Goodwood
☎(01243) 774968, Pro 774994
Goodwood, Chichester, W Sussex PO18 0PN
On A286 5 miles N of Chichester.
Downland/parkland course.
18 holes, 6401 yards, S.S.S.71
Designed by James Braid.
Founded 1891
Visitors: not before 9am weekdays and 10am weekends; phone Pro shop for details.
Green Fee: WD £28; WE £38.
Societies: Wed, Thurs; essential to book early.
Catering: full catering by booking except Mon.
Snooker table.
Hotels: Goodwood Park; Chichester Resort; Dolphin & Anchor.

C53 Goodwood Park Hotel G & CC
☎(01243) 775987, Fax 533802
Goodwood, Nr Chichester, W Sussex PO18 0QB
A27-M27 E of Chichester, in the grounds of Goodwood House.
Parkland course.
18 holes, 6530 yards, S.S.S.71
Designed by Donald Steel.
Founded 1989
Visitors: welcome with h/cap cert and correct attire.
Green Fee: £35
Societies: welcome by prior arrangement.
Catering: full catering and bar facilities, inc. private rooms.

Tennis, swimming, squash, snooker, gym, sauna etc.
Hotels: Goodwood Park, golf and leisure breaks available, conference venue.

C54 Gosport & Stokes Bay
☎(01705) 527941 (Sec), Pro 582220, Club 581625
Fort Rd, Haslar, Gosport, Hants PO12 2AT
S on A32 from Fareham, E to Haslar.
Links course.
9 holes, 5999 yards, S.S.S.69
Founded 1885
Visitors: welcome except Sun am.
Green Fee: WD £15; WE £18.
Societies: by arrangement. Tues.
Catering: full facilities.
Hotels: Anglesey.

C55 Great Salterns
☎(01705) 664549, 699519 Fax 650525
Portsmouth Golf Centre, Eastern Rd, Portsmouth PO3 5HH
2 miles from A27 on A2030 into Southsea.
Public seaside/parkland course.
18 holes, 5737 yards, S.S.S.71
Founded 1914
Visitors: welcome, booking system 7 days.
Green Fee: £10
Societies: welcome by prior arrangement.
Catering: at Farmhouse pub adjacent to course.
Driving range.
Hotels: Inn Lodge next to Farmhouse.

C56 Ham Manor
☎(01903) 783288, Pro/Fax 783732
Angmering, W Sussex BN16 4JE
3 miles E of Littlehampton.
Gently undulating parkland course.
18 holes, 6267 yards, S.S.S.70
Designed by H.S. Colt.
Founded 1936
Visitors: welcome after 8.45 am by arrangement; h/cap certs required.
Green Fee: WD £28; WE £35.
Societies: by arrangement.
Catering: lunch except Mon.
Snooker.

C57 Hampshire
☎(01264) 357555
Winchester Road, Goodworth Clatford, Nr Andover, Hants, SP11 7TB

From Andover take the Stockbridge road A3057. 0.5 miles south of Andover
Downland course
18 holes 6338 yards S.S.S. 70
Par 3 9 hole course
Designed by T Fiducia & A Mitchell
Founded 1993
Visitors: welcome
Green Fee: WD £12; WE £16
Societies: welcome
Catering: clubhouse opened March 96 with full facilities
Driving range (extended in 96)
Hotels: White Hart (Andover)

C58 Hartley Wintney
☎(01252) 844211 (Sec), Pro 843779, Club 842214
London Rd, Hartley Wintney, Hants RG27 8PT
On A30 8 miles NE of Basingstoke.
Parkland course.
9 holes, 6096 yards, S.S.S.69
Founded 1891
Visitors: weekdays; Bank Holidays and weekends with member only; restrictions on Wed.
Green Fee: on application.
Societies: full catering except Mon, snacks 7 days.
Catering: snacks and full catering 6 days.
Hotels: Lismoyne; Lamb.

C59 Hassocks
☎(01273) 846630, Pro 846990
London Road, Hassocks, Sussex BN6 9NA
At Hassocks on the A23 London Road
Parkland course
18 holes, 5754 yards, S.S.S. 68
Designed by P Wright
Founded Aug 1995
Visitors: welcome
Green Fee: WD £11.25; WE £14.75
Societies: welcome
Catering: full facilities available.

C60 Hastings
☎(01424) 852981 (club/fax)
Battle Rd, St Leonards-on-Sea, E Sussex TN38 0TA
A2100 from Battle to Hastings, 3 miles NW of Hastings.
Municipal undulating parkland course.
18 holes, 6248 yards, S.S.S.71
Designed by Frank Pennink.
Founded 1973
Visitors: no restrictions; tee booking system.

Green Fee: WD £10.30; WE £13.
Societies: welcome Mon-Fri.
Catering: full facilities.
Driving range
Hotels: Beauport Park.

C61 Hayling
☎(01705) 464446 (Sec/fax), Pro 464491, Steward: 463712
Links Lane, Hayling Island, Hants PO11 0BX
5 miles S of Havant off M27 to A3023, situated at W end of the seafront.
Links course.
18 holes, 6521 yards, S.S.S.71
Designed by Tom Simpson.
Founded 1883
Visitors: private club h/cap cert required and letter of intro. from Home Club appreciated.
Green Fee: WD £30; WE £40.
Societies: Tues and Wed only by prior arrangement.
Catering: full facilities
Hotels: Post House (Northney); Newtown House.

C62 Haywards Heath
☎(01444) 414866, Sec 414457
High Beech Lane, Haywards Heath, W Sussex RH16 1SL
2 miles NE of Haywards Heath, follow B2112 towards Lindfield, then left towards Ardingly into Summerhill Lane; High Beech Lane is 4th on left.
Parkland course.
18 holes, 6204 yards, S.S.S.70
Founded 1922
Visitors: welcome subject to tee reservations.
Green Fee: WD £22 per round, £27 per day; WE £30 per round, £35 per day
Societies: Wed and Thurs only.
Catering: bar, lunch, evening catering by arrangement.

C63 Highwoods
☎(01424) 212625 (Sec), Pro 212770
Ellerslie Lane, Bexhill-on-Sea, E Sussex TN39 4LJ
Off A259 from Eastbourne or Hastings, 2 miles from Bexhill; from Battle A269 via Ninfield, turn right in Sidley.
Parkland course.
18 holes, 6218 yards, S.S.S.70
Designed by J.H. Taylor
Founded 1925
Visitors: welcome with h/cap cert; no visitors Sun before 12am unless with member.

Green Fee: WD £25; WE £30.
Societies: by arrangement.
Catering: Full facilities.
Hotels: Cooden Resort; Granville.

C64 Hill Barn
☎(01903) 237301
Hill Barn Lane, Worthing, Sussex
BN14 9QE
N of Worthing off London &
Edinburgh Building Soc roundabout
on A27, take exit directly before
Brighton exit, signposted.
Municipal downland course.
18 holes, 5809 yards, S.S.S.70
Designed by Hawtree & Son.
Founded 1935
Visitors: welcome, no restrictions.
Green Fee: WD £11.50; WE £13.50.
Juniors £5.50.
Societies: weekdays only; min 20
persons.
Catering: breakfasts, snacks, hot
meals available all day.
Hotels: Beach; Ardington &
Chatsworth.

C65 Hockley
☎(01962) 713165, Steward: 714572,
Pro 713678, Fax 713612
Twyford, Winchester, Hants SO21
1PL
2 miles S of Winchester on A335
(Twyford road).Close to junc 11 of
M3.
Downland course
18 holes, 6296 yards, S.S.S.70
Designed by James Braid.
Founded 1915
Visitors: welcome weekdays, and at
weekends with member or by
arrangement with Secretary.
Green Fee: WD £25; WE £30.
Societies: not Mon.
Catering: snacks, lunch and evening
meals; other requirements contact
Steward.
Hotels: Forte Crest (Winchester).

C66 Hollingbury Park
☎(01273) 552010, Pro 500086
Ditchling Rd, Brighton, Sussex BN1
7HS
1 mile from Brighton, astride the
Downs between A23 London Rd and
A27 Lewes Rd.
Public undulating downland course.
18 holes, 6472 yards, S.S.S.71
Designed by J. Braid and J.H. Taylor
Founded 1908
Visitors: welcome anytime.
Green Fee: WD £11; WE £15.
Societies: weekdays only.

Catering: full restaurant facilities
open 7 days.
Hotels: Old Ship; Preston Resort.

C67 Horam Park
☎(01435) 813477, Fax 813677
Chiddingly Rd, Horam, E Sussex
TN21 0JJ
0.5 mile S of Horam on road to
Chiddingly; Horam is 13 miles N of
Eastbourne on A267.
Parkland course with lakes.
9 holes (18 tees), 5970 yards,
S.S.S.68
Designed by Glen Johnson.
Founded 1985
Visitors: welcome, telephone for
bookings.
Green Fee: ring for details.
Societies: ring for brochure.
Catering: Restaurant and bar.
Driving range.
Hotels: Boship Farm (Hailsham).

C68 Horsham Golf Park
☎(01403) 271525, Fax 274528
Worthing Rd, Horsham, W Sussex
RH13 7AX
A24 Horsham bypass at Southwater
roundabout with Shell garage,
signposted to golf course and
Horsham; course entrance 200 yards
on right.
Public parkland course.
9 holes, 4122 yards S.S.S.60
Founded July 1993
Visitors: welcome; bookable on day
of play.
Green Fee: WD: £6 (9 holes), £10
(18 holes); WE £7 (9 holes), £9 (18
holes).
Societies: welcome, not weekends;
36 holes, lunch and evening meal.
Catering: bar and restaurant.
Driving range.

C69 Ifield G & CC
☎(01293) 520222, Pro 523088, Fax
612973
Rusper Rd, Ifield, Crawley, W Sussex
RH11 0LN
M23 Crawley junction; follow signs to
Brighton and A23; after 3
roundabouts take right turning; left
into Ifield Drive, 2nd right after shops,
1st left into Rusper Rd 0.5 mile then
signposted.
Parkland course.
18 holes, 6330 yards, S.S.S.70
Designed by Bernard Darwin;
constructed by F. Hawtry and J.H.
Taylor.
Founded 1927

Visitors: welcome weekdays only or
with member at weekends.
Green Fee: £20 per round, £30 per
day.
Societies: welcome Mon, Tues pm,
Wed pm, Thurs.
Catering: full facilities all week.

C70 Leckford & Longstock
☎(01264) 810320, 0860 719184
Leckford, Stockbridge, Hants
2.5 miles N of Stockbridge on
Andover road.
Downland course
Two 9-hole courses
Designed originally by John Morrison.
New course: Donald Steel
Visitors: employees of John Lewis
Partnership and guests only.
Green Fee: WD £8; WE £12
Societies: Small societies allowed.

C71 Lee-on-the-Solent
☎(01705) 551170 (Manager),
Members: 550207, Pro 551181
Brune Lane, Lee-on-the-Solent,
Hants PO13 9PB
3 miles due S of M27 junction 11.
Heathland course.
18 holes, 5933 yards, S.S.S.69
Founded 1905
Visitors: weekdays; with h/cap cert.
Green Fee: WD £25; WE £30.
Societies: Thurs, bookable in
advance.
Catering: available all week.
Hotels: Belle Vue.

C72 Lewes
☎(01273) 473245, Pro 483823
Chapel Hill, Lewes, Sussex BN7 2BB
On A27 Lewes-Eastbourne road
opposite junction of Cliffe High St and
South St.
Downland course.
18 holes, 6213 yards, S.S.S.70
Founded 1896
Visitors: welcome weekdays and
weekends after 2pm.
Green Fee: WD £16.50; WE £27.
Societies: welcome as for visitors by
arrangement.
Catering: licensed bar; restaurant
(7/8am to 6pm), evening meals by
arrangement.
Practice ground.

C73 Liphook
☎(01428) 723271 (Pro), Sec
723785, Fax 724853
Wheatsheaf Enclosure, Liphook,
Hants GU30 7EH

Liphook

For most golfers charm is a more important quality in a course than challenge. Liphook is the type which combines the two in equal measure. 6207 yards is not long these days but matching the par of 70 is another matter when the heather and trees, the hallmark of the best Surrey and Hampshire courses, place such a premium on controlled shot-making.

You certainly appreciate the lovely setting rather more if you keep straight, the countryside possessing more normal contouring than the valleys, plateaux and gulleys that characterise the land surrounding the Devil's Punchbowl at Hindhead just up the Portsmouth Road, and in terms of golf course architecture, Liphook has rightly been hailed as an example for the connoisseur.

My late senior partner, Ken Cotton, was always singing its praises but the remarkable part of the story is that its designer, A.C. Croome, was first and foremost a schoolmaster. Liphook was the only new course for which he was entirely responsible. Jack Neville keeps him notable company in this regard, Neville's lone masterpiece being Pebble Beach. It was ill health rather than lack of demand that prevented Croome from pursuing the final chapter of a working life that had more variety than most.

In addition to being a housemaster at Radley College, he wrote about cricket and golf for several newspapers, both games at which he excelled himself. He was founder member of the Oxford and Cambridge Golfing Society donating the Croome Shield for annual competition among College pairs at the President's Putter, and was a regular competitor in the Amateur and other championships.

It was J.F. Abercromby, the designer of Addington, among other courses, who persuaded him to join forces in the firm of Fowler, Abercromby, Simpson and Croome – as elite a quartet as anyone could muster. At first, Croome's role was mainly administrative, but inside every golfer is a golf course architect clamouring to get out, and Liphook was to be the ultimate expression of Croome's talents.

No clubhouse gets a better view of its 1st and 18th holes, the work of John Morrison who wanted to provide a fine long short hole to get players moving, but, apart from the difficulty of the opening tee shot, Liphook is quick to let golfers know what is expected of them. There are three par 4s of well over 400 yards in the first six holes, the 4th, High View, being particularly demanding. It leads to the first crossing of the busy road and on to the first of three par 5s where thorn trees feature in the drive.

The 6th, with its little grassy hollow behind the green, doubles back on the 5th, the attractive short 7th starting the section of 10 holes on the other side of the railway. The railway is not the feature it is on some courses although the 7th and 8th run roughly parallel to it. The 9th, 438 yards, another demanding 4, prompts a long uphill second over a road and a heathery dell but the 10th offers a more inviting drive even if a ditch lurks on the approach to the green.

A large central bunker dominates the short 11th, in a visual sense, and the 12th, Forest Mere, completes the long par 4s, always claiming a victim or two. A nice downhill drive and a slightly uphill second give the long hitters a chance of a birdie at the 13th, and, for those negotiating the dogleg successfully, a good pitch can do the same at the 14th.

Then it is a deep breath and a mad dash to the 15th where the drive takes us up over a steep ridge with the temptation to cut off more than is good for us. The 16th is the reverse of the 15th, a quarry and the corner of a wood awaiting any poorly struck or mis-directed second. The walk to the 17th is a last reminder of the Portsmouth Road which explains in part the club's traditionally strong links with the Navy; the 17th's tee shot across a diagonal, corrugated bank of gorse and heather makes the fifth and last short hole difficult to judge, enhancing Liphook's reputation that it's not just nautical men who are all at sea.

1 mile S of Liphook off old A3.
Heath/heatherland course.
18 holes, 6247 yards, S.S.S.70
Designed by Arthur Croome.
Founded 1921
Visitors: h/cap cert required; phone in advance; after 2pm Sun & BH.
Green Fee: WD £27 per round, £35 per day; WE Sat £35 per round, £45 per day; Sun & BH: £45.
Societies: Wed, Thurs & Fri, min 16, max 36.
Catering: bar and bar snacks daily; 3 course lunch and dinner available.
Hotels: Links

C74 Littlehampton
☎(01903) 717170, Fax 726629; Pro 716369
170 Rope Walk, Riverside, Littlehampton, W Sussex BN17 5DL
From Littlehampton take A259 Bognor Regis road; take 1st left after new river bridge, signs To Golf Club.
Seaside links course.
18 holes, 6245 yards, S.S.S.70
Founded 1898
Visitors: welcome 7 days; after 12 noon on Sun.
Green Fee: WD £24; WE £30.
Societies: not weekends.
Catering: full catering facilities daily.
Hotels: Bailiff's Court, Norfolk Arms

C75 Mannings Heath
☎(01403) 210228, Fax 270974
Fullers, Hammerpond Rd, Mannings Heath, Horsham, W Sussex RH13 6PG
M23 junc 11, through Pease Pottage to Grouse Lane on left, 3.5 miles to T junction, right then 1st left to club
Undulating parkland course, many feature holes.
Waterfall course18 holes, 6378 yards, S.S.S.70; Kingfisher course 18 holes, 6305 yards, S.S.S. 69
Founded 1908. New course 1995
Visitors: welcome by arrangement.
Green Fee: WD £27 per round, £36 per day; WE £35 per round, £54 per day.
Societies: weekdays.
Catering: full catering facilities.
Hotels: South Lodge (Lower Beeding).

C76 Meon Valley Hotel Golf & Country Club
☎(01329) 833455, Pro 832184, Fax 834411
Sandy Lane, Shedfield, Southampton SO32 2HQ

On A334 8 miles E of Southampton between Botley and Wickham.
Parkland courses.
Meon course, 18 holes, 6519 yards, S.S.S.71; Valley course, 9 holes, 2885 yards, S.S.S.68
Designed by J. Hamilton Stutt.
Founded 1978
Visitors: welcome with h/cap cert. Valley course closed to visitors at weekends.
Green Fee: Meon course, WD £25; WE £35; Valley course, WD only £10
Societies: by arrangement, residents only at weekends.
Catering: meals and snacks. Squash, tennis, snooker, indoor swimming pool, health and beauty facilities (residents only).
Hotels: Meon Valley, residential golf packages available.

C77 Mid-Sussex
☎(01273) 846567 (Club)
Spatham Lane, Ditchling, Sussex BN6 8XJ
Take A23 to A2873 Hastings-Haywards Heath road to Ditchling then take Lewes Rd from Ditchling and course is 1 mile away
Parkland course
18 holes, 6410 yards S.S.S 71
Designed by D Williams Partnership
Founded 1995
Visitors: weekdays
Green Fee: £20
Societies: weekdays
Catering: full club house facilities
Hotels: Hickstead resort

C78 Moors Valley Golf Centre
☎(01425) 479776, Fax 472057
Moors Valley Country Park, Horton Rd, Ashley Heath, Nr Ringwood, Hants BH24 2ET.
A31 through Ringwood, right at roundabout signposted Ashley Heath, 2 miles on right of entrance to parkland, course inside Country Park.
Municipal parkland/heathland course.
18 holes, 6270 yards S.S.S. 70
Designed by Martin Hawtree.
Founded 1988, extended 1992
Visitors: no restrictions, bookings one week in advance.
Green Fee: WD £3.50 (7 holes), £5 (11 holes), £8.50 (18 holes); WE £4.50 (7 holes), £6 (11 holes), £11 (18 holes).
Societies: contact Pro shop
Catering: Bar and catering facilities in clubhouse
Driving range.

C79 New Forest
☎(01703) 282752 (Office)
Southampton Rd, Lyndhurst, Hants SO43 7BU
On A35 Southampton-Bournemouth road between Ashurst and Lyndhurst.
Heathland course.
18 holes, 5742 yards, S.S.S.68
Designed by Peter Swann.
Founded 1888
Visitors: welcome from 8.30am Mon-Fri, from 10am Sat, from 1.30pm Sun.
Green Fee: WD £10; WE £12.
Societies: welcome; to be booked and confirmed in advance.
Catering: bar from 11am Mon-Sat, from 12am to 3pm Sun; snacks and meals available 11.30am-4pm Mon-Sat.
Hotels: Crown; Lyndhurst Park; Carey's Manor.

C80 Newport
☎(01983) 525076
St George's Down, Newport, Isle of Wight PO30 3BA
A3056 Newport-Sandown road 0.5 mile from Newport.
Undulating parkland course.
9 holes, 5660 yards, S.S.S.68
Designed by Guy Hunt.
Founded 1896
Visitors: welcome by prior arrangement except before 3pm Sat and on Sun mornings.
Green Fee: WD £15; WE £17.50.
Societies: Mon-Fri by arrangement with Sec.
Catering: bar meals on request to Stewardess before round.

C81 North Hants
☎(01252) 616443, Fax 811627, Pro 616655
Minley Rd, Fleet, Hants GU13 8RE
0.5 mile N of Fleet Station on B3013, Junction 4A M3.
Heathland course.
18 holes, 6257 yards, S.S.S.70, Par 69
Designed by James Braid.
Founded 1904
Visitors: by prior arrangement with Sec; letter of intro and h/cap cert required.
Green Fee: £24 per round, £30 per day.
Societies: welcome Tues and Wed by arrangement.
Catering: lunch, tea, dinner; pre-booking required.
Hotels: various in Fleet, Camberley and Farnborough.

C82 **Old Thorns**
☎(01428) 724555, Fax 725036
Old Thorns, Longmoor Rd, Griggs
Green, Liphook, Hants GU30 7PE
Take Griggs Green exit off A3 (1st
exit past Liphook from London); Old
Thorns is situated 500 yards on right
of Longmoor Rd.
Public parkland course.
18 holes, 6533 yards, S.S.S.71
Designed by Commander John
Harris, adapted by Peter Alliss and
Dave Thomas
Founded 1982
Visitors: all welcome.
Green Fee: WD £25; WE £35.
Societies: Society Day £58;
minimum 12 persons.
Catering: full a la carte menu
available, terrace buffet and
Japanese restaurant.
Driving range, putting green, indoor
swimming, sauna, tennis, shiatsu.
Hotels: Old Thorns.

C83 **Osborne**
☎(01983) 295421 (Sec/Manager)
Osborne, East Cowes, Isle of Wight
PO32 6JX
A3052 Newport to East Cowes road,
situated in the grounds of Osborne
House.
Parkland course.
9 holes, 6372 yards, S.S.S.70
Founded 1903
Visitors: welcome by arrangement;
not before 12am Sat & Sun or
1.30pm Tues.
Green Fee: WD £16; WE £19.
Societies: by arrangement with
Sec/Manager.
Catering: available.
Hotels: Crossway.

C84 **Osiers Farm**
☎(01798) 344097
Petworth, W Sussex GU28 9LX
2.5 miles N of Petworth on A283
Guildford road.
Public course over farmland, hedges,
trees etc.
9 holes, 5220 yards, S.S.S.64
Designed by Chris Duncton.
Founded 1991
Visitors: welcome at any time.
Green Fee: £9.
Societies: as required, not Sun,
Bank Holidays or Sat am.
Catering: light refreshments only at
present.
Driving range.
Hotels: B&B on course, telephone for
details; Angel, Masons Arms
(Petworth).

C85 **Otterbourne GC**
☎(01962) 775225
Poles Lane, Otterbourne, Nr
Winchester, Hants
M3 junct Eastleigh North or
Winchester. Take signs to
Otterbourne then Hursley Rd; Poles
Lane is off roundabout
9 holes, 1939 yards, par 30
Founded July 1995
Visitors: welcome
Green Fee: WD £3.50; WE £4.50
Societies: welcome
Catering: Light snacks available

C86 **Paultons Golf Centre**
☎(01703) 813345, Fax 813993
Old Salisbury Rd, Ower, Nr Romsey,
Hants SO51 6AN
Exit 2 off M27 in direction of Ower,
left at 1st roundabout, then right at
Heathlands Hotel; then signposted.
Parkland course.
18 holes, 6238 yards S.S.S.70. 9 hole
course par 3
Founded 1993
Visitors: all welcome at all times.
Green Fee: WD £17.50 (18 holes),
£6.50 (9 holes); WE £18.50.
Societies: welcome by arrangement.
Catering: bars and restaurant.
Driving range.
Hotels: Heathlands (500 yards).

C87 **Paxhill Park**
☎(01444) 484467, Pro 482709, Fax
484000
East Mascalls Lane, Lindfield, W
Sussex RH16 2QN
2 miles outside Haywards Heath near
Lindfield village
Parkland course.
18 holes, 6117 yards, S.S.S.69
Designed by Patrick Tallack.
Founded Oct 1990
Visitors: welcome; not before 12am
weekends.
Green Fee: WD £15; WE £20.
Societies: daily.
Catering: full restaurant and bar
facilities; banqueting.
Hotels: Birch Hotel (Haywards
Heath); Roebuck (Wych Cross).

C88 **Peacehaven**
☎(01273) 514049, Pro 512602
Brighton Rd, Newhaven, E Sussex
BN9 9UH
On A259 1 mile W of Newhaven.
Undulating downland course.
9 holes, 5333 yards, S.S.S.66
Designed by James Braid
Founded 1895

Visitors: welcome weekdays, after
11.30am weekends and Bank
Holidays.
Green Fee: WD £11; WE £17.
Societies: catered for Mon-Fri.
Catering: available weekends, by
arrangement Mon-Fri.

C89 **Pease Pottage GC & Driving Range**
☎(01293) 521706
Horsham Rd, Pease Pottage,
Crawley RH11 8AL
Leave M23 at junction 11, then
signposted from large roundabout.
Public parkland course.
9 holes, 3511 yards, S.S.S. 57
Designed by Adam Lazar.
Founded 1986
Visitors: welcome.
Green Fee: WD £8.50 (18 holes);
WE £11.
Societies: welcome by prior
arrangement.
Catering: bar and restaurant facilities
available.
Driving range.

C90 **Petersfield**
☎(01730) 262386 (Sec/Fax), Pro
267732
Heath Rd, Petersfield, Hants GU31
4EJ
Turn off A3 to E at town centre (Red
Lion), clubhouse 1 mile past lake.
Planning to move to Tankerdell Lane,
Adhurst, Hampshire (1996)
Heathland/parkland course.
18 holes, 5603 yards, S.S.S.67. New
course 18 hole par 72
Founded 1892
Visitors: welcome weekdays,
weekends after 12am.
Green Fee: WD £15; WE £21.
Societies: Wed, Thurs and Fri (no
evening catering).
Catering: bar and dining area; lunch
available Mon-Sat; evening meals by
prior booking.
Hotels: Concorde; Red Lion.

C91 **Piltdown**
☎(01825) 722033 (Club/fax), Pro
722389
Piltdown, Uckfield, E Sussex TN22
3XB
1 mile W of Maresfield off A272
signposted Isfield.
Undulating gorse and heather.
18 holes, 6070 yards, S.S.S.69
Designed by J. Rowe, G.M. Dodd,
Frank Pennink.
Founded 1904

Visitors: not before 9.30am (2pm Sun); various other restrictions, essential to phone; h/cap cert or letter of intro. required; jacket and tie in clubhouse.
Green Fee: £27.50 per round, £32 per day.
Societies: by arrangment Mon, Wed and Fri only.
Catering: bar snacks and full catering daily.
Hotels: Roebuck (Forest Row). Chequers (Maresfield)

C92 Pyecombe

☎(01273) 845372, Pro 845398, Fax 843338
Clayton Hill, Pyecombe, Sussex BN45 7FF
On A273, 0.5 mile from junction with A23 at Pyecombe, 5 to 6 miles N of Brighton.
Downland course.
18 holes, 6278 yards, S.S.S.70
Founded 1894
Visitors: welcome weekdays after 9.15am; Sat after 10.30 am; Sun after 2pm.
Green Fee: WD £17; WE £30.
Societies: catered for Mon, Wed, Thurs.
Catering: full services available.

C93 Romsey

☎(01703) 734637 (Manager), Steward: 732218, Pro 736673, Fax 741036
Romsey Rd, Nursling, Southampton, Hants SO16 0XW
2 miles SE of Romsey on A3057 Southampton road; near M27/M271 junction 3.
Wooded parkland course.
18 holes, 5851 yards, S.S.S.68
Designed by Charles Lawrie.
Founded 1900
Visitors: welcome Mon-Fri.
Green Fee: WD £20 per round, £25 per day.
Societies: Mon, Tues and Thurs.
Catering: full licensed bar, full restaurant facilities.
Hotels: White Horse (Romsey); Travel Inn (Nursling), Novotel (Southampton).

C94 Rowlands Castle

☎(01705) 412784 (Sec), Pro 412785
Links Lane, Rowlands Castle, Hants PO9 6AE
7 miles S of Petersfield; leave A3(M) junction left to Havant/Rowlands Castle.

Parkland course.
18 holes, 6618 yards, S.S.S.72
Founded 1902
Visitors: welcome weekdays; not Sat; restricted numbers Sun, advisable to ring.
Green Fee: WD £25; WE £30.
Societies: catered for Tues and Thurs, details on application.
Catering: service until 6pm.
Hotels: Brookfield (Emsworth); Bear (Havant); Fountain Inn (Rowlands Castle).

C95 Royal Ashdown Forest

☎(01342) 822018, Pro 822247
Chapel Lane, Forest Row, East Grinstead, E Sussex RH18 5LR
A22 East Grinstead-Eastbourne road, 4.5 miles S of East Grinstead turn left in Forest Row opposite church onto B2110, after 0.5 mile turn right into Chapel Lane, top of hill turn left, over heath to clubhouse.
Undulating moorland course with views over forest.
18 holes, 6477 yards, S.S.S.71
Founded 1888
Visitors: welcome, restricted weekends, Bank Holidays; essential to phone beforehand.
Green Fee: WD £28; WE £34.
Societies: Wed-Fri normal catering; Mon limited catering.
Catering: lunch, tea; casual visitors requested to book in advance or before teeing off.
Hotels: Ashdown Forest; Brambletye (E Grinstead); Chequers.

C96 Royal Eastbourne

☎(01323) 729738 (Sec), Pro/Fax 736986
Paradise Drive, Eastbourne, Sussex BN20 8BP
0.5 mile from Town Hall.
Parkland/downland course.
Devonshire course: 18 holes, 6132 yards, S.S.S.69; Hartington course: 9 holes, 4294 yards, S.S.S.61
Founded 1887
Visitors: h/cap cert required for 18 hole course, advisable to telephone 3-4 days in advance.
Green Fee: Devonshire: WD £20; WE £25; Hartington: WD £10; WE £12.
Societies: by arrangement.
Catering: full facilities daily. Snooker.
Hotels: Grand; Lansdowne; self-catering golf cottage (sleeps 4) adjacent to clubhouse, includes free golf.

C97 Royal Winchester

☎(01962) 852462, Pro 862473, Fax 865048
Sarum Rd, Off Romsey Rd, Winchester, Hants SO22 5QE
Leave Winchester on Romsey road.
Downland course.
18 holes, 6212 yards, S.S.S.70
Designed by H.S. Colt and A.P. Taylor.
Founded 1888
Visitors: weekdays (h/cap cert required).
Green Fee: £28
Societies: Mon, Wed.
Catering: every day, liaise with Manager.
Hotels: Royal; Lainston House (Winchester).

C98 Rustington Golf Centre

☎(01903) 850790, Fax 850982
Golfers Lane, Rustington, W Sussex BN16 4NB
A259 at Rustington, between Worthing and Chichester.
Public parkland course.
9 holes (18 tees) 5735 yards, S.S.S. 70; 9 hole Par 3 course; 3 hole academy course
Designed by David Williams Partnership.
Founded 1995
Visitors: 9am to 9pm 7 days a week. Bookings taken
Green Fee: WD £10.50 (9 holes), £15.50 (18 holes); WE £15.50 (9 holes), £20.50 (18 holes).
Catering: coffee shop serving hot and cold lunches.
Driving range.

C99 Ryde

☎(01983) 614809 (Club/fax), Pro 562088
Binstead Rd, Ryde, Isle of Wight PO33 3NF
Main Ryde-Newport road.
Parkland course.
9 holes, 5287 yards, S.S.S.66
Founded 1895. Present site 1921
Visitors: not Wed pm, Sun am.
Green Fee: WD £15; WE £20.
Societies: Weekdays except Wed, contact Sec for details.
Catering: by arrangement
Hotels: Newlands.

C100 Rye

☎(01797) 225241, Pro 225218, Fax 225460
Camber, Rye, E Sussex TN31 7QS

A259 from Rye towards Folkestone, turn right after 0.5 mile at signpost Camber, course 3 miles on right.
Links course.
18 holes, 6310 yards, S.S.S.71; Jubilee course: 9 holes, 6141 yards, S.S.S.70
Designed by H.S. Colt.
Founded 1894
Visitors: only on introduction by a member.
Green Fee: apply for details
Societies: none.
Catering: lunch every day except Tues.
Hotels: George; Mermaid; Broomhill Lodge; Playden Oasts; Hope Anchor; Top of the Hill; Queens Head.

C101 Sandford Springs
☎(01635) 297881, Tee bookings: 297883, Fax 298065
Wolverton, Nr Basingstoke, Hants RG26 5RT
Beside A339 at Kingsclere between Basingstoke and Newbury.
Picturesque and varied course overlooking 5 counties.
27 holes, 3 courses Parks, Woods & Lakes. Parks & Woods 6143 S.S.S. 69; Woods & Lakes 6222 S.S.S. 70; Lakes & Parks 6005 yards, S.S.S.69
Designed by Hawtree & Son.
Founded 1988
Visitors: welcome weekdays; booking system in operation.
Green Fee: £15 per 9 holes, £23 per round, £29 per day.
Societies: Society and Company Days welcome.
Catering: full bar and restaurant facilities available; parties, wedding receptions and business gatherings catered for.
Hotels: Hilton National (Basingstoke and Newbury); special rates agreed.

C102 Seaford
☎(01323) 892442, Pro 894160
East Blatchington, Seaford, E Sussex BN25 2JD
Off A259 N of Seaford.
Downland course.
18 holes, 6551 yards, S.S.S.69
Designed by J.H. Taylor.

Founded 1887
Visitors: welcome weekdays after 9.30am; telephone first.
Green Fee: WD £25.
Societies: welcome after 9.30am by prior arrangement.
Catering: breakfast, lunch, tea and dinner available.
Hotels: Dormy House on course.

C103 Seaford Head
☎(01323) 894843 (Sec), Pro 890139
Southdown Rd, Seaford, E Sussex BN25 4JS
S of A259, 12 miles from Brighton.
Public seaside course.
18 holes, 5848 yards, S.S.S.68
Founded 1887
Visitors: welcome at all times.
Green Fee: WD £11.50; WE £14.
Societies: welcome.
Catering: light snacks, Societies catered for.

C104 Sedlescombe (Aldershaw)
☎(01424) 870898
Sedlescombe, E Sussex TN33 0SD
On main A21 near Sedlescombe.
Parkland course.
18 holes, 6500 yards, S.S.S.68
Founded 1991
Visitors: Visitors accepted.
Green Fee: WD £12.50; WE £14.
Societies: on application.
Catering: bar and snacks.
Driving range.
Hotels: Brickwall.

C105 Selsey
☎(01243) 606442 (Sec), Pro 602203
Golf Links Lane, Selsey, Chichester, W Sussex PO20 9DR
On B2145 7 miles S of Chichester.
Seaside course.
9 holes, 5834 yards, S.S.S.68
Founded 1909
Visitors: welcome if member of recognised club.
Green Fee: WD £15 per round, £17 per day; WE £15 per round, £20 per day
Societies: small societies welcome.
Catering: lunch and snacks.

C106 Shanklin & Sandown
☎(01983) 403217, Pro/Fax 404424, Members: 403170
The Fairway, Lake, Sandown, Isle of Wight PO36 9PR
On A3055 to Lake, down The Fairway.
Heathland course.
18 holes, 6063 yards, S.S.S.69
Designed by Dr. J. Cowper, James Braid.
Founded 1900
Visitors: members of affiliated clubs only with h/cap certs; after 1pm weekends.
Green Fee: WD £20; WE £25.
Societies: by arrangement, not Tues am, 20-40 players.
Catering: available from 10am all day.

C107 Singing Hills Golf Course
☎(01273) 835353, Fax 835444
Albourne, E Sussex, BN6 9EB
Between Henfield and Hurstpierpoint on B2117 adjacent to A23.
Downland courses; Lake 3rd is exact replica of 17th at Sawgrass USA.
3 x 9 holes played in 3 different combinations of 18; Lake/River, Lake/Valley, River/Valley; 6200-6300 yards, S.S.S.71
Designed by Richard Hurd (Sandow).
Founded 1992
Visitors: pay-as-you-play; computerised booking; h/cap certs or membership of recognised club required.
Green Fee: WD £20; WE £28.
Societies: welcome 7 days a week.
Catering: 2 bars, 2 restaurants, conference facilities in Pavillion.
Driving range; extensive practice area.
Hotels: Hickstead Resort.

C108 Slinfold Park Golf & Country Club
☎(01403) 791154 (Clubhouse), Shop/Range: 791555, Fax 791465
Stane Street, Slinfold, Horsham, W Sussex RH13 7RE
A29 S of junction with A281.

Wooded parkland course.
18 holes, 6407 yards, S.S.S. 71; 9
hole course (pay-as-you-play) 1315
yards Par 28
Designed by John Fortune.
Founded 1992
Visitors: welcome.
Green Fee: WD £20; WE £25; 9 hole
course £4 (9 holes), £6.50 (18 holes).
Societies: apply for details.
Catering: full facilities.
Driving range, putting green, practice
ground.
Hotels: Random Hall.

C109 **South Winchester**
☎(01962) 877800 (Club/Manager),
Pro 840469, Fax 877900 Pitt,
Winchester, Hants SO22 5QW
In village of Pitt on Romsey-Hursley
road.
Championship links style course.
18 holes, 6729 yards, S.S.S. 73
Designed by Dave Thomas, Peter
Alliss, Clive Clark.
Founded 1993
Visitors: Guests of members only.
Green Fee: WD £14; WE £22.50.
Societies: by prior arrangement with
General Manager.
Catering: golfers bar, club bar, dining
room.
Driving range

C110 **Southampton**
☎(01703) 767996, Pro 768407 Golf
booking: 760456, Restaurant: 767996
Golf Course Rd, Bassett,
Southampton, Hants SO16 7AY
N end of city, off Bassett Ave,
halfway between Chilworth
roundabout and Winchester Rd
roundabout.
Municipal parkland course.
18 holes, 6213 yards, S.S.S.69; 9
holes, 2385 yards Par 32.
Founded 1935
Visitors: welcome.
Green Fee: WD £8.20; WE £11.30
Societies: by arrangement
Catering: breakfast, lunch, bar
snacks available.

C111 **Southsea**
☎(01705) 664549, 699519
Portsmouth Golf Centre, Great
Salterns GC, Burfields Rd,
Portsmouth PO3 5HH
2 miles off M27/A27/A3 on E road
into Portsmouth.
Municipal meadowland course.
18 holes, 6000 yards, S.S.S.70
Founded 1935

Visitors: welcome.
Green Fee: Summer £9.90; Winter
£7.25
Societies: by arrangement.
Catering: available in adjacent
Farmhouse public house.
Driving range

C112 **Southwick Park**
☎(01705) 380131, Pro 380442
Pinsley Drive, Southwick, Fareham,
Hants PO17 6EL
A333 7 miles N of Portsmouth, follow
signs to HMS Dryad.
Parkland course.
18 holes, 5972 yards, S.S.S.69
Designed by Charles Lawrie.
Founded 1977
Visitors: weekdays, weekends guest
of member.
Green Fee: WD £14
Societies: welcome Tues.
Catering: available.
Hotels: Marriott (Cosham).

C113 **Southwood**
☎(01252) 548700 (Pro), Club
515139
Ively Rd, Cove, Farnborough, Hants
GU14 0LJ
1 mile W of A325 Farnborough.
Public parkland course.
18 holes, 5738 yards, S.S.S.68
Designed by Hawtree & Son.
Founded 1977
Visitors: welcome, bookable at all
times.
Green Fee: WD £11.50; WE £14.
Societies: weekdays only.
Catering: bar snacks, tea and lunch
available.
Hotels: Queens Hotel (Aldershot)

C114 **Stoneham**
☎(01703) 768151, Sec 769272, Pro
768397
Monkswood Close, Off Bassett Green
Rd, Bassett, Southampton, Hants
SO16 3TT
From A33 turn left at Chilworth
roundabout, 0.5 mile on left side of
A27; from M27 exit 5 follow signposts
to Southampton then Bassett.
Heather and peat parkland course.
18 holes, 6310 yards, S.S.S.70
Designed by Willie Park.
Founded 1908
Visitors: any time tee is available
after 9am in midweek; restricted
weekends.
Green Fee: WD £27; WE £30
Societies: Mon, Thurs, Fri by
arrangement.

Catering: full catering by day, bar
11.30am-10pm; evening meals by
arrangement.
Hotels: Wessex; Northlands; Crest;
Post House; Hilton.

C115 **Test Valley**
☎(01256) 771737
Micheldever Rd, Overton, Nr
Basingstoke, Hants RG25 3DS
2 miles S of Overton village junction
with B3400; or 1.5 miles N of A303
from Overton turn off.
Inland links course.
18 holes, 6811 yards, S.S.S.73
Designed by D. Wright (E. Darcy).
Founded May 1992
Visitors: weekdays and weekends;
prior telephone booking advisable.
Green Fee: WD £14; WE £20.
Societies: welcome 7 days; from £18
for golf and meal.
Catering: full bar and dining facilities;
dining room for up to 100.
Extensive practice facilities.

C116 **Tidworth Garrison**
☎(01980) 842301 (Sec), Club
842321, Pro 842393
Bulford Rd, Tidworth, Wiltshire SP9
7AF
From Salisbury, A338 to Tidworth,
turn left at traffic lights, 1st left into
Bulford Rd, course 1 mile on right.
Tree-lined downland course with
scenic views.
18 holes, 6110 yards, S.S.S.69
Founded 1908
Visitors: welcome by arrangement.
Green Fee: £18
Societies: catered for Tues, Thurs.
Catering: hot and cold meals daily
except Mon when sandwiches only.
Hotels: Antrobus Arms; George.

C117 **Tilgate Forest Golf Centre**
☎(01293) 530103, Fax 523478
Titmus Drive, Tilgate, Crawley, W
Sussex RH10 5EU
M23, junction 11 for Pease Pottage,
follow main road to Crawley, at 1st
roundabout turn right, follow signs.
Public parkland course.
18 holes, 6359 yards, S.S.S.70; 9
holes, 1136 yards par 27.
Designed by Huggett and Coles.
Founded 1983
Visitors: welcome.
Green Fee: WD £11.85; WE £16.25.
Societies: Mon-Thurs.
Catering: restaurant and bar all day.
Driving range.

C118 Tylney Park
☎(01256) 762079
Rotherwick, Basingstoke, Hants
RG27 9AY
Off A30 at Nately Scures, follow signs
for Rotherwick; approx 1.5 miles.
Parkland course.
18 holes, 6200 yards, S.S.S.69
Designed by W. Wiltshire.
Founded 1974
Visitors: welcome; h/cap cert
required at weekends.
Green Fee: WD £21; WE £28.
Societies: welcome Mon to Thurs.
Catering: meals served.
Hotels: Tylney Hall; Raven (Hook).

C119 Ventnor
☎(01983) 853326, Sec 566456
Steephill Down Rd, Ventnor, Isle of
Wight
A3055 to Ventnor, course on downs
above at Upper Ventnor.
Undulating downland course.
12 holes, 5767 yards, S.S.S.68
Founded 1892
Visitors: welcome except 12am-
3.30pm Weds, not before 1pm Sun.
Green Fee: WD £12; WE £14.
Societies: not Sun am, catering by
arrangement.
Catering: snacks at bar.
Pool table.
Hotels: Eversly; Bonchurch Manor,
Mayfair (Shanklin)

C120 Waterhall
☎(01273) 508658
Off Devils Dyke Rd, Brighton, E
Sussex BN1 8YN
N of the town, 3 miles from centre,
towards Devil's Dyke.
Hilly downland course.
18 holes, 5773 yards, S.S.S.68
Founded 1923
Visitors: welcome.
Green Fee: WD £10.50 per round,
£16 per day; WE £14.50.
Societies: welcome weekdays.
Catering: available

C121 Waterlooville
☎(01705) 263388 (Sec/Manager),
Pro 256911
Cherry-Tree Ave, Cowplain,
Waterlooville, Hants PO8 8AP
Off A3 in Cowplain, 10 miles N of
Portsmouth.
Tree-lined parkland course.
18 holes, 6647 yards, S.S.S.72
Designed by Henry Cotton.
Founded 1907
Visitors: welcome Mon to Fri.

Green Fee: WD £20 per round, £30
per day.
Societies: Thurs only.
Catering: Bar facilities.
Hotels: Post House (Hayling Island);
Bear (Havant).

C122 Wellow
☎(01794) 322872 (Sec), Pro 323833
Ryedown Lane, East Wellow,
Romsey, Hants SO51 6BD
M27 exit 2 onto A36 towards
Salisbury, after 1 mile right to East
Wellow, after 1 mile right into
Ryedown Lane.
Parkland course.
27 holes, divided into 3 nines
Ryedown; Embley, Blackwater.
Ryedown/ Embley 5966 yards SSS
69; Embley/Blackwater 6320 yards
SSS 70; Ryedown/Blackwater 5844
yards SSS 69
Designed by W. Wiltshire.
Founded May 1991
Visitors: welcome 7 days.
Green Fee: WD £15 per round, £17
per day; WE £18 per round, £20 per
day.
Societies: welcome, not weekends.
Catering: bar and restaurant open all
day.

C123 Wellshurst Golf & Country Club
☎(01435) 813636 (Office), Pro
813456, Fax 812444
North St, Hellingly, E Sussex BN27
4EE
2 miles N of Boship roundabout on
A22 at Hailsham, on A267.
Pay-as-you-Play parkland course,
with views of South Downs.
18 holes 5717 yards S.S.S. 68
Designed by Golf Corporation.
Founded 1991
Visitors: welcome 7 days; must have
golf shoes, no denims.
Green Fee: WD £12; WE £16.
Societies: welcome, terms agreed on
requirements.
Catering: full bar & catering facilities.
Driving range.
Hotels: Boship; many in Eastbourne.

C124 West Chiltington
☎(01798) 813574 (Sec), Pro
812115, Fax 812631
Broadford Bridge Road, West
Chiltington, W Sussex RH20 2YA
Turn left off A283 1 mile E of
Pulborough; from West Chiltington
village take Broadford Bridge Rd
opposite Queen's Head public house.

Parkland course.
18 holes, 5900 yards, S.S.S.69; 9-
hole Par 3.
Designed by Brian Barnes and Max
Faulkner
Founded July 1988
Visitors: welcome at all times.
Green Fee: 18 holes: WD £12.50;
WE £15. 9 holes: WD £5; WE £7.50.
Societies: welcome by arrangement.
Catering: full catering and bar
facilities.
Driving range; putting green.
Hotels: The Mill House (Ashington).

C125 West Hove
☎(01273) 419738 (Manager), Pro
413494, Fax 439988
Church Farm, Hangleton, Hove,
Sussex. BN3 8AN
New course and clubhouse off new
by-pass, 2nd junction from A23
flyover going W.
Undulating downland course
overlooking the sea.
18 holes, 6237 yards, S.S.S.70
Designed by Hawtree
Founded 1910, re-located 1990.
Visitors: weekdays, weekends pm on
application.
Green Fee: WD £16; WE £20.
Societies: catered for weekdays.
Catering: available daily.
Snooker.
Hotels: Old Ship; Bedford; Sackville
(Brighton).

C126 West Sussex
☎(01798) 872563, Pro 872426, Fax
872033
Pulborough, West Sussex RH20 2EN
1.5 miles E of Pulborough on A283.
Heathland course.
18 holes, 6221 yards, S.S.S.70
Designed by Sir Guy Campbell, Major
C.K. Hutchison.
Founded 1931
Visitors: welcome weekdays only
except Fri (members only) with letter
of intro. and h/cap cert.
Green Fee: WD £33 per round, £42
per day
Societies: Wed and Thurs.
Catering: lunch and tea.
Hotels: Amberley Castle; The
Roundabout.

C127 Westridge
☎(01983) 613131
Brading Rd, Ryde, Isle of Wight,
PO33 1QS
Take A3055 and the course is next to
the Supermarket superstore in Ryde

Par 3 9 hole course
Public
Visitors: welcome; pay and play
Green Fee: WD £6 (9 holes); £9 (18 holes); WE £7 (9 holes), £10 (18 holes)
Societies: welcome
Catering: full facilities, bar.
Driving range

C128 **Weybrook Park**
☎(01256) 20347
Aldermarston Rd, Sherborne St John, Basingstoke, Hants RG24 9ND
2 miles NW of Basingstoke town centre; situated between A339 Basingstoke/Newbury road and A340 Basingstoke/Aldermarston road.
Parkland course.
18 holes, 5988 yards, S.S.S.70
Founded 1971
Visitors: welcome; restrictions at weekends during competitions.
Green Fee: WD £14; WE £18.
Societies: weekdays
Catering: bar.

C129 **Wickham Park**
☎(01329) 833342
Titchfield Lane, Wickham, Nr Fareham, Hants PO17 5PJ
From M27, Alton and Wickham exit, head to Wickham Square and at top of hill turn left to club 200 yards away.

Parkland course
18 holes, 6022 yards, S.S.S. 69
Designed by J Payne
Founded Sept 1995
Visitors: welcome; no jeans.
Green Fee: WD £8; WE £11.
Societies: welcome, society packages available.
Catering: Greens Restaurant provides meals for societies. Coffee and snacks at club.

C130 **Willingdon**
☎(01323) 410981 (Sec), Pro 410984, Fax 411510
Southdown Rd, Eastbourne, E Sussex BN20 9AA
2 miles N of Eastbourne off A22.
Downland course.
18 holes, 6118 yards, S.S.S.69
Designed by J.H. Taylor, modernised by Dr Mackenzie 1925.
Founded 1898
Visitors: welcome weekdays.
Green Fee: WD £24; WE £27.
Societies: by arrangement, weekdays except Tues.
Catering: by arrangement.
Hotels: Grand; Queens; Lansdown.

C131 **Worldham Park**
☎(01420) 543151
Caker Lane, E Worldham, Nr Alton, Hants GU34 3AG

Take B3004 from Alton to Bordon and course is situated on right after Alton by-pass
Parkland course
18 holes, 5836 yards, S.S.S. 71
Designed by F Whidbourne
Founded 1994
Visitors: welcome; pay-and-play
Green Fee: WD £8; WE £10
Societies: welcome by arrangement
Catering: Bar and full catering facilities
Hotels: Alton House

C132 **Worthing**
☎(01903) 260801(Sec), Pro 260718
Links Rd, Worthing, W Sussex BN14 9QZ
At top of hill on A27 0.25 mile E of Offington roundabout at junction with A24 London road.
Downland course.
Lower, 18 holes, 6530 yards, S.S.S.72; Upper, 18 holes, 5243 yards, S.S.S.66
Designed by H.S. Colt.
Founded 1906
Visitors: by prior arrangement, must produce h/cap certificate.
Green Fee: WD Lower £25, Upper £20; WE £30 per round on both, £40 per day
Societies: weekdays except Tues.
Catering: lunch served daily except Mon.

SURREY, KENT, SOUTH LONDON

Whatever geological quirk of fate decreed that Surrey should possess so much ground so utterly perfect for golf, the fact remains that lovers of inland courses regard it as their idea of heaven. Where else in the world (with the exception perhaps of Melbourne) is there such a cluster of first class places to play – most portraying the virtues of the pine, heather and silver birch country?

Until Woking was founded in 1893 "by a few mad barristers", the game around London had largely been confined to public commons and muddy parks. Woking celebrated its centenary in 1993. But, within the space of a few years, at the end of the last century, a whole new dimension opened up introducing names now familiar the world over. Sunningdale, Walton Heath, New Zealand, Worplesdon, West Hill, West Byfleet, and St George's Hill were all in existence before the Great War. West Hill owes its creation to a woman, Mrs Geoffrey Lubbock, who tired of being unable to play on Sunday and enlisted Willie Park and Jack White, Open champion in 1904, to pioneer a Club which forms part of the famous trinity of W's with Worplesdon and Woking. A fourth W in Windlesham has now appeared, a course that has quickly proved popular although different in character.

Everyone has his or her own particular favourite course in Surrey , the pleasant nature of the challenge they offer and the fact that a number have 36-holes, make them enormously popular with visitors and visiting Societies.

Today, Wentworth, not founded until 1924, features prominently on the list, their Edinburgh course, opened in 1990, adding considerably to an already established reputation. But the county map is festooned with famous names – Royal Wimbledon, Coombe Hill, Addington, Hankley Common, Camberley Heath, Farnham, Guildford, Burhill and Effingham. Hoebridge has boosted the public amenities while, at the other end of the scale, Wisley was opened in 1991, funded by an expensive debenture scheme. Another notable newcomer is Wildwood; and Royal Mid-Surrey remains the standard bearer of Surrey's relatively small amount of parkland golf.

To illustrate how quickly soil conditions change, Kent enjoys none of the heather courses so widespread in Surrey.

Its focal point is centred firmly on the coastal links of Royal St George's, Royal Cinque Ports and Princes; and, to a slightly lesser degree, on Littlestone between Folkestone and Rye. Royal St George's is still the only Open championship venue south of Lancashire.

North Foreland is a course within easy reach of Sandwich and one used for the Open championship qualifying rounds but the Medway coastline has courses in most of its towns while, in addition to Canterbury, that city also has Broome Park, opened in 1979. A more recent addition is Tudor Park Hotel Golf and Country Club, a stone's throw from the more senior Leeds Castle which has undergone something of a facelift. However, two of the most recent additions are The London Club near Brands Hatch, which has 36 holes, and Chart Hills, designed by Nick Faldo.

Knole Park and Wildernesse are highly respected names as well as excellent courses around Sevenoaks; West Kent, Rochester and Cobham, and Langley Park come in the same category along with Sundridge Park at Bromley which has two courses, and a word for Homelands Bettergolf Centre at Ashford, an ideal place to learn or enjoy a nine-hole course of more modest demands than, say, Deal.

D1 Abbey Moor
☎(01932) 570741
Green Lane, Addlestone, Surrey
KT15 2XV
Leave M25 at junction 11 and
proceed on St Peters Way towards
Weybridge; take rt turn at large
roundabout towards Addlestone on
A318, then over railway bridge; take
2nd turning rt at small roundabout
into Green Lane; course 0.5 mile on
rt.
Public pay-and-play parkland course.
9 holes, 5164 yards S.S.S.65
Designed by David Taylor.
Founded Sept 1991
Visitors: welcome weekdays and
weekends; advisable to book early.
Green Fee: WD £7; WE £8.
Societies: weekdays only.
Catering: bar and restaurant
facilities.
Hotels: White Lodge

D2 The Addington
☎(0181) 777 6057 (Sec), Pro 777
1701, Club 777 1055
205 Shirley Church Rd, Croydon,
Surrey CR0 5AB
2.5 miles from East Croydon Station.
Heathland course.
18 holes, 6242 yards, S.S.S.71
Designed by J.F. Abercromby.
Founded 1914
Visitors: welcome weekdays only;
h/cap cert required.
Green Fee: £30
Societies: weekdays; terms on
application.
Catering: bar and restaurant.
Practice hole.
Hotels: Selsdon Park

D3 Addington Court
☎(0181) 657 0281
Featherbed Lane, Croydon, Surrey
CR0 9AA
Undulating public heathland course
Championship, 18 holes, 5577 yards,
S.S.S.67; Falconwood, 18 holes,
5513 yards, S.S.S.66; 9 holes, 1733
yards.
Designed by F. Hawtree Snr.
Founded 1931
Visitors: welcome.
Green Fee: WD Championship
£11.50, Falconwood £9.99; WE
Championship £12.50, Falconwood
£11.50. 9 holes £6.95
Societies: welcome by prior
application.
Catering: full catering facilities.
18 hole Pitch & Putt,
Hotels: Selsdon Park.

D4 Addington Palace
☎(0181) 654 3061
Gravel Hill, Addington Park, Croydon,
Surrey CR0 5BB
2 miles from East Croydon station.
Parkland course
18 holes, 6274 yards, S.S.S.71
Founded 1923
Visitors: welcome weekdays; with
member weekends.
Green Fee: £30
Societies: Tues, Wed, Fri.
Catering: snacks, meals; not Mon.
Hotels: Selsdon Park

D5 Aquarius
☎(0181) 693 1626
Marmora Rd, Honor Oak, London
SE22 0RY
Set around a reservoir.
9 holes, 5426 yards, S.S.S.66
Founded 1912
Visitors: welcome with member only.
Green Fee: £10
Societies: on request.
Catering: on request.

D6 Ashford (Kent)
☎(01233) 622655
Sandyhurst Lane, Ashford, Kent
TN25 4NT
off A20, 1.5 miles W of Ashford.
Parkland course.
18 holes, 6263 yards, S.S.S.70
Designed by C.K. Cotton.
Founded 1924
Visitors: welcome, h/cap certs
required.
Green Fee: WD £30 per day.
Societies: Tues and Thurs by
arrangement.
Catering: full facilities (functions,
banquets etc).
Hotels: The Croft.

D7 Austin Lodge
☎(01322) 863000, Bookings:
868944, Fax 862406
Eynsford, Nr Swanley, Kent DA4 0HU
A225 to Eynsford station, past station
along cul-de-sac to course.
Peaceful countryside course.
18 holes, 7118 yards, S.S.S.73
Designed by Peter Bevan & Mike
Walsh.
Founded July 1991
Visitors: by telephone booking.
Green Fee: WD £16; WE £23.
Societies: welcome, bookings
required. After 2pm at weekends.
Catering: light meals and bar all day.
Golf academy.
Hotels: The Castle

D8 Banstead Downs
☎(0181) 642 2284
Burdon Lane, Belmont, Sutton,
Surrey SM2 7DD
100 yards E of junc A217 and B2230.
Downland course
18 holes, 6194 yards, S.S.S.69
Founded 1890
Visitors: welcome with letter of intro.
Mon-Fri; Bank Holidays and
weekends with member only.
Green Fee: WD £30 before 12 noon;
£20 after noon
Societies: by arrangement.
restrictions Thurs and Tues am
Catering: 11am-6pm, dinner by
arrangement.
Hotels: Thatched House (Cheam);
Drift Bridge (Epsom).

D9 Barnehurst
☎(01322) 523746
Mayplace Rd East, Bexley Heath,
Kent DA7 6JU
To Bexleyheath Clock Tower then to
Mayplace Rd East, golf club on left.
Mature inland course.
9 holes (18 tees), 5320 yards,
S.S.S.66
Designed by James Braid.
Founded 1904
Visitors: welcome.
Green Fee: WD £7; WE £11.
Societies: welcome.
Catering: full facilities; function room.
Hotels: Post House(Bexley).

D10 Barrow Hills
☎(01932) 848117
Longcross, Chertsey, Surrey KT16
0DS
4 miles W of Chertsey.
Parkland course.
18 holes, 3090 yards, S.S.S.53
Founded 1970
Visitors: with member only.
Green Fee: members responsibility

D11 Bearsted
☎(01622) 738198
Ware St, Bearsted, Kent ME14 4PQ
Off M20 at A249; turn right at large
roundabout, take left slipway to
Bearstead Green, left at roundabout,
on under bridge; 400 yards on left.
Parkland course.
18 holes, 6437 yards, S.S.S.70
Designed by Golf Landscapes.
Founded 1895
Visitors: must be member of bona
fide club with current h/cap; not
weekends unless with member;
advisable to phone.

Green Fee: WD £24 per round, £30 per day; WE £30.
Societies: Tues-Fri by arrangement with Sec.
Catering: bar, restaurant, snacks; business lunches by arrangement.
Hotels: Tudor Park Hotel G & CC.

D12 **Beckenham Place Park**

☎(0181) 650 2292
Beckenham Hill Rd, Beckenham, Kent BR3 2BP
1 mile from Catford towards Bromley, right at Homebase.

Parkland course.
18 holes, 5722 yards, S.S.S.68
Founded 1932
Visitors: welcome.
Green Fee: WD £8.40; WE £12.50
Societies: welcome by arrangement
Catering: meals and snacks.
Hotels: Bromley Court

D13 **Betchworth Park**

☎(01306) 882052
Reigate Rd, Dorking, Surrey RH4 1NZ
1 mile E of Dorking on A25, entrance opposite horticultural gardens.

Parkland course
18 holes, 6266 yards, S.S.S.70
Designed by H. Colt.
Founded 1913
Visitors: welcome except Tues am, Sat and Sun am.
Green Fee: WD £31; WE £43.
Societies: Mon and Thurs.
Catering: lunch and tea available.
Hotels: White Horse.

D14 **Bexleyheath**

☎(0181) 303 6951
Mount Rd, Bexleyheath, Kent DA6 8JS

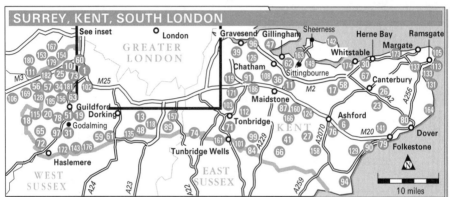

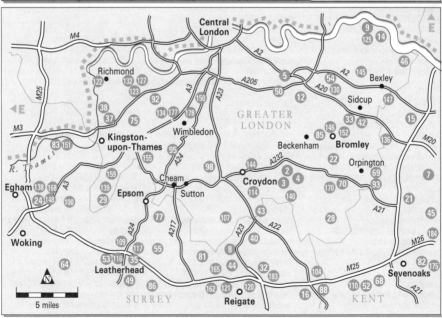

1 mile from Bexleyheath station, off Upton Rd.
Undulating course.
9 holes, 5239 yards, S.S.S.66
Founded 1907
Visitors: welcome 8am-4pm Mon-Fri.
Green Fee: £20.
Societies: weekdays by prior arrangement.
Catering: lunch, snacks and evening meals, except Mon.
Hotels: Swallow.

D15 Birchwood Park
☎(01322) 660554
Birchwood Rd, Wilmington, Dartford, Kent DA2 7HJ
Off A20 or M25 at Swanley turn off.
Meadowland course.
18 holes, 6364 yards, S.S.S.71; 9 holes, 1356 yards, Par 29
Designed by Howard Swan.
Founded 1990
Visitors: welcome.
Green Fee: WD £14; WE £23.
Societies: welcome weekdays, weekends limited; contact Sec.
Catering: full facilities.
Driving range.
Hotels: Stakis.

D16 Bletchingley
☎(01833) 744666, Pro 744848, Fax 744284
Church Lane, Bletchingley, Surrey RH1 4LP
Exit junc 6 on M25 and take A25 course is 3 miles along that road
Parkland course
18 holes, 6504 yards, S.S.S. 71
Founded 1993
Visitors: weekdays
Green Fee: WD £18; WE £25.
Societies: welcome on application.
Catering: Bar and restaurant.
Hotels: Priory (Redhill).

D17 Boughton
☎(01227) 752277
Brickfield Lane, Boughton, Nr Faversham, Kent ME13 9AJ
At intersection of the A2/M2 follow signs for Boughton and Dunkirk.
Upland course.
18 holes, 6452 yards, S.S.S. 71
Designed by P Sparks
Founded 1993
Visitors: welcome
Green Fee: WD £16; WE £22
Societies: welcome
Catering: bar and restaurant facilities

D18 Bowenhurst
☎(01252) 851695
Mill Lane, Crondall, Nr Farnham, Surrey GU10 5RP
Take A287 from Farnham, course 2.5 miles from town on right
Parkland/lakes course
9 holes, 2100 yards, S.S.S. 60
Founded 1994
Visitors: welcome pay as you play
Green Fee: WD £5; WE £6.50
Societies: welcome
Catering: clubhouse planned late 1996. Coffee lounge available until then.
Driving range.

D19 Bramley
☎(01483) 892696 (Sec), Steward: 893042, Pro 893685, Fax 894673
Bramley, Nr Guildford, Surrey GU5 0AL
Situated 4 miles S of Guildford on A281 Guildford-Horsham road, between Shalford and Bramley.
Parkland course
18 holes, 5990 yards, S.S.S.69
Designed by Charles Mayo, redesigned by James Braid.
Founded 1913

KEY								
	38	Coombe Wood	76	Homelands B'golf C	114	Purley Downs	152	Sundridge Park
1 Abbey Moor	39	Corinthian	77	Horton Park CC	115	Puttenham	153	Sunningdale
3 Addington Court	40	Coulsdon Manor	78	Hurtmore	116	Pyrford	154	Sunningdale Ladies
4 Addington Palace	41	Cranbrook	79	Hythe Imperial	117	RAC Country Club	155	Surbiton
2 The Addington	42	Cray Valley	80	Jack Nicklaus GC	118	Redhill & Reigate	156	Sutton Green
5 Aquarius	43	Croham Hurst	81	Kingswood (Surrey)	119	Redlibbets	157	Tandridge
6 Ashford (Kent)	44	Cuddington	82	Knole Park	120	Reigate Heath	158	Tenterden
7 Austin Lodge	45	Darenth Valley	83	Laleham	121	Reigate Hill	159	Thames Ditton &
8 Banstead Downs	46	Dartford	84	Lamberhurst	122	Richmond		Esher
9 Barnehurst	47	Deangate Ridge	85	Langley Park	123	Richmond Park	160	Tudor Park CC
10 Barrow Hills	48	Dorking	86	Leatherhead	124	The Ridge	161	Tunbridge Wells
11 Bearsted	49	Drift	87	Leeds Castle	125	Riverside	162	Tyrrells Wood
12 Beckenham Place Pk	50	Dulwich & Syd'm Hill	88	Limpsfield Chart	126	Rochester & Cob. Pk	163	Upchurch River Valley
13 Betchworth Park	51	Dunsfold Aerodrome	89	Lingfield Park	127	Roehampton	164	Walmer & Kingsdown
14 Bexleyheath	52	Edenbridge G & CC	90	Littlestone	128	Roker Park	165	Walton Heath
15 Birchwood Park	53	Effingham	92	London Scottish	129	Romney Warren	166	Weald of Kent
16 Bletchingley	54	Eltham Warren	91	The London	130	Royal Blackheath	167	Wentworth
17 Boughton	55	Epsom	93	Lullingstone Park	131	Royal Cinque Ports	168	West Byfleet
18 Bowenhurst	56	Farnham	94	Lydd	132	Royal Mid-Surrey	169	West Hill
19 Bramley	57	Farnham Park	95	Malden	133	Royal St George's	170	West Kent
20 Broadwater Park	58	Faversham	96	Mid-Kent	134	Royal Wimbledon	171	West Malling
21 Broke Hill	59	Fernfell G & CC	97	Milford	135	Rusper	172	West Surrey
22 Bromley	60	Foxhills	98	Mitcham	136	Ruxley	173	Westgate &
23 Broome Park CC	61	Gatton Manor	99	Moatlands	137	St Augustine's		Birchington
24 Burhill	62	Gillingham	100	Moore Place	138	St George's Hill	174	Whitstable &
25 Camberley Heath	63	Goal Farm Par 3	101	Nevill	139	Sandown Golf Centre		Seasalter
26 Canterbury	64	Guildford	102	New Zealand GC	140	Selsdon Pk H & GC	175	Wildernesse
27 Chart Hills	65	Hankley Common	103	Nizels	141	Sene Valley	176	Wildwood
28 Cherry Lodge	66	Hawkhurst	104	North Downs	142	Sheerness	177	Wimbledon Common
29 Chessington	67	Herne Bay	105	North Foreland	143	Shillinglee Park	178	Wimbledon Park
30 Chestfield	68	Hever	106	Oak Park (Crondall)	144	Shirley Park	179	Windlemere
31 Chiddingfold	69	Hewitts Golf Centre	107	Oaks Sports Centre	145	Shooters Hill	180	Windlesham
32 Chipstead	70	High Elms	108	Oastpark	146	Shortlands	181	The Wisley
33 Chislehurst	71	Hilden	109	Pachesham GC	147	Sidcup	182	Woking
34 Chobham	72	Hindhead	110	Park Wood	148	Silvermere	183	Woodcote Park
35 Clandon Regis	73	Hoebridge Golf Centre	111	Pine Ridge GC	149	Sittingbourne & MiReg	184	Woodlands Manor
36 Cobtree Manor Park	74	Holtye	112	Poult Wood	150	Springfield Park	185	Worplesdon
37 Coombe Hill	75	Home Park	113	Prince's	151	Sunbury	186	Wrotham Heath

Visitors: welcome Mon-Fri; guests of members only at weekends.
Green Fee: £25 per round, £30 per day.
Societies: Mon-Fri by prior arrangement with Sec.
Catering: bar snacks and grill menu daily.
Driving range
Hotels: Bramley Grange.

D20 **Broadwater Park**
☎ (01483) 429955
Guildford Rd, Farncombe, Nr Godalming, Surrey GU7 3BU
A3100 between Godalming and Guildford opposite Manor Inn.
Public parkland course.
9 holes Par 3, 1287 yards.
Designed by K.D. Milton.
Founded 1989
Visitors: no restrictions. Book at weekends
Green Fee: WD £3.75 (9 holes); WE £4.25 (9 holes)
Societies: welcome weekdays.
Catering: bar, snacks.
Driving range.
Hotels: Manor Inn.

D21 **Broke Hill**
☎ (01959) 533225, Fax 532880
Sevenoaks Road, Halstead, Kent TN14 7HR
Close to junction 4 of M25 opposite Knockholt station.
Meadowland course
18 holes, 6454 yards, S.S.S 71
Designed by D Williams
Founded May 1993
Visitors: weekdays only
Green Fee: £25
Societies: weekdays only
Catering: full bar and restaurant facilities. Comprehensive menu.

D22 **Bromley**
☎ (0181) 462 7014
Magpie Hall Lane, Bromley, Kent BR2 8JF
A21 2 miles S of Bromley.
Public parkland course.
9 holes, 5490 yards, S.S.S.69
Visitors: welcome except Tues am or Sun am
Green Fee: WD £4.75; WE £6.25
Societies: apply
Catering: snacks available.

D23 **Broome Park CC**
☎ (01227) 831701, Fax 821973
Barham, Canterbury, Kent CT4 6QX

Off M2 onto A2 then Folkestone road A260, 700 yards on right hand side, 8 miles from Canterbury.
Parkland course.
18 holes, 6610 yards, S.S.S.72
Designed by Donald Steel.
Founded 1979
Visitors: weekdays with h/cap cert; start times to be booked in advance.
Green Fee: WD £26 per round, £32.50 per day; WE £32, £37.50
Societies: Mon-Fri.
Catering: 2 bars, 2 restaurants, 7 days, Dizzy's Jazz Bar & Creole Restaurant.
Tennis, squash, snooker, putting green, croquet, clay pigeon shooting, health & fitness centre.
Hotels: Club has apartments & villas; telephone for details.

D24 **Burhill**
☎ (01932) 227345
Walton-on-Thames, Surrey KT12 4BL
Off A3 on A245 towards Byfleet,turn right into Seven Hills Rd and again into Burwood Rd, entrance to course is 2nd on right.
Parkland course
18 holes, 6224 yards, S.S.S.70
Designed by Willie Park.
Founded 1907
Visitors: weekdays by arrangement, h/cap cert required.
Green Fee: £44 per day.
Societies: catered for Wed and Thur only.
Catering: lunch, snack bar facilities available except Mon.
Squash and Badminton.
Hotels: Oatlands Park (Weybridge).

D25 **Camberley Heath**
☎ (01276) 23258, Fax 692505
Golf Drive, Camberley, Surrey GU15 1JG
On A325 to Camberley, near M3 exit 4, follow signs to Bagshot and Frimley.
Undulating heathland course.
18 holes, 6337 yards, S.S.S.70
Designed by H. S. Colt.
Founded 1913
Visitors: welcome weekdays, but must have h/cap cert from recognised golf club and should phone for tee reservation.
Green Fee: £33 per round, £55 per day
Societies: welcome by prior arrangement.
Catering: meals and snacks served; Japanese restaurant.
Hotels: Frimley Hall.

D26 **Canterbury**
☎ (01227) 453532
Scotland Hills, Canterbury, Kent CT1 1TW
A257 1 mile from Canterbury.
Parkland course.
18 holes, 6249 yards, S.S.S.70
Designed by H.S. Colt.
Founded 1927
Visitors: welcome on weekdays.
After 3pm at weekends by arrangement.
Green Fee: WD £27 per round, £36 per day; WE £36 per round (after 3pm) Sat and Sun.
Societies: Tues, Thurs only, by arrangement.
Catering: full menu available Mon-Sat.
Hotels: Ebury; Canterbury; Abbots Barton.

D27 **Chart Hills**
☎ (01580) 292222, Fax 292233
Weeks Lane, Biddenden, Kent TN27 8JX
Off A274 from Leeds Castle to Tenterden.
Parkland course.
18 holes, 7086 (Oaks) yards, S.S.S.72
Designed by Nick Faldo.
Founded 1993
Visitors: welcome; h/cap cert needed.
Green Fee: WD £50 per round; £80 per day; WE £60 per round, £90 per day.
Societies: welcome.
Catering: full facilitiesavailable.
Restaurant
Snooker, health centre.
Hotels: Tudor Park (Maidstone).

D28 **Cherry Lodge**
☎ (01959) 572550 (Office), Pro 572989
Jail Lane, Biggin Hill, Kent TN16 3AX
Off A233 by RAF Biggin Hill.
Undulating downland course.
18 holes, 6652 yards, S.S.S.72
Designed by John Day.
Founded 1969
Visitors: welcome Mon-Fri only by arrangement.
Green Fee: £18 per round, £23 per day.
Societies: Mon-Fri, min 18; full catering facilities available by prior booking.
Catering: à la carte restaurant open Mon-Sat, Sun lunches, 2 bars.
Banqueting.
Hotels: Bromley Court (Bromley).

D29 **Chessington**
☎(0181) 391 0948 (Pro), Office: 974 1705
Garrison Lane, Chessington, Surrey KT9 2LW
Opposite Chessington South station, very near to Chessington zoo.
Parkland course.
9 holes, 1353 yards, Par 3 course, S.S.S.25
Designed by Patrick Tallack.
Founded 1983
Visitors: welcome.
Green Fee: WD £4; WE £4.90.
Societies: welcome.
Catering: full catering facilities.
Driving range.
Hotels: Seven Hills; Oatlands Park.

D30 **Chestfield**
☎(01227) 794411 (Sec/Manager), Pro 793563
103 Chestfield Rd, Whitstable, Kent CT5 3LU
0.5 mile S of Thanet Way at Swalecliffe/Chestfield roundabout.
Parkland/seaside course.
18 holes, 6181 yards, S.S.S.70
Founded 1925
Visitors: must have current h/cap certs; not weekends or Bank Holidays.
Green Fee: £18 per round, £28 per day.
Societies: by arrangement Mon, Tues, Wed and Fri.
Catering: full facilities.
Hotels: Marine.

D31 **Chiddingfold**
☎(01428) 685888
Petworth Rd, Chiddingfold, Surrey GU8 4SL
Take A283 off the A3 and course is 10 mins away 50 yards south of Chiddingfold
Downland course
18 holes, 5482 yards, S.S.S. 67
Designed by J Gaunt & P Alliss
Founded May 1994
Visitors: welcome
Green Fee: WD £14; WE £18
Societies: welcome; society packages available
Catering: full facilities. Conference suite
Snooker

D32 **Chipstead**
☎(01737) 555781
How Lane, Coulsden, Surrey CR3 3PR
Follow signs to Chipstead from A217.
Undulating parkland course.
18 holes, 5491 yards, S.S.S.68
Founded 1906
Visitors: welcome weekdays.
Green Fee: £25 per day, £20 after 2pm.
Societies: catered for on weekdays.
Catering: lunch served except Mon; prior booking required.
Hotels: Reigate Manor

D33 **Chislehurst**
☎(0181) 467 2782
Camden Place, Camden Park Rd, Chislehurst, Kent BR7 5HJ
0.5 mile from Chislehurst station, on A222 to Bromley.
Parkland course.
18 holes, 5106 yards, S.S.S.65
Founded 1894
Visitors: welcome weekdays only.
Green Fee: £25.
Societies: by arrangement with Sec.
Catering: lunch each day. Full facilities
Hotels: Bromley Court.

D34 **Chobham**
☎(01276) 855584, Fax 856243
Chobham Rd, Knaphill, Woking, Surrey GU21 2TZ
5 minutes from Woking and M3 junction 3, between Knaphill and Chobham villages.
Parkland course.
18 holes 5821 yards S.S.S 68
Designed by Clive Clark and Peter Alliss.
Founded 1994
Visitors: welcome with advance booking.
Green Fee: WD £22; WE £30.
Societies: welcome.
Catering: bars, restaurant, function room.
Hotels: Worplestone Place Hotel

D35 **Clandon Regis**
☎(01483) 224888 (Club), Pro 223922
Epsom Road, West Clandon Nr Guildford, Surrey GU4 7TT
Take either junc 9 or 10 from M25 and take A246 towards Guildford
Parkland course
18 holes, 6412 yards, S.S.S. 71
Designed by D Williams
Founded 1994
Visitors: restricted to members guests
Green Fee: members responsibility
Societies: none
Catering: full bar and restaurant

D36 **Cobtree Manor Park**
☎(01622) 753276 (Pro)
Chatham Rd, Maidstone, Kent ME14 3AZ
Take A229 from M20.
Municipal parkland course.
18 holes, 5586 yards, S.S.S.68
Designed by F. Hawtree.
Founded 1984
Visitors: welcome, pay and play
Green Fee: WD £11; WE £16
Societies: on application.
Catering: available.

D37 **Coombe Hill**
☎(0181) 942 2284
Golf Club Drive, Kingston, Surrey KT2 7DG
0.25 mile W of A3 on A238.
Parkland course.
18 holes, 6293 yards, S.S.S.71
Designed by J.F. Abercromby.
Founded 1911
Visitors: welcome by appointment only weekdays, telephone Pro for details.
Green Fee: £50.
Societies: welcome weekdays, telephone Pro for details.
Catering: lunches served every day.
Hotels: Hilton

D38 **Coombe Wood**
☎(0181) 942 0388, Pro 942 6764
George Rd, Kingston Hill, Kingston-on-Thames, Surrey KT2 7NS
1 mile N of Kingston-on-Thames, off Kingston Hill.
Parkland course.
18 holes, 5295 yards, S.S.S.66
Designed by T. Williamson.
Founded 1904
Visitors: weekdays only.
Green Fee: £21 per round, £32 per day.
Societies: welcome Wed, Thurs and Fri.
Catering: available.
Hotels: Kingston Lodge (adjoining course).

D39 **Corinthian**
☎(01474) 707559
Gay Dawn Farm, Fawkham, Longfield, Kent DA3 8LZ
4 miles S of Dartford Tunnel, E of Brands Hatch along Fawkham road.
Parkland course (with grass green during summer, artificial greens during winter).
9 holes, 18 tees, 6323 yards, S.S.S.72
Founded 1987

Visitors: unrestricted weekdays, pm only weekends and Bank Holidays.
Green Fee: £15 per day.
Societies: welcome by arrangement with Sec.
Catering: bar evenings and Sat and Sun lunch.
Tennis, squash, sauna, gymnasium.

D40 **Coulsdon Manor**

☎(0181) 668 0414 (Hotel), Pro 668 6083
Coulsdon Rd, Coulsdon, Surrey CR5 2LL
Just off A23, 2 miles S of Croydon, 2 miles N of M25 and M23.
Parkland course.
18 holes, 6037 yards, S.S.S.69
Designed by H.S. Buck.
Founded 1926
Visitors: welcome.
Green Fee: WD £13; WE £16.
Societies: welcome by prior arrangement.
Catering: full facilities.
Hotels: Coulsdon Manor

D41 **Cranbrook**

☎(01580) 712833
Benenden Rd, Cranbrook, Kent TN17 4AL
Take A262 Ashford/Cranbrook turning off A21 just N of Lamberhurst; turn right at Bull public house in Sissinghurst, over crossroads (1.5 miles), course is located 1 mile on left.
Heavily wooded parkland course.
18 holes, 6351 yards, S.S.S.70
Designed by John D. Harris.
Founded 1969
Visitors: welcome weekdays, not before 10.30am Tues & Thurs, times limited at weekends.
Green Fee: WD £19; WE £27.50.
Societies: on application Mon, Wed, Fri; specialists on company golf days.
Catering: full bar and restaurant facilities.
Hotels: Tudor Court.

D42 **Cray Valley**

☎(01689) 839677 (Sec), Pro 837909, Club 831927
Sandy Lane, St Paul's Cray, Orpington, Kent BR5 3HY
A20 to Ruxley roundabout, junction with A233.
Undulating meadowland course.
18 holes, 5649 yards, S.S.S.67; 9 hole course.
Designed by Golf Centres Ltd.
Founded 1972

Visitors: weekdays unlimited, weekends restricted.
Green Fee: WD £11; WE £16.80.
Societies: welcome
Catering: telephone in advance.

D43 **Croham Hurst**

☎(0181) 657 5581, Pro 657 7705
Croham Rd, South Croydon, Surrey CR2 7HJ
1 mile from S Croydon; from M25 exit 6 N onto A22, take B270 to Warlingham at roundabout, then B269 to Selsdon; at traffic lights turn left into Farley Rd, clubhouse 1.75 miles on left.
Parkland course.
18 holes, 6286 yards, S.S.S.70
Designed by Hawtree & Sons.
Founded 1911
Visitors: welcome, h/cap cert required; with member only at weekends.
Green Fee: £33 per round/day.
Societies: Wed, Thurs, Fri by arrangement.
Catering: full catering facilities available every day 10am-6pm; banqueting.

D44 **Cuddington**

☎(0181) 393 0952
Banstead Rd, Banstead, Surrey SM7 1RD
200 yards from Banstead station.
Parkland course.
18 holes, 6394 yards, S.S.S.70
Designed by H.S. Colt.
Founded 1929
Visitors: welcome by appointment; h/cap or letter of introduction.
Green Fee: WD £30; WE £35.
Societies: Thurs only.
Catering: available weekdays by appointment.
Hotels: Heath Side

D45 **Darenth Valley**

☎(01959) 522944 (Manager), Pro 522922, Fax 525089
Station Rd, Shoreham, Kent TN14 7SA
Along A225 Sevenoaks-Dartford road, 4 miles N of Sevenoaks.
Public meadowland course.
18 holes, 6327 yards, S.S.S.71
Founded 1973 by M.F.C. Cross.
Visitors: welcome; bookings daily.
Green Fee: WD £12; WE £16.
Societies: welcome, prices on application to the Manager.
Catering: bar meals, society catering, functions (100).

D46 **Dartford**

☎(01322) 223616, Sec 226455, Pro 226409
Dartford Heath, Dartford, Kent DA1 2TN
On Dartford Heath, 2 miles from Dartford town centre.
Heathland course.
18 holes, 5914 yards, S.S.S.68
Founded 1897
Visitors: welcome weekdays if member of recognised club, at weekends only with member; h/cap certs required.
Green Fee: £20 per round, £28 per day.
Societies: Mon and Fri, booked well in advance.
Catering: full restaurant service.
Hotels: Black Prince.

D47 **Deangate Ridge**

☎(01634) 251180
Hoo, Rochester, Kent ME3 8RZ
A228 from Rochester to Isle of Grain, then road signposted to Deangate Ridge, 4 miles NE of Rochester.
Municipal parkland course.
18 holes, 6300 yards, S.S.S.70
Designed by Hawtree & Sons.
Founded 1972
Visitors: welcome any time, bookings essential weekends.
Green Fee: WD £6.60 (9 holes), £9.60 (18 holes); WE £9.60 (9 holes), £12.70 (18 holes).
Societies: welcome.
Catering: lunch and dinner served, bookings essential weekends.

D48 **Dorking**

☎(01306) 886917
Chart Park, Dorking, Surrey RH5 4BX
A24 0.5 mile S of Dorking between A25 and N Holmwood roundabouts.
Undulating parkland course.
9 holes (18 tees), 5163 yards, S.S.S.65
Designed by James Braid.
Founded 1897
Visitors: welcome weekdays, members only weekends and Bank Holidays; Ladies' Day Wed am.
Green Fee: £16 per day.
Societies: by arrangement.
Catering: full meals and snacks except Mon.
Hotels: Burford Bridge.

D49 **Drift**

☎(01483) 284641
The Drift, East Horsley, Surrey KT24 5HD

Turn off A3 onto B2039 signposted East Horsley, 2 miles on left, club signposted.
Woodland course.
18 holes, 6425 yards, S.S.S.72
Designed by H. Cotton
Founded 1975
Visitors: welcome weekdays only. Ring in advance.
Green Fee: £30 per day.
Societies: welcome weekdays except Tues am.
Catering: bar and restaurant.
Hotels: Thatchers.

D50 Dulwich & Sydenham Hill
☎(0181) 693 3961
Grange Lane, College Rd, London SE21 7LH
Off S Circular road at Dulwich College and College Rd.
Parkland course.
18 holes, 6008 yards, S.S.S.69
Founded 1894
Visitors: welcome weekdays only by prior booking.
Green Fee: £25 per round, £30 per day.
Societies: weekdays by arrangement.
Catering: lunch daily, dinner by arrangement.

D51 Dunsfold Aerodrome
☎(01483) 265472, Sec 276118
British Aerospace, Dunsfold Aerodrome, Nr Godalming, Surrey GU8 4BS
12 miles S of Guildford on A281.
Parkland course.
9 holes (18 tees), 6099 yards, S.S.S.69
Designed by John Sharkey.
Founded 1965
Visitors: with member only.
Green Fee: members responsibility.
Societies: from British Aerospace.
Catering: bar, snacks.

D52 Edenbridge G & CC
☎(01732) 865097
Crouch House Rd, Edenbridge, Kent TN8 5LQ
Travelling N through Edenbridge High St, turn left into Stangrove Rd (30 yards before railway station), at end of road turn right, course is on left.
Undulating meadowland course.
Old, 18 holes, 6646 yards, S.S.S.71;
New, 18 holes, 5763 yards, S.S.S.67;
9 hole Beginner's Course, Par 31
Founded 1975

Visitors: welcome, members only on Old Course weekends.
Green Fee: Old course: WD £15; New course: WD £10; WE £14 am; £12 pm
Societies: weekdays only.
Catering: lunch and bar snacks served daily.
Driving range.
Hotels: Langley Arms (Tonbridge).

D53 Effingham
☎(01372) 452203, Fax 459959
Guildford Rd, Effingham, Surrey KT24 5PZ
On A246 8 miles E of Guildford.
Downland course.
18 holes, 6550 yards, S.S.S.71
Designed by H.S. Colt.
Founded 1927
Visitors: Mon-Fri only by arrangement, h/cap certs required.
Green Fee: £35 per day, £27.50 after 2pm.
Societies: Wed, Thurs and Fri.
Catering: lunch, tea, evening meal, snacks etc.
Tennis, squash, snooker (must be accompanied by member).
Hotels: Thatchers (East Horsley); Preston Cross (Great Bookham).

D54 Eltham Warren
☎(0181) 850 1166, Sec 850 4477
Bexley Rd, Eltham, London SE9 2PE
Continuation of Eltham High St, 0.5 mile E.
Parkland course.
9 holes, 5840 yards, S.S.S.68
Founded 1890
Visitors: weekdays only; must be member of recognised club.
Green Fee: £25
Societies: welcome weekdays; restrictions Thurs.
Catering: bar snacks; full catering by arrangement except Mon.
Snooker.
Hotels: Swallow (Bexley).

D55 Epsom
☎(01372) 721666 (Sec), Pro 741867
Longdown Lane South, Epsom, Surrey KT17 4JR
0.5 mile S of Epsom Downs Station, next to Epsom College heading towards the downs.
Downland course.
18 holes, 5701 yards, S.S.S.68
Founded 1889
Visitors: welcome on weekdays from 8am, except Tues from 12.30pm; Sat and from 12am Sun.

Green Fee: WD £16.50 per round, £26 per day; WE £18.50.
Societies: Wed and Fri on written application, min 12, max 40.
Catering: meals and snacks except Mondays
Hotels: Drift Bridge

D56 Farnham
☎(01252) 782109 (Sec), Pro 782198
The Sands, Farnham, Surrey GU10 1PX
1 mile E of Farnham on A31, turning to The Sands signposted.
Parkland/heathland course.
18 holes, 6325 yards, S.S.S.70
Founded 1896
Visitors: welcome weekdays with h/cap cert; guests of members only at weekends.
Green Fee: WD £27 per round, £32 per day.
Societies: welcome by arrangement.
Catering: full catering on request.
Hotels: Hogs Back.

D57 Farnham Park
☎(01252) 715216
Folly Hill, Farnham, Surrey GU9 0AV
0.75 mile N of Farnham, next to castle in Farnham Park.
Par 3 parkland course.
9 holes, 1163 yards, S.S.S.54
Designed by Henry Cotton.
Founded 1963
Visitors: welcome at all times; weekends and Bank Holidays booking only.
Green Fee: WD £3.25; WE £4.25.
Societies: welcome (limit on size)
Catering: hot or cold snacks as required.
Hotels: The Bush (Farnham).

D58 Faversham
☎(01795) 890561
Belmont Park, Faversham, Kent ME13 0HB
Leave M2 at junction 6, A251 to Faversham, then A2 to Sittingbourne for 0.5 mile, turn left at Brogdale Rd, and follow signs.
Parkland course.
18 holes, 6030 yards, S.S.S.69
Founded 1902
Visitors: only with member weekends and public holidays.
Green Fee: £25 per round, £30 per day.
Societies: Wed and Fri only
Catering: by arrangement with Steward.
Hotels: Granary; Porch House.

D59 **Fernfell G & CC**
☎(01483) 268855, Pro 277188
Barhatch Lane, Cranleigh, Surrey
GU6 7NG
take A281 out of Guildford; 1 mile
through Cranleigh take Ewhurst road,
then turn into Barhatch
Road/Barhatch Lane.
Parkland course.
18 holes, 5561 yards, S.S.S.68
Founded 1985
Visitors: welcome
weekdays.Restricted weekends.
Green Fee: WD £20; WE £25.
Societies: welcome weekdays.
Catering: bar, restaurant, snacks,
banquets.
Tennis, snooker, swimming pool,
Leisure club opening late 1996.
Hotels: Bramley Grange (Bramley).

D60 **Foxhills**
☎(01932) 872050, Pro 873961, Fax
874762
Stonehill Rd, Ottershaw, Surrey KT16
0EL
Off A320 at Otter public house, turn
right and right again into Foxhills Rd;
1 mile from M25 exit 11.
Heathland courses.
Chertsey, 18 holes, 6374 yards,
S.S.S.70; Longcross, 18 holes, 6429
yards, S.S.S.71; 9 hole Par 3
Designed by F. Hawtree.
Founded 1973
Visitors: welcome Mon-Fri.
Green Fee: £45 per round, £65 per
day.
Societies: only by appointment.
Packages available.
Catering: 3 restaurants plus bars.
Driving range, tennis (10), squash (4),
indoor and outdoor pools, gym, health
suite, snooker, banqueting, clay
shoot.
Hotels: 16 suites on the complex.

D61 **Gatton Manor**
☎(01306) 627555, Pro 627557, Fax
627713
Ockley, Dorking, Surrey RH5 5PQ
A29 1.5 miles SW of Ockley.
Undulating parkland course.
18 holes, 6653 yards, S.S.S.73
Designed by D.B. & D.G. Heath.
Founded 1969
Visitors: welcome except Sun am.
Green Fee: WD £18; WE £25
Societies: weekdays.
Catering: meals and snacks, à la
carte restaurant.
Bowls, tennis, coarse and trout
fishing, practice range, putting green.
Hotels: Gatton Manor.

D62 **Gillingham**
☎(01634) 853017 (Sec), Pro
855862, Bar: 850999, Fax 574749
Woodlands Rd, Gillingham, Kent ME7
2AP
On A2 at Gillingham, about 2 miles
from M2 turn off to Gillingham.
Meadowland course.
18 holes, 5863 yards, S.S.S.68
Designed by James Braid.
Founded 1908
Visitors: must be member of another
club or hold current h/cap cert; only
with member weekends.
Green Fee: £18 per round, £25 per
day.
Societies: any day except Thurs;
min. 24 Mon/Tues.
Catering: Wed-Sun lunch and
evening meals.
Hotels: The Crest.

D63 **Goal Farm Par 3**
☎(01483) 473183, Owner: 473205
Gole Rd, Pirbright, Surrey GU24 0PZ
1 mile from Brookwood station off
A322 towards Pirbright
9 holes Par 3, 1273 yards
Founded 1977
Visitors: not Thurs am or Sat am.
Green Fee: WD £3.25; WE £3.50.
Societies: welcome
Catering: bar and bar snacks.

D64 **Guildford**
☎(01483) 63941 (Sec), Pro 66765,
Steward/Caterer: 31842, Fax 453228
High Path Rd, Merrow, Guildford,
Surrey GU1 2HL
2 miles E of Guildford on A246.
Downland course.
18 holes, 6090 yards, S.S.S.70
Designed by James Braid.
Founded 1886
Visitors: welcome on weekdays,
weekends with member only.
Green Fee: £25 per round, £35 per
day.
Societies: welcome by arrangement.
Catering: bar snacks, restaurant by
arrangement.
Practice ground, snooker.
Hotels: White Horse.

D65 **Hankley Common**
☎(01252) 792493 (Sec), Pro 793761
Tilford Rd, Tilford, Farnham, Surrey
GU10 2DD
4 miles SE of Farnham; from
Farnham dual carriageway A31
southbound, turn left at traffic lights,
over railway crossing, fork right to
Tilford.
Heathland course.
18 holes, 6438 yards, S.S.S.71
Designed by James Braid
Founded 1896
Visitors: welcome weekdays, by
arrangement with Sec weekends;
h/cap cert required.
Green Fee: WD £30 per round, £38
per day; WE £38.
Societies: welcome if booked in
advance.
Catering: always available.
Practice ground.
Hotels: Devil's Punch Bowl
(Hindhead).

D66 **Hawkhurst**
☎(01580) 752396, Pro 753600
High St, Hawkhurst, Cranbrook, Kent
TN18 4JS
On A268, 2 miles from A21 at
Flimwell, 0.5 mile from junction with
A229.
Undulating parkland course.
9 holes, 5751 yards, S.S.S.68
Designed by Rex Baldock.
Founded 1968
Visitors: welcome; only with member
weekends.
Green Fee: £9 (9 holes), £12 (18
holes).
Societies: welcome on application;
mostly Fri.
Catering: by arrangement.
Hotels: Royal Oak; Tudor Court;
Queens.

D67 **Herne Bay**
☎(01227) 373964, Pro 374727
Eddington, Herne Bay, Kent CT6
7PG
Take Thanet Way at Herne Bay
towards Canterbury, immediately turn
right.
Parkland course.
18 holes, 5535 yards, S.S.S.66
Founded 1895
Visitors: welcome, restrictions
weekends and Bank Holidays.
Green Fee: WD £15; WE £20
Societies: welcome any time by
arrangement.
Catering: full facilities, full meals by
prior arrangement.
Hotels: Carlton

D68 **Hever**
☎(01732) 700771, Fax 700775
Hever, Kent TN8 7NP
10 mins from M25 or A21; course
between Sevenoaks and Edenbridge
adjacent to Hever Castle.
Parkland course with 5 lakes.

18 holes, 6761 yards, S.S.S.73
Designed by Dr Peter Nicholson.
Founded May 1992
Visitors: societies only. Must book.
Societies: Mon-Fri only; must have h/caps.
Catering: main bar, spike bar, Silver Service restaurant (à la carte), snacks and sandwiches.
Snooker, tennis, health club.
Hotels: Chaser Inn (Stumble Hill).

D69 Hewitts Golf Centre

☎(01689) 896266, Fax 824577
Court Rd, Orpington, Kent BR6 9BX
From M4 junction 4 follow A224 to Orpington; 2 mins from motorway.
Public downland course.
Chelsfield Downs, 18 holes, 6077 yards, S.S.S.69; Warren, 9 holes Par 3.
Designed by MRM Leisure.
Founded 1993
Visitors: welcome at all times (book one week in advance).
Green Fee: Chelsfield Downs, WD £14; WE £17; Warren, WD £5; WE £5.50.
Societies: welcome Mon-Fri (up to one year advance booking).
Catering: bar, restaurant, society room (private, seats 40).
Driving range.
Hotels: The Thistle (Brands Hatch).

D70 High Elms

☎(01689) 858175
High Elms Rd, Downe, Kent, BR6 7SZ
5 miles out of Bromley off the A21 to Sevenoaks.
Public parkland course.
18 holes, 6210 yards, S.S.S.69
Designed by Fred Hawtree
Founded 1969
Visitors: welcome.
Green Fee: WD £9,50; WE £12.50.
Societies: weekdays only.
Catering: full meals and snacks.
Hotels: Bromley Court.

D71 Hilden

☎(01732) 833607
Rings Hill, Hildenborough, Kent TN11 8LX
Off A21 towards Tunbridge Wells adjacent to Hildenborough Station
9 hole, 1558 yards, par 30.
Founded 1994
Visitors: welcome.
Green Fee: WD £4.75; WE £6.75.
Societies: welcome.
Catering: full facilities.

D72 Hindhead

☎(01428) 604614/Fax, Pro 604458
Churt Rd, Hindhead, Surrey GU26 6HX
1.5 miles N of Hindhead on A287 towards Farnham.
Heathland course.
18 holes, 6373 yards, S.S.S.70
Founded 1904
Visitors: weekdays subject to availability, weekends by appointment (h/cap cert required, 20 or less).
Green Fee: WD £27 per round, £38 per day; £40 WE.
Societies: Wed and Thurs only.
Catering: bar, restaurant, snack bar.
Snooker, practice ground, putting green.
Hotels: Devil's Punch Bowl.

D73 Hoebridge Golf Centre

☎(01483) 722611, Fax 740369
Old Woking Rd, Old Woking, Surrey GU22 8JH
On B382 Old Woking road between Old Woking and West Byfleet.
Public parkland course.
Hoebridge, 18 holes, 6536 yards, S.S.S.71; Shey Copse, 9 holes, 2294 yards, Par 33; Maybury, Par 3, 9 holes, 2230 yards;
Designed by John Jacobs.
Founded 1982
Visitors: welcome any time, must book at weekends.
Green Fee: £14 per round Hoebridge, £6.75 per round Shey Copse (9 holes), £6 per round Par 3.
Societies: welcome by arrangement.
Catering: restaurant and snack bar open all day.
Driving range; snooker (members).
Hotels: Post House (Guildford).

D74 Holtye

☎(01342) 850635, Sec 850576
Holtye Common, Cowden, Edenbridge TN8 7ED
A264 between East Grinstead and Tunbridge Wells, 5 miles W of East Grinstead, 4 miles S of Edenbridge.
Testing forest/heathland course.
9 holes, 5325 yards, S.S.S.66
Founded 1893
Visitors: welcome weekdays; restricted Thurs am and weekends am; telephone first.
Green Fee: WD £15 per day; WE £18 (afternoons only).
Societies: Tues and Fri.
Catering: lunchtimes, 7 days a week. Large practice ground.
Hotels: White Horse Inn (adjacent).

D75 Home Park

☎(0181) 977 2423 (Office), Pro Shop 977 2658, Fax 977 4414
Hampton Wick, Richmond-upon-Thames,
From Kingston over Kingston Bridge, turn left at roundabout, 50 yards on left through iron gates at The Old Kings Head public house, straight road to club.
Parkland course in park of Hampton Court Palace.
18 holes, 6611 yards, S.S.S.71
Founded 1895
Visitors: welcome. WE before 8 am and after 1 pm.
Green Fee: WD £20; WE £25 (after 1pm £15).
Societies: weekdays.
Catering: lunches and bar snacks served; dinner bookings taken on request.
Hotels: Lion Gate.

D76 Homelands Bettergolf Centre

☎(01233) 661620
Ashford Rd, Kingsnorth, Nr Ashford Kent TN26 1NJ
Take exit 10 off M20 and follow A2070. Course signposted from secound roundabout to Kingsnorth
Parkland course
9 holes, 2205 yards, S.S.S. 62
Designed by D Steel
Founded July 1995
Visitors: pay as you play course
Green Fee: WD £7 (9 holes), £10.50 (18 holes); WE £8 (9 holes), £14 (18 holes).
Societies: welcome by prior arrangement.
Catering: bar and bar snacks available.
Driving range, practice area, 4 hole pitch and putt.

D77 Horton Park Country Club

☎(0181) 393 8400 (office), Shop 394 2626
Hook Road, Epsom, Surrey KT19 8QG
Off Hook Rd through Epsom to Chessington.
Public parkland course.
18 holes, 5100 yards, Par 70
Founded 1987
Visitors: proper golf shoes, no jeans
Green Fee: apply for details.
Societies: welcome weekdays only.
Catering: 2 bars, restaurant, function suite.
Hotels: Driftbridge.

D78 **Hurtmore**
☎(01483) 426492, Fax 426121
Hurtmore Rd, Hurtmore, Godalming,
Surrey GU7 2RN
Off A3, 3 mile S of Guildford.
Parkland course, 7 lakes.
18 holes, 5514 yards, S.S.S.69
Designed by Peter Alliss & Clive
Clark.
Founded 1990
Visitors: pay-as-you-play on booking
system (book 7 days in advance).
Green Fee: WD £8 per round; WE
£12 per round.
Societies: welcome any time.
Catering: restaurant and bar.
Putting green, small practice area.
Hotels: Post House.

D79 **Hythe Imperial**
☎(01303) 267554 (Sec), Pro 267441
Princes Parade, Hythe, Kent CT21
6AE
Turn off M20 to Hythe, to E end of
seafront.
Seaside course.
9 holes, 5560 yards, S.S.S.66
Founded 1950
Visitors: welcome, must be member
of a club; h/cap cert required.
Green Fee: WD £10 (£8 with
member); WE £15 (£10 with
member).
Societies: welcome by prior
arrangement.
Catering: hotel/club bar.
Hotels: Hythe Imperial.

D80 **Jack Nicklaus Golf Centre**
☎(0181) 308 1610, Bookings: 309
0181
Sidcup By-pass, Chislehurst, Kent
BR7 6RP
On the main A20 London road
9 hole par 3 1055 yards
Designed by M Gillett
Founded June 1995
Visitors: pay as you play
Green Fee: WD £5; WE £6
Societies: welcome
Catering: full facilities

D81 **Kingswood (Surrey)**
☎(01737) 832188
Sandy Lane, Tadworth, Surrey KT20
6NE
4 miles S of Sutton on A217, M25
junction 8.
Parkland course.
18 holes, 6880 yards, S.S.S.71
Designed by James Braid.
Founded 1928

Visitors: welcome by arrangement
when space available. WE not before
11 am.
Green Fee: WD £30 per round; WE
£42 per round.
Societies: welcome weekdays by
arrangement.
Catering: full restaurant facilities.
Snooker, squash.
Hotels: Burford Bridge.

D82 **Knole Park**
☎(01732) 452150
Seal Hollow Rd, Sevenoaks, Kent
TN15 0HJ
From M25 onto A21 Hastings road,
after 1 mile bear left onto A25
Maidstone road; at 2nd set of lights
turn right into Seal Hollow Rd, 0.5
mile before entering Seal village. Club
1.25 miles on left.
Parkland course of great beauty.
18 holes, 6259 yards, S.S.S.70
Designed by J.A. Abercromby.
Founded 1924
Visitors: weekdays only by
appointment; h/cap certs required.
Weekends & Bank Holidays only as
guests of member.
Green Fee: WD £32 per round; £42
(2 rounds).
Societies: Tues, Thurs, Fri by
appointment only; maximum of 2
per week.
Catering: lunch, tea, dinner.
Squash, snooker.
Hotels: Sevenoaks Park.

D83 **Laleham**
☎(01932) 564211, Pro 562877
Laleham Reach, Chertsey, Surrey
KT16 8RP
A320 between Staines and Chertsey,
opposite Thorpe Water Park. Follow
signs for Thorpe Park.
Testing meadowland course with
water hazards.
18 holes, 6211 yards, S.S.S.70
Founded 1907
Visitors: welcome weekdays only
before 4.30pm.
Green Fee: on application
Societies: Mon, Tues, Wed and Fri
only.
Catering: full facilities.

D84 **Lamberhurst**
☎(01892) 890241, Sec 890591, Pro
890552, Fax 891140
Church Rd, Lamberhurst, Kent TN3
8DT
Entrance from A21 on outskirts of
Lamberhurst village to N.

Undulating parkland course.
18 holes, 6345 yards, S.S.S.70
Designed by Frank Pennink.
Founded 1920
Visitors: welcome any day; after
12am at weekends and Bank
Holidays unless accompanied by
member; h/cap certs required.
Green Fee: WD £36 (£20 in Winter);
WE £36.
Societies: Tues-Thurs only.
Catering: lunch, dinner and snacks.
Hotels: George & Dragon.

D85 **Langley Park**
☎(0181) 658 6849, Pro 650 1663
Barnfield Wood Rd, Beckenham, Kent
BR3 2SZ
At lights near Bromley South station
turn into Westmoreland Rd,
clubhouse 1.75 miles on left.
Gently undulating parkland course.
18 holes, 6488 yards, S.S.S.71
Designed by J.H. Taylor
Founded 1910
Visitors: weekdays; not at weekends
unless accompanied by member;
telephone Pro for bookings.
Green Fee: £35 (£15 with member).
Societies: welcome Wed and Thurs
only.
Catering: full facilities every day.
Hotels: Bromley Court.

D86 **Leatherhead**
☎(01372) 843966
Kingston Rd, Leatherhead, Surrey
KT22 0EE
From M25 junction 9 take A243
towards London, entrance 500 yards.
Parkland course.
18 holes, 6203 yards, S.S.S.69
Founded 1903
Visitors: welcome by appointment;
WE not before 12 am.
Green Fee: WD £25 per round, £35
per 2 rounds; WE £35 per round.
Societies: welcome.
Catering: restaurant, brasserie, bar.
Practice ground.
Hotels: Woodlands Park (Oxshott).

D87 **Leeds Castle**
☎(01622) 880467, 765400 ext 4329
Leeds Castle, Maidstone, Kent ME17
1PL
On A20 from Maidstone towards
Ashford, signposted to Leeds Castle.
Public parkland course.
9 holes, 2880 yards, Par 34
Designed by Neil Coles (4 new holes,
1988)
Founded 1928

Visitors: bookings taken (9 holes only) 6 days in advance; correct dress, no denim jeans.
Green Fee: WD £8.50 (9 holes); WE £9.50.
Societies: welcome and company bookings weekdays only.
Catering: snacks and hot drinks only. Practice nets, putting green.
Hotels: Stakis.

D88 Limpsfield Chart
☎(01883) 723405 (Sec), Steward: 722106
Limpsfield, Oxted, Surrey RH8 0SL
On A25 between Oxted and Westerham, over traffic lights 300 yards on right, E of Oxted.
Heathland course.
9 holes, 5718 yards, S.S.S.68
Founded 1889
Visitors: weekends by appointment or with a member.
Green Fee: WD £18; WE £20
Societies: can be arranged.
Catering: meals served.
Hotels: Kings Arms (Westerham).

D89 Lingfield Park
☎(01342) 834602
Racecourse Road, Lingfield, Surrey RH7 6PQ
M25 Junction 6; through Lingfield village towards Edenbridge; course is on right next to racecourse before railway bridge.
Parkland course.
18 holes, 6473 yards, S.S.S.72
Founded May 1987
Visitors: welcome weekdays
Green Fee: WD £25 per round, £35 per day.
Societies: welcome by arrangement with Manager.
Catering: full bar facilities, bar snacks; other catering by arrangement.
Driving range.
Hotels: Copthorne; Jarvis Selbridge Hotel

D90 Littlestone
☎(01679) 363355 (Sec), Club 362310, Pro 362231
St Andrews Rd, Littlestone, New Romney, Kent TN28 8RB
M20 to Ashford, B2070 to New Romney, 1.5 miles from New Romney.
Seaside links course.
18 holes, Littlestone course 6460 yards, S.S.S.72; Romney Warren course 5126 yards

Designed by Laidlaw Purves.
Founded 1888
Visitors: Littlestone no visitors; Romney Warren pay as you play
Green Fee: Romney Warren: WD £10; WE £15.
Societies: weekdays by arrangement with Sec.
Catering: bar and restaurant facilities.
Hotels: Broadacre (New Romney).

D91 The London
☎(01474) 879899, Fax 879912
South Ash Manor Estate, Ash, Nr Sevenoaks, Kent TN15 7EN
Leave M25 at junction 3 or M20 at junction 1 and take A20 towards Brands Hatch; after passing under M20, turn left into Stansted lane; from M26 exit 2a, follow signs to Brands Hatch, turn right at Stansted Lane; club is 100 yards on left.
Inland links course.
Heritage, 18 holes, 6771 yards S.S.S.72 ; International, 18 holes, 6574 yards S.S.S.71
Designed by Jack Nicklaus (Heritage), Ron Kirby (International).
Founded Sept 1993
Visitors: no visitors, members' guests only.
Societies: Corporate days can be arranged
Catering: 2 bars, excellent restaurant, teppanyaki restaurant. Extensive practice facilities.
Hotels: Thistle (Brands Hatch)

D92 London Scottish
☎(0181) 788 0135 (Club), Sec 789 7517
Windmill Enclosure, Wimbledon Common, London SW19 5NQ
1 mile from Putney Station (S.R.).
Parkland course.
18 holes, 5443 yards, S.S.S.67
Founded 1865
Visitors: welcome weekdays, except Bank Holidays; must wear red upper garment.
Green Fee: £10
Societies: all year; not weekends or Mon.
Catering: lunch served, evening meals if ordered
Hotels: Wayfarer.

D93 Lullingstone Park
☎(01959) 533793, **Catering:** 532928
Park Gate, Chelsfield, Orpington, Kent BR6 7PX

Signposted from M25 junction 4.
Municipal parkland course.
18 holes, 6068 yards, S.S.S.72; 9 holes, 2432 yards
Designed by Fred Hawtree.
Founded 1923
Visitors: welcome.
Green Fee: WD: summer £9, winter (9 holes) £5.80; WE; summer £11, winter £7.80 (9 holes)
Societies: welcome by prior arrangement.
Catering: bar, snacks always available; meals by arrangement.
Hotels: Thistle (Brands Hatch)

D94 Lydd
☎(01797) 320808, Pro 321921
Romney Road, Lydd, Romney Marsh, Kent TN29 9LS
Take Ashford exit off M20 and follow A2070 signs to Lydd Airport. At Brenzett turn left and take B2075 club is on left
Links type course
18 holes, 6517 yards, S.S.S. 71
Designed by M Smith
Founded 1993, extended May 1995
Visitors: welcome
Green Fee: WD £16; WE £20
Societies: welcome by prior arrangement
Catering: Bar & restaurant.

D95 Malden
☎(0181) 942 0654 (Sec), Pro 942 6009, Fax 336 2219
Traps Lane, New Malden, Surrey KT3 4RS
0.5 mile from New Malden station, near A3 between Wimbledon and Kingston.
Parkland course.
18 holes, 6295 yards, S.S.S.70
Founded 1926
Visitors: weekdays unrestricted, weekends restricted.
Green Fee: WD £25 per round, £35 per day; WE £45.
Societies: Wed, Thurs, Fri.
Catering: all week, bar.
Hotels: Kingston Lodge

D96 Mid-Kent
☎(01474) 568035, Fax 564218
Singlewell Rd, Gravesend, Kent DA11 7RB
A2 S of Gravesend, turn off at Tollgate Moathouse Hotel.
Parkland course.
18 holes, 6199 yards, S.S.S.69
Designed by Frank Pennink.
Founded 1909

Visitors: weekdays, weekends with member, h/cap cert required
Green Fee: WD £20 per round, £30 per day.
Societies: Tues only.
Catering: lunch 7 days, dinner by arrangement.
Snooker.
Hotels: Manor Hotel

D97 Milford
☎(01483) 419200
Milford, Nr Guildford, Surrey GU8 5HS
Off A3 close to Godalming.
Woodland/meadowland course with water hazards.
18 holes, 5912 yards, S.S.S. 69
Designed by Peter Alliss & Clive Clark.
Founded 1993
Visitors: contact in advance, h/cap certs required; restricted at weekends.
Green Fee: WD £19.50 per round, £25 per day; WE & BH £25 per round, £25 per day.
Societies: by prior arrangement.
Catering: full facilities.
Practice ground.
Hotels: Frencham Ponds

D98 Mitcham
☎(0181) 648 1508, Pro 640 4280
Carshalton Rd, Mitcham Junction, Surrey CR4 4HN
A237 off A23, by Mitcham Junction station.
Meadowland course.
18 holes, 5935 yards, S.S.S.68
Founded 1886
Visitors: weekdays, restrictions weekends.
Green Fee: £11.
Societies: on application.
Catering: full facilities.
Hotels: Hilton.

D99 Moatlands
☎(01892) 724400
Watermans Lane, Brenchley, Kent TN12 6ND
A21 past Sevenoaks, Tonbridge and Tunbridge Wells; left at roundabout onto B2160 to Matfield and Paddock Wood; through Matfield, down steep hill, the right at bottom, signposted.
Undulating parkland course with views over weald.
18 hole championship course, 6693 yards, S.S.S.74
Designed by K. Saito.
Founded Nov 1993

Visitors: welcome not before 10am (winter), 11am (summer), ring Pro shop for weekend times.
Green Fee: WD £27 per round, £43 per day; WE £37 per round, £53 per day.
Societies: welcome 2 days a week; ring Pro shop for details.
Catering: restaurant (a la carte), bar food all day.
Snooker and health club (members only); driving range for lessons.
Hotels: Spa Hotel.

D100 Moore Place
☎(01372) 463533
Portsmouth Rd, Esher, Surrey KT10 9LN
On A3 Portsmouth road, 0.5 mile from centre of Esher towards Cobham.
Public undulating parkland course.
9 holes, 4186 yards, S.S.S.58
Designed by David Allen.
Founded 1926
Visitors: welcome any time, no restrictions.
Green Fee: WD £5.50; WE £7.40.
Societies: weekdays, phone for information.
Catering: full facilities.
Hotels: Haven

D101 Nevill
☎(01892) 525818
Benhall Mill Rd, Tunbridge Wells, Kent TN2 5JW
Turn into Forest Rd from A267 out of Tunbridge Wells.
Parkland/heathland course.
18 holes, 6349 yards, S.S.S.70
Designed by C.K. Cotton
Founded 1914
Visitors: accepted with h/cap cert.
Green Fee: WD £25 per round, £33 per day; WE £46.
Societies: welcome
Catering: 7 days a week.
Hotels: Spa.

D102 New Zealand Golf Club
☎(01932) 345049, Pro 349619
Woodham Lane, Addlestone, Surrey KT15 3QD
At junction of Woodham Lane and Sheerwater Rd in West Byfleet.
Heathland course.
18 holes, 6012 yards, S.S.S.69
Designed by Mure-Fergusson.
Founded 1895
Visitors: by arrangement.
Green Fee: on application.

Societies: weekdays only, by arrangement.
Catering: bar and restaurant (no evening meals).

D103 Nizels
☎(01732) 833138 (Club), Pro 838926, Fax 833764
Nizels Lane, Hildenborough, Nr Tonbridge, Kent TN11 8NX
From A21 take Tonbridge North B245; 5 mins from M25.
Parkland course.
18 holes, 6408 yards, S.S.S.71
Designed by Pocock Developments Ltd.
Founded Sept 1992
Visitors: booking up to 3 days in advance. Not before 12 noon at weekends in summer
Green Fee: WD £25; WE £35.
Societies: weekdays.
Catering: bar and restaurant open all day, breakfast from 7.30am.
Hotels: Nizels

D104 North Downs
☎(01883) 652057, 653298, 653004, Fax 652832
Northdown Rd, Woldingham, Caterham, Surrey CR3 7AA
2 miles N of M25 junction 6 to roundabout, 5th exit to Woldingham (2 miles); clubhouse 0.5 mile through village on left.
Downland course.
18 holes, 5843 yards, S.S.S.68
Designed by J.J. Pennink
Founded 1899
Visitors: welcome weekdays, h/cap cert required or prior enquiry to Manager.
Green Fee: £20 before 1pm, £28 after 1pm.
Societies: catered for weekdays, half or full day (half day only Thurs).
Catering: full restaurant, snacks.
Hotels: Kings Arms.

D105 North Foreland
☎(01843) 862140 (Sec), Pro 8696280
Convent Rd, Broadstairs, Kent CT10 3PU
A28 from Canterbury, or A2/M2/A299 from London to Kingsgate via Broadstairs, course 1.5 miles from Broadstairs station.
Seaside/clifftop course.
18 holes, 6430 yards, S.S.S.71; Short Course, 18 holes, 1752 yards, Par 54
Designed by Fowler and Simpson.
Founded 1903

Visitors: main course by prior booking, not Sun, Mon, Tues am, h/cap cert required; short course unrestricted.
Green Fee: Main course, WD £25 per round, £35 per day; WE £35. Short course £5.50 per round, £6.50 per day.
Societies: By arrangement.
Catering: available; private functions by arrangement.
Tennis.
Hotels: Castle Keep.

D106 Oak Park (Crondall)

☎(01252) 850880, Pro 850066
Heath Lane, Crondall, Nr Farnham, Surrey GU10 5PB
Off A287 Farnham-Odiham road 3 miles SE of M3 junction 5.
Gently undulating parkland course.
18 holes, 6437 yards, S.S.S.71.
Extending to 27 holes in June 1996.
Designed by Patrick Dawson.
Founded 1984
Visitors: welcome every day; tee reservations at weekends and public holidays.
Green Fee: WD £16; WE £22.50.
Societies: welcome every day by reservation.
Catering: bar, bar snacks, à la carte restaurant every day; restaurant closed Sun/Mon evenings.
Conference and banqueting facilities, driving range.
Hotels: Bishops Table (Farnham), THF Golfing Breaks.

D107 Oaks Sports Centre

☎(0181) 643 8363, Fax 770 7303
Woodmansterne Rd, Carshalton, Surrey SM5 4AN
On the B2032 past Carshalton Beeches station, Oaks Sports Centre signposted N of A2022, half way between A217 and A237.
Public meadowland course.
18 holes, 6033 yards, S.S.S.69; 9 holes, 1590 yards, S.S.S.28
Designed by Alphagreen.
Founded 1972
Visitors: welcome (public course).
Green Fee: WD 18 holes £11, 9 holes £4.50; WE 18 holes £13, 9 holes £5.50.
Societies: welcome by prior arrangement.
Catering: Licenced restaurant (no smoking), lunchtime Carvery, evening à la carte, refreshments available all day, public bar (normal licensing hours).
Driving range, 5 squash courts.

D108 Oastpark

☎(01634) 242661
Malling Rd, Snodland, Kent ME6 5LG
A228 West Malling to Rochester rd.
Public parkland course.
18 holes, 6173 yards S.S.S.69
Designed by Terry Cullen
Founded June 1992
Visitors: welcome any time, proper dress required.
Green Fee: WD £8.50; WE £12.
Societies: welcome any time.
Catering: bar, restaurant.
Large practice area.
Hotels: Trust House (Wrotham).

D109 Pachesham Golf Centre

☎(01372) 843453, Fax 844076
Oaklawn Road, Leatherhead, Surrey KT22 0BT
M25 junction 9, A244 towards Esher.
Public parkland course.
9 holes, 5608 yards, S.S.S.56
Designed by Phil Taylor.
Founded June 1991
Visitors: welcome except Sat & Sun am, bookings 2 days in advance.
Green Fee: WD 9 holes £7.50, 18 holes £12.50; WE 9 holes £9, 18 holes £15.
Societies: welcome pre-booked.
Catering: bar and restaurant.
Driving range, putting green, chipping area.
Hotels: Travel Inn (Chessington).

D110 Park Wood

☎(01959) 577744
Chestnut Avenue, Westerham, Kent TN16 2EG
From the centre of Westerham take Oxted Road then turn right into Croydon Road, go under M25 to small cross roads. Course is right and immediate right
Parkland and lakes course
18 holes, 6835 yards, S.S.S. 72
Designed by L Smith & R Goldsmith
Founded May 1993
Visitors: welcome
Green Fee: WD £20; WE £30.
Societies: Mon- Sat.
Catering: 120 seat restaurant, full bar facilities
Hotels: Kings Arms, Westerham.

D111 Pine Ridge Golf Centre

☎(01276) 20770 (Bookings), Club 678825, Fax 678837
Old Bisley Rd, Frimley, Camberley, Surrey GU16 5NX

5 mins from M3 junction 3; location map available on request.
Public, pine forested course.
18 holes, 6458 yards, S.S.S.71
Designed by Clive D. Smith
Founded June 1992
Visitors: welcome at all times, bookings taken up to 7 days in advance.pay and play
Green Fee: WD £16; WE £20.
Societies: welcome Mon-Fri, min 12; advisable to book well in advance.
Catering: large bar and restaurant; food and drink available all day.
Driving range, putting green.
Hotels: Lakeside; Frimley Hall.

D112 Poult Wood

☎(01732) 364039 (Bookings), **Catering:** 366180
Higham Lane, Tonbridge, Kent TN11 9QR
1 mile N of Tonbridge off A227.
Municipal wooded course.
18 holes, 5569 yards, S.S.S.67
Designed by Fred Hawtree
Founded 1972
Visitors: welcome casual times WD, booking for registered users.
Green Fee: WD £7.90; WE £12.10.
Societies: Mon-Fri with booking;
Catering: restaurant and lounge bar overlooking 18th green; spikes snack bar.
4 squash courts, practice area, small conference room.
Hotels: Langley; Rose & Crown.

D113 Prince's

☎(01304) 611118, Pro 613797
Sandwich Bay, Sandwich, Kent CT13 9QB
4 miles from Sandwich railway station via St George's Rd and Sandown Rd.
Traditional links course.
3 x 9-hole interconnecting loops, 3 combinations of 18 holes, 6500-7000 yards, S.S.S.72/71/71
Designed by Sir Guy Campbell & John Morrison.
Founded 1904
Visitors: welcome 7 days, no jeans or training shoes.
Green Fee: WD £36 per round, £42 per day; Sat £39 per round, £47 per day; Sun £40 per round, £52 per day.
Societies: by arrangement, no restrictions.
Catering: full bar and restaurant; banqueting.
Driving range, full practice facility, snooker.
Hotels: Bell, golf/accomodation packages on request.

D114 **Purley Downs**

☎(0181) 657 8347 (Sec)
106 Purley Downs Rd, South
Croydon CR2 0RB
3 miles S of Croydon on A235, fork
left onto Purley Downs Rd.
Downland course.
18 holes, 6212 yards, S.S.S.70
Founded 1894
Visitors: weekdays, weekends if
accompanied by a member; must
have h/cap cert.
Green Fee: £30
Societies: Mon, Thurs, Fri on
occasion.
Catering: 19th (informal), lounge bar,
dining room.
Snooker (members only).
Hotels: Selsdon Park.

D115 **Puttenham**

☎(01483) 810498, Pro 810277, Fax
810988
Heath Rd, Puttenham, Guildford,
Surrey GU3 1AL
Just off A31, Farnham to Guildford
road (Hog's Back), 4 miles W of
Guildford.
Heathland course.
18 holes, 6210 yards, S.S.S.70
Founded 1894
Visitors: welcome weekdays only by
prior arrangement
Green Fee: £23 per round, £30 per
day.
Societies: welcome
Catering: full facilities available.
Hotels: Mariners

D116 **Pyrford**

☎(01483) 723555
Warren Lane, Pyrford, Woking,
Surrey GU22 8XR
From A3 take Ripley junction and
follow signs to Pyrford.
Hilly meadowland course with water
hazards.
18 holes, 6230 yards, S.S.S.70
Designed by Peter Allis & Clive Clark.
Visitors: welcome any time.
Green Fee: WD £35; WE £50.
Societies: welcome by prior
arrangement.
Catering: full facilities.
Practice range, chipping area.
Hotels: Hilton (Cobham).

D117 **RAC Country Club**

☎(01372) 276311
Woodcote Park, Epsom, Surrey KT18
7EW
A24, 1.75 miles from Epsom.
Parkland courses.

Coronation, 18 holes, 5474 yards,
S.S.S.67; Old, 18 holes, 6709 yards,
S.S.S.72
Founded 1913
Visitors: with member only
Green Fee: apply for details.
Societies: on request.
Catering: full services available.
Hotels: Woodcote Park

D118 **Redhill & Reigate**

☎(01737) 240777 (Sec), Club
244626, Pro 244433
Clarence Lodge, Pendleton Rd,
Redhill, Surrey RH1 6LB
1 mile S of Reigate (A217), at traffic
lights turn left (A2044), after 0.25
mile, turn left into Pendleton Rd.
Moorland course.
18 holes, 5272 yards, S.S.S.66
Designed by James Braid.
Founded 1887
Visitors: welcome Mon-Fri; Sat and
Sun after 11am.
Green Fee: WD £11; WE £16.
Societies: weekdays by prior
arrangement.
Catering: full facilities available.

D119 **Redlibbets**

☎(01474) 872278
New Park Farm, Manor Lane,
Fawkham, DA3 8ND
Take A20 off M25 towards Brands
Hatch, course is on Paddock side
next to Fawkham Manor Hospital. 8
miles from Sevenoaks
Parkland course
18 holes, 6637 yards, Par 72
Designed by J Gaunt
Founded May 1996
Visitors: playing with a member.
Societies: Corporate days
Tues/Thurs in 1997.
Catering: full facilities in new
clubhouse.

D120 **Reigate Heath**

☎(01737) 242610, Sec 226793
Reigate Heath, Reigate, Surrey RH2
8QR
0.5 mile S of A25 to W of Reigate.
Heathland course.
9 holes, 5658 yards, S.S.S.67
Founded 1895
Visitors: welcome weekdays, but
telephone first. Not Tues am or
weekends unless with a member.
Green Fee: WD £16 before 12, £12
in pm, £20 per day
Societies: Wed and Thurs.
Catering: full facilities except Mon.
Hotels: Reigate Manor.

D121 **Reigate Hill**

☎(01883) 346373
Gatton Bottom, Reigate, Surrey RH2
0TU
2 miles off junc 8 of the M25
Parkland course
18 holes, 6175 yards, S.S.S. 70
Designed by D. Williams
Founded 1995
Visitors: welcome but weekend
restrictions
Green Fee: WD £25; WE £35.
Societies: by arrangement.
Catering: full catering facilities.

D122 **Richmond**

☎(0181) 940 4351(Sec), Club 940
1463, Pro 940 7792
Sudbrook Park, Richmond, Surrey
TW10 7AS
On A307 1 mile S of Richmond, look
for Sudbrook Lane on left.
Parkland course.
18 holes, 6007 yards, S.S.S.69
Designed by Tom Dunn.
Founded 1891
Visitors: weekdays by arrangement.
Green Fee: £38.
Societies: Tues, Thurs and Fri.
Catering: bar snacks and lunches
available every day.
Hotels: Petersham; Richmond Gate.

D123 **Richmond Park**

☎(0181) 876 3205, 876 1795
Roehampton Gate, Richmond Park,
London SW15 5JR
Just inside Roehampton Gate in
Richmond Park.
Public parkland course
Prince's 18 holes, 5909 yards,
S.S.S.70; Duke's 18 holes, 6100
yards, S.S.S.68
Designed by Hawtree & Sons
Founded 1923
Visitors: welcome, dawn to dusk
depending on Park Gate opening
hours; must wear golf shoes; booking
system at weekends.
Green Fee: WD £9.25; WE £13.
Societies: welcome weekdays.
Catering: pavilion cafe.
Driving range, practice area.
Hotels: Richmond Hill.

D124 **The Ridge**

☎(01622) 844382 (Sec), Pro
844243, Fax 844168
Chartway St, East Sutton, Maidstone,
Kent ME17 3DL
From M20 exit 8, take B2163 and
A274 to Sutton Valence, then 1st left
into Chartway St.

Parkland course.
18 holes, 6229 yards, S.S.S.70
Designed by Tyton Design Ltd.
Founded June 1993
Visitors: h/cap certs required. Not weekends
Green Fee: WD £18.
Societies: Tues and Thurs only.
Catering: 3 bars, 80-seat restaurant, private function room.
Practice facilities; driving range.
Hotels: Shant Hotel.

D125 Riverside

☎(0181) 310 7975, Fax 312 3441
Summerton Way, Thamesmead, SE28 8PP
Off A2, 10 mins from Blackheath, 15 mins Bexleyheath; just by Woolwich.
Pay-as-you-play course on reclaimed marshland.
9 holes, 5482 yards, Par 70
Designed by Heffernan & Heffernan
Founded 1991
Visitors: welcome subject to reasonable standard of golf.
Green Fee: WD 9 holes £5, 18 holes £9; WE 9 holes £6.50, 18 holes £10.50.
Societies: welcome by arrangement weekdays, only very small societies weekends.
Catering: 2 bars, à la carte.
Driving range.
Hotels: Black Prince (Bexleyheath), Swallow.

D126 Rochester & Cobham Park

☎(01474) 823411, Pro 823658, Fax 824446
Park Pale by Rochester, Kent ME2 3UL
Situated on A2, turn left onto B2009 and follow signs to clubhouse.
Undulating parkland course.
18 holes, 6440 yards, S.S.S.71
Founded 1891
Visitors: weekdays (unaccompanied) h/cap cert required; weekends with member before 5pm.
Green Fee: £26 per round, £36 per day.
Societies: Tues and Thurs.
Catering: full facilities available
Hotels: Inn on the Lake; Tollgate Motel.

D127 Roehampton

☎(0181) 876 1621, Sec 876 5505, Pro 876 3858, Fax 392 2386
Roehampton Lane, London SW15 5LR

Off A306 at bottom of Roehampton Lane.
Parkland course.
18 holes, 6054 yards, S.S.S.69
Founded 1901
Visitors: with member only.
Green Fee: WD £18; WE £25.
Societies: limited 32 players, must be introduced by a member.
Catering: full 7 day service.
Tennis, croquet, bowls, snooker, squash and indoor/outdoor pools.

D128 Roker Park

☎(01483) 236677
Holly Lane, Aldershot Rd, Guildford, Surrey GU3 3PB
3 miles from Guildford on A323 Aldershot road.
Public parkland course.
9 holes, 6074 yards S.S.S.70
Designed by W.V. Roker.
Founded June 1992
Visitors: any day by arrangement.
Green Fee: WD £6.50; WE £8.
Societies: weekdays, booking in advance.
Catering: bar and restaurant.
Driving range.
Hotels: Worplesdon Place.

D129 Romney Warren

☎(01679) 363355 Sec, 362231 Pro
St Andrews Rd, Littlestone, New Romney, Kent TN28 8RB
M20 to Ashford, B2070 to New Romney, 1.5 miles E of New Romney.
Pay-as-you-Play, links course.
18 holes, 5126 yards, S.S.S.65
Designed by J.D. Lewis, B.M. Evans.
Founded 1993
Visitors: welcome, no restrictions; all times bookable in advance.
Green Fee: WD £10; WE £15.
Societies: welcome weekdays by arrangement with Sec.
Catering: bar and restaurant.
Practice ground.
Hotels: Broadacre (New Romney).

D130 Royal Blackheath

☎(0181) 850 1795 (Club), Pro 850 1763
Court Rd, Eltham, London SE9 5AF
8 miles central London; take A2, turn off for Eltham, club 400 yards left on Court Rd after Eltham High St; from M25 exit 3 (A20) towards London, right at 2nd lights, club 600 yards on right; 5 mins Mottingham Station.
Parkland course with Georgian clubhouse.

18 holes, 6219 yards, S.S.S.70
Designed by James Braid.
Founded 1608
Visitors: weekdays with h/cap cert.
Green Fee: £30 per round, £40 per day.
Societies: weekdays only Tues-Fri
Catering: dining room, bar. Snacks on Mondays
Museum of Golf.
Hotels: Post House (Bexley Heath)

D131 Royal Cinque Ports

☎(01304) 374007 (Office), Pro 374170, Sec 367856
Golf Rd, Deal, Kent CT14 6RF
Follow coast road through Deal to end, turn left onto Godwyn Rd, at end turn right onto Golf Rd to club.
Seaside links course.
Medal, 18 holes, 6785 yards, S.S.S.72
Designed by Tom Dunn, Guy Campbell.
Founded 1892
Visitors: welcome weekdays, reservations required; must be members of recognised golf club and have h/cap below 20 (Men), 26 (Ladies).
Green Fee: WD £35per round, £45 per day; WE £55.
Societies: by arrangement Mon-Fri.
Catering: full facilities; jacket and tie required.
Hotels: Royal; Kings Head (Deal); Bell (Sandwich).

D132 Royal Mid-Surrey

☎(0181) 940 1894 (Clubhouse/Office), Pro 940 0459, Fax 332 2957
Old Deer Park, Richmond, Surrey TW9 2SB
On A316, 300 yards before Richmond roundabout heading into London.
Parkland courses.
Inner, 18 holes, 5544 yards, S.S.S.68; Outer, 18 holes, 6384 yards, S.S.S.70
Designed by J.H. Taylor.
Founded 1892
Visitors: weekdays with letter of intro. from own club, membership or h/cap cert, or playing with member; weekends and Bank Holidays members' guests only.
Green Fee: £45.
Societies: recognised societies welcome by arrangement with Sec.
Catering: lunch served except Mon, snack lunch served every day.
Hotels: Richmond Hill; Richmond Gate.

D133 **Royal St George's**
☎(01304) 613090 (Sec), Pro
615236, Fax 611245
Sandwich, Kent CT13 9PB
1 mile from Sandwich to Sandwich
Bay.
Links course.
18 holes, 6860 yards, S.S.S.74
Designed by Dr Laidlaw Purves.
Founded 23 May 1887
Visitors: Mon-Fri only with h/cap
certs. Max 18 (Men), 15 (Ladies).
Green Fee: WD £55 per round, £75
per day.
Societies: details available on
request.
Catering: bar, restaurant and snack
bar; dinners by arrangement for large
groups.
Hotels: Bell (Sandwich)..

D134 **Royal Wimbledon**
☎(0181) 946 2125
29 Camp Rd, Wimbledon, SW19
4UW
0.75 mile W of War Memorial in
Wimbledon village.
Parkland course.
18 holes, 6362 yards, S.S.S.70
Founded 1865
Visitors: none.
Societies: Wed, Thurs only.
Catering: full facilities.

D135 **Rusper**
☎(01293) 871456, 871871 (Pro),
Fax 871987
Rusper Rd, Newdigate, Surrey RH5
5BX
From M25 take exit 9 towards
Dorking and A24; on A24 at Beare
Green roundabout take signpost to
Newdigate; in village take signpost
Rusper, course 2 miles on right. From
Crawley, on Horsham rd at Faygate
turn right for Rusper, course 1.5 miles
on left.
Parkland course.
9 holes, 6069 yards, S.S.S.69
Designed by S. Hood.
Founded Aug 1992
Visitors: welcome at all times,
bookable 1 day in advance; no jeans
allowed.
Green Fee: WD £11.50 (18 holes);
WE £15.50 (18 holes).
Societies: welcome weekdays,
various packages available on
request.
Catering: bar and bar snacks every
day; society meals bookable in
advance.
Driving range, pool table.
Hotels: Guild Manor

D136 **Ruxley**
☎(01689) 871490
Sandy Lane, St Paul's Cray,
Orpington, Kent BR5 3HY
A20 to Ruxley roundabout, into
Sandy Lane.
Undulating parkland course.
18 holes, 5793 yards, S.S.S.68
Founded 1973
Visitors: welcome weekdays from
7am, weekends after 11.30am. No
jeans.
Green Fee: WD £8 before 9am,
£10.50 before 3pm, £7 after 3pm; WE
£15.50 before 2pm, £10 after 2pm.
Societies: welcome by prior
arrangement.
Catering: breakfasts and lunch daily;
evening meals by arrangement.
Driving range.
Hotels: Crest (Bexley).

D137 **St Augustine's**
☎(01843) 590333 (Sec), Pro 590222
Cottington Rd, Cliffsend, Ramsgate,
Kent CT12 5JN
Entrance at railway bridge on B2048
off Ramsgate-Sandwich road.
Parkland course.
18 holes, 5197 yards, S.S.S.65
Designed by Tom Vardon.
Founded 1907
Visitors: welcome with h/cap cert
weekdays and after 10am weekends.
Green Fee: WD £20; WE £22
Societies: weekdays except Mon;
prior booking essential.
Catering: available.
Hotels: Mariners, Bell (Sandwich)

D138 **St George's Hill**
☎(01932) 847758 (Club), Pro
843523, Fax 821564
St George's Hill, Weybridge, Surrey
KT13 0NL
B374 from station towards Cobham,
0.5 mile on left.
Heathland course.
3 x 9 hole courses, 3 combinations of
18; 6569 yards, S.S.S.71; 6097
yards, S.S.S.69; 6210 yards,
S.S.S.70
Designed by H.S. Colt.
Founded 1913
Visitors: welcome Wed-Fri only (Mon
members and guests only, Tues
Ladies Day), must book tee time in
advance.
Green Fee: £40 per round, £50 per
day.
Societies: catered for Wed-Fri.
Catering: full restaurant lunch and
bar snacks served.
Hotels: Oaklands Park; Ship; Hilton.

D139 **Sandown Golf Centre**
☎(01372) 461234
More Lane, Esher, Surrey KT10 8AN
1 mile from Esher station, in centre of
Sandown Park racecourse, off
Portsmouth road; follow brown signs
to Sandown Park Leisure Centre.
Public parkland course.
9 holes, 5656 yards, S.S.S.67; 9
holes Par 3
Designed by John Jacobs.
Founded 1967
Visitors: welcome at any time;
booking at weekends.
Green Fee: WD main course £5.50;
WE £7.25; Par 3, WD £3.40; WE
£4.25.
Societies: by prior arrangement.
Catering: available.
Driving range, 9-hole Pitch & Putt.
Hotels: Hilton National (Cobham).

D140 **Selsdon Park Hotel and GC**
☎(0181) 657 8811, Fax 651 6171
Sanderstead, South Croydon, Surrey
CR2 8YA
B274 from Croydon, A2022 at
Selsdon.
Parkland course.
18 holes, 6429 yards, S.S.S.71
Designed by J.H. Taylor.
Founded 1929
Visitors: welcome, contact golf
administration.
Green Fee: WD £15 per round; WE
£25 per day.
Societies: welcome by prior
arrangement.
Catering: full service available.
Driving range, putting green.
Hotels: Selsdon Park, residential
golfing breaks.

D141 **Sene Valley**
☎(01303) 268513
Sene, Folkestone, Kent CT18 8BL
Off B2065, 1 mile from Hythe.
Undulating downland course with
magnificent sea views.
18 holes, 6196 yards, S.S.S.70
Designed by Henry Cotton.
Founded 1888
Visitors: by arrangement with
Manager, h/cap cert required.
Green Fee: WD £20 per round, £30
per day; WE £25 per round, £32 per
day.
Societies: Wed, Thurs, Fri.
Catering: facilities available every
day except Mon.
Snooker
Hotels: Burlington; Burstin.

D142 Sheerness
☎(01795) 662585
Power Station Rd, Sheerness, Kent
ME12 3AE
9 miles from Sittingbourne on A249.
Seaside course.
18 holes, 6460 yards, S.S.S.71
Founded 1906
Visitors: welcome weekdays,
weekends with member.
Green Fee: WD £15 per round, £20
per day.
Societies: welcome Tues, Weds,
Thurs.
Catering: except Mon.
Hotels: Royal; Abbey (Minster).

D143 Shillinglee Park
☎(01428) 653237, Fax 644391
Chiddingfold, Godalming, Surrey GU8
4TA
Leave A3 at Milford, S on A283 to
Chiddingfold; at top end of Green turn
left along local road, then after 2
miles turn right signposted Shillinglee;
entrance to course located on left
after 0.5 mile.
Public, undulating parkland course.
9 holes, 5032 yards, S.S.S.64
Designed by Roger Mace.
Founded 1980
Visitors: welcome, advisable to book
in advance; telephone bookings
accepted.
Green Fee: WD £11; WE £13.
Societies: and company golf days
welcome.
Catering: bar and restaurant facilities
available daily from 8.30am-6pm
(3pm Sun); evening meals and
parties by arrangement.
Pitch & Putt, £3 unlimited play.
Hotels: Lythe Hill.

D144 Shirley Park
☎(0181) 654 1143, Pro 654 8767
194 Addiscombe Rd, Croydon, Surrey
CR0 7LB
On a A232 approx 1 mile E of East
Croydon station, near Shirley.
Parkland course.
18 holes, 6210 yards, S.S.S.70
Founded 1914
Visitors: welcome 8.30-12am, 1.30-
4pm wekdays; with member only
weekends.
Green Fee: £29
Societies: half-day pm, Mon, Thurs,
Fri; full day Tues.
Catering: breakfast, snack lunch
menu and afternoon tea daily;
banqueting and functions (sponsored
by member).
Hotels: Croydon Court; Brierley.

D145 Shooters Hill
☎(0181) 854 6368, Pro 854 0073
Lowood, Eaglesfield Rd, London
SE18 3DA
Off A207.
Very hilly parkland/woodland course.
18 holes, 5721 yards, S.S.S.68
Founded 1903
Visitors: weekdays only with
recognised golf club h/cap.
Green Fee: £20 per round, £25 per
day.
Societies: Tues and Thurs only.
Catering: daily.
Hotels: Clarendon (Blackheath).

D146 Shortlands
☎(0181) 460 2471, Pro 464 6182
Meadow Road, Shortlands, Kent BR2
0PB
9 holes, 5261, S.S.S.66
Founded 1894
Visitors: only with member.
Green Fee: apply for details.
Societies: bar and catering for
members and guests.

D147 Sidcup
☎(0181) 300 2150 (Sec), Pro 309
0679
7 Hurst Rd, Sidcup, Kent DA15 9AE
A222 off A2, 400 yards N of station.
Parkland course.
9 holes, 5722 yards, S.S.S.68
Designed by James Braid and H.
Myrtle.
Founded 1891
Visitors: welcome, with member only
weekends; h/cap certs required;
smart casual dress except after 7pm.
Green Fee: £18
Societies: welcome.
Catering: bar and restaurant facilities
except Mon. Snooker.
Hotels: Bickley Arms; Swallow.

D148 Silvermere
☎(01932) 867275
Redhill Rd, Cobham, Surrey KT11
1EF
At junction 10 of M25 and A3 take
A245 to Byfleet; Silvermere is 0.5
mile on left.
Woodland/parkland/meadowland
course.
18 holes, 6377 yards, S.S.S.71
Founded 1976
Visitors: book 7 days in advance;
members only am Sat and Sun.
Green Fee: WD £18.50; WE £25.
Societies: weekdays only.
Catering: full facilities from 8am.
Hotels: Hilton National.

**D149 Sittingbourne &
Milton Regis**
☎(01795) 842261
Wormdale, Newington, Sittingbourne,
Kent ME9 7PX
1 mile N of exit 5 off M2 on A249.
Undulating course.
18 holes, 6279 yards, S.S.S.70
Designed by Harry Hunter.
Founded 1929
Visitors: welcome weekdays with
letter of intro. or h/cap cert.
Green Fee: £20 per round, £32 per
day
Societies: welcome Tues and Thurs.
Catering: facilities available Tues to
Sat.
Hotels: Coniston (Sittingbourne),
Newington Manor.

D150 Springfield Park
☎(0181) 871 2468, Fax 871 2221
Burntwood Lane, Wandsworth,
London SW18 0AT
Off Garrett Lane between Tooting
and Wandsworth, in former grounds
of Springfield Hospital.
Inland links course in rural setting in
heart of London.
9 holes, 18 tees, 4451 yards S.S.S.62
Designed by Patrick Tallack
Founded 1993
Visitors: welcome except Sat and
Sun am when members only.
Green Fee: on application
Societies: as for visitors.
Catering: fully licensed bar and
catering facilities.
Bowls club, snooker room, large
function room.

D151 Sunbury
☎(01932) 772898, Club 770298
Charlton Lane, Shepperton,
Middlesex TW17 8QA
2 miles from M3 junction 1.
Public parkland course.
18 holes, 6210 yards S.S.S 69; 9
holes, Par 33
Visitors: welcome, no restrictions.
Green Fee: WD £10; WE £12.
Societies: welcome by prior
arrangement.
Catering: 16th century clubhouse.
Driving range.
Hotels: Moat House.

D152 Sundridge Park
☎(0181) 460 1822, Sec 460 0278,
Pro 460 5540, Fax 466 1072
Garden Rd, Bromley, Kent BR1 3NE
5 minutes walk from Sundridge Park
station.

Parkland courses.
East, 18 holes, 6516 yards, S.S.S.71;
West, 18 holes, 6016 yards, S.S.S.69
Designed by James Braid and Jack
Randall.
Founded 1902
Visitors: welcome weekdays only;
official club h/cap required.
Green Fee: £36.
Societies: weekdays on application.
Catering: full facilities daily.
Hotels: Bromley Court.

D153 Sunningdale

☎(01344) 21681, Pro 20128, Fax
24154
Ridgemount Rd, Sunningdale, Ascot,
SL5 9RW
Ridgemount Rd is 50 yards W of
Sunningdale railway station crossing
on the A30.
Heathland courses.
Old, 18 holes, 6609 yards, S.S.S.70;
New, 18 holes, 6703 yards, S.S.S.72
Designed by Willie Park.
Founded 1901
Visitors: Mon-Fri by prior
arrangement, max h/cap 18.
Green Fee: £80.
Societies: by arrangement.
Catering: full catering facilities except
Mon.
Hotels: Runnymede.

D154 Sunningdale Ladies

☎(01344) 20507
Cross Rd, Sunningdale, Surrey SL5
9RX
2nd turning left on A30 going W from
Sunningdale level crossing.
Heathland course
18 holes, 3616 yards, S.S.S.60
Designed by Edward Villiers.
Founded 1902
Visitors: welcome, phone first. Valid
h/cap cert needed, not before 11am
weekends
Green Fee: WD £17 (Ladies), £22
(Men); WE £19 (Ladies), £27 (Men)
Societies: catered for, Ladies only.
Catering: lunch and tea every day
except Sun.

D155 Surbiton

☎(0181) 398 3101, Fax 339 0992
Woodstock Lane, Chessington,
Surrey KT9 1UG
From A3 westbound, take
Esher/Chessington turn off, turn left
to Claygate, club 400 yards on right.
Parkland course.
18 holes, 6055 yards, S.S.S.70
Founded 1896

Visitors: welcome weekdays only;
h/cap certs required; members'
guests only at weekends.
Green Fee: £27 per round, £40.50
per day.
Societies: welcome by prior
arrangement. Packages available,
apply for details
Catering: full catering facilities
available.
Hotels: Haven (Esher); Travelodge.

D156 Sutton Green

☎(01483) 747898, Bookings:
766849
New Lane, Sutton Green, Nr
Guildford, Surrey GU4 7OF
Take the A320 Guildford to Woking
road and turn right at Mayford.
American style parkland course
18 holes, 6271 yards, S.S.S. 70
Designed by Laura Davies (touring
pro)/D Walker
Founded Dec 1994
Visitors: welcome except weekends
am.
Green Fee: WD £25; WE £30
Societies: welcome by prior
arrangement.
Catering: Bar, restaurant facilities
available.
Driving range, putting green
Hotels: Travelodge.

D157 Tandridge

☎(01883) 712273, Sec 712274, Pro
713701, Fax 730537
Oxted, Surrey RH8 9NQ
Off A25 by Oxted, 2 miles E of
Godstone; junction 6 from M25.
Parkland course.
18 holes, 6250 yards, S.S.S.70
Designed by H.S. Colt
Founded 1923
Visitors: welcome on Mon, Wed and
Thurs only, unless with member; prior
arrangement essential.
Green Fee: £31.
Societies: catered for on Mon, Wed
and Thurs.
Catering: lunches served daily
except Tues, Gallery bar food
available all day
Hotels: Kings Arms (Westerham).

D158 Tenterden

☎(01580) 763987, Pro 762409
Woodchurch Rd, Tenterden, Kent
TN30 7DR
1 mile E of Tenterden on B2067.
Undulating parkland course.
18 holes, 6050 yards, S.S.S.69
Founded 1905

Visitors: welcome except Sat, Sun
and Bank Holidays.
Green Fee: £20.
Societies: by arrangement on Thurs
& Fri
Catering: light meals served, other
catering by arrangement.
Hotels: Vine Inn.

D159 Thames Ditton & Esher

☎(0181) 398 1551
Scilly Isles, Portsmouth Rd, Esher,
Surrey
off A3 by Scilly Isles roundabout (0.25
mile from Sandown Park Race
Course).
Parkland course.
9 holes, 5419 yards, S.S.S.65
Founded 1892
Visitors: welcome, Sun afternoon.
Green Fee: WD £10.50; WE £12.50
Societies: max 28 booked in
advance with Sec.
Catering: snacks, buffet for societies.

D160 Tudor Park Country Club

☎(01622) 734334, Pro 739412, Fax
735360
Ashford Rd, Bearstead, Maidstone,
Kent ME14 4NQ
follow A20, Ashford road, on right, 3
miles from Maidstone centre.
Parkland course.
18 holes, 6041 yards, S.S.S.69.
Designed by Donald Steel.
Founded 1988
Visitors: welcome with h/cap cert.
Green Fee: WD £20; WE £30.
Societies: weekdays by prior
arrangement.
Catering: full facilities.
Leisure club and conference facilities
available.
Hotels: Tudor Park Marriott.

D161 Tunbridge Wells

☎(01892) 523034, Pro 541386, Sec
536918
Langton Rd, Tunbridge Wells, Kent
TN4 8XH
Behind Marchants Garage next to
Spa Hotel.
Undulating parkland course.
9 holes, 4560 yards, S.S.S.62
Founded 1889
Visitors: welcome; h/cap cert
required.
Green Fee: WD £15; WE £25.
Societies: by arrangement with Sec.
Catering: by arrangement.
Hotels: Spa; Periquito; Royal Wells.

D162 **Tyrrells Wood**

☎(01372) 376025, Pro 375200
Tyrrells Wood, Leatherhead, Surrey
KT22 8QP
Exit 9 from M25, A24 to Dorking, past
permanent AA caravan site, turn left
to Tyrrells Wood, signposted.
Undulating parkland course.
18 holes, 6282 yards, S.S.S.70
Designed by James Braid.
Founded 1922
Visitors: welcome weekdays by prior
appointment; h/cap certs.
Green Fee: £32
Societies: welcome, enquiries to
manager.
Catering: available all day.
Hotels: Burford Bridge; White Horse
(Dorking); Woodlands Park.

D163 **Upchurch River Valley**

☎(01634) 360626 (General/Socs),
Pro 379592, Fax 387784
Oak Lane, Upchurch, Sittingbourne,
Kent ME9 7AY
From M2 junction 4 take A278
Gillingham road, right at 3rd
roundabout onto A2 to Rainham,
course 2.5 miles on left.
Public moorland/seaside type course.
18 holes, 6237 yards, S.S.S.69; 9
holes Par 3, 1596 yards.
Designed by David Smart.
Founded June 1991.
Visitors: no restrictions, bookings
available daily.
Green Fee: WD £10.45; WE £13.45.
Societies: Mon-Fri, min. 12, no max.
By prior arrangement.
Catering: Rivers restaurant, full a la
carte, Sun lunches; 19th Hole bars,
daily specials.
Driving range, golfers only swimming
pool.
Hotels: Newington Manor, Rank
Motor Lodge.

D164 **Walmer & Kingsdown**

☎(01304) 373256, Pro 363017
The Leas, Kingsdown, Deal, Kent
CT14 8EP
Off A258, 2.5 miles S of Deal;
signposted at Ringwould village.
Undulating meadowland course.
18 holes, 6437 yards, S.S.S.71
Designed by James Braid
Founded 1909
Visitors: welcome weekdays and
after 12am weekends and Bank
Holidays; must produce h/cap cert.
Green Fee: WD £22 per round, £28
per day; WE £24 per round.

Societies: by arrangement weekdays
only.
Catering: full facilities.
Hotels: Royal; Clarendon; Kingsdown
Country House.

D165 **Walton Heath**

☎(01737) 812380 (Sec), Club
812060, Pro 812152, Caddies:
812974
Off Deans Lane, Walton-on-the-Hill,
Tadworth, Surrey KT20 7TP
2 miles north of M25 junction 3; off
A217 towards Sutton at 3rd
roundabout turn left onto B2032 to
Dorking; Clubhouse 0.75 mile,
signposted off Deans Lane.
Heathland course.
Old, 18 holes, 6801 yards, S.S.S.73;
New, 18 holes, 6609 yards, S.S.S.72
Designed by Herbert Fowler/James
Braid.
Founded 1904
Visitors: Mon-Fri, not WE or BH;
h/cap certificate required, advance
bookings to be made by phone or
letter.
Green Fee: WD £65 before 11.30am,
£55 after 11.30am.
Societies: Mon-Fri only, standard
package, terms available on request
from Sec.
Catering: 2 lounge bars, dining room
(140), separate private dining room
(36).
Large practice area, small target
practice ground.
Hotels: Bridge House; Chalk Lane.

D166 **Weald of Kent**

☎(01622) 890866, Pro 863163
Maidstone Rd, Headcorn, Kent TN27
9PT
On A274 5 miles S of Maidstone.
Parkland course.
18 holes, 6240 yards, S.S.S.69
Designed by John Millen.
Founded 1991
Visitors: welcome, bookings taken 3
days in advance.
Green Fee: WD £14.50; WE £18.50.
Societies: welcome except Sat and
Sun.
Catering: full facilities all day;
conferences, banqueting.
Shooting, fishing, riding.
Hotels: Shant (East Sutton).

D167 **Wentworth**

☎(01344) 842201, Fax 842804, Pro
843353
Wentworth Drive, Virginia Water,
Surrey GU25 4LS

21 miles SW of London at A30/A329
junction; M25 exit 13, 8 miles.
Heathland courses.
West, 18 holes, 6957 yards,
S.S.S.74; East, 18 holes, 6176 yards,
S.S.S.70; Edinburgh, 18 holes, 6979
yards, S.S.S.73; 9 holes, 1902 yards,
Par 27
Designed by H.S. Colt (East and
West); J.R.M. Jacobs (Edinburgh).
Founded 1924
Visitors: weekdays only with prior
booking; h/cap certs required.
Green Fee: on application.
Societies: Mon-Fri, limited to 50 max
per course. Min 20
Catering: breakfast, lunch, dinner
and banqueting.
Tennis, outdoor heated pool.
Hotels: Pennyhill Park; Royal
Berkshire; Runnymede.

D168 **West Byfleet**

☎(01932) 343433 (Sec), Club
345230, Pro 346584
Sheerwater Rd, West Byfleet, Surrey
KT14 6AA
M25 exit 10 onto A245 to about 0.75
mile W of West Byfleet.
Heathland/parkland course.
18 holes, 6211 yards, S.S.S.70
Designed by Cuthbert Butchart.
Founded 1904
Visitors: welcome weekdays only.
Green Fee: WD £29 per round, £36
per day.
Societies: Tues and Wed only.
Catering: snacks, lunch and tea
served; evening meals by
arrangement; lunch only on Sun.
Hotels: Northfleet (Woking); Hilton
International (Cobham).

D169 **West Hill**

☎(01483) 474365, Pro 473172, Fax
474252
Bagshot Rd, Brookwood, Surrey
GU24 0BH
On A322 Guildford-Bagshot road,
club entrance next to railway bridge
at Brookwood.
Heathland course.
18 holes, 6368 yards, S.S.S.70
Designed by Willie Park and Jack
White.
Founded 1909
Visitors: Mon, Tues, Thurs, Fri only.
Green Fee: £35 per round, £45 per
day.
Societies: Mon-Fri by application to
Sec.
Catering: full facilities available.
Hotels: Worplesdon Place
(Worplesdon); Northfleet (Woking).

D170 **West Kent**

☎(01689) 851323, Pro 856863.
West Hill, Downe, Orpington, Kent
BR6 7JJ
A21 to Orpington, head for Downe
village; leave on Luxted Lane for 300
yards then right into West Hill.
Parkland/downland course.
18 holes, 6399 yards, S.S.S.70
Founded 1916
Visitors: welcome weekdays with
letter from Sec or h/cap cert; must
phone in advance.
Green Fee: £24.
Societies: by arrangement Tues,
Wed, Thurs.
Catering: full facilities.
Hotels: Bromley Continental.

D171 **West Malling**

☎(01732) 844785 (Sec), Enquiries:
844795, Pro 844022
London Rd, Addington, Maidstone,
Kent ME19 5AR
Off A20, 8 miles NW of Maidstone.
Parkland course.
Spitfire Course, 18 holes, 6142 yards,
Par 70; Hurricane Course, 18 holes,
6268 yards, Par 70
Founded 1974
Visitors: welcome weekdays; after
12am weekends.
Green Fee: WD £20 per round, £30
per day; WE £30.
Societies: welcome by prior
arrangement.
Catering: full facilities.
Hotels: Larkfield.

D172 **West Surrey**

☎(01483) 421275, Pro 417278
Enton Green, Godalming, Surrey
GU8 5AF
0.5 mile from Milford station.
Parkland course.
18 holes, 6247 yards, S.S.S.70
Designed by Herbert Fowler.
Founded 1909
Visitors: welcome preferably by
arrangement to avoid reservations or
restrictions (including weekends);
collar and tie in dining room.
Green Fee: WD £35; WE £43.
Societies: normally Wed (pm), Thurs
and Fri by arrangement. Min 16.
Catering: restaurant by arrangement.
Hotels: Inn on the Lake (Godalming).

D173 **Westgate & Birchington**

☎(01843) 831115
176 Canterbury Rd, Westgate-on-
Sea, Kent CT8 8LT

A27, 0.25 mile from Westgate station.
Seaside links course.
18 holes, 4926 yards, S.S.S.64
Founded 1892
Visitors: welcome if members of
recognised clubs.Not before 10 am
weekdays; not before 11 weekends.
Green Fee: WD £12; WE £15.
Societies: by arrangement. Thurs
only.
Catering: by arrangement.
Hotels: Ivyside.

D174 **Whitstable & Seasalter**

☎(01227) 272020
Collingwood Rd, Whitstable, Kent
CT5 1EB
From A299 Thanet Way turn off at
Long Reach roundabout, drive down
Borstal Hill, under railway bridge, take
2nd left into Nelson Rd and 2nd left
again along unmade road.
Seaside links course.
18 holes, 5284 yards, S.S.S.63
Founded 1910
Visitors: welcome weekdays;
weekends only with member.
Green Fee: £12
Societies: by application
Catering: bar snacks.
Hotels: Marine.

D175 **Wildernesse**

☎(01732) 761526, Sec 761199, Pro
761527
Seal, Sevenoaks, Kent TN15 0JE
Off A25 in Seal village.
Rolling parkland course.
18 holes, 6438 yards, S.S.S.72
Designed by W. Park.
Founded 1890
Visitors: letter of intro. required.
Green Fee: on application to sec.
Societies: on application to sec.
Catering: bar and restaurant.

D176 **Wildwood**

☎(01403) 753255, Fax 752005
Horsham Rd, Alfold, Surrey GU6 8JE
On A281, 10 miles S of Guildford, 10
miles NW of Horsham, on
Surrey/Sussex border.
Wooded parkland course.
18 holes, 6655 yards, S.S.S.72; 9
hole extension under development.
Designed by Martin Hawtree.
Founded 1992
Visitors: Mon-Fri, weekends
afternoons only.
Green Fee: WD £21 per round, £25
per day; WE £30 per round, £35 per
day.

Societies: welcome weekdays only;
ring for details.
Catering: breakfast, lunch and dinner
available in restaurant.
Teaching Academy.
Hotels: Bramley Grange.

D177 **Wimbledon Common**

☎(0181) 946 7571 (Sec), Pro 946
0294
Camp Rd, Wimbledon Common,
London SW19 4UW
1 mile NW of War Memorial, past Fox
& Grapes on right in Camp Rd.
Moorland course.
18 holes, 5438 yards, S.S.S.66
Designed by Tom and Willie Dunn.
Founded 1908
Visitors: welcome weekdays.
Green Fee: £15 per round, £22 per
day.
Societies: Tues-Fri by arrangement.
Catering: light meals available
except Monday.

D178 **Wimbledon Park**

☎(0181) 946 1002, Pro 946 4053
Home Park Rd, Wimbledon, London
SW19 7HR
250 yards from Wimbledon station
(District Line).
Parkland course.
18 holes, 5492 yards, S.S.S.66
Founded 1898
Visitors: weekdays only with h/cap
cert or letter of intro.
Green Fee: £30.
Societies: usually Tues and Thurs.
Catering: full facilities except Mon.
Hotels: Canizaro House.

D179 **Windlemere**

☎(01276) 858727
Windlesham Rd, West End, Woking,
Surrey GU24 9QL
take A322 from Bagshot towards
Guildford; turn left on A319 towards
Chobham; course is on left opposite
the Gordon Boys' School.
Gently undulating public parkland
course.
9 holes, 2673 yards, S.S.S.34
Designed by Clive D. Smith.
Founded 1978
Visitors: open to public on payment
of green fees.
Green Fee: WD £8; WE £9.50.
Societies: as arranged with Pro at
club.
Catering: bar snacks always
available.
Driving range, pool tables.

D180 **Windlesham**
☎(01276) 452220, Fax 452290
Grove End, Bagshot, Surrey GU19
5HY
At junction of A30 and A322.
Parkland course.
18 holes, 6564 yards S.S.S.72
Designed by Tommy Horton.
Founded July 1994
Visitors: welcome except before
11am at weekends, h/cap certs
required.
Green Fee: WD £30; WE £40
Societies: welcome Mon-Thurs
Catering: full bar and restaurant
facilities.
Practice range.
Hotels: Berrystead

D181 **The Wisley**
☎(0483) 211022, Pro 211213, Fax
211662
Mill Lane, Ripley, Nr Woking, Surrey
GU23 6QU
M25 juncion 10 take A3 to Guildford,
off at exit marked Ockham, Send and
Ripley, 3rd exit from roundabout, 1st
left into Mill Lane; signs to club.
Parkland course (members only).
3 x 9 holes; Church, 3355 yards;
Garden 3385 yards; Mill, 3473 yards;
any combination gives 18 hole
course, S.S.S.73
Designed by Robert Trent Jones Jr.
Founded Jan 1990
Visitors: with member only.
Catering: bar, restaurant.

D182 **Woking**
☎(01483) 760053 (Sec/Bookings),
Pro 769582 Pro
Pond Rd, Hook Heath, Woking,
Surrey GU22 0JZ
Just S of 1st road bridge over railway,
W of Woking station (Woking-
Brookwood line), take Hollybank Rd;
then immediately right into Golf Club
Rd and right at end to clubhouse;
avoid Woking town centre.

Heathland course.
18 holes, 6322 yards, S.S.S.70
Designed by Tom Dunn.
Founded 1893
Visitors: book in advance; not
weekends and public holidays.
Green Fee: £33 per round, £50 per
day.
Societies: book in advance.
Catering: lunch available every day if
ordered in advance.
Hotels: Mayford Manor; Glen Court;
Worplesdon Place.

D183 **Woodcote Park**
☎(0181) 668 2788/Fax
Meadow Hill, Bridleway, Coulsden,
Surrey CR5 2QQ
At far end of Meadow Hill, off
Woodcote Grove Road (A237),
Purley, main road from Coulsden to
Wallington.
Slightly undulating parkland course.
18 holes, 6669 yards, S.S.S.72
Founded 1912
Visitors: welcome on weekdays with
h/cap cert.
Green Fee: £25.
Societies: Mon-Thurs by
arrangement.
Catering: bars, bar snacks, a la carte
menu daily.
Snooker.
Hotels: Trust House Forte (Purley
Way)

D184 **Woodlands Manor**
☎(01959) 523805, Sec 523806, Pro
524161
Tinkerpot Lane, Sevenoaks, Kent
TN15 6AB
Off A225, 4 miles NE of Sevenoaks,
5 miles S of M25 junction 3.
Undulating parkland course in AONB.
18 holes, 6000 yards, S.S.S.68
Designed by N. Coles, J. Lyons.
Founded 1928
Visitors: welcome weekdays; not
weekends.

Green Fee: on application
Societies: welcome Mon-Fri by
arrangement.
Catering: meals served.
Practice ground, tennis.
Hotels: Thistle (Brands Hatch).

D185 **Worplesdon**
☎(01483) 489876, Sec 472277, Pro
473287, Fax 473303
Heath House Rd, Woking, Surrey
GU22 0RA
Leave Guildford on A322 to Bagshot,
after 6 miles turn right into Heath
House Rd.
Heathland course.
18 holes, 6440 yards, S.S.S.71
Designed by J.F. Abercromby.
Founded 1908
Visitors: welcome with introduction
from Club Sec; weekdays only.
Green Fee: £40 per round, £50 per
day.
Societies: Mon, Wed, Thurs, Fri by
arrangement.
Catering: bar every day, lunch
served except Tues.
Hotels: Worplesdon Place

D186 **Wrotham Heath**
☎(01732) 884800, Pro 883854
Seven Mile Lane, Comp, Sevenoaks,
Kent TN15 8QZ
Off A20 near junction with A25.
Woodland/heathland course.
18 holes 5954 yards, S.S.S.69
Designed by Donald Steel (new 9
holes).
Founded 1906
Visitors: welcome weekdays with
h/cap cert; not bank holidays or
weekends without a member
Green Fee: £22 per round, £32 per
day.
Societies: Fri only.
Catering: full catering facilities by
arrangement with Steward except
Mon
Hotels: Post House.

DD

NORTHERN FRANCE

In spite of the considerable influx of new French courses in the last ten years, the two best in the Northern region remain the traditional masterpieces, Hardelot and Le Touquet. Le Touquet is as near as you can get to a true links outside Britain or Ireland while the Les Pins Course at Hardelot is very much in the mould of Sunningdale or The Berkshire.

Lille is well served with places to play, notably Golf de Bondues, in a glorious park, and Golf de Brigode. Calais and Dunkirk are more barren, but a number of the best courses around Paris lie to the north and the road from Calais is excellent and direct.

Golf d'Amiens is worth a stop on the way, but most sights are set on Golf de Chantilly, International Club du Lys and Golf de Morfontaine although access to Morfontaine is by introduction only. Chantilly, Hardelot and du Lys, like many older courses in France, were the work of Tom Simpson, Chantilly frequently being ranked among the best in Europe.

Other Parisian courses of similar vintage include St Cloud and St Germain but the modern foil of French golf is symbolised by Golf National, owned by the French Golf Federation, and staging post for the most recent French Opens. It is in the Guyancourt region of the city.

DD1 Amiens
☎(00 33) 22 930426, Fax 930461
Route d'Albert, 80115 Querrieu
7km North East of the Picardy town of Amiens. Take the A1 Lille to Paris road and exit on the D929 towards Amiens
Old Parkland course
18 holes, 6110 metres, S.S.S. 72
Founded 1951
Visitors: welcome by arrangement but h/cap cert needed. Closed Tuesdays
Green Fee: £17-£30
Hotels: Grand; Le Prieure.

DD2 Chantilly
☎(00 33) 445 70443, Fax 572654
Allee de la Menagerie, 60500 Vineuil St Firmin
Located 1.5km north of Chantilly. Take A1 Lille-Paris and exit towards Chantilly on the D924
Two championship courses
Longeres, 18 holes 6597m S.S.S. 72
Vineuil, 18 holes, 6480m S.S.S. 71
Founded 1908
Visitors: welcome by prior arrangement on both courses but maximum handicap men 24, ladies 28 on Longeres and at weekends an introduction is required. Vineuil is open except Thurs.
Green Fee: £42-£48
Hotels: Chateau de la Tour; Domaine de Chantilly.

DD3 Chantilly-Apremont
☎(00 33) 44 256111, Fax 251172
Golf d'Apremont, 60300 Apremont
Located 5km north of Chantilly on the D606 in the village of Apremont
New parkland course
18 holes, 6436m, S.S.S. 74
Founded 1993
Visitors: welcome but closed on Mon in winter
Green Fee: £47-£70

DD4 Chantilly-International Club du Lys
☎(00 33) 44 212600, Fax 213552
Rond-Point du Grand Cerf, Lys-Chantilly, 60269 Lamorlaye.
Exit A1 Lille-Paris at Senlis then take D924 to Chantilly and then N16 to Lamorlaye and course
Woodland course
Les Chenes, 18 holes, 6022m S.S.S.70
Les Bourleaux, 18 holes 4789m S.S.S.66
Founded 1929
Visitors: welcome with h/cap cert and at weekends by introduction only. Les Bouleaux closed Tuesday.
Green Fee: £32-£55
Hotels: du Lys

DD5 Douai
☎(00 33) 20 865 898
Bois Lenglart, 59239 Thumeries

15km north to Douai on D8.
Old Parkland course
18 holes 5675m S.S.S. 70
Founded 1935 (18 holes in 1993)
Visitors: welcome except Tues
Green Fee: £17-£25
Hotels: in Douai

DD6 Hardelot
☎(00 33) 21 837310, Fax 832433
Avenue du Golf, 62152 Neufchatel-Hardelot
Located 1km east of Hardelot off the N1 Boulogne-Amiens road at Hardelot-Plage
Les Pins is a wooded course while Les Dunes has water features
Les Pins, 18 holes 5870m S.S.S. 72
Les Dunes, 18 holes, 6052m S.S.S. 72
Founded 1931 (second course opened 1989)
Visitors: Les Pins closed in Feb and Les Dunes in Jan
Green Fee: £23-£38
Hotels: Regina; du Parc.

DD7 Le Touquet
☎(00 33) 21 056847
Avenue du Golf, 62520 Le Touquet
At Berck-Plage 2km south of Le Touquet
Forest, 18 holes, 5912m S.S.S. 71
Sea, 18 holes, 6082m S.S.S. 72
Manor, 9 holes 1300m

Sea a links course; Forest parkland.
Founded 1904
Visitors: welcome with h/cap cert
Green Fee: £23-£42
Hotels: Golf reductions at Le Manoir

DD8 **Lille**

☎(00 33) 20 232062, Fax 232411
Chateau de la Vigne, 59910 Bondues
10km north of Lille, take A1 exit for
Marcq-en-Baroeul on N217 to N17, in
Halluin take second left after airfield
18 holes, 6260m S.S.S. 73; 18 holes,
6000m S.S.S 72
Founded 1956
Visitors: welcome but not on
Tuesdays or without handicap cert on
second course
Green Fee: £23-£28
Hotels: special rates at Novotel;
telephone for details.

DD9 **Lille-Brigode**

☎(00 33) 20 911786
Ave du Golf, 59650 Villeneuve-d'Ascq
9km east of Lille. Take A1 to Ghent,
exit Pont-de-Bois
Parkland course
18 holes, 6202m S.S.S. 72
Founded 1969
Visitors: welcome except Tues;
h/cap cert required.
Green Fee: £23-£28
Hotels: Hotel Le Relais d'Hermes.

DD10 **Lille-du Sart**

☎(00 33) 20 729251
Rue J-Jaures, 59650 Villeneuve
d'Ascq
7km east of Lille exit A1 at junc 9 and
head for Wasquehal
Parkland course
18 holes, 5750m S.S.S. 71
Founded 1910
Visitors: welcome with handicap cert
except·Mon
Green Fee: £23-£28
Hotels: Reducations at Mercure;
Royal in Lille

DD11 **Paris**

☎(00 33) 30 433600, Fax 438558
Golf National, Avenue du Golf, 78280
Guyancourt
Take exit at Bois d'Arcy. Take N286
to Viroflay and then D91 to
Guyancourt
Championship courses owned by the
French Golf Federation
Albatross, 18 holes, 6155m S.S.S 73
Eagle, 18 holes 5936m S.S.S. 72
Founded 1990

Visitors: Albatross maximum
handicap 24, closed Mon; Eagle
closed Friday
Green Fee: £23-£28
Hotels: Novotel

DD12 **Senlis**

☎(00 33) 44 546827
Golf du Morfontaine, 60128 Plailly
10km south of Senlis off the D607
towards Thiers in Morfontaine
Championship course
19 holes, 6033m S.S.S. 70; 9 holes
2588m
Founded 1926
Visitors: by introduction only on the
championship course; 9 holes closed
Tues
Green Fee: on application
Hotels: Le Prieure

DD13 **Valenciennes**

☎(00 33) 27 463010
Rue du Chemin Vert, 59770 Marly-
les-Valenciennes

In Valenciennes-E off A2 Paris-
Brussels road at Valenciennes-
sud/Marly
Parkland course
9 holes, 4738m S.S.S 65
Founded 1910
Visitors: welcome except on
Tuesday
Green Fee: £16-£23
Hotels: Auberge du Bon Fermier

DD14 **Wimereux**

☎(00 33) 21 324320,
Fax 336221
Route d'Ambleteuse, 62930
Wimereux
Take N940 Boulogne-Calais road and
the course is 2km north of Wimereux
town.
Links course
18 holes, 6150m S.S.S 72
Founded 1906
Visitors: welcome by arrangement,
with h/cap cert.
Green Fee: £20-£33
Hotels: several in Wimereux.

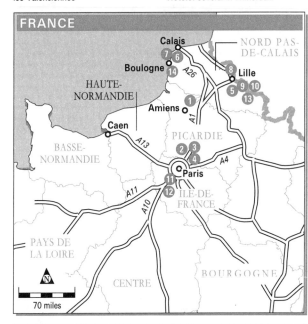

KEY
1 Amiens
2 Chantilly
3 Chantilly- Apremont
4 Chantilly- International Club du Lys
5 Douai
6 Hardelot
7 Le Touquet
8 Lille
9 Lille-Brigode
10 Lille-du Sart
11 Paris
12 Senlis
13 Valenciennes
14 Wimereux

E

HERTFORDSHIRE, ESSEX, MIDDLESEX, NORTH LONDON

Essex has seen a significant number of new courses in the last few years and even more applications for permission to build. It is a big county but the greatest demand lies around the fringe of London where the supply of land is scarcer. West Essex, Romford, Ilford, Wanstead and Chigwell are all bastions of suburban golf, while public facilities are exemplified by Hainault Forest, Chingford and Belhus Park (Thurrock). But the sense of freedom that the countryside brings is reflected in the character of the golf.

Clacton-on-Sea, Frinton and Quietwaters remind travellers how far Essex's limits extend from the sound of Bow Bells, but the best of the county's golf focuses on Chelmsford, Thorndon Park and Orsett. Thorpe Hall at Southend has the proud boast of having for years been the home Club of Michael Bonallack; and a word for Skips, newly extended and re-named Stapleford Abbots, and Channels, both less than 20 years old.

Neighbouring Hertfordshire is more densely populated with golf courses even if the majority of them are in the south.

Most are parkland in character although two of the exceptions are undoubtedly among the best. Ashridge and Berkhamsted enjoy a lofty perch on the Hertfordshire ridge of the Chilterns. Ashridge is where Henry Cotton was once the professional, and Berkhamsted is a course on a delightful common, famous for the absence of sand bunkers.

In keeping with many Clubs which started life in an exposed, open environment, Berkhamsted is now much more enclosed, making accuracy from the tee a definite prerequisite of good scoring. It is rightly popular.

The northern boundary of Hertfordshire is marked by Royston on undulating heathland on which little has changed in a hundred years. The Club's annual fixture with Cambridge is the University's oldest in continuous existence.

Letchworth and Knebworth are divided by the Great North Road which also took land from Welwyn Garden City, the course on which Nick Faldo's talents were shaped. It highlights what can be done on a limited acreage. Nearer to London, Sandy Lodge, Hadley Wood, Porters Park, Brookmans Park and Moor Park (with 36-holes) are among the best known.

There are South Herts, Mid Herts, East Herts and West Herts with a worthy mention for Verulam and Batchwood Hall on opposite sides of St Albans. Elstree offers a variety of facilities while, at the more private end of the scale, is Hanbury Manor and its sumptuous hotel. Brickendon Grange is worthy of mention and there are two courses, full of character, at Harpenden.

The Middlesex courses, as you might expect, are altogether more confined, although wonderful oases for the city dweller. From planes approaching Heathrow, it is all too clear how great are their land values. So, too, further north, where Enfield, Crews Hill and Bush Hill Park, once out in the countryside, are close to the Hertfordshire border.

Middlesex, county champions for the first time in 1989, won the title again in 1991 and have been indebted for some time to several fine golfers from Ealing. Ricky Willison, who won the 1981 English championship, later turned professional. Ealing fronts the A40 Western Avenue, a stone's throw from Sudbury and West Middlesex. Highgate, Hampstead and Hendon form as tight a cluster but Ashford Manor and Fulwell, almost into Surrey, are perhaps Middlesex's finest along with Northwood.

E1 Abbey View

☎(01727) 868227
Holywell Hill, Westminster Lodge, St
Albans, Herts AL1 2DL
In centre of St Albans.
Public parkland course.
9 holes, 1440 yards
Designed by Jimmy Thomson.
Founded 1990
Visitors: open to public at all times.
Green Fee: £4.50.
Societies: welcome, club has own
society.
Catering: available on request.

E2 Abridge G & CC

☎(01708) 688396
Epping Lane, Stapleford Tawney,
Essex RM4 1ST
M11 from London exit 5 via Abridge;
from the N, M11 exit 7 via Epping.
Parkland course.
18 holes, 6692 yards, S.S.S.72
Designed by Henry Cotton.
Founded 1964
Visitors: weekdays only; h/cap cert
required.
Green Fee: £30 per day.
Societies: Mon and Wed.
Catering: every day except Fri (no
evening meals).
Hotels: Post House Epping.

E3 Airlinks

☎(0181) 561 1418
Southall Lane, Hounslow TW5 9PE
M4 junction 3 onto A312 and A4020;
next to David Lloyd Tennis Centre.
Public meadowland/parkland course.
18 holes, 6001 yards, S.S.S.69
Designed by P. Alliss.
Founded 1984
Visitors: welcome, some restrictions
at weekends.
Green Fee: WD £10.75; WE £13.50
Societies: Mon-Fri; fees negotiable.
Catering: licensed bar, snacks, hot
and cold meals.
Diving range.
Hotels: London Airport hotels nearby.

E4 Aldenham G & CC

☎(01923) 853929, Pro 857889, Fax
858472
Church Lane, Aldenham, Nr Watford,
Herts WD24 8AL
Leave M1 at junction 5, A41 towards
S Watford, turn left at 1st roundabout
towards Radlett, club 0.25 mile.
Parkland course.
18 holes, 6480 yards, S.S.S.71; 9
holes, 2350 yards, S.S.S.29
Founded 1975

Visitors: welcome weekdays, after
1pm weekends. No restrictions on 9
holes.
Green Fee: WD £20; WE £25. 9
holes: £10.
Societies: Mon-Fri by arrangement.
Catering: snack bar, restaurant.
Hotels: London Hilton.

E5 Aldwickbury Park

☎(01582) 760112, Fax 760113
Piggottshill Lane, Harpenden, Herts
AL5 1AB
E of Harpenden on Wheathampstead
road, junc 9 of the M1 is 8 mins
away, junc 4 A1M 8 mins away.
Mature undulating parkland
18 holes Park course, 6352 yards,
S.S.S. 70, 9 hole par 3 Manor Course
1000 yards.
Designed by K Brown and M Gillett
Founded 1995
Visitors: welcome
Green Fee: on application
Societies: weekdays; packages
available on application
Catering: Restaurant; function room
for 100, bars etc
Hotels: Glen Eagles; Harpenden
House.

E6 Arkley

☎(0181) 449 0394
Rowley Green Rd, Barnet, Herts EN5
3HL
Off A1 at Stirling Corner to A411;
signposted at Rowley Lane on left.
Parkland course.
2 x 9 holes, 6045 yards, S.S.S.69
Designed by James Braid.
Founded 1909
Visitors: weekdays restricted;
weekends with member; (Tues Ladies
Day). H/caps cert required all times.
Green Fee: WD £7.50 (9 holes), £15
(18 holes).
Societies: welcome by arrangement,
min 10 players.
Catering: meals daily.
Hotels: Elstree Post House.

E7 Ashford Manor

☎(01784) 257687
Fordbridge Rd, Ashford, Middx TW15
3RT
Staines by-pass A308, 2 miles E of
Staines.
Parkland course.
18 holes, 6343 yards, S.S.S.70
Founded 1898
Visitors: must be member of
recognised golf club; weekends by
arrangement or as guest of member.

Green Fee: WD £25; WE £30.
Societies: weekdays by
arrangement.
Catering: available.

E8 Ashridge

☎(01442) 842244, Fax 843770
Little Gaddesden, Berkhamsted,
Herts HP4 1LY
A41 to Berkhamsted, turn right at
Northchurch on B4506.
Parkland course.
18 holes, 6547 yards, S.S.S.71
Designed by Sir Guy Campbell,
Colonel Hotchkin and Cecil
Hutchinson.
Founded 1932
Visitors: telephone Sec for booking.
H/cap cert required. Not weekends
Green Fee: £30.
Societies: telephone Sec for
booking. Not Thurs.
Catering: morning coffee, lunch,
afternoon tea, sandwiches always
available; dinners for societies.
Large practice ground.
Hotels: Bell Inn; The Stocks.

E9 Ballards Gore

☎(01702) 258917 (Sec), Pro 258924
Gore Rd, Canewdon, Rochford,
Essex SS4 2DA
From London via A127 to Southend
Airport, then through Rochford onto
Great Stambridge road; course 1.5
miles from Rochford centre.
Parkland course.
18 holes, 7062 yards, S.S.S.74
Designed by D. and J.J. Caton.
Founded 26 July 1980
Visitors: welcome weekdays;
weekends guest of member only,
after 12.30pm summer, 11.30am
winter.
Green Fee: WD £22
Societies: weekdays by arrangement
with Sec, subject to availability.
Catering: bar and restaurant
facilities; private functions.
Hotels: Renouf.

E10 Basildon

☎(01268) 533297, Pro 533532
Clay Hill Lane, Basildon, Essex SS16
5JP
On A176 off A13 or A127, Kingswood
roundabout, Sparrows Herne.
Public undulating parkland course.
18 holes, 6153 yards, S.S.S.69
Designed by Frank Pennink.
Founded 1967
Visitors: welcome at all times,
booking weekends.

Green Fee: WD £7.50; WE £14.50.
Societies: WD by arrangement.
Catering: full facilities.
Hotels: Crest.

E11 **Batchwood**
☎(01727) 844250, Fax 850586
Batchwood Tennis and Golf Centre,
Batchwood Drive, St Albans, Herts
AL3 5XA
NW corner of St. Albans; 5 miles S of
M1 junction 9.
Public parkland course.
18 holes, 6487 yards, S.S.S.71
Designed by J.H. Taylor.
Founded 1935
Visitors: welcome

Green Fee: WD £8; WE £10.50.
Societies: Oct-Apr, Mon-Fri only.
Catering: Public bar and restaurant.
4 indoor, 5 outdoor tennis courts, 2
squash courts, putting green, fitness
gym, dance studio.
Hotels: Aubrey Park.

E12 **Belfairs Park (Southend-on-Sea)**
☎(01702) 525345 (Starter),
Members: 526911
Starter's Hut, Eastwood Rd North,
Leigh-on-Sea, Essex SS9 4LR
4.5 miles from Southend centre;
Eastwood Rd links A127 and A13.
Private clubs playing on public course

set in Belfairs Park; parkland front 9,
heavily wooded back 9.
18 holes, 5795 yards, S.S.S.68
Designed by H.S. Colt.
Founded 1926
Visitors: unrestricted; bookings
Thurs am, weekends, public holidays.
Green Fee: WD £8.50; WE £13.
Societies: welcome
Catering: Public restaurant.
Hotels: Westcliff Hotel.

E13 **Belhus Park (Thurrock)**
☎(01708) 854260
Belhus Park, South Ockendon, Essex
RM15 4QR

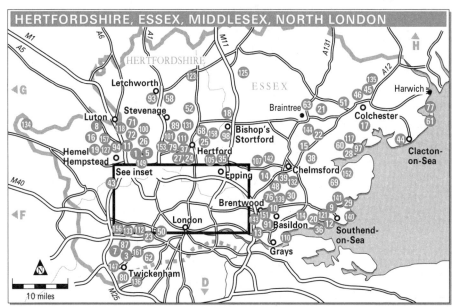

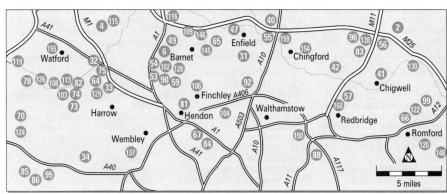

A13 to Avely.
Public parkland course.
18 holes, 5527 yards, S.S.S.68
Designed by Frank Pennink.
Founded 1972
Visitors: bookings can be made at course weekdays, in advance by telephone at weekends (booking card required).
Green Fee: WD £8; WE £12.
Societies: telephone manager.
Catering: bar and restaurant.
Driving range, squash, swimming pool, leisure centre.
Hotels: Thurrock Hotel.

E14 **Bentley**

☎(01277) 373179
Ongar Rd, Brentwood, Essex CM15 9SS
4 miles from Brentwood on A128 to Ongar.
Parkland course.
18 holes, 6709 yards, S.S.S.72
Designed by Alec Swan.
Founded 1972
Visitors: welcome Mon-Fri with letter of intro. or h/cap cert. After 11.30 Weds
Green Fee: £21 per round, £27 per day.
Societies: welcome weekdays with prior arrangement.

Catering: snacks all day, hot food lunch times, evening meals by arrangement.
Hotels: Post House.

E15 **Benton Hall**

☎(01376) 502454, Fax 521050
Wickham Hill, Witham, Essex CM8 3LH
2 mins from Witham exit off A12.
Parkland course.
18 hole Championship course 6520 yards S.S.S. 72, 9 hole Par 3 course
Designed by Alan Walker and Charlie Cox.
Founded 12th Jan, 1990
Visitors: pre-booking times.
Green Fee: WD £16; WE £20.
Societies: midweek information package on request.
Catering: bar snacks, a la carte restaurant overlooking lake; all functions catered for.
Driving range.
Hotels: Rivenhall Resort; White Hart; Marks Tey.

E16 **Berkhamsted**

☎(01442) 865832 (Manager), Pro 865851
The Common, Berkhamsted, Herts HP4 2QB

Take junction 8 off M1 to Hemel Hempstead, at roundabout take Leighton Buzzard road; after about 3 miles take Potten End turn and follow road for approx. 3 miles to club.
Heathland course, not suitable for novice golfers.
18 holes, 6605 yards, S.S.S.72
Designed by G.H. Gowring (1890/2 Founder), 1912 C.J. Gilbert with advice from Harry Colt, 1927 extension with advice from James Braid
Founded 1890
Visitors: welcome, must be member of a golf club with h/cap; not before 12.30pm Tues, not before 11.30am Sat, Sun and Bank Holidays. Not on club comp days
Green Fee: WD £22.50 per round, £35 per day; WE £35.
Societies: Wed and Fri.
Catering: full facilities
Hotels: Post House.

E17 **Birch Grove**

☎(01206) 734276
Layer Rd, Colchester CO2 0HS
2 miles S of Colchester on B1026.
Meadowland course.
9 holes, 4108 yards, S.S.S.60
Founded 1970
Visitors: welcome except Sun am.

KEY		34	C & L Golf & Country	66	Hainault Forest	98	Manor of Groves Golf	132	Stock Brook Manor
1	Abbey View		Club	67	Hampstead		& Country Club		Golf & Country Club
2	Abridge G & CC	35	Canons Brook	68	Hanbury Manor Golf	99	Maylands Golf &	133	Stockley Park
3	Airlinks	36	Castle Point		and Country Club		Country Club	134	Stocks Hotel &
4	Aldenham G & CC	37	Chadwell Springs	69	Hanover	100	Mid-Herts		Country Club
5	Aldwickbury Park	38	Channels	70	Harefield Place	101	Mill Green	135	Stoke-by-Nayland
6	Arkley	39	Chelmsford		(Uxbridge)	102	Mill Hill	136	Strawberry Hill
7	Ashford Manor	40	Cheshunt	71	Harpenden	103	Moor Park	137	Sudbury
8	Ashridge	41	Chigwell	72	Harpenden Common	104	Muswell Hill	138	Theydon Bois
9	Ballards Gore	42	Chingford	73	Harrow Hill	105	The Nazeing	139	Thorndon Park
10	Basildon	43	Chorleywood	74	Harrow School	106	North Middlesex	140	Thorpe Hall
11	Batchwood	44	Clacton-on-Sea	75	Hartsbourne G & CC	107	North Weald Golf Club	141	Three Rivers Golf and
12	Belfairs Park	45	Colchester	76	Hartswood	108	Northwood		Country Club
	(Southend-on-Sea)	46	Colne Valley (Essex)	77	Harwich & Dovercourt	109	Old Fold Manor	142	Toothill
13	Belhus Park	47	Crews Hill	78	Haste Hill	110	Orsett	143	Top Meadow
	(Thurrock)	48	Crondon Park	79	Hatfield London	111	Panshanger	144	Towerlands
14	Bentley	49	Dyrham Park		Country Club	112	Perivale Park	145	Trent Park
15	Benton Hall	50	Ealing	80	Hazelwood	113	Pinner Hill	146	Tudor Park Sports
16	Berkhamsted	51	Earls Colne Golf &	81	Hendon	114	Pipps Hill		Ground
17	Birch Grove		Country Club	82	The Hertfordshire	115	Porters Park	147	Twickenham Park
18	Bishop's Stortford	52	East Herts	83	High Beech	116	Potters Bar	148	Upminster
19	Boxmoor	53	Edgewarebury	84	Highgate	117	Quietwaters	149	Verulam
20	Boyce Hill	54	Elstree	85	Hillingdon	118	Redbourn	150	Wanstead
21	Braintree	55	Enfield	86	Horsenden Hill	119	Rickmansworth	151	Warley Park
22	Braxted Park	56	Epping Forest Golf &	87	Hounslow Heath	120	Risebridge (Havering)	152	Warren
23	Brent Valley		Country Club	88	Ilford	121	Rochford Hundred	153	Welwyn Garden City
24	Brickendon Grange	57	Fairlop Waters	89	Knebworth	122	Romford	154	West Essex
25	Briggens House Hotel	58	The Family Golf	90	Laing Sports Club	123	Royston	155	West Herts
26	Brocket Hall		Centre	91	Langdon Hills	124	Ruislip	156	West Middlesex
27	Brookmans Park	59	Finchley	92	Lee Valley	125	Saffron Walden	157	Whipsnade Park
28	Bunsay Downs	60	Forrester Park	93	Letchworth	126	Sandy Lodge	158	Whitehill
29	Burnham-on-Crouch	61	Frinton	94	Little Hay Golf	127	Shendish House	159	Whitewebbs
30	The Burstead	62	Fulwell		Complex	128	South Herts	160	Woodford
31	Bush Hill Park	63	Gosfield Lake	95	London Golf Centre	129	Stanmore	161	Wyke Green
32	Bushey G & CC	64	Grim's Dyke	96	Loughton	130	Stapleford Abbotts		
33	Bushey Hall	65	Hadley Wood	97	Maldon	131	Stevenage		

Green Fee: £10
Societies: weekdays catering for 60.
Catering: meals available during opening hours; parties by prior arrangement.
Hotels: Kingsford Park.

E18 Bishop's Stortford

☎(01279) 654715 (Sec), Pro 651324
Dunmow Rd, Bishop's Stortford, Herts CM23 5HP
Exit 8 from M11, follow signs to town centre/hospital, course is on left next to Nag's Head on E edge of town.
Parkland course.
18 holes, 6404 yards, S.S.S.71
Founded 1912
Visitors: weekdays except Tues only; weekends with member.
Green Fee: £22.
Societies: by appointment weekdays except Tues only.
Catering: lunch and dinner by appointment; bar meals until 9.30pm.
Hotels: Hilton (Stanstead Airport).

E19 Boxmoor

☎(01442) 242434
18 Box Lane, Hemel Hempstead, Herts HP3 0DJ
0.75 mile from Hemel Hempstead station on A41.
Undulating parkland course.
9 holes, 4854 yards, S.S.S.64
Founded 1890
Visitors: welcome weekdays, not Sun; suitable attire and golf shoes.
Green Fee: WD £10; WE £15.
Societies: welcome with 4 weeks notice.
Catering: limited service; Meals available on request. Pool.
Hotels: Boxmoor Lodge.

E20 Boyce Hill

☎(01268) 793625
Vicarage Hill, South Benfleet, Essex SS7 1PD
7 miles W of Southend-on-Sea; A127 to Rayleigh Weir (3 miles from course); A13 to Victoria House Corner (1 mile from course).
Undulating parkland course.
18 holes, 5956 yards, S.S.S.68
Designed by James Braid.
Founded 1922
Visitors: welcome weekdays; weekends with member. H/cap cert required and 24 hrs notice.
Green Fee: £25.
Societies: Thurs only.
Catering: service 7.30am-8pm.
Hotels: Crest; Maisonwyck.

E21 Braintree

☎(01376) 324117 (Members), Sec 346079, Pro 343465
Kings Lane, Stisted, Braintree, Essex CM7 8DA
A120 eastbound after Braintree bypass, 1st left, 1 mile to course, signposted.
Parkland course.
18 holes, 6199 yards, S.S.S.69
Designed by Hawtree and Son.
Founded 1891 (1971 at present site).
Visitors: welcome; h/cap cert required Fri, Sat & Sun.
Green Fee: WD £18 per round, £25 per day; WE £40.
Societies: by arrangement on Mon, Wed and Thurs (Tues Ladies Day).
Catering: meals served.
Hotels: White Hart.

E22 Braxted Park

☎(01621) 892305
Braxted Park, Witham, Essex CM8 3EN
M25-A12 between Chelmsford and Colchester; left at sign to Silver End and Great Braxted, right at T-junction, 0.5 mile to brick wall, follow round to main gates marked Golf Course.
Parkland course in 18th C listed park with lake, pay-and-play Mon-Fri.
9 holes, 2940 yards, Par 30
Founded 1958
Visitors: welcome weekdays.
Green Fee: £9 (9 holes), £12 (18 holes).
Societies: exclusive use of course available.
Catering: full facilities
Hotels: Rivenhall Resort.

E23 Brent Valley

☎(0181) 567 4230, Pro 567 1287
Church Rd, Hanwell, London W7 3BE
A4020 Uxbridge Rd, Hanwell, on to Church Rd by Brent Lodge Animal Centre.
Public meadowland course.
18 holes, 5440 yards, S.S.S.66
Designed by P. Alliss and D. Thomas
Founded 1938
Visitors: welcome 7 days.
Green Fee: WD £8.70; WE £12.95.
Societies: organised via the Pro.
Catering: restaurant from 8am.

E24 Brickendon Grange

☎(01992) 511258 (Sec/Manager), Bar: 511228, Pro 511218, Fax 511411
Brickendon, Nr Hertford, Herts SG13 8PD

3 miles S of Hertford near Bayford BR station.
Undulating parkland course.
18 holes, 6315 yards, S.S.S.70
Designed by C.K. Cotton.
Founded 1968
Visitors: welcome weekdays, h/cap cert required.
Green Fee: £24 per round, £30 per day.
Societies: weekdays except Wed.
Catering: bar lunches
Hotels: White Horse.

E25 Briggens House Hotel

☎(01279) 793742 (Pro), **Hotels:** 792416
Stanstead Abbots, Ware, Herts SG12 8LD
Just off A414 between St Albans and Harlow.
Parkland course.
9 holes, 5800 yards, S.S.S.72
Founded 1988
Visitors: welcome, not Sun am; usual dress rules apply.
Green Fee: WD £6.50 (9 holes), £10.50 (18 holes); WE £9.50 (9 holes), £15 (18 holes)
Societies: apply to Pro.
Catering: full facilities.
Putting green, croquet, tennis, swimming pool.
Hotels: Briggens House, free golf for residents, golfing weekends/breaks.

E26 Brocket Hall

☎(01707) 390055
Brocket Hall, Welwyn Garden City, Herts AL8 7XG
A1(M) exit 4, then via A6129 and B653 to course.
Picturesque parkland course, set in 18th C listed estate.
Melbourne course, 18 holes, 6584 yards, S.S.S.72
Designed by Peter Alliss and Clive Clark.
Founded 1992
Visitors: members and guests only; no societies.
Catering: full facilities (7.30am-9.30pm)
Hotels: Homestead Court.

E27 Brookmans Park

☎(01707) 652487 (Sec), Pro 652468, Fax 661851
Golf Club Rd, Hatfield, Herts AL9 7AT
Junction 24 off M25 (Potters Bar); course located at top of Mymms Drive, off A1000, 1 mile N of Potters Bar, 3 miles S of Hatfield.

Parkland course.
18 holes, 6460 yards, S.S.S.71
Designed by Hawtree & Taylor.
Founded 1930
Visitors: welcome weekdays except Tues by arrangement with Pro, h/cap certs required; weekends only as guest of member.
Green Fee: £27 per round, £32 per day.
Societies: Wed, Thurs, some Fri, by arrangement with Sec's office.
Catering: bar and restaurant.
Hotels: Crest (S Mimms).

E28 Bunsay Downs
☎(01245) 222648
Little Baddow Rd, Woodham Walter, Nr Maldon, Essex CM9 6RW
Leave A414 at Danbury (signposted Woodham Walter), course 0.5 mile to W of village.
Public, gently undulating meadowland course.
9 holes, 2932 yards, S.S.S.68; 9 holes Par 3, 1319 yards
Founded 1982
Visitors: welcome.
Green Fee: WD £10; WE £11. Par 3 £8; 9 holes on each course £10.
Societies: weekdays only, not BH
Catering: available all week from 8am.
Driving range, petanque.

E29 Burnham-on-Crouch
☎(01621) 785508, Sec 782282
Ferry Rd, Creeksea, Burnham-on-Crouch, Essex CM0 8PQ
turn right off B1010 2 miles after Althorne (at 40mph limit for Burnham-on-Crouch).
Undulating meadowland course along R Crouch.
18 holes, 6056 yards, S.S.S.68
Designed by Howard Swan (2nd 9).
Founded 1923
Visitors: welcome
Green Fee: £22.
Societies: catered for Tues, Fri.
Catering: lunches, bar snacks except Mon.
Hotels: White Hart.

E30 The Burstead
☎(01277) 631171, Fax 632766
Tythe Common Rd, Little Burstead, Billericay, Essex CM12 9SS
Off A127 at Fortunes of War roundabout towards Billericay, turn left just before entering Billericay at wooden sign into Laindon Common Rd; at centre of Little Burstead follow

road round to right of War Memorial, entrance 200 yards.
Farmland course with woods, hedgerows, ponds and streams.
18 holes, 6177 yards, S.S.S.69
Designed by Patrick Tallack.
Founded 1993
Visitors: welcome Mon-Fri with proof of membership of bona fide golf club.
Green Fee: £18 per round, £25 per day.
Societies: weekdays except BH.
Catering: bar and bar snacks; restaurant for members and guests only.
Practice ground.

E31 Bush Hill Park
☎(0181) 360 5738
Bush Hill, Winchmore Hill, London N21 2BU
0.5 mile S of Enfield town.
Parkland course.
18 holes, 5825 yards, S.S.S.68
Founded 1895
Visitors: welcome weekdays except Weds am.
Green Fee: £24 per round, £32 per day.
Societies: on application except Wed.
Catering: bar snacks, full restaurant.
Hotels: West Lodge.

E32 Bushey G & CC
☎(0181) 950 2283 (Manager), Pro 950 2215
High St, Bushey, Herts WD2 1BJ
On A411 1.5 miles from M1/A411 junction.
Parkland course.
9 holes, 3000 yards, S.S.S.69
Designed by Donald Steel.
Founded 1980
Visitors: weekdays; weekends and Bank Holidays after 2.30pm; no visitors Wed.
Green Fee: WD £7 (9 holes), £10 (18 holes); WE £9 (9 holes), £14 (18 holes).
Societies: max 50 by arrangement, not Wed.
Catering: meals served.
Driving range, squash, function room.
Hotels: Ladbrokes..

E33 Bushey Hall
☎(01923) 222253 (Sec), Pro 225802, Fax 229759
Bushey Hall Drive, Bushey, Herts WD2 2EP
1 mile SE of Watford.
Undulating parkland course.

18 holes, 6099 yards, S.S.S.69
Designed by Robert Stewart Clouston.
Founded 1886
Visitors: welcome, must book with Pro shop; h/cap certs required.
Green Fee: WD £10; WE £17.
Societies: welcome Mon, Tues, Thurs only.
Catering: full facilities.

E34 C & L Golf & Country Club
☎(0181) 845 5662, Fax 841 5515
Junction of West End Road & A40, Northolt, Middlesex UB5 6RD
A40 from London; opposite Northolt Airport.
Parkland course.
9 holes, 4438 yards, S.S.S.62
Designed by Patrick Tallack.
Founded Jan 1991
Visitors: Public days Mon, Wed, Fri; no jeans or T-shirts; golf shoes only.
Green Fee: WD £5; WE £8.
Societies: any day during the week.
Catering: main bar, restaurant; banqueting hall.
Tennis, snooker, bowls, squash and health and fitness facilities.
Hotels: Master Brewer.

E35 Canons Brook
☎(01279) 421482
Elizabeth Way, Harlow, Essex CM19 5BE
M11 to Harlow, Edinburgh Way then Elizabeth Way.
Parkland course.
18 holes, 6728 yards, S.S.S.73
Designed by Sir Henry Cotton.
Founded 1963
Visitors: welcome weekdays.
Green Fee: £25.
Societies: welcome weekdays.
Catering: lunch, dinners except Sun.
Hotels: Churchgate.

E36 Castle Point
☎(01268) 510830
Somnes Avenue, Canvey Island, Essex SS8 9FG
A13 to Southend, right on A130 to Canvey Island at Saddler's Farm roundabout, over Waterside Farm roundabout to Somnes Ave, course on left.
Public seaside links course.
18 holes, 6176 yards, S.S.S.69
Designed by Golf Landscapes.
Founded June 1988
Visitors: no restrictions. Booking required at weekends.

Green Fee: WD £8.10; WE £12.20.
Societies: on request, telephone in advance.
Catering: bar and restaurant facilities.
Driving range.
Hotels: Crest (Basildon); The Oyster Fleet.

E37 Chadwell Springs

☎(01920) 461447
Hertford Rd, Ware, Herts SG12 9LE
On A119 half way between Hertford and Ware.
Parkland course.
9 holes, 3209 yards, S.S.S.71
Designed by J.H. Taylor.
Founded 1975
Visitors: welcome weekdays, guests of member only weekends.
Green Fee: £20.
Societies: welcome on Mon and Wed.
Catering: full facilities.
Hotels: Moat House (Ware).

E38 Channels

☎(01245) 440005, Pro 441056, Starter/tee res: 443311, Fax 442032
Belsteads Farm Lane, Little Waltham, Chelmsford, Essex CM3 3PT
2 miles NE of Chelmsford on A130.
Undulating course on restored gravel workings, lakes and wildlife.
Channel course 18 holes, 6272 yards, S.S.S.70; Belsteads 9 hole course
Designed by Henry Cotton.
Founded 1974
Visitors: welcome weekdays, weekends with member only. No restrictions on 9 hole course.
Green Fee: Channel course £15 per round, £28 per day. Belsteads £9 (9 holes), £15 (18 holes)
Societies: weekdays only.
Catering: excellent table d'hote, a la carte.
Restored Essex barn available for weddings and corporate days.
Hotels: County; South Lodge.

E39 Chelmsford

☎(01245) 256483, Pro/Bookings: 257079
Widford Rd, Chelmsford, Essex CM2 9AP
A1016 to Wood St roundabout, Chelmsford, turn right (from London) and right again.
Undulating parkland course.
18 holes, 5981 yards, S.S.S.68
Founded 1893

Visitors: welcome weekdays if members of recognised club; weekends with member only.
Green Fee: £25 per round, £35 per day.
Societies: limited number by arrangement.
Catering: lunch except Mon, dinners Fri, Sat only, bar snacks daily.
Hotels: South Lodge.

E40 Cheshunt

☎(01992) 629777, Bookings: 624009
Park Lane, Cheshunt, Herts EN7 6QD
From M25 junction 25 towards Hertford, at 2nd lights turn left to mini-roundabout, turn right then signposted.
Municipal parkland course.
18 holes, 6613 yards, S.S.S.71
Founded 1976
Visitors: welcome weekdays and by arrangement at weekends.
Green Fee: WD £9.50; WE £12.50.
Societies: catered for any time by arrangement.
Catering: cafeteria service all day.
Hotels: Marriott.

E41 Chigwell

☎(0181) 500 2059, Pro 500 2384
High Rd, Chigwell, Essex IG7 5BH
On A113, 13.5 miles NE of London.
Undulating parkland course.
18 holes, 6279 yards, S.S.S.70
Founded 1925
Visitors: by prior appointment; weekdays only unless with member.
Green Fee: £28 per round, £39 per day.
Societies: Mon, Wed and Thurs; early booking essential.
Catering: bar and catering facilities.
Hotels: Prince Regent; Roebuck.

E42 Chingford

☎(0181) 529 5708, Royal Epping Forest GC: 529 2195
Bury Rd, Chingford, London E4 7QJ
Off Station Rd, 300 yards S of Chingford station.
Public parkland course.
18 holes, 6400 yards, S.S.S.70
Designed by James Braid.
Founded 1888
Visitors: welcome, red outer garment must be worn.
Green Fee: WD £9; WE £12.50.
Societies: by appointment.
Catering: snacks, no bar. Cafeteria next to club.

E43 Chorleywood

☎(01923) 282009
Common Rd, Chorleywood, Herts WD3 5LN
0.5 mile from Chorleywood station near Sportsman Hotel.
Well-wooded heathland course on common land.
9 holes, 5676 yards, S.S.S.67
Founded 1890
Visitors: welcome weekdays except Tues and Thurs am.
Green Fee: WD £14; WE £17.50.
Societies: small societies, limited.
Catering: bar and catering; snooker.
Hotels: The Sportsman.

E44 Clacton-on-Sea

☎(01255) 421919
West Rd, Clacton-on-Sea, Essex CO15 1AJ
On A133 16 miles from Colchester, 1 mile W of pier next to old Butlins Holiday Camp.
Undulating seaside course.
18 holes, 6494 yards, S.S.S.71
Designed by Jack White.
Founded 1892
Visitors: weekdays subject to availability; Sat am, Sun pm and Bank Holidays on application; h/cap certs required at all times.
Green Fee: WD £20 per round, £26 per day; WE £30.
Societies: by arrangement with Sec.
Catering: full except Mon.
Hotels: Royal.

E45 Colchester

☎(01206) 852946, Sec 853396
Braiswick, Colchester, Essex CO4 5AV
0.75 mile up Bergholt Rd from Colchester North station.
Parkland course.
18 holes, 6319 yards, S.S.S.70
Designed by James Braid.
Founded 1907
Visitors: welcome weekdays, weekends only with member.
Green Fee: on application.
Societies: weekdays by arrangement.
Catering: available.
Hotels: Marks Tey; George; Mill.

E46 Colne Valley (Essex)

☎(01787) 224233, Fax 224452
Station Road, Earls Colne, Essex CO6 2LT
Leave A12 at Colchester, take A604 for 8 miles through Earls Colne village, Station Rd is 1st on right.

Parkland course in the Colne valley, river and 6 lakes.
18 holes, 6301 yards, S.S.S.70
Designed by Howard Swan.
Founded May 1990
Visitors: WD and after 10am WE and BH; restrictions Thurs (Ladies day).
Green Fee: WD £15 per round, £22 per day; WE £20.
Societies: welcome weekdays by arrangement.
Catering: full facilities.
Hotels: The Drum.

E47 **Crews Hill**

☎(0181) 363 6674, Fax 364 5641
Cattlegate Rd, Crews Hill, Enfield, Middx EN2 8AZ
Off A1005 Enfield to Potters Bar road into East Lodge Lane, turn right into Cattlegate Rd.
Parkland course.
18 holes, 6250 yards, S.S.S.70
Designed by H. Colt
Founded 1921
Visitors: must be members of recognised club; weekends and Bank Holidays only with member.
Green Fee: WD £25 per round (£14 with member), £30 per day (£20 with member); WE
Societies: welcome with advance booking.
Catering: full facilities except Mon.
Hotels: Royal Chase.

E48 **Crondon Park**

☎(01277) 841115, Pro 841887
Stock Road, Stock, Essex CM4 9DP
Between Chelsford and Billericay off the B1007 on the north side of Stock, 2 miles from junction of A12 and 10 miles from junction 28 of M25
Undulating parkland valley course
18 holes Championship course, 6585 yards, S.S.S. 71
Designed by M Gillett
Founded May 1994
Visitors: welcome weekdays and weekend afternoons
Green Fee: WD £19; WE £25
Societies: weekdays on application
Catering: licenced bar, restaurant.
Hotels: Post House Brentwood; Miami Chelmsford; Heybridge Moat House, Ingatestone.

E49 **Dyrham Park**

☎(0181) 440 3361 (Sec), Pro 440 3904
Galley Lane, Barnet, Herts EN5 4RA.
2 miles outside Barnet near Arkley, off A1 and M25.

Parkland course.
18 holes, 6422 yards, S.S.S.70
Designed by C.K. Cotton.
Founded 1963
Visitors: only as guest of member or member of Golf Society.
Green Fee: on application.
Societies: Wed only; two rounds golf, light lunch and dinner or lunch and afternoon tea.
Catering: full restaurant facilities.
Hotels: Post House.

E50 **Ealing**

☎(0181) 997 0937, Bookings: 997 3959
Perivale Rd, Greenford, Middx UB6 8SS
Off A40 W opposite Hoover building (Tesco).
Parkland course.
18 holes, 6216 yards, S.S.S.70
Designed by H. Colt.
Founded 1898
Visitors: welcome weekdays only phone for advance booking.
Green Fee: £30 (£15 with member).
Societies: Mon, Wed and Thurs only.
Catering: full facilities.
Hotels: The Bridge (Greenford).

E51 **Earls Colne Golf & Country Club**

☎(01787) 224466
Earls Colne, Nr Colchester, Essex CO6 2NS
On B1024 Earls Colne-Coggeshall road, 4 miles N of A12, 1 mile S of A604.
Landscaped and tree-planted course on converted farmland.
18 hole championship course, 6879 yards, Par 73; 9 holes, 1520 yards, Par 30; 4 hole Academy course for tuition.
Designed by Reg Plumbridge.
Founded 1991
Visitors: welcome.
Green Fee: WD £16; WE £20.
Societies: welcome.
Catering: full bar and restaurant.
Driving range; leisure, health and beauty, tennis, bowls, flying school, business and conference facilities.
Hotels: Own hotel ready in May 1996 (40 bed).

E52 **East Herts**

☎(01920) 821978 (Sec)
Hamels Park, Buntingford, Herts SG9 9NA
A10 between Buntingford and Ware, just N of Puckeridge roundabout.

Parkland course.
18 holes, 6456 yards, S.S.S.71
Founded 1898
Visitors: Mon-Fri only; h/cap cert required; not weekends unless with member.
Green Fee: £24 per round, £30 per day.
Societies: welcome by arrangement.
Catering: full facilities.
Hotels: Vintage Corner Motel.

E53 **Edgewarebury**

☎(0181) 958 3571
Edgeware Way, Edgeware, Middlesex
On A41 between Edgeware and Elstree.
Par 3 Pitch & Putt course.
9 holes, 1045 yards, Par 27
Founded 1946
Visitors: welcome 9am until dusk; no booking necessary.
Green Fee: £4, £6.50 (2 rounds).
Societies: welcome.
Catering: no facilities.
Hotels: Edgewarebury Hotel.

E54 **Elstree**

☎(0181) 953 6115 (Office), Bookings: 207 5680, Fax 207 6390
Watling St, Elstree, Herts WD6 3AA
On A5183 (A5) just outside Elstree village; close to M1, M25, A41, A1; nearest rail station Elstree & Borehamwood.
Parkland course.
18 holes, 6603 yards, S.S.S.72
Founded 1984
Visitors: welcome weekdays, after 2pm weekends (subject to availability).
Green Fee: WD £20 per round; WE £25 (after 2pm.)
Societies: Mon, Tues, Thurs, Fri by prior arrangement; phone for details.
Catering: restaurant, bar, conservatory all day.
Driving range.
Hotels: Hilton International.

E55 **Enfield**

☎(0181) 363 3970, Pro 366 4492, Fax 342 0381
Old Park Rd South, Enfield, Middx EN2 7DA
Leave M25 at Junction 24 (Potters Bar); take A1005 to Enfield (4 miles) to roundabout with Church on left; turn right down Slades Hill, then 1st left into Old Park View; Club at end of road on right in Old Park Road South.
Parkland course.

ENFIELD GOLF CLUB

Old Park Road South, Enfield, Middlesex EN2 7DA Tel: 0181-363 3970

A warm welcome awaits you at Enfield. Course designed by James Braid.
Casual green fees (with Handicap Certificate) and Society Days welcome.
Call secretary for details.

18 holes, 6154 yards, S.S.S.70
Designed by James Braid
Founded 1893
Visitors: welcome weekdays (excl
Bank Holidays); 24 hours notice, with
h/cap and if member of another club;
not weekends unless guest of
member.
Green Fee: WD £22 per round, £30
per day; WE (only with member £12).
Societies: welcome Mon, Wed and
Fri, excluding Bank Holidays.
Catering: meals available every day.
Hotels: Royal Chase.

E56 Epping Forest Golf & Country Club

☎(0181) 500 2549 (Dir of Golf), Pro
559 8272, Fax 559 8409
Woolston Hall, Abridge Rd, Chigwell,
Essex IG7 6BX
Alongside M11; take
Loughton/Debden exit 5 (northbound
only) to Chigwell and Abridge.
Parkland course with numerous water
hazards.
18 holes, 6408 yards, Par 72
Designed by Neil Coles.
Founded 1994
Visitors: members and guests only;
no casual visitors or societies.
Hotels: Trust House Forte.

E57 Fairlop Waters

☎(0181) 500 9911, Pro 501 1881
Forest Rd, Barkingside, Ilford, Essex
IG6 3JA
Signposted from M11 and along A12;
near Fairlop station (Central Line).
Public heathland course.
18 holes, 6281 yards, S.S.S.69; 9
hole Par 3, 1167 yards
Designed by John Jacobs.
Founded Jan 1988
Visitors: welcome; tidy dress
required.
Green Fee: WD £7.75: WE £11.25.
Societies: weekdays by
arrangement.
Catering: bar, Daltons American
Diner, 2 banqueting suites.
Driving range, sailing, children's play
area, country park.
Hotels: Granada Travel Inn
(Redbridge)

E58 The Family Golf Centre

☎(01462) 482929
Jack's Hill, Graveley, Herts SG4 7EQ
Just off Junction 8 or 9 of A1(M),
approx. 1.5 miles along B197 N of
village of Graveley.
Pay-as-you-play, inland
links/downland course.
Chesfield Downs, 18 holes, 6646
yards, S.S.S.72; Lannock Links, 9
holes Par 3, 975 yards, S.S.S.27
Designed by Jonathan Gaunt.
Founded Jan 1991
Visitors: welcome; advance booking
system to reserve tee-off times, 1
week's notice preferred.
Green Fee: Chesfield Downs, WD
£14.75; WE £21. Lannock Links, WD
£2; WE £3.
Societies: catered for by
arrangement.
Catering: 19th Hole bar and bistro;
coffee shop.
Driving range.
Hotels: Novotel (Knebworth Park,
Stevenage); special rates available.

E59 Finchley

☎(0181) 346 2436 (Sec), Pro 346
5086
Nether Court, Frith Lane, Mill Hill,
London NW7 1PU
Near junction of A1 and A41, Mill Hill
East underground 5 min walk.
Parkland course.
18 holes, 6411 yards, S.S.S.71
Designed by James Braid.
Founded 1929
Visitors: welcome weekdays except
Thurs and Tues am or am at
weekends.
Green Fee: WD £24; WE £30.
Societies: Wed and Fri.
Catering: full service on request.
Hotels: Hendon Hall.

E60 Forrester Park

☎(01621) 891406 (Bookings), Pro
893456
Beckingham Rd, Great Totham, Nr
Maldon, Essex CM9 8EA
5 miles NE of Maldon on B1022,
between S and N villages of Great
Totham; from A12, turn off at

Rivenhall End, follow signs to Great
Braxted, at B1022 turn right towards
Maldon, after 1.8 miles turn left.
Parkland course.
18 holes, 6073 yards, S.S.S.69
Designed by D.A.H. Everett & T.R.
Forrester-Muir.
Founded 1975
Visitors: not before 12.30pm Sat,
Sun.
Green Fee: on application.
Societies: with prior reservation Mon,
Thurs, Fri.
Catering: bar 8am until dark, snacks
8am-6pm daily; lunches 10.30am-
2pm Mon-Sat; dinners for parties on
request.
4 all-weather tennis courts,
banqueting/conferences for 80.
Hotels: Rivenhall

E61 Frinton

☎(01255) 674618 (Tel/Fax), Pro
671618
1 The Esplanade, Frinton-on-Sea,
Essex CO13 9EP
A133 Colchester to Weeley village,
B1033 to Frinton, right at seafront.
Seaside links course.
18 holes, 6265 yards, S.S.S.70; 18
hole short course, 2508 yards, Par 66
Designed by Tom Dunn.
Founded 1895
Visitors: welcome weekdays and
weekends by arrangement with Sec;
h/cap cert for main course.
Green Fee: £22 per day; short
course £7.50 per day.
Societies: Wed and Thurs only.
Catering: meals available except
Mon; snooker.
Hotels: Maplin; The Rock.

E62 Fulwell

☎(0181) 977 2733, Pro 977 3844
Wellington Rd, Hampton Hill, Middx
TW12 1JY
2 miles S of Twickenham on A311,
opposite Fulwell railway station.
Meadowland course.
18 holes, 6544 yards, S.S.S.71
Designed by D. Morrison.
Founded 1904
Visitors: welcome weekdays, book
through Pro shop.

Green Fee: WD £30; WE £35.
Societies: welcome by prior arrangement.
Catering: full service for societies but advisable to phone.
Hotels: The Winning Post.

E63 Gosfield Lake
☎(01787) 474747
Hall Drive, Gosfield, Halstead, Essex CO9 1SE
1 mile W of village of Gosfield which is 7 miles N of Braintree on A1017.
Parkland course.
Lakes, 18 holes, 6707 yards, S.S.S.72; Meadows, 9 holes, 4037 yards (for 18)
Designed by Sir Henry Cotton, Howard Swan.
Founded 1988
Visitors: h/cap cert required for Lakes course; with member only or by arrangement from 12am weekends.
Green Fee: Lakes, WD £20 per round, £25 per day; WE £25. Meadows £10 per day.
Societies: welcome by arrangement.
Catering: bar, snack bar, restaurant from 12am; conference facilities, private functions, company days.
Hotels: Bull.

E64 Grim's Dyke
☎(0181) 428 4539
Oxhey Lane, Hatch End, Pinner, Middx HA5 4AL
Between Harrow and Watford on A4008.
Parkland course.
18 holes, 5598 yards, S.S.S.67
Designed by James Braid.
Founded 1910
Visitors: weekdays; h/cap cert required.
Green Fee: £20 per round, £25 per day.
Societies: Tues-Fri.
Catering: lunch except Mon; dinner by arrangement.
Hotels: Grim's Dyke Mansion House.

E65 Hadley Wood
☎(0181) 449 4328, Pro 449 3285, Fax 364 8633
Beech Hill, Barnet, Herts EN4 0JJ
From M25 junction 24, A111 towards Cockfosters, 3rd right into Beech Hill, entrance 400 yards on left.
Parkland course with water hazards.
18 holes, 6457 yards, S.S.S.71
Designed by A Mackenzie.
Founded 1922

Visitors: weekdays except Tues am, require h/cap cert or proof of club membership; at weekends limited..
Green Fee: on application.
Societies: by arrangement.
Catering: morning coffee, lunch, dinner for functions and societies, breakfast by arrangement.
Large practice area.
Hotels: West Park Lodge.

E66 Hainault Forest
☎(0181) 500 2097, Sec 500 0385, Pro 500 2131
Chigwell Row, Hainault, Essex IG7 4QW
On A217 12 miles Central London.
Public parkland course.
18 holes, 5754 yards, S.S.S.67; 18 holes, 6600 yards, S.S.S.71
Founded 1912
Visitors: welcome.
Green Fee: WD £9.80; WE £12.20.
Societies: by prior arrangement.
Catering: meals served.

E67 Hampstead
☎(0181) 455 0203, Pro 455 7089
Winnington Rd, Hampstead, London N2 0TU
1 mile down Hampstead Lane from Highgate Village or Hampstead, course adjacent to Spaniards Inn.
Undulating parkland course.
9 holes, 5822 yards, S.S.S.68
Founded 1893
Visitors: welcome weekdays (not Tues) by prior booking with Pro; restricted times weekends.
Green Fee: WD £25 per round, £30 per day; WE £32, £20 after 1pm.
Societies: small societies by arrangement.
Catering: bar, bar snacks, teas.
Hotels: La Gaffe.

E68 Hanbury Manor Golf and Country Club
☎(01920) 487722, Fax 487692
Ware, Herts SG12 0SD
22 miles N of London on A10, 8 miles N of M25 junction 25.
Parkland course.
18 holes, 7011 yards, S.S.S.74
Designed by Jack Nicklaus II.
Founded 1990
Visitors: hotel and member's guests only; h/cap certs required.
Green Fee: £35
Societies: Welcome over 12 people. Corporate days available.
Catering: bars, 3 restaurants (overseen by Albert Roux).

Practice ground, tennis, squash, gymnasium, swimming pool and full range of leisure club facilities.
Hotels: Hanbury Manor, special golfing packages available.

E69 Hanover
☎(01702) 232377
Hullbridge, Rayleigh, Essex SS6 9QS
Undulating course.
18 hole championship course, 6523 yards S.S.S.71 ; 18 hole pay-and-play course, 3700 yards Par 63
Designed by Reg Plumbridge.
Founded 1991
Visitors: guests of members only.
Green Fee: on application
Societies: PGA affiliated society enquiries only.
Catering: full service
Hotels: The Watermill

E70 Harefield Place (Uxbridge)
☎(01895) 231169, Pro 237287, Fax 810262
The Drive, Harefield Place, Uxbridge, Middx UB10 9PA
2 miles N of Uxbridge; off M40 at B467.
Public parkland course.
18 holes, 5711 yards, S.S.S.68
Visitors: welcome 7 days.
Green Fee: WD £10; WE £15.
Societies: welcome 7 days, pm only at weekends.
Catering: full facilities; function rooms, weddings etc.
Hotels: all airport hotels.

E71 Harpenden
☎(01582) 712580, Pro 767124, Fax 712725
Hammonds End, Redbourn Lane, Harpenden, Herts AL5 2AX
Off A1081 4 miles N of St Albans on B487 Redbourn road.
Parkland course.
18 holes, 6381 yards, S.S.S.70
Designed by Hawtree and Taylor
Founded 1894
Visitors: weekdays except Thurs.
Green Fee: £24
Societies: weekdays except Thurs.
Catering: by arrangement.

E72 Harpenden Common
☎(01582) 715959
East Common, Harpenden, Herts AL5 1BL
Adjacent A1081, 4 miles N of St Albans, 1 mile S of Harpenden.

Heathland course.
18 holes, 5664 yards, S.S.S.67
Founded 1931
Visitors: welcome Mon, Wed, Thurs,
Fri; h/cap certs required.Weekends
with a member.
Green Fee: £22 per round, £27 per
day.
Societies: by prior arrangement.
Catering: full bar facilities; lunches,
teas and snacks; dinner to order.
Hotels: Gleneagles.

E73 Harrow Hill
☎(0181) 864 3754
Kenton Road, Harrow, Middlesex
HA1
Off Harrow main by-pass road at
Northwick Park roundabout. ·
Public parkland course.
9 holes beginner Par 3, 950 yards
Designed by S. Teahan.
Founded 1982
Visitors: welcome.
Green Fee: £3.50 (adults), £3
(juniors); club hire available.
Catering: soft drinks.

E74 Harrow School
☎(0181) 422 2196
Harrow School, 5 High Street,
Harrow-on-the-Hill, Middlesex HA1
3JE
Parkland course.
9 holes, 3690 yards, S.S.S.57
Designed by Donald Steel.
Founded 1979
Visitors: no visitors.

E75 Hartsbourne G & CC
☎(0181) 950 1133
Hartsbourne Ave, Bushey Heath,
Herts WD2 1JW
Turn S off A411 at entrance to
Bushey Heath village 5 miles SE of
Watford.
Parkland course.
18 holes, 6305 yards, S.S.S.70; 9
holes, 5432 yards, S.S.S.66
Designed by Hawtree and Taylor.
Founded 1946
Visitors: with member only.
Green Fee: WD £18; WE £23
Societies: welcome Mon and Fri.
Catering: daily catering and bar.
Hotels: Hilton National.

E76 Hartswood
☎(01277) 218850 (Sec)
King George's Playing Fields, Ingrave
Rd, Brentwood, Essex CM 14 5AE
1 mile S of Brentwood on A128.

Municipal parkland course.
18 holes, 6160 yards, S.S.S.69
Founded 1964
Visitors: welcome.
Green Fee: WD £7.50; WE £11.50.
Societies: welcome weekdays by
arrangement.
Catering: full facilities by
arrangement.
Hotels: Post House.

E77 Harwich & Dovercourt
☎(01255) 503616
Station Rd, Parkeston, Harwich,
Essex CO12 4NZ
A120 towards Parkeston Quay, after
last roundabout 200 yards on left.
Meadowland course.
9 holes, 5742 yards, S.S.S.68
Founded 1903
Visitors: welcome, h/cap cert
required.
Green Fee: £16 (18 holes), £10 with
member; weekly ticket available £52
and monthly ticket £90.
Societies: welcome by arrangement.
Catering: bar snacks or full catering
as required except Thurs.
Hotels: Cliff, Towers (Dovercourt).

E78 Haste Hill
☎(01923) 826078
The Drive, Northwood, Middx HA6
1HN
On A404.
Public parkland course.
18 holes, 5787 yards, S.S.S.68
Founded 1930
Visitors: welcome; book in advance.
Green Fee: WD £10; WE £15.
Societies: welcome by arrangement.
Catering: meals served daily.

E79 Hatfield London Country Club
☎(01707) 642624, 642626
Bedwell Park, Essendon, Hatfield,
Herts AL9 6JA
A1000 from Potters Bar, B158
towards Essendon.
Undulating parkland course.
18 holes, 6385 yards, S.S.S.73
Designed by Fred Hawtree.
Founded 1976
Visitors: welcome; by advance
booking only.
Green Fee: WD £13 (Mon), £16
(Tues-Fri); WE £28 per round, £32
per day.
Societies: welcome.
Catering: full facilities.
Hotels: The Oak.

E80 Hazelwood
☎(01932) 770981, Pro 770932
Croysdale Ave, Sunbury-on-Thames
TW16 6QU
M3 Junction 1 exit towards Lower
Sunbury, 1 mile on right, off Green
Street
Parkland course
9 holes, 5660 yards, S.S.S. 67
Designed by Jonathan Gaunt
Founded in August 1993
Visitors: welcome
Green Fee: WD £7 (9 holes), £10 (18
holes); WE £8.50 (9 holes), £12 (18
holes).
Societies: welcome.
Catering: bar and restaurant
facilities, catering for societies of 50,
buffet and function facilities for 100
Hotels: Shepperton Moat House;
Flower Pot; Warren Lodge.

E81 Hendon
☎(0181) 346 6023, Pro 346 8990,
Fax 343 1974
off Sanders Lane, Mill Hill, London
NW7 1DG
From Hendon Central take Queens
Rd through Brent St, continue to
roundabout, take 1st exit on left, club
0.5 mile on left in Devonshire Rd;
from junction 2 M1 southbound, turn
left at 1st traffic lights and continue to
roundabout, then as above.
Parkland course.
18 holes, 6266 yards, S.S.S.70
Designed by H.S. Colt.
Founded 1903
Visitors: not Sat/Sun morning, Mon
limited; Tues-Fri all day.
Green Fee: WD £25 per round, £30
per day; WE & BH £35.
Societies: welcome Tues-Fri by
arrangement.
Catering: snacks only Mon; other
days lunch, snacks, high tea to 6pm.
Hotels: Hendon Hall.

E82 The Hertfordshire
☎(01992) 466666, Fax 470326
Broxbournebury Mansion, White
Stubbs Lane, Broxbourne, Herts
EN10 7PY
Off junc 25 of M25, take A10 towards
Cambridge. Take A10 exit for
Turnford and then A1170 to Bell
Lane. Turn left, Bell Lane becomes
White Stubbs Lane. Course on right
Parkland course
18 holes, 6410 yards, S.S.S. 70
Designed by Jack Nicklaus (his first
pay and play course in Europe).
Founded 1995
Visitors: welcome

Green Fee: WD £18 per round, £27 per day; WE £22 per round, £33 per day.
Societies: welcome; corporate days available
Catering: restaurant and bar facilities
Health club, tennis club, driving range, USGA Golf academy with chipping green, putting green, fairway bunkers, greenside bunker practice area. 40-bay grass tee practice area.

E83 High Beech
☎(0181) 508 7323
Wellington Hill, Loughton, Essex IG10 4AH
B1393 (old A11) to Robin Hood roundabout take turning signed to Conservation Centre and Youth Hostel; follow YH sign, course just past YH next Duke of Wellington pub.
Public parkland course
Red course, 9 holes Par 3; yellow course, 9 holes Par 3
Founded 1963
Visitors: Red course open to public 7 days a week, yellow course members only weekends and Bank Holidays and after 5pm.
Green Fee: Red course £2.60 (9 holes); yellow course £3 (9 holes), membership fees £15 pa, £10 joining fee.
Societies: by application
Catering: snack bar only; public house next door
5 practice nets.
Hotels: Trust House Forte.

E84 Highgate
☎(0181) 340 1906, 340 3745
Denewood Rd, London N6 4AH
Off Hampstead Lane near Kenwood House, turn into Sheldon Ave then 1st left into Denewood Rd.
Parkland course.
18 holes, 5985 yards, S.S.S.69
Founded 1904
Visitors: Mon, Tues, Thurs, Fri only; no visitors weekends.
Green Fee: WD £27 per round.
Societies: welcome Tues, Thurs, Fri by arrangement.
Catering: full, 12am-8pm.

E85 Hillingdon
☎(01895) 233956 (Sec), Pro 251980
18 Dorset Way, Hillingdon, Middx UB10 0JR
Turn off A40 to Uxbridge, past RAF Station, up Hillingdon Hill to left turn at Vine public house into Vine Lane, club gates 0.75 mile on left.

Undulating parkland course.
9 holes, 5490 yards, S.S.S.68
Designed by Harry Woods & Chas E. Stevens.
Founded 1892
Visitors: welcome weekdays except Thurs afternoon. Weekends only with a full member after 12.30pm; must be members of golf club with h/cap cert.
Green Fee: WD £19.
Societies: Mondays; packages available between £20- £44
Catering: bar and catering facilities.
Hotels: Master Brewer Motel; The Old Cottage.

E86 Horsenden Hill
☎(0181) 902 4555
Woodland Rise, Greenford, Middx UB6 0RD
Signposted off Whitton Ave East, rear of Sudbury Golf club.
Public undulating parkland course.
9 holes, 3264 yards, S.S.S.56
Founded 1935
Visitors: welcome, no restrictions.
Green Fee: WD £4.40; WE £6.50.
Societies: welcome any time.
Catering: bar, restaurant

E87 Hounslow Heath
☎(0181) 570 5271
Staines Rd, Hounslow, Middx TW4 5DS
A315 main road between Hounslow and Bedfont, on left hand side.
Public parkland course.
18 holes, 5901 yards, S.S.S.68
Designed by Fraser Middleton.
Founded 1979
Visitors: welcome.
Green Fee: WD £7.50; WE £10.50.
Societies: welcome by arrangement.
Catering: snacks, soft drinks, no bar.
Hotels: Hounslow.

E88 Ilford
☎(0181) 554 2930, Pro 554 0094
291 Wanstead Park Rd, Ilford, Essex IG1 3TR
0.5 mile from Ilford railway station.
Parkland course.
16 holes, 5414 yards, S.S.S.68
Founded 1906
Visitors: welcome with advance booking; restricted Tues and Thurs; Sat, Sun and Bank Holidays limited to members and guests.
Green Fee: WD £13.50 per round, £20 per day; WE £16 per round.
Societies: welcome weekdays.
Catering: restaurant most days.
Hotels: Woodford Moat House.

E89 Knebworth
☎(01438) 812752
Deards End Lane, Knebworth, Herts SG3 6NL
1 mile S of Stevenage on B197.
Parkland course.
18 holes, 6492 yards, S.S.S.71
Designed by Willie Park.
Founded 1908
Visitors: weekdays unaccompanied; weekends, Bank Holidays with member only; club h/cap cert required.
Green Fee: WD £29.
Societies: Mon, Tues, Thurs only.
Catering: facilities daily except after 6 on Sunday.
Hotels: Post House.

E90 Laing Sports Club
☎(0181) 441 6051
Rowley Lane, Arkley, Barnet, Herts EN5 3HW.
Off A1 S at Borehamwood.
9 holes, 4178 yards, S.S.S.60
Designed by employees of John Laing and members only.
Visitors: only if accompanied by a member.
Green Fee: £6.
Societies: limited.
Catering: limited.
Tennis, bowls, hockey, snooker.

E91 Langdon Hills
☎(01268) 548444, Fax 548065
Lower Dunton Road, Bulphan, Essex RM14 3TY
8 miles from M25 junction 30, A13 E towards Tilbury, after approx 7 miles turn off on B1007 towards Horndon on the Hill; after approx 1 mile turn left into Lower Dunton Rd.
Parkland course.
18 holes, 6485 yards, S.S.S.71; 9 hole course
Designed by MRM Sandow
Founded June 1991
Visitors: 18 hole course, welcome with h/cap cert, not before 12am weekends; 9 hole course unrestricted.
Green Fee: 18 hole course, WD £18.50 per round, £26.50 per day; WE £25 per round after 12 noon; 9 hole course WD £4 (9 holes), £6 (18 holes); WE £7.50 (18 holes).
Societies: welcome weekdays.
Catering: bars and restaurant; function suite.
Driving range, practice ground, 3 practice holes played as 9-hole Par 34; home of European School of Golf.
Hotels: Langdon Hills.

E92 **Lee Valley**

☎(0181) 803 3611, 345 6666
Lee Valley Leisure Golf Course,
Picketts Lock Lane, Edmonton,
London N9 0AS
1 mile N of North Circular road,
junction with Montagu Rd.
Public parkland course with large lake
and river hazard.
18 holes, 4902 yards, S.S.S.64
Founded 1974, extended 1993
Visitors: open to public every day, no
restrictions except dress code in
operation.
Green Fee: WD £10 per round (£5
OAPs and jnrs); WE & BH £13.
Societies: welcome weekdays only,
30 max.
Catering: breakfast until midday, bar
and bar snacks daily.
Driving range, full sporting facilities at
leisure centre.
Hotels: Holt Whites Hotel (Enfield).

E93 **Letchworth**

☎(01462) 683203 (Sec), Pro
682713, Fax 484567
Letchworth Lane, Letchworth, Herts
SG6 3NQ
2 miles from A1(M) near village of
Willian, adjacent to Letchworth Hall
Hotel.
Parkland course.
18 holes, 6181 yards, S.S.S.69
Designed by Harry Vardon.
Founded 1905
Visitors: weekdays, h/cap cert
required; weekends accompanied by
member only.
Green Fee: WD £24 per round, £33
per day.
Societies: welcome Wed, Thurs, Fri.
Catering: except Mon.
Hotels: Letchworth Hall.

E94 **Little Hay Golf Complex**

☎(01442) 833798
Box Lane, Bovingdon, Hemel
Hempstead, Herts HP3 0DQ
Just off A41, turn left at 1st traffic
lights, past Hemel Hempstead station,
up hill; course on right, signposted.
Public parkland course.
18 holes, 6678 yards, S.S.S.72
Designed by Hawtree & Son.
Founded 1977
Visitors: welcome.
Green Fee: WD £8; WE £12.
Societies: welcome by prior
arrangement.
Catering: full meal facilities.
Driving range.
Hotels: Bobsleigh.

E95 **London Golf Centre**

☎(0181) 845 3180
Ruislip Rd, Northolt, Middx UB5 6QZ
500 yards S of Polish War Memorial
roundabout on A40.
Public parkland course.
9 holes (18 tees), 5836 yards,
S.S.S.71
Founded 1975
Visitors: welcome any time, no
restrictions.
Green Fee: WD £5 (9 holes), £9 (18
holes); WE £6.75 (9 holes), £12.75
(18 holes).
Societies: welcome.
Catering: 2 bars, bistro; function hall.
Driving range, golf superstore.

E96 **Loughton**

☎(0181) 502 2923
Clay's Lane, Loughton, Essex IG10
2RZ.
From M25 junction 26 take A121
towards Loughton; 3rd exit at
roundabout, 1st turning on left.
Public parkland course.
9 holes, 4652 yards, S.S.S.63
Founded 1981
Visitors: welcome, book after Thurs
for weekends.
Green Fee: WD £5 (9 holes), £8 (18
holes); WE £6 (9 holes), £10 (18
holes) (reductions for members).
Societies: welcome, limited catering.
Catering: bar.
Hotels: Swallow; St Olaves.

E97 **Maldon**

☎(01621) 853212
Beeleigh, Langford, Maldon, Essex
CM9 6LL
2 miles NW of Maldon on B1019, turn
off at Essex Waterworks in Langford.
Meadowland course.
9 holes, 6197 yards, S.S.S.69
Founded 1891
Visitors: welcome weekdays,
(preferably with member evenings)
with h/cap cert.
Green Fee: £15 (£10 with member).
Societies: Mon and Thurs by
arrangement.
Catering: bar; catering by
arrangement.
Hotels: Blue Boar.

E98 **Manor of Groves Golf & Country Club**

☎(01279) 722333 (Club), **Hotels:**
600777
High Wych, Sawbridgeworth, Herts
CM21 0LA
1 mile N of Harlow.

Parkland course.
18 holes, 6280 yards, S.S.S.70
Designed by S. Sharer.
Founded 1991
Visitors: welcome any time Mon-Fri,
after 12am weekends; must play of
yellow tees unless professional
arrangement made.
Green Fee: WD £18 per round, £30
per day; WE £25.
Societies: any day; numbers
restricted weekends; corporate days
a speciality.
Catering: restaurant, function room
for 200, banqueting.
Snooker, swimming pool.
Hotels: Own hotel on site; weekend
golfing breaks available, reduced
rates for residents.

E99 **Maylands Golf & Country Club**

☎(01708) 373080, 346466
Colchester Rd, Harold Park, Romford,
Essex RM3 0AZ
On A12 between Romford and
Brentwood; M25 exit 28 towards
London, take next U-turn for
entrance.
Undulating parkland course.
18 holes, 6351 yards, S.S.S.70
Designed by Colt, Alison and
Morrison.
Founded 1936
Visitors: welcome weekdays with
member or with letter of introduction
or membership certificate.
Green Fee: WD £20 per round, £30
per day (half price with member); WE
£30 per round (£14 with member),
£40 per day (£18 with member).
Societies: welcome Mon, Wed, Fri;
min 20, max 40; includes meals and
36 holes.
Catering: restaurant and bar.
Hotels: Post House, Marygreen
Lodge.

E100 **Mid-Herts**

☎(01582) 832242
Gustard Wood, Wheathampstead, St
Albans, Herts AL4 8RS
On B651 6 miles N of St Albans.
Heathland/parkland course.
18 holes, 6060 yards, S.S.S.69
Founded 1893
Visitors: Tues not before 1pm;
weekends, Bank Holidays only with
member.
Green Fee: WD £21 per round, £31
per day.
Societies: welcome Thurs, Fri only.
Catering: full facilities.
Hotels: St Michaels Manor.

E101 Mill Green

☎(01707) 276900
Gypsy Lane, Welwyn Garden City,
Herts AL7 4TY
Between Welwyn and Hatfield via
A1(M), A404 and A1000.
Parkland/woodland course.
18 holes, 6615 yards, Par 72; 9 holes
Par 3.
Designed by Peter Alliss and Clive
Clark.
Founded 1994
Visitors: welcome.
Green Fee: WD £27.50 per round,
£50 per day; WE & BH £32.50 per
round.
Societies: welcome by arrangement;
prices on application.
Catering: bar and bar snacks, à la
carte restaurant.
Hotels: The Comet.

E102 Mill Hill

☎(0181) 959 2282, Sec 959 2339,
Pro 959 7261, Fax 906 0731
100 Barnet Way, Mill Hill, London
NW7 3AL
From junction of A1/A41; going N,
immediately filter right and cross into
Marsh Lane, after 0.5 mile turn left
into Hankins Lane, leading to
clubhouse; going S, 1 mile from
Stirling Corner turn left into
clubhouse.
Parkland course.
18 holes, 6247 yards, S.S.S.70
Designed by J.F. Abercromby (1931
remodelled by H.S. Colt)
Founded 1925
Visitors: welcome weekdays,
weekends reservations only.
Green Fee: WD £21 per round, £27
per day; WE £30.
Societies: welcome Mon, Wed, Fri.
Catering: daily.
Snooker, practice ground.
Hotels: Jarvis; Hilton National.

E103 Moor Park

☎(01923) 773146
(Sec/reservations), Pro 774113, Fax
777109
Rickmansworth, Herts WD3 1QN
Situated on A404 between
Rickmansworth and Northwood, 0.75
mile from Moor Park tube station).
Undulating parkland course.
High, 18 holes, 6700 yards, S.S.S.72;
West, 18 holes, 5700 yards, S.S.S.68
Designed by H.S. Colt.
Founded 1923
Visitors: welcome weekdays but
must book in advance, h/caps
required; not weekends.

Green Fee: High £30, West £25.
Societies: welcome weekdays by
arrangement.
Catering: full facilities.
Hotels: Bedford Arms.

E104 Muswell Hill

☎(0181) 888 1764 (Sec), Pro 888
8046
Rhodes Ave, Wood Green, London
N22 4UT
1 mile from Bounds Green tube
station, 1.5 miles from N Circular Rd.
Undulating course.
18 holes, 6438 yards, S.S.S.71
Founded 1893
Visitors: weekdays restricted;
weekends and Bank Holidays limited
bookings through Pro.
Green Fee: WD £23 per round, £33
per day.
Societies: welcome weekdays by
arrangement.
Catering: meals and snacks, bar.
Hotels: Ragland Hall.

E105 The Nazeing

☎(01992) 893798 (Bookings),
Clubhouse 893915
Middle St, Nazeing, Essex EN9 2LW
From M25 exit 26 take B194 N to
Nazeing, then right at lights, course is
on left. From A10 at Broxbourne
lights, take Nazeing road to course,
approx. 10 mins.
Parkland course.
18 holes, 6598 yards, S.S.S.71
Designed by Martin Gillett.
Founded 1990
Visitors: weekdays after 8.30 am,
experienced golfers only; strict dress-
code required; weekends pm only.
Green Fee: WD £20; WE £28.
Societies: welcome Mon, Tues,
Thurs and Fri, details on application.
Catering: lounge bar, spike bar,
restaurant, snacks available all day.
Open-air continental style driving
range, 9-hole putting green.
Hotels: Moat House (Harlow).

E106 North Middlesex

☎(0181) 445 1604 (Manager), Pro
445 3060
The Manor House, Friern Barnet
Lane, Whetstone, London N20 0NL
A1000 5 miles N of Finchley; 5 miles
S of M25 junction 23 via A1081.
Undulating parkland course (with 2
large ponds).
18 holes, 5611 yards, S.S.S.67
Designed by Willie Park Jnr.
Founded 1928

Visitors: welcome weekdays, h/cap
cert desirable; weekends pm only
(phone in advance).
Green Fee: WD £22 per round,
£27.50 per day; WE £30.
Societies: welcome weekdays by
arrangement.
Catering: full facilities (old manor
house with terrace overlooking 18th).
Hotels: Raglan Hall (Muswell Hill).

E107 North Weald Golf Club

☎(01992) 522118, Fax 522881
Rayley Lane, North Weald, Essex
CM16 6AR
From M25 exit 27 N on M11 to
junction 7 Harlow turn off, E for 1 mile
on A414; course sits astride A414.
Parkland course.
18 holes, 6265 yards, S.S.S.71
Designed by Peter Alliss and Clive
Clark.
Founded 1995
Visitors: welcome weekdays on
application.
Green Fee: on application.
Societies: welcome by prior
arrangement.
Catering: full facilities.

E108 Northwood

☎(01923) 821384
Rickmansworth Rd, Northwood,
Middx HA6 2QW
On main road between Northwood
Hills and Rickmansworth A404.
Parkland course.
18 holes, 6553 yards, S.S.S.71
Designed by James Braid.
Founded 1891
Visitors: welcome weekdays only.
Green Fee: £24 per round, £31 per
day.
Societies: Mon and Thursday by
arrangement.
Catering: restaurant facilities
available.
Hotels: Tudor Lodge (Eastcote).

E109 Old Fold Manor

☎(0181) 440 9185, Pro 440 7488
Hadley Green, Barnet, Herts EN5
4QN
On Potters Bar road (A1000) 0.25
mile from Barnet; M25 junction 23.
Parkland course.
18 holes, 6481 yards, S.S.S.71
Founded 1910
Visitors: welcome on weekdays, with
member only at weekends; Public
Days Mon and Wed; h/cap certs
required.

Moor Park and Sandy Lodge

In one of the popular television programmes which John Betjeman narrated towards the end of his life, he highlighted the Metropolitan line and the station of Moor Park and Sandy Lodge, shared in its earliest days largely for the convenience of golfers. While the walk to Moor Park involves quite a lengthy climb, Sandy Lodge is no more than a long pitch shot from the station which, until it was elaborately modernised, was a somewhat odd looking basic wooden structure. Sandy Lodge is a most pleasant course, remembered by most golfers for the carry over large, deep bunkers to the 1st green, a prominent sleeper-faced bunker at the 2nd, consecutive short holes at the 7th and 8th and a short hole to finish across a quarry that is much less stark than it used to be.

It also has its 16th green beside the railway and a par 5 17th alongside a wood. Laddie Lucas and Alec Hill were its best known members and John Jacobs its best known professional. It was at Sandy Lodge that Jacobs built up his considerable reputation as a teacher. In the days when he was a regular figure on the tournament circuit, the opening tournament of what was then a more truncated season, was invariably at Moor Park. The architectural splendour of the clubhouse makes it one of the most photographed in the world.

In addition to the professional tournaments which were always attractions for school boys in the Easter holidays, the Carris Trophy was certainly one of the blue riband events of junior golf.

It involved a round on each of the High and West courses, the High regarded as the sterner of the tests, like Sandy Lodge ending with a short hole at which Harold Henning once earned £1,000, a small fortune in the 1960s, during the Esso Round Robin event.

The High and West epitomise the characteristics of parkland golf although the High is unusually undulating, a factor that adds to the problems it presents. The West dominates the front of the clubhouse, the 1st tee and 18th green on the High being quite a step from its noble pillars. The 1st, crossing the road, has a narrow-looking fairway, lined on the right by stately trees, while the 2nd has another demanding drive. If it is not held up sufficiently on the left, it will fall to the right, adding suitable problems to the second shot. But the problem of guardian bunkers at the green is nothing compared to the short 3rd, whose green is virtually encircled.

From the 4th green, one of the lowest points, the next couple of fairways border elegant houses into which it is easy to slice. The 8th green lies beside a pond which, before water features became so fashionable, caused quite a stir. The 9th is one of the best holes, with an awkward green to hit and an expensive one to miss. The inward nine begins near one of the main entrances to the park with a short hole, where I once saw Arthur Havers, the Club's professional, hole-in-one during a tournament.

The 11th, 12th and 13th confront some of the severer slopes and hollows while the 14th green is remembered for being very much wider than it is deep. There is an inviting downhill second to the 15th, an up and back element about the 16th and 17th and finally a downhill short hole where out of bounds lurks on the right.

It is a hole which, mercifully, cannot be lengthened by more than a few yards. The modern giants may rarely need more than a lofted iron from the tee but it is not always easy to judge, the fear of being short often leading to being just that. It is plain to see what must be done but last holes impose a pressure all their own and many a bold ambition has been ambushed in the quest for glory.

Green Fee: WD £10 (Mon/Wed), £20 (Tues/Thurs/Fri); WE £25.
Societies: welcome Thurs, Fri only.
Catering: meals served except Mon and Wed.
Snooker room.
Hotels: The Hadley.

E110 Orsett
☎(01375) 891352
Brentwood Rd, Orsett, Essex RM16 3DS
On A128 400 yards from A13 towards Chadwell St Mary.
Heathland course.
18 holes, 6614 yards, S.S.S.72
Designed by James Braid.
Founded 1899
Visitors: weekdays by prior arrangement; h/cap certificates required.
Green Fee: WD £20 per round, £30 per day.
Societies: Mon, Tues, Wed (min. 20, max. 40).
Catering: full facilities.
Hotels: White Crofts; Plough Motel; Stifford Moat House; Orsett Hall.

E111 Panshanger
☎(01707) 333350
Old Herns Lane, Welwyn Garden City, Herts AL7 2ED.
Off B1000 close to A1, 1 mile NE of town.
Public undulating parkland course.
18 holes, 6347 yards, S.S.S.70
Founded 1976
Visitors: unrestricted.
Green Fee: WD £10.50, WE £12.50.
Societies: welcome by prior arrangement.
Catering: lunch every day.
Hotels: Homestead Court.

E112 Perivale Park
☎(0181) 575 7116
Stockdove Way, Argyle Road, Greenford, Middx UB6 8EN
On Ruislip Rd East between Greenford and Perivale, entrance from Argyle Rd.
Public parkland course.
9 holes, 2648 yards, S.S.S.65
Founded 1932
Visitors: welcome, no restrictions.
Green Fee: WD £4.40 (9 holes), £8.80 (18 holes); WE £6.50 (9 holes), £11.95 (18 holes).
Societies: none.
Catering: cafeteria serving meals, tea, coffee etc; no bar.
Hotels: Kenton (Hanger Hill).

E113 Pinner Hill
☎(0181) 866 0963, Pro 866 2109
Southview Rd, Pinner Hill, Middx HA5 3YA
From Pinner Green take Pinner Hill Rd, follow signs to residential estate.
Hilly parkland course with views over London and Harrow on the Hill.
18 holes, 6266 yards, S.S.S.70
Designed by J.H. Taylor and Hawtree.
Founded 1928
Visitors: Wed and Thurs unrestricted; Mon, Tues, Fri with h/cap cert; Sat h/cap 23 or less, by arrangement; no visitors Sun.
Green Fee: WD £25; WE £32.
Societies: welcome Mon, Tues, Fri by arrangement; full catering inc evening meal.
Catering: full except Wed and Thurs (stud bar only).
Hotels: The Barn (Ruislip).

E114 Pipps Hill
☎(01268) 271571; Golfers Arms: 523456
Cranes Farm Rd, Basildon, Essex SS14 3DG
A127 or A13, Basildon turnoff; off A1235.
Public meadowland course; part of Pipps Hill Leisure Complex.
9 holes, 2829 yards, S.S.S.67
Visitors: welcome, 18 holes only at weekends.
Green Fee: £5.50 (9 holes), £9.50 (18 holes).
Societies: welcome weekdays.
Catering: full catering facilities available; bars, restaurant, private rooms seating up to 750.
Driving range, swimming, squash, snooker, tennis.
Hotels: Forte Posthouse (in same complex)

E115 Porters Park
☎(01923) 854127 (Manager)
Shenley Hill, Radlett, Herts WD7 7AZ
From M25 junction 22 to Radlett via A5183, turn at rail station, 0.5 mile to top of Shenley Hill.
Undulating parkland course.
18 holes, 6313 yards, S.S.S.70
Founded 1899
Visitors: welcome weekdays; h/cap cert required, telephone 24 hours in advance; members guests only at weekends.
Green Fee: £28 per round, £42 per day.
Societies: Wed, Thurs only, min 20 max 50, £68 inclusive.

Catering: own chef, full catering for societies; breakfast (ordered in advance), comprehensive bar menu.
2 Practice grounds
Hotels: Red Lion.

E116 Potters Bar
☎(01707) 652020, Fax 655051
Darkes Lane, Potters Bar, Herts EN6 1DE
M25 exit 24, follow signs Potters Bar; turn right at 2nd lights into Darkes Lane; entrance 400 yards on left.
Undulating parkland course.
18 holes, 6279 yards, S.S.S.70
Designed by James Braid.
Founded 1923
Visitors: welcome weekdays, must have current h/cap cert; members guests only at weekends.
Green Fee: £20 per round, £30 per day.
Societies: Mon, Tues and Fri by arrangement.
Catering: lunch served daily.
Hotels: South Mimms Crest.

E117 Quietwaters
☎(01621) 868888
Colchester Rd, Tolleshunt Knights, Maldon, Essex CM9 8HX
B1026 S of Colchester.
Seaside courses.
Links, 18 holes, 6250 yards, S.S.S.70; Lakes, 18 holes, 6767 yards S.S.S.72
Founded 1974 (extended 1990)
Visitors: welcome at most times; not Sun am on Links.
Green Fee: WD £18 (Links), £25 (Lakes); WE £22.50 (Links), £30 (Lakes).
Societies: welcome weekdays only.
Catering: full facilities, bars and dining room.
Indoor and outdoor tennis, bowls, squash, health and fitness, banqueting.
Hotels: Fivelakes Hotel.

E118 Redbourn
☎(01582) 793493 (Pro), Sec 792150, Bar: 793363
Kinsbourne Green Lane, Redbourn, Herts AL3 7QA
S of Ml at junction 9 to A5, turn left after 1 mile down Luton Lane.
Parkland courses.
18 holes, 6506 yards, S.S.S.71; 9 holes, 1361 yards, Par 27 (public course)
Designed by H. Stovin.
Founded 1971

Visitors: welcome weekdays; weekends pm only.
Green Fee: WD £14 (£11 with member); WE & BH £18.
Societies: Mon-Thurs.
Catering: fully licensed bar, bar snacks; restaurant meals daily by arrangement; functions catered for. Driving range.
Hotels: Aubrey Park.

E119 Rickmansworth
☎(01923) 775278
Moor Lane, Rickmansworth, Herts WD3 1QL
A4145, 0.5 mile S of town.
Undulating municipal parkland course.
18 holes, 4469 yards, S.S.S.62
Visitors: welcome.
Green Fee: WD £8.50; WE £12.
Societies: catered for weekdays.
Catering: meals all day, licensed.
Hotels: Bedford Arms.

E120 Risebridge (Havering)
☎(01708) 741429
Risebridge Chase, Lower Bedfords Rd, Romford, Essex RM1 4DG
2 miles from Gallows Corner and Romford station.
Public parkland course.
18 holes, 5310 yards, S.S.S.70
Visitors: welcome; bookings for weekends.
Green Fee: WD £9.20; WE £11.20.
Societies: welcome by prior arrangement.
Catering: snacks daily.
Pitch & Putt.
Hotels: Brentwood Post Hotel.

E121 Rochford Hundred
☎(01702) 544302, Pro 548968
Rochford Hall, Hall Rd, Rochford, Essex SS4 1NW
A127 to Southend, follow signs to airport, then to Rochford; bypass Rochford, turn left under railway bridge, club 400 yards on left.
Parkland course
18 holes, 6302 yards, S.S.S.69
Designed by James Braid.
Founded 1893
Visitors: welcome weekdays with h/cap certificate (Tues Ladies Day); with member only at weekends.
Green Fee: £21 (£10 with member).
Societies: by arrangement on Wed or Thurs.
Catering: lunch only Mon-Fri.
Hotels: Renouf.

E122 Romford
☎(01708) 740986
Heath Drive, Gidea Park, Romford, Essex RM2 5QB
1.5 miles Romford centre, off A12.
Parkland course
18 holes, 6389 yards, S.S.S.70
Designed by Mackintosh (redesigned by H.S.Colt 1921)
Founded 1894
Visitors: weekdays with h/cap certificate and by arrangement with Pro; with member only at weekends.
Green Fee: £23 per round, £32 per day.
Societies: welcome by arrangement.
Catering: available.
Hotels: Coach House.

E123 Royston
☎(01763) 242696, Pro 243476
Baldock Rd, Royston, Herts SG8 5BG
On A505 on outskirts of town to E, course on Therfield Heath.
Undulating heathland course.
18 holes, 6052 yards, S.S.S.69
Founded 1892
Visitors: welcome weekdays; weekends with member only.
Green Fee: £20 per day.
Societies: by arrangement with Sec.
Catering: full facilities available. Snooker table.
Hotels: Old Bull Inn; The Banyers.

E124 Ruislip
☎(01895) 638835
Ickenham Rd, Ruislip, Middx HA4 7DQ
1 mile N of A40, Hillingdon.
Public parkland course.
18 holes, 5702 yards, S.S.S.68
Designed by Sandy Herd.
Founded 1936
Visitors: welcome, telephoned tee bookings can be made; restricted times weekends for juniors.
Green Fee: WD £10, WE £15.
Societies: catered for every day; booking essential.
Catering: breakfast, lunch, snacks, à la carte menu daily until 10pm. Driving range, snooker (8 tables).
Hotels: Master Brewer.

E125 Saffron Walden
☎(01799) 522786 (Sec), Pro 527728
Windmill Hill, Saffron Walden, Essex CB10 1BX
Take B184 from Stumps Cross roundabout on M11 (junction 9), entrance just before entering town.

Parkland course.
18 holes, 6585 yards, S.S.S.72
Founded 1919
Visitors: welcome weekdays with h/cap certificate; with member weekends and Bank Holidays.
Green Fee: £30.
Societies: welcome Mon, Wed, Thurs.
Catering: lunch available weekdays; evening meals for societies.
Hotels: Saffron.

E126 Sandy Lodge
☎(01923) 825429, Pro 825321
Sandy Lodge Lane, Northwood, Middx HA6 2JD
2 miles S of Watford and 2 miles N of Northwood, immediately adjoining Moor Park station, Metropolitan Line.
Links course.
18 holes, 6347 yards, S.S.S.71
Designed by Harry Vardon.
Founded 1910
Visitors: weekdays; weekends and Bank Holidays with member; h/cap cert required.
Green Fee: WD £28 per round £38 per day.
Societies: welcome Mon, Thurs, Fri.
Catering: full facilities.
Hotels: National Hilton.

E127 Shendish House
☎(01442) 251806
Shendish House, Apsley, Hemel Hempstead, Herts HP3 0AA
M25 junction 20, just before Apsley on A4125.
Parkland course.
9 holes (extending to 18), 6076 yards, S.S.S.69
Designed by Henry Cotton, extension 1994 by Donald Steel.
Founded 1989
Visitors: welcome Mon-Fri, after 12pm weekends; no jeans.
Green Fee: WD £10; WE £14..
Societies: welcome, preferably weekdays.
Catering: full facilities.
9 hole Pitch & Putt, tennis, practice ground.
Hotels: Kings Langley.

E128 South Herts
☎(0181) 445 2035
Links Drive, Totteridge, London N20 8QU
In Totteridge Lane (A5109), 0.5 mile W of junction with High Rd, Whetstone (A1000).
Undulating parkland course.

An 18th Century Georgian Mansion set amidst 182 acres of beautiful parkland just outside the lovely village of Aldbury.

Our championship standard Golf Course has spectacular views of Ashridge Forest & due to its high build specification has not closed due to rain in the last 2.5 years.

Societies, Company Days and Residential Golfing Breaks are our speciality any time of year.

Hotel Golf & Country Club

Stocks Road, Aldbury, Nr. Tring
Herts HP23 5RX
Tel: 01442 851341 Fax: 01442 851253
Professional Shop: 01442 851491

- 18 hole Golf Course
- Resident PGA Golf Professional
- Golf Academy with Golf Range, Chipping & Putting Greens
- Conference Facilities
- Gymnasium
- Heated Outdoor Swimming Pool (May–September)
- Jacuzzi, Steam Room & Sauna
- Tennis Courts • Riding Stables
- Full size Snooker Table
- Two Restaurants

---

18 holes, 6432 yards, S.S.S.71; 9 hole short course.
Designed by Harry Vardon.
Founded 1899
Visitors: weekdays only, recognised h/cap cert required (max. 24); weekends only with member.
Green Fee: £30.
Societies: Wed–Fri; apply in writing.
Catering: full facilities available Tues–Fri.
Hotels: Queen's Moat House (Boreham Wood); The Crest.

E129 Stanmore
☎ (0181) 954 2599
Gordon Ave, Stanmore, Middx HA7 2RL
E of Harrow; entrance off Gordon Ave, via Old Church Lane.
Parkland course.
18 holes, 5860 yards, S.S.S.68
Founded 1893
Visitors: welcome weekdays (Mon and Fri public days); not weekends or Bank Holidays.
Green Fee: WD £10 (Mon and Fri), £25 (Tues, Wed, Thurs).
Societies: welcome weekdays; package available (£50).
Catering: full facilities daily.
Hotels: Grimsdyke; Hilton (Watford).

E130 Stapleford Abbotts
☎ (01708) 370040 (Abbotts tee reservations), Priors Tee: 381103
Horseman's Side, Tysea Hill, Stapleford Abbotts, Essex RM4 1JU
3 miles from M25 Junction 28, off B175 Romford to Ongar, left at Stapleford Abbotts up Tysea Hill.
Parkland course.
Abbotts: 18 holes, 6501 yards, S.S.S.71. Priors: 18 holes, 6129 yards, S.S.S.69. Friars: 9 holes, 1140 yards, Par 3
Designed by Howard Swan.
Founded 1972

Visitors: welcome weekdays by phoning starter.
Green Fee: on application.
Societies: any day by arrangement.
Catering: bar and other facilities, function room.
Sauna.
Hotels: Post House (Harlow).

E131 Stevenage
☎ (01438) 880424
Aston Lane, Aston, Stevenage, Herts SG2 7EL
Leave A1(M) Stevenage South, then on A602 to Hertford, course signposted about 1.5 miles.
Public parkland/meadowland course.
18 holes, 6341 yards, S.S.S.71
Designed by John Jacobs.
Founded 1980
Visitors: welcome every day, but necessary to book at weekends.
Green Fee: WD £8.80; WE £10.80.
Societies: welcome weekdays.
Catering: full meals and bar snacks.
Hotels: Roebuck.

E132 Stock Brook Manor Golf & Country Club
☎ (01277) 653616, 633063
Queens Park Avenue, Stock, Billericay, Essex CM12 0SP
M25 exit 28, A12 to Galleywood/ Stock exit, then B1007 to Stock.
Parkland course.
18 holes, 6728 yards, S.S.S.72; 8 holes, 2997 yards, S.S.S.69.
Designed by Martin Gillett.
Founded 1992
Visitors: welcome; apply for details.
Green Fee: WD £25 (£20 with member); WE £30 (£20 with member).
Societies: welcome; apply for information pack.
Catering: available
Country club, bowls, tennis, croquet.
Hotels: Trust House Forte (Basildon).

E133 Stockley Park
☎ (0181) 813 5700
Uxbridge, Middx UB11 1AQ
5 mins from Heathrow, 2 mins M4 junction 4 towards Uxbridge.
Hilly parkland championship course with young trees.
18 holes, 6548 yards, S.S.S.71
Designed by Robert Trent Jones Snr.
Founded June 1993
Visitors: welcome 7 days, pay-as-you-play; correct dress, no denims, golf shoes required.
Green Fee: WD £26 per round (£14.50 Mon/Tues); WE £33.
Societies: and corporate days, welcome weekdays, booked in advance.
Catering: bar and restaurant.
Hotels: Novotel.

E134 Stocks Hotel & Country Club
☎ (01442) 851341, Pro 851491, Fax 851253
Stocks Rd, Aldbury, Nr Tring, Herts HP23 5RX
In Aldbury village, 2 miles E of Tring.
Parkland course.
18 holes, 6804 yards, S.S.S.73
Designed by Mike Billcliffe.
Founded 1993
Visitors: welcome weekdays, guest of member after 12am weekdays.
Green Fee: WD £30; WE (after 2pm) £40.
Societies: only by appointment.
Catering: 2 restaurants and bar; breakfast, lunch, dinner, banqueting. Health suite, gymnasium, tennis, riding, outdoor heated pool (May–Sept), snooker; practice academy.
Hotels: 18 bed (6 suite) hotel on site.

E135 Stoke-by-Nayland
☎ (01206) 262836
Keepers Lane, Leavenheath, Colchester, Essex CO6 4PZ

A134 from Colchester for 7 miles, B1068 to Stoke-by-Nayland.
Parkland/meadowland course.
18 holes, 6475 yards, S.S.S.71, 18 holes, 6544 yards, S.S.S.71
Founded 1972
Visitors: unrestricted during week; after 11am weekends; must have h/cap cert and club membership.
Green Fee: WD £15 (£10 with member); WE £17.50 (£10 with member); £1.50 meal voucher with visitors rates.
Societies: weekdays only by arrangement.
Catering: full facilities available.
Hotels: The Mill; The Bull.

E136 Strawberry Hill
☎(0181) 894 0165, Pro 898 2082
Wellesley Rd, Twickenham, Middx TW2 5SB
Adjacent to Strawberry Hill station.
Parkland course.
9 holes, 4762 yards, S.S.S.62
Designed by J.H. Taylor.
Founded 1900
Visitors: welcome weekdays only.
Green Fee: WD £20 per round, £25 per day.
Societies: 24 max number considered on application.
Catering: full facilities.
Hotels: several hotels in Richmond.

E137 Sudbury
☎(0181) 902 3713 (Sec), Pro 902 7910
Bridgewater Rd, Wembley, Middx HA0 1AL
At junction of Bridgewater Rd (A4005) and Whitton Ave East (A4090).
Undulating parkland course.
18 holes, 6282 yards, S.S.S.70
Designed by H. Colt.
Founded 1920
Visitors: welcome weekdays with h/cap certificate; Monday open day (no h/cap cert required); weekends with member only.
Green Fee: WD £20 (£10 Mon).
Societies: welcome Tues pm, Wed, Thurs and Fri by appointment.
Catering: full catering service, bar.
Hotels: The Cumberland (Harrow).

E138 Theydon Bois
☎(01992) 813054 (Sec/Fax), Pro 812460
Theydon Rd, Epping, Essex CM16 4EH
Off B172 1 mile S of Epping; M25 exit 26 Waltham Abbey (3 miles).

Undulating woodland course.
18 holes, 5480 yards, S.S.S.68
Designed by James Braid.
Founded 1897
Visitors: must have proof of membership of recognised golf club or society; not Wed, Thurs am; not Sat am, after 2pm on Sun.
Green Fee: WD £23 per round; WE (after 2pm) £20 (phone Pro).
Societies: welcome weekdays by arrangement.
Catering: full facilities available.
Hotels: The Bell.

E139 Thorndon Park
☎(01277) 811666, Sec 810345, Pro 810736
Ingrave, Brentwood, Essex CM13 3RH
2 miles SE of Brentwood on A128.
Parkland course.
18 holes, 6481 yards, S.S.S.71
Designed by H. Colt.
Founded 1920
Visitors: welcome weekdays and with member weekends; h/cap certificates required at all times.
Green Fee: WD £30; WE £45.
Societies: catered for Tues and Fri.
Catering: meals served weekdays.
Hotels: Post House.

E140 Thorpe Hall
☎(01702) 582205
Thorpe Hall Ave, Thorpe Bay, Essex SS1 3AT
On seafront, about 2 miles E of Southend Pier.
Parkland/meadowland course.
18 holes, 6286 yards, S.S.S.71
Founded 1907
Visitors: welcome weekdays with club h/cap; not weekends unless with member.
Green Fee: WD £30.
Societies: catered for Fri only by arrangement.
Catering: lunch served except Mon.
Snooker, squash, sauna.
Hotels: Roslyn.

E141 Three Rivers Golf and Country Club
☎(01621) 828631, Fax 828060
Stow Rd, Cold Norton, Nr Chelmsford, Essex CM3 6RR
10 miles from Chelmsford on B1012 via A12, A130, A132.
Parkland course.
Kings 18 holes, 6536 yards, Par 73; Queens 9 holes, 2142 yards, Par 54
Designed by Fred Hawtree.

Founded 1973
Visitors: welcome weekdays (advisable to phone); weekends only with member.
Green Fee: WD £19 per round, £25 per day; WE £17 with member.
Societies: welcome weekdays by arrangement.
Catering: full restaurant facilities. Squash, tennis, snooker, sauna.
Hotels: Three Rivers (limited); The Lodge; Oakland Hotel.

E142 Toothill
☎(01277) 365747
School Road, Toot Hill, Ongar, Essex CM5 9PU
Between Ongar and Epping.
Parkland course.
18 holes, 6053 yards, S.S.S.69
Designed by Martin Gillett.
Founded Sept 1991
Visitors: welcome weekdays, h/cap card necessary; weekends only with member.
Green Fee: WD £25 (£15 with member), WE (with member) £20.
Societies: welcome Tues and Thurs.
Catering: full facilities.
Hotels: Trust House Forte (Brentwood).

E143 Top Meadow
☎(01708) 852239, Pro 859545
Fen Lane, North Ockendon, Essex RM14 3PR
Off B186 in North Ockendon.
Parkland course.
18 holes, 5734 yards, S.S.S. 67
Founded 1986
Visitors: welcome weekdays; only with member at weekends.
Green Fee: WD £12.
Societies: welcome weekdays by advance booking.
Catering: bar and restaurant. Driving range.
Hotels: Top Meadow Guest House.

E144 Towerlands
☎(01376) 347951
Panfield Rd, Braintree, Essex CM7 5BJ
Course on B1053 out of Braintree.
Undulating meadowland course.
9 holes, 5406 yards, S.S.S.66
Designed by G.R. Shiels.
Founded 1985
Visitors: welcome anytime, not before 12.30pm Sat, Sun.
Green Fee: on application.
Societies: welcome any time by arrangement.

Catering: full bar and restaurant.
Driving range, 3 squash courts,
sports hall, equestrian centre, indoor
bowls.

E145 **Trent Park**

☎(0181) 366 7432
Bramley Rd, Oakwood, London N14
4UW.
Near Oakwood tube station
(Piccadilly Line).
Public parkland course.
18 holes, 6085 yards, S.S.S.69
Founded 1973
Visitors: welcome anytime; booking
required (members book 7 days in
advance; non-members 2 days)
Green Fee: WD £10.60; WE £13.50.
Societies: Mon-Fri only; brochure
available on request.
Catering: bar, snacks, meals by
arrangement.
Diving range.
Hotels: West Lodge (Hadleywood).

E146 **Tudor Park Sports Ground**

☎(0181) 441 2261, Manager: 203
4187, Ticket Office: 449 0282
Clifford Rd, New Barnet, Herts
Off Potters Rd.
Public parkland course.
9 holes, 1836 yards, S.S.S. 57
Visitors: welcome.
Green Fee: apply for details.
Catering: clubhouse for members
only.

E147 **Twickenham Park**

☎(0181) 783 1698
Staines Rd, Twickenham, Middx TW2
5JD
On A305 near Hope & Anchor
roundabout.
Municipal parkland course.
9 holes, 3109 yards, S.S.S.69
Designed by Charles Lawrie.
Founded 1977
Visitors: welcome.
Green Fee: WD £6 (9 holes); WE £7.
Societies: welcome by arrangement.
Catering: full licensed bar, snacks;
function room.
Driving range.
Hotels: Richmond Gate.

E148 **Upminster**

☎(01708) 222788
114 Hall Lane, Upminster, Essex
RM14 1AU
A127 towards Southend; M25
junction 29.

Parkland course.
18 holes, 6076 yards, S.S.S.69
Designed by H.A. Colt.
Founded 1927
Visitors: weekdays by arrangement if
member of recognised club with
h/cap certificate.
Green Fee: WD £25 per round, £30
per day.
Societies: welcome Wed-Fri by
arrangement; Ladies Day Tues; small
societies possibly on Mon and Tues.
Catering: meals except Mon.
Hotels: Marygreen Manor
(Brentwood); Trust House Forte; Post
House.

E149 **Verulam**

☎(01727) 853327, Fax 812201
London Rd, St Albans, Herts AL1
1JG
A1081 to St Albans, near M25, M10,
M1.
Parkland course.
18 holes, 6448 yards, S.S.S.71
Designed by James Braid
Founded 1905
Visitors: welcome weekdays, except
Wed am.
Green Fee: WD £25 per round, £30
per day (Mon £12 per round, £20 per
day).
Societies: Tues, Thurs, Fri.
Catering: bar snacks available.
Hotels: Sopwell House.

E150 **Wanstead**

☎(0181) 989 3938
Overton Drive, Wanstead, London
E11 2LW
Off A12 at Wanstead station, right
into The Green into St Mary's Ave,
left at T-junction at St Mary's Church.
Parkland course.
18 holes, 6004 yards, S.S.S.69
Founded 1893
Visitors: welcome Mon, Tues, Fri by
prior arrangement; not weekends.
Green Fee: £25 per day.
Societies: welcome by arrangement
Mon, Tues, Fri only.
Catering: bar and restaurant.
Hotels: Prince Regent (Woodford
Bridge); Travel Lodge.

E151 **Warley Park**

☎(01277) 224891, Pro 200441
Magpie Lane, Little Warley,
Brentwood, Essex CM13 3DX
Off M25 junction 29, A127 Southend,
immediately left Gt Warley, left, 1st
right, right into Magpie Lane (6 mins
from M25).

Undulating parkland course.
27 holes (3 x 9), played 1-2,1-3,2-3;
1, 2988 yards, 2, 2979 yards, 3, 3244
yards.
Designed by R. Plumbridge.
Founded 1975
Visitors: welcome with h/cap cert.
Green Fee: £24 per round, £36 per
day.
Societies: welcome by arrangement.
Catering: 1st class restaurant.
Large practice ground.
Hotels: Brentwood Post House.

E152 **Warren**

☎(012454) 223258, Pro 224662,
Fax 223989
Woodham Walter, Maldon, Essex
CM9 6RW
A414 6 miles E of Chelmsford
towards Maldon.
Undulating parkland course.
18 holes, 6250 yards, S.S.S.70
Founded 1934
Visitors: welcome weekdays and
weekends after 2pm; booking
essential.
Green Fee: WD £25 per round, £30
per day; WE £30.
Societies: Mon, Tues, Thurs, Fri.
Catering: full facilities 7 days.
Hotels: Pontlands Park; Blue Boar.

E153 **Welwyn Garden City**

☎(01707) 325243
Mannicotts, High Oaks Rd, Welwyn
Garden City, Herts AL8 7BP
Leave A1(M) at junction 4, take B197
Stanborough to Valley Road.
Undulating parkland course.
18 holes, 6074 yards, S.S.S.69
Designed by Hawtree and Son.
Founded 1922
Visitors: welcome weekdays; not
Sun.
Green Fee: WD £25 (£15 with
member); Sat £33 (£20 with
member).
Societies: welcome Wed and Thur
only.
Catering: bar snacks, lunches,
dinners.
Hotels: The Clock.

E154 **West Essex**

☎(0181) 529 7558, Pro 529 4367,
Catering: 529 0517
Bury Rd, Sewardstonebury,
Chingford, London E4 7QL
Off A11, 1.5 miles from Chingford
station; M25 junction 26.
Parkland course.
18 holes, 6289 yards, S.S.S.70

Designed by James Braid.
Founded 1900
Visitors: welcome weekdays; with member only Thurs pm, Tues after 11am and weekends.
Green Fee: £25 per round, £30 per day, (£12.50 with member).
Societies: welcome Mon, Wed, Fri.
Catering: lunches by arrangement.
Hotels: Roebuck.

E155 **West Herts**

☎(01923) 236484
Cassiobury Park, Watford, Herts WD1 7SL
2 miles from Watford on A412; right fork at Two Bridges Inn, right into Linksway, right at end and right into Rouseborn Lane; entrance 200 yards on left.
Parkland course.
18 holes, 6488 yards, S.S.S.71
Designed by Tom Morris & Harry Vardon.
Founded 1890
Visitors: welcome weekdays with h/cap certificate; weekends with member only.
Green Fee: £20 per round, £30 per day.
Societies: welcome Wed and Fri.
Catering: full facilities.
Hotels: Dean Park.

E156 **West Middlesex**

☎(0181) 574 3450 (Sec), Pro 574 1800
Greenford Rd, Southall, Middx UB1 3EE
A40 from Central London to Greenford, take left exit off roundabout, 2 miles straight down road.
Undulating parkland course.
18 holes, 6242 yards, S.S.S.70
Designed by James Braid.
Founded 1891
Visitors: welcome on weekdays, Mon and Wed are Public days.
Green Fee: Mon and Wed £10, Tues, Thurs, Fri £15.50.

Societies: welcome weekdays by arrangement.
Catering: hot and cold snacks daily, 3 course meals booked in advance.

E157 **Whipsnade Park**

☎(01442) 842330
Studham Lane, Dagnall, Herts HP4 1RH.
Off M1 at junction 9 between villages of Dagnall and Studham.
Parkland course.
18 holes, 6800 yards, S.S.S.72
Founded 1974
Visitors: welcome weekdays; only with member at weekends.
Green Fee: £21 per round, £31 per day.
Societies: welcome except Mon and weekends.
Catering: restaurant and bar snacks, except Mon.
Hotels: Post House (Hemel Hempstead).

E158 **Whitehill**

☎(01920) 438495
Dane End, Ware, Herts SG12 0JS
Turn left at Happy Eater on A10 from London.
Undulating course.
18 holes, 6681 yards, S.S.S.72
Designed by Golf Landscapes.
Founded May 1990
Visitors: official club h/cap required or competence certificate from Whitehill Pros.
Green Fee: WD £15; WE £18.
Societies: any time by appointment.
Catering: licensed bar, restaurant.
Driving range, practice bunker and grass practice area; beginners classes; snooker.
Hotels: Vintage Corner Hotel.

E159 **Whitewebbs**

☎(0181) 363 2951, Booking Office: 363 4454
Beggars Hollow, Clay Hill, Enfield, Middx EN2 9JN

1 mile N of Enfield town.
Public parkland course.
18 holes, 5800 yards, S.S.S.68
Founded 1932
Visitors: welcome; very busy course, queuing for playing times.
Green Fee: WD £10.60; WE £12.60.
Societies: welcome by arrangement.
Catering: Public cafe on site.
Nature trails and horse riding.
Hotels: Royal Chase.

E160 **Woodford**

☎(0181) 504 0553, Sec 504 3330, Pro 504 4254
2 Sunset Ave, Woodford Green, Essex IG8 0ST
A11 to Woodford Green, near Castle public house; M11 to junction 4.
Parkland course.
9 holes, 5806 yards, S.S.S.68
Founded 1890
Visitors: welcome weekdays except Tues, Sat and Sun am (phone in advance).
Green Fee: £15 per round (£10 after 12 am).
Societies: welcome by arrangement.
Catering: snacks served and meals by arrangement.
Hotels: The Castle.

E161 **Wyke Green**

☎(0181) 560 8777 (Sec), Pro 847 0685
Syon Lane, Isleworth, Middx TW7 5PT
From Gillette Corner on A4 Great West Rd, turn NW into Syon Lane; club 0.5 mile on right.
Parkland course.
18 holes, 6211 yards, S.S.S.70
Designed by W.H. Tate.
Founded 1928
Visitors: welcome by arrangement, h/cap cert required.
Green Fee: WD £28; WE £42.
Societies: welcome by prior appointment.
Catering: full facilities.
Hotels: Master Robert.

F

BERKSHIRE, BUCKINGHAMSHIRE, OXFORDSHIRE

In the early days of county golf, Berkshire, Buckinghamshire and Oxfordshire were so thin on the ground in terms of courses that an amalgamation was approved. Nowadays, they can boast as many Clubs as Surrey and more than any other county except Lancashire and Yorkshire but, as you would expect from an area which stretches from the verge of London to Gloucestershire,there is plenty of variety.

Castle Royle, Harleyford, Mill Ride, Mentmore, Waterstock, Lambourne, Ryehill and the Oxfordshire represent the newer front, although the Oxfordshire does not admit casual green fee payers. It is part of the Nitto Kogyo Company which owns Turnberry and lies in the heart of the countryside near Thame, a stone's throw from the M40. Opened in 1993, it has already housed a major event on the Women's professional tour and early in 1995 was preparing for the Benson and Hedges tournament on the men's European tour.

Another established venue for both men's and women's tours is Woburn with its Duke's and Duchess courses now twenty years old. Not far away, Abbey Hill and Windmill Hill extol the virtues of the more public type of operation. There is Downshire near Bracknell, Farnham Park and Wexham Park near Slough, Hawthorn Hill near Maidenhead and Cherwell Edge near Banbury. More and more such courses are necessary if the demands of the army of new golfers can come close to being met.

There is nothing better than a day's golf over the Red and Blue courses at the Berkshire with a marvellous lunch to rebuild the spirits if the heather has taken its toll. The same goes for Swinley Forest across the road where the Walter Mitty in you imagines it to be your own private course while the character of heather and birch is echoed by East Berks at Crowthorne, another delightful place to play.

Stoke Poges, Denham and Beaconsfield form a convenient triangle for those staying in the area and seeking a change of scene, the clubhouses at Denham and Beaconsfield lending a cosy, rural air unusual so close to London. Out beyond Harewood Downs and Amersham, the Vale of Aylesbury beckons, where Ellesborough, near Chequers, offers an ideal stopping place for 18-holes with an unmistakable feeling of having got away from it all.

Over in Berkshire again, Maidenhead, Sonning, Temple and Calcot are always worth a visit while Newbury Crookham is one of the oldest courses in England. Mill Ride at North Ascot, a mile or so from the Berkshire, is now well established. Travellers through Pangbourne along the Thames Valley should look out for Goring & Streatley. Oxfordshire's best known names are Huntercombe and Frilford Heath, the latter with three courses of charm and challenge. Frilford has housed a number of important events including the 1987 English championship for men. Since its earliest days, Huntercombe has assumed a more enclosed look, the appearance of the common now liberally laced with trees and bushes. Its distinctive greens bear the hallmark of Willie Park, designer of the Old course at Sunningdale who used to declare that "a man who can putt is a match for anyone".

One of the most attractive new courses is Harleyford,on the road out of Marlow towards Henley. It is part of the Harleyford Estate which runs down to the Thames, the higher part looking out across the river to Temple which is situated on the Henley road out of Maidenhead.

F1 **Abbey Hill**
☎(01908) 562566 (Club), Pro shop 563845
Monks Way, Two Mile Ash, Stony Stratford, Milton Keynes MK8 8AA
2 miles S of Stony Stratford.
Public meadowland course.
18 holes, 6143 yards, S.S.S.69
Founded 1975
Visitors: unrestricted.
Green Fee: apply for details.
Societies: on application.
Catering: meals and bar snacks.
Driving range.

F2 **Aspect Park**
☎(01491) 577562, Sec 578306
Remenham Hill, Henley on Thames, Oxon RG9 3EH
On A423 E of Henley, off M4 junction 8/9.
Parkland course.
18 holes, 6283 yards, S.S.S.71
Visitors: welcome Mon-Fri.
Green Fee: apply for details.
Societies: Mon-Fri by prior arrangement.
Catering: available; function rooms.
Driving range (12 open bays, green fee payers only).
Hotels: Red Lion (Henley).

F3 **Aylesbury Golf Centre**
☎(01296) 393644
Hulcott Lane, Bierton, Aylesbury, Bucks HP22 5GA
Just off A418 1 mile N of Aylesbury.
Public parkland course.
9 holes, S.S.S.68
Designed by A.R. Taylor.
Founded May 1991
Visitors: welcome any day.
Green Fee: WD £9; WE £10.
Societies: Mon-Fri.
Catering: licensed bar and restaurant.
Driving range.
Hotels: Watermead; Forte Crest.

F4 **Aylesbury Park**
☎(01296) 399196 (Club/Fax)
Oxford Road, Aylesbury, Bucks HP17 8QQ
Parkland course
18 holes, 6146 yards, S.S.S.69
Designed by Hawtree & Son
Founded 1996

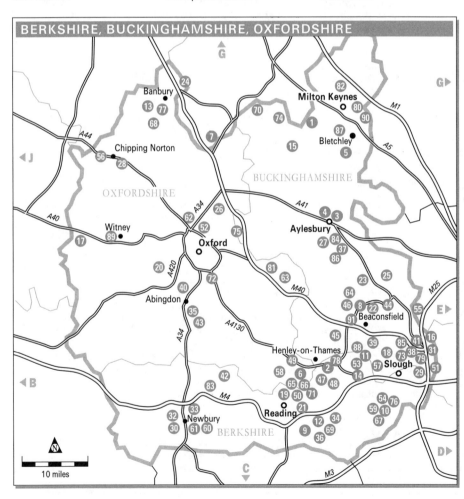

BERKSHIRE, BUCKINGHAMSHIRE, OXFORDSHIRE

10 miles

Visitors: welcome, book up to 7 days in advance.
Green Fee: apply for details.
Societies: by arrangement.
Catering: light snacks available.

F5 Aylesbury Vale
☎(01525) 240196 (Sec), Pro 240197
Stewkley Rd, Wing, Leighton Buzzard, Beds LU7 0UJ
Countryside location between Milton Keynes, Aylesbury and Leighton Buzzard; from village of Wing on A418 turn N towards Stewkley; travel for 1.75 miles and course is on right.
Undulating parkland course.
18 holes, 6622 yards, S.S.S.72
Designed by Don Wright and Mick Robinson.
Founded 1991
Visitors: welcome at all times but please phone in advance; h/cap certs not necessary but no hackers please; normal dress standards - no jeans, T-shirts or trainers.
Green Fee: WD £12; WE & BH £18.50.
Societies: welcome weekdays, 36 holes £19; please phone Sec.
Catering: first floor and downstairs bars, light snacks and home-made dishes.
Driving range.
Hotels: Village Green (Northall).

F6 Badgemore Park
☎(01491) 572206 (Sec), Club 573667, Pro 574175.
Badgemore Park, Henley-on-Thames, Oxon RG9 4NR
Leave M4 at junction 8/9 on Henley and Oxford spur, over river into Henley, straight through town (leaving Town Hall on right), after 0.75 mile on right hand side.

Parkland course.
18 holes, 6112 yards, S.S.S.69
Designed by Bob Sandow.
Founded July 1972
Visitors: welcome weekdays only.
Green Fee: WD £27 per day; £21 per round.
Societies: weekdays only, by arrangement.
Catering: full facilities available.
Hotels: Red Lion; Royal; Little White Hart.

F7 Banbury
☎(01295) 810419 (Club), Fax 810056
Aynho Road, Adderbury, Banbury, Oxon OX17 3NT
5 miles S of Banbury on the B4100.
10 mins from J10 M40.
Parkland course.
18 holes, 6365 yards, S.S.S.70
Founded 1994
Visitors: welcome.
Green Fee: WD £8 (18 holes); WE £10 (18 holes).
Societies: welcome.
Catering: by arrangement; telephone in advance.
Practice ground.

F8 Beaconsfield
☎(01494) 676545, Pro 676616, Fax 681148.
Seer Green, Beaconsfield, Bucks HP9 2UR
Off M40 onto A355 Amersham road, right at Jordans sign,course is adjacent to Seer Green/Jordans railway halt.
Parkland course.
18 holes, 6469 yards, S.S.S.71
Designed by H.S. Colt.
Founded 1914
Visitors: welcome weekdays.

Green Fee: WD £48 per day, £36 per round.
Societies: Tues and Wed by prior arrangement.
Catering: full facilities.
Hotels: The Bellhouse.

F9 Bearwood
☎(01734) 760060 (Sec), Pro shop 760156.
Mole Rd, Sindlesham, Berks RG11 5DB
On B3030 1.5 miles N of Arborfield Cross.
Parkland course.
9 holes, 5624 yards, S.S.S.68
Founded 1986
Visitors: weekdays only; h/cap cert required.
Green Fee: WD £8 (9 holes); £15 (18 holes).
Societies: none.
Catering: meals and bar snacks available.
9-hole Pitch & Putt course.
Hotels: The Moat House.

F10 The Berkshire
☎(01344) 21495/6
Swinley Rd, Ascot, Berks SL5 8AY
Situated on A332 between Ascot and Bagshot.
Heathland course.
Red course, 18 holes, 6369 yards, S.S.S.70; Blue course, 6260 yards, S.S.S.70
Designed by Herbert Fowler.
Founded 1928
Visitors: on request to Sec.
Green Fee: WD £50 per round; £65 per day.
Societies: book with Sec.
Catering: lunch available.
Hotels: Berystede; Cricketers; Royal Foresters.

KEY							
1	Abbey Hill	18	Burnham Beeches	36	East Berkshire	55	Little Chalfont	75	Studley Wood
2	Aspect Park	19	Calcot Park	37	Ellesborough	56	Lyneham	76	Swinley Forest
3	Aylesbury Golf Centre	20	Carswell Golf &	38	Farnham Park (Bucks)	57	Maidenhead	77	Tadmarton Heath
4	Aylesbury Park		Country Club	39	Flackwell Heath	58	Mapledurham	78	Temple
5	Aylesbury Vale	21	Castle Royle	40	Frilford Heath	59	Mill Ride	79	Thorney Park
6	Badgemore Park	22	Chalfont Park	41	Gerrards Cross	60	Newbury & Crookham	80	Three Locks
7	Banbury	23	Chartridge Park	42	Goring & Streatley	61	Newbury Golf Centre	81	Waterstock
8	Beaconsfield	24	Cherwell Edge	43	Hadden Hill	62	North Oxford	82	Wavenden Golf
9	Bearwood	25	Chesham & Ley Hill	44	Harewood Downs	63	The Oxfordshire		Centre
10	The Berkshire	26	Chesterton	45	Harleyford Golf	64	Princes Risborough	83	Weston Turville
11	Bird Hills (Hawthorn	27	Chiltern Forest	46	Hazlemere G & CC	65	Reading	84	Wexham Park
	Hill)	28	Chipping Norton	47	Henley	66	Richings Park	85	Whiteleaf
12	Blue Mountain Golf	29	Datchet	48	Hennerton	67	Royal Ascot	86	Windmill Hill
	Centre	30	Deanwood Park	49	Huntercombe	68	Rye Hill	87	Winter Hill
13	Brailes	31	Denham	50	Hurst	69	Sandmartins	88	Witney
14	Braywick	32	Donnington Grove CC	51	Iver	70	Silverstone	89	Woburn Country
15	Buckingham	33	Donnington Valley	52	Kirtlington	71	Sonning	90	Club
16	The Buckinghamshire		Hotel	53	Lambourne	72	Southfield	91	Wycombe Heights
17	Burford	34	Downshire	54	Lavender Park Golf	73	Stoke Poges		Golf Centre
		35	Drayton Park		Centre	74	Stowe		

F11 **Bird Hills (Hawthorn Hill)**

☎(01628) 771030, Fax 31023
Drift Rd, Hawthorn Hill, Nr
Maidenhead, Berks SL6 3ST
Leave M4 at exit 8/9; take A330
towards Bracknell for 2.5 miles;
course on right at crossroads (Drift
Rd).
Public undulating parkland course set
around lakes and ponds.
18 holes, 6176 yards, S.S.S.69
Designed by Clive D. Smith.
Founded 1984
Visitors: welcome subject to club
competitions; pay-as-you-play.
Green Fee: WD £12 (18 holes); WE
£15.
Societies: weekdays only; special
packages available.
Catering: extensive restaurant and
bar facilities available; baronial
function suite.
Driving range, and 1 bunker,
snooker.

F12 **Blue Mountain Golf Centre**

☎(01344) 300200, Pro shop 300220,
Fax 360039
Wood Lane, Binfield, Berks RG42
4EX
Off B3408 Bracknell/Wokingham
road.
Public Pay-and-Play parkland course.
18 holes, 6097 yards, S.S.S.70
Founded 1st April 1993
Visitors: any day, no restrictions.
Green Fee: WD £14; WE & BH £18.
Societies: Mon-Fri, must be booked
in advance.
Catering: modern air-conditioned
clubhouse with bar, restaurant,
conference and banqueting facilities
for up to 500.
Driving range, golf academy.
Hotels: Edward Court (Wokingham).

F13 **Brailes**

☎(01608) 685336, Pro 685633
Sutton Lane, Brailes, Banbury, Oxon
OX15 5BB
Off B4035, Shipston-on-Stour 4 miles,
Banbury 10 miles.
Parkland course.
18 holes, 6270 yards, S.S.S.70
Designed by Brian A. Hull
Founded 1992
Visitors: welcome.
Green Fee: WD £20 per day, £13 per
round; WE £22 per day, £15 per
round.
Societies: welcome.
Catering: full facilities.

F14 **Braywick**

☎(01628) 76910 (Club)
Braywick Road, Maidenhead, Berks
SL6 1DH
On A308 Maidenhead to Windsor
road.
Parkland course.
9 holes, 1660 yards, S.S.S.29
Designed by Mike Upcott
Founded 1992
Visitors: with member only.
Green Fee: £10.
Catering: by arrangement.
Driving range.
Hotels: Oakley Court.

F15 **Buckingham**

☎(01280) 815566, Pro 815210, Fax
821812
Tingewick Rd, Buckingham MK18
4AE
2 miles from Buckingham on A421
towards Oxford, 8 miles from M40
junction 10 via A43, B4031 to
Finmere then A421.
Undulating parkland course.
18 holes, 6082 yards, S.S.S.69
Founded 1914
Visitors: weekdays; members' guests
only at weekend.
Green Fee: £28.
Societies: pre-booking with Sec;
Tues and Thurs only.
Catering: lunch, dinner 7 days.
Snooker.
Hotels: Villiers; Buckingham Lodge.

F16 **The Buckinghamshire**

☎(01895) 835777, Fax 835210
Denham Court, Denham Court Drive,
Denham, Bucks UB9 5BG
Off M40 E of M25, N onto A40; turn
into Denham Court Drive at mini-
roundabout and sign to club.
Parkland course.
18 holes, 6880 yards, S.S.S.73
Designed by John Jacobs.
Founded 1992
Visitors: by invitation only.
Societies: by invitation only.
Catering: full range of bar snacks,
restaurant and private rooms
available.
Putting green, practice area, chipping
green.

F17 **Burford**

☎(01993) 822583, Pro 822344, Fax
822801
Burford, Oxon OX18 4JG
19 miles W of Oxford at junction of
A40 and A361, at Burford
roundabout.

Parkland course.
18 holes, 6414 yards, S.S.S.71
Founded 1936
Visitors: by arrangement.
Green Fee: apply for details.
Societies: limited.
Catering: full facilities available.

F18 **Burnham Beeches**

☎(01628) 661448, Pro 661661, Fax
667055
Green Lane, Burnham, Bucks SL1
8EG
M40 exit Beaconsfield, follow signs to
Slough, turn right and follow Burnham
signs (not Burnham Beeches) to
Green Lane.
Parkland course.
18 holes, 6449 yards, S.S.S.71
Founded 1891
Visitors: Mon to Fri; weekends guest
of member.
Green Fee: WD £27 per round,
£40.50 per day.
Societies: Wed, Thurs, Fri.
Catering: full facilities except Mon.

F19 **Calcot Park**

☎(01734) 427124, Pro 427797, Fax
453373
Bath Rd, Calcot, Reading, RG31 7RN
From junction 12 on M4 take A4 to
Reading for 1 mile, entrance on left.
Undulating parkland course.
18 holes, 6283 yards, S.S.S.70
Designed by H.S. Colt.
Founded 1930
Visitors: welcome weekdays only,
except Bank Holidays; h/cap cert
required.
Green Fee: on application.
Societies: Tues, Wed, Thurs.
Catering: full catering available daily.
Hotels: Calcot; Ramada.

F20 **Carswell Golf & Country Club**

☎(01367) 870422 (Club/Pro shop)
Carswell, Nr. Faringdon, Oxon SN7
8PU
Off A420 near Faringdon.
Parkland course.
18 holes, 6133 yards. S.S.S.70
Designed by Ely Brothers.
Founded 1993/4
Visitors: welcome at all times.
Green Fee: WD £12 per round, £18
per day; WE £15 per round, £22.50
per day.
Societies: welcome.
Catering: facilities available.
Covered floodlit driving range.
Hotels: Sudbury House.

F21 Castle Royle

☎(01628) 829252, Fax 829299
Knowl Hill, Reading, Berks RG10 9XA
From M4 junction 8/9 follow signs to
Reading on A4, approx 2.5 miles on
left.
Parkland course.
18 holes, 6785 yards, Par 72
Designed by Neil Coles.
Founded 1992
Visitors: members' guests only.
Green Fee: WD £30 per day, £20 per
round.
Catering: bar and restaurant
facilities.
Hotels: Bird in Hand.

F22 Chalfont Park

☎(01494) 876293 (Pro shop)
Bowles Farm, Three House Holds,
Chalfont St. Giles,
Bucks HP8 4LW
Beaconsfield junction off M40, off
main A413 towards Amersham.
Parkland course.
18 holes, 5800 yards, S.S.S.68
Founded 1994
Visitors: welcome.
Green Fees: apply for details.
Societies: welcome.
Catering: full facilities.
Driving range, lessons available;
telephone for details.
Hotels: Crest (High Wycombe).

F23 Chartridge Park

☎(01494) 791772, Fax 786462
Chartridge, Chesham, Bucks HP5
2TF
3 miles W of town centre.
Parkland course.
18 holes, 5270 yards, S.S.S.69
Designed by John Jacobs.
Founded 1989
Visitors: always welcome.
Green Fee: WD £16; WE £20.
Societies: always welcome
Catering: 2 bars, spacious
restaurant, banqueting and function
facilities.
Practice ground.
Hotels: Accommodation and golf
packages at Chartridge Centre.

F24 Cherwell Edge

☎(01295) 711591, Fax 712404
Chacombe, Banbury, Oxon OX17
2FN
3 miles E of Banbury, A442 to
Northampton; 1.5 miles E of M40
junction 11.
Parkland course.
18 holes, 5848 yards, S.S.S.68

Designed by Richard Davies.
Founded 1983
Visitors: welcome 7 days.
Green Fee: WD £9.50; WE £13.
Societies: 7 days.
Catering: lunches, bar snacks,
evening meals.
Hotels: Whatley Arms; Thatched
House.

F25 Chesham & Ley Hill

☎(01494) 784541
Ley Hill, Chesham, Bucks HP5 1UZ
Turn off A41 on to B4505 at
Boxmoor, at Bovingdon follow signs
for Ley Hill.
Wooded heathland course.
9 holes, 5240 yards, S.S.S.66
Founded 1900
Visitors: welcome Mon, Wed (after
12am), Thurs, Fri (after 1pm); Tues,
weekends and Bank Holidays with
member only.
Green Fee: apply for details.
Societies: Thurs by arrangement.
Catering: snacks except Mon.

F26 Chesterton

☎(01869) 241204, Pro shop/
bookings: 242023
Chesterton, Bicester, Oxon OX6 8TE
1 mile from M40 exit 9 by A41
towards Bicester, 2nd left, left again
at Red Cow, 500 yards on right; from
Oxford take Northampton road, then
Chesterton sign at Weston-on-the-
Green for 1 mile.
Meadowland course.
18 holes, 6229 yards, S.S.S.71
Designed by R.R. Stagg.
Founded 1973/74
Visitors: no restrictions.
Green Fee: £12-£24.
Societies: welcome weekdays
except Tues by arrangement (£12-
£35 per head).
Catering: licensed bar open daily,
full catering service available by
arrangement.
Snooker.

F27 Chiltern Forest

☎(01296) 630899 (Clubhouse), Sec
631267, Pro 631817
Aston Hill, Halton, Aylesbury, Bucks
HP22 5NQ
Off A4011 between Wendover and
Aston Clinton, 5 miles E of Aylesbury.
Hilly woodland course.
18 holes, 5765 yards, S.S.S.70
Visitors: welcome weekdays;
weekends and Bank Holidays with
member only.

Green Fee: £22.
Societies: welcome by arrangement,
usually Wed.
Catering: limited food Tues, Thurs.
Hotels: Bell Inn; West Lodge.

F28 Chipping Norton

☎(01608) 642383, Pro 643356, Fax
645422
Southcombe, Chipping Norton, Oxon
OX7 5QH
0.5 mile S of town centre on London
road or junction of A3400/A44 on left
driving N.
Downland course.
18 holes, 6241 yards, S.S.S.70
Founded 1890
Visitors: welcome weekdays; only
with member weekends and Bank
Holidays.
Green Fee: WD £17 (£11 with
member).
Societies: weekdays.
Catering: full facilities.
Hotels: Crown & Cushion; White
Hart.

F29 Datchet

☎(01753) 543887, Sec 541872, Pro
542755
Buccleuch Rd, Datchet, Slough,
Berks SL3 9BP
2 miles from Slough and Windsor,
easy access from M4.
Parkland course.
9 holes, 5978 yards, S.S.S.69
Founded 1890
Visitors: welcome weekdays 9am-
3pm.
Green Fee: £16 per round, £24 per
day.
Societies: small societies welcome
on Tues only.
Catering: bar snacks and lunches
available.
Hotels: The Manor.

F30 Deanwood Park

☎(01635) 48772 (Club)
Stockcross, Newbury, Berks RG20
8JS
On B4000, 300m off A4.
Parkland course.
9 holes, 2200 yards, S.S.S.61
Designed by Dion Beard
Founded 1995
Visitors: welcome.
Green Fee: WD £6 (9 holes); WE £8
(9 holes).
Societies: welcome.
Catering: available.
Practice area.
Hotels: Foley Lodge (adjoining).

F31 **Denham**

☎(01895) 832022, Pro 832801, Fax 835340
Tilehouse Lane, Denham, Bucks UB9 5DE
From M40 take Uxbridge/Gerrards Cross turn off, A40 towards Gerrards Cross, right onto A412 towards Watford, 2nd turning left to club.
Parkland course.
18 holes, 6451 yards, S.S.S.71
Designed by H.S. Colt.
Founded 1910
Visitors: Mon-Thurs by arrangement.
Green Fee: £50 (36 holes), £35 (18 holes).
Societies: Tues, Wed, Thurs.
Catering: lunches served daily.
Hotels: The Bull (Gerrards Cross).

F32 **Donnington Grove Country Club**

☎(01635) 581000 (Club), Fax 552259
Grove Road, Donnington, Newbury, Berks RG13 2LA
Follow signs to Donnington Castle off A34, 2.5 miles, Grove Rd. on right.
Moorland/Parkland course.
18 holes, 7050 yards, S.S.S.74
Designed by Dave Thomas.
Founded Sept. 1993
Visitors: need to become day member.
Green Fee: £5 (day membership); WD £15 per round, £25 per day; WE £25 per round, £40 per day.
Societies: welcome.
Catering: Japanese restuarant.
Tennis courts, lake, fishing.
Hotels: on site.

F33 **Donnington Valley Hotel**

☎(01635) 550464 (Sec), Pro shop 32488, **Hotels:** 551199
Oxford Road, Donnington, Newbury, Berks RG16 9AG
N of Newbury off old Oxford road.
Parkland course.
18 holes, 4215 yards, S.S.S.62
Founded 1985
Visitors: welcome.
Green Fee: apply for details.
Societies: welcome.
Catering: full facilities.
Hotels: Donnington Valley.

F34 **Downshire**

☎(01344) 302030, 422708, Fax 301020
Easthampstead Park, Wokingham, Berks RG11 3DH
Between Bracknell and Wokingham off Nine Mile Ride.
Municipal parkland course.
18 holes, 6382 yards, S.S.S.70
Designed by F. Hawtree.
Founded 1973
Visitors: welcome 7 days, bookings required.
Green Fee: on application.
Societies: welcome by arrangement.
Catering: full bar and restaurant.
9 hole Pitch & Putt, driving range.
Hotels: Ladbroke Mercury; St Annes Manor.

F35 **Drayton Park**

☎(01235) 550607 (Pro shop/ bookings), Clubhouse 528989
Fax 525731
Steventon Rd, Drayton, Oxon OX14 2RR
Off A34 2 miles S of Abingdon.
Membership Pay-as-you-Play parkland course.
18 holes, 5503 yards, S.S.S.67; 9 hole Par 3 course
Designed by Hawtree & Co.
Founded 1992
Visitors: welcome, dress rules apply, no jeans/tracksuit bottoms, must wear golf shoes.
Green Fee: WD £12 per round; WE £15 per round.
Societies: very welcome, packages available on request.
Catering: bar, bar snacks, formal and informal dinner facility (seats 120).
Driving range, 9 hole Pitch & Putt, putting green.

F36 **East Berkshire**

☎(01344) 772041, Fax 777378
Ravenswood Ave, Crowthorne, Berks RG45 6BD
SW of Bracknell on A3095 and B3348.
Heathland course.
18 holes, 6315 yards, S.S.S.70
Designed by P. Paxton.
Founded 1903
Visitors: weekdays, h/cap essential.
Green Fee: £35.
Societies: Thurs/Fri.
Catering: lunch and snacks daily.
Hotels: Waterloo.

F37 **Ellesborough**

☎(01296) 622114 (Gen Mgr/bookings), Pro 623126
Butlers Cross, Aylesbury, Bucks HP17 0TZ
1 mile W of Wendover on B4010.
Undulating downland course.
18 holes, 6283 yards, S.S.S.71
Designed by James Braid.
Founded 1906
Visitors: weekdays (excluding Tues), h/cap cert required.
Green Fee: on application.
Societies: welcome Wed & Thur only, £55 per day.
Catering: lunches served.
Hotels: Red Lion (Wendover).

F38 **Farnham Park (Bucks)**

☎(01753) 643332 (Pro), Sec 647065
Park Rd, Stoke Poges, Bucks SL2 4PJ
Junction 5 off M4 (Slough Central), A355 signposted Beaconsfield, at Farnham Pump pub 2 mini roundabouts, turn right at 2nd roundabout into Park Road (B416); course 0.5 mile on left.
Municipal parkland course.
18 holes, 6172 yards, S.S.S.69
Designed by Hawtree & Sons.
Founded 1977
Visitors: Municipal course.
Green Fee: WD £8 per round; WE £11; reductions Jnrs, OAPs and unemployed.
Societies: bookable in advance Tues and Thur.
Catering: grill etc.
Hotels: Burnham Beeches.

F39 **Flackwell Heath**

☎(01628) 520929 (Sec), Club 520027, Fax 530040
Treadaway Rd, Flackwell Heath, Bucks HP10 9PE
From London, exit 3 M40 (1.5 miles); from Oxford, exit 4 M40 (1 mile); turn off A40 High Wycombe-Beaconsfield road at Loudwater roundabout, up Treadaway Hill, on left before apex of hill into Treadaway Rd.
Undulating heathland course.
18 holes, 6207 yards, S.S.S.70
Founded 1905
Visitors: welcome Mon-Fri; h/cap cert required.
Green Fee: £27.
Societies: Wed, Thurs only.
Catering: full facilities Tues-Sun, restricted Mon.
Hotels: Bell House (Beaconsfield); Crest (High Wycombe).

F40 **Frilford Heath**

☎(01865) 390864/5/6, Fax 390823
Frilford Heath, Abingdon, Oxon OX13 5NW
A338 Oxford to Wantage road, 3 miles W of Abingdon.

Harleyford

Harleyford is the most recent addition to the expanding list of courses within Berks Bucks and Oxon, and a handsome addition, too. Traditional golf in historic surroundings is the best summary of a course from whose high ground the beauty of the Thames valley is everywhere apparent.

Harleyford's marina is one of a variety of amenities around Harleyford Manor, a resplendent Georgian house visited by Napoleon and Disraeli, which may also have been the inspiration for Kenneth Grahame's *The Wind in the Willows*. There is an elegance and grandeur about an estate approached down an avenue of mature trees and rhododendrons, a sure signal that the setting is special.

Ancient parkland provides the start and finish to a course free from affectation. There are no forbidding carries from the tee, no greens in the middle of lakes and no impossible shots. It is demanding without being daunting, enjoyable without being easy. It makes the most of natural, rolling contours which give the feeling of pleasant rise and fall although nowhere is there the sense of hard climbing. In order to preserve the natural look and show an awareness of a sensitive environment, the number of bunkers is minimal – 23 in total – but they are not needed.

Situated a mile or so out of Marlow on the Henley road, Harleyford is located most strategically. This, together with an instant ability to impress, gives it a magnetic appeal that is highly marketable. The main merit of the golf is the range of shotmaking that awaits. The principal aim is to encourage the old style running version as far as possible and deflect from the undue emphasis on power that can spoil the game.

The 1st and 2nd offer a comfortable introduction, two par fours lent character by the park trees, although they are not necessarily a sign of things to come. A cut through the woodland frames the tee shot on the short 3rd in preparation for more open surroundings at the 4th. Here, the more daring drive up the left leaves plenty of options and enables players to skirt the deep chalk pit to the right of the green and not play over it.

After the rigours of the par five 5th, from a tee beside the old parish boundary, the 6th turns back in the form of another stout short hole. The attraction of the 7th is the note of aggression struck by a drive whose target is a valley fairway plunging still further to a well guarded green position. The second shot will undoubtedly be one of the most popular.

Another charming green setting is to be found on the 9th, a giant chestnut proving a notable backdrop, but the inward half is just as full of holes to tease and delight. These include the sharply doglegged 11th where a mighty drive is required and the short 12th, an example of what the Americans would describe as a signature hole, although it rather designed itself.

Apart from lending the opportunity to relish the best view of the river valley, the tee shot, a medium to long iron, must carry to the green on the site of an old quarry.

The 13th has to negotiate a long, gradual climb with two good shots thrown in while the next two complement each other nicely. The 14th poses the age-old dilemma over boldness or caution, an adventurous drive carrying most of the way to the green although a deep bunker waits to snap up anything less than perfection.

The restoration of the Temple by the 15th tee is a further reminder of historic surroundings but, again, the mood changes, switching back to a wooded fairway on the 15th. This is followed by the par 3 16th, part open and part enclosed. Finally reaching the solitude of the park are the 17th, a par five reachable in two in spite of a cunningly angled green, and the 18th, curving right round a thick copse to a green looked over by a clubhouse in the shape of old Victorian barns, an imaginative touch entirely in character.

Wooded heathland course.
18 holes, 6843 yards, S.S.S.73; 18 holes, 6006 yards, S.S.S.69; 18 holes, 6726 yards, S.S.S.73.
Designed by J.H. Taylor, C.K. Cotton and S. Gidman.
Founded 1908
Visitors: welcome but must have h/cap cert; advisable to phone in advance.
Green Fee: WD £45; WE & BH £55.
Societies: by previous arrangement Mon-Fri.
Catering: cooked meals provided with prior arrangement, snacks served at any time.
Hotels: Dog House; Crown & Thistle; The Abingdon Lodge.

F41 **Gerrards Cross**
☎(01753) 883263 (Sec), Pro 885300, Fax 883593
Chalfont Park, Gerrards Cross, Bucks SL9 0QA
Leave A40 by A413, continue to 1st roundabout (approx 1 mile) and leave by 3rd exit onto private road.
Parkland course.
18 holes, 6295 yards, S.S.S.70
Designed by Len Holland.
Founded 1922
Visitors: welcome weekdays; phone Pro in advance and bring h/cap cert.
Green Fee: on application
Societies: welcome Wed pm and all day Thur and Fri.
Catering: bar snacks always available; lunches to order.
Hotels: Bull; Greyhound; Bellhouse.

F42 **Goring & Streatley**
☎(01491) 873229, Pro 873715, Fax 875224
Rectory Rd, Streatley-on-Thames, Berks RG8 9QA
On A417 Wantage road, 0.25 mile from Streatley crossroads.
Parkland course.
18 holes, 6255 yards, S.S.S.70
Founded 1895
Visitors: welcome Mon-Fri; weekend with member only.
Green Fee: £28 (£19 after 4pm).
Societies: apply for details.
Catering: full, a la carte and table d'hote restaurant.

F43 **Hadden Hill**
☎(01235) 510410
Wallingford Rd, Didcot, Oxon OX11 9BJ
Just E of Didcot on A4130 Wallingford road.

Members and Public parkland course.
18 holes, 6563 yards, S.S.S.71
Designed by Michael V. Morley.
Founded May 1990
Visitors: no restrictions, all starting times bookable by phone.
Green Fee: WD £12; WE £16.
Societies: welcome weekdays.
Catering: full bar and restaurant facilities all day.
Floodlit driving range.
Hotels: George, Springs (Wallingford); George, White Hart (Dorchester).

F44 **Harewood Downs**
☎(01494) 762184, Pro 764102
Cokes Lane, Chalfont St Giles, Bucks HP8 4TA
Off A413 3 miles E of Amersham.
Parkland course.
18 holes, 5958 yards, S.S.S.69
Founded 1907
Visitors: welcome.
Green Fee: WD £25 per day; WE £30 per day.
Societies: weekdays only.
Catering: daily.
Hotels: Crown; Greyhound.

F45 **Harleyford Golf**
☎(01628) 487878 (Club)
Henley Road, Marlow, Bucks SL7 2DX
On A4155 Marlow to Henley road, 2 miles from Marlow town centre.
Downland course.
18 holes, 6700 yards, S.S.S.72
Designed by Donald Steel
Open summer 1996
Visitors: with member as guest only.
Green Fees: apply for details
Catering: restaurant/bar in clubhouse.
Extensive practice ground.
Hotels: Danesfield House (adjacent).

F46 **Hazlemere G & CC**
☎(01494) 714722, Pro shop/bookings: 718298, Fax 713914
Penn Rd, Hazlemere, Bucks HP15 7LR
On B474, 0.5 mile from junction with A404 between High Wycombe and Amersham.
Undulating parkland course
18 holes, 5873 yards, S.S.S.68
Designed by Terry Murray.
Founded 1982
Visitors: weekdays only; no jeans or trainers allowed.
Green Fee: £25 per round; £34 per day.

Societies: welcome by prior arrangement weekdays only.
Catering: bar and restaurant facilities, bar snacks and full meals.
Hotels: White Hart (Beaconsfield); Crest (High Wycombe); Crown (Amersham); Bellhouse (Gerrards X).

F47 **Henley**
☎(01491) 575742, Pro 575710, Fax 412179
Harpsden, Henley-on-Thames, Oxon RG9 4HG.
M4 to junction 9 Reading, follow A4155 to Caversham/Henley, turn left to Harpsden village 1 mile before reaching Henley, clubhouse on left.
Parkland course.
18 holes, 6329 yards, S.S.S.70
Designed by James Braid.
Founded 1908
Visitors: welcome weekdays, weekends with member.
Green Fee: £30 (per round/day).
Societies: Wed and Thurs.
Catering: bar snacks daily; other by arrangement.
Hotels: Red Lion; Flohr's.

F48 **Hennerton**
☎(01734) 401000 (Sec), Pro shop 404778, Fax 401042
Crazies Hill Rd, Wargrave, Reading, Berks RG10 8LT
6 miles from M4 exits 8/9 & 10 and M40 High Wycombe; at Wargrave on A321 take Wargrave Hill turning next to garage, after 0.25 mile take 1st left towards Crazies Hill; course 0.5 mile on left.
Parkland course with extensive views of Thames valley.
9 holes, 5460 yards, S.S.S.67
Designed by Col. Dion Beard.
Founded May 1992
Visitors: welcome, up to 50% of tee times available weekdays, up to 25% at weekends.
Green Fee: WD £12 (18 holes); WE & BH £18.
Societies: welcome weekdays, from £24 per head; details on application.
Catering: bar and restaurant.
Driving range.
Hotels: Bird in Hand.

F49 **Huntercombe**
☎(01491) 641207, Pro 641241, Fax 642060
Nuffield, Henley-on-Thames, Oxon RG9 5SL.
A4130, 6 miles from Henley towards Oxford.

Woodland/heathland course.
18 holes, 6108 yards, S.S.S.70
Designed by Willie Park Jnr.
Founded 1902
Visitors: weekdays; no 3 balls or 4 balls; jackets and neckwear required in clubhouse.
Green Fee: apply for details.
Societies: Tues and Thurs only.
Catering: full meals or bar snacks.

F50 Hurst
☎(01734) 345143, 344355
Sandford Lane, Hurst, Berks RG10 0SQ
Between Reading and Twyford, signposted from Hurst village.
Public parkland course
9 holes, 3154 yards, S.S.S.70
Founded 1977
Visitors: welcome, advisable to book.
Green Fee: apply for details.
Societies: welcome.
Catering: bar facilities.

F51 Iver
☎(01753) 655615
Hollow Hill Lane, Langley Park Rd, Iver, Bucks SL0 0JJ
near Langley Station, Slough.
Parkland course.
9 holes, 6214 yards, S.S.S.70
Designed by David Morgan.
Founded 1984
Visitors: always welcome.
Green Fee: apply for details.
Societies: welcome.
Catering: meals always available.
Hotels: Holiday Inn (Langley).

F52 Kirtlington
☎(01869) 351133 (Club), Fax 351143
Kirtlington, Oxon OX5 3JY
M40 Junc 9 onto A34 follow signs Kirtlington
18 holes, 5100 metres
Designed by Graham Webster.
Founded 1995
Visitors: welcome.
Green Fee: WD £12 per round; WE £18 per round.
Societies: welcome.
Catering: available.
Driving range.

F53 Lambourne
☎(01628) 666755, 662936, Fax 663301
Dropmore Rd, Burnham, South Bucks SL1 8NF
M4 exit 7 or M40 exit 2.

Parkland course.
18 holes, 6764 yards, S.S.S.72
Designed by Donald Steel.
Founded 1991
Visitors: by arrangement, h/cap cert required.
Green Fee: WD £30 per day, £18 (with member).
Societies: no society meetings.
Catering: full facilities every day, breakfast, lunch and dinner; half-way hut refreshments.
Driving range, hairdressing, massage room.
Hotels: Cliveden; Grovefield House.

F54 Lavender Park Golf Centre
☎(01344) 884074 (Admin/Fax), Golf shop 886096
Swinley Rd, Ascot, Berks SL5 8BD
Between Ascot and Bracknell on A329 opposite Royal Foresters Hotel.
Public parkland course
9 holes Par 3, 1124 yards
Founded 1974
Visitors: welcome any time, no restrictions.
Green Fee: WD £3.25 (9 holes), £4.50 (18 holes); WE £4.50 (9 holes), £7 (18 holes).
Societies: welcome.
Catering: lunch 7 days, buffets on request.
Driving range, snooker hall (10 tables), bar.
Hotels: Royal Foresters.

F55 Little Chalfont
☎(01494) 764877, Fax 762860
Lodge Lane, Little Chalfont, Bucks
200 yards from A404 at Little Chalfont.
Undulating parkland course.
9 holes, 6800 yards, S.S.S.68
Designed by re-designed by James Dunne.
Founded 1980
Visitors: welcome.
Green Fee: WD £10; WE & BH £12.
Societies: welcome weekdays.
Catering: full facilities.
Hotels: Sportsman (Chorley Wood).

F56 Lyneham
☎(01993) 831841 (Sec), Fax 831775
Lyneham, Chipping Norton, Oxon OX7 6QQ
4 miles W of Chipping Norton off A361 Chipping Norton-Burford road.
Parkland course.
18 holes, 6669 yards, S.S.S.72

Designed by D. Carpenter, A. Smith.
Founded July 1991
Visitors: unrestricted, can book 3 days in advance including weekends.
Green Fee: WD £13 per round, £19 per day; WE & BH £16 per round, £26 per day.
Societies: welcome.
Catering: available.
Driving range.
Hotels: Mill (Kingham); White Hart, Crown and Cushion (Chipping Norton); Kings Arms Hotel (Chipping Norton); Hillsborough (Milton under Wychwood).

F57 Maidenhead
☎(01628) 24693 (Sec), Club 20545, Pro 24067, **Catering:** 35321
Shoppenhangers Rd, Maidenhead, Berks SL6 2PZ
Off A308, adjacent to Maidenhead railway station.
Parkland course.
18 holes, 6364 yards, S.S.S.70
Founded 1896
Visitors: Mon-Thurs, Fri am only; h/cap cert required.
Green Fee: £28 per day, £20 per round.
Societies: welcome by arrangement.
Catering: snack lunch, tea available; full lunch, dinner by arrangement.
Hotels: Frederick's; Holiday Inn.

F58 Mapledurham
☎(01734) 463353, Fax 463363
Chazey Heath, Mapledurham, Reading, Berks RG4 7UD
Off A4074 NW of Reading 1.5 miles from village of Mapledurham.
Gently undulating parkland course.
18 holes, 5624 yards, Par 69
Designed by MRM Sandow
Founded 1992
Visitors: welcome.
Green Fee: WD £14; WE £17.
Societies: welcome, apply for details.
Catering: bar and restaurant.
Practice ground, Pitch & Putt, practice bunkers, putting green
Hotels: Holiday Inn (Caversham).

F59 Mill Ride
☎(01344) 886777 (Pro shop), Sec 891494, Fax 886820
Mill Ride Estate, Mill Ride, North Ascot, Berkshire SL5 8LT
Turn right into Fernbank Rd at 1st traffic lights on A329 between Ascot and Bracknell. Mill Ride is 0.5 mile on left.
Parkland/inland links course.

18 holes, 6752 yards, S.S.S.72
Designed by Donald Steel
Founded 1990
Visitors: welcome, but must book in advance.
Green Fee: WD £35 per round; WE £50.
Societies: weekdays, occasional weekends.
Catering: morning coffee, lunch, tea, dinner, bar snacks; private dining room.
Practice ground, saunas, steam bath (men only).
Hotels: Royal Berkshire (Ascot); Berystede (Sunningdale); 4 guest bedrooms on site.

F60 Newbury & Crookham
☎(01635) 40035 (Sec), Pro 31201, Fax 40045
Bury's Bank Rd, Greenham, Newbury, Berks RG19 8BZ
2 miles SE of Newbury off A34.
Parkland course.
18 holes, 5940 yards, S.S.S.68
Designed by J.H. Turner.
Founded 1873
Visitors: weekdays members of other clubs; weekends with members only.
Green Fee: £25 (£12.50 with member).
Societies: Wed, Thurs and Fri.
Catering: lunch, snacks and evening meals.
Hotels: Bacon Arms; Chequers; Hilton.

F61 Newbury Golf Centre
☎(01635) 551464 (Pro)
The Racecourse, Newbury, Berks RG14 7NZ
Signposted off A34 for Racecource/Conference centre.
Parkland course.
18 holes, 6249 yards, S.S.S.70
Founded 1994
Visitors: welcome.
Green Fee: WD £7.50 (9 holes), £10 (18 holes); WE £9 (9 holes), £12.50 (18 holes).
Societies: welcome.
Catering: facilities available.
Driving range.

F62 North Oxford
☎(01865) 54924, Pro 53977, Fax 515921
Banbury Rd, Oxford OX2 8EZ
Between Kidlington and N Oxford, 2.5 miles N of city centre.
Parkland course.

18 holes, 5805 yards, S.S.S.67
Founded 1907
Visitors: welcome weekdays.
Green Fee: on application.
Societies: book with Sec.
Catering: facilities available.
Hotels: Moat House; Linton Lodge; Randolph.

F63 The Oxfordshire
☎(01844) 278300, Fax 278003
Rycote Lane, Milton Common, Thame, Oxon OX9 2PU
From M40 northbound, exit 7, turn right for Thame on A329; from M40 southbound, exit 8, 1st right onto A40, then left at A329.
Part parkland, part links style course with American water features.
18 holes, 7187 yards, S.S.S.74
Designed by Rees Jones.
Founded July 1993
Visitors: restricted to members and their guests, or by introduction only; h/cap cert required.
Green Fee: on application.
Societies: not available.
Catering: spike bar, lounge bar, restaurant, halfway house.
26-bay driving range, putting greens, practice bunkers.
Hotels: The Belfry; Hartwell House; Le Manoir au Quat Saisons; Randolph; Spread Eagle.

F64 Princes Risborough
☎(01844) 346989
Lee Rd, Saunderton Lee, Princes Risborough, Bucks HP27 9NX
M40 to High Wycombe, follow A4010 signposted Aylesbury; 2 miles before Princes Risborough turn left at Rose & Crown inn; club 1 mile on right.
Parkland course.
9 holes, 5410 yards, S.S.S.66
Designed by Guy Hunt.
Founded 1991
Visitors: welcome any time.
Green Fee: WD £10 (9 holes), £14 (18 holes); WE £10 (9 holes), £18 (18 holes).
Societies: welcome, min 8 players.
Catering: bar, restaurant and lounge.
Hotels: Rose & Crown.

F65 Reading
☎(01734) 472909 (Bookings), Pro 476115
Kidmore End Rd, Emmer Green, Reading, Berks RG4 8SG
2 miles N of Reading off Peppard Rd (B481).
Parkland course.

18 holes, 6212 yards, S.S.S.70
Founded 1910
Visitors: Mon to Thurs (unless with member)
Green Fee: £27 (per day/round).
Societies: Tues, Thurs unlimited; Wed 25 max.
Catering: full facilities available.
Hotels: Ramada; Rainbow Corner (Caversham).

F66 Richings Park
☎(01753) 655352 (Pro shop)
North Park, Iver, Bucks SL0 9DL
M4 J5 (Langley) towards Colnbrook, turn left at lights to Iver.
Parkland course.
18 holes, 6094 yards, S.S.S.69
Designed by Alan Higgins
Founded 1995
Visitors: welcome Mon-Fri.
Green Fee: £15 per round.
Societies: welcome weekdays (except Wed).
Catering: restaurant and function room.
Driving range, 5 hole academy course.
Hotels: Marriott.

F67 Royal Ascot
☎(01344) 25175, Pro 24656
Winkfield Rd, Ascot, Berks SL5 7LJ
Ascot Heath (in centre of racecourse) on A329.
Heathland course.
18 holes, 5716 yards, S.S.S.68
Designed by J.H. Taylor.
Founded 1887
Visitors: members' guests only.
Green Fee: on application.
Societies: Wed and Thurs by arrangement.
Catering: available all week by arrangement.
Hotels: Berystede.

F68 Rye Hill
☎(01295) 721818 (Club), Pro 720066, Fax 720889
Milcombe, Banbury, Oxon OX15 4RU
Off A361 between Banbury and Chipping Norton, signposted Bloxham.
Links style.
18 holes, 6692 yards, S.S.S.71
Founded 1993
Visitors: welcome.
Green Fee: WD £10; WE £12.
Societies: welcome.
Catering: bar snacks, full facilities April 1996.
Hotels: White Horse.

F69 Sandmartins

☎(01734) 792711 (Sec), Pro shop 770265, Fax 770282
Finchhampstead Rd, Wokingham, Berks RG11 3RQ
M4 junction 10 or M3 junction 3; 1 mile S of Wokingham off Nine Mile Ride.
Parkland course.
18 holes, 6204 yards, S.S.S.70
Designed by E.T. Fox.
Founded 15 May, 1993
Visitors: weekdays only.
Green Fee: £20 per round, £35 per day.
Societies: welcome by arrangement with Sec.
Catering: bar, restaurant, halfway house.
Practice area – driving, bunker, pitching.
Hotels: St Anne's Manor – Stakis (Wokingham).

F70 Silverstone

☎(01280) 850005, Fax 850080
Silverstone Rd, Stowe, Buckingham, MK18 5LH
On Silverstone road from Buckingham and Stowe, 1.5 miles beyond racing circuit.
Farmland course.
18 holes, 6194 yards, S.S.S.72
Designed by David Snell.
Founded 1992
Visitors: welcome weekdays and weekends, pay-as-you-play; smart/casual dress required.
Green Fee: WD £7.50 per round; WE £12.
Societies: welcome by prior arrangement.
Catering: full bar and restaurant, lounge, private dining room.
Driving range, putting greens, 9 hole pitching course, swing analyser etc.
Hotels: White Hart (Buckingham); Green Man (Syresham); Forte Travelodge (Towcester).

F71 Sonning

☎(01734) 693332, Pro 692910, Fax 448409
Duffield Rd, Sonning-on-Thames, Berks RG4 6GJ
A4 Maidenhead/Reading road, behind Readingensians Rugby Ground.
Parkland course.
18 holes, 6366 yards, S.S.S.70
Founded 1914
Visitors: weekdays with h/cap cert.
Green Fee: on application
Societies: by prior arrangement.
Catering: full service available.

F72 Southfield

☎(01865) 242158 (Sec/Fax)
Hill Top Rd, Oxford OX4 1PF
Cowley Rd, Southfield Rd, then right into Hill Top Rd; between Headington and Cowley.
Undulating parkland course.
18 holes, 6230 yards, S.S.S.70
Designed by James Braid (1875), redesigned H. Colt (1923)
Visitors: welcome weekdays.
Green Fee: on application
Societies: welcome weekdays.
Catering: daily except Mon.

F73 Stoke Poges

☎(01753) 717171, Pro shop 717172, Fax 717181
North Drive, Park Rd, Stoke Poges, Slough, Bucks SL2 4PG
Off M4 or A4 at Slough into Stoke Poges Lane, then turn into Park Road, then 0.5 miles on left.
Parkland course.
18 holes, 6654 yards, S.S.S.72
Designed by H.S. Colt.
Founded 1908
Visitors: weekdays by arrangement with Pro, weekends and Bank Holidays with member only; letter of intro. or h/cap cert required.
Green Fee: WD £39 per round, £58 per day.
Societies: Mon, Wed, Thurs, Fri.
Catering: full service available.
Hotels: Marriotts, Bull (Gerards Cross); Copthorne (Slough).

F74 Stowe

☎(01280) 813650 (Sec)
Stowe, Buckingham, Bucks MK18 5EH
Parkland course.
9 holes, 4573 yards, S.S.S.63
Founded 1974
Visitors: with member only.
Green Fee: £10 (visitors – with member).
Catering: clubhouse.

F75 Studley Wood

☎(01865) 351144 (Club), Fax 351166
The Straight Mile, Horton-Cum-Studley, Oxon OX33 1BF
From M40 J6 take A40 to Headington roundabout, follow signs Horton-Cum-Studley.
Woodland course.
18 holes, 6711 yards, S.S.S.73
Designed by Simon Gidman
Founded May 1996
Visitors: welcome.

Green Fee: WD £18 per round; WE £25 per round.
Societies: welcome by prior arrangement.
Catering: restaurant and function room available.
14 bay floodlit driving range.
Hotels: Studley Priory.

F76 Swinley Forest

☎(01344) 20197 (Club), Pro 874811, Fax 874733
Coronation Rd, South Ascot, Berks SL5 9LE
1.5 miles from Ascot station, through S Ascot village, right into Coronation Rd and 4th right to club.
Undulating heathland course
18 holes, 5952 yards, S.S.S.69
Designed by H.S. Colt.
Founded 1909
Visitors: welcome only by invitation of member.
Green Fee: on application.
Societies: apply to Sec.
Catering: lunch served.
Hotels: Berystede; Royal Foresters; Brockenhurst.

F77 Tadmarton Heath

☎(01608) 737278, Pro shop 730047
Wigginton, Banbury, Oxon OX15 5HL
5 miles W of Banbury off B4035 Shipston-on-Stour road at Tadmarton village.
Heathland course.
18 holes, 5917 yards, S.S.S.69
Designed by Major C.K. Hutchison.
Founded 1922
Visitors: weekdays only; must be members of other clubs with h/cap certs.
Green Fee: on application.
Societies: Tues, Wed, Fri.
Catering: full facilities.
Hotels: Banbury Moat House.

F78 Temple

☎(01628) 824795 (Sec), Steward: 824248, Pro 824254, Fax 828119
Henley Rd, Hurley, Maidenhead, Berks SL6 5LH
A4130 Maidenhead to Henley from M4 or A404 from M40.
Undulating parkland course.
18 holes, 6207 yards, S.S.S.70
Designed by Willie Park Jnr.
Founded 1909
Visitors: welcome on weekdays; must have proof of h/cap.
Green Fee: Mon - Sat £25 per round; Sun £40 per round.

Societies: catered for Mon, Tues, Wed, Fri; max 40.
Catering: full catering.
Squash.
Hotels: Eurocrest (Maidenhead); Compleat Angler (Marlow).

F79 Thorney Park

☎(01895) 422095 (Club), Fax 431307
Thorney Mill Lane, Iver, Bucks SL0 9AL
From M4 junction 5 follow signs to Iver and West Drayton.
Municipal parkland course.
9 holes, 3000 yards, S.S.S.34
Designed by Grundon Leisure Ltd.
Founded Sept 1992
Visitors: welcome.
Green Fee: WD £6 (9 holes), £9 (18 holes); WE £9
(9 holes), £13 (18 holes).
Societies: weekdays.
Catering: fully licensed bar and restaurant.
Practice ground.
Hotels: in Heathrow area (5 mins).

F80 Three Locks

☎(01525) 270050 (Pro shop),
Hotels: 270470
Great Brickhill, Milton Keynes, Bucks MK17 9BH
Between Little Brickhill on A5 and A4146; from Leighton Buzzard towards Bletchley turn off right just before The Three Locks public house.
Converted farmland course.
18 holes, 5453 yards, S.S.S.69.
Designed by MRM Sandow/ P. Critchley.
Founded April 1992
Visitors: welcome, no restrictions except weekend tee times must be booked.
Green Fee: WD £9.50 (18 holes), £16 per day; WE £11
(18 holes), £20 per day.
Societies: welcome at any time by arrangement with management; fees dependent on requirements.
Catering: club bar, bar meals, lunches and breakfast.
Extensive practice area, snooker room, pool tables.
Hotels: B & B executive hotel on site, free golf for guests; telephone for details.

F81 Waterstock

☎(01844) 338093, Fax 338036
Thame Rd, Waterstock, Oxford OX33 1HT

Direct access from M40 junction 8 onto A418 Thame road; less than 5 miles from Oxford and Thame.
Public parkland course.
18 holes, 6482 yards, Par 72; further 9 under construction for 1996
Founded April 1994
Visitors: welcome, etiquette and clothing restrictions only.
Green Fee: WD £12 per round, WE £16 per round.
Societies: welcome; attractive fees.
Catering: spike bar, bar and grill; full meals for societies, up to 70.
Driving range, practice bunkering and putting area.
Hotels: The Belfry (Milton); Country Inn, Travelodge (Wheatley); accommodation in local pubs.

F82 Wavenden Golf Centre

☎(01908) 281811, Fax 281257
Lower End Road, Wavendon, Milton Keynes MK17 8DA
From M1 Junction 13 take A421 to Milton Keynes, 1st left at roundabout, 1st left into Lower End Rd.
Public parkland course.
18 holes, 5361 yards, S.S.S.67; 9 holes Par-3, 1424 yards, S.S.S.25
Designed by John Drake/Nick Elmer
Founded Nov 1989
Visitors: welcome 7 days.
Green Fee: WD £10, WE £13.50.
Societies: welcome weekdays and weekends.
Catering: carvery, downstairs bar, bar meals.
Driving range.
Hotels: The Bell (Woburn); The Bell (Winslow).

F83 West Berks

☎(01488) 638574, Fax 638781
Chaddleworth, Newbury, Berks RG16 0HS
Off M4 at junction 14, follow signs to RAF Welford.
Downland course.
18 holes, 7059 yards, S.S.S.74
Founded 1978
Visitors: welcome weekdays with prior reservation.
Green Fee: £24.
Societies: by arrangement.
Catering: full service available.

F84 Weston Turville

☎(01296) 24084/ 25949, Fax 395376
New Rd, Weston Turville, Aylesbury, Bucks HP22 5QT

A41 or A312, situated 2 miles from Aylesbury town centre between Aston Clinton and Wendover.
Parkland course.
18 holes, 6002 yards, S.S.S.69
Founded 1975
Visitors: welcome except Sun am.
Green Fee: on application
Societies: weekdays, occasional weekends.
Catering: lunches, evening snacks.

F85 Wexham Park

☎(01753) 663271, Pro 663425, Fax 663318
Wexham St, Wexham, Slough, Berks SL3 6ND
2 miles from Slough towards Gerrards Cross, follow signs to Wexham Park Hospital and club is 0.5 mile further on.
Parkland courses.
18 holes, 5890 yards, S.S.S.66; 9 holes, 2851 yards, S.S.S.34; 9 holes, 2283, S.S.S.32
Designed by Emil Lawrence and David Morgan.
Founded 1976
Visitors: welcome.
Green Fee: on application.
Societies: welcome.
Catering: full service available.
Hotels: Wexham Park Hall, weekend golfing breaks and midweek packages inc. hotel, golf & tuition; telephone for details.

F86 Whiteleaf

☎(01844) 274058 (Sec)
The Clubhouse, Whiteleaf, Princes Risborough, Bucks HP27 0LY
1.5 miles from Princes Risborough on Aylesbury road, turn 2nd right (The Holloway) for Whiteleaf; at T-junction turn left, then right after 250 yards into private road for club.
Undulating course.
9 holes, 5391 yards, S.S.S.66
Founded 1904
Visitors: not weekends.
Green Fee: £18 (18 holes), £25 per day.
Societies: catered for on Thurs only.
Catering: lunch served daily except Mon.
Hotels: Bernard Arms; Thatchers.

F87 Windmill Hill

☎(01908) 648149, Pro shop 378623, Fax 271478
Tattenhoe Lane, Bletchley, Milton Keynes, Bucks MK3 7RB

M1 exit 13/14, take A421 through Milton Keynes towards Buckingham; 10 mins from M1.
Public parkland course.
18 holes, 6773 yards, S.S.S.72
Designed by Henry Cotton.
Founded 1972
Visitors: welcome at all times.
Green Fee: on application.
Societies: welcome any time.
Catering: by prior arrangement.
Driving range.
Hotels: Forte Crest (Milton Keynes); Shenley (Bletchley).

F88 **Winter Hill**

☎(01628) 527613
Grange Lane, Cookham, Maidenhead, Berks SL6 9RP
4 miles from Maidenhead via M4; 6 miles from M40 via Marlow.
Parkland course.
18 holes, 6408 yards, S.S.S.71
Designed by Charles Lawrie.
Founded 1976
Visitors: welcome weekdays only.
Green Fee: WD £24.
Societies: welcome, main day Wed.
Catering: full service available.
Hotels: Eurocrest.

F89 **Witney**

☎(01993) 779000 (Club), Fax 778866
Downs Road, Witney, Oxon OX8 5SY
Off the old A40.
Pay and play course.
18 holes, 6675 yards, S.S.S.71
Designed by Simon Gidman
Founded Oct 1994
Visitors: welcome (must book in advance).
Green Fee: WD £12 per round; WE £15 per round.
Societies: welcome (must book in advance, min 8 players).
Catering: restaurant.
32 bay driving range.
Hotels: Oxford Moat House.

F90 **Woburn CC**

☎(01908) 378436
Bow Brickhill, Milton Keynes MK17 9LJ
M1 exit 13, into Woburn Sands, left to Woburn, after 0.5 mile right at sign.
Dukes, 18 holes, 6940 yards, S.S.S.74; Duchess, 18 holes, 6641 yards, S.S.S.72
Designed by Charles Lawrie.
Founded 1976

Visitors: weekdays only by arrangement.
Green Fee: on application.
Societies: company days by prior arrangement.
Catering: meals served.
Hotels: available on request.

F91 **Wycombe Heights Golf Centre**

☎(01494) 816686, Bookings: 812862, Fax 816728
Rayners Ave, Loudwater, High Wycombe, Bucks HP10 9SW
M40 Junction 3, off A40
Pay-as-you-play parkland course.
18 holes, 6253 yards, S.S.S.72; 18 hole Par 3, 1955 yards
Designed by John Jacobs
Founded 1991
Visitors: welcome, pay-as-you-play.
Green Fee: WD £10.80; WE £13.90.
Societies: Mon-Fri with prior arrangement.
Catering: bar, restaurant, family room.
Driving range.
Hotels: Post House Forte; Cressex; Alexandria.

BEDFORDSHIRE, NORTHAMPTONSHIRE, CAMBRIDGESHIRE, LEICESTERSHIRE

In the last six or seven years, Northampton has gained two new courses on opposite sides of the city. Collingtree is an example of the American style of design and construction while the relocation of the Northampton Golf Club on Lord Spencer's Estate at Althorp epitomises the harmonious blending of courses into a lovely, natural landscape.

Johnny Miller planned Collingtree on the lines of excavating a great lake and using the material to create a series of hills and mounds to balance an area that hitherto was a trifle barren. The lake itself has given rise to a par 5 18th hole with an island green. An impressive part of the development is the extensive teaching and practice facilities.

Harlestone Lake is equally a feature of the new home of the Northampton Golf Club, the 16th and 18th holes playing across it in full view of a delightful clubhouse that enjoys a magnificent position. Close by lies the Northamptonshire County Club at Church Brampton which upholds a justifiably high reputation as amongst the best inland courses in England. It has the capacity to test all departments of a golfer's game as well as appealing to the aesthetic senses of those who care more about where they play than how they play.

Cold Ashby and Staverton Park are among Northamptonshire's other new courses in the last 20 years but the mantle of seniority belongs to Kettering Golf Club which in 1991 celebrated its Centenary in spite of the new by-pass running beside one corner of the course.

Gog Magog, east of Cambridge, is the pick of Cambridgeshire's Clubs with its 27 holes but Ramsey, St Ives and St Neots boast a countryside whose largely agricultural character has been little eroded by the spread of the game. Large, open fen-like fields are not ideal for golf but a word for Ely City and Cambridgeshire Moat House Hotel which meet local needs adequately enough.

Bedfordshire was the birthplace of Henry Longhurst who played most of his early golf at the Bedfordshire Golf Club then known a little less grandly as the Bedford G.C. Bedford & County followed in 1912. Nowadays Bedford has a public course called Mowsbury. Memories of Dunstable Downs, South Bedfordshire at Luton and the excellent John O'Gaunt (36 holes) at Biggleswade involve county matches with BB and O in the south-eastern group but Northamptonshire falls in the Midlands Group along with Leicestershire, where golf revolves around the county town of Leicester itself.

Rothley Park, Glen Gorse, Leicestershire and Kirby Muxloe are all based on pleasant parkland but, though only 9 holes, one of the most charming courses is Charnwood Forest near the M1 at Loughborough. Hinckley and Market Harborough are established courses, Hinckley starting life as Burbage Common. Humberstone Heights and Kibworth are more recent while Rushcliffe and Willersley Park deserve a visit.

The stock of Leicestershire golf was enhanced considerably by the crowning in 1991 as Amateur champion of Gary Wolstenholme who learned and played all his early golf in the county.

G1 Abbotsley

☎(01480) 215153,Course: 474000, Fax 403280
Eynesbury Hardwicke, St Neots, Cambs PE19 4XN
3 miles E of A1(M) through St Neots, 12 miles W of Cambridge on A45; easy access along A45 from M11 junction 13
Undulating parkland/meadowland course.
Old course(Abbotsley), 18 holes, 6311 yards, S.S.S.71; New course (Cromwell), 18 holes, 6087 yards, S.S.S.69
Designed by Derek Young, Vivien Saunders, Jenny Wisson.
Founded 1986
Visitors: welcome every day; no h/cap necessary.
Green Fee: WD: Old course, £20, New course £8; WE £25, New course £12.
Societies: weekdays and off-peak weekends.
Catering: snacks, meals served 7 days; restaurant and bar facilities.
Driving range, squash (6 courts), practise facilities, pool table, Vivien Saunders residential golf school.
Hotels: 17-bed country Hotel on site.

G2 Aspley Guise & Woburn Sands

☎(01908) 583596 (Sec), Club 582974
West Hill, Aspley Guise, Milton Keynes MK17 8DX
2 miles W of M1 junction 13, between Aspley Guise and Woburn Sands.
Parkland course.
18 holes, 6135 yards, S.S.S.70
Designed by Sandy Herd.
Founded 1914
Visitors: welcome weekdays with h/cap cert; with members weekends.
Green Fee: £22 per round; £28 per day.
Societies: Wed and Fri.
Catering: full facilities available except Mon.
Hotels: Bedford Arms; Moore Place; Broughton.

G3 Barkway Park

☎(01763) 848215
Nuthampstead Rd, Barkway, Nr Royston, Herts SG8 8EN
On B1368 approx 5 miles S of Royston.
Gently undulating woodland course.
18 holes, 7000 yards, S.S.S 74.
Designed by Vivien Saunders.
Founded 1991

Visitors: welcome; weekend tee times cannot be booked until Fri pm; no non h/cap players before 11am.
Green Fee: WD £12; WE £17.
Societies: very welcome, terms to be arranged.
Catering: full facilities.
Practice area. Driving range 1996.

G4 Beadlow Manor Hotel, Golf & Country Club

☎(01525) 860800, Fax 861345
Beadlow, Nr Shefford, Beds SG17 5PH
On A507 between Ampthill and Shefford, 1.5 miles W of Shefford.
Parkland course.
Baron Manhatten, 18 holes, 6619 yards, S.S.S.72; Baroness Manhatten, 18 holes, 6072 yards, S.S.S.69
Founded 1973
Visitors: welcome.
Green Fee: WD Baroness £16.50, Baron £9; WE Baroness £27.50, Baron £15.
Societies: welcome anytime, selection of packages available.
Catering: Public bar serving snacks; 2 restaurants; Italian restaurant, private golf members bar.
Driving range, health club, 5 conference rooms.
Hotels: 30-bedroom hotel on site.

G5 Bedford & County

☎(01234) 352617, Pro 359189, Club 354010, Fax 357195
Green Lane, Clapham, Beds MK41 6ET
Off A6 N of Bedford before Clapham village.
Parkland course.
18 holes, 6399 yards, S.S.S.70
Founded 1912
Visitors: welcome weekdays, advisable to phone; with member weekends.
Green Fee: WD £22.50.
Societies: Mon, Tues, Thurs and Fri.
Catering: available.

G6 Bedfordshire

☎(01234) 261669 (Sec), Members: 353241, Pro 353653
Bromham Rd, Biddenham, Bedford MK40 4AF
1.5 miles from town centre on A428, NW of town boundary.
Parkland course.
18 holes, 6305 yards, S.S.S.70
Designed by Tom Dunn
Founded 1891

Visitors: welcome weekdays only.
Green Fee: £20 per round, £24 per day.
Societies: catered for on weekdays by arrangement.
Catering: lunch daily; full bar and evening meals.

G7 Beedles Lake

☎(0116) 2606759
Broome Lane, East Goscote, Leics LE7 3NQ
Take A46 from Leicester to the village of East Goscote.
Parkland course
18 holes 6573 yards S.S.S. 71
Founded 1993
Visitors: welcome
Green Fee: WD £6; WE £8
Societies: Welcome except Fri, Sat, Sun.
Catering: Full facilities, conservatory for societies
Driving range, putting green

G8 Birstall

☎(0116) 2674322, Pro 2675245
Station Rd, Birstall, Leicester LE4 3BB
3 miles N of town just off A6.
Parkland course.
18 holes, 6222 yards, S.S.S.70
Founded 1901
Visitors: not weekends.
Green Fee: £25.
Societies: Wed and Fri by prior arrangement; reduction in green fees for parties over 20.
Catering: not Mon.
Snooker, billiards.

G9 Blaby

☎(0116) 2784804
Lutterworth Rd, Blaby, Leics LE8 3DP
From Leicester, through Blaby village, course on left hand side.
9 holes, 5132 yards, S.S.S 66
Founded 1991
Visitors: welcome, pay-as-you-play.
Green Fee: WD £4; WE £6.
Societies: also specialists in company days.
Catering: bar, bar meals.
Driving range.

G10 Bourn

☎(01954) 718057, Pro 718958
Toft Rd, Bourn, Cambridge CB3 7TT
From Cambridge take road to Sandy, branch off on B1046; from M11 junction 12 take A603 to Sandy then B1046.

Parkland course.
18 holes, 6273 yards, S.S.S.70. To
be extended summer 96
Designed by J. Hull and S. Bonham.
Founded Sept 1991
Visitors: welcome; dress code
applies.
Green Fee: WD £15; WE £25.
Societies: welcome weekdays.
Catering: bar snacks and restaurant
meals.

G11 **Brampton Heath**
☎(01604) 843939
Sandy Lane, Church Brampton,
Northants NN6 8AX
3 miles north of Northampton off the
A50
Parkland/Meadowland course
18 holes, 6084 yards, S.S.S. 69
Founded May 1995
Designed by D Snell
Visitors: welcome
Green Fee: WD £10; WE £14
Societies: welcome

Catering: full facilities
Driving range

G12 **Brampton Park**
☎(01480) 434700 (Sec), Pro
434705, Fax 434705
Buckden Rd, Brampton, Huntingdon,
Cambs PE18 8NF
0.5 mile E of A1; Northbound take 1st
Huntingdon turning, Southbound take
turning signposted RAF Brampton.
Picturesque meadowland course by
river with wooded lakes section.
18 holes, 6403 yards, S.S.S.73
Designed by Simon Gidman of
Hawtree & Sons.
Founded 1990
Visitors: Welcome.
Green Fee: WD £18 per round, £24
per day; WE £36.
Societies: Welcome by arrangement
with Sec except Sat and Sun.
Catering: Members bar; bar snacks
and à la carte restaurant for lunch
and dinner.

Hotels: Limited overnight
accommodation on site; bargain
break weekend and single night
packages at Lion, Buckden.

G13 **Cambridge Meridian**
☎(01223) 264700, Pro 264702, Fax
264701
Comberton Road, Toft, Cambs CB3
7RY
Junction 12 off the M11 to Barton,
then Comberton and Toft. The course
is in the village.
Traditional parkland/links style course
18 holes, 6651 yards, S.S.S. 72
(extension planned)
Founded March 1994
Designed P Alliss & C Clark
Visitors: welcome
Green Fee: WD £16; WE £25
Societies: welcome weekdays by
prior arrangement
Catering: full golf club facilities
available.
Hotels: B&B in village of Toft.

BEDFORDSHIRE, NORTHAMPTONSHIRE,
CAMBRIDGESHIRE, LEICESTERSHIRE

G14 Cambridge

☎(01954) 789388
Station Road, Longstanton, Cambs
CB4 5DR
Take the A14 from Cambridge and
then turn into the B1050 at
Longstanton.10 mins from City
Centre
Parkland course
9 holes (18 holes by Aug 96) 6908
yards, S.S.S. 72
Founded 1992
Designed by G Huggett
Visitors: Welcome, pay and play
course
Green Fee: WD £6 (9 holes), £7.50
(18 holes); WE £7.50 (9 holes), £11
(18 holes)
Societies: welcome by prior
arrangement
Catering: Full facilities
Driving range, practice ground, pool
table

G15 Cambridgeshire Moat House Hotel

☎(01954) 780555, Pro 780098, Fax
780010
Bar Hill, Cambs CB3 8EU
Adjacent to A14, 4 miles NW of
Cambridge.
Undulating parkland course.
18 holes, 6734 yards, S.S.S.72
Founded 1974
Visitors: must be members of a golf
club with letter of intro. or
membership card (unless hotel
residents); phone to check course
availability.
Green Fee: WD £20; WE £30.
Societies: welcome by prior
arrangement; only resident societies
at weekends.

Catering: full facilities.
Leisure facilites for Hotel residents.
Hotels: Cambridgeshire Moat House,
bargain breaks/inclusive packages.

G16 Chalgrave Manor

☎(01525) 876556
Dunstable Road, Chalgrave,
Toddington, Beds LU5 6JN
Close to M1 junction 12 exit for
Toddington
Parkland course
18 holes, 6342 yards, S.S.S. 71
Founded May 1994
Visitors: welcome weekdays
Green Fee: £10
Societies: welcome weekdays
Catering: Bar, clubhouse facilities.

G17 Charnwood Forest

☎(01509) 890259
Breakback Rd, Woodhouse Eaves,
Loughborough, Leics LE12 8TA
B591 off A6 at Quorndon, signs to
Woodhouse Eaves; M1 junction 23.
Undulating heathland course.
9 holes, 5960 yards, S.S.S.69
Founded 1890
Visitors: appointments required.
Green Fee: WD £15; WE £25.
Societies: weekdays.
Catering: full facilities; light catering
Mon and Thur.
Hotels: Kings Head; Quorn Country
Club; Johnscliffe.

G18 Cold Ashby

☎(01604) 740548, Pro 740099
Cold Ashby, Northampton NN6 6EP
5 miles E of M1 junction 18, just off
A50 Northampton-Leicester road.

Undulating meadowland course.
27 holes Winnick, Ashby, Elkington.
Winnick/Ashby 6004 yards, S.S.S.69;
Ashby/ Elkington 6308 yards S.S.S
70; Elkington/Winnick 6250 S.S.S. 70
Designed by John Day. Extension: D
Croxton 1995
Founded 1973
Visitors: welcome weekdays; not
before 2pm weekends; no h/cap
restrictions.
Green Fee: WD £14; WE £16.
Societies: welcome weekdays.
Catering: full bar and restaurant
facilities daily.
Hotels: Post House (Crick); Broomhill
(Spratton).

G19 Collingtree Park

☎(01604) 700000, 702600,
Reservations: 701202
Windingbrook Lane, Northampton
NN4 0XN
From M1 Junction 15, follow A508 to
Northampton
Parkland course, 18th hole is an
Island Green.
18 holes, 6692 yards, S.S.S.72
Designed by Johnny Miller.
Founded 1987
Visitors: welcome, bookings taken 1
week in advance.
Green Fee: WD £30; WE £40.
Societies: welcome Mon-Fri by
arrangement, please ring for
corporate brochure.
Catering: bar snacks at all times;
Conservatory Restaurant, a la carte
and table d'hote, banqueting.
Golf Academy; driving range, practice
grounds etc.
Hotels: Stakis (adjacent to 15th
fairway).

G20 Colmworth
☎(01234) 378181, Pro 378822, Fax 376235
Mill Cottage, New Rd, Colmworth, Beds MK44 2NV
5 miles NE of Bedford, off B660.
Undulating farmland course.
18 holes, 6559 yards, S.S.S.69. Par 3 9 hole course.
Designed by John Glasgow.
Founded 1991
Visitors: welcome after 8am every day.
Green Fee: Mon-Weds £6; Thurs/Fri £10; WE £15.
Societies: by prior arrangement.
Catering: Restaurant.
Practice green. Snooker. Driving range under construction.
Hotels: Holiday homes under construction

G21 Colworth
☎(01234) 781781
Unilever Research, Colworth House, Sharnbrook, Bedford MK44 1LQ
10 miles N of Bedford off A6 through village of Sharnbrook.
Parkland course.
9 holes, 2500 yards, S.S.S.32
Founded 1985
Visitors: with member only.
Green Fee: on application.

G22 Corby
☎(01536) 260756
Stamford Rd, Weldon, Northants
A43 Corby to Stamford road, 2 miles E of Weldon.
Municipal parkland course.
18 holes, 6677 yards, S.S.S.72
Founded 1965
Visitors: unlimited.
Green Fee: WD £7; WE £9.
Societies: welcome weekdays.
Catering: snacks and meals.
Hotels: Stakis

G23 Cosby
☎(0116) 2864759, Pro 2848275, Fax 2864484
Chapel Lane, off Broughton Rd, Cosby, Leics LE9 1RG
A46 or A426 out of Leicester, in Cosby village take Broughton Rd.
Undulating parkland course.
18 holes, 6417 yards, S.S.S.71
Founded 1895
Visitors: welcome weekdays before 4pm; with member only weekends and Bank Holidays.
Green Fee: £22.
Societies: book with Sec in advance.

Catering: bar and meals except Mon; book with Steward.
Snooker.
Hotels: Time Out (Blaby).

G24 Daventry & District
☎(01327) 702829, Sec 703204
Norton Rd, Daventry, Northants NN11 5LS
1 mile N of town, next to BBC Station.
Undulating meadowland course.
9 holes, 5812 yards, S.S.S.68
Founded early 1922
Visitors: welcome, not before 11am Sun in winter.
Green Fee: WD £9; WE £12
Societies: contact Pro.
Catering: societies only. Bar

G25 Delapre Park
☎(01604) 764036, Fax 706378
Eagle Drive, Nene Valley Way, Northampton NN4 7DU
3 miles from M1 junction 15 on A508.
Public parkland course.
18 holes, 6269 yards, S.S.S.70; Hardingstone 9 holes, 2109 yards, S.S.S.32
Designed by J. Jacobs and J. Corby.
Founded 1976
Visitors: welcome.
Green Fee: WD £7.30; WE £9.50
Societies: welcome most days, applications in writing.
Catering: daily 9am to 9.30pm.
Driving range.
Hotels: Swallow; Moat House (preferential rates for socs, golf schools).

G26 Dunstable Downs
☎(01582) 604472 (Sec), Pro 662806, Fax 478700
Whipsnade Rd, Dunstable, Beds LU6 2NB
2 miles from Dunstable on Whipsnade road B4541; from London via M1 junction 9, then A5 to town centre, left onto A505, left onto B4541; from N via M1 junction 11, A505 and B4541.
Downland course.
18 holes, 6255 yards, S.S.S.70
Designed by James Braid.
Founded 1907
Visitors: welcome weekdays if member of recognised club; h/cap cert required.
Green Fee: £28.
Societies: welcome Tues and Thurs by arrangement.
Catering: full facilites except Mon.
Hotels: Old Palace Lodge; Kitts Inn.

G27 Elton Furze
☎(01832) 280189 (Pro)
Bullock Rd, Haddon, Peterborough, Cambs PE7 3TT
From A1 take exit signposted Alwalton/Showground onto old A605; approximately 4 miles W of Peterborough.
Parkland course.
18 holes, 6315 yards, S.S.S.70
Designed by Roger Fitton.
Founded April 1993
Visitors: welcome Tues and Thurs; h/cap cert required.
Green Fee: £20.
Societies: Tues and Thurs, contact Pro shop for details.
Catering: full facilities.
Practice ground.

G28 Ely City
☎(01353) 662751 (Sec), Pro 663317, Fax 668636
Cambridge Rd, Ely, Cambs CB7 4HX
On A10, on S outskirts of Ely going towards Cambridge.
Parkland course.
18 holes, 6627 yards, S.S.S.72
Designed by Henry Cotton.
Founded 1962
Visitors: h/cap cert required at all times unless playing with member.
Green Fee: WD £24; WE £30.
Societies: welcome Tues-Fri inclusive.
Catering: full facilities; restaurant, bar and bar snacks.
Hotels: Fenland Lodge; Nyton House; Lamb; Highways Motel.

G29 Embankment
(01933) 228465
The Embankment, Wellingborough, Northants NN8 1LD
In the Embankment area of the city alongside the river
Parkland course
9 holes 3374 yards S.S.S. 55
Founded 1977
Designed: H Neal
Visitors: with members only
Green Fee: on application
Societies: not allowed
Catering: Bar and limited food

G30 Enderby
☎(0116) 2849388
Mill Lane, Enderby, Leics LE9 5LH
From M1 junction 21 to Enderby, then follow signposts to Leisure Centre.
Municipal heathland course.
9 holes, 4232 yards, S.S.S.61
Founded 1986

Visitors: no restrictions.
Green Fee: WD £3.95 (9 holes), £4.95 (18 holes); WE £4.95 (9 holes), £6.95 (18 holes)
Societies: welcome by arrangement.
Catering: bar and bar snacks.
Leisure Centre.

G31 Farthingstone Hotel G & LC

☎(01327) 361291(Bookings), Pro 361533, Fax 361645
Farthingstone, Towcester, Northants NN12 8HA
Junction 16 off M1, W off A5 between Weedon and Towcester, 3 miles from Weedon.
Undulating parkland course.
18 holes, 6300 yards, S.S.S.71
Designed by M. Gallagher.
Founded 1974
Visitors: welcome at all times.
Green Fee: WD £10; WE £15.
Societies: welcome at all times.
Catering: full facilities.
Snooker, squash.
Hotels: Farthingstone.

G32 Forest Hill

☎(01455) 824800
Markfield Lane, Botcheston, Leics LE9 9FJ
2 miles from Botcheston, 3 miles SW of A50; 10 mins from M1 junction 21.
Well-wooded parkland course.
18 holes, 6111 yards, S.S.S.69
Founded March 1991 (Changed name 1995)
Visitors: welcome any time, pay-as-you-play; advisable to book tee times in advance.
Green Fee: WD £10; WE £15.
Societies: any time by prior arrangement.
Catering: bar, restaurant. proposed 1996
Driving range.

G33 Girton

☎(01223) 276169, Pro 276991, Fax 277150
Dodford Lane, Girton, Cambs CB3 0QE
3 miles N of Cambridge on A604.
Flat open course.
18 holes, 6085 yards, S.S.S.69
Founded 1936
Visitors: welcome weekdays.
Green Fee: £16 per round
Societies: weekdays.
Catering: lunches, dinners served except Mon.
Hotels: Post House (Impington).

G34 Glen Gorse

☎(0116) 2714159 (Sec/Manager), Pro 2713748
Glen Rd, Oadby, Leicester LE2 4RF
A6 towards Market Harborough, club between Oadby and Great Glen.
Parkland course.
18 holes, 6603 yards, S.S.S.72
Founded 1933
Visitors: welcome weekdays, weekends only with member.
Green Fee: £23
Societies: weekdays; £25/day.
Catering: snack meals, sandwiches, full meals served except Mon.
Snooker room.
Hotels: Leicester Moat House.

G35 Gog Magog

☎(01223) 247626, Pro 246058, Fax 414990
Shelford Bottom, Cambridge CB2 4AB
2 miles S of Cambridge on A1307 Colchester road
Undulating course.
18 holes, 6398 yards, S.S.S.70; 9 holes, 5873 yards, S.S.S.68
(Extending to 18 in 1997)
Designed by Hawtree
Founded 1972
Visitors: weekdays with h/cap cert, weekends with member.
Green Fee: £30 per round, £37.50 per day (£19 with a member at weekends).
Societies: welcome Tues and Thurs.
Catering: daily
Hotels: University Arms; Garden House; Gonville.

G36 Greetham Valley

☎(01780) 460444 (Club), Pro 460666, Fax 460623
Wood Lane, Greetham, Nr Oakham, Leics LE15 7RG
1 mile off A1, 8 miles from Oakham on B668; 10 mins from Stamford.
Parkland course.
27 holes, Ash, Beech, Chestnut. Ash/Beech 6362 S.S.S.71; Beech/Chestnut 5875 SSS 68; Ash/Chestnut 5875 S.S.S. 68; 9 holes 1374 yards, Par 3
Founded Oct 1991-April 1992
Visitors: welcome any time, no bookings, h/caps required.
Green Fee: WD £15; WE £20; Par 3 course, £3 WD, £4 WE.
Societies: welcome.
Catering: Clubhouse open to non-members, bar snacks available; restaurant lunchtime and evenings.
Driving range, bowling green.

G37 Griffen

☎(01582) 415573
Caddington, Luton, Beds LU1 4AX
From M1 junction 11 head towards Dunstable, left at 1st roundabout (Tesco), left at next roundabout onto A505, turn right to Caddington after 0.75 mile; signposted from Caddington village.
Meadowland course.
18 holes, 6161 yards, S.S.S.69
Founded 1982
Visitors: welcome, not before 2pm weekends; half set per person, golf shoes, no jeans.
Green Fee: WD £12.
Societies: by arrangement.
Catering: bar and snacks, meals to order.

G38 Hellidon Lakes Hotel and Country Club

☎(01327) 262550, Pro 262551, Fax 262559
Hellidon, Nr Daventry, Northants NN11 6LN
15 miles from M1 junction 16 by A45 and A361 Banbury road, turn right before village of Charwelton; 15 miles from M40 junction 11 by A361.
Undulating parkland course.
27 holes, 18 hole Lakes 6587 yards, S.S.S. 72; 9 hole Holywell 2791 S.S.S. 67
Designed by David Snell.
Founded Jan 1991
Visitors: welcome but must book through Pro shop; bona fide h/cap certs required at weekends.
Green Fee: on application.
Societies: welcome by arrangement.
Catering: full facilities, restaurant, bar meals, conference and banqueting rooms.
Driving range, fly fishing, tennis, snooker, health studio, swimming pool.
Hotels: Own 4-star hotel (45 bedroom), inclusive golfing packages available.

G39 Hemingford Abbots

☎(01480) 495000, Fax 496000
Cambridge Rd, Hemingford Abbots, Cambs PE18 9HQ
Alongside A604 between Huntingdon and St Ives.
Public parkland course.
9 holes, 5468 yards, S.S.S.68
Designed by Advanced Golf Services Ltd.
Founded 1991
Visitors: welcome.
Green Fee: WD £10; WE £15.

Societies: small meetings welcome by arrangement.
Catering: bar, snacks etc.
Affiliated driving range.
Hotels: St Ives; The Bridge.

G40 Heydon Grange Golf & Country Club

☎(01763) 208988, Fax 208926
Heydon, Royston, Herts SG8 7NS
M11 junction 10 onto A505 towards
Royston, take 2nd left to Hayden,
course signposted.
Downland/parkland course with lakes.
27 holes (3 x 9-hole loops) played in
3 18-hole combinations:
Essex/Cambs, 6512 yards, S.S.S.71;
Essex/Herts, 6387 yards, S.S.S.70;
Cambs/Herts, 6623 yards, S.S.S.72.
Designed by Alan Walker.
Founded 1994
Visitors: welcome at all times; book
in advance; correct dress required.
Green Fee: £15.
Societies: and Company Days,
welcome by arrangement; packages
available.
Catering: lounge bar, cocktail and
wine bar, Grange Restaurant (Indian
and SE Asian cuisine), Lakeside
Restaurant (a la carte, carvery on
Sun); conferences and functions
catered for.
Driving range, extensive practice
grounds.

G41 Hinckley

☎(01455) 615124, Pro 615014, Fax
890841
Leicester Rd, Hinckley, Leics LE10
3DR
NE boundary of Hinckley on A47.
Lakeside parkland course.
18 holes, 6517 yards, S.S.S.71
Founded 1894 (as Burbage Common;
name changed 1981).
Visitors: Mon, Wed, Thurs and Fri;
limited at weekends.
Green Fee: £25.
Societies: Mon and Wed only by
arrangement.
Catering: daily except Sun evenings.
2 snooker rooms
Hotels: Sketchley Grange; Hinckley
Island; Three Pots Inn.

G42 Humberstone Heights

☎(0116) 2761905 (Office), Pro
2764674
Gipsy Lane, Leicester LE5 0TB
Off the Uppingham road opposite
Towers Hospital.
Municipal parkland course

18 holes, 6343 yards, S.S.S.70
Designed by Hawtree & Son.
Founded 1978
Visitors: no restrictions.
Green Fee: WD £6.80; WE £7.95
Societies: weekdays only.
Catering: bar snacks; meals by
arrangement.
Pitch & Putt course. Driving range

G43 Ivinghoe

☎(01296) 668696
Wellcroft, Ivinghoe, Leighton Buzzard,
Beds LU7 9EF
Behind The Kings Head in Ivinghoe
village, 4 miles from Tring and 6 miles
from Dunstable.
Meadowland course.
9 holes, 4508 yards, S.S.S.62
Designed by R. Garrad & Sons.
Founded 1967
Visitors: after 9am weekdays, after
8am weekends.
Green Fee: WD £7 (18 holes); WE
£8 (18 holes). 9 holes £5
Societies: weekdays.
Catering: lunches except Mon.
Hotels: Rose & Crown (Tring);
Stocks (Aldbury).

G44 John O'Gaunt

☎(01767) 260360, Pro 260094, Fax
261381
Sutton Park, Sandy, Beds SG19 2LY
On B1040 between Potton and
Biggleswade.
Undulating parkland courses.
John O'Gaunt, 18 holes, 6513 yards,
S.S.S.71; Carthagena, 18 holes, 5869
yards, S.S.S.69
Designed by Hawtree.
Founded 1948
Visitors: welcome, advisable to
contact club.
Green Fee: WD £40; WE £50
Societies: weekdays only.
Catering: full catering available.
Hotels: Stratton House
(Biggleswade); Rose & Crown
(Potton), Holiday Inn (Sandy).

G45 Kettering

☎(01536) 512074, Sec 511104, Pro
81014
Headlands, Kettering, Northants
NN15 6XA
Headlands joins Bowling Green Rd,
on which are the Council Offices;
continue along Headlands for about
0.5 mile, past Fire Station on left, club
is over railway bridge on right.
Meadowland course.
18 holes, 6081 yards, S.S.S.69

Designed by Tom Morris.
Founded 1891
Visitors: welcome weekdays;
weekends and Bank Holidays with
member.
Green Fee: £22 (£10 with member).
Societies: Wed and Fri; apply for
details.
Catering: lunch and evening meal
except Mon.
Hotels: George Hotel; Royal Hotel;
Park.

G46 Kibworth

☎(0116) 2792301 (Sec/fax), Pro
2792283
Weir Rd, Kibworth, Beauchamp, Leics
LE8 0LP
8 miles SE of Leicester on A6.
Meadowland course.
18 holes, 6333 yards, S.S.S.70
Founded 1962
Visitors: welcome weekdays.
Green Fee: £22 per round, £25 per
day
Societies: Mon, Wed, Thurs.
Catering: full facilities; special all-in
package for societies including
morning coffee, lunch and dinner.
Driving range, snooker
Hotels: Three Swans (Market
Harborough); The Yews (Great Glen);
Hermitage.

G47 Kilworth Springs

☎(01858) 575082, Pro 575974
North Kilworth, Lutterworth, Leics
LE17 6HJ
5 miles E of M1 junction 20, just off
A427 towards Market Harborough.
Front 9 links, back 9 parkland/lake
setting.
18 holes Championship course, 6718
yards, S.S.S 72
Founded August 1993
Visitors: all welcome when tee times
available; members have 7-day
booking advantage.
Green Fee: WD £17; WE £21.
Societies: welcome any time
provided tee times available.
Catering: full catering and bar
facilities; function room and
board/meeting rooms available.
Floodlit driving range.
Hotels: Sun Inn (Marston Trussell);
Wharf House (Welford); Denby
(Lutterworth).

G48 Kingfisher Lakes

(01908) 562332
Buckingham Rd, Deanshanger,
Northants MK 19 6DG

On A422 Buckingham road 7 miles from Milton Keynes opposite the village of Deanshanger
Parkland course with lakes
9 holes 2600 yards (Extension planned 1996)
Founded Aug 1994
Visitors: welcome, pay as you play course
Green Fee: £5 (9 holes), £10 (18 holes)
Societies: welcome. Corporate days organised.
Catering: Full facilities, 2 restaurants, 2 bars, function room.
Driving range, clay pigeon shooting, fishing, model steam railway
Hotels: Shires (opposite club)

G49 Kingstand

☎(0116) 2387908, Fax 2388087
Beggars Lane, Leicester Forest East, Leicester LE3 3NQ
Off main A47 Hinckley road; 5 mins M1 junction 21.
Parkland course.
9 holes, 5380 yards, Par 66
Designed by S. Chenia.
Founded 1991
Visitors: welcome; dress code applies.
Green Fee: WD £4 (9 holes), £6 (18 holes); WE £5 (9 holes), £7 (18 holes).
Societies: times to be arranged with Pro; flexible terms.
Catering: restaurant; also excellent Indian restaurant on site..
Driving range, gymnasium.

G50 Kingsthorpe

☎(01604) 710610 (Sec), Club 711173, Pro 719602
Kingsley Rd, Northampton NN2 7BU
2 miles from town centre, off A508 to Market Harborough.
Undulating parkland course.
18 holes, 5918 yards, S.S.S.69
Designed by Charles Alison
Founded 1908
Visitors: welcome weekdays by arrangement, not weekends.
Green Fee: £25.
Societies: welcome by arrangement.
Catering: lunches, dinners served.
Hotels: Moat House; Swallow, Stakis.

G51 Kingsway

☎(01763) 262727, Fax 263289
Cambridge Rd, Melbourne, Royston, Herts SG8 6EY
On A10, N of Royston, S of Cambridge.

Pay-and-Play course on landscaped farmland.
9 holes 4910 yards, S.S.S. 64
Founded April 1991
Visitors: welcome any time.
Green Fee: £5.50 (9 holes), £9.50 (18 holes).
Societies: welcome by prior arrangement.
Catering: bar and restaurant.
Driving range, 9 hole Pitch & Putt.

G52 Kirby Muxloe

☎(0116) 2393457 (Sec), Pro 2392813
Station Rd, Kirby Muxloe, Leicester LE9 9EN
On A47 3 miles W of Leicester.
Parkland course.
18 holes, 6351 yards, S.S.S.70
Founded 1893
Visitors: not Tues, must have valid h/cap cert; Captains permission required at weekends.
Green Fee: £20 per round, £25 per day.
Societies: weekdays except Tues on application.
Catering: full facilities.
Snooker room, banqueting.
Hotels: Red Cow, Forest Park

G53 Lakeside Lodge

☎(01487) 740540 (Sec), Pro 741541
Fen Road, Pidley, Huntingdon, Cambs PE17 3DD
Pidley is on B1040 Ramsey-St Ives road.
Modern, challenging public course; suits all standards of golfer.
18 holes, 6821 yards, S.S.S.73; 9 holes Par-3
Designed by Alistair Headley.
Founded 1991
Visitors: welcome at any time.
Green Fee: WD: £9; WE £15.
Societies: welcome weekdays.
Catering: full facilities available.
Driving range.
Hotels: Slepe Hall (St Ives), George (Ramsey).

G54 Langton Hall

☎(01858) 545134
Langton Hall, Leicester LE16 7TY
11 miles S of Leicester on A6, turn left after Kibworth, course 1.5 miles on left.
Parkland course.
9 holes, 6742 yards, S.S.S 72
Designed by Hawtree & Co.
Founded 1993
Visitors: welcome.

Green Fee: WD £9 (9 holes), £13.50 (18 holes); WE £9 (9 holes), £18 (18 holes).
Societies: welcome.
Catering: bar and light snacks.
Practice area.

G55 Leicestershire

☎(0116) 2738825 (Club), Pro 2736730
Evington Lane, Leicester LE5 6DJ
Evington village in SE district of Leicester, 2 miles from city centre.
Parkland course.
18 holes, 6312 yards, S.S.S.70
Founded 1891
Visitors: welcome.
Green Fee: WD £23 per round, £28 per day; WE £29 per round, £34 per day
Societies: welcome weekdays by prior arrangement.
Catering: lunches and teas daily.
Hotels: Daval; Rowans; Thornwood; Stanfre House; Gordon Lodge.

G56 Leighton Buzzard

☎(01525) 372143 (Pro), Sec 373811, Steward: 373812
Plantation Rd, Leighton Buzzard, Beds LU7 7JF
1 mile N of Leighton Buzzard off A418, take left fork at Stag Inn; or M1 junction 12 Toddington to Heath and Reach via Hockliffe.
Parkland course.
18 holes, 6101 yards, S.S.S.70
Founded 1925
Visitors: welcome weekdays except Tues with h/cap cert.
Green Fee: WD £20 per round, £27 per day.
Societies: welcome except Tues and weekends, £45 full day package.
Catering: available 7 days.
Hotels: Cock Horse (Heath and Reach)

G57 Lingdale

☎(01509) 890035 (Club), Sec 890703, Pro 890684
Joe Moore's Lane, Woodhouse Eaves, Loughborough, Leics LE12 8TF
5 miles S of Loughborough on B5330.
Undulating parkland course.
18 holes 6545 yards, S.S.S.71
Designed by D.W. Tucker & G. Austin.
Founded 1967
Visitors: welcome.
Green Fee: WD £16 per round, £20 per day; WE £23.

Societies: Mon to Fri by prior arrangement with Secretary.
Catering: full catering facilities.
Hotels: Kings Head; De Montford.

G58 **Links**
☎(01638) 663000 (Sec), Pro 662395
Cambridge Rd, Newmarket, Suffolk
CB8 0TG
1 mile S of Newmarket High St.
Undulating parkland course.
18 holes, 6574 yards, S.S.S.71
Founded 1902
Visitors: not before 11.30am Sun unless with member; h/cap certs required.
Green Fee: WD £26; WE £30.
Societies: by arrangement.
Catering: full service except Mon.
Hotels: White Hart.

G59 **Longcliffe**
☎(01509) 239129, Pro 231450
Snell's Nook Lane, Nanpantan,
Loughborough, Leics LE11 3YA
1 miles from M1 junction 23 off A512
towards Loughborough.
Heathland course.
18 holes, 6611 yards, S.S.S.72
Founded 1904
Visitors: weekdays 9am-4.30pm except Tues with h/cap cert; weekends with member only.
Green Fee: £22 per round, £30 per day
Societies: Mon-Fri excluding Tues, Ladies day.
Catering: bar, restaurant, bar snacks.
Hotels: Friendly Hotel

G60 **Lutterworth**
☎(01455) 552532 (Sec), Pro 557199
Rugby Rd, Lutterworth, Leics LE17
5HN
0.5 mile from M1 exit 20 on A4114.
Undulating course.
18 holes, 6431 yards, S.S.S.71
Designed by D. Snell.
Founded 1904
Visitors: welcome weekdays; weekends with member only.
Green Fee: £16
Societies: Mon to Fri.
Catering: full facilities 7 days.

G61 **March**
☎(01354) 52364 (Pro)
Frogs Abbey, Grange Rd, March,
Cambs PE15 0YH
A141, W off March by-pass, signposted.
Parkland course.

9 holes, 6204 yards, S.S.S.70
Founded 1920
Visitors: weekdays only.
Green Fee: £15 (£7.50 with member)
Societies: welcome Mon to Fri with prior booking.
Catering: bar, normal hours; meals with prior booking.
Pool table.
Hotels: Griffin.

G62 **Market Harborough**
☎(01858) 463684
Great Oxendon Rd, Market
Harborough, Leics LE16 8NB
1 mile S of town on A508
Northampton road.
Parkland course.
18 holes, 6622 yards, S.S.S.69
Founded 1898
Visitors: welcome weekdays; with member only weekends.
Green Fee: £16
Societies: welcome with prior arrangement.
Catering: facilities available.
Hotels: Three Swans.

G63 **Melton Mowbray**
☎(01664) 62118
(Clubhouse/office/fax), Pro 69629
Thorpe Arnold, Melton Mowbray,
Leics LE14 4SD
2 mile NE of Melton Mowbray on
A607 Grantham road.
Undulating course.
18 holes, 6222 yards, S.S.S.70
Founded 1925
Visitors: welcome before 3pm.
Green Fee: WD £20; WE £25.
Societies: weekdays by arrangement, £29.50 for 27 holes inc meals etc.
Catering: bar and restaurant.
Hotels: Grange; George;
Harborough; Stapleford Park.

G64 **Mentmore**
☎(01296) 662020, Fax 662592
Mentmore, Leighton Buzzard, Beds
LU7 0QN
On B488 4 miles SW of Leighton
Buzzard.
Rolling parkland course with lakes and trees.
Roseberry, 18 holes, 6763 yards,
S.S.S 72; Rothschild, 18 holes, 6777
yards, S.S.S. 72
Designed by Bob Sandow
Founded Oct 1992
Visitors: welcome; apply for details.
Green Fee: £30 per round, £45 per day.

Societies: apply for details.
Catering: bar, restaurant; function suite for 120.
Practice ground, indoor swimming pool, sauna, steamroom, jacuzzi.
Hotels: Peadley Manor (Tring), special arrangements for golfers.

G65 **Millbrook**
☎(01525) 840252 (Office), Pro
402269 Fax 406249
Millbrook, Beds MK45 2JB
Just E of M1 between junctions 12 and 13; from S take junction12 and proceed to Flitwick, Steppingley and Millbrook: from N take junction13, immediately right to Ridgmont and left at main Ampthill-Woburn road; course access opposite Chequers Pub in Millbrook.
Links course.
18 holes, 7051 yards, S.S.S.73
Designed by W. Sutherland.
Founded 1980
Visitors: at 24 hrs notice, weekdays except Thurs, weekends after noon.
Green Fee: WD £15; WE £25
Societies: weekdays except Thurs; Sun after 12 noon.
Catering: bar and restaurant.
Hotels: White Hart; The Firs GH.

G66 **Mount Pleasant**
☎(01462) 850999
Station Rd, Lower Stondon, Henlow,
Beds SG16 6JL
0.75 mile W of Stondon/Henlow
Camp roundabout off A600 Hitchin to Bedford road.
Undulating meadowland course.
9 holes, 6172 yards, S.S.S.69
Designed by Derek Young.
Founded July 1992
Visitors: welcome at all times, booking advisable weekends and also evenings May-Sept. Visitors can book 2 days in advance.
Green Fee: WD £5.50 (9 holes), £10
(18 holes); WE £7.50 (9 holes), £14
(18 holes).
Societies: welcome, weekdays preferred.
Catering: bar snacks only, full catering by prior arrangement.
Putting green, pitching green, bunker and undercover nets.
Hotels: Bird in Hand.

G67 **Mowsbury**
☎(01234) 771041 (Sec), Pro
216374, Bar: 771493
Cleat Hill, Kimbolton Rd, Bedford
MK41 8DQ

Northampton

Histories of Golf Clubs show that a great many of them began life on sites different to those which they now enjoy. Some early beginnings are recorded on photographs and plans that adorn clubhouse walls. Though moves have become rarer, one recent exception has been Northampton GC which forsook its old home in the centre of the city in favour of an exciting future at Harlestone on the edge of Lord Spencer's estate near Althorp.

It came about as a result of intricate negotiations involving the Estate, the Club and a company wishing to develop the city site. Similar deals elsewhere have been discussed but Northampton is one of the few that have brought hope to life. Having faced the increasing problem of existing within four rigid boundaries, the new-found sense of spaciousness and rural splendour is profound. However, an equally attractive part of the deal is a fine new clubhouse looking out over Harlestone Lake and three finishing holes which are unusual to say the least. The short 16th and 18th demand shots to carry the water while the 17th is a teasing hole where courage with the drive reaps a telling reward.

As the approach to the clubhouse dips down and up again past the church, it is immediately clear that the modern Northampton has a special character that combines challenge with enjoyment – the principle requirements of any good course. There is a pleasant start with a second shot at the 1st to a green below, a short hole over water to a clearing in the wood at the 2nd and a par 5 3rd from a high tee which needs a controlled drive in order to obtain the correct line for a second shot which is attractively tree lined. This formed part of a clearance operation and the piping of a small stream that supplies the lake on the 2nd.

There are three or four changes of character in the layout which next introduces a dogleg round the perimeter of the wood and then, after another short hole, ventures forth into more open territory where the main features are a few large established trees and the boundary walls of mellow Northamptonshire stone.

Before the turn is reached back near the clubhouse, the 8th has another dropping second shot down a shallow valley while the 9th threads its way between ancient trees that are more trunk than foliage – a haven for owls and insects. The 10th scales a slight crest, leading back to the open ground where several holes run parallel, the par 5 12th carrying the added threat of out of bounds to sliced shots. Bunkers guard the short 13th but gradually Harlestone Lake looms, the 15th carrying players down a long slope to a green in front of the old boat house, reconstructed as a condition of planning approval. The 15th green lies close to the 18th. And before the round is complete, there is a searching test of skill, nerve and decision, a climax that will be the centre of much debate, much gnashing of teeth and much jubilation.

Water holes are becoming more commonplace in British golf although few are more teasing than the par 3 16th with its green far wider than it is deep. Clearing the lake is one thing but there are penalties for overshooting the green. Trees and sharp banks surround a sloping putting surface. Position from the tee is important on the 17th but, in spite of a formidable carry from the 18th and an undulating fairway on the other side, the pitch to the green can be quite demanding. Together with Collingtree and Overstone, on the other side of town, the new Northampton has added a powerful dimension to the county's golf.

On Kimbolton Rd, from Bedford 2 miles N of city centre.
Municipal parkland course.
18 holes, 6514 yards, S.S.S.71
Designed by Hawtree.
Founded 1975
Visitors: welcome.
Green Fee: on application
Societies: on application
Catering: snacks, meals, drinks available; functions.
Driving range, squash.

G68 Northampton
☎(01604) 845155, Bar: 845102, Pro 845167, Fax 820262
Harlestone, Northampton NN7 4EF
On A428 Rugby road, approx 4 miles out of Northampton.
Parkland course.
18 holes, 6555 yards, S.S.S.71
Designed by Donald Steel.
Founded 1893
Visitors: weekdays only.
Green Fee: £25.
Societies: weekdays, not Wed.
Catering: full facilities available.
Snooker, banqueting.
Hotels: Northampton Moat House; Heyford Manor.

G69 Northamptonshire County
☎(01604) 843025 (Sec), Club 842170, Pro 842226
Golf Lane, Church Brampton, Northampton NN6 8AZ
Off A50 Northampton-Leicester road, 4.5 miles from Northampton.
Undulating heathland/parkland course.
18 holes, 6503 yards, S.S.S.71
Designed by H.S. Colt.
Founded 1909
Visitors: by arrangement; h/cap certs needed.
Green Fee: £37.50.
Societies: normally Wed only.
Catering: 11am-9pm summer; 11am-6pm winter, otherwise by arrangement.
Hotels: Broomhill (Spratton); Pytchley (West Haddon); Red Lion (East Haddon).

G70 Oadby
☎(0116) 2709052, Steward: 2700215
Leicester Rd, Oadby, Leicester LE2 4AB
On A6 from Leicester, just outside city limits, inside Leicester Race Course.

Public meadowland course.
18 holes, 6376 yards, S.S.S.70
Founded 1975
Visitors: welcome.
Green Fee: WD £6; WE £9.
Societies: on application to Oadby and Wigston Borough Council.
Catering: apply to Steward.

G71 Old Nene Golf & Country Club
☎(01487) 815622 (Clubhouse), Sec 813519, Pro 710122
Muchwood Lane, Bodsey, Ramsey, Cambs PE17 1XQ
1 mile N of Ramsey, between Ramsey and Ramsey Mereside.
Pay-as-you-Play, flat parkland course with water features.
9 holes, 5524 yards, S.S.S.67
Designed by Richard Edrich.
Founded Aug 1992
Visitors: no restrictions subject to tee reservations.
Green Fee: WD £7 (9 holes), £10 (18 holes); WE £9 (9 holes), £13 (18 holes)..
Societies: welcome; book with Sec.
Catering: lounge, dining room, bar.
Driving range, snooker table, coarse fishing.
Hotels: George, Yesteryear GH (Ramsey); Swallow, Orton Hall (Peterborough).

G72 Orton Meadows
☎(01733) 237478
Ham Lane, Orton Waterville, Peterborough, Cambs PE2 0UU
On A605 Peterborough-Oundle road, 2 miles W of Peterborough at entrance to Ferry Meadows Country Park.
Municipal parkland course.
18 holes, 5664 yards, S.S.S.67
Designed by Dennis & Roger Fitton.
Founded 1987
Visitors: advance bookings welcome.
Green Fee: WD £8.50; WE £11..
Societies: welcome except before 11am Sun.
Catering: adjoining steakhouse The Granary.
Hotels: Travelodge next to The Granary.

G73 Oundle
☎(01832) 273267 (Sec/fax); Pro 272273
Benefield Rd, Oundle, Northants PE8 4EZ
On A427 Oundle-Corby road, 1.5 miles from Oundle.

Undulating parkland course.
18 holes, 6235 yards, S.S.S.70
Founded 1893
Visitors: after 10.30am weekends and Bank Holidays, otherwise no restriction.
Green Fee: WD £20; WE £30..
Societies: welcome except Tues and weekends.
Catering: full service available, except Mon.
Hotels: Talbot; Bridge (Thrapston).

G74 Overstone Park
☎(01604) 671471, Pro 643555, Fax 671109
Billing Lane, Northampton NN6 0AP
Take A45 Northampton road, Billing Lane is off the main A45.
Parkland course, set in 800 acre Victorian walled estate.
18 holes, 6602 yards, S.S.S.72
Designed by Donald Steel.
Founded July 1993
Visitors: guests accompanying members only.
Green Fee: £25
Catering: bar and brasserie.
Health and leisure club; practice area.

G75 Park Hill
(01509) 815454 (Sec/Club), Pro 815775
Park Hill, Seagrave, Leics LE12 7NG
A46 Leicester-Newark road; after 5 miles take turning into Seagrave
Meadowland course
9 holes (extending to 18 in May 1996)
7101 yards, S.S.S. 74
Founded May 1995
Visitors: welcome by prior arrangement
Green Fee: on application
Societies: welcome weekdays and some at weekends
Catering: full facilities, function room
Practice area
Hotels: Willoughby

G76 Pavenham Park
☎(01234) 822202
Pavenham Park, Pavenham, Beds MK43 7PE
5 miles outside Bedford on A6.
Parkland course
18 holes, 6353 yards, S.S.S. 70
Founded Oct 94
Visitors: weekdays only
Green Fee: £13
Societies: weekdays by prior arrangement
Catering: Clubhouse opening 1996.
Limited facilities until then.

G77 Peterborough Milton
☎(01733) 380489 (Sec/fax), Pro 380793
Milton Ferry, Peterborough
PE6 7AG
On A47 2 miles W of Peterborough.
Parkland course.
18 holes, 6456 yards, S.S.S.72
Designed by James Braid.
Founded June 1938
Visitors: weekdays only by prior arrangement with Sec.
Green Fee: £20 per round, £30 per day.
Societies: weekdays only by prior arrangement with Sec.
Catering: full facilities.
Hotels: Haycock Inn; Moat House.

G78 RAF Cottesmore
☎(01572) 812241 ext 7760
Oakham, Leicester LE15 7BL
7 miles N of Oakham off B668.
Parkland course.
9 holes, 5622 yards, S.S.S.67
Founded 1980
Visitors: with member only.
Green Fee: on application

G79 RAF Henlow
☎(01462) 851515 ext 7083/7873.
Henlow Camp, Beds SG16 6DN
3 miles SE of Shefford on A505,
follow signs to RAF Henlow.
Meadowland course.
9 holes, 5618 yards, S.S.S.67
Founded 1985
Visitors: only with member.
Green Fee: on application
Societies: can be arranged through Sec.
Catering: light refreshment.
Hotels: Bird in Hand.

G80 RAF North Luffenham
☎(01780) 720041 ext 7523.
North Luffenham, Oakham, Leics
LE15 8RL
Follow signposts for RAF North
Luffenham from A606, station is close
to Rutland Water.
Meadowland course.
9 holes, 6010 yards, S.S.S.70
Founded 1975
Visitors: with member or by
appointment through Sec.
Green Fee: on application.
Societies: can be arranged through
Sec.
Catering: bar and restaurant
facilities.
Hotels: George; Crown.

G81 Ramsey
☎(01487) 812600, Pro 813022
4 Abbey Terrace, Ramsey,
Huntingdon, Cambs PE17 1DD
12 miles SE of Peterborough, off
B1040.
Parkland course.
18 holes, 6123 yards, S.S.S.70
Designed by J. Hamilton Stutt.
Founded 1965
Visitors: weekdays only, on
production of h/cap cert.
Green Fee: £22.
Societies: weekdays by arrangement
except Thurs.
Catering: full facilities.
6-rink outdoor bowling green.
Hotels: George (Ramsey).

G82 Rothley Park
☎(0116) 2302019 (Clubhouse), Sec
2302809, Pro 2303023
Westfield Lane, Rothley, Leicester
LE7 7LH
6 miles N of Leicester, W of A46.
Parkland course.
18 holes, 6477 yards, S.S.S.71
Founded 1912
Visitors: welcome if member of
recognised club with h/cap; members'
guests only Tues, weekends and
Bank Holidays.
Green Fee: WD £25 per round, £30
per day; WE £30.
Societies: Wed and Thurs.
Catering: full catering except Mon.
Hotels: Rothley Court.

G83 Rushcliffe
☎(01509) 852959, Pro 852701
Stocking Lane, East Leake,
Loughborough, Leics LE12 5RL
Between Gotham and East Leake 6
miles N of Loughborough; easy reach
of M1 junction 24.
Well-wooded heathland course.
18 holes, 6013 yards, S.S.S.69
Founded 1910
Visitors: welcome, properly dressed
and preferably club golfers.
Green Fee: £22
Societies: Mon-Fri, April 1 to Oct 31.
Catering: bar and restaurant.

G84 Rushden
☎(01933) 312581 (Club), Sec
418511
Kimbolton Rd, Chelveston,
Wellingborough, Northants NN9 6AN
On A45 2 miles E of Higham Ferrers.
Undulating meadowland course.
10 holes, 6335 yards, S.S.S.70
Founded 1919

Visitors: welcome weekdays except
Wed pm; weekends with member
only.
Green Fee: £15 (£10 with member).
Societies: bookable in advance,
weekdays only, not Weds pm
Catering: any time except Mon..

G85 St Ives
☎(01480) 468392, Pro 466067
Westwood Rd, St Ives, Cambs PE17
4RS
B1040 off A45 in St Ives
Parkland course.
9 holes, 6100 yards, S.S.S.69
Founded 1923
Visitors: welcome weekdays; with
member only weekends.
Green Fee: £20 per day
Societies: not weekends.
Catering: full facilities
Hotels: Slepe Hall.

G86 St Neots
☎(01480) 472363 (Sec/fax), Club
474311, Pro 476513
Crosshall Rd, St Neots, Huntingdon,
Cambs PE19 4AE
On B1048 off A1.
Parkland course with water hazards.
18 holes, 6027 yards, S.S.S.69
Designed by Harry Vardon (original
9).
Founded 1890
Visitors: welcome any day;
weekends with member; h/cap cert
required.
Green Fee: £20 per round, £30 per
day.
Societies: welcome except Fri, Sat,
Sun, Mon.
Catering: full service available in
clubhouse.
Snooker.
Hotels: Eaton Oak; Kings Head.

G87 Scraptoft
☎(0116) 2418863, Pro 2419138
Beeby Rd, Scraptoft, Leicester LE7
9SJ
Turn off A47 main Leicester-
Peterborough road to Scraptoft at
Thurnby.
Meadowland course.
18 holes, 6166 yards, S.S.S.69
Founded 1928
Visitors: welcome; jacket, collar and
tie in clubhouse.
Green Fee: WD £20.50; WE £25.50
Societies: Mon-Fri.
Catering: meals served every day
except Mon.
Hotels: White House.

G88 Shelthorpe
☎(01509) 267766
Poplar Road, Loughborough, Leics
From Leicester on A6 turn left at 1st
traffic lights, over island, then 2nd left,
signposted.
Municipal parkland course.
18 holes Par 3, 2080 yards
Visitors: welcome.
Green Fee: £2.85

G89 South Bedfordshire
☎(01582) 591500 (Sec), Pro 591209
Warden Hill Rd, Luton, LU2 7AA
3 miles N of Luton on A6, signposted
(right) into Warden Hill Rd; left at end,
slip road to right of School.
Undulating course; some trees,
hawthorn hedges; dries well.
Galley course, 18 holes, 6389 yards,
S.S.S.71; Warden course, 9 holes,
4914 yards, S.S.S.64
Founded 1892
Visitors: welcome; Galley weekdays
only with h/cap cert unless by prior
arrangement; Warden any time.
Green Fee: WD: Galley, £18,
Warden £9; WE: Galley £25, Warden,
£12.
Societies: mainly Wed, Thurs.
Catering: snacks from 10.30am-
9.30pm; set lunch, dinner by
arrangement.
Snooker.
Hotels: Chiltern; Strathmore; many
small hotels.

G90 Staverton Park
☎(01327) 302000, Pro 705506
Staverton, Daventry, Northants NN11
6JT
On A425 Daventry to Leamington
road, 1 mile S of Daventry; near M1
junctions 16/18 and M40 junctions
11/12.
Undulating meadowland course.
18 holes, 6661 yards, S.S.S.72
Designed by Comm. John Harris.
Founded 1978
Visitors: welcome.
Green Fee: WD £19; WE £22.50
Societies: welcome Mon-Fri.
Catering: full facilities at all times.
Snooker, solarium, sauna,
trimnasium, banqueting suites.
Driving range
Hotels: Staverton Park offers golfing
weekends

G91 Stockwood Park
☎(01582) 413704 Pro
Stockwood Park, London Rd, Luton,
Beds LU1 4LX

M1 junction 10, turn left towards town
centre, then left at 1st set of traffic
lights into Stockwood Park.
Meadowland course.
18 holes, 6049 yards, S.S.S.69
Designed by Charles Lawrie.
Founded 1973
Visitors: welcome at all times.
Green Fee: WD £7.30; WE £9.60.
Societies: Mon/Tues/Thurs, contact
Pro
Catering: breakfast and lunch; dinner
for societies by arrangement.
Driving range, 9-hole Pitch & Putt.
Hotels: Strathmore.

G92 Stoke Albany
☎(01858) 535208
Ashley Rd, Stoke Albany, Market
Harborough, Leics LE16 8PL
Take A6 towards Dingley, then the
B669 from Dingley
Parkland course
18 holes 6132 yards S.S.S. 69
Designed Hawtree & Sons
Founded 1995
Visitors:welcome
Green Fee: WD £12; WE £15
Societies: welcome
Catering: Clubhouse planned 1996
Practice ground

G93 Thorney Golf Centre
☎(01733) 270570
English Drove, Thorney,
Peterborough, Cambs PE6 0TJ
A47 E of Peterborough.
Municipal fenland course.
18 holes, 6104 yards S.S.S. 69; 9
holes, Par 3.
Also Thorney Lakes 18 hole
members course 6402 yards, S.S.S
71
Designed by A. Dow. Thorney Lakes
opened June 1995.
Founded May 1991
Visitors: unlimited.
Green Fee: Municipal: WD £5.50;
WE £7.50. Thorney Lakes: WD £10;
WE £16.
Societies: any time.
Catering: bar and restaurant.
Driving range.

G94 Thorpe Wood
☎(01733) 267701, Fax 332774
Nene Parkway, Peterborough PE3
6SE
On A47 to Leicester 2 miles W of
Peterborough, next to Moat House
Hotel.
Parkland course.
18 holes, 7086 yards, S.S.S.74

Designed by Peter Alliss and Dave
Thomas.
Founded 1975
Visitors: unrestricted.
Green Fee: WD £8.80; WE £11.
Societies: by arrangement up to a
year in advance.
Catering: at Greenkeeper.
Hotels: The Moat House.

G95 Tilsworth
☎(01525) 210721, **Catering:**
210722
Dunstable Rd, Tilsworth, Leighton
Buzzard, Beds LU7 9PU
On A5, 1 mile N of Dunstable.
Parkland course.
18 holes, 5306 yards, S.S.S.66
Founded 1972
Visitors: welcome all times except
Sun 7.30-9.30am.
Green Fee: WD £8; WE £10.
Societies: welcome weekdays.
Catering: hot and cold food available
lunchtimes Mon-Sat, also Thurs, Fri,
Sat evenings.
Driving range.
Hotels: Swan; Crest (Luton).

G96 Ullesthorpe
☎(01455) 209023, Fax 202537
Frolesworth Rd, Ullesthorpe,
Lutterworth, Leics LE17 5BZ
B577 off A5 to Claybrooke and
Ullesthorpe, follow signs to course.
Meadowland course.
18 holes, 6650 yards, S.S.S.72
Visitors: weekdays.
Green Fee: £13.50 per round, £21.50
per day
Societies: weekdays.
Catering: bar snacks and restaurant.
Leisure facilities at hotel.
Hotels: 39-bed hotel on site.

G97 Waterbeach Barracks
☎(01223) 861048 (Sec)
39th Engineering Regiment,
Waterbeach, Cambs CB5 9PA
Fenland course.
9 holes, 6237 yards, S.S.S. 70
Founded 1972
Visitors: HM Forces welcome,
civilians must be introduced by and
play with member.
Green Fee: apply for details.
Catering: limited bar.

G98 Wellingborough
☎(01933) 677234, Pro 678752
Harrowden Hall, Great Harrowden,
Wellingborough, Northants NN9 5AD

1 mile NE of Wellingborough to right of A509.
Parkland course.
18 holes, 6617 yards, S.S.S.72
Designed by Hawtree & Sons.
Founded 1893
Visitors: welcome weekdays except Tues with h/cap cert.
Green Fee: £25 per round, £30 day.
Societies: Wed, Thurs, Fri by prior arrangement; with h/cap certs.
Catering: bar, snacks, restaurant. Snooker, swimming pool.
Hotels: Hind; Oak House; Tudor Gate.

G99 West Park Golf & Country Club

☎(01327) 858092, Pro 858588, Fax 858009
Whittlebury, Nr Towcester, Northants NN12 8XW
On A413, 15 mins from M1 junction 15a, M40 junction 10.
Parkland/lakeland course.
4 x 9 hole loops (1905, Royal Whittlewood, Grand Prix, Wedgewood Academy), giving 6700 yard, Par 72 combinations.
Designed by Cameron Sinclair.
Founded June 1992
Visitors: welcome; h/cap certs not required but h/cap standard expected.
Green Fee: WD £25; WE £30.
Societies: welcome at all times subject to availability.
Catering: bars, bistros, restaurant; function suite.
9 hole indoor course, clay pigeon shoot, archery, cricket ground, croquet lawn; corporate hospitality.

G100 Western Park

☎(0116) 2872339
Scudamore Rd, Braunstone Frith, Leicester LE3 1UQ

Off A47, 2 miles W of city centre.
Public parkland course.
18 holes.6518 yards, S.S.S. 70
Designed by F.W. Hawtree.
Founded 1920
Visitors: welcome; book at weekends.
Green Fee: WD £4.95; WE £5.95.
Societies: welcome by prior arrangement.
Catering: facilities available 7 days a week.

G101 Whaddon Golf Centre

☎(01223) 207325
Church St, Whaddon, Nr Royston, Herts SG8 5RX
4 miles N of Royston, 9 miles S of Cambridge off A603.
Public parkland course.
9 holes Par 3795 yards
Designed by Richard Green
Founded 1987
Visitors: welcome.
Green Fee: WD £2.50; WE £3.
Catering: bar snacks.
Driving range, putting green.Crazy golf. Fishing.

G102 Whetstone

☎(0116) 2861424 (Sec/fax)
Cambridge Rd, Cosby, Leicester LE9 5SH
4 miles from M1 junction 21, SE of Leicester; take A46 to Narborough, then signposts to Whetstone.
Wooded parkland course with water features.
18 holes, 5795 yards, S.S.S.68
Designed by Nick Leatherland.
Founded 1963
Visitors: welcome; restricted weekends, book in advance.
Green Fee: WD £12; WE £13
Societies: by arrangement.

Catering: bar and food available.
Driving range.
Hotels: Time Out (Blaby).

G103 Willesley Park

☎(01530) 414596, Pro 414820
Tamworth Rd, Ashby-de-la-Zouch, Leics LE65 2PF
On B5006 approx 1.5 miles from centre of Ashby-de-la-Zouch S towards Tamworth; from M42 junction 11, 2 miles N towards Ashby-de-la-Zouch on B5006.
Undulating parkland/heathland course.
18 holes, 6304 yards, S.S.S.70
Designed by C.K. Cotton.
Founded 1921
Visitors: with reservation, must be bona fide members of another club.
Green Fee: WD £27.50; WE £32.50.
Societies: welcome Wed, Thurs, Fri (April-Sept) by prior arrangement.
Catering: full facilities except Mon. Snooker.
Hotels: Royal; Fallen Knight.

G104 Wyboston Lakes

☎(01480) 223004
Wyboston Lakes, Wyboston, Beds MK44 3AL
Off A1 S of St Neots.
Public parkland course round lakes.
18 holes, 5310 yards, S.S.S.69
Designed by Neil Oackden.
Founded 1981
Visitors: welcome; weekend bookings 1 week in advance through Pro.
Green Fee: WD £10; WE £14.
Societies: welcome.
Catering: full catering
Hotels: Hotel on site with special reduced rates offered to societies. (Telephone for details: Wyboston Lakes 212625).

H

SUFFOLK, NORFOLK

Suffolk and Norfolk provide all the ingredients for a perfect golfing holiday, any number of excellent courses – seaside and inland – in settings that give golfers a special sense of escape.

Journeys from London have been considerably assisted by new roads plus a bridge over the River Orwell at Ipswich which is spectacular. But East Anglia remains something of a quiet backwater, which contributes greatly to its popularity. Felixstowe Ferry, the place where Bernard Darwin learned to play, is the oldest, retaining a measure of its quaintness in spite of many changes since the clubhouse was based around its famous Martello Tower.

The best holes are those nearest the sea, those on the other side of the road filling the flatter land, although perhaps the most unusual hole, the short 12th, straddles the road with the tee shot having to clear a safety net to protect the passers-by – motorised and pedestrian.

Further up the coast lie Aldeburgh and Thorpeness, contrasting Clubs and courses that, nevertheless, can conveniently be taken together. For all of the nearness of the sea, neither can be classed as seaside, Thorpeness, with a profusion of heather, and Aldeburgh, weaving its crafty way between the gorse across the common.

Woodbridge is another Suffolk delight in an area around Ipswich which includes Purdis Heath and Rushmere.

Crossing the county boundary into Norfolk, the coastal path heads for Great Yarmouth & Caister, founded in 1882, Sheringham, Brancaster and Hunstanton. Lovers of racing will have identified Great Yarmouth & Caister from the stands, the first and last holes hurdling the rails and several others enclosed by the track.

The best is very good after a slightly mundane start but the focus for the connoisseur is fixed on Hunstanton and the Royal West Norfolk links at Brancaster which occupy as remote a tract as any on which the game is played. Hunstanton, one hundred years old in 1991, is a full-blown championship test divided by a central ridge of dunes that gives it a bit of a Jekyll and Hyde character.

Brancaster, on the other hand, derives its character more from deep sleepered bunkers, sandy turf, a unique stretch of marshland and a rich variety in the size, angling, shaping and defence of its greens. A year junior to Hunstanton, it rubs shoulders with nature in all its aspects, adverse weather adding a wild, bleak dimension that, for all its ferocity, can add appeal.

On more modern lines are the two courses and varied leisure facilities at Barnham Broom on the outskirts of Norwich which gain in popularity.

Cambridge University golfers have an understandably soft spot for East Anglia, fixtures, in addition to Hunstanton, including Royal Norwich and, in the old days, a final trial at Thetford which has a fine new clubhouse and a changed course since then. The changes, dictated by the Thetford-by-pass, necessitated intrusion into the forest or, at least, what was forest until the terrible storm of October 1987. Only a few scraggy pines survived the blast but Thetford, ancient and modern, is full of charm that deserves to be sampled.

From Thetford, it is relatively plain sailing to Cambridge either through or round Newmarket. On the way, there is a port of call at Royal Worlington & Newmarket which you overlook at your peril.

Given the accolade by Bernard Darwin of "the sacred nine", it is a masterpiece of simple design, a triumph in fitting a quart into a pint pot. In winter, it is a veritable haven that offers the ideal of a day of foursomes with the lure of characteristic refreshment to re-fuel the system. Throughout the world, I have enjoyed nothing better.

H1 Aldeburgh

☎(01728) 452890, Pro 453309, Fax 452937
Saxmundham Rd, Aldeburgh, Suffolk IP15 5PE
6 miles E of A12 midway between Ipswich and Lowestoft.
Heathland course.
18 holes, 6330 yards, S.S.S.71; 9 holes, 4228 yards, S.S.S.64
Designed by John Thompson and Willie Fernie.
Founded 1884
Visitors: welcome weekdays; weekends by arrangement with Sec; h/cap required for 18 hole course; no 3 or 4 ball games permitted on 18 hole course, 2 ball or foursomes only.
Green Fee: on application.
Societies: welcome by arrangement with Sec.
Catering: lunches served.
Hotels: Wentworth; White Lion; Brudenell; Uplands.

H2 Alnesbourne Priory

☎(01473) 727393/Fax
Priory Park, Ipswich, Suffolk IP10 0JT
Leave A14 Ipswich southern by-pass at exit marked Ransomes Europark, Nacton; follow signs to Industrial Estate; take 1st left after 200 yards, follow single lane road for 1 mile to reception.
Pretty parkland course fronting Orwell estuary.
9 holes, 1760 yards, S.S.S.58
Founded 1987
Visitors: always closed Tues, experienced golfers in correct attire welcome any other time.
Green Fee: between £9 and £12 for afternoon or day ticket.
Societies: restricted to Tues only by arrangement.
Catering: bar and restaurant; function room.
Tennis, heated outdoor swimming pool in summer, Adventure Playground, nature trails.
Hotels: log cabin accommodation on site; also 50 executive touring sites.

H3 Barnham Broom Hotel Golf & Country Club

☎(01603) 759393, Fax 758224
Honingham Rd, Barnham Broom, Norwich, Norfolk NR9 4DD
10 miles SW of Norwich between A11 and A47.
Valley and Hill courses.
Hill, 18 holes, 6628 yards, S.S.S.72; Valley, 18 holes, 6470 yards, S.S.S.71
Designed by Frank Pennink (Valley), Donald Steel (Hill).
Founded 1977
Visitors: welcome weekdays, booking preferred; residents 7 days; proof of club membership required.
Green Fee: £25 per round, £30 per day.
Societies: welcome, details on application.
Catering: restaurant and snack bar. Leisure centre, squash, tennis, snooker etc.
Hotels: Barnham Broom, golf getaway breaks, details on request.

H4 Bawburgh

☎(01603) 740404, Pro 742323, Fax 740403
Long Lane, Bawburgh, Norfolk NR9 3LX
To S of Royal Norfolk Showground; take Bawburgh exit off A47 Norwich southern bypass.
Parkland/heathland course.
18 holes, 6224 yards, S.S.S.70
Designed by S. Manser.
Founded 1978, extended 1992
Visitors: welcome by arrangement.
Green Fee: WD £15; WE £20.
Societies: by arrangement only.
Catering: full facilities.
Driving range.
Hotels: Park Farm.

H5 Bungay & Waveney Valley

☎(01986) 892337
Outney Common, Bungay, Suffolk NR35 1DS
A143 Bury St Edmunds to Great Yarmouth road, about 0.5 mile from town centre.
Heathland course.
18 holes, 6026 yards, S.S.S.69
Designed by James Braid.
Founded 1889
Visitors: welcome weekdays only; with member at weekends.
Green Fee: £18 per day/round.
Societies: arranged by writing to club; weekdays only except Tues.
Catering: full (snacks Mon).
Hotels: The Swan; King's Head.

H6 Bury St Edmunds

☎(01284) 755979, Fax 763288
Tuthill, Bury St Edmunds, Suffolk IP28 6LG
1st exit eastbound off A14 for Bury St Edmunds, 0.25 mile down B1106 to Brandon on right.
Parkland course.
18 holes, 6678 yards, S.S.S.72; 9 holes, 4434 yards, S.S.S.62
Designed by Hawtree (9 hole), Ray (18 hole).
Founded 1924
Visitors: welcome weekdays inc. Bank Holidays; only with member weekends.
Green Fee: 18 hole course, £24; 9 hole course, WD £11, WE £12.
Societies: weekdays by arrangement; not weekends or Bank Holidays.
Catering: full service available.
Hotels: Butterfly.

H7 Caldecott Hall

☎(01493) 488488
Caldecott Hall, Beccles Road, Fritton, Great Yarmouth NR31 9EY
On the A143 road to Great Yarmouth
Links style
9 holes (18 tees) 6842 yards, S.S.S. 73
Founded 1994
Visitors: welcome
Green Fee: WD £15 (18 holes); WE £20
Societies: by arrangement
Catering: snacks available, Bar 200 yards away
9 hole par 3 course, 9 hole pitch and putt

H8 Costessy Park

☎(01603) 746333
Old Costessy, Norwich, Norfolk NR8 5AL
3 miles W of Norwich, turn off A47 Southern by-pass on to 1074, turn at Round Well public house.
Parkland/river valley course.
18 holes, 5964 yards, S.S.S.69
Designed by Frank Macdonald.
Founded 1983
Visitors: welcome, not before 11.30am weekends.
Green Fee: apply for details.
Societies: by arrangement.
Catering: full catering and bar facilities.
Practice area; golf cart hire for physically handicapped.

H9 Cretingham

☎(01728) 685275, Fax 685037
Cretingham, Woodbridge, Suffolk IP13 7BA
2 miles from A1120 at Earl Soham; 10 miles N of Ipswich.
Parkland course.
9 holes, 4552 yards, S.S.S.64
Founded 1984

We are the **ROYAL CROMER GOLF CLUB's** officially appointed Hotel. Only 1 mile away we are in an ideal setting for your holiday. We offer a service to arrange your golfing holiday for you. Golfing during the day and in the evening special dinners and dances, theme evenings or even excursions to local attractions. **SPECIAL GROUP DISCOUNTS ARE GIVEN.**
This recently refurbished Edwardian Hotel is overlooking the sea on the beautiful North Norfolk coast. We have 30 en-suite bedrooms all with seaviews, an all day Bar and Coffee Shop, and Bolton's Seafood Bistro open 12noon-2pm & 6-10pm. Please telephone for our Golf pack.
CLIFTONVILLE HOTEL, SEAFRONT, CROMER, NORFOLK NR27 9AS (Tel: 01263 512543)

Visitors: welcome every day from 8am until dusk; h/caps not required.
Green Fee: WD £8 per day; WE & BH £10 per day.
Societies: by arrangement.
Catering: full restaurant and licensed bar, catering for groups.
Practice range, 5-hole Pitch & Putt, snooker, outdoor swimming pool, tennis, caravan park.

H10 **Dereham**
☎(01362) 695900, Pro 695631
Quebec Rd, Dereham, Norfolk NR19 2DS
Take B1110 from Dereham.
Parkland course.
9 holes, 6225 yards, S.S.S.70
Founded 1934
Visitors: welcome with h/cap cert; only with member weekends.
Green Fee: WD £20; WE £10 (with member).
Societies: by arrangement.
Catering: meals and snacks on demand, sandwiches only on Mon.
Hotels: Phoenix; George; Kings Head.

H11 **Diss**
☎(01379) 642847, Sec 641025, Pro 644399
Stuston Common, Diss, Norfolk IP22 3JB
Half way between Norwich and Ipswich, 2 miles W of A140 (turn at Scole).
Commonland course.
18 holes, 6238 yards, S.S.S.70
Founded 1903
Visitors: welcome, weekends after 4pm in summer; no restrictions Oct-March.
Green Fee: £20 per day.
Societies: very welcome weekdays.
Catering: full facilities, excellent restaurant in refurbished clubhouse.
Driving range nearby.

H12 **Dunham Golf Club (Granary)**
☎(01328) 701718
Little Dunham, Nr Swaffham, King's Lynn, Norfolk PE32 2DF

Off A47 at Necton/Dunham crossroad.
Parkland course with lakes.
9 holes, 4422 yards, Par 64
Founded 1987
Visitors: welcome.
Green Fee: WD £9; WE £12.
Societies: welcome by prior arrangement.
Catering: bar snacks available.

H13 **Dunston Hall**
☎(01508) 470178. **Hotels:** 470444.
Dunston Hall, Ipswich Road, Norwich NR14 8PQ
On the main A140 Ipswich road, 10 minutes drive from Norwich city centre
Meadowland course
10 holes (18 tees), 6053 yards S.S.S. 69
Founded July 1994
Visitors: welcome; priority to hotel guests
Green Fee: WD £15; WE £18

Societies: welcome by prior arrangement
Catering: full facilities in club house. Hotel has conference suite.
Leisure centre, driving range.
Hotels: Dunston Hall

H14 **Eagles**
☎(01553) 827147
39 School Road, Tilney All-Saints, King's Lynn, Norfolk PE34 4RS
On A47 between King's Lynn and Wisbech, 5 miles from King's Lynn.
Public moorland course.
9 holes, 4284 yards, S.S.S.61; 9 holes Par 3
Designed by David Wilson Horn.
Founded Nov 1990
Visitors: welcome any time.
Green Fee: WD £5.75 (9 holes); WE £6.75.
Societies: ring for details.
Catering: bar facilities.
Driving range.
Hotels: Butterfly; Globe.

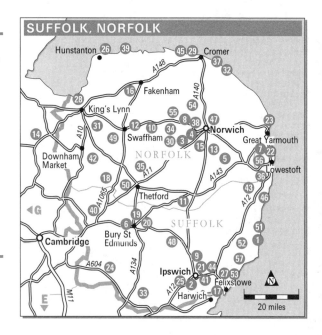

H15 **Eaton**

☎(01603) 451686/Fax, Club 452881
Newmarket Rd, Norwich NR4 6SF
Off A11 into Sunningdale, signposted;
approx 1.5 miles from centre of
Norwich.
Undulating course.
18 holes, 6135 yards, S.S.S.69
Founded 1910
Visitors: welcome all week but not
before 11.30 at weekends.
Green Fee: WD £28 (£15 half day);
WE £35 (£20 half day).
Societies: by arrangement.
Catering: snacks served weekdays;
teas all week.
Hotels: Post House; Hotel Norwich.

H16 **Fakenham**

☎(01328) 862867, Pro 863534
Sports Centre, The Race Course,
Fakenham, Norfolk
B1146 from Dereham or A1067 from
Norwich.
Parkland course.
9 holes, 5992 yards, S.S.S.69
Designed by Charles Lawrie.
Founded 1981
Visitors: welcome.
Green Fee: WD £14; WE £18 (pm
only).
Societies: by arrangement.
Catering: in Sports Centre.
Hotels: Crown; Limes; The Mill.

H17 **Felixstowe Ferry**

☎(01394) 286834
Ferry Rd, Felixstowe, Suffolk IP11
9RY
A14 to Felixstowe, avoid turning right
off A14; follow signs to Yatching
Centre.
Links course.
18 holes, 6042 yards, S.S.S.70
Designed by Henry Cotton & Sir Guy
Campbell.
Founded 1880
Visitors: welcome weekdays.
Green Fee: £22 per day
Societies: Tues, Wed and Fri.

Catering: lunch available 7 days;
evening meals by arrangement.
Hotels: Orwell Moat House, also own
s/c flats available.

H18 **Feltwell**

☎(01842) 827644, 827762
Thor Ave, Feltwell, Thetford, Norfolk
IP26 9XX
0.5 mile S of Feltwell on B1112; right
towards 2 large 'golf balls' (satellite
tracking station).
Open inland links course.
9 holes (18 tees), 6256 yards,
S.S.S.70
Founded 1972
Visitors: Welcome, sometimes
restricted at weekends.
Green Fee: WD £12; WE £20.
Societies: Any weekday.
Catering: Bar; catering 6 days/ week.
Hotels: Brandon House (Brandon).

H19 **Flempton**

☎(01284) 728291
Flempton, Bury St Edmunds, Suffolk
IP28 6EQ.
4 miles NE of Bury St Edmunds on
A1101 to Mildenhall.
Breckland course.
9 holes, 6240 yards, S.S.S.70
Designed by J. H. Taylor.
Founded 1895
Visitors: welcome weekdays, h/cap
cert required; with members only at
weekends and Bank Holidays.
Green Fee: WD £20 (18 holes), £26
per day.
Societies: very limited.
Catering: excellent by arrangement.
Hotels: The Priory and Angel Hotel;
The Riverside (Mildenhall).

H20 **Fornham Park Golf & Country Club**

☎(01284) 706777, Fax 706721
St John's Hill Plantation, The Street,
Fornham All Saints, Bury St
Edmunds, Suffolk IP28 6JQ

Off A45 to Bury St Edmunds (2
miles), B1101 to Brandon; or A134
Bury-Thetford road at Fornham St
Martin.
Parkland course.
18 holes, 6209 yards, S.S.S.70
Founded 1976
Visitors: welcome anytime.
Green Fee: WD £10 per round, £16
per day; WE £12 per round, £19 per
day.
Societies: welcome.
Hotels: Butterfly, Suffolk, Angel,
Priory, Bell (Thetford).

H21 **Fynn Valley**

☎(01473) 785463, Fax 785632
Witnesham, Ipswich, Suffolk IP6 9JA
On B1077, 2 miles due N of Ipswich.
Parkland course.
18 holes, 5807 yards, S.S.S.67; 9
holes Par 3, 1000 yards.
Designed by Tony Tyrrell.
Founded April 1991
Visitors: not Sun or Wed am
(Ladies); proper golf equipment and
clothing on main course.
Green Fee: WD £8 for 9 holes, £14
for 18 holes, £18 per day; WE £9 for
9 holes, Par 3 course, £3.50 per
round, £5 per day; discounts for jnrs.
Societies: any weekday except Wed.
Catering: bar and light refreshments,
full restaurant and lounge.
Driving range, multi-level practice
bunkers, chipping and putting greens.

H22 **Gorleston**

☎(01493) 661911
Warren Rd, Gorleston, Great
Yarmouth, Norfolk NR31 6JT
Off A12 Yarmouth to Lowestoft road,
Yarmouth end of dual carriageway,
follow signs down Links Rd to Squash
Club, entrance 200 yards on left.
Seaside course.
18 holes, 6404 yards, S.S.S.71
Founded 1906
Visitors: welcome all times, phone
call advisable; h/cap cert required.

KEY		11	Diss	22	Gorleston	34	Reymerston	46	Southwold
1	Aldeburgh	12	Dunham Golf Club	23	Great Yarmouth &	35	Richmond Park	47	Sprowston Park
2	Alnesbourne Priory		(Granary)		Caister	36	Rookery Park	48	Stowmarket
3	Barnham Broom Hotel	13	Dunston Hall	24	Haverhill	37	Royal Cromer	49	Swaffham
	G & CC	14	Eagles	25	Hintlesham Hall	38	Royal Norwich	50	Thetford
4	Bawburgh	15	Eaton	26	Hunstanton	39	Royal West Norfolk	51	Thorpeness
5	Bungay & Waveney	16	Fakenham	27	Ipswich	40	Royal Worlington &	52	Ufford Park Hotel
	Valley	17	Felixstowe Ferry	28	King's Lynn		Newmarket	53	Waldringfield Heath
6	Bury St Edmunds	18	Feltwell	29	Links Country Park	41	Rushmere	54	Wensum Valley
7	Caldecott Hall	19	Flempton	30	Mattishall	42	Ryston Park	55	Weston Park
8	Costessy Park	20	Fornham Park Golf &	31	Middleton Hall	43	St Helena	56	Wood Valley (Beccles)
9	Cretingham		Country Club	32	Mundesley	44	Seckford	57	Woodbridge
10	Dereham	21	Fynn Valley	33	Newton Green	45	Sheringham		

Green Fee: apply for details.
Societies: welcome weekdays, by prior arrangement.
Catering: available.
Hotels: Cliff; St Edmunds.

H23 Great Yarmouth & Caister

☎(01493) 728699
Beach House, Caister-on-Sea, Great Yarmouth, Norfolk NR31 5TD
About 1 mile N of Great Yarmouth on A149 take right turn at roundabout, then right into signposted lane.
Seaside links course.
18 holes, 6330 yards, S.S.S.70
Founded 1882
Visitors: welcome, advisable to telephone in advance.
Green Fee: WD £23.50; WE £28.
Societies: welcome by prior arrangement.
Catering: coffee, lunch and evening meals always available.
Hotels: Imperial.

H24 Haverhill

☎(01440) 61951, Pro 712628, Fax 714883
Coupals Rd, Haverhill, Suffolk CB9 7UW
Leave Haverhill on A604 travelling towards Colchester, pass under railway viaduct, 2nd left into Chalkstone Way, 1st right into Coupals Road.
Parkland course.
9 holes, 5717 yards, S.S.S.68
Designed by Charles Lawrie.
Founded 1973
Visitors: welcome
Green Fee: WD £12 per round, £15 per day (half price with member); WE & BH £16 per round, £20 per day (half price with member).
Societies: welcome by prior arrangement.
Catering: bar facilities; no catering.
Hotels: Woodlands Hotel.

H25 Hintlesham Hall

☎(01473) 652761, Fax 652750
Hintlesham, Ipswich, Suffolk IP8 3NS
4 miles W of Ipswich, 10 mins from A12, A14.
Parkland course.
18 holes, 6638 yards, S.S.S.72.
Designed by Hawtree & Sons.
Founded Sept 1991
Visitors: welcome.
Green Fee: WD £26; WE £45.
Societies: Mon-Fri by prior booking with Sec.

Catering: Stud bar, lounge bar, restaurant.
Private 10-bay driving range, spa, sauna, steam room, outside swimming pool.
Hotels: Hintlesham Hall.

H26 Hunstanton

☎(01485) 532811 (Sec/bookings), Pro 532751, Fax 532319
Golf Course Rd, Old Hunstanton, Norfolk PE36 6JQ
Off A149 in Old Hunstanton (signposted to club), 1 mile N of Hunstanton.
Links course.
18 holes, 6670 yards, S.S.S.72
Founded 1891
Visitors: welcome with h/cap cert, except on Bank Holiday weekends; booking advisable; no 3/4 ball play.
Green Fee: WD £40 per day; WE £50; special rates after 4pm and discounted rates in winter season on application.
Societies: welcome by prior arrangement with Sec.
Catering: available.
Hotels: Le Strange Arms; Lodge; Titchwell Manor; The Lifeboat Inn.

H27 Ipswich

☎(01473) 728941, Fax 715236
Purdis Heath, Bucklesham Rd, Ipswich, Suffolk IP3 8UQ
3 miles E of Ipswich off A14, at roundabout by St Augustine's Church turn into Bucklesham Rd.
Heathland course.
18 holes, 6435 yards, S.S.S.71; 9 holes, 3860 yards, S.S.S.59
Designed by James Braid, Hawtree & Taylor.
Founded 1895
Visitors: only by advance agreement.
Green Fee: WD £30 per day/round; WE £36 per day/round; 9 hole, WD £10; WE £12.
Societies: Mon, Thurs, Fri by advance booking.
Catering: full facilities available.
Hotels: Suffolk Grange.

H28 King's Lynn

☎(01553) 631654 (Sec), Pro 631655, Steward: 631656, Fax 631036
Castle Rising, King's Lynn, Norfolk PE31 6BD
On A149 from King's Lynn to Hunstanton, at Castle Rising sign turn left, continue about 0.75 mile on left hand side.

Parkland course.
18 holes, 6646 yards, S.S.S.72
Designed by Alliss & Thomas.
Founded 1923
Visitors: welcome weekdays except Tues.
Green Fee: WD £32; WE & BH £40.
Societies: Thurs, Fri only.
Catering: lunches daily weekdays; evening meals by arrangement.
Snooker.
Hotels: Red Cat; Dukes Head; Knights Hill.

H29 Links Country Park

☎(01263) 837691, Pro 838215
West Runton, Norfolk NR27 9QH
In West Runton village 2 miles from Sheringham, turn for railway station, over the bridge; course is located 100 yards on right.
Undulating downland course.
9 holes, 2421 yards, S.S.S.32
Founded 1899
Visitors: welcome.
Green Fee: WD £20; WE £25.
Societies: welcome by prior arrangement.
Catering: full facilities.
Tennis, saunas, swimming etc.
Hotels: Links Country Park (free golf for residents).

H30 Mattishall

☎(01362) 850111
South Green, Mattishall, Dereham, Norfolk
B1063 to Mattishall, right at church, 1 mile on left.
Parkland course.
9 holes, 2953 yards, S.S.S.68; 9 hole Pitch & Putt
Founded June 1990
Visitors: all welcome.
Green Fee: apply for details.
Hotels: Phoenix (East Dereham).

H31 Middleton Hall

☎(01553) 841800, Pro 841801
Hall Orchards, Middleton, Nr Kings Lynn, Norfolk PE32 1RH
Off A47 4 miles from King's Lynn, between church and station in Middleton then 1st left.
Parkland course.
9 holes, 5570 yards, S.S.S.67
Extended to 18 holes June 1996
Founded 1989
Visitors: welcome with h/cap cert.
Green Fee: on application.
Societies: welcome by prior booking.
Catering: bar, bar snacks.
Driving range, putting green.

H32 Mundesley

☎(01263) 720279/Fax, Sec 720095,
Links Rd, Mundesley, Norwich,
Norfolk NR11 8ES
Turn off the Mundesley-Cromer road
by Mundesley Church, signposted as
you enter the village.
Undulating course with panoramic
views.
9 holes, 5377 yards, S.S.S.66
Designed by Harry Vardon (in part).
Founded 1903
Visitors: welcome except 11.30-
3.30pm Wed or until 11.30am Sat &
Sun; h/cap cert not required but strict
dress code.
Green Fee: on application.
Societies: welcome by prior
arrangement.
Catering: available daily.

H33 Newton Green

☎(01787) 377217 (Sec), Pro/Fax
313215
Newton Green, Sudbury, Suffolk
CO10 0QN
On A134, 3 miles E of Sudbury.
Moorland course.
18 holes, 5934 yards, S.S.S.67.
Founded 1907
Visitors: weekdays; after 12 noon
weekends
Green Fee: £14 per round, £20 per
day
Societies: welcome by prior
arrangement
Catering: bar and restaurant.

H34 Reymerston

☎(01362) 850297, Pro 850778
(bookings), Fax 850614
Hingham Rd, Reymerston, Norwich,
Norfolk NR9 4QQ
12 miles W of Norwich off B1135
Dereham to Wymondham road.
Farmland course.
18 holes, 6609 yards, S.S.S.72
Designed by ADAS
Founded June 1993
Visitors: welcome any time, h/cap
certs required.
Green Fee: WD £20 per round, £30
(2 rounds); WE £25 per round, £35 (2
rounds).
Societies: welcome any day, min 12;
various options available; telephone
for details.
Catering: bar and snacks available,
Fairway restaurant, function room for
120 persons.
9 hole Pitch & Putt with own catering
facilities.
Hotels: Hotel Norwich; Phoenix
(Dereham).

H35 Richmond Park

☎(01953) 881803, Fax 881817
Saham Road, Watton, Thetford,
Norfolk IP25 6EA
A11 to Thetford, then A1075 to
Watton, turn left at top of High St,
Saham Rd at bottom.
Parkland/meadowland course.
18 holes, 6300 yards, S.S.S.70
Designed by R. Jessup, R. Scott.
Founded July 1990
Visitors: welcome; h/cap cert
weekends to 11am.
Green Fee: WD £15 per round, £20
per day; WE £20 per day/round.
Societies: welcome, bookings only
Catering: bar meals 7 days, a la
carte restaurant Tues-Sat.
Putting green, practice ground/driving
range, mini gym.

H36 Rookery Park

☎(01502) 560380/Fax
Carlton Colville, Lowestoft, Suffolk
NR33 8HJ
2 miles W of Lowestoft on A146.
Parkland course.
18 holes, 6779 yards, S.S.S.72
Designed by Charles Lawrie.
Founded 1975
Visitors: welcome all year.
Green Fee: WD £20; WE & BH £25.
Societies: any weekday except Tues
am.
Catering: full facilities 7 days.
9-hole Par 3 course, snooker.
Hotels: Hedley House; Broadlands.

H37 Royal Cromer

☎(01263) 512884/Fax
145 Overstrand Rd, Cromer, Norfolk
NR27 0JH
1 mile E of Cromer on B1159 coast
road, adjoins Cromer lighthouse.
Undulating seaside course.
18 holes, 6508 yards, S.S.S.71
Designed by James Braid.
Founded 1888
Visitors: accepted weekdays and
after 11am most weekends; booking
essential 1st April-31st Oct.
Green Fee: WD £27; WE & BH £32.
Societies: accepted weekdays.
Catering: daily.
Hotels: Cliftonville; Cliff House;
Anglia Court; Red Lion.

H38 Royal Norwich

☎(01603) 429928 (Sec), Pro 408459
Drayton High Rd, Hellesdon, Norwich
NR6 5AH
500 yards down A1067 Fakenham
road from ring road.

Parkland course.
18 holes, 6603 yards, S.S.S.72
Founded 1893
Visitors: must have h/cap.
Green Fee: on application.
Societies: book in advance.
Catering: restaurant facilities.

H39 Royal West Norfolk

☎(01485) 210223, Sec/Fax 210087
Brancaster, King's Lynn, Norfolk
PE31 8AX
7 miles E of Hunstanton on A149,
take Beach Rd from Brancaster.
Seaside links course.
18 holes, 6428 yards, S.S.S.71
Designed by Holcombe Ingleby.
Founded 1892
Visitors: must be members of
recognised golf club, hold official
h/cap cert and make prior
arrangements with Sec; no visitors,
unless with member, in August.
Green Fee: WD £37.50; WE £46.50.
Societies: small societies by
arrangement; no new visiting
societies at weekends.
Catering: snacks daily; other meals
by arrangement.
Hotels: The Manor (Titchwell); Hoste
Arms (Burnham Market).

H40 Royal Worlington & Newmarket

☎(01638) 712216, 717787
Golf Links Rd, Worlington, Bury St
Edmunds, Suffolk IP28 8SD
6 miles NE of Newmarket, A14 then
A11 towards Thetford; follow signs to
Worlington.
Inland links course.
9 holes, 3105 yards, S.S.S.70
Designed by H.S. Colt.
Founded 1893
Visitors: weekdays only, phone first;
h/cap cert required.
Green Fee: WD £35.
Societies: Tues, Thurs by
appointment; limited 24 players.
Catering: lunch and tea only.
Hotels: Bull Inn (Barton Mills);
Riverside (Mildenhall).

H41 Rushmere

☎(01473) 725648 (Sec), Pro 728076
Rushmere Heath, Ipswich, Suffolk IP4
5QQ
3 miles E of Ipswich off Woodbridge
road A1214.
Heathland course (some common
land).
18 holes, 6262 yards, S.S.S.70
Founded 1927

Thorpeness

Thorpeness combines a whiff of sea air with a touch of rural England. There is no hint of dune or links but the classic golfing terrain is reminiscent of the inland glories of Sunningdale or Woodhall Spa, and that is high praise.

A seaside heath might be the description that most accurately fits the bill although it is trivial to split hairs. What is far more important is conveying the sense of escape, pleasure and challenge that a round inspires. There is little better.

Dealing with the challenge first, this is more than enough to keep the best at full stretch. In make-up, comparisons can be made with Rye or West Sussex which consist basically of a set of excellent short holes, a string of testing fours and one par five. Thorpeness has one less short hole than Rye or West Sussex but there is no doubting the difficulty of keeping a good round together.

It is an excellent driving course with always the knowledge that heather or gorse will engulf the slightest deviation from the straight and narrow. Hitting the ball straight is the hardest part of the game. More golf takes place off the fairway than on it but the thought processes that derail the best intentions are invariably more active when control is essential.

Thorpeness and Aldeburgh are delightful little towns on the Suffolk coast with a pleasant road connecting the two but, for such close neighbours, the golf is nicely different. Thorpeness breaks you in fairly gently with a shortish four whose relative innocence is only unmasked when the pin is tucked behind the dominant bunker guarding the green. However, after the first of the par 3s, and a tough shot at that, the mind is concentrated fully by the 3rd, 4th and 5th.

The 3rd, characterised by having its tee outside the dining room window, demands position from the tee if the second shot from the left is not to be shut out. The jutting-in of a tributary of the Meare offers little margin for error, often making discretion the better part of valour. The 4th and 5th, running in opposite directions, vary according to the wind, some bestowing the 4th with the accolade of the hardest hole and others the 5th.

At 449 yards, the 4th is the longer but, on the 5th, the gorse encroaches alarmingly on the left by the green, and a ridge or bank running across the fairway invariably coincides with the landing area of a good drive. The feature of the 6th is a second from an elevated fairway across a definite dip in front of the green and, on the short 7th, players have to negotiate a carry across water, the best of them from a small tiger tee that adds about 35 yards.

The 8th marks something of a change of scenery on the other side of the road and the disused railway, although the nature of the ground raises the tempo of the challenge and maintains it until the road is recrossed for the 17th and 18th. The 9th is full of subtlety from the drive which angles slightly to the left to a green sloping noticeably from right to left.

A distant view of Sizewell detracts from the aesthetic merits of the short 10th but the five holes from the 12th offer the best of Thorpeness in terms of charm and remoteness; nor is there any let-up in the task in hand. The 12th, 13th and 15th are fours, the pick of them being the 15th, a sharp dogleg to a green with the back lower than the front.

Preceding it is the only par 5, the main decision for the fortunate few lying in whether to treat it as a five or whether to aim directly for a raised green across the scrub and silver birch which tends to obscure the target. The 16th, over the bracken, is the longest of the par 3s but the 17th, up a sharp slope, is the shortest of the par 4s, a balance immediately remedied by the 18th which, besides focusing on a green broader than it is deep, enjoys the background of the old windmill and the strange House in the Clouds, a converted water tower.

The clubhouse itself is also an architectural flight of fancy with its four turrets shaped like golf tees, but it keeps a warm welcome and possesses the added blessing of a hotel or dormy house. Would that more Clubs had the same.

Visitors: weekdays only; h/cap cert or bona fide member of golf club.
Green Fee: £20.
Societies: when dates available.
Catering: full facilities.

H42 Ryston Park
☎(01366) 383834 (Sec), Steward: 382133
Denver, Downham Market, Norfolk PE38 0HH
A10 towards Kings Lynn, before Denver 1 mile S of Downham Market.
Parkland course.
9 holes, 6310 yards, S.S.S.70
Founded 1933
Visitors: weekdays.
Green Fee: £20.
Societies: weekdays.
Catering: full facilities except Mon.

H43 St Helena
☎(01986) 875567, Fax 874565
Bramfield Rd, Halesworth, Suffolk IP19 9XA
1 mile from Halesworth off A144.
Parkland course.
18 holes, 6580 yards, S.S.S.72; 9 holes, 3059 yards, S.S.S.36
Designed by J.W. Johnson
Founded 1990
Visitors: welcome, no restrictions.
Green Fee: 18 holes: WD £15 per round, £18 per day; WE £18 per round; 9 holes £7.50 per round (pay-as-you-play).
Societies: welcome.
Catering: full facilities.
Driving range.

H44 Seckford
☎(01394) 388000, Fax 382818
Seckford Hall Rd, Great Bealings, Woodbridge, Suffolk IP13 6NT
A12, next door to Seckford Hall Hotel.
Pay-and-Play, parkland course.
18 holes, S.S.S.67
Designed by Johnny Johnson.
Founded Aug 1991
Visitors: experienced golfers only, h/caps not required.
Green Fee: £12 per round.
Societies: always welcome; play all day inc. lunch £15.
Driving range, Pitch & Putt.
Hotels: Seckford Hall.

H45 Sheringham
☎(01263) 823488, Pro 822980, Fax 825189
Weybourne Rd, Sheringham, Norfolk NR26 8HG

0.5 mile from Sheringham on A149.
Clifftop course.
18 holes, 6464 yards, S.S.S.71
Designed by Tom Dunn.
Founded 1891
Visitors: welcome with h/cap; phone first.
Green Fee: WD £32.50; WE & BH £37.50.
Societies: by arrangement with Sec weekdays.
Catering: available all week.
Hotels: Beaumaris, Southlands (Sheringham); The Links (West Runton).

H46 Southwold
☎(01502) 723234, Pro 723790
The Common, Southwold, Suffolk IP18 6TB
From A12 follow A1095 signposted Southwold, turn right at Kings Head Hotel, proceed across Common, golf club about 0.5 mile on right.
Common land course.
9 holes, 6050 yards, S.S.S.69
Founded 1884
Visitors: welcome except on competition days; phone in advance.
Green Fee: WE £14; WE £18.
Societies: by arrangement.
Catering: bar and catering facilities.

H47 Sprowston Park
☎(01603) 410657 (Sec), Pro 417264, Fax 788884
Wroxham Rd, Sprowston, Norwich, Norfolk NR7 8RP
1.5 miles from ring road on A1151 Wroxham road; follow Sprowston Park signs.
Parkland course
18 holes, 5985 yards, S.S.S.69
Founded Oct 1980
Visitors: welcome.
Green Fee: WD £12 per round; WE & BH £15.
Societies: welcome 7 days.
Catering: snacks, meals, dinners, Sun lunch; spacious dining room, daily specialities.
East Anglian Academy of Golf; driving range, 18-hole putting green.
Hotels: Sprowston Manor; bargain breaks and golf breaks on application (01603) 410871.

H48 Stowmarket
☎(01449) 736473 (Sec), Pro 736392
Lower Rd, Onehouse, Stowmarket, Suffolk IP14 3DA
2.5 miles SW of Stowmarket, off B1115 Stowmarket-Bidlestone road;

look for Shepherd & Dog public house at junction with Lower Rd.
Parkland course.
18 holes, 6101 yards, S.S.S.69
Founded reformed in 1962
Visitors: welcome weekdays, not Wed am; weekends must have h/cap cert at all times.
Green Fee: WD £20 per round, £25 per day; WE £27 per round, £35 per day.
Societies: Thurs and Fri.
Catering: meals usually available at all times.
Hotels: Cedars (Stowmarket).

H49 Swaffham
☎(01760) 721611
Cley Rd, Swaffham, Norfolk PE37 8AE
1 mile out of town on Cockley Cley road, signposted in market place.
Heathland course.
9 holes, 6252 yards, S.S.S.70
Founded 1922
Visitors: welcome weekdays, weekends only with member.
Green Fee: £18 per round/day.
Societies: welcome by arrangement.
Catering: snacks 7 days, full catering except Mon and Tues.
Hotels: George.

H50 Thetford
☎(01842) 752258, Sec 752169, Pro 752662
Brandon Rd, Thetford, Norfolk IP24 3NE
Take B1107 signposted Brandon from roundabout on A11 Thetford by-pass, course 0.5 mile on left.
Wooded, heathland course.
18 holes, 6879 yards, S.S.S.73
Designed by C.H. Mayo, Donald Steel.
Founded 1912
Visitors: welcome weekdays with current h/cap cert; weekends and Bank Holidays with member only.
Green Fee: WD £30.
Societies: Wed, Thurs, Fri only.
Catering: available daily.
Hotels: Bell; Thomas Paine; Wereham House.

H51 Thorpeness
☎(01728) 452176
Thorpeness, Suffolk IP16 4NH
Leave A12 at Saxmundham, on to B119, then B1353.
Moorland course.
18 holes, 6271 yards, S.S.S.71
Designed by James Braid.

Founded 1923
Visitors: welcome weekdays.
Green Fee: apply for details.
Societies: catered for weekdays only.
Catering: full catering service.
Hotels: Thorpeness Golf Club.

H52 **Ufford Park Hotel**

☎(01394) 383555
Yarmouth Road, Ufford, Woodbridge, Suffolk IP12 1QW
Approx 2 miles N of Woodbridge on B1438.
Parkland course in Deben valley.
18 holes, 6300 yards, S.S.S.70
Designed by Phil Pilgrim.
Founded Oct 1991
Visitors: welcome at any time.
Green Fee: WD £14 per round, £20 per day; WE & BH £18 per round, £27 per day.
Societies: welcome at any time.
Catering: bar, bar snacks, restaurant.
Driving nets, indoor swimming pool, sauna, health, fitness and beauty facilities; conferences, banqueting.
Hotels: Own hotel and Leisure Centre; weekend breaks, tuition breaks, golfing packages available.

H53 **Waldringfield Heath**

☎(01473) 736768 (Sec/Manager), Pro 736417
Newbourne Road, Waldringfield, Woodbridge, Suffolk IP12 4PT
3 miles NE of Ipswich.
Heathland course
18 holes, 5868 yards, S.S.S.69
Designed by P. Pilgrim.
Founded 1 April 1983
Visitors: welcome weekdays, after 12am weekends.

Green Fee: WD £12; WE £15.
Societies: weekdays.
Catering: full facilities.
Hotels: Marlborough (Ipswich).

H54 **Wensum Valley**

☎(01603) 261012
Beech Avenue, Taverham, Norwich, Norfolk NR8 6HP
4 miles NW of Norwich on A1067.
Parkland course.
18 holes, 6000 yards, S.S.S.69; 9 holes, 2953 yards, S.S.S.68
Designed by B.C. Todd.
Founded July 1989
Visitors: welcome.
Green Fee: WD £12 per day; WE £15 per day.
Societies: welcome at all times.
Catering: full bar and catering facilities.
Driving range, snooker, bowls.
Hotels: Accommodation at club; golf breaks arranged; phone for details.

H55 **Weston Park**

☎(01603) 871842 (Bar), Pro 872998
Weston Longville, Norwich, Norfolk NR9 5JW
Off Norwich-Fakenham road; 8 miles from Norwich turn left to Weston Longville then 1st right into Morton Lane, course 500 yards on right.
Parkland course.
18 holes, 6603 yards, S.S.S.72
Founded June 1993
Visitors: welcome at any time, h/cap certs required.
Green Fee: WD £17; WE £22.
Societies: welcome.
Catering: full facilities.
Putting green, practice area, snooker.
Hotels: Lenwade House.

H56 **Wood Valley (Beccles)**

☎(01502) 712244
The Common, Beccles, Suffolk NR34 9BX
1 mile off A146, 18 miles Norwich, 10 miles Lowestoft.
Heathland course.
9 holes, 2781 yards, S.S.S.67
Founded 1899
Visitors: welcome, weekdays unrestricted, weekends with member or phone.
Green Fee: WD £11; WE £13.
Societies: welcome, not Sunday.
Catering: bar and bar snacks; meals to order.
Hotels: Kings Head; Waveney House; Broadland.

H57 **Woodbridge**

☎(01394) 382038
Bromeswell Heath, Woodbridge, Suffolk IP12 2PF
Leave A12 N of Woodbridge on A1152 signposted to Melton; after traffic lights follow road to Orford.
Heathland course.
18 holes, 6314 yards, S.S.S.70; 9 holes, S.S.S.31
Designed by F. Hawtree.
Founded 1893
Visitors: weekdays only, h/cap certs required, advance phone call advisable; 9 hole course open all week, no h/cap cert required.
Green Fee: 18 holes, WD £30 per round/day; 9 holes, WD £14 per round/day; WE £15.
Societies: by advance booking only, Mon-Fri.
Catering: bar and dining room.
Hotels: Melton Grange; Seckford Hall.

GLOUCESTERSHIRE, WARWICKSHIRE, HEREFORD & WORCESTER

The Three Choirs Festival, the province of the cathedrals of Hereford, Worcester and Gloucester, was close to the heart of Sir Edward Elgar, the most English of all composers. Less well known was his love of golf and, in particular, his connections with the Worcestershire Golf Club at Malvern Wells although how much inspiration his musical scores owed to the latter is not clear.

Judging by the excellent centenary history of the Club, it can be assumed that his game was based more on hope than glory – perhaps even enigmatic and variable but the beauty of the Malvern Hills has been solace to many and it is appropriate therefore to head an introduction to this section with mention of the most senior Club in the area. Almost 20 years later came the Alister Mackenzie-designed Worcester Golf and County Club on more parkland surroundings. A still later addition, and one of Worcestershire's most attractive courses, is undoubtedly Blackwell near Bromsgrove. Also more modern is Abbey Park at Redditch which is a valuable addition to the county's facilities. As an example of true dedication and private enterprise, there is nothing in the entire country, to match the tale of Ross-on-Wye. Having existed for almost 60 years as a nine-hole course, they built themselves a new 18-hole home in pleasant woodland in the 1960s. What is more, the cost of course and clubhouse did not exceed £50,000 although the sacrifices and contributions of the original course committee, a gallant, cheerful band, never featured in the calculations.

In those days, golf in Herefordshire was confined to Kington, the highest course in the land, one at Raven's Cause-way and the nine holes at Ross. But Ross emerged from a wilderness of roots, scrub, thickets, marsh and typical red earth that, at first, Ken Cotton believed to be unsuitable but his skill, allied to the faith, patience and determination of the small committee, worked a minor miracle in a corner of England still blessed with meadows, orchards and green hills.

Ross is a short drive from Gloucester, a county not as well populated with courses as its size or the playing strength of its men's county team in recent years might suggest. From Tewkesbury Park and the new Puckrup Hall in the north to Cotswold Edge and Westonbirt in the south, the setting is generally one of pasture and park with the exception of the higher reaches of Gloucester itself and the ancient common at Minchinhampton.

Two Ryder Cup matches at the Belfry have done a lot to publicise golf in the Birmingham area in recent years but Warwickshire, particularly in the area around Birmingham, is full of variety. Some of the older clubs include Handsworth, Edgbaston, Harborne, Moseley, Kidderminster, Robin Hood and Sandwell Park, a stone's throw from the home of West Bromwich Albion F.C.

Olton and Copt Heath are the pride of Solihull, both ideal as enjoyable, if stiff, tests but, besides the Belfry, there is a fine, new hotel complex at Forest of Arden. The Arden course was bought by Country Club Hotels who added both hotel and a second course, the Arden dramatically upgraded in 1992 to host The Murphy's English Open .

The Belfry built a third course in 1995 but Forest of Arden has a second course, as has Minchinhampton with Kings Norton enjoying 27 holes.

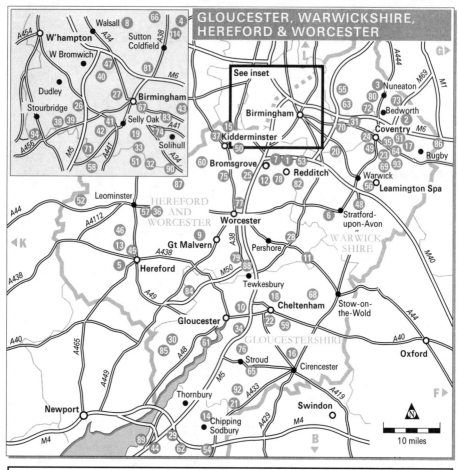

GLOUCESTER, WARWICKSHIRE, HEREFORD & WORCESTER

KEY		22	Cotswold Hills	45	Hereford Municipal	70	North Warwickshire	96	Stratford-upon-Avon
1	Abbey Park G & CC	23	Coventry	46	Herefordshire	71	North Worcestershire	97	Streamleaze
2	Ansty Golf Centre	24	Coventry Hearsall	47	Hill Top	72	Nuneaton	98	Sutton Coldfield
3	Atherstone	25	Droitwich G & CC	48	Ingon Manor G & CC	73	Oakridge	99	Tewkesbury Park
4	The Belfry	26	Dudley	49	Kenilworth	74	Olton		Hotel
5	Belmont Lodge and	27	Edgbaston	50	Kidderminster	75	Ombersley	100	Thornbury Golf Centre
	Golf Club	28	Evesham	51	Kings Norton	76	Painswick	101	Tolladine
6	Bidford Grange	29	Filton	52	Kington	77	Perdiswell	102	Tracy Park Country
7	Blackwell	30	Forest Hills	53	Ladbrook Park	78	Pitcheroak		Club
8	Boldmere	31	Forest of Arden Hotel	54	Lansdown	79	Puckrup Hall Hotel	103	The Vale G & CC
9	Bransford (Pine		Golf & Country Club	55	Lea Marston Hotel &	80	Purley Chase G & CC	104	Walmley
	Lakes)	32	Fulford Heath		Leisure Complex	81	Pype Hayes	105	Warley
10	Brickhampton Court	33	Gay Hill	56	Leamington & County	82	Redditch	106	Warwick
11	Broadway	34	Gloucester	57	Leominster	83	Robin Hood	107	Warwickshire
12	Bromsgrove Golf	35	Grange (GPT Golf	58	Lickey Hills (Rose Hill)	84	Ross-on-Wye	108	Welcombe Hotel
	Centre		Club)	59	Lilley Brook	85	Royal Forest of Dean	109	Westonbirt
13	Burghill Valley	36	Grove Golf Centre	60	Little Lakes	86	Rugby	110	Wharton Park
14	Chipping Sodbury	37	Habberley	61	Lydney	87	Sapey Golf	111	Whitefields
15	Churchill & Blackdown	38	Hagley Country Club	62	Mangotsfield	88	Sherdons	112	Widney Manor
16	Cirencester	39	Halesowen	63	Maxstoke Park	89	Shirehampton Park	113	Windmill Village Hotel
17	City of Coventry	40	Handsworth	64	Memorial Park	90	Shirley	114	Wishaw
	(Brandon Wood)	41	Harborne	65	Minchinhampton	91	Sphinx	115	Woodlands
18	Cleeve Hill	42	Harborne Church	66	Moor Hall	92	Stinchcombe Hill	116	Woodspring
19	Cocks Moor Woods		Farm	67	Moseley	93	Stoneleigh Deer Park	117	Worcester G & CC
20	Copt Heath	43	Hatchford Brook	68	Naunton Downs	94	Stourbridge	118	Worcestershire
21	Cotswold Edge	44	Henbury	69	Newbold Comyn	95	Stratford Oaks	119	Wyre Forest*

J1 Abbey Park G & CC
☎(01527) 63918
Dagnell End Rd, Redditch, Worcs
B98 7BD
A441 Redditch-Birmingham Road.
Parkland course.
18 holes, 6411 yards, S.S.S.71
Designed by Donald Steel.
Founded 1985
Visitors: welcome subject to
available tee times (bookings
required).
Green Fee: WD £10; WE £12.50.
Societies: by arrangement.
Catering: 3 bars, restaurant; meals
all day.
Snooker, swimming pool, gym, sauna
etc.
Hotels: Abbey Park (32 beds),
bargain breaks available.

J2 Ansty Golf Centre
☎(01203) 621341 (Pro shop),
Fax & 24-hr ans service: 602671
Brinklow Rd, Ansty, Coventry CV7
9JH
From M6 junction 2 take B4065
signposted to Ansty; through Ansty,
take 1st turn rt into B4029 Brinklow
rd; Golf Centre is 500 yards on left.
Pay-and-Play parkland course.
18 holes, 5773 yards, Par 71
Designed by D. Morgan.
Founded August 1990
Visitors: always welcome.
Green Fee: WD £9; WE £11.
Societies: welcome any time, 24 hrs
notice required.
Catering: bar and catering 7 days a
week.
Driving range.
Hotels: Ansty Hall; Hilton National.

J3 Atherstone
☎(01827) 713110
The Outwoods, Atherstone, Warwicks
CV9 2RL
Coleshill Rd out of Atherstone, 0.5
mile on left approached by private
road.
Undulating parkland course.
11 holes (18 tees), 6030 yards,
S.S.S.70
Founded 1894
Visitors: welcome weekdays; Sat
with member only, Sun after 5pm
only.
Green Fee: WD £17 (£8 with
member); BH £22 (£7 with member);
Sun after 5pm £7.
Societies: weekdays by prior
arrangement.
Catering: full facilities.
Hotels: Old Red Lion; Three Tuns.

J4 The Belfry
☎(01675) 470301
Lichfield Rd, Wishaw, N Warwicks
B76 9PR
M6 junction 4, follow signs to Lichfield
along A446, sited at the apex of
A4091 to Tamworth and A446 to
Lichfield; or exit 9 from M42.
Parkland course, Championship
courses.
Brabazon, 18 holes, 7220 yards,
S.S.S.72 (handicap required 24 max);
Derby, 18 holes, 6103 yards,
S.S.S.70
Designed by Peter Alliss & Dave
Thomas.
Founded 1977
Visitors: welcome at all times.
Green Fee: apply for details.
Societies: welcome at all times
(packages available).
Catering: full facilities within Hotel.
Hotels:

J5 Belmont Lodge and GC
☎(01432) 352666
Belmont House, Belmont, Hereford
HR2 9SA
2 miles S of Hereford on
Abergavenny road, A465.
Undulating meadowland course.
18 holes, 6490 yards, S.S.S.71
Designed by R. Sandow.
Founded 1983
Visitors: welcome.
Green Fee: WD £10; WE £16.
Societies: welcome (advisable to
book).
Catering: restaurant and bar snacks.
Fishing, tennis, bowls, snooker.
Hotels: hotel on course.

J6 Bidford Grange
☎(01789) 490319, Fax 778184
Stratford Rd, Bidford on Avon,
Warwicks B50 4LY
B439 5 miles W of Stratford on Avon.
Full USGA spec, all sand greens.
18 holes, 7233 yards, S.S.S.74
Designed by Howard Swan and Paul
Tillman.
Visitors: welcome.
Green Fee: WD £12; WE £15.
Societies: catered for on weekdays.
Catering: refreshment available.

J7 Blackwell
☎(0121) 445 1994 (Sec), Steward:
445 1781, Pro 445 3113
Blackwell, Bromsgrove, Worcs B60
1PY
3 miles E of Bromsgrove; from
Blackwell village centre, along Station
Rd and under railway bridge, club
entrance on left after 40 yards.
Parkland course.
18 holes, 6212 yards, S.S.S.71
Designed by H. Fowler and T.
Simpson
Founded 1983
Visitors: unrestricted weekdays; with
member only weekends and Bank
Holidays.
Green Fee: WD £45 per day.
Societies: Wed, Thurs, Fri by
arrangement with Sec.
Catering: full by prior arrangement.
Hotels: Perry Hall, Bromsgrove.

J8 Boldmere
☎(0121) 354 3379
Monmouth Drive, Sutton Coldfield, W
Midlands B73 6JL
A452 Chester road, 6 miles NE of
Birmingham City centre.
Municipal parkland course.
18 holes, 4482 yards, S.S.S.62
Founded 1936
Visitors: welcome any time.
Green Fee: WD £8; WE £8.50.
Societies: weekdays only.
Catering: available.
Hotels: Parson & Clerk.

J9 Bransford (Pine Lakes)
☎(01886) 833551 (Sec), Pro
833621, Fax 832461
Bank House Hotel, Bransford,
Worcester WR6 5JD
M5 junction 7 to Worcester; take
A4103 Hereford road out of
Worcester for 3.5 miles, hotel is on
left off roundabout.
'Florida' style course.
18 holes, 6101 yards, S.S.S.70
Designed by Bob Sandow.
Founded April 1993
Visitors: welcome.
Green Fee: apply for details.
Societies: welcome all week;
residential availability at hotel.
Catering: 3 bars, restaurant, bar
meals.
Driving range, flat green, 9-lane
championship bowling green
(outdoor); fitness centre.
Hotels: Bank House (70 beds).

J10 Brickhampton Court
☎(01452) 859444, Fax/ans: 859333
Brickhampton Court, Cheltenham
Road, Churchdown, Glos GL2 9QF
Midway between Cheltenham and
Gloucester on B4063,
3 miles from J11 M5.
Parkland course.

18 holes, Spa 6387 yards, S.S.S.70
9 holes, Glevum 1859 yards, Par 31
Designed by S. Gidman.
Founded August 1995
Visitors: welcome; evidence of
golfing ability for Spa course.
Green Fee: Spa: WD £14.50 per
round, £22.50 per day; WE £18.50.
Glevum: £6.50 (9holes), £10 (18
holes).
Societies: welcome.
Catering: full bar and restaurant.

J11 Broadway
☎(01386) 853683 (Sec), Pro 853275
Willersey Hill, Broadway, Worcs
WR12 7LG
1.25 miles E of Broadway off A44.
Undulating parkland course.
18 holes, 6216 yards, S.S.S.70
Designed by James Braid.
Founded 1896
Visitors: must book, h/cap cert
required; WE by prior arrangement.
Green Fee: WD £27 per round, £33
(36 holes);
WE £33 per round.
Societies: welcome.
Catering: Apr - Oct.
Hotels: Dormy House.

J12 Bromsgrove Golf Centre
☎(01527) 575886, Bookings:
570505
Stratford Road, Bromsgrove,
Worcestershire B60 1LD
At junction of A38 Bromsgrove
eastern by-pass and A448 Redditch
road; take A38 from M5 Junction 4 or
5, or M42 Junction 1.
Public, pay-as-you-play, course;
grade 2 undulating farmland.
9 holes, 5820 yards, S.S.S.36
Designed by Hawtree & Sons
Founded 1992
Visitors: welcome (advised to book).
Green Fee: WD £6 (9 holes), £10 (18
holes); WE £7 (9 holes), £12 (18
holes).
Societies: welcome.
Catering: None
Driving range.
Hotels: Stakis Club (A38); Pine
Lodge; Perry Hall.

J13 Burghill Valley
☎(01432) 760456
Tillington Road, Burghill, Hereford
HR4 7RW
A4110 from Hereford, at Three Elms
Inn take Tillington road for 2 miles,
club on left.

Parkland course.
18 holes, 6239 yards, S.S.S. 70.
Founded July 1991
Visitors: welcome any time.
Green Fee: apply for details.
Societies: welcome.
Catering: bar and light meals all day.
Hotels: Priory (Stretton Sugwas,
01432 760264), golfing packages
available.

J14 Chipping Sodbury
☎(01454) 319042 (Sec), Pro 314087
Chipping Sodbury, Bristol BS17 6PU
Leave M4 at exit 18 and M5 at exit
14; from Chipping Sodbury take
Wickwar road, first turn on right.
Parkland course.
18 holes, 6912 yards, S.S.S.73; 9
holes, 3076 yards
Designed by Fred Hawtree.
Visitors: welcome, but after 12 noon
at weekends (with handicap
certificates).
Green Fee: WD £25 (27 holes), £36
(36 holes); WE £30.
Societies: welcome by arrangement
on weekdays.
Catering: meals served.
Practice ground.
Hotels: Moda; Cross Hands.

J15 Churchill & Blackdown
☎(01562) 700018, Pro 700454
Churchill Lane, Blakedown,
Kidderminster, Worcs
DY10 3NB
Off A456 3 miles NE of
Kidderminster, turn under railway
viaduct in village of Blakedown.
Undulating parkland course.
9 holes, 6472 yards, S.S.S.71
Founded 1926
Visitors: welcome weekdays;
weekends and Bank Holidays with
member only.
Green Fee: WD £17.50 (£7.50 with
member); WE £10 (with member).
Societies: welcome by arrangement.
Catering: lunch, evening meals
except Mon.
Hotels: Cedars.

J16 Cirencester
☎(01285) 652465 (Sec/bookings),
Members: 653939, **Catering:**
659987, Pro 656124, Fax 650665
Cheltenham Rd, Bagendon,
Cirencester, Glos GL7 7BH
Adjoins A435 Cirencester-
Cheltenham road, 1.5 miles from
Cirencester.

Undulating course.
18 holes, 6020 yards, S.S.S.69
Designed by James Braid.
Founded 1893
Visitors: welcome (except comp.
days); h/cap certs required.
Green Fee: WD £20; WE & BH £25.
Societies: welcome.
Catering: lunches and evening
meals.
Hotels: Kings Head.

J17 City of Coventry (Brandon Wood)
☎(01203) 543141
Brandon Lane, Brandon, Coventry
CV8 3GQ
On A45 6 miles S of Coventry, 120
yards S of London Rd roundabout.
Public parkland course.
18 holes, 6610 yards, S.S.S.71
Designed by Frank Pennink.
Visitors: welcome.
Green Fee: WD £8.45; WE £11.25.
Societies: welcome but booking
essential.
Catering: meals served every day
(Mar-Oct).
Driving range.
Hotels: Brandon Hall.

J18 Cleeve Hill
☎(0242) 672025 (Club), Pro shop
672592
Cheltenham, Glos GL52 3PW
Approx 6 miles N from M5, 4 miles N
of Cheltenham off A46.
Municipal heathland course.
18 holes, 6411 yards, S.S.S.71
Founded 1891
Visitors: welcome anytime weekday;
8-11am and 3pm onwards on Sat,
11.30am onwards Sun.
Green Fee: WD £8 per round; WE
£10 per round.
Societies: welcome.
Catering: snacks and packages.
Skittles, pool table.
Hotels: The Rising Sun.

J19 Cocks Moor Woods
☎(0121) 444 3584
Alcester Rd South, Kings Heath,
Birmingham B14 6ER
On A435, near city boundary.
Public parkland course.
18 holes, 5819 yards, S.S.S.68
Founded 1924
Visitors: welcome.
Green Fee: WD £8; WE £8.50.
Societies: welcome by prior
arrangement.
Catering: available.

J20 Copt Heath

☎(01564) 772650, Pro 776155
1220 Warwick Rd, Knowle, Solihull,
W Midlands B93 9LN
On A4141 0.25 mile S of M42
junction 5.
Parkland course.
18 holes, 6500 yards, S.S.S.71
Designed by H. Vardon.
Founded 1910
Visitors: members of recognised
clubs with official club h/cap welcome,
intro by member required at
weekends.
Green Fee: WD £35 per round, £40
per day.
Societies: welcome by arrangement
with Sec.
Catering: full facilities except Mon.
Hotels: Greswolde.

J21 Cotswold Edge

☎(01453) 844167 (Sec), Pro 844398
Upper Rushmire, Wotton-under-Edge,
Gloucestershire GL12 7PT
On B4058 Wotton-Tetbury road, 8
miles from M5 junction 14.
Meadowland course.
18 holes, 6170 yards, S.S.S.68
Founded 1980
Visitors: welcome weekdays, phone
in advance; with member only
weekends.
Green Fee: WD £15; WE £20.
Societies: by prior arrangement with
Sec.
Catering: full facilities available.
Hotels: Egypt Mill.

J22 Cotswold Hills

☎(01242) 515264 (Sec), Pro 515263
Ullenwood, Cheltenham, Glos GL53
9QT
3 miles S of Cheltenham, between
A436 and B4070.
Undulating course.
18 holes, 6889 yards, S.S.S.74
Designed by M.D. Little.
Founded 1902
Visitors: members of recognised
clubs welcome (h/cap. certs.
required)
Green Fee: WD £21 per round, £26
per day; WE £26 per round, £31 per
day.
Societies: Wed and Thurs.
Catering: full services.
Hotels: Royal George (Birdlip).

J23 Coventry

☎(01203) 414152, Pro 411298
St Martin's Rd, Finham Park,
Coventry, Warwicks CV3 6PJ

2 miles S of Coventry off A45 on
A444 Stoneleigh-Leamington Spa
road.
Parkland course.
18 holes, 6613 yards, S.S.S.72
Founded 1887
Visitors: welcome weekdays only.
Green Fee: £30.
Societies: welcome by arrangement.
Catering: full facilities.
Hotels: Windmill Farm.

J24 Coventry Hearsall

☎(01203) 713470 (Sec), Pro 713156
Beechwood Ave, Earlsdon, Coventry
CV5 6DF
Just off A45 on Kenilworth-Coventry
road.
Parkland course.
18 holes, 5983 yards, S.S.S.69
Founded 1894
Visitors: welcome Mon-Fri; Sat, Sun
with member only (before 12).
Green Fee: on application.
Societies: Tues or Thurs by prior
arrangement.
Catering: lunches, sandwiches
available lunchtime, evening meals by
prior arrangement.
Hotels: Post House (Allesley).

J25 Droitwich G & CC

☎(01905) 774344
Westford House, Ford Lane,
Droitwich WR9 0BQ
Junction 5 off M5, off A38 1 mile N of
town.
Undulating meadowland course.
18 holes, 6058 yards, S.S.S.69
Founded 1897
Visitors: welcome Mon to Fri with
h/cap cert; weekends with member
only.
Green Fee: £24 per day.
Societies: Wed and Fri.
Catering: bar, bar meals, restaurant.
Snooker.
Hotels: Raven.

J26 Dudley

☎(01384) 254020 (Pro), Sec 233877
Turners Hill, Rowley Regis, Warley,
W Midlands B65 9DP
1 mile S of town centre.
Undulating parkland course.
18 holes, 5704 yards, S.S.S.68
Founded 1893
Visitors: weekdays only.
Green Fee: £18 per day.
Societies: by arrangement.
Catering: lunch and evening meals
available.
Hotels: Travelodge.

J27 Edgbaston

☎(0121) 454 1736 (Sec), Pro 454
3226, Fax 454 8295
Church Rd, Edgbaston, Birmingham
B15 3TB
From Birmingham City centre take
A38 (Bristol road), after 1 mile and at
3rd set of lights turn right into Priory
Rd, then left at end into Church Rd;
Club entrance 100 yards on left.
Parkland course.
18 holes, 6118 yards, S.S.S.69
Designed by H.S. Colt.
Founded 1896
Visitors: h/cap cert required;
members only before 9.30am and
12.30-1.30pm daily. Book in advance.
Green Fee: WD £40 per day; WE
£50 per day.
Societies: weekdays only by prior
arrangement.
Catering: bar and bar lunches, other
meals by arrangement; catering for
business meetings, seminars etc.
Snooker.
Hotels: Norfolk; Copthorne.

J28 Evesham

☎(01386) 860395 (Club), Pro
861144
Craycombe Links, Old Worcester Rd,
Fladbury, Pershore, Worcs WR10
2QS
3 miles from Evesham on B4084, 4
miles from Pershore on A4538.
Parkland course.
9 holes (18 tees), 6415 yards,
S.S.S.71
Founded 1894
Visitors: welcome weekdays;
weekends only with member; avoid
Tues (Ladies Day); h/cap cert.
required.
Green Fee: £15 per day (£7 with
member).
Societies: by arrangement, max 24.
Catering: bar snacks always
available; special meals by
arrangement.
Hotels: Northwick (Evesham).

J29 Filton

☎(0117) 969 4169
Golf Course Lane, Filton, Bristol
BS12 7QS
From Almondsbury interchange
(M4/M5) take A38 towards Bristol;
after 2 miles turn right at roundabout
(Southmead Rd) and right at lights
(Golf Course Lane).
Parkland course.
18 holes, 6312 yards, S.S.S.69
Designed by F. Hawtree & Son.
Founded 1909

Visitors: welcome on weekdays; weekends when accompanied by a member only.
Green Fee: £20 per round, £25 per day, (£12 with member).
Societies: catered for on weekdays by arrangement.
Catering: available all day.
Hotels: Crest Hotel; Stakis.

J30 Forest Hills

☎(01594) 562899, 810620
Mile End Road, Coleford, Gloucestershire GL16 7BY
On road from Coleford centre to Mile End on left hand side.
Parkland course.
18 holes, 5674 yards, S.S.S.68
Designed by Adrian Stiff.
Founded 1992
Visitors: welcome.
Green Fee: WD £10; WE £13.
Societies: welcome by prior arrangement.
Catering: full facilities.
Hotels: Angel.

J31 Forest of Arden Hotel G & CC

☎(01676) 22335, 23721
Maxstoke Lane, Meriden, Coventry, Warwicks CV7 7HR
Off A45 10 miles NW of Coventry, 2.5 miles E of Birmingham International Airport; take Maxstoke turn off from A45 and follow lane for 2 miles.
Parkland course.
Aylesford, 18 holes, 6525 yards, S.S.S.69; Arden, 6792 yards, S.S.S.71
Designed by Donald Steel.
Founded 1970 (Hotel opened 1989)
Visitors: welcome with h/cap cert except Sat, Sun am; only 2 days advance booking for weekends.
Green Fee: Aylesford £20; Arden £30.
Societies: welcome weekdays by prior arrangement with golf co-ordinator (weekends residential only).
Catering: restaurant 10am-10pm, bar and lounge; private facilities available. Tennis (3 floodlit), snooker, swimming pool, squash (2), health and beauty facilities.
Hotels: Forest of Arden (153 beds), golf breaks, details on request.

J32 Fulford Heath

☎(01564) 822806 (Kitchen), Office: 824758, Pro 822930
Tanners Green Lane, Wythall, Birmingham B47 6BH
1 mile from main Alcester Rd, signposted to Tanners Green.
Parkland course.
18 holes, 6216 yards, S.S.S.70
Founded 1933
Visitors: welcome weekdays.
Green Fee: £30.
Societies: Tues or Thurs by arrangement.
Catering: lunches and evening meals served except Mon.
Hotels: George; Regency.

J33 Gay Hill

☎(0121) 430 6523, 430 8544, 430 7077, Pro 474 6001,
Fax 436 7796
Hollywood Lane, Hollywood, Birmingham B47 5PP
On A435, 7 miles from Birmingham city centre and 3 miles from M42 junction 3.
Meadowland course.
18 holes, 6532 yards, S.S.S.71
Founded 1913 (1921 on present course).
Visitors: weekdays; weekends only if accompanied by a member; after 12.30pm Sun.
Green Fee: WD £28.50 (£7.50 with member); WE £12 (if accompanied by a member).
Societies: Thurs only, with prior arrangement.
Catering: meals available.
Hotels: George (Solihull).

J34 Gloucester

☎(01452) 411331
Robinswood Hill, Matson Lane, Gloucester GL4 9EA
2 miles S of Gloucester city centre on B4073 to Painswick.
Parkland course.
18 holes, 6170 yards, S.S.S.69; 9 holes Par 3, 990 yards
Designed by Donald Steel.
Founded 1976
Visitors: welcome any time; phone for tee times.
Green Fee: WD £19; WE £25.
Societies: welcome.
Catering: full facilities available. Driving range, snooker.
Hotels: Gloucester Hotel at course, special weekend and weekday golfing breaks.

J35 Grange (GPT Golf Club)

☎(01203) 451465
Copsewood, Coventry, W Midlands CV3 1HS
2.5 miles from Coventry centre on Binley Rd, A428
Meadowland course.
9 holes, 6002 yards, S.S.S.69
Designed by re-designed by T.J. McAuley.
Founded 1924
Visitors: welcome weekdays before 2pm (except Wed); Sun after 11am; not Sat.
Green Fee: WD £10; Sun £15.
Societies: welcome by arrangement with Sec.
Catering: none; may arrange for Societies.
Hotels: Hilton (M1/M6 link road).

J36 Grove Golf Centre

☎(01568) 610602
Fordbridge, Leominster, Herefordshire HR6 0LE
Parkland course
9 holes, 3560 yards
Designed by J Gaunt/R Sandow
Visitors: welcome
Green Fee: WD £4 (9 holes), £6 (18 holes); WE & BH £5 (9 holes), £8 (18 holes).

J37 Habberley

☎(01562) 745756
Habberley, Kidderminster, Worcs DY11 5RG
3 miles N of Kidderminster on Trimpley Road.
Hilly parkland course.
9 holes, 5487 yards, S.S.S.69
Founded 1924
Visitors: welcome weekdays if member of recognised club; weekends and Bank holidays with member only.
Green Fee: WD £10.
Societies: Mon-Fri by prior arrangement.
Catering: facilities available daily except Tue.
Hotels: Heath.

J38 Hagley Country Club

☎(01562) 883701 (Clubhouse), Pro 883852
Wassell Grove, Hagley, W Midlands DY9 9JW
4 miles S of Birmingham on A456, turn right into Wassell Grove, 0.5 mile.
Undulating parkland course.
18 holes, 6353 yards, S.S.S.72
Founded 1979
Visitors: welcome weekdays; weekends with member only, after 10am.

Green Fee: £20 per round, £25 per day.
Societies: welcome weekdays; prior arrangement essential through Club Manager.
Catering: bar and full restaurant facilities.
Squash (4).

J39 Halesowen

☎(0121) 501 3606
The Leasowes, Halesowen, W Midlands B62 8QF
M5 junction 3 to Kidderminster, then to Halesowen.
Parkland course.
18 holes, 5754 yards, S.S.S.67
Founded 1902
Visitors: welcome; weekends with member only; Bank Holidays by arrangement.
Green Fee: WD £18 per round, £25 per day.
Societies: welcome by prior arrangement.
Catering: facilities available daily except Mon.
Hotels: Cobden.

J40 Handsworth

☎(0121) 554 0599 (Clubhouse),
Office: 554 3387,
Pro 523 3594
11 Sunningdale Close, Handsworth Wood, Handsworth, Birmingham B20 1NP
M5 junction 1 towards Birmingham, lft at lights into Island Rd, Oxhill Rd, lft at lights into Friary Rd, 2nd lft Greystone Ave, 2nd lft Sunningdale Close; M6 junction 7, take A34 through lights, 1st rt Old Walsall Rd, up Hamstead Hill, rt into Vernon Ave
Parkland course.
18 holes, 6267 yards, S.S.S.70
Founded 1895
Visitors: welcome weekdays; h/cap certs required; weekends with member only.
Green Fee: on application.
Societies: weekdays by arrangement; special packages available.
Catering: lunch and dinner except Mon.
Squash.
Hotels: Post House.

J41 Harborne

☎(0121) 427 3058, Pro 427 3512
40 Tennal Rd, Birmingham B32 2JE
Via Harborne village and War Lane, SW of Birmingham.

Undulating parkland/moorland course.
18 holes, 6235 yards, S.S.S.70
Designed by H.S. Colt.
Founded 1893
Visitors: welcome weekdays; Bank Holidays and weekends with member only; h/cap cert. required.
Green Fee: £30 per round, £35 per day.
Societies: by arrangement.
Catering: available 7 days, parties on request.
Hotels: Claremont; Apollo.

J42 Harborne Church Farm

☎(0121) 427 1204 (Tel/Fax)
Vicarage Rd, Harborne, Birmingham B17 0SN
From Birmingham, via Broad St, Harborne Rd and War Lane to Vicarage Rd.
Municipal parkland course.
9 holes, 4914 yards, S.S.S.62
Founded 1926
Visitors: welcome.
Green Fee: WD £4.50 (9 holes), £6.50 (18 holes); WE £5 (9 holes), £8 (18 holes).
Catering: snacks and meals served in cafe.

J43 Hatchford Brook

☎(0121) 743 9821
Coventry Rd, Sheldon, Birmingham B26 3PY
Almost on Birmingham city boundary adjacent to Airport, on main A45 Coventry road.
Public parkland course.
18 holes, 6202 yards, S.S.S.69
Founded 1969
Visitors: all welcome.
Green Fee: WD £8; WE £8.50.
Societies: welcome, book 2 weeks in advance.
Catering: canteen facilities while course open.
Hotels: Metropole; Post House (Forte).

J44 Henbury

☎(0117) 950 0044
Henbury Hill, Westbury-on-Trym, Bristol BS10 7BQ
Leave M5 at junction 17, 2nd exit from roundabout, right at 3rd roundabout into Crow Lane, left at T-junction, course is situated at top of hill on right.
Parkland course.
18 holes, 6039 yards, S.S.S.70
Founded 1891

Visitors: welcome weekdays with h/cap cert.
Green Fee: £21 per round, £28 per day.
Societies: catered for on Tues and Fri by arrangement.
Catering: full range available.
Hotels: Henbury Lodge; Ship (Bristol).

J45 Hereford Municipal

☎(0432) 278178, Fax 266281
Holmer Road, Hereford HR4 9UD
A49 through Hereford towards Leominster.
Public course in middle of race course.
9 holes, 3060 yards, S.S.S.69
Founded 1983
Visitors: welcome, closed on race days.
Green Fee: on application.
Societies: welcome with advance booking.
Catering: bar and restaurant facilities available.
Practice ground, adjacent leisure centre.
Hotels: Beefeater Starting Gate Travel Inn.

J46 Herefordshire

☎(01432) 830219 (Sec/bookings)
Ravens Causeway, Wormsley, Hereford HR4 8LY
6 miles NW of Hereford on road to Weobley; turn left off B4110 at Three Elms Inn.
Undulating parkland course.
18 holes, 6036 yards, S.S.S.69
Designed by Major Hutchison.
Founded 1898 (at Wormsley from 1932)
Visitors: welcome weekdays; weekends by arrangement.
Green Fee: WD £15 per round, £26 per day; WE £18 per round, £26 per day.
Societies: welcome by arrangement, apply to Sec.
Catering: restaurant meals served, licensed bar with bar snacks available.
Hotels: Pilgrim; Green Dragon (Hereford).

J47 Hill Top

☎(0121) 554 4463
Park Lane, Handsworth Wood, Birmingham B21 8LJ
Public parkland course.
18 holes, 6254 yards, S.S.S.69
Founded 1980

Visitors: welcome; Link card system allows bookings 8 days in advance; no telephone bookings without card.
Green Fee: WD £8 (Link £7); WE £8.50 (Link £7.50).
Societies: welcome Mon-Fri, not at peak times.
Catering: available.
Hotels: Post House (W Bromwich).

J48 Ingon Manor Golf & Country Club

☎(01789) 731857 (Club), Fax 731657
Ingon Lane, Snitterfield, Nr Stratford Upon Avon,
Warwickshire CV37 0QE
Approx 2 miles NE of Stratford, between A439 and A46,
5 mins from J15 M40.
Undulating parkland course.
18 holes, 6600 yards, Par 72
Designed by David Hemstock Associates & Colin Geddes.
Founded 1993
Visitors: welcome.
Green Fee: WD £15; WE & BH £20.
Societies: welcome; corporate days.
Catering: restaurant; function rooms.
Practice area, chipping and putting.
Hotels: Ingon Manor on site; golfing breaks.

J49 Kenilworth

☎(0926) 58517, Pro 512732,
Catering: 54038
Crew Lane, Kenilworth, Warwicks CV8 2EA
A429 Kenilworth road, then via Common Lane, Knowle Hill and Crew Lane to clubhouse.
Undulating course.
18 holes, 6413 yards, S.S.S.71
Founded 1889
Visitors: welcome daily; advisable to ring Pro beforehand.
Green Fee: WD £26; WE £37.
Societies: apply in writing; society days Weds.
Catering: full facilities daily, advisable to contact Caterer.
Hotels: De Montfort; Avonside; Chesford Grange.

J50 Kidderminster

☎(01562) 822303
Russell Rd, Kidderminster, Worcs DY10 3HT
Course signposted off A449, within 1 mile of town centre.
Parkland course.
18 holes, 6405 yards, S.S.S.71
Founded 1909

Visitors: welcome weekdays only; weekends with member only; proof of membership of recognised golf club must be provided; Ladies day Tues.
Green Fee: £22 per round, £30 per day.
Societies: welcome by prior arrangement Thurs only.
Catering: full facilities except Mon. Snooker
Hotels: The Collingdale; Stone Manor.

J51 Kings Norton

☎(01564) 826789, Pro 822822, Manager: 826789, Office: 826706
Brockhill Lane, Weatheroak, Alvechurch, Birmingham B48 7ED
8 miles from centre of Birmingham between A435 and A441; from M42 junction 3 turn towards Birmingham, signs to club on left after 200 yards.
Parkland course
27 holes (3 loops of 9); Blue 9 holes, 3382 yards; Red 9 holes, 3372 yards; Yellow 9 holes, 3290 yards; S.S.S.72: also 12 hole Par 3 course.
Designed by F. Hawtree & Son.
Founded 1892
Visitors: weekdays only, with member only at weekends; accredited h/cap required.
Green Fee: £27 (18 holes), £29.50 (27 holes).
Societies: weekdays only.
Catering: full facilities; conferences and banqueting.
Hotels: Westmead.

J52 Kington

☎(01544) 230340, Pro 231320
Bradnor, Kington, Herefordshire HR5 3RE
Take B4355 from A44 Kington by-pass, turn left after 150 yards.
Moorland course; highest 18 hole course in England.
18 holes, 5753 yards, S.S.S.68
Designed by C.K. Hutchinson.
Founded 1925
Visitors: welcome.
Green Fee: WD £13 per round, £16 per day; WE & BH £16 per round, £20 per day.
Societies: welcome esp. weekdays.
Catering: available.
Hotels: Burton; Oxford Arms.

J53 Ladbrook Park

☎(01564) 742264 (Sec), Pro shop 742581, Steward: 742722
Poolhead Lane, Tanworth-in-Arden, Warwicks B94 5ED

M42 junction 3; S on A435 forking left after 500 yards to Tanworth/Penn Lane, continue to T-junction, turn left into Broad Lane, then 1st left into Poolhead Lane; clubhouse 50 yards on left; approx 2.5 mile from M42.
Undulating parkland course.
18 holes, 6427 yards, S.S.S.71
Designed by H.S. Colt.
Founded 1908
Visitors: welcome weekdays (except Tues a.m.) by prior arrangement, contact Pro shop.
Green Fee: WD £35 (£10 with member).
Societies: by prior arrangement, contact Sec.
Catering: daily except Mon by prior arrangement.
Hotels: George; Moat House.

J54 Lansdown

☎(01225) 422138 (Sec), Clubhouse/Steward: 425007, Pro 420242, Fax 339252
Lansdown, Bath, Avon BA1 9BT
From M4 junction 18 take A46 towards Bath; at roundabout take A420 towards Bristol, take 1st left and club is approx 2 miles on right by Bath Racecourse.
elevated parkland course.
18 holes; White Course, 6316 yards, S.S.S.70; Yellow Course, 6007 yards, S.S.S.69
Designed by Harry Colt.
Founded 1894/5
Visitors: welcome weekdays, with h/cap weekends; not competition days; smart casual dress (no jeans).
Green Fee: WD £18 per round; WE & BH £30.
Societies: welcome by prior arrangement.
Catering: full range of snacks and meals available.
Hotels: Hilton.

J55 Lea Marston Hotel & Leisure Complex

☎(01675) 470468
Haunch Lane, Lea Marston, Warwickshire B76 0BY
1 mile from M42 Junction 9 on A4097 Kingsbury road; 2 miles from Belfry golf course.
Public parkland course.
9 holes, 783 yards, Par 3
Designed by J.R. Blake
Founded 1983
Visitors: smart casual dress.
Green Fee: WD £3 (9 holes), WE £4.75 (9 holes).
Societies: welcome.

Catering: 6 bars, 100 place restaurant.
Driving range, tennis, crown green bowls, pool etc, health club, indoor swimming pool.
Hotels: Lea Marston on site; special golfing breaks.

J56 Leamington & County
☎(01926) 425961, Pro 428014
Golf Lane, Whitnash, Leamington Spa, Warwicks CV31 2QA
2 miles S of town centre, off A452.
Undulating parkland course.
18 holes, 6488 yards, S.S.S.71
Designed by H.S. Colt.
Founded 1908
Visitors: welcome.
Green Fee: WD £28 per round, £30 per day; WE £40 per round.
Societies: welcome Wed, Thurs.
Catering: lunch and evening meal served except Mon.
Snooker.
Hotels: Hilton.

J57 Leominster
☎(01568) 612863 (Clubhouse), Pro 611402, Sec 610055
Ford Bridge, Leominster, Hereford HR6 0LE
On A49 Leominster bypass 3 miles S of Leominster, clearly signposted.
Undulating meadowland course.
18 holes, 6029 yards, S.S.S.69
Designed by Bob Sandow.
Founded 1967
Visitors: welcome weekdays; weekends by prior arrangement.
Green Fee: WD £14.50 per round, £17 per day; WE & BH £21.
Societies: welcome by prior arrangement.
Catering: bar facilities daily; restaurant and snacks except Mon.
Driving range adjacent to course, coarse fishing on River Lugg.
Hotels: Talbot; Castle Pool (Hereford).

J58 Lickey Hills (Rose Hill)
☎(0121) ☎(0121) 453 7600, Pro 453 3159
Lickey Hills, Rednal, Birmingham B45 8RR
Junc 4 off M5 or Junc1 off M42 signposted to Lickey Hall Park
Public parkland course.
18 holes, 5866 yards, S.S.S.69
Designed by Carl Bretherton.
Founded 1927
Visitors: welcome.

Green Fee: £8.50.
Societies: by arrangement.
Catering: snacks served.
Hotels: Westmead.

J59 Lilley Brook
☎(01242) 526785
Cirencester Rd, Charlton Kings, Cheltenham, Glos GL53 8EG
3 miles from centre of Cheltenham on Cheltenham-Cirencester road, A435.
Parkland course.
18 holes, 6212 yards, S.S.S.70
Founded 1922
Visitors: bona fide members of golf club with official h/cap; weekend subject to availability.
Green Fee: WD £20 per round, £25 per day; WE £25 per round, £30 per day.
Societies: weekdays.
Catering: lunches, dinners served.
Hotels: Queens; Cheltenham Park.

J60 Little Lakes
☎(01299) 266385
Lye Head, Rock, Bewdley, Worcs DY12 2UZ
A456 2 miles W of Bewdley, turn left at Greenhouse and Garden Centre, proceed for 0.5 mile.
Undulating parkland course.
18 holes, 5644 yards, S.S.S.72
Designed by Michael Cooksey.
Founded 1975
Visitors: welcome weekdays; weekends with member only.
Green Fee: WD £12 (£7 with member), WE £15 (£12 with member).
Societies: weekdays by arrangement.
Catering: lunches served.
Hotels: Heath.

J61 Lydney
☎(01594) 842614, Sec 843940
off Lakeside Ave, Lydney, Glos GL15 5QA
Entering Lydney on A48 from Gloucester, turn left at bottom of Highfield Hill and look for Lakeside Ave, 7th turning on left.
Parkland course.
9 holes, 5298 yards, S.S.S.66
Founded 1909
Visitors: welcome; weekends and Bank Holidays with member only.
Green Fee: £12.
Societies: small societies welcome, full facilities available, lunch, dinner.
Catering: bar and snacks available.
Hotels: Speech House.

J62 Mangotsfield
☎(0117) 956 5501
Carson's Rd, Mangotsfield, Bristol BS17 3LW
M32, leave at junction Filton/Downend, follow sign for Downend and Mangotsfield.
Hilly meadowland course.
18 holes, 5300 yards, S.S.S.66
Founded 1975
Visitors: welcome.
Green Fee: WD £9; WE £11.
Societies: welcome.
Catering: meals served.
Hotels: Crest.

J63 Maxstoke Park
☎(01675) 464915, Fax 466743
Castle Lane, Coleshill, Warwicks B46 2RD
3 miles NE of Coleshill, M6 junction 4.
Parkland course.
18 holes, 6442 yards, S.S.S.71
Founded 1898
Visitors: welcome weekdays; with member only weekends and Bank Holidays.
Green Fee: £25 per round, £35 per day.
Societies: welcome.
Catering: full bar and restaurant.
Hotels: Lea Marston.

J64 Memorial Park
☎(01203) 675415
Memorial Park Golf Office, Leamington Road, Coventry, W Midlands
About 1 mile from city centre; access from Leamington Rd car park at Memorial Park.
18 hole Par 3 municipal course.
Visitors: welcome.
Green Fee: pay and play.
Societies: welcome.
Catering: cafe in park in summer.
Bowling greens, 10 tennis courts, playground, aviary.

J65 Minchinhampton
☎(01453) 833840 (New), 836382 (Old)
New Course, Minchinhampton, Stroud, Glos GL6 9BE; Old Course, Minchinhampton, Stroud, Glos GL6 9AQ
Leave M5 at junction 13; New Course, 3 miles E of Minchinhampton on Avening road; Old Course, 1 mile W of Minchinhampton on Common.
Parkland course (Avening/Cherington), common land course (Old).

Old, 18 holes, 6205 yards, S.S.S.71;
Avening, 18 holes, 6244 yards S.S.S.
70; Cherington, 18 holes, 6270 yards,
S.S.S. 70.
Designed by F.W. Hawtree
(Avening/Cherington), Robert Wilson
(Old)
Founded 1889
Visitors: welcome at all times with
prior notice; h/cap certs required.
Green Fee: on application.
Societies: by prior arrangement.
Catering: available most times;
limited hours in winter.
Hotels: Bear at Rodborough;
Burleigh Court; Amberley Inn; Hare
and Hounds (Tetbury).

J66 Moor Hall
☎(0121) 308 6130 (Sec), Pro 308
5106
Moor Hall Park, Sutton Coldfield, W
Midlands B75 6LN
From M42 take A446 to Bassets Pole
roundabout, follow Sutton Coldfield
road to 1st traffic lights, entrance 200
yards on left.
Parkland course.
18 holes, 6249 yards, S.S.S.70
Founded 1932
Visitors: welcome weekdays (except
Thur before 1.0).
Green Fee: £27 per round, £37 per
day.
Societies: Tues and Wed only.
Catering: available.
Hotels: Moor Hall.

J67 Moseley
☎(021) 444 4957 (Sec 10am-
4.30pm), Club 444 2115,
Fax 441 4662
Springfield Rd, Kings Heath,
Birmingham B14 7DX
On Birmingham ring road, 0.5 mile E
of Alcester Rd.
Parkland course.
18 holes, 6300 yards, S.S.S.70
Founded 1892
Visitors: reference to Sec, letter of
intro, official (Club) h/cap cert.
Green Fee: £37.
Societies: Wed only, book via Sec.
Catering: available.

J68 Naunton Downs
☎(01451) 850090, Pro 850092,
Bar/restuarant: 850093, Fax 850091
Naunton, Cheltenham,
Gloucestershire GL54 3AE
Off B4068 Stow-on-the-Wold/
Cheltenham road adjacent Naunton.
Downland course.

18 holes, 6078 yards, S.S.S.69
Designed by Jacob Pott.
Founded July 1993
Visitors: welcome, weekends book in
advance.
Green Fee: £19.95 per day.
Societies: welcome.
Catering: lounge bar, spike bar,
drawing room, restaurant, limited on
Mondays.
Hotels: Washbourne Court.

J69 Newbold Comyn
☎(01926) 421157
Newbold Terrace East, Leamington
Spa, Warwicks CV32 4EW
Off B4099 Willes Road.
Parkland course.
18 holes, 6315 yards, S.S.S.70
Founded 1972
Visitors: welcome.
Green Fee: WD £7.30; WE £9.50.
Societies: welcome.
Catering: bar and restaurant.

J70 North Warwickshire
☎(01676) 22259 (Pro), Sec 22915
Hampton Lane, Meriden, W Midlands
CV7 7LL
6 miles N of Coventry on A45.
Parkland course.
9 holes, 6390 yards, S.S.S.70
Founded 1894
Visitors: weekdays except Thur
(Ladies Day); weekends with member
only.
Green Fee: WD £18 (£8 with
member); WE £10 (with member
only).
Societies: by arrangement.
Catering: bar snacks.
Snooker.
Hotels: Manor Hotel (Meriden).

J71 North Worcestershire
☎(0121) 475 1047 (Sec), Pro 475
5721
Frankley Beeches Rd, Northfield,
Birmingham B31 5LP
7 miles S of Birmingham City centre,
just off A38, approx 4 miles from M5
junction 4.
Meadowland course.
18 holes, 5950 yards, S.S.S.69
Designed by James Braid.
Founded 1907
Visitors: welcome weekdays;
weekends with member only.
Green Fee: £18.50 per round, £27
per day.
Societies: Tues and Thurs.
Catering: full facilities.
Hotels: Norwood.

J72 Nuneaton
☎(01203) 347810, Pro 340201
Golf Drive, Whitestone, Nuneaton,
Warwicks CV11 6QF
Leave M6 at junction 3 on A444, 2
miles S of Nuneaton.
Wooded undulating meadowland
course.
18 holes, 6428 yards, S.S.S.71
Founded 1906
Visitors: welcome weekdays, with
member only weekends.
Green Fee: £20 (Oct - Mar £15).
Societies: welcome on application,
(Fri max 24).
Catering: full facilities available
except Mon.
Hotels: Long Shoot; Chase.

J73 Oakridge
☎(0167) 541389 (Sec), Pro 540542
Arley Lane, Ansley Village, Nuneaton,
Warwicks CV10 9PH
Off B4112, 3 miles W of Nuneaton.
Parkland course.
18 holes, 6242 yards, S.S.S.71
Founded 1993
Visitors: welcome Mon-Fri, h/cap
cert required; WE and competition
days with member only.
Green Fee: WD £10 (£8 with
member); WE £10 (with member).
Societies: welcome Mon-Thur and
Fri a.m.
Catering: full à la carte, set meals,
snacks (except Mon).
Practice range, snooker.
Hotels: Forest of Arden.

J74 Olton
☎(0121) 705 1083, Fax 711 2010,
Pro 705 7296
Mirfield Rd, Solihull, W Midlands B91
1JH
2 miles off junction 5 M42 - A41 to
Birmingham.
Parkland course.
18 holes, 6265 yards, S.S.S.71
Founded 1893
Visitors: welcome weekdays except
Wed; weekends with member only.
Green Fee: £30 (£10 with member).
Societies: welcome weekdays by
arrangement.
Catering: available.
Snooker.
Hotels: St Johns.

J75 Ombersley
☎(01905) 620747, Fax 620047
Bishops Wood Road, Lineholt,
Ombersley, Droitwich, Worcs WR9
0LE

Off A449 between Worcester and Kidderminster; at Mitre Oak pub roundabout take A4025 to Stourport, after 400 yards turn 1st left.
Parkland course with views over Severn Valley.
18 holes, 6139 yards, Par 72
Designed by On Course Design (David Morgan).
Founded Sept 1991
Visitors: no restrictions.
Green Fee: WD £10 per day; WE £13.30.
Societies: welcome by arrangement, not weekends.
Catering: full facilities.
Driving range, putting green, practice bunker; disabled facilities.
Hotels: Mitre Oak.

J76 Painswick
☎(01452) 812180
Painswick Beacon, Painswick, Stroud, Glos GL6 6TL
1 mile N of Painswick village on A46.
Commonland course.
18 holes, 4680 yards, S.S.S.64
Founded 1891
Visitors: welcome weekdays & Sat; Sun with member only.
Green Fee: WD £10; Sat £15.
Societies: by prior arrangement with Sec; special packages.
Catering: by arrangement with Steward; selection of snacks normally available.
Hotels: Moat House.

J77 Perdiswell
☎(01905) 457189, Pro 754668
Bilford Road, Worcester, Worcs WR3 8DX
In north of Worcester off main Droitwich road.
Meadowland course
9 holes, 2935 yards, S.S.S. 68 (expanding to 18 in 1997)
Visitors: welcome
Green Fee: WD £4.30 (9 holes), £6.90 (18 holes); WE £5.70 (9 holes), £8 (18 holes).
Societies: welcome
Catering: bar and snacks.

J78 Pitcheroak
☎(0527) 541054
Plymouth Rd, Redditch, Worcs B97 4PB
In centre of Redditch, signposted.
Municipal parkland course
9 holes (18 tees), 4561 yards, S.S.S.62
Founded 1973

Visitors: welcome any time.
Green Fee: WD £4.25 (9 holes), £5.75 (18 holes); WE £4.75 (9 holes), £6.75 (18 holes).
Societies: welcome.
Catering: bar and restaurant.
Hotels: Mount Ville.

J79 Puckrup Hall Hotel
☎(01684) 296200, Fax 850788
Puckrup, Tewkesbury, Glos GL20 6EL
4 miles N of Tewkesbury on A38, 0.5 mile from M50 junction 1.
Parkland course.
18 holes, 6431 yards, S.S.S.71
Designed by Simon Gidman.
Founded Oct 1992
Visitors: welcome.
Green Fee: WD £15 (winter), £22 (summer); WE £20 (winter), £25 (summer).
Societies: welcome; by arrangement on Tues and Thurs.
Catering: full services.
Hotel Leisure Club.
Hotels: Puckrup Hall.

J80 Purley Chase G & CC
☎(01203) 393118 (office), Club 397468, Pro shop 395348
Ridge Lane, Nr Nuneaton, N Warwicks CV10 0RB
4 miles W of Nuneaton, 2 miles SW of Atherstone, signposted.
Parkland course.
18 holes, 6772 yards, S.S.S.72
Designed by B. Tomlinson.
Founded 1976
Visitors: welcome weekdays, at weekends subject to availability.
Green Fee: WD £13; WE £20.
Societies: welcome weekdays.
Catering: full facilities.
Driving range.
Hotels: Hinkley Island.

J81 Pype Hayes
☎(0121) 351 1014
Eachelhurst Rd, Walmley, Sutton Coldfield, W Midlands B76 8EP
Off M6 at Spaghetti Junction, onto Tyburn Rd, 1 mile to Eachelhurst Rd.
Public parkland course.
18 holes, 5964 yards, S.S.S.68
Founded 1932
Visitors: welcome.
Green Fee: WD £7.50; WE £8.50.
Societies: welcome by prior arrangement except weekends & Bank Holidays.
Catering: cafeteria.
Hotels: Pens Hall.

J82 Redditch
☎(01527) 543309, Pro 546372
Lower Grinsty Lane, Callow Hill, Redditch, Worcs B97 5JP
3 miles W of town centre; take Heathfield rd off A448 Redditch-Bromsgrove rd, left into Green Lane.
Parkland (1st 9), woodland (2nd 9) course.
18 holes, 6671 yards, S.S.S.72
Designed by F. Pennink.
Founded 1913
Visitors: members of recognised golf club welcome weekdays; with member weekends.
Green Fee: £27.50 per day (£8 with member).
Societies: weekdays by arrangement.
Catering: full service except Mon.
Snooker.
Hotels: Southcrest; Hotel Montville.

J83 Robin Hood
☎(0121) 706 0061 (Sec), Pro 706 0806
St Bernards Rd, Solihull, W Midlands B92 7DJ
From Olton station (6 miles S of Birmingham on A41) travel NE up St Bernards Rd for 1 mile, drive to clubhouse on right.
Parkland course.
18 holes, 6635 yards, S.S.S.72
Designed by H.S. Colt.
Founded 1893
Visitors: welcome weekdays except BH; weekends with member only.
Green Fee: £29 per round, £35 per day.
Societies: welcome weekdays only.
Catering: full services except Mon..
Hotels: George.

J84 Ross-on-Wye
☎(01989) 720439 (Pro)
Two Park, Gorsley, Ross-on-Wye, Hereford HR9 7UT
Adjacent M50 junction 3, 5 miles N of Ross.
Parkland course.
18 holes, 6451 yards, S.S.S.73
Designed by C.K. Cotton.
Founded 1903
Visitors: h/cap cert. required; phone in advance.
Green Fee: £30 per round, £35 per day.
Societies: welcome by prior arrangement.
Catering: full bar and restaurant facilities.
2 snooker tables.
Hotels: Chase; Travel Lodge.

Ross-on-Wye

In the summer of 1961, Ken Cotton was busy building two new courses, one in the stately old deer park of St Pierre beside the Newport Road out of Chester and the other in rather damp woodland on the outskirts of Ross-on-Wye. Both were adventurous, new ventures at a time when golf course building had only just begun to revive after the War.

It was a happy day therefore when Cotton phoned to extend an invitation to visit the site and see the construction work in progress. But not the least remarkable part of a remarkable tale is that it very nearly did not happen at all.

At the behest of a small group of men who had formed a special committee of the existing nine hole Ross-on-Wye Club, he inspected the land in question only to report that he felt it unsuitable. It was only when the committee drove to Cotton's house near Pangbourne to plead with him to give it a try that he relented. The committee had previously searched high and low for a suitable site and saw this as their last chance. The decision to start was an act of faith by all concerned because the first steps involved a comprehensive clearance operation unsurpassed even with the making of Woburn a dozen or so years later.

My first memory was the sight of the head woodsman, then in his eighties, fuelling a woodland fire with fresh scrub and branches and cooking a lunch of bacon and eggs on the back of a carefully cleaned shovel. Even after working on many, many new courses, it is still something of a marvel that it all took shape as, indeed, was the speed with which Cotton conceived his layout. After walking round the perimeter in pouring rain, and cogitating later in his bath, he presented the committee with a plan that needed virtually no change, although the patience needed to implement it requires almost as much praise as Cotton's initial inspiration.

Without the enormous personal contribution and sacrifice of the committee, it would undoubtedly have failed; certainly, neither before nor since has there been such a shining example of unselfish enterprise. The only aim in mind was of assuring the future of Ross-on-Wye Golf Club, an aspiration they achieved with flying colours. The new course was more than just a notable addition in an area virtually devoid of golf, it now ranks as one of the best inland courses in Britain. It has a handful of blind shots and there is a high demand on control from the tee but, from an enclosed, dark woodland, has emerged a beautiful setting for the game, one in which the distant beauty enhances the aesthetic pleasures of trees and pretty flowers.

It is hard nowadays to believe the problems faced at the outset but it needs a realisation of them to judge the success achieved and to pay tribute to the vision and skill which brought it about. It made the official opening on May 7th 1967 an auspicious occasion. For one thing, new courses were far rarer then than they are nowadays and, for another, the opening ceremony was performed by one of Cotton's partners, Frank Pennink, in his capacity as President of the English Golf Union.

It was a happy gathering that followed the exhibition game, marvelling how the course had been so patiently moulded from the forest and how the entire operation, including the purchase of the land and the building of the clubhouse, had only cost £41,000. Nearly thirty years later, that would have provided no more than a couple of new greens – on some expensive enterprises, not even that.

J85 Royal Forest of Dean

☎(01594) 832583, Pro 833689
Lords Hill, Coleford, Glos GL16 8BD
Between M4, M5 and M50; from M5,
M50 4 miles Monmouth, 8 miles
Ross, from M4 8 miles Chepstow.
Parkland/meadowland course.
18 holes, 5813 yards, S.S.S.69
Designed by John Day of Alphagreen
Ltd.
Founded 1973
Visitors: welcome.
Green Fee: WD £12; WE £14.
Societies: book through hotel.
Catering: full services.
Outdoor swimming pool, tennis,
bowls.
Hotels: Bells Hotel.

J86 Rugby

☎(01788) 542306, Pro 575134
Clifton Rd, Rugby, CV21 3RD
On Rugby-Market Harborough road,
on right just past railway bridge as
leaving town.
Parkland course.
18 holes, 5614 yards, S.S.S.67
Founded 1891
Visitors: welcome weekdays;
weekends and Bank Holidays with
member.
Green Fee: WD £20 (£7 with
member); WE £9 (with member)
Societies: weekdays by
arrangement.
Catering: meals except Tues & Sun.
Hotels: Carlton.

J87 Sapey Golf

☎(01886) 853288, 853567, Fax
853485
Upper Sapey, Nr Worcester, Worcs
WR6 6XT
Midway between Bromyard and
Stourport on B4203.
Open parkland course.
18 holes, 5935 yards, S.S.S.68
Founded July 1990
Visitors: welcome.
Green Fee: WD £15 per round, £22
per day; WE & BH £20 per round,
£25 per day.
Societies: welcome.
Catering: restaurant Wed-Sun
inclusive; snacks Mon-Tue.
Driving range.
Hotels: The Granary (Collington);
The Elm.

J88 Sherdons

☎(01684) 274782
Manor Farm, Tredington,
Tewkesbury, GL20 7BP
2 miles out of Tewkesbury on the
A38, turn off at Odessa Inn and the
course is signposted
Parkland course
9 holes, 2654 yards, S.S.S. 66
Founded 1995
Visitors: welcome; pay-as-you-play
Green Fee: WD £6 (9 holes), £9 (18
holes); WE £7.50 (9 holes), £12 (18
holes).
Societies: weekdays preferred; by
arrangement at weekends
Catering: limited
Driving range
Hotels: Gubshill Manor

J89 Shirehampton Park

☎(0117) 982 2083 (Sec), Club 982
3059, Pro 982 2488
Park Hill, Shirehampton, Bristol BS11
0UL
1.5 miles from M5 junction 18, B4018
through village of Shirehampton;
course at top of hill overlooking River
Avon.
Undulating parkland course.
18 holes, 5521 yards, S.S.S.67
Founded 1907
Visitors: welcome.
Green Fee: WD £18 (£13 with
member); WE £25 (£15 with
member).
Societies: welcome.
Catering: snacks, lunch always
available; evening meals by
arrangement.

J90 Shirley

☎(0121) 744 6001, Pro 745 4979
Stratford Rd, Monkspath, Shirley,
Solihull, W Midlands B90 4EW
From M42 junction 4, 500 yards on
left towards Birmingham.
Parkland course.
18 holes, 6507 yards, S.S.S.71
Founded 1953
Visitors: welcome weekdays, h/cap
cert required; weekends with member
only.
Green Fee: £25 per round, £35 per
day.
Societies: Mon-Fri by arrangement.
Catering: meals and snacks daily.
Snooker.
Hotels: St John's (Solihull).

J91 Sphinx

☎(01203) 458890, 451361 after 7pm
Siddeley Ave, Coventry, W Midlands
CV3 1FZ
Approx 4 miles S of centre of
Coventry, close to main Binley Rd.
Parkland course

9 holes, 4262 yards, S.S.S.60.
Founded 1948 (as Rolls Royce
Sports Club).
Visitors: welcome; with member only
weekends.
Green Fee: on application.
Societies: recognised societies
welcome.
Catering: bar and bar meals.

J92 Stinchcombe Hill

☎(01453) 542015
Stinchcombe Hill, Dursley, Glos GL11
6AQ
1 mile along narrow lane (signposted)
off A4135 Tetbury-Dursley road; or
approach direct from Dursley town
centre, 0.5 mile up hill past bus
station.
Meadowland/downland course.
18 holes, 5734 yards, S.S.S.68
Founded 1889
Visitors: welcome any day; restricted
weekends and Bank Holidays except
with member.
Green Fee: WD £12.50 per round,
£20 per day; WE £25.
Societies: weekdays by
arrangement.
Catering: full facilities available.
Hotels: Hare and Hounds; Prince of
Wales; Amberley Inn; Stonehouse
Court.

J93 Stoneleigh Deer Park

☎(01203) 639991/639912 (tee
times), Fax 511533
The Old Deer Park, Coventry Rd,
Stoneleigh, Warwicks CV8 3DR
A46 Stoneleigh exit, course 1 mile S
of village.
Parkland course on banks of River
Avon.
Tantara, 18 holes, 6083 yards
(changing 1996), S.S.S.68; Avon, 9
holes, 1251 yards, Par 3
Designed by K. Harrison.
Founded 1991
Visitors: welcome; book starting
times through shop.
Green Fee: WD £12.50; WE £20.
Societies: welcome.
Catering: bar, restaurant.

J94 Stourbridge

☎(01384) 395566
Worcester Lane, Stourbridge DY8
2RB
2 miles from Stourbridge town centre
on Worcester road.
Parkland course.
18 holes, 6231 yards, S.S.S.70
Founded 1892

Visitors: welcome weekdays; with member only weekends.
Green Fee: £25.
Societies: welcome by prior arrangement.
Catering: facilities available daily except Mon.
Hotels: Pedmore House.

J95 Stratford Oaks
☎(01789) 731571
Bearley Road, Snitterfield, Stratford-upon-Avon, Warwicks CV37 0EZ
5 miles M40 junction 15, or A34 to Stratford and follow signs for Snitterfield.
Parkland course.
18 holes, 6100 yards, S.S.S.71
Designed by Howard Swan.
Founded 1989
Visitors: welcome any time; must book at WE.
Green Fee: on application.
Societies: welcome Mon-Fri by arrangement.
Catering: bar, restaurant.
Driving range, putting greens, practice chipping area, practice grass area.
Hotels: Arden Valley; Alveston Manor.

J96 Stratford-upon-Avon
☎(01789) 205749, Pro 205677, Club 297296
Tiddington Rd, Stratford-upon-Avon, Warwicks CV37 7BA
0.5 mile from river bridge on B4089.
Parkland course.
18 holes, 6311 yards, S.S.S.70
Founded 1894 (1928 on present site)
Visitors: weekdays.
Green Fee: WD £25 per round, £28 per day; WE £35 per round.
Societies: Tues and Thurs by arrangement.
Catering: snacks and meals.

J97 Streamleaze
☎(01453) 843128
Canons Court Farm, Bradley, Wotton-under-Edge, Glos GL12 7PN
Turn left off B4058 3 miles from M5 junction 14.
Farmland course.
9 holes, 5173 yards, S.S.S.65
Founded 1982
Visitors: welcome.
Green Fee: WD £7; WE £8.50.
Societies: welcome.
Catering: bar and bar snacks.
Hotels: Gables Hotel; Newport Towers.

J98 Sutton Coldfield
☎(0121) 353 9633, (Sutton Coldfield Ladies GC (0121) 353 1682)
110 Thornhill Rd, Streetly, Sutton Coldfield B74 3ER
9 miles NE of Birmingham on B4138; M6 junction 6; car park on opposite side of Thornhill Rd to course.
Heathland course.
18 holes, 6541 yards, S.S.S.71
re-designed by Dr Mackenzie.
Founded 1889
Visitors: welcome weekdays; wekends with member only.
Green Fee: £35 per day, reductions with member.
Societies: welcome.
Catering: lunches, snacks daily.
Snooker.
Hotels: Sutton Court; Post House.

J99 Tewkesbury Park Hotel
☎(01684) 295405
Lincoln Green Lane, Tewkesbury, GL20 7DN
0.5 mile S of town on A38, 3 miles from junction 9 off M5.
Parkland course.
18 holes, 6533 yards, S.S.S.72
Designed by Frank Pennink.
Founded 1976
Visitors: welcome with h/cap cert.
Green Fee: WD £15; WE £25.
Societies: welcome.
Catering: snacks and meals.
Hotels: Tewkesbury Park.

J100 Thornbury Golf Centre
☎(01454) 281144, Fax: 281177
Bristol Rd, Thornbury, Avon BS12 2SL
On S side of Thornbury from A38.
Newly landscaped parkland course.
18 holes, 6154 yards, S.S.S.69; 18 holes par 3, c.2800 yards.
Designed by Hawtree.
Founded 1992
Visitors: welcome; book in advance up to 6 days.
Green fee: £12.50 per round.
Societies: welcome.
Catering: full facilities.
Driving range.
Hotels: Lodge on site.

J101 Tolladine
☎(01905) 721074, Pro shop 726180
Tolladine Rd, Worcester WR4 9BA
Leave M5 at junction 6 Warndon, about 1 mile from city centre opposite Virgin Tavern.
Meadowland course.
9 holes, 5432 yards, S.S.S.67
Founded 1898
Visitors: welcome weekdays, weekends accompanied by member only.
Green Fee: WD £10 per round, £15 per day, £7 (with member); WE £8 (with member).
Societies: welcome.
Catering: limited, by arrangement.
Hotels: The Star.

J102 Tracy Park Country Club
☎(0117) 937 2251
Bath Rd, Wick, Bristol BS15 5RN
Junction 18 off M4, S on A46 for 4 miles, right on A420 for 2 miles.
Parkland course.
3 x 9 holes; Avon, 6423 yards, S.S.S.71; Bristol, 6430 yards, S.S.S.71; Cotswold, 6189 yards, S.S.S.69
Designed by Grant Aitken.
Founded 1975
Visitors: welcome; h/cap cert. required.
Green Fee: WD £20; WE £30.
Societies: welcome 7 days by arrangement.
Catering: lunch, dinner, bar snacks.
Squash, tennis, swimming, croquet, snooker.
Hotels: Lansdown Grove; Linden; Manor House.

J103 The Vale Golf & Country Club
☎(01386) 462781, 462427, Pro shop 462520
Hill Furze Rd, Bishampton, Pershore, Worcs WR10 2LZ
Off B4084 near Bishampton village, 7 miles M5 junction 6, 6 miles Evesham, 5 miles Pershore.
Parkland/downland course.
International, 18 holes, 7114 yards, S.S.S.74; Lenches, 9 holes, 5836 yards, S.S.S.68
Founded June 1991
Visitors: welcome, phone Pro to book.
Green Fee: WD £18 (winter); WE £24 (winter).
Societies: welcome, book in advance.
Catering: Vale bar, Spikes bar, snacks and brunch, full à la carte restaurant and carvery; function room (140), conference room.
Driving range.
Hotels: Chequers (Fladbury), golf packages available.

J104 **Walmley**

☎(021) 373 0029 (Club), Pro shop 373 7103
Brooks Rd, Wylde Green, Sutton Coldfield, W Midlands B72 1HR
6 miles N of Birmingham, turn off Birmingham to Sutton Coldfield road 0.25 mile N of Chester Rd (Yenton Pub), right into Greenhill Rd, Brooks Rd continues from this.
Parkland course.
18 holes, 6559 yards, S.S.S.72
Founded 1902
Visitors: welcome weekdays; weekend with member only.
Green Fee: £25 per day.
Societies: weekdays.
Catering: available.
Hotels: Penns Hall (Wylde Green).

J105 **Warley**

☎(0121) 429 2440
Lightwoods Hill, Smethwick, Warley, W Midlands B67 5ED
Off A456 4.5 miles W of centre of Birmingham, behind Dog pub.
Municipal parkland course.
9 holes, 2685 yards, S.S.S.68
Founded 1921
Visitors: welcome at all times, phone bookings in operation.
Green Fee: WD £4.50 (9 holes), £7.50 (18 holes); WE £5.50 (9 holes), £8 (18 holes).
Catering: available.

J106 **Warwick**

☎(01926) 494316
The Racecourse, Warwick, CV34 6HW
Centre of Warwick Racecourse.
Public meadowland course.
9 holes, 2682 yards, S.S.S.66
Designed by D.G. Dunkley.
Founded 1886
Visitors: welcome except race days.
Green Fee: WD £4 (9 holes); WE £5.50 (9 holes).
Societies: welcome.
Catering: bar only.
Driving range.
Hotels: Tudor House.

J107 **Warwickshire**

☎(01926) 409409, Fax 408409
Leek Woolton, Warwick CV35 7QT
J15 M40 take A46 towards Coventry, 2nd exit Leek Woolton
Inland Links/Parkland water
36 holes of championship golf in 4 loops of 9 between 6000-7400 yards, course can be catered for individual needs; 9 hole par 3 course.

Designed by K. Litten
Founded 1993
Visitors: welcome.
Green Fee: £40 (18 holes).
Societies: corporate days.
Catering: full facilities.
Driving range.
Hotels: numerous hotels in area.

J108 **Welcombe Hotel**

☎(01789) 295252, 299012 (Clubhouse), Fax 414666
Warwick Rd, Stratford-upon-Avon, Warwicks CV37 0NR
5 miles from M40 junction 15, 1.5 miles from Stratford on A439.
Parkland course.
18 holes, 6217 yards, S.S.S.70
Designed by T.J. McCauley.
Founded 1980
Visitors: advance telephone booking essential.
Green Fee: WD £30 per round, £40 per day; WE £35 per round, £45 per day.
Societies: welcome; packages available for 12 or more.
Catering: available.
Floodlit tennis, snooker.
Hotels: Welcombe, golf breaks available.

J109 **Westonbirt**

☎(01666) 880242
Tetbury, Glos GL8 8QG
Turn off A433 3 miles SW of Tetbury, through Westonbirt village, take turning opposite Westonbirt Arboretum entrance.
Parkland course.
9 holes, 4504 yards, S.S.S.61
Designed by Monty Hearn.
Visitors: welcome.
Green Fee: apply for details.
Societies: weekdays by arrangement.
Catering: available at Holford Arms, teas and snacks on course.
Hotels: Hare & Hounds.

J110 **Wharton Park**

☎(01299) 405222, 405163 (Pro shop), Fax 405121
Long Bank, Bewdley, Worcs DY12 2QW
On A456 at W end of Bewdley by-pass.
Undulating parkland course in Wyre Forest.
18 holes, 6603 yards, S.S.S.72
Founded 1992
Visitors: welcome.
Green Fee: WD £15; WE £22.

Societies: welcome by prior arrangement.
Catering: full facilities, conferences, function room.
snooker, driving range.
Hotels: The Heath.

J111 **Whitefields**

☎(01788) 521800, Fax 521695
Coventry Rd, Thurlaston, Nr Rugby, Warwicks CV23 9JR
Just off M45 on A45 to Coventry; within easy reach from M6, M40, M69, M1.
Parkland course.
18 holes, 6433 yards, S.S.S.70
Founded Aug 1992
Visitors: welcome.
Green Fee: WD £16; WE £20.
Societies: welcome Mon-Fri.
Catering: bars, spike bar, restaurant, catering for over 100.
Driving range.
Hotels: Own 15 room hotel.

J112 **Widney Manor**

☎(0121) 711 3646, Fax 711 3691
Saintbury Drive, Widney Manor, Solihull, West Midlands B91 3SZ
Off junc 4 of M42 take Stratford road and then turn right into Monkshall Path Road, then signposted to Widney Manor
Parkland course
18 holes, 5103 yards, S.S.S. 63
Designed by Golf Design Group
Founded 1993
Visitors: welcome
Green Fee: WD £8; WE £11.50
Societies: welcome some restrictions at weekends
Catering: full facilities.

J113 **Windmill Village Hotel**

☎(01203) 407241
Birmingham Road, Allesley, Coventry, W Midlands CV5 9AL
Off A45 westbound Coventry-Birmingham road.
Part flat, part hilly course.
18 holes, 5169 yards, S.S.S.66
Designed by Robert Hunter & John Harrhy.
Founded 1990
Visitors: welcome.
Green Fee: WD £9.95; WE £13.95.
Societies: welcome.
Catering: available.
Swimming pool, 8 snooker tables, fitness gym, sauna, conference facilities.
Hotels: Windmill Village.

J114 **Wishaw**

☎(0121) 313 2110
Bulls Lane, Wishaw, Sutton Coldfield
B76 9QN
M42 junc 9, go towards Belfry and
then take second on left at Belfry to
the Cock at Wishaw, club 0.75m on
left
Parkland course
18 holes, 5481 yards, S.S.S. 67
Founded 1993
Visitors: welcome
Green Fee: WD £10; WE £15
Societies: welcome weekdays by
arrangement
Catering: full range, bar snacks and
meals servrd and Sunday lunches
also available
Hotels: Belfry; Moor Hall.

J115 **Woodlands**

☎(01454) 619319, Fax 619397
Woodlands Lane, Almondsbury,
Bristol BS12 4JZ
M5 take exit 16 to large roundabout,
then left exit signposted Woodlands
Lane.
Public parkland course.
18 holes, 6068 yards, Par 70
Designed by C Chapman
Founded 1989
Visitors: pay-as-you-play.
Green Fee: WD £12; WE £15.
Societies: welcome by prior
arrangement.
Catering: full facilities.
Hotels: The Grange, Starkeys, Aztec
West (Bradley Stoke).

J116 **Woodspring**

☎(01275) 394378, Fax 394473
Yanley Lane, Long Ashton, Bristol,
Avon BS18 9LR
On A38 near Bristol Airport
Parkland course
27 holes Avon 2942 yards & Brunell
3320 yards play as 18 S.S.S. 70,
Severn 3340 yards opened April 1996
to form 3 courses
Designed by P Alliss & C Clark
Founded 1994
Visitors: welcome
Green Fee: WD £18; WE £24.
Societies: welcome weekdays
Catering: full facilities
Driving range, snooker, sauna
Hotels: Town and Country Lodge

J117 **Worcester G & CC**

☎(01905) 422555 (Sec), Pro
422044, **Catering:** 421132
Boughton Park, Worcester WR2 4EZ
1.5 miles from town centre on
Bransford Rd (A4103); from M5
junction 7 follow signs for Hereford.
Parkland course.
18 holes, 6251 yards, S.S.S.70
Designed by Dr. A. Mackenzie.
Founded 1898
Visitors: welcome with h/cap cert;
with member only at weekends;
phone Pro.
Green Fee: £25.
Societies: welcome.
Catering: available.
Tennis, squash, snooker.
Hotels: The Gifford.

J118 **Worcestershire**

☎(01684) 575992, 573905
Wood Farm, Malvern Wells, Worcs
WR14 4PP
2 miles S of Great Malvern, turn off
A449 on to B4209, follow signs.
Meadowland/parkland course.
18 holes, 6449 yards, S.S.S.71
Designed by Colt, Mackenzie, Braid
and later Jiggins and Hawtree.
Founded 1879
Visitors: members of recognised club
with h/cap certs, no play before 10am
weekends.
Green Fee: WD £25; WE £30.
Societies: Thurs and Fri.
Catering: full facilities.
2 snooker tables.
Hotels: Abbey; Foley Arms.

J119 **Wyre Forest**

☎(01299) 822682
Zortech Ave, Kidderminster, Worcs
DY11 7EX
On the main A451 Kidderminster-
Stourport road, 2 miles from the town
centre
Parkland
18 holes 5790 yards, S.S.S. 68
Designed by Golf Design Group
Founded 1994
Visitors: welcome
Green Fee: WD £8.50; WE £12
Societies: welcome with some
restrictions at weekends
Catering: full bar facilities 8am-11pm
Driving range.
Hotels: Gainsborough.

Golf in Wales can be divided very clearly into North and South with one or two notable exceptions in the central region like Borth & Ynyslas, which is well worth a break in any journey.

Road access to the Principality is usually by way of the Severn Bridge, the coast road from Chester to Bangor or into the mountain heart by way of Shrewsbury, Llangollen or Dolgellau. Bernard Darwin, who always favoured the train, made the latter a much publicised route, and was able to recite from memory the stations that came between Shrewsbury and his beloved Aberdovey where he spent an annual holiday.

The station at Aberdovey is right beside the clubhouse and little time need be lost in launching a round across an historic piece of land which Darwin described with sentimental love and warmth. Although two years Aberdovey's junior, Royal St David's enjoys an even more resplendent setting under the historic shadow of Harlech Castle with more distant views of Snowdonia. It is a well trodden favourite for the staging of Welsh championships.

The north coast is well served by Conwy (Caernarvonshire) and by Prestatyn which, after a somewhat flat beginning, blossoms into ideal duneland territory. Llandudno G.C. at Maesdu and North Wales G.C. next door are familiar names.

For an instant introduction to Welsh golf in the south, nothing beats the convenience of St. Pierre which was one of the first new courses to be built in the wake of World War II and undoubtedly one of the best. It weaves a most pleasant path through stately trees of ancient origin, a sheltered home for the game that contrasts sharply with the exposed reaches of Royal Porthcawl, Southerndown, Pyle & Kenfig, Ashburnham and Tenby.

Temptation to reach Porthcawl may make travellers overlook the charms of Newport at Rogerstone but Newport now has the added attraction of Celtic Manor, right by the M4, which has been very well received. However, Porthcawl is the pride of Wales particularly after the stirring victory of the Great Britain and Ireland team, captained by a Welshman, in the Walker Cup in 1995. It is a classic links. Porthcawl is sandwiched by Southerndown, one of the finest examples of downland golf, and Pyle & Kenfig, a course split in two by a road which also acts as a division of character. The best is true links.

Pennard beyond Swansea is a lovely, remote links that never attracts the praise it warrants while Gower GC above Gowerton is a new attraction with spectacular views, but this is more the province of West Wales with the attractions of Ashburnham and Tenby, which combine a stern challenge with more scenic blessings.

Ashburnham is as well known for golf as the neighbouring town of Llanelli is for rugby but Tenby beckons for those who look upon themselves as connoisseurs of glorious places to play. Host to countless championships, it is a seaside links of unrivalled joy and beauty and, for the historically minded, it has an important additional qualification – it is the oldest constituted Club in the principality.

It is golf on the grand scale, frequently influenced by the wind and calling for an ability to flight the ball low and indulge in the art of the chip and run which many in other parts of the world regard as a relic of a lost age.

This section has been dominated by north and south but Cradoc at Brecon, Knighton and Llandrindod Wells are some contrasting courses in contrasting settings for those desirous of exploring more central parts.

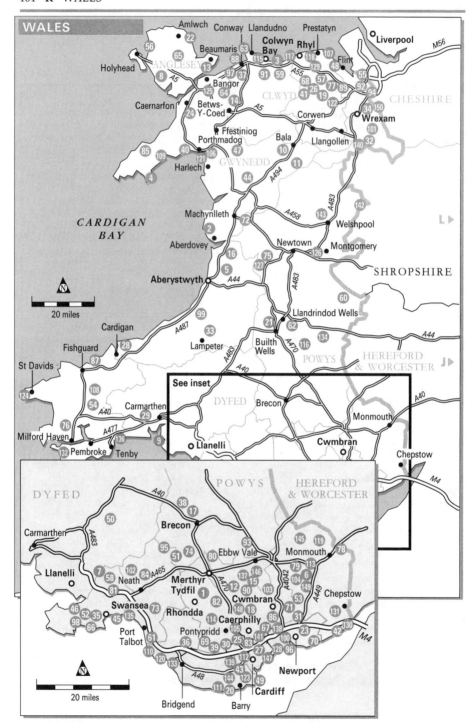

K1 Aberdare

☎(01685) 871188, Sec 872797, Pro 878735
Abernant, Aberdare, Mid-Glam CF44 0RY
0.5 mile from town centre (A4059), past General Hospital.
Mountain course with parkland features.
18 holes, 5875 yards, S.S.S.69
Founded 1921
Visitors: members of recognised golf club welcome weekdays with h/hap cert; Sat with member only; Sun and Bank Holidays advance notice to Sec.
Green Fee: WD £14; WE & BH £18.
Societies: welcome on application to Sec.
Catering: full range of bar snacks and meals; not Mon.
Snooker.
Hotels: Baverstock; Ty Newydd.

K2 Aberdovey

☎(01654) 767210, Sec 767493
Aberdovey, Gwynedd LL35 0RT
On main A493 immediately W of Aberdovey.
Seaside links course.
18 holes, 6445 yards, S.S.S.71
Amendments by James Braid.
Founded 1892
Visitors: welcome; h/cap certs required.

Green Fee: £17 - £27 per round.
Societies: weekdays only.
Catering: daily 10.30am-8.30pm; bar 11am-11pm.
Hotels: list available from Sec.

K3 Abergele & Pensarn

☎(01745) 824034, Fax 823813
Tan-y-Gopa Rd, Abergele, Clwyd LL28 8DS
Through Abergele from A55, turn left in direction of Llanddulas; course below Gwrych Castle.
Parkland course.
18 holes, 6450 yards, S.S.S.71
Designed by Hawtree & Sons.
Founded 1910
Visitors: welcome.
Green Fee: WD £22; WE & BH £28.
Societies: by prior arrangement.
Catering: restaurant except Mon.
Snooker.

K4 Abersoch

☎(01758) 712622
Golf Rd, Abersoch, Gwynedd LL53 7EY
6 miles from Pwllheli; 1st left through village.
Seaside links course.
18 holes, 5819 yards, S.S.S.68
Designed by Harry Vardon.
Founded 1910

Visitors: welcome with h/cap cert; booking required.
Green Fee: WD £18; WE £20.
Societies: by arrangement.
Catering: meals served.
Hotels: Egryn; Wylfa; Riverside; Neigwl; Deugoch, Carisbrook.

K5 Aberystwyth

☎(01970) 615104, Pro 625301
Bryn y-Mor, Aberystwyth, Dyfed SY23 3QD
N end of promenade behind sea front hotels, access road adjacent to Cliff Railway, 1 mile from town centre.
Undulating meadowland course.
18 holes, 6109 yards, S.S.S.71
Designed by Harry Vardon.
Founded 1911
Visitors: limited at weekends.
Green Fee: £15.
Societies: by appointment.
Catering: bar and restaurant.
Hotels: apply to Sec for details.

K6 Alice Springs

☎(01873) 880772, 880244
Bettws Newydd, Usk, Gwent NP5 1JY
A449 into Usk, N on B4598, after 1.5 miles take right to Bettws Newydd, course (Queens) 1.5 miles on left; for Kings course take same B4598, do not turn off, course 3 miles N on right.

Parkland course.
Queens, 18 holes, 6041 yards,
S.S.S.69; Kings, 6868 yards,
S.S.S.71
Designed by Keith R. Morgan.
Founded Aug 1989
Visitors: phone for tee time
weekends and Bank Holidays.
Green Fee: WD £12.50; WE £15.
Societies: Mon-Fri; weekends by
arrangement.
Catering: bar and snacks all day,
restaurant with phone booking.

K7 **Allt-y-Graban**

☎(01792) 885757, 883279
Allt-y-Graban Rd, Pontlliw, Swansea,
West Glam SA4 1DT
From M4 exit 47 follow A48 through
Penllergaer and Pontlliw; take 1st
turning left after Glamorgan Arms
onto Allt-y-Graban Rd; course
opposite garden centre.
Parkland course.
9 holes, 6 Par 4, 3 Par 3
Designed by F.G. Thomas.
Founded August 1993
Visitors: welcome 9.30am to 1 hour
before dusk.
Green Fee: £6 (9 holes), £9 (18
holes).
Societies: weekdays; contact club for
terms.
Catering: clubhouse with refreshment
and changing facilities.
Hotels: Fforest Motel (Fforestfach);
Diplomat (Llanelli).

K8 **Anglesey**

☎(01407) 810930 (Manager), Pro
811202, Steward: 810219
Station Rd, Rhosneigr, Gwynedd
LL64 5QT
S off A5 about 8 miles from Holyhead
onto A4080, in 3 miles turn right at
Llanfaelog church, under railway
bridge, about 200yds to course.
Seaside links course.
18 holes, 6300 yards, S.S.S.68
Founded 1914
Visitors: h/cap cert required,
preferable to phone.
Green Fee: WD £15; WE & BH £20.
Special rates in winter.
Societies: by arrangement, reduction
for 10+.
Catering: meals served.
Hotels: Maelog Lake (Rhosneigr).

K9 **Ashburnham**

☎(01554) 832466 (Sec)
Cliffe Terrace, Burry Port, Dyfed
SA16 0HN
9 miles from Llanelli exit on M4, 4
miles from Llanelli on A484.
Championship links course.
18 holes, 6916 yards, S.S.S.73; 18
holes, 6627 yards, S.S.S.72
Founded 1894
Visitors: weekdays; some weekends.
Green Fee: apply for details.
Societies: welcome weekdays by
arrangement.
Catering: full facilities.

K10 **Bala**

☎(01678) 520359 (9am-3pm April-
Sept, 9am-10am Oct-March,
evenings all year)
Penlan, Bala, Gwynedd LL23 7YD
Take A494 out of Bala to Dolgellau,
turn 1st right on leaving Bala.
Upland course.
10 holes, 4962 yards, S.S.S.64
Founded 1973
Visitors: welcome, some restrictions
Sat and Sun pm.
Green Fee: on application.
Societies: welcome by prior
arrangement.
Catering: bar; catering by prior
arrangement.
Snooker, pool.
Hotels: Plas Goch; White Lion; Pale
Hall.

K11 **Bala Lake Hotel**

☎(01678) 520344
Bala, Gwynned, LL23 7YF
Off B4403 1.5 miles from Bala.
Public parkland course.
9 holes, 4281 yards, S.S.S.61
Founded 1960
Visitors: welcome.
Green Fee: apply for details.
Societies: welcome.
Catering: full facilities.
Open air swimming pool.
Hotels: Bala Lake Hotel.

K12 **Bargoed**

☎(01443) 830143
Heolddu, Bargoed, Mid-Glam
20 miles from Cardiff on A469 to town
centre; moorland road.
Moorland course.
18 holes, 6213 yards, S.S.S.70
Founded 1912
Visitors: welcome weekdays;
weekends with member only.
Green Fee: WD £17 (£10 with
member).
Societies: by arrangement.
Catering: bar snacks and evening
meals served.
Hotels: Park Hotel; Maes Manor.

K13 **Baron Hill**

☎(01248) 810231
Beaumaris, Anglesey, Gwynedd LL58
8YN
Follow A545 Menai Bridge-
Beaumaris, course is signposted on
left when approaching Beaumaris.
Undulating moorland.
9 holes, 5564 yards, S.S.S.67
Founded 1895
Visitors: welcome, h/cap preferred,
parties contact Sec; Tues Ladies day,
Sun competitions until mid-afternoon).
Green Fee: £12 per day, £40 per
week (reduced with member).
Societies: booking necessary, not
Sun.
Catering: new clubhouse due to
open Spring 1996.
Hotels: Bulkeley Arms; Bishopsgate;
Bull.

K14 **Betws-y-Coed**

☎(01690) 710556
Betws-y-Coed, Gwynedd
Just off main A5 road in the middle of
village of Betws-y-Coed.
Parkland course.
9 holes, 4996 yards, S.S.S.63
Founded 1977
Visitors: welcome.
Green Fee: WD £15; WE £20.
Societies: arrangements to be made
in writing to Sec or phone (01492)
641663 after 6pm..
Catering: everyday except Mon.
Hotels: Royal Oak; Plas Hall.

K15 **Blackwood**

☎(01495) 223152
Cwmgelli, Blackwood, Gwent NP2
1EL
0.75 mile N of Blackwood on A4048,
Tredegar road.
Meadowland course.
9 holes, 5304 yards, S.S.S.66
Founded 1914
Visitors: welcome weekdays,
weekends by arrangement.
Green Fee: WD £13; WE & BH £16.
Societies: weekdays by prior
arrangement.
Catering: golf societies only by
arrangement.
Hotels: Maes Manor; Plas Inn.

K16 **Borth & Ynyslas**

☎(01970) 871202 (Sec), Pro 871557
Borth, Dyfed SY24 5JS
8 miles N of Aberystwyth; travel N
from Aberystwyth to Machynlleth and
turn left N side of village of Bow
Street.

Aberforeshire, Caernarfon, Gwynedd LL54 5RP
Tel: 01286 678359

Less than a mile from the historic royal town of Caernarfon we can offer a delightful, 18-hole, 5746yd parkland course. Designed to provide panoramic views of Snowdonia, the Menai Straits & Anglesey, come & relax & enjoy our beautifully sculptured & well manicured course. Full tuition & equipment is always available from our resident PGA professional, & a warm Welsh welcome & hot meal awaits you in the clubhouse.

Traditional links course (oldest in Wales).
18 holes, 6116 yards, S.S.S.70
Founded 1885
Visitors: members of a golf club with club h/cap.
Green Fee: WD £18; WE £22.
Societies: and properly constituted parties catered for after consultation with Sec; allow 7 days notice at all tiimes, but weekends may often be difficult.
Catering: full facilities, prior booking necessary.
Hotels: Railway; Glanmor (Borth); Ynyshir Country House (Eglwysfach); Black Lion (Talybont).

K17 **Brecon**
☎(01874) 622004, Sec (home): 625547
Newton Park, Llanfaer, Brecon, Powys LD3 8PA
300 yards from roundabout on bypass S of town.
Meadowland course.
9 holes, 5256 yards, S.S.S.66
Founded 1902
Visitors: welcome.
Green Fee: £10 per day.
Societies: welcome by prior arrangement.
Hotels: Peterstone Court Hotel (Brecon).

K18 **Bryn Meadows G & CC**
☎(01495) 225590 or 227276, Pro 221905
The Bryn, Hengoed, Mid-Glam CF8 7SM
A469 15 miles from Cardiff, turn up Bryn Lane near Crown Hotel.
Parkland course.
18 holes, 6156 yards, S.S.S.70
Designed by E. Jefferies & B. Mayo.
Founded 1973
Visitors: welcome weekdays.
Green Fee: WD £17.50 (£12.50 with member); WE £22.50 (£17.50 with member).
Societies: welcome weekdays by arrangement.
Catering: full facilties except Sun; banqueting.

Indoor heated pool, jacuzzi, pool table, full leisure facilities; Wales Tourist Board 5 Crown and Gold Medal award winners.
Hotels: Bryn Meadows, special 2-day packages.

K19 **Bryn Morfydd Hotel**
☎(01745) 890280
The Duchess Course, Llanrhaeadr, Nr Denbigh LL16 4NP
2.5 miles E of Denbigh on A525.
Mature parkland course.
Dukes Course, 18 holes, 5601 yards, S.S.S.68, Par 71; Duchess, 9 holes, 1200 yards, Par 27
Designed by Alliss/Thomas (Duchess Course); Muirhead/Henderson(Dukes Course).
Founded 1982 (Duchess); 1993 (Dukes)
Visitors: welcome, no h/cap cert required.
Green Fee: Duchess Course £5; Dukes Course WD £12; WE & BH £16.
Societies: welcome, rates on application.
Catering: full hotel facilities, separate golf clubhouse
British School of Golf, practice ground, swimming pool.
Hotels: Bryn Morfydd (on site).

K20 **Brynhill**
☎(01446) 735061, Sec 720277
Port Rd, Barry, S Glam CF6 7PH
M4 junct 33, follow signs to Barry and Cardiff (Wales) Airport; golf club on Port Rd near Colcot Arms Hotel.
Undulating meadowland course.
18 holes, 5949 yards, S.S.S.68
Designed by G.K. Cotton.
Founded 1921
Visitors: welcome Mon-Sat, membership or h/cap cert required; no visitors Sun.
Green Fee: WD £20 (£9 with member); £25 Sat (£9 with member).
Societies: catered for weekdays by arrangement.
Catering: lunches, dinners served except Mon.
Hotels: Mount Sorrel; International; Copthorne (Culverhouse Cross).

K21 **Builth Wells**
☎(01982) 553296
Golf Club Rd, Builth Wells, Powys LD2 3NF
A483 immediately W of Builth Wells.
Parkland course.
18 holes, 5376 yards, S.S.S.67
Founded 1923
Visitors: welcome anytime.
Green Fee: WD £16 per day, £12 per round; WE & BH £22 per day, £18 per round.
Societies: welcome any time by arrangement.
Catering: available, societies by arrangement.
Hotels: send for brochure.

K22 **Bull Bay**
☎(01407) 830960, Pro 831188
Bull Bay Rd, Amlwch, Anglesey LL68 9RY
A5025 18 miles from Menai Bridge.
Undulating coastal heathland course – the northernmost golf course in Wales.
18 holes, 6217 yards, S.S.S.70
Designed by Herbert Fowler and Walton Heath.
Founded 1913
Visitors: welcome, h/cap cert preferred.
Green Fee: WD £15; WE £20.
Societies: by arrangement with Sec; discount for parties over 12; telephone for details.
Catering: full facilities available in new clubhouse.
Hotels: Bull Bay; Dinorben; Lastra Farm; Trecastell.

K23 **Caerleon**
☎(01633) 420342
Broadway, Caerleon, Newport, Gwent NP6 1AY
3 miles from M4 junction 25.
Public parkland course.
9 holes, 3092 yards, S.S.S.34
Designed by D. Steel.
Founded 1974
Visitors: welcome.
Green Fee: WD £3.30 (9 holes); WE £4.10.
Catering: snack bar.
Driving range, pool.

K24 **Caernarfon**

☎(01286) 678359 (Sec/Pro)
Aberforeshore, Llanfaglan,
Caernarfon LL54 5RP
2 miles S of town off Caernarfon-
Pwllheli road.
Parkland course.
18 holes, 5870 yards, S.S.S.69
Founded 1905
Visitors: welcome.
Green Fee: WD £18 per day, £15 per
round; WE £22 per day, £20 per
round.
Societies: welcome by prior
arrangement.
Catering: full facilities.
Hotels: Caerlyr Hall; Bryn Eisteddfod;
Erw Fair; Caeau Capel; Black Boy;
Deugoch; Seiont Manor.

K25 **Caerphilly**

☎(01222) 883481, Sec 863441, Pro
869104
Pencapel, Mountain Rd, Caerphilly,
Mid-Glam CF8 2SY
7 miles from Cardiff centre on A469;
12 miles from Newport; 6 miles from
M4 on A470 N; 250 yards from
bus/rail station.
Mountain/parkland course; 2 holes on
steep gradient.
14 holes (further 4 under
construction), 6059 yards, S.S.S.71
Designed by Fernie (original 9).
Founded 1905
Visitors: welcome weekdays with
proof of club membership and h/cap
cert; not Sun or Bank Holidays unless
with member.
Green Fee: £20 per day, (£10 with
member); jnrs £6.
Societies: Mon-Fri only.
Catering: bar; restaurant meals by
arrangement.
Snooker.
Hotels: Mount; Greenhill; Moat
House; Cedar Tree.

K26 **Caerwys Nine Of Clubs**

☎(01352) 720692
Caerwys, Mold, Clwyd CH7 5AQ
1.5 miles S of A55 expressway
midway between Holywell and St
Asaph.
Undulating parkland course.
9 holes, 3088 yards, Par 60
Designed by Eleanor Barlow.
Founded May 1988
Visitors: welcome; pay-as-you-play.
Green Fee: WD £4.50 (18 holes) £7
(day ticket); WE & BH £5.50 (18
holes) £8 (day ticket); Juniors WD
£2.50, WE & BH £4.50.

Societies: by booking only.
Catering: light refreshments.
Putting green, snooker, table tennis.
Hotels: Holywell; also self-catering
accomodation (4-6 persons) on site;
telephone for details.

K27 **Cardiff**

☎(01222) 753320 (Sec), Pro
754772, Clubhouse 753067
Sherborne Ave, Cyncoed, Cardiff, S
Glam CF2 6SJ
Take A48M off the M4, 3 miles to
Pentwyn exit, take industrial road for
2 miles to village, turn left at
roundabout and again left at Spar
shop, club 150 yards.
Undulating parkland course.
18 holes, 6016 yards, S.S.S.70
Founded 1921
Visitors: welcome weekdays
arranged in advance, restricted Tues
am (Ladies Day); with member only
at weekends.
Green Fee: on application.
Societies: Thurs by advance
booking.
Catering: full facilities available.
Hotels: Post House; Stakis Inn.

K28 **Cardigan**

☎(01293) 612035
Gwbert-on-Sea, Cardigan, Dyfed
SA43 1PR
3 miles NW of Cardigan, take left fork
at Cardigan Cenotaph at N end of
town.
Seaside meadowland course.
18 holes, 6687 yards, S.S.S.72
Founded 1928
Visitors: unrestricted.
Green Fee: WD £15 per day; WE &
BH £20 per day.
Societies: welcome any day with
previous arrangement.
Catering: full facilities.
Squash, pool.
Hotels: Cliff; Castell Malgwyn
(Llechryd); Gwbert.

K29 **Carmarthen**

☎(01267) 281588
Blaenycoed Rd, Carmarthen, Dyfed
SA33 6EH
4 miles NW of Carmarthen.
Undulating parkland course.
18 holes, 6212 yards, S.S.S.70
Founded 1929
Visitors: welcome, Tues ladies day
(tee reserved 12am-2.30pm).
Green Fee: WD £18; WE £25.
Societies: welcome by prior
arrangement.

Catering: full bar 12am-11pm; no
catering Wed otherwise 12am-2pm
and 4.30pm-10pm.
Hotels: Falcon; Ivy Bush.

K30 **Castell Heights**

☎(01222) 886666 (Bookings), Club
886686, Fax 861128
Blaengwynlais, Caerphilly, Mid-
Glamorgan CF8 1NG
4 miles from M4 junction 32 on
Tongwynlais-Caerphilly road, by
Mountain Lakes Golf Club.
Public, mountainside course.
9 holes, 2688 yards, S.S.S.66
Founded 1982
Visitors: welcome, pay-as-you-play.
Green Fee: apply for details.
Societies: welcome by prior
arrangement.
Catering: bar and bar snacks
available.
Mountain Lakes Driving Range.

K31 **Celtic Manor Golf Course**

☎(01633) 413000
Catsash Road, Coldra Woods,
Newport, Gwent NP6 2YQ
M4 junction 24. A48 to Newport, 200
yards on RH side.
2 courses: Parkland.
18 holes, 7001 yards, S.S.S. 74
18 holes, 4094 yards, Par 61
Designed by Robert Trent-Jones Snr.
Founded 1995
Visitors: welcome.
Green Fees: on application.
Societies: welcome.
Catering: full facilities; largest
clubhouse in Britain.
Other facilities include Ian Woosnam
Golf Academy; two leisure clubs,
conference facilities etc.
Hotels: Celtic Manor.

K32 **Chirk**

☎(01691) 774407
Chirk, Nr Wrexham, Clwyd LL14 5AD.
Take A483 from Wrexham to A5; 1
mile.
Parkland course.
18 holes, 7045 yards, S.S.S. 73
Founded 1992
Visitors: welcome.
Green Fees: WD £15 per round; £22
per day; WE £22 per round; £28 per
day.
Societies: welcome.
Catering: full clubhouse facilities
available.
Driving range.
Hotels: Hand (Chirk).

CRADOC GOLF CLUB invites you to the beautiful Brecon Beacons National Park. Our 18 hole, Parklands Course will delight individual golfers and golf societies alike.

Cradoc offers spectacular views of the Beacons, a superb, manicured course, a separate practice ground, and a friendly welcome & home cooked food in the clubhouse.

Just 2 miles from Brecon, Cradoc Golf Club is within easy reach of South Wales, the South West, &The Midlands. **For bookings or more details call 01874-623658.**

K33 Cilgwyn
☎(01570) 493286
Llangybi, Lampeter, Dyfed SA48 8NN
5 miles NE of Lampeter on A485 in village of Llangybi.
Parkland course.
9 holes, 5327 yards, S.S.S.67
Founded 1905
Visitors: welcome.
Green Fee: WD £10; WE & BH £15; £60 per week
Societies: catered for throughout year.
Catering: restaurant and bar meals available Tues to Sun.
Pool table
Hotels: Black Lion; Falcondale (Lampeter).

K34 Clay`s Farm Golf Centre
☎(01978) 661406 (Pro), Fax 661417, Catering: 661416
Bryn Estyn Road, Wrexham, Clwyd LL13 9UB
Nantwich road off Wrexham by-pass; turn for Wrexham Industrial Estate; club is signposted.
Parkland course.
18 holes, 5624 yards, S.S.S. 67
Founded 1991
Visitors: welcome anytime; booking advisable.
Green Fees: WD £11 per round; WE £14 per round.
Societies: welcome anytime by arrangement.
Catering: full facilities.
Hotels: Holt Lodge.

K35 Clyne
☎(01792) 401989
120 Owls Lodge Lane, Mayals, Black Pill, Swansea SA3 5DP
Take coast road from Swansea to Blackpyl (3 miles); turn right into Mayals Rd.
Moorland course.
18 holes, 6312 yards, S.S.S.71
Designed by H.S. Colt.
Founded 1921
Visitors: welcome.
Green Fee: apply for details.
Societies: weekdays by arrangement; not weekends.

Catering: full facilities available except Mon.
Hotels: Osborne; Forte Crest; Swansea Marriott.

K36 Coed-y-Mwster Golf Club
☎(01656) 862121
The Club House, Coychurch, Nr Bridgend, Mid Glamorgan CF35 6AF
1.5 miles off junction 35 of M4.
Parkland course.
9 holes (12 tees), 5758 yards, S.S.S. 68
Founded July 1994
Visitors: welcome anytime.
Green Fees: £15 (18 holes)
Societies: welcome by prior arrangement.
Catering: bar meals available at all times.
Hotels: Coed-y-Mwster Hotel (adjacent).

K37 Conwy (Caernarvonshire)
☎(01492) 593400, Sec 592423, Pro 593225
Morfa, Conwy, Gwynedd LL32 8ER
Follow signs for Conwy Marina off A55 Chester-Bangor expressway; course adjacent to Marina.
Championship links course.
18 holes, 6936 yards, S.S.S.74
Founded 1890
Visitors: times restricted, contact Pro in advance.
Green Fee: WD £23; WE & BH £28.
Societies: catered for on application to Sec.
Catering: available except Mon evening and Tues all day.
Hotels: Castle Bank; Bryn Cregin; Caerlyr.

K38 Cradoc
☎(01874) 623658 (Sec), Pro 625524
Penoyre Park, Cradoc, Brecon, Powys LD3 9LP
2 miles N of Brecon on B4520.
Parkland course.
18 holes, 6318 yards, S.S.S.71
Designed by C.K. Cotton.
Founded 1974

Visitors: welcome; not Sun.
Green Fee: WD £18; WE & BH £20.
Societies: welcome with prior arrangement; not Sun.
Catering: full facilities daily except Mon by special arrangement.
Snooker, practice ground.
Hotels: Wellington; Castle of Brecon; George; Bishops Meadow; Lake (Llangammarch Wells).

K39 Creigiau
☎(01222) 890263
Creigiau, Cardiff, S Glam CF4 8NN
4 miles NW of Cardiff towards Llantrisant.
Parkland course.
18 holes, 5979 yards, S.S.S.69, Par 71
Founded 1926
Visitors: welcome weekdays; Tues Ladies Day.
Green Fee: £26.
Societies: welcome weekdays by arrangement.
Catering: lunch, dinner.
Hotels: Friendly Hotel, Miskin Manor; Park; Royal; Angel.

K40 Criccieth
☎(01766) 522154
Ednyfed Hill, Criccieth, Gwynedd A497, 4 miles from Portmadoc, turn right past Memorial Hall, 0.5 mile up hill.
Undulating hilltop course.
18 holes, 5787 yards, S.S.S.68
Founded around 1904
Visitors: welcome.
Green Fee: WD & Sat £12; Sunday & BH £15.
Societies: welcome.
Catering: meals and snacks served by arrangement with Steward.
Hotels: George IV; Bron Eifion; Marine; Lion.

K41 Denbigh
☎(01745) 816669 (Sec), Pro 814159, Caterer: 816664
Henllan Rd, Denbigh, Clwyd B5382 Denbigh to Henllan road, 1 mile out of Denbigh.
Undulating parkland course.

18 holes, 5712 yards, S.S.S.67
Designed by John Stockton
Founded 1922
Visitors: welcome; phone Pro shop for reservation.
Green Fee: WD £19; WE & BH £25.
Societies: daily.
Catering: full facilities 7 days, licenced bar.
Snooker.
Hotels: Oriel House (St Asaph); Tan y Gyrt Hall (Nantglyn)

K42 **Dewstow**
☎(01291) 430444, Fax 425816
Caerwent, Newport, Gwent NP6 4AH
On A48 between Newport and Chepstow, turn off at Caerwent, course signposted; 4 miles W of Chepstow.
Parkland course.
Park Course: 18 holes, 6100 yards, S.S.S.69. Valley Course: 6100 yards, S.S.S.70.
Founded 1988
Visitors: welcome any time, normal dress standards, no h/cap cert required.
Green Fee: WD £11; WE & BH £15.
Societies: anytime by prior arrangement but weekends may be limited; from £16.50 including 1-course meal.
Catering: lounge, bar, restaurant (full menu), bar snacks
Driving range.

K43 **Dinas Powis**
☎(01222) 512727 (Sec), Club 512157
Golf House, Old Highwalls, Dinas Powis, S Glam CF6 4AJ
M4 junction 33, on A4055 to Dinas Powis via Barry (Cardiff Airport).
Parkland course.
18 holes, 5486 yards, S.S.S.67
Founded 1914
Visitors: welcome with h/cap cert and proof of club membership.
Green Fee: WD £20; WE £27.
Societies: welcome by arrangement, limited to 40.
Catering: bar and restaurant.
Hotels: Star.

K44 **Dolgellau**
☎(01341) 422603
Pencefn, Golf Rd, Dolgellau, Gwynedd LL40 1SL
Turn off town by-pass onto old A494 road, turn right just after main bridge, signposted from there on; 0.5 mile from town centre.

Parkland course.
9 holes (18 tees), 4671 yards, S.S.S.63
Founded 1911
Visitors: welcome weekdays; ring Sat.
Green Fee: WD £13; WE £16.
Societies: by arrangement.
Catering: available through year.
Hotels: Royal Ship; Bontoon Hall; Dolserau Hall.

K45 **Earlswood**
☎(01792) 321578
Earlswood Golf Course, Jersey Marine, Neath SA10 6JP
Turn off A483 Neath-Swansea road onto B4290, proceed towards Jersey Marine village, then 1st right; club signposted.
Public course.
18 holes, S.S.S.68
Founded May 1993
Visitors: welcome. no restrictions.
Green Fee: £8.
Societies: welcome.

K46 **Fairwood Park**
☎(01792) 203648, Sec 297849, Pro 299194
Blackhills Lane, Upper Killay, Swansea SA2 7JN
From central Swansea follow signs for Sketty and Killay then Swansea Airport; take left turn opposite Airport entrance; course 0.5 mile up Blackhills Lane on left.
Parkland championship course.
18 holes, 6741 yards, S.S.S.72
Founded 1969
Visitors: welcome with h/cap cert; advisable to phone in advance.
Green Fee: WD £25; WE & BH £30.
Societies: welcome weekdays and weekends by prior arrangement.
Catering: breakfast, lunch, dinner, tea, coffee, snacks; licensed bar.
Snooker, pool, darts.
Hotels: In Swansea.

K47 **Ffestiniog**
☎(01766) 762637
Clwb Golff Ffestiniog, Y Cefn, Ffestiniog, Gwynedd
1 mile from Ffestiniog on Bala road.
Scenic mountain course.
9 holes, 5032 metres, S.S.S.65
Founded 1893
Visitors: hardly any restrictions.
Green Fee: on application.
Societies: by arrangement only.
Catering: bar only.
Hotels: Abbey Arms.

K48 **Flint**
☎(01352) 732327, Steward: 733461
Cornist Park, Flint, Clwyd CH6 5HJ
Take A548 coast road, or M56/A55; course is 1 mile from town centre; from Town Hall, follow signs to Cornist Park.
Parkland course.
9 holes, 5953 yards, S.S.S.69
Founded 1966
Visitors: welcome weekdays.
Green Fee: £12 per day.
Societies: catered for Mon-Fri by arrangement.
Catering: prior arrangement for catering and bar.
Snooker.
Hotels: Chequers; Northop Hall; Springfield; Pentre; Halkyn.

K49 **Glamorganshire**
☎(01222) 701185 (Sec), Pro 707401, Members: 707048
Lavernock Rd, Penarth, S Glam CF6 2UP
Take junction 33 off M4, join A4232 and then A4267 which passes club.
Parkland course.
18 holes, 6181 yards, S.S.S.70
Founded 1890
Visitors: welcome except on competition days, Bank Holidays and other days when Societies on course; must have bona fide h/cap cert from own club.
Green Fee: WD £24; WE & BH £30.
Societies: welcome on application to Sec.
Catering: first class facilities, à la carte menus, bar snacks; lunches every day.
Snooker, practice area.
Hotels: Walton House.

K50 **Glynhir**
☎(01269) 850472
Glynhir Rd, Llandybie, Ammanford, Dyfed SA18 2TF
1.25 miles from Ammanford on A483 Llandybie road, turn right up Glynhir Rd and continue for almost 2 miles to club.
Undulating parkland/meadowland course.
18 holes, 5952 yards, S.S.S.69
Designed by F.W. Hawtree.
Founded 1964 – moved from previous course at Llandeilo.
Visitors: bona fide members of recognised golf clubs with current membership and h/cap certs welcome weekdays and by permission Saturday and holidays in summer(no visitors Sunday).

The Mill at Glynhir

Llandybie, Dyfed SA18 2TE

♛ ♛ ♛ ♛ W.T.B.

Ashley Courtney Hotel of **distinction** originally 17th Century waterdriven cornmill, tastefully converted into a luxury 11 bedroom country house hotel. Idyllic situation overlooking the Brecon National Park yet convenient for the famous Gower and Pembrokeshire coast, every convenience in your room even a spa bath, indoor heated swimming pool, 2 ½ acres of grounds bounded by our own trout river. **Free Golf** can be enjoyed at adjacent Glynhir and many other courses. From £27.50 p.p.p. night to include dinner B&B & Golf. Alas no under 11's

Tel/fax 01269 850672

Green Fee: WD £15; WE £20.
Societies: weekdays welcome, Sat only on occasions, not Sun or holidays; all by prior appointment.
Catering: restaurant, bar meals available daily.
Hotels: The Mill at Glynhir; Glynhir Golf Clubhouse; Cawdor, White Hart (Llandeilo); The Plough (Llandeilo).

K51 Glynneath
☎(01639) 720452
Pen-y-craig, Pontneathvaughan (Powys), Nr Glynneath, W Glam SA11 5UH
11 miles N of Neath, 2 miles NE of Glynneath on B4242.
Picturesque woodland course overlooking Vale of Neath.
18 holes, 5533 yards, S.S.S.67
Designed by Cotton, Pennink, Lawrie & Partners.
Founded 1931
Visitors: no restrictions.
Green Fee: WD £12 per round, £15 per day; WE £18.
Societies: weekdays by prior arrangement.
Catering: by arrangement; bar from 12am.
Snooker.
Hotels: Plas-y-Felin.

K52 Gower
☎(01792) 872480
Cefn Goleu, Three Crosses, Gowerton, Swansea SA4 3HS
Exit M4 at junction 47, take A483 to Swansea, at 1st roundabout turn onto A484 signposted to Llanelli, at 3rd roundabout B4296 signposted to Gowerton, go straight ahead at traffic lights and then continue up the hill for 1 mile.
9 holes, 3305 yards
Designed by Donald Steel.
Founded 1995
Visitors: welcome.

Green fee: WD £9 (9 holes), £12 (18 holes); WE £9 (9 holes), £15 (18 holes).
Societies: welcome by prior arrangement.
Catering: bar and food available.

K53 Greenmeadow
☎(01633) 869321, Pro 862626
Treherbert Road, Croesyceiliog, Cwmbran, Gwent NP44 2BZ
Off A4042.
Parkland course.
14 holes, 5597 yards, S.S.S.67 (18 holes from Spring 1996, 6300 yds)
Founded 1978
Visitors: welcome.
Green Fee: apply for details.
Societies: welcome.
Catering: full facilities.
Hotels: Parkway; Commodore.

K54 Haverfordwest
☎(01437) 764523 (Sec), Pro 768409, Clubhouse 763565
Arnolds Down, Haverfordwest, Dyfed SA61 2XQ
1 mile E of town on A40.
Parkland course.
18 holes, 6005 yards, S.S.S.69
Founded 1904
Visitors: bona fide golfers welcome.
Green Fee: WD £17 per day; WE £24 per day.
Societies: welcome by prior arrangement.
Catering: restaurant; hot and cold bar snacks; licensed bars.
Hotels: Hotel Mariners; St Brides (Saundersfoot); County.

K55 Hawarden
☎(01244) 531447
Groomsdale Lane, Hawarden, Deeside, Clwyd CH5 3EH
A55 9 miles W of Chester, 3rd left after Hawarden station.

Parkland course.
18 holes, 5894 yards, S.S.S.68
Founded 1911
Visitors: with member only or with prior arrangment with the Sec.
Green Fee: WD £12 per round, £15 per day; WE £16 per round.
Societies: by arrangement in advance with Sec.
Catering: full facilities.
Hotels: St Davids (Ewloe).

K56 Holyhead
☎(01407) 763279 (Sec), Pro 762022, Bar: 762119
Trearddur Bay, Holyhead, Gwynedd LL65 2YG
Follow A5 from Bangor, turn left at Valley traffic lights, continue approx 4 miles, course is on left.
Undulating heathland course.
18 holes, 6058 yards, S.S.S.70
Designed by James Braid.
Founded 1912
Visitors: welcome, particularly weekdays and residential; h/cap cert required.
Green Fee: apply for details.
Societies: recognised societies welcome subject to prior arrangement with Sec.
Catering: lunchtime bar snacks; evening meals by arrangement.
Hotels: Trearddur Bay; Anchorage; Beach; Dormie residence on site.

K57 Holywell
☎(01352) 713937 (Sec/Fax), Pro 710040
Brynford, Nr Holywell, Clwyd CH8 8LQ
Turn off A55 onto A5026, turn to Brynford at traffic lights, 1 mile to crossroads turn right.
Undulating moorland/parkland links-type course.
18 holes, 6073 yards, S.S.S.70
Founded 1906

LLANDUDNO GOLF CLUB (MAESDU) LTD.

Maesdu Golf Club is a seaside course with panoramic views of Conwy Harbour, The Snowdonia Mountain Range & Anglesey.

Green Fees: £22 weekdays. £30 weekends & Bank Holidays.
Call The Secretary on: 01492 876450 (Fax: 01492-871570).

Visitors: welcome weekdays except on competition days, weekends accompanied by a member or by prior arrangement.
Green Fee: WD £15; WE £20.
Societies: by prior arrangement with Sec.
Catering: lunch and evening meals, bar facilities.
Snooker.
Hotels: Fielding Arms; Beaufort Hotel; Stamford Gate; Old Mill (Nannerch).

K58 Inco
☎(01792) 844216, Sec 843336
Clydach, Swansea, W Glamorgan
2 miles N of M4 junction 45.
Flat parkland course with river and trees.
12 holes, 6273 yards, S.S.S.70 (18 holes planned from May 1997)
Founded 1965
Visitors: welcome.
Green Fee: telephone in advance for details.
Societies: welcome by prior arrangement.
Catering: bar and snacks (evenings only).

K59 Kinmel Park Golf Complex
☎(01745) 833548
Bodelwyddan, Clwyd, N Wales LL18 5SR
Just off main A55 expressway at Bodelwyddan between Abergele and St Asaph.
9 hole Par 3 course, transformed at dusk into Britain's first night-time course – 'lightsticks' and luminous balls. Also school of golf.
Designed by Peter Stebbings
Founded 1988
Visitors: welcome; booking essential for night-time through Peter Stebbings Golf.
Green Fee: from £3 per round.
Societies: welcome by prior arrangement.
Catering: bar facilities and restaurant.
Driving range.
Hotels: Kinmel Manor (Abergele).

K60 Knighton
☎(01547) 528646
The Ffrydd, Knighton, Powys LD7 1EF
0.5 mile S of Knighton.
Undulating course.
9 holes, 5320 yards, S.S.S.66
Designed by Harry Vardon.
Founded 1913
Visitors: welcome.
Green Fee: WD £8; WE £10.
Societies: by prior arrangement with Sec.
Catering: snacks available weekends, other by prior arrangement.
Hotels: Red Lion; Knighton Hotel.

K61 Lakeside
☎(01639) 883486, 899959
Water St, Margam, Port Talbot, West Glam SA13 2PA
Just off M4 junction 38.
Parkland course.
9 holes, approx. 1900 yards (18 holes from Summer 1996).
Designed by D.T. Thomas.
Founded May 1992
Visitors: all welcome; good dress sense required, golf shoes or trainers only.
Green Fee: £5.
Catering: bar facilities and restaurant meals available; also facilities for the disabled.

K62 Llandrindod Wells
☎(01597) 82210, Sec/Manager: 823873
Llandrindod Wells, Powys LD1 5NY
Signposted from A483, 0.5 mile E of town, above lake.
Mountain course.
18 holes, 5759 yards, S.S.S.68
Designed by Harry Vardon.
Founded 1905
Visitors: welcome at all times.
Green Fee: WD £12; WE £20.
Societies: welcome by prior arrangement.
Catering: bar and restaurant facilities.
Hotels: Severn Arms; Metropole; Commodore; Glen Usk; Llanerch; Bell Inn; Pencerrig; Guidfa House.

K63 Llandudno (Maesdu)
☎(01492) 876450, Fax 871570
Hospital Rd, Llandudno, Gwynedd LL30 1HU
Alongside main Llandudno Hospital, approx 1 mile from town centre.
Seaside parkland course.
18 holes, 6545 yards, S.S.S.72
Designed by Tom Jones.
Founded 1915
Visitors: members of recognised clubs.
Green Fee: WD £22; WE £30.
Societies: accepted any day; max 32 players weekends.
Catering: facilities available with prior booking.
Snooker
Hotels: Royal; Bryn Cregin; Imperial.

K64 Llanfairfechan
☎(01248) 680144, Sec 680524
Llannerch Road, Llanfairfechan, Gwynned LL33 0EB
In Llanfairfechan between Conwy and Bangor.
Parkland course.
9 holes, 3119 yards, S.S.S.57
Founded 1972
Visitors: welcome any time except during competitions (mostly Sun).
Green Fee: WD £10; WE & BH £15.
Societies: write to Sec.
Catering: bar open all evenings, all day from 11am on Sat, 11.30am-2pm Sun.
Hotels: Split Willow.

K65 Llangefni (Public)
☎(01248) 722193
Llangefni, Anglesey, N Wales
On outskirts of Llangefni heading towards Amlwch.
Parkland course.
9 holes, 1467 yards, S.S.S.28
Designed by Hawtree & Sons.
Founded 1983
Visitors: welcome.
Green Fee: £2.20 (9 holes).

K66 Llangland Bay
☎(01792) 366023, Sec 361721
Llangland Bay, Swansea, W Glam SA3 4QR

M4 to Swansea, 6 miles W.
Seaside parkland course.
18 holes, 5827 yards, S.S.S.69
Founded 1904
Visitors: welcome if member of recognised club.
Green Fee: apply for details.
Societies: welcome if booked in advance, max 36.
Catering: bar meals; cooked meals to order before playing.
Hotels: Osborne.

K67 Llanishen

☎(01222) 755078
Cwm, Lisvane, Cardiff CF4 5UD
5 miles to N of Cardiff city centre, 1.5 miles N of Llanishen church via Heol Hir.
Parkland course.
18 holes, 5296 yards, S.S.S.66
Founded 1905
Visitors: weekdays unlimited; weekends and Bank Holidays accompanied by member only; h/cap cert required.
Green Fee: £22.
Societies: Thurs only by previous arrangement.
Catering: full facilities available except Mon.
Hotels: Phoenix (Cardiff), Manor Parc Hotel.

K68 Llannerch Park

☎(01745) 730805
North Wales Golf Range and Course, Llannerch Park, St Asaph, Clwyd LL17 0BD
On A525 Denbigh-St Asaph road, Tourist Board signposted.
Parkland course.
9 holes, 1587 yards, Par 30
Founded 1988
Visitors: welcome 10am until dusk; pay-as-you-play.
Green Fee: £2 (9 holes).
Societies: by prior arrangement, start before 10am.
Catering: light refreshments.
Driving range.

K69 Llantrisant & Pontyclun

☎(01443) 222148, Sec 224601, Pro 228169
Lanlay Rd, Talbot Green, Mid-Glam CF7 8HZ
M4 junction 34, then A4119 to Talbot Green.
Parkland course.
12 holes, 5712 yards, S.S.S.68
Founded 1927

Visitors: welcome weekdays.
Green Fee: £20 (£10 with member).
Societies: welcome weekdays by arrangement, max 25.
Catering: by prior arrangement with Steward.
Hotels: Heronstone; New Inn; City Inn.

K70 Llanwern

☎(01633) 412029 (Sec), Pro 413233
Tennyson Ave, Llanwern, Newport, Gwent NP6 2DY
1 mile from M4 junction 24.
Parkland course.
18 holes, 6115 yards, S.S.S.69
Founded 1928
Visitors: weekdays with proof of h/cap and membership of recognised club. Only with member at weekends.
Green Fee: WD £20 (£10 with member); WE £25.
Societies: Wed and Thurs by arrangement.
Catering: full bar and restaurant facilities.
Snooker table.
Hotels: Stakis Country Court.

K71 Llanyrafon Golf Course

☎(01633) 874636
Llanfrechfa Way, Cwmbran, Gwent
M4 junction 26, head N to Pontypool, turn left into Llanfrechfa Way.
Municipal parkland course.
9 holes Par 3
Founded 1981
Visitors: no restrictions.
Green Fee: WD £2.30 per round; WE £3.15 per round; reductions for jnrs and OAPs.
Hotels: Commodore; Park Way; Central.

K72 Machynlleth

☎(01654) 702000
Ffordd, Drenewydd, Machynlleth, Powys SY20 8UH
Approaching Machynlleth on A489 turn left before the speed restriction signs.
Undulating course.
9 holes, 5726 yards, S.S.S.67
Designed by James Braid.
Founded 1907
Visitors: welcome apart from competition days; welcome Sun.
Green Fee: WD £12; WE £15.
Societies: welcome by prior arrangement.
Catering: by arrangement.
Hotels: Wynnstay; White Lion.

K73 Maesteg

☎(01656) 734106 (Sec), Pro 735742, Clubhouse 732037
Mount Pleasant, Neath Rd, Maesteg, Mid-Glam CF34 9PR
Adjacent to main Maestag to Port Talbot road; 0.5 mile from Measteg town centre on B4282.
Reasonably flat hilltop course with forest views overlooking valleys down to sea at Swansea.
18 holes, 5900 yards, S.S.S.69
Designed by James Braid (1945).
Founded 1912
Visitors: no restrictions; over 12 visitors in group by arrangement.
Green Fee: WD £17 (£12 with member); WE £20 (£14 with member).
Societies: by arrangement.
Catering: bar meals available daily.
Hotels: Heronstone Hotel (Bridgend); Aberavon Hotel (Port Talbot); Greenacres (Maesteg B&B).

K74 Merthyr Tydfil

☎(01685) 723308
Cilsanws Mountain, Cefn Coed, Merthyr Tydfil, Mid-Glam CF48 2NU
Take turning to Pontsticill off A470 at Cefn Coed, then 1st left.
Mountain course in Brecon Beacons Nat. Park.
11 holes, 5951 yards, S.S.S.69
Founded 1908
Visitors: welcome at all times except Sun.
Green Fee: WD £12; WE £16.
Societies: apply in writing.
Catering: evenings only.

K75 Mid-Wales Golf Centre

☎(01686) 688303
Maesmawr, Caersws, Nr Newtown, Powys
38 miles W of Shrewsbury, 6 miles W of Newtown; 0.75 mile off main road clearly signposted.
Public farmland course.
9 holes Par 3, 1277 yards.
Designed by Jim Walters.
Founded July 1992
Visitors: no restrictions unless competition being played; advisable to ring beforehand; reasonable standard of dress and etiquette.
Green Fee: WD £6; WE £8.
Societies: welcome by prior arrangement.
Catering: licensed bar and light refreshments.
Driving range, children's play area.
Hotels: Maesmawr Hall.

K76 Milford Haven

☎(01646) 692368
Woodbine House, Hubberston,
Milford Haven
Follow road to Dale 0.75 mile to W of
town.
Meadowland course.
18 holes, 6071 yards, S.S.S.70
Designed by David Snell.
Founded 1913
Visitors: welcome at all times.
Green Fee: WD £13; WE & BH £18.
Societies: welcome at all times; fees
negotiable on numbers.
Catering: full restaurant facilities
available.
Hotels: Lord Nelson; Sir Benfro; Little
Haven.

K77 Mold

☎(01352) 740318, 741513
Cilcain Rd, Pantymwyn, Mold, Clwyd
3 miles from Mold; leave on Denbigh
road, turn left 100 yards before
Drovers and club is 2.5 miles on left.
Undulating parkland course.
18 holes, 5528 yards, S.S.S.67
Designed by Hawtree.
Founded 1909
Visitors: welcome.
Green Fee: on application.
Societies: welcome by prior
arrangement.
Catering: bar snacks, full facilities
available.
Hotels: Bryn Awel; Chequers.

K78 Monmouth

☎(01600) 712212, Sec 712941
Leasebrook Lane, Monmouth, Gwent
1 mile along A40 Monmouth to Ross
road.
Parkland course.
18 holes, 5698 yards, S.S.S.69
Founded 1896
Visitors: welcome weekdays and
weekends.
Green Fee: £15 per day.
Societies: by arrangement with Sec.
Catering: every day.
Hotels: The Riverside Motel; Pilgrim
(Much Birch).

K79 Monmouthshire

☎(01873) 852606 (Sec), Pro 852532
Llanfoist, Abergavenny, Gwent NP7
9HE
M4 to Newport then A4042, take road
to Llanfoist at Llanellen.
Parkland course.
18 holes, 6054 yards, S.S.S.70.
Designed by James Braid.
Founded 1892

Visitors: must have proof of
membership of recognised club and
h/cap cert.
Green Fee: WD £21; WE & BH £26.
Societies: Mon and Fri only, apply
before Dec preceding year.
Catering: full facilitiesavailable daily
except Tues.
Hotels: Angel; Llanwenarth Arms.

K80 Morlais Castle

☎(01685) 722822
Pant, Dowlais, Merthyr Tydfil, Mid-
Glam CF48 2UY
Follow signs for Brecon Mountain
Railway.
Moorland course.
18 holes, 6320 yards, S.S.S.71
Founded 1900
Visitors: welcome except Sat pm
and Sun am.
Green Fee: WD £14 per day (£8 with
member); WE £16 (£10 with
member).
Societies: apply to Sec.
Catering: bar/snacks; lunches and
evening meals served to order.
Hotels: Tregenna; Baverstocks.

K81 Morriston

☎(01792) 771079
160 Clasemont Rd, Morriston,
Swansea, W Glam SA6 6AJ
3 miles N of Swansea city centre on
A4067, then 0.5 mile W along A48;
from M4 junction 46, 0.75 mile E.
Parkland course.
18 holes, 5734 yards, S.S.S.70
Founded 1919
Visitors: welcome at all times.
Green Fee: WD £25; WE & BH £30;
one-third reduction with member.
Societies: on application.
Catering: lunch served except Mon.
Hotels: Dragon; Dolphin; Forest
Motel; Hilton; Holiday Inn.

K82 Mountain Ash

☎(01443) 479459
Cefnpennar, Mountain Ash, Mid-Glam
CF45 4DT
A470 Cardiff to Abercynon, then
A4059 to Mountain Ash.
Mountain course.
18 holes, 5553 yards, S.S.S.67
Founded 1908
Visitors: welcome; with member only
weekends.
Green Fee: WD £15 (£10 with
member).
Societies: welcome.
Catering: full facilities except Mon.
Hotels: Baverstock.

K83 Mountain Lakes

☎(01222) 861128, Fax 869030
Blaengwynlais, Nr Caerphilly, Mid-
Glam CF8 1NG
4 miles from M4 junction 32 on
Tongwynlais-Caerphilly road, by
Castell Heights golf course.
Moorland/parkland course with water
hazards.
18 holes, 6800 yards, S.S.S.74
Designed by Bob Sandow.
Founded 1988
Visitors: must ring in advance to
check availability; h/cap certs
required.
Green Fee: £15 per round, £20 per
day.
Societies: brochure available on
request.
Catering: day restaurant and bar;
banqueting, conference and function
rooms.
Driving range
Hotels: list available on request;
telephone for details.

K84 Neath

☎(01639) 633693 (Clubhouse/Pro
shop), Sec 632759
Cadoxton, Neath, W Glam SA10 8AH
2 miles from Neath town centre,
opposite Cadoxton Church.
Mountain course.
18 holes, 6593 yards, S.S.S.72
Designed by James Braid.
Founded 1934
Visitors: welcome on weekdays.
Must be accompanied by a
member at weekends and Bank
Holidays.
Green Fee: £20 (£12 with member).
Societies: welcome by arrangement;
reduced terms for 20+, Wed-Fri h/cap
certs required.
Catering: full except Mon.
Snooker.

K85 Nefyn & District

☎(01758) 720966 (Sec), Pro
720102, Steward: 720218, Fax
720476
Morfa Nefyn, Pwllheli, Gwynedd LL53
6DA
1 mile W of Nefyn, 20 miles W of
Caernarfon on B4417.
Seaside clifftop course.
18 holes, 6537 yards, S.S.S.71; 9
holes, 2979 yards, S.S.S. 34
Founded 1907
Visitors: h/cap certs required April-
Oct incl.
Green Fee: WD £20 per round, £25
per day; WE £25 per round, £35 per
day.

Societies: by prior arrangement with Sec, limited weekends.
Catering: full facilities.
Snooker.
Hotels: Caeau Capel; Linksway; Woodlands Hall; Nanhoran Arms; Llys Olwen GH.

K86 Newport
☎(01633) 892643, 896794
Great Oak, Rogerstone, Newport, Gwent NP1 9FX
From M4 junction 27 take B4591 for 1 mile, across roundabout then right at Bosch services.
Parkland course.
18 holes, 6431 yards, S.S.S.71
Founded 1903
Visitors: welcome weekdays, members of recognised club only.
Green Fee: WD £30; WE & BH £40.
Societies: Wed, Thurs, Fri.
Catering: bar (men's), mixed lounge, dining room.
Hotels: Country Court; Lodge; Harris; Celtic Manor.

K87 Newport (Pembs)
☎(01239) 820244
Newport, Dyfed SA42 0NR
Follow signs to Newport Sands from Newport.
Seaside course.
9 holes, 5815 yards, S.S.S.68
Designed by James Braid
Founded 1925
Visitors: welcome.
Green Fee: £15
Societies: by arrangement.
Catering: full bar and restaurant facilities.
Hotels: self-catering holiday flats adjacent clubhouse; Golden Lion.

K88 North Wales
☎(01492) 875325 (Sec), Pro 876878, Steward: 875342, Members: 875881
72 Bryniau Rd, West Shore, Llandudno, Gwynedd LL30 2DZ
On A496, 1 mile from Llandudno town centre overlooking Conway Bay
Seaside links course.
18 holes, 6247 yards, S.S.S.71
Founded 1894
Visitors: by prior reservation.
Green Fee: WD £22 per day; WE & BH £28.
Societies: welcome by prior reservation.
Catering: full facilities available.
Snooker.
Hotels: Bryn Cregin; Royal.

K89 Northop Country Park
☎(01352) 840440, Fax 840445
Northop, Nr Chester, Clwyd CH7 6WA
Take A55 North Wales Coast road and exit at Northop/Connahs Quay. Northop Country Park is left on exit road
Parkland course.
18 holes, 6735 yards, S.S.S.73
Designed by John Jacobs.
Founded June 1994
Visitors: welcome, prior booking required.
Green Fee: WD £25; WE £35.
Societies: welcome weekdays.
Catering: bar and restaurant.
Tennis, gym, sauna, snooker.
Hotels: St David's Park. (Ewloe)

K90 Oakdale
☎(01495) 220044, Pro 220440
Llwynon Lane, Oakdale, Gwent NP2 0NF
M4 junction 28, A467 to Crumlin, then B4251 to Oakdale.
Public parkland course.
9 holes, 1344 yards, S.S.S.28
Designed by Ian Goodenough.
Founded 1990
Visitors: welcome
Green Fee: £3.75 (9 holes) any day, £2.75 jnrs.
Societies: welcome, bookings only.
Catering: snacks in clubhouse (no license).
Driving range.
Hotels: The Old Forge.

K91 Old Colwyn
☎(01492) 515581
Woodland Ave, Old Colwyn, Clwyd LL29 9NL
200 yards off A55 in Old Colwyn, turn into Boddelwyddan Ave between chapel and M & K Garage.
Undulating meadowland course.
9 holes, 5243 yards, S.S.S.66
Founded 1907
Visitors: welcome except Sat pm and Tues and Wed evenings.
Green Fee: WD £10; WE £15.
Societies: by arrangement except Sat.
Catering: by arrangement.

K92 Old Padeswood
☎(01244) 547401
Station Rd, Padeswood, Mold, Clwyd CH7 4JL
2.5 miles S of Mold, 8 miles W of Chester on A5118.
Meadowland course.
18 holes, 6685 yards, S.S.S.72; 9 holes, Par 3
Designed by Arthur Joseph.
Founded 1933
Visitors: welcome except Competition Days.
Green Fee: WD £18; WE & BH £20; Par 3, £2 (£1 jnr).
Societies: weekdays only by appointment; phone (01244) 550414.
Catering: bar and restaurant facilities at all times.
Hotels: Bryn Awel; St David's Park.

K93 Old Rectory Hotel
☎(01873) 810373
Llangattock, Crickhowell, Powys NP8 1PH
Off A40 to Crickhowell between Abergavenny and Brecon.
Parkland course.
9 holes, 2360 yards, S.S.S.54
Founded 1979
Visitors: welcome.
Green Fee: £10 per day.
Societies: welcome.
Catering: bar, restaurant, function suites.
Outdoor swimming pool.
Hotels: Old Rectory.

K94 Padeswood & Buckley
☎(01244) 550537, Pro and Members: 543636
The Caia, Station Lane, Padeswood, Mold, Clwyd CH7 4JD
Off A5118, 3 miles E of Mold, 2 miles S of Buckley, 2nd club on right.
Parkland/meadowland course.
18 holes, 5982 yards, S.S.S.70
Founded 1933
Visitors: welcome weekdays 9.30am-4.30pm; permission of Sec or Captain required on Sun.
Green Fee: WD £20 per round, £25 per day.
Societies: weekdays.
Catering: snacks, lunches and evening meals.
Hotels: The Druid; Chequers; Beaufort Palace, St David's Park.

K95 Palleg
☎(01639) 842193
Palleg Rd, Lower Cwmtwrch, Swansea, W Glam SA9 1QT
15 miles N of Swansea on Brecon road A4067, left at Aubrey Arms roundabout, 1 mile.
Meadowland/moorland course.
9 holes, 3209 yards, S.S.S.72

Designed by C.K. Cotton.
Founded 1930
Visitors: welcome weekdays.
Green Fee: apply for details.
Societies: welcome by arrangement;
not Bank Holidays.
Catering: by arrangement except
Mon.

K96 **Parc Golf**
☎(01633) 680933
Church Lane, Coedkernew, Newport,
Gwent NP1 9TU
M4 junction 28, onto A48 towards
Cardiff for 1.5 miles, then signposted.
Parkland course.
18 holes, 5600 yards, S.S.S.67
Designed by B. Thomas & T. Hicks.
Founded 1989
Visitors: welcome weekdays and by
prior arrangement weekends.
Green Fee: WD £10 per round; WE
£12 per round.
Societies: welcome by prior
arrangement.
Catering: full facilities.
Driving range
Hotels: Coach & Horses (Castleton).

K97 **Penmaenmawr**
☎(01492) 623330
Conway Rd, Penmaenmawr,
Gwynedd LL34 6RD
Main A55 expressway from Colwyn
Bay taking Bangor signs; at 1st
roundabout after tunnels take left exit
and sharp left again; 1st right
thereafter to top of hill (crossing
intersection); turn left, clubhouse
within 20 yards of corner.
Undulating parkland course.
9 holes (18 tees), 5031 yards,
S.S.S.65
Founded 1910
Visitors: welcome.
Green Fee: WD & Sat £12; Sun £18.
Societies: welcome; fees by
arrangement.
Catering: every day except Tues.
Hotels: Caerlyr; Sychnant Pass
(Conway); Split Willow
(Llanfairfechan).

K98 **Pennard**
☎(01792) 233131, Pro 233451
2 Southgate Rd, Southgate,
Swansea, W Glam SA3 2BT
8 miles W of Swansea, on A4067 and
B4436 to Pennard Church, then
unclassified to club.
Undulating seaside course.
18 holes, 6265 yards, S.S.S.71
Founded 1896

Visitors: welcome at all times.
Green Fee: WD £24 (£10 jnrs); WE
£30 (£15 jnrs).
Societies: Weekdays only, h/cap cert
required, 12 or more, £16 each.
Catering: bar snacks; lunches and
evening meals by prior arrangement.
Snooker, squash.
Hotels: Osborne; Winston;
Nicholaston; Cefn Goleua Park; Fairy
Hill.

K99 **Penrhos Golf &
Country Club**
☎(01974) 202999
Llanrhystud, Nr Aberystwyth, Dyfed,
SY23 5AY
Between Aberystwyth and Aberaeron,
just off A487 on B4337.
Parkland course.
18 holes, 6641 yards, S.S.S.72, 9
hole practice course, 1827 yards.
Designed by Jim Walters
Founded July 1991
Visitors: welcome; booking advised.
Green Fee: WD £15; WE £18.
Societies: welcome by arrangement,
Sat included.
Catering: full facilities.
Leisure complex, tennis, driving
range.
Hotels: Conrah County; Marine
(Aberystwyth); self catering available-
please ring for details.

K100 **Peterstone G & CC**
☎(01633) 680009, Fax 680563
Peterstone Wentlooge, Cardiff CF3
8TM
Off A48, turning to Marshfield.
Seaside parkland course.
18 holes, 6497 yards, S.S.S.71
Designed by Bob Sandow.
Founded May 1990
Visitors: welcome.
Green Fee: apply for details.
Societies: welcome.
Catering: bar, a la carte restaurant,
conference room.
Hotels: accommodation (2 rooms) in
Country Club.

K101 **Plassey**
☎(01978) 780020
The Plassey Golf Course, Eyton,
Wrexham, Clwyd LL13 0SP
From Wrexham take Bangor-on-Dee
exit off A483 Chester-Ruabon
bypass, follow tourist board anvil
signs to `The Plassey'.
Public parkland course.
10 holes, extending to 18, 1994/5
Founded April 1992

Visitors: welcome, no restrictions.
Green Fee: WD £4 (9 holes), £6 (18
holes); WE £5 (9 holes), £8 (18
holes).
Societies: welcome by arrangement,
8-20 players; from £10 for 18 holes
and 3-course lunch.
Catering: Ham Bank Inn offering
special golfers' lunches, dinner,
parties; Plassey real ale brewed on
site.
Leisure facilities at caravan park on
complex.

K102 **Pontardawe**
☎(01792) 863118, Sec 830041, Pro
830977
Cefn Llan, Pontardawe, Swansea, W
Glam SA8 4SH
4 miles N of M4 on A4067.
Meadowland course.
18 holes, 6038 yards, S.S.S.70
Founded 1924
Visitors: welcome weekdays, h/cap
cert required
Green Fee: WD £19
Societies: on application.
Catering: full facilities available
except Mon (bookable).
Snooker.
Hotels: Pen-yr-Allt; Pink Geranium.

K103 **Pontnewydd**
☎(01633) 482170
West Pontnewydd, Cwmbran, Gwent
NP4 4AR
Follow signs for West Pontnewydd or
Upper Cwmbran, W slopes of
Cwmbran.
Meadowland course.
10 holes, 5353 yards, S.S.S.67
Founded 1875
Visitors: welcome weekdays,
weekends only with member.
Green Fee: apply for details.
Catering: available.
Hotels: Parkway; Commodore.

K104 **Pontypool**
☎(01495) 763655
Lasgarn Lane, Trevethin, Pontypool,
Gwent NP4 8TR
1 mile N of Pontypool.
Heathland/parkland course.
18 holes, 6046 yards, S.S.S.69
Founded 1903
Visitors: welcome; h/cap certs
required.
Green Fee: WD £18; WE £24.
Societies: welcome; h/cap certs
required.
Catering: available daily.
Hotels: Commodore; Parkway.

Estab. 1902

18 HOLE PAR 70 SSS 71 6330 YARDS

Individual Golfing visitors and Societies welcomed by arrangement.

Green Fees £18.00 per weekday, £25.00 weekends and Bank Holidays.

1996 Open Week June 29–July 6 write for details.

Wellstocked professional's shop, expert tuition, snooker room 2 bars & restaurant

· PORTHMADOG · GOLF CLUB ·

Club House, Morfa Bychan, Porthmadog
Tel: 01766 514124 Fax: 01766 514638
Professional 513828 Steward 512037

K105 Pontypridd
☎(01443) 402359, Sec 409904, Pro 491210
Ty-Gwyn, The Common, Pontypridd, Mid-Glam CF37 4DJ
9 miles from Cardiff, take A470 N to Pontypridd and Merthyr.
Wooded undulating mountain course.
18 holes, 5721 yards, S.S.S.68
Designed by Bradbeer.
Founded 1905
Visitors: welcome weekdays if bona fide member of another club; only if accompanied by member weekends and Bank Holidays, h/cap certs required.
Green Fee: WD £20 (£14 with member); WE & BH £20.
Societies: weekdays only, prior arrangement with Sec.
Catering: bar, lounge, dining room, meals and bar snacks available; no meals Thurs.
Snooker.

K106 Porthmadog
☎(01766) 512037, 514638, Sec 514124, Pro 513828
Morfa Bychan, Porthmadog, Gwynedd LL49 9UU
2 miles W of Porthmadog, take road to Morfa Bychan and Black Rock Sands; turn at Woolworths in High St.
Seaside heathland course.
18 holes, 6330 yards, S.S.S.71
Founded 1900
Visitors: welcome.
Green Fee: WD £18; WE & BH £25
Societies: by arrangement with Sec.
Catering: meals and snacks served.
Extended clubhouse, snooker room.
Hotels: Royal Sportsman; Tyddyn Lywyn; Plas Gwyn.

K107 Prestatyn
☎(01745) 854320
Marine Rd East, Prestatyn, Clwyd LL19 7HS

Follow A548 coast road to Prestatyn, cross railway bridge and turn right at Pontins, Prestatyn Sands.
Links championship course.
18 holes, 6764 yards, S.S.S.73
Designed by S. Collins.
Founded 1905
Visitors: welcome, except Sat and Tues mornings.
Green Fee: WD £20; WE & BH £25.
Societies: by arrangement with Sec only; no Sats or Tues.
Catering: full facilities.
Hotels: Bryn Gwalia; Nant Hall; Kinmel Manor (Abergele); Royal (Llandudno).

K108 Priskilly Forest Golf Club
☎(01348) 840276
Castle Morris, Haverfordwest, Pembrokeshire SA62 5EH
A40 to Fishguard, left at Letterston; golf course 1.5 miles.
Parkland course.
9 holes, 5712 yards, S.S.S. 68
Founded 1992
Designed by J. Walters
Visitors: welcome.
Green Fees: £5 (9 holes), £8 (18 holes), £10 per day.
Societies: welcome; small societies preferred.
Catering: on request.
Hotels: B&B available at the course.

K109 Pwllheli
☎(01758) 612520, 701633, Sec 701644
Golf Rd, Pwllheli, Gwynedd LL53 5PS
Turn into Cardiff Rd in town centre, bear right at 1st fork, course is signposted.
Parkland/links course.
18 holes, 6091 yards, S.S.S.69
Designed by Tom Morris extended by James Braid
Founded 1900

Visitors: welcome.
Green Fee: WD £20 per day; WE & BH £25
Societies: any day by prior arrangement with Sec.
Catering: full facilities.
Snooker table.
Hotels: Caeau Capel (Nefyn); Bryn Eisteddfod (Clynnnogfawr); Nanhoron Hotel (Morfa).

K110 Pyle & Kenfig
☎(01656) 783093 (Sec), Pro 772446
Waun-y-Mer, Kenfig, Mid-Glam CF33 4PU
Leave M4 at junction 37, follow Porthcawl signs; 1st right after 3rd roundabout.
Seaside links and downland course.
18 holes, 6650 yards, S.S.S.73
Designed by H. Colt.
Founded 1922
Visitors: welcome weekdays, advisable to phone in advance; with member only weekends and Bank Holidays.
Green Fee: £25 per round, £35 per day (£20 with member).
Societies: by prior arrangement with Sec.
Catering: full facilities available.
Hotels: Seabank; Rose and Crown; Fairways; Atlantic.

K111 RAF St Athan
☎(01446) 751043, Manager: 797186
St Athan, Barry, S Glam
1st right after St Athan village on the Cowbridge road.
Public parkland course.
9 holes, 6452 yards, S.S.S.71
Founded 1982
Visitors: welcome any time except Sun am.
Green Fee: WD £10; WE £15.
Societies: welcome by arrangement; apply to Sec.
Catering: available.

The St. David's Hotel
Harlech, Gwynedd LL46 2PT
TEL: (01766) 780 366   FAX: (01766) 780 820

W.T.B. 4 Crowns – Logis of Great Britain 2 Fireplaces
Ideally situated overlooking the Royal St. David's Golf Course, and the Llyn Peninsula. A perfect base for your Golfing Holiday. Welcoming hotel, all en-suite rooms with WC bath/shower, TV's, tea/coffee facilities, radio and direct dial telephone. Good Food.

★ SPECIAL BREAKS ★ GOLF PACKAGES ★

K112 Radyr
☎(01222) 842408 (Manager),
Members: 842442
Drysgol Rd, Radyr, Cardiff CF4 8BS
M4 junction 32, off A470 at Taffs
Well.
Parkland course.
18 holes, 6015 yards, S.S.S.70
Founded 1902
Visitors: weekdays with h/cap cert; weekends with member only.
Green Fee: £28 per day.
Societies: Wed, Thur and Fri.
Catering: full facilities available 7 days a week. In winter by prior arrangement.
Snooker.

K113 Raglan Parc Golf Club
☎(01291) 690077
Parc Lodge, Raglan, Gwent NP5 2ER
0.5 mile from village of Raglan; junction of A40 and A449.
Undulating Parkland course.
18 holes, 6400 yards, S.S.S. 72
Founded 1994
Visitors: welcome anytime; booking advisable.
Green Fees: £15 per day.
Societies: welcome (maximum 30) by prior arrangement; packages available.
Catering: Spike bar, snacks and light meals available.

K114 Rhondda
☎(01443) 441384 (Sec)
Golf House, Penrhys, Rhondda CF43 3PW
On Cardiff to Rhondda road 3 miles from Porth.
Mountaintop course.
18 holes, 6205 yards, S.S.S.70
Founded 1904/1910
Visitors: welcome weekdays, weekends with member.
Green Fee: WD £20; WE £25.

Societies: weekdays by prior arrangement.
Catering: meals, bar snacks available except Mon.
Snooker.
Hotels: Heritage.

K115 Rhos-on-Sea
☎(01492) 549641, 549100
Penrhyn Bay, Llandudno, Gwynedd LL30 3PU
A55 to Old Colwyn, follow coast road to Penrhyn Bay, course by sea.
Parkland course without trees.
18 holes, 6064 yards, S.S.S.69
Founded 1899
Visitors: welcome anytime, pre-booking required for large parties and weekends.
Green Fee: WD £17; WE £22.
Societies: welcome any day by booking.
Catering: lounge bar daily, breakfasts, bar snacks; restaurant. Snooker tables.
Hotels: Dormy House Hotel on site.

K116 Rhosgoch
☎(01497) 851251
Rhosgoch, Builth Wells, Powys LD2 3JY
5 miles N of Hay-on-Wye.
Parkland course.
9 holes, 4842 yards, S.S.S.64
Designed by Herbie Poore.
Founded 1984
Visitors: welcome.
Green Fee: WD £7 per day; WE £10 per day.
Societies: welcome.
Catering: bar, snacks; dinner by arrangement.

K117 Rhuddlan
☎(01745) 590217, Pro 590898
Meliden Rd, Rhuddlan, Clwyd LL18 6LB

Off A55 3 miles N of St Asaph.
Parkland course.
18 holes, 6482 yards, S.S.S.71
Designed by Hawtree & Co.
Founded 1930
Visitors: welcome; guests of members only on Sun.
Green Fee: WD £24; Sun & BH £30.
Societies: welcome Mon-Fri by arrangement.
Catering: lunch and dinner daily.
Snooker.
Hotels: Kinmel Manor (Abergele); Royal Hotel (Llandudno); The Esplanade (Llandudno).

K118 Rhyl
☎(01745) 353171, Sec 334136 (home)
Coast Rd, Rhyl, Clwyd LL18 3RE
1 mile from station on A548 road to Prestatyn.
Seaside links course.
9 holes, 6153 yards. S.S.S.70
Designed by Redesigned by James Braid
Founded 1890
Visitors: welcome except competition days.
Green Fee: WD £12; WE & BH £15.
Societies: by prior arrangement with Sec.
Catering: bar snacks and meals all day.
Snooker.
Hotels: Grange; Marina.

K119 The Rolls of Monmouth
☎(01600) 715353, Fax 713115
The Hendre, Monmouth, Gwent NP5 4HG
3.25 miles W of Monmouth on B4233 (Abergavenny road).
Undulating parkland course.
18 holes, 6733 yards, S.S.S.73
Designed by Urbis Planning.
Founded 1982

Visitors: no restrictions
Green Fee: WD £30; WE £35. Mon £25 (including coffee and light lunch).
Societies: welcome weekdays and weekends.
Catering: full facilities 7 days.
Hotels: Riverside Hotel, Talocher (farmhouse hotel).

K120 **Royal Porthcawl**
☎(01656) 782251, Pro 773702, Fax 771687
Rest Bay, Porthcawl, Mid-Glam CF36 3UW
Leave M4 at junction 37 to Porthcawl seafront, turn right, follow to Locks Common and bear left.
Links course.
Championship course 18 holes, 6685 yards, S.S.S.74
Designed by Charles Gibson.
Founded 1891
Visitors: welcome, h/cap cert required (max h/cap for man 20, max h/cap for lady 30).
Green Fee: WD £45 per day; WE & BH £50 per day.
Societies: by arrangement (no weekends).
Catering: lunches, teas and dinner by arrangement.
Hotels: Atlantic; Seabank; Fairways.

K121 **Royal St David's**
☎(01766) 780857 (Pro), Sec/Manager and tee bookings: 780361
Harlech, Gwynedd LL46 2UB
Between Barmouth and Porthmadog on A496.
Links championship seaside course.
18 holes, 6427 yards, S.S.S.72
Founded 1894
Visitors: welcome weekdays and weekends, prior arrangement advisable; must have regular h/cap.
Green Fee: WD £25; WE & BH £30.
Societies: catered for.
Catering: full catering facilities available.
Hotels: St David's; Maes y Newydd; Talsarnau; Noddfa; Rum Hole; Castle; Castle Cottage; Byrdir GH.

K122 **Ruthin Pwllglas**
☎(01824) 703427
Ruthin Pwllglas, Ruthin, Clwyd
2.5 miles S of Ruthin in A494, right fork before Pwllglas village.
Parkland/moorland course.
10 holes, 5418 yards, S.S.S.66
Designed by David Lloyd Rees.
Founded 1906

Visitors: welcome.
Green Fee: WE £12.50; WE £18.
Societies: welcome by prior arrangement.
Catering: parties by prior arrangement.
Hotels: Ruthin Castle.

K123 **St Andrews Major**
☎(01446) 722227
Coldbrook Rd East, Nr Cadoxton, Barry, S Glam CF6 3BB
From M4 exit 33 follow signs to Barry and Rhoose Airport, take left turn to Sully just after Wenvoe Golf Club, turn left on Coldbrook Road East.
Pay-as-you-Play, parkland course.
9 holes, 5862 yards, S.S.S.68
Designed by MRM Leisure.
Founded 1993
Visitors: no restrictions, but usually very busy at weekends and public holidays.
Green Fee: Members £6 (9 holes), £10 (18 holes); Non-members £8 (9 holes), £13 (18 holes).
Societies: no restrictions.
Catering: bar and restaurant facilities available.
Hotels: Copthorne.

K124 **St Davids City**
☎(01437) 721751, Sec/bookings: 720312 (home)
Whitesands, St Davids, Pembrokeshire
2 miles W of St Davids, follow signs for Whitesands Bay.
Links course with views of Whitesands Bay and St Davids Head, most westerly course in Wales.
9 holes (18 tees), 6121 yards, S.S.S.70
Founded 1902
Visitors: welcome, no restrictions but Ladies day Fri pm and club competitions Sat.
Green Fee: £13 per day.
Societies: welcome by prior arrangement with Sec.
Catering: at Whitesands Bay Hotel, adjacent to Course.
Hotels: Whitesands Bay; Old Cross; St Nons; Warpool Court; numerous guest houses and self-catering cottages.

K125 **St Deiniol**
☎(01248) 353098
Bangor, Gwynedd LL57 1PX
Off A5/A55 junction on to A5122 for 1 mile into Bangor; on E outskirts of town, golf club signposted.

Undulating parkland course.
18 holes, 5068 yards, S.S.S.67
Designed by James Braid.
Founded 1905
Visitors: welcome at any time; parties by arrangement.
Green Fee: WD £12 per day; WE & BH £16 per day.
Societies: welcome by prior arrangement.
Catering: full catering service. Snooker; Shop.
Hotels: British Hotel; Eryl Mor.

K126 **St Giles**
☎(01686) 625844, Sec 622223
Pool Rd, Newtown, Powys SY16 3AJ
0.5 mile E of Newtown on main Welshpool to Newtown road, A483.
Parkland course.
9 holes, 5936 yards, S.S.S.69
Founded 1910
Visitors: welcome weekdays, some weekends.
Green Fee: on application.
Societies: must write to Sec for booking.
Catering: meals except Mon.

K127 **St Idloes**
☎(01686 41) 2559
Penrallt, Llanidloes, Powys SY18 6LG
Off A470 at Llanidloes, 1 mile B4569.
Slightly undulating course on hill plateau with superb views.
9 holes, 5510 yards, S.S.S.66
Designed by members
Founded 1920
Visitors: welcome with club h/cap cert.
Green Fee: WD £10.50; WE £12.50.
Societies: very welcome by appointment with Sec.
Catering: available on request; banqueting, functions.
Hotels: Unicorn; Lion; Mount Inn.

K128 **St Mellons**
☎(01633) 680408 (Sec), Pro 680101, Club 680401
St Mellons, Cardiff, S Glam CF3 8XS
On A48 between Newport and Cardiff on left, follow yellow sign for St Mellons Country Club.
Parkland course.
18 holes, 6275 yards, S.S.S.70
Founded 1964
Visitors: welcome.
Green Fee: £25.
Societies: weekdays only by arrangement.
Catering: available.
Hotels: St Mellons Country Club.

St Pierre

In the summer of 1987, St Pierre celebrated its 25th anniversary. In a game which goes back centuries, that might not seem much of a landmark but St Pierre earned itself pride of place by being the first post-war championship course to be built in Britain – the herald of a new era.

When it comes to personal sentiment, it was the first new course I saw under construction. In the winter of 1961-2, Ken Cotton was invited to design two courses in the border country of England and Wales, one in the old deer park alongside the main road from Chepstow to Newport and the other in unpromising woodland at Ross-on-Wye. He thought a visit to see how it was done would be a good experience for a young writer – and how right he was.

The two courses could not possibly have been more of a contrast. St Pierre was largely ready-made in terms of fairways whereas Ross-on-Wye, a miracle of enterprise by a devoted band, had to be stripped root by root before the holes took shape.

That Cotton succeeded in both instances showed that he was a master of his craft. You can only judge the results if you knew the original terrain, the difficulties encountered and the budgets available. Both St Pierre and Ross-on-Wye were built on the thinnest of shoe-strings. Bill Graham, who had dreamed of a course in the lovely park at St Pierre, drove past one day, and discovering that it was on the market, proved himself a man of action by buying it.

The land, the ancient manor house where the Crown Jewels were stored during the Battle of Agincourt, and the cost of construction of the course came to something under £30,000. However absurdly modest that seems nowadays, one or two sacrifices had to be made but Graham's reasons for purchasing had to be commercially based and there he showed how valid his instincts were.

Floodlit golf proved to be one of his few ideas to misfire. When St Pierre was built the motorway systems were already well launched, and the opening of the Severn Bridge only a few years away. St Pierre was, and is, wonderfully accessible from London, Birmingham and Bristol, as well a South Wales.

It wasn't given long to settle down before it was much in demand. Dunlop made it a frequent home for their much lamented Masters and in 1980 the Ladies Golf Union paid it the ultimate compliment by holding the Curtis Cup there. Regular calls have been made upon it by organisers of small tournaments and company days, all of whom flock to take advantage of its residential amenities and a host of other sporting facilities. The latest compliment was paid to it by the announcement of the staging of the 1996 Solheim Cup, the ladies' equivalent of the Ryder Cup which the Europeans won at Dalmahoy in 1992.

The addition of the second course brought alteration to Cotton's original design, and more land was purchased on higher ground. However, nothing destroyed Cotton's first impression that, for Club golfers at large, it is a delightful place to play.

Stately ancient trees feature strongly. After a mild introduction to them at the 1st, the 2nd is dominated by them, although there follows a break on the loftier reaches of the 3rd to the 6th. At the 6th, the eye is caught by the distant sights but, with the 7th, the trees return and, from then on, there is no let-up.

Several recent changes and a few new back tees have made the professionals flex their muscles a little more. However, one hole where no change is contemplated, and certainly none required, is the 18th across the lake. One of golf's oldest cliches is that nothing is certain until the last putt is holed; nowhere is it more apt than at St Pierre.

K129 St Melyd

☎ (01745) 854405, Sec 853574 (home), Shop 888858
The Paddock, Prestatyn Clwyd LL19 9NB
Between Prestatyn and Meliden village on main road A547.
Undulating parkland course.
9 holes, 6017 yards, S.S.S.68
Founded 1922
Visitors: welcome any time except Sat.
Green Fee: WD £15; WE & BH £19.
Societies: welcome any time except Sat.
Catering: facilities available at any time
Hotels: Pontins Holiday Village; Nant Hall; Bryn Gwalia; Graig Park Hotel.

K130 St Pierre Hotel Golf & Country Club

☎ (01291) 625261, Fax 629975
St Pierre Park, Chepstow, Gwent NP6 6YA
On A48 Chepstow-Newport road, 2 miles from Chepstow.
Old course parkland, New course (Mathern) parkland.
Old, 18 holes, 6700 yards, S.S.S.73; New, 18 holes, 5762 yards, S.S.S.68
Old course designed by C.K. Cotton, New course by Bill Cox.
Founded 1962
Visitors: h/cap cert required; booking advised.
Green Fee: on application
Societies: Mon to Fri; weekends residential only.
Catering: full facilities available. Conferences (catering for up to 220 delegates), extensive leisure facilities also available.
Hotels: St Pierre.

K131 Shirenewton Golf Club

☎ (01291) 641642
Shirenewton, Nr Chepstow, Gwent NP6 6RL
Off the M4 take A48 towards Newport; on reaching Chirk turn right towards Shirenewton (3 miles).
Parkland course.
18 holes, 6820 yards, S.S.S. 72
Designed by M. Weeks/Tony Davies
Founded March 1995
Visitors: welcome
Green Fees: WD £16; WE £18.
Societies: welcome.
Catering: bar and restaurant facilites available.
Hotels: Old Course (Chepstow).

K132 South Pembrokeshire

☎ (01646) 621453 (Sec)
Defensible Barracks, Pembroke Dock, Dyfed
1.5 miles S of Hobbs Point at W end of A477, 0.5 mile from Pembroke Dock.
Seaside parkland course.
9 holes, 5804 yards, S.S.S.69 (a further 9 holes due to open Spring 96 with new clubhouse)
Founded 1970
Visitors: welcome.
Green Fee: £10 per day.
Societies: by prior arrangement; apply to Sec.
Catering: bar except Mon, meals by arrangement.

K133 Southerndown

☎ (01656) 880476, 880326 Pro, Fax 880317
Ewenny, Bridgend, Mid-Glam CF32 0QP
4 miles from Bridgend on the coast road from Bridgend to Ogmore-by-Sea; turn off at Pelican Inn opposite Ogmore Castle.
Links/downland course.
18 holes, 6417 yards, S.S.S.72
Designed by W. Herbert Fowler, Willie Park, H.S. Colt.
Founded Feb 1906
Visitors: weekdays; weekends only if accompanied by a member; h/cap certs required.
Green Fee: WD £30; WE £36.
Societies: welcome weekdays only by prior arrangement; contact Sec.
Catering: facilities daily. Snooker.
Hotels: Sea Lawns; Sea Bank; Heronston; The Great House.

K134 Summerhill Golf Club

☎ (01497) 820451/Fax
Hereford Road, Clifford, Hay-on-Wye HR3 5EW
Out of Hay town centre on B4352 towards toll bridge; signposted on RH side.
Parkland course.
9 holes, 5825 yards, S.S.S. 68
Founded 1994
Visitors: welcome anytime.
Green Fees: WD £8; WE £10.
Societies: welcome by prior arrangement.
Catering: full facilities available; function room.
Hotels: The Kilvert; The Swan.

K135 Swansea Bay

☎ (01792) 814153, 812198, Pro 816159
Jersey Marine, Neath, W Glam SA10 6JP
Off B4290, Jersey Marine turning off A483 dual carriageway between Neath and Swansea.
Links course.
18 holes, 6605 yards, S.S.S.72
Founded 1892
Visitors: welcome.
Green Fee: WD £16; WE & BH £22.
Societies: catered for.
Catering: meals served.

K136 Tenby

☎ (01834) 842978 (Sec), Pro 844447
The Burrows, Tenby, Dyfed SA70 7NP
A40 from Carmarthen to St Clears, then A477 on W of Tenby town centre.
Seaside links course.
18 holes, 6232 yards, S.S.S.71
Founded 1888 (oldest in Wales)
Visitors: welcome with h/cap cert.
Green Fee: WD £20; WE & BH £24.
Societies: welcome with prior booking.
Catering: full facilities, bar snacks available; restaurant meals to be pre-booked.
Hotels: contact Sec for list.

K137 Tredegar & Rhymney

☎ (01685) 840743
Cwmtysswg, Rhymney, Mid-Glam B4256 1.5 miles from Rhymney.
Undulating mountain course.
9 holes, 2788 yards, S.S.S.67
Founded 1921
Visitors: welcome.
Green Fee: on application.
Societies: weekdays only by prior arrangement.
Catering: no catering daytime; evenings by arrangement.
Hotels: Red Lion Inn (Tredegar).

K138 Tredegar Park

☎ (01633) 894433 (Sec), Club 895219, Pro 894517, Fax 897152
Bassaleg Rd, Newport, Gwent NP9 3PX
Leave M4 at junction 27, to Newport, 1st right in Western Ave and right at end of Western Ave.
Parkland course.
18 holes, 6097 yards, S.S.S.70
Designed by James Braid.
Founded 1923

Visitors: must be member of affiliated club and produce evidence thereof.
Green Fee: on application.
Societies: welcome by prior arrangement.
Catering: for members and visitors only.
Hotels: The Kings; Celtic Manor.

K139 Vale of Glamorgan Golf and Country Club

☎(01443) 222221, Fax 222220
Hensol Park, Hensol, South Glamorgan CF7 8JY
M4 junction 34 and follow signs (about 600 yards).
Parkland course.
18 holes (Lake), 6507 yards, S.S.S. 72
9 holes (Hensol), 3115 yards, S.S.S. 36
Designed by P. Johnson.
Founded 1993.
Visitors: welcome weekdays with h/cap certificate, must be accompanied by a member at weekends.
Green Fees: WD £20; WE £25.
Societies: weekdays by prior arrangement.
Catering: full facilities.
Driving range, putting and chipping greens.
Hotels: under construction; telephone for details.

K140 Vale of Llangollen

☎(01978) 860906 (Sec), Pro 860040
Llangollen, Clwyd LL20 7PR
On A5, 1 mile S of Llangollen.
Parkland course.
18 holes, 6673 yards, S.S.S.73
Founded 1908
Visitors: welcome weekdays and some weekends.
Green Fee: WD £20; WE £25.
Societies: weekdays by prior arrangement with Sec.
Catering: full catering facilities available.
Hotels: Royal; The Hand; Tyn y Wern; Bryn Howel.

K141 Virginia Park

☎(01222) 863919, Fax 863113
Virginia Park, Caerphilly, Mid Glam CF8 3SW
In centre of town, next to Caerphilly recreation centre.
Municipal parkland course.
9 holes, S.S.S.66
Founded Aug 1992

Visitors: welcome, h/cap cert required.
Green Fee: £6 (9 holes), £11 (18 holes).
Societies: welcome by prior arrangement.
Catering: bars, full refreshments available.
Driving range.

K142 Welsh Border Golf Complex

☎(01743) 884247
Bulthy Farm, Bulthy, Middletown, Nr Welshpool, Powys SY21 8ER
Via A458 Shrewsbury/Welshpool road, turn off to club signposted in Middletown.
Parkland course.
9 holes, 3006 yards, S.S.S.69; 9 holes Par 3, 1614 yards
Designed by Andrew Griffiths.
Founded 1991
Visitors: proper dress, h/cap certs not required; no restrictions for Par 3 course.
Green Fee: £7 (9 holes), £10 (18 holes), £15 per day; Par 3 course, £4 (9 holes), £6 (18 holes).
Societies: welcome any time by arrangement with Sec.
Catering: bar and restarant facilities available.
Driving range.
Hotels: Rowlon Castle; Bulthy Farm GH.

K143 Welshpool

☎(01938) 850249
Golfa Hill, Welshpool, Powys
4 miles from Welshpool on A458.
mountain course.
18 holes, 5708 yards, S.S.S.69
Designed by James Braid.
Founded 1929
Visitors: welcome.
Green Fee: apply for details.
Societies: welcome by prior arrangement.
Catering: facilities available.
Hotels: Golfa Hall; Royal Oak.

K144 Wenvoe Castle

☎(01222) 594371 (Sec), Pro 593649
Wenvoe, Cardiff CF5 6BE
A48 W from Cardiff, left after 3 miles onto A4050, course 2 miles on right.
Parkland course.
18 holes, 6422 yards, S.S.S.71
Founded 1936
Visitors: Mon-Fri with h/cap cert; Sat/Sun with member only.
Green Fee: £24.

Societies: Mon-Fri by prior application; reduction for 16 plus.
Catering: bars, lunches, dinner, snacks.
Snooker.
Hotels: Copthorne (Culverhouse Cross).

K145 Wernddu Golf Centre

☎(01873) 856223/Fax
Abergavenny, Gwent NP7 8NG
1.5 miles E of Abergavenny on B4521 off A465
Public parkland course.
9 holes, Par 31; 9 holes Par 36
Designed by G. Watkins.
Founded 1992
Visitors: 8am to dusk every day; correct dress required.
Green Fee: £6 (9 holes), £10 (18 holes).
Societies: by arrangement weekdays.
Catering: bar, light refreshments.
Driving range, 9-hole Pitch & Putt, practice putting area.
Hotels: self-catering holiday cottages available.

K146 West Monmouthshire

☎(01495) 310233, Sec (home): 310126, Pro 313052
Golf Road, Nantyglo, Gwent NP3 4QT
Heads of Valley road A465, western valley A467 to Semtex roundabout, follow Winchestown signs.
Heathland course (14th tee highest in Great Britain, 1450ft).
18 holes, 6118 yards, S.S.S.69
Founded 1906
Visitors: welcome, Mon-Sat; Sun guests only.
Green Fee: WD £18 (£13 with member).
Societies: by appointment Mon-Fri. Special rates for 16+.
Catering: bar and restaurant.

K147 Whitchurch (Cardiff)

☎(01222) 620985 (Sec), Club 620125, Fax 529860
Pantmawr Rd, Whitchurch, Cardiff, S Glam CF4 6XD
Off M4 at exit 32, 200 yards on A470 to Cardiff.
Parkland course.
18 holes, 6317 yards S.S.S.71
Designed by re-designed by James Braid
Founded 1915

Visitors: welcome; h/cap cert required.
Green Fee: WD £30 (£10 with member); WE & BH £35 (£15 with member).
Societies: Thurs only by prior arrangement.
Catering: facilities available every day.
Hotels: Travelodge; Masons Arms; The Friendly Hotel.

K148 Whitehall

☎(01443) 740245
The Pavilion, Nelson, Treharris, Mid-Glam CF46 6ST
Take Treharris and Nelson exit at roundabout on A470, turn right and head S for 0.25 mile, take 1st left turning up Mountain Rd.
Mountain course.
9 holes, 5666 yards, S.S.S.68
Founded 1922
Visitors: welcome weekdays; accompanied by a member at weekends.
Green Fee: on application

Societies: welcome by arrangement with Sec.
Catering: available with prior arrangement.
Hotels: Llechwen Hall (Pontypridd).

K149 Woodlake Park Golf Club

☎(01291) 673933, Fax 673811
Glascoed, Pontypool, Gwent NP4 0TE
Situated on eastern bank of Llandegfedd Reservoir 3 miles from Usk; 10 miles M4 junction 24, 8 miles junction 26.
Parkland course.
18 holes, 6278 yards, S.S.S.70
Designed by M.J. Wood and H.N. Wood.
Founded August 1993
Visitors: welcome at any time; must be member of bona fide club.
Green Fee: £20 per round, £27.50 per day.
Societies: packages from £20 per person; weekends available; booking essential.

Catering: spikes bar seating 60; function room and restaurant seating 120.
Indoor Golf Academy; pitching/chipping and bunkers; 9-hole putting green; driving into nets.
Hotels: 3 Salmons (Usk); Cwrt Bleddyn (Llangibby); Parkway (Cwmbran).

K150 Wrexham

☎(01978) 364268, 261033, 351476
Holt Rd, Wrexham, Clwyd LL13 9SB
Situated on A534 2 miles E of Wrexham.
Undulating sandy course.
18 holes, 6233 yards, S.S.S.70
Designed by James Braid.
Founded 1906 (present location 1923)
Visitors: welcome.
Green Fee: on application.
Societies: welcome Mon, Thurs, Fri by arrangement.
Catering: full facilities.
Snooker.
Hotels: Holt Lodge.

SHROPSHIRE, STAFFORDSHIRE, CHESHIRE

In the last few years, Staffordshire and Shropshire have made the headlines on account of their golfing sons and daughters. Diane Bailey and Geoffrey Marks became the first to captain victorious Curtis and Walker Cup teams on American soil. David Gilford, a member of Trentham Park, won a place in the Ryder Cup teams in 1991 and 1995 along with Ian Woosnam whose county golf as an amateur was played for Shropshire in company with Sandy Lyle who was raised at Hawkstone Park. Hawkstone is part of a hotel complex that provides popular golfing facilities about 14 miles north of Shrewsbury in an area that is full of largely rural delights. It has recently seen significant change with the addition of a much upgraded second course.

In Shropshire, Bridgnorth is a delight with several holes along the river. But while Shropshire's courses are relatively few and far between, Staffordshire enjoys quantity as well as quality. It includes Little Aston, Penn, home of the late and great Charlie Stowe, and South Staffordshire at Wolverhampton, as well as the delights of Beau Desert, Drayton Park, Leek, Trentham, Trentham Park, Enville, Uttoxeter (which the locals pronounce Uttcheter), Patshull Park and Newcastle-under-Lyme.

Enville was the home course as a girl of Diane Bailey (née Robb) while Geoffrey Marks has remained loyal all his playing days to Trentham – to the south of Stoke-on-Trent. Enville's two contrasting courses are very good while Trentham is a parkland course with nice changes of level, very much like its neighbour Trentham Park.

Newcastle Municipal is a relatively recent public course that is much used. But probably the best courses in this section are Whittington Barracks (a slightly forbidding name for a moorland retreat that has championship status) and Little Aston which epitomises the very best of parkland golf, the main hazards taking the form of characteristically large bunkers, a couple of lakes, some majestic trees and a degree of undulation which tests one's judgement of distance.

South of the Mersey, the first ports of call after emerging from the tunnel, are the celebrated links of Wallasey and Royal Liverpool. Wallasey is less well known in spite of its association in bygone days with Dr Frank Stableford, mastermind of the excellent scoring system that bears his name – a system less cruel than the rigours of undiluted medal play.

Maybe, he devised the idea from his battles with Wallasey's glorious seaside links and the winds that plague golfers even more. The latest version of the course incorporates rather more of the flat, plain land than it used to, but flatness is also a feature of Royal Liverpool at Hoylake which few have seen fit to criticise in an area that has changed hardly at all in character since the Club was founded in 1869.

As the second oldest seaside course in England, Royal Liverpool wears the local crown but Caldy and Heswall are other Wirral landmarks not far off the road back to Chester where most of the best golfing country lies to the east and to the south-east.

Sandiway, Delamere Forest, Mere and Eaton at Waverton are all redoubtable courses in beautiful settings, as, indeed, is Portal at Tarporley which opened its doors for the first time in 1991 although an even more recent creation is Carden Park at Malpas which has fine teaching facilities.

L1 Adlington Golf Centre

☎(01625) 850660, Fax 850960
Sandy Hey Farm, Adlington,
Macclesfield, Cheshire SK10 5NG
Just off A523 midway between
Macclesfield & Stockport
Meadowland course
Par 3 Academy course
9 holes, 632 yards
Designed by Hawtree
Founded 1995
Visitors: pay & play
Green Fee: WD £3.50; WE £4.50
Societies: welcome by prior
arrangement
Catering: light refreshments
available.
24 bay floodlit driving range.

L2 Alder Root Golf Club

☎(01925) 291919, Pro 291932
Alder Root Lane, Winwick,
Warrington, Cheshire WA2 8RZ
Junction 9, M62, north A49, turn left
at 1st set of traffic lights, then 1st
right into Alder Root Lane. (1 mile
from motorway)
Parkland course
9 holes, 5820 yards, S.S.S. 68
Founded 1993
Visitors: by arrangement
Green Fee: WD £16 per day; WE
£18 per day
Societies: by arrangement,
weekdays only.
Catering: Bar snacks
Hotels: Bulls Head

L3 Alderley Edge

☎(01625) 585583
Brook Lane, Alderley Edge, Cheshire
SK9 7RU
From Alderley Edge, turn left off A34
opposite Tower Garage towards
Mobberley/Knutsford, B5085.
Undulating parkland course.
9 holes, 5839 yards, S.S.S.68
Designed by T. G. Renouf.
Founded 1907
Visitors: welcome subject to proof of
h/cap; restricted Wed, weekends.
Green Fee: apply for details.
Societies: catered for Thurs.
Catering: full catering facilities except
Mon.
Hotels: De Trafford Arms.

L4 Aldersey Green Golf Club

☎(01829) 782157, Pro shop 782480,
Club 782453
Aldersey, Chester, Cheshire CH3
9EH
On A41 Whitchurch Road.
Parkland course.
18 holes, 6159 yards, S.S.S.70
Founded 1993
Visitors: welcome
Green Fee: WD £15 per round; WE
£20 per round.
Societies: welcome by prior
arrangement.
Catering: bar and bar meals
available.

L5 Alsager Golf & Country Club

☎(01270) 875700, Fax 882207
Audley Rd, Alsager, Stoke-on-Trent
ST7 2UR
Leave M6 at junction 16, take A500
towards Stoke-on-Trent for 1 mile,
leave at 1st turn left for Alsager;
course 2 miles.
Parkland course.
18 holes, 6206 yards, S.S.S.70
Founded 1976
Visitors: correct dress required, no
jeans, ties and jackets after 7pm.
Green Fee: on application
Societies: Mon, Wed, Thurs, by
arrangement.
Catering: available.
Banqueting, snooker, bowls.

L6 Altrincham

☎(0161) 928 0761
Stockport Rd, Timperley, Altrincham,
Cheshire WA15
On A560 1 mile W of Altrincham.
Public undulating parkland course.
18 holes, 6162 yards, S.S.S.69
Founded 1935
Visitors: welcome; advance bookings
at all times.
Green Fee: apply for details.
Catering: no facilities at club;
Beefeater restaurant next door.
Hotels: Cresta Court; Woodlands
Park.

L7 Alvaston Hall Golf Club

☎(01270) 624341/629444
Middlewich Road, Nantwich, Cheshire
CW5 6PD
M6 junction 16, A500 signposted
Chester, at roundabout take A534 to
Middlewich, quarter of a mile on left
hand side.
Meadowland course
9 holes, 3612 yards, S.S.S. 57
Founded 1992
Visitors: welcome
Green Fee: £6 (9 holes)
Societies: welcome
Catering: full catering facilities, bar,
40 seater lounge, 16 bay driving
range.
Hotels: Alvaston Hall Hotel & Country
Club (133 bedrooms), golf clinics.

L8 Antrobus Golf Club

☎(01925) 730890, Pro 730900
Foggs Lane, Antrobus, Northwich,
Cheshire CW9 6JQ
M56 junction 10, on A49 between
Northwich - Warrington.
Meadowland course
18 holes, 6153 yards, S.S.S. 69
Designed by Mike Slater
Founded 1993
Visitors: welcome
Green Fee: £14 (18 holes)
Societies: welcome
Catering: bar snacks
driving range - 12 bays undercover/6
outside
Hotels: Lord Daresbury; Park Royal;
Premier Lodge.

L9 Aqualate

☎(01952) 811699
Stafford Rd, Newport, Shropshire
TF10 9DB.
Off A518 Newport to Stafford Rd, 300
yards from junction with A41.
Parkland course
9 holes (18 tees), 5963 yards, S.S.S.
TBA (69 par)
Designed by M D Simmons/T Juhre
Founded Sept 1994
Visitors: welcome all days, 'tee
times' via booking system
Green Fee: WD £5 (9 holes), £9 (18
holes); WE £7 (9 holes), £12 (18
holes).
Societies: welcome by arrangement,
packages available.
Catering: light refreshments only, no
clubhouse at present.
20 bay floodlit driving range
Hotels: Royal Victoria (Newport)

L10 Arrowe Park

☎(0151) 677 1527 (Pro)
Arrowe Park, Woodchurch,
Birkenhead, Merseyside L49 5LW
3 miles from town centre, take
Borough Rd, Woodchurch Rd and
then opposite Landicon Cemetery;
M53 junction 3, 1 mile.
Municipal parkland course.
18 holes, 6377 yards, S.S.S.70
Founded 1932
Visitors: welcome, phone first.
Green Fee: £6
Societies: arrange with Pro.
Catering: restaurant

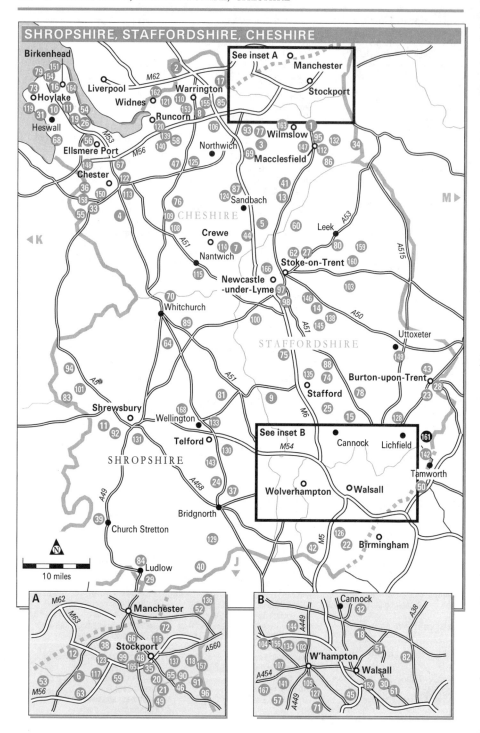

L11 Arscott

☎(01743) 860114, Pro 860881
Arscott, Pontesbury, Shropshire SY5
0XP
4 miles SW of Shrewsbury on A488,
midway between Hanwood and
Pontesbury.
Elevated parkland course with
extensive views.
18 holes, 6025 yards, S.S.S.69
Designed by Martin Hamer.
Founded 1992
Visitors: welcome at all times;
bookings required, Mar-Oct.
Green Fee: WD £14 per day, WE
£18 per day.
Societies: weekdays and some
weekends, bookings advised; rates
on request.
Catering: full bar and restaurant
facilities at all times.
Hotels: Boar's Head (Bishops
Castle); Sandford House, Rowton
Castle (Shrewsbury).

L12 Ashton on Mersey

☎(0161) 973 3220, Pro 962 3727
Church Lane, Sale, Cheshire M33
5QQ
2 miles from Sale station.
Parkland course.

9 holes, 6202 yards, S.S.S.69
Founded 1897
Visitors: welcome, except Tues after
3pm (Ladies Day).
Green Fee: apply for details.
Societies: by arrangement.
Catering: snacks, lunches, evening
meals.
Hotels: Mersey Farm (Travelodge)

L13 Astbury

☎(01260) 272772, Office: 279139,
Pro 298663
Peel Lane, Astbury, Nr Congleton,
Cheshire CW12 4RE
On outskirts of Congleton; leave A34
Congleton-Newcastle road at Astbury
village.
Parkland/meadowland course.
18 holes, 6296 yards, S.S.S.70
Founded 1922
Visitors: members of recognised golf
clubs welcome; must be
accompanied by member at
weekends.
Green Fee: £25 per day (£8 with
member).
Societies: Thurs only, £20 per
person per day.
Catering: by prior arrangement only.
Hotels: Bulls Head; Lion and Swan.

L14 Barlaston

☎(01782) 372867 Sec, Pro shop
372795
Meaford Rd, Stone, Staffs ST15 8UX
From M6 junction 14 take A34
towards Stoke-on-Trent; over Warton
roundabout at Stone, past Wayfarers
public house on left and turn right
0.25 mile after traffic lights; club is
300 yards beyond power station.
Moorland course.
18 holes, 5800 yards, S.S.S.68
Designed by Peter Alliss.
Founded 1977
Visitors: welcome weekdays, not
before 10am weekends.
Green Fee: WD £18; WE £22.50.
Societies: welcome weekdays only
by arrangement.
Catering: bar daily, meals by
arrangement.
Hotels: Stonehouse.

L15 Beau Desert

☎(01543) 422626
Rugeley Road, Hazel Slade,
Cannock, Staffs WS12 5PJ
Take A460 from Cannock through
Hednesford, right at signpost to Hazel
Slade, and next left.
Moorland course.

KEY		34	Chapel-en-le-Frith	69	Heyrose	102	Oxley Park	134	South Staffordshire
1	Adlington Golf Centre	35	Cheadle	70	Hill Valley G & CC	103	Parkhall	135	Stafford Castle
2	Alder Root Golf Club	36	Chester	71	Himley Hall Golf	104	Patshull Park Hotel	136	Stamford
3	Alderley Edge	37	Chesterton Valley Golf		Centre		Golf and Country Club	137	Stockport
4	Aldersey Green Golf		Club	72	Houldsworth	105	Penn	138	Stone
	Club	38	Chorlton-cum-Hardy	73	Hoylake Municipal	106	Peover	139	Styal
5	Alsager G & CC	39	Church Stretton	74	Ingestre Park	107	Perton Park Golf	140	Sutton Hall
6	Altrincham	40	Cleobury Mortimer	75	Izaak Walton		Centre	141	Swindon
7	Alvaston Hall Golf	41	Congleton	76	Knights Grange	108	Portal G & CC	142	Tamworth Municipal
	Club	42	Corngreaves		Sports Complex		Premier Course	143	Telford Golf & Country
8	Antrobus Golf Club	43	The Craythorne	77	Knutsford	109	Portal G & CC		Moat House
9	Aqualate	44	Crewe	78	Lakeside (Rugeley)	110	Poulton Park	144	Three Hammers Golf
10	Arrowe Park	45	Dartmouth	79	Leasowe	111	Prenton		Complex
11	Arscott	46	Davenport	80	Leek	112	Prestbury	145	Trentham Park
12	Ashton on Mersey	47	Delamere Forest	81	Lilleshall Hall	113	Pryors Hayes Golf	146	Trentham
13	Astbury	48	Didsbury	82	Little Aston		Club	147	TheTytherington
14	Barlaston	49	Disley	83	Llanymynech	114	Queen's Park	148	Upton-by-Chester
15	Beau Desert	50	Drayton Park	84	Ludlow	115	Reaseheath	149	Uttoxeter
16	Bidston	51	Druids Heath	85	Lymm	116	Reddish Vale	150	Vicars Cross
17	Birchwood	52	Dukinfield	86	Macclesfield	117	Ringway	151	Wallasey
18	Bloxwich	53	Dunham Forest G &	87	Malkins Bank	118	Romiley	152	Walsall
19	Brackenwood		CC	88	The Manor Golf Club	119	Royal Liverpool	153	Walton Hall
20	Bramall Park	54	Eastham Lodge		(Kingstone) Ltd	120	Runcorn	154	Warren
21	Bramhall	55	Eaton	89	Market Drayton	121	St Michael Jubilee	155	Warrington
22	Brand Hall	56	Ellesmere Port	90	Marple	122	St Thomas's Priory	156	Wergs
23	Branston G & C C	57	Enville	91	Mellor & Townscliffe		Golf Club	157	Werneth Low
24	Bridgnorth	58	Frodsham	92	Meole Brace	123	Sale	158	Westminster Park
25	Brocton Hall	59	Gatley	93	Mere G & CC	124	Sandbach	159	Westwood (Leek)
26	Bromborough	60	Goldenhill	94	Mile End	125	Sandiway	160	Whiston Hall
27	Burslem	61	Great Barr	95	Mottram Hall Hotel	126	Sandwell Park	161	Whittington Heath
28	Burton-on-Trent	62	Greenway Hall	96	New Mills	127	Sedgley Golf Centre	162	Widnes
29	Cadmore Lodge	63	Hale	97	Newcastle Municipal	128	Seedy Mill	163	Wilmslow
30	Calderfields Golf	64	Hawkstone Park Hotel	98	Newcastle-under-	129	Severn Meadows	164	Wirral Ladies
	Academy	65	Hazel Grove		Lyme	130	Shifnal	165	Withington
31	Caldy	66	Heaton Moor	99	Northenden	131	Shrewsbury	166	Wolstanton
32	Cannock Park	67	Helsby	100	Onneley	132	Shrigley Hall Hotel	167	Worfield
33	Carden Park	68	Heswall	101	Oswestry	133	The Shropshire	168	Wrekin

18 holes, 6300 yards, S.S.S.71
Designed by H. Fowler.
Founded 1921
Visitors: welcome weekdays; Sat and Sun phone Pro.
Green Fee: £35 per day.
Societies: welcome.
Catering: available.
Hotels: Cedar Tree (Rugeley); Roman Way (on A5 Cannock).

L16 Bidston

☎(0151) 638 3412, Sec 638 3412, Pro 630 6650
Bidston Link Road, Wallasey, Merseyside. L46 2HR
Just off J1 M53
Parkland course.
18 holes, 6207 yards, S.S.S.70
Founded 1913
Visitors: welcome weekdays.
Green Fee: on application
Societies: weekdays only.
Catering: full facilities.
Hotels: Leasowe Castle (Moreton).

L17 Birchwood

☎(01925) 818819, Fax 822403
Kelvin Close, Birchwood, Warrington, Cheshire WA3 7PB
M62 junction 11; follow A574 for Risley/Birchwood (entrance opposite Digital).
Parkland course.
18 holes, 6850 yards, S.S.S.73
Designed by T. J. McAuley.
Founded 1979
Visitors: welcome weekdays.
Green Fee: £24-£32.
Societies: Mon, Wed, Thurs; send for brochure.
Catering: A la carte, bar snacks, carvery, 7 days.
Banqueting, snooker.
Hotels: Lord Daresbury; Garden Court.

L18 Bloxwich

☎(01922) 476593 (Sec), Pro 476889, Club 405724
136 Stafford Rd, Bloxwich, Walsall, W Midlands WS3 3PQ
Off main Walsall-Cannock road (A34), 4 miles N of Walsall centre.
Semi-parkland course.
18 holes, 6286 yards, S.S.S.70
Designed by J. Sixsmith.
Founded 1924
Visitors: welcome with or without reservation except weekends and Bank Holidays.
Green Fee: £20 per round, £25 per day (£5 with member).

Societies: catered for, preferably weekdays; reduced rates over 20 players.
Catering: bar, restaurant (except Mon); lunches by arrangement. Snooker.
Hotels: Barons Court; County; Beverley; Royal.

L19 Brackenwood

☎(0151) 608 3093
Bracken Lane, Bebington, Wirral, Merseyside L63 2LY
M53 junction 4, to Clatterbridge and Bebington.
Public parkland course.
18 holes, 6285 yards, S.S.S.70
Founded 1933
Visitors: welcome.
Green Fee: £6.
Societies: by arrangement.
Hotels: Thornton Hall; Village, Dibinsdale (Bromborough).

L20 Bramall Park

☎(0161) 485 3119
20 Manor Rd, Bramhall, Stockport SK7 3LY
8 miles S of Manchester, A6 to Bramhall Lane, then A5102 to Carrwood Rd.
Parkland course.
18 holes, 6214 yards, S.S.S.70
Founded 1894
Visitors: welcome.
Green Fee: on application.
Societies: Tues/Thurs pm, other days on enquiry.
Catering: full except Mon.
Hotels: Oakley Manor (Cheadle Hulme); Alma Lodge.

L21 Bramhall

☎(0161) 439 4057, Sec 439 6092, Pro 439 1171
Ladythorn Rd, Bramhall, Stockport, Cheshire SK7 2EY
Near Bramhall station, 8 miles S of Manchester on A5102.
Parkland course.
18 holes, 6280 yards, S.S.S.70
Founded 1905
Visitors: welcome, subject to members competitions, book with Pro.
Green Fee: WD £23 per round, £27 per day; WE £30 per round, £37 per day.
Societies: catered for Wed, book with Sec.
Catering: a la carte, bar snacks.
Hotels: Moat House; Oakley Manor; Etrop Grange.

L22 Brand Hall

☎(0121) 552 2195, Fax 544 5088.
Heron Road, Oldbury, Warley, W Midlands B68 8AQ
6 miles NW of Birmingham, 1.5 miles from M5 junction 2.
Public parkland course.
18 holes, 5734 yards, S.S.S.68
Visitors: welcome.
Green Fee: apply for details.
Societies: welcome.
Catering: cafe, clubhouse, bar. Putting green.

L23 Branston Golf & Country Club

☎(01283) 543207, Fax 566984
Burton Rd, Branston, Burton-on-Trent DE14 3DP
Take A5121 off the A38 towards Burton-on-Trent, past church on right, over railway bridge, past petrol station on right, small island, turn right, then first on the left.
Parkland course.
18 holes, 6632 yards, S.S.S.71
Founded 1976
Visitors: welcome on weekdays.
Green Fee: apply for details.
Societies: weekdays.
Catering: 7 days a week.
Hotels: Riverside; Dog & Partridge; Mackwoth Hotel.

L24 Bridgnorth

☎(01746) 763315, Pro 762045
Stanley Lane, Bridgnorth, Shropshire WV16 4SF
Through High St, along Broseley Rd for 400 yards, right into Stanley Lane.
Parkland course.
18 holes, 6668 yards, S.S.S.72
Founded 1889
Visitors: daily except Mon and Wed.
Green Fee: WD £24 per day, £18/round; WE & BH £25, (half price with member).
Societies: catered for weekdays by arrangement with Sec.
Catering: available except Mon.
Hotels: Falcon; Kings Head; Croft; Whitburn Grange.

L25 Brocton Hall

☎(01785) 662627, Manager: 661901
Brocton, Stafford ST17 0TH
4 miles S of Stafford on A34, turn left at crossroads signposted Brocton, club entrance 300 yards on left.
Parkland course.
18 holes, 6095 yards, S.S.S.69
Designed by Harry Vardon.
Founded 1894

Visitors: accepted.
Green Fee: WD £25; WE & BH £30.
Societies: bookings accepted on Tues and Thurs.
Catering: by arrangement with the caterer.
Hotels: Tillington Hall.

L26 Bromborough

☎(0151) 334 2155, Pro 334 4499
Raby Hall Rd, Bromborough, Wirral, Merseyside L63 0NW
0.5 mile from Bromborough station, 0.75 mile from A41 Birkenhead-Chester road; M53 junction 5.
Parkland course.
18 holes, 6650 yards, S.S.S.73
Founded 1904
Visitors: welcome weekdays; check with Pro
Green Fee: WD £26 (£10 with member); WE & BH £30 (£10 with member).
Societies: Wed; early booking essential.
Catering: extensive snack menu, meals by arrangement.
Hotels: Dibbinsdale; Thornton Hall.

L27 Burslem

☎(01782) 837006
Wood Farm, High Lane, Tunstall, Stoke-on-Trent ST6 7JT
4 miles N of Hanley, situated on High Lane.
Moorland course.
11 holes, 5527 yards, S.S.S.67
Founded 1907
Visitors: welcome weekdays; not weekends.
Green Fee: apply for details.
Societies: weekdays.
Catering: apply to Steward.

L28 Burton-on-Trent

☎(01283) 544551
43 Ashby Rd East, Burton-on-Trent DE15 0PS
3 miles E of Burton-on-Trent on A50.
Undulating wooded parkland course.
18 holes, 6579 yards, S.S.S.71
Designed by H.S. Colt.
Founded 1894
Visitors: welcome, letter of intro, h/cap cert required; phone reservation advisable.
Green Fee: £28 per day, £22 per round.
Societies: weekdays.
Catering: full facilities except Mon. Snooker.
Hotels: Stanhope Arms (Bretby); Newton Park (Newton Solney).

L29 Cadmore Lodge

☎(01584) 810044
Berrington Green, Tenbury Wells, Worcester WR15 8TQ
Off A456 20 miles W of Kidderminster.
Parkland course with lakes.
9 holes, 5129 yards, S.S.S.66
Designed by John Weston.
Founded 1990
Visitors: welcome, no restrictions.
Green Fee: WD £7 per day; WE £10 per day.
Societies: welcome, book in advance.
Catering: full facilities.
Bowls, Tennis, Fishing.

L30 Calderfields Golf Academy

☎(01922) 640540 (Sec),
Rec/bookings: 32243
Aldridge Rd, Walsall, W Midlands WS4 2JS
From M6 junction 10, take A454 Aldridge-Walsall road; entrance to course is by Dilke Arms (Brewers Fayre).
Parkland course.
18 holes, 6700 yards, S.S.S.72
Designed by Roy Winter.
Founded 1983
Visitors: welcome any time.
Green Fee: £10 per round.
Societies: welcome.
Catering: full bar and restaurant facilities.
Pool tables, darts, 27 bay floodlit driving range, putting green, practise bunkers, golf superstore.
Hotels: Crest; Post House; Barons Court.

L31 Caldy

☎(0151) 625 5660, Fax 625 7394.
Links Hey Rd, Caldy, Wirral, Merseyside, L48 1NB
A540 from Chester turn left at Caldy crossroads.
Seaside/parkland course.
18 holes, 6675 yards, S.S.S.73
Designed by James Braid, John Salvesen.
Founded 1907
Visitors: welcome weekdays; Tues Ladies Day; weekends if accompanied by member.
Green Fee: WD £33 per round, £38 per day.
Societies: Thurs by prior arrangement.
Catering: bar snacks available all day, dinner served by prior arrangement.

L32 Cannock Park

☎(01543) 578850 (Phone/Fax)
Stafford Rd, Cannock, Staffs WS11 2AL
On A34 Stafford road, 0.5 mile from Cannock centre on left hand side, course situated behind Leisure Centre.
Municipal parkland course playing over Cannock Chase.
18 holes, 5048 yards, S.S.S.65
Designed by John Mainland.
Founded 1988
Visitors: welcome; busy course, phone bookings on the day or by letter for societies.
Green Fee: WD £6.50; WE £7.50.
Societies: welcome by arrangement; write to Sec.
Catering: full facilities.
Putting green, swimming, badminton, gym etc.

L33 Carden Park

☎(01829) 731199, Fax 731133
Carden Park, Chester, Cheshire CH3 9DQ
On A534 towards Wrexham, 1.5 miles from junction with A41.
Park and woodland course.
18 holes, 6828 yards, S.S.S.73; 9 hole Par 3 short course
Designed by Alan Higgins.
Founded Aug 1993
Visitors: welcome, h/cap certs required for 18 hole course, please ring for reservations.
Green Fee: WD £25 per round, £35 per day; weekend fees on application.
Societies: welcome, details on application.
Catering: restaurant and full bar facilities.
Driving range.
Hotels: Birches Hotel.

L34 Chapel-en-le-Frith

☎(01298) 813943 (Sec), Club 812118.
Manchester Rd, Chapel-en-le-Frith, Stockport, Cheshire SK12 6UH
1 mile N of Chapel-en-le-Frith on B5470 almost opposite Hanging Gate public house.
Meadowland course.
18 holes, 6054 yards, S.S.S.69
Founded 1906
Visitors: welcome, small numbers without reservation.
Green Fee: WD £20; WE & BH £30.
Societies: welcome by prior arrangement.
Catering: all meals daily
Hotels: Kings Arms.

L35 Cheadle
☎(0161) 491 4452 (Sec), Club 428
2160, Steward: 491 3878, Pro 428
9878
Shiers Drive, Cheadle, Cheshire SK8
1HW
1.5 miles from junction 11 M63, follow
signs for Cheadle; 1 mile S of
Cheadle village, 1.5 miles from
Cheadle Hulme railway station.
Undulating parkland course.
9 holes, 5006 yards, S.S.S.65
Designed by R. Renouf.
Founded 1885
Visitors: members of golf club with
official h/cap; not Tues or Sat.
Green Fee: on application.
Societies: by written application to
Sec; no parties Sat, Sun or Tues.
Catering: bar and lunches daily
except Thur, at other times by
arrangement with Steward.
Snooker.
Hotels: The Village; Alma Lodge.

L36 Chester
☎(01244) 677760
Curzon Park North, Chester CH4 8AR
1 mile from centre of Chester, off
A55, course located behind Chester
Racecourse.
Parkland course.
18 holes, 6508 yards, S.S.S.71
Founded 1901
Visitors: welcome by arrangement.
Green Fee: WD £23; WE £28.
Societies: by arrangement.
Catering: full facilities.

L37 Chesterton Valley Golf Club
☎(01746) 783682
Chesterton, Nr. Worfield, Bridgnorth,
Shropshire WV15 5NX
On B4176 Dudley - Telford road
Meadowland course
9 holes, 3129 yards, S.S.S.70
Founded 1993
Visitors: welcome, telephone first.
Green Fee: £6.50
Societies: welcome

L38 Chorlton-cum-Hardy
☎(0161) 881 3139, Sec 881 5830,
Pro 881 9911
Barlow Hall Rd, Chorlton, Manchester
M21 7JJ
3 miles from city centre, off A5103,
near Southern Cemetery.
Meadowland course.
18 holes, 6004 yards, S.S.S.69
Founded 1903
Visitors: telephone Pro.

Green Fee: WD £20; WE £25.
Societies: Thurs.
Catering: snacks and meals daily
(limited hours), Mon sandwiches etc
only; evening meals to order.
Hotels: Longford Park; Trust House;
Post House; Northenden.

L39 Church Stretton
☎(01694) 722281, Sec/bookings:
722633
Hunters Moon, Trevor Hill, Church
Stretton, Shropshire SY6 6JH
0.25 mile W of town centre, off
Cardingmill Valley Rd, up the winding
Trevor Hill.
Hillside course on lower slopes of
Longmynd.
18 holes, 5020 yards, S.S.S.65
Designed by James Braid.
Founded 1898
Visitors: welcome weekdays; Sat not
9-10.30am or 1.30-2.30pm; Sun not
before 10.30am or 1.30-2.30pm.
Green Fee: WD £12; WE & BH £18.
Societies: by arrangement, not Sun.
Catering: bar and catering.
Hotels: Denehurst; Longmynd;
Stretton Hall.

L40 Cleobury Mortimer
☎(01299) 271112, Club 271320, Fax
271468
Wyre Common, Cleobury Mortimer,
Shropshire DY14 8HQ
10 miles west of Kidderminster on the
A4117 and 11 miles east of Ludlow
Parkland course
18 holes, 6450 yards, S.S.S. 71
Founded 1993
Visitors: welcome
Green Fee: WD £10; WE £15
Societies: welcome by prior
arrangement with the pro
Catering: Spike bar, snooker room
and restaurant; snakcs available
everyday except Monday

L41 Congleton
☎(01260) 273540
Biddulph Rd, Congleton, Cheshire
CW12 3LZ
1 mile SE of Congleton station on
main Congleton-Biddulph road A527.
Parkland course.
9 holes, 5103 yards, S.S.S.65
Founded 1898
Visitors: welcome, Tues Ladies day.
Green Fee: WD £14; WE & BH £20
(half price with member).
Societies: Mon and Thurs.
Catering: snacks; phone for full
meals; not Mon.

L42 Corngreaves
☎(01384) 567880
Corngreaves Road, Cradley Heath,
W Midlands
2 miles E of Dudley.
Public parkland course.
Full length 9 holes
Founded 1985
Visitors: welcome.
Green Fee: apply for details.

L43 The Craythorne
☎(01283) 564329, Pro 533745, Fax
511908
Craythorne Rd, Stretton, Burton-on-
Trent, Staffs DE13 0AZ
Take N exit for Burton-on-Trent from
A38, into Stretton village, turn right at
church.
Parkland course.
18 holes, 5255 yards, (being
extended '96) S.S.S.67, Par 68; 9
hole pitch & putt.
Designed by Cyril Johnson.
Founded 1972
Visitors: welcome any time; booking
at weekends.
Green Fee: WD £17 per round, £25
per day; WE & BH £22 per round,
£30 per day.
Societies: anytime.
Catering: bar and restaurant.
Driving range.

L44 Crewe
☎(01270) 584099 (Sec), Pro
585032, Steward: 584227
Fields Rd, Haslington, Crewe,
Cheshire CW1 5TB
1 mile SW of A534 at Haslington,
between Crewe and Sandbach.
Parkland course.
18 holes, 6259 yards, S.S.S.70
Founded 1911
Visitors: weekdays only unless with
member.
Green Fee: £27, £22 after 1pm (£10
with member, WD, and £14, WE).
Societies: Tues only by prior
arrangement.
Catering: bar snacks, lunches,
dinners.
Snooker.
Hotels: Crewe Arms; Saxon Cross
Motel; Lamb (Nantwich).

L45 Dartmouth
☎(0121) 588 2131
Vale St, West Bromwich, W Midlands
B71 4DW
1.5 miles from M5/6 junction 1.
Undulating meadowland/parkland
course.

9 holes (16 tees), 6036 yards,
S.S.S.69
Founded 1910
Visitors: welcome weekdays, h/cap
cert preferred; with member only
some weekends.
Green Fee: approx £16.50 per day
(£8 per day with member).
Societies: by prior arrangement any
weekday.
Catering: by arrangement.
Snooker.
Hotels: Moat House; Albion.

L46 **Davenport**
☎(01625) 877321 (Club), Sec
876951, Pro 877319
Worth Hall, Middlewood Rd, Poynton,
Stockport, Cheshire SK12 1TS
From Stockport take A6 to Rising Sun
at Hazel Grove, then A523
Macclesfield road, at Poynton traffic
lights turn left into Park Lane, club is
approx 1.5 miles.
Undulating parkland course.
18 holes, 6066 yards, S.S.S.69
Designed by Fraser Middleton.
Founded 1913
Visitors: welcome most days other
than Sat, phone Pro to check.
Green Fee: WD £24; WE & BH £30;
one -third price if accompanied by
member.
Societies: Tues and Thurs, £32.50
(package).
Catering: by arrangement with
Steward; fixed hours for snacks.
Hotels: Belfry; Belgrade.

L47 **Delamere Forest**
☎(01606) 882807 (Steward), Sec
883264, Pro 883307
Station Rd, Delamere, Northwich,
Cheshire CW8 2JE
From A556 Manchester-Chester road
take B5152 towards Frodsum; lane to
club is on right, approx 1 mile from
A556, immediately by Delamere
station.
Undulating heathland course.
18 holes, 6305 yards, S.S.S.70
Designed by Herbert Fowler.
Founded 1910
Visitors: welcome; 2 balls only
weekends and Bank Holidays.
Green Fee: WD £25 per round, £35
per day; WE & BH £30 per round;
£10 if playing with member.
Societies: Tues and Thurs by
arrangement.
Catering: bar snacks; restaurant if
booked in advance.
Hotels: Hartford Hall; Swan;
Willington Hall.

L48 **Didsbury**
☎(0161) 998 9278 (Sec), Pro 998
2811
Ford Lane, Northenden, Manchester
M22 4NQ
Off M63 junction 9, near Northenden
Church, club sign on wall.
Parkland course.
18 holes, 6273 yards, S.S.S. 70
Founded 1891
Visitors: welcome; Ladies day Tues;
weekends by arrangement.
Green Fee: WD £22 (£9 with
member); WE £25 (£10 with
member).
Societies: Thurs and Fri by prior
arrangement.
Catering: restaurant and snacks
available.
Hotels: Post House; Britannia.

L49 **Disley**
☎(01663) 762071
Stanley Hall Lane, Jackson's Edge,
Disley, Cheshire SK12 2JX
A6, 6 miles S of Stockport.
Moorland/meadowland course.
18 holes, 6015 yards, S.S.S.69
Designed by James Braid.
Founded 1889
Visitors: Mon, Tues and Wed.
Green Fee: apply for details.
Societies: Tues and Wed.
Catering: bar; catering all days
except Mon.
Hotels: Stakis Moorside.

L50 **Drayton Park**
☎(01827) 251139, Fax 284035
Drayton Park, Tamworth, Staffs B78
3TN
2 miles S of Tamworth on A4091.
Parkland course.
18 holes, 6214 yards, S.S.S.71
Designed by James Braid.
Founded 1897
Visitors: by arrangement weekdays.
Green Fee: £28.
Societies: Tues and Thurs with prior
arrangement.
Catering: full facilities from 10.30am.
Snooker.
Hotels: Gungate; Castle; Beafeater.

L51 **Druids Heath**
☎(01922) 55595, Pro 59523
Stonnall Rd, Aldridge, Walsall WS9
8JZ
Off A452 6 miles NW of Sutton
Coldfield.
Undulating course.
18 holes, 6914 yards, S.S.S.73
Founded 1973

Visitors: welcome weekdays.
Green Fee: on application.
Societies: weekdays.
Catering: by prior arrangement.
Hotels: Barons Court; Fairlawns.

L52 **Dukinfield**
☎(0161) 338 2340
Yew Tree Lane, Dukinfield, Cheshire
SK10 5DB
From Ashton Rd 1 mile then right into
Yew Tree Lane, club 1 mile on right,
on hill behind Senior Service factory.
Hillside course.
18 holes, 5303 yards, S.S.S.66
Founded 1913
Visitors: weekdays.
Green Fee: on application.
Societies: by prior arrangement with
Sec.
Catering: meals by arrangement.
Hotels: The Village.

L53 **Dunham Forest G & CC**
☎(0161) 928 2605, Pro 928 2727
Oldfield Lane, Altrincham, Cheshire
WA14 4TY
2 miles N of M56 junction 7, proceed
in direction of Manchester, course is
on left of main road.
Parkland course.
18 holes, 6636 yards, S.S.S.72
Founded 1961
Visitors: welcome.
Green Fee: on application.
Societies: welcome weekdays
except Wed.
Catering: bar and restaurant.
Hotels: Bowdon; Cresta Court.

L54 **Eastham Lodge**
☎(0151) 327 3008 (Pro), Sec 327
3003, Club 327 1483
117 Ferry Rd, Eastham, Wirral L62
0AP
Off A41 Birkenhead-Chester road,
follow signs for Eastham Country
Park, club on left of Ferry Rd
approaching Country Park.
Parkland course.
15 holes, 5953 yards, S.S.S.69
Designed by Hawtree & Sons.
Founded 1975
Visitors: welcome on weekdays, at
weekends only with member.
Green Fee: £22, £9 with member.
Societies: Tues only.
Catering: bar snacks or full meal pre-
ordered.
Snooker.
Hotels: Village Hotel & Leisure
Centre (Bromborough).

Delights of Enville and Bridgnorth

Enville and Bridgnorth lie to the west of Wolverhampton and Stourbridge, marking the start of the rural tapestry which continues its spread across the border counties with Wales. Enville is closer to the industrial pulse of the West Midlands but its two courses, the Highgate and Lodge, are unexpectedly remote, a woodland setting not so very far removed from the famous courses of Surrey and Berkshire.

Of the two, the Highgate might be termed the old and the Lodge the new. The extension to 36-holes is relatively recent, long after, in fact, Diane Bailey (née Robb) developed her skills there in the 1950s. The Highgate is also my favourite largely because of the quality and beauty of the holes on either side of the turn.

The 7th and 8th, two relatively short par 4s, are sandwiched between the difficult par 4 6th and the magnificent dogleg par 5 9th where some majestic trees make bunkers redundant. Another of the par 5s is the 10th which curves the opposite way to the 9th. But the pleasant part of both courses is the contrast in character between the more open, heathland holes and those dominated by trees. The latter typify the new holes on the Lodge on the other side of the road but many prefer the less inhibited start and finish although the demands are almost as exacting.

Bridgnorth is also a combination of old and new, the Club existing for most of its life on the edge of the attractive town as nine holes, starting and finishing (they still do) with a couple of holes memorable for their eccentricity. Both are dominated by the same prominent ridge or hill over which the drive and the first and the second shot at the 18th are played,

opinion of them ranging from praise to condemnation.

Maybe modern machinery would sculpt them differently, the long slopes down to both greens calling for a nice mixture of luck and judgement. The 18th is the longer and more demanding, a tough finish in any context, but, variety being the spice of life, both add an unusual note in a golfing world that is often dully predictable. Something of the same theme surrounds the 2nd although the second shot to the elevated green has to be truly struck and judged to the inch, the opening triangle of three holes' then completed by an inviting downhill par 3.

The next 14 holes occupy the flatter land between the road and the river, the best part of the outward half being the 6th, 7th and 8th, the 8th a most challenging hole with a raised green that is stoutly defended. Its nomination as Stroke Index 1 tells its own story.

The 6th and 7th are flanked on the right by the river but on the 13th the river awaits the hook, the second of three par 5s in four holes. A long tee shot is required to find the green on the 14th but the toughest drive is perhaps the 15th between the road on the left and the trees that characterise the right hand side. The fairway is emphatically the place to be.

After that, the drive at the 17th enjoys considerably greater latitude but it is really a second shot hole calling for a high iron over a horseshoe bunker around the front of the green. Then, it is back over the road for a climax that, whatever its critics may say, rewards the art of positional play; the better placed the drive the greater the chance of attacking the flag, even if a proper assessment of its success has to await the scaling of the central rise.

L55 Eaton
☎(01244) 335885 (Sec), Pro
335826, Fax 335782
Guy Lane, Waverton, Chester, CH3
7PH
3 miles SE of Chester off the A41.
Parkland course.
18 holes, 6562 yards, S.S.S.71
Designed by Donald Steel.
Founded 1965 (Club), 1993 (Course)
Visitors: h/caps required; by prior
arrangement.
Green Fee: on request.
Societies: weekdays only, by prior
arrangement.
Catering: full catering facilities
available.

L56 Ellesmere Port
☎(0151) 339 7689
Chester Rd, Childer Thornton, S
Wirral, Cheshire L66 1QF
W on M53, take A41 turning S
towards Chester for 2 miles, club at
rear of St Paul's Church, Hooton.
Municipal parkland/meadowland
course.
18 holes, 6432 yards, S.S.S.71
Designed by Cotton, Pennink, Lawrie
& Partners.
Founded 1971
Visitors: welcome.
Green Fee: WD £5.40; WE & BH
£6.30.
Societies: weekdays and weekends,
booking fee £1.20 per head.
Catering: full facilities, bar and
restaurant all day.
Squash centre, smart golf.
Hotels: Brook Meadow; Chimney
(Hooton); Village Hotel and Leisure
Club (Bromborough).

L57 Enville
☎(01384) 872074 (Sec/Manager),
Club 872551, Pro 872585
Highgate Common, Enville,
Stourbridge, W Midlands DY7 5BN
5 miles W of Stourbridge; from A449
follow A458 Bridgenorth road for 1.8
miles; club signposted.
Heathland/woodland course.
Highgate, 18 holes, 6556 yards,
S.S.S.72; Lodge, 18 holes, 6217
yards, S.S.S.70
Founded 1935
Visitors: welcome weekdays and
with member at weekends.
Green Fee: £25 (18 holes), £30 (27
holes), £36 (36 holes).
Societies: by arrangement a year in
advance if possible; weekdays only.
Catering: full facilites.
Hotels: Anchor.

L58 Frodsham
☎(01928) 732159
(Office/Sec/Manager), Pro shop
739442
Simons Lane, Frodsham, Cheshire
WA6 6HE
10 minutes from M56 junction 12; turn
left at lights in Frodsham centre onto
B5152, 0.75 mile turn right after
pedestrian crossing, 0.5 mile up hill
turn right, club is 1st on left.
Parkland course.
18 holes, 6289 yards, Par 70
Designed by John Day.
Founded July 1990
Visitors: welcome all days except
competition days; tee times booked
through shop.
Green Fee: WD £20 per day; WE &
BH £25 per day.
Societies: welcome weekdays only,
contact office for details.
Catering: full bar and wide selection
of food served throughout the day.
Hotels: Forest Hills.

L59 Gatley
☎(0161) 437 2091, Pro 436 2830
Waterfall Farm, off Styal Rd, Heald
Green, Cheadle, Cheshire SK8 3TW
Off Yew Tree Grove and Styal Rd 2
miles from Cheadle, 1 mile from
Manchester Airport.
Parkland course.
9 holes, 5934 yards, S.S.S.68
Founded 1912
Visitors: welcome weekdays except
Tues.
Green Fee: £20 per day
Societies: apply to Sec.
Catering: full facilities.

L60 Goldenhill
☎(01782) 784715
Mobberley Rd, Goldenhill, Stoke-on-
Trent, Staffs ST6 55S
On A50 between Tunstall and
Kidsgrove.
Public parkland/meadowland course
(in old open-cast mine basin).
18 holes, 5957 yards, S.S.S.68
Founded 1983
Visitors: welcome; booking system.
Green Fee: WD £6 per round, WE £7
per round.
Societies: welcome by arrangement.
Catering: bar and restaurant.
Practice ground, putting green.

L61 Great Barr
☎(0121) 357 5270 (Pro)
Chapel Lane, Great Barr, Birmingham
B43 7BA
Adjacent to exit 7, off M6, 6 miles NW
of Birmingham.
Meadowland course.
18 holes, 6545 yards, S.S.S.72
Designed by J. Hamilton Stutt.
Founded 1961
Visitors: weekdays.
Green Fee: apply for details.
Societies: Tues, Thurs, by prior
arrangement.
Catering: by arrangement.
Hotels: Post House.

L62 Greenway Hall
☎(01782) 503158
Stanley Road, Stockton Brook, Stoke-
on-Trent ST9 9LI
Off A53 Stoke to Leek road, approx 5
miles from Stoke.
Meadowland course.
18 holes, 5676 yards, S.S.S.67
Founded 1908
Visitors: with member only, not
weekends.
Green Fee: £14 per day.
Societies: by appointment only.
Catering: available by prior
arrangement.

L63 Hale
☎(0161) 980 4225, Pro 904 0835
Rappax Rd, Hale, Altrincham,
Cheshire WA15 0NU
2 miles SE of Altrincham.
Undulating parkland course.
9 holes, 5780 yards, S.S.S.68
Founded 1903
Visitors: weekdays except Thurs;
weekends and Bank Holidays only
with member.
Green Fee: WD £20.
Societies: by arrangement with Hon
Sec.
Catering: lunch except Tues and
Thurs by arrangement with Steward.
Hotels: Bowdon; Ashley.

L64 Hawkstone Park Hotel
☎(01939) 200611, Fax 200311
Weston-under-Redcastle,
Shrewsbury, Shropshire SY4 5UY
Off A49, 12 miles N of Shewsbury; off
A442, 12 miles N of Telford (M54
junction 6); off A53, 12 miles SW of
Newcastle-under-Lyme (M56 junction
15).
Parkland course
Hawkstone, 18 holes, 6491 yards,
S.S.S.72
Windmill, 18 holes, 6764 yards,
S.S.S.72
Founded 1935

Visitors: h/cap required, must book in advance.
Green Fee: from £25 per round
Societies: book through reservation office.
Catering: terrace bar/restaurant, Hawkstone restaurant.
Golf centre, practice range, putting and pitching green, 6 hole/Par 3 Academy course.
Hotels: own hotel on site, residential golf breaks from £59.95 per person; telephone for details.

L65 Hazel Grove

☎(0161) 483 3978 (Manager/Sec), Pro 483 7272, Steward: 483 3217
Buxton Rd, Hazel Grove, Stockport, Cheshire SK7 6LU
Buxton Rd is on A6.
Parkland course.
18 holes, 6310 yards, S.S.S.71
Founded 1913
Visitors: welcome weekdays.
Green Fee: on application
Societies: Thurs and Fri by prior arrangement.
Catering: daily.

L66 Heaton Moor

☎(0161) 432 2134, Pro 432 0846
Heaton Mersey, Stockport, Cheshire SK4 3NX
2 miles from Stockport.
Parkland course.
18 holes, 5876 yards, S.S.S.68
Founded 1892
Visitors: welcome except Tues and Wed.
Green Fee: apply for details.
Societies: by arrangement.
Catering: meals served.

L67 Helsby

☎(01928) 722021 (Sec), Pro 725457
Towers Lane, Helsby, Cheshire WA6 0JB
M56 junction 14 to Helsby; through traffic lights, take 1st right into Primrose Lane; 1st right into Towers Lane.
Parkland course.
18 holes, 6262 yards, S.S.S.70
Designed by James Braid.
Founded 1902
Visitors: welcome weekdays.
Green Fee: £20 per round, £27 per day.
Societies: catered for Tues and Thurs only.
Catering: full service available except Mon.
Hotels: Chester Grosvenor; Queens.

L68 Heswall

☎(0151) 342 1237, Pro 342 7431
Cottage Lane, Gayton, Heswall, Wirral, Cheshire L60 8PB
From M53 take exit 4; at roundabout turn into Well Lane, leads into Cottage Lane.
Parkland course.
18 holes, 6472 yards, S.S.S.72
Founded 1901
Visitors: not Tues and Thurs; phone call advisable.
Green Fee: WD £30 per round, £40 per day; WE £35 per round, £45 per day; winter package available.
Societies: Wed and Fri only; full catering.
Catering: bar snacks available every day.
Large practice area, 2 snooker tables.
Hotels: Craxton Wood; Crabwell Manor; Mollington Banastre; Thornton Hall; Woodhey; Victoria.

L69 Heyrose

☎(01565) 733664 (Sec/Fax/Bar), Pro 734267
Budworth Rd, Tabley, Knutsford, Cheshire WA16 0HY
4 miles W of Knutsford, 0.5 mile along Budworth Rd, off Pickmere Lane; M6 junction 19 1 mile.
Wooded converted farmland with water features.
18 holes, 6510 yards, S.S.S.73
Designed by E.L.C.N. Bridge.
Founded June 1990
Visitors: welcome except before 2pm Sat.
Green Fee: WD £19 per round, £24 per day; WE £24 per round, £29 per day.
Societies: weekdays only by arrangement.
Catering: clubhouse with bar and restaurant.
Practice ground, practice bunker, putting green, driving net.
Hotels: Cottons (Knutsford); Swan (Bucklow Hill); The Old Vicarage (Tabley), Travelodge.

L70 Hill Valley G & CC

☎(01948) 663584, Fax 665927
Terrick Rd, Whitchurch, Shropshire SY13 4JZ
Off A49/A41 bypass, 1 mile from centre of Whitchurch.
Undulating parkland course.
West course: 18 holes, 6050 yards, S.S.S.69; East course: 18 holes, 5300 yards, S.S.S.65.
Designed by P. Alliss & D. Thomas.
Founded 1975

Visitors: welcome at all times.
Green Fee: on application.
Societies: at all times.
Catering: open 8am-11pm; breakfast, lunch, dinner served daily; conferences, leisure centre.
Health & beauty centre, snooker, tennis courts.
Hotels: Terrick Hall; Dodington Lodge; motel accommodation within clubhouse.

L71 Himley Hall Golf Centre

☎(01902) 895207
Log Cabin, Himley Hall Park, Dudley, W Midlands DY3 4DF
From A449 Wolverhampton-Kidderminster road turn at traffic lights signposted Dudley onto B4176, then turn into Himley Hall Park on left.
Public parkland course.
9 holes, 6215 yards, S.S.S.70
Designed by D.A. Baker.
Founded 1980
Visitors: welcome.
Green Fee: WD £4.50 (9 holes), £6.50 (18 holes); WE & BH £4.80 (9 holes), £7 (18 holes); reductions for juniors & OAPs.
Societies: by prior arrangement.
Catering: cafe, hot meals available all day.
Hotels: Himley House; Park Hall.

L72 Houldsworth

☎(0161) 442 9611/1714/1712
Houldsworth Park, Reddish, Stockport SK5 6BN
M63 to junction 13 turn left, up to roundabout, take road to Reddish, turn left at Houldsworth pub.
Parkland course.
18 holes, 6078 yards, S.S.S.69
Designed by T.G. Renouf.
Founded 1911
Visitors: welcome weekdays (Ladies Day Tues 1.30-3.30pm).
Green Fee: on application
Societies: advance booking only.
Catering: full facilities.

L73 Hoylake Municipal

☎(0151) 632 2956, 632 4883
Carr Lane, Hoylake, Merseyside L47 4BG
Off M53 10 miles SW of Liverpool, follow signs for Hoylake, 100 yards from Hoylake station.
Municipal parkland course.
18 holes, 6313 yards, S.S.S.70
Designed by James Braid.
Founded 1933

Visitors: unrestricted; phone for weekends 1 week in advance; Sat from 8.30am.
Green Fee: on application
Societies: welcome, after 1.30pm weekends; phone Pro.
Catering: hot snacks, meals, bar meals.

L74 Ingestre Park

☎(01889) 270845, Pro 270304, Bar: 270061
Ingestre, Stafford ST18 0RE
6 miles E of Stafford off A51 via Great Haywood and Tixall Rd; M6 junctions 13 and 14.
Undulating parkland course in former estate of Earl of Shrewsbury.
18 holes, 6334 yards, S.S.S.70
Designed by Hawtree & Son.
Founded 1977
Visitors: welcome with h/cap cert weekdays; only if accompanied by member weekends and Bank Holidays.
Green Fee: WD £21 per round, £26 per day (£8 with member); WE £10 with member.
Societies: Mon, Tues, Thurs, Fri by arrangement with Manager.
Catering: snacks and meals available daily.
Snooker.
Hotels: Dower House; Garth; Tillington Hall; Happy Eater Motel.

L75 Izaak Walton

☎(01785) 760900
Eccleshall Rd, Cold Norton, Stone, Staffs ST15 0NS
M6 junction 14, A34 to Stone, B5206 towards Eccleshall for 2 miles.
Meadowland course.
18 holes, S.S.S.72
Designed by Mike Lowe
Founded May 1993
Visitors: welcome weekdays
Green Fee: WD £12 per round; WE £17 per round.
Societies: welcome
Catering: bar and restaurant.
Practice facilities.
Hotels: Stone House (Stone); St George's (Eccleshall).

L76 Knights Grange Sports Complex

☎(01606) 552780
Grange Lane, Winsford, Cheshire
In centre of Winsford.
Public meadowland course
9 holes, 2995 metres, S.S.S.68;
Founded 1983

Visitors: no restrictions.
Green Fee: WD £2.70 (9 holes), £3.50 (18 holes); WE & BH £3.95 (9 holes), £5.10 (18 holes).
Societies: apply in writing to the Manager.
Catering: Hot drinks & snacks.
Tennis, bowls, practice area, caravan site etc.

L77 Knutsford

☎(01565) 633355
Mereheath Lane, Knutsford, Cheshire
2 miles from junction 19 on M6, make for Knutsford entrance to Tatton Park, club a few yards on right down Mereheath Lane.
Parkland course.
9 holes, 6288 yards, S.S.S.70
Founded 1891
Visitors: welcome weekdays except Wed by arrangement with Sec.
Green Fee: on application.
Societies: catered for on Thurs by arrangement.
Catering: by arrangement with Steward.
Hotels: George; Angel; Cottons; Rose & Crown; Swan.

L78 Lakeside (Rugeley)

☎(01889) 575667.
Rugeley Power Station, Armitage Rd, Rugeley, Staffs WS15 1PR
Between Lichfield and Stafford.
Parkland course.
18 holes, 5534 yards, S.S.S.67
Founded 1969
Visitors: only with member.
Green Fee: on application.
Societies: by arrangement.
Catering: evening only.

L79 Leasowe

☎(0151) 677 5852, Pro 678 5460
Leasowe Rd, Moreton, Wirral L46 3RD
Take Wallasey turn off M53 1 mile after Queensway tunnel, 1 mile W of Wallasey village.
Links course.
18 holes, 6227 yards, S.S.S.71
Designed by John Ball Jnr.
Founded 1891
Visitors: welcome weekdays, weekends by arrangement.
Green Fee: WD £20; WE & BH £25.
Societies: welcome by arrangement any day except Sat, min 16 players.
Catering: restaurant, bar, snacks available.
2 snooker tables, large practice area.
Hotels: Leasowe Castle.

L80 Leek

☎(01538) 384779 (Sec), Club 385889
Cheddleton Rd, Leek, Staffs ST13 5RE
0.75 mile S of Leek on A520.
Semi-moorland course.
18 holes, 6240 yards, S.S.S.70
Founded 1892
Visitors: welcome weekdays before 3pm.
Green Fee: WD £24; WE £30.
Societies: Wed only.
Catering: lunches served except Sun; evening meals except Sun and Mon.
Snooker.
Hotels: Abbey Inn; Three Horseshoes; Jester.

L81 Lilleshall Hall

☎(01952) 604776, 603840
Lilleshall, Newport, Shropshire TF10 9AS
5 miles from Newport turn off A41 into Sheriffhales Rd, after 2 miles right into Abbey Rd, course is to N..
Parkland course.
18 holes, 5789 yards, S.S.S.68
Designed by H.S. Colt.
Founded 1937
Visitors: weekdays unaccompanied; weekends with members only.
Green Fee: apply for details.
Societies: by prior arrangement.
Catering: 9am-6.00pm daily.
Hotels: Royal Victoria; White House (Donnington).

L82 Little Aston

☎(0121) 353 2942 (Sec/Pro), Clubhouse 353 2066.
Streetly, Sutton Coldfield B74 3AN
Off A454, 3 miles N of Sutton Coldfield in Little Aston Park.
Parkland course.
18 holes, 6670 yards, S.S.S.73
Designed by Harry Vardon.
Founded 1908
Visitors: welcome weekdays.
Green Fee: on application.
Societies: weekdays only.
Catering: lunches served to order except Mon.
Hotels: Fairlawns.

L83 Llanymynech

☎(01691) 830983 (Sec), Pro 830879, Club 830542.
Pant, Oswestry, Shropshire SY10 8LB
1 mile W of A483 Welshpool-Oswestry road and 6 miles S of

Oswestry, turn by Cross Guns Inn, signposted to club in village of Pant. Upland course; holes 4,5,6 in England, remainder in Wales.
18 holes, 6114 yards, S.S.S.69
Founded 1933
Visitors: welcome.
Green Fee: WD £15 per round, £22 per day; WE £20 per round, £25 per day.
Societies: by prior arrangement; apply to Sec.
Catering: 7 days.

L84 Ludlow
☎(01584) 856285 (Sec), Pro 856366.
Bromfield, Ludlow, Shropshire SY8 2BT
Take A49 Shrewsbury road, turn right 2 miles N of Ludlow, signposted.
Parkland course.
18 holes, 6331 yards, S.S.S.70
Founded 1889
Visitors: welcome, ring Pro in advance.
Green Fee: WD £18.50 per day; WE £24.50 per day.
Societies: weekdays April-Oct by arrangement.
Catering: bar and restaurant facilities.

L85 Lymm
☎(0192 575) 5020 (Sec), Pro 5054, Clubhouse 2177.
Whitbarrow Rd, Lymm, Cheshire WA13 9AN
5 miles SE of Warrington.
Parkland course.
18 holes, 6304 yards, S.S.S.70
Founded 1907
Visitors: welcome weekdays; Thurs Ladies Day, no visitors before 2.30pm; only with member weekends and Bank Holidays.
Green Fee: £20.
Societies: usually on Wed.
Catering: meals available.
Hotels: Lymm; Statham Lodge; Dingle.

L86 Macclesfield
☎(01625) 615845 (Sec), Club 423227
Hollins Rd, Macclesfield, Cheshire SK11 7EA
Turn into Windmill St at traffic island in Leek Rd (A527).
Hilly course.
18 holes, 5625 yards, S.S.S.69
Designed by Hawtree & Son.
Founded 1889

Visitors: welcome most days.
Green Fee: WD £17; WE £20.
Societies: by arrangement.
Catering: bar and restaurant, not Tues.
Hotels: Sutton Hall.

L87 Malkins Bank
☎(01270) 765931, Clubhouse 767878
Betchton Rd, Sandbach, Cheshire
1.5 miles from M6 junction 17.
Municipal parkland course.
18 holes, 5971 yards, S.S.S.69
Designed by Hawtree & Son.
Founded 1980
Visitors: welcome 7 days; booking system in operation 7 days.
Green Fee: on application.
Societies: catered for daily.
Catering: bar and catering daily.
Hotels: Old Hall (Sandbach); Saxon Cross Motel (M6 junction 17).

L88 The Manor Golf Club (Kingstone) Ltd
☎(01889) 563234
Leese Hill, Kingstone, Uttoxeter, Staffordshire ST14 8QT
On the main Uttoxeter - Stafford road
18 holes, 6200 yards, S.S.S.69
Designed by David Gough.
Founded 1992
Visitors: welcome.
Green Fee: WD £10 per round; WE £15 per round; half price with member.
Societies: welcome.
Catering: bar snacks.
5 bay driving range, putting green.

L89 Market Drayton
☎(01630) 652266
Sutton, Market Drayton, Shropshire
1.5 miles S of town.
Undulating meadowland course.
18 holes, 6266 yards, S.S.S.70
Founded 1911
Visitors: welcome except Sun and Bank Holidays.
Green Fee: £20.
Societies: welcome on application to Sec.
Catering: available all day.
Hotels: Corbet Arms; Bear Inn; bungalow (sleeps 6) available for rent.

L90 Marple
☎(0161) 427 2311, Pro 449 0690
Hawk Green, Marple, Stockport, Cheshire SK6 7EL

Off A6 at High Lane for 2 miles, left at Hawk Green.
Parkland/meadowland course.
18 holes, 5700 yards, S.S.S.67
Founded 1892
Visitors: welcome excluding competition days.
Green Fee: apply for details.
Societies: Mon, Tues and Fri only; special inclusive package for societies of 12 or more.
Catering: full facilities.
Hotels: West Towers.

L91 Mellor & Townscliffe
☎(0161) 427 2208, Pro 427 5759
Tarden, Gibb Lane, Mellor, Stockport, Cheshire SK6 5NA
Off A626 opposite Devonshire Arms on Longhurst Lane, Mellor.
Parkland/moorland course.
22 holes, 5925 yards, S.S.S.69
Founded 1894
Visitors: welcome, except Sat when must be with member.
Green Fee: WD £20 per day (£8 with member); WE & BH £27.50 (£10 with member).
Societies: welcome
Catering: full facilities, except Tues.
Hotels: Pack Horse Inn.

L92 Meole Brace
☎(01743) 364050
Meole Brace, Shrewsbury, Shropshire SY2 6QQ
S of Shrewsbury at junction of A5/A49.
Municipal parkland course with water features.
12 holes, 3335 yards, S.S.S.68
Founded 1976
Visitors: welcome.
Green Fee: apply for details.
Societies: welcome, booking weekends.

L93 Mere Golf & Country Club
☎(01565) 830155, Fax 830518
Chester Rd, Mere, Knutsford, Cheshire WA16 6LJ
From M6 junction 19 take A556 for 1 mile; from M56 junction 7 take A556 past Swan at Bucklow Hill.
Parkland course.
18 holes, 6817 yards, S.S.S.73
Designed by George Duncan and James Braid.
Founded 1934
Visitors: by prior arrangement Mon, Tues and Thurs.
Green Fee: £60.

Societies: Mon, Tues, Thurs.
Catering: very extensive; breakfast, lunch and dinner 7 days.
Driving range with floating golf balls (only open to golfing visitors).
Hotels: Swan (Bucklow Hill); Kilton Inn; Lord Daresbury; all offer discounted rates.

L94 Mile End

☎(01691) 670580 (Sec), Pro shop 671246.
Mile End, Oswestry, Shropshire SY11 4JE
1 mile SE of Oswestry, just off A5, well signposted.
Parkland/converted farmland course.
9 holes, 3065 yards, S.S.S.69 (18 holes from May)
Designed by Michael Price.
Founded June 1992
Visitors: all welcome with h/cap cert or proof of membership of recognised club; restrictions when members competitions in progress, please ring.
Green Fee: WD £10 (18 holes), £14 per day; WE £14/£18.
Societies: on application; discounts available.
Catering: lunchtime bar and meals except Wed.
Driving range.

L95 Mottram Hall Hotel

☎(01625) 820064, Bookings: 828135
Wilmslow Road, Mottram St Andrew, Prestbury, Cheshire SK10 4QT
From M56 junction 6 follow A538 through Wilmslow into Prestbury.
Parkland/woodland course.
18 holes, 7006 yards, S.S.S.74
Designed by David Thomas.
Founded May 1991
Visitors: welcome with h/cap cert.
Green Fee: apply for details.
Societies: welcome.
Catering: bar and restaurant, on course drink/food buggy,
Putting green, practice facilities, leisure centre at the hotel.
Hotels: Mottram Hall (133 beds).

L96 New Mills

☎(01663) 743485 (Club), Pro 746161
Shaw Marsh, New Mills, Stockport, Cheshire
Take St Mary Rd from centre of New Mills, about 0.75 miles.
Moorland course.
9 holes, 5707 yards, S.S.S.67
Founded 1907

Visitors: welcome weekdays and Sat am except competition days.
Green Fee: apply for details.
Societies: welcome weekdays by arrangement with Sec.
Catering: snacks and meals served.
Hotels: Pack Horse and Sportsman; Moorside.

L97 Newcastle Municipal

☎(01782) 627596
Newcastle Rd, Keele, Staffs ST5 2QB.
Off M6 at junction 15 onto A525 for 2 miles.
Public parkland course.
18 holes, 6256 yards, S.S.S.70
Founded 1975
Visitors: rounds bookable any time.
Green Fee: apply for details.
Societies: on application to Newcastle B.C. (01782) 717717.
Catering: bar/bar meals.
Driving range.
Hotels: Keele University Hospitality (opposite).

L98 Newcastle-under-Lyme

☎(01782) 618526 (Pro), Steward: 616583
Whitmore Rd, Newcastle under Lyme, Staffs ST5 2QB
1.5 miles SW of Newcastle under Lyme on A53.
Parkland course.
18 holes, 6229 yards, S.S.S.70
Founded 1908
Visitors: welcome weekdays; h/cap cert required.
Green Fee: apply for details.
Societies: catered for Mon all day and Thurs pm.
Catering: bar and restaurant.
Snooker.
Hotels: Post House; Borough Arms.

L99 Northenden

☎(0161) 998 4738 (Sec), Pro 945 3386, Steward/Members: 998 4079, Fax 945 5592.
Palatine Rd, Northenden, Manchester M22 4FR
M63 exit 9, 1 mile into Northenden.
Parkland course.
18 holes, 6503 yards, S.S.S.71
Founded 1913
Visitors: no restrictions, but phone.
Green Fee: £25 (£12 with member).
Societies: Tues and Fri.
Catering: bar and restaurant.
Snooker.
Hotels: Britannia; Post House.

L100 Onneley

☎(01782) 750577, Sec 846759
Onneley, Crewe, Cheshire CW3 5QF
1 mile from Woore on A51 to Newcastle.
Undulating meadowland course.
9 holes, 5584 yards, S.S.S.67
Founded 1968
Visitors: Mon - Fri; Sat only with member.
Green Fee: £15 per round (£8 with member)
Societies: welcome by prior booking with Sec; £18 per day including meal.
Catering: by arrangement with Stewardess (01782) 750577
Hotels: Wheatsheaf Inn.

L101 Oswestry

☎(01691) 610221, Sec 610535
Aston Park, Oswestry, Shropshire SY11 4JJ
NW of Shrewsbury, just off A5, 3 miles from Oswestry.
Parkland course.
18 holes, 6024 yards, S.S.S.69
Designed by James Braid.
Founded 1930
Visitors: welcome, must be member of club and hold h/cap cert or play with member.
Green Fee: WD £18; WE £25; reduction if playing with member.
Societies: Wed and Fri only.
Catering: every day.
Hotels: Wynstay; Sweeney Hall; Ashfield Country.

L102 Oxley Park

☎(01902) 25892 (Sec), Fax 712241
Bushbury, Wolverhampton WV10 6DE
A449, 1 mile N of Wolverhampton.
Parkland course.
18 holes, 6168 yards, S.S.S.69
Founded 1913
Visitors: welcome, booking advisable at weekends.
Green Fee: WD £20 per round, £24 per day.
Societies: Wed by arrangement.
Catering: breakfast, lunch, dinner.
Snooker.
Hotels: Mount; Goldthorn; Park Hall.

L103 Parkhall

☎(01782) 599584 Course Manager.
Hulme Road, Weston Coyney, Stoke-on-Trent, Staffs ST3 5BH
1 mile outside Longton on main A50.
Public moorland course.
18 holes, 2335 yards, Par 54
Founded Nov 1989

Visitors: welcome.
Green Fee: apply for details.
Societies: booking times: weekends and Bank Holidays only.

L104 **Patshull Park Hotel Golf and Country Club**

☎(01902) 700100 (Golf administrator), Fax 700874
Pattingham, Wolverhampton, WV6 7HR
M54 junction 3 onto A41 (Wolverhampton); right into Albrighton, right at Crown Inn cross-road, 1 mile to A464; right (Shifnal), 1st left to Patshull & Pattingham (via Burnhill Green): or A41 from W'ton/Whitchurch road, left to Pattingham.
Lakeside, parkland course.
18 holes, 6412 yards, S.S.S.72
Designed by John Jacobs.
Founded 1979
Visitors: welcome, telephone for tee reservation, h/cap preferred,
Green Fee: WD £22.50; WE £27.50; 2 day golf breaks from £105 (3 rounds, bed & breakfast, lunch and dinner)
Societies: full range of golf packages available from £30/head; telephone for details.
Catering: restaurant, coffee shop, golfers bar, banqueting/conferences catered for.
Snooker, practice ground, swimming, leisure club, gymnasium, trout & coarse fishing.
Hotels: own hotel group, residential bargain breaks.

L105 **Penn**

☎(01902) 341142
Penn Common, Penn, Wolverhampton, W Midlands WV4 5JN
2 miles SW of Wolverhampton off A449.
Heathland course.
18 holes, 6465 yards, S.S.S.71
Founded 1908
Visitors: welcome weekdays.
Green Fee: £20.
Societies: weekdays.
Catering: lunch weekdays except Mon; dinner weekdays except Mon and Wed.
Hotels: Goldthorn; Park Hall.

L106 **Peover**

☎(01565) 723337
Plumley Moor Road, Lower Peover, Nr Knutsford WA16 9SE
M6 junction 19 towards Chester, take A56 signposted Lower Peover turn left into Plumley Moor Road.
Parkland course
9 holes, 5487 yards, Par 70
Designed by P Naylor
Founded 1996
Visitors: pay & play
Green Fee: on application
Societies: Corporate days by arrangement.
Catering: Clubhouse opening summer 96
Hotels: Cottons Hotel (Knutsford)

L107 **Perton Park Golf Centre**

☎(01902) 380073
Wrottesley Park Road, Perton, Wolverhampton, W Midlands WV6 7HL
6 miles from Wolverhampton, just off A454 Bridgnorth to Wolverhampton road: or A41 Wolverhampton to Newport road 4 miles from Wolverhampton.
Flat meadowland course in open countryside.
18 holes, 6620 yards, S.S.S.70
Founded 1990
Visitors: welcome.
Green Fee: Mon - Fri £8 per round; WE & BH £15 per round; bookings advisable.
Societies: welcome by prior arrangement.
Catering: new club house with fully licensed bar and restaurant.
Driving range, snooker, bowling green.

L108 **Portal G & CC Premier Course**

☎(01829) 733884, Pro shop 733703, Fax 733666
Forest Rd, Tarporley, Cheshire CW6 0JA
Approx 15 miles S of Warrington on main A49, 0.5 mile N of Tarporley village.
Undulating parkland course.
18 holes, 6508 yards, S.S.S.72.
Founded May 1990
Visitors: welcome Mon-Fri.
Green Fee: WD £22 per round, £30 per day; WE £30 per round.
Societies: Mon-Fri by prior arrangement.
Catering: full restaurant and bar facilities.
Sauna, snooker; function room, banqueting for up to 200.
Hotels: Swan (Tarporley); Wild Boar (Beeston).

L109 **Portal G & CC**

☎(01829) 733933
Cobblers Cross, Tarporley, Cheshire CW6 0DJ
0.5 mile N of Tarporley village on A49, 10 miles N of Chester.
45 hole complex.
Public parkland course.
18 holes, 7145 yards, S.S.S.73.
Designed by Donald Steel
Founded May 1991
Visitors: welcome, no restrictions.
Green Fee: on application.
Societies: and corporate business days, catered for 7 days a week.
Catering: full facilities 7 days a week; 3 banqueting suites.
Hotels: Nunsmere Hall (Tarporley); Wild Boar (Beeston).

L110 **Poulton Park**

☎(01925) 812034, 825220
Dig Lane, Cinnamon Brow, Warrington
Off A574, turn into Crab Lane, 3 miles from Warrington.
Meadowland course.
9 holes, 5256 metres, S.S.S.66
Founded 1978
Visitors: welcome weekdays, restricted weekends.
Green Fee: on application.
Societies: weekdays.
Catering: meals served except Mon.
Hotels: Paddington House; Garden Court.

L111 **Prenton**

☎(0151) 608 1053, 608 1461, Pro 608 1636
Golf Links Rd, Prenton, Birkenhead, Wirral L42 8LW
2 miles W of Birkenhead off A552; M53 junction 3.
Flat parkland course.
18 holes, 6411 yards, S.S.S.71
Designed by Colt Mackenzie & Co.
Founded 1905
Visitors: welcome any day except competition days (Sat in summer).
Green Fee: WD £25 (£10 with member); WE & BH £30.
Societies: Wed and Fri by prior arrangement.
Catering: full service available.
Snooker.
Hotels: Leasowe Castle; Crabwell Manor; Riverhill; Bowler Hat.

L112 **Prestbury**

☎(01625) 828241
Macclesfield Rd, Prestbury, Cheshire SK10 4BJ

2 miles NW of Macclesfield on Macclesfield Rd leaving Prestbury village.
Undulating parkland course.
18 holes, 6359 yards, S.S.S.71
Designed by Colt & Morrison.
Founded 1920
Visitors: welcome weekdays, with member at weekends; advisable to phone in advance.
Green Fee: apply for details.
Societies: Thurs only, by prior arrangement.
Catering: lunches, dinners and bar snacks
Hotels: The Bridge; Edge; Mottram Hall.

L113 **Pryors Hayes Golf Club**

☎(01829) 741250 (Sec), 740140
Willington Road, Oscroft, Tarvin, Nr Chester, Cheshire CH3 8NL
Just off A51 - 6 miles from Chester
Parkland course.
18 holes, 5993 yards, S.S.S.69
Designed by John Day
Founded 1993
Visitors: welcome
Green Fee: WD £15 per round; WE £20 per round.
Societies: packages available.
Catering: full facilities.
Putting green
Hotels: Willington Hall

L114 **Queen's Park**

☎(01270) 666724
Queen's Park Drive, Crewe, Cheshire, CW2 7SB.
Just off Victoria Ave to S of Crewe centre.
Public meadowland course
9 holes, 2460 yards, S.S.S.64
Founded 1985
Visitors: welcome except Sun before 10.30am.
Green Fee: on application
Societies: welcome by arrangment.
Catering: bar and bar meals available.
Bowls, tennis.
Hotels: Crewe Arms; Hunter's Lodge.

L115 **Reaseheath**

☎(01270) 625131
Reaseheath College, Nantwich, Cheshire
Research course, approved centre for greenkeeper training.
9 holes 3332 yards, S.S.S.54
Designed by D. Mortram
Founded 1987

Visitors: small parties and societies only, min 8; by prior arrangement; April-Oct preferred
Green Fee: £3 (18 holes).
Catering: at local hostelry.

L116 **Reddish Vale**

☎(0161)480 2359, Pro 480 3824.
Southcliffe Rd, Reddish, Stockport, Cheshire SK5 7EE
1.5 miles N of Stockport, off Reddish road B6167.
Undulating course in valley.
18 holes, 6086 yards, S.S.S.69
Designed by Dr A. Mackenzie.
Founded 1912
Visitors: welcome weekdays (not 12.30-1.30pm), with member only at weekends.
Green Fee: £22.
Societies: weekdays by prior arrangement.
Catering: generally available during normal bar opening hours.
Hotels: Belgrade; Old Rectory, Haughton Green.

L117 **Ringway**

☎(0161) 980 8432 (Pro), Sec 980 2630, **Catering:** 904 0940.
Hale Rd, Hale Barns, Altrincham, Cheshire WA15 8SW
8 miles S of Manchester, 1 mile from juction 6 - M56 on the A538 towards Altrincham just through Hale Barns village.
Parkland course.
18 holes, 6494 yards, S.S.S.71
Designed by Harry Colt and James Braid.
Founded 1909
Visitors: welcome, but not Friday; Tues and Sat are Club competition days.
Green Fee: WD £28; WE £34.
Societies: Thur only, May-Sep, by prior arrangement.
Catering: full facilities available by arrangement with Catering Manageress.
Snooker.
Hotels: Cresta Court; Four Seasons; Unicorn.

L118 **Romiley**

☎(0161) 430 2392
Goosehouse Green, Romiley, Stockport SK6 4LJ
On B6104 off A560, 0.75 mile from Romiley station.
Undulating parkland course.
18 holes, 6335 yards, S.S.S.70
Founded 1897

Visitors: welcome except Thurs (Ladies Day).
Green Fee: apply for details.
Societies: by prior arrangement; apply to Sec.
Catering: full service.

L119 **Royal Liverpool**

☎(0151) 632 3101 (Sec), Starter: 632 6757, Pro 632 5868 Fax 632 6737
Meols Drive, Hoylake, Wirral, Merseyside L47 4AL
On A553 from M53 junction 2.
Championship links course.
18 holes, 6835 yards, S.S.S.74
Founded 1869
Visitors: welcome by prior arrangement with Sec or Starter.
Members priority to 9.30am and 1-2pm; Thurs am Ladies.
Green Fee: WD £47.50 per round, £65 per day; WE £65 per round, £95 per day.
Societies: Tue-Fri (not Thurs am) by arrangement.
Catering: soup/sandwiches available daily, dining room (jacket and tie required) for lunches or dinners by prior arrangement (minimum 20 persons)
Snooker, practice range.
Hotels: Crabwall Manor (Chester); Thornton Hall (Thronton Hough); Bowler Hat (Oxton).

L120 **Runcorn**

☎(01928) 572093, Sec 574214
Clifton Rd, Runcorn, Cheshire WA7 4SU
Signposted The Heath off A557.
High parkland course.
18 holes, 6035 yards, S.S.S.69
Founded 1909
Visitors: welcome weekdays except Tues; not Sat/Sun unless with member; bona fide h/cap cert required.
Green Fee: WD £18 per day; WE & BH £21 per day.
Societies: Mon and Fri.
Catering: bar and dining room, meals by arrangement.
Snooker.
Hotels: Crest.

L121 **St Michael Jubilee**

☎(0151) 424 6230, 423 6461
Dundalk Rd, Widnes, Cheshire
Close to Widnes centre.
Public parkland course
18 holes, 5668 yards, S.S.S.67
Founded 1977

Visitors: welcome weekdays, with booking at weekends.
Green Fee: apply for details.
Societies: welcome by arrangement.
Catering: full facilities.
Practice area.
Hotels: Hillcrest.

L122 St Thomas's Priory Golf Club
☎(01543) 491911/491116, Pro Shop 492096, Fax 492244
Armitage Lane, Armitage, Nr. Rugeley, Staffordshire WS15 1ED
On A513 between Armitage and Rugeley, entrance to club opposite Ash Tree public house.
Undulating parkland course
18 holes, 6150 yards, S.S.S.71
Designed by Paul Mulholland
Founded 1995
Visitors: with members only
Green Fee: £10 with member
Societies: on application
Catering: Restaurant
Practice facilities

L123 Sale
☎(0161) 973 1730 (Pro), Manager: 973 1638, **Catering:** 973 3404.
Sale Lodge, Golf Rd, Sale, Cheshire M33 2XU
Edge of Sale, 1 mile from station, half mile from M63 junction 8.
Parkland course.
18 holes, 6352 yards, S.S.S.70
Founded 1913
Visitors: welcome any day, phone for confirmation.
Green Fee: WD £24; WE & BH £30.
Societies: by arrangement with Manager.
Catering: bar and catering 7 days.
Snooker.
Hotels: Post House; Normanhurst; Lennox Lea.

L124 Sandbach
☎(01270) 762117, Steward: 759227
117 Middlewich Rd, Sandbach, Cheshire CW11 1FH
1 mile N of town centre on A533 Middlewich Rd. off M6 junction 17.
Meadowland course.
9 holes, 5598 yards, S.S.S.67
Founded 1921
Visitors: welcome weekdays; weekends and Bank Holidays by invitation only.
Green Fee: £16 per round per day.
Societies: limited to a few each year.
Catering: except Mon and Thurs.
Hotels: Saxon Cross Motel; Old Hall.

L125 Sandiway
☎(01606) 883247 (Sec), Pro 883180, Fax 888548
Chester Rd, Sandiway, Northwich, Cheshire CW8 2DJ
On A556 14 miles E of Chester, 4 miles from Northwich.
Undulating parkland course.
18 holes, 6435 yards, S.S.S.72
Designed by Ted Ray.
Founded 1921
Visitors: weekdays and certain weekends with letter of intro.
Green Fee: WD £30; WE & BH £35.
Societies: catered for Tues.
Catering: meals daily by arrangement.
Hotels: Hartford Hall; Oaklands.

L126 Sandwell Park
☎(0121) 553 4637 (Sec), Pro 553 4384
Birmingham Rd, West Bromwich, W Midlands B71 4JJ
M5 junction 1, 0.25 mile from West Bromwich Albion Football Ground.
Parkland/heathland course.
18 holes, 6422 yards, S.S.S.72
Founded 1897
Visitors: weekdays unlimited; weekends with member.
Green Fee: Apr-Oct £25 (18 holes); £27.50 (27 holes); £35 (36 holes).
Societies: any weekday, £27.50 (27 holes), £32.50 (36 holes).
Catering: full facilities except Mon.
Hotels: Moat House.

L127 Sedgley Golf Centre
☎(01902) 880503
Sandyfields Rd, Sedgeley, Dudley, W Midlands DY3 3DL
0.5 mile from Sedgley town centre near Cotwall End Nature Centre, just off A463.
Pay-as-you-play course; wooded, undulating with extensive views.
9 holes, 3147 yards, Par 37.
Designed by W.G. Cox.
Founded Sept 1989
Visitors: booking required at weekends.
Green Fee: WD £4.50 (9 holes), £6.50 (18 holes); WE £5.00 (9 holes), £7.00 (18 holes).
Societies: weekdays preferred by prior arrangement.
Catering: meals available for societies by arrangement; all day breakfasts Sat, am only Sun.
Driving range.
Hotels: Himley House, Park Hall (Wolverhampton); Station, Ward Arms (Dudley).

L128 Seedy Mill
☎(01543) 417333
Elm Hurst, Lichfield, Staffs WS13 8HE
1.5 miles N of Lichfield off A515.
Undulating parkland course.
18 holes, 6247 yards, S.S.S.70; also 9 hole Par 3 course.
Designed by Hawtree & Sons.
Founded 1991
Visitors: welcome; pay-as-you-play.
Green Fee: WD £16 per round; WE £22 per round.
Societies: welcome
Catering: full facilities.
Hotels: Little Barrow (Lichfield).

L129 Severn Meadows
☎(01746) 862212
Highley, Nr Bridgnorth, Shropshire WV16 6HZ
10 miles N of Bewdley via B4194, B4363, B4555; 8 miles S of Bridgenorth.
Hilly parkland course in Severn Valley.
9 holes, 5258 yards, S.S.S.67
Founded 1989
Visitors: welcome weekdays, pay-as-you-play, must book at weekends.
Green Fee: apply for details.
Societies: booking only.
Catering: clubhouse and bar, meals to order.
Putting green, practice nets.
Hotels: Bull (Chelmarsh).

L130 Shifnal
☎(01952) 460330
Decker Hill, Shifnal, Shropshire TF11 8QL
On B4379 1 mile from Shifnal; from M54 junction 4 turn left, left again, travel with motorway for 2 miles, left again, 500 yards left again.
Parkland course.
18 holes, 6422 yards, S.S.S.71
Designed by Frank Pennink.
Founded 1929
Visitors: weekdays; weekends only with member.
Green Fee: WD £22 per round, £30 per day.
Societies: Tues, Wed or Fri.
Catering: lunch and evening meals available.
Hotels: Park House; Jerningham Arms.

L131 Shrewsbury
☎(01743) 872977 (Sec), Pro 873751, Club 872976
Condover, Shropshire SY5 7BL

4 miles SW of Shrewsbury, follow signs for Condover and golf club. Parkland course. 18 holes, 6178 yards, S.S.S.69 Designed by C.K. Cotton, Pennink, Lawrie & Partners. Founded 1890
Visitors: must have h/cap certs.
Green Fee: WD £16.50 per round, £21.50 per day; WE & BH £20.50 per round, £26.50 per day.
Societies: apply to Pro.
Catering: full facilities available. Snooker.
Hotels: Deanhurst.

L132 **Shrigley Hall Hotel**
☎(01625) 575757, Fax 573323
Shrigley Park, Pott Shrigley, Macclesfield, Cheshire SK10 5SB.
From M63 Stockport take A6 towards Hazel Grove and Buxton, then A523 towards Macclesfield; turn left at Lee Arms in Adlington, signposted Pott Shrigley, 2 miles.
Parkland course.
18 holes; 6305 yards, S.S.S.71
Designed by Donald Steel.
Founded 2 May 1989
Visitors: welcome.
Green Fee: WD £20 per round; WE £30 per round.
Societies: welcome by prior arrangement.
Catering: bars and restaurants. Pitch & Putt, swimming, tennis, squash, fishing and other leisure facilities.
Hotels: Shrigley Hall (weekend golfing packages available).

L133 **The Shropshire**
☎(01952) 677800 (Bookings), Pro shop 677866, Fax 677622
Muxton Grange, Muxton, Telford, Shropshire TF2 8PQ
5 miles NE of Telford; 5 mins from M54 junction 4 on B5060, signposted off Granville roundabout and located next to Granville Country Park.
Pay-as-you-Play, variable undulating course.
27 holes, 3 loops of 9 (Blue, Silver, Gold), Par 71-72
Designed by Martin Hawtree
Founded July 1992
Visitors: open 7 days a week, booking up to 7 days in advance; correct dress required.
Green Fee: WD £7.50 (9 holes), £12 (18 holes); WE £12 (9 holes), £18 (18 holes); reductions for jnrs.
Societies: 7 days a week with prior booking.

Catering: 2 traditional bars, snack bar, 80-seat restaurant, 5 function rooms, 240-seat permanent marquee. Driving range, 12 hole Pitch & Putt, 18-hole and 9-hole putting greens.
Hotels: details on request.

L134 **South Staffordshire**
☎(01902) 751065
(Sec/Manager/bookings), Pro 754816
Danescourt Rd, Tettenhall, Wolverhampton WV6 9BQ
A41 from Wolverhampton to Tettenhall, clubhouse and course behind cricket club.
Parkland course.
18 holes, 6513 yards, S.S.S.71
Designed by Harry Vardon (original); H.S. Colt.
Founded 1892
Visitors: weekdays except Tues am.
Green Fee: WD £30 per round, £35 per day; WE £40
Societies: welcome except Tues am and weekends.
Catering: snacks, lunches, dinners available.
Hotels: Mount; Connaught (Wolverhampton).

L135 **Stafford Castle**
☎(01785) 223821
Newport Rd, Stafford
0.5 mile from Stafford main street.
Meadowland course.
9 holes, 6832 yards, S.S.S.70
Founded 1907
Visitors: welcome weekdays.
Green Fee: £14
Societies: by prior arrangement.
Catering: bar meals daily, others by arrangement
Hotels: Swan; Tillington Hall; Vine.

L136 **Stamford**
☎(01457) 832126, Pro 834829
Oakfield House, Huddersfield Rd, Heyheads, Stalybridge, Cheshire SK15 3PY
On B6175 Huddersfield Rd, 3 miles from Ashton-under-Lyne off A6108.
Undulating moorland course.
18 holes, 5701 yards, S.S.S.68
Founded 1900
Visitors: welcome weekdays (Ladies Day Tues afternoon); restricted weekends.
Green Fee: WD £20 per day, £10 with member.
Societies: weekdays except Mon and Tues.
Catering: meals served except Mon.
Hotels: York House (Ashton-u-Lyne).

L137 **Stockport**
☎(0161) 427 2001/Fax, Sec 427 8369, Pro 427 2421
Offerton Rd, Offerton, Stockport SK2 5HL
1 mile along A627 from Hazel Grove to Marple.
Parkland course.
18 holes, 6326 yards, S.S.S.71
Founded 1906
Visitors: members of other clubs welcome.
Green Fee: on application
Societies: Wed and Thur.
Catering: restaurant (closed Mon).

L138 **Stone**
☎(01785) 813103
Filleybrooks, Stone, Staffs ST15 0NB
0.5 mile N of Stone on A34 next to Wayfarer Hotel.
Meadowland course.
9 holes, 6299 yards, S.S.S.70
Founded 1896
Visitors: welcome weekdays.
Green Fee: £15 per round, £20 per day.
Societies: welcome weekdays by prior arrangement.
Catering: lunches and evening meals available.
Hotels: Stonehouse (on A34); Crown.

L139 **Styal**
☎(01625) 530063
Station Road, Styal SK9 4JN
Alongside Styal railway station
Parkland course
18 holes, 6312 yards, S.S.S.70
Founded 1994
Visitors: pay & play
Green Fee: WD £12; WE £16
Societies: welcome
Catering: no clubhouse

L140 **Sutton Hall**
☎(01928) 714872
Sutton Hall, Aston Lane, Sutton Weaver, Nr Frodsham WA7 3ED
Off junction 12 - M56 towards Frodsham.
Parkland course
18 holes, 6547 yards, S.S.S.71
Founded Oct 1995
Visitors: not before Summer 96
Societies: not before Summer 96
Catering: telephone for details.

L141 **Swindon**
☎(01902) 897031
Bridgnorth Road, Swindon, Dudley, West Midlands DY3 4PU

On B4176 Bridgnorth road, 5 miles from Wolverhampton; just off A449 Stourbridge to Wolverhampton road. Woodland/parkland course; exceptional views.
18 holes, 6091 yards, S.S.S.69; 9 holes Par-3, 1135 yards.
Founded 1974
Visitors: welcome, booking not required.
Green Fee: WD £18 per round, £28 per day; WE & BH £27 per round, £40 per day.
Societies: by arrangement weekdays only.
Catering: fully licensed bar and restaurant.
Driving range, snooker table.

L142 **Tamworth Municipal**
☎(01827) 53850
Eagle Drive, Amington, Tamworth, Staffs B77 4EG
M42 junction 10, proced towards Tamworth, signposted round town; off B5000 Polesworth road.
Municipal parkland course.
18 holes, 6605 yards, S.S.S.72
Founded 1975
Visitors: welcome 7 days.
Green Fee: £8.50/adult, £4.50 jnrs/OAPs.
Societies: Mon to Fri.
Catering: bar and daily catering; special functions by prior arrangement.
Practice area, snooker (club members).
Hotels: Canada Lodge (M42).

L143 **Telford Golf & Country Moat House**
☎(01952) 429977 (Tel/Fax)
Great Hay, Telford, Shropshire TF7 4DT
Off A442 at Sutton Hill, S of Telford.
Undulating meadowland course.
18 holes, 6274 yards, S.S.S.70
Designed by John Harris.
Founded 1981
Visitors: welcome with h/cap cert.
Green Fee: apply for details.
Societies: by arrangement.
Catering: meals served every day.
Driving range, squash, swimming pool, snooker, sauna etc.
Hotels: Telford Hotel Country Club.

L144 **Three Hammers Golf Complex**
☎(01902) 790428
Old Stafford Rd, Coven, Staffordshire WV10 7PP

M54 junction 2, N on A449, course 1 mile on right.
Public 18 hole Par 3 short course.
Designed by Henry Cotton.
Visitors: welcome.
Green Fee: on application.
Societies: welcome weekdays and Sat.
Catering: bar and bistro, à la carte restaurant, private dining facilities.
Driving range.

L145 **Trentham Park**
☎(01782) 658800, Pro 642125
Trentham Park, Trentham, Stoke-on-Trent ST4 8AE
4 miles S of Newcastle under Lyme on A34, 1 mile from M6 junction 15.
Parkland course.
18 holes, 6422 yards, S.S.S.71
Founded 1936
Visitors: h/cap and club membership required.
Green Fee: WD £22.50 per round, £25 per day; WE & BH £30
Societies: Wed and Fri.
Catering: full facilities.
Snooker.
Hotels: Clayton Lodge; Post House.

L146 **Trentham**
☎(01782) 658109, Pro 657309
14 Barlaston Old Rd, Trentham, Stoke-on-Trent ST4 8HB
Off M6 junction 15 towards Stoke, follow A34 to Trentham Gardens, turn left, 1st right.
Parkland course.
18 holes, 6644 yards, S.S.S.72
Founded 1894
Visitors: welcome with h/cap cert; not Sat or Sun am.
Green Fee: £30.
Societies: Wed, Thurs, max 40.
Catering: bar and restaurant.
Squash, snooker.
Hotels: Post House; Clayton Lodge; Stonehouse (Stone).

L147 **The Tytherington**
☎(01625) 434562
Macclesfield, Cheshire, SK10 2JP
Approx 2 miles from Macclesfield on A523 Stockport road.
Modern championship parkland course.
18 holes, 6765 yards, S.S.S.73
(Ladies 5592 yards, S.S.S.75).
Designed by Dave Thomas, Patrick Dawson.
Founded Oct 1986
Visitors: h/cap certs required.
Green Fee: on application

Societies: weekdays.
Catering: bar, conservatory, restaurant, private rooms available.
Tennis, snooker, pool, health club.
Hotels: special arrangments with local hotels.

L148 **Upton-by-Chester**
☎(01244) 381183 (Sec), Pro 381333
Upton Lane, Chester CH2 1EE
Off A41 Liverpool-Chester road, near Upton zoo.
Parkland course.
18 holes, 5808 yards, Par 69
Founded 1934
Visitors: Unlimited except competition days.
Green Fee: WD £20 per day; WE £25.
Societies: Wed, Thurs, Fri.
Catering: full restaurant facilities available.
Hotels: Mollington Banastre; Dene; Euro Hotel.

L149 **Uttoxeter**
☎(01889) 565108, Pro 564884, Sec 566552
Wood Lane, Uttoxeter, Staffs ST14 8JR
Off B5017 Uttoxeter-Marchington road, about 0.5 mile along Wood Lane, just past race course.
Moorland course
18 holes, 5468 yards, S.S.S.68
Founded 1972
Visitors: welcome except invitation days etc; subject to availability.
Green Fee: WD £15; WE £20; half price with member and jnrs.
Societies: all year by arrangement; £30 per person, min 4.
Catering: available except Mon.
Pool.
Hotels: White Hart.

L150 **Vicars Cross**
☎(01244) 335174, Pro 335595
Tarvin Rd, Great Barrow, Chester CH3 7HN
A51 3 miles E of Chester.
Undulating parkland course.
18 holes, 6243 yards, S.S.S.70
Designed by E. Parr.
Founded 1939
Visitors: welcome Mon-Thurs all day; course closed for major competitions, advisable to ring beforehand for availability.
Green Fee: £22 per day.
Societies: Tues, Thurs.
Catering: full facilities.
Hotels: Oaklands; Hoole Hall.

L151 **Wallasey**

☎(0151) 691 1024, Pro 638 3888
Bayswater Rd, Wallasey, Merseyside
L45 8LA
From Liverpool through Wallasey
Tunnel to junction 1; follow signs to
New Brighton.
Seaside links course.
18 holes, 6607 yards, S.S.S.73
Designed by Tom Morris Snr.
Founded 1891
Visitors: welcome weekdays, limited
weekends.
Green Fee: WD £32 per day; WE
£37 per day; £15 with member.
Societies: Mon-Fri by arrangement.
Catering: full facilities.
Snooker.
Hotels: Leasowe Castle; Grove
House.

L152 **Walsall**

☎(01922) 613512
The Broadway, Walsall, W Midlands
WS1 3EY
1 mile S of Walsall centre, 400 yards
from the Boundary; take A34 from M6
junction 7.
Parkland/meadowland course.
18 holes, 6232 yards, S.S.S.70
Founded 1907
Visitors: welcome weekdays, with
member weekends.
Green Fee: on application
Societies: welcome.
Catering: full service.

L153 **Walton Hall**

☎(01925) 266775 (Club), Pro
shop/bookings: 263061
Warrington Rd, Higher Walton,
Warrington WA4 5LU
1 mile from M56 junction 11; turn right
at 2nd set of traffic lights.
Municipal, scenic parkland course.
18 holes, 6801 yards, S.S.S.73
Designed by Dave Thomas.
Founded 1972
Visitors: welcome unrestricted; 6am
onwards in summer, 8am onwards in
winter.
Green Fee: WD £6.50; WE £8.00.
Societies: by arrangement through
Pro shop.
Catering: full service available 1st
April to 31st Oct.

L154 **Warren**

☎(0151) 639 5730
The Grange, Grove Rd, Wallasey,
Merseyside
500 yards up Grove Rd, beyond
Grove Rd station.

Municipal links course.
9 holes, 2945 yards, S.S.S.36
Founded 1911
Visitors: welcome weekdays; phone
first at weekends.
Green Fee: apply for details.
Hotels: Grove House.

L155 **Warrington**

☎(01925) 265431 (Pro), Sec 261775
London Rd, Appleton, Warrington,
Cheshire WA4 5HR
On A49 from M56 or S on A49
through town, 3 miles S of
Warrington.
Undulating parkland course.
18 holes, 6217 yards, S.S.S.70
Designed by James Braid.
Founded 1902
Visitors: welcome.
Green Fee: on application
Societies: welcome by prior
arrangement; apply to Sec.
Catering: available except Mon.

L156 **Wergs**

☎(01902) 742225
Keepers Lane, Tettenhall,
Wolverhampton WV6 8UA
Follow A41 Telford road out of
Wolverhampton for approx 2.5 miles;
turn right (course signposted) into
Keepers Lane, course is 0.5 mile
on right.
Public parkland course.
18 holes, 6949 yards, S.S.S.73
Designed by C.W. Moseley.
Founded June 1990
Visitors: pay-as-you-play.
Green Fee: WD £12.50; WE & BH
£15.
Societies: at all times.
Catering: lounge/spike bar and
restaurant.
Large practice area.
Hotels: Novotel (W'hampton).

L157 **Werneth Low**

☎(0161) 368 2503
Werneth Low Rd, Hyde, Cheshire
SK14 3AF
2 miles from Hyde town centre via
Gee Cross and Joel Lane.
Hill top course.
11 holes, 6113 yards, S.S.S.70
Designed by Peter Campbell.
Founded 1912
Visitors: welcome except Sun.
Green Fee: £12
Societies: weekdays by
arrangement.
Catering: facilities available daily,
except Wed.

L158 **Westminster Park**

☎(01244) 680231
Hough Green, Chester, Cheshire
CH4 8JQ
In Saltney on SW outskirts of
Chester.
Public parkland course
9 holes Par 3, 900 yards, S.S.S.27
Visitors: welcome.
Green Fee: apply for details.

L159 **Westwood (Leek)**

☎(01538) 398897 (Pro), Sec 398385
Wallbridge, Newcastle Rd, Leek,
Staffs ST13 7AA
0.5 mile S of Leek on A53.
Moorland/parkland course.
18 holes, 6207 yards, S.S.S.69
Founded 1923
Visitors: welcome weekdays, only if
accompanied by a member Sat; not
Sun.
Green Fee: £18 (£7 with member).
Societies: Mon and Thurs or other
days by prior arrangement, contact
Mr C Plant.
Catering: available.
Snooker, pool.

L160 **Whiston Hall**

☎(01538) 266260, (0850) 903815
Whiston, Nr Cheadle, Staffs ST10
2HZ
A52 midway between Stoke-on-Trent
and Ashbourne, 3 miles from Alton
Towers.
Challenging course set in beautiful
countryside.
18 holes, 5784 yards, S.S.S.69
Designed by Thomas Cooper.
Founded 1971
Visitors: welcome, but please avoid
7am-10am Sun, and 10.30am-
1.30pm Sat.
Green Fee: WD £10; WE & BH £14.
Societies: welcome any time by prior
arrangement.
Catering: bar and catering at
weekends all year, some weekdays in
summer.
snooker, fly fishing lakes.
Hotels: Stakis Grand (Stoke-on-
Trent)

L161 **Whittington Heath**

☎(01543) 432317 (Sec/admin), Pro
432261, Steward: 432212
Tamworth Rd, Lichfield, WS14 9PW
On A51 2.5 miles from Lichfield
station.
Heathland course.
18 holes, 6458 yards, S.S.S.71
Founded 1886

Visitors: welcome weekdays with h/cap cert or letter of intro.
Green Fee: £32 per day per round.
Societies: Wed, Thurs max 40.
Catering: snack lunches, evening meals available except Mon.
Hotels: George; Little Barrow; Swan.

L162 **Widnes**
☎(0151) 424 2995
Highfield Rd, Widnes, Cheshire
Near town centre.
Parkland course.
18 holes, 5688 yards, S.S.S.67
Founded 1924
Visitors: welcome weekdays.
Green Fee: apply for details.
Societies: weekdays, except Tues.
Catering: meals by arrangement.

L163 **Wilmslow**
☎(01565) 872148 (Sec), Pro 873620
Great Warford, Mobberley, Knutsford, Cheshire WA16 7AY
2 miles from Wilmslow on B5085 Knutsford road, turn at Warford Lane.
Parkland course.
18 holes, 6607 yards, S.S.S.72
Founded 1889
Visitors: welcome Mon-Fri; restricted weekends, Wed after 2pm.
Green Fee: WD £30 per round, £40 per day; WE £40 per round, £50 per day.
Societies: Tues and Thurs.
Catering: full facilities.
Hotels: Edge; The Belfry.

L164 **Wirral Ladies**
☎(0151) 652 1255
93 Bidston Rd, Oxton, Birkenhead, Merseyside L43 6TS
On A41 adjacent to M53 exit 3.
Moorland course.
18 holes, 4966 yards, S.S.S.69
Designed by H. Hilton.
Founded 1894
Visitors: welcome anytime.
Green Fee: £20 per round.
Societies: apply to Sec.
Catering: meals at all times.

L165 **Withington**
☎(0161) 445 9544, Pro 445 4861,
Catering: 434 8716
243 Palatine Rd, West Didsbury, Manchester M20 8UD
From Manchester S on A5103 then B5166 through Northenden.
Parkland course.
18 holes, 6424 yards, S.S.S.71
Founded 1892
Visitors: weekdays; weekends with member
Green Fee: £24 per round, £27 per day.
Societies: welcome
Catering: full facilities; phone caterer in advance.
Hotels: Britania Ringway.

L166 **Wolstanton**
☎(01782) 622413 (Sec), Clubhouse 616995, Pro 622718
Dimsdale Old Hall, Hassam Parade, Newcastle under Lyme, Staffs ST5 9DR
1.5 miles NW of Newcastle under Lyme on A34, turn off at The Sportsman Hotel into Dimsdale Parade, then 1st right into Hassam Parade.
Meadowland/parkland course.
18 holes, 5807 yards, S.S.S.68
Founded 1904

Visitors: welcome weekdays.
Green Fee: on application.
Societies: welcome Mon, Wed, Thurs and Fri.
Catering: lunches served Mon-Sat.
Hotels: The Friendly Hotel

L167 **Worfield**
☎(01746) 716372 (Sec), Pro 716541
Roughton, Nr Bridgnorth, Shropshire WV15 5HE
On A454 Bridgenorth-Wolverhampton road.
Parkland course.
18 holes, 6798 yards, S.S.S.73
Designed by T. Williams.
Founded Sept 1987
Visitors: welcome Mon-Fri, after 10am Sat/Sun; h/cap cert required.
Green Fee: WD £15 per round, £20 per day; WE £20 per round, £25 per day.
Societies: welcome at all times.
Catering: bars and restaurant, all catering available.
Practice area.
Hotels: Vicarage (Worfield); Pengwern (Shrewsbury).

L168 **Wrekin**
☎(01952) 244032 (Sec/club), Pro 223101
Ercall Woods, Wellington, Telford TF6 5BX
Off M54 back along B5061 to Golf Links Lane.
Parkland course.
18 holes, 5699 yards, S.S.S.67
Founded 1905
Visitors: welcome weekdays.
Green Fee: apply for details.
Societies: weekdays except Mon.
Catering: booked in advance.

DERBYSHIRE, NOTTINGHAMSHIRE, LINCOLNSHIRE

The greatest news for the region came with the announcement early in 1995 that the English Golf Union is to establish a national headquarters at Woodhall Spa. This includes the setting up of offices, the design of a second course and the building of the finest teaching centre in the land. In a beautiful setting of sylvan splendour will be a driving range and a separate short game practice area. Construction of the second course began in July 1995 with an opening date projected for 1998, a year after the driving range.

Lincolnshire can also boast rare coastal delights in the shape of Seacroft at Skegness. Golfers place a high premium on tranquillity particularly when seeking a leisurely round and Seacroft fits that bill admirably. Its true seaside qualities may be slow to blossom as the opening holes are flanked on the right by trim avenues and typically large Lincolnshire fields. Out of bounds, in fact, is an obvious threat most of the way to the turn but, from the moment that the short 10th turns back, diagonally to the line of play hitherto, there are inspiring sights of the sea and many memorable holes.

Seacroft lies on the opposite side of The Wash from Hunstanton on the edge of the Gibraltar Road wildlife sanctuary which epitomises its joyous remoteness. It is the only true seaside links between Hunstanton and Seaton Carew, a pick of the Eastern seaboard and a perfect foil for Woodhall Spa which highlights the best of inland golf, a stout championship challenge among glorious heathland, deep bunkers and handsome trees. A word too, for Luffenham Heath near Stamford which is almost as good and a welcome to Forest Pines, a new neighbour to Scunthorpe Golf Club and Holme Hall.

Moving westwards, the Notts Golf Club at Hollinwell is a rival to Woodhall Spa in its severity as a test and in a pleasant setting that largely obscures evidence of the mining community that surrounds it. It lies in a gentle valley fringed by pine trees and boasts a collection of par 4s which are notably good. There is also a little climbing to be done which tends to be enlightening rather than exhausting. Hollinwell has distinguished neighbours in Sherwood Forest and Coxmoor, courses that enjoy similarly appealing golfing terrain with problems to match.

Part of Lindrick falls in Nottinghamshire although I am inclined to think the bulk of it is in Yorkshire – or used to be. However, wherever its loyalties are directed, it is a superb course that has rightly attracted its share of big events including victory in the 1957 Ryder Cup at a time when Great Britain and Ireland were not used to winning. Newark is worthy of recommendation and Wollaton Park in Nottingham has housed professional events.

If Derbyshire, the third county in this particular trinity, lacks the outstanding courses of the other two, some of them bear the signature of famous architects. Cavendish at Buxton is the work of Alister Mackenzie while James Braid and John Morrison had a hand in Kedleston Park. To Harry Colt goes the credit for Chesterfield and Frank Pennink made changes at Mickleover. Chevin is another Derbyshire gem, a mile or two across the moor from Breadsall Priory Hotel Golf and Country Club and its two contrasting courses.

The first course, opened in 1977, indulges in a good deal of up and down but the second course, which opened in 1992, commands marvellous views with exactly the same feeling of escape that can be experienced on the distant coast at Seacroft.

M1 **Alfreton**

☎(01773) 832070, Pro 831901
Highfields, Wingfield Rd, Oakthorpe,
Derbys DE5 7DH
Matlock road from Alfreton, 0.75 mile.
Parkland course.
11 holes, 5074 yards, S.S.S.65
Founded 1892
Visitors: welcome; Sat, Sun and Mon
with member only.
Green Fee: £13 per round, £17 per
day.
Societies: weekdays; consult Sec.
Catering: full facilities except Mon.
Hotels: Swallow (S Normanton);
Granada (Swanwick).

M2 **Allestree Park**

☎(01332) 550616 (Pro), Clubhouse
552971, Fax 541195
Allestree Hall, Allestree, Derbys

Leave Derby on A6, 4 miles from city
centre, signposted Allestree Park.
Undulating parkland course.
18 holes, 5774 yards, S.S.S.68
Founded 1940
Visitors: welcome at all times, except
for competition days or Sun
mornings.
Green Fee: on application.
Societies: welcome.
Catering: by prior arrangement;
(01332) 552971.
Hotels: Clovelly (Derby); Mickleover
Court; Travelodge.

M3 **Ashbourne**

☎(01335) 342078
Clifton, Nr Ashbourne, Derbys DE6
4BN
1 mile S of Ashbourne on A515 to
Sudbury and Lichfield.

Undulating parkland course.
9 holes, 5359 yards, S.S.S.66
Designed by Frank Pennink.
Founded 1910
Visitors: welcome.
Green Fee: WD £14; WE £18.
Societies: by prior arrangement.
Catering: by arrangement.

M4 **Bakewell**

☎(01629) 812307
Station Rd, Bakewell, Derbys DE45
1GB
0.75 mile from Bakewell Square,
cross River Wye on A619 Sheffield-
Chesterfield road, right up Station Rd,
right before Industrial Estate.
Hilly parkland course.
9 holes, 5240 yards, S.S.S.66
Designed by George Low.
Founded 1899

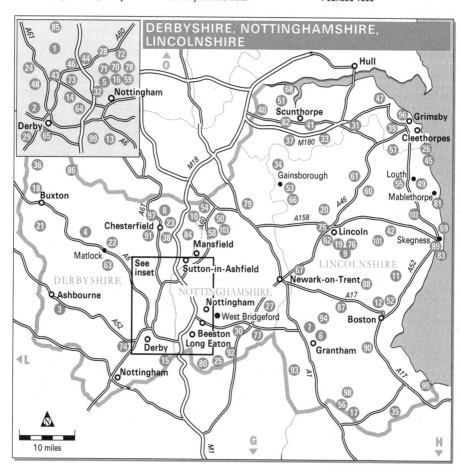

DERBYSHIRE, NOTTINGHAMSHIRE, LINCOLNSHIRE

Visitors: welcome weekdays; Ladies' Day Thurs; weekends by prior arrangement.
Green Fee: £14.
Societies: welcome by prior arrangement.
Catering: meals and bar except Mon.
Hotels: Rutland Arms.

M5 Beeston Fields
☎(0115) 9257062, Pro 9220872, Fax 9254280
Beeston Fields, Nottingham NG9 3DD
Off A52 4 miles W of Nottingham, 4 miles from M1 exit 25.
Parkland course.
18 holes, 6404 yards, S.S.S.71
Designed by Tom Williamson.
Founded 1922
Visitors: daily by arrangement.
Green Fee: on application.
Societies: catered for Mon and Wed by arrangement.
Catering: meals served every day.
Hotels: The Priory; Novotel; The Post House.

M6 Belton Park
☎(01476) 67399
Belton Lane, Londonthorpe Rd, Grantham, Lincs NG31 9SH
A607 from Grantham signposted to Sleaford and Lincoln, turn right at traffic lights at Park signposted Londonthorpe, club is 1 mile on left.
Parkland courses.
Brownlow, 18 holes, 6420 yards, S.S.S.71; Belmont, 18 holes, 6016 yards, S.S.S.69; Ancaster, 18 holes, 6252 yards, S.S.S.70

Designed by Dave Thomas & Peter Alliss.
Founded 1890
Visitors: welcome, preferably with h/cap cert; no jeans or collarless shirts, proper golf shoes required.
Green Fee: WD £22 per round, £27.50 per day; WE £27 per round, £33 per day.
Societies: not Tues or weekends.
Catering: full facilities at all times.
2 practice fairways.
Hotels: Angel & Royal; King's; The Swallow Hotel.

M7 Belton Woods Hotel & Country Club
☎(01476) 593200
Belton, Nr Grantham, Lincolnshire NG32 2LN
2 miles E of A1 via Gonerby Moor services; 2 miles N of Grantham on A607 to Lincoln.
Rolling parkland courses with mature trees and adjacent woodland.
Lakes, 18 holes, 6808 yards, S.S.S.73; Woodside, 18 holes, 6834 yards, S.S.S.73; Spitfire, 9 holes Par 3, 1184 yards
Founded Jan 1991
Visitors: welcome any day; 10 days advance booking only.
Green Fee: £20 (£2.50 Spitfire); special winter rates and reductions for residents.
Societies: Mon-Fri by prior arrangement; special Company and Society Golf Days.
Catering: leisure restaurant 7am-10pm, bar snacks available 11am-10pm; à la carte restaurant, banqueting for 240.

Driving range, putting green, full range of health, sports, leisure and conference facilities.
Hotels: Belton Woods, golfing breaks for individuals and groups; golf tuition holidays.

M8 Birch Hall
☎(01246) 291979, Manager: 291934
Sheffield Rd, Unstone, Sheffield S18 5DH
3 miles from Chesterfield, 7 miles from Sheffield on old A61 Sheffield-Chesterfield road.
Parkland course.
18 holes, 6409 yards, S.S.S.74
Designed by David Tucker.
Founded Oct 1992
Visitors: welcome except Sat and Sun am.
Green Fee: £14 per round.
Societies: welcome 7 days with prior arrangement.
Catering: bar and restaurant; bar has public house license, named The Inn on the Green.
Hotels: Sandpiper Motel adjoining course; Sheffield Moat House.

M9 Blankney
☎(01526) 320263 (Sec), Pro 320202, Fax 322521
Blankney, Lincoln, Lincs LN4 3AZ
10 miles from Lincoln, 1 mile past Metheringham on B1188.
Parkland course.
18 holes, 6479 yards, S.S.S.71
Designed by Cameron Sinclair (updated design).
Founded 1903

KEY							
1	Alfreton	19	Canwick Park	41	Holme Hall	61	Market Rasen Race Course
2	Allestree Park	20	Carholme	42	Horncastle		
3	Ashbourne	21	Cavendish	43	Horsley Lodge	62	Martin Moor
4	Bakewell	22	Chatsworth	44	Hucknall	63	Matlock
5	Beeston Fields	23	Chesterfield	45	Humberston Park	64	Maywood
6	Belton Park	24	Chevin	46	Ilkeston Borough (Pewit)	65	Mickleover
7	Belton Woods Hotel & Country Club	25	Chilwell Manor			66	Millfield
		26	Cleethorpes	47	Immingham	67	Newark
8	Birch Hall	27	Cotgrave Place Golf & Country Club	48	Kedleston Park	68	Normanby Hall
9	Blankney			49	Kenwick Park	69	North Shore
10	Bondhay Golf & Country Club	28	Coxmoor	50	Kilton Forest	70	Nottingham City
		29	Derby	51	Kingsway	71	Notts (Hollinwell)
11	Boston	30	Edwalton Municipal	52	Kirton Holme	72	Oakmere Park (Oxton)
12	Boston West	31	Elsham	53	Lincoln	73	Ormonde Fields Country Club
13	Bramcote Hills Golf Course	32	Erewash Valley	54	Lindrick		
		33	Forest Pines	55	Louth Golf & Squash Club	74	Pastures
14	Breadsall Priory Hotel Golf & Country Club	34	Gainsborough			75	Pottergate
		35	Gedney Hill	56	Luffenham Heath	76	RAF Waddington
15	Breedon Priory	36	Glossop & District	57	The Manor Golf Course	77	Radcliffe-on-Trent
16	Bulwell Forest	37	Grange Park			78	Ramsdale Park Golf Centre
17	Burghley Park	38	Grassmoor Golf Centre	58	Mansfield Woodhouse		
18	Buxton & High Peak	39	Grimsby	59	Mapperley	79	Retford
		40	Hirst Priory	60	Market Rasen & District	80	Ruddington Grange
						81	Sandilands
82	Scunthorpe
83	Seacroft
84	Sherwood Forest
85	Shirland
86	Sickleholme
87	Sleaford
88	South Kyme
89	Southview
90	Spalding
91	Stanedge
92	Stanton-on-the-Wolds
93	Stoke Rochford
94	Sudbrook Moor
95	Sutton Bridge
96	Swingtime (Grimsby)
97	Tapton Park Municipal
98	Toft Hotel
99	Trent Lock Golf Centre
100	Wollaton Park
101	Woodhall Spa
102	Woodthorpe Hall
103	Worksop

Visitors: phone General Manager/Pro in advance.
Green Fee: WD £17 per round, £25 per day; WE £25 per round, £30 per day.
Societies: weekdays and weekends.
Catering: full facilities.
Snooker.
Hotels: Self-catering bungalow for up to 6 available; £15 pp per night.

M10 Bondhay Golf & Country Club
☎(01909) 723608, 724709, Fax 720226
Bondhay Lane, Whitwell, Worksop, Notts S80 3EH
Just off A619, 5 mins from M1 junction 30.
Parkland course.
18 holes, 6800 yards, Par 72; 9 hole family course.
Designed by Donald Steel.
Founded 1991
Visitors: welcome, no restrictions; book in advance.
Green Fee: £14.95; family course £3.95 (9 holes).
Societies: book in advance.
Catering: full facilities.
Driving range, Health club.
Hotels: Vandykes (Worksop); Beeches (Rotherham).

M11 Boston
☎(01205) 362306, Sec 350589
Cowbridge, Horncastle Rd, Boston, Lincs PE22 7EL
2 miles N of Boston on B1183, look for sign on right crossing 1st bridge.
Parkland course; water on 10 holes.
18 holes, 6490 yards, S.S.S.71
Designed by B.S. Cooper, extended by Donald Steel.
Founded 1962
Visitors: welcome.
Green Fee: WD £17 per round, £22 per day.
Societies: welcome weekdays.
Catering: full facilities every day.
Hotels: White Hart (Bridgefoot); New England (Wide Bargate).

M12 Boston West
☎(01205) 290540 (Office), Pro 290670
Hubbert's Bridge, Boston, Lincs PE20 3QX
At the crossroads of the B1192and A1121 at Hubbert's Bridge. 1 mile from the A52 Boston-Grantham road and 3 miles from the A17 Sleaford-Kings Lynn road

Lowland course with challenging water holes
9 holes, 6346 yards, S.S.S. 72
Designed by Michael Zara
Founded in Sept 1995
Visitors: welcome; pay and play course
Green Fee: WD £5.50 (9 holes); WE £6.50
Societies: welcome by prior arrangement.
Catering: full facilities for visitors and societies
Golf academy, driving range
Hotels: White Hart; New England.

M13 Bramcote Hills Golf Course
☎(0115) 9281880
Thoresby Rd, off Derby Rd, Bramcote, Nottingham NG9 3EP
Leave M1 at junction 25, take A52 towards Nottingham, past Bramcote Leisure Centre, turn left 0.25 mile further on.
Parkland course.
18 holes Par 3, 1501 yards
Founded 1981
Visitors: pay-as-you-play.
Green Fee: WD £5.40; WE £5.90, reductions for jnrs.
Societies: bookings welcomed.
Catering: refreshments only.

M14 Breadsall Priory Hotel G & CC
☎(01332) 832235, Fax 833509
Moor Rd, Morley, Derbys DE7 6DL
3 miles NE of Derby off A61, towards Breadsall, turn left into Rectory Lane and right onto Moor Rd.
Priory course, parkland; Moorland course, moorland.
Priory, 18 holes, S.S.S.68; Moorland, 18 holes, S.S.S.68
Founded 1977 (Priory), 1992 (Moorland)
Visitors: welcome weekdays; by prior arrangement weekends.
Green Fee: on application.
Societies: welcome at all times.
Catering: 5 bars, 2 restaurants; breakfast, lunch and dinner.
Tennis, pool, snooker, etc.
Hotels: Breadsall Priory.

M15 Breedon Priory
☎(01332) 863081/Fax
The Clubhouse, Wilson, Nr Derby, DE7 1AT
1 mile E of A 453 between East Midlands Airport and Ashby-de-la-Zouche.

Parkland course.
18 holes, 5530 yards, S.S.S.67
Founded 1990
Visitors: Welcome Mon-Fri; weekends pm only and by arrangement.
Green Fee: WD £14; WE £16.
Societies: weekdays by arrangement; also catering for Corporate Days.
Catering: bar, bar snacks, à la carte restaurant.
Hotels: Park Farmhouse (Nr Castle Donnington).

M16 Bulwell Forest
☎(0115) 9770576, Pro 9763172
Hucknall Rd, Bulwell, Nottingham NG5 9LQ
4 miles N of city centre, follow signs for Bulwell or Hucknall, 3 miles from M1 junction 26.
Moorland course.
18 holes, 5572 yards, S.S.S.67
Founded 1902
Visitors: welcome.
Green Fee: WD £9; WE £11.
Societies: welcome by prior arrangement.
Catering: facilities available by arrangement.

M17 Burghley Park
☎(01780) 53789, Pro 62100
St Martins Without, Stamford, Lincs PE9 3JX
Leave A1 at roundabout S of town, course entrance is 1st gateway on the right, 1 mile S of Stamford.
Parkland course.
18 holes, 6236 yards, S.S.S.70
Designed by the Rev. J.D. Day.
Founded 1890
Visitors: welcome weekdays only; h/cap certs essential.
Green Fee: £20.
Societies: welcome weekdays by arrangement.
Catering: lunches and teas served, dinner for Societies and by arrangement.
Hotels: George of Stamford; Crown; Cavalier, Collyweston; Lady Anne's; Garden House.

M18 Buxton & High Peak
☎(01298) 23453, 26263/Fax
Waterswallows Rd, Fairfield, Buxton, Derbys
1 mile N from Buxton station on A6.
Meadowland course.
18 holes, 5954 yards, S.S.S.69
Founded 1887

Visitors: welcome.
Green Fee: WD £20; WE & BH £25.
Societies: by arrangement with House Manageress; full and half-day packages, Mon-Fri full day inc lunch and dinner, 36 holes £35.
Catering: full facilities and supper licence.
Hotels: Buckingham; Palace; Portland; Egerton; Grovesnor House; Givenchy GH; Barms Farm; Hawthorn Farm.

M19 Canwick Park

☎(01522) 522166, Sec 542912, Pro 536870
Canwick Park, Washingborough Road, Lincoln LN4 1EF
2 miles E of city centre.
Parkland course.
18 holes, 6237 yards, S.S.S.70
Designed by Hawtree & Partners.
Founded 1893, new course 1974
Visitors: welcome weekdays.
Green Fee: WD £15 per round, £22 per day; WE £19 per round, £22 per day.
Societies: welcome weekdays by arrangement.
Catering: lunches and evening meals every day except Mon (unless by arrangement).
Hotels: Eastgate; Brierley House.

M20 Carholme

☎(01522) 523725 (Sec), Pro 536811
Carholme Rd, Lincoln LN1 1SE
On A57, 1 mile from city centre.
Parkland course.
18 holes, 6243 yards, S.S.S.70
Founded 1906
Visitors: welcome weekdays, weekends if accompanied by a member.
Green Fee: WD £13 (£8 with member); WE £16 (£9 with member).
Societies: weekdays only by arrangement.
Catering: lunches served.

M21 Cavendish

☎(01298) 23494, Pro 25052, Sec 79708
Gadley Lane, Buxton, Derbys SK17 6XD
0.75 mile from town centre going W on A53 Leek road, right on Carlisle Rd, then left on Watford Rd signposted.
Parkland/downland course.
18 holes, 5833 yards, S.S.S.68
Designed by Dr Alister MacKenzie.
Founded 1925

Visitors: welcome.
Green Fee: WD £25 (£10 with member); WE £35 (£15 with member).
Societies: catered for weekdays by arrangement with Pro.
Catering: snacks available at all times and other meals served by arrangement.
Snooker table.
Hotels: Lee Wood; Buckingham; Portland; Egerton.

M22 Chatsworth

☎(01246) 582204
Chatsworth Park, Bakewell, Derbys
Parkland course.
9 holes (18 tees), 5248 yards, S.S.S.66
Visitors: none; members and guests only.

M23 Chesterfield

☎(01246) 279256, Pro 276297, Fax 276622
Walton, Chesterfield, Derbys S42 7LA
2 miles from town centre on Matlock Rd A632.
Parkland course.
18 holes, 6057 yards, S.S.S.70
Designed by H. Colt.
Founded 1897
Visitors: welcome weekdays.
Green Fee: apply for details.
Societies: catered for weekdays if booked in advance.
Catering: lunch and dinner served every day.
Hotels: Chesterfield; Portland.

M24 Chevin

☎(01332) 841864, Pro 841112
Golf Lane, Duffield, Derbys DE6 4EE
5 miles N of Derby on A6, just outside Duffield.
Hilly parkland course.
18 holes, 6057 yards, S.S.S.69
Founded 1894
Visitors: welcome weekdays, not before 9.30am nor 12.30-2pm; with member at weekends.
Green Fee: apply for details.
Societies: not weekends; no meals Mon.
Catering: meals served except Mon.
Snooker.
Hotels: Strutt Arms adjacent.

M25 Chilwell Manor

☎(0115) 9258958, Pro 9258993
Meadow Lane, Chilwell, Nottingham NG9 5AE

4 miles W of Nottingham, near Beeston, on A6005.
Parkland course.
18 holes, 6395 yards, S.S.S.69
Founded 1906
Visitors: welcome weekdays, restricted to 4 per hour.
Green Fee: WD £18 per round/day; WE (not BH) £20.
Societies: catered for Mon, Wed, Fri.
Catering: lunches served weekdays; evening meals by arrangement.
Hotels: Post House; Novotel; The Village Hotel.

M26 Cleethorpes

☎(01472) 812059, Sec/Pro 814060
Kings Rd, Cleethorpes, S Humberside DN35 0PN
Off A1031 1 mile S of Cleethorpes.
Meadowland course.
18 holes, 6349 yards, S.S.S.70
Designed by Harry Vardon (now vastly altered).
Founded 1894 (altered 1994)
Visitors: must be members of recognised club (Ladies only, Wed pm).
Green Fee: WD £20 (£15 with member); WE £25 (£16 with member).
Societies: by arrangement.
Catering: full facilities available by arrangement with Steward.
Hotels: Kingsway; Wellow.

M27 Cotgrave Place Golf & Country Club

☎(0115) 9335500, Pro 9334686, Fax 9334567
Stragglethorpe, Nottingham NG12 3HB
Approx 3.5 miles from Nottingham on A52 Grantham road, take right turn to Cotgrave.
Parkland course, lake bestrewn.
3 x 9 holes, A:Lakeside, 3186 yards, S.S.S. 70; B:Parkland, 3117 yards, S.S.S. 70; C:Fox Covert, 2755 yards.
Founded May 1992
Visitors: welcome by arrangement.
Green Fee: WD £22 per day; WE £35 per day.
Societies: welcome; apply for details; company days a speciality.
Catering: full facilities.
Floodlit driving range.

M28 Coxmoor

☎(01623) 559878, Office: 557359, Pro 559906, Fax 557359
Coxmoor Rd, Sutton-in-Ashfield, Notts NG17 5LF.

LUXURY HOTEL & 27 HOLE GOLF COURSE

Facilities include 50 en-suite bedrooms, conference rooms, a la carte restaurant. All weather floodlit driving range. Societies welcome. Golfing breaks from £75.00. Call for details. Just off junction 4, M180.

Country Hotel **AA★★★RAC**

Highly commended *Championship Golf Course*

Forest Pines Golf Club, Briggate Lodge Inn, Ermine Street, Broughton, Near Brigg, Lincolnshire, DN20 0AQ **Tel: 01652 650770 Fax: 01652 650495**

On A611 5 miles from M1 junction 27, 2 miles SW of Mansfield.
Heathland course. County Championship Course.
18 holes, 6571 yards, S.S.S.72
Founded 1913
Visitors: weekdays except Tues (Ladies' Day); must book tee time in advance.
Green Fee: WD £25 per round, £34 per day.
Societies: welcome by arrangement with Sec.
Catering: full facilities.
Hotels: Pine Lodge; Carr Bank Manor; Dalestorth GH; Hole in the Wall; Swallow.

M29 Derby

☎(01332) 766462 (Pro), **Catering:** 766323
Shakespeare St, Sinfin, Derby DE24 9HD
1 mile off A5111 at Sinfin, vehicle access via Wilmore Rd.
Municipal parkland course.
18 holes, 6165 yards, S.S.S.69
Founded 1923
Visitors: welcome.
Green Fee: on application.
Societies: weekdays by prior arrangement.
Catering: bar and catering available daily.

M30 Edwalton Municipal

☎(0115) 9234775
Edwalton Village, Nottingham NG12 4AS
Left at A606 from Nottingham at Edwalton Hall Hotel.
Parkland course.
Main course, 9 holes, 3336 yards, S.S.S.36; Par 3, 9 holes, 1563 yards, S.S.S.27
Designed by Frank Pennink.
Founded 1981
Visitors: welcome
Green Fee: Main (9 holes) £4.40; Par 3 (9 holes) £2.50.
Societies: welcome weekdays by arrangement.
Catering: lunches and evening meals served.
Hotels: Edwalton Hall.

M31 Elsham

☎(01652) 680291 (Manager), Pro 680432
Barton Rd, Elsham, Brigg, S Humberside DN20 0LS
Situated on E side of Brigg to Barton road, B1206, 3 miles N of Brigg.
Parkland course.
18 holes, 6411 yards, S.S.S.71
Founded 1901
Visitors: welcome weekdays.
Green Fee: on application.
Societies: by arrangement weekdays except Thurs.
Catering: full bar all day.

M32 Erewash Valley

☎(0115) 9322984 (Sec), Pro 9324667
Golf Club Road, Stanton-by-Dale, Ilkeston, Derbys DE7 4QR
From M1 junction 25 follow signs to Stanton Ironworks Co Ltd, through Sandiacre.
Meadowland/parkland course.
18 holes, 6492 yards, S.S.S.71; Par 3 course
Founded 1905
Visitors: welcome except competition days.
Green Fee: WD £22.50 per round, £27.50 per day; WE & BH £27.50 per round/day.
Societies: catered for weekdays by arrangement.
Catering: lunches, evening meals by arrangement.
Snooker, bowling green.
Hotels: Post House; Novotel.

M33 Forest Pines

☎(01652) 650770, Pro 650706
Briggate Lodge Inn, Ermine Street, Nr Brigg, Lincs DN20 0AQ
Take M180 exit junc 4 and then A15 towards Scunthorpe, at first roundabout the club is opposite
Forest courco
27 holes, Forest-Pines (Championship course) 6882 yards S.S.S. 73; Pines-Beeches 6694 yards S.S.S 71; Forest-Beeches 6394 yards, S.S.S. 70
Designed by J Morgan
Founded May 1996

Visitors: From July 1996, h/cap cert required
Green Fee: WD £25 per round, £35 per day; WE £30 per round, £40 per day.
Societies: welcome; special packages on offer (27 holes, coffee, lunch, evening meal and driving range £40).
Catering: Full facilities available including restaurant and bars. Leisure complex opening in club house with swimming pool and fitness suite etc
Driving range, golf schools, accommodation courses
Hotels: 50 bedroom hotel on site offering golf packages and weekend breaks.

M34 Gainsborough

☎(01427) 613088, 612278
Thonock, Gainsborough, Lincs DN21 1PZ
1 mile NE of Gainsborough.
Parkland course.
18 holes, 6266 yards, S.S.S.70; additional 18 holes due to open Autumn 1996.
Founded 1985
Visitors: welcome weekdays.
Green Fee: £20 per round, £25 per day.
Societies: Mon-Fri, must book in advance.
Catering: bar, restaurant, coffee shop all day.
Driving range, practice putting green, snooker.
Hotels: Black Swan; Hickman Hill.

M35 Gedney Hill

☎(01406) 330922 (Pro)
West Drove, Gedney Hill, Nr Holbeach, Lincs PE12 0NT
6 miles from Crowland on B1166, 6 miles from Thorney by A47 and B1167.
Public links type course, reasonably flat, small greens.
18 holes, 5357 yards, S.S.S.66
Designed by C. Britton.
Founded 1988
Visitors: welcome; smart dress on and off course.

Green Fee: WD £5.75; WE £8.75; reductions for Jnrs and OAPs.
Societies: welcome weekdays by arrangement.
Catering: casual bar, bar snacks available; restaurant for meals and functions.
Driving range, snooker, heated swimming pool.

M36 Glossop & District
☎(01457) 865247, Pro 853117
Hurst Lane, off Sheffield Rd, Glossop, Derbys SK13 9PU
1 mile out of town on A57 Sheffield road.
Moorland course.
11 holes, 5800 yards, S.S.S.68
Founded 1895
Visitors: welcome.
Green Fee: apply for details.
Societies: welcome by prior arrangement.
Catering: meals served by arrangement.
Hotels: Hurst Lee Guest House.

M37 Grange Park
☎(01724) 762945
Butterwick Rd, Messingham, Scunthorpe, S Humberside DN17 3PP
Signposted from Messingham.
Public parkland course.
13 holes, 4122 yards, Par 49; 9 holes Par 3.
Designed by Ray Price.
Founded July 1991
Visitors: welcome, no restrictions.
Green Fee: WD £5; WE £7; jnrs half price.
Catering: coffee bar.
Driving range.

M38 Grassmoor Golf Centre
☎(01246) 856044, Fax 853933
North Wingfield Rd, Grassmoor, Chesterfield, Derbys S42 5EA
M1 junction 29; 2 miles S of Chesterfield.
Moorland course.
18 holes, 5723 yards, S.S.S.69
Designed by Michael Shattock.
Founded Nov 1992
Visitors: all welcome, phone to reserve time.
Green Fee: WD £7.50; WE £9.
Societies: welcome weekdays and weekends.
Catering: bar and restaurant facilities available.
Driving range, sauna.

M39 Grimsby
☎(01472) 342630 (Sec), Clubhouse 342823, Pro 356981
Littlecoates Rd, Grimsby, S Humberside DN34 4LU
1 mile W of Grimsby town centre; turn left off A18 at 1st roundabout, course is 0.75 mile on left, next to Forte Post House.
Undulating parkland course.
18 holes, 6098 yards, S.S.S.69
Founded 1922
Visitors: members of golf clubs only; Ladies Day Tues.
Green Fee: WD £18; WE £25.
Societies: Mon and Fri only.
Catering: available; full meals by arrangement, except Wed.
Bridge.
Hotels: Forte Posthouse.

M40 Hirst Priory
☎(01724) 711621, Pro 711619
Hirst Priory Park, Crowle, Nr Scunthorpe, S Humberside
Exit M180 at junc 2; take A1161 to Crowle and Goole, 0.5m on left
Parkland course
18 holes, 6119 yards, S.S.S. 69
Founded May 1994
Visitors: welcome
Green Fee: WD £11.75; WE £14.50
Societies: welcome
Catering: full facilities.

M41 Holme Hall
☎(01724) 862078 (Sec/bookings), Club 840909, Pro 851816
Holme Lane, Bottesford, Scunthorpe, S Humberside DN16 3RF
2 miles SE of Scunthorpe near M180 exit 4.
Heathland course.
18 holes, 6475 yards, S.S.S.71
Founded 1908
Visitors: welcome weekdays, not weekends or Bank Holidays.
Green Fee: £20 per round/day.
Societies: welcome weekdays except Mon.
Catering: meals by arrangement (01724 282053), bar snacks daily except Mon.
Hotels: Royal; Wortley; Beverley; Briggate Lodge.

M42 Horncastle
☎(01507) 526800
West Ashby, Horncastle, Lincs LN9 5PP
Just off A158 between Lincoln and Skegness; down hill at Edlington, follow AA signs.

Heathland course with trees and water features.
18 holes, 5717 yards, S.S.S.70
Designed by Ernie Wright.
Founded July 1990
Visitors: welcome.
Green Fee: WD £12 per round, £18 per day; WE & BH £15 per round, £20 per day.
Societies: 7 days a week.
Catering: bars and restaurant; conferences, ballroom.
Floodlit driving range, coarse fishing.
Hotels: Petwood; Admiral Rodney (Horncastle).

M43 Horsley Lodge
☎(01332) 780838 Clubhouse, Pro 781400, Fax 781118
Horsley Lodge, Smalley Mill Road, Horsley, Derbys DE21 5BL.
4 miles from Derby on A608 Derby-Heanor road turn left at Rose & Crown then 2nd left.
Undulating parkland course.
18 holes, 6443 yards, S.S.S.71
Designed by George 'Bill' White.
Founded 1990
Visitors: welcome, not during weekend competitions.
Green Fee: £18 per round £25 per day.
Societies: welcome any week day or non-competition Sat.
Catering: 2 bars, à la carte restaurant, function room, banqueting.
Driving range, sauna etc.
Hotels: Own luxury hotel on site; free golf for residents, bargain breaks; telephone for details.

M44 Hucknall
☎(0115) 9642037
Wigwam Lane, Hucknall, Notts NG15 7TA
Just off junc 27 of M1 in direction of Hucknall, 0.5m from centre of town
Parkland course
18 holes, 6233 yards, S.S.S. 72
Founded 1994
Visitors: welcome
Green Fee: WD £8.50; WE £9.50.
Societies: welcome
Catering: bar, snacks and meals available

M45 Humberston Park
☎(01472) 210404
Humberston Ave, Humberston, S Humberside DN36 4SJ
Humberstone Avenue at back of Cherry Garth Scouts Field.

Parkland course.
9 holes, 1836 yards, S.S.S. 58
Founded 1970
Visitors: welcome, not before 12am weekends.
Green Fee: WD £6 (9 holes), £8 (18 holes); WE £7 (9 holes), £10 (18 holes).
Societies: welcome by prior arrangement.
Catering: bar facilities available; snacks served.

M46 **Ilkeston Borough (Pewit)**
☎(0115) 9307704, 9304550
West End Drive, Ilkeston, Derbyshire DE7 5GH
0.5 mile E of Ilkeston town centre.
Municipal meadowland course.
9 holes, 4116 yards, S.S.S.60
Founded 1920
Visitors: welcome.
Green Fee: £6 (18 holes)
Societies: welcome, weekdays only, by arrangement.

M47 **Immingham**
☎(01469) 575298, Pro 575493, Fax 577636
Church Lane, Immingham, Grimsby, S Humberside DN40 2EU
A180 Immingham exits, Pelham Rd; Bluestone Lane or Washdyke Lane both lead into Church Lane.
Parkland course.
18 holes, 6190 yards, Par 71
Designed by Hawtree & Son (1st 9), F. Pennink (2nd 9).
Founded 1974
Visitors: welcome weekdays, restrictions at weekends; advisable to telephone.
Green Fee: WD £15 per round.
Societies: weekdays by prior arrangement.
Catering: snacks, bar meals, arranged with Steward.

M48 **Kedleston Park**
☎(01332) 840035, Pro 841685
Kedleston, Quarndon, Derby DE6 4JD
From A38 follow signs to Kedleston Hall.
Parkland course.
18 holes, 6611 yards, S.S.S.71
Designed by James Braid and Morrison & Co.
Founded 1947
Visitors: weekdays only by appointment.
Green Fee: £25 per round.

Societies: weekdays only by appointment.
Catering: restaurant and bar. Snooker.
Hotels: Kedleston; Midland; Mundy Arms.

M49 **Kenwick Park**
☎(01507) 605134, Pro 607161
Kenwick, Nr Louth, Lincs LN11 8NY
On Mablethorpe road out of Louth.
Woodland/parkland course.
18 holes, 6815 yards, S.S.S.73
Designed by Patrick Tallack.
Founded 1992
Visitors: members and guests only unless resident at Kenwick Hall.
Catering: bar and restaurant. Practice ground.
Hotels: Kenwick Hall.

M50 **Kilton Forest**
☎(01909) 472488, Pro 486563
Blyth Rd, Worksop, Notts S81 0TL
2 miles NE of town centre on B6045; on by-pass follow signs for Blyth.
Public parkland course
18 holes, 6444 yards, S.S.S.71
Founded 1978
Visitors: welcome, booking system in operation weekends and Bank Holidays.
Green Fee: WD £7; WE £8.35.
Societies: by arrangement, Club competitions WE and some BH.
Catering: bar meals every day. Bowling green adjacent.
Hotels: Regency.

M51 **Kingsway**
☎(01724) 840945
Kingsway, Scunthorpe, S Humberside DN15 7ER
S of A18 between Berkeley and Queensway roundabouts.
Undulating parkland course.
9 holes, 1915 yards, S.S.S.59
Designed by R.D. Highfield.
Founded 1971
Visitors: welcome every day.
Green Fee: WD £2.95; WE £3.45.
Catering: snacks available.

M52 **Kirton Holme**
☎(01205) 290669
Holme Rd, Nr Boston, Lincs PE20 1SY
2 miles W of Boston off A52.
Parkland course.
9 holes, 2884 yards, Par 35
Designed by D.W. Welberry.
Founded 1992

Visitors: welcome, no restrictions.
Green Fee: WD £4.40 per round, £7.70 per day; WE & BH £5.50 per round, £8.80 per day.
Societies: welcome by prior arrangement.
Catering: light snacks; bar and bar meals.
Hotels: Poachers Inn.

M53 **Lincoln**
☎(01427) 718721, Pro 718273
Torksey, Lincoln LN1 2EG
Off A156, 12 miles NW of Lincoln.
Undulating meadowland course.
18 holes, 6438 yards, S.S.S.71
Founded 1891
Visitors: welcome with reservation weekdays only.
Green Fee: £22 per round, £28 per day.
Societies: weekdays by prior arrangement.
Catering: meals served by arrangement.
Hotels: White Hart; Grand; Crest; Hume Arms (Torksey).

M54 **Lindrick**
☎(01909) 475282, Pro 475820, Fax 488685
Lindrick, Worksop, Notts S81 8BH
On A57, 4 miles W of Worksop.
Heathland course.
18 holes, 6612 yards, S.S.S.72
Designed by Tom Dunn, Willie Park and H. Fowler.
Founded 1891
Visitors: welcome weekdays, prior notice required.
Green Fee: WD Nov-Mar £25 per round/day; Apr-Oct £40 per round/day; WE £45 per round.
Societies: weekdays except Tues.
Catering: lunches served most days; evening meals can be prepared for visiting societies/parties, prior notice required.
Hotels: Red Lion (Todwick); Fourways, Charnwood (Blyth); Olde Bell (Barnby Moor).

M55 **Louth Golf & Squash Club**
☎(01507) 602554, Pro 604648, Fax 603681
Crowtree Lane, Louth, Lincs LN11 9LJ
W of Louth in triangle between A157 Louth by pass and A153.
Undulating parkland course in AONB.
18 holes, 6477 yards, S.S.S.71
Founded 1965

Visitors: welcome.
Green Fee: WD £16 per round, £20 per day; WE & BH £25 per round, £30 per day.
Societies: weekdays; £5 deposit when booking.
Catering: full catering provided. Squash courts.
Hotels: Priory; Kings Head; Masons Arms; Brakenborough Arms; Beaumont Hotel.

M56 Luffenham Heath
☎(01780) 720205 (Sec), Pro 720298, **Catering:** 721095
Ketton, Stamford, Lincs PE9 3UU
6 miles SW of Stamford on A6121 by Fosters Bridge, off A47 at Morcott onto A6121.
Undulating heathland course.
18 holes, 6253 yards, S.S.S.70
Designed by James Braid.
Founded 1911
Visitors: by prior arrangement; h/cap certs required.
Green Fee: WD £30; WE £35.
Societies: Wed, Thurs, Fri, bookings through Sec.
Catering: by arrangement.
Hotels: George (Stamford); Monkton Arms (Glaston).

M57 The Manor Golf Course
☎(01472) 873468
Laceby Manor, Laceby, Grimsby, S Humberside DN37 7EA
Approx. 1 mile from Laceby roundabout on A18, on left hand side; large green and white sign.
Parkland course.
18 holes, 6354 yards, S.S.S. 70
Designed by Sir Charles Nicholson and Rushton.
Founded June 1992
Visitors: welcome any time except when club competitions are being played; restricted play every Tues morning.
Green Fee: £12.
Societies: telephone Sec to discuss details.
Catering: bar; coffee etc available all opening hours.
Hotels: Oaklands (0.75 mile).

M58 Mansfield Woodhouse
☎(01623) 23521
Leeming Lane North, Mansfield Woodhouse, Notts NG19 9EU
On A60 Mansfield-Worksop road, 2 miles N of Mansfield.

Public parkland course
9 holes, 2411 yards, S.S.S.65
Founded 1973
Visitors: welcome any time except Sat before 11am.
Green Fee: apply for details.
Catering: full facilities.

M59 Mapperley
☎(0115) 9265611, Pro 9202227
Central Ave, Mapperley Plains, Nottingham NG3 5RH
From Nottingham take B684 Woodborough Rd, Central Ave is about 4 miles NE of Nottingham, turn right at Speeds (Volvo) Garage.
Hilly meadowland course.
18 holes, 6283 yards, S.S.S.70
Founded 1905
Visitors: welcome; Tues Ladies Day.
Green Fee: WD £12 per round, £15 per day; WE £18 per round, £21 per day.
Societies: weekdays.
Catering: lunch and evening meals served except Wed, when only snacks available.

M60 Market Rasen & District
☎(01673) 842416
Legsby Rd, Market Rasen, Lincs LN8 3DZ
B1202 off A46, 1 mile S of racecourse.
Moorland course.
18 holes, 6043 yards, S.S.S.69
Founded 1922
Visitors: welcome weekdays; with member weekends.
Green Fee: £16 per round, £24 per day..
Societies: Tues and Fri by arrangement with Sec.
Catering: lunch served every day.

M61 Market Rasen Race Course
☎(01673) 843434, Fax 844532
Market Rasen Race Course, Legsby Road, Market Rasen, Lincs LN8 3EA
Off A631.
Public pay-as-you-play course.
9 holes, 2377 yards, Par 33
Founded May 1989
Visitors: welcome, not race days.
Green Fee: WD £4 (9 holes), £6 (18 holes); WE £5 (9 holes), £8 (18 holes); reductions for jnrs and OAPs.
Societies: welcome.
Catering: available on race course. Children's playground.
Hotels: The Limes.

M62 Martin Moor
☎(01526) 378243
Blankney Rd, Martin Moor, Metheringham, Lincs
9 miles south of Lincoln on the Metheringham and Billhay road
Parkland course
9 holes, 3357 yards, S.S.S. 72
Designed by S Harrison
Founded June 1992
Visitors: welcome
Green Fee: WD £4 (9 holes), £5.50 (18 holes); WE & BH £5 (9 holes), £7.50 (18 holes)
Societies: weekdays by prior arrangement
Catering: bar; buffet for societies by arrangement
Practice area.

M63 Matlock
☎(01629) 582191, Pro 584934
Chesterfield Rd, Matlock, Derbys DE4 5LF
On A632 Matlock-Chesterfield road, 1.5 miles out of Matlock.
Moorland/parkland course.
18 holes, 5991 yards, S.S.S.69
Founded 1907
Visitors: welcome weekdays, weekends with member only.
Green Fee: WD £25; WE & BH £12.50 (with member only).
Societies: catered for weekdays by arrangement.
Catering: snacks available, meals to order except Mon.
Hotels: Peacock; New Bath.

M64 Maywood
☎(0115) 9392306
Rushy Lane, Risley, Draycott, Derbys DE72 3ST
Off M1 junction 25; then off A52 to Risley by Post House Hotel.
Wooded course with water features.
18 holes, 6424 yards, S.S.S.72
Founded 1990
Visitors: welcome.
Green Fee: WD £15; WE £20.
Societies: by arrangement.
Catering: bar facilities and snacks available.
Hotels: Post House; Novotel.

M65 Mickleover
☎(01332) 513339, Pro 518662
Uttoxeter Rd, Mickleover, Derby
3 miles W of Derby; take A516 out of Derby, join B5020 to Mickleover.
Meadowland course.
18 holes, 5708 yards, S.S.S.68
Founded 1923

Visitors: welcome.
Green Fee: WD £20; WE & BH £25.
Societies: Tues, Thurs, £22.
Catering: facilities available.
Hotels: Mickleover Court; Crest; International.

M66 Millfield
☎(01427) 718473 (Club/Fax)
Laughterton, Torksey, Nr Lincoln, Lincs LN1 2LB
8 miles E of Lincoln between A57 and A158 on A113, 10 miles from Gainsborough.
Inland links course.
18 holes, 5986 yards, S.S.S.69; 9 holes Par 3, 1500 yards; further 15 hole intermediate course, 4100 yards.
Founded 1984
Visitors: no restrictions, pay-as-you-play.
Green Fee: £7 (18 hole course), £4 (15 hole course).
Societies: weekdays by arrangement.
Catering: light refreshments.
Driving range, tennis, bowls.
Hotels: self-catering apartments.

M67 Newark
☎(01636) 626282 (Sec/Manager), Club 626241
Kelwick, Coddington, Newark, Notts NG24 2QX
On A17 between Newark and Sleaford, just past Coddington roundabout.
Parkland course.
18 holes, 6421 yards, S.S.S.71
Founded 1901
Visitors: welcome any time; h/cap cert required; Tues Ladies' Day.
Green Fee: WD £22; WE £27.
Societies: welcome except Tues and weekends; catering with booking.
Catering: bar and meals all day.
Snooker.
Hotels: Robin Hood; George Inn (Leadenham).

M68 Normanby Hall
☎(01724) 720252, Sec 844303, Pro 720226
Normanby Park, Normanby, Scunthorpe, S Humberside DN15 9HU
5 miles N of Scunthorpe adjacent to Normanby Hall.
Parkland course.
18 holes, 6548 yards, S.S.S.71
Designed by H.F. Jiggens, Hawtree & Sons.
Founded 1978

Visitors: welcome, telephone Pro for times.
Green Fee: WD £10 per round, £16 per day; WE £12.
Societies: not after 2.30pm Fri, weekends or Bank Holidays; book on (01724) 280444 Ext 852.
Catering: full facilities; including banqueting etc at Normanby Hall and Country Park adjacent to course.
Hotels: Royal; Wortley House.

M69 North Shore
☎(01754) 763298, Fax 761902
North Shore Rd, Skegness, Lincs PE25 1DN
1 mile N of town on seaward side of Ingoldmells Rd.
Links/parkland course.
18 holes, 6254 yards, S.S.S.71
Designed by James Braid.
Founded 1910
Visitors: welcome if member of recognised club with h/cap cert.
Green Fee: WD £17 per round, £24 per day; WE & BH £25 per round, £35 per day.
Societies: as for visitors, special package available.
Catering: normal hotel services provided.
Snooker, tenpin bowls, banqueting.
Hotels: North Shore on site, special golf breaks.

M70 Nottingham City
☎(0115) 9278021, Pro/individual bookings: 9272767, Sec/party bookings (am only): 9276916
Lawton Drive, Bulwell, Nottingham NG6 8BL
2 miles off M1 at junction 26.
Municipal parkland course.
18 holes, 6120 yards, S.S.S.70
Founded 1910
Visitors: welcome weekdays and by booking at weekends.
Green Fee: on application.
Societies: welcome by prior arrangement.
Catering: meals served.

M71 Notts (Hollinwell)
☎(01623) 753225, Fax 753655
Hollinwell, Derby Rd, Kirkby-in-Ashfield, Notts NG17 7QR
Leave M1 at junction 27, then 2 miles N on A611.
Undulating heathland course.
18 holes Championship, 7020 yards, S.S.S.74
Designed by Willie Park Jnr.
Founded 1887

Visitors: reserved for members 12am-1pm Mon/Tues, 12am-2pm Wed/Thurs, and until 1pm Fri.
Green Fee: £35 per round, £45 per day.
Societies: welcome by prior arrangement.
Catering: full facilities every day.
Hotels: Swallow; Pine Lodge.

M72 Oakmere Park (Oxton)
☎(0115) 9653545, Fax 9655628
Oaks Lane, Oxton, Notts NG25 0RH
On A614 and A6097 8 miles NE of Nottingham.
Parkland course.
18 holes, 6046 metres, S.S.S.72; 9 holes, 3193 metres, Par 37.
Designed by Frank Pennink.
Founded 1974
Visitors: welcome but should make reservation at weekends.
Green Fee: on application; special WD rates, phone for details.
Societies: welcome 7 days; but max possible notice required for weekends.
Catering: clubhouse bar, spike bar, restaurant (resident chef).
Driving range.

M73 Ormonde Fields Country Club
☎(01773) 742987 (Pro), Sec 570043
Nottingham Rd, Codnor, Ripley, Derbys DE5 9RG
Off M1 at junction 26, take A610 towards Ripley for about 2 miles.
Undulating course.
18 holes, 6011 yards, S.S.S.69
Founded 1906
Visitors: welcome weekdays; by arrangement with Sec weekends.
Green Fee: WD £17.50.
Societies: by arrangement.
Catering: full facilities.

M74 Pastures
☎(01332) 367270 (Sports club)
Pastures Hospital, Mickleover, Derby DE3 5DQ
On A516 4 miles W of Derby.
Undulating meadowland course.
9 holes, 5005 yards, S.S.S.64
Designed by Frank Pennink.
Founded 1969
Visitors: with member only.
Green Fee: on application.
Societies: weekdays by special arrangement.
Catering: facilities provided for societies only.

Seacroft

For years, the temptation to get to Woodhall Spa blinded me from some of the other attractions of Lincolnshire's golf, notably the links of Seacroft which lie between Skegness and the nature reserve at Gibraltar Point. The British coastline is dotted with a profusion of courses with many qualities although settings that are off the beaten track are denied the championship recognition of the Birkdales, Formbys and Muirfields. However, remoteness is a characteristic to be cherished rather than despised and at Seacroft adds to the appeal of a course that typifies the virtues of seaside links.

From the clubhouse, doubts may be formed by the road and row of houses that line the opening holes but very soon a firm impression is formed that the threat of out of bounds cannot be shirked by cowardly play to the left. There are limiting factors there, too.

A central spine of dunes divides the course at two levels and there is the added feature, one unique in my experience, of a huge host of thorn bushes that are punishing in more senses than one. The 3rd, blind from the back tee, is a short par 4 with a little pitch to an elevated green that is unwise to miss on the right. But the 4th introduces us to a series of short holes that are first class, the 4th involving another elevated green and a tee shot that needs to be solidly hit to negotiate the hint of a valley in between.

After the 5th, where there is little fruitful option to hitting the fairway, the 6th offers the first significant change of direction but the 7th, 8th and 9th continue the journey to the furthest point from the clubhouse with sandhills offering the main hazards and providing a series of interesting shots. The second half begins with another beautifully, simple short

hole, but it is the 225 yard 12th, which heads towards the sea, that introduces a stretch of 4 or 5 holes that are quite delightful both in the challenge and enjoyment they present and in giving us views of the sea. On a clear day, the outline of Hunstanton can be detected across the Wash. The 13th demands the closest attention, a hole that can be approached in a number of different ways.

The green stands on a small plateau and is guarded by a big bunker in the face of the hill. It needs two of the best to get home and discretion is often the better part of valour. The more conservative way is to hit over a prominent ridge and launch a high pitch at the green.

Beyond the green is a marshy lagoon separating the course from the beach but the genuine seaside nature of the links is maintained by the third par 3 in five holes and a drive over a hill at the 15th followed by a nasty second in a cross wind to a green standing back to back with the 3rd. All the attributes of a good dogleg are embraced by the 16th and the need for proper control is highlighted by the 17th and 18th which become increasingly overlooked by houses.

However, the last word must belong to Bernard Darwin who, writing in his famous book *The Golf Courses of the British Isles* reminded readers of the posters, familiar in the early years of the century, which proclaimed "Skegness is so bracing".

In closing his chapter on East Anglia with a description of Seacroft, he lauded the fact that there was good turf and plenty of sand and the sea itself, although he added "we do not often see it. Neither do we see – and this is an unmixed blessing – the teeming swarms of trippers that come to Skegness to be braced".

THE SHERWOOD FOREST GOLF CLUB LTD

EAKRING ROAD, MANSFIELD, NOTTS NG18 3EW

Secretary/Professional: Mr K. Hall Tel: 01623 26689
Catering Manageress: Mrs D. McCart Tel: 01623 23327

Full catering service available with dining for up to 100 persons at one sitting.
Course is heathland, set in the very heart of Robin Hood country, and was designed
by James Braid. Yellow markers distance is 6,294 yds. SSS 71.
White markers distance is 6,714 yds. SSS 73.

The Course was the venue for the
Midland Qualifying Round for the Open Championship 1990–1995
Green Fees on application.
All applications to be made to the secretary.
Within a few miles of places of interest – such as the Major Oak (Robin Hood's Larder),
Newstead Abbey, Thoresby Hall, Clumber Oark, and 14 miles from the
centre of Nottingham.

M75 **Pottergate**
☎(01522) 794867
Moor Lane, Branston, Nr Lincoln,
Lincs
In the village of Branston on B1188
Parkland course
9 holes, 2519 yards, S.S.S 66
Designed by W Bailey
Founded 1992
Visitors: welcome
Green Fee: £5.50 (9 holes), £7.50
(18 holes)
Societies: welcome
Catering: bar and snacks available

M76 **RAF Waddington**
☎(01522) 720271
Waddington, Lincoln, LN5 9NB
4 miles S of Lincoln.
Airfield course.
9 holes, 5519 yards, S.S.S.69
Founded 1973
Visitors: if introduced by member.
Green Fee: apply for details.
Catering: limited bar facility.

M77 **Radcliffe-on-Trent**
☎(0115) 9333000 (Sec/Manager),
Pro 9332396, Steward: 9335771
Dewberry Lane, Cropwell Rd,
Radcliffe on Trent, Notts NG12 2JH

From Nottingham take A52 to
Grantham, turn right at 1st set of
lights after dual carriageway ends,
entrance 400 yards up Cropwell Rd
on left.
Undulating parkland course.
18 holes, 6434 yards, S.S.S.71
Designed by Frank Pennink.
Founded 1909
Visitors: welcome any weekday
except Tues, h/cap cert must be
produced.
Green Fee: WD £23; WE £28.
Societies: apply in writing or phone
Sec; Wed only.
Catering: bar, restaurant and bar
snacks.
Hotels: Bridgford Lodge,
(Nottingham).

M78 **Ramsdale Park Golf Centre**
☎(0115) 9655600, Fax 9654105
Oxton Rd, Calverton, Notts NG14
6NU.
NE Nottingham on the B6386 Oxton
to Calverton road.
Pay-as-you-Play parkland course.
18 holes, 6546 yards, S.S.S.71; 18
holes, 2844 yards, Par 3
Designed by Hawtree & Son.
Founded May 1992

Visitors: welcome
Green Fee: £12.50 (main course),
£6.80 (Par 3 course).
Societies: anytime by arrangement.
Catering: full facilities.
Driving range.

M79 **Retford**
☎(01777) 703733 (Pro), Sec 860682
Ordsall, Retford, Notts DN22 7VA
S off A620.
Woodland course.
18 holes, 6301 yards, S.S.S.70
Founded 1920
Visitors: welcome weekdays, with
member at weekends.
Green Fee: £19 per round, £23 per
day, (£10 with member).
Catering: full meal facilities.

M80 **Ruddington Grange**
☎(0115) 9846141, 9241391
Wilford Road, Ruddington,
Nottingham NG11 6NB
S of Nottingham via M1 junction 24,
A453, A52 Grantham road.
Parkland course.
18 holes, 6543 yards, S.S.S.72
Designed by Eddie McCausland,
David Johnson.
Founded 1988

Visitors: welcome with h/cap certs; not Sat.
Green Fee: WD £15 per day; WE £20 per day.
Societies: welcome, advance bookings only.
Catering: bars, restaurant, function rooms.
Practice ground, putting green.
Hotels: The Nottingham Night Lodge.

M81 Sandilands

☎(01507) 441432, Sec 441617
Sea Lane, Sandilands, Sutton-on-Sea, Mablethorpe, Lincs LN12 2RJ
4 miles S of Mablethorpe on A52 coast road, course runs next to sea wall.
Seaside links course.
18 holes, 6000 yards, S.S.S.69
Founded 1901
Visitors: welcome any time.
Green Fee: WD £15; WE & BH £20.
Societies: special weekday rate, £25 (2 rounds golf and evening meal).
Catering: bar meals available at all times.
Hotels: Grange & Links, 3-day golf breaks, societies welcome, phone (01507) 441334.

M82 Scunthorpe

☎(01724) 866561, Pro 868972
Burringham Rd, Scunthorpe, S Humberside DN17 2AB
On B1450, adjoining Mallard Hotel.
Parkland course.
18 holes, 6281 yards, S.S.S.71
Founded 1936
Visitors: Mon to Fri.
Green Fee: £16 per round, £20 per day.
Societies: Mon to Fri.
Catering: full facilities Mon to Fri.
Hotels: Mallard.

M83 Seacroft

☎(01754) 763020, Pro 769624/Fax
Drummond Rd, Skegness, Lincs PE25 3AU
1 mile S of Skegness alongside road to Gibraltar Road Bird Sanctuary.
Undulating seaside links course.
18 holes, 6479 yards, S.S.S.71
Founded 1895
Visitors: welcome from bona fide club with h/cap.
Green Fee: WD £25 per round, £35 per day; WE £30 per round, £40 per day.
Societies: as for visitors.
Catering: available except Tues.
Hotels: Vine; Crown.

M84 Sherwood Forest

☎(01623) 26689 (Sec), Pro 27403, Club 23327, Fax 27403
Eakring Rd, Mansfield, Notts NG18 3EW
M1 junction 27, take Mansfield exit from roundabout, left at T-junction, left at next T-junction (5 miles), right at next lights, right at next T-junction, left at lights, right at 3rd mini-roundabout, course two-thirds mile on left.
Heathland course, Championship standard.
18 holes, 6714 yards, S.S.S.73
Designed by H.S. Colt, redesigned by James Braid.
Founded 1895
Visitors: must be members of golf club with h/cap; only with member at weekends.
Green Fee: WD £35 per round, £45 per day.
Societies: Mon, Thurs, Fri, by prior arrangement.
Catering: full facilities daily.
Hotels: Pine Lodge; Midland; Swallows; The Fringe.

M85 Shirland

☎(01773) 834935 (Pro), Club 834969
Lower Delves, Shirland, Derbys DE5 6AU
1 mile N of Alfreton off A61; 3 miles from M1 junction 28 via A38.
Tree-lined rolling parkland course
18 holes, 6072 yards, S.S.S.69
Founded 1976
Visitors: no restrictions weekdays, book through Pro at weekends.
Green Fee: WD £15 per round, £25 per day; WE £20 per round.
Societies: welcome weekdays, book through Pro.
Catering: full facilities.
practice grounds, county standard bowling green.

M86 Sickleholme

☎(01433) 651306, Pro 651252
Saltergate Lane, Bamford, Sheffield S30 2BH
On A625, 14 miles W of Sheffield, near Marquis of Granby.
Hillside meadowland course.
18 holes, 6064 yards, S.S.S.69
Founded 1898
Visitors: welcome but not Wed am; preferably phoned in advance.
Green Fee: WD £25; WE £32.
Societies: catered for on weekdays by arrangement.
Catering: by arrangement.

M87 Sleaford

☎(01529) 488273, Pro 488644
Willoughby Rd, South Rauceby, Sleaford, Lincs NG34 8PL
Signposted off A153 Sleaford-Grantham road, 2 miles W of Sleaford.
Heathland course.
18 holes, 6443 yards, S.S.S.71
Designed by Tom Williamson.
Founded 1905
Visitors: welcome except winter Sun.
Green Fee: WD £21; WE £28; reductions when playing with member.
Societies: Mon-Fri by prior arrangement.
Catering: full bar; meals and snacks except Mon.
Hotels: Carre Arms.

M88 South Kyme

☎(01526) 861113
Skinners Lane, South Kyme, Lincoln LN4 4AT
On B1395 off A17 and A153.
Fenland course.
18 holes, 6597 yards, S.S.S.71
Designed by Graham Bradley.
Founded July 1990
Visitors: welcome.
Green Fee: WD £10; WE £12.
Societies: welcome booked in advance.
Catering: bar and bar menu, hot drinks and snacks all day; lunch and dinner for larger parties by prior arrangement.
Hotels: Golf, Petwood (Woodhall Spa).

M89 Southview

☎(01754) 760589
Burgh Rd, Skegness, Lincs PE25 2LA
On outskirts of Skegness on the A158 signposted Southview Leisure Park
Parkland course
9 holes, 2408 yards, S.S.S. 64
Founded 1990
Visitors: welcome at all times
Green Fee: £6 (18 holes)
Societies: welcome at all times
Catering: full service in the Leisure park
Video tuition, swimming pool, sauna, sunbeds, snooker
Hotels: North Shore; Crown; Links.

M90 Spalding

☎(01775) 680386 (Sec), Club 680234, Pro 680474
Surfleet, Spalding, Lincs PE11 4EA

4 miles N of Spalding off A16; course is approx 1 mile off A16, well signposted.
Meadowland course.
18 holes, 6478 yards, S.S.S.71
Founded 1908
Visitors: members of recognised clubs; h/cap cert required unless accompanied by member.
Green Fee: WD £24 (£12 with member); WE £30 (£15 with member).
Societies: welcome Thurs only on application.
Catering: full facilities available daily except Tues.
Extensive practice area.

M91 **Stanedge**
☎(01246) 566156
Walton Hay Farm, Stanedge, Chesterfield, Derbys S45 0LW
5 miles SW of Chesterfield, at top of long hill on A632, turn on to B5057; club 300 yards W of Red Lion Inn.
Undulating moorland course.
9 holes, 4867 yards, S.S.S.64
Founded 1931
Visitors: welcome weekdays before 2pm; anytime if accompanied by a member.
Green Fee: WD £15 (£7.50 with member); WE & BH £15 (with member only).
Societies: by prior arrangement only.
Catering: provided for parties by prior arrangement.
Hotels: The Chesterfield; Portland; Glen Stuart; Olde House.

M92 **Stanton-on-the-Wolds**
☎(0115) 9372044, Pro 9372390, Steward: 9372264
Stanton-on-the-Wolds, Keyworth, Notts NG12 5BH
Off A606 at Blue Star Garage 8 miles SE of Nottingham.
Meadowland course.
18 holes, 6437 yards, S.S.S.71
Designed by Tom Williamson.
Founded 1906
Visitors: weekdays if no club competitions in progress; weekends and Bank Holidays if accompanied by a member only.
Green Fee: £20 per round/day; societies £25 per round/day.
Societies: write to Sec, H.G. Gray FCA, 2 Golf Rd, Stanton-on-the-Wolds, Notts. NG12 5BH, (0115) 9372006.
Catering: ring Steward in advance.
Hotels: Edwalton (Nottingham).

M93 **Stoke Rochford**
☎(01476) 530275, 530245
Stoke Rochford, Grantham, Lincs
Off A1 northbound carriageway 5 miles S of Grantham, entrance at A.J.S. Service area.
Parkland course.
18 holes, 6251 yards, S.S.S.70
Designed by C. Turner.
Founded 1926
Visitors: welcome weekdays, not before 10.30am Sat or Sun unless accompanied by a member; advisable to telephone Pro before visiting.
Green Fee: on application.
Societies: catered for Mon, Tues and Fri only.
Catering: lunches and evening meals served upon request.
Snooker.

M94 **Sudbrook Moor**
☎(01400) 250796 (Pro), Catering/Enquiries: 250876
Carlton Scroop, Nr Grantham, Lincs NG32 3AT
On A607 8 miles N of Grantham.
Parkland course.
9 holes, 4566 yards, S.S.S.62
Designed by Tim Hutton.
Founded 1986
Visitors: welcome.
Green Fee: WD £5 per day; WE & BH £7.
Societies: welcome by prior arrangement.
Catering: coffee shop.
Practice ground.
Hotels: phone for details.

M95 **Sutton Bridge**
☎(01406) 350323, Pro 351080
New Rd, Sutton Bridge, Spalding, Lincs
On A17 10 miles W of Kings Lynn.
Parkland course.
9 holes, 5820 yards, S.S.S.68
Founded 1914
Visitors: weekdays only.
Green Fee: £16.
Catering: meals, sandwiches; not Mon.

M96 **Swingtime (Grimsby)**
☎(01472) 250555, Fax 267447
Cromwell Rd, Grimsby, S Humberside DN31 2BH
Next to Leisure Centre and auditorium in town
Parkland course
9 holes, 2426 yards, S.S.S. 33
Founded 1994

Visitors: welcome; pay-as-you-play
Green Fee: WD £6 (9 holes), £9 (18 holes); WE £7 (9 holes), £11 (18 holes)
Societies: welcome
Catering: limited
Driving range, golf superstore
Hotels: St James; Post House.

M97 **Tapton Park Municipal**
☎(01246) 273887, Bookings: 239500
Murray House, Crow Lane, Chesterfield, Derbys S41 0EQ
Near centre of Chesterfield, signposted.
Municipal parkland course.
18 holes, 6025 yards, S.S.S.69; 9 holes, 2613 yards, Par 34
Founded 1934
Visitors: welcome any time; booking system all week, up to 6 days in advance.
Green Fee: apply for details.
Societies: welcome by prior arrangement.
Catering: bar and restaurant facilities.
Pitch & Putt.

M98 **Toft Hotel**
☎(01778) 590616, **Hotels:** 590614
Toft, Nr Bourne, Lincs PE10 0XX
6 miles N of Stamford on A6121.
Undulating parkland course with water features.
18 holes, 6486 yards, S.S.S.71
Designed by Derek and Roger Fitton.
Founded 1988
Visitors: welcome; standard dress etiquette; tees bookable 14 days in advance.
Green Fee: WD £10 per round, £18 per day; WE £15 per round, £25 per day.
Societies: welcome by arrangement.
Catering: full bar, bar snack and restaurant facilities in adjacent hotel; function room (120).
Hotels: Toft, weekend/bargain breaks with reduced green fees for residents.

M99 **Trent Lock Golf Centre**
☎(0115) 9464398
Lock Lane, Sawley, Long Eaton, Notts NG10 3DD
2 miles off M1 junction 25.
Parkland course.
18 holes, 6211 yards, S.S.S.70
Designed by E.W. McCausland.
Founded 1991

Visitors: welcome any day, essential to book at weekends.
Green Fee: £10 (£8.50 with member); juniors & OAPs £6.50.
Societies: by prior arrangement.
Catering: bar snacks and restaurant, 11am to 10pm; private function room. Driving range.

M100 **Wollaton Park**
☎(0115) 9787574 (Sec), Pro 9784834, **Catering:** 9787341
Wollaton Park, Nottingham NG8 1BT
Off A614 Nottingham ring road at junction of A52 and Derby road.
Parkland course.
18 holes, 6494 yards, S.S.S.71
Designed by T. Williamson.
Founded 1927
Visitors: contact Sec or Pro.
Green Fee: WD £23 per round, £30 per day; WE £25 per round, £36 per day.
Societies: Tues and Fri.
Catering: limited on Mon.
Snooker, pitch & putt.

M101 **Woodhall Spa**
☎(01526) 352511
The Broadway, Woodhall Spa, Lincs LN10 6PU

On B1191 6 miles SW of Horncastle, 18 miles SE of Lincoln, 18 miles NE of Sleaford.
Heathland course.
18 holes, 6907 yards, S.S.S.73
Designed by Col S.V. Hotchkin.
Founded 1905
Visitors: welcome all week by prior arrangement with Sec, max h/cap 20, ladies 30.
Green Fee: If members of clubs affliated to EGU WD £25 per round, £40 per day; If not (and ladies) WD £35 per round, £55 per day.
Societies: welcome all week by prior arrangement with Sec, max h/cap 20, ladies 30.
Catering: full facilities available 7 days a week.
Hotels: Golf; Petwood; Dower House; Eagle Lodge; Village Limits.

M102 **Woodthorpe Hall**
☎(01507) 450294, Sec 463664/Fax
Woodthorpe, Alford, Lincs LN13 0DD
3.5 miles from Alford off B1371.
Parkland course.
18 holes, 5020 yards, S.S.S.65
Founded 1986
Visitors: welcome weekdays; by arrangement at weekends.
Green Fee: £10 per round.

Societies: by prior arrangement with Sec.
Catering: facilities available. Inn on site.
Fishing, snooker, bowls, shop.
Hotels: self-catering accommodation available at Woodthorpe Leisure Park.

M103 **Worksop**
☎(01909) 477731 (Sec), Pro 477732, Members: 472696
Windmill Lane, Worksop, Notts S80 2SQ
On SE of town, from new by-pass (A57) take A6005, follow local signposts for Sherwood Forest, turn immediately left into Windmill Lane.
Sandy heathland course.
18 holes, 6651 yards, S.S.S.73
Founded 1904
Visitors: welcome, but telephone first.
Green Fee: WD £22.50 per round, £30 per day; WE & BH £30 per round.
Societies: by arrangement, not weekends, Bank Holidays.
Catering: full, with notice.
Hotels: Van Dyk; Regancy; Aston Hall; Red Lion; Clumber Park; Travelodge.

LANCASHIRE, ISLE OF MAN, CUMBRIA

Lancashire encompasses the great chain of coastal courses between Liverpool and Southport that, for the championship status many possess, is as prolific a stretch as any in the world. West Lancashire is the most senior, the modern clubhouse conveniently served by Hall Road Station on the electric railway line that also gets a good view of Formby, Southport & Ainsdale, and Hillside. West Lancashire is noble seaside terrain although the rugged dimension of the dunes grow a cubit or two as they approach Southport.

Royal Birkdale, scene of seven Opens, provides a succession of avenues between sandhills, its fairways possessing few of the eccentric humps and hollows which golfers either love or hate. Royal Birkdale's fame is very much postwar, its reputation fairly galloping after it had staged its first Open in 1954 but its neighbour, Hillside, has come even more recently to the distinction of hosting championships.

Jack Nicklaus made his professional debut in Britain there in 1962 but the course has undergone major change since then, the alterations enabling it to graduate to higher realms. It needs no stressing that Birkdale and Hillside constitute mighty days' golf and that Formby, more secluded, keeps them company. Hesketh and Southport & Ainsdale should also be included in select itineraries of the Southport area, the latter having staged two pre-war Ryder Cup matches – that in 1933 resulting in a rare home victory.

Of the Lancashire courses north of Southport, Royal Lytham & St Annes is a pillar of strength, a championship links renowned for the severity of its challenge. Although visitors always retire battered and bruised, it does not stop them coming.

Royal Lytham is a relentless test but the Lytham area has other notable attractions. St Annes Old Links, next to Blackpool Airport, and Fairhaven, are demanding enough to have hosted qualifying rounds for the Open but there is plenty of variety in a part of the world where golf is as popular as black pudding. Knott End, near Fleetwood, Blackpool North Shore and Lytham Green Drive offer enjoyable detours while Ormskirk and Pleasington stand out in Lancashire's heartland.

Castletown, in the Isle of Man, is only a short hop from Blackpool Airport and the links and their lovely hotel only a short taxi ride from the terminal buildings at Ronaldsway, which are remarkably free of the unattractive bustle of bigger airports.

But the Isle of Man has other golfing temptations that may be more to the liking of those less anxious to grapple with such a stern task. Not the least of the scenic delights of the island are the distant views of the lakeland hills conjuring up thoughts of fell walkers, poets, climbers and relaxation on a boat.

Golf is secondary in the minds of the majority of Cumbria's visitors but Seascale and Silloth occupy an important place as fine seaside courses. Seascale is the more remote, a small town south of Whitehaven and Workington just off the road that makes a grand sweep around the Lake District. Furness and Grange over Sands are worthy of a short detour, but Seascale is true links with more undulation than some.

Then it is up past St Bees Head to the edge of the Solway Firth and Silloth on Solway which is an authentic championship setting in a town well known for its flour mill and the little harbour that serves it.

N1 Accrington & District

☎(01254) 232734, Sec/Fax 381614, Pro 231091
New Barn Farm, Devon Ave, West End, Oswaldtwistle, Accrington, Lancs BB5 4LS
On A679 5 miles from Blackburn.
Moorland course.
18 holes, 6028 yards, S.S.S.69
Designed by James Braid.
Founded 1893
Visitors: welcome at any time.
Green Fee: on application.
Societies: by arrangement.
Catering: full facilities.
Hotels: Kendal; Moat House, Duncan House.

N2 Allerton Municipal

☎(0151) 428 1046
Allerton, Liverpool 18
From city centre on Allerton Rd.
Undulating parkland course.
9 holes, 1847 yards, S.S.S.34; 18 holes, 5494 yards, S.S.S.67
Visitors: welcome; book times for 18 hole course by phone or in person.
Green Fee: on application.
Societies: on application.
Catering: by arrangement.

N3 Alston Moor

☎(01434) 381675
The Hermitage, Alston, Cumbria CA9 3DB
1.75 miles from Alston on B6277 to Middleton in Teesdale.
Parkland course.
10 holes, 5380 yards, S.S.S.66
Founded 1906
Visitors: welcome anytime.
Green Fee: on application.
Societies: any time by arrangement.
Catering: by prior arrangement.
Hotels: George & Dragon; Hillcrest; Bluebell Inn; Nenthall.

N4 Appleby

☎(017683) 51432
Brackenber Moor, Appleby-in-Westmorland, Cumbria CA16 6LP
2 miles E of Appleby on A66.
Moorland course.
18 holes, 5913 yards, S.S.S.68
Designed by Willie Fernie of Troon.
Founded 1903
Visitors: welcome at any time.
Green Fee: WD £12; WE & BH £16.
Societies: welcome by arrangement.
Catering: by arrangement.
Snooker.
Hotels: Tufton Arms; Royal Oak; Appleby Manor; The Gate.

N5 Ashton & Lea

☎(01772) 726480, Fax 735762
Tudor Ave, off Blackpool Rd, Lea, Preston PR4 0XA
3 miles from Preston centre on Blackpool road, turn opposite Pig and Whistle.
Parkland course.
18 holes, 6346 yards, S.S.S.70
Designed by J. Steer.
Founded 1913
Visitors: phone (01772) 735282 for tee reservations.
Green Fee: WD £20; WE & BH £23.
Societies: weekdays on application to Sec.
Catering: full facilities daily.
Snooker.
Hotels: Crest; Tickled Trout; Travel Inn.

N6 Ashton-in-Makerfield

☎(01942) 727267, Sec 719330
Garswood Park, Liverpool Rd, Ashton-in-Makerfield WN4 0YT
On A58, off M6 0.5 mile to course.
Parkland course.
18 holes, 6205 yards, S.S.S.70
Designed by F.W. Hawtree.
Founded 1902
Visitors: welcome weekdays except Wed; accompanied by member at weekends.
Green Fee: WD £22.
Societies: Tues and Thurs.
Catering: meals except Mon.
Hotels: The Thistle.

N7 Ashton-under-Lyne

☎(0161) 330 1537
Gorsey Way, Ashton-under-Lyne, Lancs OL6 9HT
From Ashton take Mossley Rd, left at Queens Rd, right at St Christophers Road.
Moorland course.
18 holes, 6209 yards, S.S.S.70
Founded 1913
Visitors: welcome if member of golf club; Sat and Sun only with member.
Green Fee: apply for details.
Societies: by arrangement, not Wed or weekends.
Catering: full facilities except Mon.
Snooker.
Hotels: York House; Birch Hall (Oldham).

N8 Bacup

☎(01706) 873170
Maden Rd, Bacup, Lancs OL13 8HM
Off A671, 7 miles N of Rochdale, 0.5 mile from Bacup centre.
Meadowland course.
9 holes, 5652 yards, S.S.S.67
Founded 1911
Visitors: welcome weekdays, except Mon, Tues, and at weekends after competitions.
Green Fee: apply for details.
Societies: welcome by prior arrangement weekdays except Mon and Tues.
Catering: full facilities.
Snooker.

N9 Barrow

☎(01229) 825444, Pro 832121
Rakesmoor Lane, Hawcoat, Barrow-in-Furness, Cumbria LA14 4QB
Turn left into Bank Lane to Hawcoat off Dalton by-pass (opposite Scotts Paper Mill) on entering boundary of Barrow.
Undulating meadowland course.
18 holes, 6209 yards, S.S.S.70
Founded 1922
Visitors: welcome, ladies day Fri.
Green Fee: WD £15; WE & BH £25.
Societies: by arrangement.
Catering: by arrangement.
Hotels: Abbey House, Glen Garth; Lisdoonie.

N10 Baxenden & District

☎(01254) 234555
Top-o'-the Meadow, Wooley Lane, Baxenden, Nr Accrington, Lancs
Take Accrington exit from M65, follow signs for Baxenden, course signposted in village.
Moorland course.
9 holes, 5717 yards, S.S.S.68
Founded 1913
Visitors: welcome weekdays, with member only weekends.
Green Fee: apply for details.
Societies: welcome weekdays by arrangement.
Catering: bar and bar snacks available, meals provided if ordered in advance.

N11 Beacon Park

☎(01695) 622700, Fax 633066
Beacon Lane, Dalton, Up Holland, Wigan, Lancs WN8 7RU
Signposted from centre of Up Holland on A577 and from A5209 near Parbold, located on side of Ashurst Beacon Hill overlooking Skelmersdale.
Public hilly parkland course.
18 holes, 5996 yards, S.S.S.69
Designed by Donald Steel.
Founded 1982

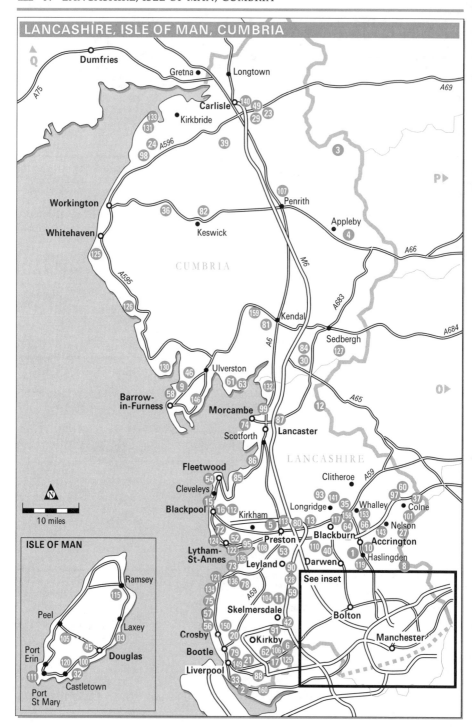

LANCASHIRE, ISLE OF MAN, CUMBRIA

Dumfries

Gretna
Longtown

Carlisle
Kirkbride

Workington

Whitehaven

Keswick

CUMBRIA

Penrith

Appleby

Kendal

Sedbergh

Ulverston

Barrow-in-Furness

Morcambe

Scotforth
Lancaster

Fleetwood

Cleveleys

Blackpool

Kirkham

Clitheroe

Longridge

Whalley
Colne

Nelson

Preston

Blackburn

Accrington

Haslingden

Lytham-St-Annes

Leyland

Darwen

See inset

Skelmersdale

Bolton

Manchester

Crosby

Kirkby

Bootle

Liverpool

10 miles

ISLE OF MAN

Ramsey

Peel

Laxey

Port Erin

Douglas

Port St Mary

Castletown

Visitors: welcome at any time.
Green Fee: apply for details.
Societies: welcome weekdays, by arrangement weekends.
Catering: bar meals during bar hours; other meals by arrangement. Driving range.
Hotels: Lancashire Lodge (Skelmersdale).

N12 Bentham

☎(015242) 61018, Sec 62455
Robin Lane, Bentham, Lancaster LA2 7AG
Between Lancaster and Settle on B6480, 13 miles E of M6 junction 34.
Undulating meadowland course.
9 holes, 5760 yards, S.S.S.69
Founded 1922

Visitors: welcome.
Green Fee: apply for details.
Societies: welcome by prior arrangement.
Catering: snacks.
Hotels: Bridge Hotel (Ingleton); Post House (Lancaster).

N13 Blackburn

☎(01254) 51122 (Sec/Club), Pro 55942
Beardwood Brow, Blackburn, Lancs BB2 7AX
Easy access from M6, M61 and M65; in W end of Blackburn off Revidge Rd, from Moat House Hotel on A677 turn left at traffic lights, left at Dog Hotel.
Undulating meadowland course.
18 holes, 6140 yards, S.S.S.70
Founded 1894
Visitors: welcome weekdays (restricted Tues).
Green Fee: WD £19 (£7 with member); WE & BH £22 (£8 with member).
Societies: welcome by prior arrangement; contact Sec for special terms.
Catering: daily except Mon.
Snooker.
Hotels: Moat House (Blackburn); Dunkenhalgh (Clayton-le-Moors).

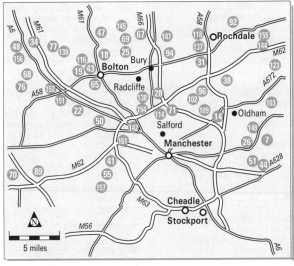

5 miles

N14 Blackley

☎(0161) 643 2980, Sec 654 7770, Pro 643 3912
Victoria Ave East, Blackley, Manchester M9 6HW
5 miles N of city centre.
Parkland course.
18 holes, 6237 yards, S.S.S.70
Founded 1907
Visitors: weekdays only. Weekends and Bank Holidays with member only.
Green Fee: £18.
Societies: Mon, Tues, Wed and Fri, special all-in fee including bar lunch and evening meal £29.
Catering: all types available.
Hotels: Periquito (Oldham).

N15 Blackpool North Shore

☎(01253) 352054 (Sec), Pro 354640, bar/**Catering:** 351017
Devonshire Rd, Blackpool FY2 0RD
N of town centre 0.5 mile from Promenade.
Undulating parkland course.
18 holes, 6400 yards, S.S.S.71
Founded 1906
Visitors: restricted Thurs and Sun; not Sat.
Green Fee: WD £25; WE £30.
Societies: Mon, Tues, Wed, Fri; special package rates.
Catering: bar and full catering.
Snooker.
Hotels: Sheraton; Doric.

N16 Blackpool Park

☎(01253) 397916
North Park Drive, Blackpool, Lancs FY3 8LS
1.5 miles E of centre of Blackpool.
Parkland course.
18 holes, 6060 yards, S.S.S.69
Designed by Dr Mackenzie.
Founded 1926
Visitors: welcome anytime.
Green Fee: apply for details.
Societies: welcome weekdays by arrangement.
Catering: facilities available every day except Tues.

N17 Blundells Hill

☎(0151) 426 9040, Pro 430 0100
Blundells Lane, Rainhill, Liverpool L35 6NA
Two minutes from M62 junction 7
Parkland course
Founded 1994
18 holes, 6256 yards, S.S.S. 71
Visitors: welcome; book in advance through pro.

Green Fee: WD £20; WE £30
Societies: welcome by prior arrangement with Sec (01744 24892)
Catering: full facilities; function room for 200
Snooker room.

N18 Bolton Old Links

☎(01204) 842307 (Office am), Club 840050, Pro 843089
Chorley Old Rd, Bolton BL1 5SU
On B6226 just N of A58 from M61 junction 5.
Moorland course.
18 holes, 6406 yards, S.S.S.72
Designed by Dr A. MacKenzie.
Founded 1891
Visitors: welcome except competition days; telephone for information.
Green Fee: WD £25; WE & BH £35.
Societies: by prior arrangement on weekdays.
Catering: daily except Mon.
Snooker.
Hotels: Crest; Pack Horse; Last Drop; Bolton Moat House.

N19 Bolton

☎(01204) 843278, Sec 843067, Pro 843073
Lostock Park, Chorley New Rd, Bolton BL6 4AJ
Leave M61 at exit 6, off main road half way between Bolton and Horwich.
Parkland course.
18 holes, 5978 yards, S.S.S.70
Founded 1891
Visitors: welcome weekdays except Tues.
Green Fee: £34 Mon, Thurs, Fri; £38 Wed, Sat, Sun, BH.
Societies: Thurs by arrangement.
Catering: all day.
Hotels: Crest.

N20 Bootle

☎(0151) 928 6196, Bookings: 928 1371
Dunnings Bridge Rd, Bootle, Merseyside L30 2PP
A565, 5 miles from Liverpool.
Municipal seaside links course.
18 holes, 6362 yards, S.S.S.70
Designed by F. Stephens.
Founded 1934
Visitors: welcome.
Green Fee: WD £4.80; WE & BH £6.40.
Societies: welcome by prior arrangement.
Catering: meals served.
Hotels: Park.

N21 Bowring

☎(0151) 489 1901
Bowring Park Golf Course, Roby Rd, Huyton, Liverpool L36 4HD
6 miles N of Liverpool city centre.
Municipal parkland course.
18 holes, 5620 yards, S.S.S.70
Founded 1913
Visitors: welcome, 8am-4pm winter, 8am-9pm summer.
Green Fee: £4.55 per round.
Societies: welcome, book in advance.
Catering: snacks.

N22 Brackley

☎(0161) 790 6076
Bullows Rd, Little Hulton, Worsley, Manchester M38 9TR
9 miles from Manchester on A6, turn right at White Lion Hotel into Highfield Rd, left into Captain Fold Rd, left into Bullows Rd.
Parkland course.
9 holes, 3003 yards, S.S.S.69
Founded 1976
Visitors: welcome by prior arrangement.
Green Fee: £3.50 per round.

N23 Brampton

☎(016977) 2255, Pro 2000
Brampton, Cumbria CA8 1HN
1.75 miles from Brampton on B6413 Castle Carrock road.
Moorland course.
18 holes, 6420 yards, S.S.S.71
Designed by James Braid.
Founded 1907
Visitors: welcome; standard tee bookings 9.30-10.30am Mon, Wed and Thurs.
Green Fee: WD £18; WE & BH £22.
Societies: welcome by prior arrangement weekdays; limited at weekends.
Catering: full bar and catering facilities available.
Snooker.
Hotels: reduced green fees are offered by numerous local hotels and guest houses; details available on request.

N24 Brayton Park Golf Course

☎(0169 73) 20840
Brayton, Aspatria, Carlisle, Cumbria CA5 3TD
Off A596, W of Carlisle.
Parkland course.
9 holes, 2521 yards, Par 32
Founded 1978

Visitors: welcome, no restrictions.
Green Fee: WD £5 (9 holes), £7 (18 holes); WE £6 (9 holes), £8 (18 holes).
Societies: by prior booking.
Catering: full facilities.
Driving range.
Hotels: Kelsey (Mealsgate); Wheyrigg (Abbeytown), Green Hill Hotel.

N25 Breightmet
☎(01204) 527381
Red Bridge, Ainsworth, Bolton, Lancs BL2 5PA
From Bolton 3 miles on main road to Bury and turn left to Red Bridge.
Parkland course.
9 holes, 6448 yards, S.S.S.71
Designed by Alliss & Thomas.
Founded 1911
Visitors: weekdays except Wed.
Green Fee: WD £15 (£8 with member); WE & BH £18 (£10 with member).
Societies: welcome Tues, Thurs, Fri.
Catering: every day except Mon.
Snooker.
Hotels: Pack Horse.

N26 Brookdale
☎(0161) 681 4534, Pro 681 2655
Ashbridge
, Woodhouses, Failsworth, Manchester M35 9WM
5 miles N of Manchester.
Parkland, meadowland course.
18 holes, 6040 yards, S.S.S.68
Founded 1962
Visitors: welcome.
Green Fee: apply for details.
Societies: welcome by prior arrangement with Sec; special package can be arranged.
Catering: facilities available daily except Mon.

N27 Burnley
☎(01282) 421045, Sec 451281
Glen View, Burnley BB11 3RW
Off A56 to Glen View Rd, after 300 yards turn right.
Moorland/meadowland course.
18 holes, 5899 yards, S.S.S.69
Founded 1905
Visitors: weekdays and Sun; limited Sat.
Green Fee: WD £20; WE & BH £25.
Societies: weekdays, Sun.
Catering: snacks and full meals except Mon and Wed pm.
Hotels: Kierby; Rosehill House; Oaks.

N28 Bury
☎(0161) 766 4897, Pro 766 2213
Unsworth Hall, Blackford Bridge, Bury BL9 9TJ
On A56 7 miles N of Manchester.
Undulating moorland course.
18 holes, 5961 yards, S.S.S.69
Founded 1890
Visitors: welcome with reservation; h/cap cert required.
Green Fee: WD £22; WE & BH £28.50.
Societies: catered for Wed, Thurs and Fri.
Catering: daily except Mon.
Hotels: Red Hall; Village Leisure.

N29 Carlisle
☎(01228) 513029, Sec/Fax 513303, Pro 513241
Aglionby, Carlisle CA4 8AG
2 miles E of Carlisle, leave M6 at exit 43 and take A69 for about 0.75 mile.
Parkland course.
18 holes, 6278 yards, S.S.S.70
Designed by Tom Simpson, Mackenzie Ross and (latterly) Frank Pennink.
Founded 1909
Visitors: welcome weekdays and Sundays, check availability by telephone; Saturday members only.
Green Fee: WD £20 per round, £30 per day; Sunday £35.
Societies: Mon, Wed and Fri; party rates for 12 or more.
Catering: meals and snacks daily.
Hotels: Queens Arms; Bridge; Kilorran; Cumbria Park.

N30 Casterton
☎(01524) 271592
Sedburgh Rd, Casterton, Carnforth, Lancs LA6 2LA
Take M6 junc 36 and head on A65 for 4 miles towards Skipton then 1 mile along A683
Picturesque upland course.
9 holes, 5774 yards, S.S.S. 68
Designed by W Adamson.
Founded 1946
Visitors: welcome.
Green Fee: WD £8 per round; £12 per day; WE £10 per round, £15 per day.
Societies: on application
Catering: full facilities but no bar.
Hotels: Pheasant; Whoop Hall; Royal (Kirkby Lonsdale).

N31 Castle Hawk
☎(01706) 40841, Fax 860587
Heywood Rd, Castleton, Rochdale

Leave Rochdale on Castledon road, in Castledon turn right directly before railway station, follow until reach Heywood Rd (dirt track).
Undulating parkland/meadowland course.
18 holes, 5389 yards, S.S.S.68; 9 holes, 3158 yards, S.S.S.55
Designed by T. Wilson.
Founded 1965
Visitors: welcome.
Green Fee: WD £6; WE £8.
Societies: welcome.
Catering: snacks and lunches available; evening meals by arrangement.

N32 Castletown
☎(01624) 822201, Sec 825435
Fort Island, Castletown, Isle of Man
1 mile from airport.
Seaside course.
18 holes, 6711 yards, S.S.S.72
Designed by Mackenzie Ross.
Founded 1 June 1892
Visitors: welcome.
Green Fee: WD £20; WE & BH £25. Residents £18.
Societies: welcome by prior arrangement.
Catering: bar snacks served all day; full à la carte lunch and dinner.
Snooker, indoor swimming pool, sauna, solarium.
Hotels: Castletown Golf Links adjoining course, DBB/Golf & flight packages available.

N33 Childwall
☎(0151) 487 0654, Pro 487 9871, Fax 487 0882
Naylor's Rd, Liverpool L27 2YB
2 miles M62 exit 6, 5 miles from Liverpool city centre.
Parkland course.
18 holes, 6425 yards, S.S.S.71
Designed by James Braid.
Founded 1922
Visitors: 9.45am and 2pm, Mon, Wed, Thurs, Fri.
Green Fee: WD £22; WE £31.50.
Societies: as for visitors (not weekends).
Catering: bars and restaurant facilities.
Snooker.
Hotels: Logwood Mill; Derby Lodge.

N34 Chorley
☎(01257) 480263, Pro 481245, Fax 480722
Hall o' th'Hill, Heath Charnock, Nr Chorley, Lancs PR6 9HX

Castletown, Isle of Man

When the weather is fine, the greens holding and there is no wind, seaside links often present fewer problems than other types of course; but the moment the wind stirs it is another matter.

Tales of the 1979 P.G.A. Cup match at Castletown in the Isle of Man centred largely on days of sunshine, the ball running a mile, and agreement that it was an idyllic spot. My baptism was a little more severe, a near gale springing up overnight and rain slanting in from the Irish Sea. The clear outline of mountain peaks disappeared and there was a remoteness, almost a loneliness, on the little peninsula. but not even a princely soaking could dampen my admiration. Castletown's position as one of the great courses of the British Isles is undoubted.

Its modern version owes everything to Mackenzie Ross whose restoration after the war was similar to the miracle he wrought at Turnberry. Good driving is essential. On such as the 7th and 8th, the fairway is the only place to be; yet the line from the championship tees involves quite a carry.

Castletown's hazards are all natural – gorse, bracken, rough, rocks and a beach which gives the course more coastal frontage than perhaps any other in the world. Apart from a clump of forlorn palms behind the 8th green, and some planting to mask the wall behind the 4th there isn't a tree to be seen. Though the golfer has nothing to shield him, there is nothing to obscure the magnificent array of views either; the sea, two great sweeps of bay, the landmark of the castle and, on a good day, the Cumbrian Hills.

In days gone by, it was the residence of the Earl of Derby who, as Lord of Man, started the Derby at Castletown prior to taking it to Epsom. The 10th was the actual site, the hole not surprisingly assuming the name 'Racecourse'.

Castletown deserves undivided attention, although the start is no indication of what lies ahead. The 1st is a short, uphill par 4, one yard, in fact, over the par 3 limit, and the 2nd a somewhat plain two

shotter. It is when you turn away down the long 5th, a dogleg round the corner of a stone wall, with a second shot (or third or fourth) between a large mound and an old pill box, that the course really begins.

The 5th, not quite such a good par 5 as the 3rd, sandwiches the 4th, where the drive must be left to obtain the correct angle to negotiate the slope of the green and to miss the guardian bunkers on the right. Castletown's short holes make a wonderful set, the 6th, the shortest of them, providing an inviting shot even if the green is encircled by trouble. The same applies to the drive at the 7th and the second shot to a green typical of Mackenzie Ross's imaginative designs.

The 8th is no easier. The fairway may present a nice target at a lower level but it is also alarmingly narrow and the road is only a thin strip separating errant drives from the beach on which balls, pebbles and boulders are indistinguishable. The drive at the 9th must be aimed at the outline of King William's College, a fortress of Manx stone. And at what may have been the home turn in the first Derby down by the 10th green, Castletown Bay hoves in sight.

At the delightful short 11th and the next two par 4s, it is all too simple to let a tee shot drift to the right and, if the 14th is a shade less of a threat in this regard, the tee marker tells the bad news that it is 468 yards. On the 15th, a stone wall denotes out of bounds and the contouring of the greens foils those playing too safe to the left; but the best is yet to come – notably the 17th with its gaping gorge in front of the tee and resplendent rocks to the right. The 18th is a challenging finish, set against the square form of the welcoming Links Hotel.

Those who originally spied out the land knew what they were doing; but a question must be asked of the island's emblem of the Three Legs of Man and its motto 'whichever way you throw me, I shall stand'. Did they ever experiment on the championship tee at the 17th with a gale off the sea?

On A673 100 yards S of junction with A6 at Skew Bridge traffic lights. Heathland course. 18 holes, 6307 yards, S.S.S.70 Designed by J.A. Steer. Founded 1898
Visitors: welcome by prior arrangement with Sec, Tues-Fri only (not Bank Holidays).
Green Fee: £25.
Societies: as for visitors.
Catering: full bar and restaurant facilities; societies by prior arrangement. Snooker.
Hotels: Yarrow Bridge Hotel; Parkville; Hartwood Hall; Gladmar.

N35 Clitheroe
☎(01200) 22618, Sec 22292, Pro 24242
Whalley Rd, Pendleton, Clitheroe BB7 1PP
Off A59 2 miles S of Clitheroe. Undulating parkland course. 18 holes, 6326 yards, S.S.S.71 Designed by James Braid. Founded 1891
Visitors: welcome subject to competition days on Sun and Thurs (Ladies Day). No visitors on Sat.
Green Fee: WD £27; WE & BH £32.
Societies: welcome by arrangement; max 48 Mon, Tues, Wed; max 24 Thurs, Fri, Sun (not Sat).
Catering: bar and restaurant.
Hotels: Post House; Swan and Royal; Brooklyn GH; Stirk House.

N36 Cockermouth
☎(017687) 76223, Sec (home): (01900) 822650
Embleton, Cockermouth, Cumbria CA13 9SG
4 miles E of Cockermouth. Fell land course. 18 holes, 5496 yards, S.S.S.67 Designed by James Braid. Founded 1896
Visitors: weekdays unrestricted before 5pm except Wed; not Sun before 11am and 2-3.15pm.
Green Fee: WD £15; WE & BH £20.
Societies: apply to Sec.
Catering: snacks and meals by arrangement with Stewardess. Snooker.
Hotels: Armathwaite Hall; Globe.

N37 Colne
☎(01282) 863391
Law Farm, Skipton Old Rd, Colne, Lancs BB8 7EB

Leave end of M65, straight on 0.75 mile to roundabout, take small road in left hand corner signposted Lothersdale; club at top of hill. Moorland course. 9 holes, 5961 yards, S.S.S.69 Founded 1901
Visitors: welcome except competition days; 2 balls only Thurs; no parties weekends April-Oct; normal dress and equipment requirements.
Green Fee: WD £15; WE & BH £20 (half price with member).
Societies: by appointment.
Catering: snacks or full meals; parties (to 100) by negotiation with Steward. Snooker tables.

N38 Crompton & Royton
☎(0161) 624 2154, 624 0986
Highbarn, Royton, Oldham, Lancs OL2 6RW
Off A627 at Royton centre. Moorland course. 18 holes, 6222 yards, S.S.S.70 Founded 1908
Visitors: welcome.
Green Fee: WD £24 (£10 with member); WE & BH £30 (£10 with member).
Societies: welcome by arrangement, package deals available.
Hotels: Avant, Periquito (Oldham).

N39 Dalston Hall
☎(01228) 710165
Dalston, Nr Carlisle, Cumbria CA5 7JX
M6 junction 42, through Dalston village, course 0.5 mile on right. Parkland course. 9 holes, 5294 yards, S.S.S.67 Designed by David Pearson. Founded May 1990
Visitors: tee booking required at weekends and after 4pm weekdays.
Green Fee: WD £5 (9 holes), £8 (18 holes); WE £6 (9 holes), £11 (18 holes).
Societies: throughout the season, booking required.
Catering: bar and restaurant. Fly fishing.
Hotels: Dalston Hall caravan park; tourers and tents welcome.

N40 Darwen
☎(01254) 701287, Sec 704367, Pro 776370
Winter Hill, Darwen, Lancs BB3 0LB
1.5 miles from Darwen town centre, off A666 Bolton-Blackburn road.

Moorland course. 18 holes, 5752 yards, S.S.S.68 Founded Sept 1893
Visitors: welcome weekdays and with advance bookings at weekends.
Green Fee: WD £13 (£6 with member); WE £20 (£8 with member).
Societies: catered for except Mon, Tues, Sat.
Catering: full, except Mon.
Hotels: Red House Motel; Whitehall Country Club.

N41 Davyhulme Park
☎(0161) 748 2856, Sec/bookings: 748 2260, Pro 748 3931
Gleneagles Rd, Davyhulme, Urmston, Manchester M41 8SA
8 miles S of Manchester, adjacent to Trafford Hospital, Moorside Rd, Davyhulme. Parkland course. 18 holes, 6237 yards, S.S.S.70 Founded 1910
Visitors: welcome except competition days.
Green Fee: on application.
Societies: Mon, Tues, Thurs.
Catering: all week. Snooker.

N42 Dean Wood
☎(01695) 622219, Pro 622980
Lafford Lane, Up Holland, Skelmersdale, Lancs WN8 0QZ
M6 exit 26, 1.5 miles on A577 to Up Holland. Undulating parkland course. 18 holes, 6137 yards, S.S.S.70 Designed by James Braid. Founded 1922
Visitors: welcome weekdays, preferably by arrangement; weekends by introduction.
Green Fee: WD £24; WE & BH £30.
Societies: weekdays only by arrangement.
Catering: daily. Snooker.
Hotels: Holland Hall.

N43 Deane
☎(01204) 651944, Sec 651808
Broadford Rd, Bolton, Lancs BL3 4NB
M61 exit 5, 1 mile towards town centre, Dealey Rd on left leads directly to club. Undulating parkland course. 18 holes, 5595 yards, S.S.S.67 Founded 1906
Visitors: members of other clubs only unless playing with member.

Green Fee: WD £20; WE & BH £25.
Societies: Tues, Thurs, Fri.
Catering: full facilities daily except Mon.
Hotels: Crest; Pack Horse; Moat House.

N44 Denton

☎(0161) 336 3218 (Sec), Pro 336 2070
Manchester Rd, Denton, Manchester M34 5NU
A57, 5 miles SE of Manchester; also M66 Denton roundabout from Stockport.
Parkland course.
18 holes, 6541 yards, S.S.S.71
Founded May 1909
Visitors: welcome weekdays, and at weekends if accompanied by a member.
Green Fee: WD £22; WE & BH £27 (£10 with member).
Societies: catered for Mon, Wed, Thurs and Fri; book in advance through Sec.
Catering: lunches served except Mon.

N45 Douglas

☎(01624) 675952, Pro 661558
Pulrose Rd, Douglas, Isle of Man
1 mile from Douglas town centre, clubhouse situated near to large cooling tower for Electricity Dept Power Station.
Municipal parkland course.
18 holes, 5922 yards, S.S.S.68
Designed by Dr A. Mackenzie.
Founded 1927
Visitors: welcome; advisable to phone.
Green Fee: on application.
Societies: welcome; advisable to phone.
Catering: full meals and snacks served from 11am to 11pm from May to end September by prior arrangement.

N46 Dunnerholme

☎(01229) 462675
Duddon Rd, Askam-in-Furness, Cumbria LA16 7AW
A590 to Askam, turn left over railway line into Duddin Rd, continue down towards seashore over cattle grid on right.
Links course.
10 holes, 6154 yards, S.S.S.70
Founded 1905
Visitors: welcome but not Sun until after 4.30pm.

Green Fee: WD £12; WE & BH £15.
Societies: welcome almost any time if telephoned in advance.
Catering: facilities available. Pool.
Hotels: Railway; White Water; Clarence; Wellington; Abbey House.

N47 Dunscar

☎(01204) 303321, Pro 592992
Longworth Lane, Bromley Cross, Bolton BL7 9QY
N of Bolton about 2 miles off A666 Blackburn road, course signed to left at Dunscar Bridge.
Parkland/moorland course.
18 holes, 6085 yards, S.S.S.69
Founded 1908
Visitors: welcome, steward's day off Mon; weekends by arrangement.
Green Fee: WD £20 (£10 with member); WE & BH £30 (£10 with member).
Societies: details from Sec.
Catering: lunch and dinner served daily except Mon.
Hotels: Last Drop; Egerton House; Moat House.

N48 Duxbury Park

☎(01257) 267380, Fax 241378
Duxbury Park, Chorley, Lancs PR7 4AS
1.5 miles S of Chorley, off A6, 200 yards along A5106.
Municipal parkland course.
18 holes, 6270 yards, S.S.S.70
Founded 1970
Visitors: municipal course, booking accepted by phone.
Green Fee: on application.
Societies: booked in writing, not Sat or Sun.
Catering: separate facilities from the club.
Hotels: Hartwood Hall; Kilhey Court.

N49 Eden

☎(01228) 573003, Fax 818435
Crosby-on-Eden, Carlisle, Cumbria CA6 4RA
2 miles E of Carlisle, 3 miles from M6; for full directions telephone Pro shop.
Parkland course.
18 holes, 6368 yards, S.S.S.72
Designed by E. MacCauslin
Founded June 1992
Visitors: welcome.
Green Fee: WD £15; WE £20.
Societies: by prior arrangement.
Catering: full facilities.
Driving range.

N50 Ellesmere

☎(0161) 790 2122 (Club), Pro 790 8591
Old Clough Lane, Worsley, Manchester M28 5HZ
5 miles W of Manchester, on A580, adjacent to junction 14 on M62.
Undulating parkland course.
18 holes, 6248 yards, S.S.S.70
Founded 1913
Visitors: members of recognised club welcome by arrangement with Pro, except during club competitions and Bank Holidays.
Green Fee: WD £18 per round, £24 per day; WE £25.
Societies: catered for weekdays; apply in writing to Hon Sec.
Catering: available at all times by arrangement with Steward's wife.
Hotels: Novotel.

N51 Fairfield Golf & Sailing Club

☎(0161) 370 1641, Pro 370 2292
Booth Rd, Audenshaw, Manchester M34 5GA
A635 6 miles from city centre.
Parkland course.
18 holes, 5654 yards, S.S.S.68
Founded 1892
Visitors: welcome weekdays; club competitions Wed pm, Thurs and weekends am.
Green Fee: WD £17 per round, £25 per day; WE £23.
Societies: by arrangement Mon. Tues, Fri.
Catering: full facilities can be provided by prior arrangement, but limited on Mon.
Hotels: Village (Hyde).

N52 Fairhaven

☎(01253) 736976
Lytham Hall Park, Ansdell, Lytham-St-Annes FY8 4JU
On B5261 2 miles from Lytham, next to Fylde Rugby Ground.
Semi-links course.
18 holes, 6883 yards, S.S.S.73
Designed by James Braid.
Founded 1895
Visitors: welcome by arrangement.
Green Fee: WD £30 per round, £35 per day; WE £35.
Societies: welcome by prior arrangement.
Catering: meals served daily except Mon (sandwiches available from bar). Snooker, card room, banqueting facilities.
Hotels: Clifton Arms; Grand; Dalmeney; Fearnlea.

N53 **Fishwick Hall**
☎(01772) 798300, Pro 795870
Glenluce Drive, Farringdon Park,
Preston, Lancs PR1 5TD
From M6 junction 31 take A59
towards Preston, past Tickled Trout
Motel, Glenluce Drive is 1st left at top
of hill.
Undulating meadowland/parkland
course.
18 holes, 6092 yards, S.S.S.69
Founded 1912
Visitors: welcome between 9.30 and
11.30am and after 2pm.
Green Fee: WD £20; WE & BH £25;
reduction Nov-Feb and if
accompanied by a member.
Societies: by arrangement
weekdays.
Catering: full catering facilities
available.
Hotels: Tickled Trout Motel.

N54 **Fleetwood**
☎(01253) 873661 (Pro and
Catering), Sec 773573, Club
873114
Princes Way, Fleetwood, Lancs FY7
8AF
On A587, 7 miles N of Blackpool.
Links course alongside beach.
18 holes, 6723 yards, S.S.S.72
Designed by Edwin Steer.
Founded 1932
Visitors: welcome weekends and any
weekday except Tues, h/cap cert
required.
Green Fee: WD £20; WE £25.
Societies: welcome weekdays; also
at weekends by prior arrangement
only.
Catering: full bar facilities 11.30am-
11pm (restricted Sun), catering 7
days as required.
Snooker.
Hotels: Boston; North Euston.

N55 **Flixton**
☎(0161) 748 2116 (Club), Pro 746
7160, **Catering:** 748 7545
Church Rd, Flixton, Urmston,
Manchester M41 6EP
0.5 mile from Flixton village on
B5213.
Meadowland course.
9 holes, 6410 yards, S.S.S.71
Founded 1896
Visitors: welcome weekdays except
Wed, weekends if accompanied by
member only.
Green Fee: £15 per day.
Societies: welcome by prior
arrangement all weekdays except
Wed.

Catering: bar snacks available; full
meals provided by arrangement made
in advance.
Snooker.
Hotels: Novotel (Worsley).

N56 **Formby Ladies**
☎(01704) 874127 (Club), Sec
873493
Golf Rd, Formby, Liverpool L37 1YH
6 miles S of Southport off A565.
Seaside course.
18 holes, 5374 yards, S.S.S.71
Founded 1896
Visitors: welcome except Thurs, ring
first.
Green Fee: WD £28; WE £33.
Societies: welcome by prior
arrangement.
Catering: bar snacks and salads
served.
Hotels: Prince of Wales; Royal
Clifton; Scarisbrick; Bold.

N57 **Formby**
☎(01704) 872164
Golf Rd, Formby, Liverpool L37 1LQ
1 mile W of A565, adjacent to
Freshfield station.
Links course.
18 holes, 6701 yards, S.S.S.73
Designed by Willie Park.
Founded 1884
Visitors: visitors welcome by
arrangement with Sec; not before
9.30am; some extra restrictions on
Wed/Sun; not Sat.
Green Fee: £50.
Societies: weekdays by
arrangement.
Catering: lunches except Mon.
Hotels: Tree Tops.

N58 **Furness**
☎(01229) 471232
Central Drive, Walney Island, Barrow-
in-Furness, Cumbria LA14 3LN
A590 to Barrow, towards Walney
Island, over bridge, through lights, 0.5
mile on right.
Seaside links course.
18 holes, 6363 yards, S.S.S.71
Founded 1872
Visitors: welcome, h/cap cert
required; parties booked in advance.
Green Fee: £17 per day (£10 with
member).
Societies: advance booking; not
competition days.
Catering: bar meals available, Sun
lunch and evening dinner.
Snooker, darts.
Hotels: White House; Abbey House.

N59 **Gathurst**
☎(01257) 252861, Sec 255235
Miles Lane, Shevington, Wigan WN6
8EW
1 mile S of M6 junction 27, 0.25 mile
W of Shevington village centre.
Meadowland course.
9 holes, 6308 yards, S.S.S.70
Founded 1913
Visitors: Mon, Tues, Thurs and Fri.
Green Fee: £20 per day.
Societies: by arrangement.
Catering: lunch except Mon, Tues.
Hotels: Lindley (Parbold); The
Beeches (Standish).

N60 **Ghyll**
☎(01282) 842466
Ghyll Brow, Barnoldswick, Colne,
Lancs BB8 6JQ
M65 then A56 to Thornton-in-Craven,
turn left on B6252, 1 mile on left.
Scenic parkland course.
9 holes, 5796 yards, S.S.S.68
Founded 1907
Visitors: not Tues am, not Fri after
4.30pm, not Sun; h/cap certificates
not required.
Green Fee: WD £14 (£7 with
member); WE & BH £18 (£12 with
member).
Societies: welcome at same times as
visitors, £14/day per person; parties
above 8 ring Sec.
Catering: bar (evenings only),
catering by arrangement.
Hotels: Stirk House (Gisburn);
Tempest (Elslack).

N61 **Golf Centre**
Wigan Rd, Westhoughton, Nr Bolton,
BL8 2BX
M61 junction 5, travel through
Westhoughton towards Hindley
Parkland
18 holes, 6400 yards, S.S.S. 73
Designed M Shattock
Founded May 1996
Visitors: welcome
Green Fee: WD £6.50; WE £10.
Societies: welcome
Catering: club house opening 1997.

N62 **Grange Fell**
☎(01539) 532536
Fell Rd, Grange-over-Sands, Cumbria
LA11 6HB
On main road to Cartmel from
Grange at top of the hill.
Hillside course with panoramic
Lakeland views.
9 holes, 4826 metres, S.S.S.66
Founded 1952

Visitors: welcome; closed most Sun in the season.
Green Fee: WD £10; WE & BH £15.
Hotels: Grange; Netherwood; Cumbria Grand.

N63 **Grange Park**
☎(01744) 26318 (Sec)
Prescot Rd, St Helens, Merseyside WA10 3AD
On A58 1 mile from town centre towards Prescot.
Parkland course.
18 holes, 6422 yards, S.S.S.71
Founded 1891
Visitors: welcome weekdays (Ladies Day Tues), by arrangement weekends.
Green Fee: WD £23; WE £35.
Societies: Mon, Wed, Thur, Fri by arrangement.
Catering: full restaurant facilities available.
Hotels: Post House; Chalon Court; Haydock Thistle.

N64 **Grange-over-Sands**
☎(015395) 33180, Sec 33754, Pro 35937
Meathop Rd, Grange-over-Sands, Cumbria LA11 6QX
Leave A590 at roundabout signposted Grange, golf course located on left just before entering Grange.
Flat parkland course.
18 holes, 5958 yards, S.S.S.69
Founded 1921
Visitors: welcome at any time (Thurs Ladies day).
Green Fee: WD £15 per round, £20 per day; WE £20 per round, £25 per day.
Societies: by arrangement weekdays and weekends.
Catering: facilities available daily except Tues.
Hotels: Grange; Cumbria Grand; Berners Close; Netherwood.

N65 **Great Harwood**
☎(01254) 884391
Harwood Bar, Great Harwood, Lancs BB6 7TE
Between Blackburn and Burnley, off A680 Accrington-Whalley road.
Parkland course.
9 holes, 6411 yards, S.S.S.71
Founded 1896 (1928 present site)
Visitors: welcome any time except competition days; must be member of recognised club.
Green Fee: WD £16; WE £22.

Societies: on application.
Catering: bar and restaurant facilities except Mon.
Snooker.
Hotels: Duncan House.

N66 **Great Lever & Farnworth**
☎(01204) 656137 (Sec), Pro 656650
Off Plodder Lane, Great Lever, Bolton BL3 3EN
1.5 miles from town centre.
Meadowland course.
18 holes, 5986 yards, S.S.S.69
Founded 1917
Visitors: welcome weekdays.
Green Fee: WD £15; WE & BH £25.
Societies: weekdays by prior arrangement.
Catering: lunch served daily except Mon.
Hotels: Crest (Bolton).

N67 **Green Haworth**
☎(01254) 237580
Green Haworth, Accrington, Lancs BB5 3SL
From Accrington town centre take main road to Blackburn, turn left on Willows Lane, follow road for 2 to 3 miles, sign for course just past Red Lion Hotel.
Moorland course.
9 holes, 5513 yards, S.S.S.68
Founded 1914
Visitors: welcome weekdays; restrictions Wed (Ladies Day); Sat with reservation.
Green Fee: apply for details.
Societies: catered for with prior arrangement.
Catering: provided by prior arrangement.
Hotels: Moat House (Blackburn).

N68 **Greenmount**
☎(01204) 883712
Greenhalgh Fold Farm, Greenmount, Bury BL8 4LH
Exit M66 Bury, follow signs for Ramsbottom, at lights in Holcombe village turn left, 0.25 mile turn left into Holcombe Rd, 1 mile turn right into Holhouse Lane, over speed bumps, turn right approaching Convent into Clubhouse.
Undulating parkland course.
9 holes, 4920 yards, S.S.S.64 (extension planned).
Founded 1920
Visitors: welcome weekdays and with member at weekends.
Green Fee: £16.

Societies: Mon, Wed, Thurs, Fri only, book in advance.
Catering: full service except Mon.
Snooker.
Hotels: Red Hall; Old Mill; Red Lion.

N69 **Haigh Hall**
☎(01942) 833337, Pro 831107
Haigh Country Park, Aspull, Wigan, Lancs WN2 1PE
M6 exit 27, B5239 to Standish, 6 miles NE of Wigan.
Municipal parkland course.
18 holes, 6423 yards, S.S.S.71
Founded 1973
Visitors: welcome any time by arrangement; make telephone bookings via Pro.
Green Fee: WD £5.95; WE £8.50.
Societies: welcome with prior arrangement, contact Pro.
Catering: cafeteria.
Hotels: Brocket; Oak; Almond Brook Moathouse.

N70 **Harwood**
☎(01204) 522878
Springfield, Roading Brook Rd, Harwood, Bolton BL2 4JD
On B6391 off A666 4 miles NE of Bolton town centre.
Undulating parkland course.
9 holes, 5958 yards, S.S.S.69 (18 hole extension planned)
Founded 1926
Visitors: welcome weekdays, must be members of recognised club.
Green Fee: £15 (£6 with member).
Societies: on application.
Catering: by prior arrangement.
Snooker.
Hotels: Last Drop (Bromley Cross); Grants Arms (Ramsbottom).

N71 **Haydock Park**
☎(01925) 228525 (Sec), Bar Manager: 224389
Golborne Park, Newton-le-Willows, Merseyside WA12 0HX
M6 to A580, then 1 mile E.
Parkland course.
18 holes, 6043 yards, S.S.S.69
Founded 1877
Visitors: weekdays except Tues.
Green Fee: £25 per round/day.
Societies: weekdays except Tues.
Catering: on request.
Hotels: Kirkfield.

N72 **Heaton Park**
☎(0161) 798 0295
Prestwich, Manchester M25 2SW

Leave M62 at exit 19, right at A576, 200 yards on right.
Public undulating parkland course.
18 holes, 5766 yards, S.S.S.68
Designed by J.H. Taylor.
Founded 1912
Visitors: welcome, advance booking weekend only.
Green Fee: WD £6.50; WE £7.50.
Societies: welcome by prior arrangement.

N73 Hesketh
☎(01704) 536897 (Sec), Pro 530050
Cockle Dick's Lane, off Cambridge Rd, Southport, Merseyside PR9 9QQ
1 mile N of Southport town centre on main Preston road, A565.
Links course.
18 holes, 6407 yards, S.S.S.72
Designed by J.O.F. (Jamie) Morris.
Founded 1885
Visitors: welcome weekdays, occasionally weekends; telephone for information; advance booking needed for societies.
Green Fee: WD £25 per round, £35 per day; WE £40.
Societies: by prior arrangement, catered for weekdays except Tues am.
Catering: bar snacks served and full dining room facilities always available.
Hotels: The Metropole.

N74 The Heysham
☎(01524) 851011 (Sec/Manager), Pro 852000
Trumacar Park, Middleton Rd, Heysham, Lancs LA3 3JH
3 miles from M6, 2 mile S of Morecambe on right of road to Middleton.
Parkland course.
18 holes, 6258 yards, S.S.S.68
Designed by H. Vardon.
Founded 1910
Visitors: welcome.
Green Fee: WD £20; WE £25.
Societies: by arrangement with Sec/Manager.
Catering: full facilities provided every day.
Snooker.
Hotels: Midland; Clarendon; Strathmore; Post House.

N75 Hillside
☎(01704) 567169 (Sec), Pro 568360, Fax 563192
Hastings Rd, Hillside, Southport PR8 2LU

Take A565 Southport-Liverpool road, turn right before Hillside railway station, club located at end of Hastings Road.
Championship links course.
18 holes, 6850 yards, S.S.S.74
Designed by Fred Hawtree.
Founded 1909 (1923 on present site)
Visitors: welcome weekdays except Tues, advance booking recommended, limited times Sun; no visitors Sat.
Green Fee: WD £35 per round, £45 per day; WE £45.
Societies: by appointment.
Catering: facilities all day, 100 seat restaurant.
Snooker.
Hotels: Prince of Wales; Scarisbrick.

N76 Hindley Hall
☎(01942) 255131, Pro 255991
Hall Lane, Hindley, Wigan, Lancs WN2 2SQ
M61 junction 6 onto A6, take Dicconson Lane, then after 1 mile left at church into Hall Lane, club just after lake.
Moorland course.
18 holes, 5913 yards, S.S.S.68
Founded 1895
Visitors: welcome if member of recognised club, advisable to check with Sec in advance.
Green Fee: WD £20; WE & BH £27.
Societies: welcome by prior arrangement.
Catering: meals served by arrangement with chef.
Hotels: Georgian House.

N77 Horwich
☎(01204) 696980
Victoria Rd, Horwich, Bolton BL6 5PH
1.5 miles from M61.
Parkland course.
9 holes, 5404 yards, S.S.S.67
Founded 1895
Visitors: welcome if accompanied by member only.
Green Fee: on application.
Societies: catered for weekdays only by application.
Catering: full facilities.

N78 Hurlston Hall
☎(01704) 840400, bookings 841120, Fax 841404
Hurlston Lane, Scarisbrick, Lancashire L40 8JD
6 miles from Southport, 2 miles from Ormskirk, along A570 trunk road; 8 miles from M58.

Lake and parkland course.
18 holes, 6746 yards, S.S.S.72
Designed by Donald Steel.
Founded 1994.
Visitors: welcome; h/cap cert or letter of intro from club required; advance booking preferred.
Green Fee: WD £25 per round, £30 per day, WE & BH £30 per round, £35 per day; winter course £20 per round.
Societies: registered gplf societies welcome by arrangement.
Catering: full facilities
18 bay floodlit driving range.
Hotels: Scarisbrick; Prince of Wales

N79 Huyton & Prescot
☎(0151) 489 3948
Hurst Park, Huyton Lane, Huyton, Liverpool L36 1UA
Approx 10 miles from Liverpool city centre, just off M57.
Parkland course.
18 holes, 5779 yards, S.S.S.68
Founded 1905
Visitors: must be members of recognised golf clubs; only if accompanied by a member at weekends.
Green Fee: £22.
Societies: by arrangement on weekdays only.
Catering: every day.
Hotels: Derby Lodge; Hillcrest.

N80 Ingol Golf & Squash Club
☎(01772) 734556
Tanterton Hall Rd, Ingol, Preston, Lancs PR2 7BY
Leave M6 junction 32, turn left towards Preston, follow signpost on left marked Ingol.
Parkland course.
18 holes, 6296 yards, S.S.S. 71
Designed by Cotton, Pennink, Lawrie & Partners.
Founded 1980
Visitors: welcome any day.
Green Fee: WD £15; WE £20.
Societies: by arrangement.
Catering: full facilities.
Squash, snooker, banqueting.
Hotels: Barton Grange; Broughton Park; Fulwood Park.

N81 Kendal
☎(01539) 724079 (Clubhouse), Sec 733708, Pro 723499
The Heights, Kendal, Cumbria LA9 4PQ
To Kendal on A6 signposted in town.

KENDAL GOLF CLUB The Heights, Kendal

Situated on the edge of the Lake District, we can offer spectacular views of the Lakeland Fells, including Scarfell Pike, and a fine, challenging course fringed by woodland. Golf societies & visitors are welcome (weekdays £16) with special packages for 8 or more, & company days by negotiation. Telephone the manager on 01539 733708 or professional on 01539 723499

A course with a challenge

Moorland course.
18 holes, 5515 yards, S.S.S.66
Founded 1891
Visitors: welcome any time except Sat competition days; prior application suggested.
Green Fee: WD £16; WE £20.
Societies: catered for any time subject to availability and by prior arrangement.
Catering: full facilities available except Mon.
Hotels: County; Woolpack.

N82 Keswick
☎(017687) 79324 (Sec), Pro 79010
Threlkeld Hall, Threlkeld, Keswick, Cumbria CA12 4SX
Off A66 4 miles E of Keswick.
Moorland/parkland course.
18 holes, 6225 yards, S.S.S.72
Designed by Eric Brown.
Founded 1975
Visitors: welcome even at most weekends and Bank Holidays; advisable to telephone.
Green Fee: WD £15; WE £20.
Societies: apply to sec; some weekends and Bank Holidays.
Catering: bar and dining facilities available.
Hotels: Lodore Swiss; Keswick; Borrowdale; Wordsworth; all have free midweek golf.

N83 King Edward Bay (Howstrake)
☎(01624) 620430, Pro 672709, Sec 676794
Howstrake, Groudle Rd, Onchan, Isle of Man IM3 2JR
2 miles NE of Douglas.
Moorland/seaside course.
18 holes, 5485 yards, S.S.S.65
Founded 1893
Visitors: welcome Mon-Sat; Sun after 10am by arrangement; h/cap cert required.
Green Fee: WD £10; WE £12.
Societies: weekdays; weekends by arrangement.
Catering: 10am-10pm daily except Mon.
Putting green, driving net, sauna, sunbed.

N84 Kirkby Lonsdale
☎(015242) 76365, Pro 76366
Scalebar Lane, Barbon, Carnforth, Cumbria LA6 2LE
2.5 miles N of Kirkby Lonsdale on A368 to Sedbergh; Clubhouse on Backfoot Lane.
Parkland course next to River Lune.
18 holes, 6472 yards, S.S.S.72
New course founded 1991
Visitors: no restrictions except Sun.
Green Fee: WD £16; WE £20.
Societies: Tues and Thurs with prior arrangement.
Catering: available.
Hotels: Whoop Hall.

N85 Knott End
☎(01253) 810576 (Sec), Pro 811365 Pro
Wyreside, Knott End on Sea, Blackpool FY6 0AA
Take A585 Fleetwood road off M55, and then B2588 to Knott End.
Meadowland course.
18 holes, 5789 yards, S.S.S.68
Designed by James Braid.
Founded 1911
Visitors: welcome weekdays, not before 9.30am or between 12.30-1.30pm.
Green Fee: WD £18 per round, £21 per day; WE £20 per round, £24 per day.
Societies: by arrangement.
Catering: every day.
Hotels: Bourne Arms; Seven Stars.

N86 Lancaster
☎(01524) 751247, **Catering:** 751105, Pro 751802
Ashton Hall, Ashton-with-Stodday, Lancaster LA2 0AJ
On A588 2.5 miles SW of Lancaster.
Undulating parkland course.
18 holes, 6465 yards, S.S.S.71
Designed by James Braid.
Founded 1933
Visitors: welcome weekdays only.
Green Fee: WD £28.
Societies: welcome by prior arrangement.
Catering: meals served.
Hotels: Post House; residential dormy house (18 persons).

N87 Lansil
☎(01524) 39269
Caton Rd, Lancaster, Lancs LA1 3PE
2 miles E of Lancaster on A683.
Parkland/meadowland course.
9 Holes, 5608 yards, S.S.S.67
Founded 1947
Visitors: welcome but not before 1pm Sun.
Green Fee: £12.
Societies: weekdays.
Catering: meals and bar snacks available; parties by prior arrangement.
Hotels: Farmers Arms; Post House.

N88 Lee Park
☎(0151) 487 3882 (Sec)
Childwall Valley Rd, Gateacre, Liverpool L27 3YA
On B5171 off A562, next to Lee Manor High School.
Parkland course.
18 holes, 6125 yards, S.S.S.69
Designed by Frank Pennink.
Founded 1950
Visitors: welcome.
Green Fee: WD £21; WE £26.
Societies: Mon, Thur, Fri by arrangement with Sec.
Catering: bar snacks served and meals.
Hotels: Gateacre Hall.

N89 Leigh
☎(01925) 763130, Pro 762013, Sec 762943
Kenyon Hall, Broseley Lane, Culcheth, Warrington WA3 4BG
2 mins from Culcheth centre; from A580 (East Lancs road) A574 or B5207.
Parkland course.
18 holes, 5892 yards, S.S.S.68
Founded 1906
Visitors: anytime except during club competitions.
Green Fee: WD £26; WE £33.
Societies: Mon and Tues on application.
Catering: bar snacks/full catering available.
Snooker.
Hotels: Greyhound Motel (Leigh); Thistle (Haydock).

N90 Leyland

☎(01772) 436457
Wigan Rd, Leyland, Lancs PR5 2UD
On A49, 0.25 mile from M6 exit 28.
Meadowland course.
18 holes, 6123 yards, S.S.S.69
Founded 1923
Visitors: weekdays unrestricted, weekends with member.
Green Fee: £25.
Societies: apply to Sec.
Catering: full facilities daily.
Hotels: Jarvis.

N91 Liverpool Municipal (Kirkby)

☎(0151) 546 5435
Ingoe Lane, Kirkby, Liverpool 32, L32 4SS
M57 junction 6, 300 yards on right of B5192.
Municipal meadowland course.
18 holes, 6706 yards, S.S.S.72
Founded 1966 (1967 Kirkby GC).
Visitors: welcome every day, tee bookings available.
Green Fee: £6.20
Societies: welcome every day, tee booking required weekends 1 week in advance.
Catering: bar and cafeteria.
Practice ground.
Hotels: Golden Eagle (Kirkby).

N92 Lobden

☎(01706) 343228
Lobden Moor, Whitworth, Nr Rochdale OL12 8XJ
A671 4 miles from Rochdale, 0.5 mile from centre of village.
Moorland course.
9 holes, 5770 yards, S.S.S.68
Founded 1888
Visitors: weekdays and Sun.
Green Fee: apply for details.
Catering: by arrangement with Steward.
Snooker.

N93 Longridge

☎(01772) 783291
Fell Barn, Jeffery Hill, Longridge, Preston, Lancs PR3 2TU
Off B6243 8 miles NE of Preston, follow signs to Jeffery Hill.
Moorland course with panoramic views.
18 holes, 5920 yards, S.S.S.69
Founded 1877
Visitors: welcome; check by phone or letter.
Green Fee: £18 per day Mon-Thurs, £21 Fri, Sat, Sun and BH.

Societies: apply in writing to Sec; packages £25.
Catering: bar and meals at reasonable times.
Snooker.
Hotels: Shireburn Arms (Hurst Green); Gibbon Bridge (Chipping); Black Moss GH.

N94 Lowes Park

☎(0161) 764 1231
Hill Top, Bury, Lancs BL9 6SU
A56 Walmersley Rd, right into Lowes Rd, follow signs to club; approx 1.5 miles from Bury centre, right at General Hospital.
Moorland course (usually windy).
9 holes, 6009 yards, S.S.S.69
Founded 1914
Visitors: welcome weekdays, except Wed (Ladies Day), Sat and competition days; Sun by appointment only.
Green Fee: WD £15; WE £20.
Societies: contact Sec.
Catering: full facilities except Mon.
Hotels: Red Hall.

N95 Lytham Green Drive

☎(01253) 737390, Fax 731350
Ballam Rd, Lytham, Lancs FY8 4LE
0.75 mile from Lytham centre.
Parkland course.
18 holes, 6157 yards, S.S.S.69
Founded 1922
Visitors: welcome weekdays, h/cap cert required; limited at weekends.
Green Fee: WD £24 per round, £30 per day; WE £35.
Societies: apply to Sec.
Catering: full service except Mon.
Hotels: Clifton Arms.

N96 Manchester

☎(0161) 643 3202
Hopwood Cottage, Rochdale Rd, Middleton, Manchester M24 2QP
7 miles N of city on A664, 2 miles from exits 19 and 20 off M62.
Undulating moorland course.
18 holes, 6540 yards, S.S.S.72
Designed by H.S. Colt
Founded 1882
Visitors: weekdays and limited Sundays, h/cap certs required.
Green Fee: WD £30 per round, £40 per day; WE £45.
Societies: weekdays except Wed.
Catering: full facilities available.
Driving range (for visitors paying green fees or taking lessons only), snooker, banqueting.
Hotels: Norton Grange; Midway.

N97 Marsden Park

☎(01282) 617525
Downhouse Rd, Belson, Lancs BB9 8DG
Off A56, 8 miles N of Burnley.
Undulating meadowland course.
18 holes, 5806 yards, S.S.S.68
Designed by C.K. Cotton & Partners.
Founded 1968
Visitors: welcome.
Green Fee: WD £7; WE £8.25.
Societies: welcome by prior arrangement.
Catering: full restaurant and bar service.
Hotels: The Oaks.

N98 Maryport

☎(01900) 812605
Bank End, Maryport, Cumbria CA15 6PA
N of Maryport, turn left off A596 onto B5300 (Silloth), course 1 mile.
Seaside links course.
18 holes, 6088 yards, S.S.S.69
Founded 1905
Visitors: welcome at any time.
Green Fee: WD £7.50; WE £10.
Societies: catered for.
Catering: by prior arrangement.
Hotels: Ellenbank; The Waverley.

N99 Morecambe

☎(01524) 412841 (Sec), Members: 418050, Pro 415596
Bare, Morecambe, Lancs LA4 6AJ
5 miles from M6 at Carnforth, follow signs to Morecambe.
Seaside/parkland course.
18 holes, 5770 yards, S.S.S.68
Designed by Dr Clegg.
Founded 1922
Visitors: welcome at all times except before 9.30am or 12am-1.30pm Mon-Sat and before 1.30pm Sun; h/cap certs required.
Green Fee: WD £17; WE £22.
Societies: welcome by arrangement with Sec, if members of recognised golf clubs; packages available from £13.50.
Catering: full catering available except Mon when bar snacks only.
Hotels: Elms.

N100 Mount Murray

☎(01624) 661111
Santon, Isle of Man IM4 2HT
On the main Castletown to Douglas road, 2 miles from Douglas
Parkland course
18 holes, 6709 yards, S.S.S. 73
Founded in 1994

Visitors: welcome
Green Fee: WD £18; WE £24.
Societies: welcome by prior arrangement
Catering: Bistro and restaurant facilities available.
Driving range.
Hotels: Mount Murray (offers golf packages).

N101 **Nelson**

☎(01282) 611834
King's Causeway, Brierfield, Nelson, Lancs BB9 0EU
Off A682 2 miles E of Brierfield.
Moorland course.
18 holes, 5967 yards, S.S.S.69
Founded 1902
Visitors: welcome weekdays except Thurs afternoons; weekends and Bank Holidays by application.
Green Fee: WD £25; WE £30.
Societies: by arrangement.
Catering: lunches served except Mon, evening meals served except Mon or Fri.
Hotels: The Higher Trapp.

N102 **North Manchester**

☎(0161) 643 2941 (Clubhouse), Sec 643 9033, Pro 643 7094
Rhodes House, Manchester Old Rd, Middleton, Manchester M24 4PE
5 miles N of Manchester, exit 18 off M62.
Moorland/parkland course.
18 holes, 6498 yards, S.S.S.72
Founded 1894
Visitors: welcome weekdays and by arrangement at weekends.
Green Fee: WD £22 per round, £25 per day.
Societies: welcome weekdays except Tues.
Catering: full service 7 days.
Hotels: Bower (Oldham); Birch (Heywood).

N103 **Oldham**

☎(0161) 624 4986, Pro 626 8346
Lees New Rd, Oldham OL4 5PN
Just off minor road between Oldham and Ashton-under-Lyne or on A669 turn right at Lees.
Moorland/parkland course.
18 holes, 5122 yards, S.S.S.65
Founded registered 1891
Visitors: unlimited, but telephone for arrangements on competitions being played.
Green Fee: WD £16; WE £22.
Societies: by arrangement.
Catering: full facilities.

N104 **Ormskirk**

☎(01695) 572112, Sec 572227
Cranes Lane, Lathom, Ormskirk, Lancs L40 5UJ
2 miles E of Ormskirk.
Parkland course.
18 holes, 6358 yards, S.S.S.70
Founded 1899
Visitors: advanced booking advised; restrictions Wed.
Green Fee: WD £30 per round, £35 per day; WE & Wed £35 per round, £40 per day.
Societies: book in advance.
Catering: full facilities.
Hotels: Briars Hall.

N105 **Peel**

☎(01624) 843456 (Mon-Fri am)
Rheast Lane, Peel, Isle of Man IM5 1BG
On A1, signposted on outskirts of Peel, coming from Douglas.
Moorland course.
18 holes, 5914 yards, S.S.S.68
Designed by A. Herd.
Founded 1895
Visitors: welcome weekdays; by arrangement weekends (after 10.30am).
Green Fee: WD £15; WE £18.
Societies: apply to Sec.
Catering: meals and snacks to order by arrangement with Steward.
Hotels: Stakis, Ascot.

N106 **Pennington**

☎(01942) 682852
Pennington Country Park, St Helen's Road, Leigh, Greater Manchester WN7 3PA
Off A572 to S of town centre; M6 junctions 22/23.
Public parkland course with ponds and streams.
9 holes, 5838 yards, S.S.S.68
Visitors: welcome.
Green Fee: WD £2.70 (9 holes); WE £3.90 (9 holes).
Societies: weekdays by arrangement.
Catering: snack bar.
Fishing, bird watching.

N107 **Penrith**

☎(01768) 891919
Salkeld Rd, Penrith, Cumbria CA11 8SG
0.5 mile NE of Penrith, M6 junction 41.
Parkland course.
18 holes, 6047 yards, S.S.S.69
Founded 1890

Visitors: must be member of golf club with h/cap.
Green Fee: WD £20 per round, £25 per day; WE £25 per round, £30 per day.
Societies: welcome by prior arrangement.
Catering: facilities available all day 7 days a week.
Snooker.
Hotels: George; Edenhall.

N108 **Penwortham**

☎(01772) 744630
Blundell Lane, Penwortham, Preston, Lancs PR1 0AX
Off A59 at Penwortham traffic lights, 1 mile from Preston.
Parkland course.
18 holes, 6056 yards, S.S.S.69
Founded 1908
Visitors: weekdays (not Tues).
Green Fee: WD £22 per round, £25 per day; WE £28.
Societies: weekdays (not Tues) by arrangement.
Catering: lunches and evening meals.
Hotels: Crest.

N109 **Pike Fold**

☎(0161) 740 1136
Cooper Lane, Victoria Ave, Blackley, Manchester M9 2QQ
4 miles N of city centre off Rochdale road; off Victoria Ave from M62 junction 18.
Undulating meadowland course.
9 holes, 5789 yards, S.S.S.68
Founded 1909
Visitors: welcome weekdays.
Green Fee: £15.
Societies: welcome by appointment.
Catering: full facilities by prior arrangement with Steward.
Snooker.
Hotels: Piccadilly; Midland.

N110 **Pleasington**

☎(01254) 202177, Pro 201630
Pleasington, Blackburn, Lancs BB2 5JF
3 miles from Blackburn off A674.
Undulating parkland course.
18 holes, 6423 yards, S.S.S.71
Founded 1891
Visitors: Mon, Wed, Fri by prior arrangement; h/cap cert required.
Green Fee: WD £30; WE £35.
Societies: Mon, Wed, Fri by prior arrangement.
Catering: full facilities.
Hotels: Moat House Motel.

N111 Port St Mary Golf Pavilion

☎(01624) 834932
Port St Mary, Isle of Man IM9 5EJ
Just outside town of Port St Mary heading towards the sea, course is signposted.
Public seaside links course.
9 holes, 5418 yards, S.S.S.68
Designed by George Duncan.
Founded 1936
Visitors: welcome any time; in summer not before 10.30 am or weekends.
Green Fee: WD £10; WE £12.50.
Societies: welcome by prior arrangement, discount for 10 players or more.
Catering: bar, cafeteria and restaurant.
Putting green, outdoor chessboard.
Hotels: Port Erin (free golf); Bay View.

N112 Poulton-le-Fylde

☎(01253) 892444
Myrtle Farm, Breck Rd, Poulton-le-Fylde, Lancs FY6 7HJ
0.5 mile N of Poulton town centre.
Municipal meadowland course.
9 holes, 6056 yards, S.S.S.69
Founded 1974
Visitors: welcome, no restrictions.
Green Fee: WD £5.50 (9 holes), £8.50 (18 holes); WE £7.50 (9 holes), £11 (18 holes).
Societies: welcome by prior arrangement.
Catering: bar, snacks and lunches daily.
Snooker, games room.

N113 Preston

☎(01772) 700011, Pro 700022
Fulwood Hall Lane, Fulwood, Preston, Lancs PR2 8DD
From M6, leave at junction 31 take Blackpool Road, turn right at Deepdale Road, turn left at Watling St Road, then turn right at Fulwood Hall Lane.
Undulating course.
18 holes, 6212 yards, S.S.S.69
Designed by James Braid.
Founded 1892
Visitors: welcome weekdays.
Green Fee: WD £22 per round, £27 per day.
Societies: welcome weekdays; no visiting parties weekends or Bank Holidays.
Catering: lunches, breakfast, dinner, snacks.
Hotels: Broughton Park.

N114 Prestwich

☎(0161) 773 4578, Pro 773 2544
Hilton Lane, Prestwich, Manchester M25 8SB
On A4066 0.25 mile W of junction with A56.
Parkland course.
18 holes, 4806 yards, S.S.S.63
Founded 1908
Visitors: not before 5pm Sat, 3pm Sun or Tues am; h/cap certs required.
Green Fee: WD £16; WE £18.
Societies: welcome except Tues (Ladies Day).
Catering: by arrangement with Steward, except Mon.
Hotels: Village Squash; Hazel Dean.

N115 Ramsey

☎(01624) 812244
Brookfield, Ramsey, Isle of Man IM8 2AH
12 miles N of Douglas, 5 minutes walk from town centre.
Parkland course.
18 holes, 5960 yards, S.S.S.69
Designed by James Braid.
Founded 1890
Visitors: welcome; phone in advance.
Green Fee: WD £16; WE £20.
Societies: welcome by arrangement; apply to Sec.
Catering: lunches daily.
Hotels: Grand Island.

N116 Reach

(01253) 766156, **Hotels:** 838866, Fax 798800
De Vere Hotels, East Park Drive, Blackpool FY3 8LL
Leave M55 at junc 4, follow signs for Blackpool on A583 and at fourth set of lights turn right into South Park Drive, take second exit on mini roundabout and course is 0.25m on right
Parkland course with links characteristics
18 holes, 6431 yards, S.S.S. 72
Designed by Peter Alliss and Clive Clark
Founded 1993
Visitors: welcome after 10am
Green Fee: WD £20; WE £30.
Reductions for residents.
Societies: welcome all year round.
Catering: Spikes Bar, three restaurants.
Leisure club, swimming pool and gym. Tennis and squash courts
Driving range, chipping green and putting green.
Hotels: De Vere Blackpool.

N117 Regent Park (Bolton)

☎(01204) 844170 (Club), Pro 842336
Links Rd, Lostock, Bolton, Lancs BL6 4AF
M61 exit 6 to Bolton, entrance on right after 1 mile approx.
Municipal parkland course.
18 holes, 6130 yards, S.S.S.69
Founded 1932
Visitors: welcome 7 days; restrictions every alternate time on Sat.
Green Fee: WD £6; WE £8.
Societies: Mon-Fri by arrangement.
Catering: bar, take-away, restaurant.
Practice fairway.
Hotels: Forte-Crest; Swallowfield.

N118 Rishton

☎(01254) 884442
Eachill Links, Hawthorne Drive, Rishton, Blackburn, Lancs BB1 4HG
3 miles E of Blackburn, signposted from church in village.
Meadowland course.
9 holes, 6097 yards, S.S.S.69
Founded 1928
Visitors: welcome weekdays; weekends and Bank Holidays with member; restricted Wed (Ladies day).
Green Fee: £13.
Societies: welcome with prior arrangement, letter to Sec.
Catering: lunch and evening meals, closed Mon.
Snooker.
Hotels: Dunkenhalgh.

N119 Rochdale

☎(01706) 43818 (Sec), Club 46024, Pro 522104
Edenfield Rd, Bagslate, Rochdale OL11 5YR
3 miles from M62 exit 20 on A680.
Parkland course.
18 holes, 6002 yards, S.S.S.69
Founded 1888
Visitors: welcome but restricted.
Green Fee: WD £23; WE £27.
Societies: Wed and Fri.
Catering: coffee, lunch and evening meals served.
Snooker.
Hotels: The Broadfield; Midway.

N120 Rossendale

☎(01706) 831339 (Sec)
Ewood Lane Head, Haslingden, Rossendale, Lancs BB4 6LH
16 miles from Manchester off M66.
Moorland/meadowland course.
18 holes, 6293 yards, S.S.S.70
Founded 1903

METROPOLE HOTEL, SOUTHPORT

Portland Street, Southport PR8 1LL   Tel 01704 536836   Fax 01704 549041

RAC/AA 2-star hotel. Centrally situated and close to Royal Birkdale and 5 other championship courses.
Fully licensed with late bar facilities for residents. Full sized snooker table.
Golfing proprietors will assist with tee reservations.

Visitors: welcome except Sat.
Green Fee: WD £22.50; Sun £27.50.
Societies: welcome by prior arrangement.
Catering: full facilities except Mon. Snooker, banqueting.
Hotels: Red Hall; Sykeside.

N121 Rowany
☎(01624) 834072 (Manager), Steward: 834108
Rowany Drive, Port Erin, Isle of Man IM9 6LN
4 miles W of Castletown, located at end of Port Erin promenade.
Parkland/seaside course.
18 holes, 5840 yards, S.S.S.69
Founded 1895
Visitors: welcome, no restrictions.
Green Fee: £10 per round, £15 per day.
Societies: always welcome; arrangements to be made with Manager (available 8am - 12 noon weekdays).
Catering: bar, bar snacks, lunches, evening meals.
Hotels: Port Erin Royal; Cherry Orchard.

N122 Royal Birkdale
☎(01704) 569913, Sec 567920, Pro 568857
Waterloo Rd, Birkdale, Southport, Merseyside PR8 2LX
1.5 miles S of Southport on A565.
Seaside course; Open Championship venue.
18 holes, 6690 yards, S.S.S.73
Designed by Hawtree & Taylor.
Founded 1889
Visitors: letter of intro required from visitor's home club with confirmation of handicap; must book in advance with Sec; not Sat or mornings on Sun.
Green Fee: WD £55 per round, £75 per day; WE £75.
Societies: welcome Wed and Thurs by prior arrangement.
Catering: light lunches and afternoon teas served, full lunches and dinners by arrangement for societies.
Hotels: various available in Southport.

N123 Royal Lytham & St Annes
☎(01253) 724206
Links Gate, St Annes on Sea, Lancs FY8 3LQ
1 mile from centre of St Annes on Sea.
Links course; Open Championship venue 1996.
18 holes, 6685 yards, S.S.S.74
Founded 1886
Visitors: weekdays by arrangement; weekends, dormy visitors only.
Green Fee: £75.
Societies: welcome by prior arrangement.
Catering: full catering and bar facilities available.
Snooker.
Hotels: Dormy house available.

N124 Saddleworth
☎(01457) 873653
Mountain Ash, Ladcastle Rd, Uppermill, Oldham OL3 6LT
5 miles from Oldham, signposted off A670 Ashton-Huddersfield road at bend where road crosses railway bridge.
Scenic moorland course.
18 holes, 5976 yards, S.S.S.69
Designed by Dr A. Mackenzie.
Founded 1904
Visitors: welcome.
Green Fee: WD £23; WE £26.
Societies: catered for weekdays; packages from £33.
Catering: facilities daily.

N125 St Annes Old Links
☎(01253) 723597 (Sec), Pro 722432
Highbury Rd, St Annes, Lytham St Annes, Lancs FY8 2LD
Leave M6 at junction 32;Leave M55 at junction 4, follow signs to Blackpool Airport; continue past airport, turn left at A584 coast road to St Annes; continue 1 mile to traffic lights, then turn left into Highbury Rd, course is situated immediately over railway bridge.
Championship links course.
18 holes, 6616 yards, S.S.S.72
Designed by James Herd.
Founded 1901

Visitors: welcome weekdays; restricted Tues and weekends.
Green Fee: WD £30; WE £40.
Societies: apply to Sec.
Catering: lunches, teas, dinner daily. Men's bar, snooker, practice ground.
Hotels: St Ives; Warwick (Blackpool).

N126 St Bees
☎(01946) 824300
Station Rd, St Bees, Cumbria CA27 0EJ
On B5345, 4 miles S of Whitehaven.
Seaside course.
9 holes, 5122 yards, S.S.S.65
Founded 1942/43
Visitors: welcome except on competition days in summer.
Green Fee: £12.
Societies: by arrangement with school.
Catering: none available.
Hotels: Queens.

N127 Seascale
☎(01946) 728202/Fax
The Banks, Seascale, Cumbria CA20 1QL
On coast to N of village; clubhouse at top of hill.
Seaside links course.
18 holes, 6416 yards, S.S.S.71
Founded 1893
Visitors: unrestricted.
Green Fee: WD £20; WE £25.
Societies: apply to Sec, terms for parties of 12 or more.
Catering: full facilities except Mon, Tues (by arrangement).
Hotels: Calder House; 3-day bargain breaks available.

N128 Sedbergh
☎(01539) 620993 (Hon Sec), Club 621551
Catholes-Abbot Holme, Dent Rd, Sedbergh, Cumbria LA10 5SS
1.5 miles S of Sedbergh on road to Dent; 5 miles from M6 junction 37.
Scenic undulating parkland course, easy walking.
9 holes, 5588 yards, S.S.S.68
Designed by W.G. Squires
Founded 1896 (new site 1991)

Visitors: welcome except Sun am; advisable to phone; h/cap certificate may be requested.
Green Fee: WD £14 per round, £20 per day; WE £18 per round, £25 per day.
Societies: welcome by prior arrangement, company days available.
Catering: good facilities, licenced bar.
Hotels: bargain breaks arranged, ring Sec for details.

N129 Shaw Hill Hotel Golf & Country Club
☎(01257) 269221, Fax 261223
Preston Rd, Whittle-le-Woods, Nr Chorley, Lancs PR6 7PP
From M6 exit 28, just off A6 towards Chorley; from M61 exit 8, just off A6 towards Preston.
Parkland course.
18 holes, 6424 yards, S.S.S.73
Designed by T. McCauley.
Founded 1925
Visitors: welcome with proof of h/cap.
Green Fee: Mon-Thurs £30; Fri-Sun £40.
Societies: weekdays only with prior arrangement.
Catering: bar facilities, full à la carte restaurant and function rooms available.
Sauna, solarium, snooker room.
Hotels: own 3 star hotel, golf inclusive packages available.

N130 Sherdley Park
☎(01744) 815518 (Club), Pro 813149
Sherdley Park, St Helens, Merseyside WA9 5DE
2 miles S of town centre on Warrington road.
Public undulating parkland course.
18 holes, 5974 yards, S.S.S.68
Designed by P.R. Parkinson.
Founded 1973
Visitors: welcome.
Green Fee: WD £6.20; WE £7.20.
Societies: welcome by prior arrangement.
Catering: bar and cafeteria.

N131 Silecroft
☎(01229) 774250Sec 774342
Silecroft, Cumbria LA18 4NX
On A5093 3 miles N of Millom, through Silecroft village towards shore.
Seaside course.
9 holes (18 tees), 5712 yards, S.S.S.68
Founded 1903
Visitors: normally unrestricted weekdays (unless club competition in progress); weekends and Bank Holidays often restricted 12am-5.30pm.
Green Fee: WD £10; WE £15.
Societies: welcome by prior arrangement.
Catering: by prior arrangement for visiting groups.
Hotels: Bankfield; Miners Arms; John Bull.

N132 Silloth on Solway
☎(016973) 31304
Silloth on Solway, Carlisle, Cumbria CA5 4BL
B5302 at A596 at Wigton, 18 miles W of Carlisle.
Undulating seaside course.
18 holes, 6614 yards, S.S.S.72
Designed by Willie Park jnr.
Founded 1892
Visitors: welcome any time; limited at weekends.
Green Fee: WD £25; WE £30.
Societies: welcome; packages from £35.
Catering: full facilities available daily except Mon.
Hotels: Golf; Queens; Skinburness.

N133 Silverdale
☎(01524) 701300
Redbridge Lane, Silverdale, Carnforth, Lancs LA5 0SP
Off M6 at Carnforth, course opposite Silverdale railway station via Carnforth and Warton.
Hilly heathland course.
12 holes, 5463 yards, S.S.S.67
Founded 1906
Visitors: welcome, not club competition days (Sun Men, Wed Ladies).

Green Fee: WD £12; WE £17 (£40 per week).
Societies: by arrangement.
Catering: full facilities weekdays.
Hotels: Wheatsheaf; Silverdale.

N134 Solway Village Golf Centre
☎(016973) 31236
Solway Village, Silloth-on-Solway, Cumbria CA5 4QQ
Easily located in village of Silloth.
Scenic parkland course.
9 holes, 2000 yards, Par 3 course
Founded 1988
Visitors: welcome any time.
Green Fee: on application.
Catering: bar and restaurant.
Driving range, pool, indoor bowls.

N135 Southport & Ainsdale
☎(01704) 578000, Pro 577316, Fax 570896
Bradshaws Lane, Ainsdale, Southport, Merseyside PR8 3LG
3 miles S of Southport on A565, 0.5 mile from Ainsdale station.
Championship links course.
18 holes, 6612 yards, S.S.S.73
Designed by James Braid.
Founded 1907
Visitors: weekdays only, must be members of a golf club; advance booking recommended.
Green Fee: £30 per round, £40 per day.
Societies: weekdays only, must be members of a golf club; advance booking essential.
Catering: full facilities.
Snooker.
Hotels: Prince of Wales; Scarisbrick; Royal Clifton.

N136 Southport Municipal
☎(01704) 535286, Park GC: Sec 579093, Club 530133.
Park Rd West, Southport, Merseyside PR9 0JS
N end of Promenade.
Public seaside course.
18 holes, 6139 yards, S.S.S.69
Founded 1914 (as Park Golf Club)

Standish Court Golf Club
Rectory Lane, Standish, WIGAN WN6 0XD
Phone 01257 425777 Fax 01257 425888

The North West's newest golfing venue, delightful 18 hole course in mature parkland. Superb clubhouse offering all day food and drink in either Hogan's Bar or Bistro. Societies very welcome. Five and ten year or annual memberships available. Professionally designed, professionally built and professionally managed

---

Visitors: welcome.
Green Fee: WD £5.50; WE £7.50.
Societies: welcome by prior arrangement.
Catering: meals served.
Hotels: Scarisbrick (special golf packages with Park GC; telephone for details).

Visitors: welcome weekdays; restricted weekends.
Green Fee: WD £25; WE £30
Societies: weekdays; Wed and Fri preferred.
Catering: lunches/snacks served, except Mon.
Hotels: Hawthorne

Visitors: welcome except weekends; phone Bayley Arms.
Green Fee: £10
Societies: by letter to Sec.
Catering: at Bayley Arms; snacks, la carte always available.
Hotels: Bayley Arms.

N137 **Southport Old Links**
☎(01704) 28207
Moss Lane, Southport, Merseyside PR9 7QS
From town centre take Lord St to roundabout at Law Courts, turn right into Manchester Rd, into Roe Lane and into Moss Lane.
Seaside course.
9 holes, 6244 yards, S.S.S.71
Founded 1920
Visitors: preferably not Wed or weekends.
Green Fee: WD £18 per round, £25 per day; WE £25
Societies: by arrangement if party of 12 or more.
Catering: snacks or light cooked meals can be provided as arranged with Steward.

N138 **Springfield Park**
☎(01706) 56401
Springfield Park, Bolton Rd, Rochdale, Lancs OL11 4RE
3 miles from M62.
Parkland course.
18 holes, 5337 yards, S.S.S.66
Founded 1927
Visitors: welcome anytime.
Green Fee: WD £5; WE £6.
Societies: welcome by prior arrangement
Catering: none.

N139 **Stand**
☎(0161) 766 3197 (Sec), Club 766 2388
The Dales, Ashbourne Grove, Whitefield, Manchester M45 7NL
1 mile N of M62, exit 17.
Undulating parkland course.
18 holes, 6426 yards, S.S.S.72
Designed by Alex Herd.
Founded 1904

N140 **Standish Court Golf Club**
☎(01257) 425777 Fax 425888
Rectory Lane, Standish, Wigan WN6 0XD
Leave M6 at junction 27, course is 5 mins from motorway on B5239 between Wigan & Chorley.
Undulating parkland course.
18 holes, 5609 yards, S.S.S.66
Designed by Patrick Dawson.
Founded 1995
Visitors: welcome, phone in advance for tee times.
Green Fee: WD £12.50; WE £15.
Societies: welcome by prior arrangement.
Catering: available all day.
Hotels: Kilhey Court

N141 **Stonyholme Municipal**
☎(01228) 34856 (Pro), Club 33208
St Aidans Rd, Carlisle, Cumbria CA1 1LF
Off A69, 1 mile W of M6, junction 43.
Flat meadowland course.
18 holes, 5787 yards, S.S.S.68
Designed by Frank Pennink.
Founded 1974
Visitors: welcome.
Green Fee: WD £6.50; WE £8.
Societies: welcome.
Catering: meals served.

N142 **Stonyhurst Park**
☎(01200) 23089, Sec (01772) 717650
c/o The Bayley Arms, Hurst Green, Blackburn BB7 9QB
On B6243 Clitheroe-Longridge road.
Parkland course.
9 holes, 5529 yards, S.S.S.66
Founded 1979

N143 **Swinton Park**
☎(0161) 794 1785, Sec 794 0861
East Lancashire Rd, Swinton, Manchester M27 5LX
On A580 Manchester-Liverpool road, about 4 miles from Manchester.
Parkland course.
18 holes, 6726 yards, S.S.S.72
Designed by Braid & Taylor.
Founded 1926
Visitors: welcome weekdays only.
Green Fee: on application.
Societies: by arrangement Tues, Wed and Fri.
Catering: bar snacks, meals throughout day (excluding Mon).
Snooker.
Hotels: Gay Willows Hotel.

N144 **Towneley**
☎(01282) 38473
Todmorden Rd, Burnley, Lancs BB11 3ED
Off Todmorden Rd approx 2 miles from town centre.
Public parkland course.
18 holes, 5811 yards, S.S.S.69; 9 holes Par 3
Designed by Burnley Council.
Founded 1932
Visitors: welcome anytime; normal dress rules; booking required.
Green Fee: WD £7; WE £8.
Societies: any weekday by arrangement with Pro.
Catering: bar, restaurant, lunchtimes weekdays; all day weekends.
Snooker table.

N145 **Tunshill**
☎(01706) 342095
Kiln Lane, Milnrow, Lancs
M62 junction 21 to Milnrow; follow Kiln Lane out of Milnrow town centre and continue along narrow lane to clubhouse.

Moorland course.
9 holes, 5742 yards, S.S.S.68
Founded 1943
Visitors: welcome weekdays except
Tues evening; with special permission
at weekends.
Green Fee: apply for details.
Societies: welcome weekdays.
Catering: by prior arrangement.
Snooker, pool.

N146 Turton
☎(01204) 852235
Wood End Farm, Chapeltown Rd,
Bromley Cross, Bolton BL7 9QH
4 miles NW of Bolton, use Hospital
Rd, Bromley Cross, Bolton; near Last
Drop Hotel.
Moorland course.
18 holes, 5907 yards, S.S.S.69
Designed by James Braid.
Founded 1908
Visitors: welcome except Wed
11.30-3pm, Sat, Sun and special
competition days.
Green Fee: WD £15; WE (when
available) £20.
Societies: by arrangement.
Catering: every day except Mon,
resident Steward and Stewardess.
Hotels: Last Drop; Egerton House.

N147 Ulverston
☎(01229) 582824, Sec 587806, Pro
582806
The Club House, Bardsea Park,
Ulverston, Cumbria LA12 9QJ
From Ulverston town centre to
Bardsea on B5087.
Parkland course.
18 holes, 6201 yards, S.S.S.71
Designed by H. Colt.
Founded 1895 (present course 1910)
Visitors: welcome; introduction card
or h/cap cert preferred; Tues Ladies
Day; not Sat if Men's Competition.
Green Fee: on application.
Societies: welcome by prior
arrangement.
Catering: full meals, bar snacks
daily; full time Steward.
Hotels: Virginia House; Sefton
House; White Water (Backbarrow).

N148 Walmersley
☎(0161) 764 1429 (Club), Sec 764
5057
Garretts Close, Walmersley, Bury
BL9 6TE
On A56 about 2.5 miles N of Bury;
M66 junction 1, then 0.5 mile S; turn
into Old Rd at Walmersley Post
Office.

Moorland course.
9 holes, 5341 yards, S.S.S. 67
Founded 1906
Visitors: Mon, Wed, Thurs and Fri;
Sun (with member).
Green Fee: £20 per day.
Societies: by arrangement Wed-Fri.
Catering: available except Mon.
Snooker.
Hotels: Old Mill; Red Hall.

N149 Werneth (Oldham)
☎(0161) 624 1190
Green Lane, Garden Suburb,
Oldham, Lancs OL8 3AZ
5 miles from Manchester, take A62 to
Hollinwood and then A6104.
Moorland course.
18 holes, 5363 yards, S.S.S.66
Founded 1908
Visitors: welcome weekdays only.
Green Fee: £16.50.
Societies: weekdays.
Catering: lunch and evening meals
served except Mon.
Snooker.
Hotels: Periquito (Oldham).

N150 West Derby
☎(0151) 254 1034 (Sec), Pro 220
5478
Yew Tree Lane, Liverpool L12 9HQ
4 miles E of Liverpool centre, 1 mile
S of West Derby village.
Parkland course.
18 holes, 6239 yards, S.S.S.70
Founded 1896
Visitors: welcome weekdays.
Green Fee: WD £25; WE £30.
Societies: welcome by prior
arrangement.
Catering: full facilities.
Hotels: Logwood Mill.

N151 West Lancashire
☎(0151) 924 1076
Hall Rd West, Blundellsands,
Liverpool L23 8SZ
M57 to Aintree, A5036 to Seaforth,
then A565 to Crosby, follow signs to
club, by Hall Rd station.
Seaside links course.
18 holes, 6767 yards, S.S.S.73
Designed by C.K. Cotton.
Founded 1873
Visitors: welcome with h/cap cert
except competition days.
Green Fee: WD £28 per round, £40
per day; WE £50.
Societies: Mon, Wed, Thurs, Fri.
Catering: lunch daily, other by
arrangement.
Hotels: Blundellsands.

N152 Westhoughton
☎(01942) 811085
Long Island, Westhoughton, Bolton,
Lancs BL5 2BR
4 miles SW of Bolton on A58.
Meadowland course.
9 holes, 5772 yards, S.S.S.68
Founded 1929
Visitors: welcome weekdays, with
member only at weekends.
Green Fee: £12.
Societies: by arrangement.
Catering: snacks, meals except Mon.
Snooker.
Hotels: The Georgian House.

N153 Whalley
☎(01254) 822236
Portfield Lane, Whalley, Blackburn,
Lancs BB6 9DR
A59 to Whalley, course on left of road
to Accrington.
Parkland course.
9 holes, 6258 yards, S.S.S.70
Founded 1912
Visitors: welcome except Thurs
12.30-4pm (Ladies Day) and Sat
during April-Sept.
Green Fee: WD £18; WE £25.
Societies: by arrangement.
Catering: lunches, teas and dinners
except Mon.
Snooker.
Hotels: Moat House; Dunkenhalgh.

N154 Whitefield
☎(0161) 766 2904
81/83 Higher Lane, Whitefield,
Manchester M25 7EZ
Leave M62 at exit 17 onto A56, club
is 200 yards on left in Higher Lane.
Parkland course.
18 holes, 5714 yards, S.S.S.68
Founded 1932
Visitors: welcome.
Green Fee: WD £25; WE £30.
Societies: Tues-Fri.
Catering: meals served.
Hotels: Bolton Crest; Hazeldean.

N155 Whittaker
☎(01706) 378310
Shore Lane, Littleborough, Lancs
OL15 0LH
1.5 miles from town centre.
Moorland course.
9 holes, 5606 yards, S.S.S.68
Founded 1906
Visitors: not Sun and Tues pm.
Green Fee: WD £10; WE £15.
Societies: apply to Sec.
Catering: none, bar can be arranged.
Hotels: Dearnley Cottage.

N156 **Wigan**

☎(01257) 421360
Arley Hall, Haigh, Wigan WN1 2UH
Leave M6 at exit 27, through
Standish on B5239, turn left at traffic
lights at Canal Bridge, opposite
Crawford Arms public house.
Parkland course.
9 holes, 6036 yards, S.S.S.69
Founded 1898
Visitors: welcome any day except
Tues, Wed and Sat.
Green Fee: WD £25; WE £30.
Societies: on application, special
package available.
Catering: available.
Hotels: Bellingham; Brockett Arms;
Kilhey Court.

N157 **William Wroe**

☎(0161) 748 8680
Pennybridge Lane, Flixton,
Manchester M41 3DX
Leave M63 at exit 4, take B5124,
then B5158 to Flixton road; course
is 12 miles N of Manchester city
centre.
Municipal parkland course.
18 holes, 4395 yards, S.S.S.61
Visitors: welcome, (bookings 7 days
in advance) 8am-4.30pm.
Green Fee: WD £6.30; WE £8.40.
Societies: welcome, book 7 days in
advance.
Catering: local pub.

N158 **Wilpshire**

☎(01254) 248260
72 Whalley Rd, Wilpshire, Blackburn,
Lancs BB1 9LF
On A666 4 miles N of Blackburn.
Moorland course.
18 holes, 5911 yards, S.S.S.69
Founded 1890
Visitors: welcome weekdays.
Green Fee: WD £25; WE £30.
Societies: catered for weekdays.
Catering: lunches daily, evening bar
snacks.
Hotels: Moat House; Trafalgar
(Salmesbury).

N159 **Windermere**

☎(01539) 443123
Cleabarrow, Windermere, Cumbria
LA23 3NB
1.25 miles from Bowness on Kendal
road B5284.
Undulating parkland course.
18 holes, 5006 yards, S.S.S.67
Designed by George Low.
Founded 1891
Visitors: welcome; must be members
of recognised golf club and have
official handicaps.
Green Fee: WD £23; WE £28.
Societies: by arrangement, numbers
12-60.
Catering: bar daily, bar meals 12am-
2pm, 6.30-9pm except Mon.
Snooker.
Hotels: Wild Boar (Crook).

N160 **Woolton**

☎(0151) 486 2298 (Sec), Pro 486
1298
Doe Park, Speke Rd, Woolton,
Liverpool L25 7TZ
6 miles from City centre.
Parkland course.
18 holes, 5717 yards, S.S.S.68
Founded 1901
Visitors: welcome.
Green Fee: WD £20; WE £30.

Societies: catered for weekdays; not
Tues.
Catering: by arrangement.
Hotels: Logwood Mill.

N161 **Workington**

☎(01900) 603460 (Steward), Pro
67828
Branthwaite Rd, Workington, Cumbria
CA14 4SS
Off A595 2 miles SE of town centre.
Undulating meadowland course.
18 holes, 6217 yards, S.S.S.70
Designed by James Braid.
Founded 1893
Visitors: welcome, must be members
of golf club and hold current h/cap
cert.
Green Fee: WD £17; WE £22.
Societies: apply to Sec.
Catering: full except Mon and Thurs
pm.
Hotels: Washington Central.

N162 **Worsley**

☎(0161) 789 4202
Stableford Ave, Monton, Eccles,
Manchester M30 8AP
1 mile from junction of M62/M63.
Parkland course.
18 holes, 6252 yards, S.S.S.70
Designed by James Braid.
Founded 1894
Visitors: welcome if member of golf
club with official h/cap.
Green Fee: WD £20 per round, £25
per day; WE £25 per round, £30 per
day.
Societies: welcome weekdays.
Catering: available from 12am.
Snooker.
Hotels: Novotel.

O

YORKSHIRE

Crossing the Pennines and approaching Yorkshire on the M62 gives a perfect impression of the wild loneliness of the countryside, an impression that can only be reinforced as you travel north.

Nevertheless, the area around Leeds is the one most blessed with the quality of its golf and its courses. Few courses, if any, are as much dominated by a river as Ilkley, particularly the opening holes which have a habit of destroying a score before it has taken shape. For all its modest length, Ilkley is quite a handful.

Alwoodley, Moor Allerton, Moortown and Sand Moor formed a distinguished cluster until Moor Allerton sold up and moved out towards Wike. The development of houses on the old course and on part of Sand Moor meant that Moortown became so surrounded that a redesign of their layout was essential. Sand Moor relocated their clubhouse on the other side of Alwoodley Lane and added several new holes but both Moortown and Sand Moor have preserved their considerable reputations.

Alwoodley, handiwork of the legendary Alister Mackenzie, is undoubtedly one of his finest, an elegant, demanding course in a wonderful setting that is not as well known as it should be. The latest version of Moor Allerton lies close by, the creation of Robert Trent Jones, while the outlying areas of Yorkshire's county town have pleasant golfing attractions, notably Headingley, Scarcroft, Garforth and the new Leeds Golf Centre between Moor Allerton and Alwoodly.

Neighbouring Bradford boasts West Bowling and the Bradford Club while Halifax is well served and Huddersfield claims Crosland Heath, Woodsome Hall and the Huddersfield GC at Fixby which is probably the pick. Bradley Park, on the edge of the M62 is a well used public course. Moving south-east, the Sheffield district is full of good things. Hallamshire, Hallowes, Dore & Totley, Abbey-dale, Lees Hall and Phoenix constitute the pick; nor must one forget Doncaster Town Moor, Wheatley and the Doncaster Club as thoughts move to the East Riding.

Of the old North Riding courses, Ganton surely wears the crown. Lying in the midst of the lovely Vale of Pickering, it is without doubt one of the finest inland courses in Britain and the only one to have housed the British Amateur championship, which it did for the first time in 1964. Michael Bonallack's "impertinence" in going round in 61 in the final of the 1968 English Championship should not deceive anyone into thinking that it is short or straightforward.

A round at Ganton is always a boost to the spirits, but Pannal at Harrogate and Fulford, York, are other courses that have welcomed their share of professional tournaments. From a clubhouse position close to the Leeds/Harrogate road, Pannal rises onto higher ground but Fulford is almost entirely flat, the stiffest climb being over the bridge that crosses the York by-pass. It splits the course virtually in two, a layout more on the lines of ancient seaside links which take the golfer straight out for six holes, then after a pleasant loop, straight back.

Scarborough has both North Cliff and South Cliff, the one designed by James Braid, the other by Alister Mackenzie. North Cliff is the sterner but Braid also had a hand in Bridlington, while Filey is a course of which I retain happy memories of a pleasant round many years ago.

Further south, Beverley & East Riding and Driffield form convenient stopping-off spots for travellers to the area of Hull which has a municipal course at Springhead Park, plus the Hull GC and Hessle. Boothferry is another municipal course while up in the north of the county Catterick Garrison and Richmond stand out along with Bedale and, just to the south, the pleasant 9 holes of Ripon City.

KEY

1	Abbeydale	24	Brough	49	Fardew	74	Hickleton
2	Aldwark Manor	25	Calverley	50	Ferrybridge 'C'	75	Hillsborough
3	Allerthorpe Park	26	Castle Fields	51	Filey	76	Hornsea
4	Alwoodley	27	Catterick Garrison	52	Flamborough Head	77	Horsforth
5	Ampleforth College	28	Cave Castle Hotel	53	Forest Park	78	Howley Hall
6	Austerfield Park CC	29	Cherry Burton	54	Forest of Galtres	79	Huddersfield (Fixby)
7	Baildon	30	City of Wakefield	55	Fulford	80	Hull
8	Barnsley	31	Clayton	56	Fulneck	81	Ilkley
9	Beauchief	32	Cleckheaton & District	57	Ganstead Park	82	Keighley
10	Bedale	33	Cocksford	58	Ganton	83	Kirkbymoorside
11	Ben Rhydding	34	Concord Park	59	Garforth	84	Knaresborough
12	Beverley & East	35	Cottingham	60	Gott's Park	85	Lakeside
	Riding	36	Crimple Valley	61	Grange Park	86	Leeds (Cobble Hall)
13	Bingley St Ives	37	Crookhill Park	62	Hainsworth Park	87	Leeds Golf Centre
14	Birley Wood	38	Crosland Heath	63	Halifax	88	Lees Hall
15	Boothferry	39	Crows Nest Park	64	Halifax Bradley Hall	89	Lightcliffe
16	Bracken Ghyll	40	Dewsbury District	65	Hallamshire	90	Lofthouse Hill
17	Bradford	41	Doncaster	66	Hallowes	91	Longley Park
18	Bradford Moor	42	Doncaster Town Moor	67	Hanging Heaton	92	Low Laithes
19	Bradley Park	43	Dore & Totley	68	Harrogate	93	Malton & Norton
20	Brandon	44	Drax	69	Headingley	94	Marsden
21	Branshaw	45	Driffield	70	Headley	95	Masham
22	Bridlington	46	Easingwold	71	Hebden Bridge	96	Meltham
23	Bridlington Links	47	East Bierley	72	Hessle	97	Mid Yorkshire
		48	Elland	73	Heworth	98	Middleton Park

99	Moor Allerton
100	Moortown
101	Normanton
102	Northcliffe
103	Oakdale
104	Otley
105	Oulton Park
106	Outlane
107	Owston Park
108	Painthorpe House G & CC
109	Pannal
110	Phoenix
111	Phoenix Park
112	Pike Hills
113	Pontefract & District
114	Pontefract Park
115	Queensbury
116	Rawdon
117	Renishaw Park
118	Richmond
119	Riddlesden
120	Ripon City
121	Romanby

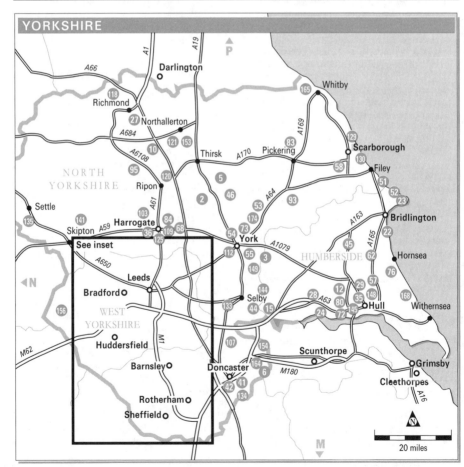

YORKSHIRE

122	Rotherham	136	Shay Grange	149	Swallow Hall	162	West End
123	Roundhay		Golf Centre The	150	Swingtime		(Halifax)
124	Roundwood	137	Shipley		(Leeds)	163	Wetherby
125	Rudding Park	138	Silkstone	151	Tankersley Park	164	Wheatley
126	Ryburn	139	Silsden	152	Temple	165	Whitby
127	Sand Moor	140	Sitwell Park		Newsam	166	Whitwood
128	Sandhill	141	Skipton	153	Thirsk &	167	Willow Valley G
129	Scarborough	142	South Bradford		Northallerton		& CC
	North Cliff	143	South Leeds	154	Thorne	168	Withernsea
130	Scarborough	144	Spaldington	155	Tinsley Park	169	Wombwell
	South Cliff	145	Springhead	156	Todmorden		(Hillies)
131	Scarcroft		Park	157	Wakefield	170	Woodhall Hills
132	Scathingwell	146	Springmill	158	Waterton Park	171	Woodsome Hall
133	Selby	147	Stocksbridge &	159	Wath	172	Woolley Park
134	Serlby Park		District	160	West Bowling	173	Wortley
135	Settle	148	Sutton Park	161	West Bradford	174	York

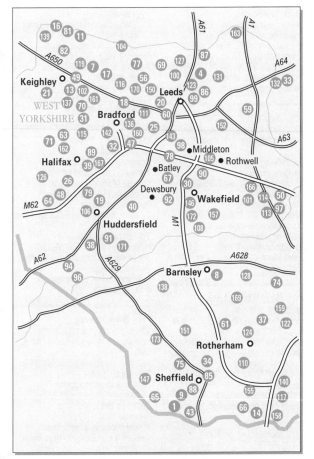

O1 **Abbeydale**
☎(0114) 2360763, Pro 2365633
Twentywell Lane, Dore, Sheffield S17
4QA
Off A621 5 miles S of Sheffield.
Parkland course.
18 holes, 6419 yards, S.S.S.71
Founded 1895
Visitors: welcome by arrangement;
not before 9.30am, or 12am-1.30pm.
Green Fee: WD £25 per round, £30
per day; WE £35.

Societies: welcome by prior
arrangement.
Catering: bar and restaurant all day.
Snooker.
Hotels: Beauchief; Sheffield Moat
House.

O2 **Aldwark Manor**
☎(01347) 838353, Fax 838867
Aldwark, Alne, York YO6 2NF
12 miles N of York in village of
Aldwark off A19; 5 miles SE of
Boroughbridge off A1.
Parkland course, easy walking.
18 holes, 6171 yards, S.S.S.70
Founded 1978
Visitors: welcome weekdays,
weekends by arrangement.
Green Fee: WD £16 per round, £20
per day; WE £20 per round, £24 per
day.
Societies: welcome by prior
arrangement.
Catering: snacks and full restaurant;
facilities available for banqueting and
private parties.
Hotels: Aldwark Manor on course.

O3 **Allerthorpe Park**
☎(01759) 306686, Fax 304308
Allerthorpe, York YO4 4RL
Situated 0.5m off A1079 York-Hull
road in village of Allerthorpe
Parkland course
9 hole (18 tees), 5510 yards, S.S.S.
67
Founded in 1994
Visitors: welcome by arrangement
Green Fee: £13 (18 holes)
Societies: welcome, corporate days
available
Catering: Full facilities
Hotels: Feathers (Pocklington)

O4 **Alwoodley**
☎(0113) 2681680 (Club), Pro
2689603
Wigton Lane, Alwoodley, Leeds LS17
8SA
5 miles N of Leeds on A61.
Heathland/moorland course.
18 holes, 6686 yards, S.S.S.72
Designed by Dr A. Mackenzie/H. Colt.
Founded 1907
Visitors: weekdays only by
arrangement, not before 3pm on Sat
or between 10.30-11.30 Sun or
before 3pm.
Green Fee: £50
Societies: by arrangement.
Catering: bar and restaurant facilities
by arrangement.
Hotels: Harewood Arms.

O5 Ampleforth College
☎(01439) 788485
c/o Sec, Beckdale Cottage, 56 High
St, Helmsley, York YO6 5AE
In Gilling East, 20 miles N of York.
Parkland course.
10 holes, 4018 yards, S.S.S.63
Founded 1962
Visitors: welcome but must give way
to College pupils 2-4pm during term
time; apply for play and pay green
fees at Fairfax Arms in Gilling East.
Green Fee: on application
Societies: apply to Sec.
Catering: at Fairfax Arms in village.

O6 Austerfield Park CC
(01302) 710841 (Club/Fax), 710850
Cross Lane, Austerfield, Doncaster, S
Yorks DN10 6RF
On roundabout, A614 2 miles N of
Bawtry.
Parkland course.
18 holes, 6859 yards, S.S.S.73
Designed by E. and M. Baker Ltd.
Founded 1974
Visitors: welcome any day.
Green Fee: WD £15; WE £19
Societies: welcome, packages WD
£28; WE £32.
Catering: full bar and restaurant.
Driving range, Pitch & Putt Par 3, flat
green bowls.
Hotels: Crown; Mount Pleasant;
Punches; Three Counties.

O7 Baildon
☎(01274) 584266, Pro 595162
Moorgate, Baildon, Shipley, W Yorks
BD17 5PP
5 miles N of Bradford, A6037 to
Shipley, 0.75 mile NE on A6038, left
at Junction Hotel.
Moorland course.
18 holes, 6225 yards, S.S.S.70
Founded 1896
Visitors: welcome weekdays and at
weekends by arrangement.
Green Fee: WD £16; WE £20
Societies: welcome by prior
arrangement.
Catering: lunches available except
Mon.

O8 Barnsley
☎(01226) 382856, Pro 382954
Wakefield Rd, Staincross, Nr
Barnsley, S Yorks S75 6JZ
On A61 3 miles from Barnsley.
Public undulating meadowland
course.
18 holes, 6042 yards, S.S.S.69
Founded 1928
Visitors: welcome.
Green Fee: WD £7.50; WE £8.50
Societies: welcome by arrangement
with Pro.
Catering: bar meals.
Hotels: Queens; Ardley Moat House.

O9 Beauchief
☎(0114) 2620040, Pro 2367274
Abbey Lane, Sheffield S8 0DB
5 miles from city centre, Abbeydale
Rd is on A625 to Baslow.
Municipal meadowland course.
18 holes, 5452 yards, S.S.S.66
Founded 1925
Visitors: welcome.
Green Fee: WD £8; WE £8.70
Societies: weekdays only, by
arrangement with City of Sheffield
Recreation Dept, Meersbrook Park,
Sheffield S8 9FL.(0114 2431253)
Catering: meals served daily.
Hotels: Beauchief adjacent to course.

O10 Bedale
☎(01677) 422568, Pro 422443
Leyburn Rd, Bedale, N Yorks DL8
1EZ
On A684 on leaving Bedale.
Parkland course.
18 holes, 6565 yards, S.S.S.71
Founded 1894
Visitors: welcome.
Green Fee: WD £16; WE £28.
Societies: weekdays only.
Catering: served daily.
Hotels: Leeming Motel
(Northallerton); Old Vicarage
(Bedale).

O11 Ben Rhydding
☎(01943) 608759
High Wood, Ben Rhydding, Ilkley, W
Yorks LS29 8SB
Keep left after passing Wheatley
Hotel to top of hill, left to golf course.
Moorland course.
9 holes, 4711 yards, S.S.S.64
Founded 1947
Visitors: on application.
Green Fee: on application.

O12 Beverley & East Riding
☎(01482) 868757, Pro 869519
Anti Mill, Westwood, Beverley HU17
8RG
On Beverley-Walkington road.
Undulating course.
18 holes, 6127 yards, S.S.S.69
Designed by Dr J.J. Fraser.
Founded 1889
Visitors: welcome weekdays.
Restricted weekends
Green Fee: WD £11 per round, £15
per day; WE £15.
Societies: weekdays.
Catering: lunches and evening meals
served.
Hotels: Beverley Arms; Lairgate.

O13 Bingley St Ives
☎(01274) 562436, Pro 562506
The Golf Clubhouse, St Ives Estate,
Bingley, W Yorks BD16 1AT
Turn off A650, Bingley town centre on
Harden-Cullingworth road; 0.5 mile on
right, turn right into Estate.
Wooded parkland/moorland course.
18 holes, 6485 yards, S.S.S.71
Designed by A Mackenzie.
Founded 1931
Visitors: welcome weekdays.
Green Fee: £24
Societies: weekdays.
Catering: meals daily except Mon.
Hotels: Bankfield.

O14 Birley Wood
☎(0114) 2647262
Birley Lane, Sheffield S12 3BP
4 miles S of Sheffield off A616
towards Mosborough; M1 junctions
30 take A616 towards Sheffield
Public open course.
18 holes, 5088 yards, S.S.S.66
Founded 1974
Visitors: no restrictions.
Green Fee: WD £7.75; WE £8.10.
Societies: welcome, phone Sheffield
Recreation Dept.
Catering: meals at Fairways Inn
adjoining course.

O15 Boothferry
☎(01430) 430364, Club 430371
Spaldington, Howden, Goole DN14
7NG
A63 towards Howden then B1228 to
Bubwith for 3 miles.
Public meadowland course.
18 holes, 6651 yards, S.S.S.72
Designed by Donald Steel.
Founded 1982
Visitors: welcome weekdays,
weekends and Bank Holidays except
Christmas Day.
Green Fee: WD £8.50; WE £12.50
Societies: catered for any day except
certain club competitions days;
reduced rates for societies of 12
players or more.
Catering: meals and snacks served
all lunchtimes, and summer season
evenings

O16 Bracken Ghyll

☎(01943) 831207
Skipton Rd, Addingham, Nr Ilkley
LS29 0SL
On the A65 Skipton-Leeds road in the
village of Addingham
Undulating parkland
9 holes, 6560 yards, S.S.S 71
(possible extension 1996; telephone
for details)
Designed by OCM Associates
Founded in 1993
Visitors: welcome; phone to check
availability.
Green Fee: WD £12; WE £15.
Societies: welcome; packages
available.
Catering: bar and bar snacks
available except Mondays unless by
special arrangement.
Indoor practice area, video tuition
available.
Hotels: Craiglands; Devonshire
Country House; Randells.

O17 Bradford

☎(01943) 875570 (Sec), Pro 873719
Hawksworth Lane, Guiseley, Leeds
LS20 8NP
From Shipley 3.5 miles NE on A6038,
left to Hawksworth Lane.
Moorland/parkland course.
18 holes, 6303 yards, S.S.S.71
Founded 1891
Visitors: weekdays unlimited;
weekends Sunday only.
Green Fee: WD £20; WE £30
Societies: welcome weekdays by
arrangement.
Catering: full facilities available;
functions catered for.
Snooker.
Hotels: Chevin Lodge; Hollins Hall.

O18 Bradford Moor

☎(01274) 638313, Pro 626107
Scarr Hall, Pollard Lane, Bradford
BD2 4RW
2 miles from Bradford city centre.
Undulating meadowland course.
9 holes, 5900 yards, S.S.S.68
Founded 1907
Visitors: welcome weekdays only
Green Fee: £12
Societies: welcome weekdays by
arrangement.
Catering: meals served.
Snooker.

O19 Bradley Park

☎(01484) 539988
Bradley Rd, Huddersfield, W Yorks
HD2 1PZ

M62 runs alongside course between
junctions 24 and 25, boundary
borders on A6107 Bradley Rd,
entrance to course signposted
midway along Bradley Rd.
Public undulating parkland course.
18 holes, 6220 yards, S.S.S.70; 9
holes Par 3
Designed by Donald Steel.
Founded 1977
Visitors: welcome weekdays and
weekends.
Green Fee: WD £9; WE £11.
Societies: Mon-Fri, not weekends;
contact Pro.
Catering: full facilities.
Driving range.
Hotels: Forte Crest (Brighouse) Golf
House.

O20 Brandon

☎(0113) 2737471
Holywell Lane, Shadwell, Leeds, W
Yorks LS17 8EZ
NW of Leeds, 1 mile from N Leeds
ring road at Roundhay Park.
Parkland course.
18 holes, 3601 yards, S.S.S.62
Designed by George Eric Allamby.
Founded 1967
Visitors: 8am-dusk 7 days, must
have set of clubs each and
appropriate footwear.
Green Fee: WD £5; WE £6..
Societies: welcome weekdays, 10
days notice.
Catering: snacks available all day.
New clubhouse, scheduled opening
spring 1996
Hotels: White House; Rydal Bank.

O21 Branshaw

☎(01535) 647441 (Bookings),
Clubhouse 643235
Branshaw Moor, Oakworth, Keighley,
W Yorks BD22 7ES
B6143 2 miles SW of Keighley.
Moorland course.
18 holes, 5858 yards, S.S.S.69
Designed by James Braid, Alister
MacKenzie.
Founded 1912
Visitors: welcome any time but must
phone Pro for time; h/cap cert
required.
Green Fee: WD £12 per round, £15
per day; WE £15 per round, £20 per
day.
Societies: weekdays, package
available from Pro.
Catering: facilities available every
day except Mon.
Hotels: Beeches (Keighley) Old Hall;
White Lion.

O22 Bridlington

☎(01262) 672092, Office: 606367,
Pro 674721
Belvedere Rd, Bridlington, E
Yorkshire YO15 3NA
1.5 miles S of Bridlington station, off
A165 from Hull.
Seaside course.
18 holes, 6491 yards, S.S.S.71
Designed by James Braid.
Founded 1905
Visitors: welcome.
Green Fee: WD £12 per round, £18
per day; WE £20.
Societies: welcome by arrangement
with Hon Sec.
Catering: full facilities.
Hotels: Marine; The Spa; Monarch.

O23 Bridlington Links

☎(01262) 401584, Fax 401702
Flamborough Road, Marton,
Bridlington, E Yorks YO15 1DW
Between Bridlington and
Flamborough on the B1255
Clifftops links course
18 holes, 6719 yards, S.S.S. 72; 9
hole Sir Henry Cotton Foundation
course, 1349 yards
Designed by Howard Swan
Founded May 1993
Visitors: welcome
Green Fee: WD £10 per round, £15
per day; WE £12.50 per round,
£17.50 per day
Societies: welcome every day by
arrangement.
Catering: Large clubhouse with
views over Bridlington Bay,
restaurant, carvery, speciality Sunday
lunches, funtion suite, lounge bar with
balconies.
Three hole academy course, driving
range
Hotels: Flaneburgh; Sewerby
Grange; North Star; Timonger; Manor
Court.

O24 Brough

☎(01482) 667291 (Sec), Club
667374, Pro 667483
Cave Rd, Brough, N Humberside
HU15 1HB
10 miles W of Hull off A63.
Parkland course.
18 holes, 6139 yards, S.S.S.69
Founded 1893
Visitors: weekdays only; Wed after
2.30pm only.
Green Fee: WD £30; WE £40
Societies: Tues and Fri by prior
arrangement.
Catering: available.
Hotels: Cave Castle; Crest (Hull).

O25 Calverley
☎(0113) 2569244 (Pro), Club 2564362
Woodhall Lane, Pudsey, Leeds LS28 5QY
7 miles from Leeds centre, 4 miles from Bradford centre.
Parkland course, 18 holes private, 9 holes public.
18 holes, 5527 yards, S.S.S.67; 9 holes, 2137 yards, Par 33
Founded 1983
Visitors: welcome; h/cap cert required for 18 hole course; 9 hole course unrestricted.
Green Fee: 18 hole course: WD £12; WE £17; 9 hole course, £6 (18 holes).
Societies: any time by prior arrangement.
Catering: bar and restaurant facilities available.

O26 Castle Fields
☎(01484) 712108
Rastrick Common, Rastrick, Brighouse, W Yorks
Parkland course.
6 holes, 2406 yards, S.S.S.50
Founded 1903
Visitors: only if accompanied by a member.
Green Fee: apply for details.

O27 Catterick Garrison
☎(01748) 833268 (Sec), Pro 833671, Fax 833263
Leyburn Rd, Catterick Garrison, N Yorks DL9 3QE
6 miles SW of Scotch Corner, turn off A1 at Catterick Garrison and follow signs (2.5 miles).
Undulating moorland/parkland course.
Designed by Arthur Day.
Founded 1932
Visitors: welcome.
Green Fee: WD £12.50; WE £25.
Societies: on application.
Catering: restaurant and bar snacks.
Hotels: Bridge House (Catterick Bridge); Golden Lion (Leyburn).

O28 Cave Castle Hotel
☎(01430) 421286 (Golf), Hotels: 422245
South Cave, Brough, E Yorks HU15 2EU
10 miles from city of Kingston upon Hull, junction of A63/M62 East.
Parkland course.
18 holes, 6409 yards, S.S.S.71
Founded July 1989

Visitors: welcome.
Green Fee: WD £12.50; WE £18
Societies: weekdays and after 10.30 at weekends, special rates by arrangement.
Catering: full facilities; conference and banqueting up to 300, à la carte.
Hotels: Cave Castle, weekday and weekend golfing breaks.

O29 Cherry Burton
☎(01964) 550924
Leconfield Road, Cherry Burton, Beverley, HU17 7RB
Close to Beverley on the B1248
Parkland course
9 holes, 2278, S.S.S. 62 (extension planned June 1996)
Designed by W Adamson
Founded Sept 1993
Visitors: welcome, no restrictions.
Green Fees: WD £5 (9 holes), £7 (18 holes); WE £6 (9 h), £9 (18 h).
Societies: welcome everyday.
Catering: bar snacks.
Hotels: Beverley; Lairgate.

O30 City of Wakefield
☎(01924) 360282 (Pro)
Lupset Park, Horbury Rd, Wakefield, W Yorks WF2 8QS
Approx 2 miles from M1 junctions 39 or 40, course situated on A642 Huddersfield road.
Public parkland course.
18 holes, 6419 yards, S.S.S.70
Founded 1936
Visitors: welcome.
Green Fee: WD £7.60; WE £9.60
Societies: apply to Stewardess (01924) 367242.
Catering: meals and snacks for groups, arrange with Stewardess.
Hotels: Swallow; Post House; Cedar Court.

O31 Clayton
☎(01274) 880047
Thornton View Rd, Clayton, Bradford, W Yorks BD14 6JX
On A647 from Bradford, then turn right and follow signs to Clayton.
Moorland course.
9 holes, 5467 yards, S.S.S.67
Founded 1906
Visitors: welcome weekdays and Sat unless tee closed for competition.
Green Fee: WD/WE £10; BH £20 .
Societies: apply to Sec.
Catering: bar and bar snacks except Mon; other by arrangement.
Snooker.
Hotels: Pennine Hilton.

O32 Cleckheaton & District
☎(01274) 874118, Sec 851266, Pro 851267
Bradford Rd, Cleckheaton, W Yorks BD19 6BU
M62 exit 26 onto A638 towards Bradford.
Parkland course.
18 holes, 5860 yards, S.S.S.68
Founded 1900
Visitors: welcome.
Green Fee: WD £22; WE £28.
Societies: catered for weekdays.
Catering: morning coffee, lunches, teas, dinner every day except Mon.
Hotels: Novotel (Bradford).

O33 Cocksford
☎(01937) 834253
Stutton, Tadcaster, N Yorkshire LS24 9NG
1.5 miles S of Tadcaster near village of Stutton.
Parkland course.
27 holes, 3 courses Old, Plews, Quarry High; Old & Plews 5570 yards, S.S.S.69; Plews & Quarry High 5559 yards S.S.S. 68; Old & Quarry High 4951 yards S.S.S. 65
Designed by Townend and Brodigan.
Founded 1991
Visitors: welcome, correct dress, tee times from Pro shop.
Green Fee: WD £16 per round, £20 per day ;WE £22 per round, £25 per day.
Societies: welcome weekdays by prior arrangement, £27 per package phone for details. Corporate membership available.
Catering: lounge bar, bar snacks, Sparrows Restaurant, open to non-members.
Hotels: 4 luxury cottages on site.

O34 Concord Park
☎(0114) 2570111
Shiregreen Lane, Sheffield, S Yorks
Off A6135, 3.5 miles N of Sheffield, next to Concord Sports Centre.
Public undulating parkland course.
18 holes, 4321 yards, S.S.S.62
Founded 1952
Visitors: welcome by arrangement.
Green Fee: £5.20.
Catering: available in adjacent sports centre.

O35 Cottingham
☎(01482) 842394
Spring Park Farm, Park Lane, Cottingham HU16 5RZ

Just off main Beverley road. Take Cottingham signs and the course is 60 yards on left
Parkland course
18 holes, 6230 yards, S.S.S. 69
Designed by J Wiles
Founded 1994
Visitors: welcome
Green Fee: WD £12; WE £18.
Societies: welcome weekdays by arrangement.
Catering: bar and full catering.
Driving range.

O36 **Crimple Valley**
☎(01423) 883485, Fax 881018
Hookstone Wood Rd, Harrogate, N Yorks HG2 8PN
1 mile S of Harrogate town centre; turn off A61 at crossroads at Appleyards Garage, after 0.75 mile signposted to right.
Gently sloping fairways in rural setting.
9 holes, 2500 yards, S.S.S.33
Founded 1976
Visitors: welcome at all times.
Green Fee: WD £4.50 (9 holes), £7.50 (18 holes); WE £5
Catering: licensed bar, lunches available weekdays, breakfasts at weekends.

O37 **Crookhill Park**
☎(01709) 862979 (Pro/Manager), Clubhouse 862974
Conisbrough, Nr Doncaster, S Yorks DN12 2AH
Between Conisbrough and Edlington; turn off A630 Doncaster-Rotherham road onto B6094, then course is signposted.
Public parkland course.
18 holes, 5839 yards, S.S.S.68
Founded 1975
Visitors: welcome, no restrictions.
Green Fee: WD £8.25; WE £9/50.
Societies: welcome any time by arrangement; written confirmation required.
Catering: bar and bar snacks.
Hotels: Consort Suite (Thurcroft); Moat House (Doncaster).

O38 **Crosland Heath**
☎(01484) 653216, Sec 653262, Pro 653877
Felk Stile Rd, Crosland Heath, Huddersfield HD4 7AF
Take A62 Huddersfield-Oldham road for 3 miles, then follow signs for Goodalls Caravans.
Moorland course.

18 holes, 6004 yards, S.S.S.70
Founded 1913
Visitors: welcome by arrangement; h/cap cert required.
Green Fee: on application
Societies: welcome except Sat; contact Sec.
Catering: full facilites available except Mon.
Hotels: Dryclough (Crosland Moor); Durker Roods (Meltham).

O39 **Crows Nest Park**
☎(01422) 201216/Fax
Coach Road, Brighouse, W Yorks HD6 2LN
From East, M62 exit 26, A58 towards Halifax, after 3m take Brighouse turn, rt at next lights, at brow of hill turn into Smith House La, right after Harrison's Fm. From West, M62 exit 25, signs to Brighouse, then signs from Bradford, at 2nd roundabout left after Ritz. Club is 1.5m on Couch Rd.
Undulating parkland
9 holes, 6020 yards, S.S.S 71
Designed by W Adamson
Founded June 1995
Visitors: welcome.
Green Fees: WD £7 (9 holes0, £12 (18 holes); WE £8 (9 holes), £15 (18 holes).
Societies: welcome; packages available.
Catering: clubhouse with views over lakes and course offers full catering facilities.
Driving range, putting green and practice bunkers.
Hotels: Lane Head; Sacha Court; Forte Crest.

O40 **Dewsbury District**
☎(01924) 492399, Pro 496030
The Pinnacle, Sands Lane, Mirfield, W Yorks WF14 8HJ
Off A644, 2.5 miles from Dewsbury, at Swan Hotel turn left into Steanard Lane, sign at Sands Lane.
Undulating meadowland/moorland course.
18 holes, 6267 yards, S.S.S.71
Redesigned by Peter Alliss & Dave Thomas (1970).
Founded 1891
Visitors: welcome weekdays by prior arrangement, weekends after 4pm.
Green Fee: WD £16 per round, £20 per day; WE £18
Societies: welcome.
Catering: full facilites available except Mon.
Hotels: Flowerpot Motel; The Woolpack.

O41 **Doncaster**
☎(01302) 865632 (Office), Fax 865994, Pro 868404
278 Bawtry Rd, Bessacarr, Doncaster, S Yorks DN4 7PD
Easy to locate between Doncaster and Bawtry on A638.
Undulating heathland course.
18 holes, 6220 yards, S.S.S.69
Founded 1894
Visitors: welcome
Green Fee: WD £14; WE £16.
Societies: weekdays except Wed, by arrangement with Sec.
Catering: main meals available by prior arrangement daily.
Hotels: Punches; Danum.

O42 **Doncaster Town Moor**
☎(01302) 535286 (Pro), Clubhouse/Sec 533167
Bawtry Rd, Belle Vue, Doncaster, S Yorks DN4 5HU
400 yards S of racecourse roundabout on A638 travelling towards Bawtry; entrance as for Doncaster Rovers Football Ground.
Parkland course.
18 holes, 6072 yards, S.S.S.69
Founded 1895
Visitors: welcome except Sun before 11.30am.
Green Fee: WD £14;WE £16.
Societies: apply to Competition Sec.
Catering: available; contact club
Hotels: Danum; Earl of Doncaster; Rockingham.

O43 **Dore & Totley**
☎(0114) 2360492, Pro 2366844, Sec 2369872
Bradway Rd, Sheffield, S Yorks S17 4QR
Off A61 Sheffield-Chesterfield road on Holmesfield Rd.
Parkland course.
18 holes, 6256 yards, S.S.S.70
Founded 1913
Visitors: welcome by prior arrangement.
Green Fee: £25
Societies: welcome weekdays except Wed.
Catering: full facilities except Mon. Snooker.
Hotels: Beauchief.

O44 **Drax**
☎(01405) 860533 Sec
Drax, Nr Selby, N Yorks YO8 8PQ
Off A1041 6 miles S of Selby, opposite Drax Power Station.

Parkland course with many trees.
9 holes, 5510 yards, S.S.S.67
Founded 1989
Visitors: only if introduced by
member.
Green Fee: WD £5; WE £7
Catering: at Drax Sports and Social
Club.

O45 **Driffield**
☎(01377) 253116 (Clubhouse), Sec
254167, Pro 240448
Sunderlandwick, Driffield, N
Humberside YO25 9AD
1 mile from Driffield town centre
towards Hull on A164.
Parkland course.
18 holes, 6222 yards, S.S.S.70
Founded 1935
Visitors: welcome, h/cap certs
required.
Green Fee: WD £18; WE £25.
Societies: catered for weekdays by
arrangement.
Catering: not Mon, except parties by
arrangement.
Hotels: Bell.

O46 **Easingwold**
☎(01347) 821486, Pro 821964
Stillington Rd, Easingwold, N Yorks
YO6 3ET
0.75 mile off A19, entering
Easingwold from York turn right
immediately past garage.
Parkland course.
18 holes, 6285 yards, S.S.S.70
Founded 1930
Visitors: welcome.
Green Fee: WD £25; WE £30.
Societies: by prior arrangement with
Sec (not weekends or Bank
Holidays).
Catering: bar lunches, lunches,
dinners except Mon.
Hotels: George.

O47 **East Bierley**
☎(01274) 681023, Steward: 680450
South View Rd, Bierley, Bradford, W
Yorks BD4 6TJ
3 miles SE of Bradford on Wakefield-
Heckmondwike Rd.
Undulating moorland course.
9 holes, 4692 yards, S.S.S.63
Founded 1909
Visitors: no restrictions except Mon
evening and Sun.
Green Fee: WD £12; WE £15
Societies: write for details.
Catering: bar and restaurant open
daily.
Snooker.

O48 **Elland**
☎(01422) 372505, Pro 374886
Hammerstones, Leach Lane, Elland,
W Yorks HX5 0TA
Leave M62 at junction 24, look for
Blackley sign, approx 1 mile.
Parkland course.
9 holes, 5630 yards, S.S.S.66
Founded 1912
Visitors: welcome weekdays.
Green Fee: WD £14; WE £25
Societies: by arrangement.
Catering: meals, bar snacks except
Mon.
Hotels: Hilton National; The Rock.

O49 **Fardew**
☎(01274) 561229
Nursery Farm, Carr Lane, East
Morton, Keighley BD20 5RY
On north side of Leeds/ Liverpool
canal between Bingley and Keighley
Parkland course
9 holes, 6208, S.S.S. 70
Founded July 1993
Visitors: welcome; pay-as-you-play
Green Fee: WD £6 (9 holes), £10 (18
holes); WE £7 (9 holes), £12 (18
holes)
Societies: welcome but catering in
local pubs.

O50 **Ferrybridge 'C'**
☎(01977) 674188 extn 2852
Ferrybridge 'C' P.S. Golf Club, P.O.
Box 39, Strangland Lane, Knottingley,
W Yorks WF11 8SQ
400 yards to W side of A1, on
Castleford-Knottingley road.
9 holes, 5138 yards, S.S.S.65
Designed by N.E. Pugh.
Founded 1976
Visitors: with member only.
Green Fee: by arrangement
Societies: welcome by arrangement.

O51 **Filey**
☎(01723) 513293 (Sec), Pro 513134
West Ave, Filey, N Yorks YO14 9BQ
Private road off end of West Ave in S
end of town.
Seaside course.
18 holes, 6112 yards, S.S.S.69
Founded 1897
Visitors: unaccompanied with proof
of membership of a golf club and/or
h/cap cert.
Green Fee: WD £20; WE £25.
Societies: by arrangement, not Bank
Holidays.
Catering: all year.
Snooker.
Hotels: White Lodge.

O52 **Flamborough Head**
☎(01262) 850333
Lighthouse Rd, Flamborough,
Bridlington, N Humberside YO15 1AR
5 miles NE of Bridlington on B1255,
near lighthouse at Flamborough.
Undulating course.
18 holes, 5436 yards, S.S.S.66
Extension planned 1996
Founded 1932
Visitors: welcome; restricted Sun
am, Wed 10.30am-1.30pm.
Green Fee: WD £15; WE £18.
Societies: apply to Sec.
Catering: full facilities
Snooker table.
Hotels: Flaneburg; Timoneer.

O53 **Forest Park**
☎(01904) 400425
Stockton on Forest, York, N Yorks
YO3 9UW
2 miles from E end of York by-pass,
in village of Stockton on Forest.
Parkland course.
18 holes, 6660 yards, S.S.S.72; 9
holes, 6372 S.S.S.70
Founded 1991
Visitors: welcome, telephone for tee
times.
Green Fee: 18 holes: WD £14.50;
WE £20; 9 holes: WD £7; WE £10.
Societies: welcome by arrangement.
Catering: bar, dining room; snacks
and full catering.
Driving range.

O54 **Forest of Galtres**
☎(01904) 766198, Club 750287
Skelton Lane, Wigginton, York YO3
3RF
In the Forest of Galtres, 2 miles from
the northern section of the York ring
road off the A19
Parkland course
18 holes, 6312 yards, S.S.S. 70
Designed by S Gidman
Founded 1993
Visitors: welcome at all times
Green Fees: WD £15 per round, £20
per day; WE & BH £18.50 per round,
£22.50 per day.
Societies: welcome
Catering: Bar, lounge and dining
room. Full range of snacks and meals
available.
Hotels: Fairfield Manor; Jacobean
Lodge.

O55 **Fulford**
☎(01904) 413579 (Sec), Pro 412882
Heslington Lane, Heslington, York
YO1 5DY

Off A19 from York, follow signs to University.
Parkland course.
18 holes, 6775 yards, S.S.S.72
Designed by Dr A. Mackenzie.
Founded 1906
Visitors: by prior arrangement. Weekdays only.
Green Fee: WD £30 per round, £35 per day
Societies: welcome by arrangement; contact Sec at above address and telephone number.
Catering: morning coffee, lunch and evening meal.
Hotels: Alfreda.

O56 Fulneck
☎(0113) 2565191
The Clubhouse, Fulneck, Pudsey, W Yorks LS28 8NT
Between Leeds and Bradford. At Pudsey cenotaph turn right then first left into Bankhouse Lane and follow signs
Undulating wooded parkland course.
9 holes, 5330 yards, S.S.S.67
Founded 1892
Visitors: welcome weekdays, with member only weekends.
Green Fee: £14 (£6 with member).
Societies: welcome by arrangement in advance.
Catering: by arrangement in advance.

O57 Ganstead Park
☎(01482) 811280 (Sec), Pro 811121
Longdales Lane, Coniston, Hull HU11 4LB
On A165 E of Hull, 2 miles from city boundary.
Parkland course.
18 holes, 6801 yards, S.S.S.73
Designed by Peter Green.
Founded 1976
Visitors: any day except Weds and before lunch Sun.
Green Fee: WD £15; WE £24.
Societies: by arrangement.
Catering: lunches, evening meals.
Hotels: Hull Marina; Beverley Arms.

O58 Ganton
☎(01944) 710329, Pro 710260
Ganton, Scarborough, N Yorks YO12 4PA
11 miles from Scarborough on A64.
Heathland course.
18 holes, 6720 yards, S.S.S.74
Designed by Dunn, Vardon, Colt, C.K. Cotton.
Founded 1891

Visitors: by prior arrangement.
Green Fee: WD £40; WE £45.
Societies: by prior arrangement.
Catering: available.
Hotels: Hackness Grange; Crown).

O59 Garforth
☎(0113) 2862021, Sec 2863308, Pro 2862063
Long Lane, Garforth, Leeds LS25 2DS
6.5 miles E of Leeds on A63, then left onto A642 towards Wakefield.
Parkland course.
18 holes, 6304 yards, S.S.S.70
Founded 1913
Visitors: welcome weekdays.
Green Fee: WD £22
Societies: during the week.
Catering: full facilities.

O60 Gott's Park
☎(0113) 2310492
Armley Ridge Rd, Leeds LS12 2QX
About 3 miles W of city centre.
Public parkland course.
18 holes, 4960 yards, S.S.S.64
Founded 1933
Visitors: welcome.
Green Fee: WD £7.50; WE £7.95
Societies: apply to Council.
Catering: meals served.

O61 Grange Park
☎(01709) 559497 Pro
Upper Wortley Rd, Rotherham S61 2SJ
2 miles W of Rotherham town on A629.
Municipal parkland course.
18 holes, 6421 yards, S.S.S.71
Founded 1971
Visitors: no restrictions.
Green Fee: WD £8; WE £9.50.
Catering: full catering Tues-Sun, sandwiches Mon.

O62 Hainsworth Park
☎(01964) 542362
Brandesburton, Driffield, E Yorks YO25 8RT
Just off A165 8 miles N of Beverley.
Parkland course.
18 holes, 6003 yards, S.S.S.69
Founded 1983
Visitors: some restrictions. phone beforehand.
Green Fee: WD £12; WE £15.
Societies: any time.
Catering: bar and restaurant facilities available.
Hotels: Burton Lodge on course.

O63 Halifax
☎(01422) 244171, Pro 240047
Union Lane, Ogden, Halifax HX2 8XR
4 miles from town centre on A629.
Moorland course.
18 holes, 6037 yards, S.S.S.70
Designed by W.H. Fowler, James Braid.
Founded 1895
Visitors: welcome weekdays.
Green Fee: WD £15; WE £30.
Societies: weekdays and limited weekends.
Catering: full range, à la carte and table d'hôte, except Mon.
Hotels: Holdsworth House (Holmfield); Princess (Halifax).

O64 Halifax Bradley Hall
☎(01422) 374108, Pro 370231
Stainland Rd, Holywell Green, Halifax, W Yorks HX4 9AN
Half-way between Halifax and Huddersfield on B6112.
Moorland course.
18 holes, 6213 yards, S.S.S.70
Founded 1924
Visitors: welcome.
Green Fee: WD£16 with h/cap cert, £18 without; WE £24 with h/cap cert. £28 without.
Societies: on application.
Catering: full except Mon and Tues. Snooker.
Hotels: Old Golf House (Outlane), Rock Inn (Holywewll Green).

O65 Hallamshire
☎(0114) 2302153 (Sec), Club 2301007, Pro 2305222, Fax 2305656
The Clubhouse, Sandygate, Sheffield S10 4LA
A57 from centre of Sheffield, left fork at Crosspool, 1 mile to course.
Moorland course.
18 holes, 6359 yards, S.S.S.71
Founded 1897
Visitors: weekdays and limited weekends.
Green Fee: WD £30; WE £35.
Societies: weekdays except Weds.
Catering: full facilities. Snooker.
Hotels: Hallam Tower; Rutland.

O66 Hallowes
☎(01246) 413734 Sec, 411196 Pro
Hallowes Lane, Dronfield, Sheffield S18 6UA
Take A61 Sheffield-Chesterfield road into Dronfield (do not take by-pass), turn sharp left under railway bridge, club signposted.

Undulating moorland course.
18 holes, 6342 yards, S.S.S.70
Founded 1892
Visitors: weekdays only, unless with member.
Green Fee: £20.
Societies: limited.
Catering: by arrangement with the Stewardess.

O67 **Hanging Heaton**
☎(01924) 461606, Pro 467077, Sec 430100
White Cross Rd, Bennett Lane, Dewsbury, W Yorks WF12 7DT
On A653 1 mile from Dewsbury centre.
Parkland course.
9 holes, 5902 yards, S.S.S.67
Founded 1922
Visitors: welcome weekdays by arrangement.
Green Fee: WD £12.
Societies: welcome weekdays.
Catering: lunch except Mon.

O68 **Harrogate**
☎(01423) 862999 (Sec), Pro 862547, Steward: 863158 Steward, Caterer/Chef: 860278, Fax 860073
Forest Lane Head, Harrogate, N Yorks HG2 7TF
On right of A59, 2.5 miles from Harrogate towards Knaresborough.
Undulating parkland course.
18 holes, 6241 yards, S.S.S.70
Designed by Sandy Herd.
Founded 1892
Visitors: welcome.
Green Fee: WD £28 per round, £32 per day; WE £40.
Societies: weekdays only by arrangement, parties over 12.
Catering: bar and restaurant, chef catering.
Snooker.
Hotels: Dower House; Newton House (Knaresborough).

O69 **Headingley**
☎(0113) 2679573 (Sec), Pro 2675100
Back Church Lane, Adel, Leeds LS16 8DW
At roundabout on Leeds ring road take A660 towards Otley, turn right after 1 mile at lights, then left, course is just past Adel Church.
Undulating parkland course.
18 holes, 6298 yards, S.S.S.70
Founded 1892
Visitors: members of other clubs welcome, prior reservation preferred.

Green Fee: WD £25 per round, £30 per day; WE £36.
Societies: recognised societies welcome if previous arrangements made with Sec.
Catering: full facilities
2 snooker tables.
Hotels: Post House; Parkway.

O70 **Headley**
☎(01274) 833481
Headley Lane, Thornton, Bradford, W Yorks BD13 3LX
4 miles W of Bradford, on B6145 Thornton road, in village of Thornton.
Moorland course.
9 holes, 4914 yards, S.S.S.64
Founded 1906
Visitors: unlimited, not Sat.
Green Fee: £10.
Societies: by arrangement. Special packages available.
Catering: by arrangement.
Hotels: Guide Post Hotel

O71 **Hebden Bridge**
☎(01422) 842896
Wadsworth, Hebden Bridge, W Yorkshire HX7 8PH
1 mile N of Hebden Bridge past Birchcliffe Centre.
Moorland course.
9 holes, 5064 yards, S.S.S.65
Founded 1930
Visitors: weekdays no restrictions, weekends check first.
Green Fee: WD £12; WE £15.
Societies: welcome by arrangement.
Catering: meals and bar snacks except Mon.
Hotels: Carlton (reduced green fees); Hebden Lodge, Old Civic Hall; White Lion.

O72 **Hessle**
☎(01482) 650171, Pro 650190
Westfield Rd, Cottingham, Hull, N Humberside HU16 5YL
3 miles SW of Cottingham, off A164.
Undulating meadowland course.
18 holes, 6700 yards, S.S.S.72.
Designed by Peter Alliss & Dave Thomas.
Founded 1906; new course opened June 1975
Visitors: not Tues, 9.15am-1pm. After 11am weekends
Green Fee: WD £18; WE £25.
Societies: recognised golfing societies welcome by prior arrangement with Sec.
Catering: available every day during summer months.

O73 **Heworth**
☎(01904) 422389 (Pro)
Muncaster House, Muncastergate, York YO3 9JX
1.5 miles from city centre, on A1036 York-Scarborough road.
Meadowland/parkland course.
11 holes, 6434 yards, S.S.S.69
Founded 1911
Visitors: weekdays, weekends restricted availability.
Green Fee: WD £20; WE £25
Societies: weekdays.
Catering: full facilities except Mon

O74 **Hickleton**
☎(01709) 896081 (Sec), Club 892496, Pro 895170.
Hickleton, Nr Doncaster, S Yorks DN5 7BE
7 miles out of Doncaster on B6411, off A635 to Barnsley.
Undulating parkland course.
18 holes, 6434 yards, S.S.S.71
Designed by Huggett, Coles & Dyer.
Founded 1909
Visitors: welcome if members of recognised club; after 2.30pm weekends and Bank Holidays.
Green Fee: WD £20; WE £25.
Societies: weekdays; annual society open day in Sept.
Catering: full facilities

O75 **Hillsborough**
☎(0114) 2349151 (Sec), Pro 2332666
Worrall Rd, Sheffield S6 4BE
Moorland/parkland course.
18 holes, 6216 yards, S.S.S.70
Founded 1920
Visitors: welcome weekdays.
Green Fee: WD £28; WE £35.
Societies: by arrangement.
Catering: soup/sandwiches any lunch time except Fri; full meals by prior arrangement.
Snooker.
Hotels: Grosvenor; Rutland.

O76 **Hornsea**
☎(01964) 532020 (Sec), Pro 534989, Clubhouse 535488
Rolston Rd, Hornsea, N Humberside HU18 1XG
Follow sign for Hornsea Pottery in Hornsea, clubhouse is approx 600 yards further along on road to Withernsea.
Parkland/moorland course.
18 holes, 6685 yards, S.S.S.72
Designed by Sandy Herd.
Founded 1898

River setting at Ilkley

St. Andrews, Carnoustie and Prestwick have their famous burns, a fame publicised by their influence in shaping golfing history. Water hazards take many other forms. In fact, lakes are now the rule rather than the exception on most new courses throughout the world. Sadly, some developers and golf course architects view lake building as essential but a few Clubs such as Ilkley have the grandest and most natural of all water features – a river frequently in full spate.

What makes it even more dramatic is that the Wharfe casts its spell at Ilkley on the opening holes when actions have not yet matched intentions and errors are often beyond redemption. River, Bridge and Island, the names of the first three holes, express the mood although they do not convey the complete picture, a quiet valley set back from a bustling town beneath the vastness and bleakness of the Moor.

It is an inspiring setting that occupies the thoughts as the walk back to the first tee is made but it masks the impact of the immediate tasks. The 1st is 410 yards between trees and the river and the 2nd and 3rd are two consecutive short holes which test nerve and skill. The tee shot on the 2nd plays over the tributary of the river that creates the island while the 3rd, 206 yards, has river on both flanks.

The admirable 4th, the first of two par 5s in three holes, calls for a short carry on the drive over the tributary of the river as it returns to the main stream which then lingers as far as the 7th, not quite as much of a threat as hitherto although its presence nags. The 5th, 200 yards, and romantically named Kingfisher, maintains the demands of the short holes. Direction then changes with the 7th, an attractive looking hole with a pleasant raised setting for the green.

As the river pursues its meanderings, its duty done, the 8th turns back, announcing a different tenor to the holes, if no lessening of their appeal or challenge. Trees gradually substitute for the river as the principal danger to wayward shots on a succession of par 4s. The 4s are interrupted by the 13th, a short hole of character, but, after that, a finish begins that strikes another change of scene.

The 14th, 433 yards, is rated the hardest hole of the inward half in spite of a lack of fairway bunkers to plague the drive and the 15th is a quaint short hole with an alarming slope from the back of the green. A putt down the hill on a well shaved surface would have a stimpmeter dancing with joy. Drives from elevated tees are always to be remembered and that from the 16th offers an exciting shot as well as some handsome views.

There is a rural hint to the holes either side of the turn but the 16th and 17th lie in the shadow of a wood, dropping down again to river level. The last three are ideal holes when you need three fours to win the medal or a match, the 18th, back across the road, doglegging gently to the left to a green situated below a charming clubhouse.

Much of what you see today is the result of the architectural genius of Harry Colt and Alister Mackenzie, the latter based just down the road at Alwoodley. It also served as a base during the formative years of Colin Montgomerie, very much an adopted Yorkshireman, who sharpened his competitive skills on a course that helped make him the best player in Europe.

Ilkley is a shining example of a delightful place to play with a course, testing and enjoyable, that is rightly popular with visitors and well respected in a county of high expectations.

Visitors: every day; after 3pm Sat and Sun, after 2pm Tues and not before 9.30 Thurs.
Green Fee: WD £18 per round, £25 per day; WE £30 per round, £37 per day.
Societies: by arrangement with Sec, not weekends.
Catering: Steward's day off Mon, catering available by prior arrangement.
Snooker.
Hotels: Tickton Grange; Burton Lodge.

O77 **Horsforth**

☎(0113) 2586819, Pro 2585200
Layton Rd, Horsforth, Leeds, W Yorks LS18 5EX
On A65 Leeds-Ilkley road, Layton Rd is on right after crossing A6120 Leeds ring road, and after passing Rawdon Crematorium on left.
Undulating pastureland course.
18 holes, 6205 yards, S.S.S.70
Founded 1905
Visitors: welcome, not weekends.
Green Fee: WD £20; WE £30.
Societies: weekdays and Sun with arrangement.
Catering: full service available.
Hotels: Post House (Bramhope).

O78 **Howley Hall**

☎(01924) 472432, Pro 473852
Scotchman Lane, Morley, Leeds LS27 0NX
From A650 Bradford-Wakefield road, take B6123, situated in between Morley and Batley.
Parkland course.
18 holes, 6346 yards, S.S.S.71
Founded 1900
Visitors: welcome except Sat am.
Green Fee: WD £21 per round, £25 per day; WE £30.
Societies: welcome weekdays and Sundays
Catering: facilities available every day except Mon.
Snooker.
Hotels: Post House(Ossett).

O79 **Huddersfield (Fixby)**

☎(01484) 426203 (Sec), Clubhouse 420110, Pro 426463, Fax 424623.
Fixby Hall, Lightridge Rd, Huddersfield HD2 2EP
Take M62 exit 24 to roundabout, 3rd exit A643 Brighouse, 1 mile to lights (Sun Inn), right, after 0.75 mile right on Lightridge Rd, course is 500 yards on right.

Heathland course.
18 holes, 6432 yards, S.S.S.71
Designed by Herbert Fowler, amendments by Hawtree.
Founded 1891
Visitors: societies and companies to book in advance; starting sheets; tee reservation recommended.
Green Fee: WD £30 per round, £40 per day; WE £40 per round, £50 per day.
Societies: Mon, Wed, Thurs, Fri only.
Catering: lunch, à la carte restaurant by prior arrangement.
Snooker.
Hotels: Pennine Hilton; Forte; Clifton; Brighouse.

O80 **Hull**

☎(01482) 658919, Pro 653074
The Hall, 27 Packman Lane, Kirkella, Hull HU10 7TJ
5 miles W of Hull, off A164.
Parkland course.
18 holes, 6242 yards, S.S.S.70
Designed by James Braid.
Founded 1921
Visitors: Mon to Fri only.
Green Fee: £22.
Societies: by prior arrangement.
Catering: prior arrangement if possible, lunches served Mon to Fri.
Snooker.
Hotels: Willerby Manor; Grange Park.

O81 **Ilkley**

☎(01943) 600214 (Sec), Steward: 607277, Pro 607463
Myddleton, Ilkley, W Yorks LS29 0BE
On A65 18 miles NW of Leeds.
Parkland course.
18 holes, 6262 yards, S.S.S.70
Founded 1890
Visitors: welcome by arrangement.
Green Fee: WD £35; WE £40.
Societies: weekdays only.
Catering: full facilities.
Hotels: Rombalds; Grove.

O82 **Keighley**

☎(01535) 604778 (Manager), Clubhouse 603179; Pro 665370
Howden Park, Utley, Keighley, W Yorks BD20 6DH
1 mile W of Keighley on old Kelghley/Skipton road.
Parkland course.
18 holes, 6141 yards, S.S.S.70
Founded 1904
Visitors: not before 9am or 12.30-1.30pm weekdays; Ladies' Day Tues; no visitors Sat, by arrangement Sun.
Green Fee: WD: £21.

Societies: welcome by arrangement with Manager.
Catering: bar and catering 12-2pm and 4.30-10.30pm every day except Mon.A la carte menu, carvery.
Hotels: Dalesway; Beeches.

O83 **Kirkbymoorside**

☎(01751) 431525
Manor Vale, Kirkbymoorside, N Yorks YO6 6EG
On A170 Thirsk to Scarborough road; Helmsley 7 miles, Pickering 7 miles.
Undulating moorland course.
18 holes, 6000 yards, S.S.S.69
Founded 1905
Visitors: welcome but not before 9.30am, advisable to telephone first.
Green Fee: WD £17; WE £25.
Societies: by arrangement.
Catering: meals and snacks daily.
Snooker.
Hotels: George and Dragon; Feversham Arms; Feathers; Kings Head; Worsley Arms (Hovingham).

O84 **Knaresborough**

☎(01423) 862690 (Sec), Club 863219, Pro 864865
Butterhills, Boroughbridge Rd, Knaresborough HG5 0QQ
1.5 miles N of Knaresborough off main Boroughbridge road.
Parkland course.
18 holes, 6481 yards, S.S.S.71
Designed by Hawtree & Son.
Founded 1920
Visitors: welcome, few restrictions.
Green Fee: WD £18.50 per round, £25 per day; WE £25 per round, £30 per day.
Societies: catered for.
Catering: every day except Mon.
Hotels: Dower House; Newton House.

O85 **Lakeside**

☎(0114) 2473000
Rother Valley GC, Mansfield Rd, Wales Bar, Sheffield S31 8PE
Take exit 30 or 31 from M1 and follow signs to the Rother Valley
Parkland course with water features
The Blue Monster,18 holes, 6602 yards, S.S.S. 73; 9 hole par 3 course.
Designed by M Rose
Founded May 1996
Visitors: welcome
Green Fee: WD £8; WE £14.
Societies: welcome.
Catering: bar, restaurant.
Driving range, putting green.
Hotels: Swallow (Rotherham).

O86 Leeds (Cobble Hall)

☎(0113) 2658775, Sec 2659203, Pro:2658786
Elmete Lane, Leeds LS8 2LJ
Off A58 Wetherby road, 4 miles from Leeds.Next to Roundhay Park.
Parkland course.
18 holes 6078 yards, S.S.S.69
Founded 1896
Visitors: weekdays with prior booking, weekends only with member.
Green Fee: WD £22 per round, £25 per day.
Societies: by advance booking; weekdays only.
Catering: full catering and bar facilities.
Snooker.
Hotels: Queens; Metropole; Bramhope Post House.

O87 Leeds Golf Centre

☎(0113) 2886186
Wike Ridge Lane, Shadwell, Leeds LS17 9JW
Follow signs on A61 towards Harrogate, take Harewood turn off and course is 60 yards away
Heathland course.
18 holes, 6620 yards, S.S.S. 72; 9 holes, 1350 yards, Par 3
Designed by Donald Steel.
Founded 1993
Visitors: welcome 7 days, no restrictions.
Green Fee: WD £12.50; WE £15.
Societies: welcome weekdays by arrangement.
Catering: full catering all day.
Driving range.
Hotels: Marriott (Leeds);Woodhall Hotel

O88 Lees Hall

☎(0114) 2554402 (Club), Sec 2552900, Steward: 2551526, Pro 2507868
Hemsworth Rd, Norton, Sheffield S8 8LL
3 miles S of Sheffield, A61 then A6054 towards Gleadless, 1st exit at roundabout, follow road to next roundabout passing water tower on left, take 1st exit, course 300 yards on right.
Parkland course.
18 holes, 6171 yards, S.S.S.69
Founded 1907
Visitors: always welcome.
Green Fee: WD £20 per round, £27 per day; WE £30.
Societies: weekdays subject to prior booking.

Catering: no catering on Tues.
Snooker.
Hotels: Grosvenor House; Hallam Towers; Sheffield Moat House.

O89 Lightcliffe

☎(01422) 202459
Knowle Top Rd, Lightcliffe, Halifax HX3 8RG
On A58 Leeds-Halifax road, on left entering Lightcliffe/Hipperholme village 4 miles E of Halifax.
Parkland course.
9 holes, 5388 yards, S.S.S.68
Founded 1907
Visitors: welcome apart from Wed and Sat.
Green Fee: WD £15; WE £20
Societies: catered for on weekdays except Wed.
Catering: lunch and evening meals except Mon.
Hotels: Clifton Trust House.

O90 Lofthouse Hill

(01924) 823703/Fax
Leeds Road, Lofthouse, Wakefield WF3 3LR
A61 out of Wakefield 4 miles; situated halfway between Leeds and Wakefield.
Links style course.
9 holes, 3167 yards, S.S.S. 70
(further 9 holes due to be completed 1996)
Founded 1994
Designed by B J Design
Visitors: welcome.
Green Fees: WD £10; WE £15.
Societies: welcome after extension completed; telephone for latest information.
Catering: 2 bars and restaurant facilities available.
Driving range; practice ground; putting green.

O91 Longley Park

☎(01484) 426932 (Club), Pro 422304
Maple St, off Somerset Rd, Huddersfield HD5 9AX
0.5 mile from town centre.
Parkland course.
9 holes, 5269 yards, S.S.S.66
Founded 1911
Visitors: welcome weekdays; restricted weekends.
Green Fee: WD £13; WE £16.
Societies: by arrangement except Thurs and Sat.
Catering: except Mon by arrangement.

O92 Low Laithes

☎(01924) 273275 (Club), Pro 274667
Parkmill Lane, Flushdyke, Ossett, W Yorks WF5 9AP
Leave M1 at exit 40, signposted on Dewsbury road, 1st turning from northbound exit M1.
Parkland course.
18 holes, 6463 yards, S.S.S.71
Designed by Mackenzie.
Founded 1925
Visitors: dress rules and reasonable golfers.
Green Fee: WD £18 per round, £22 per day; WE £30.
Societies: by prior arrangement, not weekends.
Catering: full facilities daily.
Hotels: Post House; Mews; Swallow.

O93 Malton & Norton

☎(01653) 692959 (Club), Sec 697912, Pro 693882
Welham Park, Malton, N Yorks YO17 9QE
From Malton and Norton level crossing, S on Welham road for 0.75 mile, turn right.
Parkland course.
27 holes: Welham & Park course, 6456 yards, S.S.S.71; Park & Derwent course, 6242 yards, S.S.S.70; Derwent & Welham course, 6286 yards, S.S.S.70
Designed by Hawtree & Son.
Founded 1910
Visitors: welcome, restricted on club competition days.
Green Fee: WD £22; WE £27.
Societies: apply to Sec.
Catering: full facilities, breakfast by arrangement.
Hotels: Talbot; The Mount; Burythorpe House; Oakdene CH.

O94 Marsden

☎(01484) 844253
Mount Rd, Hemplow, Marsden, Huddersfield HD7 6NN
Off A62 8 miles out of Huddersfield towards Manchester.
Moorland course.
9 holes, 5702 yards, S.S.S.68
Designed by Dr A. Mackenzie.
Founded 1920
Visitors: welcome weekdays.
Green Fee: £10.
Societies: catered for by arrangement weekdays.
Catering: lunches served daily except Tues, evening meals by prior arrangement.
Hotels: Durker Roods (Meltham).

O95 Masham

☎(01765) 689379, Sec 689491
Swinton Rd, Masham, Ripon, N Yorks
HG4 4HT
9 miles N of Ripon on A6108.
Parkland course.
9 holes, 6102 yards, S.S.S.69
Founded 1895
Visitors: welcome weekdays,
weekends and Bank Holidays with
member only.
Green Fee: £15
Societies: apply to Sec.
Catering: bar all day, catering
daytime only.
Hotels: Kings Head.

O96 Meltham

☎(01484) 850227, Pro/Bookings:
851521
Thick Hollins, Meltham, Huddersfield
HD7 3DQ
5 miles from Huddersfield on B6108,
in Meltham take B6107; from
Holmfirth take A635 and turn right at
Ford Inn.
Moorland/parkland course.
18 holes, 6305 yards, S.S.S.70
Founded 1908
Visitors: any day except Wed, Sat.
Green Fee: WD £20; WE £25.
Societies: weekdays and Sun.
Catering: available every day.
Hotels: Durker Roods; Old Bridge.

O97 Mid Yorkshire

☎(01977) 704522, Fax 600823, Pro
600844
Havercroft Lane, Darrington, Nr
Pontefract, Yorks WF8 3BP
400 yards on A1 S from M62/A1
intersection.
Parkland course.
18 holes, 6466 yards, S.S.S.71
Designed by Steve Marnoch.
Founded May 1993
Visitors: welcome weekdays;
restrictions before noon at weekends.
Green Fee: Mon-Tues & Thurs £18;
Wed & Fri £20; WE £30.
Societies: unrestricted weekdays by
prior booking; weekends 1-4.30pm by
arrangement.
Catering: public bar, lounge bar,
function suite for up to 200.
Conference facilities.
Driving range, golf clinic.
Hotels: Darrington (300 yards).

O98 Middleton Park

☎(0113) 2700449, Pro 2709506
Ring Rd, Beeston, Leeds 10, LS10
3TN

3 miles S of city centre.
Public parkland course.
18 holes, 5263 yards, S.S.S.66
Designed by Leeds City Council.
Founded 1932
Visitors: welcome weekdays.
Green Fee: £7.50.
Societies: can be booked.

O99 Moor Allerton

☎(0113) 2661154 (Admin), Pro
2665209, Fax 2371124
Coal Rd, Wike, Leeds LS17 9NH
Take A61 Harrogate Rd, about 1 mile
past intersection with A6120 ring road
turn right onto Wigton Lane, at T-
junction take 1st left, then 1st right
then signposted.
Championship undulating parkland
course.
1-18 The Lakes, 6470 yards,
S.S.S.72; 10-27 Blackmoor, 6673
yards, S.S.S.73; 1-9/19-27 High
Course, 6841 yards, S.S.S.74
Designed by Robert Trent Jones.
Founded 1923
Visitors: welcome weekdays and Sat
subject to numbers and prior booking.
Green Fee: WD £26; WE £40
Societies: any weekday, small
groups accepted Sat subject to prior
booking.
Catering: lunches every day; dinner
Tues, Wed, Thurs, unlimited
numbers; Mon, Fri min 40 required;
banqueting for up to 250.

O100 Moortown

☎(0113) 2686521 (Sec), Club
2681682, Pro 2683636, Fax 2686521
Harrogate Rd, Leeds LS17 7DB
Course is located on A61 approx 5
miles N of Leeds.
Moorland course.
18 holes, 6782 yards, S.S.S.73
Designed by Dr A. Mackenzie.
Founded 1909
Visitors: welcome weekdays, apply
to Sec/Pro weekends.
Green Fee: WD £40 per round, £45
per day; WE £45 per round, £50 per
day.
Societies: weekdays by arrangement
with Sec.
Catering: lunches served except
Mon; other meals by arrangement.
Snooker.
Hotels: Harewood Arms; Post House.

O101 Normanton

☎(01924) 892943
Snydale Rd, Normanton, Wakefield,
W Yorks WF6 1PA

Off M62 at junction 31, 0.5 mile from
Normanton centre.
Flat meadowland course.
9 holes, 5400 yards, S.S.S.66
Founded 1903
Visitors: weekdays and Sat,
members only Sun.
Green Fee: apply for details.
Societies: weekdays only.
Catering: full facilities.

O102 Northcliffe

☎(01274) 584085 (Club), Sec
596731, Pro 587193
High Bank Lane, Shipley, W Yorks
BD18 4LJ
Take A650 Bradford-Keighley road to
Saltaire roundabout, turn up
Moorhead Lane, leading to High Bank
Lane, club 0.5 mile on left.
Parkland course.
18 holes, 6104 yards, S.S.S.69
Designed by James Braid and Harry
Vardon.
Founded 1920
Visitors: welcome except Sat and
Sun; (Tues Ladies Day).
Green Fee: WD £20.
Societies: welcome Wed-Fri.
Catering: bar, snacks except Mon;
dinner by arrangement with Steward.
Hotels: Bankfield.

O103 Oakdale

☎(01423) 567162, Pro 560510
Oakdale, Harrogate HG1 2LN
From Ripon Rd, Harrogate, turn into
Kent Rd, follow signs.
Undulating parkland course with
panoramic views.
18 holes, 6456 yards, S.S.S.71
Designed by Dr A. Mackenzie.
Founded 1914
Visitors: welcome.
Green Fee: WD £25 per round, £30
per day; WE £30.
Societies: weekdays.
Catering: full dining facilities except
Mon lunchtime, dinner by
arrangement.
Hotels: Crown; Fern; Majestic;
Studley; Old Swan; Balmoral.

O104 Otley

☎(01943) 465329 (Sec), Club
461015, Pro/Fax 463403
West Busk Lane, Otley, W Yorks
LS21 3NG
On Otley-Bradford road 1.5 miles
from Otley.
Parkland course.
18 holes, 6225 yards, S.S.S.70
Founded 1906

Visitors: welcome.
Green Fee: WD £24; WE £30
Societies: by arrangement.
Catering: full facilities except Mon.
Hotels: Post House; Devonshire Arms.

O105 **Oulton Park**

☎(0113) 2823152
Rothwell, Leeds LS26 8EX
M62 junction 30, A642 to Rothwell, over 1st roundabout (1 mile), immediately left at 2nd roundabout.
Municipal parkland course.
18 holes, 6479 yards, S.S.S.71; 9 holes, 3287 yards, S.S.S.35
Designed by Peter Alliss & Dave Thomas.
Founded 1990
Visitors: no restrictions, pay-and-play course, must book at weekends.
Green Fee: 18 hole course, £10; 9 hole course £5.
Societies: any time during week, after 1pm weekends.
Catering: bar and bar meals all day; restaurant 9am-6pm.
Driving range, pool table.
Hotels: Oulton Hall.

O106 **Outlane**

☎(01422) 374762
Slack Lane, Outlane, Huddersfield, W Yorks HD3 3YL,
Off A640 Rochdale road, 4 miles out of Huddersfield, through village of Outlane, turn left under motorway.
Semi-moorland course.
18 holes, 6010 yards, S.S.S.70
Founded 1906
Visitors: welcome.
Green Fee: WD £18; WE £27
Societies: by arrangement with Mrs C. Hirst (on above number).
Catering: meals daily except Mon.
Hotels: Old Golf House; Pennine Hilton .

O107 **Owston Park**

☎(01302) 330821
Owston Hall, Owston, Nr Carcroft, Doncaster, S Yorks DN6 9JF
Off A19, 10 mins N of Doncaster.
Parkland course.
9 holes (18 tees) 6148 yards, S.S.S.71
Designed by Michael Parker.
Founded 1988
Visitors: welcome, pay-as-you-play.
Green Fee: WD £3.75 (9 holes), £6.50 (18 holes); WE £7.50 (18 holes).
Societies: welcome.

O108 **Painthorpe House Golf & Country Club**

☎(01924) 255083, Fax 252022
Painthorpe Lane, Crigglestone, Wakefield, W Yorks WF4 3HE
2 mins from M1 junction 39.
Parkland course.
9 holes, 4250 yards, S.S.S.62
Founded 1961
Visitors: welcome Mon-Fri only.
Green Fee: £5
Societies: by arrangement.
Catering: 4 bars, dining room, 2 ball rooms.
Exhibitions, conferences, dinner dances (max 450), bowls.
Hotels: Cedar Court (Durkar).

O109 **Pannal**

☎(01423) 872628
(Sec/reservations), Fax 870043
Follifoot Rd, Pannal, Harrogate HG3 1ES
Just off A61 Leeds-Harrogate road at Pannal.
Parkland/moorland championship course.
18 holes, 6618 yards, S.S.S.72
Designed by Sandy Herd.
Founded 1906
Visitors: welcome weekdays, limited time at weekends.
Green Fee: WD £30 per round, £38 per day; WE £38 per round.
Societies: weekdays by arrangement with Sec.
Catering: by arrangement.

O110 **Phoenix**

☎(01709) 382624
Pavilion Lane, Brinsworth, Rotherham, S Yorks S60 5PB
1 mile along Bawtry road turning from Tinsley roundabout on M1.
Undulating meadowland course.
18 holes, 6169 yards, S.S.S. 71
Founded 1932
Visitors: welcome if member of recognised golf club.
Green Fee: WD £21; WE £28.
Societies: welcome by prior arrangement.
Catering: full on request.
Hotels: Fairways; Brinsworth; Moat House; Brecon; Swallow.

O111 **Phoenix Park**

☎(0274) 667573, Fax 610335.
Phoenix Park, Dick Lane, Thornbury, Bradford, W Yorks
From Bradford take Leeds road (A647) for 2.5 miles to Thornbury roundabout, course at roundabout.

Undulating parkland course.
9 holes, 4982 yards, S.S.S.64
Visitors: welcome weekdays only.
Green Fee: on application.
Societies: by arrangement with Sec.
Catering: by arrangement with Steward prior to visit.

O112 **Pike Hills**

☎(01904) 706566, Pro 708756
Tadcaster Rd, Askham Bryan, York YO2 3UW
Turn left towards York off A64 Leeds-Scarborough road immediately after by-pass flyover.
Parkland course.
18 holes, 6146 yards, S.S.S.69
Founded 1920
Visitors: weekdays before 4.30pm; weekends and Bank Holidays only with member.
Green Fee: WD £15 per round, £20 per day.
Societies: parties of 12+ if previously booked, correct dress essential, each member must have recognised h/cap.
Catering: full facilities.

O113 **Pontefract & District**

☎(01977) 792241, Club 798886, Pro 706806
Park Lane, Pontefract, W Yorks WF8 4QS
M62 exit 32, situated on B6134.
Parkland course.
18 holes, 6227 yards, S.S.S.70
Founded 1900
Visitors: welcome weekdays.
Green Fee: WD £25.
Societies: weekdays except Wed.
Catering: daily full facilities.
Hotels: Red Lion; Wentbridge House; Park Side Inne.

O114 **Pontefract Park**

☎(01977) 702799
Park Road, Pontefract, W Yorkshire
0.5 mile from M62 towards Pontefract beside race course.
Public parkland course.
9 holes, 2034 yards, S.S.S. 62
Visitors: welcome.
Green Fee: £2.50

O115 **Queensbury**

☎(0274) 882155, Pro 816864
Brighouse Rd, Queensbury, Bradford, W Yorks BD13 1QF
Take M62 junc 26, then A58 towards Halifax for 3.5m. Take Keighley turning for 3m. Also 4 miles from Bradford on A647.

Undulating parkland course.
9 holes, 5024 yards, S.S.S.65
Founded 1923
Visitors: bona fide golfers welcome.
Green Fee: WD £10; WE £20..
Societies: by arrangement.
Catering: Bar, à la carte menu;
functions and parties catered for
Hotels: Novotel.

O116 **Rawdon**

☎(0113) 2506040, Pro 2592017
Buckstone Drive, Rawdon, Leeds
LS19 6BD
On A65 6 miles from Leeds.
Undulating parkland course.
9 holes, 5982 yards, S.S.S.69
Founded 1896
Visitors: welcome weekdays.
Green Fee: £16
Societies: welcome weekdays by
arrangement.
Catering: lunch except Mon.
3 all-weather tennis courts, 4 grass.
Hotels: Peas Hill; Robin Hood.

O117 **Renishaw Park**

☎(01246) 432044, Pro 435484
Station Rd, Renishaw, Sheffield S31
9UZ
M1 junction 30, take the sign for
Eckington, club 1.5 miles on right.
Parkland course.
18 holes, 6253 yards, S.S.S.70
Designed by R. Sitwell.
Founded 1911
Visitors: welcome weekdays; ring
club for dress rule.
Green Fee: £20 per round, £28 per
day
Societies: by arrangement.
Catering: full bar and restaurant.
Hotels: Sitwell Arms; Mosborough
Hall.

O118 **Richmond**

☎(01748) 822457 (Pro), Sec
825319, Clubhouse 825319
Bend Hagg, Richmond, N Yorks
DL10 5EX
A6108 from Scotch Corner, turn right
at traffic lights after 4 miles.
Parkland course.
18 holes, 5769 yards, S.S.S.68
Designed by Frank Pennink.
Founded 1892
Visitors: welcome; not before
11.30am on Sun.
Green Fee: WD £18; WE £25.
Societies: catered for.
Catering: daily.
Hotels: Frenchgate; holiday cottage
on course (for up to 8 people).

O119 **Riddlesden**

☎(01535) 602148
Howden Rough, Riddlesden,
Keighley, W Yorks
A650 Keighley-Bradford road, left into
Bar Lane, left into Scott Lane 2 miles.
Moorland course.
18 holes, 4185 yards, S.S.S.61
Founded 1927
Visitors: unlimited weekdays; after
2pm Sat and Sun.
Green Fee: on application
Catering: 12am-2pm and 6-10pm
weekdays, 12am-5.30pm weekends.
Hotels: Dalesway.

O120 **Ripon City**

☎(01765) 603640, Pro 600411
Palace Rd, Ripon, N Yorks HG4 3HH
1 mile NW on A6108 towards
Masham/Leyburn.
Undulating parkland course.
18 holes, 6120 yards, S.S.S.69
Designed by ADAS,
Founded 1905
Visitors: Sat very busy, Tues and
Sun starting sheet in operation.
Green Fee: WD £18; WE £25.
Societies: package deals available
by prior arrangement.
Catering: full facilities
Hotels: Ripon Spa; Nags Head
(Pickhill); Unicorn.

O121 **Romanby**

☎(01609) 777824, Office: 778855,
Pro 779988, Fax 779084
Yafforth Road, Northallerton, N Yorks
DL7 0PE
Off A1 take A684 Northallerton-
Bedale road and at cross roads in
Ainderby Steeple turn left towards
Yafforth. Course in on right.
Parkland course
18 holes, 6657 yards, S.S.S. 72
Designed by W Adamson
Founded July 1993
Visitors: welcome.
Green Fee: WD £11.50; WE £15.
Societies: welcome every day;
packages start from £27.
Catering: full facilities. Meals served
throughout the day.

O122 **Rotherham**

☎(01709) 850812 (Sec), Club
850466, Course Manager: 854612,
Fax 855288, Pro 850480
Thrybergh Park, Doncaster Road,
Thrybergh, Rotherham S65 4NU
On A630 Doncaster-Rotherham road,
from A1M; 3 miles from M18 at
Bramley; 7 miles from M1 at junc 35.

Parkland course.
18 holes, 6324 yards, S.S.S.70
Founded 1903
Visitors: by arrangement with Pro.
Green Fee: WD £26.50; WE £31.50.
Societies: parties of 16+ players to
book with Sec; not Wed, weekends or
Bank Holidays; reductions for socs of
40+ players.
Catering: full facilities every day.
Snooker.
Hotels: Swallow; Moat House; Limes;
Brecon.

O123 **Roundhay**

☎(0113) 2662695, Pro 2661686
Park Lane, Leeds LS8 2EJ
Take A58 to Oakwood Clock, then
Princes Avenue, Street Lane, turn
right at Park Lane, course is located
4 miles from city centre.
Municipal parkland course.
9 holes, 5096 yards, S.S.S.65
Founded 1921
Visitors: unrestricted.
Green Fee: WD £7.15; WE £7.75.
Societies: by arrangement with Pro.
Catering: restaurant Tues-Sun
evenings; snacks available every day.
Hotels: Beech Wood.

O124 **Roundwood**

☎(01709) 523471
Off Green Lane, Rawmarsh,
Rotherham, S Yorks S62 6LA
2.5 miles N of Rotherham on A633.
Parkland course.
9 holes, 5600 yards, S.S.S.67
Founded 1977
Visitors: welcome, not Sat or Sun
am.
Green Fee: on application.
Societies: welcome.
Catering: bar and snacks Wed-Sat.
Practice putting green.

O125 **Rudding Park**

☎(01423) 872100
Follifoot, Harrogate, N Yorks HG3
1DJ
Off A658 Harrogate southern by-
pass, signposted.
Parkland course.
18 holes, 6871 yards, S.S.S.72
Designed by Hawtree.
Visitors: welcome at all times,
advisable to phone.
Green Fee: WD £16; WE £19.
Societies: welcome by prior
arrangement.
Catering: full facilities.
Driving range.
Hotels: Majestic.

O126 **Ryburn**

☎(01422) 831355
The Shaw, Norland, Sowerby Bridge,
W Yorkshire HX6 3QP
3 miles S of Halifax.
Moorland course.
9 holes, 4907 yards, S.S.S.65
Founded 1910
Visitors: welcome, no restrictions.
Green Fee: WD £14; WE £20.
Societies: by application only.
Catering: available.
Hotels: The Hobbit.

O127 **Sand Moor**

☎(0113) 2685180, Pro 2683925
Alwoodley Lane, Leeds LS17 7DJ
A61 N from city centre 6 miles, left
into Alwoodley La, 0.5 mile on right.
Undulating parkland/moorland course.
18 holes, 6429 yards, S.S.S.71
Designed by A Mackenzie. Founded
1926
Visitors: welcome weekdays;
members reserved times 12am-
1.30pm; Tues 9.30-10.30am; Thurs
8.30-12am.
Green Fee: WD £28.
Societies: weekdays by prior
arrangement.
Catering: full facilities
Hotels: Harewood Arms; Parkway;
Forte Crest.

O128 **Sandhill**

☎(01226) 753444
c/o Colliery Farm, Little Houghton,
Barnsley, S Yorks S72 0HW
Off A635 1 mile E of Darfield, 6 miles
E of Barnsley.
Meadowland course.
18 holes, 6214 yards, S.S.S.70
Designed by John Royston.
Founded Oct 1991
Visitors: welcome, unlimited; ring to
book tee times.
Green Fee: WD £8; WE £10.
Societies: by arrangement.
Catering: full facilities
Driving range.

O129 **Scarborough North Cliff**

☎(01723) 360786, Pro 365920
North Cliff Ave, Burniston Rd,
Scarborough YO12 6PP
2 miles N of town centre on coast
road (Burniston Rd), turn right along
North Cliff Ave.
Seaside/parkland course.
18 holes, 6425 yards, S.S.S.71
Designed by James Braid.
Founded 1928

Visitors: no restrictions except before
10am Sun; recognised golfers only.
Green Fee: on application.
Societies: mainly weekdays by prior
arrangement with Sec, parties of 8 to
36. WD £20; WE £23 for minimum 8
when also buying menus at £9-£11.
Catering: soup and sandwiches
available to 5.30pm; bar snacks
lunchtime and 7-10pm; no catering
Sun and Mon evening.
Hotels: Park Manor, Headlands.

O130 **Scarborough South Cliff**

☎(01723) 374737, Club 360522, Pro
365150
Deepdale Ave, Scarborough YO11
2UE
1 mile S of Scarborough on main
Filey road.
Parkland/seaside course.
18 holes, 6039 yards, S.S.S.69
Designed by Dr A. Mackenzie.
Founded 1903
Visitors: welcome.
Green Fee: WD £20; WE £25.
Societies: weekdays and weekends.
Catering: full catering facilities.
Hotels: Crown; St Nicholas;
Southlands; Mount House.

O131 **Scarcroft**

☎(0113) 2892311(Club), Pro
2892780
Syke Lane, Leeds LS14 3BQ
On A58 NE of Leeds in Scarcroft
village, immediately after the pub on
the left is Syke Lane.
Parkland course.
18 holes, 6426 yards, S.S.S.71
Designed by Major C. Mackenzie.
Founded 1937
Visitors: welcome weekdays,
weekends by prior arrangement only.
Green Fee: WD £25; WE £35.
Societies: welcome Tues-Fri by
arrangement, all-in rates for parties of
more than 20
Catering: meals daily except Mon.
Hotels: Harewood Arms; Swan &
Talbot (Wetherby), Windmill, Jarvis
Inn(Wetherby).

O132 **Scathingwell**

☎(01937) 557878
Scathingwell Centre, Scathingwell,
Tadcaster, Yorks LS24 9PF
On A162 3 miles south of Tadcaster
Parkland course
18 holes, 6700 yards, S.S.S. 72
Designed by I Webster
Founded April 1995

Visitors: welcome
Green Fee: WD £15; WE £17
Societies: welcome weekdays;
packages available
Catering: full club house facilities.
Hotels: Londesborough; Selby Fork
Motel.

O133 **Selby**

☎(01757) 228622, Pro 228785
Mill Lane, Brayton, Selby, N Yorks
YO8 9LD
3 miles SW of Selby, 1 mile E of A19
at Brayton village; from M62 junction
34, take A19 (Selby-Doncaster) for 5
miles N towards Selby, turn 1st left in
Brayton into Mill Lane, club is located
1 mile on right.
Links style course.
18 holes, 6246 yards, S.S.S.70
Designed by J.H. Taylor & Hawtree
Ltd.
Founded 1907
Visitors: welcome weekdays with
h/cap certs; members and guests
only at weekends.
Green Fee: WD £22 per round, £25
per day.
Societies: Wed, Thurs and Fri.
Catering: every day.
Snooker, large practice ground.
Hotels: Londesbro; Selby Fork Motel;
The Owl (Hambleton).

O134 **Serlby Park**

☎(01777) 818268 (Club), Hon Sec
(01302) 536336
Serlby, Doncaster, S Yorkshire DN10
6BA
3 miles S of Bawtry.
Parkland course
9 holes, 5376 yards, S.S.S.66
Designed by Viscount Galway.
Founded 1895
Visitors: must be with member.
Green Fee: WD£8; WE £10.
Societies: on application to sec.
Catering: available.
Hotels: Crown (Bawtry); Mount
Pleasant, Olde Bell (Barnby Moor).

O135 **Settle**

☎(01729) 825288
Buckhaw Brow, Settle, N Yorks BD24
Main A65 Settle-Kendal road,
opposite Giggleswick Quarry.
Parkland/moorland course.
9 holes, 4600 yards, S.S.S.62
Designed by Tom Vardon.
Founded 1891
Visitors: welcome, restricted Sun.
Green Fee: on application
Hotels: Falcon Manor.

O136 The Shay Grange Golf Centre

☎(01274) 483955/Fax
Long Lane, Off Bingley Road,
Bradford, W Yorks BD9 6RX
M62 Bradford turn off, follow signs for
Haworth B6144, continue to Bingley
Road, B6269; 500 yds on the right.
Municipal parkland course.
9 holes, 2000 yards, Par 29
Designed by Tim Colclough.
Founded 1996
Visitors: welcome; pay-and-play.
Green Fees: on application.
Societies: welcome by arrangement.
Hotels: Bankfield Hotel (Jarvis);
Norfolk Gardens Hotel (Bradford);
Oakwood Hall Hotel (Bingley).

O137 Shipley

☎(01274) 563212 (Clubhouse), Pro
563674, Sec 568652
Beckfoot Lane, Cottingley Bridge,
Bingley, W Yorks BD16 1LX
Situated on A650 Bradford-Keighley
road at Cottingley Bridge, Bingley.
Parkland course.
18 holes, 6218 yards, S.S.S.70
Designed by Colt, Alison and
Mackenzie assisted by James Braid.
Founded 1896
Visitors: welcome except Tues
before 2pm, Sat before 4pm.
Green Fee: WD £27; WE £36.
Societies: by arrangement with Hon
Sec.
Catering: except Mon, bar snacks
and evening meals by arrangement
with Steward.
Snooker.
Hotels: Bankfield; Oakwood Hall; Hall
Bank.

O138 Silkstone

☎(01226) 790328, Pro 790128
Field Head, Silkstone, Barnsley, S
Yorks S75 4OD
1 mile from M1 on A628 towards
Manchester.
Undulating meadowland course.
18 holes, 6069 yards, S.S.S.70
Founded 1893
Visitors: welcome weekdays.
Green Fee: £25
Societies: catered for weekdays.
Catering: full facilities except Mon.
Hotels: Ardsley Moat House;
Brooklands Motel.

O139 Silsden

☎(01535) 652998
High Brunthwaite, Silsden, Keighley
BD20 0NH

A629, 4 miles from Keighley, on to
A6034 to Silsden town centre, turn E
at canal.
Moorland/meadowland course.
14 holes, 4870 yards, S.S.S.64
Founded 1913
Visitors: welcome; restrictions Sat
pm and Sun am.
Green Fee: apply for details.
Hotels: Steeton Hall.

O140 Sitwell Park

☎(01709) 541046 (Sec/office), Pro
540961, Stewardess: 700799, Fax
703637
Shrogswood Rd, Rotherham, S Yorks
S60 4BY
From M1 exit 31, A630 and A631 to
Bawtry; M18 exit 1, A631 Sheffield rd;
2 miles SE of Rotherham.
Undulating parkland course.
18 holes, 6209 yards, S.S.S.70
Designed by Dr A. Mackenzie.
Founded 1913
Visitors: welcome.
Green Fee: WD £23; WE £27.
Societies: welcome weekdays; book
through Sec.
Catering: book through Stewardess.
Snooker.
Hotels: Brecon; Brentwood; Consort;
Limes; Swallow.

O141 Skipton

☎(01756) 795657, Pro 793257
North-West By-Pass, Skipton, N
Yorks BD23 1LL
Off NW by-pass (A59 and A65) 1 mile
from town centre.
Undulating course with panoramic
views.
18 holes, 6049 yards, S.S.S.69
Founded 1905
Visitors: welcome; phone Pro
beforehand.
Green Fee: WD £18; WE £22.
Societies: welcome, special terms for
parties of 12 or more; contact sec.
Catering: full facilities every day.
Hotels: Randell's; Herriot's;
Devonshire Arms (Bolton Abbey).

O142 South Bradford

☎(01274) 679195 (Club), Pro
673346
Pearson Rd, Odsal, Bradford BD6
1BH
From Odsal roundabout take Stadium
Rd (1st road left down Cleckheaton
Rd) then Pearson Rd to club.
Undulating meadowland course.
9 holes, 6068 yards, S.S.S.69
Founded 1906

Visitors: welcome weekdays.
Green Fee: £14 (£8 with member)
Societies: Tues-Fri by prior
arrangement
Catering: lunches and evening meals
served except Mon.
Hotels: Guide Post.

O143 South Leeds

☎(0113) 2700479, Pro 2702598
Gypsy Lane, off Middleton Ring Rd,
Leeds LS11 5TU
From M62 junction 28 take Leeds-
Dewsbury road to lights at Tommy
Wass Hotel, turn right, follow ring
road for 100 yards then left into
Gypsy Lane; approx 2 miles.
Parkland course.
18 holes, 5769 yards, S.S.S.68
Founded 1914
Visitors: welcome any time (reduced
green fees if playing with member).
Green Fee: WD £18; WE £26.
Societies: apply to Sec.
Catering: every day except Mon.
Snooker.

O144 Spaldington

☎(01757) 288262)
Spaldington Lane, Howden, N
Humberside DN12 7NP
Take B1288 out of Howden towards
Bubwith then head for Spaldington.
Club is on left just past Boothferry GC
Parkland course
Eagles 9 hole, 1741 yards, par 29
Designed by PMS Golf
Founded Aug 1995
Visitors: welcome
Green Fee: £3.50.
Societies: welcome
Driving range

O145 Springhead Park

☎(01482) 656309
Willerby Rd, Hull, Yorks HU5 5JE
4 miles W of Hull centre.
Municipal parkland course.
18 holes, 6402 yards, S.S.S.71
Founded 1930
Visitors: welcome, no restrictions,
queue to play.
Green Fee: WD £7; WE £8.
Societies: on application
Catering: Full restaurant facilities.
Hotels: Willerby Manor; Grange Park.

O146 Springmill

☎(01924) 272515
Queens Drive, Osset, W Yorks
M1 junction 40, 1 mile out of Osset
towards Wakefield.

Public parkland course.
9 holes Par 3, 1165 yards.
Visitors: welcome.
Green Fee: apply for details.
Societies: welcome.

O147 Stocksbridge & District
☎(0114) 2882003
30 Royd Lane, Townend, Deepcar,
Sheffield S30 5RZ
A616 into Deepcar, 1st left into Carr
Rd, course 1 mile on left.
Moorland course.
18 holes, 5200 yards, S.S.S.65
Designed by Peter Alliss, Dave
Thomas (extension).
Founded 1924
Visitors: welcome any time.
Green Fee: WD £15; WE £24.
Societies: weekdays on request, not
weekends.
Catering: on request except Mon.
Hotels: Grosvenor; Hallam Towers.

O148 Sutton Park
☎(01482) 374242, Ticket office:
594781
Saltshouse Rd, Holderness Rd, Hull,
N Humberside HU8 9HF
4 miles E of city centre on A165
(B1237).
Municipal parkland course.
18 holes, 6251 yards, S.S.S.70
Founded 1935
Visitors: unlimited.
Green Fee: WD £5.60; WE £7.30.
Societies: on application to ticket
office.
Catering: bar snacks lunchtime, full
meals by arrangement.
Snooker.
Hotels: Royal Station.

O149 Swallow Hall
☎(01904) 448889
Swallow Hall, Crockey Hill, York YO1
4SG
A64 York ring road, take A19 S for
Selby, after 1.5 miles left in Crockey
Hill signposted Wheldrake; course 2
miles on left.
Public parkland course.
18 holes, 3092 yards, Par 3
Founded May 1991
Visitors: welcome, dawn to dusk.
Green Fee: WD £7 (18 holes); WE
£8.
Societies: welcome any time by
arrangement.
Catering: coffee machine and cold
drinks.
Driving range.

O150 Swingtime (Leeds)
☎(0113) 2633030, Fax 2633044
Redcote Lane, Leeds LS4 2AW
1.5 miles W of Leeds town centre of
Kirkstall Road.
Parkland course.
9 holes, 2734 yards
Founded 1996
Visitors: welcome.
Green Fees: on application.
Catering: full facilities.
Driving Range.

O151 Tankersley Park
☎(0114) 2468247, Pro 2455583
High Green, Sheffield S30 4LG
Close M1 between junctions 35a
(northbound only) or 36, on A616.
Parkland course.
18 holes, 6212 yards, S.S.S.70
Designed by Hawtree
Founded 1907
Visitors: weekdays unlimited, Sat
and Sun after 3pm; must be bona fide
golfers with club h/cap.
Green Fee: WD £19.50 per round,
£24.50 per day.
Societies: Mon-Fri only.
Catering: bar and restaurant.
Snooker.

O152 Temple Newsam
☎(0113) 2645624, Pro 2647362
Temple Newsam Rd, Leeds LS15
On A64 York road, 5 miles from
Leeds centre, follow signs for Temple
Newsam House.
Public undulating parkland course.
Lord Erwin 18 holes, 6153 yards,
S.S.S.69; Lady Dorothy 18 holes,
6094 yards, S.S.S.70
Founded 1923
Visitors: welcome.
Green Fee: on application
Societies: by arrangement.
Catering: bar 7 days, carvery Sat,
Sun.
Hotels: Windmill; Mercury.

O153 Thirsk & Northallerton
☎(01845) 522170 (Club), Sec
525115, Pro 526216
Thornton-le-Street, Thirsk, N Yorks
YO7 4AB
2 miles N of Thirsk on A168, the
Northallerton spur 0.5 mile from the
dual carriageway A19.
Meadowland course.
9 holes, 6342 yards, S.S.S.70
Founded 1914
Visitors: welcome (only members
guests on Sundays)

Green Fee: WD £10 per round, £15
per day; WE £20.
Societies: weekdays, not Tues and
Wed pm; members of recognised golf
club; book in writing well in advance.
Catering: full facilites except Tues.
Hotels: Golden Fleece; Three Tuns.

O154 Thorne
☎(01405) 812084, Clubhouse
815173
Kirton Lane, Thorne, Doncaster, S
Yorks DN8 5RJ
M18 junction 6 or M180 junction 1.
Public parkland course.
18 holes, 5366 yards, S.S.S.65
Designed by Richard Highfield.
Founded 1980
Visitors: welcome, no restrictions.
Green Fee: WD £8; WE £9.
Societies: book in advance.
Catering: full facilities.

O155 Tinsley Park
☎(0114) 2560237, 2610004
High Hazel Park, Darnall, Sheffield
S9 4PE
Take A57 off M1 at junction 33, at
traffic lights turn right on Greenland
Rd and right by bus depot.
Parkland course.
18 holes, 6103 yards, S.S.S.69
Founded 1921
Visitors: unrestricted.
Green Fee: WD £7.75; WE £8.10
Societies: by arrangement with
Sheffield CC Recreation Dept.
Catering: full facilities
Hotels: Royal Victoria.

O156 Todmorden
☎(01706) 812986
Rive Rocks, Cross Stone Rd,
Todmorden OL14 7RD
1.5 miles along Halifax road, turn left.
Moorland course.
9 holes, 5878 yards, S.S.S.68
Founded 1895
Visitors: Tues-Fri no restrictions
(Thurs Ladies' Day); weekends by
prior arrangement.
Green Fee: WD £15; WE £20.
Societies: Tues-Fri.
Catering: snacks daily except Mon.
Hotels: Scaite Cliffe Hall;
Brandschatter Berghoff.

O157 Wakefield
☎(01924) 255104 (Club), Pro
255380, Sec 258778
Woodthorpe Lane, Sandal, Wakefield
WF2 6JH

3 miles S of Wakefield on A61, from
M1 exit 39.
Parkland course.
18 holes, 6613 yards, S.S.S.72
Designed by Alex (Sandy) Herd.
Founded 1891
Visitors: by arrangement.
Green Fee: WD £22; WE £30.
Societies: apply to Sec.
Catering: except Mon.
Snooker.
Hotels: Cedar Court; Swallow.

O158 **Waterton Park**
☎(01924) 259525
The Balk, Walton, Wakefield WF2
6QL
Close to junction 29 off the M1
Parkland course
18 holes, 6825 yards, S.S.S. 72
Designed by S Gidman
Founded Sept 1995
Visitors: as members' guests only.

O159 **Wath**
☎(01709) 878677 (Pro), Club
872149
Abdy, Blackamoor, Rotherham, S
Yorks S62 7SJ
Off A633 in Wath, 7 miles N of
Rotherham.
Meadowland course.
18 holes, 5886 yards, S.S.S.68
Founded 1904
Visitors: welcome weekdays, with
member at weekends.
Green Fee: £20
Societies: welcome by arrangement;
special package.
Catering: full facilities.
Hotels: Moat House (Rotherham).

O160 **West Bowling**
☎(01274) 724449 (Clubhouse), Sec
393207, Pro 728036
Newall Hall, Rooley Lane, Bradford,
W Yorks BD5 8LB
Corner of M606 and Bradford ring
road East.
Parkland course.
18 holes, 5763 yards, S.S.S.68
Founded 1898
Visitors: welcome weekdays,
restricted weekends.
Green Fee: WD £22 (£26 if not
member of a golf club); WE £32.
Societies: not weekends; apply to
manager.
Catering: full facilities except Mon
Oct-Mar.
Snooker.
Hotels: Novotel; Norfolk Gardens;
Guide Post; Tong Village; Victoria.

O161 **West Bradford**
☎(01274) 542767, Pro 542102
Chellow Grange, Haworth Rd,
Bradford, W Yorks BD9 6NP
B6144 3 miles from Bradford on
Haworth Rd.
Meadowland course.
18 holes, 5783 yards, S.S.S.68
Founded 1900
Visitors: welcome weekdays.
Green Fee: £16.50.
Societies: weekdays.
Catering: meals served except Mon.
Hotels: Norfolk Gardens.

O162 **West End (Halifax)**
☎(01422) 353608 (Clubhouse), Pro
363293, Sec/Fax 341878, Steward:
369844
Paddock Lane, Highroad Well,
Halifax, W Yorks HX2 0NT
Leave Halifax on Burnley/Rochdale
road, turn right at 1st lights by
People's Park (Parkinson Lane), over
lights to T-junction, turn right to next
T-junction and turn left, take 2nd on
right (Court Lane) to junction, turn left
into Paddock Lane.
Parkland course.
18 holes, 5951 yards, S.S.S.69
Designed by members.
Founded 1906
Visitors: welcome.
Green Fee: WD £17 per round, £22
per day; WE £20 per round, £27 per
day.
Societies: to be booked through Sec;
not Sat.
Catering: full facilities except Mon.
Snooker.
Hotels: Tower House; Holdsworth
House; Crown Imperial.

O163 **Wetherby**
☎(01937) 583375 (Pro), Sec/
Manager: 580089, Club 582527, Fax
581915.
Linton Lane, Wetherby, LS22 4JF
Off A1 at Wetherby, then travel SW;
course in village of Linton, 1 mile from
Wetherby centre.
Parkland course.
18 holes, 6235 yards, S.S.S.70
Founded 1910
Visitors: Not before 9.30 and not
between 12-1.15pm,otherwise
welcome at all times.
Green Fee: WD £23 per round, £28
per day; WE £34.
Societies: Mon, Tues pm,Wed,
Thurs, Fri. 9.30am and 2pm starting
times.
Catering: full service, 7 days.
Hotels: Linton Springs.

O164 **Wheatley**
☎(01302) 831655, Pro 834085
Armthorpe Rd, Doncaster, S Yorks
DN2 5QB
Follow S ring road from old A1 E
along boundary of St Leger
racecourse to next crossroads,
clubhouse is on right opposite large
water tower.
Undulating parkland course.
18 holes, 6405 yards, S.S.S.71
Designed by George Duncan.
Founded 1913 (relocated 1933)
Visitors: welcome.
Green Fee: WD £20 per round, £25
per day; WE £30.
Societies: weekdays only by
arrangement.
Catering: restaurant facilities
available.
Hotels: Balmoral; Earl of Doncaster;
Punches.

O165 **Whitby**
☎(01947) 602768 (Club), Sec/Fax
600660, Pro 602719
Sandsend Rd, Low Straggleton,
Whitby, N Yorks YO21 3SR
On A174 main coast road between
Whitby and Sandsend.
Seaside course.
18 holes, 6134 yards, S.S.S.69
Founded 1892.
Visitors: welcome, ring Pro shop to
arrange.
Green Fee: WD £20; WE £25.
Societies: parties over 12
(experienced golfers) by prior
arrangement.
Catering: facilities available daily
except Mon.
Hotels: Larpool; Seacliff; White
House.

O166 **Whitwood**
☎(01977) 512835
Altofts Lane, Whitwood, Castleford, W
Yorkshire WF10 5PZ
M62 junction 31, 0.5 mile towards
Castleford.
Public parkland course.
9 holes, 6282 yards, S.S.S.70
Designed by Steve Wells (Wakefield
Council).
Founded April 1986
Visitors: welcome at all times,
booking system operates at
weekends.
Green Fee: WD £5.40; WE £6.95.
Societies: address requests to
A.Conway, King Charles II House,
Pontefract, W Yorks.
Catering: local inn.
Hotels: Bridge Inn.

O167 **Willow Valley Golf & Country Club**
☎(01274) 878624
Highmoor Lane, Clifton, Brighouse, W Yorks HD6 4JB
Off M62 at junc 25 and head to Brighouse, at first mini-island turn right onto A643. After 2 miles course is on right.
Parkland course
18 holes, 6988 yards, S.S.S. 73; 9 holes, 2039 yards, S.S.S. 30.
Designed by J Gaunt
Founded April 1996
Visitors: welcome
Green Fee: 18 holes course: £15; 9 hole course £5 (9 holes), £9 (18 holes).
Societies: welcome
Catering: club house facilities; bar
Driving range
Hotels: Trust House Forte; Black Horse; Healds Hall.

O168 **Withernsea**
☎(01964) 612258 (Club), Sec 612978
Chestnut Ave, Withernsea, N Humberside HU19 2PG
20 miles NE of Hull at S end of town.
Seaside course.
9 holes, 5112 yards, S.S.S.64 (extension planned 1996)
Founded 1907
Visitors: welcome weekdays; restrictions at weekends and Bank Holidays.
Green Fee: £9.
Societies: on application to Sec.
Catering: evening meals weekdays; breakfast, lunch, evening meal weekends; private functions by arrangement with Sec.
Hotels: St Hilda GH; Vista Mar GH.

O169 **Wombwell (Hillies)**
☎(01226) 754433
Wentworth View, Wombwell, Barnsley, S Yorkshire S73 0LA
4 miles SE of Barnsley, 3 miles M1 junction 36.

Municipal meadowland course.
9 holes, 4190 yards, S.S.S.62
Founded 1981
Visitors: no restrictions.
Green Fee: WD £3 (9 holes), £5.75 (18 holes); WE £3.70 (9 holes), £7.30 (18 holes).
Societies: welcome by prior arrangement.
Catering: evening and weekend bar service.

O170 **Woodhall Hills**
☎(0113) 2554594 (Sec), Pro 2562857
Woodhall Rd, Calverley, Pudsey, W Yorks
Turn off A647 Leeds-Bradford road to Calverley, 1 mile.
Moorland course.
18 holes, 6102 yards, S.S.S.69
Founded 1905
Visitors: after 9.30am weekdays and 10.30am Sun; no visitors Sat.
Green Fee: WD £20.50; WE £25.
Societies: contact Sec.
Catering: dining room service available.
Snooker.

O171 **Woodsome Hall**
☎(01484) 602971(Club), Sec 602739, Pro 602034
Fenay Bridge, Huddersfield, W Yorks HD8 0LQ
5 miles SE of Huddersfield off A629 Sheffield-Penistone road.
Parkland course.
18 holes, 6080 yards, S.S.S.69
Founded 1922
Visitors: welcome weekdays with h/cap cert, jackets and ties; not before 4pmTues; limited at weekends.
Green Fee: WD £25 per round, £30 per day; WE £30 per round, £35 per day.
Societies: welcome weekdays by arrangement.
Catering: full facilities except Mon.
Hotels: Springfield Park.

O172 **Woolley Park**
☎(01942) 480437
Woolley Park, Wolley, Wakefield, W Yorks
Take junc 38 off M1 and drive through Haigh to Woolley. Course signposted
Parkland course
18 holes, 5900 yards, S.S.S. 70
Designed by M Shattock
Founded April 1996
Visitors: welcome
Green Fees: WD £8.50; WE £14.

O173 **Wortley**
☎(0114) 2885294 (Sec), Steward: 2882139,Pro 2886490
Hermit Hill Lane, Wortley, Sheffield S30 4DF
Off M1 at junction 35A (from S) or 36 (from N), take A629 through Wortley village, course 1st right.
Undulating wooded parkland course.
18 holes, 6037 yards, S.S.S.69
Founded 1894
Visitors: Phone for availability.
Green Fee: WD £25; WE £30.
Societies: welcom Mon (no catering provided), Wed and Fri by prior arrangement.
Catering: by arrangement except Mon.
Hotels: Hallam Towers (Sheffield); Brooklands (Barnsley).

O174 **York**
☎(01904) 490304 (Pro), Sec 491840, Fax 491852
Lords Moor Lane, Strensall, York YO3 5XF
2 miles N of A1234 (York Ring Road), exit at Earswick/Strensall roundabout.
Woodland course.
18 holes, 6312 yards, S.S.S.70
Designed by J.H. Taylor (1904).
Founded 1890
Visitors: Members' guests only.
Green Fee: on application.
Societies: catered for except Sat.
Catering: full facilities available except Fri.

NORTHUMBERLAND, DURHAM, CLEVELAND, TYNE & WEAR

Northumberland is one of the most lovely counties, a rich tapestry of seascape, woodland, lonely moor and rich, fertile farmland.

A welcome addition to the golfing map has been the development at Slaley Hall near Hexham, a comfortable drive west of Newcastle. A man-sized course is an attractive adjunct to housing although the long stretch of Northumberland's coastline, running parallel with the A1, makes it an obvious target for those who like sea air in their nostrils and golf that can be described, in the most complimentary of veins, as off-the-beaten-track.

The best is Berwick-upon-Tweed at Goswick, a true links approached along a quiet lane that crosses the main railway line and goes no further when the entrance to the Club is reached. The course divides itself neatly into two parts, the best and most enchanting being the few holes that nestle between the dunes and open up views of the hallowed, ancient ground of Holy Island.

It is the second oldest place in the county where golf is played, the distinction of being the oldest belonging to the little village 9-hole course at Alnmouth. For the golfer travelling along the coast, there are several pleasant stopping-off spots, notably at Bamburgh Castle, Dunstandburgh, Warkworth, Newbiggin-by-the-Sea and Seahouses.

The northern outskirts of Newcastle boast Ponteland, Gosforth and the Northumberland Club in High Gosforth Park, much of which is confined within the white rails of the racecourse. It is a Club that has housed the men's English amateur championship and the Women's Commonwealth tournament, testimony to its quality as a test of golf and to its convenience as a location.

Crossing the Tyne into Durham marks a distinct change of scenery although there are two outstanding courses in Seaton Carew, a magnificent links even if its backcloth is industrial, and Brancepeth Castle south west of Durham, designed by the master, Harry Colt, and of which Leonard Crawley was inordinately fond. That is enough of a recommendation, ideally situated as it is for anyone intent on breaking the journey to Scotland.

Crook and Bishop Auckland, both great names in the heyday of amateur football, are close by and Durham City was founded in 1887 but Durham's best news for some time is the opening of The Ramside, a 27-hole course attached to the well known Ramside Hall Hotel. Knotty Hill, at nearby Sedgefield, is a most enterprising project comprising 36-holes that is bound to be popular with local golfers while Elemore at Sunderland is a new public venture that is most welcome.

From Durham, there is a natural inclination to head towards the sea and sample the coastal chain of courses starting with Hartlepool, the handiwork of James Braid, and then sandwiching Seaton Carew between Hartlepool and the ancient Cleveland Club at Redcar.

Seaton Carew, host to a variety of national championships, is one of the very few seaside links on the East of England coast north of Norfolk, but there are other good ports of call. Eaglescliffe and Middlesborough are two more courses out of the Braid Stable. Moving west towards Darlington, there are Teeside, Billingham, Dinsdale Spa and in or near Darlington itself are Stressholme and Blackwell Grange.

Somewhat more remote are Barnard Castle and Allendale; but a final word for Hexham, just north of Allendale. Designed in 1907 by Harry Vardon, it occupies pleasant, undulating parkland.

P1 Allendale

☎(0191) 537 4089
High Studdon, Allenheads Rd,
Allendale, Hexham, Northumberland
N47 9DQ
1.5 miles south of Allendale on
B6295.
Moorland/parkland course.
9 holes, 5044 yards, S.S.S.65
Designed by members with advice
from EGU and Sports Council.
Founded 1907 (relocated Sept 1992)
Visitors: any time except Sun am,
August Bank Holiday and some Sat;
h/cap cert not required, competitions
have priority at all times.
Green Fee: £10.
Societies: weekdays and most Sat
by arrangement.
Catering: coffee & tea making facility.
Clubhouse planned.
Hotels: Kings Head; Golden Lion.

P2 Alnmouth

☎(01665) 830231, Fax 830922
Foxton Hall, Lesbury, Alnwick,
Northumberland NE66 3BE
Alnmouth road from Alnwick, left at
Alnmouth, Foxton 1 mile on right.
Seaside meadowland course.
18 holes, 6429 yards, S.S.S.71
Founded 1869
Visitors: welcome Mon, Tues and
Thurs; h/cap cert required.
Green Fee: £27.
Societies: by arrangement; max 30
players.
Catering: available at all times.
Hotels: Marine House; Schooner;
Dormy House, golf inclusive
packages.

P3 Alnmouth Village

☎(01665) 830370
Marine Rd, Alnmouth,
Northumberland NE66 2RZ
From Alnwick on A1 to Alnmouth on
A1068.
Undulating seaside course.
9 holes, 6078 yards, S.S.S.70
Founded 1869
Visitors: welcome. Restrictions on
comp days.
Green Fee: WD £15; WE £20.
Societies: welcome; official golf club
h/caps required.
Catering: by arrangement.
Hotels: Marine.

P4 Alnwick

☎(01665) 602632, Sec 602499
Swansfield Park, Alnwick,
Northumberland NE66 2AT

From S, 1st left off A1, course is
signposted from slip road
Parkland course.
18 holes, 6284 yards, S.S.S.70
Founded 1907
Visitors: welcome except on
competition days
Green Fee: WD £15; WE £20.
Societies: apply to Sec.
Catering: full catering service
provided.
Hotels: White Swan; The Oaks;
Plough.

P5 Arcot Hall

☎(0191) 236 2794
Dudley, Cramlington, Northumberland
NE23 7QP
1 mile E of A1 off A1068 near Holiday
Inn.
Parkland course.
18 holes, 6387 yards, S.S.S.70
Designed by James Braid.
Founded 1910
Visitors: weekdays. Weekends only
as member's guest.
Green Fee: £20 per round; £25 per
day.
Societies: by prior arrangement; not
weekends.
Catering: full facilities all day.
Hotels: Holiday Inn.

P6 Backworth

☎(0191) 268 1048
Backworth Welfare, The Hall,
Backworth, Shiremoor, Tyne and
Wear NE27 0AH
Off Tyne Tunnel link road at
Holystone roundabout.
Parkland course.
9 holes, 5825 yards, S.S.S.69
Founded 1937
Visitors: welcome with restrictions,
ring for details.
Green Fee: WD £12; WE £15.
Societies: welcome by prior
arrangement.
Catering: bar, snacks; catering by
arrangement.
Pool, bowls, banqueting.
Hotels: Moat House; Royal; Swallow.

P7 Bamburgh Castle

☎(01668) 214378
(Steward/bookings), Sec 214321
The Wynding, Bamburgh,
Northumberland NE69 7DE
Turn off A1 between Alnwick and
Berwick on B1341 or B1342 and
proceed to Bamburgh village, turn left
opposite Lord Crewe Arms and travel
along The Wynding.

Seaside course.
18 holes, 5621 yards, S.S.S.67
Designed by George Rochester.
Founded 1896
Visitors: welcome, restricted Bank
Holidays, weekends and club
competition days; h/cap certs
required.
Green Fee: WD £23; WE £30 per
round, £38 per day.
Societies: welcome by prior
arrangement.
Catering: lunches, teas and evening
meal except Tues.
Hotels: Sunningdale; Mizen Head;
Victoria; Lord Crewe Arms.

P8 Barnard Castle

☎(01833) 638355, Pro 631980
Harmire Rd, Barnard Castle, Co
Durham DL12 8QN
On N boundary of town on B6278
Barnard Castle-Eggleston road.
Undulating parkland course.
18 holes, 6406 yards, S.S.S.71
Founded 1898
Visitors: welcome except on
competition days.
Green Fee: WD £15 per round, £18
per day; WE £24.
Societies: welcome with
arrangement; max 40 players.
Catering: meals and bar snacks.
Limited on Mon.
Snooker.
Hotels: Red Well.

P9 Beamish Park

☎(0191) 370 1382
The Clubhouse, Beamish, Stanley,
Co Durham DH9 0RH
Take Chester-le-Street turn-off from
A1(M), follow signs for Beamish
Museum.
Parkland course.
18 holes, 6204 yards, S.S.S.70
Designed by Henry Cotton (part).
Founded 1950
Visitors: Not before 9am on any day.
Green Fee: WD £16 per round, £20
per day; WE £24, per round , £30 per
day.
Societies: weekdays only by prior
arrangement.
Catering: bar and restaurant;
banqueting.
Hotels: Arch

P10 Bedlingtonshire

☎(01670) 822457 (Sec), Pro 822087
Acorn Bank, Bedlington,
Northumberland NE22 6AA
0.5 mile W of Bedlington on A1068.

Public meadowland/parkland course.
18 holes, 6813 yards, S.S.S.73
Designed by Frank Pennink.
Founded April 1972
Visitors: welcome
Green Fee: WD £15 per round, £20
per day; WE £20.
Societies: on application.
Catering: Full services.
Hotels: Ridge Farm.

P11 **Belford**
☎(01668) 213433
South Rd, Belford, Northumberland,
NE70 7HY
Just off A1 approx midway between
Alnwick and Berwick upon Tweed.
Parkland course.
9 holes, 6304 yards, S.S.S.70
Designed by Nigel W. Williams.
Founded April 1993
Visitors: welcome, no restrictions.
Green Fee: WD £9 (9 holes), £13 (18
holes), £16 per day; WE £10 (9
holes), £16 (18 holes), £21 per day.
Societies: welcome at all times other
than competition days.
Catering: bar facilities, snacks and
bar meals available.
Driving range.
Hotels: Bluebell.

P12 **Bellingham**
☎(01434) 220530
Boggle Hole, Bellingham, Hexham,
Northumberland NE48 2DT
Off B6320, 16 miles NE of Hexham,
easy access from A68.
Parkland/moorland course.
9 holes (18 tees), 5245 yards,
S.S.S.66
Designed by Edward Johnson.
Founded 1893
Visitors: welcome, limited Sun (after
5pm).
Green Fee: WD £10; WE £15.
Societies: welcome, limited to 18
holes on Sat, limited Sun.
Catering: parties welcome,
individuals by arrangement.
Hotels: Riverdale Hall.

P13 **Berwick-upon-Tweed (Goswick)**
☎(01289) 387256
Beal, Berwick-upon-Tweed,
Northumberland TD15 2RW
Off A1 approx 3 miles S of Berwick-
upon-Tweed.
Links course.
18 holes, 6500 yards, S.S.S.71
Designed by James Braid.
Founded 1890

Visitors: welcome but must book at
weekends.
Green Fee: WD £18 per round, £24
per day; WE £24 per round, £32 per
day.
Societies: special rate for parties and
societies, Mon-Fri only, £25 per day
including catering.
Catering: all week; evening meals
available except Mon, soup and
sandwiches available all day.
Hotels: Blue Bell.

P14 **Billingham**
☎(01642) 554494, 557060
Sandy Lane, Billingham, Cleveland
TS22 5NA
E of A19 Billingham by-pass, near
town centre.
Undulating parkland course.
18 holes, 6460 yards, S.S.S.71
Designed by Frank Pennink.
Founded 1967

Visitors: welcome with h/cap cert..
Green Fee: WD £20 per day; WE
£33 per day.
Societies: weekdays by prior
arrangement.
Catering: facilities available daily
except Mon.
Hotels: Forum.

P15 **Birtley**
☎(0191) 410 2207
Portobello Rd, Birtley, Co Durham
DH3 2LR
A6127 off A1, 6 miles S of Newcastle.
Parkland course.
9 holes, 5154 yards, S.S.S.67
Founded 1921
Visitors: welcome weekdays only
unless accompanied by member.
Green Fee: £12
Societies: welcome by prior
arrangement.
Catering: bar facilities in evenings.

P16 Bishop Auckland

☎(01388) 602198 (Club), Sec
663648 Sec, Pro 661618
High Plains, Durham Rd, Bishop
Auckland, Co Durham DL14 8DL

Go up Durham Rd towards
Spennymoor; course on left half-way
up the bank. From Spennymoor or
Rushyford, take Canney Hill turn off,
course on right half way down bank.

Parkland course.
18 holes, 6420 yards, S.S.S.71
Founded 1894
Visitors: welcome, no visiting parties
Sat or Sun.
Green Fee: WD £20 per round, £24
per day; WE £26.
Societies: best days Wed, Thurs, Fri
(Ladies Day Tues).
Catering: full facilities except Mon.
2 snooker tables.
Hotels: Park Head; Old Manor House
(West Auckland).

P17 Blackwell Grange

☎(0325) 464464 (Club), Sec
464458, Pro 462088
Briar Close, Blackwell, Darlington, Co
Durham DL3 8QX
1 mile S of Darlington, 0.25 mile W
off A66.
Undulating parkland course.
18 holes, 5621 yards, S.S.S.67
Designed by Frank Pennink.
Founded 1930
Visitors: welcome except Wed pm
(Ladies Day). Book at weekends
Green Fee: WD £16 per round £22
per day; WE £20.
Societies: by arrangement on
weekdays.
Catering: full service Tues-Sat.
Hotels: Blackwell Grange Moat
House.

P18 Blyth

☎(01670) 367728
New Delaval & Newsham, Blyth,
Northumberland NE24 4DB
11 miles N of Newcastle, 6 miles N of
Whitley Bay.
Parkland course.
18 holes, 6533 yards, S.S.S.72
Designed by Hamilton Stutt & Co.
Founded 1905

KEY				
1	Allendale	20	Brancepeth Castle	
2	Alnmouth	21	Burgham Park	
3	Alnmouth Village	22	Castle Eden &	
4	Alnwick		Peterlee	
5	Arcot Hall	23	Chester-le-Street	
6	Backworth	24	City of Newcastle	
7	Bamburgh Castle	25	Cleveland	
8	Barnard Castle	26	Close House	
9	Beamish Park	27	Consett & District	
10	Bedlingtonshire	28	Crook	
11	Belford	29	Darlington	
12	Bellingham	30	Dinsdale Spa	
13	Berwick-upon-Tweed	31	Dunstanburgh Castle	
14	Billingham	32	Durham City	
15	Birtley	33	Eaglescliffe	
16	Bishop Auckland	34	Elemore	
17	Blackwell Grange	35	Garesfield	
18	Blyth	36	Gosforth (Bridlepath)	
19	Boldon	37	Hall Garth G & CC	
		38	Haltwhistle	

39	Hartlepool	57	Parklands	
40	Heworth	58	Ponteland	
41	Hexham	59	Prudhoe	
42	Hobson Municipal	60	Ramside	
43	Houghton-le-Spring	61	Ravensworth	
44	Huntley Hall	62	Roseberry Grange	
45	Knotty Hill Golf Centre	63	Rothbury	
46	Magdalene Fields	64	Ryhope	
47	Matfen Hall	65	Ryton	
48	Middlesbrough	66	Saltburn-by-the-Sea	
49	Middlesbrough	67	Seaham	
	Municipal	68	Seahouses	
50	Morpeth	69	Seaton Carew	
51	Mount Oswald	70	Slaley Hall	
52	Newbiggin-by-the-Sea	71	South Moor	
53	Newcastle United	72	South Shields	
54	Northumberland	73	Stocksfield	
55	Norton Golf Course	74	Stressholme Golf	
56	Oak Leaf Golf		Centre	
	Complex (Aycliffe)	75	Swarland Hall	

76	Teesside	
77	Tynedale	
78	Tynemouth	
79	Tyneside	
80	Wallsend	
81	Warkworth	
82	Washington Moat	
	House	
83	Wearside	
84	Westerhope	
85	Whickham	
86	Whitburn	
87	Whitley Bay	
88	Wilton	
89	Woodham G & CC	
90	Wooler	
91	Wynyard (The	
	Wellington)	

Visitors: weekdays only before 3pm, unless with member.
Green Fee: £18 per round, £20 per day.
Societies: welcome by arrangement (28 days in advance).
Catering: full facilities.
Hotels: Park

P19 Boldon

☎(0191) 536 5360 (Sec/Office), Club 536 4182, Pro 536 5385
Dipe Lane, East Boldon, Tyne & Wear NE36 0PQ
On A184, 1 mile E of A19/A1 junction.
Parkland course.
18 holes, 6338 yards, S.S.S.70
Founded 1912
Visitors: welcome weekdays, after 3.30 at weekends and Bank Holidays restricted.
Green Fee: WD £16; WE £20.
Societies: by arrangement.
Catering: bar snacks all day; meals by arrangement.
Snooker table.
Hotels: Friendly.

P20 Brancepeth Castle

☎(0191) 378 0075, Fax 378 3835
Brancepeth Village, Durham DH7 8EA
4 miles W of Durham city on A690 to Crook; turn left at crossroads in village of Brancepeth and take slip road to left immediately before Castle gates.
Parkland course.
18 holes, 6285 yards, S.S.S.71
Designed by H.S. Colt.
Founded 1924
Visitors: weekdays only for parties, individuals at weekends.
Green Fee: WD £27; WE £30.
Societies: weekdays, reduced green fees dependent on number of players in party. £40 golf, coffee and dinner packages.
Catering: lunches and bar snacks pm, dinners by prior booking.
Hotels: Bridge (Croxdale).

P21 Burgham Park

☎(01670) 787898, Fax 787164
Near Felton, Morpeth, Northumberland NE65 8QP
6 miles north of Morpeth, 1 mile west of the A1 on the Longhorsley road
Undulating parkland course
18 holes, 6751, S.S.S. 72
Designed by A Mair
Founded 1994

Visitors: welcome
Green Fee: on application.
Societies: welcome by prior arrangement
Catering: full bar and catering facilities
Hotels: Lindon Hall; Queens Head; Sun.

P22 Castle Eden & Peterlee

☎(01429) 836220, Sec 836510, Pro 836689.
Castle Eden, Hartlepool, Cleveland TS27 4SS
Durham-Hartlepool road off A19, follow signs to Castle Eden, course opposite Whitbread Brewery.
Parkland course.
18 holes, 6262 yards, S.S.S.70
Designed by Henry Cotton (2nd 9).
Founded 1927
Visitors: welcome 9-11.30am & 1.45-3.30pm
Green Fee: WD £20; WE £30.
Societies: weekdays.
Catering: every day.
Hotels: Crossways.

P23 Chester-le-Street

☎(0191) 388 3218, Pro 389 0157
Lumley Park, Chester-le-Street, Co Durham DH3 4NS
Leave A1(M) to Chester-le-Street, follow A167 signposted Durham, course 0.25 mile E of Chester-le-Street, beside Lumley Castle.
Parkland course.
18 holes, 6437 yards, S.S.S.69
Designed by J.H. Taylor (original 9).
Founded 1909
Visitors: welcome weekdays, not before 9.30 and not between 12-2pm; weekends not before 10am; must have letter of intro/h/cap cert.
Green Fee: WD £20; WE £25.
Societies: welcome; not weekends.
Catering: bar 11am-11pm Mon-Sat; snacks, lunches and evening meals. Snooker.
Hotels: Lumley Castle.

P24 City of Newcastle

☎(0191) 285 1775
Three Mile Bridge, Gosforth, Newcastle upon Tyne NE3 2DR
3 miles N of Newcastle city centre on left hand side of B1318 road heading N, opposite Three Mile Inn.
Parkland course.
18 holes, 6508 yards, S.S.S.71
Designed by Harry Vardon.
Founded 1892

Visitors: welcome (on men's competition days only at quiet times). Not before 10.30am Weds and weekends
Green Fee: WD £20; WE £25.
Societies: welcome on application
Catering: lunches, bar snacks, sandwiches every day. Snooker, pool.
Hotels: Gosforth Park.

P25 Cleveland

☎(01642) 483693 (Club), Sec 471798
Queen St, Redcar, Cleveland TS10 1BT
From A174 to A1042 to Coatham.
Championship links course.
18 holes, 6707 yards, S.S.S.72
Founded 1887
Visitors: welcome.
Green Fee: WD £20; WE £30.
Societies: welcome weekdays by arrangement; contact Sec for brochure.
Catering: full facilities
Hotels: Park.

P26 Close House

☎(01661) 852953, Sec 811158
Close House, Heddon-on-the-Wall, Newcastle-upon-Tyne NE15 0HT
9 miles W of Newcastle off A69.
Parkland course.
18 holes, 5605 yards, S.S.S.67
Founded 1968
Visitors: with member only
Green Fee: apply for details.
Societies: weekdays by arrangement. Packages available
Catering: full service on request
Hotels: Novotel

P27 Consett & District

☎(01207) 502186, Pro 580210, Sec 562261
Elmfield Rd, Consett, Co Durham DH8 5NN
Off A68 2 miles from Castleside or Allensford; 12 miles from Durham (A691) and Newcastle (A694).
Undulating parkland course.
18 holes, 6013 yards, S.S.S.69
Designed by Harry Vardon.
Founded 1911
Visitors: welcome, prior confirmation at weekends advisable.
Green Fee: WD £11; WE £22.
Societies: welcome by arrangement, max 40.
Catering: full catering by arrangement, limited Mon. Snooker.

P28 Crook
☎(01388) 762429
Low Jobs Hill, Crook, Co Durham
DL15 9AA
On A689 6 miles W of Durham city
between Willington and Crook.
Moorland/parkland course.
18 holes, 6102 yards, S.S.S.69
Founded 1919
Visitors: welcome; restrictions
Sunday.
Green Fee: WD £12; WE £20.
Societies: by appointment.
Catering: full facilities
Hotels: Kensington Hall

P29 Darlington
☎(01325) 463936, 355324 Sec
488126
Haughton Grange, Darlington, Co
Durham DL1 3JD
From A1M follow A167 S then A66, 1
mile on left.
Parkland course.
18 holes, 6243 yards, S.S.S.70
Designed by Mackenzie.
Founded 1908
Visitors: welcome weekdays
Green Fee: £22
Societies: welcome by prior
arrangement.
Catering: excellent bar and
restaurant facilities except Mon.
Snooker.
Hotels: Kings Head.

P30 Dinsdale Spa
☎(0325) 332297(Sec), Pro 332515,
Club 332222
Middleton-St-George, Darlington, Co
Durham DL2 1DW
From A66 or A19 follow signs for
Teeside Airport until Middleton-St-
George, club is 1.5 miles from village
on Neasham road.
Parkland course.
18 holes, 6090 yards, S.S.S.69
Founded 1906
Visitors: welcome weekdays.
Green Fee: £20
Societies: welcome by prior
arrangement.
Catering: facilities available except
Mon.
Hotels: Croft Spa.

P31 Dunstanburgh Castle
☎(01665) 576562
Embleton, Alnwick, Northumberland
NE66 3XQ
Off A1, 7 miles NE of Alnwick (follow
signs to Embleton not Dunstanburgh
Castle).

Seaside links course.
18 holes, 6298 yards, S.S.S.70
Designed by James Braid.
Founded 1900
Visitors: welcome every day (after
10am Sun). No 4 balls on Sat/Sun
am.
Green Fee: WD £15; WE £18 per
round, £22 per day.
Societies: welcome every day (after
10am Sun).
Catering: meals and snacks
available all day, licenced bar.
Hotels: Sportsman Inn.

P32 Durham City
☎(0191) 378 0069, Pro 378 0029,
Sec 386 0200
Littleburn Farm, Langley Moor,
Durham DH7 8HL
Off A690 2 miles SW of Durham City.
Meadowland course.
18 holes, 6326 yards, S.S.S.70
Designed by C.C. Stanton.
Founded 1887
Visitors: welcome weekdays.
Green Fee: on application
Societies: weekdays.
Catering: facilities available daily
except Mon.
Hotels: Royal County; Three Tuns;
Duke of Wellington.

P33 Eaglescliffe
☎(01642) 780098, Pro 790122, Sec
780284
Yarm Rd, Eaglescliffe, Stockton-on-
Tees, Cleveland TS16 0DQ
On the left of A135 from Stockton-on-
Tees to Yarm.
Undulating parkland course.
18 holes, 6278 yards, S.S.S.69
Designed by James Braid,
modification by H. Cotton.
Founded 1914
Visitors: welcome on application.
Green Fee: WD £22; WE £28.
Societies: catered for weekdays.
Catering: full facilities
Hotels: Parkmore (Eaglescliffe); Tall
Trees.

P34 Elemore
☎(0191) 526 9020
Elemore Lane, Heton-le-Hole, Tyne
and Wear
Located 8 miles south of the city
centre on the A183
Parkland course
18 holes, 5947 yards, S.S.S. 69
Founded 1994
Visitors: welcome on pay as you
play basis

Green Fee: £6. Season tickets
available
Societies: welcome
Catering: bar and function lounge in
purpose built clubhouse. Family
room. Practice facilities.

P35 Garesfield
☎(01207) 561278, Sec 561309
Chopwell, Tyne & Wear NE17 7AP
A694 Newcastle-Consett road to
Rowlands Gill, take B6315 to High
Spen, then take Chopwell road 1 mile
on left.
Parkland course.
18 holes, 6603 yards, S.S.S.72
Designed by William Woodend.
Founded 1922
Visitors: weekdays not before 3pm
on Fri, not before 4.30pm on
weekends and Bank Holidays unless
with member.
Green Fee: apply for details.
Societies: by arrangement.
Catering: full facilities except Mon.

P36 Gosforth (Bridlepath)
☎(0191) 285 3495
Broadway East, Gosforth, Newcastle
upon Tyne NE3 5ER
3 miles N of city centre; turn right at
1st main roundabout after Regent
Centre metro station.
Meadowland course.
18 holes, 6024 yards, S.S.S.69
Founded 1905
Visitors: welcome weekdays;
members' guests only before 4pm
weekends and Bank Holidays.
Green Fee: £20
Societies: weekdays.
Catering: full facilities.
Hotels: Gosforth Park.

P37 Hall Garth G & CC
☎(01325) 300400, Fax 310083
Coatham Mundeville, Nr Darlington,
Co Durham DL1 3LU
From junction 59 of the A1(M) take
A167 towards Darlington. At the top
of the hill turn left towards Brafferton
and club is 0.5m on right.
Parkland course
9 holes, 6621 yards, S.S.S. 72
Designed by B Moore
Founded May 1995
Visitors: welcome
Green Fee: WD £10; WE £12.50
Societies: welcome
Catering: Stables pub on premises;
food available from 7am-10pm
Hotels: Hall Garth (16th century
country house with leisure facilities).

P38 **Haltwhistle**

☎(016977) 47367
Banktop, Greenhead, Via Carlisle,
Northumberland CA6 7HN
3 miles W of Haltwhistle, 0.25 mile off
A69 on road to Gilsland.
Undulating parkland course.
12 holes, 5968 yards, S.S.S.69
(Extending to 18 holes in 1996)
Founded 1968
Visitors: welcome any day except
Sun am.
Green Fee: £12
Societies: welcome except Sun;
contact Secretary.
Catering: bar; catering by prior
arrangement.
Hotels: beneficial arrangements for
golfers at Greenhead Hotel, Gilsland
Spa and Manor House.

P39 **Hartlepool**

☎(01429) 274398, Pro 267473
Hart Warren, Hartlepool, Cleveland
TS24 9QF
N boundary of Hartlepool off A1086,
well signposted.
Seaside links course.
18 holes, 6215 yards, S.S.S.70
Designed by James Braid (in part).
Founded 1906
Visitors: weekdays unrestricted,
weekends limited.
Green Fee: WD £20; WE £30.
Societies: weekdays.
Catering: available except Mon by
arrangement with Steward. ▪
Snooker.
Hotels: Staincliffe; Marine.

P40 **Heworth**

☎(0191) 469 2137
Gingling Gate, Heworth, Tyne & Wear
NE10 8XY
Parkland course.
18 holes, 6404 yards, S.S.S.71
Founded 1912
Visitors: welcome but not before
10am at weekends.
Green Fee: £15
Societies: welcome by prior
arrangement.
Catering: bar and restaurant.

P41 **Hexham**

☎(01434) 603072
Spital Park, Hexham, Northumberland
NE46 3RZ
On A69, 1 mile W of Hexham centre.
Undulating parkland course.
18 holes, 6301 yards, S.S.S.68
Designed by Harry Vardon.
Founded 1907

Visitors: welcome any day by
application.
Green Fee: WD £23 per round, £28
per day; WE £30.
Societies: by arrangement, not Sat
or Sun.
Catering: full facilities every day.
Hotels: Beaumont

P42 **Hobson Municipal**

☎(01207) 570189 (Sec), **Catering:**
270941, Pro 271605
Burnopfield, Newcastle-upon-Tyne,
Tyne & Wear NE16 6BZ
On main Newcastle-Consett road.
Municipal parkland course.
18 holes, 6403 yards, S.S.S.71
Founded 1980
Visitors: restricted Sat (Club
competitions). Book in advance
Green Fee: WD £9; WE £12.
Societies: apply to Pro.
Catering: bar, lounge and restaurant.
Hotels: Harperley.

P43 **Houghton-le-Spring**

☎(0191) 584 1198, Pro 584 7421
Copt Hill, Houghton-le-Spring DH5
8LU
On A1085 Houghton-le-Spring to
Seaham Harbour road, 0.5 mile from
Houghton-le-Spring.
Undulating hillside course.
18 holes, 6443 yards, S.S.S.71
Founded 1908
Visitors: welcome any day after 9am,
restrictions at weekends and club
competition days.
Green Fee: WD £18 per round, £25
per day; WE £25 per round, £30 per
day
Societies: welcome, prior
arrangement for meals.
Catering: facilities available most
days.
Hotels: White Lion; Ramside Hall;
Rainton Lodge.

P44 **Huntley Hall**

☎(01287) 676216, Pro 677444, Fax
678250
Brotton, Saltburn-by-the-Sea,
Cleveland TS12 2QQ
15 miles from Teeside on the A174.
17 miles from Whitby on the A173.
Heritage coastline course
18 holes, 6510 yards, S.S.S. 73
Designed by J Morgan
Founded 1993
Visitors: welcome
Green Fee: WD £18; WE £25.
Societies: welcome Mon-Sat;
packages available.

Catering: restaurant and bars;
members bar and spike bar. 7 days a
week, breakfast to evening meals.
Driving range, chipping area, putting
green, tuition available, buggy hire.
Hotels: en suite bedrooms available
from summer 1996.

P45 **Knotty Hill Golf Centre**

☎(01740) 620320
Sedgefield, Stockton-on-Tees,
Cleveland TS21 2BB
A1(M) junction 60, A689; 1 mile N of
Sedgefield A177.
Undulating parkand course, Pay-as-
you-Play.
North course, 18 holes, 6584 yards,
S.S.S.72
Designed by C. Stanton.
Founded Sept 1992
Visitors: welcome at all times.
Green Fee: £7 (9 holes), £12 (18
holes).
Societies: any day except Sun,
information available on request.
Catering: restaurant and bar.
Driving range.
Hotels: Hardwick Hall adjoining
course.

P46 **Magdalene Fields**

☎(01289) 306384, Greenranger:
330700
Berwick-upon-Tweed TD15 1NE
5 minutes walk from town centre.
Seaside course (parkland fairways).
18 holes, 6407 yards, S.S.S.71
Visitors: welcome, limited weekend
tee-offs; contact Greenranger.
Green Fee: WD £15.50; WE £17.50.
Societies: by arrangement, ring Sec.
Catering: meals during summer, at
other times by arrangement.
Hotels: Cobbleyard.

P47 **Matfen Hall**

☎(01661) 886500, Fax 886146
Matfen, Northumberland NE20 0RQ
Parkland course
18 holes, 6744 yards, S.S.S 72, 9
hole par 3 course
Designed by M James/A Mair
Visitors: welcome without restrictions
Green Fee: WD £16 per round, £22
per day; WE & BH £21 per round,
£27 per day.
Societies: welcome weekdays and
after 9.45am Sat & Sun
Catering: bar service and full
catering available.
Hotels: Beaumont; Swallow; Black
Bull B&B.

P48 Middlesbrough

☎(01642) 311515, Pro 316430
Brass Castle Lane, Marton,
Middlesbrough, Cleveland TS8 9EE
5 miles S of Middlesbrough, 1 mile W
of A172.
Parkland course.
18 holes, 6215 yards, S.S.S.69
Designed by James Braid.
Founded 1908
Visitors: welcome except Sat.
Green Fee: WD £17; WE £32.
Societies: by arrangement
Catering: full facilities; 24 hours
notice for restaurant meals.
Hotels: Marton Hotel & Country Club

P49 Middlesbrough Municipal

☎(01642) 315533
Ladgate Lane, Middlesbrough,
Cleveland TS5 7YZ
Access from A19 via A174 to Acklam.
Undulating parkland course.
18 holes, 6333 yards, S.S.S.70
Designed by Middlesborough
Borough Council
Founded 1977
Visitors: welcome, but need a
starting time.
Green Fee: WD £7.75; WE £9.75
Societies: welcome
Catering: lunches and evening
meals, open to the public.
Driving range.
Hotels: Blue Bell.

P50 Morpeth

☎(01670) 504942 (Sec), Club
519980, Pro 515675
The Common, Morpeth, NE61 2BT
On A197 1 mile S of Morpeth.
Parkland course.
18 holes, 6104 yards, S.S.S.70
Designed by Harry Vardon (1922).
Founded 1906
Visitors: welcome after 9.30
weekdays, not 11.30-12.30 Sat.
Green Fee: WD £20; WE £25
Societies: weekdays; apply to Sec.
Catering: snacks, bar lunches,
dinners; booking advisable.
Hotels: Waterford Lodge; Queens
Head, Linden Hall.

P51 Mount Oswald

☎(0191) 386 7527, Fax 386 0975
Mount Oswald Manor, South Rd,
Durham DH1 3TQ
SW of Durham on A1050.
Parkland (part wooded) course.
18 holes, 6101 yards, S.S.S.69
Founded 1924

Visitors: welcome any time;
members only until 10am Sun.
Green Fee: WD £10 per round, £17
per day; WE £12 per round, £21 per
day.
Societies: welcome any time; special
rates for 12 or more inc weekends.
Catering: meals 9.30am-9.30pm;
Sun lunch; function room (75-80),
smaller rooms for other parties.
Pool table.
Hotels: Three Tuns.

P52 Newbiggin-by-the-Sea

☎(01670) 817344, Pro 817833
Clubhouse, Newbiggin-by-the-Sea,
Northumberland NE64 6DW
Off A197 16 miles N of Newcastle, 8
miles E of Morpeth; at easternmost
point of village adjacent Church Point
Caravan Park.
Seaside links course.
18 holes, 6452 yards, S.S.S.71
Founded 17 July 1884
Visitors: welcome after 10am; not
competition days.
Green Fee: WD £14; WE £19
Societies: apply to Sec.
Catering: bar meals, lunch, dinner
except Tues.
Snooker.
Hotels: Morpeth Hall

P53 Newcastle United

☎(01632) 2864693, Pro 2869998
Ponteland Rd, Cowgate, Newcastle-
upon-Tyne, Northumberland NE5
3JW
1 mile W of city centre.
Moorland course.
18 holes, 6596 yards, S.S.S.71
Founded 1892
Visitors: welcome
weekdays.Weekends after 3.30pm
Green Fee: WD £15; WE £18.
Societies: by arrangement.
Catering: meals by arrangement.
Snooker.
Hotels: Gosforth

P54 Northumberland

☎(0191) 236 2009 (Steward), Sec
236 2498
High Gosforth Park, Newcastle-upon-
Tyne NE3 5HT
Situated off A6125 4 miles N of
Newcastle-upon-Tyne city centre.
Undulating parkland course.
18 holes, 6629 yards, S.S.S.72
Designed by H.S. Colt & James
Braid.
Founded 1898

Visitors: welcome weekdays by
reservation with Sec and letter of
intro.
Green Fee: £30 per round, £35 per
day
Societies: on application.
Catering: luncheon served except
Mon.
Hotels: Gosforth Park.

P55 Norton Golf Course

☎(01642) 676385
Junction Rd, Stockton-on-Tees,
Cleveland TS20 1SU
Parkland course.
18 holes, 5855 yards, S.S.S. 71
Designed by T Harper
Founded 1989
Visitors: no jeans, correct footwear,
half set of clubs each player.
Green Fee: WD £8; WE £9.
Societies: welcome by prior
arrangement.
Catering: bar and bar meals
available in pub. No clubhouse
Hotels: Post House, Swallow

P56 Oak Leaf Golf Complex (Aycliffe)

☎(01325) 310820
School Aycliffe Lane, Newton Aycliffe,
Co Durham DL5 6QZ
Take A68 from A1(M), turn right to
Newton Aycliffe; course on left,
illuminated sign at end of road.
Municipal parkland course.
18 holes, 5334 yards, S.S.S. 71
Visitors: welcome, no restrictions.
Green Fee: WD £6; WE £7.
Societies: off peak tee times, £25
deposit on booking; min 9 or 3 X 3
balls.
Catering: bar facilities at sports
complex.
Driving range; sports and leisure
complex.
Hotels: Redworth Hall (Redworth);
Eden Arms; Gretna Hotel.

P57 Parklands

☎(0191) 236 4480
High Gosforth Park, Newcastle-upon-
Tyne NE3 5HQ
N of Newcastle on A1.
Parkland course.
18 holes, 6664 yards, S.S.S.69
Founded 1971
Visitors: no restrictions.
Green Fee: WD £17; WE £25
Societies: welcome.
Catering: bar and restaurant.
Driving range, 9-hole Pitch & Putt.
Hotels: Washington Moat House.

P58 Ponteland

☎(01661) 822689
53 Bell Villas, Ponteland, Newcastle-upon-Tyne NE20 9BD
On A696 road to Jedburgh, 1.5 miles N of Newcastle Airport.
Parkland course.
18 holes, 6524 yards, S.S.S.71
Designed by Harry Ferney.
Founded 1927
Visitors: Mon to Thurs.
Green Fee: £22.50.
Societies: Tues and Thurs, by prior arrangement.
Catering: full facilities in bar hours, by prior arrangement at other times.
Hotels: Moat House

P59 Prudhoe

☎(01661) 832466, Pro 836188
Eastwood Park, Prudhoe, Northumberland NE42 5DY
12 miles W of Newcastle on A695.
Parkland course.
18 holes, 5862 yards, S.S.S.68
Founded 1930
Visitors: welcome weekdays and weekends except comp days
Green Fee: WD £17; WE £20-25.
Societies: welcome weekdays by arrangement.
Catering: bar snacks and meals served.
Hotels: Hexham; Beaumont.

P60 Ramside

☎(0191) 386 5282
Ramside Hall, Carrville, Durham DH1 1TD
Take the Carrville signposts off the A19, past filling station in direction of Sunderland and then turn right into Ramside
Parkland course
27 holes 1-18 6851 S.S.S. 73, 10-27 6406 S.S.S 71, 1-9,19-27 6193 S.S.S. 69
Founded April 1996
Visitors: welcome
Green Fee: on application
Societies: welcome by application
Catering: full service available
Hotels: Ramside Hall

P61 Ravensworth

☎(0191) 487 6014, Pro 491 3475, Sec 488 7549
Moss Heaps, Wrekenton, Gateshead, Tyne & Wear NE9 7UU
Off A1, 2 miles S of Gateshead.
Moorland/parkland course.
18 holes, 5872 yards, S.S.S.68
Founded 1906

Visitors: welcome.
Green Fee: WD £17; WE £25.
Societies: weekdays.
Catering: facilities available every day except Mon.
Hotels: Springfield.

P62 Roseberry Grange

☎(0191) 370 2047 (Office), Pro 370 0660, Club 370 0670
Grange Villa, Chester-le-Street, Durham DH2 3NF
Off A693 from Chester-le-Street to Stanley, turn left before Beamish Museum.
Parkland course.
18 holes, 5892 yards, S.S.S.68
Founded 1986
Visitors: welcome.
Green Fee: £7.50.
Societies: welcome, book in writing via District Council.
Catering: bar, snacks daily.
Driving range, putting green.

P63 Rothbury

☎(01669) 621271 (Club), Sec 620718
Old Race Course, Rothbury, Morpeth, Northumberland NE65 7TR
Off A697, 15 miles NE of Morpeth.
Meadowland course.
9 holes, 5681 yards, S.S.S.67
Founded 1891
Visitors: weekdays except Tues pm; some weekends by arrangement only.
Green Fee: WD £11; WE £16.
Societies: as for visitors.
Catering: bar facilities, bar meals and snacks available, open weekdays 11am-3pm.
Pool table.
Hotels: Coquetvale.

P64 Ryhope

☎(0191) 523 7333
c/o Mr Winfield, 30 Rosslyn Avenue, Ryhope, Sunderland, Durham SR2 0DH
Turn off A19 at Ryhope village towards Hollycarrside.
Municipal parkland course.
9 holes, 4601 yards, S.S.S.69
Designed by Sunderland Borough Council.
Founded March 1991
Visitors: unrestricted.
Green Fee: £6
Societies: welcome by prior arrangement
Catering: full service
Hotels: Seaburn

P65 Ryton

☎(0191) 413 3737, 413 3253
Dr Stanners, Clara Vale, Ryton, Tyne & Wear NE40 3TD
Off A695 8 miles from Newcastle, follow signs from Ryton to Wylam then Clara Vale.
Moorland/parkland course.
18 holes, 6042 yards, S.S.S.69
Founded 1891
Visitors: welcome weekdays, by application at weekends.
Green Fee: WD £15 per round, £20 per day; WE £20
Societies: parties welcome by arrangement.
Catering: full facilities every day except Thurs

P66 Saltburn-by-the-Sea

☎(01287) 622812 (Sec), Pro 624653
Hob Hill, Saltburn-by-the-Sea, Cleveland TS12 1NJ
1 mile from Saltburn on A1268 Guisborough road on left.
Parkland course.
18 holes, 5897 yards, S.S.S.68
Founded 1894
Visitors: welcome; h/cap cert preferred.
Green Fee: WD £19; WE £24.
Societies: by arrangement.
Catering: full facilities except Mon.
Snooker.
Hotels: Royal York.

P67 Seaham

☎(0191) 581 2354, Pro 513 0837
Dawdon, Seaham, Co Durham SR7 7RD
Off A19, 6 miles S of Sunderland, take road to Seaham.
Heathland course.
18 holes, 6017 yards, S.S.S.69
Designed by Dr A. Mackenzie.
Founded May 1911
Visitors: welcome.
Green Fee: WD £15; WE £18.
Societies: must be booked through Sec.
Catering: Full facilities, meals to be booked.
Snooker.
Hotels: Harbour View

P68 Seahouses

☎(01665) 720794
Beadnell Rd, Seahouses, Northumberland NE68 7XT
Off A1 5 miles N of Alnwick; B1340.
Seaside course.
18 holes, 5462 yards, S.S.S.67
Founded 1913

Seaton Carew

One of the great joys of golf in the West of Ireland is the feeling of spaciousness and the fact that the views from the links are dominated by natural beauty. For those who never venture further from Donegal than Rosses Point, it might be thought such beauty is an integral part of all courses but one of the game's great strengths is the number of contrasting settings in which it is played. It strikes me therefore that the citizens of Hartlepool are every bit as ardent in counting their blessings over Seaton Carew as the Irish are in their admiration for Tralee or Lahinch.

Modern Seaton Carew is set in surroundings of industrial chimneys and chemical production plants but that has never been, and never will be, a deterrent to golfers. It is something to which you get used in the same way that, by the end of a round at Royal Mid-Surrey, you never notice the aeroplanes or, at West Hill, the trains.

Courses are judged by the challenge and enjoyment they provide and both are high on the list at Seaton Carew whose distinction is heightened by being one of the few outstanding links on the seaboard of eastern England. Its championship qualities have been recognised by the staging of the English Amateur strokeplay and British Boys' championships, events that enhanced the courses admirable and deserved reputation.

Nevertheless, one view from the course is of the swings and roundabouts of the amusement park, a reminder that Seaton Carew's attractions are not all confined to golf. All the same, Seaton Carew, founded in 1874 as the Durham and Yorkshire GC, is the oldest in either county and its seniority undoubtedly adds to its eminence.

The current course is one of 22 holes, a convenient method of giving members playing options rather than an attempt to set new fashions, although the Old Course at St Andrews started as 22 holes. Some prefer the old course which plays more or less out and back although with more variation in direction than on many seaside links but Frank Pennink's design of four new holes gave rise to the championship version of the course which makes it significantly more formidable.

An opening hole named "Rocket" calls to mind that Seaton Carew is very much in railway country but the tempo rises with the long 2nd and the short 3rd, which turns back towards the clubhouse. The short 6th also follows the line of the 3rd but the new 10th is the only hole that runs east, a timely signal that the flavour of the golf gains a piquant touch as it gets nearer to the sea.

The 10th is a straight par four but the dogleg 11th leads on to another fine par 4, aptly named "Beach" on account of its proximity to the fence guarding the shore. By now, the sea buckthorn has begun to dominate and the 13th and 14th, both par 5s, are flanked on the right by a hazard that is both statistically punishing and physically painful.

There is relief from it at the 208 yard 15th but there is no escaping the buckthorn on the last three holes which constitute quite a finish. It is particularly easy to become engulfed by it on the right of the 18th, a hole with an unusually contoured fairway but the most renowned hole is the 17th, its title of "Snag" carrying more than a hint of understatement.

It is the second shot, and more especially the distinctive green, which makes demands on our cunning although the drive can become entangled with the same central spine of hillocks encountered on the way out; and the drive can err a little too safely the other way. However, the correct angle for the second shot is essential to hold a green shaped like a scallop shell, bunkered all around and contoured ingeniously on several levels. It wouldn't do if all greens presented such problems but golf would be duller without its teasers and the 17th green at Seaton Carew is as notable an instrument of torture as man can devise.

Visitors: welcome at all times; at weekends please contact club beforehand for availability of starting times.
Green Fee: WD £16; WE £20
Societies: weekdays and most weekends.
Catering: lunches, bar meals and full à la carte.
Hotels: Bamburgh Castle; Links.

P69 Seaton Carew
☎(01429) 266249
Tees Rd, Seaton Carew, Hartlepool, Cleveland TS25 1DE
Off A178 3 miles S of Hartlepool.
Championship seaside links course.
Old, 18 holes, 6613 yards, S.S.S.72; Brabazon, 18 holes, 6855 yards, S.S.S.73
Designed by Duncan McCuaig.
Founded 1874
Visitors: on application to Hon Sec.
Green Fee: WD £26; WE £36
Societies: apply to Hon Sec.
Catering: full facilities.
Snooker.
Hotels: Seaton; Staincliffe Marine.

P70 Slaley Hall
☎(01434) 673350 (Club)
Slaley, Hexham, Northumberland NE47 0BY
Off A68 near Corbridge.
Mainly heathland course with lakes and woods.
18 holes, 7038 yards, S.S.S.73
Designed by Dave Thomas.
Founded 1989
Visitors: welcome with h/cap cert; bookings only.
Green Fee: £35.
Societies: welcome by prior appointment.
Catering: full facilities.
Practice ground, leisure complex.
Hotels: 145-bed hotel on site.

P71 South Moor
☎(01207) 232848 (Club), Pro 283525
The Middles, Craghead, Stanley, Co Durham DH9 6AG
2 miles from Stanley on B6313; 8 miles NW of Durham.
Moorland course.
18 holes, 6445 yards, S.S.S.71
Designed by Dr A. Mackenzie.
Founded 1923
Visitors: welcome but not before 9.30; only with member at weekends
Green Fee: WD £14 per round, £21 per day; WE £25.

Societies: welcome, not Sun.
Catering: lunches and evening meals served all week.
Snooker.
Hotels: Lumley Castle.

P72 South Shields
☎(0191) 456 0475 (Club), Office: 456 8942, Pro 456 0110
Cleadon Hills, South Shields, Tyne & Wear NE34 8EG
Near Cleadon Chimney, prominent landmark.
Seaside course.
18 holes, 6264 yards, S.S.S.70
Founded 1893
Visitors: welcome at all times.
Green Fee: WD £20; WE £25
Societies: by arrangement.
Catering: meals any time; bar 11am-11pm weekdays, 12am-2pm and 7pm-10.30pm Sun.
Hotels: New Crown.

P73 Stocksfield
☎(01661) 843041
New Ridley, Stocksfield, Northumberland NE43 7RE
On A695 Corbridge-Prudhoe.
Parkland/wooded course.
18 holes, 5978 yards, S.S.S.68
Designed by Frank Pennink.
Founded 1912
Visitors: welcome any time weekdays. Not Sat.
Green Fee: WD £10; WE £22
Societies: by arrangement.
Catering: Full service, meals by prior booking.
Hotels: Black Bull.

P74 Stressholme Golf Centre
☎(01325) 461002
Snipe Lane, Darlington, Co Durham DL2 2SA
About 8 miles N of Scotch Corner, 2 miles N of Darlington centre.
Municipal parkland course.
18 holes, 6432 yards, S.S.S.69
Founded 1976
Visitors: welcome, 8am-5.30pm.
Green Fee: WD £8.40; WE £10.
Societies: by arrangement with Darlington Dolphin Centre.
Catering: drinks, snacks, meals.

P75 Swarland Hall
☎(01670) 787010 (Sec), Office: 602016, Caterer: 787940
Coast View, Swarland, Morpeth, Northumberland NE65 9JG

In village of Swarland approx 1 mile W of A1 trunk road some 9 miles S of Alnwick.
Parkland course.
18 holes, 6628 yards, S.S.S.68
Founded 1993
Visitors: welcome
Green Fee: WD £12.50 per round, £17.50 per day; WE £20
Societies: welcome by prior arrangement.
Catering: bar, bar meals, dining room.
Hotels: Alnwick

P76 Teesside
☎(01642) 676249 (Club), Sec 616516, Pro 673822
Acklam Rd, Thornaby, Cleveland TS17 7JS
Off A19 take A1130 to Stockton, course 0.5 mile from A19 on right.
Meadowland course, flat and treelined.
18 holes, 6515 yards, S.S.S.71
Founded 1901
Visitors: welcome weekdays; weekends after 11am, unless with member.
Green Fee: WD £24; WE £28
Societies: weekdays. Packages for groups of more than 10.
Catering: full facilities
Hotels: Post House.

P77 Tynedale
☎(01434) 608154
Tyne Green, Hexham, Northumberland NE46 3HQ
From A69 take road into Hexham, turn right into Countryside Park, course 500 yards on S side of River Tyne.
Public parkland course.
9 holes, 5403 yards, S.S.S.67
Founded 1907
Visitors: welcome; Sun not before 11am.
Green Fee: on application.
Societies: welcome, advance bookings only.
Catering: full catering.
Hotels: Beaumont; County; Royal.

P78 Tynemouth
☎(0191) 257 4578, Pro 258 0728
Spital Dene, Tynemouth, North Shields, Tyne & Wear NE30 2ER
On A695.
Parkland course.
18 holes, 6403 yards, S.S.S.71
Designed by Willie Park.
Founded 1913

Visitors: welcome weekdays after 9.30am. Not Sat or before 12.30 on Sundays
Green Fee: £15 per round, £20 per day.
Societies: weekdays by prior arrangement.
Catering: lunches, teas and snacks served.
Hotels: Park.

P79 Tyneside
☎(0191) 413 2742 (Sec), Club 413 2177
Westfield Lane, Ryton, Tyne & Wear NE40 3QE
7 miles W of Newcastle upon Tyne on S side of River Tyne, on A695, turn N at Ryton down to Old Ryton village, turn left, past Cross Inn, and then right at end of row of old houses on right.
Parkland course.
18 holes, 6042 yards, S.S.S.69
Designed by H.S. Colt (1910).
Founded 1879
Visitors: welcome.
Green Fee: WD £20 per round, £25 per day; WE £30.
Societies: weekdays only by prior arrangement with Sec.
Catering: bar, tea/coffee, bar snacks, lunch, high tea, dinner (service 10.30am-9pm).
Hotels: Ryton Park Country House.

P80 Wallsend
☎(0191) 262 1973
Bigges Main, Wallsend-on-Tyne, Northumberland NE28 8SU
E of Newcastle on coast road to Whitley Bay.
Public parkland course.
18 holes, 6608 yards, S.S.S.72
Founded 1905
Visitors: no visitors before 10.30am weekends.
Green Fee: WD £11; WE £13.50.
Societies: on written request.
Catering: hot or cold snacks available.
Driving range.

P81 Warkworth
☎(01665) 711596
The Links, Warkworth, Morpeth, Northumberland NE65 0SW
Off A1068 to Warkworth, 10 miles N of Morpeth, 7 miles SE of Alnwick.
Seaside course.
9 holes, 5856 yards, S.S.S.68
Designed by Tom Morris.
Founded 1891

Visitors: welcome except Tues and Sat (competitions).
Green Fee: WD £12; WE £20.
Societies: apply to Sec.
Catering: by arrangement with Stewardess.
Hotels: Sun; Warkworth House.

P82 Washington Moat House
☎(0191) 402 9988
Stone Cellar Rd, High Usworth, District 12, Washington, Tyne & Wear NE37 1PH
A1M/A194M, well signposted.
Parkland course.
18 holes, 6204 yards, S.S.S.72
Founded 1990
Visitors: by appointment.
Green Fee: WD £17; WE £25.
Societies: welcome with prior appointment.
Catering: full facilities.
Driving range, Pitch & Putt, snooker.
Hotels: Washington Moat House.

P83 Wearside
☎(0191) 534 2518 (Club), Sec 534 2518, Pro 534 4269
Coxgreen, Sunderland, Tyne & Wear SR4 9JT
Take A183 going towards Chester-le-Street from A19, after 100 yards turn right at Coxgreen sign, left at small T-junction, follow road down hill to clubhouse, (2 mins from A19).
Meadowland/parkland course.
18 holes, 6373 yards, S.S.S.70
Founded 1892
Visitors: welcome except on competition days; unaccompanied visitors must show h/cap cert.
Green Fee: WD £25; WE £32
Societies: welcome on application to Sec.
Catering: full facilities, except Mon during winter.
Par 3 course and practice field.
Hotels: Seaburn.

P84 Westerhope
☎(0191) 286 9125 (Club), Sec/Bookings: 286 7636, Pro 286 0594
Whorlton Grange, Westerhope, Newcastle-upon-Tyne NE5 1PP
5 miles W of Newcastle; Airport Rd for 3 miles then follow signs to Westerhope.
Parkland course.
18 holes, 6444 yards, S.S.S.71
Designed by Alexander Sandy Herd.
Founded 1941

Visitors: Mon to Fri.
Green Fee: £16 per round, £22 per day.
Societies: catered for Mon to Fri. Apply in advance.
Catering: available.
Hotels: Stakis; Novotel (Newcastle-upon-Tyne).

P85 Whickham
☎(091) 488 7309 (Club), Sec/Manager: 488 1576
Hollinside Park, Whickham, Newcastle-upon-Tyne NE16 5BA
5 miles W of Newcastle.
Undulating parkland course.
18 holes, 5878 yards, S.S.S.68
Founded 1911
Visitors: unrestricted weekdays, by arrangement weekends.
Green Fee: WD £20; WE £25
Societies: weekdays only.
Catering: snacks, cooked meals by arrangement.
Snooker.
Hotels: Gibside (Whickham).

P86 Whitburn
☎(0191) 529 2144, Pro 529 4210, Sec 529 4944
Lizard Lane, South Shields, Tyne & Wear NE34 7AF
Half-way between Sunderland and South Shields off coast road.
Parkland course.
18 holes, 5780 yards, S.S.S.68
Founded 1932
Visitors: welcome weekdays after 9.30am (restricted Tues); at weekends phone Pro beforehand.
Green Fee: WD £17.50; WE £22.50.
Societies: weekdays except Tues. Discounts for groups of 11 or more players.
Catering: full facilities.
Hotels: Seaburn; Roker.

P87 Whitley Bay
☎(0191) 252 0180, Pro 252 5688
Claremont Rd, Whitley Bay, Tyne & Wear NE26 3UF
On A183, 10 miles NE of Newcastle; at N end of town.
Links/parkland course.
18 holes, 6500 yards, S.S.S.72
Founded 1890
Visitors: welcome
Green Fee: WD £20; WE £30.
Societies: weekdays by arrangement.
Catering: full bar and restaurant facilities except Mon.
Hotels: Windsor.

P88 **Wilton**

☎(01642) 465265 (Sec), Members: 454626, Pro 454730
Wilton, Redcar, Cleveland TS10 4QY
8 miles E of Middlesborough and 4 miles W of Redcar on A174; follow signs to Wilton Castle.
Parkland course.
18 holes, 6145 yards, S.S.S.69
Founded 1952
Visitors: welcome after 10am; no visitors Sat.
Green Fee: WD £18; WE £24.
Societies: Mon, Wed, Fri, occasional Thurs and Sun, by arrangement with Sec.
Catering: bars, dining area.
Practice ground, snooker.
Hotels: Park (Redcar); Post House (Thornaby); Wilton Castle.

P89 **Woodham G & CC**

☎(01325) 318346, Pro 315257, Restaurant: 301551
Burnhill Way, Newton Aycliffe, Durham DL5 4PN
2 miles A1(M), 1 mile N of Newton Aycliffe.

Parkland course with lakes.
18 holes, 6771 yards, S.S.S.72
Designed by J. Hamilton Stutt.
Founded 1983
Visitors: unlimited weekdays, by appointment weekends.
Green Fee: WD £18 per round, £24 per day; WE £24.
Societies: by appointment.
Catering: a la carte restaurant
Hotels: Redworth Hall; Eden Arms.

P90 **Wooler**

☎(01668) 281137
Dod Law, Doddington, Wooler, Northumberland NE71 6EA
Signposted from B6525 Wooler-Berwick road.
Moorland course with heather and bracken and panoramic views.
9 holes (18 tees), 6372 yards, S.S.S.70
Designed by club members.
Founded 1970 (present course 1976)
Visitors: welcome.
Green Fee: WD £10; WE £15.
Societies: by prior arrangement; apply to Sec

Catering: bar every night in the summer between 8-11pm; catering by arrangement May-Sept.
Hotels: Ryecroft; Tankerville Arms; Black Bull; Anchor Inn; Wheatsheaf; Loretto Guest House; St Leonards Bed & Breakfast.

P91 **Wynyard (The Wellington)**

☎(01740) 644555
Wynyard Park, Salthouses, Billingham TS22 5NQ
Between A1 and A19. Take A689 from both roads to Wynyard Park
Parkland course with mature woodlands on front 9 and lakes a feature on back 9
Designed by Hawtree & Son
Founded 1996
Visitors: restricted to members' guests.
Societies: Corporate days will be available
Catering: Full facilities, bar and restaurant
Driving range, practice facility, academy area.

Q
LOTHIAN, BORDERS, DUMFRIES & GALLOWAY

This is an area embracing the south-west of Scotland, the Borders (more famous for rugby than golf), and the part of central Scotland which incorporates East Lothian, one of the oldest and most famous regions in the expanding world of golf.

Until Muirfield was opened in 1892, Musselburgh was a regular home of the Open championship between 1874 and 1889 while North Berwick staged a number of challenge matches that are part of the game's folklore.

Today, you could stay for a week and play a different East Lothian course of championship standard, each day without having to drive for more than twenty minutes. The old Musselburgh course, now enveloped by Edinburgh racecourse, is the place to start on historical grounds although Royal Musselburgh has a more sheltered parkland home a mile or two down the road to North Berwick which bristles with golfing retreats.

Longniddry, and the shorter Kilspindie at Aberlady, provide contrasting pleasures but the true heart of East Lothian lies around Gullane Hill and the incomparable stretch of natural terrain that houses Gullane Nos 1, 2 and 3, and Luffness New which celebrated its centenary in 1994. From a distance, they are indistinguishable the one from the other, green ribbons of fairway lined by taller grass running down to the edge of Aberlady Bay – a bird sanctuary and nature reserve that profits rather than suffers from its proximity to golf.

Luffness is enchanting, neither stern nor straightforward, with magnificently true, small greens, but Gullane Hill is a dominant feature of all three Gullane courses, hiding the road from the holes bordering the Firth of Forth and a series of resplendent views. Everyone has courses for which he feels strong affection and Luffness and Gullane are two undoubted favourites of mine.

The incomparable stretch of country on which they stand was introduced to me by a kind cousin during my time at school in Edinburgh when a day's golf really was an escape but, apart from the greens, my memories are of a blind short hole across a quarry – long since abandoned – and a magnificent lunch.

On the other side of Gullane Hill lies Muirfield, the third home of the Honourable Company of Edinburgh Golfers and invariably placed top in polls on British courses. It has no enemies, a noble combination of ancient and modern. North Berwick, on the other hand, has changed very little over the years. One newcomer to join the old, established courses, is Whitekirk, close to North Berwick and the A1. The last of the coastal courses is Dunbar which, too, has many admirers.

As well as East Lothian, there are Midlothian and West Lothian which, though full of good courses, are less remarkable. Boyhood memories compel me to single out Bruntsfield, Dalmahoy and the Royal Burgess at Barnton, a mile or two from the Forth Bridge.

The Border country has several nine hole courses in scenic settings and two or three of grander dimensions. However, the county of Dumfries & Galloway deserves greater recognition than it invariably receives, particularly the countryside fringing the Solway Firth. Southerness is the flagship, a championship test which Mackenzie Ross designed and built when he was resurrecting Turnberry after the war, and where heather and gorse put a heavy onus on fine driving.

Other recommendations must include Powfoot, Thornhill, and working a path westward, the courses at Wigtownshire County, Stranraer and last but not least, Portpatrick (Dunskey).

Q1 Baberton

☎(0131) 453 4911 (Sec), Pro 453 3555
Baberton Ave, Juniper Green, Edinburgh EH14 5DU
5 miles W of Edinburgh on A70 Lanark road.
Parkland course.
18 holes, 6098 yards, S.S.S.69
Designed by Willie Park.
Founded 1893
Visitors: on introduction by a member during weekdays.
Green Fee: £18 per round, £25 per day.
Societies: Mon-Fri only by arrangement with Sec.
Catering: full facilities.

Q2 Bathgate

☎(01506) 52232 (Club), Pro 630553, Sec 630505, Fax 636775
Edinburgh Rd, Bathgate, W Lothian EH48 1BA
400 yards E from Bathgate town centre.
Parkland course.
18 holes, 6250 yards, S.S.S.70
Designed by Willie Park.
Founded 1892
Visitors: unrestricted weekdays, limited at weekends.
Green Fee: WD £15 per round, £20 per day; WE £30.
Societies: welcome by prior arrangement with Sec.
Catering: coffee, lunch, high tea available.
Hotels: Golden Circle; Fairway.

Q3 Braid Hills

☎(0131) 452 9408, Sec 445 2044, Starter: 447 6666
Braid Hills Approach Rd, Edinburgh EH10 6JY
A702 from city centre S.
Public hillside courses with panoramic views.
18 holes, 5731 yards, S.S.S.68; 18 holes, 4832 yards, S.S.S.64
Founded 1897
Visitors: unrestricted.
Green Fee: £7.40
Societies: by prior arrangement.
Catering: by prior arrangement.
Hotels: Braid Hills.

Q4 Broomieknowe

☎(0131) 663 9317
36 Golf Course Rd, Bonnyrigg, Midlothian EH19 2HZ
About 0.5 mile into Bonnyrigg from Eskbank Rd roundabout on A7.
Gently undulating parkland course.
18 holes, 6150 yards, S.S.S.69
Designed by James Braid; alterations by Hawtree and Son.
Founded 1906
Visitors: welcome but no weekend party bookings.
Green Fee: WD £17 per round, £25 per day; WE £25

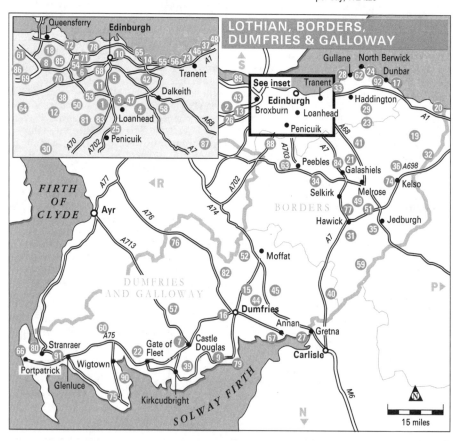

Societies: Mon-Fri.
Catering: bar lunches served, evening meals by arrangement with Steward.
Hotels: Dalhousie Castle; County; Waverley.

Q5 Bruntsfield Links

☎(0131) 336 1479 Sec, Club 336 2006, Pro 336 4050
32 Barnton Ave, Davidsons Mains, Edinburgh EH4 6JH
Off A90 in Davidsons Mains 2 to 3 miles W of Edinburgh city centre.
Parkland course.
18 holes, 6407 yards, S.S.S.71
Designed by Willie Park.
Founded 1761
Visitors: welcome weekdays by appointment.
Green Fee: WD £35 per round, £45 per day; WE £40 per round, £50 per day
Societies: by appointment.
Catering: luncheon daily, evening meals during playing season. Tues & Thurs limited service.
Hotels: Barnton; Capital Moat House.

Q6 Carrickknowe

☎(0131) 337 1096
Glendevon Park, Edinburgh EH12 5VZ
Opposite the Post House Hotel, down Balgreen Rd.
Public meadowland course.
18 holes, 6299 yards, S.S.S.70
Founded 1933
Visitors: welcome.
Green Fee: £7.40
Societies: by arrangement.
Catering: by arrangement with Sec.
Hotels: Post House, Capital Moat House; Murrayfield.

Q7 Castle Douglas

☎(01556) 502801, Sec 502099
Abercromby Rd, Castle Douglas, Kirkcudbrightshire
400 yards on Ayr road A713 from town clock.
Parkland course.
9 holes, 5408 yards, S.S.S.66
Visitors: welcome.
Green Fee: £12.
Societies: welcome.
Catering: bar facilities during summer months.
Hotels: Imperial; Douglas Arms; Kings Arms.

Q8 Cogarburn

☎(0131) 333 4718 (Starter), Club 333 4110
Hanley Lodge, Newbridge, Midlothian EH28 8NN
Westbound A8 Glasgow road, turn sharp left at commencement of airport slip road, left again at T-junction.
Parkland course.
12 holes, 5045 yards, S.S.S.65
Founded 1975
Visitors: welcome, not after 5pm.
Green Fee: £7 per round.
Societies: by arrangement with Sec.
Catering: usually available; licensed but limited facilities.
Pool table.
Hotels: Barnton; Royal Scot.

Q9 Colvend

☎(01556) 663398, Sec 610878
Sandyhills, by Dalbeattie, Kirkcubrightshire DG5 4PY
6 miles from Dalbeattie on A710 Solway coast road.
Undulating meadowland course.
9 holes, 4644 yards, S.S.S.63

Designed by Willie Fernie (Troon) 1905; extended 1982 with advice from Dave Thomas.
Founded 1905
Visitors: welcome; course closed April-Sept at 2pm Tues, 5.30pm Thurs, Sun comp days, Sat am juniors day.
Green Fee: £12day; under 18 half-price except Sat and Sun.
Societies: apply to Sec.
Catering: April-Oct full lunch and dinner facilities; winter restricted to weekends.
Hotels: Clonyard House, Craig Barons.

Q10 Craigentinny

☎(0131) 554 7501 (Starter), Club 657 4815
143 Craigentinny Ave, Edinburgh, Scotland
1 mile from Meadowbank Stadium, 2.5 miles E of city centre.
Public links course.
18 holes, 5413 yards, S.S.S.66
Founded 1891
Visitors: welcome bookings taken 24 hrs in advance.
Green Fee: £7.70
Societies: welcome by appointment.
Catering: On request

Q11 Craigmillar Park

☎(0131) 667 2837 (Club), Office: 667 0047
1 Observatory Rd, Edinburgh EH9 3HG
Approx 3 miles from city centre close to Royal Observatory, Blackford Hill.
Parkland course.
18 holes, 5859 yards, S.S.S.68
Designed by James Braid.
Founded 1895

Visitors: non-introduced visitors must produce h/cap cert, letter of intro or proof of club membership; off first tee by 3.30pm weekdays; by request at weekends or Bank Holidays.
Green Fee: WD £17 per round, £25 per day; WE on request only
Societies: on application.
Catering: bar lunches, high teas on request.
Hotels: Suffolk

Q12 Dalmahoy
☎(0131) 333 4105, Fax 335 3203
Kirknewton, Midlothian EH27 8EB
7 miles W of Edinburgh city centre on A71.
Rolling parkland course.
East, 18 holes, 6677 yards, S.S.S.72; West, 18 holes, 5185 yards, S.S.S.66
Designed by James Braid.
Founded 1922
Visitors: welcome weekdays, weekends by application. H/cap cert needed (21 and below)
Green Fee: East WD £39; West WD £24.
Societies: welcome weekdays by arrangement.
Catering: extensive facilities in country club.
Tennis, squash, swimming pool, snooker, health and beauty facilities.
Hotels: Dalmahoy; golf and leisure breaks available.

Q13 Deer Park Golf & Country Club
☎(01506) 431037, Fax 435608
Golf Course Rd, Knightsbridge, Livingston, W Lothian EH54 8PG
Leave M8 at junction 3, Livingston interchange, follow signposts to Knightsbridge, club signposted from there.
Parkland course.
18 holes, 6688 yards, S.S.S.72
Designed by Charles Lawrie.
Founded 1978
Visitors: welcome 7 days.Restrictions Sat & Sun
Green Fee: WD £16; WE £26.
Societies: welcome 7 days.
Catering: full facilities available 7 days a week.
Swimming pool, squash, snooker, pool, 10-pin bowling, saunas etc.
Hotels: Hilton; Houston House.

Q14 Duddingston
☎(0131) 661 7688, Pro 661 4301
Duddingston Rd, W Edinburgh EH15 3QD

3 miles from city centre E of A1.
Parkland course.
18 holes, 6420 yards, S.S.S.72
Founded 1895
Visitors: Mon-Fri only.
Green Fee: £22 per round, £32 per day.
Societies: Tues, Thurs only; £19 per round, £20 per day.
Catering: lunches, high teas, bar every day.
Hotels: Lady Nairne; King's Manor.

Q15 Dumfries & County
☎(01387) 253585
Edinburgh Rd, Dumfries DG1 1JX
1 mile N of Dumfries town centre on A701.
Parkland course.
18 holes, 5928 yards, S.S.S.68
Designed by Willie Fernie.
Founded 1912
Visitors: welcome except Sat in summer, restrictions Sun and comp days.
Green Fee: WD £21; WE £26.
Societies: apply to Sec.
Catering: full facilities every day.
Hotels: Station; Moreig; Cairndale; Embassy.

Q16 Dumfries & Galloway
☎(01387) 253582, Sec 263848, Pro 256902
Laurieston Ave, Dumfries DG2 7NY
On A75 W of Dumfries.
Parkland course.
18 holes, 5803 yards, S.S.S.68
Founded 1880
Visitors: welcome without reservation except competition days but booking essential at weekends in summer
Green Fee: WD £21; WE £25
Societies: catered for.
Catering: full facilities available except Mon.
Hotels: Cairndale, Station.

Q17 Dunbar
☎(01368) 862317
East Links, Dunbar EH42 1LT
0.5 mile from Dunbar centre.
Seaside course.
18 holes, 6426 yards, S.S.S.71
Founded 1794
Visitors: unrestricted except Thurs.
Green Fee: WD £30; WE £40.
Societies: by arrangement with Sec in writing.
Catering: full facilities 7 days.
Hotels: Battleblent; Hillside; Goldenstones.

Q18 Dundas Park
☎(0131) 331 5603
3 Loch Place, South Queensferry, W Lothian EH30 9NG
1 mile S of Queensferry, on right of A8000.
Parkland course (good practice course).
9 holes, 6024 yards, S.S.S.69
Founded 1957
Visitors: with member only.
Green Fee: apply for details.
Societies: welcome, written request to Sec.
Catering: self-catering snacks in clubhouse.

Q19 Duns
☎(01361) 882717 (Sec)
Hardens Rd, Duns, Berwicks TD11 3HN
1 mile W of Duns off A6105.
Undulating meadowland course.
9 holes, 5864 yards, S.S.S.68
Founded 1894
Visitors: unrestricted except on comp days and before 3pm Mon, Tues, Wed
Green Fee: £10.
Societies: welcome if previously arranged with Sec.
Catering: limited bar facilities, mainly at weekends.
Hotels: Barniken House; Freedom of the Fairways package from Scottish Borders Tourist Board.

Q20 Eyemouth
☎(01890) 750551
Gunsgreen House, Eyemouth TD14 5DY
2.5 miles E of Burmouth, off A1, signposted on A1107.
Seaside course.
9 holes, 5446 yards, S.S.S.66
Founded 1884
Visitors: unrestricted weekdays, after 10.30am Sat. No on Sundays. Construction work could lead to restrictions. Contact sec.
Green Fee: £10.
Societies: by arrangement.
Catering: bar open evenings and lunchtime weekends.
Snooker, pool.
Hotels: Home Arms; Contented Sole; Ship; Whale.

Q21 Galashiels
☎(01896) 753724 (Club), Sec 755307
Ladhope Recreation Ground, Galashiels, Selkirkshire TD1 2NJ

At N end of town off A7.
Hilly course.
18 holes, 5309 yards, S.S.S.67
Designed by James Braid.
Founded 1884
Visitors: weekends by arrangement.
Green Fee: WD £10 per round, £14 per day; WE £14 per round, £18 per day.
Societies: welcome by arrangement.
Catering: by arrangement only via Sec.
Pool table.
Hotels: Kingsknowes; Kings; Abbotsford Arms.

Q22 Gatehouse
☎(01557) 814459
Laurieston Rd, Gatehouse-of-Fleet
Turn right at War Memorial on entering town from E.
Public, undulating course with gorse in places.
9 holes, 4800 yards, S.S.S.63
Founded 1921
Visitors: welcome any time.
Green Fee: WD £10; WE £15
Societies: apply to Sec.
Catering: Masonic Arms provides catering
Hotels: Anworth; Murray Arms.

Q23 Gifford
☎(01620) 810267, Club 810591
c/o Sec, Calroust, Tweddale Ave, Gifford, E Lothian, EH41 4QN
4.5 miles S of Haddington off A6137.
Meadowland/woodland course.
9 holes, 6101 yards, S.S.S.69
Designed by Willie Wood.
Founded 1904
Visitors: welcome, except Tues and Wed from 4pm or Sat and Sun from 12 noon.
Green Fee: £10.
Hotels: Goblin Ha'; Tweddale Arms.

Q24 Glen
☎(01620) 895288
East Links, Tantallon Terrace, North Berwick EH39 4LE
22 miles NE of Edinburgh on A198, follow road along E beach, clubhouse is last building on right.

Seaside/parkland course.
18 holes, 6089 yards, S.S.S.69
Designed by Mackenzie Ross.
Founded 1906
Visitors: no restrictions.
Green Fee: WD £15.50 per round, £22 per day: WE £20 per round, £28 per day.
Societies: welcome at all times, advance booking recommended.
Catering: bar lunches, high teas, coffee.
Hotels: Blenheim House; Fairways; Nether Abbey.

Q25 Glencorse
☎(01968) 677189
Milton Bridge, Pencuik, Midlothian EH26 0RD
On A701, 9 miles S of Edinburgh.
Parkland course, burns on 10 holes.
18 holes, 5205 yards, S.S.S.66
Designed by Willie Park Jnr.
Founded 1890
Visitors: welcome most weekdays and weekends if no competitions.
Green Fee: apply for details.
Societies: most weekdays.
Catering: full facilities.
Hotels: Inveravon House (Loanhead); Original, Royal (Roslin).

Q26 Greenburn
☎(01501) 770292
6 Greenburn Rd, Fauldhouse, W Lothian EH47 9HG
Midway between Edinburgh and Glasgow, off M8 at Whitburn, 3 miles.
Moorland course.
18 holes, 6210 yards, S.S.S.70
Founded 1953
Visitors: weekdays.
Green Fee: on application.
Societies: by prior booking.
Catering: weekends and midweek when societies are booked in.
Hotels: Hillcroft (Whitburn).

Q27 Gretna
☎(01461) 338464
`Kirtle View', Gretna, Dumfriesshire DG16 5HD
0.5 mile W of Gretna on S side of A75, 1 mile from M74/A75 junction.

Parkland course.
9 holes, 3214 yards, S.S.S.71
Designed by Nigel Williams. Bothwell
Founded 1991
Visitors: welcome 7 days, no restrictions unless competition being played.
Green Fee: WD £8; WE £10, 9 holes £5.
Societies: welcome by prior arrangement, terms on application.
Catering: bar meals and refreshments available at most times.
Driving range.
Hotels: 7 recommended hotels within 1 mile.

Q28 Gullane
☎(01620) 842255, Fax 842327
Gullane, East Lothian EH31 2BB
Off A1, on A198 to Gullane.
Links courses.
No. 1, 18 holes, 6466 yards, S.S.S.71; No. 2, 18 holes, 6244 yards, S.S.S.70; No. 3, 18 holes, 5166 yards, S.S.S.65
Founded 1882
Visitors: welcome on No. 1 course Mon-Fri with h/cap cert and on Nos 2 & 3 at all times.
Green Fee: WD No. 1 course £24, No2 £21, No3 £12.50; WE No1 £53.50, No2 £26.50, No3 £16.
Societies: welcome by prior arrangement (except No. 1 at weekends).
Catering: bar meals any day, dining room lunches daily except Mon; dinners by arrangement.
Hotels: Golf Inn; Mallard; Queens.

Q29 Haddington
☎(01620) 823627, Pro 822727, Fax 826580
Amisfield Park, Whittinghame Dr, Haddington, E Lothian EH41 4PT
17 miles E of Edinburgh on A1, cross Victoria Bridge on E edge of town, golf course is 500 yards on left.
Parkland course.
18 holes, 6280 yards, S.S.S.70
Founded 1865
Visitors: welcome with pre-booking, Sat and Sun 10am-12moom, 2pm-4pm.

Green Fee: WD £15 per round, £23 per day; WE £20 per round, £27 per day.
Societies: welcome by prior arrangement.
Catering: lunches, bar snacks, bar meals, high tea.
Hotels: Mercat; Railway; Browns; Maitland Field House.

Q30 Harburn

☎(01506) 871131 (Sec), Members: 871256, Pro 871582
West Calder, West Lothian EH55 8RS
Turn S at West Calder off A71 Kilmarnock-Edinburgh road.
Parkland course.
18 holes, 5921 yards, S.S.S.68
Founded 1933
Visitors: welcome except on comp days
Green Fee: WD£16 per round, £21 per day; Fridays £19 per round, £26 per day; WE £21 per round, £32 per day.
Societies: welcome by prior arrangement.
Catering: bar snacks; full facilities by arrangement.
Hotels: Livingstone National; Dalmahoy CC.

Q31 Hawick

☎(01450) 372293 (Club), Sec 375594
Vertish Hill, Hawick, Roxburgh TD9 0NY
SE of Edinburgh on A7.
Parkland course.
18 holes, 5929 yards, S.S.S.69
Founded 1877
Visitors: welcome, phone to arrange, not Sat. Restricted to one round per day at weekends
Green Fee: WD £15 per round, £22 per day; WE £22.
Societies: telephone Sec to arrange, limited to 24 players, one round only on Sun.
Catering: full facilities.
Hotels: Kirklands; Elm House; Mansfield Park.

Q32 Hirsel

☎(01890) 882678
Kelso Rd, Coldstream, Berwickshire TS12 4LG
W end of Coldstream on A697, Edinburgh-Newcastle road.
Parkland course.
18 holes, 6092 yards, S.S.S.69
Founded 1948

Visitors: any time.
Green Fee: on application.
Societies: by arrangement.
Catering: Apr-Sept or by arrangement.
Hotels: Tillmouth Park; Newcastle Arms.

Q33 Honourable Company of Edinburgh Golfers

☎(01620) 842123
Muirfield, Gullane, East Lothian EH31 2EG
Last road on left leaving Gullane for North Berwick on A198, approx 18 miles from Edinburgh.
Links course.
Medal, 18 holes, 6941 yards, S.S.S.73
Designed by Tom Morris.
Founded 1744
Visitors: Tues and Thurs; must be members of recognised golf club and have h/cap of 18 or better if gentlemen, 24 if Ladies.
Green Fee: WD £53 per round, £77 per day.
Societies: no reduced rates or packages; same as for visitors.Max 12. Tues/Thurs only.
Catering: morning coffee (50p) lunch (£12), afternoon tea (£1); there are limited changing facilities for Ladies, but they are not allowed to eat in the Clubhouse.
Hotels: Greywalls; Open Arms (Dirleton).

Q34 Innerleithen

☎(01896) 830951, Sec 830071
Leithen Water, Leithen Road, Innerleithen EH44 6NL
1 mile from Innerleithen on Heriot road.
Heathland course.
9 holes, 5984 yards, S.S.S.69
Designed by Willie Park.
Founded 1886
Visitors: no restrictions except Medal days.
Green Fee: on application.
Societies: by arrangement.
Catering: by arrangement.

Q35 Jedburgh

☎(01835) 863587, Sec 864175
Dunion Rd, Jedburgh, Roxburghshire TD8 6DQ
0.75 mile W of Jedburgh.
Undulating parkland course.
9 holes, 5555 yards, S.S.S.67
Founded 1892

Visitors: welcome except competition days at weekends. Adviseable to book
Green Fee: £12.
Societies: booked at least 2 weeks in advance.
Catering: bar facilities and meals available April-Oct.
Hotels: Royal; Jedforest.

Q36 Kelso

☎(01573) 223009, Sec 223259.
Racecourse Rd, Kelso, Roxburgh TD5 7SL
1 mile N of Kelso town centre, golf course is within National Hunt Racecourse.
Flat parkland course.
18 holes, 6066 yards, S.S.S.69
Designed by James Braid.
Founded 1887
Visitors: welcome.
Green Fee: WD £12 per round, £20 per day; WE £18 per day, £27 per round
Societies: by arrangement.
Catering: available except Mon and Tues; societies on these days by prior arrangement.
Hotels: Cross Keys, Queens Head

Q37 Kilspindie

☎(01875) 835216
Aberlady, East Lothian EH32 0QD
Immediately E of Aberlady village, private road to left leading to club.
Seaside course.
18 holes, 5410 yards, S.S.S.66
Designed by Ross & Sayers, extended by Willie Park.
Founded 1867
Visitors: welcome subject to members' demands; advisable to enquire in advance.
Green Fee: apply for details.
Societies: welcome weekdays if booked in advance.
Catering: full facilities available except Fri.
Hotels: Kilspindie House (Aberlady).

Q38 Kingsknowe

☎(0131) 441 4030 (Pro), Sec 441 1145
326 Lanark Rd, Edinburgh EH14 2JD
W of Edinburgh on A71.
Parkland course.
18 holes, 5979 yards, S.S.S.69
Designed by Alex Herd, James Braid, J.C. Stutt.
Founded 1908
Visitors: welcome weekdays.
Green Fee: WD £15; WE £25.

Societies: welcome weekdays on application to Sec.
Catering: bar, lunch, high tea except Mon.
Snooker.
Hotels: Capital Moat House; Orwell Lodge.

Q39 Kirkcudbright
☎(01557) 330314
Stirling Crescent, Kirkcudbright DG6 4EZ
Turn left off A75 into town from Castle Douglas.
Hilly parkland course.
18 holes, 5876 yards, S.S.S.67
Founded 1893
Visitors: welcome except on competition days.H/cap cert needed, advance booking advised.
Green Fee: £15 per round, £20 per day
Societies: welcome by prior arrangement.
Catering: available.
Hotels: Arden House; Royal; Selkirk.

Q40 Langholm
☎(013873) 80265 (Enquiries), Sec 80673
Whitaside, Langholm, Dumfriesshire DG13 0MN
Between Carlisle and Hawick on A7, 400 yards E of Market Place.
Hillside course.
9 holes, 5744 yards, S.S.S.68
Founded 1892
Visitors: welcome weekdays and weekends except competitions.
Green Fee: £10
Societies: apply to Sec.
Catering: can be arranged; telephone for details.
Hotels: Eskdale

Q41 Lauder
☎(01578) 722526
Galashiels Rd, Lauder, Berwickshire
Off A68, 0.5 mile from Lauder.
Undulating course.
9 holes, 6002 yards, S.S.S.70
Designed by W. Park of Musselburgh.
Founded 1896
Visitors: welcome.
Green Fee: apply for details.
Societies: book in advance.

Q42 Liberton
☎(0131) 664 3009 (Sec), Club 664 8580, Pro 664 1056
297 Gilmerton Rd, Edinburgh EH16 5UJ

S of Edinburgh on A7.
Parkland course.
18 holes, 5299 yards, S.S.S.66
Founded 1920
Visitors: welcome except before 12 noon Sat/Sun
Green Fee: WD £15; WE £25.
Societies: welcome weekdays.
Catering: full facilities available.
Hotels: Royal Scot, Caledonian, Old Waverley, Balmoral

Q43 Linlithgow
☎(01506) 842585 (Sec), Club 671044, Pro 844356
Braehead, Linlithgow, W Lothian EH49 6QF
Approx 10 miles from Edinburgh on M9; proceed W along High Street, turn left at Preston Road (opposite Black Bitch pub), signposted.
Undulating parkland course.
18 holes, 5729 yards, S.S.S.68
Designed by Robert Simpson of Carnoustie.
Founded 1913
Visitors: welcome except Sat & comp days
Green Fee: WD £12: WE £18.
Societies: by arrangement with Sec.
Catering: curtailed during winter months, every day except Tues during season.
Hotels: Star & Garter; West Port.

Q44 Lochmaben
☎(01387) 810552
Castlehill Gate, Lochmaben, Dumfries DG11 1NT
On A709 between Dumfries and Lockerbie.
Undulating parkland course.
9 holes, 5357 yards, S.S.S.66
Designed by James Braid.
Founded 1926
Visitors: welcome except competition days.
Green Fee: WD £14 per round, £16 per day; WE £16 per day, £20 per day.
Societies: catered for on weekdays.
Catering: by arrangement for meetings.
Fishing, sailing.

Q45 Lockerbie
☎(01576) 202462
Corrie Rd, Lockerbie, Dumfriesshire DG11 2ND
A74 to Lockerbie, take Langholm road, turn left at T-junction towards Corrie, club 0.25 mile on right; signposted from town centre.

Parkland course.
18 holes, 5614 yards, S.S.S.66
Designed by James Braid (original 9).
Founded 1889
Visitors: welcome, pre-booking available. Restrictions on Sun
Green Fee: WD£12 per round, £18 per day; Sat £22; Sun £16.
Societies: by arrangement; weekday package for groups.
Catering: full bar and catering service during summer.
Hotels: Queens; Kings Arms.

Q46 Longniddry
☎(01875) 852141, Starter: 852228
Links Rd, Longniddry, E Lothian EH32 0NL
A1 from Edinburgh, at Wallyford roundabout take A198, turn left at Longniddry down Links Rd.
Links/parkland course.
18 holes, 6219 yards, S.S.S.70
Designed by Harry Colt.
Founded 1921
Visitors: welcome excluding weekends, competition days and public holidays, unless accompanied by a member; phone starter. H/cap cert required
Green Fee: WD £25 per round, £35 per day; WE £35.
Societies: Mon to Thurs.
Catering: dining room excluding Fri, bar service, snacks available.
Hotels: Marine (N Berwick); Kilspindie House (Aberlady); Golf Inn.

Q47 Lothianburn
☎(0131) 445 2206 (Club), Sec 445 5067, Pro 445 2288
106 Biggar Rd, Edinburgh EH10 7DU
S boundary of Edinburgh, adjacent to Edinburgh by-pass.
Panoramic hillside course.
18 holes, 5750 yards, S.S.S.69
Designed by James Braid.
Founded 1893
Visitors: welcome weekdays but not before 10 am Sat or Sun. Not on comp days
Green Fee: WD £12; WE £18.
Societies: welcome by arrangement with Sec on weekdays.
Catering: lunch, bar meals, high tea; dinners by prior arrangement (not Wed).
Hotels: Braid Hills.

Q48 Luffness New
☎(01620) 843114, Clubmaster: 843376, Sec 843336, Fax 842933
Aberlady, E Lothian EH32 0QA

You're guaranteed the friendliest welcome at Minto Golf Club
(Winner of Scottish Borders Tourist Board – Friendliest Welcome Award 1994)
Minto Golf Club invites you to its beautiful, 18-hole, parkland course (5,568yds).
Enjoy the panoramic views over the Teviot Valley & then curl-up with a drink or
meal in the clubhouse. Local accommodation & hotels are readily available in the
village of Denholm, Hawick 'the home of cashmere'& Jedburgh.

Minto Golf Club,
Minto, Hawick, TD9 8SH
Tel: **0145087 220**

1 mile outside Aberlady on the Gullane road, A198.
Links course.
18 holes, 6123 yards, S.S.S.69
Designed by Tom Morris (1894).
Founded 1894
Visitors: Mon to Fri only, except public and Bank Holidays; introduction by member or by own club Sec, h/caps to 24, ladies after 10am, jackets and ties obligatory in club rooms.
Green Fee: £27 per round, £40 per day.
Societies: welcome midweek by prior arrangement; no special terms.
Catering: smoke room, dining room, coffee, lunch (2/3 course) daily, no snacks, high tea/dinner (min 10) by arrangement.
Practice gound, 5-hole course.
Hotels: Marine(N Berwick); Golf, Greywalls (Gullane).

Q49 **Melrose**
☎(01896) 822855, Sec 822391.
Dingleton, Melrose, Roxburghshire
Off A68 Carlisle-Edinburgh road, 0.5 mile S of Melrose.
Parkland course.
9 holes, 5579 yards, S.S.S.68
Founded 1880
Visitors: Restrictions on Sat and Sun in summer; ladies day on Tues.
Green Fee: £15
Societies: by arrangement.
Catering: snacks available; by arrangement for parties.
Pool.

Q50 **Merchants of Edinburgh**
☎(0131) 447 1219
10 Craighill Gardens, Edinburgh EH10 5PY
S side of Edinburgh off A701.
Hilly parkland course.
18 holes, 4889 yards, S.S.S.64
Founded 1907
Visitors: weekdays before 4pm.
Green Fee: £15
Societies: welcome on weekdays by arrangement with Sec.
Catering: full service
Hotels: Braid Hills.

Q51 **Minto**
☎(01450) 870220
Minto Village, by Denholm, Hawick, Roxburghshire TD 9 8SH
5 miles NE of Hawick off A698, turn left in Denholm for Minto.
Parkland course.
18 holes, 5460 yards, S.S.S.68
Founded 1926
Visitors: welcome most days, phone at weekends.
Green Fee: WD £15 per round, £20 per day; WE £25 per round, £30 per day.
Societies: by arrangement.
Catering: full catering and bar facilities available, except limited catering on Thurs.
Hotels: Elm House; Kirklands.

Q52 **Moffat**
☎(01683) 220020
Coatshill, Moffat, DG10 9SB
On A701 between Moffat and Beattock, 1 mile off A74.
Moorland course.
18 holes, 5218 yards, S.S.S.66
Designed by Ben Sayers.
Founded 1884
Visitors: welcome; not Wed pm.
Green Fee: WD £17.50; WE £25.50.
Societies: welcome by prior arrangement except Wed.
Catering: bar, bar lunches, coffee daily.

Q53 **Mortonhall**
☎(0131) 447 6974 (Sec).
231 Braid Rd, Edinburgh EH10 6PB
2 miles S of city centre on A702, situated on S of Braid Hills.
Moorland course.
18 holes, 6557 yards, S.S.S.71
Designed by James Braid & Fred Hawtree.
Founded 1892
Visitors: welcome by prior arrangement.
Green Fee: WD 23 per round, £28 per day; WE £28 per round, £38 per day.
Societies: welcome weekdays by arrangement.
Catering: bar and catering facilities.
Hotels: Braid Hills.

Q54 **Murrayfield**
☎(0131) 337 3478
Murrayfield Rd, Edinburgh EH12 6EU
2 miles W of city centre.
Parkland course.
18 holes, 5725 yards, S.S.S.68
Founded 1896
Visitors: welcome weekdays with letter of intro.
Green Fee: £22 per round, £28 per day.
Societies: limited, only by prior arrangement.
Catering: meals served daily except Mon. Bar snacks, dining room available.
Hotels: Ellersly House; Murrayfield.

Q55 **Musselburgh**
☎(0131) 665 2005 (Sec/forward bookings), Pro/day booking: 665 7055
Monktonhall, Musselburgh, E Lothian EH21 6SA
From the A1 end of the Edinburgh city by-pass (A720) take B6415 to Musselburgh.
Parkland course.
18 holes, 6614 yards, S.S.S.72
Designed by James Braid.
Founded 1938
Visitors: on application. Advance booking required.
Green Fee: WD £17 per round, £25 per day; WE £21 per round, £30 per day.
Societies: on application.
Catering: bar and restaurant facilities.
Hotels: Kings Manor, Woodside.

Q56 **Musselburgh Old Course**
☎(0131) 665 6981
Silver Ring Clubhouse, 3b Mill Hill, Musselburgh, East Lothian EH21 7RG
7 miles E of Edinburgh.
Public seaside course.
9 holes, 5380 yards, S.S.S.67
Visitors: welcome weekdays and Bank Holidays; weekends not before 1pm.
Green Fee: apply for details.
Societies: welcome by prior arrangement.

Q57 New Galloway

☎(01644) 420737 (Sec)
New Galloway, Castle Douglas,
Kirkcudbrightshire DG7 3RN
On way out of village on A762.
Hilly panoramic moorland course.
9 holes, 5006 yards, S.S.S.65
Founded 1902
Visitors: welcome.
Green Fee: £10; Juniors (under 18)
£5.
Societies: apply to Sec.
Catering: bar; meals in village.
Hotels: Kenmure Arms; Cross Keys.

Q58 Newbattle

☎(0131) 663 2123, Pro 660 1631,
Sec 663 1819
Abbey Rd, Dalkeith, Midlothian EH22
3AD
7 miles SW of Edinburgh on A7, take
Newbattle exit at Esbank roundabout,
turn left opposite police station, club
300 yards on right.
Undulating parkland course.
18 holes, 6012 yards, S.S.S.69
Founded 1935
Visitors: Mon-Fri except Public and
Local Holidays up to 4pm.
Green Fee: £16 per round, £24 per
day.
Societies: Mon-Fri except holidays,
9-10am and 2-3pm.
Catering: full facilities on request.
Hotels: Lugton Inn; Eskbank.

Q59 Newcastleton

☎(013873) 75257
Holm Hill, Newcastleton, Roxburgh
TD9 0QD
25 miles N of Carlisle; turn right off
A7 to Canonbie, 10 miles to
Newcastleton on B6357.
Hillside course.
9 holes, 5748 yards, S.S.S.68
Designed by J. Shade.
Founded 1894
Visitors: no restrictions.
Green Fee: WD £7; WE £8.
Societies: welcome.
Catering: can be arranged in
Liddesdale Hotel.
Hotels: Grapes; Liddesdale.

Q60 Newton Stewart

☎(01671) 402172, 403847
Kirroughtree Ave, Minnigaff, Newton
Stewart, Dumfries & Galloway DG8
6PF
Off A75.
Parkland course.
18 holes, 5970 yards, S.S.S.69
Founded 1981

Visitors: welcome after 10am
Green Fee: WD £14 per round, £17
per day; WE £17 per round, £21 per
day.
Societies: by prior arrangement.
Catering: meals and bar lunches
during bar hours; other by
arrangement with Steward.
Hotels: Glencairn, Crown.

Q61 Niddry Castle

☎(01506) 891097
Castle Rd, Winchburgh, W Lothian
EH52 6RQ
2 miles NE of Broxburn.
Parkland course with large burn.
9 holes, 5514 yards, S.S.S.67
Designed by Derek Smith.
Founded 1984
Visitors: welcome except weekend
competition days.
Green Fee: WD £10; WE £15.
Societies: booking only.
Catering: limited in clubhouse.
Putting green, practice net.
Hotels: Tally Ho.

Q62 North Berwick

☎(01620) 892135
Beach Rd, North Berwick EH39 4BB
23 miles E of Edinburgh on A198.
Seaside course.
18 holes, 6420 yards, S.S.S.70
Designed by Mackenzie Ross.
Founded 1832
Visitors: unrestricted.
Green Fee: WD£27 per round, £40
per day; WE £40 per round, £55 per
day.
Societies: unrestricted weekdays.
Booking required
Catering: full facilities.
Hotels: Marine; Point Garry.

Q63 Peebles

☎(01721) 720197
Kirkland St, Peebles EH45 8EU
NW of town off A72, signposted on
main roads into town; 23 miles S of
Edinburgh.
Undulating parkland course.
18 holes, 6160 yards, S.S.S.69
Designed by James Braid, with
alterations by H.S. Colt.
Founded 1892
Visitors: welcome; no denim or golf
footwear in clubrooms.
Green Fee: WD £17 per round, £23
per day; WE £23 per round, £32 per
day.
Societies: max 36.
Catering: bar and restaurant.
Hotels: Peebles Hydro.

Q64 Polkemmet Country Park

☎(01501) 743905
Park Centre, Polkemmet Country
Park, Whitburn, Bathgate, W Lothian
EH47 0AD
On N side of B7066, midway between
Harthill and Whitburn; signs from
Whitburn exit M8.
Public parkland course (old private
estate).
9 holes, 5938 metres, S.S.S.37
Designed by W Lothian District
Council.
Founded 1981
Visitors: no restrictions; players must
have own clubs.
Green Fee: Mon-Sat: 9 holes,
summer; £2.85; Sun, £3.60
Societies: weekdays only by
arrangement.
Catering: bar snacks and meals
available, all day license; restaurant
lunches and evening meals served in
Lairds Lodge
Driving range, bowls, play fort and
play area, riverside and woodland
walks.
Hotels: Hillcroft

Q65 Portobello

☎(0131) 669 4361
Stanley St, Portobello, Edinburgh
EH15 1JJ
E of Edinburgh on A1 to Milton
Road.
Public parkland course.
9 holes, 4810 yards, S.S.S.32
Founded 1826
Visitors: no restrictions except for
Sat in summer (Medal Days).
Green Fee: £3.70 (9 holes).
Societies: no restrictions except Sat
in summer (Medal Days).
Hotels: Kings Manor.

Q66 Portpatrick (Dunskey)

☎(01776) 810273
Portpatrick, Stranraer, Wigtownshire
DG9 8TB
A77 follow signs to Stranraer, then
follow signs to Portpatrick, fork right
at War Memorial, 300 yards on right
signpost to club.
Links type course set on high cliffs.
Dunskey, 18 holes, 5882 yards,
S.S.S.68; Dinvin, 9 holes, 1504
yards, S.S.S.27
Designed by Dunskey Estate.
Founded 1903
Visitors: welcome with h/cap cert
except competition days; best to
book.

Green Fee: Dunskey course: WD £16 per round, £23 per day; WE £19 per round, £28 per day. Dinvin course: £5 per round, £10 per day.
Societies: welcome, must book in advance with Sec.
Catering: all meals in season.
Hotels: Fernhill; Portpatrick; Devonshire Arms.

Q67 Powfoot

☎(01461) 700276
Cummertrees, Annan, Dumfriesshire DG12 5ZE
3 miles W of Annan, off B724.
Seaside course.
18 holes, 6266 yards, S.S.S.70
Designed by James Braid.
Founded 1903
Visitors: welcome weekdays, not Sat, or after 2pm on Sun
Green Fee: WD £20 per round, £27 per day; Sun £20. £80 per week.
Societies: welcome weekdays only by arrangement.
Catering: full bar facilities; lunches and teas by arrangement.
Hotels: Powfoot Golf; Kirklands.

Q68 Prestonfield

☎(0131) 667 1273 (Bar), Sec 667 9665
6 Priestfield Rd N, Edinburgh EH16 5HS
Near to Commonwealth Pool, Dalkeith Rd.
Parkland course.
18 holes, 6210 yards, S.S.S.70
Designed by James Braid.
Founded 1920
Visitors: welcome; apply though sec.
Green Fee: WD £20 per round, £30 per day;WE £30 per round, £40 per day.
Societies: weekdays starting from 9.30am and 2pm.
Catering: full facilities except Mon.
Hotels: Rosehall; March Hall.

Q69 Pumpherston

☎(01506) 432869
Drumshoreland Rd, Pumpherston, Livingston EH53 0LF
1 mile S of Uphall off A89.
Undulating parkland course with water hazards.
9 holes, 5134 yards, S.S.S.66
Founded 1895
Visitors: only with member.
Green Fee: WD £4; WE £6.
Societies: weekdays only, max 24.
Catering: bar snacks.
Hotels: Houston House.

Q70 Ratho Park

☎(0131) 333 1752 (Sec/Fax), Pro 333 1252
Ratho, Newbridge, Midlothian EH28 8NX
8 miles W of Edinburgh on Glasgow road, adjacent to Edinburgh Airport.
Parkland course.
18 holes, 5900 yards, S.S.S.68
Designed by James Braid.
Founded 1928
Visitors: any day by arrangement with Pro.
Green Fee: WD £25 per round, £30 per day; WE £35.
Societies: Tues, Wed, Thurs, by arrangement.
Catering: bars and restaurant.
Snooker.

Q71 Ravelston

☎(0131) 315 2486
24 Ravelston Dykes Rd, Blackhall, Edinburgh EH4 5NZ
Turn S off A90 Queensferry road at Blackhall, on Strachan Road.
Parkland course.
9 holes, 5200 yards, S.S.S.66
Designed by James Braid.
Founded 1912
Visitors: allowed during quiet periods; h/cap certs preferred.
Green Fee: £15 (18 holes).
Societies: Not allowed
Catering: light snacks only.

Q72 Royal Burgess Golfing Society of Edinburgh

☎(0131) 339 2075 (Res)
181 Whitehouse Rd, Edinburgh EH4 6BY
W side of Edinburgh on Queensferry road, 100 yards N of Barton roundabout.
Parkland course.
18 holes, 6111 yards, S.S.S.71
Designed by Tom Morris.
Founded 1735
Visitors: weekdays only. No lady members. Not before 4pm on comp days.
Green Fee: WD £30 per round, £40 per day; WE £50.
Societies: weekdays only.
Catering: lunches and bar snacks.
Hotels: Barnton; Royal Soot.

Q73 Royal Musselburgh

☎(01875) 810276 (Clubhouse), Pro 810139, Sec 810276
Prestongrange House, Prestonpans, E Lothian EH32 9RP

7 miles E of Edinburgh, 1 mile from Wallyford roundabout on A1, take A198 North Berwick road.
Parkland course.
18 holes, 6237 yards, S.S.S.70
Designed by James Braid.
Founded 1774
Visitors: weekdays welcome, very limited weekends.
Green Fee: WD £20 per round, £35 per day; WE £35.
Societies: must book in writing in advance.
Catering: coffee, lunches, high teas, snacks; dinner all available by advance booking.
Snooker.
Hotels: Kilspindie House.

Q74 St Boswells

☎(01835) 822359, Club 822527
Ashleabank, St Boswells, Roxburghshire TD6 0DE
A68 junction with B6404 opposite Buccleuch Hotel, 0.25 mile along banks of River Tweed.
Flat parkland course.
9 holes, 5250 yards, S.S.S.65
Designed by William Park, altered by John Shade (1956).
Founded 1899
Visitors: unrestricted except for competition days.
Green Fee: £15
Societies: by prior booking.
Catering: at Buccleuch Hotel.
Hotels: Buccleuch.

Q75 St Medan

☎(01988) 700358
Monreith, Newton Stewart, Wigtownshire DG8 8NJ
3 miles S of Port William on A747.
Seaside links course.
9 holes, 4554 yards, S.S.S.63
Founded 1905
Visitors: no restrictions except competitions.
Green Fee: £12 per round, £15 per day.
Societies: welcome any day.
Catering: full bar and catering except Tues, Mar-Sept.
Hotels: Steam Packet; Corsemalzie.

Q76 Sanquhar

☎(01659) 50577, Sec 58181
Old Barr Rd, Sanquhar, Dumfries DG4 6JZ
Off A76 0.5 mile from Sanquhar.
Parkland course.
9 holes, 2572 yards, S.S.S.68
Founded 1894

Southerness

Nothing like enough golfers are acquainted with the delights of Southerness which lies on the silent, sandy stretches of the Solway Firth about 15 miles south of Dumfries. This is largely because the south-west corner of Scotland is not the best known golfing area of a country that has so much to offer although those aware of its charm find it rich in quality and enjoyment and, like me, hard to believe that its reputation has not spread further.

As with so many courses around our shores, much of its appeal lies in its out of the way position but it still makes a convenient beginning or end to any golfing tour. The drive from Carlisle is by no means arduous but, by the time that one turns off the main road down a long, narrow lane towards the sea, there is a growing impatience to see what lies beyond.

Before the days of a new clubhouse, built in 1974 close to the position of the old 6th hole, journey's end was less pretentious. The small community dominated by the Paul Jones Hotel consisted of a field of caravans, a few shops and a clubhouse which had more the look of some rustic cricket pavilion. A notice invited visitors to settle green fees with the caretaker in the village shop across the road and the path to the first tee was through some quaint little paddock.

However, one round on the course, laid out by Mackenzie Ross shortly after the last war, is sufficient to appreciate its merits and indicate, rather like Dornoch at the opposite end of the country, that it is well worthy of having won its championship spurs. By a happy coincidence, Dornoch was awarded the British Amateur Championship in 1985, the same year in which the Scottish Golf Union took the Scottish Amateur to Southerness, constructed for about £2,000 around 1947. The staging of the championship bestowed a posthumous tribute to Mackenzie Ross who resurrected Turnberry at more or less the same time as he paid his regular visits to Southerness.

By the current rating, there is only one par 5 but the weight of the challenge is marked by having eight holes between 405 and 470 yards, many with fine natural greens angled to ensure the best chance of finishing near the hole comes from drives correctly positioned. There is no great feeling that the fairways are narrow but gorse and heather can swallow up wayward shots and there is a tough start including the longest hole, the 5th, with its elevated and quaintly shaped green.

The 8th, taking aim on the lighthouse, begins the stretch along the shore but the pick of the holes are the dogleg 12th and the 13th and the old 18th, a formidable 467 yards. The 17th green, perched above the beach, also gives the best view of the splendour of the setting. Leagues of golden sand slip westwards along the coast of Kirkcudbright. The peaks of Cumberland stand strong against the peaceful waters of the Firth and, inland, the simple green landscape completes a feeling of escape that causes as much surprise as finding a golf course to match its majestic surroundings.

Visitors: welcome.
Green Fee: WD £10; WE £12.
Societies: by prior arrangement.
Catering: by prior arrangement.
Snooker, carpet bowling, darts etc.
Hotels: Blackaddie House; Glendyne;
Nithsdale; Mennock Foot Lodge.

Q77 Selkirk

☎(0750) 20621, Sec 22508
The Hill, Selkirk
1 mile S of Selkirk on A7 to Hawick.
Moorland course.
9 holes, 5640 yards, S.S.S.67
Founded 1883
Visitors: welcome weekdays, not Fri
evenings and Mon after 3pm (ladies
only).
Green Fee: £12.
Societies: by arrangement but limited
at weekends.
Catering: parties by arrangement
otherwise limited
Hotels: County.

Q78 Silverknowes

☎(0131) 336 5359, Pro 336 3843
Silverknowes, Parkway, Edinburgh
EH4 5ET
W end of Edinburgh, off Cramond
Foreshore.
Municipal course.
18 holes, 6202 yards, S.S.S.70
Founded 1958
Visitors: with reservation only.
Green Fee: £7.40
Societies: Welcome on application
Hotels: Commodore, adjacent.

Q79 Southerness

☎(01387) 880677
Southerness, Dumfries DG2 8AZ
16 miles SW of Dumfries off A710.
Links course.
18 holes, 6566 yards, S.S.S.72
Designed by Mackenzie Ross.
Founded 1947
Visitors: members of recognised
clubs only; 10-12am and 2-4pm
weekdays, 10-11.30am and 2.30-4pm
weekends.
Green Fee: WD £25; WE £35.
Societies: apply to Sec.
Catering: full bar and catering.
Hotels: Cairndale; Clonyard.

Q80 Stranraer

☎(01776) 870245, Pro 703539
Creachmore, Stranrear DG9 0LF
Take A718 from Stranraer towards
Leswalt, club is well signposted on
right.

Parkland course.
18 holes, 6308 yards, S.S.S.71
Designed by James Braid.
Founded 1905
Visitors: welcome but not before
9.30 or between 11.30-1pm
Green Fee: WD £17.50 per round,
£24 per day; WE £23 per round, £30
per day.
Societies: catered for by prior
arrangement.
Catering: not Mon.
Hotels: North West Castle.

Q81 Swanston

☎(0131) 445 2239, Pro 445 4002
111 Swanston Rd, Edinburgh EH10
7DS
S side of city on lower slopes of
Pentland Hills.
Hillside course.
18 holes, 5024 yards, S.S.S.65
Designed by Herbert More.
Founded 1927
Visitors: welcome weekdays and
with restrictions at weekends.
Green Fee: WD £10 per round, £15
per day; WE £15 per round, £20 per
day.
Societies: welcome by prior
arrangement.
Catering: full facilities.
Hotels: Braid Hills, Newland Inn.

Q82 Thornhill

☎(01848) 330546, Pro 331779
Blacknest, Thornhill, Dumfries-shire
DG3 5DW
14 miles N of Dumfries on A76 to
Thornhill, turn right at cross, 1 mile on
right.
Moorland/parkland course.
18 holes, 6011 yards, S.S.S.69
Founded 1893
Visitors: welcome without reservation
except on comp days.
Green Fee: WD £18; WE £20.
Societies: welcome; contact Club
Steward.
Catering: bar facilities available.
Hotels: George, Gillbank

Q83 Torphin Hill

☎(0131) 441 1100, Pro 441 4061
Torphin Rd, Colinton, Edinburgh
EH13 0PG
SW of Colinton, follow signposts.
Hillside course.
18 holes, 5030 yards, S.S.S.66
Founded 1895
Visitors: restricted during
competitions; no 4-balls at
weekends.

Green Fee: WD £12; WE £20.
Societies: welcome weekdays.
Catering: full facilities except Tues.
Hotels: Braid Hills; Royal Scot.

Q84 Torwoodlee

☎(01896) 752660
Galashiels, Selkirkshire
On A7 Galashiels-Edinburgh road, 1
mile from town centre.
Parkland course.
18 holes, 5800 yards, S.S.S.68
Designed by Willie Park (new layout,
John Gurner).
Founded 1895
Visitors: welcome, restricted Sat and
Thurs after 1pm.
Green Fee: on application.
Societies: welcome on application.
Catering: full facilities except Tues.
Hotels: Burts; George & Abbotsford.

Q85 Turnhouse

☎(0131) 339 1014, Pro 339 7701
154 Turnhouse Rd, Edinburgh EH12
0AD
W of city on A9080 near airport.
Parkland/heathland course.
18 holes, 6171 yards, S.S.S.69
Founded 1909
Visitors: only visiting clubs; not
weekends; Hotel visitors contact Pro.
Green Fee: £18 per round, £36 per
day.
Societies: Welcome by prior
arrangement.
Catering: lunch, high tea except
Mon.
Hotels: Royal Scot, Posthouse,
Stakis

Q86 Uphall

☎(01506) 856404 (Manager), Pro
855553
Houston Mains, Uphall, W Lothian
EH52 6JT
7 miles W of Edinburgh airport, on
A89 Edinburgh-Glasgow road in
village of Uphall.
Parkland course.
18 holes, 6268 yards, S.S.S.67
Founded 1895
Visitors: welcome, weekends
telephone Pro for booking.
Green Fee: WD £13 per round, £18
per day; WE £18 per round, £25 per
day.
Societies: welcome by arrangement
with Manager.
Catering: full catering service, hot
and cold snacks, high teas, 2 bars.
Practice ground, putting green.
Hotels: Houston.

Q87 Vogrie

☎(01875) 821716, Sec 821986
Vogrie Estate Country Park,
Gorebridge, Lothian EH23 4NN
Off A68 Jedburgh road.
Public parkland course.
9 holes, 2530 yards, Par 33
Founded 1989
Visitors: welcome, pay as you play.
Green Fee: apply for details.
Societies: welcome.
Catering: tearoom in park..

Q88 West Linton

☎(01968) 660463 (Club), Sec
660970, Pro 660256
West Linton, Peebleshire H46 7HN
15 miles from Edinburgh on A702.
Moorland course.
18 holes, 6132 yards, S.S.S.69
Founded 1890
Visitors: welcome weekdays but
restrictions at weekends and comp
days.
Green Fee: WD £15 per round, £22
per day; WE £25.
Societies: weekdays by arrangement
Catering: full facilities except Tues.
Hotels: Gordon Arms; Linton.

Q89 West Lothian

☎(01506) 826030 (Club), Pro
825060
Airngath Hill, Linlithgow, W Lothian
EH49 7RH
On hill separating Bo'ness and
Linlithgow, marked by Hope
Monument.

Undulating meadowland course.
18 holes, 6406 yards, S.S.S.71
Designed by Fraser Middleton.
Founded 1892
Visitors: no restrictions weekdays
before 4pm; after 4pm and at
weekends by arrangement only.
Green Fee: WE £8; WE £10.
Societies: catered for weekdays and
at weekends.
Catering: meals as requested.
Hotels: Earl O'Murray, Richmond
Park.

Q90 Wigtown & Bladnoch

☎(01988) 403354
Lightlands Terrace, Wigtown,
Galloway DG8 9EF
0.25 mile from town centre on A746,
signposted Whithorn.
Parkland course, part hilly.
9 holes, 5462 yards, S.S.S.67
Founded 1960
Visitors: no restrictions.
Green Fee: £10 per round, £15 per
day; week ticket (5 days) £40.
Societies: welcome by prior
arrangement.
Catering: bar and snacks 12am-
2.30pm (June-Sept); evening meals
and groups by arrangement.
Hotels: Conifers Leisure Park; Bruce;
Hill o'Burns; all offer free golf.

Q91 Wigtownshire County

☎(01581) 300420
Mains of Park, Glenluce, Newton
Stewart, Wigtownshire DG9 0NN

8 miles E of Stranraer on A75, 2
miles W of Glenluce.
Links course.
18 holes, 5847 yards, S.S.S.68
Designed by Gordon Cunningham.
Founded 1894
Visitors: welcome; members priority
times 10.30-11am, 1-1.30pm
weekdays; 8-9.30am, 1-1.40pm
weekends.
Green Fee: WD £16 per round, £20
per day; WE £18 per round, £22 per
day.
Societies: welcome at all times,
preferably pre-booked;
Catering: facilities available all year
round.
Hotels: North West Castle;
Portpatrick; Glenbay.

Q92 Winterfield

☎(01368) 62280 (Club), Pro 63562,
Sec 65119
North Rd, Dunbar, E Lothian EH42
1AU
W side of Dunbar.
Seaside course.
18 holes, 5155 yards, S.S.S.65
Founded 1935
Visitors: welcome.
Green Fee: WD £11 per round;
£13.50 per day; WE £12.50 per
round, £20 per day.
Societies: welcome by arrangement
with Pro.
Catering: 2 bars and restaurant
facilities.
Hotels: Hillside, Royal Mackintosh,
Bayswell.

STRATHCLYDE

Strathclyde casts a comprehensive net over the golfing scene as well as providing more than its share of Britain's great courses. It encompasses the remote outposts of Machrie and Machrihanish, the whole of the area around Glasgow and the veritable treasure trove of Ayrshire, a county many claim possesses more glittering, golfing jewels than any other in Britain.

Prime among its southern defences is Turnberry, one of the world's most spectacular settings for golf. There are few more stirring stretches than that between the short 4th and the short 11th on the Ailsa course, a testing clutch of holes graduating from the relative shelter of the dunes to the rugged, rocky promontory alongside the lighthouse. Wild westerly winds can be more than flesh, blood and balance can stand, one solution lying on the Arran, the Ailsa's neighbour, which is flatter, less exposed and little inferior.

Together, they comprise a wonderful day's golf, a comment pretty commonplace in Ayrshire. Old Prestwick , Royal Troon, Western Gailes, Glasgow Gailes, Barassie, Irvine, Ayr Belleisle and Prestwick St Nicholas provide a wonderfully rich assortment along with the newer delights of Brunston Castle in its lovely setting at Dailly.

As the birthplace of championship golf, Old Prestwick commands eminence, a course that has proved its freshness time and again. There are few more daunting opening tee shots, few better dogleg holes than the 4th and few more sporting tests than the 13th and 17th. It faded as a staging ground for the Open championship on account of its difficulty in handling big crowds but its demise coincided with the rise of Troon, although there were 27 years between Troon's first and second Opens, a gap attributable in part to the war.

There are five or six courses in Troon, or on its doorstep, many shrewd judges rating Western Gailes on a par with Royal Troon. It certainly ranks extremely highly with a greater share perhaps of spectacular holes and interesting greens. At one end, it is possible to hit a shot over the railway onto Kilmarnock (Barassie) and, at the other, onto Glasgow Gailes, the country "seat", so to speak, of the Glasgow GC in the city district of Killermont.

On one of the approach roads to Glasgow from the south, Eastwood, East Renfrewshire and Whitecraigs are encountered in quick succession but Glasgow is surrounded on all sides by good golf. Names to note are West Kilbride, Renfrew, Gleddoch, Old Ranfurly, Kilmacolm, Ranfurly Castle, Helensburgh, Balmore and Cawder. The ranks have been swelled recently by Loch Lomond which has received a barrage of accolades

Nor must the other courses overlooking the Clyde be forgotten or those on Arran. But if it is romance that you seek, head for Machrie on the Isle of Islay or Machrihanish on the Mull of Kintyre, both reachable by air from Glasgow airport. Machrie is an authentic links full of hidden dells and high hills – bordered on one side by lonely, sandy beaches and on the other by moor and hill.

Back on the mainland at Machrihanish, the beach comes into play on the opening drive, and a notice for non-golfers proclaims "Danger, First Tee Above, please move further along the beach" – an invigorating introduction to another superb tract of natural land, the only true setting to the game.

For those choosing the lengthy and circuitous route by road, Machrihanish rarely disappoints but journey's end is Dunaverty, ten miles south of Campbeltown and home of Belle Robertson who brought it fame and distinction. Its raw charm is hard to better although its modest length can be dramatically magnified by the breezes that frequently graduate to raging winds.

R1 Airdrie

☎(01236) 762195, Pro 754360
Rochsoles, Airdrie ML6 0PQ
From Airdrie Cross in centre of town
travel N on Glenmavis Rd.
Parkland course.
18 holes, 6004 yards, S.S.S.69
Designed by James Braid.
Founded 1877
Visitors: welcome with introduction
from own Sec.
Green Fee: £15 per round, £25 per
day.
Societies: contact Sec, not
weekends or Bank Holidays.
Catering: full catering.
Snooker.
Hotels: Tudor; Kenilworth.

R2 Alexandra Park

☎(0141) 556 1294
Alexandra Golf, Alexandra Park,
Sannox Gdns, Glasgow G31 8SE
M8 cut off before fruit market.
Hilly municipal parkland course.
9 holes, 2800 yards, Par 34
Designed by Graham McArthur.
Founded 1818
Visitors: welcome at all times.
Green Fee: on application.
Societies: welcome by prior
arrangement.
Bowling greens.
Hotels: Hospitality Inn; Copthorne;
Hilton.

R3 Annanhill

☎(01563) 521644
Irvine Rd, Kilmarnock KA1 4RT
Off main Kilmarnock-Irvine road.
Parkland course.
18 holes, 6118 yards, S.S.S.70
Designed by J. McLean.
Founded 1957
Visitors: welcome except Sat.
Green Fee: WD £10; WE £15.
Societies: by arrangement.
Catering: snacks at weekends; full
meals, breakfast, lunch, dinner or
high tea by arrangement.
Hotels: Howard Park; Holiday Inn.

R4 Ardeer

☎(01294) 464542, Pro 601327, Sec
465316
Greenhead, Stevenston, Ayrshire
Follow A78 (signs for Largs and
Greenock), on High Rd by-passing
Stevenston, turn right into Kerelaw
Rd and continue for 1 mile.
Parkland course.
18 holes, 6630 yards, S.S.S.72
Founded 1880

Visitors: welcome except Sat.
Green Fee: apply for details.
Societies: catered for Sun - Fri.
Catering: full facilities available.

R5 Auchenharvie Golf Complex

☎(01294) 603103
Moor Park Rd West, Brewery Park,
Stevenston, Ayrshire KA20 3HU
Public links/parkland course.
9 holes (18 tees), 2565 yards,
S.S.S.33
Designed by Michael Struthers.
Founded May 1981
Visitors: welcome.
Green Fee: WD £3.30; WE £5.50.
Societies: welcome.
Catering: clubhouse bar.
Driving range.

R6 Ayr Belleisle

☎(01292) 441258, Fax 442632
Belleisle Park, Doonfoot Rd, Ayr
1.5 miles S of Ayr on A719.
Parkland course.
18 holes, 6477 yards, S.S.S.71
Designed by James Braid & Stutt.
Founded 1927
Visitors: welcome.
Green Fee: Mon - Sun £17 per
round, £24 per day.
Societies: apply to Course
Administrator at address above.
Catering: meals and snacks
available in hotel.
Hotels: Belleisle House; Balgarth;
Old Racecourse.

R7 Ayr Dalmilling

☎(01292) 263893, Fax 610543
Westwood Ave, Ayr, Strathclyde KA8
0QY
1.5 miles from town centre on NE
boundary off A77.
Municipal meadowland course.
18 holes, 5752 yards, S.S.S.68
Founded 1960
Visitors: unrestricted; times bookable
in advance from 1994.
Green Fee: £10 per round, £18 per
day.
Societies: by prior arrangement.
Catering: tea, coffee, lunches, high
teas, snacks daily except Tues;
licensed bar.
Hotels: Racers.

R8 Ayr Seafield

☎(01292) 441258, Fax 442632
Belleisle Park, Doonfoot Rd, Ayr
1.5 miles S of Ayr on A719.

Parkland/seaside course.
18 holes, 5650 yards, S.S.S.68
Founded 1927
Visitors: welcome.
Green Fee: £11 per round.
Societies: apply to course
Administrator at address above.
Catering: meals and snacks
available in hotel.
Hotels: Belleisle House; Balgarth;
Old Racecourse.

R9 Ballochmyle

☎(01290) 550469, Fax 553150
Ballochmyle, Mauchline, Ayrshire KA5
6LE
1 mile S of Mauchline on B705, off
A76(T) Dumfries-Kilmarnock road.
Parkland course.
18 holes, 5952 yards, S.S.S.69
Founded 1937
Visitors: welcome weekdays.
Green Fee: on application.
Societies: weekdays by arrangement
except Wed.
Catering: bar and restaurant.
Snooker.

R10 Balmore

☎(01360) 620240, Sec (0141) 332
0392
Balmore, Torrance, Stirlingshire
2 miles N of Glasgow on A803 and
then A807.
Parkland course.
18 holes, 5530 yards, S.S.S.67
Designed by James Braid.
Founded 1906
Visitors: welcome with introduction
from member.
Green Fee: apply for details.
Catering: full catering facilities.

R11 Barshaw

☎(0141) 889 2908, 889 5400, Sec
884 2533
Barshaw Park, Glasgow Rd, Paisley,
Renfrewshire
A737 from Glasgow W to Paisley, 1
mile before Paisley Cross.
Municipal meadowland course.
18 holes, 5703 yards, S.S.S.67
Founded 1920
Visitors: welcome all week.
Green Fee: £6 (half price OAPs, jnrs
and unemployed).
Hotels: Water Mill; Brablock.

R12 Bearsden

☎(0141) 942 2351, Sec 942 2381
Thorn Rd, Bearsden, Glasgow G61
4BP

1 mile N from Bearsden Cross on Thorn Rd.
Parkland course.
9 holes, 6014 yards, S.S.S.69
Founded 1891
Visitors: to be introduced by and play with member.
Green Fee: on application.
Catering: light meals, snacks.
Hotels: Black Bull; Burnbrae.

R13 **Beith**
☎(01505) 503166
Threepwood Rd, Beith, Ayrshire, KA15 2JR
2 miles S of Linwood, about 1 mile E of Beith.
Hilly parkland course.
18 holes (from June 1996), 5800 yards, S.S.S.68
Founded 1896
Visitors: welcome.
Green Fee: £12 per round, £18 per day.
Societies: welcome; book by letter.
Catering: full facilities.

R14 **Bellshill**
☎(01698) 745124
Orbiston, Bellshill, Lanarkshire ML4 2RZ
Right turn off Bellshill/Motherwell road 10 miles SE of Glasgow.
Parkland course.
18 holes, 6315 yards, S.S.S.70
Founded 1905
Visitors: not between 4pm and 7pm, May-Aug inclusive; otherwise welcome.
Green Fee: WD £18; WE & BH £25.
Societies: by prior arrangement; not Sun.
Catering: licensed bar and lounge; meals and snacks available.

R15 **Biggar**
☎(01899) 220618
The Park, Broughton Rd, Biggar, Lanarkshire ML12 6QX
1 mile E of Biggar on Broughton Rd, opposite police station, signposted.
Municipal flat scenic parkland course.
18 holes, 5537 yards, S.S.S.68

Designed by Willie Park.
Founded 1895
Visitors: unrestricted but telephone (01899) 220319 in advance.
Green Fee: WD £12; WE £15.
Societies: welcome 36 max, advance booking essential.
Catering: all day licence and catering (smart casual dress, no jeans).
All weather tennis, boating, childrens' play area, caravan park.
Hotels: Toftcombs; Elphinstone (Biggar); Tinto (Symington).

R16 **Bishopbriggs**
☎(0141) 772 1810 (Club), Sec 772 8938
Brackenbrae Rd, Bishopbriggs, Glasgow G64 2DX
4 miles N of Glasgow on A803, turn left 200 yards short of Bishopbriggs Cross.
Parkland course.
18 holes, 6041 yards, S.S.S.69
Designed by James Braid.
Founded 1906

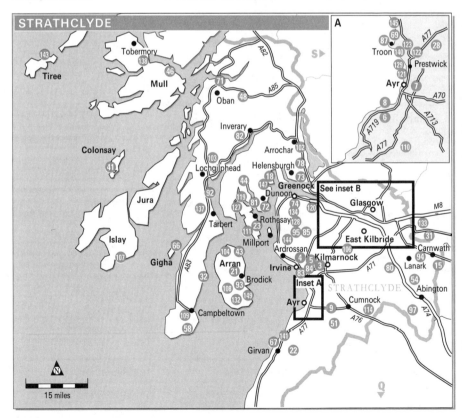

STRATHCLYDE

Visitors: welcome with member or by application to Committee.
Green Fee: on application.
Societies: Tues, Wed, Thurs only; apply to Sec at least 1 month in advance.
Catering: meals and snacks available.

2 miles S of Rutherglen via Stonelaw road, follow road signs.
Parkland course.
18 holes, 5448 yards, S.S.S.68
Founded 1910
Visitors: welcome with member.
Green Fee: on application.
Catering: by arrangement.

Undulating parkland/moorland course.
9 holes, 2112 yards, S.S.S.62
Founded 1896
Visitors: welcome; some delays likely Sat afternoons and Mon evenings.
Green Fee: apply for details.

R17 **Blairbeth**
☎(0141) 634 3355
Fernhill, Rutherglen, Glasgow G73 4XF

R18 **Blairmore & Strone**
☎(01369) 840676
Strone, By Dunoon, Argyll PA23 8TJ
0.75 mile N of Strone on A880.

R19 **Bonnyton**
☎(01355) 302781(Club), Pro 302256, Fax 303151
Eaglesham, Glasgow G76 0QA
City centre S of Eaglesham.
Moorland course.
18 holes, 6252 yards, S.S.S.71
Founded 1957
Visitors: welcome weekdays.
Green Fee: on application.
Societies: catered for by prior arrangement.
Catering: weekdays and Sun lunches and high teas available; Sat lunches and dinner served; bar lunches every day.

R20 **Bothwell Castle**
☎(01698) 853177 (Club), Sec/Fax 854052, Pro 852052
Blantyre Rd, Bothwell, Glasgow G71 8PJ
M74 junction 5 to A9071, 3 miles N of Hamilton.
Parkland course.
18 holes, 6240 yards, S.S.S.70
Founded 1922

KEY							
1	Airdrie	31	Carnwath	63	Elderslie	94	Lanark	126	Renfrew
2	Alexandra Park	32	Carradale	64	Erskine	95	Largs	127	Rothesay
3	Annanhill	33	Cathcart Castle	65	Fereneze	96	Larkhall	128	Routenburn
4	Ardeer	34	Cathkin Braes	66	Gigha	97	Leadhills	129	Royal Troon
5	Auchenharvie Golf Complex	35	Cawder	67	Girvan	98	Lenzie	130	Ruchill
6	Ayr Belleisle	36	Clober	68	Glasgow	99	Lethamhill	131	Sandyhills
7	Ayr Dalmilling	37	Clydebank & District	69	Glasgow (Gailes)	100	Linn Park	132	Shiskine
8	Ayr Seafield	38	Clydebank Overtoun	70	Gleddoch Country Club	101	Littlehill	133	Shotts
9	Ballochmyle	39	Coatbridge	71	Glencruitten	102	Loch Lomond	134	Skelmorlie
10	Balmore	40	Cochrane Castle	72	Gourock	103	Lochgilphead	135	Strathaven
11	Barshaw	41	Colonsay	73	Greenock	104	Lochranza	136	Strathclyde Park
12	Bearsden	42	Colville Park	74	Greenock Whinhill	105	Lochwinnoch	137	Tarbert
13	Beith	43	Corrie	75	Haggs Castle	106	Loudoun	138	Tobermory
14	Bellshill	44	Cowal	76	Hamilton	107	Machrie	139	Torrance House
15	Biggar	45	Cowglen	77	Hayston	108	Machrie Bay	140	Troon Municipal
16	Bishopbriggs	46	Craignure	78	Helensburgh	109	Machrihanish	141	Turnberry Hotel
17	Blairbeth	47	Crow Wood	79	Hilton Park	110	Maybole	142	Vale of Leven
18	Blairmore & Strone	48	Dalmally	80	Hollandbush	111	Millport	143	Vaul
19	Bonnyton	49	Dalmuir Municipal	81	Innellan	112	Milngavie	144	West Kilbride
20	Bothwell Castle	50	Deaconsbank	82	Inverary	113	Mount Ellen	145	Western Gailes
21	Brodick	51	Doon Valley	83	Irvine	114	New Cumnock	146	Westerwood Hotel Golf & Country Club
22	Brunston Castle	52	Dougalston	84	Irvine Ravenspark	115	Old Course Ranfurly	147	Whinhill
23	Bute	53	Douglas Park	85	Kilbirnie Place	116	Paisley	148	Whitecraigs
24	Calderbraes	54	Douglas Water	86	Kilmacolm	117	Palacerigg	149	Whiting Bay
25	Caldwell	55	Drumpellier	87	Kilmarnock (Barassie)	118	Pollok	150	Williamwood
26	Cambuslang	56	Dullatur	88	Kilsyth Lennox	119	Port Bannatyne	151	Windyhill
27	Campsie	57	Dumbarton	89	Kirkhill	120	Port Glasgow	152	Wishaw
28	Caprington	58	Dunaverty	90	Kirkintilloch	121	Prestwick		
29	Cardross	59	East Kilbride	91	Knightswood	122	Prestwick St Cuthbert		
30	Carluke	60	East Renfrewshire	92	Kyles of Bute	123	Prestwick St Nicholas		
		61	Easter Moffat	93	Lamlash	124	Ralston		
		62	Eastwood			125	Ranfurly Castle		

Visitors: welcome weekdays 9.30am-3.30pm.
Green Fee: £20 per round, £28 per day.
Societies: weekdays by written application.
Catering: snacks, lunches, high teas, dinners daily.
Hotels: Silvertrees; Bothwell Bridge.

R21 Brodick

☎(0770) 302349, Pro 302513
Brodick, Isle of Arran KA27 8BW
By car ferry from Ardrossan, Ayrshire (55 min); 0.5 mile from Brodick pier.
Seaside course.
18 holes, 4404 yards, S.S.S.62 (extending March 1996).
Founded 1897
Visitors: welcome all week.
Green Fee: £10 per round, £15 per day.
Societies: by letter to Sec, catered for at all times.
Catering: light lunches, contact Steward (01770) 302349.

R22 Brunston Castle

☎(01465) 811471, Fax 811545
Bargany, Dailly, By Girvan, Ayrshire KA26 9RH
35 mins from Prestwick Airport, S of Ayr and Turnberry (4 miles); turn left off A77 just N of Girvan on to B741; after 6 miles turn left towards Dailly; signposted.
Parkland course beside Water of Girvan.
18 holes, 6858 yards, S.S.S.73
Designed by Donald Steel.
Founded 1992
Visitors: welcome any day unless course closed for tournaments; phone for booking.
Green Fee: WD £22.50 per round, £35 per day; WE £27.50 per round, £39 per day.
Societies: welcome if times available.
Catering: clubhouse meals and snacks, bar facilities.
Practice area, putting green.
Hotels: Kings Arms; Malin Court (Turnberry); Kings Arms (Ballantrae).

R23 Bute

☎(01700) 831648 (Sec)
Kingarth, Isle of Bute, Strathclyde
In Stravanan Bay off A845 Rothesay-Kilchattan Bay road.
Links course.
9 holes, 2497 yards, S.S.S.64
Founded 1888

Visitors: welcome, not before 12.30pm Sat.
Green Fee: £6 per day.
Hotels: Kingarth; St Blanes.

R24 Calderbraes

☎(01698) 813425
57 Roundknowe Rd, Uddingston G71 7TS
Start of M74 to Carlisle, 4 miles from Glasgow.
Hilly parkland course.
9 holes, 5046 yards, S.S.S.67
Founded 1891
Visitors: weekdays only, off course by 5pm.
Green Fee: WD £12 per day.
Societies: weekdays, max 20 players.
Catering: bar and catering facilities available.
Hotels: Redstones.

R25 Caldwell

☎(01505) 850329 (Club), Pro 850616, Fax:850366
Uplawmoor, Renfrewshire G78 4AU
Off A736 5 miles SW of Barrhead, 12 miles NE of Irvine.
Moorland course.
18 holes, 6228 yards, S.S.S.70
Founded 1903
Visitors: welcome weekdays but advisable to check in advance.
Green Fee: on application.
Societies: catered for on weekdays by arrangement.
Catering: weekdays.
Hotels: Uplawmoor; Dalmeny.

R26 Cambuslang

☎(0141) 641 3130
30 Westburn Drive, Cambuslang, Glasgow G72 7NA
Off main Glasgow to Hamilton road at Cambuslang.
Parkland course.
9 holes, 6072 yards, S.S.S.69
Founded 1891
Visitors: apply in writing to Sec.
Green Fee: on application..
Catering: full facilities.
Hotels: Cambus Court.

R27 Campsie

☎(01360) 310244, Pro shop 310920
Crow Rd, Lennoxtown, Glasgow G65 7HX
N of Lennoxtown on B822.
Hillside course.
18 holes, 5517 yards, S.S.S.67
Founded 1897

Visitors: welcome weekdays and by prior arrangement at weekends.
Green Fee: on application.
Societies: apply to Sec.
Catering: bar snacks available; meals by prior arrangement.
Hotels: Glazert CHH; Kincaid House.

R28 Caprington

☎(01563) 523702
Ayr Rd, Kilmarnock KA1 4UW
S of Kilmarnock on Ayr Rd.
Municipal parkland course.
18 holes, 5718 yards, S.S.S.68
Visitors: welcome.
Green Fee: apply for details.
Societies: apply to Sec.
Catering: on request.

R29 Cardross

☎(01389) 841213 (Club), Sec 841754, Pro 841350
Main Rd, Cardross, Dumbarton G82 5LB
A814 Dumbarton-Helensburgh road.
Parkland course.
18 holes, 6469 yards, S.S.S.71
Designed by Willie Fernie of Troon and James Braid.
Founded 1895
Visitors: welcome weekdays, weekends introduced by member.
Green Fee: £22 per round, £32 per day.
Societies: by arrangement with Sec (weekdays only).
Catering: bar snacks, teas.
Hotels: Dumbuck; Commodore; Cameron House.

R30 Carluke

☎(01555) 771070
Hallcraig, Mauldslie Rd, Carluke ML8 5HG
1.5 miles from lights at town centre on road to Hamilton and Larkhall.
Tree-lined parkland course with views over Clyde valley.
18 holes, 5800 yards, S.S.S.68
Founded 1894
Visitors: weekdays only until 4.30pm; no visitors on public holidays.
Green Fee: £17 per round, £22 per day.
Societies: by written request to Sec.
Catering: full facilities.
Hotels: Popinjay (3 memberships).

R31 Carnwath

☎(01555) 840251
1 Main St, Carnwath, Strathclyde ML11 8JX

5 miles NE of Lanark.
Undulating course.
18 holes, 5860 yards, S.S.S.69
Founded 1907
Visitors: any day except Sat or after 4pm; no parties on Tues or Thur.
Green Fee: WD £18; Sun & BH £25.
Societies: catered for.
Catering: meals (snacks only Tues and Thurs).
Hotels: Tinto (Symington).

R32 Carradale
☎(01583) 431643 (Sec)
Carradale, Campbeltown, Argyll PA28 6SA
In Kintyre, Argyll, off B842 from Campbeltown.
Difficult, scenic sea view course.
9 holes, 2392 yards, S.S.S.63
Founded 1906
Visitors: welcome at all times, no introduction necessary.
Green Fee: £7 per day; extended terms on application.
Catering: at both hotels (below).
Hotels: Carradale; Ashbank.

R33 Cathcart Castle
☎(0141) 638 9449 (Sec), Pro 638 3436
Mearns Rd, Clarkston, Glasgow G76 7YL
1 mile from Clarkston on B767.
Undulating parkland course.
18 holes, 5832 yards, S.S.S.68
Founded 1895
Visitors: introduced by member.
Green Fee: £22 per round, £30 per day.
Societies: by arrangement with Sec, Tues and Thurs only.
Catering: snacks, meals, bar.
Hotels: Redhurst; McDonald; Busby.

R34 Cathkin Braes
☎(0141) 634 6605 (Sec), Pro 634 0650, Club 634 4007
Cathkin Rd, Rutherglen, Glasgow G73 4SE
SE of Glasgow on B759 between A749 and B766.
Moorland course.
18 holes, 6208 yards, S.S.S.71
Designed by James Braid.
Founded 1888
Visitors: Mon-Fri by prior arrangement.
Green Fee: £20 per round, £30 per day.
Catering: full catering to order.
Hotels: Stuart; Bruce; Burnside; Busby.

R35 Cawder
☎(0141) 772 5167 (Sec), Clubhouse 772 7101, Pro 772 7102
Cadder Rd, Bishopbriggs, Glasgow G64 3QD
0.5 mile E of Bishopbriggs cross, off A803 Glasgow-Kirkintilloch road.
Parkland course.
Cawder, 18 holes, 6229 yards, S.S.S.71; Keir, 18 holes, 5877 yards, S.S.S.68
Designed by Donald Steel (Cawder course), James Braid (Keir course).
Founded 1933
Visitors: welcome weekdays by arrangement with Sec.
Green Fee: on application.
Societies: welcome weekdays by arrangement with Sec.
Catering: full catering facilities.
Hotels: Black Bull; Glazert Country House Hotel; Crowood House.

R36 Clober
☎(0141) 956 1685 (Sec), Pro shop 956 6963
Craigton Rd, Milngavie G62 7HP
7 miles NW of Glasgow.
Parkland course.
18 holes, 5068 yards, S.S.S.65
Designed by Lyle Family.
Founded 1952
Visitors: Mon-Thurs before 4.30pm, Fri before 4pm.
Green Fee: on application.
Societies: weekdays by prior arrangement.
Catering: available Tues, Wed, Fri, Sat and Sun; snacks Mon and Thurs.
Hotels: Black Bull; Thistle.

R37 Clydebank & District
☎(01389) 873289, Pro 878686
Hardgate, Clydebank, Dunbartonshire G81 5QY
8 miles NW of Glasgow via Great Western Rd.
Parkland course.
18 holes, 5825 yards, S.S.S.68
Founded 1905
Visitors: welcome weekdays, weekends with member only.
Green Fee: on application.
Societies: by arrangement.
Catering: meals served.
Hotels: Cameron House; Boulevard; Pine Trees.

R38 Clydebank Overtoun
☎(0141) 952 6372 (Pro shop)
Overtoun Rd, Clydebank, Dunbartonshire G81 3RE
5 minutes from Dalmuir station.

Municipal parkland course.
18 holes, 5643 yards, S.S.S.67
Founded 1928
Visitors: municipal rules apply.
Green Fee: WD £4.40; Sun £4.80.
Societies: by arrangement.
Catering: cafe attached to Pro Shop.

R39 Coatbridge
☎(01236) 428975, Fax 421008
Townhead Rd, Coatbridge, Lanark ML5 2HX
In Coatbridge town.
Public parkland course.
18 holes, 6026 yards, S.S.S.69
Founded 1971
Visitors: welcome.
Green Fee: apply for details.
Societies: welcome.
Catering: full facilities.
Driving range, putting green.
Hotels: Jordanian.

R40 Cochrane Castle
☎(01505) 320146
Scott Ave, Craigston, Johnstone PA5 0HF
0.25 mile off Johnstone-Beith road to S of town, Bird in the Hand Hotel is good landmark near turning to club.
Parkland course.
18 holes, 6226 yards, S.S.S.71
Designed by Charles Hunter of Prestwick, altered by James Braid.
Founded 1895
Visitors: weekdays unrestricted, introduced by member weekends.
Green Fee: £17 per round, £25 per day.
Societies: max 32 players.
Catering: full facilities except Mon.
Pool, darts.
Hotels: Lynhurst.

R41 Colonsay
☎(01951) 200316, Fax 200353
Isle of Colonsay, Argyll, PA61 7Y
Ferry from Oban Mon/Wed/Fri (2.5 hrs); course is 2 miles W of pier.
Primitive and challenging public course on natural Hebridean machair, bearing no resemblance to modern or mainland courses.
18 holes, 4775 yards, S.S.S.72
Founded Pre 1880 (reputedly over 200 years)
Visitors: membership open to all at £5 per family per year.
Green Fee: apply for details.
Hotels: membership available through Colonsay Hotel; farm guesthouse and self-catering details on request.

R42 **Colville Park**
☎(01698) 263017 (Club/Fax)
New Jerviston House, Merry Street,
Motherwell, Lanarkshire ML1 4UG
On left hand side of A723, 1 mile N of
Motherwell Cross.
Parkland course.
18 holes, 6280 yards, S.S.S.70
Designed by James Braid.
Founded 1922
Visitors: with member only; no
weekend parties.
Green Fee: £20 per day.
Societies: Mon-Fri day ticket only.
Catering: full facilities.
Hotels: Old Mill; Moorings; Popinjay.

R43 **Corrie**
☎(01770) 810223
Sannox, Isle of Arran KA27 8JD
By A84 coast road from Brodick.
Undulating course.
9 holes, 3896 yards, S.S.S.61
Founded 1892
Visitors: welcome except Sat pm.
Green Fee: on application.
Societies: by arrangement; limited
numbers.
Catering: light meals and snacks
served.
Hotels: Ingledene (Sannox); Corrie,
Black Rock GH (Corrie).

R44 **Cowal**
☎(01369) 705673 (Club), Pro
702395
Ardenslate Rd, Kirn, Dunoon, Argyll
PA23 8LT
NE edge of Dunoon, 0.5 mile from
A815 at Kirn.
Moorland course.
18 holes, 6251 yards, S.S.S.70
Designed by James Braid.
Founded 1891
Visitors: welcome.
Green Fee: WD £16 per round, £24
per day; Mon - Fri £75; WE £24 per
round, £35 per day.
Societies: welcome by prior booking;
Sat, Sun limit 33 players; terms
available from Hon Sec.
Catering: full catering available.
International and `Home from Home'
membership available to golfers
resident outside Scotland.
Hotels: Belmont; Esplanade; Mayfair;
Rosscairn; Slatefield; St Ives; West
End.

R45 **Cowglen**
☎(0141) 632 0556, Pro shop 649
9401
301 Barrhead Rd, Glasgow G43 1EU

S side of Glasgow, following signs to
Burrell Collection, opposite Pollok golf
club.
Undulating parkland course.
18 holes, 6006 yards, S.S.S.69
Founded 1906
Visitors: introduced by member or by
letter to Sec.
Green Fee: £19 per round, £25 per
day.
Societies: apply to Sec.
Catering: lunch, dinner, bar snacks
available.
Hotels: Tinto Firs.

R46 **Craignure**
☎(01680) 812370 (Sec)
Scallastle, Graignure, Isle of Mull
PA64 5AP
1 miles from ferry at Craignure.
Links course.
9 holes, 2463 yards, S.S.S. 64
Founded 1980
Visitors: welcome, no restrictions.
Green Fee: £8.
Societies: no restrictions.
Hotels: Isle of Mull.

R47 **Crow Wood**
☎(0141) 779 4954 (Sec), Club 779
2011, Pro 779 1943
Garnkirk House, Cumbernauld Rd,
Muirhead, Glasgow G69 9JF
1 mile N of Stepps on A80.
Parkland course.
18 holes, 6249 yards, S.S.S.70
Designed by James Braid.
Founded 1925
Visitors: welcome midweek, subject
to 24 hrs minimum notice to Sec.
Green Fee: WD £17 per round, £25
per day.
Societies: weekdays by prior
arrangement.
Catering: meals served daily.
Snooker.
Hotels: Garfield; Crow Wood House;
Moodiesburn House.

R48 **Dalmally**
☎(01838) 200370 (Sec)
Old Saw Mill, Dalmally, Argyll PA33
1AS
1 mile W of Dalmally on A85.
Public flat parkland course by River
Orchy.
9 holes, 2277 yards, S.S.S.63
Founded 1987
Visitors: welcome.
Green Fee: £8 per day.
Societies: welcome with prior notice.
Catering: available with prior notice.
Hotels: Glen Orchy Lodge.

R49 **Dalmuir Municipal**
☎(0141) 952 8698 bookings
Overtoun Rd, Dalmuir, Clydebank,
Strathclyde
8 miles W of Glasgow.
Public parkland course.
18 holes, 5349 yards, S.S.S.67
Visitors: welcome.
Green Fee: apply for details.
Catering: cafe.
Practice nets.
Hotels: Radnor.

R50 **Deaconsbank**
☎(0141) 638 7044 (Golf shop), Mgr:
620 0826
Stewarton Rd, Thornliebank, Glasgow
G46 7UZ
5 miles S of Glasgow.
Public parkland course.
18 holes, 4800 yards, S.S.S.64
Founded 1922
Visitors: welcome.
Green Fee: apply for details.
Societies: welcome.
Catering: full facilities.
Driving range, putting green, pool
tables.
Hotels: The MacDonalds.

R51 **Doon Valley**
☎(01292) 531607
Hillside Park, Patna, Strathclyde KA6
7JT
10 miles S of Ayr on A713,
signposted from village of Patna.
Municipal meadowland course.
9 holes, 5700 yards, S.S.S.69
Founded 1927
Visitors: welcome.
Green Fee: £5.35 per round (annual
membership £32.55).
Societies: by arrangement.
Catering: by arrangement; bar.
Pool, darts.
Hotels: Parsons Lodge.

R52 **Dougalston**
☎(0141) 956 5750, Fax 956 6480
Strathblane Rd, Milngavie, Glasgow
G62
7 miles N of Glasgow city centre on
A879 and A81.
Public parkland course.
18 holes, 6683 yards, S.S.S.72
Designed by John Harris.
Founded 1976
Visitors: Mon - Fri.
Green Fee: £12 per round, £20 per
day.
Societies: anytime, book in advance.
Catering: all types of catering.
Hotels: Burnbrae, 1 mile.

R53 Douglas Park

☎(0141) 942 2220, Pro shop 942 1482
Hillfoot, Bearsden, Glasgow G61 2TJ
20 minutes from centre of Glasgow;
course adjacent to Hillfoot Station.
Parkland course.
18 holes, 5957 yards, S.S.S.68
Founded 1897
Visitors: with member only.
Green Fee: on request.
Societies: apply to Sec.
Catering: meals by arrangement.

R54 Douglas Water

☎(01555) 880361
Ayr Rd, Rigside, Lanark ML11 9NY
7 miles SW of Lanark on A70, 2 miles
E of A74, signposted Rigside.
Undulating parkland course.
9 holes, 2916 yards, S.S.S.69
Designed by striking coal miners
1921.
Founded 1922
Visitors: welcome.
Green Fee: apply for details.
Catering: by arrangement.

R55 Drumpellier

☎(01236) 424139 (Sec), Admin:
428723, Pro shop 432971
Drumpellier Ave, Coatbridge ML5
1RX
8 miles E of Glasgow on A89, 1 mile
from Coatbridge.
Parkland course.
18 holes, 6227 yards, S.S.S.70
Designed by W. Fernie.
Founded 1894
Visitors: welcome weekdays
excluding Bank Holidays.
Green Fee: £22 per round, £30 per
day.
Societies: weekdays.
Catering: full catering.
Pool.
Hotels: Coatbridge.

R56 Dullatur

☎(012367) 23230
Dullatur, Glasgow G68 0AR
1.5 miles from Cumbernauld village.
Undulating moorland course.
18 holes, 6195 yards, S.S.S.70
(New 18 hole course June 1996)
Founded 1896
Visitors: welcome weekdays by
arrangement.
Green Fee: £25 per day, £18 per
round.
Societies: weekdays.
Catering: full facilities available, prior
notice.

R57 Dumbarton

☎(01389) 732830 (Club)
Broadmeadows, Dumbarton,
Dumbartonshire G82 2BQ
15 miles NW of Glasgow off A82.
Meadowland course.
18 holes, 5981 yards, S.S.S.69
Founded 1888
Visitors: welcome weekdays.
Green Fee: £16 per day.
Societies: welcome by prior
arrangement.
Catering: lunches, snacks etc.

R58 Dunaverty

☎(01586) 830677
Southend by Campbeltown, Argyll
PA28 6RW
On B842, 10 miles S of
Campbeltown.
Undulating seaside course.
18 holes, 4799 yards, S.S.S.63
Founded 1889
Visitors: welcome.
Green Fee: £12 per round, £18 per
day, £48 per week.
Societies: limited; by prior
arrangement
Catering: snacks available.
Hotels: Argyll

R59 East Kilbride

☎(013552) 20913, Sec 47728
Chapelside Rd, Nerston, East Kilbride
G74 4PF
On Glasgow to East Kilbride road turn
off at Nerston opposite Commerce
Park.
Undulating meadowland course.
18 holes, 6419 yards, S.S.S.71
Designed by Fred Hawtree.
Founded 1900
Visitors: accompanied by member or
by prior arrangement.
Green Fee: £15 per round, £25 per
day.
Societies: Mon and Fri.
Catering: full catering except Tues
and Wed pm.
Hotels: Bruce; Stuart; Stakis
Westpoint.

R60 East Renfrewshire

☎(01355) 500258/6 (Clubhouse),
Pro 500206
Loganswell, Pilmuir, Newton Mearns,
Glasgow G77 6RT
A77, 1 mile from Mearns Cross.
Moorland course with panoramic
views.
18 holes, 6097 yards, S.S.S.70
Designed by James Braid.
Founded 1926

Visitors: welcome by prior telephone
call.
Green Fee: £25 per round, £30 per
day.
Societies: by arrangement.
Catering: meals served.

R61 Easter Moffat

☎(01236) 842878 (Sec), Club
842289, Pro 843015
Mansion House, Plains, by Airdrie,
Lanarkshire ML6 8NP
2 miles E of Airdrie on the old
Edinburgh-Glasgow road.
Moorland/parkland course.
18 holes, 6221 yards, S.S.S.70
Founded 1922
Visitors: welcome.
Green Fee: apply for details.
Societies: weekdays by prior
arrangement.
Catering: facilities available by
arrangement.

R62 Eastwood

☎(01355) 500261 (Club), Pro
500285, Sec 500280
Loganswell, Newton Mearns,
Glasgow G77 6RX
On A77 from Glasgow, 3 miles S of
Newton Mearns Cross at junction of
Old Mearns Rd.
Moorland course.
18 holes, 5886 yards, S.S.S.69
Designed by J. Moon.
Founded 1893
Visitors: parties welcome by prior
appointment with Sec.
Green Fee: WD £20 per round, £30
per day.
Societies: welcome by prior
arrangement.
Catering: full facilities.
Hotels: Redhurst; McDonald
(Giffnock).

R63 Elderslie

☎(01505) 323956
63 Main Rd, Elderslie, Renfrewshire
PA5 9AZ
On A737 between Paisley and
Johnstone.
Undulating parkland course.
18 holes, 6175 yards, S.S.S.70
Founded 1909
Visitors: full facilities Mon to Fri only.
Green Fee: £18 per round, £24 per
day.
Societies: Mon, Wed, Fri by
arrangement.
Catering: full facilities.
Snooker.
Hotels: Excelsior, Glasgow Airport.

R64 Erskine

☎(01505) 862108 (Pro shop), Club 862302
Bishopton, Renfrewshire PA7 5PH
N of M8 leave Erskine Toll Bridge and turn left along B815 for 1.5 miles.
Parkland course.
18 holes, 6287 yards, S.S.S.70
Founded 1904
Visitors: welcome if introduced by or playing with a member.
Green Fee: on application.
Societies: welcome by prior arrangement.
Catering: meals served to members and their guests only, or by prior arrangement.
Hotels: Erskine; Crest.

R65 Fereneze

☎(0141) 881 1519, Sec 248 6976, Pro 881 7058
Fereneze Ave, Barrhead, Glasgow G78 1HJ
9 miles SW of Glasgow near Barrhead station.
Moorland course.
18 holes, 5962 yards, S.S.S.70
Founded 1904
Visitors: by application to Pro, Sec, or accompanied by member.
Green Fee: apply for details.
Societies: weekdays only, apply to Sec.
Catering: lunches, bar snacks, evening meals all day Sat/Sun, usually by booking weekdays.
Hotels: Dalmeny Park.

R66 Gigha

☎(01583) 505287
Isle of Gigha, Kintyre, Argyll PA41 7AA
By ferry from Tayinloan (ring Whitehouse (0188 073) 253/4 for times); 2.5 hours drive from Glasgow.
Links course.
9 holes, 5026 yards, S.S.S. 66
Visitors: welcome.
Green Fee: £7 per round, £10 per day.
Catering: at Boat House and Gigha Hotel.
Hotels: Gigha.

R67 Girvan

☎(01465) 714346
Girvan, Ayrshire KA26 9HW
Off A77, main Stranraer to Ayr road.
Seaside links/parkland course.
18 holes, 5095 yards, S.S.S.64
Designed by James Braid.
Founded pre-1877

Visitors: welcome.
Green Fee: £11 per round, £18 per day.
Societies: welcome by arrangement.
Catering: meals served by arrangement (01465) 714272.
Hotels: Kings Arms; Turnberry.

R68 Glasgow

☎(0141) 942 2011 (Sec), Fax 942 0770
Killermont, Bearsden, Glasgow G61 2TW
6 miles NW of Glasgow near Killermont Bridge on A81 or A806.
Parkland course.
18 holes, 5968 yards, S.S.S.69
Designed by Tom Morris Snr.
Founded 1787 (Killermont 1905)
Visitors: catered for by application.
Green Fee: £35 per round.
Societies: on application.
Catering: lunches, high teas served by prior arrangement.
Hotels: Grosvenor; Burnbrae; Black Bull; Stakis Pond.

R69 Glasgow (Gailes)

☎(01294) 311347 (Club), Sec (0141) 942 2011, Fax (041) 942 0770
Gailes, by Irvine, Ayrshire KA11 5AE
2 miles S of Irvine on A78.
Seaside links course.
18 holes, 6502 yards, S.S.S.72
Designed by Willie Park Jr.
Founded 1787 (Gailes 1892)
Visitors: on application to Sec, or introduction by member.
Green Fee: WD £30 per round, £37 per day; WE £33 per round.
Societies: on application to Sec.
Catering: lunches and high teas; also bar snacks.
Hotels: Hospitality Inn (Irvine); Marine (Troon).

R70 Gleddoch Country Club

☎(01475) 540304 (Club), Pro 540704, Fax 540459
Langbank, Renfrewshire PA14 6YE
M8 to Greenock, first turning to Langbank Houston (B789).
Parkland/moorland course.
18 holes, 6357 yards, S.S.S.71
Designed by Hamilton Stutt.
Founded 1975
Visitors: welcome by arrangement with Pro, Keith Campbell.
Green Fee: on application.
Societies: welcome.
Catering: meals and snacks.
Hotels: Gleddoch House.

R71 Glencruitten

☎(01631) 562868 (Bar), Pro shop 564115
Glencruitten Rd, Oban, Argyll PA34 4PU
1 mile from town centre off A816; follow road signs for Rare Breeds Park.
Hilly parkland/moorland course.
18 holes, 4452 yards, S.S.S.63
Designed by James Braid.
Founded 1908
Visitors: welcome weekdays, with restrictions on Thurs and Sat.
Green Fee: WD £12 per round, £15 per day; WE £14 per round, £16 per day.
Societies: limited number of societies accepted.
Catering: meals and snacks available, licenced bar.
Pool tables.

R72 Gourock

☎(01475) 631001 (Club), Pro shop 636834
Cowal View, Gourock, Renfrewshire PA19 6HD
2 miles up hill from Gourock station.
Moorland course.
18 holes, 6547 yards, S.S.S.73
Designed by Henry Cotton.
Founded 1896
Visitors: welcome - apply via Pro shop.
Green Fee: WD £16 per round, £22 per day; Sun £20 per round.
Societies: by arrangement.
Catering: bar lunches, high teas, dinner by arrangement.
Hotels: Gantock; Contine.

R73 Greenock

☎(01475) 720793 (Club), Pro shop 787236
Forsyth St, Greenock, Renfrewshire PA16 8RE
1 mile SW of town centre, main road to Gourock away from River Clyde.
Moorland course.
18 holes, 5838 yards, S.S.S.69; 9 holes, 2149 yards, S.S.S.32
Designed by James Braid.
Founded 1890
Visitors: welcome except Sat.
Green Fee: on application.
Catering: full service except Mon.
Hotels: Tontine.

R74 Greenock Whinhill

☎(01475) 724694
Beith Rd, Greenock, Renfrewshire PA16 9LN

23 miles W of Glasgow,
Renfrewshire.
Moorland course.
18 holes, 5454 yards, S.S.S.68
Founded 1908
Visitors: welcome.
Green Fee: apply for details.
Societies: welcome by prior
arrangement.
Catering: meals provided by
arrangement.

R75 Haggs Castle
☎(0141) 427 1157 (Sec), Pro 427
3355, Club 427 0480
70 Dumbreck Rd, Glasgow G41 4SN
At end of M77 off M8.
Parkland course.
18 holes, 6464 yards, S.S.S.72
Designed by Peter Alliss & Dave
Thomas.
Founded 1910
Visitors: only when accompanied by
member.
Green Fee: £27 per round, £37 per
day.
Societies: Wed only by prior
arrangement.
Catering: all types available.
Snooker.
Hotels: Sherbrooke Castle.

R76 Hamilton
☎(01698) 282872, Sec 286131, Pro
shop 282324
Riccarton, Ferniegair, Hamilton,
Lanarkshire ML3 7UE
Off A74 between Larkhall and
Hamilton.
Parkland course.
18 holes, 6264 yards, S.S.S.70
Designed by James Braid.
Founded 1892
Visitors: welcome with member,
others by arrangement.
Green Fee: apply for details.
Societies: by arrangement with Sec.
Catering: snacks daily, meals served
by arrangement.

R77 Hayston
☎(0141) 776 1244 (Clubhouse),
Pro:775 0882,
Sec 775 0723
Campsie Rd, Kirkintilloch, Glasgow
G66 1RN
NE from Glasgow via Bishopbriggs
and Kirkintilloch, 1 mile N of
Kirkintilloch.
Parkland course.
18 holes, 6042 yards, S.S.S.69
Designed by James Braid.
Founded 1926

Visitors: weekdays only with letter of
intro.
Green Fee: on application.
Societies: Tues and Thurs.
Catering: full service from 9am;
lunch, bar snacks, high tea, dinner if
ordered in advance.

R78 Helensburgh
☎(01436) 674173 (Club), Pro shop
675505, Fax 671170
25 East Abercromby St, Helensburgh,
Dunbartonshire
G84 9JD
21 miles W of Glasgow on A82.
Moorland course.
18 holes, 6104 yards, S.S.S.69
Designed by Tom Morris.
Founded 1893
Visitors: welcome weekdays.
Green Fee: £15 per round, £23 per
day; jnrs £6 per round.
Societies: by arrangement.
Catering: bar lunches, evening meals
by arrangement.
Hotels: Commodore.

R79 Hilton Park
☎(0141) 956 4657 (Sec), Pro 956
5125
Stockiemuir Rd, Milngavie, Glasgow
G62 7HB
8 miles N of Glasgow on A809.
Moorland courses.
Allander, 18 holes, 5374 yards,
S.S.S.66; Hilton, 18 holes, 6054
yards, S.S.S.70
Designed by James Braid.
Founded 1927
Visitors: welcome weekdays by prior
arrangement.
Green Fee: £20 per round, £26 (2
rounds).
Societies: weekdays.
Catering: full facilities.
Hotels: Kirkhouse; Black Bull;
Country Club.

R80 Hollandbush
☎(01555) 893484 (Club), Sec
820222, Pro shop 893646
Acretophead, Lesmahagow,
Strathclyde ML11 0JS
Off A74 between Lesmahagow and
Coalburn.
Parkland/moorland course.
18 holes, 6223 yards, S.S.S.70
Designed by Ken Pate.
Founded 1954
Visitors: welcome.
Green Fee: on application.
Catering: full catering facilities.
Large practice ground.

R81 Innellan
☎(01369) 830242
Knockamillie Rd, Innellan, Argyll
4 miles S of Dunoon.
Parkland course.
9 holes, 4878 yards, S.S.S.63
Founded 1891
Visitors: anytime except Mon
evenings.
Green Fee: on application.
Societies: catered for weekdays and
weekends.
Catering: available.
Hotels: Esplanade; Slatefield;
Rosscairn.

R82 Inverary
☎(01499) 302508 (Sec)
Inverary, Argyll, Scotland
SW corner of town on Lochgilphead
Rd.
Parkland course.
9 holes, 5700 yards, S.S.S.68
Designed by Watt Landscaping.
Founded June 1993
Visitors: welcome any time except
during club competitions.
Green Fee: £10 per day; jnrs half
price.
Societies: by prior arrangement.
Catering: Nets, small practice area.
Hotels: Loch Fyne; George; The
Great Inn.

R83 Irvine
☎(01294) 275979
Bogside, Irvine KA12 8SN
On road from Irvine to Kilwinning, turn
left after Ravenspark Academy and
carry straight on for 0.5 mile over
railway bridge.
Links course.
18 holes, 6480 yards, S.S.S.73
Designed by James Braid.
Founded 1887
Visitors: welcome weekdays (except
Fri) and after 3pm weekends.
Green Fee: WD £30 per round, £40
per day; WE £40.
Societies: on application to Sec.
Catering: meals and snacks served.
Hotels: Hospitality Inn; Redburn;
Eglinton Arms; Golf; Annfield.

R84 Irvine Ravenspark
☎(01294) 271293, Pro 276467
13 Kidsneuk Lane, Irvine, Ayrshire
KA12 8SR
On A78 midway between Irvine and
Kilwinning.
Municipal parkland course.
18 holes, 6429 yards, S.S.S.71
Founded 6 June 1907

Visitors: welcome every day except Sat until 2.30pm.
Green Fee: WD £6.60 per round, £11 per day; WE £11 per round, £16.50 per day.
Societies: catered for Mon-Fri, Sun by arrangement with Sec.
Catering: bar open all day every day; lunches and high teas.
Hotels: Hospitality Inn; Annfield; Redburn; Golf Inn.

R85 **Kilbirnie Place**
☎(01505) 683398 (Club)
Largs Rd, Kilbirnie, Ayrshire KA25 7AJ
On outskirts of Kilbirnie on main Largs road.
Parkland course.
18 holes, 5511 yards, S.S.S.67
Founded 1922
Visitors: weekdays and Sun.
Green Fee: WD £10 per round, £18 per day; Sun £17 per round.
Societies: weekdays, apply in writing to Sec.
Catering: every day.

R86 **Kilmacolm**
☎(01505) 872139 (Club), Fax 874007
Porterfield Rd, Kilmacolm, Renfrewshire PA13 3PD
A740 to Linwood, then A761 to Bridge of Weir.
Moorland course.
18 holes, 5964 yards, S.S.S.68
Designed by James Braid.
Founded 1890
Visitors: welcome weekdays; weekends if accompanied by member only.
Green Fee: £20 per round, £26 per day.
Societies: welcome by prior arrangement.
Catering: available.
Hotels: Gryffe (Bridge of Weir).

R87 **Kilmarnock (Barassie)**
☎(01292) 311077 (Club), Sec 313920, Pro shop 311322
29 Hillhouse Rd, Barassie, Troon, Ayrshire KA10 6SY
Off A78 just N of Troon opposite Barassie station.
Seaside course.
18 holes, 6473 yards, S.S.S.72
Designed by Matthew M. Monie.
Founded 1887
Visitors: Mon, Tues, Thurs, Fri only.
Green Fee: £30 per round, £40 per day.

Societies: Tues and Thurs by prior arrangement.
Catering: full facilities available.
Hotels: Marine (Troon).

R88 **Kilsyth Lennox**
☎(01236) 823213 (Sec), Club 824115
Tak-Ma-Doon Rd, Kilsyth, Glasgow G65 0HX
12 miles from Glasgow on A80.
Moorland/parkland course.
18 holes, 5912 yards, S.S.S. 70
Founded 1907
Visitors: by arrangement with secretary.
Green Fee: on application.
Societies: on application.
Catering: facilities available.

R89 **Kirkhill**
☎(0141) 641 3083 (Club), Sec 641 8499
Greenlees Rd, Cambuslang, Glasgow G72 8YN
Follow East Kilbride road from Burnside, take first turning on left past Cathkin by-pass roundabout.
Meadowland course.
18 holes, 5875 yards, S.S.S.69
Designed by James Braid.
Founded 1910
Visitors: welcome by arrangement with Sec.
Green Fee: £15 per round, £22 per day.
Societies: welcome by prior arrangement in writing.
Catering: bar snacks, full meals provided by arrangement with Clubmistress.
Hotels: Kings Park; Burnside; Stuart; Bruce.

R90 **Kirkintilloch**
☎(0141) 776 1256 (Club), Sec 775 2387
Todhill, Campsie Rd, Kirkintilloch, Glasgow G66 1RN
1 mile from Kirkintilloch on road to Lennoxtown.
Meadowland course.
18 holes, 5269 yards, S.S.S.66
Designed by James Braid.
Founded 1895
Visitors: only if introduced.
Green Fee: £15 per round, £20 per day.
Societies: welcome only by advance booking.
Catering: full facilities except Mon and Tues.
Hotels: Garfield (Stepps).

R91 **Knightswood**
☎(0141) 959 2131
Lincoln Ave, Knightswood, Glasgow
Off Dumbarton Rd from city centre.
Parkland course.
9 holes, 2717 yards, S.S.S.64
Founded 1920s
Visitors: welcome.
Green Fee: apply for details.
Societies: welcome by prior arrangement.

R92 **Kyles of Bute**
☎(01700) 811603 (Sec)
Tighnabruaich, Argyll PA21 2EE
B836 from Dunoon to Tighnabruaich, through village to Kames Cross, then B8000 to Millhouse, club entrance on left at top of 1st rise.
Undulating moorland course.
9 holes, 2389 yards, S.S.S.32
Founded 1907
Visitors: welcome except Sun am.
Green Fee: £6 per day; £3 under 18.
Societies: by arrangement.
Catering: tea, coffee, snacks when available.
Hotels: Royal; Kames; Kyles of Bute.

R93 **Lamlash**
☎(01770) 600296 (Clubhouse), Starter: 600196
Lamlash, Brodick, Isle of Arran KA27 8JU
3 miles S of Brodick Pier on A841.
Undulating heathland.
18 holes, 4681 yards, S.S.S.64
Founded 1889
Visitors: welcome, no restrictions.
Green Fee: WD £10 per day; WE £12 per day.
Societies: booking by letter.
Catering: tearoom, club bar.
Hotels: Glenisle; Marine (unlicenced).

R94 **Lanark**
☎(01555) 663219 (Club/Sec), Pro 661456
The Moor, Whitelees Rd, Lanark ML11 7RX
Off A73 or A72, turn left in Lanark into Whitelees Rd, for 0.5 mile.
Moorland course.
18 holes, 6423 yards, S.S.S.71
Designed by Ben Sayers and James Braid.
Founded 1851
Visitors: welcome weekdays.
Green Fee: £23 per round, £35 per day.
Societies: Mon-Wed only.
Catering: full, resident chef.
Hotels: Tinto; The Popinjay.

R95 Largs

☎(01475) 673594 (Sec/Fax), Club 674681
Irvine Rd, Largs, Ayrshire KA30 8EU
1 mile S of Largs on A78, 28 miles from Glasgow.
Parkland course with sea views..
18 holes, 6237 yards, S.S.S.71
Founded 1891
Visitors: welcome.
Green Fee: £25 per round, £35 per day.
Societies: Tues and Thurs, small groups on Fri a.m.
Catering: full facilities.
Hotels: Elderslie; Haylie; South Bay; Brisbane.

R96 Larkhall

☎(01698) 881113
Burnhead Rd, Larkhall, Lanarkshire
Take M8 motorway to Larkhall exit then head SW on B7019.
Municipal course.
9 holes, 6423 yards, S.S.S.71
Visitors: all welcome.
Green Fee: £3.75
Societies: by arrangement.
Catering: Bar

R97 Leadhills

☎(01659) 74324 (Sec)
Leadhills, Biggar, Lanarkshire ML12 6XR
On B797, 6 miles from A74 at Abington, course behind hotel within Leadhills village.
Moorland course; highest in Scotland.
9 holes, 4100 yards, S.S.S.62
Founded 1935
Visitors: welcome anytime.
Green Fee: £5 per day.
Societies: welcome.
Catering: at local hotel.
Hotels: Hopetoun Arms.

R98 Lenzie

☎(0141) 776 1535 (Club),
Sec/bookings:776 6020
Pro 777 7748
19 Crosshill Rd, Lenzie, Glasgow G66 5DA
A80 to Stepps, Lenzie road turn left at traffic lights.
Moorland course.
18 holes, 5984 yards, S.S.S.69
Founded 1889
Visitors: welcome with member.
Green Fee: £16 per round, £24 per day.
Societies: welcome weekdays.
Catering: meals and snacks available except Mon.

R99 Lethamhill

☎(0141) 770 6220
Cumbernauld Rd, Glasgow G33 1AH
On A80 adjacent to Hogganfield Loch.
Municipal course.
18 holes, 5836 yards, S.S.S.70
Visitors: welcome.
Green Fee: Summer £3.70 per round; Winter £4.50 per round.

R100 Linn Park

☎(0141) 637 5871 (Club)
Simshill Rd, Glasgow G44 5EP
Off M74 S of Glasgow.
Public parkland course.
18 holes, 4952 yards, S.S.S.65
Designed by Glasgow Parks.
Founded 1925
Visitors: welcome.
Green Fee: apply for details.
Wildlife park 200 yards from clubhouse.

R101 Littlehill

☎(0141) 772 1916 (Club)
Auchinairn Rd, Bishopbriggs, Glasgow G74 1UT
3 miles N of city centre.
Municipal parkland course.
18 holes, 6228 yards, S.S.S.70
Designed by James Braid.
Founded 1924
Visitors: no restrictions.
Green Fee: apply for details.
Societies: apply to Glasgow Corporation Parks Dept.
Catering: lunches available daily except Mon.

R102 Loch Lomond

☎(01436) 860223 (Pro shop), Fax 860265
Rossdhu House, Luss by Alexandria, Dunbartonshire G83 8NT
On W bank of Loch Lomond on A82.
Parkland course.
18 holes, 7060 yards, S.S.S.72
Designed by Tom Weiskopf.
Founded Opening 1995
Visitors: with members only.

R103 Lochgilphead

☎(01546) 602340
Blarbuie Road, Lochgilphead, Argyll PA31 8LD
A82 and A83 from Glasgow to Lochgilphead; 1 mile from parish church on Hospital Rd.
Hilly parkland course.
9 holes, 4484 yards, S.S.S.63
Designed by Dr Ian MacCammond.
Founded 1891
Visitors: welcome weekdays, members competitions weekends.
Green Fee: £10 per day.
Societies: by arrangement.
Catering: bar available evenings and weekends; catering by arrangement.
Hotels: Stag; Argyll; Lochgair; Castlesween Caravan Park.

R104 Lochranza

☎(01770) 830273 (Club)
Lochranza, Isle of Arran, KA27 8HL
In village of Lochranza at N of island.
Grassland course with river and trees, 3 holes adjacent seashore.
9 holes (18 flags, 18 tees), 5564 yards, Par 70
Designed by Iain M. Robertson.
Founded course laid 1991.
Visitors: welcome 7 days.
Green Fee: £5 (9 holes), £10 (18 holes), £12 per day.
Societies: welcome any time.
Catering: snacks.
Hotels: caravan park adjacent (vans for hire); weekly golf packages inc outings to other courses; hotel/guest house packages on request.

R105 Lochwinnoch

☎(01505) 842153 (Club), Pro 843029
Burnfoot Rd, Lochwinnoch, Renfrewshire PA12 4AN.
On A760 about 10 miles S of Paisley, 1st on right after Struthers Garage, 400 yards along Burnfoot Rd.
Parkland course.
18 holes, 6243 yards, S.S.S.71
Designed by
Founded 1897
Visitors: weekdays till 4pm, no visitors weekends.
Green Fee: £15 per round, £20 per day.
Societies: by arrangement.
Catering: by arrangement.
Hotels: Lindhurst.

R106 Loudoun

☎(01563) 821993 (Sec), Club 820551
Galston, Ayrshire KA4 8PA
A77 to Kilmarnock, take Edinburgh road, club lies on main road between Galston and Newmilns.
Parkland course.
18 holes, 5844 yards, S.S.S.68
Designed by
Founded 1909

Machrie

Machrie's charm lies in its out of the way setting. Lapped on one side by the Atlantic and separated from the mainland by a sea voyage (or a short aeroplane hop from Glasgow), its delights are little known.

They are certainly not as well known as they deserve to be, because the course is in the very best tradition of seaside links. However, by developing its assets a little more than in the past, the Island of Islay is putting itself far more on the map; and without wishing to spoil a way of life by causing a golfing invasion to its shores, the recommendation for its golf is based on happy personal experience that it would be churlish not to pass on.

After years of acting as co-tenants to grazing sheep and cattle, golfers owe something of a transformation to the former owners of Bowmore Distillery who bought the course and hotel, and added a cluster of cottages alongside which are an ideal base for whatever form of holiday you seek on Islay.

It is a wide choice but, as golfers have supported the distillers' product ever since man first took three putts, there is a delicious aptness about the change. However, Machrie's new look was not confined to new management. It has six new holes which add enormously to its rating as a test of golf. Some of the eccentricities that grew up before there was much in the way of machinery or golf course architects have been reduced; gone are one or two, though not all, of the blind shots into crater-like greens – a type of hole not so favourably looked upon as it once was; in their place have arisen a new 2nd, 10th, 11th, 12th, 13th and 14th that offer, in distillers' language, a smoother blend.

The 1st, a gentle opener, has an inviting drive from a raised tee, but the 2nd quickly gets down to the real golfing business. The first of the alterations, it is a winding dogleg to the left, the dogleg taking the form of a fast flowing brook, with plans for extending the hole to par 5.

Anyone with thoughts of getting home in two will need a strong nerve as well as two good shots, although the 3rd and 4th are less stern. The 5th is a fine short hole and the 6th typical of Machrie's natural blessings with a drive to the left providing the correct approach and view of a green in a dell.

In its early days in the last century, the drive at the 7th over a vast sandhill was rather more formidable than it is now; all the same, it can still strike fear at the beginning of a stretch of three holes, all par fours, which follow the line of a glorious sandy beach. These emphasise the remoteness and the beauty and the fact that, unlike many famous seaside courses, here is the opportunity to really see the sea.

The 10th tee is a notable example even if it is not time to be distracted. A marvellous natural short hole at the furthest limit of the course marks the introduction to the new golfing country; this is nicely demanding but, at the same time, there is a pleasant scenic change to the hills and lonely peat moors.

The 11th requires a strong second to a long green with a heathery drop to the left and the not so short par 3 12th, is even tougher. The main feature of the 13th, a par 5 bending left, is the amphitheatre in which the green is situated, while the 14th is perhaps the hardest of all the par fours. A long drive is necessary for the proper view of the flag outlined against the skyline.

After a spell where stout hitting is essential, the last four holes are not quite as severe; nevertheless, the need for good judgement is paramount and, against any sort of wind, the 16th and 18th, in particular, can pose much greater problems. However, if your score doesn't turn out quite the way you planned (how many do?), there are ample consolations.

There is no shortage of spirituous assistance to help forget the bad round – and celebrate the good – and the atmosphere of the Club and hotel, as of the island as a whole, is wonderfully friendly and informal.

Visitors: welcome weekdays.
Green Fee: £17 per round, £29 per day.
Societies: welcome by prior arrangement.
Catering: facilities available.
Hotels: Broomhill; Foxbar.

R107 **Machrie**

☎(01496) 302310 (Club/Hotel), Fax 302404
The Machrie Hotel & Golf Course, Port Ellen, Isle of Islay, Argyll PA42 7AN
30 mins by air from Glasgow, 4 miles from Port Ellen.
Traditional links course.
18 holes, 6226 yards, S.S.S.70
Designed by Willie Campbell, redesigned by Donald Steel.
Founded 1891
Visitors: welcome.
Green Fee: apply for details.
Societies: at any time by arrangement.
Catering: bar lunches, grill, table d'hote, à la carte.
Banqueting. conferences, company days, own beach, salmon/sea trout fishing, snooker.
Hotels: Machrie Hotel; leisure/golf packages available, telephone for details.

R108 **Machrie Bay**

☎(01770) 850232 (Captain)
Sheeans, Pirnmill, Brodick, Isle of Arran KA27
Ferry to Brodick and via String Rd to Machrie.
Fairly flat seaside course.
9 holes, 2123 yards, S.S.S.32
Designed by William Fernie.
Founded 1900
Visitors: welcome.
Green Fee: £5 per round, £7.50 per day.
Catering: snacks served April-Sept.
Tennis.

R109 **Machrihanish**

☎(01586) 810213 (Club), Pro shop 810277
Machrihanish, Campbeltown, Argyll PA28 6PT
5 miles W of Campbeltown on B843.
Seaside links course.
18 holes, 6228 yards, S.S.S.71; also 9 hole course
Founded 1876
Visitors: welcome at all times; golf/flight day package available through Logan Air, Glasgow.

Green Fee: Sun-Fri £20 per round, £28 per day;Sat £35 per day.
Societies: welcome, certain weekends available also.
Catering: full facilities.

R110 **Maybole**

Memorial Park, Maybole, Ayrshire KA19
9 miles S of Ayr on main Stranraer route.
Public hillside course with splendid views.
9 holes, 2652 yards, S.S.S.65
Founded 1905
Visitors: no restrictions; booking available through South Ayrshire District Council.
Green Fee: apply for details.
Societies: booking as for visitors.
Hotels: many in Ayr offering golf packages.

R111 **Millport**

☎(01475) 530311 (Club), Sec 530306
Golf Rd, Millport, Isle of Cumbrae KA28 0BA
Cal-Mac car ferry Largs Slip to Cumbrae (7 minutes), thence 3 miles by car or public transport.
Seaside moorland course.
18 holes, 5828 yards, S.S.S.69
Founded 1888
Visitors: welcome at all times.
Green Fee: £20 per day max.
Societies: welcome by arrangement, inc weekends.
Catering: full facilities, including bar.
Large practice area.
Hotels: Royal George; Islands.

R112 **Milngavie**

☎(0141) 956 1619 (Club)
Laighpark, Milngavie, Glasgow G62 8EP
Off A809 NW of Glasgow.
Moorland course.
18 holes, 5818 yards, S.S.S.68
Founded 1895
Visitors: welcome by prior arrangement.
Green Fee: apply for details.
Societies: catered for Wed-Fri.
Catering: by arrangement.
Hotels: Black Bull; Burnbrae.

R113 **Mount Ellen**

☎(01236) 872277 (Clubhouse), Pro 872632
Johnstone Rd, Johnstone House, Gartcosh, Glasgow G69 8EY

Off A80 Glasgow-Stirling road.
Parkland course.
18 holes, 5525 yards, S.S.S.67
Founded 1905
Visitors: by appointment.
Green Fee: £12 per round, £20 per day.
Catering: full facilities.
Pool.

R114 **New Cumnock**

☎(01290) 338848
Lochill, Cumnock Rd, New Cumnock, Ayrshire KA18 4BQ
0.5 mile N of New Cumnock.
Parkland course.
9 holes, 5176 yards, S.S.S.65
Founded 1901
Visitors: welcome, not before 4pm Sun; restricted on competition days.
Green Fee: £8 per day.
Societies: on application in writing.
Catering: snacks.
Hotels: Lochside House.

R115 **Old Course Ranfurly**

☎(01505) 613612 (Club), Sec/Office: 613214
Ranfurly Place, Bridge of Weir, Renfrewshire PA11 3DE
7 miles W of Paisley, 10 mins from Glasgow airport.
Moorland course.
18 holes, 6089 yards, S.S.S.69
Founded 1905
Visitors: welcome weekdays by introduction, weekends with member.
Green Fee: £15 per round, £25 per day.
Societies: by special arrangement.
Catering: morning coffee, bar lunches, high tea, dinner.
Hotels: on request.

R116 **Paisley**

☎(0141) 884 4114 (Pro shop), Sec 884 3903
Braehead, Paisley PA2 8TZ
From Glasgow, A737 to Paisley, 3 miles S of Paisley centre.
Moorland course.
18 holes, 6466 yards, S.S.S.71
Founded 1895.
Visitors: weekdays before 4pm, h/cap cert or prior arrangement with Sec or Pro.
Green Fee: £20 per round, £28 per day.
Societies: by arrangement; not weekends or Bank Holidays.
Catering: full catering available.
Snooker.
Hotels: Watermill; Excelsior.

R117 **Palacerigg**
☎(01236) 734969 (Club), Starter: 721461
Palacerigg Country Park, Cumbernauld G67 3HU
Take A80 to Cumbernauld, follow signs to Country Park.
Parkland course.
18 holes, 6408 yards, S.S.S.71
Designed by Henry Cotton.
Founded 1975
Visitors: welcome weekdays.
Green Fee: WD £7.35; WE £8.90.
Societies: welcome weekdays by arrangement.
Catering: lunches and high teas available weekdays except Mon and Tues.
Hotels: Castlecary.

R118 **Pollok**
☎(0141) 632 1080 (Club), Sec 632 4351
90 Barrhead Rd, Glasgow G43 1BG
On A736, 4 miles S of city centre.
Wooded parkland course.
18 holes, 6257 yards, S.S.S.70
Founded 1892
Visitors: men only Mon-Fri.
Green Fee: £26 per round, £33 per day.
Societies: by letter to Sec.
Catering: full dining facilities.
Hotels: Albany; Macdonald; Holiday Inn; Forum.

R119 **Port Bannatyne**
☎(01700) 502009
Bannatyne Mains Rd, Port Bannatyne, Isle of Bute
2 miles N of Rothesay on A845.
Hilly seaside course.
13 holes, 5085 yards, S.S.S.65
Designed by James Braid.
Founded 1912
Visitors: unrestricted.
Green Fee: £10 per day, £30 per week; jnrs £5 per day, £15 per week.
Societies: welcome.
Catering: snacks, other catering by arrangement.
Hotels: Ardmory House; Port Royal; Ardbeg Lodge.

R120 **Port Glasgow**
☎(01475) 704181 (Club)
Devol Farm Industrial Estate, Port Glasgow, Renfrewshire PA14 5XE
SW of Glasgow on M8 towards Greenock; in town of Port Glasgow.
Undulating course.
18 holes, 5712 yards, S.S.S.68
Founded 1895

Visitors: weekdays until 3.55pm; at all other times only with introduction.
Green Fee: apply for details.
Societies: catered for on non-competition days (Sun-Fri).
Catering: meals served on request.
Hotels: Clune Brae; Star.

R121 **Prestwick**
☎(01292) 477404 (Sec), Pro 479483
2 Links Rd, Prestwick, Ayrshire KA9 1QG
1 mile from Prestwick Airport adjacent to Prestwick station.
Seaside links course.
18 holes, 6544 yards, S.S.S.73
Founded 1851
Visitors: by arrangement; prior booking essential.
Green Fee: on application.
Societies: welcome by prior arrangement.
Catering: dining room, men only; Cardinal room, mixed, casual dress, light lunches.
Hotels: Parkstone; Fairways; Golf View; North Beach.

R122 **Prestwick St Cuthbert**
☎(01292) 477101 (Sec), Fax 671730
East Rd, Prestwick, Ayrshire KA9 2SX
Off main Ayr to Prestwick Rd, at Bellevue Rd.
Parkland course.
18 holes, 6470 yards, S.S.S.71
Designed by Stutt & Co.
Founded 1899
Visitors: welcome weekdays, weekends only if introduced by member.
Green Fee: £20 per round, £27 per day.
Societies: by arrangement, not weekends or Bank Holidays.
Catering: lunch, bar lunches, dinner.
Hotels: Carlton; St Nicholas; Parkstone.

R123 **Prestwick St Nicholas**
☎(01292) 477608 (Sec), Pro 479755
Grangemuir Rd, Prestwick, Ayrshire KA9 1SN
Off A79, from Main St turn into Grangemuir Rd which runs down to sea.
Links course.
18 holes, 5952 yards, S.S.S.69
Designed by C. Hunter.
Founded 1851

Visitors: welcome weekdays.
Green Fee: £22 per round, £35 per day.
Societies: weekdays.
Catering: bar lunch, high tea, dinner.
Hotels: Parkstone; St Ninians; North Beach.

R124 **Ralston**
☎(0141) 882 1349 (Club)
Strathmore Ave, Ralston, Paisley, Renfrewshire PA1 3DT
Off main Paisley to Glasgow road.
Parkland course.
18 holes, 6100 yards, S.S.S.69
Founded 1904
Visitors: organised parties only.
Green Fee: on application.
Catering: meals served, bar snacks.
Hotels: Glynhill; Pines; Watermill; Crookston.

R125 **Ranfurly Castle**
☎(01505) 612609 (Clubhouse), Pro 614795
Golf Rd, Bridge of Weir, Renfrewshire PA11 3HN
Off M8 at sign for Linwood.
Undulating moorland course.
18 holes, 6284 yards, S.S.S.71
Designed by Andrew Kirkaldy & Willie Auchterlonie.
Founded 1889
Visitors: weekdays by introduction.
Green Fee: £25 per round, £30 per day.
Societies: Tues and Thurs.
Catering: snacks, lunches, high teas.
Hotels: Gryffe Arms.

R126 **Renfrew**
☎(0141) 886 6692 (Sec), Pro 885 1754, Fax 886 1808
Blythswood Estate, Inchinnan Rd, Renfrew RA4 9EG
Off A8 at Normandy Hotel.
Parkland course.
18 holes, 6818 yards, S.S.S.73
Designed by John Harris.
Founded 1894
Visitors: introduced by member.
Green Fee: apply for details.
Societies: welcome by arrangement, max 40.
Catering: full catering.
Hotels: Normandy; Glynhill; Dean Park.

R127 **Rothesay**
☎(01700) 503554 (Pro shop/Fax)
Canada Hill, Rothesay, Isle of Bute PA20 9HN

30 minutes by steamer from Wemyss Bay (30 miles from Glasgow). Undulating parkland course. 18 holes, 5370 yards, S.S.S.66 Designed by James Braid. Founded 1892 **Visitors:** welcome, bookings advisable Sat/Sun. **Green Fee:** on application. **Societies:** welcome by prior arrangement. **Catering:** full catering all week, April-Sept.

R128 Routenburn
☎(01475) 673230 (Club), Pro shop 687240
Largs, Ayrshire KA30 8SQ
1 mile N of Largs; 1st major left turn coming into Largs from Greenock direction.
Seaside hill course.
18 holes, 5640 yards, S.S.S.68
Designed by James Braid.
Founded 1914
Visitors: welcome weekdays.
Green Fee: on application.
Societies: welcome weekdays by arrangement.
Catering: full catering facilities except Thurs.

R129 Royal Troon
☎(01292) 311555 Office, 317578 Club Steward, 313281 Pro, 318204 Fax
Craigend Rd, Troon, Ayrshire KA10 6EP
3 miles from Prestwick Airport.
Seaside links course.
Old Course (championship), 18 holes, 7081 yards, S.S.S.73; Portland Course, 18 holes, 6274 yards, S.S.S.71
Founded 1878
Visitors: Mon, Tues and Thurs only with starting time restriction; max h/cap 18; no Ladies on Old Course; letter of intro required together with h/cap cert.
Green Fee: Old course £90; Portland £48 per day; only 1 round permitted on Old Course; lunch etc included.
Societies: max 24 persons.
Catering: full restaurant service and bar snacks by arrangement.
Hotels: Marine Highland; Piersland.

R130 Ruchill
☎(0141) 770 0519 (Glasgow Parks Dept)
Brassey Street, Maryhill, Glasgow G20

2.5 miles NW of Glasgow off Bearsden road.
Municipal parkland course.
9 holes, 2240 yards, S.S.S.61
Founded 1928
Visitors: welcome.
Green Fee: apply for details.
Societies: contact Glasgow Parks Dept.

R131 Sandyhills
☎(0141) 778 1179 (Club)
223 Sandyhills Rd, Glasgow G32 9NA
E side of Glasgow, from Tollcross Rd, left at Killin St and right into Sandyhills Rd.
Parkland course.
18 holes, 6237 yards, S.S.S.70
Founded 1905
Visitors: welcome by prior arrangement.
Green Fee: apply for details.
Societies: welcome by arrangement.
Catering: full catering.

R132 Shiskine
☎(01770) 860293 (Sec), Treasurer: 860392
Blackwaterfoot, Isle of Arran KA27 8HA
300 yards off A841 in Blackwaterfoot.
Seaside course.
12 holes, 3000 yards, S.S.S.42
Founded 1896
Visitors: welcome.
Green Fee: apply for details.
Societies: catered for by arrangement, write or phone Hon Sec or Hon Treasurer.
Catering: bar meals (not licensed) Mar-Oct.
Tennis, bowling.

R133 Shotts
☎(01501) 820431 (Club), Pro shop 822658
Blairhead, Shotts ML7 5BJ
Off M8 junction 5, B7057 Benhar road for 2 miles.
Undulating moorland course.
18 holes, 6205 yards, S.S.S.70
Designed by James Braid.
Founded 1895
Visitors: unlimited during week.
Green Fee: WD £18 per day; WE £20 per day.
Societies: weekdays only by prior booking.
Catering: full catering April-Oct.
Practice area.
Hotels: Station; Travel Inn (4 miles); New House.

R134 Skelmorlie
☎(01475) 520152 (Club)
Skelmorlie, Ayrshire PA17 5ES
1 mile from Wemyss Bay station.
Parkland/moorland course.
13 holes, 5104 yards, S.S.S.65
Additional 5 holes due 1997.
Designed by James Braid.
Founded 1891
Visitors: welcome except Sat from Mar to Oct.
Green Fee: on application.
Societies: welcome except Sat.
Catering: lunches, dinners, teas.
Hotels: Haywood.

R135 Strathaven
☎(01357) 520539 (Club), Sec 520421, Pro shop 521812
Overton Ave, Glasgow Rd, Strathaven ML10 6NL
On outskirts of town on A726.
Parkland course.
18 holes, 6226 yards, S.S.S.70
Designed by William Fernie of Troon, extended to 18 holes by J.R. Stutt.
Founded 1908
Visitors: weekdays, parties Tues only.
Green Fee: on application.
Societies: Tues only.
Catering: available all day.
Hotels: Strathaven.

R136 Strathclyde Park
☎(01698) 266155 Ext 154 (Club), Pro shop 285511
Mote Hill, Hamilton, Lanarkshire ML3 6BY
Take Hamilton turn off M74 (heading N towards Glasgow), 0.5 mile on to roundabout, 2nd exit (straight through), to next roundabout and turn right into Mote Hill, past ice rink on left, course immediately ahead; 1.5 miles from M74.
Public parkland course.
9 holes, 3175 yards, S.S.S.70
Visitors: booking system; book same day, in person 7am, phones open 8.45am.
Green Fee: £2.50 (9 holes).
Catering: by arrangement.
Driving range, putting green, practice area.
Hotels: Travelodge.

R137 Tarbert
☎(01880) 820565 (Club)
Kilberry Rd, Tarbert, Argyll PA29 6XX
1 mile on A83 to Campbeltown from Tarbert, turn right onto B8024 for 0.25 mile.

Hilly seaside course.
9 holes, 2230 yards, S.S.S.63
Visitors: welcome with restrictions.
Green Fee: £5 (9 holes), £8 (18 holes), £10 per day.
Societies: Mon-Fri.
Hotels: Stonefield Castle; Tarbert; West Loch Tarbert.

R138 **Tobermory**

☎(01688) 302493 (Sec), Shop 302020
Erray Rd, Tobermory, Isle of Mull PA75 6PR
A848 to Tobermory, course past Police Station.
Clifftop heathland course; panoramic views over Sound of Mull.
9 holes, 4890 metres, S.S.S.64
Designed by David Adams.
Founded 1896
Visitors: welcome.
Green Fee: £11 per day.
Societies: welcome.
Hotels: Western Isles, Fairways Lodge.

R139 **Torrance House**

☎(01355) 248638 (Starter's Office), Club 249720
Strathaven Rd, East Kilbride, Glasgow G75 0QZ
On A726 on outskirts of East Kilbride travelling S to Strathven; course in country park.
Municipal parkland course.
18 holes, 6640 yards, S.S.S.71
Designed by Hawtree & Sons.
Founded 1969
Visitors: welcome, may book up to 6 days in advance.
Green Fee: £16 per round.
Societies: visiting parties to book in advance (01355) 279555.
Catering: available in clubhouse.
Practice/driving area 1 mile from club

R140 **Troon Municipal**

☎(01292) 312464 (Starter)
Harling Drive, Troon, Ayrshire KA10 6NE
100 yards from railway station.
Links course.
Lochgreen, 18 holes, 6687 yards, S.S.S.72; Darley, 18 holes, 6327 yards, S.S.S.71; Fullerton, 18 holes, 4784 yards, S.S.S.63
Founded 1905
Visitors: welcome.
Green Fee: apply for details.
Societies: welcome.
Catering: full catering.

R141 **Turnberry Hotel**

☎(01655) 331000, Fax 331706
Turnberry Hotel, Turnberry, Ayrshire KA26 9LT
0.25 mile off A77 from Glasgow, 15 miles south of Ayr.
Seaside links courses.
Ailsa, 18 holes, 6440 yards, S.S.S.72; Arran, 18 holes, 6014 yards, S.S.S.69
Designed by Mackenzie Ross (Ailsa).
Founded 1897
Visitors: principally reserved for Hotel residents; non-residents must apply in writing.
Green Fee: Ailsa: £60 per round; Arran £30 per round.
Societies: not unless resident.
Catering: clubhouse restaurant and bar open all day.
Wide range of facilities within Turnberry Hotel and Spa.
Hotels: Turnberry.

R142 **Vale of Leven**

☎(01389) 752351 (Club), Sec 757691
Northfield Rd, Bonfield, Alexandria, Dunbartonshire G83 9EP.
Turn right from A82 at Bonhill; course signposted from here.
Moorland course overlooking Loch Lomond and Ben Lomond.
18 holes, 5962 yards, S.S.S.66
Founded 1907
Visitors: welcome except Sat during April-Oct; parties welcome on application to Sec.
Green Fee: WD £12 per round, £18 per day; WE £18 per round, £24 per day.
Societies: welcome except Sat.
Catering: full bar and catering facilities except Tues.
Hotels: Balloch; Tullichewan; Lomond Park; Duck Bay Marina; Dumbuck; Dumbarton.

R143 **Vaul**

☎(01879) 220562 (Captain)
Scarinish, Isle of Tiree, Argyll PA77 6XH
50 miles west of Oban by ferry; 40 minute flight from Glasgow Airport.
Public seaside course on east coast of island.
9 holes, 6300 yards, S.S.S.70
Founded 1920
Visitors: welcome.
Green Fee: apply for details.
Societies: welcome by prior arrangement.
Catering: available at nearby Lodge Hotel.
Hotels: Lodge Hotel (19th).

R144 **West Kilbride**

☎(0294) 823911
33-35 Fullerton Drive, Seamill, W Kilbride, Ayrshire KA23 9HT
On A78 Ardrossan to Largs road at Seamill.
Seaside/links course.
18 holes, 5974 yards, S.S.S.70
Designed by Tom Morris.
Founded 1893
Visitors: weekdays with introduction; not Bank Holidays or weekends.
Green Fee: £35 per day, £21 after 1.30pm
Societies: Tues and Thurs by prior arrangement.
Catering: bar and lunches, high teas and dinners.
Hotels: Hospitality Inn (Irvine).

R145 **Western Gailes**

☎(01294) 311649, 311357 (Club)
Gailes, Irvine, Ayrshire KA11 5AE
5 miles N of Troon on A78.
Links course.
18 holes, 6664 yards, S.S.S.72
Founded 1897
Visitors: welcome Mon, Tues, Wed and Fri (no Lady visitors on Tues); advisable to book in advance.
Green Fee: £45 per round, £65 per day.
Societies: welcome by arrangement Mon, Tues, Wed, Fri.
Catering: lunches, snacks and high teas available.

R146 **Westerwood Hotel Golf & Country Club**

☎(01236) 457171 (Hotel), Tee-off times: 452772, Fax 738478
St Andrews Drive, Cumbernauld, G68 0EW
Signposted off A80 13 miles from Glasgow.
Parkland course.
18 holes, 6721 yards, S.S.S.73.
Designed by Seve Ballasteros and Dave Thomas.
Founded May 1989
Visitors: welcome, no restrictions.
Green Fee: WD £22.50 per round, £35 per day; WE £27.50 per round, £45 per day.
Societies: by prior arrangement.
Catering: lunch, dinner and bar snacks available in clubhouse.
Indoor golf facility, driving range, putting green, bowls, tennis, croquet, boules, swimming, jacuzzi, gym etc.
Hotels: 49 bed hotel with business and conference facilities. Reduced green fees for residents; golfing packages available.

R147 Whinhill

☎(01475) 721064
Beith Road, Greenock, Renfrewshire, Strathclyde
Just outside Greenock on old Largs road.
Municipal parkland course.
18 holes, 5434 yards, S.S.S.68
Visitors: welcome.
Green Fee: apply for details.
Catering: small clubhouse for members only.
Putting green.

R148 Whitecraigs

☎(0141) 639 4530 (Sec)
72 Ayr Rd, Giffnock, Glasgow G46 6SW
7 miles S of Glasgow on A77.
Parkland course.
18 holes, 6230 yards, S.S.S.70
Founded 1905
Visitors: by introduction only.
Green Fee: £28 per round, £35 per day.
Societies: Wed only.
Catering: lunches available.
Hotels: Macdonald.

R149 Whiting Bay

☎(01770) 700487
Golf Course Rd, Whiting Bay, Isle of Arran, Strathclyde
8 miles S of Brodick.
Heathland and hilly, levelling out from 4th.

18 holes, 4405 yards, S.S.S.63
Founded 1895
Visitors: welcome, no restrictions.
Green Fee: £6 per day.
Societies: on application to Sec.
Catering: bar and catering from Easter to end Oct.
Snooker, pool.
Hotels: Cameronia; Grange House; Kiscadale; Viewbank; Royal.

R150 Williamwood

☎(0141) 637 1783 (Clubhouse)
Clarkston Rd, Netherlee, Glasgow G44 3YR
5 miles S of Glasgow.
Wooded parkland course.
18 holes, 5808 yards, S.S.S.68
Designed by James Braid.
Founded 1906
Visitors: by introduction only.
Green Fee: on application.
Societies: weekdays by arrangement.
Catering: lunches and evening meals served.
Hotels: MacDonald (Giffnock); Redhurst (Clarkston).

R151 Windyhill

☎(0141) 942 7157 (Pro shop),
Clubhouse 942 2349
Baljaffray Rd, Bearsden, Glasgow G61 4QQ
Take A739 from Glasgow, after 8 miles turn right onto A809, after 1

mile turn left onto A810, club 1 mile on right.
Undulating moorland course.
18 holes, 6254 yards, S.S.S.70
Designed by James Braid.
Founded 1908
Visitors: welcome on weekdays; weekends only if introduced by a member.
Green Fee: £20 per day.
Societies: only by prior arrangement with Sec.
Catering: full facilities available except Mon and Tues.
Hotels: Burnbrae; Black Bull (Milngavie).

R152 Wishaw

☎(01698) 372869 (Sec/bookings),
Pro 358247
Lower Main Street, Wishaw, Lanarkshire ML2 7PL
15 miles SW of Glasgow, 5 miles from M74 (Motherwell Junction).
Parkland course.
18 holes, 6167 yards, S.S.S.69
Designed by James Braid.
Founded 1897
Visitors: welcome weekdays before 4pm; no visitors on Sat.
Green Fee: WD £12 per round, £20 per day; Sun £25.
Societies: welcome weekdays, Sun by arrangement; not Sat.
Catering: lunches, bar snacks, high tea, dinner until 9pm.
Hotels: Wishaw Town.

St Andrews, Carnoustie, Gleneagles and Blairgowrie comprise a vivid cross section of the many varied attractions that bring golfers by the thousand every year. Fife itself, quite apart from St Andrews, is as full of good things as a Christmas hamper, the magic carpet ride concentrating on the coastal sweep round past Kirkcaldy to the point near the lovely Balcomie links at Crail and then onto the shores of St Andrews Bay.

Burntisland and Kinghorn are the first of note although Leven and Lundin Links start the historians dipping into the archives to remind the modern golfer that he is on hallowed ground. The low boundary fence shared by the two Clubs reflects the days when Leven extended as far as the present clubhouse at Lundin. Later, it found spare land nearer home to the north of the old railway thus allowing Lundin to come into being in 1857.

Now, the railway has ceased to function but the line of the track remains a feature of both courses, a little more forbidding perhaps at Lundin. Scenic landmarks are Largo Bay and the opposite shore of East Lothian but the best view of that is from the 10th green of the Golf House Club, Elie, a course in the best holiday traditions and a notable favourite.

There are good practice facilities at Elie Sports Club where children are welcome but St Andrews has completed the transformation to its facilities, facilities worthy of the Home of Golf. These include a new clubhouse close to the first tees of the New and Jubilee and a permanent driving range as an accompaniment to the new Strathtyrum and revised Balgove courses. Meanwhile, the up-to-date versions of Jubilee and Eden help

divert the demands on the Old and New. But, before focusing attention on the other side of the Tay, mention must be made of Scotscraig and Ladybank.

Downfield, home of championships, is the finest of the courses in the immediate vicinity of Dundee but, by now, sights are set on Carnoustie although not at the cost of by-passing Monifieth or Panmure at Barry which overlap on either side of the Aberdeen railway line.

Carnoustie's absence from the Open championship rota since 1975 will happily end in 1999, a decision greeted with acclaim far beyond the Angus coast. The return of the Amateur in 1992 renewed its championship connections, but a word for its neighbour Montrose, which hosted the 1991 British Boys championship, and for Letham Grange near Arbroath. It is a relative newcomer, and a worthy addition to a famous area, a soothing contrast to the links lining its coastline.

For overseas visitors who tend to prefer inland golf, Gleneagles is still an automatic favourite with its new Jack Nicklaus creation called The Monarch. Almost as popular is Blairgowrie at Rosemount in a setting that is almost as glorious.

King James VI, an island retreat in the centre of the River Tay in the middle of Perth, is a must for romantics and historians while Glenbervie between Falkirk and Stirling is a regular staging post for important events.

Further afield, the charms of Central Region are epitomised by Buchanan Castle, Callander, Crieff, Dalmunzie, Alyth, Taymouth Castle and Edzell, a gentle way of breaking in travellers to the beautiful highland country to the north.

S1 Aberdour

☎(01383) 860256, Sec 860080,
Clubmaster: 860688, Fax 860050
Seaside Place, Aberdour, Fife KY3
0TX
Right off A921 in Aberdour village
travelling from Inverkeithing; by coast
route to Burntisland.
Parkland/seaside course with
extensive views over River Forth.
18 holes, 5460 yards, S.S.S.66
Designed by Peter Robertson & Joe
Anderson.
Founded 1896
Visitors: welcome weekdays; casual
visitors should telephone Pro for tee
reservation.
Green Fee: WD £28 per day.
Societies: visiting clubs by prior
booking with Sec, except Sat.
Catering: by arrangement with
Clubmaster.
Hotels: Woodside.

S2 Aberfeldy

☎(01887) 820535
Taybridge Rd, Aberfeldy, Perthshire
PH15 2BH
10 miles off A9 at Ballinluig.
Parkland course.
18 holes, 5500 yards, S.S.S.66
Founded 1895
Visitors: welcome.
Green Fee: £14 per round, £21 per
day.
Societies: welcome by prior
arrangement.
Catering: full facilities.
Hotels: Weem; Crown; Guinach;
Breadalbane; Ailean Chraggan;
Station; Balnearn; Palace, Moness.

S3 Aberfoyle

☎(01877) 382493 (Club); Sec
382638
Braeval, Aberfoyle, Stirling FK8 3RL
1 mile from Aberfoyle on A81 Stirling
road.
Heathland course.
18 holes, 5218 yards, S.S.S.66
Designed by James Braid.
Founded 1890
Visitors: welcome but after 10.30am
at weekends.
Green Fee: WD £12; WE £16.
Societies: welcome by prior
arrangement.
Catering: full facilities.

S4 Alloa

☎(01259) 722745, Pro 724476
Schawpark, Sauchie,
Clackmannanshire FK10 3AX
On A908 1 mile N of Alloa; 8 miles E
of Stirling.
Undulating parkland course.
18 holes, 6229 yards, S.S.S.70
Designed by James Braid.
Founded 1891
Visitors: welcome.
Green Fee: WD £16; WE £20.
Societies: weekdays only by prior
arrangement.
Catering: full catering facilities.
Snooker.
Hotels: Harviestoun; Royal Oak;
Dunmar House; Claremont Lodge.

S5 Alva

☎(01259) 760431
Beauclerc St, Alva,
Clackmannanshire FK12 5LE
On A91 Stirling-St Andrews road, 7
miles from Stirling.
Undulating course at foot of Ochil
Hills.
9 holes, 2423 yards, S.S.S.64
Founded 1900
Visitors: welcome.
Green Fee: on application.
Catering: bar snacks.
Pool table.
Hotels: Alva Glen; Johnstone Arms.

S6 Alyth

☎(01828) 632268 (Sec), Starter/Pro
632411
Pitcrocknie, Alyth, Perthshire PH11
8HF
On B954 Alyth to Glenisla road about
0.5 mile from major roundabout on
A926 Blairgowrie-Kirriemuir road.
Heathland course.
18 holes, 6205 yards, S.S.S.71
Designed by James Braid.
Founded 1894
Visitors: welcome.
Green Fee: WD £18 per round, £27
per day; WE £23 per round, £32 per
day
Societies: welcome by arrangement
with Sec.
Catering: full catering facilities.
Hotels: Alyth; Lands of Loyal; Losset
Inn.

S7 Anstruther

☎(01333) 310956 (Clubhouse), Sec
312283
Marsfield, Shore Rd, Anstruther, Fife
KY10 3DZ
Turn right off main road at Craw's
Nest Hotel.
Seaside course.
9 holes, 4504 yards, S.S.S.63
Founded 1890
Visitors: welcome except on
competition days.
Green Fee: on application.
Societies: by arrangement.
Catering: snacks and lunches
served.
Hotels: Craw's Nest; Royal;
Smugglers Inn.

S8 Arbroath

☎(01241) 875837 (Pro), Club
872069
Elliot, Arbroath, Angus DD11 2PE
On A92, 1 mile S of Arbroath.
Public seaside links course.
18 holes, 6185 yards, S.S.S.69
Designed by James Braid.
Founded 1905
Visitors: unrestricted but should be a
member of a bona fide golf club; not
weekends am.
Green Fee: WD £13; WE £18.
Societies: welcome by prior
arrangement.
Catering: full bar and catering
service.
Hotels: Seaforth.

S9 Auchterarder

☎(01764) 662804, Pro 663711
Orchil Rd, Auchterarder, Perthshire
PH3 1LS
On A9 between Stirling and Perth.
Woodland and heathland course.
18 holes, 5785 yards, S.S.S.68
Designed by Bernard Sayers.
Founded 1892
Visitors: advisable to pre-book;
phone Pro shop 1 week ahead, not
after 4pm
Green Fee: WD £15; WE £22.
Societies: must be booked by letter
to secretary.
Catering: full catering and bar.
Hotels: Golf Inn; Morven; Cairn
Lodge (adjoining course).

S10 Auchterderran

☎(01592) 721579
Woodend Rd, Cardenden, Fife KY5
0NH
On main Lochgelly to Glenrothes
road at N end of Cardenden.
Public parkland course.
9 holes, 5250 yards, S.S.S.66
Founded 1904
Visitors: welcome.
Green Fee: WD £9; WE £12.50
Societies: welcome by advance
booking.
Catering: bar and snack facilities
available. Meals cooked to order.
Hotels: Bowhill; Central.

S11 **Balbirnie Park**

☎(01592) 752006
Balbirnie Park, Markinch, Glenrothes,
Fife KY7 6DD
2 miles E of Glenrothes.
Scenic parkland course.
18 holes, 6210 yards, S.S.S.70
Founded 1983
Visitors: unrestricted, but advisable
to book beforehand.
Green Fee: WD £20 per round, £27
per day; WE £28 per round, £36/day.

Societies: welcome.
Catering: coffee, lunches, snacks,
high teas; dinners by previous
arrangement.

S12 **Ballingry**

☎(01592) 860086, Fax 414345
Lochore Meadows Country Park,
Crosshill, Ballingry, Fife KY5 8BA
Between Lochgelly and Ballingry, W
of M90.

Public parkland course.
9 holes, 6484 yards, S.S.S. 71
Founded 1981
Visitors: welcome. Book tees at
weekend
Green Fee: WD £5.80; WE £8.40
Societies: welcome by prior
arrangement.
Catering: facilities available in park
centre
Angling, wind-surfing, pony trekking.
Hotels: Navitie

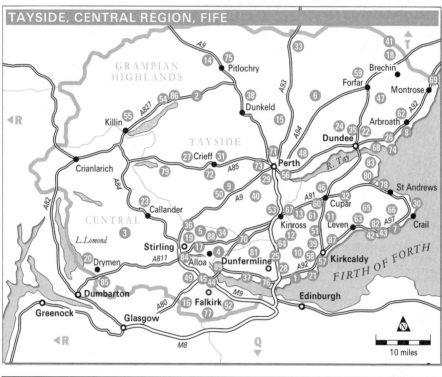

KEY		19	Bridge of Allan	37	Dunfermline	56	King James VI	75	Pitlochry
1	Aberdour	20	Buchanan Castle	38	Dunkeld & Birnam	57	Kinghorn	76	Pitreavie
2	Aberfeldy	21	Burntisland	39	Dunnikier Park	58	Kirkcaldy		(Dunfermline)
3	Aberfoyle	22	Caird Park	40	Dunning	59	Kirriemuir	77	Polmont
4	Alloa	23	Callander	41	Edzell	60	Ladybank	78	St Andrews
5	Alva	24	Camperdown	42	Elie	61	Leslie	79	St Fillans
6	Alyth		(Municipal)	43	Elie Sports Club	62	Letham Grange	80	St Michaels
7	Anstruther	25	Canmore	44	Falkirk	63	Leven	81	Saline
8	Arbroath	26	Carnoustie Golf Links	45	Falkirk Tryst	64	Lochgelly	82	Scoonie
9	Auchterarder	27	Comrie	46	Falkland	65	Lundin	83	Scotscraig
10	Auchterderran	28	Cowdenbeath	47	Forfar	66	Lundin Ladies	84	Stirling
11	Balbirnie Park	29	Craigie Hill	48	Glenalmond	67	Milnathort	85	Strathendrick
12	Bishopshire	30	Crail	49	Glenbervie	68	Monifieth	86	Taymouth Castle
13	Bishopshire	31	Crieff	50	Gleneagles Hotel	69	Montrose Links Trust	87	Thornton
14	Blair Atholl	32	Cupar	51	Glenrothes	70	Muckhart	88	Tillicoultry
15	Blairgowrie	33	Dalmunzie	52	Grangemouth	71	Murrayshall	89	Tulliallan
16	Bonnybridge	34	Dollar	53	Green Hotel	72	Muthill		
17	Braehead	35	Downfield	54	Kenmore Golf Course	73	North Inch		
18	Brechin	36	Dunblane New	55	Killin	74	Panmure		

S13 Bishopshire
☎(01592) 780203 (Sec)
Kinnesswood by Kinross, Tayside, Scotland
3 miles E of Kinross off M90.
Upland course.
10 holes, 4784 yards, S.S.S.64
Designed by W. Park.
Founded 1903
Visitors: welcome, but must be off course by 5pm Fri..
Green Fee: WD £6; WE £7.
Societies: by arrangement.
Catering: in Lomond Hotel (300 yards away)
Hotels: Lomond; Scotlandwell Inn.

S14 Blair Atholl
☎(01796) 481407 (Sec)
Blair Atholl, Perthshire PH18 5TG.
On A9 5 miles N of Pitlochry.
Parkland course.
9 holes, 5710 yards, S.S.S.69
Founded 1896.
Visitors: welcome except Sundays and comp days
Green Fee: WD £11; WE £14.
Societies: bookings only.
Catering: bar snacks and meals.
Hotels: Atholl Arms; Tilt.

S15 Blairgowrie
☎(01250) 872594, 872622
Rosemount, Blairgowrie, Perthshire PH10 6LG
A93 from Perth.
Moorland course.
Rosemount, 18 holes, 6588 yards, S.S.S.72; Lansdowne, 18 holes, 6895 yards, S.S.S.73; Wee, 9 holes, 2307 yards, S.S.S.32.5
Designed by James Braid, Thomas/Alliss.
Founded 1889
Visitors: advance booking Mon, Tues, Thur; through starter Wed, Sat.
Green Fee: WD £35; WE £40.
Societies: Mon, Tue, Thur; book in advance
Catering: full facilities.
Hotels: Kinloch House; Rosemount Golf; Altamount House.

S16 Bonnybridge
☎(01324) 812645, 812822
Larbert Rd, Bonnybridge, Stirlingshire FK4 1NY
On B816, 3 miles W of Falkirk.
Undulating moorland course.
9 holes, 6060 yards, S.S.S.69
Founded 1925

Visitors: welcome with member only or by letter of introduction.
Green Fee: £10
Catering: meals served weekends only, limited in winter.
Hotels: Royal

S17 Braehead
☎(01259) 722078, 725766
Cambus, by Alloa
On A907 on Stirling-Alloa road, about 1.5 miles W of Alloa.
Parkland course.
18 holes, 6041 yards, S.S.S.69
Founded 1891
Visitors: welcome unrestricted, although advised to phone for starting time.
Green Fee: WD £14; WE £22.
Societies: welcome 7 days; prior booking required in writing.
Catering: April-Oct, lunch, high tea 7 days.
Practice area.
Hotels: Royal Oak; Dunmar House.

S18 Brechin
☎(01356) 622326
Trinity, by Brechin, Angus DD9 7PD

Historic setting to Buchanan Castle

Scotland's celebrated reputation for the variety and quality of its golf courses is centred very largely around its coastline. Apart from Gleneagles, Blairgowrie and, more recently, Loch Lomond, there are few hidden jewels in its central heartland but the joy of exploring fresh territory lies in the pleasant surprises it brings forth.

The name of Buchanan Castle had been familiar to me for years. In the heyday of Eric Brown, the Club and his association with it was mentioned every time he played. Going back further, the connection of John M. Bannerman was even better known as the factor for the Estate of the Dukes of Montrose who allowed the course, designed by James Braid, to be opened in 1936.

Bannerman who, for a long time, held the record for the most number of Scottish rugby caps, was later Lord Bannerman after standing for Parliament as a Liberal. However, it was his influence which helped Buchanan Castle to flourish amid the scenic glories of the Trossachs which receive thousands of visitors each year. For most, there is little thought of golf but it is a convenient port of call to those heading north and one that would grace the most distinguished itinerary. It can be an easy run from Glasgow Airport by way of the Erskine Bridge.

Its charms are gentler than the championship links, its overall length, in fact, being modest by modern standards. Its character is that of a peaceful parkland with an air of antiquity lent by some handsome trees and the Castle that is reminiscent of Brancepeth in Durham.

For those with a lively imagination, it is possible to believe that the course might be in the grounds of your country home. This complies with the feeling of intimacy, but it would be wrong to suggest that it is devoid of demand or challenge. It requires thought, decision as well as the shotmaking ability and control to avoid the snares that line its path.

The 1st is a case in point, the opening drive having to negotiate the giant tree that forms the right angled dogleg. Confidence is not always an abundant commodity on the first tee and it is easy to play too safe, leaving the green out of reach although there is no respite on the 2nd and 3rd which are similarly testing par 4s, the 3rd with a stream crossing the fairway.

It is a course of fast flowing brooks, attractive bridges and strategic trees or copses, the stream on the 3rd reappearing to tease on the drive and pitch 5th which follows the first of the short holes. A drive that tempts you to cut the corner is the best feature of the par 5 6th which is a little dull near the green. However, the scene is quickly transformed on the 7th which is a classic dogleg round a majestic wood, only the most solid drive bringing the green into view or range. Fours are greatly to be prized.

Good judgement and a sound nerve are requirements of the short 8th where the tee shot is over water; and then follow two more attractive par 4s, the 9th curving right.

The 12th returns close to the clubhouse, leaving a finishing loop of six holes that offer variety and the opportunity as well as the capacity to come to grief. Length is supplied by the 13th and 14th but there is considerably less freedom on the 15th where the gap between trees on either side of the tee can seem alarmingly narrow.

There is a rural tinge to the setting of the green but the 16th which turns about, is an excellent short hole while the 17th and 18th maintain the need for strong hitting. Nevertheless, there is nothing too daunting on a course so eminently suitable for the vast legions of golfers whose enjoyment is so often eroded elsewhere by an impression of mission impossible.

Take B966 out of Brechin in Aberdeen direction, course is 1 mile away from Brechin and is clearly signposted.
Parkland/meadowland course.
18 holes, 6096 yards, S.S.S.69
Designed by James Braid.
Founded 1893
Visitors: welcome at any time; parties welcome by prior arrangement; restricted on Weds (Ladies Day).
Green Fee: WD £14 per round, £19 per day; WE £18 per round, £27.50 per day.
Societies: always welcome, parties over 8 must book through Sec. For groups of more than 8 £25 (2 rds of golf and catering)
Catering: full catering and lounge bar refreshments.
Squash.
Hotels: Northern (Brechin); Star

S19 **Bridge of Allan**

☎(01786) 832332
Sunnlaw, Bridge of Allan, Stirling
3 miles N of Stirling, at bridge over River Allan turn up hill to course for 1 mile.
Undulating course.
9 holes, 5120 yards, S.S.S.65
Founded 1895
Visitors: welcome weekdays and Sun.
Green Fee: WD £8; WE £12
Catering: bar snacks available at weekends and after 7.30pm weekdays.
Hotels: Royal.

S20 **Buchanan Castle**

☎(01360) 660369 (Clubmaster), Pro 660330, Sec 660307
Drymen, Glasgow
Off A809, 17 miles NW of Glasgow.
Parkland course.
18 holes, 6086 yards, S.S.S.69
Designed by James Braid.
Founded 1936
Visitors: by arrangement (limited).
Green Fee: WD £25 per round, £35 per day.
Societies: Thurs by arrangement with Sec.
Catering: by arrangement with Clubmaster.
Hotels: Buchanan Highland.

S21 **Burntisland**

☎(01592) 874093 (Manager), Starter/Pro 873247.
Dodhead, Burntisland, Fife KY3 9EY

On B923, 0.5 mile E of Burntisland.
Parkland course.
18 holes, 5965 yards S.S.S.69
Designed by and redesigned by James Braid.
Founded 1897
Visitors: welcome except on comp days; contact Manager for starting times; £5 per head deposit on application.
Green Fee: on application.
Societies: welcome; snacks and meals served.
Catering: morning coffee, lunch, bar lunch, high tea, dinner.
Hotels: Inchview; Kingswood.

S22 **Caird Park**

☎(01382) 453606, Club 434278, Starter: 451147
Mains Loan, Dundee, Tayside DD4 9BX
Via Kingsway to NE of town.
Municipal parkland course.
18 holes, 6303 yards, S.S.S.70
Founded 1926
Visitors: welcome.
Green Fee: WD £12.40; WE £20.60
Societies: book via Dundee District Council.
Catering: by arrangement with club; bar and spacious lounge.
Hotels: Swallow, Kingsway

S23 **Callander**

☎(01877) 330090 (Clubhouse/Sec)
Aveland Rd, Callander, Perthshire FK17 8EN
A84 from Stirling, turn right at Roman Camp Hotel about 0.5 mile from Main St, car park and clubhouse signposted.
Parkland course.
18 holes, 5151 yards, S.S.S.66
Designed by Tom Morris.
Founded 1890
Visitors: welcome any time.
Green Fee: WD £15 per round, £20 per day; WE £20 per round, £25 per day.
Societies: welcome any time, contact Sec.
Catering: full catering every day, bar open all day.
Hotels: Abbotsford Lodge; Roman Camp; Dalgair House; The Coppice.

S24 **Camperdown (Municipal)**

☎(01382) 623398, Booking: 623141, Starter: 432664.
Camperdown Park, Dundee, Tayside

Coupar-Angus road, at Kingsway junction.
Championship parkland course.
18 holes, 6305 yards, S.S.S.72
Designed by Eric Brown.
Founded 1959
Visitors: bookings only.
Green Fee: apply for details.
Societies: welcome by prior arrangement.
Catering: bar facilities available in clubhouse.
Tennis.
Hotels: Swallow.

S25 **Canmore**

☎(01383) 724969, Pro 728416
Venturefair Ave, Dunfermline, Fife
On A823, 1 mile N of Dunfermline.
Undulating parkland course.
18 holes, 5432 yards, S.S.S.66
Founded 1897
Visitors: welcome weekdays, Sat after 4pm and not on comp days
Green Fee: WD £12; WE £18 per round, £25 per day.
Societies: welcome by prior arrangement.
Catering: full catering.
Hotels: City

S26 **Carnoustie Golf Links**

☎(01241) 853789 (Reservations), Starter 853249, Fax 852720
Links Parade, Carnoustie, Angus DD7 7JE
On A630, 12 miles E of Dundee.
Seaside course.
Championship, 18 holes, 6936 yards, S.S.S.74; Burnside, 18 holes, 6020 yards, S.S.S.69; Buddon Links, 18 holes, 5420 yards, S.S.S.66
Visitors: welcome with reservation, deposit required; h/cap certs required on Championship Course. No visitors after 2pm Sat, or 11.30am Sun
Green Fee: Championship, £45; Burnside, £14 per round, £21 per day; Buddon Links, £10 per round, £15 per day.
Societies: welcome by prior arrangement.
Catering: full facilities available.
Hotels: Glencoe; Station; Carlogie.

S27 **Comrie**

☎(01764) 670055 (Clubhouse), Sec 670941
On A85 6 miles W of Crieff, on E outskirts of town.
Highland course.
9 holes, 5962 yards, S.S.S.69
Founded 1891

Visitors: welcome; tee reserved from 4.30pm Mon/Tues and 4.30pm to 6.30pm Fri.
Green Fee: WD £10; WE £12.
Societies: by prior arrangement with Sec, numbers restricted to 20 players.
Catering: coffee, light snacks during summer season.
Hotels: Comrie; Mossgeil GH.

S28 Cowdenbeath
☎(01383) 511918, 513200
Seco Place, Cowdenbeath, Nr Dunfermline, Fife KY4 8JPA
6 miles E of Dunfermline.
Municipal parkland course.
9 holes, 6552 yards, S.S.S.71
Founded 1990
Visitors: welcome, no restrictions except on comp days.
Green Fee: WD £4.60; WE £9.25 per day.
Societies: welcome, phone in advance.
Catering: licensed bar, light snacks. Practice area.
Hotels: Halfway House, Kingseat

S29 Craigie Hill
☎(01738) 620829 (Sec), Pro 622644, Club 624377
Cherrybank, Perth PH2 0NE
About 1 mile W of Perth, easy access from A9 and M90.
Hilly course.
18 holes, 5386 yards, S.S.S.66
Designed by W. Ferne and J. Anderson.
Founded 1909
Visitors: Mon to Fri unlimited; weekends telephone bookings required.
Green Fee: WD £10 per round, £15 per day; WE £20
Societies: available weekdays and Sun.
Catering: full except Mon and Tues.
Hotels: Lovat.

S30 Crail
☎(01333) 450278 (Clubhouse), Sec 450686, Pro 450960
Balcomie Clubhouse, Fifeness, Crail KY10 3XN
11 miles SE of St Andrews on A917.
Seaside links/parkland course.
18 holes, 5922 yards, S.S.S.68
Designed by Tom Morris.
Founded 1786
Visitors: welcomed, restrictions only on main competition days and members priority times.

Green Fee: WD £19 per round, £30 per day; WE £24 per round, £38 per day.
Societies: welcome, entertained as for visitors.
Catering: full service of quality catering.
Hotels: Balcomie Links; Golf; Marine (all in Crail).

S31 Crieff
☎(01764) 652909 (Bookings), Sec 652397, Pro 652909
Perth Rd, Crieff, Perthshire PH7 3LR
From Edinburgh M9 to Dunblane; from Glasgow A80/M80/M9 to Dunblane then A9 for 5km and A822 to Crieff; take A85 at town centre for 1km golf course on left; from Perth A85, golf course at entry to Crieff on right.
Parkland course.
Ferntower, 18 holes, 6405 yards, S.S.S.71; Dornoch, 9 holes, 2386 yards, S.S.S.63
Founded 1891
Visitors: welcome, advance booking advisable, must book for weekends; must have h/cap cert.
Green Fee: Ferntower, WD: £18 per round, £25 per day; WE £25 per round, £33 per day; Dornoch, WD £11 (18 holes); WE £13.
Societies: welcome but must book well in advance.
Catering: full restaurant facilities, advisable to book; bar meals also available.
Hotels: Crieff Hydro; Murray Park; Arduthie.

S32 Cupar
☎(01334) 653549
Hilltarvit, Cupar
10 miles from St Andrews off A91.
Hillside/parkland course.
9 holes, 5074 yards, S.S.S.65
Founded 1855
Visitors: welcome weekdays except after 4pm Weds. Weekends only on Sun after 10am. Course only open weekends in winter
Green Fee: WD £10; WE £12.
Societies: catered for on weekdays and Sun.
Catering: lunches and high teas by arrangement.
Hotels: Cupar Arms

S33 Dalmunzie
☎(01250) 885226
Spittal of Glenshee, Blairgowrie, Perthshire PH10 7QG

On A93 Blairgowrie-Braemar road, 18 miles N of Blairgowrie, adjacent to Dalmunzie Hotel.
Undulating course.
9 holes, 2035 yards, S.S.S.60
Designed by Alister Mackenzie.
Founded 1922
Visitors: welcome any day.
Green Fee: £5 (9 holes), £8.50 (18 holes).
Societies: please book, all welcome.
Catering: facilities in hotel.
Hotels: Dalmunzie House.

S34 Dollar
☎(01259) 742400
Brewlands House, Dollar, Clackmannanshire
On A91, 13 miles E of Stirling.
Hillside course.
18 holes, 5144 yards, S.S.S.66
Founded 1890
Visitors: welcome.
Green Fee: WD £9 per round, £13 per day; WE £17.50.
Societies: by arrangement.
Catering: meals daily except Tues.
Hotels: Strathallan.

S35 Downfield
☎(01382) 825595 (Office), Pro 89246, Fax 813111
Turnberry Ave, Dundee DD2 3QP
Turn off Kingsway (signposted A923 Coupar Angus), right at mini roundabout into Faraday St (signposted Clatto Country Park), 100 yards turn left into Harrison Rd, at T-junction turn left into Dalmahoy Drive, 0.5 mile to clubhouse.
Parkland course.
18 holes, 6822 yards, S.S.S.73
Designed by C.K. Cotton.
Founded 1932
Visitors: weekdays only between 9.30-11am and after 2pm. weekends after 3pm only
Green Fee: WD £25 per round, £36 per day; WE £30.
Societies: as for visitors Mon-Fri, Sun 2-3pm must be pre-booked through Sec.
Catering: full catering and bar facilities.
Snooker, extensive practice area.
Hotels: Stakis Earl Grey; Swallow; Angus Thistle.

S36 Dunblane New
☎(01786) 823711, Fax 825946
Perth Rd, Dunblane FK15 0LJ
On old A9 at Fourways roundabout, 6 miles N of Stirling.

Parkland course.
18 holes, 5957 yards, S.S.S.68
Founded 1923
Visitors: Mon-Fri, advisable to pre-book with Pro. Restricted weekends.
Green Fee: WD £18 per round, £27 per day; WE £27.
Societies: Mon, Thurs, Fri only.
Catering: full bar and restaurant facilities.
Tennis and squash adjacent.
Hotels: Dunblane Hydro; Stirling Arms.

S37 **Dunfermline**
☎(01383) 723534, Pro 729061
Pitfirrane, Crossford, Dunfermline KY12 8QV
2 miles W of Dunfermline on road to Kincardine Bridge, A994, on S side of main road between Crossford and Cairney Hill.
Parkland course.
18 holes, 6216 yards, S.S.S.70; Short 9 hole Par 3 course
Designed by J.R. Stutt & Sons.
Founded 1887 (course 1952)
Visitors: Mon to Fri between 10am - 12noon and 2-4pm subject to availability. Sundays only at weekends.
Green Fee: WD £20 per round, £18 per day; WE £25
Societies: Mon-Fri by arrangement.
Catering: bar and restaurant facilities.
Snooker.
Hotels: Keavil; Pitfirran Arms; The Maltings.

S38 **Dunkeld & Birnam**
☎(01350) 727524 (Club), Sec 727564
Fungarth, Dunkeld, Perthshire PH8 0HY
1 mile N of Dunkeld on A923 Blairgowrie road.
Heathland course.
9 holes, 5240 yards, S.S.S.66
Founded 1892
Visitors: welcome.
Green Fee: WD £11 per round, £13 per day; WE £16 per round, £24 per day.
Societies: catered for.
Catering: full facilities.
Hotels: Royal Dunkeld

S39 **Dunnikier Park**
☎(01592) 261599(Club), Pro 205916, Sec 200627
Dunnikier Way, Kirkcaldy, Fife KY1 3LP

N boundary of town.
Parkland course.
18 holes, 6109 yards, S.S.S.71
Founded 1963
Visitors: no restrictions.
Green Fee: WD £10 per round, £17 (36 holes); WE £12.50 per round, £19 (36 holes).
Societies: on application to Sec.
Catering: full catering facilities available.
Hotels: Dunnikier House.

S40 **Dunning**
☎(01764) 684747
Rollo Park, Dunning, Perth PH2 0RG
Off A9, 9 miles SW of Perth.
Parkland course.
9 holes, 4836 yards, S.S.S.64
Visitors: welcome except on comp days.
Green Fee: WD £10 per round £14 per day; WE £12 per round.
Societies: by application to Sec, Mr J. Slater, Kirkgate House, Tron Square, Dunning, Perth PH2 0RG.
Catering: tea, coffee, soft drinks available in clubhouse; meals and refreshments in village.
Hotels: Gleneagles

S41 **Edzell**
☎(01356) 648235 (Clubhouse), Sec 647283, Fax 648094
High St, Edzell, by Brechin, Angus DD9 7TF
Take A94 N from Forfar and turn left at N end of Brechin by-pass onto B966.
Moorland/parkland course.
18 holes, 6348 yards, S.S.S.70
Designed by Bob Simpson.
Founded 1895
Visitors: weekdays excluding 4.45-6.15pm, weekends 7.30-10am and 12am-2pm.
Green Fee: on application
Societies: by arrangement with Sec.
Catering: bar 11am-11pm, light refreshments 9am-9pm, restaurant 12am-9pm in season.
Hotels: Glenesk.

S42 **Elie**
☎(01333) 330301 (Sec), Clubhouse 330327
Golf House Club, Elie, Leven, Fife KY9 1AS
12 miles from St Andrews on A915, 6 miles from Leven on A917.
Seaside links course.
18 holes, 6273 yards, S.S.S.70
Founded 1875

Visitors: welcome except on Sundays in summer.
Green Fee: WD £28.50 per round, £40 per day; WE £36 per round, £50 per day.
Societies: by arrangement with Sec; not June, July, Aug, public holidays or weekends. Parties of 24-30 only.
Catering: lunches, soups, sandwiches, high teas by arrangement with Steward.
Hotels: Craw's Nest; Old Manor; Golf.

S43 **Elie Sports Club**
☎(01333) 330955 (Pro), Club 330301, Sec (01334) 870907
Elie, Fife KY9 1AS
10 miles S of St Andrews on A917.
Seaside course.
9 holes, 6273 yards, S.S.S.64
Visitors: welcome but restricted at weekends
Green Fee: WD £28.50; WE £36.
Societies: by arrangement.
Catering: full facilities
Driving range, tennis, bowling, putting green
Hotels: Golf; Old Manor, Lundin Links

S44 **Falkirk**
☎(01324) 611061, 612219
136 Stirling Rd, Falkirk FK2 7YP
1.5 miles W of town centre on A9.
Parkland course.
18 holes, 6230 yards, S.S.S.69
Designed by James Braid.
Founded 1922
Visitors: weekdays to 3.30pm; not Sat; Sun by arrangement.
Green Fee: WD £15 per round, £20 per day; WE £25.
Societies: not Wed or Sat or Sun
Catering: full facilities.
Hotels: Stakis Park; Red Lion, Airth Castle.

S45 **Falkirk Tryst**
☎(01324) 562415, Pro 562091
86 Burnhead Rd, Larbert FK5 4BD
On outskirts of Stenhousemuir, close to A9, 0.75 mile from Larbert Station.
Flat links course.
18 holes, 6100 yards, S.S.S.69
Founded 1885
Visitors: no unintroduced visitors Sat or before 3pm Sun.
Green Fee: £15 per round, £20 per day.
Societies: Mon-Fri only.
Catering: full facilities.
Hotels: Red Lion; Commercial; Park.

S46 Falkland

☎(01337) 857404
The Myre, Falkland, Cupar, Fife KY7
7AA
Situated in The Howe of Fife near to
villages of Freuchie and
Auchtermuchty.
Parkland course.
9 holes, 5140 yards, S.S.S.65
Founded 1976
Visitors: all welcome except on comp
days.
Green Fee: WD £8; WE £12
Societies: parties by prior
arrangement.
Catering: morning coffee, lunch, high
tea by arrangement; lunchtime bar
facilities and summer evenings and
weekends; restricted in winter.
Hotels: Hunting Lodge

S47 Forfar

☎(01307) 462120 (Sec), Pro 465683
Cunninghill, Arbroath Rd, by Forfar,
Angus DD8 2RL
1 mile from town on road to Arbroath.
Undulating moorland course.
18 holes, 6052 yards, S.S.S.69
Designed by James Braid.
Founded 1871
Visitors: welcome.
Green Fee: WD £16 per round, £24
per day; WE £32.
Societies: by arrangement with Sec.
Catering: meals served.
Hotels: Royal; James House.

S48 Glenalmond

☎(01738) 880270, Sec 880424,
Club 880275
Glenalmond, Perthshire, Tayside
Moorland course.
9 holes, 2900 yards, S.S.S.68
Founded 1923
Visitors: members only.
Green Fee: apply for details.

S49 Glenbervie

☎(0324) 562605 (Sec), Pro 562725
Stirling Rd, Larbert, Stirlingshire FK5
4SJ
On A9 between Falkirk and Stirling.
Parkland course.
18 holes, 6402 yards, S.S.S.71
Designed by James Braid.
Founded 1932
Visitors: no visitors before 4pm at
weekends.
Green Fee: WD £25 per round, £35
per round.
Societies: Tues and Thurs.
Catering: lunches, high teas, dinner.
Hotels: Park (Falkirk).

S50 Gleneagles Hotel

☎(01764) 663543, 662231, 662134
Fax
Auchterarder, Perthshire PH3 1NF
Half-way between Perth and Stirling
on A9.
Undulating moorland courses.
Kings, 18 holes, 6471 yards,
S.S.S.71; Queens, 18 holes, 5965
yards, S.S.S.69; Monarchs, 18 holes,
6551 yards, S.S.S.72
Kings and Queens courses designed
by James Braid.
Founded 1908
Visitors: restricted to members and
hotel residents.
Green Fee: £65 per round.
Societies: welcome if resident.
Catering: meals and snacks
available; 4 restaurants and bars in
hotel.
9 hole Par 3 course; Country Club;
health spa; clay target shooting
school; equestrian centre.
Hotels: Gleneagles.

S51 Glenrothes

☎(01592) 754561, 756941
Golf Course Rd, Glenrothes, Fife KY6
2LA
W end of town 8 miles from M90
junction 3, A92.
Public, undulating parkland course.
18 holes, 6444 yards, S.S.S.71
Designed by J.R. Stutt.
Founded 1958
Visitors: no restrictions except
parties of 12 and more to book in
advance through Sec.
Green Fee: £12
Societies: catered for by
arrangement with Sec 1 month in
advance, minimum 12 maximum 40
players.
Catering: all types of catering
available 7 days.
Hotels: Forum; Stakis Albany.

S52 Grangemouth

☎(01324) 711500, Pro 714355
Polmonthill, Polmont, Stirlingshire
FK2 0YA
M9 junction 4, follow signpost to
Polmont Hill.
Public parkland course.
18 holes, 6314 yards, S.S.S.71
Designed by Sportwork.
Founded 1973
Visitors: welcome.
Green Fee: WD £6; WE £7.60.
Societies: welcome by prior
arrangement.
Catering: meals by arrangement.
Hotels: Inchrya Grange; Lea Park.

S53 Green Hotel

☎(01577) 863467 (Hotel), Bookings:
863407, Pro 865125
Green Hotel, Beaches Park, Kinross
KY13 7EU
0.5 mile from M90 junction 6
(Kinross exit) 27 miles from
Edinburgh and 16 miles from Perth;
opposite Green Hotel in centre of
Kinross.
Parkland course.
Red, 18 holes, 6257 yards, S.S.S.70;
Blue, 18 holes, 6456 yards, S.S.S.71
Founded 1970/1991
Visitors: welcome, booking
advisable.
Green Fee: WD £15 per round, £25
per day; WE £25 per round, £35 per
day.
Societies: welcome by prior
arrangement.
Catering: meals served in Hotel and
Clubhouse by arrangement.
Swiiming, squash, sauna, tennis at
Green Hotel.
Hotels: Green Hotel, 200 yards from
course.

S54 Kenmore Golf Course

☎(01887) 830226, Fax 830211
Kenmore, Aberfeldy, Perthshire PH15
2HN
W off A9 at Ballinluig to Aberfeldy
6 miles past Aberfeldy on A827
through village of Kenmore, over
river on right.
Public, mildly undulating, parkland
course beside Loch Tay.
9 holes, 6052 yards, S.S.S.69
Designed by D. Menzies and
Partners.
Founded 1992
Visitors: welcome any time, no
beginners.
Green Fee: WD £10 (9 holes), £16
(18 holes); WE £12 (9 holes), £18 (18
holes).
Societies: welcome by prior
arrangement.
Catering: bar, lounge and restaurant.
Boules.
Hotels: Guinach House (Aberfeldy);
Kenmore Hotel, self-catering cottages
on site.

S55 Killin

☎(01567) 820312
Killin, Perthshire FK21 8TX
On outskirts of village on Aberfeldy
road going E.
Parkland course.
9 holes, 2508 yards, S.S.S.65
Designed by John Duncan of Stirling.
Founded 1913

Visitors: welcome weekdays and weekends.
Green Fee: on application.
Societies: welcome, max 24 per party.
Catering: bar and full range of meals and snacks.

S56 King James VI
☎(01738) 632460, 625170
Moncreiffe Island, Perth PH2 8NR
On an island in centre of Perth (River Tay); access by footbridge (15 min walk).
Inland parkland course.
18 holes, 6038 yards, S.S.S.68
Founded 1858
Visitors: welcome; not Sat unless with a member.
Green Fee: WD £15 per round, £22 per day; WE £18 per round. £28 per day.
Societies: by arrangement.
Catering: full facilities.
Hotels: Salutation; Isle of Skye.

S57 Kinghorn
☎(01592) 890345, Starter: 890978
Macduff Crescent, Kinghorn, Fife KY3 9RE
Off A92 3 miles W of Kirkcaldy.
Municipal undulating links course.
18 holes, 5269 yards, S.S.S.67
Designed by layout recommended by Tom Morris.
Founded 1887
Visitors: welcome, parties by arrangement in writing.
Green Fee: WD £9 per round, £15 per day: WE £12 per round, £15 per day.
Societies: application for parties 12-30 must be made in writing to Sec.
Catering: full catering by arrangement, snacks at weekends.
Hotels: Kingswood; Longboat, Bayview.

S58 Kirkcaldy
☎(01592) 260370, Pro: 203258
Balwearie Rd, Kirkcaldy, Fife KY2 5LT
On A92 at W end of town.
Parkland course.
18 holes, 6150 yards, S.S.S.70
Founded 1904
Visitors: welcome any day except Sat.
Green Fee: WD £15; WE £20
Societies: any day except Tues and Sat.
Catering: full catering every day.
Hotels: Parkway, Victoria.

S59 Kirriemuir
☎(01575) 572144, Pro: 573317, Fax 574608
Northmuir, Kirriemuir, Angus DD8 4PN
1 mile N of town centre.
Parkland and heathland course.
18 holes, 5510 yards, S.S.S.67
Designed by James Braid.
Founded 1908
Visitors: welcome weekdays only; available from 9.30am onwards for individual players but not for parties.
Green Fee: £15 per round, £20 per day.
Catering: full catering facilities available at clubhouse.
Hotels: Airlie Arms; Dykehead; Ogilvy Arms; Thrums Hotel (offer guest reductions; telephone for details).

S60 Ladybank
☎(01337) 830814 (Sec), Starter: 830725
Annsmuir, Ladybank, Fife KY15 7RA
6 miles W of Cupar on main Kirkcaldy to Dundee road.
Heathland course.
18 holes, 6641 yards, S.S.S.72
Designed by Tom Morris.
Founded 1879
Visitors: at any time after 9.30am Mon, Weds, Fri and 10am Tues and Thurs (no booked parties at weekend). Restricted on Sat.
Green Fee: WD £26 per round, £35 per day; WE £28 per round, £38 per day.
Societies: by arrangement with Sec but not at weekends.
Catering: full catering services available.
Practice ground.
Hotels: Balbirnie House; Fernie Castle; Glenfarg Hotel; Lomond Hills, Old Manor House.

S61 Leslie
☎(01592) 620040
Balsillie, Leslie, Fife KY6 3EZ
Leave M90 at junctions 5/7 to Leslie 11 miles.
Undulating course.
9 holes, 4940 yards, S.S.S.64
Founded 1898
Visitors: welcome.
Green Fee: WD £8; WE £10.
Societies: welcome by prior arrangement.
Catering: available with prior arrangement
Hotels: Greenside; Rescobie.

S62 Letham Grange
☎(01241) 890373, Pro: 890377, Fax 890414
Letham Grange, Colliston, by Arbroath, Angus DD11 4RL
A92 Dundee to Arbroath, at Arbroath take A933 to Brechin, at Colliston (4 miles) turn right, signposted.
Public parkland/woodland course.
Old course, 18 holes, 6968 yards, S.S.S.73; New course, 18 holes, 5528 yards, S.S.S.68
Designed by Donald Steel & G.K. Smith (Old course), T. MacAuley (New course).
Founded 1985 (Old), 1988 (New).
Visitors: welcome, not before 10.30am Sat/Sun/Tues on Old course; not before 10am Sat/Sun/Fri on New course.
Green Fee: Old, WD £21 per round, £32 per day; WE £32. New, WD £12 per round, £18 per day; WE £15.
Societies: welcome every day subject to availability.
Catering: bars and restaurants within hotel.
Practice ground, putting green, chipping green.
Hotels: Letham Grange.

S63 Leven
☎(01333) 428859 (Sec), Starter: 421390
Promanade Rd, Leven, Fife KY8 4HS
Travel E along Promenade, turn left into Church Rd, turn right into Links Rd, clubhouse at end of road on right.
Seaside course.
18 holes, 6435 yards, S.S.S.70
Founded 1820
Visitors: welcome weekdays but some restrictions at weekends Parties should contact secretary.
Green Fee: WD £20 per round, £30 per day; WE £24 per round, £36 per day.
Societies: contact Mr A Herd, Links Secretary, c/o Starters Box, Leven Links, Promenade Rd, Leven, Fife.
Catering: full meals at any time, bar snacks etc.
Snooker table.
Hotels: Old Manor; Lundin Links; Caledonian.

S64 Lochgelly
☎(01592) 780174, Starter: 782589
Cartmore Rd, Lochgelly, Fife
On A910 2 miles NE of Cowdenbeath.
Parkland course.
18 holes, 5454 yards, S.S.S.67
Founded 1911

THE OLD MANOR HOTEL
Nr. St Andrews, Lundin Links, Fife. Tel: 01333 320368

Overlooking Leven and Lundin Links Championship courses, with superb golf for individuals or groups on some of the finest courses in the world at St. Andrews, Carnoustie, Crail, Downfield, Elie, Ladybank, Rosemount and Scotscraig.
25 Rooms, 2 Restaurants, good food, fine wine.
A 'Scotland's Commended' Hotel. 4 Crown, AA★★★, AA Rosette, B & B from £30.00 (1996)

Visitors: welcome.
Green Fee: WD £11; WE £16 per round, £25 per day
Societies: welcome by arrangement
Catering: available by arrangement.
Hotels: Kirkcaldy

S65 Lundin
☎(01333) 320202; Pro: 320051
Golf Rd, Lundin Links, Fife KY8 6BA
In an easterly direction from Kirkcaldy 14 miles, from Leven 3 miles.
Seaside course.
18 holes, 6377 yards, S.S.S.71
Designed by James Braid.
Founded 1857
Visitors: Mon to Fri 9.30-3.30 (booking system) Sat afternoon only after 2.30pm. No visitors Sunday.
Green Fee: WD £20 per round, £30 per day; WE £30
Societies: By prior arrangement in writing with sec.
Catering: full facilities
Hotels: Old Manor, Lundin Links

S66 Lundin Ladies
☎(01333) 320832, 320022
Woodielea Road, Lundin Links, Fife KY8 6AR
On N side of A 915 in middle of Lundin Links (100 yards W of Lundin Links Hotel).
Short, challenging, parkland course.
9 holes, 4730 yards, S.S.S.67 (LGU criteria)
Designed by James Braid.
Founded 1891
Visitors: welcome; limited on Wed in summer.
Green Fee: WD £8; WE £9.50.
Societies: tee booking through Sec for parties.
Catering: Not available.
Hotels: Lundin Links

S67 Milnathort
☎(01577) 864069
South St, Milnathort KY13 2AW
Off M90 1.5 miles N of Kinross.
Parkland course.
9 holes, 5979 yards, S.S.S.69
Founded 1890
Visitors: welcome except comp days.

Green Fee: WD £12; WE £17.
Societies: welcome by prior arrangement with Hon Sec.
Catering: meals and snacks available by prior arrangement.
Hotels: Jolly Beggars; Royal; Thistle.

S68 Monifieth
☎(01382) 532767, Sec 535553
c/o Sec H.R.Nicoll, Medal Starter's Box, Princes St, Monifieth, Dundee DD5 4AW
6/7 miles E of Dundee along A930 to Monifieth High St; signposted.
Seaside course.
Medal, 18 holes, 6655 yards, S.S.S.71; Ashludie, 18 holes, 5123 yards, S.S.S.66
Visitors: welcome by arrangement with Starter; Sat after 2pm; Sun after 10am; party bookings through Sec; parties 12+ must have h/cap certs.
Green Fee: WD £22 per round, £32 per day; WE £26 per round, £38 per day.
Societies: welcome by arrangement with Sec, subject to weekend restrictions as above.
Catering: every day.
Hotels: Panmure; Woodlands.

S69 Montrose Links Trust
☎(01674) 672932, Pro: 672634, Fax 671800
Traill Drive, Montrose, Angus DD10 8SW
Off A92 Dundee-Aberdeen road, 1 mile from town centre.
Seaside courses.
Medal, 18 holes, 6470 yards, S.S.S.71; Broomfield, 18 holes, 4765 yards, S.S.S.63
Records of golf being played at Montrose in 1562.
Visitors: welcome. but not on Sat or comp days or before 10am Sundays
Green Fee: Medal, WD £18/round, £27.30/day; WE; £25/round, £38.50/day. Broomfield, WD £8/round, £12/day; WE £12/round, £18/day.
Societies: welcome.
Catering: can be arranged in one of the member Golf Clubs (Montrose Caledonia GC (01674) 672313;

Montrose Mercantile GC 672408; Royal Montrose GC 672376).
Hotels: Park (offers golfing package holidays); Links; George.

S70 Muckhart
☎(01259) 781423
Drumburn Rd, Muckhart, Dollar, Clackmannanshire FK14 7JH
Between A91 and A823 S of Muckhart, signposted.
Undulating moorland course.
18 holes, 6034 yards, S.S.S.70
Founded 1908
Visitors: welcome, phone weekends.
Green Fee: WD £14/round, £20/day; WE £20/round, £28/day.
Societies: daily, contact Manager.
Catering: lunches every day, evening meals by arrangement.
Hotels: B&B on perimeter of course. Gleneagles, Windleslane, Green,

S71 Murrayshall
☎(01738) 552784 (Pro), Club 551171
Scone, Perthshire PH2 7PH
Signposted off A94 from Perth/Coupar Angus, 4 miles Perth centre.
Parkland course.
18 holes, 6446 yards, S.S.S.71
Designed by J. Hamilton Stutt.
Founded 1981
Visitors: no restrictions.
Green Fee: WD £20/round, £30/day; WE £25/round, £40/day.
Societies: welcome by arrangement.
Catering: full clubhouse catering.
Tennis, bowls, croquet.
Hotels: Murrayshall House.

S72 Muthill
☎(01764) 681523 (Clubhouse), Sec 655949
Peat Rd, Muthill, Crieff PH5 2AD
500 yards off Stirling-Crieff road A822, signposted at W end of village.
Parkland course.
9 holes, 2371 yards, S.S.S.63
Founded 1935
Visitors: restricted evenings and days during club matches.
Green Fee: WD £8; WE £12.
Hotels: Drummond Arms.

S73 **North Inch**

☎(01738) 639911 (Council), Starter: 636481
c/o Perth & Kinross District Council, Old Council Chambers, 3 High Street, Perth PH1 5JU
To N of central Perth, adjacent to Gannochy Trust Sports Complex.
Public course, tree- and river-lined parkland.
18 holes, 5178 yards, S.S.S.65
Tom Morris involved in orig. design.
18 holes since 1927
Visitors: pay as you play policy.
Green Fee: WD £5.25; WE £7.50.
Societies: in summer tee occasionally reserved for local clubs.
Catering: at Bell's sports complex.

S74 **Panmure**

☎(01241) 853120 (Club), Sec 855120
Burnside Road, Barry, Angus DD7 7RT
Off A930, 2 miles W of Carnoustie.
Seaside course.
18 holes, 6317 yards, S.S.S.70
Founded 1845
Visitors: welcome except Sat.
Green Fee: £25 per round, £40 per day.
Societies: by arrangement.
Catering: full facilities 7 days.
Hotels: Carlogie; Panmure, Station, Woodlands.

S75 **Pitlochry**

☎(01796) 472792 (Pro)
Golf Course Rd, Pitlochry TH16 5QY
A9 to Pilochry, then via Atholl Rd, Larchwood Rd, and Golf Course Rd.
Hill course.
18 holes, 5811 yards, S.S.S.69
Designed by Willie Fernie of Troon, modernised by Major C. Hutchinson.
Founded 1908
Visitors: welcome.
Green Fee: WD £20; WE £25.
Societies: welcome by arrangement with Pro shop.
Catering: meals and snacks served, breakfast and dinner by arrangement with Steward.

S76 **Pitreavie (Dunfermline)**

☎(01383) 722591, Pro: 723151
Queensferry Rd, Dunfermline, Fife KY11 5PR
From A90(M) junction 2 turn off for Dunfermline to join A823, course half way between Rosyth and Dunfermline on E side of dual carriageway.
Undulating parkland course.
18 holes, 6086 yards, S.S.S.69
Designed by Dr A. Mackenzie.
Founded 1922
Visitors: welcome every day except comp days; parties and societies must reserve in advance; small parties can reserve tees through Pro.
Green Fee: WD £16 per round, £22 per day; WE £30.
Societies: must be reserved in advance through Sec.
Catering: full catering facilities, parties to be booked in advance.
Hotels: King Malcolm (Thistle Inns).

S77 **Polmont**

☎(01324) 711277
Manuelrigg Maddiston, by Falkirk, Stirlingshire FK2 0LS
4 miles S of Falkirk, 1st right after Central Region Fire Brigade HQ.
Undulating parkland course.
9 holes, 6062 yards, S.S.S.69
Founded 1904
Visitors: welcome, not on Sat.
Green Fee: WD £12; WE £15.
Societies: by arrangement.
Catering: full catering, by arrangement with Sec.
Hotels: Inchyra Grange; Polmont.

S79 **St Fillans**

☎(01764) 685312
South Loch Earn Rd, St Fillans, Perthshire PH6 2NG
12 miles W of Crieff on A85 to Crianlarich.
Parkland course.
9 holes, 5668 yards, S.S.S.68
Designed by James Braid.
Founded 1903
Visitors: welcome any day.
Green Fee: apply for details.
Societies: any time except July and Aug (max 16).
Catering: unlicensed, snacks and light meals available.
Hotels: Achray House; Four Seasons; Drummond Arms; Comrie.

S80 **St Michaels**

☎(01334) 839365
Leuchars, St Andrews, Fife KY16 0DX
On A919 6 miles from St Andrews and Dundee, at W end of Leuchars village turn over railway bridge about 200 yards out of village.
Undulating parkland course.
9 holes, 5510 yards, S.S.S.68 (18 hole course 1996, 5802 yards)
Founded 1903

S78 **St Andrews**

☎(01334) 475757 (all courses)
473107 (St Andrews Golf Club)
St Andrews Links Management Committee, Pilmour Cottage, St Andrews, Fife KY16 9JA
60 miles N of Edinburgh via A91 to St Andrews; by rail to Leuchars on Edinburgh-Dundee main line.
Public seaside courses.
Green Fee: apply for details.
Societies: welcome.
Catering: available in nearby hotels.
Hotels: full range in St Andrews from B&B to international standard.

Old Course
18 holes, 6566 yards, S.S.S.72
Open Championship course 1995
Founded circa 1400
Visitors: welcome except Sun; only with letter of intro or h/cap cert; no bookings Sat, tee times allotted by ballott.

New Course
18 holes, 6604 yards, S.S.S.72
Founded 1896
Visitors: welcome; no tee reservations Sat, first come, first served.

Jubilee Course
18 holes, 6223m, S.S.S.72
Founded 1897
Visitors: welcome; book tee 24 hours in advance.

Eden Course
18 holes, 5588m, S.S.S.70
Founded 1914
Visitors: welcome; book tee 24 hours in advance.

Balgove Course
9 holes, 1399m, Par 30
Founded 1974
Visitors: welcome.

Strathtyrum Course
18 holes, 5094 yards, S.S.S.65
Founded 1993
Visitors: welcome.

Duke's Course
18 holes 6039m
Founded 1995
Visitors: welcome

Visitors: welcome except Sun before 1pm.
Green Fee: WD £12; WE £15 per round, £22.50 per day.
Societies: welcome except Sun am by prior arrangement with Sec.
Catering: bar and lounge facilities, meals available except Wed.
Hotels: St Michaels Inn

S81 Saline
☎(01383) 852591, Sec 852344
Kinneddar Hill, Saline, Fife KY12 9LT
M90 exit 4, 7 miles on B914 to Dollar
5 miles NW of Dunfermline, off A907
Dunfermline-Stirling road.
Hillside course.
9 holes, 5402 yards, S.S.S.66
Founded 1912
Visitors: welcome without restriction except Sats.
Green Fee: WD £8; WE £12.
Societies: catered for weekdays and Sun. Maximum 24
Catering: bar, snacks, full catering by prior arrangement.
Practice nets, putting area.
Hotels: Saline; Castle Campbell., Pitbauchly

S82 Scoonie
☎(01333) 427057, Starter: 423437.
North Links, Leven, Fife KY8 4SP
10 miles SW of St Andrews.
Flat municipal parkland course.
18 holes, 4979 metres, S.S.S.66
Founded 1951
Visitors: welcome by letter to Sec (except Thurs and Sat).
Green Fee: WD £10 per round, £17 per day; WE £12.50 per round, £19 per day.
Societies: welcome by appointment, letter to Sec. min 12 max 30.
Catering: bar, snacks and full meals available.
Hotels: Caledonian (15 mins walk from course).

S83 Scotscraig
☎(01382) 552515
Golf Rd, Tayport, Fife DD6 9DZ
On B946 3 miles from S end of Tay Road Bridge, turn left 3rd street past petrol station.
Links/seaside course.
18 holes, 6495 yards, S.S.S.71
Founded 1817
Visitors: welcome weekdays and by prior arrangement at weekends. Not comp days.

Green Fee: WD £25 per round, £36 per day; WE £30 per round, £42 per day.
Societies: welcome by arrangement.
Catering: meals served except Tues.
Hotels: Seymour; Scores. Rusacks, Russell.

S84 Stirling
☎(01786) 464098 (Office), Pro: 471490
Queens Rd, Stirling FK8 3AA
1 mile W of town centre on A811 on left hand side of ring road.
Parkland course.
18 holes, 6876 yards, S.S.S.71
Designed by James Braid/Henry Cotton.
Founded 1869
Visitors: welcome weekdays, restricted weekends.
Green Fee: WD £17 per round, £25 per day.
Societies: weekdays only.
Catering: lunches, high teas, dinner available by arrangement.
Pool table.
Hotels: Golden Lion.

S85 Strathendrick
☎(01360) 440582 (Sec)
Glasgow Rd, Drymen, Stirlingshire G63 0AA
17 miles NW of Glasgow off A809.
Hilly moorland course.
9 holes, 5116 yards, S.S.S.65
Founded 1901
Visitors: with member only. Not at weekends
Green Fee: £10 per round, £16 per day.
Societies: limited
Catering: restricted
Hotels: Buchanan Arms, Winnock

S86 Taymouth Castle
☎(01887) 830228 (Club), Sec 830663
Kenmore, by Aberfeldy, Tayside PH15 2NT
6 miles W of Aberfeldy, large sign by castle gates on right of road.
Fairly flat parkland course.
18 holes, 6066 yards, S.S.S.69
Designed by James Braid.
Founded 1923
Visitors: unlimited, booking required.
Green Fee: apply for details.
Societies: welcome.
Catering: full catering, bar open all day from 11am.

S87 Thornton
☎(01592) 771111
Station Rd, Thornton, Fife KY1 4DW
1 mile E of A92 through Thornton.
Parkland course.
18 holes, 6177 yards, S.S.S.69
Founded 1921
Visitors: welcome except on competition days and before 10am on Sat and between 12noon and 2pm on Sun
Green Fee: WD £14 per round, £20 per day;WE £20 per round, £30 per day.
Societies: catered for by arrangement.
Catering: lunches, snacks and high teas. Bar.
Hotels: Rescorbie, Royal, Old Manor.

S88 Tillicoultry
☎(01259) 750124 (Sec)
Alva Rd, Tillicoultry, FK13 6BL
9 miles E of Stirling on A91.
Undulating meadowland course.
9 holes, 5358 yards, S.S.S.66
Designed by Peter Robertson, Braids Hill G.C. Edinburgh.
Founded 1899
Visitors: welcome weekdays, weekends by arrangement; restrictions on jnrs (under 15).
Green Fee: WD £9.50; WE £15.50.
Societies: by arrangement, contact Sec, R. Whitehead, 12 Stalker Ave, Tillicoultry, FK13 6EY.
Catering: bar meals all year round, catering for parties by prior arrangement.
Hotels: Castle Craig, Blairlogie, Harviestoun

S89 Tulliallan
☎(01259) 730396, Pro: 730798
Alloa Rd, Kincardine on Forth, by Alloa FK10 4BB
1.5 miles N of Kincardine Bridge on Alloa road, next to Police College.
Parkland course.
18 holes, 5965 yards, S.S.S.69
Founded 1902
Visitors: welcome by arrangement with Pro.
Green Fee: WD £15 per round, £25 per day; WE £20 per round, £30 per day
Societies: welcome by prior arrangement except Sat; weekdays max 40, Sun max 30.
Catering: meals, high teas and snacks served.
Hotels: Airth Castle

T

HIGHLANDS, GRAMPIAN

By far the fastest and most convenient road to Inverness is the much improved A9 which has no sooner bade farewell to Perth than it has, it seems, found Aviemore beckoning. The scenery along the way outshines even the postcards, although golf takes a back seat.

There are one or two courses that might tempt a stopover. Blair Atholl, Pitlochry and, on reaching Aviemore, Boat of Garten, an authentic classic in the short course mould. There has been a course of some sort at Boat of Garten for a hundred years, but it was the handiwork of James Braid which, by extending it to 18 holes, really put it on the map.

But the ardent connoisseur, who has had his card marked properly, will undoubtedly opt for the east coast route starting in Aberdeen and working north round Buchan Ness and then west along the Moray Firth to Inverness.

It will, in fact, be hard getting away from Aberdeen after acquaintance with Royal Aberdeen with its valleyed fairways between dunes and an awareness that the Club, founded in 1780, is one of the oldest in the world. The nearby Kings Links is one of the country's busiest courses, while Murcar, which rubs shoulders with Royal Aberdeen, has a lot in common with its distinguished neighbour although many holes in the second half occupy a lofty perch that marks a change in character.

A few miles to the north, Cruden Bay represents the model links with mountainous dunes and resplendent views worthy of comparison with Turnberry, Tralee and Pebble Beach. In pre-war days, it had a luxury hotel and a railway link with the south. The hotel and public railway have disappeared but its reputation remains undimmed, an example of ingenuity guiding shotmaking and one or two old-fashioned blind shots that undoubtedly enhance that reputation.

All these courses deserve a long look but time is often pressing and many good things lie ahead notably Peterhead, Fraserburgh, the Moray Club at Lossiemouth and Nairn, once known freely as the Brighton of the North. As with Cruden Bay the scenic quality of Moray and Nairn is a major part of their attraction. Nairn opens with a number of holes along the shore but both have housed their championships and left their would-be conquerors suitably contrite and chastened.

Nairn lies close to Inverness Airport, providing easier access from London for those whose sights are set on Dornoch and Skibo, both with stunning settings. It would be wrong to say that the aeroplane has been responsible for the discovery of Dornoch because its praises have been sung by many, not least Roger and Joyce Wethered who knew a thing or two about good courses.

However, it is perfectly true to say that the fashion for visiting Dornoch has grown significantly in the last thirty years particularly among Americans curious to see where Donald Ross, the most famous American golf course architect was born, and what it was about the ancient links that influenced his work so enormously. There is the added incentive to include Skibo now that the building of the bridges over the Cromarty and Dornoch Firth has shortened the approach from Inverness dramatically.

Nor are Dornoch and Skibo the end of the northern rainbow. They certainly live up to star billing but nearby Golspie is decidedly pleasant if less severe and Brora, a creation of James Braid, where the insomniac golfer can play in the famous midnight competition in June, provides the perfect foil for anyone seeking relief from trying to tame Dornoch. Even true lovers of art cannot look at one masterpiece all the time.

T1 **Abernethy**
☎(01479) 821305
Nethybridge, Inverness-shire PH 25
3EB
On B970 Grantown-on-Spey-Coylum
Bridge road, 0.25 mile N of
Nethybridge.
Undulating course.
9 holes, 2484 yards, S.S.S.66
Founded 1893
Visitors: welcome.
Green Fee: £9.
Societies: by arrangement.
Catering: meals served.
Hotels: Nethybridge; Mountview;
Heatherbrae.

T2 **Aboyne**
☎(013398) 86328 (Pro), Sec 87078
Formaston Park, Aboyne,
Aberdeenshire AB34 5HE
Travelling W on A93 from Aberdeen,
take 1st turning on right after entering
village, signposted on A93.

Undulating parkland course.
18 holes, 5910 yards, S.S.S.68
Founded 1883
Visitors: welcome except on comp
days
Green Fee: WD £16 per round, £21
per day; WE £20 per round, £25 per
day.
Societies: welcome except Sun.
Catering: full catering service
available April-Oct.
Hotels: Charleston Hotel; Birse
Lodge; Huntley Arms.

T3 **Alford**
☎(019755) 62178
Montgarrie Rd, Alford, Nr
Aberdeenshire AB33 8AE
26 miles W of Aberdeen on A944;
course in centre of village of Alford.
Parkland course.
18 holes, 5290 yards, S.S.S.66
Designed by David Hurd.
Founded 1982

Visitors: welcome; advised to
telephone for weekend play; h/cap
not required but practical knowledge
of the game preferred.
Green Fee: WD £11 per round, £15
per day; WE £17 per round, £22 per
day.
Societies: anytime by previous
booking; weekdays preferred; course
usually busy weekends in summer.
Catering: bar, dining area with
catering booked in advance, snacks.
Pool table.
Hotels: Kildrummy Castle (8 miles
W); 2 hotels in village, 1 at Bridge of
Alford.

T4 **Alness**
☎(01349) 883877
Ardross Rd, Alness, Ross-shire
On A9 10 miles N of Dingwall
9 holes, 4872 yards, S.S.S.63
Designed by John Sutherland.
Founded 1904

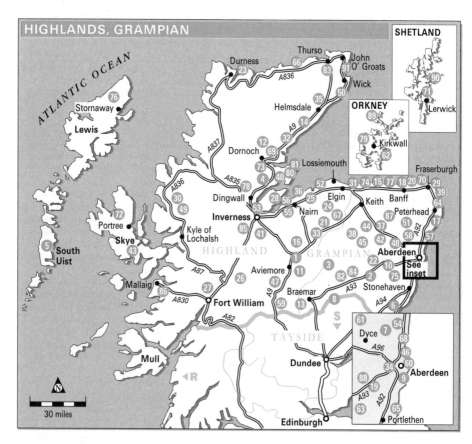

Visitors: welcome at any time except Mon evening
Green Fee: apply for details.
Societies: none.
Catering: can be arranged.

T5 Askernish
Lochboisdale, Askernish, South Uist, Western Isles
5 miles NW of Lochboisdale, ferry terminal from Oban.
Seaside course.
9 holes, 5371 yards, S.S.S.61
Designed by Tom Morris.
Founded 1891
Green Fee: apply for details.
Societies: welcome.
Hotels: Borrodale; Lochboisdale.

T6 Auchenblae
☎(01561) 320002; Starter: 320331
Auchenblae, Laurencekirk, Kincardineshire AB30 1BU.
2 miles off A94 W of Fordoun.
Parkland course.
9 holes, 2208 yards, S.S.S.63
Visitors: welcome anytime; Wed and Fri competition nights for members so restricted 5.30-9pm.
Green Fee: apply for details.
Catering: local shop for snacks etc.
Hotels: Drumtochty Arms.

T7 Auchmill
☎(01224) 714577
Bonny View, Auchmill, Aberdeen
5 miles N of Aberdeen.
Municipal course.
18 holes, 5560 yards, S.S.S.69
Visitors: all welcome.
Green Fee: £4.45
Societies: no group bookings unless through council.
Catering: limited

T8 Ballater
☎(013397) 55567 (Sec), Pro: 55658
Victoria Rd, Ballater, Aberdeenshire AB3 5QX
A93 on Deeside, 42 miles W of Aberdeen, 62 miles from Perth.
Open flat, moorland course.
18 holes, 6094 yards, S.S.S.69
Designed by James Braid.
Founded 1891
Visitors: welcome, must book at weekends and certain days during summer.
Green Fee: WD £16 per round, £24 per day; WE £19 per round, £29 per day.
Societies: welcome by arrangement with Sec.
Catering: full catering.
Putting green, tennis, bowls.
Hotels: Glenlui Hotel

T9 Balnagask
☎(01224) 876407, Nigg Bay GC: 871286
St Fitticks Rd, Balnagask, Aberdeen
2 miles SE of city centre.
Public seaside course.
18 holes, 5986 yards, S.S.S.69
Designed by Hawtree & Son.
Founded 1955
Visitors: welcome.
Green Fee: £4.45 winter; £6.30 summer
Societies: welcome by prior arrangement.
Catering: available; apply to Council for details.
Hotels: Caledonian

T10 Banchory
☎(01330) 822365 (Sec), Tee reservations: 822447
Kinneskie Rd, Banchory, Kincardineshire AB31 3TA
18 miles W of Aberdeen, on North Deeside road; 100 yards SW of Banchory shopping centre.
Parkland course.
18 holes, 5284 yards, Par 67 New course under construction.
Founded 1905
Visitors: welcome, no introduction necessary.
Green Fee: WD £19; WE £21.
Societies: welcome by prior arrangement weekdays only
Catering: full bar and restaurant facilities.
Hotels: Burnett Arms; Banchory Lodge.

T11 Boat of Garten
☎(01479) 831282
Boat of Garten, Inverness-shire PH24 3BQ
5 miles N of Aviemore on old A9 road, turn right onto B970.
Undulating course, birch tree lined fairways.
18 holes, 5866 yards, S.S.S.69
Designed by James Braid.
Founded 1898
Visitors: welcome with h/cap cert
Green Fee: WD £20; WE £25.
Starting sheet used every day.
Societies: must be booked in advance.
Catering: facilities available all day.
Hotels: Craigard; Boat.

T12 Bonar Bridge & Ardgay
☎(01549) 421248
Market Stance, Migdale Rd, Bonar Bridge IV24 3EJ
Off A9 travelling N from Inverness.
Moorland course.
9 holes, 4626 yards, S.S.S.63
Founded 1901

KEY									
1	Abernethy	18	Cullen	36	Hopeman	55	Nairn	74	Spey Bay
2	Aboyne	19	Deeside	37	Huntly	56	Nairn Dunbar	75	Stonehaven
3	Alford	20	Duff House Royal	38	Insch	57	Newburgh-on-Ythan	76	Stornoway
4	Alness	21	Dufftown	39	Inverallochy	58	Newmachar	77	Strathlene
5	Askernish	22	Dunecht House	40	Invergordon	59	Newtonmore	78	Strathpeffer Spa
6	Auchenblae	23	Durness	41	Inverness	60	Northern	79	Stromness
7	Auchmill	24	Elgin	42	Inverurie	61	Oldmeldrum	80	Tain
8	Ballater	25	Forres	43	Isle of Skye	62	Orkney	81	Tarbat
9	Balnagask	26	Fort Augustus	44	Keith	63	Peterculter	82	Tarland
10	Banchory	27	Fort William	45	Kemnay	64	Peterhead	83	Thurso
11	Boat of Garten	28	Fortrose &	46	King's Links	65	Portlethen	84	Torphins
12	Bonar Bridge &		Rosemarkie	47	Kingussie	66	Reay	85	Torvean
	Ardgay	29	Fraserburgh	48	Kintore	67	Rothes	86	Traigh
13	Braemar	30	Gairloch	49	Lochcarron	68	Royal Aberdeen	87	Turriff
14	Brora	31	Garmouth & Kingston	50	Lybster	69	Royal Dornoch	88	Westhill
15	Buckpool (Buckie)	32	Golspie	51	McDonald	70	Royal Tarlair	89	Westray
16	Carrbridge	33	Grantown-on-Spey	52	Moray	71	Shetland	90	Whalsay
17	Cruden Bay	34	Hazlehead	53	Muir of Ord	72	Skeabost	91	Wick
		35	Helmsdale	54	Murcar	73	Skibo		

Visitors: welcome at all times.
Green Fee: £10
Societies: any weekday by prior arrangement.
Catering: available May-Sept.
Hotels: Bridge; Dunroamin.

T13 **Braemar**

☎(013397) 41618 (Office), Club 41318
Cluniebank Rd, Braemar, Aberdeenshire AB35 5XX
Signposted from village of Braemar, club lies approximately 0.5 mile from Braemar on Cluniebank.
Parkland/moorland course with River Clunie running through.
18 holes, 4916 yards, S.S.S.64
Designed by Joe Anderson.
Founded 1902
Visitors: welcome by arrangement (book 24 hours in advance).
Green Fee: WD £10 per round, £14 per day; WE £13 per round, £17 per day.
Societies: welcome, prior booking required.
Catering: bar open 11am-11pm (until midnight Fri and Sat), lunch, snacks and high teas available to 7pm.
Hotels: Fife Arms; Moorfield; Invercauld Arms.

T14 **Brora**

☎(01408) 621417
Golf Rd, Brora, Sutherland KW9 6QS
75 miles N of Inverness on A9, signpost in middle of village giving direction.
Seaside links course.
18 holes, 6110 yards, S.S.S.69
Designed by James Braid.
Founded 1891
Visitors: welcome at any time, restrictions may occur on tournament days.
Green Fee: £16.
Societies: arranged by advance written application.
Catering: available Easter to Oct.
Hotels: Links; Royal Marine; Sutherland Arms.

T15 **Buckpool (Buckie)**

☎(01542) 832236
Barhill Rd, Buckie, Banffshire AB5 1DU
Leave A98 signposted Buckpool, course 1 mile at end of road before entering St Peters Rd.
Seaside links course.
18 holes, 6257 yards, S.S.S.70
Founded 1965

Visitors: welcome.Book in advance
Green Fee: WD £8 per round, £12 per day; WE £10 per round, £18 per day.
Societies: societies and groups welcome subject to prior arrangement.
Catering: weekends and daily by prior arrangement.
Squash.
Hotels: St Andrews; Cullen Bay; Marine.

T16 **Carrbridge**

☎(01479) 841623
Carrbridge, Inverness-shire PH23 3AU
About 200 yards from village on A938.
Parkland/moorland course.
9 holes, 2623 yards, S.S.S.66
Founded 1980
Visitors: welcome; Sun limited due to competitions.
Green Fee: WD £10; WE £11.
Catering: tea, coffee, light snacks available.
Hotels: Dalrachny Lodge; Carrbridge; Struan House; Cairns.

T17 **Cruden Bay**

☎(01779) 812285, Pro: 812414, Fax 812945
Aulton Rd, Cruden Bay, Peterhead, Aberdeenshire AB42 7NN
23 miles N of Aberdeen on coastal route to Peterhead.
Seaside course.
9 holes, 4710 yards, S.S.S.62; 18 holes, 6395 yards, S.S.S.71
Designed by Tom Morris & Archie Simpson.
Founded 1899
Visitors: welcome but not on competition days before 3.30pm; restricted at weekends when h/cap cert required. Must telephone in advance.
Green Fee: WD £30; WE £40.
Societies: on application, weekdays only.
Catering: full bar and restaurant facilities.
Hotels: Kilmarnock Arms, Red House (Cruden Bay); Waterside Inn (Peterhead); Udny Arms (Newburgh).

T18 **Cullen**

☎(01542) 840685
The Links, Cullen, Buckie, Banffshire, Grampian AB56 2UU
200 yards from A98 on W side of Cullen.

Links/parkland course.
18 holes, 4610 yards, S.S.S.62
Designed by Tom Morris (original 9 holes).
Founded 1879
Visitors: welcome, time restrictions on application.
Green Fee: WD £12 per day; WE £15 per day.
Societies: all months except July/August, apply for details.
Catering: bar and catering available April-Oct.
Practice nets, 18-hole putting green, sea swimming, fishing, bowls, tennis, pool, darts etc.
Hotels: Royal Oak; Grant Arms; Seafields Arms; Moray Golf Rover scheme available from Moray District Council.

T19 **Deeside**

☎(01224) 869457 (Sec), Pro: 861041
Golf Rd, Bieldside, Aberdeen AB1 9DL
3 miles W of Aberdeen on A93 North Deeside road.
Parkland course.
18 holes, 5971 yards, S.S.S.69; 9 holes, 3316 yards, S.S.S.36
Founded 1903
Visitors: welcome after 9am weekdays and 4pm on Sat if member of recognised golf club and with letter of intro from Sec.
Green Fee: WD £25; WE £30.
Societies: welcome Thurs only by arrangement.
Catering: full facilities.
Hotels: Cults; Bieldside Inn.

T20 **Duff House Royal**

☎(01261) 812062, Pro: 812075
The Banyards, Banff AB45 3SX
On A98 entering town from S.
Parkland course.
18 holes, 6161 yards, S.S.S.69
Designed by Dr A. and Major C.A. Mackenzie.
Founded 1909
Visitors: welcome at all times, h/cap cert preferred, tee times restricted to not before 11am or between 12.30-3.30pm at weekends and July/Aug.
Green Fee: WD £14 per round, £18 per day, WE £20 per round, £22 per day.
Societies: catered for at all times but weekends fully booked with waiting list.
Catering: full service.
Hotels: Banff Springs; County; Fife Lodge.

T21 Dufftown

☎(01340) 820325
Tomintoul Road, Dufftown, Banffshire
AB55 4BX
1 mile from Dufftown on B9009.
Family course with panoramic views.
18 holes, 5308 yards, S.S.S.67
Founded 1896
Visitors: unrestricted.
Green Fee: apply for details.
Societies: 7 days, by prior
arrangement.
Catering: bar, snacks etc.

T22 Dunecht House

☎(013306) 404
Dunecht, Skene, Aberdeenshire AB3
7AX
B944 to Dunecht, 1st left.
Parkland course.
9 holes, 6270 yards, S.S.S.70
Founded 1925
Visitors: with member only.
Green Fee: apply for details.

T23 Durness

☎(01971) 511364 Sec (home)
Balnakeil, Durness, Sutherland, IV27
4PN
57 miles NW of Lairg on A838.
Public seaside course with daring
finishing hole.
9 holes (18 tees), 5555 yards,
S.S.S.68
Designed by F. Keith, L. Ross, I.
Morrison.
Founded 1988
Visitors: welcome, occasionally
restricted Sun am.
Green Fee: £9.
Societies: any time.
Catering: snacks May-Sept.

T24 Elgin

☎(01343) 542338, Pro: 542884
Hardhillock, Birnie Rd, Elgin, Moray
IV30 3SX
On S edge of Elgin, turn right into
Birnie Rd from Rothes road going S.
Undulating sandy parkland course.
18 holes, 6411 yards, S.S.S.71
Founded 1906
Visitors: welcome after 9.30am
weekdays, 10am weekends; book in
advance. Tues is ladies day.
Green Fee: WD £19 per round, £26
per day; WE £25 per round, £32 per
day.
Societies: book with Sec.
Catering: full bar and catering.
Hotels: Eight Acres; Laich Moray;
Mansion House; Rothes Glen;
Sunning Hill.

T25 Forres

☎(01309) 672949 (Sec), Pro:
672250
Muiryshade, Forres, IV36 0RD
1 mile S of clock tower in town
centre, by St Leonards Rd and
Edgehill Rd.
Undulating parkland course.
18 holes, 6236 yards, S.S.S.69
Designed by James Braid.
Founded 1889
Visitors: welcome.
Green Fee: £14 per round, £20 per
day.
Societies: welcome by confirmation.
Catering: full facilities all year.
Hotels: Knockomie; Ramnee; Park.

T26 Fort Augustus

☎(01320) 366460 (Sec), Club
366660
Markethill, Fort Augustus, Inverness-
shire PH32 4DT
Off A82, entrance beyond 30mph
restriction S of village.
Moorland course.
9 holes (18 tees), 5454 yards,
S.S.S.68
Designed by Dr Lane.
Founded 1905
Visitors: tickets at clubhouse,
restrictions Sat pm.
Green Fee: £10
Societies: apply Sec, Glentarff, Fort
Augustus.
Catering: self-catering facilities.
Hotels: Lovat Arms.

T27 Fort William

☎(01397) 704464
North Rd, Torlundy, Fort William
PH33 6SW
On A82 Fort William to Inverness
road, 2 miles N of Fort William.
Moorland course.
18 holes, 6217 yards, S.S.S.68
Designed by J.R. Stutt.
Founded 1975
Visitors: welcome any time except
Sat 8-10am. Course work being
carried out
Green Fee: £10 per round, £12 per
day
Societies: welcome on application
Catering: restricted.
Hotels: Alexandra

T28 Fortrose & Rosemarkie

☎(01381) 620529 (Sec), Pro:
620733
Ness Rd East, Fortrose, Ross-shire
IV10 8SE

On Cromarty road branching off A9 N
out of Inverness, about 16 miles N of
Inverness.
Seaside links course.
18 holes, 5858 yards, S.S.S.69
Designed by re-designed by James
Braid.
Founded 1888
Visitors: welcome at all times except
comp days.
Green Fee: £15 per round, £21 per
day
Societies: catered for if possible on
written application.
Catering: available.
Hotels: Marine; Royal (Fortrose);
Royal (Cromarty).

T29 Fraserburgh

☎(01346) 518287(Club), Sec
516616
Philorth, Fraserburgh AB43 5TL
1 mile E of Fraserburgh, on A92
Aberdeen-Fraserburgh road, turn off
right on road to Cairnbulg.
Undulating seaside course.
18 holes, 6278 yards, S.S.S.70
Designed by James Braid.
Founded 1881
Visitors: no restrictions, all welcome
except comp days; telephone for
information.
Green Fee: WD £11 per round, £14
per day; WE £15 per round, £20 per
day.
Societies: welcome by prior
arrangement, no restrictions
weekdays and most Sun; small
parties on Sat subject to Club
commitments.
Catering: bar lunches daily, evening
meals to order.
Hotels: Alexandra; Royal; Tufted
Duck (St Combs).

T30 Gairloch

☎(01445) 712407
Gairloch, Ross-shire IV21 2BE
On main road A832, in Gairloch.
Seaside course.
9 holes, 4514 yards, S.S.S.63
Designed by Captain Burgess.
Founded 1898
Visitors: welcome all week with
h/cap cert
Green Fee: £12 per round, £14 per
day.
Societies: welcome on application in
advance.
Catering: shop with refreshments
during season.
Otherwise no facilities.
Hotels: Old Inn, Creagmor,
Mytlebank.

T31 Garmouth & Kingston

☎(01343) 870388, Sec 870231
Garmouth, Fochabers, Moray IV32 7LU
Off A96 8 miles E of Elgin.
Seaside course.
18 holes, 5616 yards, S.S.S.67
Founded 1931
Visitors: welcome.
Green Fee: WD £11 per round, £17 per day; WE £16 per round, £22 per day .
Societies: by arrangement with Sec; deductions for parties over 20.
Catering: by arrangement with Sec.
Hotels: Garmouth.

T32 Golspie

☎(01408) 633266, Fax 633393
Ferry Rd, Golspie, Sutherland KW10 6ST
First right in Golspie off A9 from Inverness.
Links/heathland/seaside/meadowland course.
18 holes, 5871 yards, S.S.S.68
Founded 1889
Visitors: unrestricted except at weekends when must book.
Green Fee: WD £15 per day; WE £20 per day.
Societies: welcome subject to tee reservations for competitions and tournaments.
Catering: all day during season (April-Oct).
Hotels: Stags Head; Golf Links.

T33 Grantown-on-Spey

☎(01479) 872626, Pro: 872398.
Golf Course Rd, Grantown-on-Spey, Morayshire PH26 3HY
Leave A9 at Aviemore, take A939 to Grantown, situated at end of town.
Woodland/parkland course.
18 holes, 5715 yards, S.S.S.67
Designed by Willie Park and James Braid.
Founded 1890
Visitors: welcome, not before 10am Sat/Sun.
Green Fee: WD £13 per day; WE £16 per day.
Societies: by arrangement, not before 10am Sat/Sun.
Catering: full facilities
Hotels: Grant Arms; Ben Mohr; Garth.

T34 Hazlehead

☎(01224) 317336 (Pro).
Hazlehead Park, Aberdeen AB1 8BD
4 miles NW of city centre.
Municipal moorland courses.
18 holes, 6045 yards, S.S.S.68; 18 holes, 6304 yards, S.S.S.70; 9 holes, 2770 yards, S.S.S.34
Visitors: all welcome.
Green Fee: £6.85 (18 holes).
Societies: Apply to council.
Catering: available nearby.
Hotels: Treetops; Belvedere; Queens.

T35 Helmsdale

☎(01431) 821339, Sec 621733
Golf Rd, Helmsdale, Sutherland, KW8 6JA
Off A9 into village of Helmsdale.
Moorland course.
9 holes, 3720 yards, S.S.S.60
Founded 1895
Visitors: welcome.
Green Fee: £5 per round, £10 per day, £25 per week.
Societies: welcome on application to the secretary
Catering: New clubhouse in 1996.
Hotels: Navidale; Bridge; Belgrave.

T36 Hopeman

☎(01343) 830578
Hopeman, Moray IV30 2YA
7 miles N of Elgin on B9012.
Seaside links-type course.
18 holes, 5591 yards, S.S.S.67
Designed by J. MacKenzie.
Founded 1923
Visitors: unrestricted except on Sat am comp day.
Green Fee: WD £10; WE £15.
Societies: welcome.
Catering: bar and restaurant facilities.
Pool.
Hotels: Station; Clasaich.

T37 Huntly

☎(01466) 792643, Pro: 794023; Course manager: 794181
Cooper Park, Huntly, Aberdeenshire AB54 4SH
On A96 0.5 mile from town centre, through school arch.
Parkland course.
18 holes, 5399 yards, S.S.S.66
Founded 1892
Visitors: welcome except on comp days Weds, Thurs & Sat.
Green Fee: WD £13; WE £20.
Societies: by arrangement with Sec.
Catering: facilities by arrangement.
Full service in summer.
Practice area.
Hotels: Castle; Huntly; Gordon Arms.

T38 Insch

☎(01464) 820363
Golf Terrace, Insch, Aberdeenshire
28 miles NW of Aberdeen, off A96 Inverness road.
Parkland course with water hazards.
9 holes, 5488 yards, S.S.S.67
Visitors: welcome, no restrictions.
Green Fee: apply for details.
Catering: bar; catering on request.
Snooker, darts.

T39 Inverallochy

☎(01346) 582000
Inverallochy, Nr Fraserburgh, Grampian
3 miles S of Fraserburgh on B9033.
Seaside links course.
18 holes, 5137 yards, S.S.S.65
Founded 1888
Visitors: welcome except 10.30am-2.30pm Sat.
Green Fee: £10.
Societies: welcome by prior arrangement.
Catering: limited catering available.
Bowls.
Hotels: Tufted Duck (Fraserburgh).

T40 Invergordon

☎(01349) 852715
King George St, Invergordon, Ross-shire
Off High St, Invergordon.
Parkland course.
9 holes (planned to increase to 18), 3014 yards, S.S.S.69
Designed by J Urquhart.
Founded 1893
Visitors: welcome at any time; (Mon and Wed evenings Ladies competitions; Tues and Thurs evenings Men's competitions; all day Sat Men's competitions).
Green Fee: £7.
Societies: welcome by prior arrangement.
Hotels: Marine; Kincraig.

T41 Inverness

☎(01463) 239882 (Sec), Pro: 231989, Club 233422
Culcabock Rd, Inverness IV2 3XQ
1 mile W of A9, near Raigmore Hospital.
Parkland course.
18 holes, 6226 yards, S.S.S.70
Founded 1883
Visitors: welcome, restricted Sat comp day.
Green Fee: WD £20.50 per round, £28.50 per day; WE £24.50 per round, £32.50 per day.

Societies: limited; early booking required; not Sat.
Catering: full bar facilities, meals 12-2, 5-7
2 practice areas.
Hotels: Kingsmills; Craigmonie; Caledonian.

T42 Inverurie

☎(01467) 624080, Pro: 620193, Club 620207
Blackhall Rd, Inverurie, Aberdeenshire
On A96 Aberdeen-Inverness road, off Blackhall Rd.
Wooded parkland course.
18 holes, 5711 yards, S.S.S.65
Designed by G. Smith and J.M. Stutt.
Founded 1923
Visitors: welcome but prior booking advisable.
Green Fee: WD £14; WE £21.
Societies: welcome by prior arrangement.
Catering: available daily.
Hotels: Kintore Arms; Strathburn.

T43 Isle of Skye

☎(01478) 612000
Sconser, Isle of Skye, Inverness
Between Broadford and Portree (on main road).
Seaside course.
9 holes, 4798 yards, S.S.S.63
Designed by Dr F. Deighton.
Founded 1964
Visitors: welcome at all times.
Green Fee: on application.
Hotels: Sconser Lodge.

T44 Keith

☎(01542) 882469 (Club)
Fife Park, Fife-Keith, Keith, Banffshire AB55 3DF
About 0.5 mile off A96 on Dufftown road.
Undulating parkland course.
18 holes, 5797 yards, S.S.S.68
Founded 1965
Visitors: welcome at all times, advisable to phone during playing season.
Green Fee: WD £10 per round, £12 per day; WE £12 per round, £15 per day.
Societies: welcome at all times by prior arrangement with Hon Sec.
Catering: bar every evening 5-11pm weekdays, 4-11pm weekends; full catering by arrangement.
Pool table.
Hotels: Royal, Grampian, Ugie House.

T45 Kemnay

☎(01467) 642225, 643746 Pro: 642225
Monymusk Road, Kemnay, Aberdeenshire AB51 5RA
15 mile N of Aberdeen on A96, turn onto B994.
Parkland course.
18 holes, 5903 yards, S.S.S.68
Designed by Greens of Scotland Ltd (New course).
Founded 1908
Visitors: welcome most times but check in case tee booked for competitions.
Green Fee: WD £12 per round, £17 per day; WE £14 per round, £20 per day.
Societies: welcome by prior arrangement.
Catering: Full facilities.
Hotels: Park Hill Lodge; Grant Arms (Monymusk), Burnett Arms.

T46 King's Links

☎(01224) 632269
King's Links, Aberdeen
E of city centre adjacent to Pittodrie Stadium.
Municipal seaside course.
18 holes, 6384 yards, S.S.S.71
Visitors: all welcome.
Green Fee: municipal rates.
Societies: welcome by prior arrangement.

T47 Kingussie

☎(01540) 661600 (Sec), Club 661374
Gynack Rd, Kingussie, Inverness-shire PH21 1LR
Leave A9 at N end of village, drive into village, turn right at Duke of Gordon Hotel and continue to end of road.
Hill course.
18 holes, 5500 yards, S.S.S.67
Designed by Vardon & Herd.
Founded 1891
Visitors: unrestricted but bookings advised.
Green Fee: WD £13 per round, £16 per day; WE £15 per round, £20 per day WE.
Societies: welcome by prior arrangement.
Catering: available May-Oct.
Hotels: Scot House

T48 Kintore

☎(01467) 632631
Balbithan Rd, Kintore, Inverurie, Aberdeenshire

Off A96, 12 miles N of Aberdeen.
Undulating moorland course.
18 holes, 5997 yards, S.S.S.69
Founded 1911
Visitors: welcome daily except Mon and Wed comp days 4.30-6pm and Fri after 4.30pm for boys.
Green Fee: WD £10 per round, £13 per day; WE £15 per round, £18 per day.
Societies: welcome.
Catering: if booked in advance.
Hotels: Crown; Thainstone; Torryburn.

T49 Lochcarron

☎(01520) 722257 (Sec).
Lochcarron, Rossshire
1 mile E of Lochcarron village.
Seaside/heathland course.
9 holes, 3578 yards, S.S.S.62
Founded 1910
Visitors: welcome except Sat.
Green Fee: £6
Societies: welcome on application.
Catering: no club house. Catering in local hotel.
Hotels: Lochcarron; Rock Villa.

T50 Lybster

Main St, Lybster, Caithness KW1 6BL
13 miles S of Wick on A9, turn down village main street, golf course entrance opposite football pitch.
Moorland course.
9 holes, 1898 yards, S.S.S.62
Founded 1926
Visitors: welcome, pay before play in money box provided.
Green Fee: apply for details.
Societies: any group welcome anytime except Sat evenings (club competitions).

T51 McDonald

☎(01358) 720576, Pro: 722891, Steward: 723741
Hospital Rd, Ellon, Aberdeenshire AB41 9AW
Leave Ellon by A948 Auchnagatt road and take 1st turning on left.
Parkland course.
18 holes, 5991 yards, S.S.S.69
Founded 1927
Visitors: welcome but book in advance.
Green Fee: WD £14 per round, £20 per day; WE £16 per round, £24 per day; Sun £20 per round, £30 per day
Societies: welcome by prior arrangement.
Catering: bar 7 days, full catering
Hotels: Mercury, New Inn.

T52 **Moray**
☎(01343) 812018, Pro: 813330, Fax 815102
Stotfield Rd, Lossiemouth, Moray IV31 6QS
From Elgin on A96 Aberdeen-Inverness road, travel on A941 Elgin-Lossiemouth road.
Links courses.
Old Course, 18 holes, 6667 yards, S.S.S.72; New Course, 18 holes, 6005 yards, S.S.S.69
Founded 1889
Visitors: welcome; New Course any time; Old Course, weekdays after 9.30am-12 midday and 2-5pm, advance booking required at weekend.
Green Fee: New course: WD £17 per round, £22 per day; WE £22 per round, £27 per day. Old course: WD £22 per round, £32 per day; WE £33 per round, £43 per day.
Societies: reduction of 10% for parties of 12 or more.
Catering: full facilities available during summer, weekends Oct-Mar. Book with sec.
Hotels: Stotfield; Skerrybrae.

T53 **Muir of Ord**
☎(01463) 870825 (Admin), Pro: 871311
Great North Rd, Muir of Ord, Ross-shire IV6 7SX
15 miles N of Inverness on either A862 or A9/A832.
Moorland/parkland course with links-type fairways.
18 holes, 5202 yards, S.S.S.65
Part designed by James Braid.
Founded 1875
Visitors: welcome, not before 11am weekends.
Green Fee: WD £12; WE £18.
Societies: welcome, essential to book in advance. Reductions are available for parties of more than 15 players.
Catering: bar, snacks, full meals April-Oct inc.
Practice area, putting green, snooker, pool.
Hotels: Ord Arms; Priory.

T54 **Murcar**
☎(01224) 704354, Pro/Fax 704370
Bridge of Don, Aberdeen AB23 8BD
3 miles from Aberdeen on A92, Fraserburgh road.
Seaside course.
18 holes, 6241 yards, S.S.S.70
Designed by Archie Simpson.
Founded 1909

Visitors: welcome weekdays, h/cap cert required. Restrictions Sun am, Weds pm, Sat until 4pm.
Green Fee: WD £25 per round £35 per day; WE £40
Societies: catered for weekdays. Apply to sec.
Catering: snacks, lunches, dinners.
Hotels: Mill of Mundurno

T55 **Nairn**
☎(01667) 453208, Pro: 452787, Fax 456328
Seabank Rd, Nairn IV12 4HB
1 mile N of A96, W of Nairn, turn off onto Seabank Rd at church.
Seaside links course.
18 holes, 6722 yards, S.S.S.72
Designed by Tom Morris, James Braid.
Founded 1887
Visitors: welcome.Restrictions Sat/Sun am
Green Fee: WD £35; WE £42
Societies: catered for.
Catering: summer full catering, winter restricted.
Snooker.
Hotels: Golf View; Newton.

T56 **Nairn Dunbar**
☎(01667) 452741, Pro: 453964, Fax 456897
Lochloy Rd, Nairn IV12 5AE
Off A96, 0.5 mile E of town.
Seaside course.
18 holes, 6712 yards, S.S.S.71
Founded 1899
Visitors: welcome.
Green Fee: WD £18.50 per round, £25 per day; WE £25 per round, £30 per day.
Societies: welcome.
Catering: available.
Hotels: Links; Golf View; Windsor.

T57 **Newburgh-on-Ythan**
☎(01358) 789438
c/o 51 Mavis Bank, Newburgh, Ellon, Aberdeen AB41 0FB
14 miles N of Aberdeen on Peterhead road, on entering village of Newburgh turn right at Ythan Hotel.
Seaside links course.
9 holes, 6411 yards, S.S.S.70 New 9 holes open April 1996
Founded 1888
Visitors: welcome except comp days and Tues pm in summer.
Green Fee: on application
Societies: apply to Sec.
Catering: Hotels provide full service
Hotels: Ythan; Udny.

T58 **Newmachar**
☎(01651) 863002, Pro: 862127
Swailend, Newmachar, Aberdeen AB2 0UU
12 miles N of Aberdeen on A947.
Heathland course.
18 holes, 6623 yards, S.S.S.73
Designed by Dave Thomas.
Founded 1990
Visitors: welcome weekdays; h/cap cert required.
Green Fee: WD £10 per round, £15 per day.
Societies: weekdays with prior booking.
Catering: full catering and bar facilities.

T59 **Newtonmore**
☎(01540) 673328 (Club), Sec 673878
Golf Course Rd, Newtonmore, Highland PH20 1AT
Leave A9 2 miles S of Newtonmore, course 150 yards from centre of village.
Moorland/parkland course.
18 holes, 6029 yards, S.S.S.68
Designed by James Braid.
Founded 1893
Visitors: welcome, no restrictions.
Green Fee: WD £10 per round, £14 per day; WE £14 per round, £20 per day.
Societies: apply to Sec.
Catering: meals and snacks served except Tues.
Pool.
Hotels: Glen; Balavil Sports; Mains.

T60 **Northern**
☎(01224) 636440
Golf Rd, Kings Links, Aberdeen AB2 1QB
E of city centre.
Municipal seaside course.
18 holes, 6270 yards, S.S.S.69
Visitors: welcome.
Green Fee: £6.50
Societies: by arrangement.
Catering: at weekends, by arrangement during week.

T61 **Oldmeldrum**
☎(01651) 872648, Pro: 873555
Kirk Brae, Oldmeldrum, Aberdeen, AB51 1OU
18 miles NW of Aberdeen on A947 Banff road; turn 1st right on entering village of Oldmeldrum.
Parkland course.
18 holes, 5988 yards, S.S.S.69
Founded 1885 extended1990

Visitors: phone clubhouse for tee reservation (bar hours).
Green Fee: WD £12; WE £18.
Societies: contact Sec via clubhouse.
Catering: Full facilities. Practice area.
Hotels: Meldrum Arms; Morris's; Meldrum House.

T62 Orkney

☎(01856) 872457, Sec 874165
Grainbank, Kirkwall, Orkney KW15 1RD
0.5 mile W of Kirkwall.
Parkland course.
18 holes, 5411 yards, S.S.S.68
Founded 1889
Visitors: at all times, some restrictions in summer due to competitions.
Green Fee: £10 per day; weekly and fortnightly rates available.
Societies: at all times. Book in advance.
Catering: bar lunchtime and evening during week, all day weekends.
Games room.
Hotels: Ayre.

T63 Peterculter

☎(01224) 734994 (Club/Fax)
Oldtown, Burnside Rd, Peterculter, Aberdeen AB1 0LN
On W side of Peterculter village, signposted from the main Deeside road.
Undulating, scenic parkland course.
18 holes, 5947 yards, S.S.S.69
Designed by E. Lappin.
Founded 1989
Visitors: welcome.
Green Fee: WD £16 per day; WE £21 per day.
Societies: Formal bookings only. Except Mon & WE
Catering: meals every day except Mon & WE
Practice ground.
Hotels: Ardoe House; Gordon Arms.

T64 Peterhead

☎(01779) 472149, Fax 480725
Craigewan Links, Peterhead, Aberdeenshire AB4 6LT
A92 and A975, 30 miles N of Aberdeen.
Seaside links course.
18 holes, 6173 yards, S.S.S.70; 9 holes, 2400 yards, S.S.S.60
Designed by Willie Park and James Braid.
Founded 1841

Visitors: weekdays few restrictions, weekend restrictions to tee times for competitions.
Green Fee: WD £20 per day; WE £24 per day.
Societies: by arrangement except Sat.
Catering: bar, meals by arrangement, snacks.
Pool table.
Hotels: Palace; Waterside Inn; Waverley.

T65 Portlethen

☎(01224) 782575 (Club), Pro: 782571, Sec 781090
Badentoy Rd, Portlethen, Aberdeen AB1 4YA
Alongside A92 6 miles S of Aberdeen.
Parkland course.
18 holes, 6717 yards, S.S.S.72
Designed by Donald Steel.
Founded 1981
Visitors: Welcome except Sat.
Green Fee: WD £12 per round, £18 per day; WE £18.
Societies: by prior arrangement.
Catering: bar, restaurant 9am-9pm every day.
Snooker.
Hotels: Hillside; Skean Dhu (Aberdeen).

T66 Reay

☎(01847) 881288
by Thurso, Caithness KW14 7RE
11 miles W of Thurso.
Most northerly links course on mainland Britain.
18 holes, 5865 yards, S.S.S.68
Founded 1893
Visitors: welcome anytime except comp days.
Green Fee: on application.
Societies: not Sat.
Catering: bar; lunch during summer months only.
Hotels: Forss House; Meluich.

T67 Rothes

☎(01340) 831443
Blackhall, Rothes, Aberlour, Banffshire AB38 7AN
On S side of Rothes which lies on A941 about 10 miles S of Elgin; turn right by Glen Spey distillery and follow road past Rothes castle.
Moorland course, partly surrounded by pine forest.
9 holes, 4956 yards, S.S.S.64
Designed by John Souter.
Founded 1990

Visitors: welcome.
Green Fee: WD £8; WE £10.
Societies: welcome any time by arrangement subject to club/open competitions.
Catering: bar open evenings during summer and usually lunchtimes July/Aug; catering at weekends or by arrangement.
Hotels: Seafield Arms; Station; Eastbank; Rothes Glen; Craigellachie.

T68 Royal Aberdeen

☎(01224) 702571, Pro: 702221
Balgownie, Bridge of Don, Aberdeen AB2 8AT
2 miles N of Aberdeen on A92, cross River Don, turn right at 1st set of lights, then Links Rd to course.
Seaside links courses.
18 holes, 4066 yards, S.S.S.60; 18 holes, 6372 yards, S.S.S.71
Designed by Robert Simpson and James Braid.
Founded 1780
Visitors: welcome with letter of intro or h/cap cert; not before 3.30pm Sat. Mon-Fri 10-11.30 and 2-3.30 only
Green Fee: WD £37 per round, £48 per day; WE £48.
Societies: weekdays and Sun by arrangement.
Catering: full facilities.
Hotels: Marcliffe; Udny Arms.

T69 Royal Dornoch

☎(01862) 810219, Sec 811220, Fax 810792
Golf Rd, Dornoch IV25 3LW
A9 from Inverness, via Tain and Dornoch Bridge.
Links course.
Championship 18 holes, 6514 yards, S.S.S.72; Struie 18 holes (6 from original course), 5500 yards, S.S.S.66
Designed by Tom Morris, John Sutherland, George Duncan.
Founded 1877
Visitors: welcome, tee reservations in advance; h/cap certs (max 24 Men, 35 Ladies) required for Championship course.
Green Fee: WD £40; WE £45
Societies: when requested except July/Aug; early reservations required.
Catering: full facilities except Mon.
Hotels: Castle; Mallin House; Royal Golf.

T70 Royal Tarlair

☎(01261) 832897
Buchan St, Macduff AB4 1TA

Skibo

Skibo is a highland paradise. It transports you to a world of peace and beauty, solitude and splendour. Andrew Carnegie fell in love with it at first sight and hundreds of others have done so since.

Carnegie, who left Dunfermline at the age of 13, to become the "Steel King" in America, holidayed in Scotland most summers, seeking a home for himself in old age and for his only daughter, Margaret, who was born in 1897. He renovated the Castle and Estate, building up the outdoor interests of hunting, fishing and shooting and even commissioning John Sutherland, Royal Dornoch's famous Secretary, to design a 9-hole golf course on the promontory of land nestling between Loch Evelix and the Dornoch Firth.

It is said that Carnegie had been asked to play at Dornoch but, being a non-golfer at that time, felt that he had better build his own course in order to learn to play first. After Carnegie's death in 1919, the golf course generally faded as one of Skibo's attractions, but in 1992 it was restored as the centre-piece of the Carnegie Club which Peter de Savary, who bought Skibo in 1990, established as a private residential sporting club.

In keeping with the natural glories of the surroundings, the course was made to blend with a landscape of exciting contrasts. It is part links, part heath and part meadowland, flanked on three sides by water and looked down upon by the brooding hills of Sutherland.

The course itself, which is designated a Site of Special Scientific Interest, is an object lesson of how a proper understanding can be forged between golfers and those wishing to preserve our rare, wildlife habitats. An independent voice, seeing the course at the end of construction, declared that it had transformed the appearance of the land and will certainly allow many more people to appreciate Skibo's wonders. In any event, the bestowal of a national award for its role in protecting the environment is confirmation of the impact it made in its first full year of operation.

From the time that the second shot at the 1st hole merges with low dunes until the drive at the 7th scales an attractive ridge, the flavour is essentially seaside. The par 3 3rd is worthy of the delights of Rye's short holes and, while the 4th and 5th, on the other side of the little ferry road, are par 4s of modest length, correct placement from the tee is vital. They also bring the first of the water into close proximity although gorse is more of a menace on these holes.

Having negotiated the short 6th and the gentle climb to the 7th fairway, the next six or seven holes offer a little more shelter, but the 8th, which doglegs round the shores of Loch Evelix, is the favourite of many, before the 9th, 10th, 12th, 13th and 14th involve a bout of strong hitting.

The drive on the 14th passes the old boathouse on the right and the second shot the salmon ladder below the causeway road which meanders through the woodland back to the castle. It is a fact that the castle is only visible from the 17th and 18th but these holes are part of the scenic finish which really begins with the last of the short holes at the 15th.

The 15th and 18th greens sandwich the clubhouse which possesses a suitably warm, highland character in an enchanting spot that surveys the scene in all its moods. Not that the golfing challenge is done. Far from it. The last three holes form a triangle of equal proportions in the sense of devilment and daring.

From the 16th green in the low sandhills, the 17th and 18th favour the brave, the 17th bordered all too closely by the Firth once more and the par 5 18th, a replica of the last at Pebble Beach. There is a decided advantage in cutting off as much of the marsh as possible but there is a limit to how safely you can play to the right and, from the sloping fairway, it needs care and cunning with the second and third shots if the green on the water's edge is to be reached.

SCIBERSCROSS LODGE

Classic Victorian Highland Retreat amidst spectacular scenery. **4 Golf Courses nearby** - Royal Dornoch, Skibo, Brora and Golspie. Game fishing, Riding available. For a change of scene there are castles and distilleries nearby to visit. Dinner available for non residents, prior booking only. Johansen and Taste of Scotland Recommended. Credit Cards accepted.

Strath Brora, Rogart, Sutherland IV28 3YQ. Tel: 01408 641246 Fax: 01408 641465

On A98 48 miles from Aberdeen. Seaside links course.
18 holes, 5866 yards, S.S.S.68
Designed by George Smith.
Founded 1923
Visitors: welcome any day.
Green Fee: WD £11 per round, £13 per day; WE £14 per round, £20 per day.
Societies: by arrangement.
Catering: full catering and bar.
Hotels: Devon House; Highland Haven.

T71 Shetland
☎(01595) 840369
Dale, Gott by Lerwick, Shetland
Road N from Lerwick, 3 miles.
Undulating moorland course.
18 holes, 5776 yards, S.S.S.70
Designed by Fraser Middleton.
Founded 1891
Visitors: welcome.
Green Fee: £8 per day, £25 per week.
Societies: by arrangement.
Catering: bar and snacks.
Hotels: Lerwick; Grand; Queens.

T72 Skeabost
☎(01470) 532202, 532322
Skeabost Bridge, Isle of Skye IV51 9NP
40 miles from Kyle of Lochalsh.
Parkland course.
9 holes, 3224 yards, S.S.S.59
Founded 1984
Visitors: welcome; no jeans or T-shirts, proper golf shoes.
Green Fee: apply for details.
Catering: bar and restaurant in hotel (April-Oct).
Hotels: Skeabost (26 beds).

T73 Skibo
☎(01862) 881250
Skibo Castle, Dornoch, Sutherland IV24 3RQ
Just off A9 immediately N of Dornoch Firth Bridge.
Seaside links course.
18 holes, 6671 yards, S.S.S.72
Designed by Donald Steel.
Founded 1994

Visitors: welcome on production of h/cap cert between 11am -1pm. Apply in advance.
Green Fee:. £50
Societies: Limited number welcome by prior arrangement.
Catering: meals and snacks.
Hotels: Morangie House, Royal Golf

T74 Spey Bay
☎(01343) 820424, Sec 820459
Spey Bay, Fochabers, Moray IV32 7JP
Turn off A96 near Fochabers Bridge, follow B9104 Spey Bay rd to coast.
Links course.
18 holes, 6092 yards, S.S.S.69
Designed by Ben Sayers.
Founded 1907
Visitors: welcome. Restrictions on Sun, Tues pm & Thurs pm
Green Fee: WD £10 per round, £15 per day; WE £13 per round, £18 per day.
Societies: Day packages available
Catering: meals and bar all day. Bar lunches in winter.
Driving range, tennis, petanque, putting, caravan site.
Hotels: Spey Bay, golf packages/golf outings arranged.

T75 Stonehaven
☎(01569) 762124
Cowie, Stonehaven AB3 2RH
On A92 1 mile N of town, new roundabout at Commodore Hotel, take second exit on left, pass Leisure Centre on right.
Seaside/parkland course.
18 holes, 5103 yards, S.S.S.65
Designed by A. Simpson.
Founded 1888
Visitors: welcome except Sat before 4pm.
Green Fee: WD £13; WE £18.50.
Societies: Welcome on application
Catering: full.
Hotels: Crown; Heugh; Royal.

T76 Stornoway
☎(01851) 702240, Sec 703654
Castle Grounds, Stornoway, Isle of Lewis PA87 0XP

5 mins walk from town centre, just within main entrance to castle grounds.
Parkland/moorland course.
18 holes, 5252 yards, S.S.S.66
Designed by J.R. Stutt.
Founded 1890
Visitors: welcome.
Green Fee: £10 per day, £35 per week, £60 per fortnight.
Societies: welcome by prior arrangement Mon-Fri, special rates apply.
Catering: bar snacks, full meals by arrangement.
Hotels: can be arranged, ring Sec for details.

T77 Strathlene
☎(01542) 831798, Club 831798
Portessie, Buckie, Banffshire AB56 2DJ
On A942, 2 miles E of Buckie Harbour, from main Banff to Inverness road, take turning to Strathlene 3 miles E of Buckie road sign.
Undulating moorland/seaside course.
18 holes, 5977 yards, S.S.S.69
Designed by Alex Smith.
Founded 1877
Visitors: welcome.
Green Fee: WD £10 per round; £15 per day; WE £14 per round, £18 per day.
Societies: welcome by prior arrangement.
Catering: facilities available 9am-5pm.
Hotels: St Andrews.

T78 Strathpeffer Spa
☎(01997) 421219, Pro: 421011
Strathpeffer, Ross-shire IV14 9AS
5 miles W of Dingwall, 0.25 mile N of village square (golf course is signposted).
Upland course, no sand bunkers.
18 holes, 4792 yards, S.S.S.65
Designed by W. Park.
Founded 1888
Visitors: welcome without reservation; tee reserved for members and guests until 10am Sun.

Green Fee: £12 per round, £16 per day
Societies: welcome by prior arrangement. £25 packages available.
Catering: licensed, meals, snacks 7 days.
Hotels: Ben Wyvis; Highland; Holly Lodge.

T79 Stromness
☎(01856) 850772, Sec 850622
Ness, Stromness, Orkney K16 3DU
Bordering sea at S end of town.
Parkland course.
18 holes, 4762 yards, S.S.S.64
Founded 1890
Visitors: no restrictions, bookings not necessary.
Green Fee: £12 per day.
Societies: welcome any time.
Catering: licensed bar facilities available only.
Tennis, pool, darts, bowls.
Hotels: Braes.

T80 Tain
☎(01862) 892314 (Sec/bookings), Pro: 893313
Tain, Ross-shire IV19 1PA
A9 N of Inverness, 0.5 mile from town centre.
Seaside/parkland course.
18 holes, 6246 yards, S.S.S.69
Designed by Tom Morris.
Founded 1890
Visitors: welcome except competition days
Green Fee: WD £15 per round, £22 per day; WD £18 per round, £24 per day.
Societies: welcome. Reductions available for groups of more than 10 players
Catering: Full facilities are available by prior arrangement with Club Steward.
Hotels: Royal; Morangie; Mansfield.

T81 Tarbat
☎(01862) 871236
Portmahomack, Ross-shire IV20 1YQ
B9165 off A9, 7 miles E of Tain.
Seaside links course.
9 holes, 2568 yards, S.S.S.66
Designed by J. Sutherland.
Founded 1909
Visitors: welcome at all times.
Green Fee: WD £5; WE £6.
Societies: welcome by prior arrangement.
Catering: tea and coffee.
Hotels: Castle; Caledonian.

T82 Tarland
☎(01339) 881413
Aberdeen Rd, Tarland, Aboyne, Aberdeenshire AB3 4YL
On A974, 30 miles W of Aberdeen, 6 miles N of Aboyne.
Parkland course.
9 holes, 5812 yards, S.S.S.68
Designed by Tom Morris.
Founded 1908
Visitors: no restrictions.
Green Fee: WD £12; WE £15.
Societies: not weekends.
Catering: June-Sept all day; April, May, Oct by arrangement.
Hotels: Aberdeen Arms; Balnacoil; Commercial; Pannanich Wells.

T83 Thurso
☎(01847) 893807, Sec 895024
Newlands of Geise, Thurso, Caithness KW14 7XF
2 miles SW from centre of Thurso on B870.
Parkland course.
18 holes, 5841 yards, S.S.S.69
Designed by W. Stuart.
Founded 1893
Visitors: no restrictions.
Green Fee: on application.
Catering: all day bar, catering all day during summer.
Hotels: Pentland; John O'Groats House.

T84 Torphins
☎(01339) 882115, Sec 882402
Bog Rd, Torphins, Banchory AB31 4JA
6 miles W of Banchory on A980.
Undulating heathland course.
9 holes, 4684 yards, S.S.S.63
Founded 1896
Visitors: unrestricted except during competitions.
Green Fee: WD £10; WE £12.
Societies: weekdays only.
Catering: snacks only.Limited evening meals.
Hotels: Learney Arms.

T85 Torvean
☎(01463) 225651 (Sec), Pro/Starter: 711434
Glenurquhart Rd, Inverness IB3 6JN
On A82 Fort William road, 1 mile W of city centre, on W of Caledonian Canal.
Municipal parkland course.
18 holes, 5784 yards, S.S.S.68
Founded 1962
Visitors: welcome; booking advisable, contact Starter.

Green Fee: WD £8.60; WE £10.
Societies: welcome by arrangement with Pro/Starter.
Catering: meals served by arrangement.
Hotels: Loch Ness House, opposite clubhouse, Dunain Park.

T86 Traigh
☎(01687) 450645
Traig Farm, Arisaig, Inverness-shire
3 miles W of Arisaig on A830 Fort William-Mallaig road.
Links course.
9 holes, 2405 yards, S.S.S.64
Designed by John Salvesen.
Founded redesigned 1995
Visitors: welcome, pay at course.
Green Fee: £6 per day.
Catering: snacks available at clubhouse.
Hotels: Cnoc-na-Faire.

T87 Turriff
☎(01888) 562745 (Club), Sec 562982, Pro: 563025
Rosehall, Turriff, Aberdeenshire AB53 7BB
On Aberdeen side of town, about 1 mile up Huntly Rd on B9024.
Meadowland/parkland course.
18 holes, 5877 yards, S.S.S.69
Founded 1896
Visitors: welcome with h/cap cert, book with Pro; not before 10am weekends club with member.
Green Fee: WD £13 per round, £17 per day; WE £17 per round, £22 per day.
Societies: by arrangement with Sec.
Catering: by arrangement.
Hotels: Union; White Heather.

T88 Westhill
☎(01224) 740159 (Pro)
Westhill Heights, Skene, Aberdeenshire AB32 6RY
6 miles from Aberdeen on A944 Aberdeen-Alford road, course to N of town overlooking it.
Undulating parkland/moorland course.
18 holes, 5921 yards, S.S.S.69. New course under construction
Designed by Charles Lawrie.
Founded 1977
Visitors: welcome except Sat.
Green Fee: WD £12 per round, £16 per day; WE £15 per round, £20 per day.
Societies: weekdays and Sun.
Catering: bar facilities, catering by arrangement.
Hotels: Broadstreik Inn, Westhill Inn.

T89 **Westray**

☎(01857) 677373 (Treasurer), Sec 677516
Tulloch's Shop, Westray, Orkney
In Westray.
Links course.
9 holes, 2405 yards, Par 33
Founded 1890s
Visitors: welcome 7 days.
Green Fee: on application.
Societies: welcome.
Hotels: Cleaton House.

T90 **Whalsay**

☎(01806) 566481, Sec 566450
Skaw Taing, Island of Whalsay,
Shetland ZE2 9AL

At N of island, ask directions from ferry.
Moorland/parkland course, part municipal.
18 holes, 6009 yards, S.S.S.70
Founded 1975
Visitors: welcome, unrestricted except on comp days.
Green Fee: £5.
Societies: welcome, phone in advance.
Catering: licensed bar, snacks available.

T91 **Wick**

☎(01955) 602726
Reiss, Wick, Caithness KW1 4RW

3 miles N of Wick on A9, turn right at signpost, continue 0.75 mile to clubhouse.
Seaside links course.
18 holes, 5976 yards, S.S.S.70
Designed by McCulloch.
Founded 1870
Visitors: welcome subject to club and open competitions; check in advance.
Green Fee: £15
Societies: welcome by prior arrangement.
Catering: bar, snacks at weekends. Pool.
Hotels: Queens; Nethercliffe; Mackays (free golf for residents); ; Mercury, Sinclair Bay.

NORTHERN IRELAND

Discussion on comparative merits of golf courses is always fierce although rarely conclusive. Golfers are influenced by a multitude of factors from how they played to the condition of the greens and the beauty of the setting. Where the debate surrounds courses that are near neighbours, passions are liable to be even more frenzied but, whilst Royal Portrush and Royal County Down cannot quite be classed as neighbours, they lie roughly equidistant on either side of Belfast and as a result tend to split opinion nicely.

This is not the place to fuel the argument about their merits but there is not the slightest doubt that both are in the classic mould; nobody should visit Ulster and play one without the other. Few big cities can boast two championship links within such easy reach of their centres.

Royal County Down is at Newcastle, an attractive holiday town nestling in the the romantic shadow of the Mountains of Mourne. Mountains make an imposing backcloth to golf anywhere and one is always aware of the brooding presence at Newcastle, sun and cloud casting ever changing patterns and colours. They make the 9th particularly imposing but an equally dominant impression of the course is forged by the massive sand dunes that line so many of the fairways together with the heather and gorse that magnify and punish errant shots.

They place huge demands on bold, forceful driving although the varied nature of the shots to the greens gives an important added dimension that increases the regret that circumstances beyond its control have denied Royal County Down more major championships. The British Amateur of 1970 and the Curtis Cup match two years earlier were events enhanced by the quality of its challenge; but the same applies to Royal Portrush – the only Irish Club to have housed the Open Championship – in 1951. It saw Max Faulkner emerge as champion, although his win marked the beginning of a drought where British victories were concerned, which lasted until Tony Jacklin won in 1969.

Portrush also saw the crowning of Catherine Lacoste as British Women's champion, many of the noble holes bringing out the best in a supreme striker, and in 1993 the British Men's Amateur Open returned after a gap of 33 years. The spectacular part is down by the shore not far from the Giant's Causeway. Holes entitled Purgatory and Calamity convey the true picture.

However, it must not be thought that golf in the Province is confined to Newcastle and Portrush – superb as they are. Lovers of links golf have a splendid example in Portstewart and another in Castlerock – both close to Portrush but Belfast itself is well served, Royal Belfast, with excellent views of the city, and Malone, being the pick.

There is also Balmoral, home club of the late Fred Daly, Holywood and Shandon Park which used to stage the Gallaher's Ulster Open at a time when a young Tony Jacklin was taking his first steps onto the world golfing stage.

Clandeboye and Bangor are towns on the fringe of the Belfast district with splendid courses and the best of the new courses are Blackwood, with 36 holes and a driving range, and Rockmount on rolling agricultural land. Lastly, I well remember journeys to Lurgan when Frank Pennink was redesigning the course, and a sentimental mention for Warrenpoint near the border with the Republic, the course that raised Ronan Rafferty.

U1 Aberdelghy

☎(01846) 662738
Bell's Lane, Lambeg, Co Antrim, N
Ireland
Between Dunmurry and Lambeg, just
off main Belfast-Lisburn road.
Municipal parkland course.
9 holes, 4384 yards, S.S.S.65
Founded July 1986
Visitors: welcome any time (except
Sat am).
Green Fee: WD £3.50 (9 holes),
£6.50 (18 holes); WE & BH £4.20 (9
holes), £7.50 (18 holes); reductions
for jnrs, OAPs and unemployed.
Societies: welcome, discount for 15
and over; tee times cannot be
reserved.
Hotels: Beechlawn, Forte Crest
(Dunmurry).

U2 Ardglass

☎(01396) 841219, Sec 771067, Pro:
841022,
Fax 841841
Castle Place, Ardglass, Co Down
BT30 7TP.
On B1, 7 miles from Downpatrick.
Seaside course.
18 holes, 5497 metres, S.S.S.69
Founded 1896
Visitors: welcome.
Green Fee: WD £15 (£9 with
member); WE & BH £20 (£13 with
member).
Societies: welcome by prior
arrangement.
Catering: meals served except Mon,
bar.
Snooker.
Hotels: Abbey Lodge (Downpatrick).

U3 Ashfield

☎(01693) 868180, Fax 868611
Freeduff, Cullyhanna, Co Armagh
18 holes, 5110 metres, S.S.S.67
Founded 1990
Green Fee: WD £10 (£8 with
member); WE & BH £12 (£10 with
member).

U4 Ballycastle

☎(012657) 62536, Sec 63857, Pro:
62506
Cushendall Rd, Ballycastle, Co
Antrim BT54 6QP
About 40 miles along coast road, N of
Larne Harbour.
Undulating seaside course.
18 holes, 5376 metres, S.S.S.69
Founded 1890
Visitors: welcome weekdays and
weekends by arrangement.

Green Fee: WD £15 (£8 with
member); WE & BH £20 (£9 with
member) .
Societies: catered for all year except
July/Aug (bookable).
Catering: bar snacks and meals
available.
Snooker.
Hotels: Antrim Arms; Hillsea; Marine.

U5 Ballyclare

☎(019603) 22696, Sec 40122, Bar:
24352
25 Springvale Rd, Ballycare, Co
Antrim BT 39 9JW
14 miles N of Belfast, off Larne road.
Parkland course.
18 holes, 5745 metres, S.S.S.71
Founded 1923
Visitors: welcome, not Sat.
Green Fee: WD £15 (£10 if
accompanied by a member); WE &
BH £20 (£12 if accompanied by a
member).
Societies: welcome by prior
arrangement.
Catering: restaurant and snacks
(24542).
Snooker, indoor bowls (winter).
Hotels: Chimney Corner; Dunadry
Inn.

U6 Ballyearl Golf and Leisure Centre

☎(01232) 848287
585 Doagh Rd, Newtownabbey,
Belfast BT36 8RZ
1 mile N of Mossley off B59.
Public parkland course.
9 holes 2362 yards, Par 3
Visitors: welcome.
Green Fee: WD £3; WE £4;
reductions for jnrs and OAPs.
Societies: welcome by prior
arrangement.
Catering: bar and snacks.
Squash courts, fitness centre, driving
range, 180-seat theatre.
Hotels: Chimney Corner.

U7 Ballymena

☎(01266) 861487, Pro: 861652,
Caterer: 862087
128 Raceview Rd, Ballymena, Co
Antrim BT42 4HY
2.5 miles E of town on A42 to Brough
Shane and Carnlough.
Heathland/parkland course.
18 holes, 5245 metres, S.S.S.67
Founded 1902
Visitors: welcome weekdays and
Sun; not Sat.
Green Fee: apply for details.

Societies: recognised golfing
societies by arrangement with Hon
Sec.
Catering: available daily.
Hotels: Adair Arms; Tullyglass
House; Leighinmohr; The Country
House.

U8 Balmoral

☎(01232) 381514, Pro: 667747
518 Lisburn Rd, Belfast BT9 6GX
2 miles S of Belfast city centre;
clubhouse is immediately beside
King's Hall on Lisburn Road,
opposite Balmoral Halt railway
station.
Flat parkland course.
18 holes, 5702 metres, S.S.S.70
Founded 1914
Visitors: welcome except Sat and
after 3pm Sun.
Green Fee: apply for details.
Societies: Mon and Thurs by
arrangement.
Catering: bar (01232) 668540;
restaurant (01232) 664571.
Snooker.
Hotels: Conway; Europa; Plaza;
York; Beechlawn; Balmoral.

U9 Banbridge

☎(018206) 62211, Sec 623784, Bar:
62342
116 Huntly Rd, Banbridge, Co Down
BT32 3UR
About 0.5 mile from town along
Huntly Rd, River Bann on right all the
way.
Parkland course.
18 holes, 5047 metres, S.S.S.67
Founded 1912
Visitors: welcome most days, Ladies
preference Tues, Men's competitions
Sat.
Green Fee: WD £15 (£8 with
member); WE & BH £20 (£10 with
member, except Sat).
Societies: welcome summer months
by arrangement.
Catering: can be arranged on
request.
Hotels: Bannville House; Belmont;
Downshire.

U10 Bangor

☎(01247) 270922, Pro: 462164
Broadway, Bangor, Co Down BT20
4RH
0.75 mile S from town centre.
Undulating parkland course.
18 holes, 5874 metres, S.S.S.71
Designed by James Braid.
Founded 1903

Visitors: welcome weekdays; weekends by prior arrangement.
Green Fee: WD £21 (£10 with member); WE & BH £27 (£12 with member).
Societies: Mon and Wed only by prior arrangement, min 20 players.
Catering: bar meals available 11.30am-2.30pm and 5.30-7.30pm; dining room available, contact caterer (01247) 270483; no catering Mon Oct-Mar.
Hotels: Royal; Crawfordsburn Inn.

U11 **Belvoir Park**

☎(01232) 491693, Pro: 646714, Caterer: 641159, Fax 646113
73 Church Rd, Newtownbreda, Belfast BT8 4AN
4 miles Belfast centre, off Ormean Rd (main road to Saintfield & Newcastle). Parkland course.
18 holes, 5958 metres, S.S.S.71
Designed by H.S. Colt.
Founded 1927
Visitors: welcome.
Green Fee: apply for details.

Societies: 5 per month April/Sept.
Catering: excellent facilities by Parkview Catering.
Snooker.
Hotels: La Mon House; Stormont.

U12 **Bentra**

☎(019603) 78996
1 Slaughterford Rd, Whitehead, Co Antrim BT38 9TG
5 miles N of Carrickfergus on road to Larne.

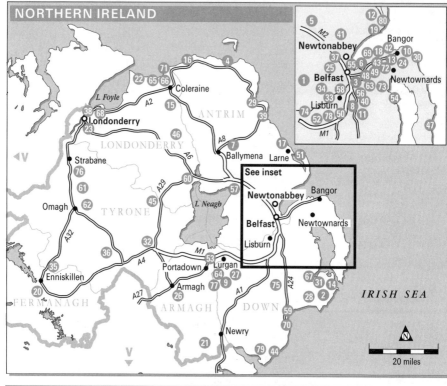

KEY		16	Bushfoot	33	Dunmurry	49	Knockbracken Golf &	65	Portstewart
1	Aberdelghy	17	Cairndhu	34	Edenmore Golf		Country Club	66	Rathmore
2	Ardglass	18	Carnalea		Course	50	Lambeg	67	Ringdufferin
3	Ashfield	19	Carrickfergus	35	Enniskillen	51	Larne	68	Roe Park
4	Ballycastle	20	Castle Hume	36	Fintona	52	Lisburn	69	Royal Belfast
5	Ballyclare	21	Castleblayney	37	Fortwilliam	53	Lurgan	70	Royal County Down
6	Ballyearl Golf and	22	Castlerock	38	Foyle	54	Mahee Island	71	Royal Portrush
	Leisure Centre	23	City of Derry	39	Garron Tower	55	Mallusk	72	Scrabo
7	Ballymena	24	Clandeboye	40	Gilnahirk	56	Malone	73	Shandon Park
8	Balmoral	25	Cliftonville	41	Greenisland	57	Massereene	74	Silverwood
9	Banbridge	26	County Armagh	42	Helen's Bay	58	Mount Ober	75	Spa
10	Bangor	27	Craigavon	43	Holywood	59	Mourne	76	Strabane
11	Belvoir Park	28	Crossgar	44	Kilkeel	60	Moyola Park	77	Tandragee
12	Bentra	29	Cushendall	46	Kilrea	61	Newtownstewart	78	Temple
13	Blackwood	30	Donaghadee	47	Kirkistown Castle	62	Omagh	79	Warrenpoint
14	Bright Castle	31	Downpatrick	48	The Knock	63	Ormeau	80	Whitehead
15	Brown Trout	32	Dungannon			64	Portadown		

Municipal parkland course.
9 holes, 6084 yards, S.S.S.68
Visitors: welcome at any time.
Green Fee: WD £6.50; WE £10, reductions are offered to jnrs and OAPs.
Societies: welcome, tee times cannot be reserved.
Catering: bar and snacks at Bentra Roadhouse adjoining course, from 11.30am (12.30am Sun).
Hotels: Magheramorne House; Coast Road, Dobbins (Carrickfergus).

U13 Blackwood
☎(01247) 853581
150 Crawfordsburn Rd, Clandeboye, Bangor BT19 1GB
On A2 towards Bangor from Belfast turn for Newtownards. then left after 1 mile; course 500 yards on right.
Heathland/parkland course.
18 holes, 6304 yards, S.S.S. 70 , Par 72; 18 holes, 2492 yards, Par 3.
Designed by Simon Gidman.
Founded Sept 1994.
Visitors: always welcome, pay-and-play; advisable to phone in advance.
Green Fee: WD £12 (£7 with member); WE & BH £15 (£9 with member).
Societies: welcome, book in advance.
Catering: bar and snacks, restaurant, dining room.
Driving range.
Hotels: Clandeboye Lodge.

U14 Bright Castle
☎(01396) 841319
14 Coniamstown Rd, Bright, Co Down, N Ireland
5 miles S of Downpatrick.
Parkland course.
18 holes, 6584 metres, S.S.S.74
Designed by Arnold Ennis.
Founded 1970
Visitors: welcome, no restrictions.
Green Fee: apply for details
Societies: welcome, contact in advance.
Catering: bar, bar snacks.
Hotels: Abbey Lodge (Downpatrick).

U15 Brown Trout
☎(01265) 868209, Sec 662545
209 Agivy Road, Aghadowey, Nr Coleraine, Co Londonderry
Intersection of the A54 and B66.
Parkland course.
9 holes, 4978 metres, S.S.S.68
Designed by Bill O'Hara Snr.
Founded 1973

Visitors: no restrictions.
Green Fee: WD £10 (£8 with member); WE & BH £12 (£10 with member).
Societies: very welcome, inc. Sat.
Catering: all-day catering, à la carte restaurant.
Horse riding, fishing.
Hotels: Brown Trout Golf and Country Inn on course.

U16 Bushfoot
☎(012657) 31317, Sec 822551
50 Bushfoot Rd, Portballintrae, Co Antrim BT57 8RR
4 miles E of Portrush on coast.
Seaside links course.
9 holes, 5876 yards, S.S.S.67
Founded 1890
Visitors: welcome on weekdays and at weekends if no official club competitions.
Green Fee: WD £12 (£7 with member); WE & BH £15 (£12 with member).
Societies: welcome by prior arrangement.
Catering: bar and restaurant facilities.
Snooker room, Pitch & Putt (summer), functions.
Hotels: Bayview; Beech; Bushmills Inn; Causeway.

U17 Cairndhu
☎(01574) 583324, Sec 279320, Pro: 583417
192 Coast Rd, Ballygally, Larne, Co Antrim BT40 2QG
4 miles N of Larne.
Parkland course.
18 holes, 5598 metres, S.S.S.69
Designed by John S.F. Morrison.
Founded 1928
Visitors: welcome except Sat.
Green Fee: WD £12 (£7 with member); WE & BH £20 (£12 with member except Sat).
Societies: welcome by prior arrangement.
Catering: meals and snacks available on weekdays (5pm-10pm), Sat (11.30am-8pm), Sun (12.30-6.30pm).
Snooker.
Hotels: Ballygally Castle; Halfway House; Drumnagreagh House.

U18 Carnalea
☎(01247) 270368, Pro: 270122, Fax 273989
Station Rd, Bangor, Co Down BT19 1EZ

Adjacent to Carnalea railway station 1.5 miles from Bangor.
Seaside meadowland course.
18 holes, 5097 metres, S.S.S.67
Founded 1927
Visitors: welcome 7 days.
Green Fee: WD £11 (£9 with member); WE & BH £15 (£11 with member).
Societies: weekdays only by arrangement.
Catering: full catering facilities except Mon.
Hotels: Royal; Crawfordsburn Inn; Tedworth.

U19 Carrickfergus
☎(019603) 63713, Pro: 51803, Public: 62203
35 North Rd, Carrickfergus, Co Antrim BT38 8LP
Off A2, 9 miles NE of Belfast;on North Rd, Carrickfergus, 1 mile from Shore Road.
Parkland/meadowland course.
18 holes, 5765 yards, S.S.S.68
Founded 1926
Visitors: welcome except Sat.
Green Fee: WD £14 (£7 with member); WE & BH £20 (£10 with member).
Societies: Mon-Fri only, by arrangement.
Catering: full facilities.
Snooker.
Hotels: Coast Road; Dobbins Inn; Glenavna House.

U20 Castle Hume
☎(01365) 327077
Castle Hume, Enniskillen, Co Fermanagh BT93 7ED
18 holes, 5941 metres, S.S.S.72
Founded 1991
Green Fee: apply for details

U21 Castleblayney
☎(0142) 46588 Sec.
Onomy, Castleblayney, Co Monaghan, Ulster
Almost in Castleblayney town centre on Derry-Dublin road.
Parkland course.
9 holes, 4923 yards, S.S.S. 66
Designed by Bobby Browne.
Founded 1984
Visitors: welcome.
Green Fee: WD £5; WE & BH £8.
Societies: welcome by prior arrangement.
Catering: full facilities; Hope Castle restaurant and bar.
Hotels: Glencarn; Central.

U22 **Castlerock**
☎(01265) 848314 (Office/Fax), Sec 848714,
Public: 848215, Caterer: 848004
65 Circular Rd, Castlerock, Co Londonderry BT51 4TJ
Off A2, 6 miles W of Coleraine.
Seaside course.
27 holes, 6687 yards, S.S.S.72
Designed by Ben Sayers.
Founded 1901
Visitors: welcome.
Green Fee: WD £15 (£8 with member); WE & BH £25 (£13 with member).
Societies: weekdays only by arrangement.
Catering: franchise at club.
Snooker.
Hotels: Golf (Castlerock); Lodge (Coleraine).

U23 **City of Derry**
☎(01504) 46369, Pro: 311496
49 Victoria Rd, Londonderry BT47 2PU
On main Londonderry-Strabane road, 3 miles from Craigavon Bridge.
Parkland course.
27 holes, 5860 metres, S.S.S.71
Founded 1912
Visitors: welcome weekdays before 4.30pm unless with member; weekends by arrangement with Pro; Dunhugh course open at all times.
Green Fee: apply for details.
Societies: catered for on weekdays and possibly at weekends, by arrangement.
Catering: full facilities available.
Hotels: Everglades (bargain break packages); Broomhill House; White Horse Inn; Waterfoot.

U24 **Clandeboye**
☎(01247) 271767, Sec 466907, Pro: 271750
Tower Rd, Conlig, Newtownards, Co Down BT23 3PN
Above Conlig village off A21 between Bangor and Newtownards.
Dufferin, parkland/heathland course; Ava, parkland/moorland course.
36 holes, 6026 metres, S.S.S.73
Designed by William Rennick Robinson and Dr Bernard von Limburger.
Founded 1933
Visitors: welcome weekdays; must be accompanied by member Sat and Sun; (Ladies Day Thurs).
Green Fee: WD £21 & £17 (£10 & £9 with member); WE & BH N/A (£13 & £12 with member).

Societies: by arrangement, Apr-Sept Mon, Tue, Wed, Fri; Oct-Mar Mon, Wed.
Catering: available, restaurant not open Mon Oct-Mar.
Hotels: Royal; Culloden; Crawfordsburn Inn; Strangford Arms.

U25 **Cliftonville**
☎(01232) 746595, Sec 710747
44 Westland Rd, Belfast BT14 6NH
From centre of Belfast take Antrim road, about 2 miles from centre, then Cavehill Rd on left and left again at Fire Station.
Parkland course.
9 holes, 5706 metres, S.S.S.70
Founded 1911
Visitors: welcome except Sat and Tues afternoons.
Green Fee: WD £12 (£8 with member); WE & BH £15 (£10 with member).
Societies: by arrangement with Council through Hon Sec, J.M. Henderson.
Catering: bar snacks available; meals by arrangement.
Hotels: Lansdowne Court.

U26 **County Armagh**
☎(01861) 525861, Sec 525425, Pro: 525864
The Demesne, Newry Rd, Armagh BT10 1EN
Off Newry Rd, 0.25 mile from city centre.
Parkland course.
18 holes, 5655 metres, S.S.S.69
Founded 1893
Visitors: welcome except 12am-2pm Sat and 12am-3pm Sun.
Green Fee: WD £12 (£8 with member); WE & BH £18 (£12 with member).
Societies: catered for by arrangement except on Sat.
Catering: full facilities; by prior arrangement Mon.
Hotels: Charlemont Arms; Drumsill House.

U27 **Craigavon**
☎(01762) 326606
Golf and Ski Centre, Turmoyra Lane, Silverwood, Lurgan, Craigavon, Co Armagh BT66 6NG
Off M1 from Belfast at A76 exit 10, continue for 500 yards from sliproad, take 1st right into Kiln Rd and 1st right again.
Public parkland course.
18 holes, 7253 yards, S.S.S. 72, Par

72; 9 holes, 1349 yards, Par 3.
Visitors: welcome any time, advisable to ring in advance weekends.
Green Fee: WD £10; WE & BH £13.
Societies: by arrangement, mainly Sun, some Sat.
Catering: snacks, bar and restaurant at Silverwood Golf & Ski Centre adjacent to course.
12-hole Pitch & Putt, driving range and putting green.
Hotels: Silverwood.

U28 **Crossgar**
☎(01396) 831523, Sec 830415
231 Derryboye Rd, Crossgar, Co. Down
9 holes, 4139 metres, S.S.S.63
Founded 1993
Green Fee: WD £8 (£6 with member); WE & BH £10 (£8 with member).

U29 **Cushendall**
☎(012667) 71318, Sec 58366
Shore Rd, Cushendall, Ballymena, Co Antrim BT44 0QQ
Turn right at Curfew Tower in village, proceed 0.25 mile to Strand.
Seaside/parkland course.
9 holes, 4386 metres, S.S.S.63
Designed by Daniel Delargy.
Founded 1937
Visitors: welcome.
Green Fee: WD £8 (£5 with member); WE & BH £10 (£7 with member).
Societies: weekdays.
Catering: summer, weekends only winter; or by prior arrangement at any time.
Hotels: Thornlea.

U30 **Donaghadee**
☎(01247) 883624, Pro: 882392, Fax 888891
84 Warren Rd, Donaghadee, Co Down BT21 0PQ
On A2 18 miles E of Belfast.
Part links/part parkland.
18 holes, 5576 metres, S.S.S.69
Founded 1899
Visitors: welcome except Sat (competition day), booking advisable.
Green Fee: WD £14 (£9 with member); WE & BH £18 (£11 with member).
Societies: Mon, Wed and Fri by arrangement.
Catering: full facilities.
Snooker.
Hotels: Copelands; Dunallen.

U31 Downpatrick
☎(01396) 615947, Sec 613557, Pro:
615167, Caterer: 615244
43 Saul Rd, Downpatrick, Co Down
BT30 6PA
A24 and A7 23 miles SE of Belfast.
Parkland course.
18 holes, 5615 metres, S.S.S.69
Designed by Hawtree & Sons.
Founded 1930
Visitors: welcome, restricted at
weekends.
Green Fee: WD £14 (£10 with
member); WE & BH £18 (£13 with
member).
Societies: welcome by prior
arrangement.
Catering: full facilities.
Snooker.
Hotels: Denvir's; Abbey Lodge.

U32 Dungannon
☎(018687) 727338, Sec 722602,
Bar: 722098
34 Springfield Lane, Mullaghmore,
Dungannon, Co Tyrone BT70 1QX
0.5 mile out of town on Donaghmore
Rd.
Parkland course.
18 holes, 5433 metres, S.S.S.68
Founded 1890
Visitors: welcome anytime.
Green Fee: WD £10 (£8 with
member); WE & BH £13 (£11 with
member).
Societies: welcome by prior
arrangement.
Catering: facilities available by
arrangement.
Hotels: Dunowen; Inn on the Park;
Glengannon Inn.

U33 Dunmurry
☎(01232) 610834, Pro: 621314, Bar:
621402
91 Dunmurry Lane, Dunmurry, Belfast
BT17 9JS
Situated between Dunmurry village
and Upper Malone Rd, Belfast.
Parkland course.
18 holes, 5348 metres, S.S.S.68
Designed by T.J. McAuley.
Founded 1905
Visitors: not before 5pm Sat, after
5pm Tues and Thurs.
Green Fee: WD £16 (£10 with
member); WE & BH £25 (£12 with
member).
Societies: not Sat, 11.30am-12.30pm
Sun.
Catering: facilities available each day
except Mon.
Hotels: Conway; Beechlawn;
Balmoral.

U34 Edenmore Golf Course
☎(01846) 611310, Sec (01762)
663152
Edenmore House, 70 Drumnabreeze
Rd, Maralin, Co. Armagh, N Ireland
BT67 0RH
From Belfast take M1 motorway, turn
off at 5th exit for Moira; pass through
Moira to Maralin (1 mile); at Maralin
turn left into New Forge Road, then
1st left into Steps Road; after small
bridge take 1st right into Orange Lane
and then 1st left into Drumnabreeze
Road.
Parkland course.
9 holes, 6143 yards, S.S.S. 70
Designed by Frank Ainsworth.
Founded June 1992
Visitors: welcome except Sun
(course closed); no h/cap
requirement; Club members have
priority booking for tee-off times on
Sat up to 12.30pm.
Green Fee: WD £10 (£8 if
accompanied by a member); WE &
BH £12 (£10 if accompanied by a
member).
Societies: welcome any time by prior
arrangement.
Catering: excellent restaurant;
morning tea or coffee, lunch (12-
2pm), afternoon tea; private functions
in evenings by prior arrangement (for
20-80).
Hotels: Seagoe (Portadown); White
Gables (Hillsborough); Silverwood
(Lurgan).

U35 Enniskillen
☎(01365) 325250, Sec 324562
Castlecoole, Enniskillen, Co
Fermanagh
1 mile from Enniskillen off Tempo
Road.
Parkland course.
18 holes, 5588 metres, S.S.S. 69
Designed by (1st 9) Dr Dixon &
George Mawhinney, (2nd 9) T.J.
McAuley.
Founded 1896
Visitors: unrestricted.
Green Fee: WD £10 (£5 if
accompanied by a member; one
guest only); WE & BH £12 (£6 with
member).
Societies: golfing societies welcome
if previous arrangements made with
Club Steward.
Catering: bar snacks available daily,
full catering facilities by prior
arrangement.
Snooker.
Hotels: Killyhevlin; Fort Lodge;
Railway, Belmore Court.

U36 Fintona
☎(01662) 840366
Ecclesville Demesne, Fintona, Co
Tyrone
9 miles SW of Omagh.
Parkland course.
9 holes, 5765 metres, S.S.S.70
Founded 1904
Visitors: welcome.
Green Fee: any day £10
Societies: welcome by prior
arrangement.
Catering: by prior arrangement.

U37 Fortwilliam
☎(01232) 370770, Pro: 770980,
Caterer: 370072,
Fax 781891
Downview Ave, Belfast B15 4EZ
On A2 3 miles N of Belfast.
Meadowland course.
18 holes, 5973 yards, S.S.S.69
Designed by Mr Buchart.
Founded 1891
Visitors: welcome except Sat.
Green Fee: apply for details.
Societies: welcome by arrangement
with Sec.
Catering: full service available.
Hotels: Lansdowne Court.

U38 Foyle
☎(01504) 352222, Fax 353967
12 Alder Road, Londonderry BT48
8DB
27 holes, 6678 metres, S.S.S.72
Founded 1994
Green Fee: WD £11 (£9 with
member); WE & BH £13 (£11 with
member).

U39 Garron Tower
☎(01232) 85202
St Macnissi's College, Carnlough, Co
Antrim BT44 0JS
Founded 1968
Playing facilities at Cushendall &
Ballycastle Golf Clubs.

U40 Gilnahirk
☎(01232) 448477
Manns Corner, Upper Bramel Rd,
Gilnahirk, Castlereagh, Belfast
3 miles from Belfast off Ballygowan
road.
Public moorland course.
9 holes, 5398 metres, S.S.S.68
Founded 1983
Visitors: welcome.
Green Fee: apply for details.
Putting green.
Hotels: Stormont.

U41 Greenisland

☎(01232) 862236, Sec 864583
156 Upper Rd, Grennisland,
Carrickfergus, Co Antrim BT38 8RW
About 9 miles N of Belfast.
Meadowland course.
9 holes, 5536 metres, S.S.S.68
Re-designed by H. Middleton.
Founded 1894
Visitors: welcome except Sat.
Green Fee: WD £10 (£5 with
member); WE & BH £15 (£7.50 with
member).
Societies: welcome by prior
arrangement.
Catering: full facilities.
Snooker.
Hotels: Glenavna, Newtownabbey.

U42 Helen's Bay

☎(01247) 852815 (Office/Fax), Sec
853226,
Public: 852601, Caterer: 852816
Golf Rd, Helen's Bay, Bangor, Co
Down BT19 1TL
Off A2, 9 miles E of Belfast.
Seaside course.
9 holes, 5176 metres, S.S.S.67
Founded 1896
Visitors: welcome Mon, Wed, Thurs
(before 2pm), Fri, Sun; with member
only Sat and Bank Holidays after
2.30pm.
Green Fee: WD £12 (£6 with
member); WE & BH £15 (£7.50 with
member).
Societies: Mon, Wed and Fri.
Catering: full facilities.

U43 Holywood

☎(01232) 423135, Pro: 425503, Fax
425040
Nuns Walk, Demesne Rd, Holywood,
Co Down BT18 9LE
On A2 6 miles E of Belfast.
Undulating course.
18 holes, 5430 metres, S.S.S.68
Founded 1904
Visitors: welcome except Sat.
Green Fee: WD £15 (£9 with
member); WE & BH £20 (£12 with
member).
Societies: catered for except Thurs,
Sat and Bank Holidays.
Catering: bar and catering facilities
(426832).
Snooker.
Hotels: Culloden.

U44 Kilkeel

☎(016937) 65095, Sec 63787
Mourne Park, Kilkeel, Co Down BT34
4LB
3 miles from Kilkeel on Newry road,
signposted.
Parkland course.
18 holes, 6615 metres, S.S.S.72
Designed by Lord Justice Babbington
(original 9), Eddie Hackett (new 9).
Founded 1948 on present site.
Visitors: welcome except Sat.
Green Fee: WD £12 (£7.50 with
member); WE & BH £16 (£10 with
member).
Societies: on application.
Catering: full facilities.
Snooker, pool.
Hotels: Kilmorey Arms; Cranfield
House.

U45 Killymoon

☎(016487) 63762, Bar: 62254
200 Killymoon Rd, Cookstown, Co
Tyrone BT80 8TW
0.5 mile off A29 on S side of
Cookstown.
Parkland course.
18 holes, 5488 metres, S.S.S.69
Designed by Hugh Adair.
Founded 1889
Visitors: all week except Sat, club
competition day.
Green Fee: apply for details.
Societies: welcome by arrangement
except Thurs and Sat.
Catering: bar, full catering available.
Hotels: Glenavon; Greenvale; Royal.

U46 Kilrea

☎(01265) 834738 Sec
38 Drumagarner Rd, Kilrea, Co
Londonderry, N Ireland
0.5 mile SW of Kilrea on road to
Maghera.
Inland links course, well-drained.
9 holes, 3956 metres, S.S.S.62
Founded 1920
Visitors: welcome 7 days, avoid
Tues, Wed evenings, Sat in summer.
Green Fee: apply for details.
Societies: welcome any day by prior
arrangement.

U47 Kirkistown Castle

☎(01247) 771233, Sec 771136, Pro:
771004,
Fax 771699
142 Main Rd, Cloughey, Co Down
BT22 1JA
A20 from Belfast to Kircubbin, follow
signs to Newtownards and Portaferry,
then B173 to Cloughey.
Links course.
18 holes, 5596 metres, S.S.S.70
Designed by B. Polley.
Founded Oct 1902
Visitors: welcome.
Green Fee: WD £13 (£9 with
member); WE & BH £25 (£12 with
member).
Societies: welcome weekdays,
except Bank Holidays; society rates
available for 16 and over.
Catering: full facilities daily 11am-
8pm.
Hotels: Portaferry.

U48 The Knock

☎(01232) 483251, Pro: 483825,
Caterer: 480915
Summerfield, Upper Newtownards
Rd, Dundonald, Belfast BT16 0QX
Travel E out of Belfast towards
Dundonald, course on left 0.5 mile
beyond Stormont Houses of
Parliament.
Parkland course.
18 holes, 6435 yards, S.S.S.71
Designed by Colt, McKenzie &
Allison.
Founded 1895
Visitors: not Sat unless with
member.
Green Fee: WD £20 (£10 with
member); WE & BH £25 (£12 with
member).
Societies: Mon and Thurs.
Catering: full facilities all week.
Snooker.
Hotels: Stormont (within 1 mile).

U49 Knockbracken Golf & Country Club

☎(01232) 795666, **Hotels:** 792108
Ballymaconaghy Rd, Knockbracken,
Belfast BT8 4SB
Near Four Winds restaurant on SE
outskirts of city.
Meadowland course.
18 holes, 5391 yards, S.S.S.68
Visitors: welcome any time but
priority tee times for members at
weekends.
Green Fee: WD: £8; WE & BH £10.
Societies: welcome by prior
arrangement.
Catering: full bar and restaurant
facilities 7 days.
Driving range, putting greens, ski
slope.
Hotels: La Mon

U50 Lambeg

☎(01846) 662738
Aberdelly, Bells Lane, Lambeg,
Lisburn, Co. Antrim
9 holes, 4384 metres, S.S.S.65
Founded 1986
Green Fee: apply for details

U51 Larne

☎(019603) 82228, Sec 72043
54 Ferris Bay Rd, Islandmagee,
Larne BT40 3RT
From Belfast, N to Carrickfergus and
6 miles from Whitehead, from Larne
S along coast road to Islandmagee;
23 miles Belfast, 7 miles Larne.
Seaside course at N tip of
Islandmagee peninsula.
9 holes, 5572 metres, S.S.S.69
Designed by Babington.
Founded 1894
Visitors: weekdays; not Sat.
Green Fee: WD £8 (£4 with
member); WE & BH £15 (£6 with
member).
Societies: open; not Sat.
Catering: available.
Hotels: Magheramorne House.

U52 Lisburn

☎(01846) 677216, Pro: 677217, Fax
603608
68 Eglantine Rd, Lisburn, Co Antrim
BT27 5RQ
3 miles S of Lisburn, near radio mast.
Meadowland/parkland course.
18 holes, 6647 metres, S.S.S.72
Designed by Hawtree & Sons.
Founded 1905
Visitors: at specified times.
Green Fee: apply for details.
Societies: Mon, Thurs, Fri.
Catering: 7 days.
Hotels: White Gables (Hillsborough).

U53 Lurgan

☎(01762) 322087 Sec 326815, Pro:
321306,
Fax 325306
The Demesne, Lurgan, Co Armagh
BT67 9BN
Centre of Lurgan to Windsor Ave and
past castle gates around lake edge.
Parkland course with lakes.
18 holes, 5836 metres, S.S.S.70
Designed by Frank Pennink.
Founded 1893
Visitors: welcome except Sat.
Green Fee: WD £15 (£7.50 with
member); WE & BH £20 (£10 with
member).
Societies: on request, not Sat.
Catering: available except Mon.
Hotels: Silverwood; Carngrove;
Seagoe.

U54 Mahee Island

☎(01238) 541234, Sec (01 247)
878219
Comber, Newtownards, Co Down,
BT23 6ET
Turn left 0.5 mile from Comber on
Comber/Killyleagh road, keep bearing
left to Mahee Island, 6 miles.
Parkland/seaside course.
9 holes, 5108 metres, S.S.S.67
Founded 1929
Visitors: restricted after 4pm Wed
and until 5pm Sat.
Green Fee: WD £10 (£5 with
member); WE & BH £15 (£7.50 with
member).
Societies: alternate Sun, weekdays
except Mon; apply in writing to Sec.
Catering: by arrangement, no bar.
Pool.
Hotels: Balloo House; La Mon
House; Strangford Arms.

U55 Mallusk

(Sec (01232) 391491
City of Belfast Golf Course, Mallusk,
Newtownabbey, Co. Antrim
9 holes, 4444 metres, S.S.S.62
Founded 1992
Green Fee: WD £4.50; WE & BH £7

U56 Malone

☎(01232) 612758, Pro: 614917, Fax
431394
240 Upper Malone Rd, Dunmurry,
Belfast BT17 9LB
5 miles from Belfast centre, take
Upper Malone Rd.
Parkland course.
27 holes, 6642 yards, S.S.S.71
Designed by Fred Hawtree.
Founded 1895
Visitors: welcome except Wed after
2pm and Sat before 5pm.
Green Fee: apply for details.
Societies: catered for Mon and
Thurs.
Catering: full facilities except Sun
after 2pm.

U57 Massereene

☎(01849) 428096, Pro: 464074
51 Lough Rd, Antrim
1 mile S of town, 3.5 miles from
Aldergrove Airport.
Parkland course.
18 holes, 6614 yards, S.S.S.71
Designed by F.W. Hawtree.
Founded 1895
Visitors: welcome weekdays and
weekends, Sat competition day.
Green Fee: WD £18 (£8 with
member); WE & BH £23 (£10 with
member).
Societies: Tues, Thurs 9-12am and
2-3.30pm; Wed 9-11.30am.
Catering: full facilities.
Hotels: Dunadry; Deerpark.

U58 Mount Ober

☎(01232) 401811, Public: 792108,
Bar: 792100,
Fax 705862
24 Ballymaconaghy, Knockbracken,
Belfast BT8 4SB
18 holes, 5391 yards, S.S.S.68
Founded 1985
Green Fee: apply for details

U59 Mourne

☎(01396) 723889, Sec 723483,
Public: 723218
36 Golf Links Rd, Newcastle, Co.
Down BT33 0AN
Playing facilities at Royal Co.Down

U60 Moyola Park

☎(01648) 68468, Pro: 68830
Shanemullagh, Castledawson,
Magherafelt, Co Londonderry BT45
8DG
Turn right half-way through
Castledawson village, continue along
Curran Rd, course entrance 400
yards on right.
Parkland course.
18 holes, 6517 yards, S.S.S.71
Designed by Don Patterson.
Founded 1976
Visitors: welcome.
Green Fee: apply for details.
Societies: welcome at all times
except Sat by prior arrangement.
Catering: full facilities, phone (01648)
68392.
Snooker.
Hotels: Moyola Lodge.

U61 Newtownstewart

☎(016626) 61466, Sec 71487, Bar:
61829
38 Golf Course Rd, Newtownstewart,
Omagh, Co Tyrone BT78 4HU
2 miles SW of Newtownstewart via
B84 Drumquin road.
Parkland course.
18 holes, 5341 metres, S.S.S.69
Designed by Frank Pennink.
Founded 1914
Visitors: welcome but advance
booking advisable.
Green Fee: WD £10 (£5 with
member); WE & BH £15 (£7.50 with
member).
Societies: welcome by prior
arrangement.
Catering: licensed bar open normal
hours, meals can be served by
arrangement.
Snooker.
Hotels: Hunting Lodge; Royal Arms;
Silver Birch; Fir Trees Lodge.

Royal County Down and Royal Portrush

Old Tom Morris's achievement in laying out Royal County Down at a cost not to exceed £4.00 is part of golf's folklore and represented remarkably good value for money even in those days. However, not much of his original work survives in the modern version of a links that many regard as perhaps the mightiest of all.

If you are lucky enough to play golf on either of Northern Ireland's two great courses, Royal County Down and Royal Portrush, somebody, sooner or later, is bound to fuel the debate about which is the better.

Rather like being asked whether Bobby Jones was superior to Ben Hogan, or Jack Hobbs a better batsman than Don Bradman, it is a provocative question, yet nearly everyone is agreed that both rank among the ten best courses in Great Britain and Eire, and no golfer visiting those parts for the first time should play the one and not the other.

Although the approach to Portrush along the coast road from Antrim can be spectacularly beautiful, one reason for giving County Down at Newcastle the edge is because its setting under the shadow of the Mountains of Mourne is so majestic and inspiring that nobody could fail to be moved by it. There is something special about playing against a backcloth of mountains, but even if you denied Newcastle the splendour of its distant views, the avenues forged by the fairways between high sandhills clad with gorse, would still be most beguiling. The quiet seaside town of Newcastle lies on a narrow strip of dune country on the edge of Dundrum Bay, its fine, natural features combining to present the severest of championship tests in which there is a big demand on long, straight driving and no end of challenging strokes to well protected greens.

It is sad that Ulster's problems have deprived it of more championship status following its staging of the Curtis Cup in 1968 and the British Amateur Championship, won for the third successive year by Michael Bonallack, in 1970. The Amateur returns there in 1999.

The first three holes along the shore make a stern beginning; then comes a long short hole from a high tee across the gorse and a classic par 4, the 5th doglegging round the hills. More holes linger in the mind notably the 9th which, following a blind drive, unveils the full panoply of the setting. It is one of the most photographed pictures in golf. The inward half continues the challenging trend, the least blemish being severely punished.

Not that Portrush offers any more relief. It, too, lies in the mist of some natural golfing country, north of Belfast, and, with the wind blowing in from the Atlantic and the rough in full bloom, good scoring is no light matter.

Bernard Darwin, on seeing it for the first time, wrote that its designer, Harry Colt, had built himself a monument more enduring than brass and it is certainly a thorough examination of a golfer's skill. The 5th, with its green by the water's edge looking away towards the Giant's Causeway, is particularly appealing along with the magnificent 1-shot 6th that follows. Then, later on, there are holes aptly termed "calamity corner" and "purgatory" and all the time, to lend a historical note, the reminder that in 1951 Max Faulkner won the Open Championship on the only occasion in which it ventured outside Scotland or England. Similarly, in 1960, Joe Carr, perhaps the best known and most loved figure in all Ireland, stood 10 up and 10 to play in the final of the Amateur Championship.

These were the supreme moments in the lives of two players who, in their respective worlds, provided more colour and entertainment than any of their contemporaries. For them, Portrush must have a warm place in their hearts, and no wonder.

U62 Omagh

☎(01662) 241442, Sec 243749, Bar: 243160
83a Dublin Rd, Omagh, Co Tyrone BT78 1HQ
On A5 on outskirts of Omagh.
Parkland course.
18 holes, 5213 metres, S.S.S.68
Founded 1910
Visitors: welcome any day except Tues, Sat and Sun.
Green Fee: WD £10 (£8 with member); WE & BH £15 (£13 with member).
Societies: welcome weekdays.
Catering: available for societies.
Snooker.
Hotels: Royal Arms.

U63 Ormeau

☎(01232) 641069, Pro: 640999
50 Park Rd, Belfast BT7 2FX
2 miles from city centre, Ravenhill Rd.
Parkland course.
9 holes, 4894 metres, S.S.S.65
Founded 1892
Visitors: welcome weekdays and Sun.
Green Fee: WD £9 (£5 with member); WE & BH £11 (£7 with member).
Societies: Thurs and Sun on application.
Catering: bar and restaurant.
Snooker.
Hotels: Drumkeen House.

U64 Portadown

☎(01762) 355356, Pro: 334655, Caterer: 352214
192 Gilford Rd, Portadown, Craigavon, Co Armagh BT63 5LF
On A59 2 miles SE of Portadown, entrance 400 yards beyond Metal Box factory on right.
Parkland course.
18 holes, 5621 metres, S.S.S.70
Founded 1900
Visitors: welcome, not Tues and Sat.
Green Fee: apply for details.
Societies: details on request.
Catering: bar daily, restaurant except Mon.
Squash, snooker.
Hotels: Seagoe; Carn.

U65 Portstewart

☎(01265) 832015, Sec 832936, Pro: 832601,
Fax 834097
117 Strand Rd, Portstewart, Co Londonderry BT55 7PG
4 miles W of Portrush.
Links course.
45 holes; Strand: 6784 yards, S.S.S. 73; Town: 4733 yards, S.S.S.62.
Founded 1894
Visitors: weekdays on application.
Green Fee: WD £25 (£10 with member); WE & BH £35 (£12 with member).
Societies: welcome weekdays, must book by phone.
Catering: every day.
Hotels: Edgewater.

U66 Rathmore

☎(01265) 822996, Sec 731998, Pro: 823335
Bushmills Rd, Portrush, Co Antrim BT56 8JG
Founded 1947
Playing facilities at Royal Portrush Golf Centre

U67 Ringdufferin

☎(01396) 828812
Ringdufferin Rd, Toye, Killyleagh, Co. Down BT30 9PH
9 holes, 4994 metres, S.S.S.66
Founded 1993
Green Fee: WD £5; WE & BH £6

U68 Roe Park

☎(015047) 22212, Sec 22612, Fax 22313
Limavaddy, Co. Londonderry BT49 9LB
18 holes, 6318 yards, S.S.S.71
Founded 1993
Green Fee: WD £16 (£13 with member); WE & BH £20 (£16 with member)

U69 Royal Belfast

☎(01232) 428165, Sec 424474, Pro: 428586,
Fax 421404
11 Station Rd, Craigavad, Holywood, Co Down BT18 0BP
2 miles E of Holywood on A2.
Parkland course.
18 holes, 6306 yards, S.S.S.71
Designed by H.C. Colt, redesigned (1988) Donald Steel.
Founded 1881
Visitors: except Wed and Sat before 4.30pm, by introduction or letter from home club.
Green Fee: WD £30 (£15 with member); WE & BH £35 (£17.50 with member).
Societies: by arrangement.
Catering: full facilities.
Hotels: Culloden.

U70 Royal County Down

☎(013967) 23314, Pro: 22419, Fax 26281
Newcastle, Co Down BT33 0AN
From Belfast take A24 to Carryduff, A7 to Ballynahinch and A2 to Newcastle, about 30 miles.
Links course.
36 holes, 6969 yards, S.S.S.73
Designed by Tom Morris Snr.
Founded 1898
Visitors: Mon, Tues, Thurs, Fri; h/cap cert required.
Green Fee: WD Winter £35, Summer £45 (£13 if accompanied by a member); WE & BH Winter £45, Summer £60 (£13 if accompanied by a member).
Societies: welcome by prior arrangement only.
Catering: Centenary Room open Mon-Fri.
Hotels: Slieve Donard; Burrendale; Glassdrumman Lodge.

U71 Royal Portrush

☎(01265) 822311, Sec 822318, Pro: 823335,
Fax 823139
Bushmills Rd, Portrush, Co Antrim BT56 8JQ
1 mile from Portrush town off A1.
Seaside links course.
27 holes, 6772 yards, S.S.S.73
Designed by H.S. Colt.
Founded 1888
Visitors: welcome Mon, Tues, Thurs, Fri am, Sun after 10am.
Green Fee: WD Dunluce £43 (£15 with member),
WD Valley £18 (£8 with member); WE & BH Dunluce £50 (£15 with member); WE & BH Valley £15 (£10 with member).
Societies: catered for; on Dunluce Mon, Tues, Thurs, Fri am, Sun 10.30-11.30am; on Valley every day except Sat/Sun am.
Catering: full catering daily, snacks, high tea and à la carte.
Hotels: Bayview (Portballatrae); Magherabuoy House.

U72 Scrabo

☎(01247) 812355, Sec 816516, Pro: 817848,
Fax 822919
233 Scrabo Rd, Newtownards, Co Down BT23 4SL
Off A20 10 miles E of Belfast; near Scrabo Tower.
Hilly parkland course.
18 holes, 5699 metres, S.S.S.71
Founded 1907

Visitors: weekdays except Wed.
Green Fee: WD £15 (£8 with member); WE & BH £20 (£11 with member).
Societies: any day except Sat, not during June.
Catering: full bar and restaurant. Snooker.
Hotels: Strangford Arms; George; La Mon House.

U73 Shandon Park

☎(01232) 401856, Sec 656974, Pro: 797859,
Fax 402773
73 Shandon Park, Belfast BT5 6NY
3 miles from city centre via Knock dual carriageway.
Parkland course.
18 holes, 6261 yards, S.S.S.70
Founded 1926
Visitors: welcome weekdays.
Green Fee: WD £22 (£9 with member); WE & BH £27 (£13 with member).
Societies: Mon and Fri only by arrangement.
Catering: meals and snacks.
Hotels: Stormont; Drumkeen.

U74 Silverwood

☎(01762) 326606, Sec (01864) 619728,
Tormoyra Lane, Silverwood, Lurgan BT66 6NG
18 holes, 6459 yards, S.S.S.71
Founded 1984
Green Fee: WD £9; WE & BH £12

U75 Spa

☎(01238) 562365, Sec (01232) 812340
20 Grove Rd, Ballynahinch, Co Down BT24 8PN
A24, 1 mile from Ballynahinch, exit at sign for Spa or Dromara.
Parkland course.
18 holes, 5938 metres, S.S.S.72
Founded 1907
Visitors: welcome.
Green Fee: WD £14 (£10 with member); WE & BH £18 (£10 with member).

Societies: Mon-Thurs and some Sun; 1st tee 10.30-11.45am.
Catering: bar; meals by arrangement.
Snooker, pool, bowls.
Hotels: Millbrook Lodge; White Horse.

U76 Strabane

☎(01504) 382007, Sec 883098, Public: 382271
Ballycolman, Strabane, Co Tyrone BT82 9PH
1 mile from Strabane on Dublin road beside church and three schools.
Parkland course.
18 holes, 5552 metres, S.S.S.69
Designed by Eddie Hackett.
Founded 1908
Visitors: welcome.
Green Fee: apply for details.
Societies: apply to Sec.
Catering: by arrangement.
Hotels: Fir Trees Lodge.

U77 Tandragee

☎(01762) 841272, Pro: 841761, Bar: 840727
Market Hill Rd, Tandragee, Co Armagh BT62 2ER
A27 from Portadown towards Newry and Dublin, right on B3 in Tandragee towards Market Hill and Clare Glen, course 200 yards on right.
Hilly parkland course.
18 holes, 4955 metres, S.S.S.69
Designed by F. Hawtree.
Founded 1920
Visitors: Mon-Wed before 4pm, Thurs before 2pm (Ladies Day), Fri before 1pm, Sun 10.30-11.30am and after 3pm.
Green Fee: WD £15 (£8 with member); WE & BH £21 (£10 with member).
Societies: Sun 10.30-11.30am, Mon-Wed before 12am and after 2pm, Fri before 12am.
Catering: full service available from 12.30pm daily; normal bar facilities 7 days (841763).
Snooker, large function room.
Hotels: Seagoe, Carn Grove (Portadown).

U78 Temple

☎(01846) 639213, Fax 638637
60 Church Rd, Boardmills, Lisburn, Co. Down BT27 6UP
9 holes, 5451 yards, S.S.S.66
Founded 1994
Green Fee: WD £8 (£6 if accompanied by a member); WE & BH £10.

U79 Warrenpoint

☎(016937) 53695, Pro: 52371, Fax 52571
Lower Dromore Rd, Warrenpoint, Co Down BT34 3LN
5 miles from Newry on main Warrenpoint road.
Parkland course.
18 holes, 5638 metres, S.S.S.70
Founded 1893
Visitors: by appointment.
Green Fee: WD £16 (£8 if accompanied by a member); WE & BH £22 (£11 if accompanied by a member).
Societies: welcome by prior arrangement.
Catering: full facilities.
Snooker, squash.
Hotels: Carlingford Bay.

U80 Whitehead

☎(019603) 53631, Pro: 53118, Bar: 53792
McCrae's Brae, Whitehead, Co Antrim BT38 9NZ
Take turning into Whitehead off main Carrickfergus-Larne road to Islandmagee road, signposted at bottom of McCrae's Brae to club.
Undulating parkland course.
18 holes, 5817 metres, S.S.S.70
Founded 1904
Visitors: any day except Sat.
Green Fee: WD £11 (£6 with member); WE & BH £17 (£11 with member).
Societies: welcome by arrangement Mon to Fri 9am-12.30pm, 1.30pm-4.30pm (Fri until 4pm), Sun 10.30-12am.
Catering: facilities may be arranged with Steward.
Hotels: Magheramorne House.

V

EIRE

The first lesson that has to be learned about golf in Ireland is that, in order to derive the greatest benefit, it is better not to be in too much of a hurry. Settle in to the pace of life. Don't plan an impossible itinerary. Travel can be slow and golfing destinations remote but that is undoubtedly part of their attraction and you will soon adapt.

This certainly applies to the coastal sweep that begins in Dublin and ends in Galway, a journey that incorporates many wonderful courses, particularly out west where giant dunes, lonely beaches and wild winds lend an accompaniment to the play that is quite uplifting. Ballybunion, Lahinch, Tralee and Waterville are fit for giants, places that pose the ultimate in challenge although beguiling enough to soften failure.

For those arriving at Shannon Airport, the decision is whether to head north or south of the great Estuary which runs into Limerick. Greater by far are the number of courses to the south-west but Lahinch, the St Andrews of Ireland, because of its discovery by officers of the Black Watch, is as fine an example of links golf as could be imagined.

Ballybunion's Old course is an undoubted monument that has brought deserved fame to the little seaside town. It involves a little more climbing than on other links although some of the high spots enhance the spectacular views. Nearby Tralee, the work of Arnold Palmer, is a course of two parts, a front nine of more open land and a back nine dominated by majestic dune country involving many demanding strokes.

Some of the greens on the outward half enjoy settings on the edge of the sea which are captivating if the wind is not severe but beauty of the setting is a recurring theme all over the south-west of Ireland, and it certainly applies to Waterville, the inspiration of a local man, J.A. Mulcahy.

Killarney, scene of the 1996 Curtis Cup, continues to be highly popular with its scenic glories. It is an ideal port of call for those enjoying the delights of Kerry but there are other inland delights such as Little Island (Cork) and Carlow, set in a lovely old deer park, and three new creations, St. Helen's Bay at Rosslare, Faithlegg in County Waterford and The European Club in County Wicklow. The European Club has been widely praised and is beautifully situated, while Mount Juliet and the K Club at Straffan, County Kildare, have hosted major events in spite of being only about five years old.

The Irish course which has seen more great events than any other is Portmarnock, many Irish Opens, the Canada Cup, British Amateur and the Walker Cup head the impressive list, a tribute to the formidable test of golf.

Royal Dublin, older than Portmarnock, is another noble links and a word for Sutton, the nine hole course famous for its association with Joe Carr. It stands on Cush Point looking across the narrow estuary to Portmarnock where Carr was born. It is such a short, compact little course that it used to be said that if Carr shouted "Fore", everybody ducked; but if it is enchantment that you want, the Island at Malahide offers the perfect retreat among its lonely dunes. Further up the coast, Baltray, or County Louth, represents as fine a tract of land as any in a country renowned for great courses.

Many of Dublin's other courses are more parkland in character but out on the west coast the feature of the courses is again one of grandeur and beauty. Connemara, Donegal, Rosapenna and Westport are the main attractions and there are few lovelier spots than County Sligo at Rosses Point, home of the late Cecil Ewing, another giant of Irish golf. In 1991, the Club housed the Home Internationals, a wonderfully friendly environment for a unique gathering.

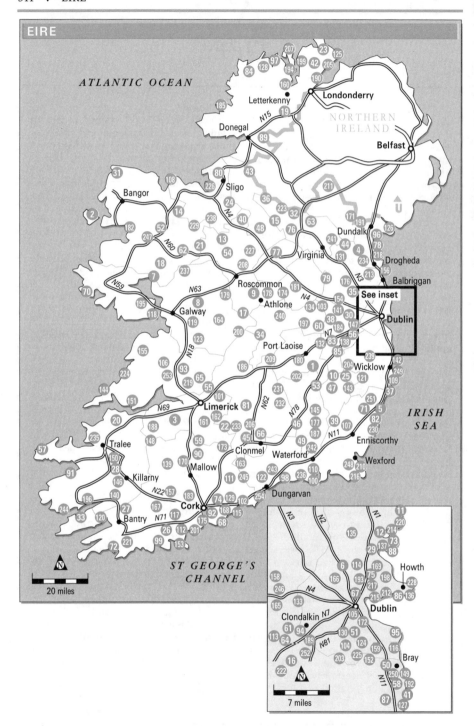

EIRE

ATLANTIC OCEAN

NORTHERN IRELAND

Londonderry

Letterkenny

Belfast

Donegal

Dundalk

Drogheda

Balbriggan

See inset

Dublin

IRISH SEA

Wicklow

Enniscorthy

Wexford

Dungarvan

Waterford

Clonmel

Mallow

Killarny

Cork

Bantry

Tralee

Limerick

Port Laoise

Athlone

Roscommon

Galway

Bangor

Sligo

Virginia

ST GEORGE'S CHANNEL

20 miles

Clondalkin

Dublin

Howth

Bray

7 miles

V1 Abbeyleix

☎(0502) 31450, Sec 31051
Abbeyleix, Co Laois
Within 0.5 mile of Main St on
Stradbally Rd.
Parkland course.
9 holes, 5626 metres, S.S.S.68
Founded 1895
Visitors: welcome.
Green Fee: WD £8 (£6 with
member); WE & BH £10 (£6 with
member).
Societies: welcome by arrangement,
usually on Sat.
Catering: by arrangement for
societies.
Hotels: Hibernian; Killeshin,
Montague (Portlaoise); Globe House
(Ballinakill).

V2 Achill Island

☎(098) 43456
Keel, Achill, Co Mayo
Via Castlebar or Westport.
Public seaside course.
9 holes, 4960 metres, S.S.S.66
Designed by P. Skerrit.
Founded 1952
Visitors: welcome.
Green Fee: any day: £5.
Societies: monthly (approx).
Hotels: Achill Sound; Wavecrest;
Atlantic; Gray's; McDowell's;
Slievemore; Achill Head; Clew Bay.

V3 Adare Manor

☎(061) 396204, Sec 396407
Adare, Co Limerick

10 miles from Limerick city on main
Killarney road.
Parkland course built round castle
and friary ruins.
18 holes, 5800 yards, S.S.S.69
Designed by Eddie Hackett.
Founded 1900
Visitors: welcome weekdays,
weekends with member or by prior
arrangement.
Green Fee: WD £15 (£10 with
member); WE & BH £20 (£15 with
member).
Societies: on club notice board; book
well in advance.
Catering: limited to chicken, fish etc
in basket; sandwiches, tea, coffee etc
available.
Hotels: Dunranen Arms; Woodlands.

V4 Ardee
☎(041) 53227, Sec 26616, Public:
56283, Fax 56137
Town Parks, Ardee, Co Louth
0.25 mile N of town on Mullinstown
Road.
Parkland course.
18 holes, 5500 metres, S.S.S.69
Designed by Eddie Hackett.
Founded 1911
Visitors: welcome at all times, Mon-
Fri.
Green Fee: any day: £15 (£7 with
member).
Societies: Mon-Sat.
Catering: available at all times.
Hotels: Gables B&B; Nuremore.

V5 Arklow
☎(0402) 32492
Abbeylands, Arklow, Co Wicklow
0.5 mile from Arklow town centre.
Seaside course.
18 holes, 5404 metres, S.S.S.67
Designed by Hawtree & Taylor.
Founded 1927
Visitors: welcome except Sun.
Green Fee: apply for details.
Societies: welcome except Sun.
Catering: by arrangement.
Hotels: Arklow Bay; Royal; Hoynes.

V6 Ashbourne
☎(01) 8352005, Sec 8350604
Archerstown, Ashbourne, Co Meath
18 holes, 5778 metres, S.S.S.70
Founded 1991
Green Fee: WD £15 (£8 with
member); WE & BH N/A

V7 Ashford Castle
☎(092) 46003
Cong, Co Mayo, EIRE
27 miles N of Galway on shores of
Lough Corrib.
Parkland course.
9 holes, 4506 yards, Par 70
Designed by Eddie Hackett.
Founded 1972
Visitors: welcome, phone for tee
times.
Green Fee: any day: £15;
(complimentary for residents at
Ashford Castle
Societies: welcome by prior
arrangement.
Catering: bar and snacks.
Hotels: Ashford Castle

V8 Athenry
☎(091) 94466, Sec 751405
Palmerstown, Oranmore, Co Galway
5 miles from Athenry on Galway-
Dublin route N6 at junction with
Athenry road.
Parkland course.
18 holes, 5552 metres, S.S.S.69
Designed by Eddie Hackett.
Founded 1902
Visitors: welcome Mon-Sat.
Green Fee: any day: £12 (£7 with
member).
Societies: welcome if booked in
advance.
Catering: full bar and catering
facilities.

V9 Athlone
☎(0902) 92073, Sec 94429, Pro:
94285, Fax 94080
Hodson Bay, Athlone, Co
Roscommon
3 miles from Athlone on Roscommon
road on shores of Lough Ree.
Undulating parkland course.
18 holes, 5922 metres, S.S.S.71
Designed by Fred Hawtree.
Founded 1892
Visitors: welcome every day except
Sun; booking advisable.
Green Fee: WD £12 (£6 with
member); WE & BH £15 (£6 with
member).
Societies: welcome except Sun.
Catering: bar and restaurant.
Snooker; driving range 2 miles from
course.
Hotels: Hodson Bay; Prince of
Wales; Royal Hoey; Shamrock
Lodge.

V10 Athy
☎(0507) 31729, Caterer: 31464
Geraldine, Athy, Co Kildare
On T6, 2 miles N of Athy.
Undulating parkland course.
18 holes, 5500 metres, S.S.S.69
Founded 1906
Visitors: welcome weekdays.
Green Fee: apply for details.
Societies: catered for Sat am.
Catering: by arrangement with Club
Steward; ring after 7.30pm.
Hotels: Leinster Arms; Kilkea Castle.

V11 Balbriggan
☎(01) 8412229, Sec 8491822,
Public: 8412173
Blackhall, Balbriggan, Co Dublin
0.5 mile S of town on main Belfast-
Dublin road, 17 miles from Dublin.
Parkland course.
18 holes, 5881 metres, S.S.S.71
Designed by R. Stilwell, J. Paramour.
Founded 1945
Visitors: welcome weekdays.
Green Fee: WD £14 (£6 with
member); WE & BH £18 (£6 with
member).
Societies: weekdays.
Catering: full restaurant facilities.
Hotels: Holmpatrick House; Skerries;
Old Well; Julianstown.

V12 Balcarrick
☎(01) 8436957, Sec 8408260,
Public: 8436228
Corballis, Donabate, Co Dublin
9 holes, 6362 metres, S.S.S. 73
Founded 1972
Green Fee: WD £10 (£5 for 1st guest
with member, £6 2nd & 3rd); WE &
BH £15 (£8 & £10).

V13 Ballaghaderreen
☎(0907) 60295, Sec 60717
Aughalista, Ballaghaderreen, Co
Roscommon
3 miles from Ballaghaderreen.
Parkland course.
9 holes, 5363 metres, S.S.S.66
Founded 1937
Visitors: welcome.
Green Fee: any day: £6.
Societies: welcome, phone in
advance.
Catering: snacks, meals by
arrangement.

V14 Ballina
☎(096) 21050, Sec 21795
Mossgrove, Shanaghy, Ballina, Co
Mayo
On outskirts of town on road to
Bonniconlon.
Inland, undulating course.
9 holes, 5212 metres, S.S.S.67
Designed by Eddie Hackett.
Founded 1910
Visitors: welcome.
Green Fee: any day: £10 (£6 with
member).
Societies: by arrangement with Sec
or Steward.
Catering: bar meals served by
arrangement.
Hotels: Downhill; American; Bartra
House.

V15 Ballinamore
☎(078) 44346, Sec 44163
Creevy, Ballinamore, Co Leitrim
1 mile from town centre, sign at
bridge.
Moorland/parkland course.
9 holes, 5204 metres, S.S.S.66
Founded 1939

Visitors: welcome at all times except some Sun.
Green Fee: any day; £5.
Societies: welcome by prior arrangement.
Catering: bar, coffee, soup and sandwiches available.
Hotels: Slieve-an-Iaraim; Commercial; McAllisters.

V16 **Ballinascorney**
☎(01) 4512082, Public: 4512516
Bohernabreena, Tallaght, Dublin 24
10 miles SW of Dublin.
18 holes, 5464 yards, S.S.S.67
Founded 1971
Visitors: welcome weekdays.
Green Fee: apply for details.
Catering: bar.

V17 **Ballinasloe**
☎(0905) 42126, Sec 43293, Fax 42538
Rossgloss, Ballinasloe, Co Galway
Turn left opposite Garbally College gates on Ballinasloe-Portumna road, 1 mile from there.
Parkland/meadowland course.
18 holes, 5868 metres, S.S.S.70
Designed by Eddie Hackett.
Founded 1894

Visitors: welcome 7 days except major competitions on Sun.
Green Fee: any day: £12 (£6 with member).
Societies: welcome 7 days by prior arrangement.
Catering: bar and full catering facilities available.
Hotels: Haydens; Lerridges Country.

V18 **Ballinrobe**
☎(092) 41448
Castlebar Road, Ballinrobe, Co Mayo
30 miles from Galway, 30 miles from Knock Airport.
Public parkland course set amid beautiful scenery.
9 holes, 5540 metres, S.S.S.68
Founded 1895
Visitors: welcome all week except Tues after 5.00pm and Sun during competitions.
Green Fee: apply for details.
Societies: welcome weekdays by arrangement.
Catering: bar and restaurant facilities; good food also at Red Door restaurant and several pubs in the vicinity.
Fishing in some of best lakes in Ireland.
Hotels: Lakeland; Valkenberg.

V19 **Ballybofey & Stranorlar**
☎(074) 31093
Stranorlar, Ballybofey, Co Donegal
14 miles from Strabane, club signposted on Strabane-Ballybofey main road; course 500 yards off main road on outskirts of Stranorlar village.
Parkland course.
18 holes, 5437 metres, S.S.S.69
Designed by P.C. Carr.
Founded 1957
Visitors: welcome all times except major competitions; check with B. Duffy, Steward.
Green Fee: apply for details.
Societies: welcome by prior arrangement.
Catering: bar facilities; snacks and meals by arrangement.
Hotels: Kee's; Jackson's.

V20 **Ballybunion**
☎(068) 27146, Fax 27387
Sandhill Rd, Ballybunion, Co Kerry
In Ballybunion, 20 miles from Tralee, 40 miles from Killaney.
Links course.
36 holes, 6241 metres, S.S.S.72
Designed by Simpson McKenna (Old), R. Trent Jones Snr (Cashen).
Founded 1893

Visitors: welcome, book in advance; min h/cap 24 (men), 36 (ladies).
Green Fee: any day: Old, £35; Cashen, £25; (Both £50).
Societies: welcome Mon-Fri.
Catering: snacks, meals, dining room, restaurant.
Practice green, steam room etc.
Hotels: Golf; Marine; Cliff House.

V21 **Ballyhaunis**
☎(0907) 30014, Sec 30013, Caterer: 30044
Coolnaha, Ballyhaunis, Co Mayo
2 miles N of Ballyhaunis on Sligo road, 6 miles from Horan International Airport; on main rail line from Dublin; main bus routes Galway/Derry, Dublin/Westport.
Undulating course.
9 holes, 5393 metres, S.S.S.68
Founded 1929
Visitors: welcome; Ladies Day Thurs, Club competitions on Sun.
Green Fee: WD £8. No visitors Sunday.
Societies: catered for; contact Hon Sec 1 week in advance.
Catering: on notification.
Fishing, shooting, clay pigeon shoot, snooker, bridge etc.
Hotels: Central; Manor House; Westway; Orina; International; also local B&B.

V22 **Ballykisteen G & CC**
☎(062) 51439, Sec 52877
Ballykisteen, Co Tipperary, EIRE
On Limerick road, 3 miles from Tipperary town.
Parkland course.
18 holes, 6765 yards, S.S.S.73
Designed by Des Smyth.
Founded April 1994
Visitors: welcome all week.
Green Fee: WD £15 (£10 with member); WE & BH £20 (£15 with member).
Societies: welcome.
Catering: full bar and restaurant facilities.
Hotels: Ballykisteen (on site).

V23 **Ballyliffin**
☎(077) 76119, Sec 74417, Fax 76672
Ballyliffin, Carndonagh P.O., Co Donegal
8 miles from Buncrana, 6 miles from Carndonagh.
Seaside links course.
21 holes, 6384 yards, S.S.S.72
Founded 1947

Visitors: welcome.
Green Fee: WD £10; WE & BH £15.
Societies: welcome by booking in advance.
Catering: bar, snacks and meals during summer (or by arrangement).
Hotels: Strand; Ballyliffin; (free golf for residents).

V24 **Ballymote**
☎(071) 83158
Carrigans, Ballymote, Co Sligo
1 mile N of Ballymote.
Parkland course.
9 holes, 5200 metres, S.S.S.65
Founded 1966
Visitors: welcome at any time.
Green Fee: any day £5.
Catering: at Corrann Restaurant.
Hotels: Castle.

V25 **Baltinglass**
☎(0508) 81350, Sec 81514
Baltinglass, Co Wicklow
40 miles S of Dublin.
Parkland course.
9 holes, 5554 yards, S.S.S.69
Designed by Dr. W.G. Lyons, Hugh Dark and Col. Mitchell.
Founded 1928
Visitors: welcome.
Green Fee: WD £10 (£6 with member); WE & BH £12 (£8 with member).
Societies: 3 outings allowed per month.
Catering: meals can be provided by arrangement.

V26 **Bandon**
☎(023) 41111, Pro: 42224, Fax 44690
Castlebernard, Bandon, Co Cork
1.5 miles W of Bandon town, 15 miles from Cork Airport.
Parkland course.
18 holes, 5663 metres, S.S.S.69
Founded 1909
Visitors: welcome every day.
Green Fee: apply for details.
Societies: welcome weekdays by prior arrangement.
Catering: full facilities.
Tennis.
Hotels: Munster Arms.

V27 **Bantry Park**
☎(027) 50579, Sec 50372
Donemark, Bantry, Co Cork
1 mile from Bantry on Glengariff road.
9 holes, 5946 metres, S.S.S.70
Founded 1975

Visitors: welcome; club h/cap required.
Green Fee: any day: £10 (£8 with member).
Societies: apply in writing.
Catering: bar, snacks, lunches available.
Hotels: West Lodge, Bantry Bay, Sea View, Reendesert, Dromkeal.

V28 **Beaufort**
☎(064) 44440, Sec 44404, Fax 44752
Churchtown, Beaufort, Killarney, Co Kerry, EIRE
7 miles W of Killarney.
Parkland course.
18 holes, 6038 metres, S.S.S.72
Designed by Arthur Spring.
Founded 1994
Visitors: welcome, phone in advance.
Green Fee: WD £25 (£15 with member); WE & BH £28 (£18 with member).
Societies: welcome, phone in advance.
Catering: tea, coffee, soup and sandwiches.

V29 **Beaverstown**
☎(01) 8436439, Sec 8475706, Fax 8436721
Beaverstown, Donabate, Co Dublin
24km (15 miles) N of Dublin, 5km N of Dublin Airport.
Parkland course.
18 holes, 5874 metres, S.S.S.71
Designed by Eddie Hackett.
Founded 1984
Visitors: welcome weekdays, with member at weekends.
Green Fee: WD £12 (£6 with member); WE & BH £20 (£10 with member).
Societies: by prior arrangement.
Catering: bar, restaurant, (snacks, lunches, evening meals).
Snooker.

V30 **Beech Park**
☎(01) 4580522, Public: 4580100, Fax 4588365
Johnstown, Rathcoole, Co Dublin
2 miles from Rathcoole village on Kilteel road.
Parkland course.
18 holes, 5738 metres, S.S.S.70
Designed by Eddie Hackett.
Founded 1973
Visitors: welcome on Mon, Thurs, Fri, subject to course availability.
Green Fee: apply for details.

Societies: by arrangement with Sec/Manager.
Catering: full bar and catering facilities (4588178).
Snooker.
Hotels: Greenisle; Ambassador.

V31 Belmullet
☎(097) 82292, Sec 81136
Carne, Belmullet, Co Mayo
1.5 miles W of Belmullet.
Seaside links course.
18 holes, 6058 metres, S.S.S.72
Designed by Eddie Hackett.
Founded 1925
Visitors: welcome
Green Fee: any day £15 (£12 with member).
Hotels: Western Strands.

V32 Belturbet
☎(049) 22287, Sec 22498
Erne Hill, Belturbet, Co Cavan
0.5 mile on Cavan road from Belturbet, on left.
Parkland course.
9 holes, 5347 metres, S.S.S.65
Founded 1950
Visitors: welcome weekdays and weekends.
Green Fee: apply for details.
Societies: welcome at all times by appointment with Sec.
Catering: full catering on request.
snooker.
Hotels: Seven Horseshoes; Slieve Russell.

V33 Berehaven
☎(027) 70700
Millcove, Castletownbere, Co Cork
On main Glengariff-Castletownbere road, 3 miles before Castletownbere.
Public seaside course.
9 holes, 4748 metres, S.S.S.64
Founded 1903
Visitors: welcome at all times with valid h/cap.
Green Fee: apply for details.
Societies: welcome at all times.
Catering: available.
Tennis, swimming, fishing, sailing.

V34 Birr
☎(0509) 20082
Glenns, Birr, Co Offaly
2 miles from Birr on road to Banager.
Undulating parkland course.
18 holes, 5727 metres, S.S.S.70
Founded 1893
Visitors: welcome, check on Sun.
Green Fee: apply for details.

Societies: every day except Sun.
Catering: by arrangement except Tues.
Hotels: County Arms, Doolys (Birr); Shannon (Banager).

V35 The Black Bush
☎(01) 8250021, Public:8250144, Fax 8250400
Thomastown, Dunshaughlin, Co Meath
0.5 mile E of Dunshaughlin on Ratoath road.
Parkland course with panoramic views.
27 holes, 6360 metres, S.S.S.73
Designed by Robert Brown.
Founded 1987
Visitors: welcome, 9 hole course any time; 18 hole course any weekday, telephone to check for availability weekends.
Green Fee: apply for details.
Societies: welcome weekdays.
Catering: bar and restaurant 11.00am-11.00pm daily.
Driving range.
Hotels: Gaulstown House.

V36 Blacklion
☎(072) 53024
Toam, Blacklion, Co Cavan, via Sligo
W on A4 from Enniskillen to Sligo; E on N16 from Sligo to Enniskillen; located beside Blacklion village.
Parkland course.
9 holes, 5605 metres, S.S.S.69
Designed by Eddie Hackett.
Founded 1962
Visitors: welcome except on President's/Captain's days etc.
Green Fee: WD £8 (£6 with member); WE & BH £10 (£8 with member).
Societies: welcome by prior arrangement.
Catering: bar, bar snacks, meals by arrangement; clubhouse open from 1.30pm daily.
Fishing.
Hotels: guest houses in Blacklion, Belcoo and Florencecourt.

V37 Blainroe
☎(0404) 68168, Sec 67022, Fax 69369
Blainroe, Co Wicklow
3 miles S of Wicklow town on coast road.
Seaside course.
18 holes, 6171 metres, S.S.S.72
Designed by Hawtree & Sons.
Founded 1978

Visitors: ring for times.
Green Fee: WD £18 (£8 with member); WE & BH £25 (£10 with member).
Societies: catered for 6 days.
Catering: lunch, dinner and bar food.
Hotels: Arklow Bay; Grand; Hunter's; Tinakilly House.

V38 Bodenstown
☎(045) 97096, Sec 76588
Bodenstown, Sallins, Co Kildare
5 miles N of Naas via N7 and R407.
Parkland course.
36 holes, 6321 metres, S.S.S.73
Founded 1973
Visitors: welcome; members only on Old Course weekends.
Green Fee: any day: £10 (£9 with member).
Societies: by arrangement.
Catering: full facilities.
Snooker.
Hotels: Ambassador (Kill).

V39 Borris
☎(0503) 73310, Sec 24213, Public: 73143
Deer Park, Borris, Co Carlow
Drive S from Carlow via Begenalstown; drive E from Kilkenny via Gowran and Goresbridge.
Parkland course.
9 holes, 5572 metres, S.S.S.69
Founded 1907
Visitors: welcome weekdays and with member on Sun.
Green Fee: any day: £10; Sun: with member only.
Societies: catered for on weekdays and Sat am between 10.00am and 12.00am.
Catering: catering available for societies by arrangement.
Hotels: New Park, Springhill, Clubhouse, Hotel Kilkenny (all Kilkenny); Royal, Seven Oaks, Lane Court (all Carlow).

V40 Boyle
☎(079) 62594, Sec 63288
Boyle, Co Roscommon
1.5 miles from Boyle on Roscommon road.
Undulating parkland course.
9 holes, 4899 metres, S.S.S.66
Designed by Eddie Hackett.
Founded 1911
Visitors: welcome.
Green Fee: any day: £5.
Societies: welcome.
Catering: bar facilities and snacks.
Hotels: Royal; Forest Park.

V41 **Bray**

☎(01) 2862484, Sec 2888435,
Public: 2862092
Ravenswell Rd, Bray, Co Wicklow
L29 from Dublin, turn left at bridge
entering town.
Parkland course.
9 holes, 5782 metres, S.S.S.70
Founded 1897
Visitors: welcome weekdays except
Mon.
Green Fee: any day: £17 (£6 with
member).
Societies: societies affiliated to
Golfing Union catered for with prior
arrangement.
Catering: only limited catering
available.
Snooker.
Hotels: Royal; Westbourne.

V42 **Buncrana**

☎(077) 62279
Buncrana, Co Donegal
9 holes, 4250 metres, S.S.S.62
Founded: 1951
Green Fee: any day: £6

V43 **Bundoran**

☎(072) 41302
Bundoran, Co Donegal
32 miles W of Enniskillen, 25 miles N
of Sligo.
Links/parkland course.
championship 18 holes, 5785 mtrs,
S.S.S.71
Designed by Harry Vardon.
Founded 1894
Visitors: welcome at all times, book
in advance.
Green Fee: apply for details.
Societies: welcome but advance
booking required.
Catering: snacks only, meals in
hotel.
Hotels: Great Northern on course;
Holyrood; Imperial; Maghery;
Atlantic.

V44 **Cabra Castle**

☎(042) 67030
Kingscourt, Co Cavan, Eire
6 miles S of Carrickmacross.
Parkland course.
9 holes, 5308 metres, S.S.S.68
Founded 1977
Visitors: welcome, only with member
Sun.
Green Fee: apply for details.
Societies: welcome except Sun,
phone in advance.
Catering: full facilities.
Snooker, horse riding.

V45 **Cahir Park**

☎(052) 41474, Sec 41601, Pro:
(062) 62111
Kilcommon, Cahir, Co Tipperary.
1 mile S of Cahir on Clogheen road.
Parkland course.
9 holes, 5446 metres, S.S.S.69
Designed by Eddie Hackett.
Founded 1965
Visitors: welcome; advisable to
check at weekends.
Green Fee: any day: £10.
Societies: catered for on Sat.
Catering: bar; group meals at 3 days
notice.
Hotels: Cahir House; Castle Court;
Kilcoran Lodge.

V46 **Callan**

☎(056) 25136, Caterer: 54362
Geraldine, Callan, Co Kilkenny
10 miles S of Kilkenny, 0.5 mile from
Callan.
Parkland course.
9 holes, 5722 metres, S.S.S.68
Designed by Des Smyth.
Founded 1929
Visitors: welcome.
Green Fee: apply for details.
Societies: welcome weekdays and
Sat am.
Catering: bar daily, food by
arrangement.
Hotels: Somers; Newpark; Hotel
Kilkenny; Club House.

V47 **Carlow**

☎(0503) 31695, Sec 31353, Pro:
41745, Fax 40065
Deerpark, Dublin Rd, Carlow, Co
Carlow
1 mile from Carlow station, take Naas
road from Dublin (52 miles).
Undulating parkland course.
18 holes, 5844 metres, S.S.S.71
Designed by Tom Simpson.
Founded 1899
Visitors: welcome.
Green Fee: WD £20 (£10 with
member); WE & BH £25 (£12.50 with
member).
Societies: weekdays only, advance
booking required.
Catering: full catering available.
Hotels: Seven Oaks; Royal; Lane
Court.

V48 **Carrick-on-Shannon**

☎(079) 67015, Sec (091) 61701,
Woodbrook, Carrick-on-Shannon, Co
Roscommon.
3 miles W of Carrick on N4 route.
Parkland course.

9 holes, 5545 metres, S.S.S.68
Designed by Eddie Hackett.
Founded 1910
Visitors: welcome at all times.
Green Fee: any day: £10 (£7 with
member).
Societies: on request to Sec.
Catering: bar facilities and snacks,
catering on request.
Hotels: County; Bush.

V49 **Carrick-on-Suir**

☎(051) 640047
Garravoone, Co Tipperary
approx 2 miles from Carrick-on-Suir
on main road to Dungarvan;
signposted on right side of road.
Undulating parkland course.
9 holes, 5948 yards, S.S.S.68
Designed by Edward Hackett.
Founded 1939
Visitors: welcome except Sun.
Green Fee: apply for details.
Societies: welcome except Sun.
Catering: by advance booking.
Hotels: Carraig; Cedarfield House.

V50 **Carrickmines**

☎(01) 2955972, Sec 4922960
off Glenamuck Rd, Carrickmines,
Dublin 18
T43, 7 miles S of Dublin, left at
Sandyford.
Heathland course.
9 holes, 6103 metres, S.S.S.69
Founded 1900
Visitors: welcome weekdays and
Sun; Sat and Bank Holidays only with
member.
Green Fee: WD £17 (£7 with
member); WE & BH £20 (£7 with
member).
Catering: very limited.

V51 **Castle**

☎(01) 4904207, Sec 2803832, Pro:
4920272,
Public: 4933444, Fax 4920264
Woodside Drive, Rathfarnham, Dublin
14
from city turn left after Terenure and
2nd right.
Parkland course.
18 holes, 5653 metres, S.S.S.69
Designed by H.S. Colt,
Founded 1913
Visitors: welcome weekdays.
Green Fee: WD £25 (£10 with
member); WE & BH N.A. (£10 with
member).
Societies: applications considered.
Catering: full lunch and dinner.
Hotels: Orwell Lodge.

V52 Castlebar

☎(094) 21649, Sec 32232
Rocklands, Castlebar, Co Mayo
1.25 miles from town centre.
Parkland course.
18 holes, 5698 metres, S.S.S.70
Founded 1910
Visitors: welcome weekdays.
Green Fee: WD £12; WE & BH £15.
Societies: welcome by arrangement
except Sun.
Catering: catering available with 3
hours notice.
Hotels: Welcome Inn; Breaffy House;
Travellers Friend; Imperial.

V53 Castlecomer

☎(056) 41139, Sec 33276
Drumgoole, Castlecomer, Co
Kilkenny
On N7 10 miles N of Kilkenny.
Parkland course.
9 holes, 5923 metres, S.S.S.71
Designed by Pat Ruddy.
Founded 1935
Visitors: welcome Mon to Sat, book
in advance.
Green Fee: WD £8 (£5 with
member); WE & BH £10 (£5 with
member).
Societies: Mon-Sat.
Catering: snacks available and
lunches to order.
Hotels: Newpark (Kilkenny).

V54 Castlerea

☎(0907) 20068
Clonalis, Castlerea, Co Roscommon
On main Dublin-Castlebar road,
course just outside town on Castlebar
side.
Parkland course.
9 holes, 4974 metres, S.S.S.66
Founded 1905
Visitors: welcome.
Green Fee: apply for details.
Societies: welcome by prior
arrangement.
Catering: available by arrangement
for societies.

V55 Castletroy

☎(061) 335753, Sec 330262, Pro:
338283, Fax 335373
Castletroy, Limerick
3 miles from Limerick city on Dublin
road, turn right at signpost in
Castletroy, course 300 yards on left.
Parkland course.
18 holes, 5793 metres, S.S.S.71
Founded 1937
Visitors: weekdays unlimited,
weekends with member only.

Green Fee: any day: £20 (£12 with
member).
Societies: Mon, Wed, Fri by
arrangement.
Catering: full catering service.
Hotels: Two Mile Inn; Castletroy
Park; Royal George.

V56 Castlewarden Golf & Country Club

☎(01) 4589254 (Office/Fax), Sec
4903015, Pro: 4588219
Castlewarden, Straffan, Co Kildare,
EIRE
Between Rathcoole and Kill; 2nd turn
after Blackchurch Inn.
Moorland course.
18 holes, 6008 metres, S.S.S.71
Designed by Tommy Halpin; re-
designed by R.J. Browne (1992)
Founded 1989
Visitors: welcome Mon. Thurs, Fri;
weekends with member only.
Green Fee: WD £10/£12 (£6 with
member); WE & BH £14 (£8 with
member).
Societies: welcome Mon, Thurs, Fri;
some Sats if no Medals or Majors.
Catering: bar, snacks, lunches,
dinners.
Practice area.
Hotels: Ambassador (Kill).

V57 Ceann Sibeal (Dingle)

☎(066) 56225, Sec 59079, Fax
56409
Ballyougheragh, Ballyferriter, Co
Kerry
Follow Ballyferriter signs from Dingle,
turn right 0.5 mile after Ballyferriter.
Seaside links course; most westerly
golf course in Europe..
18 holes, 6124 metres, S.S.S.71
Designed by Eddie Hackett.
Founded 1924
Visitors: welcome at all times.
Green Fee: WD £18 (£12 with
member); WE & BH £20 (£12 with
member).
Societies: welcome with advance
booking.
Catering: full bar and restaurant.
Sea fishing, practice ground.
Hotels: Granville, Ostan Golf Dun an
Oir (Ballyferriter); Benners, Skellig
(Dingle)

V58 Charlesland

☎(01)2876764, Sec 2875637, Fax
2873882
Charlesland, Greystones, Co Wicklow
18 holes, 6159 metres, S.S.S.72
Founded: 1991

Green Fee: WD £23 (£11 with
member); WE & BH £28 (£14 with
member).

V59 Charleville

☎(063) 81257, Public: 81274
Smiths Rd, Ardmore, Charleville, Co
Cork
On main road from Cork to Limerick,
about 35 miles from Cork, 25 miles
from Limerick.
Parkland course.
18 holes, 6430 yards, S.S.S.70
Founded 1909
Visitors: welcome weekdays; contact
office in advance.
Green Fee: apply for details.
Societies: any day except Sun,
contact office.
Catering: full bar and restaurant
facilities.
Hotels: Deer Park.

V60 Cill Dara

☎(045) 21433, Public: 21295
Kildare, Co Kildare
1 mile E of Kildare.
Moorland course.
9 holes, 5738 metres, S.S.S.70
Founded 1920
Visitors: welcome.
Green Fee: apply for details.
Societies: meals served by
arrangement.

V61 Clane

(Sec (01) 6286608
Clane, Co Kildare
Playing facilities at Clongowes Golf
Club, Naas, Co Kildare (045) 68202.
9 holes, 5400 metres, S.S.S.65
Founded 1976
Green Fee: apply for details

V62 Claremorris

☎(094) 71527, Sec 71868
Rushbrook, Castlemagarett,
Claremorris, Co Mayo
1.5 miles from Claremorris town on
Galway road.
Parkland course.
9 holes, 5600 metres, S.S.S.69
Founded 1917
Visitors: welcome any day except
Sun.
Green Fee: any day: £8 (£6 with
member).
Societies: catered for on weekdays.
Catering: by arrangement.
Swimming, squash, snooker in
Claremorris town.
Hotels: Dalton Inn; Western.

V63 Clones
☎(047) 56017
Hilton Park, Clones, Co Monaghan
3 miles S of Clones towards
Scotshouse.
Parkland course.
9 holes, 5798 metres, S.S.S.68
Founded 1913
Visitors: welcome, restricted on Sun.
Green Fee: apply for details.
Societies: welcome, except Sun.
Catering: available at all times.
Hotels: Creighton; Hibernian;
Lennard Arms; White Horse,
Cootehill.

V64 Clongowes
Naas, Co Kildare
☎(045) 68202, Sec:76690
9 holes, 5400 metres, S.S.S.65
Founded 1966
Green Fee: apply for details

V65 Clonlara
☎(061) 354141, Public: 354191, Fax
354143
Clonlara Golf and Leisure, Clonlara,
Co Clare, EIRE
7 miles W of Limerick.
Parkland course.
9 holes, 5289 metres, S.S.S.69
Founded 1993
Visitors: welcome.
Green Fee: WD Summer £7; Winter
£5 (£5 with member); WE & BH £10
(Sat £5 with member, Sun £7 with
member).
Societies: welcome weekdays,
phone in advance.
Catering: bar and bar meals.
Tennis, sauna.
Hotels: Cottages & apartments to let.

V66 Clonmel
☎(052) 24050, Sec 22201, Public:
21138
Lyreanearla, Mountain Rd, Clonmel,
Co Tipperary
On road to Comeragh Mountains, 2
miles SE of Clonmel.
Parkland course.
18 holes, 5768 metres, S.S.S.70
Designed by Eddie Hackett.
Founded 1911
Visitors: phone Sec for details.
Green Fee: WD £13 (£10 with
member); WE & BH £15 (£10 with
member).
Societies: welcome by arrangement.
Catering: full facilities.
Snooker, pool, table tennis.
Hotels: Hotel Minella; Clonmel Arms;
Hearns.

V67 Clontarf
☎(01) 8331892, Pro: 8331877,
Public: 8331520, Fax 8331933
Donnycarney House, Malahide Rd,
Dublin 3
NE of city centre, 2.5 miles from city
centre via North Strand and Fairview
to Lower Malahide Road.
Parkland course.
18 holes, 5459 metres, S.S.S.68
Founded 1912
Visitors: welcome weekdays, check
with Sec for times.
Green Fee: apply for details.
Societies: Tues and Fri.
Catering: full facilities.
Bowling green; snooker.
Hotels: Skylon; Hollybrook; Marine.

V68 Cobh
☎(021) 812399
Ballywilliam, Cobh, Co Cork
1 mile E of Cobh.
Public parkland course.
9 holes, 4366 metres, S.S.S.63
Designed by Eddie Hackett.
Founded 1987
Visitors: welcome weekdays,
booking at weekends.
Green Fee: apply for details.
Societies: welcome Mon-Sat.
Catering: bar, snacks.
Putting and pitching green.
Hotels: Commodore, Rinn Ronain
(free golf).

V69 Coldwinters
☎(01) 8640324, Fax 8341400
Newtown House, St Margaret's, Co
Dublin
18 holes, 5973 metres, S.S.S.71
Founded: 1994
Green Fee: WD £7.60; WE & BH
£11.50

V70 Connemara
☎(095) 23602, Sec 21784, Public:
23621, Fax 23662
Ballyconneely, Clifden, Co Galway
9 miles SW of Clifden.
Links course on edge of Atlantic set
amidst mountain scenery.
18 holes, 6611 metres, S.S.S.75.
Designed by Eddie Hackett.
Founded 1973
Visitors: welcome all year; must
have h/cap cert.
Green Fee: apply for details.
Societies: welcome except July/Aug.
Catering: full bar and à la carte
restaurant.
Hotels: Allbey Glen; Rock Glen;
Clifden Bay; Ballynahynch Castle.

V71 Coollattin
☎(055) 26302, Bar: 29125
Coollattin, Shillelheh, Co Wicklow,
EIRE
12 miles SW of Aughrim.
Parkland course.
9 holes, 5688 metres, S.S.S.70
Founded 1922
Visitors: welcome Mon-Fri.
Green Fee: any day £10.
Societies: welcome weekdays by
prior arrangement.
Catering: bar and snacks; full meals
by arrangement, phone (055) 29207.
Pool table.

V72 Coosheen
☎(028) 28182, Sec (021) 870823
Schull, Co Cork
18 holes, 3662 metres, S.S.S.61
Founded 1989
Green Fee: WD £6; WE & BH £8

V73 Corballis
☎(01) 8436583
Dunabate, Co Dublin
off main Dublin-Belfast road.
Public seaside links course.
18 holes, 4543 metres (4971 yards),
S.S.S.64
Founded 1971
Visitors: welcome, golf clubs for
each player, no other restrictions.
Green Fee: WD £8 (£4 for Students,
Jnrs, UE & OAP's before 2.30 pm);
WE & BH £10.
Societies: welcome by arrangement
except Sun & BH.
Catering: no bar; lunch & light
refreshments.
Pool.
Hotels: Dunes; Swords.

V74 Cork
☎(021) 353451, Pro: 353421, Fax
353410
Little Island, Cork, Co Cork
5 miles E of Cork on N25.
Championship parkland course.
18 holes, 6115 metres, S.S.S.72
Designed by Alister Mackenzie.
Founded 1888
Visitors: welcome Mon, Tues, Wed,
Fri except 12.30-2pm or after 4pm;
weekends after 2.30pm.
Green Fee: WD £23 (£10 with
member); WE & BH £26 (£10 with
member).
Societies: as for visitors.
Catering: full catering facilities.
Hotels: Silver Springs; Ashbourne
House; John Barleycorn;
Commodore; Metropole.

County Louth

There are certain courses throughout Britain and Ireland where a sense of expectancy reaches a peak at a specific point near journey's end; when turning off the main road at Wadebridge for St Enodoc, for instance, or when a long drive nears its end along the only road to Southerness, a superb links on the Solway Firth, which in 1985 hosted the Scottish Amateur for the first time.

A similar sense of anticipation accompanies the last lap to Brancaster which takes you past the church and down through the marsh lined by tall rushes; and there is a less glamorous approach beyond the level crossing to the Royal Cinque Ports Golf Club at Deal. The twisty conclusion to the journey to Rye is another example. But there are few sights as thrilling as the links of County Louth at Baltray at last coming into view.

It is a fine, challenging course in the traditional mould of dunes, undoubtedly one of my favourites and one whose rating within Ireland is not as high as it should be. It is worthy of the best, full of variety and contrast with always the magnificence of its distant views.

Although there have been modifications, one or two made necessary by moving the clubhouse some years ago, there is still an authentic touch of Tom Simpson about it that bears the unmistakable mark of quality. If I had to exemplify it, I would point to the long 3rd which, after a reasonably straightforward drive, reveals hidden talents once the brow of dunes has been scaled. Beautifully natural humps and hollows make careful placing of the second shot essential and, for those attempting to get home in two, there is only a narrow path between salvation and ruin. An attractive small green is not easy to hit.

The curving 1st and testing 2nd make a nice introduction but the 4th, a short par 4, offers some relief before the first of four first class short holes. The 5th and 7th, sandwiched around another fine par 5, demand well-controlled, truly hit iron shots while the 8th and 9th are no easy par 4s.

A sense of space becomes more apparent on the second half which, having begun with a hole alongside the clubhouse, works its way towards the sea by means of the dogleg par 5 11th. It is then that a special character is lent by the 12th, 13th and 14th which, from a combination of factors, comprise a notable trio. They emphasise the merit of great par 4s, not perhaps daunting in terms of yardage but rewarding in the satisfaction they give by being played properly, as they must be if they are to yield a par or a birdie.

Changes to the course have resulted in two short holes in the last four but the 16th is appealing and the 18th the last of five par 5s. Baltray, as the course is more conveniently called after the local fishing village, has a championship cloak without a doubt and it also has its less forbidding side which makes it so popular for a day out.

Harry Bradshaw's winning aggregate of 291 in the 1947 Irish Professional championship tells a tale or two about its full blown potential. It is also rare among Irish clubs in having two legendary Irish women golfers as members. Val Reddan, as Clarrie Tiernan, won the Irish title twice and was also the first Irish woman to play in the Curtis Cup. After the war, she was confronted by her new local rival Philomena Garvey in the final of the Irish, not, as would have been most appropriate, at Baltray, but at Lahinch. After the longest final, Garvey won at the 39th, the first of her 15 victories.

Continuing the feminine influence, Mrs Josephine Connolly founded the East of Ireland Men's championship played annually at Baltray, an event by which Irish golfers set great store. It can claim father and son winners in Joe and Roddy Carr, but when you speak of the course you speak of distinction. Its list of champions is no more than it deserves.

Courtown Golf Club
Kiltennel, Gorey, Co Wexford, Tel: 055-25166 Fax: 055-25553

Parkland course with some spectacular views of the nearby
sea through tree lined fairways.

Green Fees
High Season (June, July, August) £15 mid week £20 weekend
Remaining 9 months £13 midweek £17 weekend

Full catering facilities available. Sets of golf clubs can be hired.

V75 Corrstown
☎(01) 8640533/4, Sec 8318981,
Public: 8362836,
Fax 8640537
Corrstown, Kilsallaghan, Co Dublin
27 holes, 5584 yards, S.S.S.69
Founded 1993
Green Fee: None (£8 with member

V76 County Cavan
☎(049) 31541, Sec 32045, Public:
31283
Arnmore House, Drumelis, Cavan, Co
Cavan
1 mile from Cavan town on
Killeshandra road.
Parkland course.
18 holes, 5519 metres, S.S.S.69
Founded 1894
Visitors: welcome 7 days per week,
restricted days Wed and Sun.
Green Fee: WD £10 (£5 with
member); WE & BH £12 (£6 with
member).
Societies: Mon-Fri preferred.
Catering: full catering.
Snooker.
Hotels: Kilmore; Farnham Arms.

V77 County Longford
☎(043) 46310, Sec 45556
Glack, Longford
off Dublin to Sligo road (N4) E of
town, signposted.
Undulating course.
18 holes, 5494 metres, S.S.S.69
Designed by E. Hackett.
Founded 1894
Visitors: welcome.
Green Fee: apply for details.
Societies: welcome by arrangement.
Catering: meals served.

V78 County Louth
☎(041) 22329, Pro: 22444, Fax
22969
Baltray, Drogheda, Co Louth

4 miles NE of Drogheda, take road
along N bank of River Boyne to
Baltray village.
Seaside links course.
18 holes, 6783 yards, S.S.S.72
Designed by Tom Simpson.
Founded 1892
Visitors: on request, not Tues.
Green Fee: WD £30 (£10 with
member); WE & BH £35 (£10 with
member).
Societies: on application.
Catering: full facilities.
Tennis, snooker.
Hotels: Glenside; Neptune; Boyne
Valley.

V79 County Meath (Trim)
☎(046) 31463, Public: 31854,
Caterer: 36842
Newtownmoynagh, Trim, Co Meath
3 miles from Trim on Trim/Longwood
road.
Parkland course.
18 holes, 6720 metres, S.S.S.72
Designed by Eddie Hackett.
Founded 1898
Visitors: welcome weekdays,
restrictions Thurs, Sat, Sun.
Green Fee: apply for details
Societies: Mon-Sat inc., enquiries
welcome.
Catering: bars, restaurant; new
clubhouse.
Hotels: Wellington Court (Trim);
Harry's (Kinnegad); Wells (Enfield).

V80 County Sligo
☎(071) 77134/86, Sec 77170, Pro:
77171, Fax 77460
Rosses Point, Sligo
5 miles W of Sligo, off N15 at N edge
of Sligo town; signposted Rosses
Point.
Seaside links championship course.
18 holes, 6003 metres, S.S.S.72
Designed by Colt & Alison.
Founded 1894

Visitors: welcome weekdays; limited
times weekends and Bank Holidays,
booking essential.
Green Fee: WD £18 (£9 with
member); WE & BH £25 (£12.50 with
member).
Societies: welcome by prior
arrangement subject to availability.
Catering: bar, bar food, full
restaurant facilities.
Practice areas.
Hotels: Yeats Country; Ballincar
House; Sligo Park; Silver Swan;
Markree Castle; Southern.

**V81 County Tipperary
Golf & Country Club**
☎(062) 71116, Sec 61307, Fax
71366
Dundrum, Cashel, Co. Tipperary,
EIRE
1 mile from Dundrum village, 6 miles
W of Cashel off main Dublin/Cork
road.
Parkland course.
18 holes, 6030 metres, S.S.S.72
Designed by Philip Walton.
Founded 1993
Visitors: welcome.
Green Fee: WD £16 (£12 with
member); WE & BH £20 (£16 with
member).
Societies: welcome by arrangement.
Catering: 2 bars, 2 restaurants,
snack bar.
Snooker.
Hotels: Dundrum House on site.

V82 Courtown
☎(055) 25166, Sec (054) 89219,
Fax (055) 25553
Kiltennel, Gorey, Co Wexford
3 miles from Gorey off Dublin-
Rosslare road.
Parkland course.
18 holes, 5898 metres, S.S.S.71
Designed by Harris & Associates.
Founded 1936

IRELAND'S LARGEST GOLF COMPLEX

As the name suggests we are not just any hotel offering golf, but THE golfing hotel in Dublin offering Ireland's largest golf complex. Situated on the grounds of the Howth Castle, this 50 bedroom RAC 3 star hotel offers the choice of no less than 4 separate parkland courses, all within its grounds. Only 9 miles from Dublin city/airport. We offer exceptional value golfing breaks with guaranteed tee times 7 days a week and unlimited use of all our courses including our 6778 yard par 72 course.

For details call or write to:

Deer Park Hotel & Golf Courses

Deer Park Hotel, Howth, Co. Dublin. Tel: 010 3531 8322624

Visitors: welcome except on major competition days.
Green Fee: WD June-Aug £15, Sept-May £13 (half price with member); WE & BH £20/£17 (half price with member).
Societies: by prior arrangement except June-Aug.
Catering: snacks and full catering.
Hotels: Bayview; Marlfield House.

V83 Craddockstown
☎(045) 97610, Sec (01) 4511817
Craddockstown, Naas, Co Kildare
18 holes, 6134 metres, S.S.S.72
Founded 1983
Green Fee: WD £12 (£7 with member); WE & BH £15 (£10 with member)

V84 Cruit Island
☎(075) 43296
Kincasslagh, Co Donegal, EIRE
6 miles N of Dungloe adjacent to Viking House Hotel.
Scenic seaside links course.
9 holes, 4860 metres, S.S.S.66
Founded 1983
Visitors: welcome.
Green Fee: apply for details.
Societies: welcome.
Catering: bar and snacks weekends; daily in summer.
Hotels: through Donegal Leisure Breaks, golf inclusive (phone 075 42167).

V85 Curragh
☎(045) 41714, Pro: 41896, Bar: 41238
Curragh, Co Kildare
3 miles S of Newbridge, 28 miles SW of Dublin.
Parkland course.
18 holes, 6028 metres, S.S.S.71
Designed by David Ritchie (1852).
Founded 1883

Visitors: weekdays only; required to contact Sec before attending.
Green Fee: WD £14 (£7 with member); WE & BH £18 (£10 with member).
Societies: weekdays, limited weekends; apply to Sec in advance.
Catering: full facilities.
Hotels: Hotel Keadeen; Lumville House.

V86 Deer Park Hotel
☎(01) 8326039, Sec 8390009, Bar: 8322624
Deer Park Hotel, Howth, Co Dublin
9 miles E of city centre via Fairview, Clontarf and Sutton.
Public parkland courses.
36 holes, 6078 metres, S.S.S.73
Designed by Fred Hawtree.
Founded 1973
Visitors: welcome all week; weekends expect delays.
Green Fee: Apply for details.
Societies: Welcome weekdays.
Catering: full facilities, lounge, snack bar, restaurant.
Snooker, function room.
Hotels: Deer Park Hotel on site; golfing specials available.

V87 Delgany
☎(01) 2874536, Sec 2894149, Pro: 2874697,
Fax 2873977
Delgany, Co Wicklow
adjacent to village of Delgany off main road to Wexford.
Parkland course.
18 holes, 5414 metres, S.S.S.68
Founded 1908
Visitors: welcome except comp days.
Green Fee: WD £17 (£7 with member); WE & BH £20 (£10 with member).
Societies: welcome.
Catering: full catering facilities.
Hotels: Wicklow Arms; Glenview.

V88 Donabate
☎(01) 8436346, Sec 8341264, Public: 8436059
Donabate, Balcarrick Co Dublin
1st right 1 mile N of Swords on Dublin to Belfast road.
Parkland course.
18 holes, 5704 metres, S.S.S.69
Founded 1925
Visitors: welcome.
Green Fee: WD £18 (£9 with member); WE & BH after 6.00 pm (£12 with member).
Societies: welcome by arrangement.
Catering: meals served.

V89 Donegal
☎(073) 34054, Sec 22166, Public: 34163, Fax 34377
Murvagh, Laghey, Co Donegal
About 6 miles S of Donegal via N15.
Seaside links course.
18 holes, 6541 metres, S.S.S.75
Designed by Eddie Hackett.
Founded 1960, opened 1973
Visitors: welcome, no restrictions.
Green Fee: WD £15 (£10 with member); WE & BH £18 (£13 with member).
Societies: catered for daily.
Catering: bar and restaurant; buffet service.
Snooker.
Hotels: Sandhouse (Rossnowlagh); Abbey, Highland Central (Donegal).

V90 Doneraile
☎(022) 24137
Doneraile, Co Cork
off T11, 28 miles N of Cork, 9 miles from Mallow.
Parkland course.
9 holes, 5055 metres, S.S.S.67
Founded 1927
Visitors: welcome.
Green Fee: apply for details.
Societies: welcome.
Catering: meals served.

V91 Dooks
☎(066) 68205, Sec 61225, Fax 68476
Glenbeigh, Co Kerry
4 miles W of Killonglin, at bridge between Killonglin and Glenbeigh.
Seaside course.
18 holes, 6010 yards, S.S.S.68
Designed by Eddie Hackett.
Founded 1889
Visitors: welcome, check at weekends; evidence of handicap required.
Green Fee: any day: £16.
Societies: welcome.
Catering: restaurant facilities.
Hotels: Glenbeigh; Towers; Bianconi Inn; Canagh Lodge; Mount Brandon; And na Si; Castlerosse; Village Ho.

V92 Douglas
☎(021) 895297, Pro: 362055, Public: 891086
Douglas, Cork
Within 3 miles of Cork city, 0.5 mile beyond Douglas village.
Parkland course.
18 holes, 5664 metres, S.S.S.69
Founded 1909
Visitors: welcome, with reservation at weekends.
Green Fee: on application.
Societies: by arrangement before start of season.
Catering: snacks and meals served.

V93 Dromoland Castle
☎(061) 368144, Sec 361564, Fax 363355
Newmarket-on-Fergus, Co Clare
On main Limerick-Galway road, 1.5 miles through Newmarket-on-Fergus.
Public parkland course.
18 holes, 5719 metres, S.S.S.71
Designed by Whittaker (USA).
Founded 1961
Visitors: welcome.
Green Fee: WD £20 (£15 with member); WE & BH £25 (£15 with member).
Societies: welcome, fees negotiable.
Catering: available.
Tennis, banqueting.
Hotels: Dromoland Castle.

V94 Dublin Mountain
☎(01) 4582622, Sec 4593329
Gortlum, Brittas, Co Dublin
18 holes, 5433 metres, S.S.S.69
Founded 1993
Green Fee: WD £6 (£5 with member); WE & BH £8 (£7 with member).

V95 Dun Laoghaire
☎(01) 2803916, Sec 2953590, Pro: 2801694,
Fax 2804868
Eglinton Park, Tivoli Rd, Dun Laoghaire, Co Dublin
7 miles from Dublin, 0.5 mile from Dun Laoghaire town centre and ferry port.
Parkland course.
18 holes, 5272 metres, S.S.S.68
Founded 1910
Visitors: Mon, Tues, Wed am, Fri; reserved for members 12.30-2.00pm.
Green Fee: any day £25 (£10 with member).
Societies: Tues and Fri by prior booking only.
Catering: full service provided during season.
Hotels: Royal Marine; Fitzpatricks Castle; Hotel Victor.

V96 Dundalk
☎(042) 21731, Sec 34790, Pro: 22102, Public: 22270, Fax 22022
Blackrock, Dundalk, Co Louth
Off T1 3 miles S of Dundalk on Dundalk Bay.
Parkland course.
18 holes, 6160 metres, S.S.S.72
Designed by Dave Thomas & Peter Allis.
Founded 1905
Visitors: welcome except Sun (competition day).
Green Fee: WD £16 (£8 with member); WE & BH £20 (£10 with member).
Societies: welcome; booking essential.
Catering: full catering, dinners, snacks every day.
Hotels: Fairways; Imperial; Ballymascanlon; Derryhale; Carrickdale; Lorne.

V97 Dunfanaghy
☎(074) 36335, Pro: 36488
Dunfanaghy, Letterkenny, Co Donegal
On main Letterkenny-Dunfanaghy road 0.5 mile E of Dunfanaghy.
Public seaside links course.
18 holes, 5066 metres, S.S.S.66
Founded 1906
Visitors: welcome except Sun.
Green Fee: WD £11 (£7 with member); WE & BH £13 (£7 with member).
Societies: by arrangement.
Catering: bar, snacks.
Hotels: Arnold's; Shandon; Carrig Rua; Port-na-blagh.

V98 Dungarvan
☎(058) 43310, Sec 42342, Pro: 44707, Public: 41605, Fax 44113
Knocknagranagh, Dungarvan, Co Waterford
Take N25, approx 2 miles E of Dungarvan turnright to club.
Meadowland course.
18 holes, 6134 metres, S.S.S.73
Designed by Maurice Fives.
Founded 1924
Visitors: welcome any time.
Green Fee: WD £12 (£10 with member); WE & BH £15 (£12 with member).
Societies: apply in advance.
Catering: full dining facilities.
Hotels: Clonea Strand; Gold Coast Holiday Homes; Park.

V99 Dunmore
☎(023) 33352, Sec 34552
Dunmore House, Muckross, Clonakilty, Co Cork
3 miles from Clonakilty, signposted.
Hilly open course.
9 holes, 4464 yards, S.S.S.61
Designed by E. Hackett.
Founded 1967
Visitors: welcome any time.
Green Fee: WD £10 (£5 with member); WE & BH £10 (£5 with member).
Societies: welcome by prior arrangement.
Catering: bar and restaurant facilities in Dunmore House.

V100 Dunmore East Golf & Country Club
☎(023) 83151
Dunmore East, Co Waterford, EIRE
Take 1st left at entrance to Dunmore village, left at the strand, then 1st right; course signposted.
Parkland course.
9 holes, 4402 metres, S.S.S.64
Designed by Eamon Condon & Assoc.
Founded 1993
Visitors: welcome.
Green Fee: Apply for details.
Societies: welcome by prior arrangement.
Catering: bar and snacks all day; meals arranged at local hotels.

V101 East Clare
☎(061) 921322
Bodyke, Co Clare
9 holes, 5676 metres, S.S.S.70
Founded 1992
Green Fee: any day: £7

V102 East Cork
☎(021) 631687, Sec 632819
Gortacrue, Midleton, Co Cork
On main Cork to Waterford road 10
miles E of Cork city, turn left at
roundabout in Midleton, signposted
about 1.5 miles.
Parkland course.
18 holes, 5207 metres, S.S.S.67
Designed by Edward Hackett.
Founded 1969
Visitors: welcome except Sun am.
Green Fee: any day: £12.
Societies: welcome by arrangement;
telephone for details.
Catering: lunches served except
Sun.
Snooker, horse riding etc, details on
request.
Hotels: Commodore, Garryvoes
(special golf packages); Middleton
Park.

V103 Edenderry
☎(0405) 31072, Sec 31534
Kishavanny, Edenderry, Co Offaly
1 mile before town on road from
Dublin; turn right just before River
Boyne, clubhouse 0.5 mile on left.
Public parkland/moorland course,
quick drying.
18 holes, 6121 metres, S.S.S.72
Founded 1948
Visitors: restricted Thurs and
weekends; apply for details.
Green Fee: WD £8 (£5 with
member); WE & BH £10 (£6 with
member).
Societies: on application except Sun
and Thurs.
Catering: bar, good quality catering
by arrangement.

V104 Edmondstown
☎(01) 4931082, Sec 4946555, Pro:
4941049,
Restaurant: 4933205, Fax 4933152
Rathfarnham, Dublin 16
T42 S of Dublin, Rathfarnham 1 mile.
Parkland course.
18 holes, 5663 metres, S.S.S.69
Designed by Eddie Hackett.
Founded 1944
Visitors: welcome, dress code in
operation.
Green Fee: WD £20 (£10 with
member); WE & BH £25 (£10 with
member).
Societies: Mon, Thurs, Fri, Sat, to
11.30am.
Catering: full facilities.
Snooker.
Hotels: Jury's; Christchurch; Orwell
Lodge.

V105 Elm Park
☎(01) 2693438, Pro: 2692650, Fax
2694505
Nutley Lane, Donnybrook, Dublin 4
2 miles from city centre beside
Montrose television studios and St
Vincents Hospital.
Parkland course.
18 holes, 5422 metres, S.S.S.68
Designed by Fred Davies.
Founded 1925
Visitors: welcome but phone in
advance.
Green Fee: on application.
Societies: catered for Tues only.
Catering: full facilities.

V106 Ennis
☎(065) 24074, Sec 20045, Pro:
20690, Fax 41848
Drumbiggle, Ennis, Co Clare
1 mile W of N18 Limerick-Galway at
Ennis.
Gently rolling parkland course.
18 holes, 5316 metres, S.S.S.68
Founded 1907
Visitors: not before 12.00am Sun;
please book in advance.
Green Fee: any day: £15 (£7.50 with
member).
Societies: not Sun.
Catering: bar, excellent daylong
catering.
Snooker.
Hotels: Auburn Lodge; Queens; West
County; Old Ground; (concessionary
green fee scheme).

V107 Enniscorthy
☎(054) 33191, Sec 35257, Public:
34519
Knockmarshal, Enniscorthy, Co
Wexford
1.5 miles from town on New Ross
road.
Parkland course.
18 holes, 5697 metres, C.S.S.70
Designed by E. Hackett.
Founded 1925
Visitors: welcome except Tues
(Ladies Day); prior arrangement at
weekends.
Green Fee: WD £10; WE & BH £12.
Societies: most welcome.
Catering: full catering.
Hotels: Murphy Floods.

V108 Enniscrone
☎(096) 36297, Sec 36243, Fax
36657
Enniscrone, Co Sligo
8 miles N of Ballina, 0.5 mile from
Enniscrone.
Seaside course.
18 holes, 6044 metres, S.S.S.73
Designed by E. Hackett.
Founded 1918
Visitors: weekdays unrestricted,
phone for weekend times.
Green Fee: £12 (Low season); £18
(£6 with member).
Societies: welcome if arranged in
advance.
Catering: bar and restaurant
facilities, order before play.
Hotels: Atlantic, Benbulben, Castle
Arms, (Enniscrone); Downhill,
Imperial, Beleek Castle, (Ballina).

V109 The European Club
☎(0404) 47415
Brittas Bay, Co Wicklow, EIRE
N11 S from Dublin; turn left for Brittas
Bay at Jack White's Inn; turn right at
beach and proceed 1.5 miles.
Links course.
18 holes, 6729 yards, S.S.S.72
Designed by Pat Ruddy
Founded 1987
Visitors: welcome every day; h/cap
cert desired.
Green Fee: WD £25; WE & BH £30
Societies: welcome every day.
Catering: light refreshments
available.
Practice range.
Hotels: Grand (Wicklow); Tinakilly
House (Rathnew); Glenview (Glen of
Downs); Jack White's Inn (Brittas
Bay).

V110 Faithlegg
☎(051) 382241/688, Sec 73181,
Public: 382202,
Fax 382664
Faithlegg House, Co. Waterford,
EIRE
6 miles from Waterford city centre, on
banks of River Suir; from Waterford,
take Dunmore East Rd towards
Cheekpoint village.
Parkland course.
18 holes, 6057 metres, S.S.S.72
Designed by Patrick Merrigan.
Founded May 1993
Visitors: always welcome.
Green Fee: WD £20, before 9.00 am
£16 (£12 if accompanied by a
member).
Societies: always welcome, rates
negotiable.
Catering: full bar and restaurant
facilities; phone (051) 382155.
Practice area and putting green.
Hotels: Tower; Jury's; Granville;
Dooley's; Candlelight; B&B readily
available.

V111 Fermoy
☎(025) 31472
Corrin, Fermoy, Co Cork
2 miles from Fermoy off Cork-Dublin road.
Undulating course.
18 holes, 5795 metres, S.S.S.70
Designed by Commander Harris.
Founded 1893
Visitors: welcome weekdays.
Green Fee: apply for details.
Societies: weekdays and Sat am by arrangement.
Catering: snacks served.
Hotels: Grand.

V112 Fernhill
☎(021) 373103, Fax 371011
Carrigaline, Co Cork
18 holes
Founded 1994
Green Fee: apply for details

V113 Finnstown Fairways
☎(01) 6280644, Sec 6241151, Fax 6281088
Finnstown Fairways Country House Hotel and Golf Course, Newcastle Rd, Lucan, Co Dublin, EIRE
From Dublin take M50 for 7 miles to Lucan crossraods, then left onto Newcastle Rd.
Parkland course.
9 holes, 4654 yards, S.S.S.66
Designed by Bobby Brown.
Founded 1991
Visitors: welcome with h/cap cert.
Green Fee: WD £10 (£8 if accompanied by a member); WE & BH £12 (£10 if accompanied by a member).
Societies: welcome, phone in advance.
Catering: bar and restaurant facilities available.
Gym.

V114 Forrest Little
☎(01) 8401763, Pro: 8407670, Fax 8401000
Forest Little, Cloghran, Co Dublin
0.5 mile beyond Dublin Airport on Dublin-Belfast road, take 1st turn left.
Parkland course.
18 holes, 5865 metres, S.S.S.70
Designed by Fred Hawtree.
Founded 1940
Visitors: welcome weekdays.
Green Fee: apply for details.
Societies: catered for on Mon and Thurs afternoons.
Catering: snacks always available; à la carte menu from 5.00pm daily.

V115 Fota Island
☎(021) 883700, Pro: 883710, Public: 883871,
Fax 883713
Fota Island, Carrigtwohill, Co Cork, EIRE
9 miles E of Cork City on N25 Waterford and Roslaire road; take right turn at sign for Fota Island and Cobh, entrance immediately over bridge on right.
Gently rolling parkland course set amidst woodland; traditional design with pot bunker, double greens etc.
18 holes, 6197 metres, S.S.S.74
Designed by Peter McEvoy and Christy O'Connor Jnr.
Founded Sept 1993
Visitors: welcome 9am-12.30pm and 2-5pm weekdays, 10.30am-12.30pm and 2-5pm weekends and holidays; h/caps not required but visitors must be golfers.
Green Fee: apply for details.
Societies: welcome.
Catering: bar and light meals, full restaurant.
Driving range.
Hotels: Ashbourne House; Silver Springs; Ballymaloe House; Arbutus Lodge.

V116 Foxrock
☎(01) 2893992, Public: 2895668, Bar: 2897523,
Caterer: 2895668, Golf shop 2893414, Fax 2894943
Torquay Rd, Dublin 18
About 6 miles from Dublin; turn right off T7 just past Stillergan on to Leopardstown Rd, then left into Torquay Rd.
Parkland course.
9 holes, 5667 metres, S.S.S.69
Founded 1893
Visitors: welcome Mon, Wed am, Thurs, Fri; Sun only with member.
Green Fee: WD £20 (£8 with member); WE & BH n/a (£10 with member).
Societies: catered for Mon & Thurs.
Catering: soup, sandwiches, coffee.

V117 Frankfield
☎(021) 363124
Frankfield, Douglas, Co Cork, EIRE
10 miles S of Cork.
Parkland course.
9 holes, 4621 metres, S.S.S.65
Founded 1984
Visitors: welcome.
Green Fee: apply for details.
Societies: phone in advance.
Catering: lunch served Mon-Fri.

V118 Galway
☎(091) 22033, Sec 592587, Pro: 23038, Caterer: 21827
Blackrock, Salthill, Co Galway
On L100 2 miles W of Galway.
Tight, tree-lined, parkland course.
18 holes, 5816 metres, S.S.S.71
Founded 1895
Visitors: welcome Mon, Wed, Thurs, Fri.
Green Fee: WD £15 (£10 with member).
Societies: accepted, with advance booking.
Catering: full facilities.
Snooker.

V119 Galway Bay Golf & Country Club
☎(091) 90500, Sec 21159, Pro: 90503, Bar: 90507, Fax 90510
Renville, Oranmore, Co Galway
From Galway take coast road through Oranmore, signposted from there.
Seaside parkland course.
18 holes, 6533 metres, S.S.S.72
Designed by Christy O'Connor Jnr.
Founded 1993
Visitors: welcome, must have h/cap cert.
Green Fee: WD £20 (£15 with member); WE & BH £25 (£20 with member).
Societies: welcome, phone in advance.
Catering: restaurant, bar, spikes bar.
Practice bays.

V120 Glengarriff
☎(027) 63150
Glengarriff, Co Cork
On T65, 55 miles W of Cork.
Seaside course.
9 holes, 4094 metres, S.S.S.66
Founded 1936
Visitors: welcome.
Green Fee: apply for details.
Societies: special rates for societies.

V121 Glenmalure
☎(0404) 46679, Sec (01) 2826963, Fax (0404) 46783
Greenane, Rathdrum, Co. Wicklow
2 miles W of Rathdrum, towards the Glenmalure.
Moorland course.
18 holes, 4783 metres, S.S.S.66
Designed by Pat Suttle.
Founded May 1993
Visitors: welcome, no restrictions.
Green Fee: WD £12 (£6 with member); WE & BH £15 (£7.50 with member).

Societies: welcome, no restrictions.
Catering: bar lunches, no dinner as yet.
Hard tennis courts.
Hotels: Vale View, Woodenbridge (Avoca).

V122 Gold Coast Golf and Leisure

☎(058) 42249, Sec 41811, Fax 43378
Ballinacourty, Dungarvan, Co. Waterford, EIRE
On the edge of Dungarvan Bay.
Links course
9 holes, 5786 metres, S.S.S.70
Designed by Capt. R. Hewson
Founded 1993
Visitors: any time, subject to availability; official h/cap cert required.
Green Fee: any day: £12 (£8 with member).
Societies: any time subject to availability.
Catering: at Gold Coast Restaurant (on course) or Clonea Strand Hotel.
Driving range; indoor leisure centre at Clonea Strand Hotel.
Hotels: Clonea Strand; Gold Coast Cottages; Gold Coast Golf Hotel.

V123 Gort

☎(091) 31336, Sec 31281
Laughty Shaughnessy, Gort, Co Galway
Tubber road, Gort, 24 miles S of Galway.
Parkland course.
9 holes, 5174 metres, S.S.S.67
Designed by E. Hackett.
Founded 1924
Visitors: welcome all week except Wed evenings and Sun am; Ladies' Day Thurs.
Green Fee: any day: £9
Societies: apply to Hon Sec or bar manager.
Catering: light snacks April-Sept.
Hotels: Sullivans; Glynn's; O'Gradey's Rest.

V124 Grange

☎(01) 4932889, Sec 4979266, Pro: 4932299, Caterer: 4931404, Locker room: 4935800, Fax 4939490
Rathfarnham, Dublin 16
7 miles S from city centre, near Rathfarnham village.
Parkland course.
24 holes, 5517 metres, S.S.S.69
Designed by James Braid.
Founded 1910

Visitors: welcome weekdays except Tues and Wed afternoons.
Green Fee: WD £28 (£8 with member); WE & BH n/a (£12 with member).
Societies: welcome Mon and Thurs by arrangement.
Catering: full facilities.

V125 Greencastle

☎(077) 81013, Sec 82280
Greencastle, Moville, Co Donegal
On L85 23 miles NE of Londonderry through Moville.
Public seaside course.
18 holes, 5211 metres, S.S.S.67
Designed by Eddie Hackett (new 9 holes).
Founded 1892
Visitors: welcome.
Green Fee: WD £10 (£8 with member); WE & BH £15 (£10 with member).
Societies: welcome by prior arrangement.
Catering: bar and catering facilities.
Hotels: Fort; McNamaras, Foyle (Moville).

V126 Greenore

☎(042) 73678, Public: 73212
Greenore, Co Louth
From Belfast, take 1st left on Dundalk road out of Newry to Omeath and Carlingford, course 2 miles on from Carlingford; from Dublin, through Drogheda, take 1st right on Newry road out of Dundalk, then 15 miles to Greenore.
Wooded seaside course.
18 holes, 6506 yards, S.S.S.71
Designed by Eddie Hackett.
Founded 1896
Visitors: welcome weekdays and most weekends; advisable to phone Sec at weekends.
Green Fee: apply for details.
Societies: welcome any day with arrangement.
Catering: daily.
Hotels: Ballymascanlon; McKevitts Village; Park; Granvue.

V127 Greystones

☎(01) 2874136, Sec 2828684, Pro: 2875308,
Caterer: 2877479, Fax 2873749
Greystones, Co Wicklow, EIRE
N11 out of Dublin towards Wexford, signposted.
Parkland course.
18 holes, 5401 metres, S.S.S.68
Founded 1895

Visitors: welcome Mon, Tues, Fri; phone in advance.
Green Fee: WD £20 (£5 with member); WE & BH £24 (£6 with member).
Societies: by arrangement, phone in advance.
Catering: full facilities; summer every day, winter Wed-Sun inclusive.
Hotels: La Touche.

V128 Gweedore

☎(075) 31140, Fax 31666
Derrybeg, Letterkenny, Co Donegal
L82 from Letterkenny or T72 from Donegal.
Seaside course.
9 holes, 6150 metres, S.S.S.69
Designed by Eddie Hackett.
Founded 1926
Visitors: always welcome, reasonable rates, excellent service.
Green Fee: WD £7 (£5 with member); WE & BH £8 (£5 with member).
Societies: catered for weekends.
Catering: lunches served at weekends.

V129 Harbour Point

☎(021) 353094, Sec 361813, Fax 354408
Little Island, Cork, Co Cork
Take Rosslare road out of Cork; after 2.5 miles at 2nd roundabout take Little Island exit and watch for 'Harbour Point' signposts.
Undulating parkland championship course overlooking harbour.
18 holes (2 natural loops of 9), 6063 yards, S.S.S.72
Designed by Paddy Merrigan.
Founded June 1991
Visitors: welcome any time.
Green Fee: WD £20 (£10 with member), e/bird: £10;
WE & BH £20 (£10 with member).
Societies: by arrangement.
Catering: full bar and restaurant.
Driving range.
Hotels: Fitzpatricks Silversprings; Ashbourne House; John Barleycorn.

V130 Hazel Grove

☎(01) 4520911, Sec 4522931,
Mt Seskin Rd, Jobstown, Tallaght, Dublin 24, EIRE
On Blessington road, 2.5 miles from Tallaght.
Parkland course.
11 holes, 5030 yards, S.S.S.67.
Designed by Jim Byrne.
Founded 1988

Visitors: welcome Mon, Wed, Fri; not after 12am Tues, not after 11am Sat, not Sun; Thurs Ladies' Day.
Green Fee: any day: £10 (£7 with member).
Societies: by arrangement, maximum 50 players (Sat am maximum 40 players).
Catering: bar, function room available (seating 140); catering by arrangement.
Large practice area.

V131 Headfort
☎(046) 40857, Sec 40831, Pro: 40639, Public: 41204, Bar: 40146
Kells, Co Meath
0.25 mile from Kells on main Kells-Dublin road.
Parkland course.
18 holes, 5973 metres, S.S.S.70
Founded 1928
Visitors: welcome Mon, Wed, Thurs, Fri; limited weekends.
Green Fee: WD £15 (£5 with member); WE & BH £18 (£7 with member).
Societies: mornings only weekdays (except Tues); limited number of Sat mornings.
Catering: full service.
Hotels: Headfort Arms.

V132 Heath
☎(0502) 46533, Pro: 46622
The Heath, Portlaoise, Co Laois
4 miles NE of Portlaoise, just off main Dublin to Cork/Limerick road.
Heathland course.
18 holes, 5721 metres, S.S.S.70
Founded 1930
Visitors: welcome, by prior arrangement with Hon Sec at weekends.
Green Fee: apply for details.
Societies: welcome, apply in advance to Sec.
Catering: full facilities available by arrangement with Steward.
Driving range.
Hotels: Killeshin; Montague; Regency.

V133 Hermitage
☎(01) 6268491, Sec 8382571, Pro: 6268072
Lucan, Co Dublin
T3 W from Dublin, 1 mile from Lucan.
18 holes, 6032 metres, S.S.S.71 (Championship)
Founded 1905
Visitors: welcome Mon, Thurs, Fri most mornings.

Green Fee: WD £25 (£9 with member); WE & BH £35 (£15 with member).
Societies: weekdays.
Catering: every day.
Hotels: Ashling; Spa; Springfield.

V134 Highfield
☎(0405) 31021, Sec (01) 6270196
Carbury, Co Kildare
18 holes, 5707 metres, S.S.S.70
Founded 1992
Green Fee: WD £7 (£5 with member); WE & BH £10 (£7 with member)

V135 Hollywood Lakes
☎(01) 8433406/7, Public: 8433009, Fax 8433002
Hollywood, Ballyboughal, Co Dublin
12 miles N of Dublin city off Dublin/Belfast road.
Public parkland course with all-weather elevated greens.
18 holes, 6246 metres, S.S.S.73
Designed by Mel Flanagan.
Founded 1990
Visitors: welcome any time.
Green Fee: WD £12 (£7 with member); WE & BH £15 (£7 with member).
Societies: booking necessary.
Catering: bar, restaurant.
Hotels: Trust House Forte (Dublin Airport); Grand (Malahide); Skylon (Drumcondra).

V136 Howth
☎(01) 8323055, Sec 8324836, Pro: 8392617, Caterer: 8324553, Fax 8321793
Carrickbrack Rd, Sutton, Dublin 13
9.5 miles NE of city centre, 1.5 miles from Sutton Cross towards Howth summit.
Heathland course.
18 holes, 5628 metres, S.S.S.69
Designed by James Braid.
Founded 1911
Visitors: welcome weekdays.
Green Fee: WD £16 (Fri £18), (£8 with member); WE & BH n/a (£10 with member).
Societies: weekdays except Wed.
Catering: snacks and bar service.
Hotels: Marine; Howth Lodge.

V137 Island
☎(01) 8436462, Sec 8453418, Public: 8436852, Bar: 8436104, Fax 8436860
Corballis, Donabate, Co Dublin

From Dublin leave N1 approx 1 mile beyond Swords at Donabate signpost, then L91 for 3 miles and turn right at sign.
Seaside course.
18 holes, 6053 metres, S.S.S.72
Designed by F. Hawtree & Eddie Hackett.
Founded 1890
Visitors: weekdays.
Green Fee: WD £27 (£10 with member); WE & BH £30 (£10 with member).
Societies: Mon, Tues, Fri, by prior arrangement.
Catering: available.
Hotels: Grand (Malahide); The Dunes (Donabate).

V138 The K Club
☎(01) 6273987, Caterer, 6273111, Fax 6273990
Straffan, Co Kildare
22 miles from Dublin city centre via N7 Naas dual carriageway, or Lucan/Celbridge route.
Parkland course
18 holes, 6519 metres, S.S.S.74
Designed by Arnold Palmer
Founded 1991
Visitors: welcome, advance booking essential
Green Fee: apply for details
Societies: welcome by prior arrangement
Catering: restaurant, snack bar, full bar facilities.
Indoor and outdoor tennis courts, river and lake fishing, exercise centre, croquet
Hotels: Kildare Hotel & Country Club

V139 Kanturk
☎(029) 50534, Sec (022) 47238, Caterer: (029) 50587
Fairyhill, Kanturk, Co Cork, EIRE
Parkland course
9 holes, 5527 metres, S.S.S.69
Founded 1971
Visitors: welcome any time.
Green Fee: WD £10.
Catering: bar refreshments.

V140 Kenmare
☎(064) 41291, Sec 41069, Fax 42061
Kenmare, Co Kerry
On N71, 20 miles S of Killarney, 100 yards out of town.
Parkland course.
18 holes, 6003 yards, S.S.S.69
Designed by Eddie Hackett.
Founded 1903, extended 1993

Visitors: welcome, no restrictions.
Green Fee: WD £12.50 (£6.25 with member); WE & BH £15 (£7.50 with member, exc Sat)
Societies: apply to Sec.
Catering: bar, snacks available on request.
Hotels: Park; Sheen Falls Lodge; Kenmare Bay.

V141 Kilcock
☎(01) 6284074, Public: 6287592
Gallow, Kilcock, Co Meath, EIRE
2 miles N of Kilcock.
Parkland course.
18 holes, 5775 metres, S.S.S.70
Designed by Eddie Hackett.
Founded 1985
Visitors: welcome weekdays unrestricted, weekends by prior arrangement.
Green Fee: apply for details.
Societies: welcome, £20 deposit; phone in advance.
Catering: bar snacks.
Hotels: The Wells (Enfield).

V142 Kilcoole
☎(01) 2872066, Sec 2877387, Public: 2872070
Kilcoole, Co Wicklow, EIRE
21 miles S of Dublin on E coast.
Parkland course.
9 holes, 5506 metres, S.S.S.69, Par 70
Founded 1992
Visitors: welcome except Sat and Sun am.
Green Fee: WD £12 (£6 with member); WE & BH £14 (£8 with member).
Societies: welcome, book in advance.
Catering: drinks, snacks, meals by arrangement.

V143 Kilkea Castle
☎(0503) 45156
Castle Dermot, Co Kildare, EIRE
40 miles from Dublin.
Parkland course.
18 holes, 6200 metres, Par 70
Designed by McDadd & Cassidy.
Founded summer 1994
Visitors: welcome but advisable to book.
Green Fee: Mon-Thurs £25; Fri-Sun £30
Societies: welcome; necessary to book in advance.
Catering: full facilities.
Leisure centre, tennis, horse riding, archery.

V144 Kilkee
☎(065) 56048
East End, Kilkee, Co Clare
Within 400 metres of town.
Meadowland course.
9 holes, 5537 metres, S.S.S.69
Designed by McAllister.
Founded 1941
Visitors: welcome.
Green Fee: apply for details.
Societies: May, June and from mid-Aug to end of Sept.
Catering: snacks always available; meals for societies by arrangement.
Hotels: Strand; Victoria; Stella Maris; Bay View.

V145 Kilkenny
☎(056) 65400, Sec 22510, Pro: 61730, Caterer: 61830
Glendine, Kilkenny, Co Kilkenny
1 mile NW of mediaval city of Kilenny off the Castlecomer road.
Parkland course.
18 holes, 5857 metres, S.S.S.70
Founded 1896
Visitors: welcome, few restrictions.
Green Fee: WD £16 (£8 with member); WE & BH £18 (£9 with member).
Societies: mostly Sat mornings.
Catering: at clubhouse.
Snooker and pool.
Hotels: Newpark; Hotel Kilkenny; Springhill Court.

V146 Killarney
☎(064) 31034, Pro: 31615, Public: 31528/34527
Mahony's Point, Killarney, Co Kerry
3 miles W of Killarney on Killorglin road.
Parkland/lakeside courses.
Killeen, 18 holes, 6378 metres, S.S.S.73;
Mahony's Point, 18 holes, 6152 metres, S.S.S.72
Designed by Eddie Hackett and Dr W. Sullivan (Killeen), Sir Guy Campbell (Mahony's).
Founded 1893
Visitors: welcome, h/cap cert required.
Green Fee: any day: £28.
Societies: at all times.
Catering: all day every day.
Hotels: green fee discounts at numerous local hotels.

V147 Killeen
☎(045) 66003, Public: 66045, Fax 75881
Kill, Co Kildare

N7 to Kill village, turn right off carriageway leading for Straffan, turn left at next junction, 2 miles on left.
Parkland course.
18 holes, 4989 metres, S.S.S.66
Founded 1991
Visitors: Welcome weekdays and weekends.
Green Fee: WD £11 (£9 with member); WE & BH £13 (£11 with member).
Societies: welcome.
Catering: full bar and catering facilities.
Hotels: Green Isle; Ambassador.

V148 Killeline
☎(069) 61600, Sec 62515, Caterer: 61011, Fax 62853
Newcastle West, Co. Limerick, Eire
On the town (Newcastle West) boundary, 500 yards off main Limerick-Killarney road.
Parkland course.
9 holes, 6100 metres, S.S.S.68
Founded 1993
Visitors: welcome all day Mon-Sat, Sun by arrangement only.
Green Fee: any day: £10 (£7.50 with member).
Societies: all days except Sun.
Catering: lounge bar and restaurant.
Hotels: River Room; Devon Inn.

V149 Killiney
☎(01) 2852823, Sec 2887462, Pro: 2856294,
Bar/Caterer: 2851983, Public: 2851027
Ballinclea Rd, Killiney, Co Dublin
3 miles from Dun Laoghaire town centre.
Parkland course.
9 holes, 5626 metres, S.S.S.69
Founded 1903
Visitors: welcome; not Thurs, Sat, Sun am.
Green Fee: WD £17 (£8 with member); WE & BH £20 (£10 with member).
Societies: by arrangement only.
Catering: snacks at all times, full catering by arrangement.
Hotels: Killiney Castle; Killiney Court; Victor.

V150 Killorglin
☎(066) 61979, Sec 61151, Public: 62078, Fax 61437
Steelroe, Killorglin, Co. Kerry, EIRE
3km from Killorglin on raod to Tralee; 25km from Tralee, 22km from Killarney.

Parkland course.
18 holes, 6400 yards, S.S.S.72
Designed by Eddie Hackett.
Founded 1993
Visitors: welcome at all times; pre-booking advisable at weekends.
Green Fee: WD £12; WE & BH £14
Societies: society/group rates available on request.
Catering: bar, restaurant, meals and snacks.
Hotels: numerous in area; details on request by fax.

V151 **Kilrush**
☎(065) 51138
Parknamoney, Kilrush, Co Clare
On main road into town from Ennis.
Parkland course.
9 holes, 5009 metres, S.S.S.67
Founded 1934
Visitors: welcome.
Green Fee: apply for details.
Societies: catered for by arrangement.
Catering: bar facilities only.

V152 **Kilternan G & CC**
☎(01) 2955559, Sec 2885531, Fax 2955670
Kilternan Hotel, Enniskerry Road, Co Dublin
10 miles S of Dublin centre.
Hilly course.
18 holes, 4914 metres, S.S.S.67
Founded 1987
Visitors: welcome weekdays, and afternoon weekends; restricted Mon (Ladies').
Green Fee: WD £12 (£6 with member); WE & BH £16 (£8 with member).
Societies: by arrangement.
Catering: full facilities.
Extensive leisure and health facilities.
Hotels: Own hotel on site; special packages for individuals and societies.

V153 **Kinsale**
☎(021) 772197, Sec 772687
Ringenane, Belgooly, Co Cork
On main Cork-Kinsale road, 2 miles short of Kinsale signposted on left, 10 miles from Cork Airport.
Parkland course.
9 holes, 5332 metres, S.S.S.68
Founded 1912
Visitors: welcome weekdays.
Green Fee: £12 (£5 with member).
Societies: welcome by appointment.
Catering: bar and full catering.
Hotels: Trident, Actons, Blue Hand.

V154 **Knockanally G & CC**
☎(045) 69322, Sec (01) 6287433, Public: (045) 69391
Donadea, North Kildare
3 miles off main Dublin-Galway road between Kilcock and Enfield.
Parkland course.
18 holes, 6424 yards, S.S.S.72
Designed by Noel Lyons.
Founded 1985
Visitors: welcome, no restrictions.
Green Fee: WD £15 (£10 with member); WE & BH £20 (£10 with member).
Societies: every day.
Catering: full facilities.
Hotels: Moyglare Manor (Maynooth); Curryhills House (Prosperous); Wells (Enfield).

V155 **Lahinch**
☎(065) 81003, Fax 81592
Lahinch, Co Clare
34 miles from Shannon Airport.
Seaside courses.
Old, 18 holes, 6123 metres, S.S.S.73; Castle, 18 holes, 5138 metres, S.S.S.70
Designed by Tom Morris, revised by Dr A. MacKenzie; Castle Course, Commander J.D. Harris, revised by Donald Steel.
Founded 1892
Visitors: welcome weekdays; weekends except from 9-10am and 1-2pm Sat; 9-10.30am and 1-2pm Sun.
Green Fee: Old £30 (£24 with member); Castle £20 (£16 with member).
Societies: Old, Mon-Sat; Castle, every day.
Catering: full facilities.
Hotels: Aberdeen Arms; Sancta Maria; Liscannor Golf; Atlantic; Claremont; Falls.

V156 **Laytown & Bettystown**
☎(041) 27170, Public: 27563, Bar: 27534
Bettystown, Co Meath
On L125 off T1, 26 miles N of Dublin, 4 miles from Drogheda.
Seaside links course.
18 holes, 5653 metres, S.S.S.69
Founded 1909
Visitors: welcome weekdays.
Green Fee: apply for details.
Societies: most days; every effort made.
Catering: full bar and restaurant facilities.
Hotels: Neptune; Boyne Valley; Rosnaree; Mosney Holiday Centre.

V157 **Lee Valley**
☎((021) 331721, Sec 872646, Pro: 331758, Fax 331695
Clashanure, Ovens, Co Cork, EIRE
On main Cork-Killarney road.
Parkland course.
18 holes, 6131 metres, S.S.S.72
Designed by Christy O'Connor Jnr.
Founded 1993
Visitors: welcome.
Green Fee: WD £20 (£10 with member); WE & BH £25 (£10 with member).
Societies: welcome by prior arrangement.
Catering: bar and restaurant.
Driving range.

V158 **Leixlip**
☎(01) 6246185, Sec 4902916, Public: 6244978
Leixlip, Co Kildare
18 holes, 5550 metres, S.S.S.69
Founded 1994
Green Fee: WD £10; WE & BH £13 (£10 with member).

V159 **Leopardstown Golf Centre**
☎(01) 289 5341
Foxrock, Dublin 18
5 miles S of Dublin.
Public parkland course.
18 holes, 5384 yards, Par 67
Visitors: welcome.
Green Fee: apply for details.
Societies: Sun am only.
Catering: cafe, restaurant.
Driving range.

V160 **Letterkenny**
☎(074) 21150
Barnhill, Letterkenny, Co Donegal
On T72, 2 miles N of Letterkenny.
18 holes, 6239 metres, S.S.S.71
Designed by E. Hackett
Founded 1913
Visitors: welcome.
Green Fee: apply for details.
Societies: welcome.
Catering: snacks served, meals by arrangement.

V161 **Limerick**
☎(061) 415146, Sec 340174, Pro: 412492, Public: 414083
Ballyclough, Limerick
Take Fedamore road S of city.
Parkland course.
18 holes, 5938 metres, S.S.S.71
Founded 1891

Visitors: welcome before 4pm Mon, Wed, Thurs, Fri; no visitors weekends.
Green Fee: WD £20 (£12 with member); WE & BH n/a (£12 with member).
Societies: Mon, Wed, Fri before lunch.
Catering: full facilities.
Hotels: Woodfield House.

V162 Limerick County Golf & Country Club
☎(061) 351881, Fax 351384
Bellyneety, Co Limerick, EIRE
5 miles from Limerick on Kilmallock road.
Parkland course.
18 holes, 6712 yards, S.S.S.72
Designed by Des Smith.
Founded 1993
Visitors: welcome 9am-5pm weekdays, 10am-1.30pm weekends.
Green Fee: apply for details.
Societies: very welcome, phone in advance.
Catering: full facilities.
Golf school, putting greens, 3 practice holes.
Hotels: 12 holiday cottages to let.

V163 Lismore
☎(058) 54026, Sec 54222
Lismore, Co Waterford
0.5 mile from Lismore on Killarney road.
Parkland course.
9 holes, 5291 metres, S.S.S.67
Designed by Eddie Hackett.
Founded 1965
Visitors: welcome all days, some Sun reserved.
Green Fee: WD £8; WE & BH £10
Societies: by arrangement, all days except Sun.
Catering: prior booking needed.
Hotels: Lismore; Ballyraeter House.

V164 Loughrea
☎(091) 41049
Loughrea, Co Galway
On L11, 1 mile N of Loughrea.
Meadowland course.
18 holes, 5176 metres, S.S.S.68
Designed by Eddie Hackett.
Founded 1924
Visitors: unrestricted.
Green Fee: apply for details.
Societies: welcome by prior arrangement.
Catering: availableby prior arrangement.
Hotels: O'Deas; Meadow Court.

V165 Lucan
☎(01) 6282106, Sec 4974509, Public: 6280246,
Fax 6282929
Celbridge Rd, Lucan, Co Dublin
0.5 mile past Lucan village on road to Celbridge from Dublin.
Parkland course.
18 holes, 5994 metres, S.S.S.71
Founded 1897
Visitors: weekdays only, Wed to 1pm.
Green Fee: WD £16 (£8 with member).
Societies: Mon, Wed, Fri.
Catering: full bar and restaurant.

V166 Luttrellstown Castle
☎(01) 8208210, Sec 2888667, Fax 8208427
Clonsilla, Dublin 15, EIRE
W of Co Dublin.
Parkland course.
18 holes, 6384 metres, S.S.S.73, Par 72
Designed by Dr Nick Bielenberg.
Founded 1993
Visitors: welcome.
Green Fee: WD £30 (£18 with member); WE & BH £35 (£23 with member).
Societies: welcome, phone in advance.
Catering: full facilities.

V167 Macroom
☎(026) 41072
Lackaduv, Macroom, Co Cork
Situated on outskirts of town on main Cork/Killarney road; entrance to clubhouse through cattle gates in centre of Macroom town.
Parkland course.
18 holes, 5469 metres, S.S.S.69
Designed by J. Kennealy (new 9 holes).
Founded 1924
Visitors: welcome except specified weekends, phone to check; prior booking during golf season recommended.
Green Fee: apply for details.
Societies: by prior booking or arrangement with Sec.
Catering: full facilities.
Hotels: Castle, Victoria (reduced green fees for residents).

V168 Mahon
☎(021) 362480, Sec 362727
Clover Hill, Blackrock, Co Cork
2 miles SE of Cork on Douglas road.
Municipal course.

18 holes, S.S.S.62, Par 64
Founded 1980
Visitors: welcome weekdays, advance booking weekends.
Green Fee: WD £8.50; WE & BH £9.50.
Catering: bar, snacks, lunch, dinner by arrangement.

V169 Malahide
☎(01) 8461611, Sec 8322199, Pro: 8460002,
Public: 8461493, Caterer: 8461067, Fax 8461270
Beechwood, The Grange, Malahide, Co Dublin
1 mile off coast road at Portmarnock, 15 mins by road from Dublin Airport.
Parkland course.
3 x 9 holes, 3 courses with S.S.S.70/70/71, 6018 metres.
Designed by Eddie Hackett.
Founded 1892 (new course 1990).
Visitors: welcome at all times but please book in advance; jacket and tie after 7.30pm.
Green Fee: WD £21 (£6 with member); WE & BH £31 (£6 with member).
Societies: on application.
Catering: bar and restaurant.
Snooker.
Hotels: Grand, Grove (Malahide); Sands, Country Club (Portmarnock).

V170 Mallow
☎(022) 42501, Sec 21573, Pro: 43424, Public: 20180
Ballyellis, Mallow, Co Cork
1 mile from town on Killavullen road.
Public parkland course.
18 holes, 5874 metres, S.S.S.71
Designed by Commander J.D. Harris.
Founded 1892
Visitors: weekdays except Tues (Ladies Day), weekends members only.
Green Fee: WD £15; WE & BH £17.
Societies: prior booking, not Sun.
Catering: bar and restaurant.
Tennis, squash, snooker.
Hotels: Longueville House; Central; Hibernian; Springport Hall.

V171 Mannan Castle
☎(042) 63195, Sec 61805 (office), Fax 63308
Donaghmoyne, Carrickmacross, Co Monaghan
9 holes, 5804 metres, S.S.S.71
Founded 1993
Green Fee: WD £5; WE & BH £8 (£5 with member)

V172 Milltown
☎(01) 4976090, Sec 4975579, Pro: 4977072, Fax 4976008
Lower Churchtown Rd, Dublin 14
3 miles S of city centre, via Ranelagh village.
Parkland course.
18 holes, 5638 metres, S.S.S.69
Founded 1907
Visitors: welcome except Tues, Wed pm and Sat.
Green Fee: WD £30 (£14 with member); WE & BH n/a.
Societies: by arrangement.
Catering: lunch and dinner served.
Hotels: Orwell Lodge; Montrose; Jurys; Berkley Court.

V173 Mitchelstown
☎(025) 24072
Mitchelstown, Co Cork
1 mile from Mitchelstown off N1 Dublin to Cork road.
Parkland course.
15 holes (due to extend to 18), 5148 metres, S.S.S.67
Designed by David Jones.
Founded 1908
Visitors: welcome.
Green Fee: £10 (£7 with member).
Societies: welcome except Sun.
Catering: full catering for societies by arrangement.
Hotels: Clongibbon House; Firgrove; Castle Park.

V174 Moate
☎(0902) 81271, Sec 81270, Caterer: 81335
Moate, Co Westmeath
On T4, 8 miles E of Athlone.
Parkland course.
18 holes, 5742 metres, S.S.S.70
Founded 1900
Visitors: welcome.
Green Fee: WD £7 (£5 with member); WE & BH £10 (£5 with member).
Societies: catered for.
Catering: meals by arrangement.

V175 Monkstown
☎(021) 841376, Pro: 841686, Public: 841225
Parkgariffe, Monkstown, Co Cork
On L68 7 miles SE of Cork; on entering Monkstown village from Cork, turn right up hill at signpost to club, at crossroads at top of hill turn left, Club 200 yards on right.
Parkland course (89 new bunkers).
18 holes, 5669 metres, S.S.S.69
Founded 1908

Visitors: welcome except Tues.
Green Fee: WD (M-T) £20; Soc £18 (£7 with member); WE & BH £23; Soc £20 (£8 with member).
Societies: welcome.
Catering: full meals all day; phone (021) 841098.
Practice ground.
Hotels: Rochestown Park; Norwood Court.

V176 Moor Park
☎(046) 27661, Fax 29575
Mooretown, Navan, Co Meath
18 holes, 5600 metres, S.S.S.69
Founded 1993
Green Fee: apply for details

V177 Mount Juliet
☎(056) 24455, Sec 63988, Fax 24642
Thomastown, Co Kilkenny
1 mile from Thomastown on main Dublin-Waterford road.
Parkland course.
18 holes, 6555 metres, S.S.S.74, Par 72; 3 hole Teaching Academy
Designed by Jack Nicklaus.
Founded 1992
Visitors: welcome every day, please book in advance.
Green Fee: WD £65 (£35 with member); WE & BH £70 (£35 with member).
Societies: every day, book in advance.
Catering: full bar and restaurant facilities.
Driving range, riding, fishing, clay shooting, archery, tennis, swimming pool, spa and leisure centre.
Hotels: Mount Juliet House.

V178 Mount Temple
☎(0902) 81545, Sec 81132, Fax 81957
Campfield Lodge, Moate, Co Westmeath
In Mount Temple village just off main Dublin/Galway N6 Route, 5 miles from Athlone, 4 miles from Moate.
Parkland course, built in old traditional style.
18 holes, 5872 yards, S.S.S.71
Designed by Robert J. Brown and Michael Dolan.
Founded Oct 1991
Visitors: all welcome, open competitions available throughout the year; Sat play by arrangement.
Green Fee: WD £10; WE & BH £12.
Societies: welcome by prior acknowledgement to management.

Catering: home-cooked farmhouse refreshment; bar; village pub 100 yards.
Hotels: Grand (Moate); Prince of Wales, Hudson Bay, Royal (Athlone).

V179 Mountbellew
☎(0905) 79259, Sec 79622
Shankhill, Mountbellew, Co Galway
On T4, 28 miles E of Galway
Undulating meadowland course.
18 holes, 5143 metres, S.S.S.66
Founded 1929
Visitors: welcome.
Green Fee: any day: £8 (£6 with member).
Societies: by arrangement with Sec.
Catering: teas, soup, sandwiches, full meals on notification.

V180 Mountrath
☎(0502) 32558, Sec 32421
Knockinina, Mountrath, Co Laois
1.5 miles on Limerick side of Mountrath off Dublin-Limerick road.
Undulating parkland course.
18 holes, 5493 metres, S.S.S.69
Founded 1929
Visitors: welcome.
Green Fee: any day: £8 (£6 with member).
Societies: contact Sec.
Catering: on request for outings etc.
Hotels: Killeshin; Leix County.

V181 Mullingar
☎(044) 48366, Sec 42753, Pro: 40085, Fax 41499
Belvedere, Mullingar, Co Westmeath
3 miles from Mullingar on Tullamore road.
Parkland course.
18 holes, 590 metres, S.S.S.70
Designed by James Braid.
Founded 1894 (1994 centenary year).
Visitors: welcome, no restrictions.
Green Fee: WD £16 (£10 with member); WE & BH £23 (£10 with member).
Societies: welcome by arrangement.
Catering: full bar and restaurant facilities.
Hotels: Bloomfield House; Greville Arms.

V182 Mulranny
☎(098) 36262, Sec 41568
Mulranny, Westport, Co Mayo
N59, 10 miles W of Newport.
Undulating seaside links.
9 holes, 5729 metres, S.S.S.69
Founded 1968

Visitors: welcome.
Green Fee: any day: £7
Societies: welcome.
Catering: at Mulranny Bay Hotel.
Hotels: Mulranny Bay; Newport House; Achill Sound.

V183 Muskerry
☎(021) 385297, Sec 542554, Pro: 381445
Carrigrohane, Co Cork
7 miles W of city centre, near Blarney village.
Parkland course.
18 holes, 5786 metres, S.S.S.71
Founded 1897
Visitors: welcome on weekdays except Wed afternoons, Thurs mornings before 12.30pm and Fri after 3.30pm; phone in advance.
Green Fee: WD £17 (£8 with member 1st guest; £10 2nd; £12 3rd); WE & BH £20 (same as before).
Societies: as for visitors.
Catering: snacks available; meals by arrangement before play.
Hotels: Christys; Blarney Park.

V184 Naas
☎(045) 74644, Sec 76737, Bar: 97509
Kerdiffstown, Naas, Co Kildare
Between Johnstown and Sallins.
Parkland course.
18 holes, 5660 metres, S.S.S.69
Designed by Arthur Spring.
Founded 1886
Visitors: Mon, Wed, Fri and Sat.
Green Fee: WD £12 (£6 with member); WE & BH £15 (£7.50 with member).
Societies: Mon, Wed, Fri, Sat am.
Catering: bar; meals by prior arangement.
Snooker.
Hotels: Harbour View; Town House; Ambassador.

V185 Narin & Portnoo
☎(075) 45107, Bar: 45332
Portnoo, Co Donegal
From Donegal via Ardara, then 6 miles N.
Seaside course.
18 holes, 5322 metres, S.S.S.68
Founded 1930
Visitors: welcome, restricted July/Aug.
Green Fee: apply for details.
Societies: by arrangement.
Catering: bar and light snacks.
Snooker.
Hotels: Nesbitt Arms; Highlands.

V186 Nenagh
☎(067) 31476, Sec 32547, Pro: 33242, Public: 33383
Beechwood, Nenagh, Co Tipperary
4 miles NE of Nenagh town, well signposted.
Parkland course.
18 holes, 5491 metres, S.S.S.68
Designed by Alister Mackenzie (original 9), E. Hackett (additional 9).
Founded 1892, extended 1972
Visitors: welcome every day but advisable to ring Steward for availability on Sat/Sun.
Green Fee: WD £12; WE & BH £15
Societies: welcome by prior arrangement.
Catering: full facilities.
22-acre practice ground.
Hotels: Nenagh Lodge; Lakeside (Killalde).

V187 New Ross
☎(051) 21433, Sec 98145, Public: 25231
Tinneranny, New Ross, Co Wexford
from town centre take Waterford Rd, turn right at Albatros factory, about 1 mile.
Parkland course.
9 holes, 5172 metres, S.S.S.69
Founded 1905
Visitors: welcome except Sun if there is a competition.
Green Fee: WD £8 (£5 with member); WE & BH £12 (£8 with member).
Societies: welcome by prior arrangement.
Catering: snacks always available, meals by arrangement.

V188 Newcastle West
☎(069) 62105
Ardagh, Co Limerick
2 miles off main Limerick/Killarney roadway N21, 23 miles from Limerick city.
Parkland course.
9 holes, 5013 metres, S.S.S.67
Designed by Arthur Spring.
Founded 1939, 1994 on present site.
Visitors: welcome most times by arrangement; not Sun.
Societies: welcome by prior arrangement most days except Sun; reduced green fees subject to numbers.
Catering: bar and bar snacks available.
Hotels: Dunraven Arms, Woodlands (Adare); River Room (Newcastle West); Devon (Templeglantine).

V189 Newlands
☎(01) 4593157, Sec 4513436, Pro: 4593538,
Public: 4592903, Fax 4593498
Clondalkin, Dublin 22
6 miles from city centre on main southern Cork road.
Parkland course.
18 holes, 5696 metres, S.S.S.70
Designed by James Braid.
Founded 1926
Visitors: welcome weekdays.
Green Fee: any day: £25 (£9 with member).
Societies: welcome weekdays.
Catering: full facilities.
Hotels: Green Isle.

V190 North West
☎(077) 61715, Public: 61027, Caterer: 61841
Lisfannon, Fahan, Co Donegal
2 miles S of Buncrana.
Seaside links course.
18 holes, 5968 metres, S.S.S.69
Founded 1892
Visitors: welcome, no restrictions.
Green Fee: WD £10 (£8 with member); WE & BH £15 (£12 with member).
Societies: welcome weekdays, weekends in summer.
Catering: bar and restaurant every day.
Snooker room.
Hotels: White Strand; Roneragh House; Lake of Shadows.

V191 Nuremore
☎(042) 61438, Sec 62125
Carrickmacross, Co Monaghan
1 mile S of Carrickmacross on main Dublin to Derry road.
Parkland course.
18 holes, 6246 metres, S.S.S.74
Designed by Eddie Hackett.
Founded 1964, new course July 1991
Visitors: welcome any time.
Green Fee: WD £15; WE & BH £18.
Societies: welcome any time.
Catering: meals and snacks at hotel or clubhouse.
Hotels: Nuremore.

V192 Old Conna
☎(01) 2826055/2826766, Sec 2985876, Pro: 2820822,
Caterer: 2820038, Fax 2825611
Ferndale Road, Bray, Co Dublin
12 miles from Dublin city.
18 holes, 5590 metres, S.S.S.71, Par 72
Founded 1977

Visitors: welcome Mon, Thurs, Fri.
Green Fee: WD £20 (£10 with member).
Catering: bar, snacks, lunch and dinner served.

V193 The Open Golf Centre

☎(01) 864 0324, Fax 8341400
Newtown House, St Margaret's, Co Dublin
6 miles from Dublin city centre on main Derry road, adjacent to Dublin Airport.
Public parkland course.
27 holes, 6533 yards, Par 71
Designed by Martin Hawtree.
Founded May 1993
Visitors: all welcome.
Green Fee: WD £7.60; WE & BH £11.50.
Societies: welcome.
Catering: snacks.
Driving range.
Hotels: numerous in city centre

V194 Otway

☎(074) 58319
Saltpans, Rathmullan, Co Donegal
On W shore of Loch Swilly.
Seaside course.
9 holes, 4234 yards, S.S.S.60
Founded 1893
Visitors: welcome.
Green Fee: apply for details.
Societies: welcome by prior arrangement.
Hotels: Pier; Rathmullan House; Fort Royal.

V195 Oughterard

☎(091) 82131
Gortreevagh, Oughterard, Co Galway
1 mile from Oughterard on N59, 15 miles from Galway.
Mature parkland course with elevated greens.
18 holes, 6089 metres, S.S.S.69
Designed by Hawtree/Hackett.
Founded 1973
Visitors: welcome.
Green Fee: apply for details.
Societies: welcome weekdays (avoid Wed).
Catering: bar, snacks, lunch, dinners, all available; full à la carte menu each day.
International Angling and Golf competition held annually during 1st weekend in May.
Hotels: Connemara Gateway; Rosslake; Boat Inn; Corrib; Lake; Mountain View.

V196 Parknasilla

☎(064) 45122
Parknasilla, Sneem, Co Kerry
2 miles E of Sneem on Ring of Kerry road.
Undulating seaside course.
9 holes, 4652 metres, S.S.S.65
Founded 1974
Visitors: welcome.
Green Fee: apply for details.
Hotels: Parknasilla Great Southern, 15 mins walk.

V197 Portarlington

☎(0502) 23115
Garryhinch, Portarlington, Co Offaly
3 miles from Portarlington on Mountmellick road.
Tree-lined parkland course.
18 holes, 5496 metres, S.S.S.68
Founded 1909
Visitors: welcome.
Green Fee: WD £10 (£5 with member); WE & BH £12 (£6 with member).
Societies: welcome except Sun.
Catering: bar and restaurant facilities.
Snooker.
Hotels: East End (for special arrangements phone 23225); Hazel; Montague.

V198 Portmarnock

☎(01) 8462968, Pro: 8462634, Public: 8462794,
Bar: 8462957, Caterer: 8462783, Fax 8462601
Portmarnock, Co Dublin
from Dublin along coast road to Baldoyle, on to Portmarnock, right at Jet Garage, 1 mile up private road.
Seaside links course.
27 holes, 6497 metres, S.S.S.75
Designed by W.G. Pickeman & George Ross.
Founded 1894
Visitors: welcome.
Green Fee: WD £40 (£10 with member); WE & BH £50 (£15 with member).
Societies: welcome by arrangement Mon, Tues, Fri according to availability.
Catering: full facilities; jackets and ties must be worn.
Hotels: Portmarnock Country Club.

V199 Portsalon

☎(074) 59459, Sec 53459
Portsalon, Fanad, Co Donegal
Letterkenny to Ramelton to Milford to Kennykeel to Portsalon.
Seaside links course.
18 holes, 5354 metres, S.S.S.68
Designed by Mr Thompson of Portrush.
Founded 1891
Visitors: welcome.
Green Fee: WD £10 (£6 with member); WE & BH £12 (£6 with member).
Societies: welcome booked in advance.
Catering: bar and restaurant facilities.
Hotels: Claggan House; Portsalon House; Fort Royal, Rathmullan House, Pier (Rathmullan).

V200 Portumna

☎(0509) 41059, Sec 41442, Caterer: 41158
Woodford Rd, Portumna, Co Galway
1.5 miles from Portumna on Woodfood road.
Parkland course.
18 holes, 5205 metres, S.S.S.67
Founded 1913
Visitors: welcome.
Green Fee: £10 (£6 with member, one at any time).
Societies: by arrangement.
Catering: light refreshments, dinner by arrangement.
Hotels: Westpark; Clonwyn House; Portland House.

V201 Raffeen Creek

☎(021) 378430, Sec 372937, Public: 378170
Ringaskiddy, Co Cork
1 mile from Ringaskiddy (Cork) Ferryport.
Seaside/parkland course with water.
9 holes, 5098 metres, S.S.S.68
Designed by Eddie Hackett.
Founded 1988
Visitors: unrestricted weekdays, afternoons at weekends.
Green Fee: WD £10 (£7 with member).
Societies: By arrangement.
Catering: bar food.
Snooker.

V202 Rathdowney

☎(0505) 46170, Sec 46233
Rathdowney, Portlaoise,Co. Laois
Take N7 to Abbeyleix, turn left for town of Rathdowney, follow signposts from square in Rathdowney.
Meadowland course.
9 holes, 5642 metres, S.S.S.69
Designed by Eddie Hackett.
Founded 1930

Visitors: welcome.
Green Fee: any day: £6
Societies: by arrangement.
Catering: by arrangement with Hon Sec giving one week notice.

V203 Rathfarnham
☎(01) 4931201, Sec 2954793,
Public: 4939156,
Fax 4931561
Newtown, Rathfarnham, Dublin 16
2 miles from Rathfarnham village.
Parkland course.
9 holes, 5833 metres, S.S.S.70
Designed by John Jacobs.
Founded 1899
Visitors: welcome except Tues, Sat, Sun.
Green Fee: WD £20 (£10 with member); WE & BH n/a).
Societies: by arrangement only.
Catering: lunch and dinners by arrangement.
Hotels: Marley Park.

V204 Rathsallagh House
☎(045) 403316, Fax 4033295
Dunlavin, Co Wicklow, EIRE
32 miles SW of Dublin.
Parkland course.
18 holes, 6916 yards, S.S.S. 74
Designed by Peter McEvoy.
Founded 1994
Visitors: welcome, especially weekdays.
Green Fee: Summer: Mon £25, Tues-Thurs £29, WE & BH £35; Winter: WD £20; WE & BH £25. Early bird special rates - apply for details.
Societies: by arrangement.
Catering: new club restaurant open 1st April 1996 with full facilities, also available at Rathsallagh House.
Practice range, snooker, pool, tennis, horse riding.
Hotels: Rathsallagh House

V205 Redcastle
☎(077) 82073, Sec (08 01 504) 350510
Redcastle, Moville, Co Donegal
9 holes, 6032 yards, S.S.S.70
Founded 1983
Gree Fee: WD £7 (£5 with member); WE & BH £10 (£9 with member)

V206 Rockwell
☎(062) 61444, Sec 61444
Cashel, Co Tipperary
9 holes, 3782 metres, S.S.S.60
Founded 1964
Green Fee: apply for details

V207 Rosapenna
☎(074) 55301, Fax 55128
Rosapenna Hotel, Downings, Co Donegal
25 miles N of Letterkenny.
Championship links course.
18 holes, 6271 yards, S.S.S.71
Designed by Tom Morris (1893), re-designed by Braid & Vardon (1906)
Founded 1893
Visitors: welcome.
Green Fee: any day: £15.
Catering: at Rosapenna Hotel.
Hotels: Rosapenna; Carrigart.

V208 Roscommon
☎(0903) 26382, Sec 26062
Mote Park, Roscommon, Co Roscommon
On N61, 95 miles W of Dublin, 0.5 mile S of Roscommon town.
Public parkland course.
9 holes 5784 metres, S.S.S.69
Founded 1904
Visitors: welcome.
Green Fee: any day: £10.
Societies: by arrangement with Hon Sec (0903) 26100 office, 26062 home, £6 per person.
Catering: bar and limited restaurant facilities.
Practice area.
Hotels: Royal; Abbey.

V209 Roscrea
☎(0505) 21130, Public: 22620
Derryvale, Roscrea, Co Tipperary
2 miles E of Roscrea on N7 Dublin road.
Public parkland course.
18 holes, 5708 yards, S.S.S.70
Designed by A. Spring.
Founded 1892
Visitors: no restrictions.
Green Fee: apply for details.
Societies: by appointment.
Catering: bar and restaurant facilities available.
Snooker.
Hotels: Racket Hall; Pathe; Leix County.

V210 Rosslare
☎(053) 32203, Sec 23010, Pro: 32238, Bar: 32113
Rosslare Strand, Co Wexford
10 miles S of Wexford, 6 miles N of Rosslare Harbour.
Seaside links course.
27 holes, 6572 yards, S.S.S.71
Designed by Hawtree & Taylor (Old), Christy O'Connor Jnr (New).
Founded 1908 (Old), 1992 (New).

Visitors: welcome most days, ring for availability; time sheets in operation Tues (Ladies Day), Sat, Sun.
Green Fee: WD £18 (£9 with member, exc July/Aug); WE & BH £23 (£11.50 with member, exc July/Aug).
Societies: ring office for bookings.
Catering: full bar and restaurant facilities Tel 32460.
Practice ground, snooker.
Hotels: Kellys Strand; Cedars; Burrow Park.

V211 Rossmore
☎(047) 81316, Sec 81473
Rossmore Park, Cootehill Road, Monaghan
2 miles from Monaghan, Cootehill rd.
Undulating parkland course.
18 holes, 5277 metres, S.S.S.68
Designed by Des Smyth.
Founded 1916
Visitors: welcome; check by phone at weekends.
Green Fee: any day: £10 (£7 with member).
Societies: catered for.
Catering: full facilities 7 days.
Snooker, bridge club.
Hotels: Hillgrove; Four Seasons; Westenra; Lakeside.

V212 Royal Dublin
☎(01) 8336346, Sec 8451315, Pro: 8336477,
Bar: 8337153, Fax 8336504.
Bull Island, Dollymount, Dublin 3
4 miles NE of city centre on coast road to Howth.
Seaside links course.
18 holes, 6267 metres, S.S.S.73
Designed by H.S. Colt.
Founded 1885
Visitors: welcome weekdays; weekends and Bank Holidays by arrangement with Sec/Manager.
Green Fee: WD £40 (£10/£15/£20 with member); WE & BH £50 (£15/£25 with member).
Societies: weekdays except Wed.
Catering: full service (Tel: 8333370).
Hotels: Marine; Howth Lodge.

V213 Royal Tara
☎(046) 25508, Sec 25732, Pro: 26009, Bar: 25244
Bellinter, Navan, Co Meath
30 miles N of Dublin off N3.
Public parkland course.
27 holes, 5904 metres, S.S.S.71
Designed by Des Smyth Golf Design
Founded 1923

ST. HELEN'S BAY GOLF & COUNTRY CLUB.

St. Helen's, Kilrane, Rosslare Harbour, Co. Wexford, Ireland. Tel: 053-33669/33234. Fax: 053-33803.

Located beside beautiful St. Helen's Bay, 14 holes actually overlook the coast. The course is designed to be at one with nature, taking advantage of onshore winds & gently sloping land. St. Helen's incorporates 9 water features, 5000 trees and even offers on site accommodation in the course cottages.

Visitors: welcome by arrangement.
Green Fee: WD £14 (£8 with member); WE & BH £18 (£9 with member).
Societies: Mon, Thurs, Fri, Sat by arrangement.
Catering: full facilities (Tel 25968).

V214 Rush
☎(01) 8438177, Sec 8437977, Public: 8437548
Rush, Co Dublin
Dublin to Belfast road, turn right at Blakes Cross.
Seaside links course.
9 holes, 5598 metres, S.S.S.69
Founded 1943
Visitors: preferably not Wed, Thurs, Sat, Sun and Bank Holidays.
Green Fee: WD £15 (£6 with member); WE & BH n/a.
Societies: catered for.
Catering: full facilities.
Hotels: Argyle Lodge B&B.

V215 St Annes
☎(01) 8336471, Sec; 8323786, Pro: 8314138,
Public: 8352797, Caterer: 8530144
North Bull Island, Dollymount, Dublin 5
4 miles NE of Dublin off Howth road.
Seaside course.
18 holes, 5797 metres, S.S.S.70
Designed by Eddie Hackett
Founded 1921
Visitors: no restrictions except competitions; prior enquiry advised.
Green Fee: WD £20 (£10 with member); WE & BH £25 (£10 with member).
Societies: on application.
Catering: by arrangement.

V216 St Helen's Bay
☎(053) 33234/33669, Fax 33803
St Helen's, Kilrane, Rosslare Harbour, Co. Wexford, EIRE
On main Wexford/Rosslare Harbour road, 1.5 miles Rosslare Harbour.
Links and parkland course.
18 holes, 6091 metres, S.S.S.72
Designed by Philip Walton.
Founded 1993

Visitors: welcome all times including weekends.
Green Fee: apply for details.
Societies: welcome at all times.
Catering: full time catering and bar available.
Practice and tuition area.
Hotels: 6 local hotels are corporate members; own accommodation on site.

V217 St Margaret's Golf & Country Club
☎(01) 8640400, Fax 8640289
St Margaret's, Co Dublin
4 miles W of Dublin Airport.
Parkland course.
18 holes, 6917 yards, S.S.S.73
Designed by Ruddy & Craddock.
Founded 1992
Visitors: welcome.
Green Fee: £40 per round.
Societies: and company days, welcome, £25 per round for parties over 20.
Catering: full facilites, 2 bars, 2 restaurants.
Hotels: Forte Crest; Grand (Malahide).

V218 Seapoint
☎(041) 22333, Fax 22331
Termonfeckin, Co. Louth, EIRE
35 mins from Dublin Airport, 70 miles from Belfast; from Dublin, take N1 to Drogheda, cross Boyne river and turn right for Termonfeckin; in Termonfeckin turn right after bridge for Seapoint.
Championship links course.
18 holes, 6339 metres, S.S.S.74
Designed by Des Smyth, Declan Branigan
Founded June 1993
Visitors: welcome at all times; booking required.
Green Fee: WD £20 (£8 with member); WE & BH £25 (£10 with member).
Societies: most welcome weekdays, reduced rates for groups.
Catering: bar and restaurant facilities available.
Driving range, putting green.
Hotels: Westcourt; Boyne Valley.

V219 Shannon
☎(061) 471849, Sec (065) 22653, Pro: (061) 471551, Public: 471020, Fax 471507
Shannon Airport, Co Clare
0.5 mile from Shannon Airport terminal.
Woodland/parkland course.
18 holes, 6186 metres, S.S.S.74
Founded 1966
Visitors: welcome weekdays.
Green Fee: WD £20 (£10 with member); WE & BH £25 (£10 with member).
Societies: by arrangement.
Catering: bar, snacks, lunch, dinner.

V220 Skerries
☎(01) 8491567, Sec 8490135, Pro: 8490925, Public: 8491148, Bar: 8491204, Fax 8491591
Hacketstown, Skerries, Co Dublin
Take Belfast road N out of Dublin, past Airport and Swords, fork right for Lusk and Skerries after end of Swords by-pass.
Undulating parkland course.
18 holes, 6113 metres, S.S.S.72
Founded 1905
Visitors: welcome.
Green Fee: WD £17 (£8 with member); WE & BH £22 (£10 with member).
Societies: Mon, Thurs and Fri.
Catering: full facilities.
Snooker.
Hotels: Pier House; Anna Villa.

V221 Skibbereen & West Cabbery
☎(028) 21227
Licknavar, Skibbereen, Co Cork
off T65, 52 miles SW of Cork City.
Moorland course.
18 holes, 5900 metres, S.S.S.68
Designed by Eddie Hackett.
Founded 1905
Visitors: welcome, advisable to ring in advance.
Green Fee: apply for details.
Societies: welcome by arrangement.
Catering: bar, pub food available at all times.
Driving net, putting green.
Hotels: West Cork; Eldon.

V222 Slade Valley

☎(01) 452739, Sec 4565299, Pro: 4582183,
Bar: 4582207, Fax 4582784
Lynch Park, Brittas, Co Dublin
off N1 Dublin to Naas road.
Undulating course.
18 holes, 5388 metres, S.S.S.68
Designed by W.D. Sullivan and D. O'Brien.
Founded 1970
Visitors: by arrangement with Sec.
Green Fee: WD £16 (£8 with member).
Societies: apply to Sec.
Catering: meals at weekends, also Tues and Wed during summer.
Hotels: Green Isle; Downshire House (Blessington).

V223 Slieve Russell

☎(049) 26444, Pro: 26458, Fax 26474
Ballyconnell, Co Cavan, EIRE
approx 90 miles SW of Belfast.
Parkland course.
18 holes, 6413 metres, S.S.S.74
Designed by Paddy Merrigan.
Founded 1992
Visitors: visitors always welcome, but book in advance.
Green Fee: apply for details.
Societies: welcome, booking required.
Catering: full facilities.

V224 Spanish Point

☎(065) 84198
Spanish Point, Miltown Malbay, Co Clare
2 miles from Milton Malbay, 8 miles from Lahinch.
Seaside course.
9 holes, 3574 metres, S.S.S.58
Founded 1896
Visitors: welcome.
Green Fee: apply for details.
Societies: welcome except Sun.
Catering: only on special occasions; light snacks at bar (eg sandwiches).
Hotels: Central.

V225 Stackstown

☎(01) 4941993, Sec (045) 77751, Pro: (01) 4944561, Public: 4934466, Bar: 4942338
Kellystown Road, Rathfarnham, Dublin 16
8 miles S of Dublin via N81 and R115.
Hilly course with panoramic views.
18 holes, 5789 metres, S.S.S.71
Founded 1976

Visitors: welcome weekdays; advisable to phone for weekends.
Green Fee: WD £14 (£7 with member); WE & BH £18 (£9 with member).
Societies: welcome by prior arrangement.
Catering: bar, snacks, lunch, dinner.

V226 Strandhill

☎(071) 68188, Sec 69734, Fax 68438
Strandhill, Co Sligo
5 miles W of Sligo city, 1 mile from Strandhill Airport; course is situated in resort of Strandhill, well signposted.
Seaside links course.
18 holes, 5516 metres, S.S.S.68
Founded 1931
Visitors: welcome weekdays and most weekends.
Green Fee: WE £12 (£10 with member); WE & BH £15 (£13 with member).
Societies: welcome, group rates available.
Catering: snacks available, meals by arrangement.
Sea fishing, surfing.
Hotels: Ocean View (Strandhill); Southern, Silver Swan, Yeats Country Ryan, Sligo Park (Sligo town).

V227 Strokestown

☎(078) 33100
Strokestown, Co Roscommon
9 holes, 5226 metres, S.S.S.67
Founded 1992
Green Fee: apply for details

V228 Sutton

☎(01) 8322965, Pro: 8321703, Fax 8321603
Cush Point, Sutton, Dublin 13
7 miles NE of city centre.
Seaside links course.
9 holes, 5226 metres, S.S.S.67
Founded 1890
Visitors: welcome except competition days (Tues and Sat).
Green Fee: WD £15 (£8 with member); WE & BH £20 (£8 with member).
Societies: by arrangement only.
Catering: by arrangement only.

V229 Swinford

☎(094) 51378, Sec 81321
Brabazon Park, Swinford, Co Mayo
Beside town, opposite Western Health Board complex; 3.5 hours W of Dublin on N5.

Public parkland course.
9 holes, 5573 metres, S.S.S.68
Founded 1922
Visitors: welcome any time.
Green Fee: any day: £7
Societies: welcome at all times.
Catering: licensed bars, bar snacks available.
Hotels: Heather Lodge.

V230 Tara Glen

☎(055) 25413
Ballymoney, Courtown, Co Wexford
9 holes
Founded 1993
Green Fee: apply for details

V231 Templemore

☎(0504) 31400, Fax 31913.
Manna South, Templemore, Co Tipperary
0.5 mile from town centre beside the Thurles road.
Parkland course.
9 holes, 5112 metres, S.S.S.67
Founded 1970
Visitors: no restrictions except on special event days.
Green Fee: apply for details.
Societies: by appointment with Hon Sec.
Catering: no bar, light refreshments provided on request, catering at local Inns.
Hotels: Hayes, Anner (Thurles).

V232 Thurles

☎(0504) 21983, Sec 23787, Public: 22466
Turtulla, Thurles, Co Tipperary
1 mile S of Thurles on Cork road.
Parkland course.
18 holes, 5904 metres, S.S.S.71
Founded 1909
Visitors: welcome except Sat/Sun.
Green Fee: any day: £15 (£8 with member).
Societies: catered for on weekdays and Sat.
Catering: full catering.
Driving range, championship squash courts.
Hotels: Hayes; Anner; Hotel Munster.

V233 Tipperary

☎(062) 51119, Sec 52335
Rathanny, Tipperary
1 mile from town on Glen of Aherlow road.
Parkland course.
18 holes, 5805 metres, S.S.S.71
Founded 1896

Visitors: welcome weekdays, Sun by prior arrangement.
Green Fee: any day: £10
Societies: by arrangement.
Catering: bar, snacks.
Hotels: Glen; Royal; Aherlow House.

V234 Townley Hall
☎(041) 42229, Sec 37843
Townley Hall, Tullyallen, Drogheda, Co Louth
18 holes, 4978 metres, Par 70
Founded 1994
Green Fee: any day: £5.

V235 Tralee
☎(066) 36379, Sec 26417, Public: 36355, Fax 36008
West Barrow, Ardfert, Co Kerry
8 miles NW of Tralee; from Tralee through Spa and Churchill to Barrow.
Links course.
18 holes, 6252 metres, S.S.S.73
Designed by Arnold Palmer Design.
Founded 1896
Visitors: weekdays by arrangement with Sec; not Weds June-Aug; 11am-12.30pm weekends; h/cap certs may be required; max 28 men, 36 ladies..
Green Fee: WD £25 (£12.50 with member); WE & BH £30 (£15 with member).
Societies: weekdays.
Catering: full facilities.
Hotels: Mount Brandon; Grand.

V236 Tramore
☎(051) 386170, Sec 381436, Pro: 381706
Newtown Hill, Tramore, Co Waterford
Via Waterford, 1 mile beyond Tramore.
Parkland course.
18 holes, 5998 metres, S.S.S.73
Designed by Tibbett (1936/7)
Founded 1894
Visitors: welcome.
Green Fee: WD £17 (£8.50 with member); WE & BH £21 (£10 with member).
Societies: by arrangement.
Catering: meals served.
Hotels: Majestic; Grand; Sea View.

V237 Tuam
☎(093) 28993
Barnacurragh, Tuam, Co Galway
1.5 miles from town on the Athenry road which is off Dublin road.
Parkland course.
18 holes, 6503 metres, S.S.S.71
Founded 1907

Visitors: welcome weekdays.
Green Fee: apply for details.
Societies: catered for on weekdays and Sat by arrangement.
Catering: full restaurant and bar.
Hotels: Hermitage; Imperial.

V238 Tubbercurry
☎(071) 85849
Tubbercurry, Co Sligo, EIRE
Within 1.5 miles of Tubercurry on Ballymote road.
Parkland course.
9 holes, 5478 metres, S.S.S.69
Designed by Eddie Hackett.
Founded 1990
Visitors: welcome at all times.
Green Fee: apply for details.
Catering: new clubhouse.

V239 Tulfarris Hotel & CC
☎(045) 64612, Caterer: 64574
Blessington, Co Wicklow
6 miles from Blessington off N81.
9 holes, 5612 metres, S.S.S.69
Designed by Eddie Hackett.
Founded 1989
Visitors: welcome; limited Sun.
Green Fee: apply for details.
Societies: by arrangement.
Catering: restaurant, bar, bar snacks.
Banqueting, conference centre, tennis, indoor pool, gym, snooker.
Hotels: Tulfarris Hotel & CC, special golfing packages on request.

V240 Tullamore
☎(0506) 21439, Sec 51317, Pro/Fax 51757
Brookfield, Tullamore, Co Offaly
2.5 miles from town centre, 1 mile off Birr road, on Kinnity road.
Parkland course.
18 holes, 5779 metres, S.S.S.70
Designed by James Braid.
Founded 1886
Visitors: welcome except during club competitions on Sun.
Green Fee: WD £12 (£7 with member); WE & BH £15 (£10 with member).
Societies: weekdays and Sat.
Catering: available, large numbers (eg societies) by prior arrangement.
Hotels: Phoenix Arms.

V241 Virginia
☎(049) 47235
Virginia, Co Cavan
50 miles N of Dublin on main Cavan-Dublin road, within Park Hotel, by Lough Ramor.

Meadowland course.
9 holes, 4900 metres, S.S.S.62
Founded 1946
Visitors: welcome.
Green Fee: apply for details.
Catering: in Park hotel.
Hotels: Park.

V242 Waterford
☎(051) 76748, Sec 75597, Pro: 54256, Fax 53405
Newrath, Waterford
0.25 mile from city centre.
Parkland course.
18 holes, 5722 metres, S.S.S.70
Designed by Cecil Barcroft and Willie Park.
Founded 1912
Visitors: welcome weekdays.
Green Fee: WD £15 (£10 with member); WE & BH £18 (£12 with member).
Societies: catered for weekdays.
Catering: full facilities available.
Hotels: Jurys; Bridge; Granville; Dooleys; Tower.

V243 Waterford Castle Golf & Country Club
☎(051) 71633, Sec 381616, Public: 50902, Fax 79316
The Island, Ballinakill, Co. Waterford
2 miles out of Waterford on Dunmore East road; 4th left after Hospital roundabout; own car ferry to island.
Parkland course on island in R. Suir.
18 holes, 6209 metres, S.S.S.73, Par 72
Designed by Des Smyth and Declan Brannigan.
Founded 1993
Visitors: welcome; book in advance.
Green Fee: WD £18 (£10 with member); WE & BH £20 (£10 with member).
Societies: welcome by arrangement.
Catering: teas, coffee, snacks; meals by prior arrangement.
Tennis, indoor swimming pool.
Hotels: Waterford Castle (051) 78203.

V244 Waterville House & Golf Links
☎(066) 74102, Public: 74237, Bar: 74102, Fax 74482
Rink of Kerry, Waterville, Co Kerry
N70 to Waterville, then coastal road for 1 mile W of town.
Seaside links course.
18 holes, 7184 yards, S.S.S.74
Designed by E. Hackett.
Founded 1901

Visitors: welcome at all times except major tournaments; all players must produce h/cap cert before signing in.
Green Fee: any day: £40 (£20 with member).
Societies: group rates available, 7 days; society must be affiliated and members must have club h/caps.
Catering: bar and restaurant.
Practice range, putting green.
Hotels: Waterville House; Butlers Arms; Bay View; Jolly Swagman; Villa Maria; Club Med.

V245 West Waterford

☎(058) 43216, Fax 44343
Coolcormack, Dungarvan, Co Waterford, EIRE
2.5 miles W of Dungarvan off N25 on Aglish Road.
Parkland course.
18 holes, 6162 metres, S.S.S.74
Designed by Eddie Hackett.
Founded July 1992
Visitors: welcome.
Green Fee: apply for details.
Societies: welcome by arrangement.
Catering: bar and restaurant all day every day.
Practice ground; guest house.

V246 Westmanstown

☎(01) 8205817, Sec 8210562, Bar: 8207888,
Fax 8207891
Clonsilla, Dublin 15
Coming from Dublin to Lucan village turn right and follow sign for Clonsilla, course on right.
Flat parkland course.
18 holes, 5819 metres, S.S.S.70
Designed by Eddie Hackett.
Founded 1988
Visitors: welcome Mon-Fri.
Green Fee: WD £15 (£7 with member); WE & BH £20 (£7 with member).
Societies: by prior arrangement.
Catering: Tel (01) 8208063.
Hotels: Spa (Lucan).

V247 Westport

☎(098) 25113, Sec 26134, Pro: 27481, Fax 27217
Carrowholly, Westport, Co Mayo
2 miles from Westport, continue for 0.5 mile on Newport road then left.
Parkland course.
18 holes, 6959 yards, S.S.S.73
Designed by Hawtree & Son.
Founded 1908

Visitors: welcome.
Green Fee: WD £12 Oct-March, £19 April-Sept (£10 with member); WE & BH £15 Oct-March, £22 April-Sept (£10 with member).
Societies: welcome; special rates by arrangement.
Catering: lounge bar; snacks and meals in dining room.
Hotels: Railway; Clewbay; Central; Castlecourt; Woods; Hotel Westport.

V248 Wexford

☎(053) 42238, Sec 44611, Pro: 46300, Public: 45095
Mulgannon, Wexford
Within Wexford town.
Parkland course.
18 holes, 5578 metres, S.S.S.70
Designed by J. Hamilton Stutt & Co (original), Des Smyth (new course).
Founded 1960
Visitors: weekdays; avoid Wed evening and Thurs (Ladies Day).
Green Fee: WD £14 (£8 with member); WE & BH £15 (£8 with member).
Societies: by booking; reduced green fees depending on numbers.
Catering: bar and snacks.
Pool table, darts.
Hotels: Talbot; Whites; Kelly's Strand; Cedars.

V249 Wicklow

☎(0404) 67379, Sec 69386, Pro: 66122, Public: 69558
Dunbur Rd, Wicklow, Co Wicklow
On L29 32 miles from Dublin.
Seaside course.
18 holes, 5695 metres, S.S.S.70
Founded 1904
Visitors: welcome weekdays.
Green Fee: any day: £15 (£10 with member).
Catering: meals served except Tues.

V250 Woodbrook

☎(01) 2824799, Sec 2896803, Fax 2821950
Dublin Rd, Bray, Co Wicklow
11 miles S of Dublin centre on N11.
Parkland course.
18 holes, 5996 metres, S.S.S.71
Founded 1921
Visitors: by arrangement.
Green Fee: WD £25 (£10 with member); WE & BH £35 (£10 with member).
Societies: Mon, Thurs, Fri by arrangement.

Catering: bar, snacks, dinner, à la carte.
Hotels: Royal; Victor; Killiney Castle.

V251 Woodenbridge

☎(0402) 35202, Sec 31571, Fax 31402
Woodenbridge, Arklow, Co Wicklow
45 miles S of Dublin on route N11 to Arklow; 4 miles NW of Arklow.
Parkland course.
18 holes 6316 yards, S.S.S.70
Founded 1884
Visitors: welcome except Thurs and Sat.
Green Fee: any day £20 (£10 with member).
Societies: weekdays by arrangement.
Catering: full restaurant facilities available.
Practice ground.
Hotels: Woodenbridge; Valley; Vale View.

V252 Woodlands

☎(045) 60777, Public: 70150
Coill Dubh, Naas, Co Kildare
9 holes, 5202, S.S.S.68
Founded 1985
Green Fee: WD £6 (£5 with member); WE & BH £7 (£6 with member)

V253 Woodstock

☎(065) 29463, Sec 22148, Public: 42408, Bar: 42407,
Caterer: 42406, Fax 20304
Woodstock House, Shanaway Road, Ennis, Co Clare
18 holes, 5879 metres, S.S.S.71
Founded 1993
Green Fee: any day: £18 (£10 with member)

V254 Youghal

☎(024) 92787, Sec 93091, Pro: 92590, Fax 92641
Knockaverry, Youghal, Co Cork
Overlooking Youghal town and bay.
Meadowland course.
18 holes, 5664 metres, S.S.S.70
Designed by Commander Harris.
Founded 1898
Visitors: welcome.
Green Fee: any day £14 (£7 with member).
Societies: welcome.
Catering: full bar and restaurant facilities in new clubhouse.

INDEX

Make the CSMA work for you.

Please send me more details of CSMA Services ☐

My CSMA number is | | | | | | | | | | |

OR

I may be eligible for CSMA membership and would also like further information on the many benefits of membership ☐

Name _____

Address _____

_____ Postcode _____

Employer/Previous Employer _____

ZCC1

Please send to CSMA,
Britannia House, 21 Station Street, Brighton BN1 4DE.

**NOW WE CAN
WORK FOR YOU**